LANDSCAPE PLANTS
for
EASTERN NORTH AMERICA

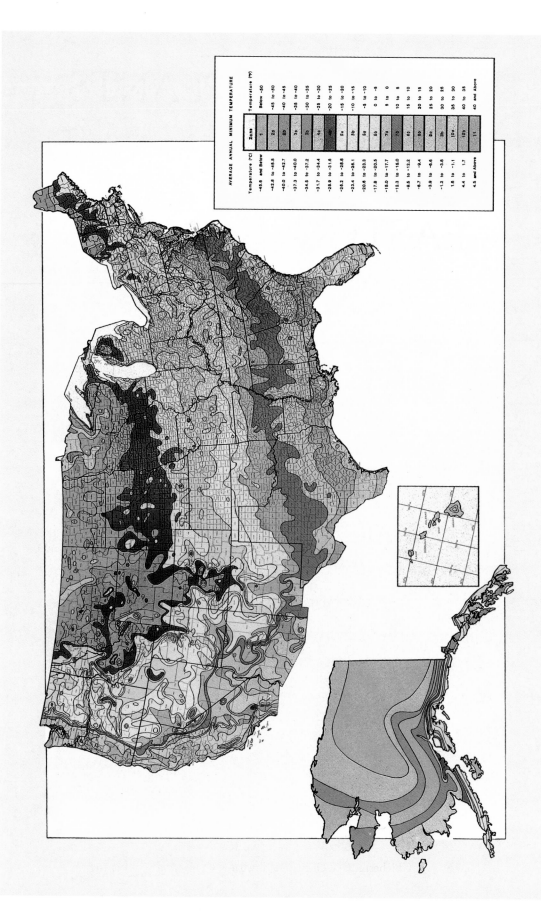

AVERAGE ANNUAL MINIMUM TEMPERATURE

Temperature (°C)	Zone	Temperature (°F)
-45.6 and Below	1	Below -50
-42.8 to -45.5	2a	-45 to -50
-40.0 to -42.7	2b	-40 to -45
-37.3 to -40.0	3a	-35 to -40
-34.5 to -37.2	3b	-30 to -35
-31.7 to -34.4	4a	-25 to -30
-28.9 to -31.6	4b	-20 to -25
-26.2 to -28.8	5a	-15 to -20
-23.4 to -26.1	5b	-10 to -15
-20.6 to -23.3	6a	-5 to -10
-17.8 to -20.5	6b	0 to -5
-15.0 to -17.7	7a	5 to 0
-12.3 to -15.0	7b	10 to 5
-9.5 to -12.2	8a	15 to 10
-6.7 to -9.4	8b	20 to 15
-3.9 to -6.6	9a	25 to 20
-1.2 to -3.8	9b	30 to 25
1.6 to -1.1	10a	35 to 30
4.4 to 1.7	10b	40 to 35
4.5 and Above	11	40 and Above

LANDSCAPE PLANTS
for
EASTERN NORTH AMERICA

Exclusive of Florida
and the Immediate Gulf Coast

SECOND EDITION

HARRISON L. FLINT
Purdue University

Drawings by
Jenny M. Lyverse

John Wiley & Sons, Inc.
New York · Chichester · Weinheim · Brisbane · Singapore · Toronto

This text is printed on acid-free paper.

This publication is designed to provide accurate and
authoritative information in regard to the subject
matter covered. It is sold with the understanding that
the publisher is not engaged in rendering legal, accounting,
or other professional services. If legal advice or other
expert assistance is required, the services of a competent
professional person should be sought.

Library of Congress Cataloging in Publication Data:
Flint, Harrison L. (Harrison Leigh), 1929–
    Landscape plants for eastern North America : exclusive of Florida
  and the immediate Gulf Coast / Harrison L. Flint ; drawings by Jenny
  M. Lyverse.—2nd ed.
      p. cm.
  Includes index.
    ISBN 0-471-59919-0 (cloth : alk. paper)
    1. Landscape plants—East (U.S.) 2. Landscape plants—Canada.
I. Lyverse, Jenny M. II. Title.
SB435.5.F56 1997
635.9'0974—dc20   96-34306

Printed in the United States of America
10 9 8 7 6 5 4 3

To my students,
and to you, the reader—
if you will take the time
to read the Introduction before proceeding,
your patience will be repaid by time saved later.

PREFACE

Use of landscape plants in the United States and probably Canada as well has changed significantly since publication of the first edition of this book in 1983. Many cultivars newly in use then have received wide acceptance, and many new ones have appeared. Interest in native plants has continued to increase, along with landscape use of herbaceous perennial plants.

Commercial availability of landscape plants has also grown, in response to renewed interest in plant diversity within the landscape industry and among the general public. Availability has also been better communicated, in part through new directories to commercial sources of plants, especially the relatively comprehensive *Source List of Plants and Seeds*, published triennially by the Andersen Horticultural Library of the Minnesota Landscape Arboretum.

With resources such as these, it is more difficult to dismiss a plant as being "unavailable" merely to avoid the effort and expense of searching for sources. Now retailers, landscape designers, and contractors have easy access to large numbers of landscape plants (admitting that there are still some plants that are very difficult to locate, especially in a desired size and number). Likewise, the practice of a few plant-minimalist landscape architects in reducing plant palettes to the absolute minimum has become an anachronism. Unity and continuity are still important design principles, but so also are diversity and visual interest, and problems of "unavailability" are no longer the effective excuse that they might have been a decade or two ago.

In part because of these trends, several changes have been made in this revised edition of *Landscape Plants for Eastern North America* (LPENA). Cultivar listings have been updated and expanded. Additional species have been included, primarily to make LPENA more useful in the western parts of its domain, and appendix listings have been expanded. There has also been an element of "fine-tuning" to better reflect my own learning and experience.

Inevitably, there have been nomenclatural changes since the first edition of LPENA. Initially, this does not appear to be good news, since it requires adjustment and learning new plant names. But, as Liberty Hyde Bailey wrote in his classic, *How Plants Get Their Names* (Dover Publications), we should be thankful that the plant has finally (one may hope) been properly named. Just as "taxes are what we pay for civilized society" (Chief Justice Oliver Wendell Holmes, Jr., 1904), a scientific system of plant nomenclature is the price we pay for orderly commerce in plants.

Scientific names used herein for most plant species native to North America north of Mexico follow *A Synonymized Checklist of the Vascular Flora of the United States, Canada, and Greenland*, by John T. Kartesz (Timber Press, Portland, Oregon, 1994). For most plant species native elsewhere, I have followed *The New Royal Horticulture Dictionary of Gardening* (Stockton Press, New York, 1992). A few departures have been made from these to acknowledge different authorities or more recent treatment or opinion. Family names have been brought into conformity with the "type" system, in which the suffix -aceae is added to the stem of the type-genus. For example, Compositae becomes Asteraceae, Cruciferae becomes Brassicaceae, Gramineae becomes Poaceae, Labiatae becomes Lamiaceae, Leguminosae becomes Fabaceae, Palmae becomes Arecaceae, Umbelliferae becomes Apiaceae, and so on. In such cases in this book, the older family names are also appended.

I continue to be indebted to many people, including several of those listed in the preface to the first edition as well as many others. Special thanks go to Tom Dodd, Jr., Edward R. Hassel-kus, the late Robert C. Simpson, and George Ware, who have been of great help on many occasions. Others include Clayton J. Antieau, Kris Bachtel, David J. Beattie, Peter Bristol, the late Jim Cross, Earl Cully, Rick Darke, the late Donald Egolf, Claire and David Erlinger, Galen Gates, Thomas L. Green, Josephine Henry, Dale Herman, C. E. "Buddy" Hubbuch, Barbara and Michael Kaczorowski, Gary Koller, David G. Leach, Robert W. Lighty, Paul W. Meyer, the late Edmund J. "Ed" Mezitt, Kris Medic, the late Brian Mulligan, Elwin R. Orton, Jr., John Pair, Harold Pellett, Norman Pellett, J. C. Raulston, Wilbert G. Ronald, Claire Sawyers, Don Shadow, Guy Sternberg, Charles E. Tubesing, Mark Widrlechner, and undoubtedly several others who belong on this list.

Last but most important, I am indebted to my wife, Terrie Kercher, whose support and forebearance, especially over the last three years, have literally made this edition possible.

HARRISON L. FLINT

West Lafayette, Indiana
April 1996

PREFACE
TO THE FIRST EDITION

It is my intention that this book serve two primary functions. First, it is a source of selection-related information about landscape plants useful within the stated geographical limits, for landscape designers and others having responsibility for the selection of landscape plants. Second, it is a text and reference book for students of horticulture and landscape architecture who are building their knowledge of landscape plant materials. Its distinctiveness lies in its orientation to the design-related selection process, its broad geographical coverage, and the distinctiveness of its illustrations.

Since identification and selection of landscape plants are largely separate functions, information on plant identification has been omitted deliberately, although some of the photographs will be of incidental use for this purpose. Moreover, little or no attempt has been made to deal with botanical systematics other than when interrelatedness of plants impinges on the selection process or when it is necessary for nomenclatural clarity.

Botanical nomenclature follows that of *Hortus Third* (New York: Macmillan, 1976) in most instances, with rare departures to acknowledge different authorities or more recent treatment. The same has been done with family names; even though this is not always consistent with most recent phylogenetic treatment, it is presently the path of least confusion for most readers. This book has been written for professional landscape architects and plantsmen, but at the same time a serious attempt has been made to minimize specialized botanical terms and other technical jargon so that serious amateurs might find it useful as well.

I have worked in the northeastern and mid-western United States and have studied and photographed landscape plants throughout most of the geographical area covered by this book. But I also rely heavily on the expertise and local and regional experience of many knowledgeable amateur and professional plantsmen throughout the region.

A complete acknowledgment of help received would be most difficult, since a great many colleagues, teachers, and former students have had a hand in this book. But there is a smaller, special group of people who have tolerated my incessant questioning over a substantial number of years and whose patient answers have contributed in a major way to my education and to the content of this book. They include Fred M. Abbey, North Ferrisburgh, Vermont; Jack W. Caddick, Kingston, Rhode Island; Eugene Cline, Canton, Georgia; John F. Cornman, Ithaca, New York; W. A. Cumming, Morden, Manitoba; Tom Dodd, Jr., Semmes, Alabama; Alfred J. Fordham, Westwood, Massachusetts; Edward R. Hasselkus, Madison, Wisconsin; Case Hoogendoorn, Middletown, Rhode Island; E. J. Horder, Mobile, Alabama; the late Alfred Johnson, St. Paul, Minnesota; Clarence E. Lewis, East Lansing, Michigan; J. C. McDaniel, Urbana, Illinois; and Robert G. Mower, Ithaca, New York.

I am indebted to others for ideas gained by reading their writings and in most instances through personal conversation as well: A. R. Buckley, Ottawa, Canada; Michael A. Dirr, Athens, Georgia; Fred Galle, Pine Mountain, Georgia; the late Donald Hoag, Fargo, North Dakota; Richard Jaynes, New Haven, Connecticut; Neil G. Odenwald, Baton Rouge, Louisiana; Lawrence Sherk, Etobicoke, Ontario; the late

F. L. Skinner, Dropmore, Manitoba; Brooks Wigginton, Wheeling, West Virginia; Donald Wyman, Weston, Massachusetts; and others.

Special appreciation goes to Ruth V. Kvaalen, who reviewed the manuscript in great detail and contributed many suggestions, especially concerning nomenclature. Additional suggestions on the text were made by Jenny M. (Lyverse) Smith, whose illustrations have also given this book distinctive character. The manuscript was thoroughly reviewed at completion by Edward R. Hasselkus, Henry P. Orr, Harry Ponder, Lawrence G. Sherk, and Brooks Wigginton, whose efforts I greatly appreciate.

Assistance with unappealing tasks such as proofreading of typescript and general encouragement were given by Elsie S. Flint, John H. Flint, and Sarah B. Lowe.

Photographs on pages 32 and 343 were furnished, respectively, by Sarah B. Lowe and Theodore D. Walker. Other photographs are my own.

Finally, the encouragement of my colleagues at Purdue University and that of the University administration in providing a climate conducive to activities such as this is greatly appreciated.

It may be true that no book is ever finished. Revised editions regularly contain information and insights not included in first writings. I welcome suggestions and criticisms toward this end.

HARRISON L. FLINT

West Lafayette, Indiana
December 1982

CONTENTS

LANDSCAPE PLANTS
for
EASTERN NORTH AMERICA

INTRODUCTION

PURPOSE OF THE BOOK

The selection of landscape plants is a two-part process involving compilation of information on site requirements and landscape characteristics of prospective plant choices together with a creative process of matching plant traits with design needs. Some designers follow an orderly sequence of steps leading to selection. Others work more informally and intuitively. Whether the process is orderly and stepwise or seemingly random, planting designers all need a basic fund of information with which to begin the design process. This book is intended to fill that need.

CONTENT OF THE BOOK

Scope

This book is designed to be useful in the eastern half of the North American continent with the exception of the Florida peninsula and the southern tip of Texas (areas south of USDA Hardiness Zone 9a). Many statements herein will be qualified as relating to "our area." This refers to the area limited by the Atlantic Ocean on the east, the 30° north latitude parallel on the south, and the 98–100° west longitude meridians on the west (grading from 98° in the southwestern corner to 100° in the northwestern corner). Corners are located near Jacksonville, Florida in the southeast, Austin, Texas in the southwest, and some point north of Brandon, Manitoba in the northwest, as well as in the northeast so as to include the Maritime Provinces of Canada.

Species included are mostly trees, shrubs, woody vines, climbers, and groundcovers, but a few subshrubs and functional herbaceous groundcover plants are also included. Relating information on more than 1500 species and 2500 cultivars to a land mass of more than a million square miles precludes a high degree of geo-graphic resolution. More detailed information relating to specific localities can be found in local and regional publications on landscape plants and native flora or can be obtained from nurserymen, landscape designers, contractors, and other professionals with local experience.

Primary and Secondary Species

Decisions as to primary and secondary, or "related species," status are based on several considerations.

1. As a general rule, in spite of the following exceptions, the primary species is closely related to the related species listed under it and generally preferred over them, more commonly used, or more easily available.
2. When several species are similar in most of their characteristics and requirements, usually only one has been given primary status, even though those relegated to "related species" status sometimes are more important landscape plants than other species that have received primary status. For example, *Betula papyrifera* (paper birch) and *B. pendula* (European white birch) are so similar in general effect and requirements that it would be repetitious to give both primary status. Because of this, *B. pendula* is treated as a related species even though it is more important in our area than *Betula alleghaniensis* (yellow birch), which is given primary status because of its distinctness.
3. When there is little to recommend either of two similar species, one native and the other exotic (nonnative), over the other, the native species usually is given primary status and the exotic is treated as a related species (illustrated by the case of *Betula papyrifera* and *B. pendula*).
4. Included in the related species category are species of different genera related within a

1

family to the primary species—for example, inclusion of *Broussonetia papyrifera* (paper mulberry) under *Morus alba* (white mulberry).

In some instances, species treated as related species are not very closely related botanically. For example, *Atriplex canescens*, a member of the Goosefoot Family (Chenopodiaceae), is listed with *Baccharis halimifolia*, a relative of the Composite or Aster Family (Asteraceae), only because of similarity in site requirements and landscape function. In another instance, *Cliftonia* and *Cyrilla*, members of the Cyrillaceae, are treated as related species under *Clethra* even though they belong not only to different families but even different taxonomic orders. The relationship here is one of function and landscape character rather than botanical relationship. It should not be assumed that related species are invariably closely related botanically to the primary species under which they are listed, even though that usually is the case.

NOMENCLATURE

Scientific Names

Botanical or scientific names are called *binomials* because they consist of two names. The first name, always initially capitalized, is the *genus* (plural *genera*) name, describing the kind of plant, for instance, maple (*Acer*), dogwood (*Cornus*), or yew (*Taxus*). The second name, never capitalized in most modern usage, is the *species* (plural also *species*) name, describing the individual type within the kind, for instance, red maple (*Acer rubrum*), flowering dogwood (*Cornus florida*), or Japanese yew (*Taxus cuspidata*). In technical writings, a third name or abbreviation designating the author of the plant name is added to the binomial. In the context of this book, the usefulness of author designations is deemed insufficient to justify their inclusion.

Plant species sometimes are subdivided into lesser categories of *subspecies* (ssp.), *variety* (var.), and *forma* (f.). These names, when applicable, are appended to the binomial following the appropriate abbreviation: for instance, *Acer saccharum* ssp. *floridanum* (Florida sugar maple), *Rhododendron catawbiense* var. *album* (white-flowered Catawba rhododendron), and *Cercis*

canadensis f. *alba* (white-flowered redbud). Subspecies and varieties (not to be confused with horticultural varieties or cultivars) occur as natural subpopulations within species populations, having their own geographic ranges and tending to breed true to type, whereas forms are more or less individual occurrences, sometimes repeated, appearing randomly rather than in a geographical pattern, and usually not breeding true. Since many forms (*formae*) are reproduced in cultivation more than in nature, many have been given cultivar names, sometimes identical with old form names except for the notation used (see Cultivars). For instance, *Cercis canadensis* f. *alba* is often listed as *Cercis canadensis* 'Alba.' This practice can be confusing and is not recommended, but does occur.

Synonyms

In botanical nomenclature, a synonym is an illegitimate botanical name, incorrect either in form or application. Therefore it is not acceptable to interchange it with the correct name, as is true for synonyms outside scientific context. Legitimacy of botanical names is determined by application of the International Code of Botanical Nomenclature (ICBN), an agreement among botanists around the world. Since plant classification and nomenclature is an ongoing field of scientific inquiry, names that previously have been considered correct sometimes must be discarded in the face of new evidence and replaced by different names. When this happens, the previously accepted name becomes a synonym. Since there may be a great time lag between such name changes and their commercial acceptance, many synonyms are still in use in nursery catalogs. To reduce the resulting confusion, such commonly used synonyms are listed here following the corresponding legitimate name.

Cultivars

The *cultivar*, a contraction of "*cultivated variety*," is the primary taxonomic unit of cultivated plant nomenclature. Cultivated plants are subject to the same rules of botanical nomenclature that wild plants are, and additionally they are subject to a separate set of regulations governing the naming of cultivars, the International Code of Nomenclature for Cultivated Plants (ICNCP). Cultivars, unlike botanical categories, are not italicized in printed text and are either enclosed in single quotation marks or preceded by the abbreviation cv. For example, compact winged euonymus can be written either *Euonymus alatus* 'Compacta' or *Euonymus alatus* cv. Compacta. Cultivar names are always initially capitalized, and those named since January 1, 1959 must be written in the vernacular of the country of origin, although Latinized cultivar names applied before that date are accepted as correct.

Occasionally two or more cultivar names are applied to the same clone or to plants too similar to justify their separation. There are ways of determining which cultivar name should receive priority, but they are sometimes uncertain and usually tedious as well as costly. In part because of the difficulty in dealing with cultivated plant nomenclature, cultivars have received relatively little attention from plant taxonomists. Consequently, when synonymous cultivar names are listed here, no final judgment of priority or legitimacy is intended, even though the cultivar name listed first usually is accepted by the author as correct.

Common Names

Common names are simply colloquial names in more or less common usage, but there is a tendency in some writings to coin appropriate vernacular names in cases where a common name is not known to be in use. This causes confusion, so an attempt has been made here to refrain from coining new common names and as much as possible to use names that are known or thought to be in common usage.

In general, common names are not arbitrated by either national or international bodies, and so there are no "correct" or "incorrect" common names in the same sense as scientific names. An exception is that the forestry profession in the United States has agreed to specific common names for a few important forest species.

Plant Patents

New cultivars can be patented in much the same way as devices and processes, and for the same time period: 17 years. A considerable number of the plants included here have been under patents that have since expired.

Because of legislation pending at this writing which, if enacted, would extend the patent pe-riod from 17 to 20 years, plants still under patent in 1996 are indicated as such by patent number and year in this edition.

Trademarked Names

Trademarked names have been used for groups of plants, such as Brownell Sub-zero Roses®, for many years but now are increasingly being applied to individual plants as tradenames. Currently, individual plant entities to be trademarked must also be given "generic" cultivar names, but a few older trademarked names are still listed without generic names in some catalogs.

Sometimes an originator or introducer has patented a plant under an existing cultivar name and later, when the patent has expired, has trademarked the existing cultivar name and coined a new cultivar name to serve as the generic name required by the Office of Trademarks. The confusion caused by this practice is obvious. In this book, plants are listed by the cultivar names considered to be current by the author, and any trademarked names are appended along with patent information. The author has listed all names in this book as carefully as possible, but neither the author nor the publisher can guarantee complete accuracy. It is the responsibility of patent and trademark holders to inform users of such patents and trademarks, and the responsibility of users to respect them, ascertaining "official" status as necessary.

PLANT SIZE GROUPS

In the 1920s, a size-group numbering system was devised by Professor Ralph W. Curtis of Cornell University. This system has been adopted by a generation of Curtis' former students, many of whom have been teachers in the area of landscape plant materials, and at least one additional generation, including the present author. For the purposes of this book, the Curtis system has been modified by (a) converting to the metric system, (b) eliminating gaps between numbers, and (c) adding a category to classify tree sizes more closely. The modified version used here is outline in Table I-1. These numbers, appended to the scientific name of the species listed, give a quick reference to functional size.

TABLE I-1.   Plant Size Group Designations

| Size Group Number | Height | | | Description |
	Meters	Approximate Equivalent (ft)	Human Scale	
1	Depends partially on support provided			Climber
2	to 0.5	to 1½	Ankle height	Groundcover
3	0.5–1	1½–3	Knee height	Dwarf shrub
4	1–2	3–6½	Chest height	Small shrub
5	2–4	6½–13	Overhead	Medium shrub
6	4–8	13–26	Overhead	Large shrub or small tree
7	8–16	26–52	Overhead	Medium tree
8	16+	52+	Overhead	Large tree

GEOGRAPHIC RANGES

Native Range

Plant species grow wild in well-defined areas. In some cases, these coincide closely with the areas where the species are adapted to landscape use—for example, *Cornus florida* (flowering dogwood). But native range limits depend on factors other than those that limit landscape use, such as the ability to reproduce naturally without human help. Because of this, many species can be used far outside their native ranges. An extreme example is *Taxodium distichum* (bald cypress), confined by its reproductive needs to areas near watercourses in the Deep South and northward on the Atlantic Coast to southern Delaware and in the Mississippi basin to southwestern Indiana, but successfully used in landscape plantings in many upland sites, some 400 miles north of its northernmost native stands. In spite of such discrepancies between natural and useful ranges, knowledge of the natural range of a native species can be useful in predicting its adaptability to landscape use. Sensitive landscape designers and plant specialists look closely at native habitats, observing their extent and character, to predict their performance in the landscape.

Native ranges of species from other parts of the world often are not known in North America with as much resolution as those of our native species, but they can be useful in predicting the success of those species in our area if their native ranges are known to have a climate analogous to

that of the area in which they will be used. For example, the climate of Manchuria is similar enough to that of much of the northeastern United States and adjacent Canada that many Manchurian species are well adapted to this area.

Some landscape plants have no native range because they have arisen by hybridization of other species. Such hybrids may be given a collective name, indicated as a species name preceded by "×," as in *Berberis ×mentorensis* (Mentor barberry), which is not a species but rather a collection of all hybrids of *B. julianae* (wintergreen barberry) × *B. thunbergii* (Japanese barberry).

Useful Range

The area in which a particular plant species is adapted to landscape use is defined primarily by plant hardiness zones, which are based on average annual minimum temperatures. Several different hardiness zone maps have been published. Since they differ in numbering systems, it is essential to use plant hardiness zone ratings only with the map that was used in assigning the ratings. The map used in assigning plant ratings in this book is that prepared at the U.S. National Arboretum and published by the U.S. Department of Agriculture* (Figure I-1).

To define useful range only by hardiness zones

---

*U.S.D.A. Plant Hardiness Zone Map, Misc. Pub. No. 1475, Agr. Res. Service, U.S. Dept of Agriculture, 1990.

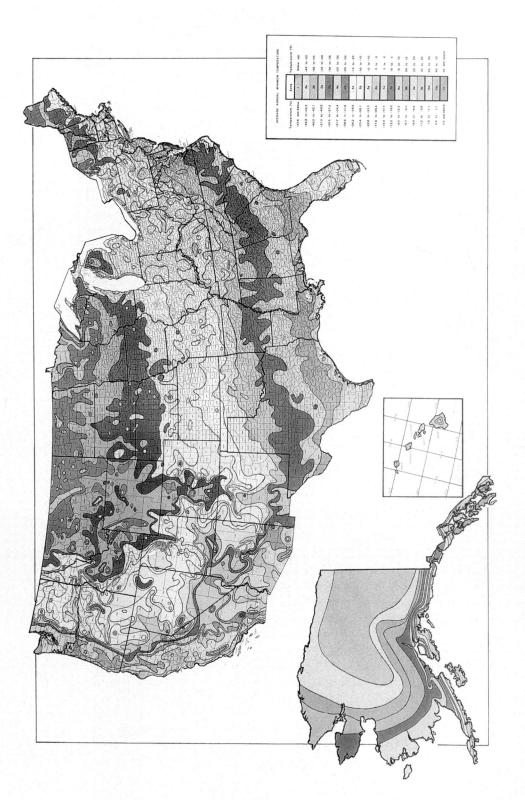

FIGURE I-1. Adapted from the Plant Hardiness Zone Map, U.S. Department of Agriculture.

is convenient but a great oversimplification. Even though temperature is the dominant factor determining useful ranges, other components of climate and soils play important roles in limiting the useful ranges of many species. Often more detailed information on soil and climate is available from state, provincial, or federal agricultural research stations or extension services. Such information, as well as the advice of experienced local plantsmen, can add greatly to a designer's confidence in specifying plant material.

PLANT FUNCTION

The first consideration in selecting landscape plants is to know the purpose for which a plant is being selected. Plants function in many ways. The functions listed under individual species are not intended to be all-inclusive but represent most common usage. Since they are described in a single word or a few words at most, they are intended to serve only as reminders. Much more information will be found in books on planting design.

SIZE AND HABIT

Plant size groups are useful for classifying plants by functional height, but size and shape are ever-changing characteristics of most landscape plants. Because of this, two form drawings are included for most of the primary species—one at an early functional size, the second at mature or ordinary maximum size for the species. It is not intended that the two drawings represent the same individual plant at different ages, in the same season, or pruned alike. In some instances, two different seasonal aspects are deliberately included. For instance, the young plant of *Chionanthus virginicus* (fringetree) is represented in flower in late spring, while the mature plant is shown in summer condition. Or, a tree that can be trained to a single or multiple trunks or a shrub that can also function as a small tree may be shown in both ways. The addition of time notations gives information about early growth rate and at least suggests something about longevity. Oversimplification once more is necessary. Inherent variation among individuals within most woody plant species is considerable.

Not all plants will look like the examples shown, and site variables can also greatly affect both growth rate and longevity. For example, street trees planted in relatively small soil pockets seldom even approach the maximum size that the same trees would reach in a lawn planting, and their useful life sometimes is shortened greatly by their environment.

Maximum sizes shown are related to plant performance in eastern North America. Trees introduced to our area from the Pacific Northwest such as *Sequoiadendron giganteum* (giant sequoia) and *Thuja plicata* (giant arborvitae) never assume the proportions that they would in their native habitats.

ADAPTABILITY

Information on site requirements is summarized in the bar graphs under each primary species. Tolerance is indicated by the blackened portion of each bar. For example, the hypothetical plant described in Figure I-2 will do well in any light condition except full shade and perhaps full sun in summer, but needs at least half shade in winter. The shaded (stippled) area in the first bar indicates qualified tolerance, and the nature of the qualification in each case is explained in the text preceding the bar graphs. In this case, the tolerance of full sun might hold only for part of the useful range, with light shade necessary in the South and perhaps in the Midwest. The full range of light conditions that exists in landscape sites cannot be represented adequately by a single bar graph. The difference between the full shade cast by mature tree canopies far overhead and that under the low, dense canopy of *Acer plat-*

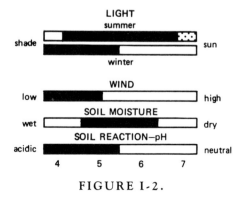

FIGURE I-2.

anoides (Norway maple), for example, is profound, and many other variations exist in landscape sites. The bar notation is useful for developing pools of plants from which to make choices for specific situations, but final selection should be based on firsthand observation and local experience.

Our hypothetical plant tolerates little wind. The reason for this and the degree of wind tolerated in each instance is stated or implied in the accompanying text. Possible reasons include soft-wooded branches that are prone to storm damage, fragile leaves such as those of *Acer palmatum* (Japanese maple) or *Magnolia macrophylla* (bigleaf magnolia) that may be damaged by strong summer winds, or evergreen foliage that is prone to winter dehydration. Plants that are more susceptible to diseases in humid or poorly circulated air may be shown as having a requirement for wind rather than merely tolerating it.

Soil moisture tolerances also require further explanation. A bar blackened all the way to the wet end indicates a plant such as *Cephalanthus occidentalis* (buttonbush) or *Taxodium distichum* (bald cypress) that will grow in standing water for at least part of the year; and a bar blackened to about halfway between the wet end and the center, as shown in our hypothetical example, can be considered to represent an "average" landscape plant, requiring good soil drainage but perhaps tolerating brief periods of flooding. A bar blackened to halfway between the center and dry end represents a plant that would tolerate occasional brief drought but not prolonged dry periods, and a bar blackened to the dry end represents a highly drought-tolerant plant. But soil moisture tolerances are seen to be even more complex than this when the differences between wet soil in a peat bog and that in a heavy clay soil are considered. As with light conditions, the bar notation is useful for initial sorting, but final selection should be based on more sophisticated appraisal of the site and prospective choices.

The final bar in Figure I-2 indicates the range of soil acidity in which our hypothetical plant can be expected to grow well. Our plant is clearly an "acid-soil" plant, performing best below pH 5.5. The largest number of such species included are members of the Ericaceae (Heath Family), but other acid-soil plants are also included. Some plants perform poorly in very acidic soil, and those that are known to have a requirement for higher soil pH are indicated. Currently available information on soil acidity requirements of landscape plants is not complete, and careful designers will rely on their own observations and other local experience rather than a simplistic comparison of a soil test with the bar notation. Soil pH is a common limiting factor in selection with only a relatively small number of species in most parts of our area, since the great majority of plants show wide tolerance of soil acidity. But for those species with narrower requirements, proper soil acidity makes the difference between success and failure.

In summary, it can be seen from the bar graphs that our hypothetical species performs well in any light conditions in summer except full shade and perhaps full sun (more explanation in the text). But in winter it must be at least half shaded for protection against dehydration. It needs acidic soil (pH not exceeding 5.5) that is reasonably well drained yet not excessively dry. From this much information alone, it is apparent that this plant would be a poor choice for a windswept site or a calcareous (high limestone content) soil unless major modification of microclimate or soil were practicable.

In many instances, more detailed information or qualification about environmental tolerances will be included in the text. But the designer's accumulated experience will provide the ultimate confidence in selection of plants.

SEASONAL INTEREST

Colorful flowers, foliage, and fruits provide obvious seasonal interest. The more subtle attractions of colorful or corky winter twigs, patterned or bicolored bark, conspicuous winter buds, and unusual form, texture, or branching patterns all contribute to a plant's character in the landscape. The creative designer will come to know plants in all seasons and will learn to combine them skillfully into a year-round, interesting landscape. This can be done without introducing strong color at any one season, if that is the objective. In any case, seasonal color perhaps should be biased by the time factor. How does one rate *Syringa vulgaris* (common lilac), for

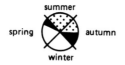

FIGURE I-3.

example, with a week or two of fragrant, colorful flowers and little other seasonal interest, against a shrub such as *Cornus racemosa* (gray dogwood), which is quietly colorful over the greater part of the year?

The seasonal "clock" accompanying each primary species is intended for quick reference to duration and intensity of seasonal color. The hypothetical species represented in Figure I-3 is shown by the blackened sectors to be highly colorful or otherwise interesting in late spring and late autumn, perhaps in the form of flowers and either fruits or autumn foliage. It is mildly interesting during summer and early autumn, as shown by the stippled area, perhaps because its foliage has character. The absence of any shading during winter and early spring suggests that this species is not an evergreen and has no other winter interest. If it were an evergreen with undistinguished foliage it would be represented by a stipple, or if the evergreen foliage were colorful or richly textured, the entire clock face would be blackened.

Timing of the seasons obviously varies over our area, and how a season is defined is arbitrary at best. For example, *Cornus florida* (flowering dogwood) may reach its flowering peak by mid-March in the southern extremes of our area (Zone 9a), whereas trees in the northern extremes of the useful range for that species (Zone 5b) flower nearly two months later. There is a rule of thumb that spring advances about one degree of latitude every five to seven days, but this also depends upon longitude and elevation, closeness to water, and weather variations in individual years. It is probably more meaningful to delineate the seasons according to plant developmental events than by the calendar. For example, *Cornus mas* (cornelian-cherry dogwood) flowers close to April 1 in most years in Lafayette, Indiana. One could consider this the beginning of spring or instead could use the flowering of *Viburnum farreri* (fragrant viburnum), which usually comes closer to the vernal equinox

at this location. Any attempt to refine the boundaries of the seasons beyond observation of phenological (developmental) events probably will result in frustration. As constant as the seasons are in the long run, they are notably fickle on an annual basis.

PROBLEMS AND MAINTENANCE

Without question, the need for maintenance is an important criterion in selecting landscape plants, and it appears to be growing in importance. But willingness and ability to provide maintenance is a highly variable characteristic of people, which any serious grower of hybrid tea roses knows. It seems that there is a place for both low-maintenance and high-maintenance landscape plants. The important thing is to know which is which and to select according to the situation. Maintenance is dealt with here only as it is related to plant selection. Detailed information on maintenance is included in other books and can be obtained from state, provincial, or local extension service offices. It is especially important to obtain reliable, up-to-date information on the use of pesticides because of the potential hazards involved and the fact that pesticides and their regulation are subject to change.

One of the most serious limitations to plant selection is that of commercial availability. Most landscape nurseries offer a limited array of landscaped plants, and these vary from year to year. Many plants are available only from a few nurseries specializing in unusual plants or in select groups such as rhododendrons, heaths, or groundcovers. Moreover, some plants that were once unavailable are being reintroduced into commerce, and some formerly available are no longer.

Commercial availability is an ever-changing picture. Because of this and the continuous proliferation of new cultivars, planting designers who want to make effective use of the rich body of landscape plants that are available in eastern North America have no choice but to maintain a library of at least a few nursery catalogs and a ready hand on the telephone to update their information on sources as necessary.

ALPHABETICAL LIST
of
PLANTS

Abelia ×grandiflora 4–5

GLOSSY ABELIA
Evergreen or semievergreen shrub
Caprifoliaceae (Honeysuckle Family)

Hybrid Origin.   A. chinensis × A. uniflora.

Size and Habit.   Height is limited by winterkill of stems in Zones 5b–7a.

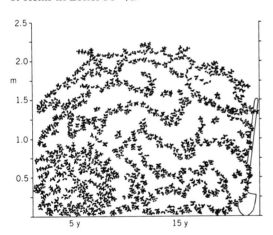

Abelia ×grandiflora.

Adaptability

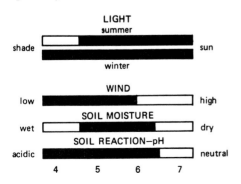

Useful Range.   USDA Zones 5b–9a+.

Function.   Border, hedge, foundation, massing, specimen, screen (Zones 7b–9a+).

Seasonal Interest.   *Flowers:* Pale pink to white, 2 cm/0.8 in. long, numerous, in leafy clusters (panicles), opening gradually through middle and late summer. *Foliage:* Glossy, evergreen (semievergreen in Zones 5b–7a), 2.5 cm/1 in. long, fine-textured, bright to dark green, bronzing in winter.

Problems and Maintenance.   Annual pruning is required to remove deadwood in Zones 5b–7a.

Cultivars.   'Edward Goucher' (hybrid of A. ×grandiflora × A. schumanii) is similar to A. ×grandiflora except with larger, deeper rose-purple flowers, slightly lower stature, and slightly less cold hardiness. It is inferior to A. ×grandiflora in landscape effect in spite of its larger flowers. 'Francis Mason' (='Variegated') has yellow-variegated foliage and remains below 1.5 m/5 ft in height, even in warm climates. 'Sherwoodii' is an excellent semidwarf selection of A. ×grandiflora, not exceeding 1 m/3.3 ft in height, with slightly finer foliage texture.

9

Abies concolor 8

WHITE FIR
Evergreen tree
Pinaceae (Pine Family)

Native Range. Southwestern United States and adjacent Mexico.

Useful Range.   USDA Zones 4a–8b.

Function.   Specimen, hedge, massing, screen.

Size and Habit

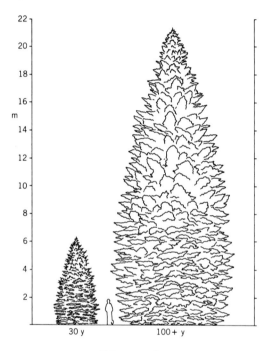

Abies concolor.

Adaptability. Better adapted to hot, dry summers than most *Abies* species.

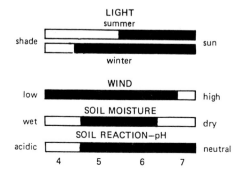

Seasonal Interest. *Foliage:* Evergreen, highly glaucous on both sides. The flat, curved needles, about 5 cm/2 in. long, give a pleasing texture. Color and form are reminiscent of the bluer forms of Colorado spruce but less positive in effect and more versatile in design.

Problems and Maintenance. Little or no maintenance normally is required.

Cultivars. 'Candicans' has striking, silvery blue foliage. 'Compacta' is slower growing than the species type. 'Conica' is also slower growing, with more compact pyramidal form. 'Pyramidalis' is very narrowly pyramidal and compact in form, making a striking vertical accent. A few compact and weeping cultivars are occasionally available.

Related Species

Abies balsamea 8 (balsam fir).   Usually sparse growing and poorly adapted to cultivation except in areas close to its native range from Labrador to Minnesota and south to West Virginia (Zones 2a–5a).

Abies fraseri 8 (Fraser fir).   This southern counterpart of *A. balsamea,* is sometimes called southern balsam fir. It is subject to the same limitations as *A. balsamea,* but more useful in somewhat warmer zones (5a–7a) in areas close to its native range. Inferior to *A. concolor* and the better Asian and European firs in landscape effect in most of that useful range.

Abies lasiocarpa 8 (Rocky Mountain fir).   This large tree, native from Alaska to New Mexico, has needles shorter than those of *A. concolor* but equally glaucous. The species type, like some other conifers from the Pacific Northwest, has not performed well in most of eastern North America, but ssp. *arizonica* (cork or Arizona fir) has done somewhat better in our area, making a compact, small tree with strong bluish foliage. The semidwarf form 'Compacta' is even more compact and is useful as a specimen in Zones 5a–7b, and perhaps in colder and warmer zones as well.

Abies procera 8 (synonym: *A. nobilis;* noble fir). This large tree from the Pacific Northwest grows slowly in our area but is better adapted to warm climates than most firs, useful in Zones 6a–7b. The selection 'Glauca' has silvery blue-green foliage.

Abies homolepis 8

NIKKO FIR

Evergreen tree

Pinaceae (Pine Family)

Native Range.   Japan.

Useful Range.   USDA Zones 5a–6b.

Function.   Massing, screen, specimen.

Size and Habit

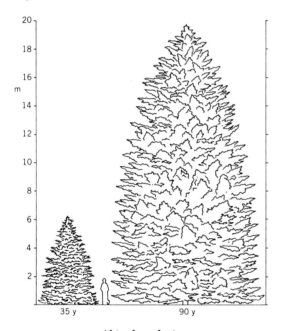

Abies homolepis.

Adaptability.   Light shade helps in establishment in the Midwest and South.

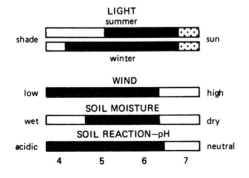

Seasonal Interest. *Foliage:* Evergreen, dark green needles, about 2.5 cm/1 in. long, with broad white stomatal bands underneath. Foliage is denser than that of many firs. *Cones:* Purplish to 10 cm/4 in. long, borne erectly on branches, add interest early in the growing season, then turn brown at maturity.

Problems and Maintenance. Little or no maintenance is required in areas where this tree is adapted.

Related Species

Abies firma 8 (Momi fir).   Another handsome Japanese species, better than most firs in the South (Zones 6b–9a), but seldom available.

Abies holophylla 8 (needle or Manchurian fir). A seemingly widely adapted fir from Manchuria and Korea (Zones 5a–7a) with bright green foliage, it needs wider trial to assess adaptability more accurately.

Keteleeria davidiana 8 (David keteleeria).   This evergreen tree from China is closely related to *Abies* and resembles a fir while young, eventually becoming rounded or flat-topped and open in habit. It is so seldom used in our area that its limitations are not well known, but it is worth trying more widely in Zones 7b–9a+.

Keteleeria fortunei 8 (Fortune keteleeria).   This close relative of *K. davidiana* is similar in all respects but probably less cold-hardy and rarer in cultivation in our area. It is worthy of trial at least in Zone 9a and southward.

Abies koreana 7

KOREAN FIR
Evergreen tree
Pinaceae (Pine Family)

Native Range.   Korea.

Useful Range.   USDA Zones 5a–7a, perhaps also Zone 4b.

Function.   Specimen, screen.

Size and Habit

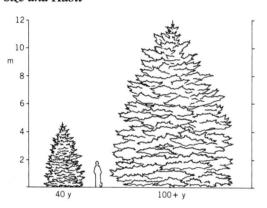

Abies koreana.

Adaptability

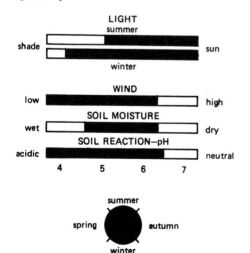

Seasonal Interest. *Foliage:* Evergreen, dark green needles, to 2 cm/0.8 in. long, with broad white stomatal bands underneath. Foliage appears dense, in part because of compact growth. *Cones:* Violet-purple, about 5 cm/2 in. long, borne erectly on branches, beginning when the tree is young, 1–2 m/3.3–6.6 ft tall.

Problems and Maintenance. Little or no maintenance is required in areas where this tree is adapted.

Cultivars. 'Prostrate Beauty,' also known as f. *prostrata* and 'Compact Dwarf,' probably is nothing more than the result of propagation by cuttings from lower branches of trees of the species. It is an excellent, hardy, dense shrub, grows to at least 2 to 3 times wide as high, and is useful for massing and foundation planting over at least as wide an area as the species (Zones 4b–7b). Commercial availability is limited, but ease of cutting propagation and growing popularity of the plant suggests greater availability in the future. Leaders (vertical shoots) occasionally develop in older plants, and must be removed to preserve the low form of the plant.

Abies koreana **'Prostate Beauty.'**

Related Species

Abies veitchii 8 (Veitch fir).   A handsome fir from Japan for northern climates, this does not do well in even marginally southern areas, presumably because of less drought resistance than some other Asian firs. This graceful tree with handsome dark green foliage, white underneath, and bluish purple cones is useful in Zones 3b–5b and relatively cool, moist sites in Zone 6.

Abies nordmanniana 8

NORDMANN FIR
Evergreen tree
Pinaceae (Pine Family)

Native Range.   Caucasus Mountains.

Useful Range.   USDA Zones 5b–7b.

Function.   Specimen, screen.

Size and Habit

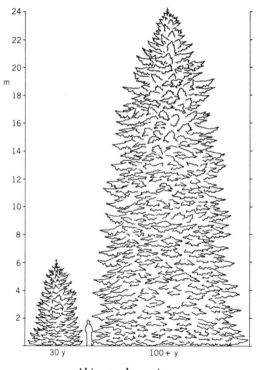

Abies nordmanniana.

Adaptability

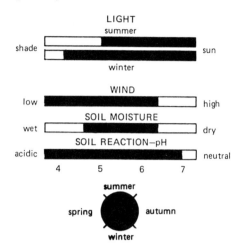

Seasonal Interest. *Foliage:* Evergreen, dark green needles, 2.5 cm/1 in. or longer, with prominent stomatal lines underneath, among the most handsome firs under good conditions.

Problems and Maintenance. Little or no maintenance is required in areas where this tree is adapted.

Related Species

Abies cephalonica 8 (Greek fir). A widely adapted fir with deep green, pointed needles, white underneath, it tolerates extremes of heat and drought better than most firs (Zones 5a–8a).

Abies pinsapo 8 (Spanish fir). This distinctive tree with short, blunt needles is one of the better firs for southern areas (Zones 6b–8a). The selection 'Glauca,' with blue-green foliage, is fairly well known on the East Coast, and is distinctive in color and texture.

Acer buergerianum 7

TRIDENT MAPLE
Deciduous tree
Aceraceae (Maple Family)

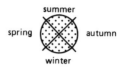

Native Range.   Japan.

Useful Range.   USDA Zones 6a–8a, and at least marginally in Zone 5b.

Function.   Street, shade, or patio tree, specimen.

Size and Habit

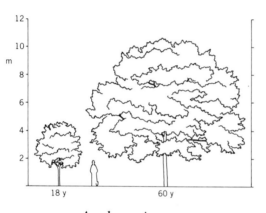

Acer buergerianum.

Adaptability.   Individual trees may be adapted to colder zones than indicated. Further testing is needed to determine limits of hardiness more accurately.

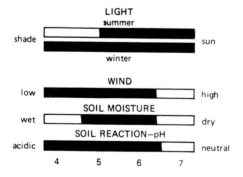

Seasonal Interest.   *Foliage:* Bright green leaves, 3–8 cm/1–3 in. long, have distinctive shape and texture, turning yellow-orange in some years before falling. *Bark:* Multicolored flaking lends mild interest at all seasons.

Acer buergerianum.

Problems and Maintenance.   Little or no maintenance is required in areas where this tree is adapted.

Cultivars.   Several selections for form, foliage color, and texture are available from nurseries specializing in Japanese maples.

Acer campestre 7

HEDGE MAPLE
Deciduous tree
Aceraceae (Maple Family)

Native Range. Europe and western Asia.

Useful Range. USDA Zones 5a–8b with selection of appropriate genetic material.

Function. Shade or patio tree, tall hedge or screen.

Size and Habit

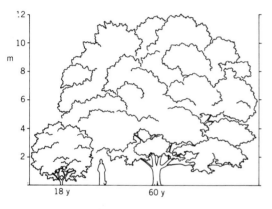

Acer campestre.

Adaptability. Its extensive natural range in Europe suggests a wide variation in adaptation. When possible, use material that has been grown successfully in the local area for some time. Selection of superior cultivars from this highly variable species should be worthwhile.

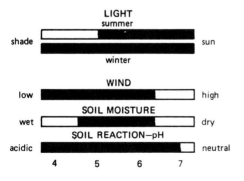

Seasonal Interest. *Foliage:* Dark green leaves, 5–10 cm/2–4 in. across with characteristic rounded lobes, give a clean, crisp texture during summer and remain green late, occasionally turning dull yellow-gold before falling.

Problems and Maintenance. This tree is relatively maintenance-free.

Cultivars. 'Evelyn' (Queen Elizabeth®, Plant Patent No. 4392, 1981) is reportedly faster growing and more upright than typical for the species, potentially useful for street planting in Zones 6b–7b. Other useful cultivars probably could be selected from the range of variation in form, foliage retention, autumn color, and adaptation that exists in this species.

Related Species

Acer miyabei 7 (miyabe maple). This low-branching tree, to 10–15 m/33–50 ft tall, is open in habit and useful in Zones 5a–7b+. 'Morton' (State Street®) is a mature tree in the Morton Arboretum, about 18 m/60 ft tall and 15 m/50 ft wide, with superior form and good yellow autumn foliage color. It may prove to be a more cold-hardy substitute for *A. campestre* but has not yet been released at this writing.

Acer griseum 6

PAPERBARK MAPLE
Deciduous tree
Aceraceae (Maple Family)

Native Range.   China.

Useful Range.   USDA Zones 5a–7b+.

Function.   Patio tree, specimen.

Size and Habit

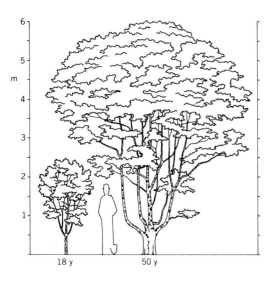

Acer griseum.

Adaptability.   Once thought not hardy north of Zone 6a, but with further trial at least some genetic material has been found hardy in southern Wisconsin (Zone 5a). Southern limits are not clearly established.

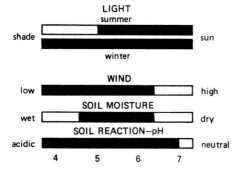

Seasonal Interest.   *Foliage:* Trifoliolate leaves of interesting texture, soft green, changing little in autumn before falling in most years and locations, but sometimes turn a good red color. *Bark:* Cinnamon-brown bark, exfoliating or smoothly polished on old trunks, by far the outstanding landscape feature of this tree, accentuated by the relatively open branching habit of mature trees.

Problems and Maintenance.   Relatively maintenance-free; some careful pruning may be desirable on some specimens to open the branching and display the bark to better advantage in summer. Availability is limited by propagation problems, but is improving with better techniques and the considerable attention this tree is now receiving.

Acer griseum, mature tree.

Cultivars.   Little or no selection of cultivars has been carried out because of problems in vegetative propagation. Virtually all trees from seedling lots have significant bark interest, another reason that little attention has been given to the selection of superior types. A few hybrids of *A. griseum* with other Asian trifoliate maples are handsome and promising, but not yet available.

Acer maximowiczianum 7

Synonym: *A. nikoense*
NIKKO MAPLE
Deciduous tree
Aceraceae (Maple Family)

Native Range.   Japan, China.

Useful Range.   USDA Zones 5a–7a.

Function.   Shade tree, specimen.

Size and Habit

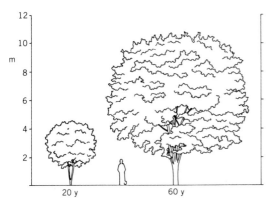

Acer maximowiczianum.

Adaptability

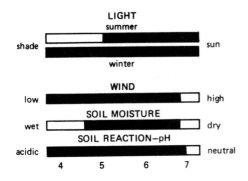

Seasonal Interest.   *Flowers:* Yellow with unfolding foliage, not conspicuous. *Foliage:* Trifoliolate, with leaflets 5–10 cm/2–4 in. long, medium green, fuzzy underneath, turning bright to deep red in autumn, on some trees, in some years.

Problems and Maintenance.   This tree is trouble-free and needs little maintenance.

Related Species

Acer diabolicum 6 (devil or horned maple). This Japanese maple seems better adapted to the South than many other maples and becomes a graceful and attractive small tree. It is seldom available and then only as the *f. purpurascens*, which has red flowers and fruits, and foliage that is reddish on emergence. It is useful, on a trial basis, in Zones 6a–8b.

Acer mandshuricum 6 (Manchurian maple). Another cold-hardy (Zones 4b–6b), round-topped, small shade tree with trifoliolate, dark green leaves, whitish underneath and with red petioles, turning bright red in autumn. As yet, it is seldom available.

Acer triflorum 6 (three-flower maple). Another small, trifoliolate maple, distinguished by attractive striped and flaking bark, similar in most other respects, including hardiness, to A. *maximowiczianum*.

Acer negundo 7

BOX ELDER, MANITOBA MAPLE
Deciduous tree
Aceraceae (Maple Family)

Native Range.   Eastern United States and adjacent Canada.

Useful Range.   USDA Zones 2a–8a.

Function.   Shade tree.

Size and Habit

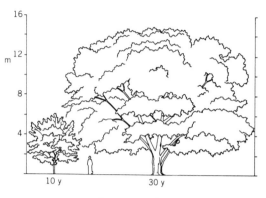

Acer negundo.

Adaptability.   This is one of the most cold-hardy of all shade trees, thus valued in cold regions where few other trees will grow. It is surprisingly widely adapted in the South but is not a high-priority tree in any but cold regions, because of weak wood and short life.

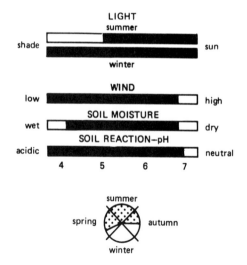

Seasonal Interest.   *Flowers:* Pale yellow, in early spring; not showy but with fleeting landscape interest. *Foliage:* Strikingly white variegated in the cultivar listed, but with little or no landscape value in the species.

Problems and Maintenance.   The most serious maintenance problem is pruning to remove storm damaged wood, sufficient reason for not growing the tree when alternatives are available. This seems to be less of a problem in the northern prairies, where the tree has specific value because of its adaptability, but box-elder bug remains a problem in many areas.

Acer negundo 'Variegatum.'

Cultivars.   'Baron' is a nonfruiting Canadian selection. 'Flamingo' has pink immature foliage, which develops into white and pink variegated green leaves. 'Sensation' (Plant Patent applied for) has stronger branching than typical for this species and is reported to have bright red autumn foliage. 'Variegatum,' with white-margined leaves, has long been used for outstanding summer effect, but is reliably cold-hardy only to Zone 5a.

Acer palmatum 6

JAPANESE MAPLE
Deciduous tree
Aceraceae (Maple Family)

Native Range.   Korea, Japan.

Useful Range.   USDA Zones 5b–9a, with selection of appropriate genetic material.

Function.   Specimen, patio tree, accent in border.

Size and Habit

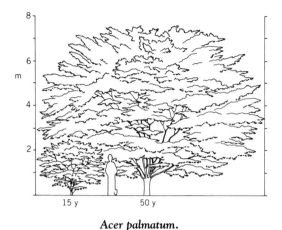

Acer palmatum.

Adaptability. Cold-hardiness varies with the cultivar. Most are cold-hardy to Zone 6b, only a few to Zone 5b. Young foliage is susceptible to drying in full sun and strong wind. Plant in protected sites.

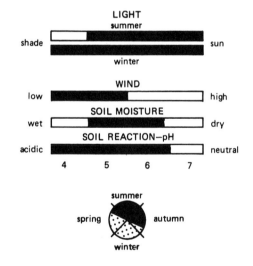

Seasonal Interest. *Foliage:* Handsomely textured, 5–10 cm/2–4 in. across, regularly palmately lobed in the species and some cultivars, incised to the petiole (effectively compound) in other cultivars, with many intermediates; medium green in summer (in the species) to pale green, yellow, or red-purple, that of most cultivars turns red in autumn. *Twigs:* Green to full or deep red in most cultivars; smooth, with a polished appearance. One cultivar has brilliant scar-let twigs, especially in late winter and early spring.

Problems and Maintenance. This tree is relatively trouble-free and needs little maintenance.

Cultivars. More than 200 cultivars of *A. palmatum* are available from nurseries in the United States and Canada. These vary in plant form, foliage color, degree of leaf dissection and number of lobes, and winter twig color. Since most nurseries carry only a few cultivars, it is necessary to know which cultivars are available locally, as well as to be aware of nurseries outside the local area that specialize in Japanese maples. Hardiness of cultivars varies, another reason for being in touch with local nurseries. A few of the more common cultivars are listed here:

'Atropurpureum' may once have been a distinct clone, but now represents a group of several clones with red foliage in spring and summer. Some of these lose much of their color as summer progresses, eventually becoming bronze or dull green before coloring again in autumn.

'Bloodgood' is considered by some to be the best of the red-leaved Japanese maples, with foliage opening bright crimson in spring, gradually turning a darker purple and fading little before fall.

'Burgundy Lace' has dark red, deeply divided and toothed, ribbonlike foliage, and grows into a wide-spreading tree to 4 m/13 ft tall and nearly as wide. It performs best in partial shade.

'Higasayama' (sometimes incorrectly called 'Roseo-marginata') has deeply divided leaves with seven variably twisted lobes, marginally rose-variegated in spring and early summer, changing to creamy-white later.

'Kagiri-nishiki' (synonym: 'Roseo-marginata') has deeply divided leaves, usually with five irregularly toothed and curved lobes, white-margined in early summer, the white turning to rose later.

'Osakazuki' has rather large yellow to yellow-green leaves in summer, turning brilliant red in autumn.

'Senkaki' (= 'Sango Kaku'; red-twigged Japanese maple) has light green foliage and brilliant coral-red twigs, especially effective in late winter and spring. In time it grows into a tree at least 7 m/23 ft tall.

The Dissectum Group of Japanese maple cultivars, once collectively called var. *dissectum,* includes cultivars having deeply incised, yellow-green to dark red leaves with very narrow, threadlike lobes. Most of the cultivars in this group are weeping and moundlike, or cascading if they are grafted on a high standard (rootstock trunk about 1.5 m/ 5 ft high), or staked up, or both. A few of the more popular ones are listed here:

'Crimson Queen' has a beautiful cascading habit and the most durable red foliage of any Dissectum cultivar, holding a deep red color until it turns brighter red in autumn.

'Ornatum' forms a mound of coppery red foliage from spring to midsummer, then fades to greenish by early autumn, when it turns bright red. It is said to be among the most cold-hardy of *A. palmatum* cultivars (to Zone 5b).

'Red Filigree Lace' has the most delicately threadlike red foliage of all these cultivars, holding its deep purple-red color until autumn, when it turns bright crimson. As might be expected for a plant with so little leaf area, it grows more slowly than the other cultivars listed.

'Seiryu' is unusual in the Dissectum Group for its treelike growth habit, to at least 3 m/10 ft in height. Its bright green foliage turns gold in autumn, sometimes flushed with red.

'Viridis' is not really a single cultivar, but a collective name for any of the better thread-leaved maples with green foliage. Plants sold under this name are usually weeping and mound-like, and most have yellow-gold foliage in autumn.

'Waterfall' is a cascading form when grafted high or staked, with light green foliage, yellow-ish at growing tips, turning to clear gold flushed with crimson tints in autumn.

Related Species

Acer circinatum 6 (vine maple). This small tree, native to the Pacific Northwest, is similar to *A. palmatum* except in having more showy flowers, greater shade tolerance, and twisted growth habit in its forest habitat. In cultivation it is upright in habit, reminiscent of *A. palmatum,* with handsome, smooth soft-green bark. Useful in Zones 6a–8b in the Pacific Northwest but not widely tested in eastern North America.

Acer japonicum 6 (fullmoon maple). This small tree is similar in effect to *A. palmatum,* but with nearly circular leaves having 7–11 lobes. The hardiest cultivars are useful in Zones 5a–8b, and perhaps even Zone 4b. Several cultivars have been selected, including the following:

f. *aconitifolium* (fernleaf fullmoon maple) is sometimes listed as 'Aconitifolium,' but is actually a collection of clones with deeply dissected leaves rather than a single cultivar. Most plants so-labeled have medium green leaves, turning bright crimson in autumn, and grow to 5 m/16 ft tall.

'Aureum' has bright yellow new foliage, turning green later in the summer, then orange and red in autumn. This tree grows slowly to 3 m/10 ft, and becomes broader than tall.

'Green Cascade' resembles a Dissectum type of *A. palmatum* more than the other forms of *A. japonicum,* with its deeply dissected foliage and cascading growth habit, when grafted high or staked.

Acer pseudo-sieboldianum 6 (Korean maple). This small tree from Manchuria and Korea resembles *A. palmatum,* but is considerably more cold-hardy, at least to Zone 4b, so it is an appropriate substitute in colder climates.

Acer pensylvanicum 7

STRIPED MAPLE, MOOSEWOOD
Deciduous tree
Aceraceae (Maple Family)

Native Range. Eastern United States and adjacent Canada.

Useful Range. USDA Zones 3b–7a.

Function. Specimen (in shade), woodland borders, naturalizing.

Size and Habit

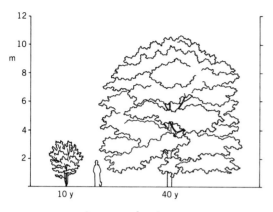

Acer pensylvanicum.

Adaptability. Grows best in at least partial shade.

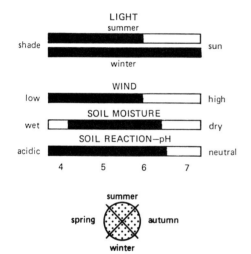

Seasonal Interest. *Flowers:* Small, yellow, in pendulous, chainlike clusters (racemes) to 15 cm/6 in. long, in late spring. *Foliage:* Coarse, pale green in spring, medium green in summer, and turning yellow in autumn. *Bark:* Young branches are longitudinally striped whitish and green, the outstanding landscape feature of this tree.

Problems and Maintenance. This tree is relatively trouble-free, given a proper site, and needs little or no maintenance.

Cultivars. 'Erythrocladum' has bright red twigs in winter, but seldom is available.

Related Species

Acer capillipes 7 (Japanese striped maple). This tree is similar to *A. pensylvanicum,* but has smaller leaves with red-petioles. It is more tolerant of full sun, less cold-hardy (Zone 5b–7b+).

Acer davidii 7 (David maple). Similar to the above species, with even more striking green and white striped bark and foliage that turns yellow to purple in autumn, this Chinese species is better adapted to southern conditions than *A. pensylvanicum* (Zones 7a–9a+), but not tolerant of full sun.

Acer rufinerve 7 (redvein maple). Another Japanese counterpart of *A. pensylvanicum,* this tree has somewhat finer-textured, darker green foliage, turning deep red in autumn. It is less cold-hardy (Zones 6a–8a+) than *A. pensylvanicum* but somewhat more satisfactory in sun.

Acer tegmentosum 6 (Manchurian striped maple). This small tree has the same striped bark that characterizes all the maples in this group. It is almost as cold-hardy (Zones 5a–7a) as *A. pensylvanicum,* more tolerant of sun, and has finer-textured foliage. 'White Tigress' is believed to be either a selection or a hybrid of *A. tegmentosum.* It has outstanding landscape interest and is more tolerant of sun and heat than most of the striped maples.

Acer tegmentosum.

Dipteronia sinensis 6. This rare small tree from central China, the only non-maple in the Aceraceae, grows with gracefully arching branches to 6–10 m/20–33 ft tall, with large, pinnately compound leaves, to 20–30 cm/8–12 in. long and composed of 9–13 leaflets. Its inconspicuous white flowers, opening in early to midsummer, are followed by interesting disklike, 2.5 cm/1 in. winged fruits. Potentially useful in Zones 6b–9a, but rarely available at this writing.

Acer platanoides 8

NORWAY MAPLE
Deciduous tree
Aceraceae (Maple Family)

Native Range. Europe, Caucasus Mountains.

Useful Range. USDA Zones 4a–7b with selection of appropriate genetic material.

Function. Shade, street tree.

Size and Habit

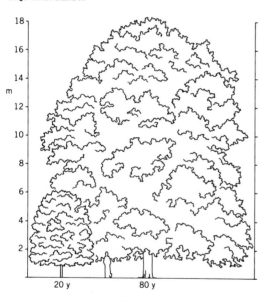

Acer platanoides.

Adaptability. Not as well adapted to city conditions as some maples.

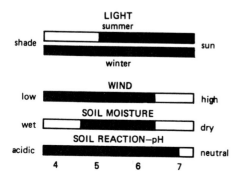

Seasonal Interest. *Flowers:* Yellow-green to bright yellow in early spring, in loose, rounded clusters, 5 cm/2 in. across, among the most colorful of any of the maples. *Foliage:* Dark green (white-variegated or deep red in cultivars) and coarse-textured, individually 10–18 cm/4–7 in. across, turning dull yellow in late autumn in some years.

Problems and Maintenance. Little or no maintenance is required except for removal or pruning of diseased or storm damaged trees. Verticillium wilt has been a problem in some areas, requiring removal and substitution. This tree's shallow roots and dense canopy make it impossible to maintain turfgrass or groundcovers underneath, and mulches are the best solution. Frost-cracking of trunks is sometimes a problem in Zone 4. Has not performed well as a street tree in small soil volumes.

Cultivars. 'Cleveland' is an excellent street tree with narrow oval form (taller than wide) not requiring as much lateral space as most trees of the species.

'Columnare' is much narrower than 'Cleveland' (height about twice its width), useful for small urban spaces or for vertical accent.

'Crimson King' and 'Royal Red' have dark red foliage during the entire growing season. They are cold-hardy to Zone 4b.

'Crimson Sentry' is a bud sport of 'Crimson King', with very upright, narrowly oval form, finer foliage texture, and brighter red color.

'Deborah' (Plant Patent No. 4944, 1978), 'Fairview'™, and 'Schwedleri' have deep red foliage in early summer, gradually fading to bronze and then green by late summer. 'Deborah' and 'Fairview' are better structurally than 'Schwedleri'.

'Drummondii' (= 'Variegatum'; harlequin maple) has striking white-margined foliage, making it a strong accent in any landscape. As is true for many variegated plants, it grows more slowly than its green counterparts.

'Emerald Queen' is a "standard" cultivar, against which others might be measured, with good oval to broadly rounded form, good site tolerances, especially for A. *platanoides*, and better-than-average golden autumn foliage.

'Erectum' is a tightly columnar tree, with height about three times its breadth, but probably no longer available.

'Ezestre' (Easy Street™), a bud sport of 'Columnare,' is reported to be faster growing than that cultivar, to about 12 m/40 ft tall and half as wide, with a narrowly pyramidal habit.

'Globosum' is low growing and broad spreading, with globose form, especially when young. It seldom exceeds 5 m/16 ft, so fits under utility wires.

'Greenlace' and Oregon Pride® ('Bailpride') have finely dissected foliage that gives a light, airy appearance and allows more light to reach the ground underneath. 'Greenlace' is probably no longer commercially available.

'Pond' (Emerald Lustre™, Plant Patent No. 4837, 1980), 'Jade Glen'™, 'Summershade'®, and 'Superform' (= 'Miller's Superform') are among the better types with broad rounded shape and green foliage. Of these, 'Superform' is outstanding for its symmetrical structure; 'Summershade' has heavy, leathery foliage and is unusually heat-tolerant; and 'Pond' (Emerald Lustre™) is very cold-hardy (Zone 4a), with lustrous foliage and red growing tips.

Related Species

Acer mono 7 (mono maple). This handsome intermediate-sized tree, to 15 m/50 ft, resembles an oversized Japanese maple, with foliage and form vaguely reminiscent of A. *palmatum*. Its foliage is bright light green when first expanding, then darker green, sometimes turning yellow in autumn. Useful in Zones 5a–7b+.

Acer pseudoplatanus 8 (sycamore maple). One of relatively few native European trees useful in our area, this makes a fine shade tree, similar in habit to A. *platanoides*, but with more leathery foliage and irregularly scaly, orange-brown bark.

It is less cold-hardy than A. *platanoides*, but useful in Zones 5b–7b and unusually salt-tolerant. In Zone 5b, trunks of young trees should be wrapped to reduce trunk scald during establishment. Several foliage variants have been named in Europe, where this is a popular shade tree. Leaves of 'Brilliantissimum' emerge pink, then turn yellow and finally green. Leaves of 'Atropurpureum' (= 'Spaethii') are deep purple underneath (many trees of the species are lightly tinged purple). Those of 'Variegatum' are white variegated, and those of 'Worleei' golden yellow with red petioles. Few of these variants are very widely available in the United States.

Acer pseudoplatanus.

Acer truncatum 6 (Shantung maple). This small tree from northern China is closely related to A. *mono* and A. *platanoides* in flower and foliage, but smaller than either. It is probably useful in Zones 4a–7b, but the species is seldom available. Recently, hybrids of A. *platanoides* × A. *truncatum* have been introduced: 'Keithsform' (Norwegian Sunset™; Plant Patent No. 7529, 1991) and 'Warrenred' (Pacific Sunset™; Plant

Patent No. 7433, 1991). Assuming a growth rate intermediate between the parents, they can be expected to function in size group 7. They have produced good fall color in Oregon, and they show initial promise as small street or patio trees.

Acer rubrum 8

RED OR SWAMP MAPLE
Deciduous tree
Aceraceae (Maple Family)

Native Range. Eastern United States and adjacent Canada, from the Gulf Coast and most of peninsular Florida to 49° north latitude in Canada.

Useful Range. USDA Zones 3b–9a with selection of appropriate genetic material.

Function. Shade, street tree.

Size and Habit

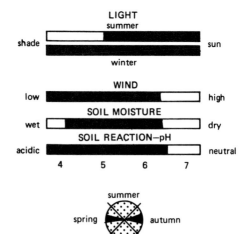

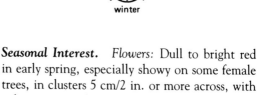

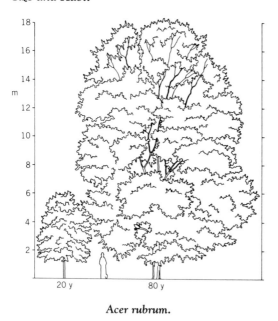

Acer rubrum.

Adaptability. Especially valued for its tolerance of poorly drained soil and even soil that is alternately wet and dry.

Seasonal Interest. *Flowers:* Dull to bright red in early spring, especially showy on some female trees, in clusters 5 cm/2 in. or more across, with color continued by the developing fruits. In general, flower color is more showy in the South than in the North. *Foliage:* Medium texture, whitish beneath, with red petioles, 5–10 cm/2–4 in. long, turning bright scarlet to yellow in autumn. *Trunks and branches:* Silvery gray branches add winter color and are interesting in contrast with flowers in spring.

Problems and Maintenance. Little maintenance is required except for pruning following storm damage, since this tree is weaker-wooded than A. platanoides and A. saccharum (but less prone to such damage than A. saccharinum).

Cultivars. Because of the wide variation in adaptability and seasonal interest in this species, there is a continuing selection of cultivars, some of which are too new to have been adequately tested. Delayed incompatibility has been seen in grafted trees in the past, but the increasing availability of own-root (cutting propagated) trees should eliminate this problem. A few of the most popular cultivars at this writing, as well as the following botanical variety, are included here.

Variety *drummondii* is a native population in the lowlands along the southeastern coast and lower Mississippi River Basin. These trees have unusually colorful red flowers and large red fruits (on females), pubescent foliage, coloring late but effectively in autumn, and scaly bark. They are very tolerant of wet soil, and they are favored over the more northern forms of this species in the coastal areas of the Deep South (at least in Zones 7a–9a+).

'Autumn Flame' was selected for its small leaves, giving fine foliage texture, early but persistent fall foliage color, cold-hardiness (Zone 3b), and compact, rounded form.

'Autumn Spire' (Plant Patent No. 7803, 1992) was selected for cold-hardiness, red fall foliage, and narrowly oval form (height $1\frac{1}{2}$ to 2 times width).

'Bowhall' (= 'Scanlon,' = 'Pyramidale') was selected for its good orange fall color, and especially for its narrowly oval to columnar form (height 2 to 3 times width). It is an excellent choice where space is at a premium.

'Columnare' is truly columnar in form, more so than either of the above (height close to 4 times width), with deep red-purple autumn foliage, but may no longer be available.

'Magnificent Magenta' (Plant Patent No. 7222, 1990; Burgundy Belle®), originating as a wild tree in northeastern Kansas and introduced by Earl Cully of Jacksonville, Illinois, is unusually drought-tolerant for this species, with bright red to intense burgundy autumn foliage and a densely oval head, growing to 14 m/45 ft tall and nearly as wide. It has withstood temperatures as low as −34° C/−30°F and is useful in at least Zones 5b–8b, probably also Zone 5a.

'Northwood' (Plant Patent No. 5053, 1980) is extremely cold-hardy (Zone 3b, perhaps even 3a) and has reasonably good fall color. It is most useful in the far north, where many cultivars of red maple fail.

'PNI 0268' (October Glory®) and 'Franksred' (Red Sunset®) are selections for outstanding late autumn foliage color. 'PNI 0268' (October Glory®) is especially late in coloring, an indication of late acclimation for winter that is confirmed by winter damage in Zones 3b–5. It is a superior selection for milder climates, however. 'Franksred' (Red Sunset®) starts to color earlier yet holds its foliage late. It is more cold-hardy than 'PNI 0268' (October Glory®), but not hardy in the colder parts of Zone 4.

'Schlesingeri' was selected for its early development of soft red-orange autumn foliage and broadly vase shaped form.

Related Hybrids. For many years, hybrids between *Acer rubrum* × *A. saccharinum* have been known, or at least suspected, but have been of only academic interest. In recent years, though, several selections have been made from these hybrids, collectively called *A.* × *freemanii*. These cultivars tend to have some of the characteristics of each parent, which could result in trees more widely adaptable than *A. rubrum* and more colorful than *A. saccharinum*, especially in autumn. These hybrids are dioecious like their *A. rubrum* parent, so may include potentially seedless cultivars. The well-known cultivars 'Armstrong' and 'Armstrong Two' have been in commerce for more than 40 years, and their usefulness is well known. Several others show promise, and their long-range prospects will become more clear in time.

'Celzam' (= Celebration®; Plant Patent No. 7279, 1991) is seedless, compact, and upright-pyramidal in habit, to 13–15 m/43–49 ft tall and 6–8 m/20–26 ft wide, with strong branching angles and golden-yellow fall foliage.

'Jeffersred' (Autumn Blaze®; Plant Patent No. 4864, 1982) has bright orange-red fall foliage, the best in this group, compact oval form, and tolerance of a wide range of site conditions. At least as a young tree it seems to flower sparsely, if at all. If that proves true in the long run it will, of course, be seedless but devoid of spring flowering interest.

'D.T.R. 102' (Autumn Fantasy®; Plant Patent No. 7655, 1991) has very good red fall color in most sites and broadly oval form.

'Lee's Red' and 'Morgan' (= 'Indian Summer') are both Canadian selections with excellent red autumn foliage. 'Morgan' is broadly globose and not as large as the above cultivars, but reputedly very cold hardy.

'Armstrong Two,' 'Celebration,' 'Marmo,' and 'Scarlet Sentinel' may all be useful, but do not have consistently good autumn color. 'Celebrity' is advertised as seedless.

Acer saccharinum 8

SILVER MAPLE
Deciduous tree
Aceraceae (Maple Family)

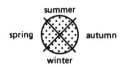

Native Range. Eastern United States and adjacent Canada, extending westward into the Central Plains, but rarely to the Gulf or southeastern Atlantic coasts.

Useful Range. USDA Zones 3a–9a with selection of appropriate genetic material.

Function. Shade tree, especially for quick, temporary effect.

Size and Habit

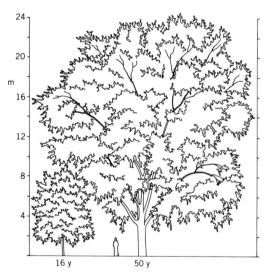

Acer saccharinum.

Adaptability. Especially valued for its tolerance of both dry and relatively wet soil and for its fast growth.

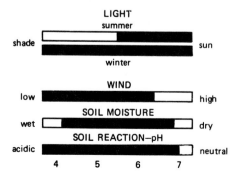

Seasonal Interest. *Flowers:* Dull reddish orange, not as showy as those of *A. platanoides* or *A. rubrum,* in early spring. *Foliage:* Medium- to fine-textured (in cutleaved forms), silvery gray underneath, 10–12 cm/4–5 in. across, sometimes turning clear, soft yellow in autumn but more often falling with little color change. *Trunk and branches:* Silvery gray branches add winter color, along with orange inner bark displayed as the bark flakes from trunks.

Problems and Maintenance. This is a high-maintenance tree because of several unfortunate characteristics. Its fast growth results in relatively soft wood, making it unusually susceptible to storm damage. This is often aggravated in street trees by topping (severe pruning allegedly done to reduce storm breakage). Unusually soft growth follows severe pruning, making the tree more susceptible to storm injury than if no pruning had been done. Furthermore, silver maple is shallow-rooted, causing lawn maintenance problems, and seeds freely, giving rise to weed seedlings.

Cultivars. There is always demand for this tree in spite of its faults, and cultivars have been selected to maximize the beauty of this species and to lessen the problems of storm breakage and weed seedlings.

'Beebe Cutleaf Weeping' has pendulous branches and deeply incised leaves.

'Blair' was selected in Blair, Nebraska, for its good form and structure and better fall color than average.

'Silver Queen' has mostly staminate (male) flowers and is reputedly seedless, but apparently not completely so.

'Skinneri' (Skinner's Cutleaf) was selected in Kansas more than 50 years ago for its incised leaves and gracefully horizontal to semi-weeping form. It produces the best developed central leader and widest crotches of any *A. saccharinum*

Problems and Maintenance. This plant is trouble-free but can be invasive, and it always should be bounded by pavement, buildings, or steel edging to contain it and prevent it from becoming a serious weed problem.

Cultivars. 'Variegatum' has irregularly white-margined leaves, is slightly less aggressive than the green-leaved species type, and is much more common.

Aesculus ×*carnea* 8

RED HORSE CHESTNUT
Deciduous tree
Hippocastanaceae (Horse Chestnut Family)

Hybrid Origin.   *A. hippocastanum* × *A. pavia.*

Useful Range.   USDA Zones 5a–8b.

Function.   Specimen, shade tree.

Size and Habit

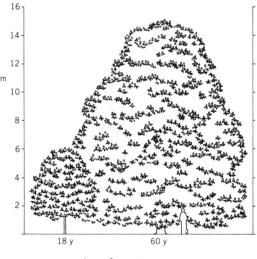

Aesculus ×*carnea.*

Seasonal Interest. *Flowers:* Pink to red flowers in erect pyramidal clusters, 12–20 cm/5–8 in. long, in late spring. *Foliage:* Dark green, coarse, palmately compound with leaflets to 25 cm/10 in. long. *Fruits:* Glossy brown nuts in large husks.

Problems and Maintenance. Leaf, twig, and fruit litter makes this tree a poor choice for street or urban use. Leaf scorch disease is less serious than with *A. hippocastanum,* but it can be a problem in some areas. Sun-scald of trunks also can be a problem in Zone 5a.

Cultivars. 'Briotii' (ruby horse chestnut) eventually grows to 15 m/50 ft tall, with bright rose-red flowers and deep green foliage. 'O'Neill Red' is similar but with double red flowers and lighter green foliage. *A.* ×*plantierensis,* until recently called *A.* ×*carnea* f. *plantierensis,* grows to 20 m/66 ft tall, and has pale pink flowers and fruits that develop husks but not seeds. This form has been separated from *A.* ×*carnea* because it is

Adaptability. This hybrid is somewhat more drought-tolerant than *A. hippocastanum.*

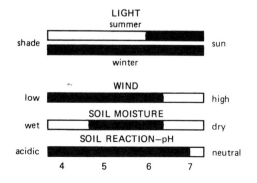

Aesculus hippocastanum 'Baumannii.'

triploid and sterile (parentage: *A. hippocastanum* pollinated by *A. ×carnea*), whereas *A. ×carnea* is tetraploid and fertile.

Related Species and Hybrids

Aesculus hippocastanum 8 (common horse chestnut). This Balkan tree is similar to its hybrid, *A. ×carnea*, except slightly larger at maturity, to 25 m/82 ft tall, and more susceptible to drought injury and leaf scorch disease. Its white flowers have red and yellow markings inside. There is little reason for using this species in preference to *A. ×carnea* other than its slightly greater cold-hardiness (Zone 4). When this species is used, the sterile, double-flowered selection 'Baumanii' (Bauman horse chestnut) may be preferred, because it is not pollinated and thus holds its flowers a little longer than the species type and is free of fruit litter.

Aesculus pavia 6 (red buckeye). This small, shrubby tree, to 6–8 m/20–26 ft tall, native to the southeastern United States coastal plain, has dark red tubular flowers. It is susceptible to a serious leaf spot disease in some areas, but otherwise useful in Zones 5b–9a.

Aesculus splendens 5 (flame or Louisiana buckeye). This is an irregularly growing upright shrub native to the south-central United States. It has tubular flowers somewhat brighter red than those of *A. pavia*, and it is similar in other respects. Most authorities now consider it to be a variant of *A. pavia* rather than a separate species, but in any case it is recognized as an entity in landscape use because of its unusually showy flowers and slightly smaller stature. It is useful in the same range as *A. pavia*.

Aesculus sylvatica 4 (*A. georgiana*; painted or Georgia buckeye). This is a small shrubby buckeye from the southeastern United States Piedmont, with creamy, pale yellow, or yellow-green flowers, sometimes over-tinted with pink or red. It is seldom available, but it is probably useful in Zones 5b–8b.

Aesculus glabra 7

OHIO BUCKEYE
Deciduous tree
Hippocastanaceae (Horse Chestnut Family)

Native Range. Central midwestern United States and southwestward to Texas.

Useful Range. USDA Zones 3a–8b.

Function. Specimen, shade tree.

Size and Habit

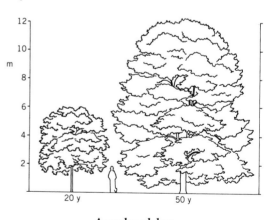

Aesculus glabra.

Adaptability. This tree is more drought-resistant than the horse chestnuts and better adapted to the Midwest.

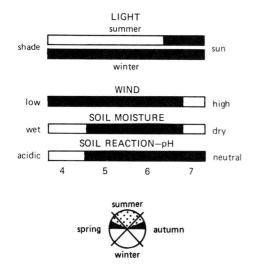

LIGHT
summer
shade | sun
winter

WIND
low | high
SOIL MOISTURE
wet | dry
SOIL REACTION—pH
acidic | neutral
4   5   6   7

summer
spring ⊗ autumn
winter

Seasonal Interest. *Flowers.* Small, pale yellow flowers in erect, pyramidal clusters, 10–15 cm/ 4–6 in. long, in middle spring. *Foliage:* Medium green, palmately compound, not as coarse as that of the horse chestnuts, with leaflets 8–12 cm/3–5 in. long, turning yellow or orange-red in autumn. *Fruits:* Smooth brown nuts in husks.

Problems and Maintenance. Leaf, twig, and fruit litter is messy, but this is not as great a problem as it is with the horse chestnuts because all plant parts are smaller. This tree is considered difficult to transplant.

Varieties. Var. *arguta* is a shrub or small shrubby tree, 3–6 m/10–20 ft, native to the southwestern part of its natural range from Arkansas to Texas, and presumably better adapted to cultivation than the species would be in that region, but not functional as a shade tree.

Related Species and Hybrids

Aesculus californica 6 (California buckeye). This wide-spreading shrubby tree is primarily of landscape interest outside our range, namely, in the drier climates of California and Texas; but there also has been considerable interest within our range, namely, East Texas to the Carolinas. It differs from other *Aesculus* species in its tolerance of dry soils (it drops its leaves early in extreme drought, then returns after spring rains) and in its silvery trunk and branches. Flowers are fragrant and creamy white with red and yellow markings, in late spring. *A. californica* is hardy in Zones 7b–9a, perhaps colder zones as well.

Aesculus flava 8 (synonym: *A. octandra*; yellow or sweet buckeye). This large tree is native to central Appalachia and westward through the Ohio River valley. Like the smaller *A. glabra*, it is better adapted and more trouble-free in the central United States (USDA Zones 5a–8a) than *A. hippocastanum*, which has been more widely used in the past. The pink-flowered variety *virginica* is not widely available.

Most *Aesculus* species hybridize readily when their ranges overlap in the wild, and in cultivation the opportunities for hybridization are even greater because of the proximity of trees from many parts of the world. Only a few hybrids are presently of interest, but others are potentially useful.

A. ×hybrida (*A. flava × A. pavia*) 8 is thought to be a natural hybrid and includes large trees with flowers that are yellow, red, or both. This hybrid is not well known in commerce, but is of interest because of its involvement in the following complex hybrid.

A. ×arnoldiana (probably *A. glabra × A. ×hybrida*) 7 was first selected in the Arnold Arboretum. The recent introduction from the Minnesota Landscape Arboretum, 'Autumn Splendor,' is thought to belong to *A. ×arnoldiana* (although it is sometimes listed in catalogs as a cultivar of *A. sylvatica*). This is a medium-sized tree about the same size and appearance as *A. glabra*. It has yellow flowers with an orange-red blotch and glossy dark green, scorch-free foliage in summer, turning maroon-red in autumn, much more colorful than other buckeyes.

Aesculus parviflora 5

BOTTLEBRUSH BUCKEYE
Deciduous shrub
Hippocastanaceae (Horse Chestnut Family)

Native Range. Southeastern United States.

Useful Range. USDA Zones 5a–9a.

Size and Habit

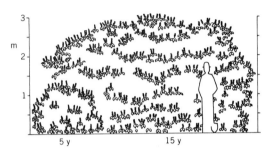

Aesculus parviflora.

Adaptability

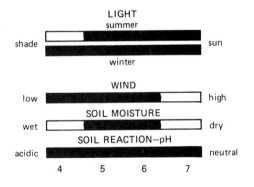

Function. Specimen, massing. Because of its tendency to spread to a great width, this plant should be reserved for relatively large-scale situations.

Seasonal Interest. *Flowers:* White flowers in cylindrical clusters to 25 cm/10 in., in midsummer. *Foliage:* Dark green, palmately compound, with leaflets 10–20 cm/4–8 in. long, producing a distinctively coarse texture and falling with little color change in autumn. *Fruits:* Smooth brown nuts in husks.

Problems and Maintenance. This impressive plant is relatively maintenance-free, since the fruit and foliage litter remain hidden beneath the moundlike form, and leaf-scorch is not usually a serious problem. In all but very large-scale situations, pruning and digging out sucker shoots may be necessary to control size.

Varieties and Cultivars. The variety *serotina*, from Alabama, flowers about three weeks later than average for the species type: in late summer. The selection 'Rogers' is intermediate in flowering time, with much larger flower clusters, to 45 cm/18 in. long.

Ailanthus altissima 7–8

Synonym: *A. Glandulosa*
TREE OF HEAVEN
Deciduous tree
Simaroubaceae (Quassia Family)

Native Range. Northern China; naturalized in the eastern United States.

Useful Range. USDA Zones 5a–9a.

Function. Fast-growing shade tree in situations where other trees will not grow.

Size and Habit

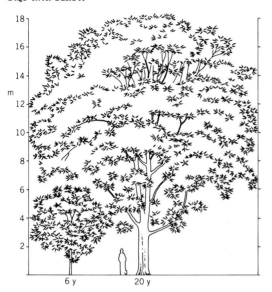

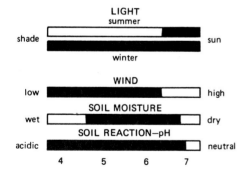

Ailanthus altissima.

Adaptability. This is among the most widely adaptable of all trees, growing rapidly even in poor soil, in warm and moderately cold climates, and in proximity to salt at the seashore or near salted roads in the North. Its adaptability has made it both a noxious weed in good soils and a useful shade tree in many inner city environments. Individual trees are short-lived.

LIGHT
summer
shade ▭ sun

winter
shade ▭ sun

WIND
low ▭ high

SOIL MOISTURE
wet ▭ dry

SOIL REACTION–pH
acidic ▭ neutral
4   5   6   7

Seasonal Interest. *Flowers:* Dioecious plant, relatively inconspicuous in bloom, but staminate (male) flowers give off a disagreeable odor. *Foliage:* Handsome, dark green, pinnately compound leaves, to 0.8 m/2.6 ft long, give this tree a coarse, "tropical" appearance. *Fruits:* Dull yellow to bright red on individual female trees, ornamental in late summer and early autumn.

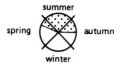

Problems and Maintenance. When both male and female trees are present, seedlings will germinate and grow in any available space, becoming a serious weed problem. This tree is short-lived with soft wood easily damaged by wind and ice, and it produces considerable foliage and twig litter.

Varieties. Var. *erythrocarpa* has dark green foliage, whitened underneath, and bright red fruits in late summer and early autumn.

Related Species

Toona sinensis 6–7 (synonym: *Cedrela sinensis*; Chinese toon). This Chinese tree is reminiscent of *Ailanthus* in form, even though it is not of the same family, but rather the Meliaceae (mahogany family), with very large (to 60 cm/2 ft) pinnately compound leaves and conspicuous clusters of whitish flowers in midsummer. Foliage is pink or red as it emerges. The selection 'Flamingo' has unusually showy bright pink expanding foliage, which turns briefly yellow, then bright green until autumn, when it turns yellow again before dropping. Useful in Zones 7a–9a+, and sheltered sites in Zone 6b.

Melia azedarach 6 (chinaberry tree). This fast-growing but short-lived tree in the Meliaceae is adapted to poor growing conditions, but only in the Deep South or the Southwest (Zones 8b–9a+). It is native to the Himalayas but naturalized throughout the tropics and subtropics, including the warmest areas of the continental United States. Seasonal interest includes fragrant, pale purple flowers in middle spring, dense, dark green foliage all summer, and, in autumn, small, pale yellow fruits that are toxic to animals, including humans.

Picrasma ailanthoides 7 (synonym: *Picrasma quassioides*; Korean bitternut). This small tree (to 10 m/33ft) is similar in form and foliage to *Ailanthus* and belongs to the same family, but is slower growing, with reddish brown bark and red to yellow autumn foliage. It is hardy in Zones 6b–9a+ but probably not commercially available.

Ajuga reptans 2

CARPET BUGLE, BUGLEWEED
Evergreen or semievergreen groundcover
Lamiaceae (Labiatae; Mint Family)

Native Range. Europe, naturalized locally in North America.

Useful Range. USDA Zones 3b–9a.

Function. Groundcover.

Size and Habit

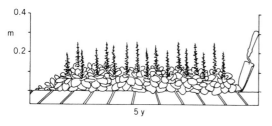

Ajuga reptans.

Adaptability. Protection from full sun is necessary for best results in the Midwest and South.

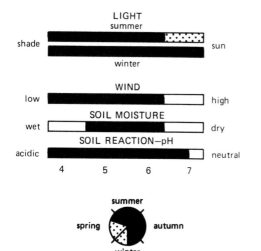

Seasonal Interest. *Flowers:* Blue, rose-pink, or white, small but borne in large numbers in spikelike clusters to 15 cm/6 in. tall, very showy in late spring. *Foliage:* Nearly evergreen, lustrous leaves make a solid mat of interesting texture, but in the North become dull and dingy by late winter.

Problems and Maintenance. This excellent groundcover is unusually trouble-free and requires little maintenance after establishment, or even during establishment, since it grows rapidly. Its rapid growth can be a problem, however, and planting beds sometimes are best enclosed in edging to prevent encroachment into turf areas.

Cultivars. The following are a few of the most popular cultivars: 'Alba' has creamy white flowers and light green foliage; 'Bronze Beauty' is vigorous, with bronze foliage and blue flowers; 'Burgundy Glow' has silvery white and green foliage, partly flushed with red-purple, making a most unusual color combination with its light blue flowers; 'Catlin's Giant' is taller and larger in all respects, with large bronzed leaves, an effective groundcover plant; 'Emerald Green' has bright green foliage and a clump-forming growth habit; 'Pink Beauty and 'Rosy Spires' have rosy pink flowers and bright green foliage; 'Silver Beauty' has a refined growth habit, with silvery green and white foliage and light blue flowers.

Related Species

Ajuga genevensis 2 (Geneva or alpine bugleweed). This Eurasian species differs from A. *reptans* in that it does not spread as vigorously and so is less invasive, but it may be a little less effective as a groundcover.

Ajuga pyramidalis 2 (pyramidal bugleweed). This European species has larger leaves and flower spikes than those of A. *reptans* and tends to remain more in a clump than most of the more invasive A. *reptans* cultivars. It is usually seen as the selection 'Metallica Crispa,' which has deeply bronzed leaves and rich blue flowers.

Akebia quinata 1 and 2

Deciduous or semievergreen vine or groundcover
Lardizabalaceae (Lardizabala Family)

Native Range.   China, Korea, and Japan.

Useful Range.   USDA Zones 4b–9a.

Function.   Screen (with support), groundcover.

Size and Habit.   This fine-textured vine climbs rapidly by twining and makes an effective screen on a trellis, chain-link fence, or similar support. Its neat texture makes it a good choice for small-scale situations, provided that its growth can be kept within bounds.

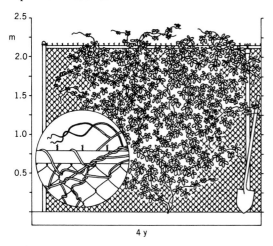

Akebia quinata.

Adaptability.   Grows rapidly on good soil.

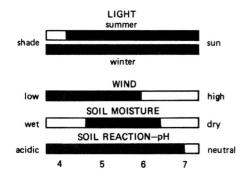

Seasonal Interest.   *Flowers:* Small, fragrant, but inconspicuous, deep red-purple flowers in early spring. *Foliage:* Dark green, fine-textured, palmately compound foliage gives neat textural interest and persists well into winter. *Fruits:* Interesting purplish pods that open to show black seeds. Fruits seldom are formed in cultivation without hand cross-pollination between clones.

Problems and Maintenance.   This vine requires little or no maintenance except when it is necessary to prune it to prevent it from overgrowing the planting site. When it is used as a groundcover, initial mulching or weeding is necessary, but in good soil it covers rapidly and little further weed control is necessary. At times it may be overly aggressive, climbing over adjacent shrubs.

Cultivars.   None are available.

Related Species

Akebia trifoliata 1 and 2 and *Akebia* ×*pentaphylla* 1 and 2 (*A. quinata* × *A. trifoliata*).   These are similar to *A. quinata* in adaptability and landscape effect, but they are slightly less handsome and rarely available.

Decaisnea fargesii 5 (blue bean shrub).   This large, rather coarse shrub in the Lardizabalaceae (Lardizabala Family) from western China, grows to about 3 m/10 ft tall and at least as wide, with compound leaves 50–80 cm/20–32 in. long. Its 2.5 cm/1 in. yellowish green flowers hang in drooping clusters, 25–50 cm/10–20 in. long, and are followed, when fertilization takes place, by dull metallic blue pods, resembling thick bean pods, 5–10 cm/2–4 in. long and 2 cm/0.8 in. thick. Useful in average to moist soil and full sun to half-shade, in Zones 6a–9a.

Holboellia coriacea 1.   This vigorous evergreen vine in the Lardizabalaceae from central China climbs by twining to heights of at least 6 m/ 20 ft, perhaps twice that in favorable sites. Its compound leaves are composed of three leaflets, each 6–15 cm/2.4–6 in. long. This vigorous climber is useful for year-round screening in Zones 8a–9a+, but not widely available.

Stauntonia hexaphylla 1. This vigorous evergreen vine from Japan and Korea is closely related to *Holboellia* and similar in appearance, but differing in having three to seven leaflets. Probably useful in about the same areas as *Holboellia* but not widely available.

Albizia julibrissin 6

SILK TREE, MIMOSA
Deciduous tree
Fabaceae (Leguminosae; Pea Family)

Native Range.   Central Asia: Iran to China.

Useful Range.   USDA Zones 6a–9a+ with selection of appropriate genetic material (see Cultivars).

Function.   Specimen, patio tree, border accent. Used primarily for its seasonal color and texture, secondarily for function.

Size and Habit

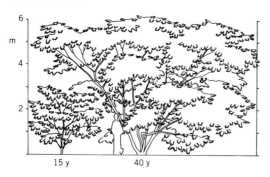

Albizia julibrissin.

Adaptability.   This tree is unusually well adapted to hot, dry summers.

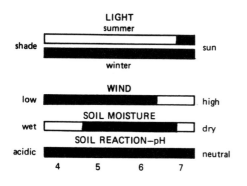

Seasonal Interest.   *Flowers:* Pale to rosy pink flowers in fluffy round clusters from early to midsummer in the South and mid- to late summer in the North, remaining colorful for a month or more. *Foliage:* Extremely fine-textured, bright green, doubly compound leaves give striking contrast to most other foliage and add to the gracefulness of the plant. *Fruits:* Flat pods add interest in late summer and early autumn.

Albizia julibrissin.

Albizia julibrissin.

Problems and Maintenance. This tree is subject to mimosa webworm and requires a spray program to avoid disfiguring of foliage in some areas. Many trees are susceptible to a serious disease, mimosa wilt, but there are resistant clones (see Cultivars). It is subject to topkill in some winters in the northern part of its useful range and to wind damage, but it returns to good form in a few years with corrective pruning. As a result of these problems, this tree is a short-lived, high-maintenance plant. But in spite of this, it is widely used for its unique interest.

Cultivars. 'Charlotte' and 'Tryon' have been selected by the U.S. Department of Agriculture as resistant to mimosa wilt disease. They are useful in Zones 7b–9a+.

'Ernest Wilson' is an unusually hardy and low-growing form selected from seed collected by E. H. Wilson in Korea in 1918 and released as a cultivar by the Arnold Arboretum 50 years later. It is useful in Zones 6a–9a+ and can be propagated easily by juvenile softwood cuttings forced from root pieces.

F. rosea is a collective name without current botanical standing that includes individual trees having unusual hardiness and deep pink flower color, among them 'Ernest Wilson.'

Alnus glutinosa 7–8

EUROPEAN OR BLACK ALDER
Deciduous tree
Betulaceae (Birch Family)

Native Range. Northern Eurasia and southward to Caucasus.

Useful Range. USDA Zones 4a–8b.

Function. Fast-growing shade tree, specimen, naturalizing.

Size and Habit

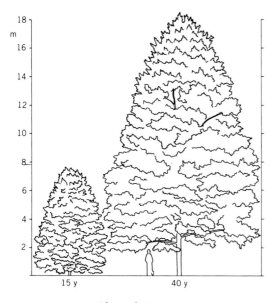

Alnus glutinosa.

Adaptability. Alders are unusual in that they combine a tolerance of wet soils and the ability to use atmospheric nitrogen with the help of nitrogen-fixing bacteria. In this way, they grow quickly in soils that are both infertile and poorly drained, as well as in drier sites, making them useful for urban planting.

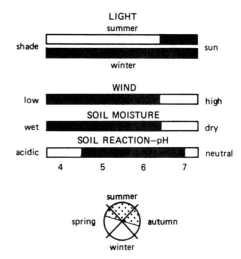

Seasonal Interest. *Flowers:* Dormant flower catkins of two distinct types (male and female) add quiet interest in winter, especially when the male catkins expand and open in late winter and spring. *Foliage:* Leaves, rounded and 5–10 cm/ 2–4 in. long, remain dark green all summer (when not infested with leaf miners or tent caterpillars) and into autumn, when they fall with little color change.

Problems and Maintenance.   Alders are relatively short-lived in most situations, and their foliage may be disfigured by leaf miners, tent caterpillars, and woolly alder aphids if a spray program is not provided. Their broad adaptability makes them useful in some situations in spite of their problems.

Cultivars.   'Imperialis' and 'Laciniata' both have deeply cut foliage, giving much finer texture than the species type. 'Laciniata' is the more vigorous of the two, with better growth habit, but it seems likely that not all plants of 'Laciniata' are true to name. 'Pyramidalis' has a narrowly pyramidal shape and is somewhat denser and lower branching than the species type. Several other cultivars have been selected in Europe but are seldom, if ever, used in North America.

Related Species

Alnus incana 6 (European white alder).   This is smaller and slower growing than *A. glutinosa* and extremely cold-hardy. It has escaped into the wild in parts of the northeastern United States, and often assumed to be native. It may be available for landscape use, but is used much less than *A. glutinosa.*

Alnus rubra 7 (synonym: *A. oregona;* red alder). This native of the Pacific Northwest is at least as large as *A. glutinosa.* It is said to be more susceptible to tent caterpillars than other alders, and in any case is probably of little landscape interest in eastern North America.

Alnus rugosa 6 (speckled alder) and *A. serrulata* 6 (smooth or hazel alder).   These are smaller North American species, probably of interest only for naturalizing in wet sites.

Amelanchier laevis 6–7

ALLEGHENY SERVICEBERRY
Deciduous tree or large shrub
Rosaceae (Rose Family)

Native Range.   Northeastern United States and adjacent Canada, west to Iowa, south to northern Georgia.

Useful Range.   USDA Zones 3b–8a.

Function.   Specimen or patio tree or shrub, border, naturalizing.

Size and Habit

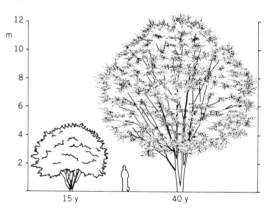

Amelanchier laevis.

Adaptability.   Serviceberries are widely adapted, but there are some differences among species. *A. laevis* as well as *A. alnifolia, A. canadensis,* and *A. ×grandiflora* grow well in moist and shady locations, while *A. arborea* and the low species *A. humilis, A. spicata,* and *A. stolonifera* are more tolerant of dry, open sites. When possible, select plants from material native to the region where they will be used.

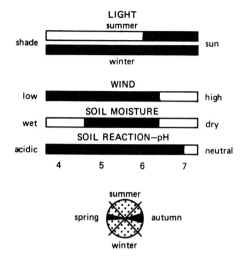

LIGHT
summer
shade ▭ sun
winter

WIND
low ▭ high

SOIL MOISTURE
wet ▭ dry

SOIL REACTION–pH
acidic ▭ neutral
4   5   6   7

spring · summer · autumn · winter

Amelanchier laevis.

Amelanchier laevis.

Seasonal Interest. *Flowers:* Small but numerous in early spring, in nodding clusters, contrasting with the reddish bronze young foliage, lasting for only a few days. *Foliage:* Leaves are red-bronze as they unfold, green when fully expanded (3–8 cm/1–3 in. long), turning red-orange to russet-gold in autumn and falling early. *Fruits:* Briefly red, ripening purple-black, and usually taken quickly by birds, but valued highly for pie and preserve making. *Bark:* Silvery gray with subtle darker gray longitudinal striping on trunks and larger branches.

Problems and Maintenance. *Amelanchier* species are subject to several troubles common to species in the pome-fruit subfamily of the rose family, especially fire blight and mites. These can be controlled without difficulty provided the basic site requirements of the trees are met. Scale insects can also be a problem in warmer areas. In spite of such troubles, serviceberries are not considered high-maintenance trees, especially in naturalized plantings.

Cultivars. All have outstanding white flowers and red to bronze new growth, but differ in habit, autumn foliage, and duration of color in spring foliage. 'Cumulus' is fast growing and broadly columnar, its width more than half its height, with orange autumn foliage. 'Flambeau' is distinctive for its striking bronze-purple young leaves in spring; its autumn foliage is a delicate, soft orange. 'Prince Charles' (Plant Patent No. 6039, 1987) is more oval in shape and early flowering, with deep orange fall foliage.

Related Species and Hybrids

Amelanchier alnifolia 4–5 (saskatoon, juneberry, serviceberry). This is the common serviceberry of the Northwest and Canadian prairies. There its large fruits are valued for preserves and pies, and several cultivars have been selected for both fruiting and landscape value. There is little to recommend it in eastern North American, since it is disease-prone in humid climates, and in any case there are excellent alternatives in A. *laevis* and A. ×*grandiflora.*

Amelanchier arborea 7 (synonym: often called A. *canadensis,* a name properly given to a different species (see below); most plants sold today as A. *canadensis* are really A. *arborea;* shadblow, downy serviceberry, juneberry). This is the largest species of *Amelanchier,* eventually reaching heights up to 20 m/66 ft, and trunk diameters to 40 cm/1.3 ft., slightly larger than most trees of A. *laevis.* Even though these two species are interchangeable for flowering effect in many situ-

Amelanchier arborea.

ations, A. *arborea* is sometimes at a disadvantage because it tends to "sucker" more heavily, making it harder to maintain in tree form. Moreover, its yellow autumn foliage is usually much inferior to the orange or red foliage of A. *laevis*. A. *arborea* is equally showy in flower, however, with a short-lived but beautiful billowy effect, and differs from A. *laevis* in its silvery green, downy new foliage and fruits that ripen red-purple, drier and more insipid than the juicy purple-black berries of A. *laevis*. Useful in Zones 3b–8a. Few, if any, cultivars are available.

Amelanchier canadensis 5–6. This is not to be confused with A. *arborea*, which is often sold as A. *canadensis*. It is an upright thicket-forming shrub growing to 3 m/10 ft tall and nearly as wide. Its flowers are borne in upright clusters unlike the nodding ones of A. *arborea*, A. *laevis*, and A. ×*grandiflora*, and with age it becomes more moundlike than treelike. Useful in Zones 4b–8a. The original plant of 'Prince William' (Plant Patent No. 6040, 1987) which grew to a

mass nearly 10 feet tall and wide in 20 years in Wisconsin, belongs to this species. An unusual cultivar that *may* (or may not) belong to A. *canadensis* is 'Silver Fountain,' a beautiful, strongly pendulous tree with pure white flowers, to perhaps 3–6 m/10–20 ft tall.

Amelanchier ×*grandiflora* 6–7 (apple serviceberry). This is a group of tetraploid, naturally occurring hybrids between the two large *Amelanchier* species, A. *arborea* and A. *laevis*, and is similar to them in landscape effect. The foliage is not as downy as that of A. *arborea* nor as red at emergence as A. *laevis*, and the flowers are larger and more showy than either parent. In general, A. ×*grandiflora* is more similar to A. *laevis* than to A. *arborea* in its relative freedom from "suckering," and it is useful in Zones 3b–8a. In general, A. ×*grandiflora* cultivars are useful in the same way as flowering crabapples and hawthorns. Several excellent cultivars have been selected, including the following.

'Autumn Brilliance' (Plant Patent No. 5717, 1986) has exceptional red-orange fall color. 'Cole's Select' (= 'Cole') has excellent red autumn foliage. 'Forest Prince' is a promising newer selection for its vigor and outstanding foliage. 'Princess Diana' (Plant Patent No. 6041, 1987) has the brightest red autumn foliage of all and has the usual flowering interest. 'Robin Hill' and 'Rubescens' are distinctive for their pink and purple-pink flower buds, respectively. In both cases, the flowers open white or faintly pink. 'Robin Hill' is narrower than average in overall shape and is the earliest serviceberry to flower. 'Strata' is most striking in flower because of its horizontally layered branching, and it also has good fall color.

Amelanchier humilis 3–4 (low serviceberry), *Amelanchier spicata* 3–4 (low serviceberry), and *Amelanchier stolonifera* 3–4 (running serviceberry). These species are all relatively low, thicket-forming shrubs with upright branches and inflorescences. They offer hardiness and seasonal interest similar to that of the larger serviceberries, but with little of their gracefulness. Their usefulness is limited to massing on dry soil, or for fruit production.

Amelanchier ×*lamarckii* 6 (A. *canadensis* × A. *laevis*; Lamarck serviceberry). This naturally occurring hybrid group is not greatly different from *A.* ×*grandiflora* and is often confused with it. The selection 'Ballerina' is unusually vigorous, with large clusters of pure white flowers, slightly later than *A.* ×*grandiflora* cultivars, and slightly narrower elliptical leaves that turn red-bronze in autumn.

Amorpha canescens 3

LEADPLANT

Deciduous shrub

Fabaceae (Leguminosae; Pea Family)

Native Range. Central North America: Manitoba and Saskatchewan to Louisiana and northern Mexico.

Useful Range. USDA Zones 3a–9a.

Function. Border, specimen.

Size and Habit. *A. canescens* is a subshrub, killing to the ground each winter over most of its useful range and returning to flower in a single growing season.

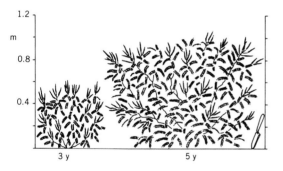

Amorpha canescens.

Adaptability. This shrub is unusually well adapted to hot climates and dry, infertile soils, probably the principal reason to consider it for landscape use.

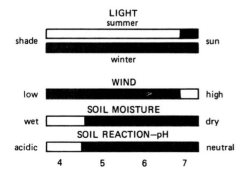

Seasonal Interest. *Flowers:* Small, blue in fairly colorful spikes to 15 cm/6 in. long, from early to middle summer. *Foliage:* Gray, hairy, compound with many small leaflets, producing fine texture. *Fruits:* Small pods, not conspicuous.

Problems and Maintenance. Leadplant is one of the most trouble-free of shrubs, requiring little or no maintenance other than annual removal of the winterkilled top when necessary.

Related Species

Amorpha fruticosa 6 (false indigo). Unlike *A. canescens,* this large shrub, native to much of our area, does not regularly winterkill to the ground except from Zone 4 northward. Since it becomes too large and ungainly to be useful, it should be given radical renewal pruning every year or two. Even then it lacks the interest of *A. canescens,* and in most situations other shrubs perform more effectively. Still, it does tolerate difficult site conditions and it is widely adapted as a native plant from New England to Saskatchewan and southward to Florida and Mexico in Zones 3b–9a.

Amorpha nana 3 (dwarf false indigo). This tidy dwarf shrub with very fine-textured green foliage, native from Manitoba and Saskatchewan to northern Mexico, is useful as a border shrub for its foliage and purple flowers, in spikes to 10 cm/4 in. long in late spring, in Zones 3a–9a.

Ampelopsis brevipedunculata 1

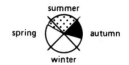

PORCELAIN OR AMUR AMPELOPSIS
Deciduous vine
Vitaceae (Grape Family)

Native Range.   Northeastern Asia.

Useful Range.   USDA Zones 5a–9a.

Function.   Screen (with support), specimen.

Size and Habit.   Grows vigorously and climbs by tendrils to heights of 5 m/16 ft or greater.

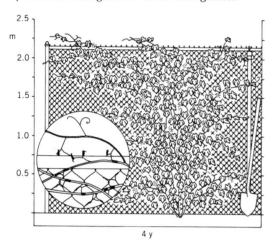

Ampelopsis brevipedunculata.

Adaptability.   This widely adapted vine grows well in most soil, but it can be slow in establishment.

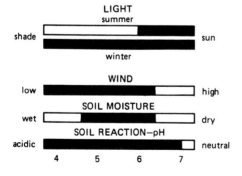

Seasonal Interest.   *Foliage:* Bright green, lobed, handsomely textured. *Fruits:* Small berries that appear to be made of porcelain, progressing through pastel shades of yellow, lilac, green, and blue, all colors sometimes appearing in a single cluster.

Problems and Maintenance.   This vine is relatively trouble-free, but can become weedy, and the foliage may be chewed by insects such as Japanese beetle.

Varieties and Cultivars.   'Elegans' has smaller, white and pink variegated leaves and slower growth, is less useful for screening, but is interesting for specimen use. Var. *maximowiczii* has more finely dissected foliage than the species type and predominantly blue fruits.

Related Species

Ampelopsis arborea 1 (peppervine).   This vigorous vine is graceful but not dense enough to be very functional as a screen. The foliage is doubly compound and semievergreen, the flowers are fairly large but not conspicuous, and the fruits are about the same size as those of *A. brevipedunculata* but dark purple. It may need to be pruned for restraint in warmer areas. Hardy in Zones 7b–9a+.

Several other species of *Ampelopsis* have been cultivated, most with no advantage over those listed here. *Ampelopsis humulifolia* may have advantages for screening and handsome foliage, but lacks the strong fruiting interest of *A. brevipedunculata* and probably is not commercially available.

Aralia elata 6–7

JAPANESE ANGELICA TREE,
DEVIL'S WALKING STICK
Deciduous shrub or tree
Araliaceae (Aralia Family)

Native Range.   Japan, Korea, Manchuria.

Useful Range.   USDA Zones 4a–9a.

Function.   Distinctive specimen shrub or tree, of umbrellalike form and coarse texture, branching sparsely.

Size and Habit

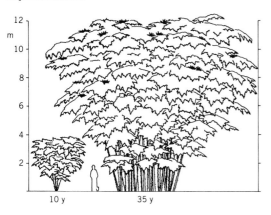

Aralia elata.

Adaptability.   Unusually tolerant of widely varying soil and environmental conditions, including dry city sites.

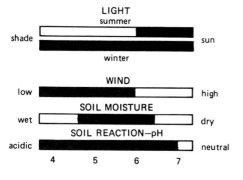

Seasonal Interest.   *Flowers:* Small, creamy white, in huge clusters (compound umbels) to 45 cm/18 in. across, in midsummer. *Foliage:* Huge, coarse-textured, doubly compound leaves, to 1 m/3.3 ft long, turning dull reddish in autumn.

Problems and Maintenance.   Fast-growing sucker shoots must be removed if this plant is to be used in tree form; otherwise it becomes a thicket. Branches, petioles, and even leaf surfaces have sharp prickles, a problem around small children. There are few other problems.

Cultivars.   'Aureovariegata' has yellow variegated leaf margins. 'Variegata' has white variegated leaf margins.

Related Species

Aralia spinosa 6–7 (Hercules' club, angelica tree, devil's walking stick).   This is the American counterpart of *A. elata*, native from Pennsylvania to Florida, Texas, and Iowa. Similar in landscape use to, and interchangeable with, *A. elata*, except in Zone 4, where it is not fully hardy.

Arctostaphylos uva-ursi 2

BEARBERRY, KINNIKINICK
Evergreen groundcover
Ericaceae (Heath Family)

Native Range. Circumpolar: northern parts of Asia, Europe, and North America, farther south at high elevations.

Useful Range. USDA Zones 3a–7a with selection of appropriate genetic material, and with snow cover in Zones 3–5.

Function. Excellent evergreen groundcover.

Size and Habit

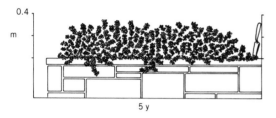

Arctostaphylos uva-ursi.

Adaptability. This groundcover is unusually well adapted to very infertile, sandy, dry soils and cold climates, but is best in areas with fairly cool summers. It is subject to desiccation in winter sun and wind.

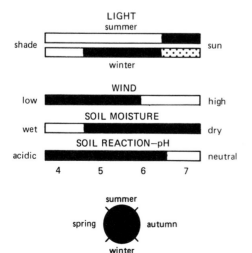

Seasonal Interest. *Flowers:* Small, pink, in midspring. *Foliage:* Evergreen, neatly fine-textured, lustrous, turning bronze-purple in winter. *Fruits:* Bright red berries in summer.

Arctostaphylos uva-ursi.

Problems and Maintenance. This plant is trouble-free, requiring little maintenance once established. Transplanting can be a problem unless pot-grown plants are specified, but large sods also can be moved successfully.

Cultivars. 'Massachusetts' and 'Vancouver Jade' are excellent mat-forming selections 15–30 cm/6–12 in. high, resistant to leaf spot diseases, and cold-hardy at least to Zone 4a, perhaps colder areas as well.

Related Species

Arctostaphylos manzanita 5 (Parry manzanita). This large shrub bears little superficial resemblance to *A. uva-ursi.* It has an interesting open, twisted form, with polished-looking red-brown trunks and branches, handsome evergreen foliage, white or pink flowers in spring, and ornamental red fruits that are useful for preserves. It is one of several species of *Arctostaphylos* native to the West Coast and Southwest United States and valued for planting there. Worthy of wider trial in the Southeast in localities with moderate summer temperatures and acidic soil in Zones 7b–9a.

Arctostaphylos patula 4 (green manzanita). This shrub is similar to A. *manzanita* in overall appearance and flowers, fruits, and bark, but a little smaller. It is the only *Manzanita* species that in its natural distribution crosses the Sierra Nevada mountains and continues eastward to the Rockies, and it may be of landscape interest in the eastern Rockies as well. Useful at least to Zone 5a, perhaps Zone 4 as well.

Ardisia crenata 4

CORAL ARDISIA, CORALBERRY, SPICEBERRY, CHRISTMAS BERRY

Evergreen shrub

Myrsinaceae (Myrsine Family)

Native Range. India to Japan.

Useful Range. USDA Zone 9a+.

Function. Specimen, mass planting, naturalizing.

Size and Habit. Upright in form, spreading by underground shoots but not making a dense mass.

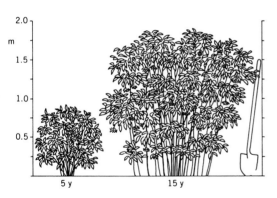

Ardisia crenata.

Adaptability

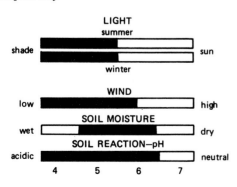

Seasonal Interest. *Flowers:* Small, pink or white, in terminal clusters on branches, not highly conspicuous. *Foliage:* Leathery, evergreen leaves, to 8 cm/3 in. long, lustrous with glandular-crisped margins. *Fruits:* Long-lasting bright red (or white) berries, about 1.2 cm/0.5 in. across.

Problems and Maintenance. This plant is generally trouble-free and requires little or no maintenance when used in good sites.

Cultivars. 'Alba' has white flowers.

Related Species

Ardisia crispa 3–4 (Chinese ardisia). Very similar to A. *crenata,* often confused with it, and equivalent in landscape use. Differs from A. *crenata* in having slightly pubescent young growth. There is a white-fruited selection, 'Alba,' and one with white-variegated foliage, 'Variegata.'

Ardisia japonica 2 (marlberry, Japanese ardisia). This low growing plant is useful as a woodland groundcover. Like A. *crenata* and A. *crispa,* it grows best in reasonably fertile, well-drained soil in partial shade. Its seasonal interest consists of evergreen foliage and bright red fruits. It is notably more cold-hardy than the other two species, useful in Zones 7a–9a+. Several variants with foliage variegated in white, silver, gold, and pink, have been selected in Japan and are becoming available in the United States.

Aristolochia macrophylla 1

Synonyms: *A. Durior, A. Sipho*
DUTCHMAN'S PIPE
Deciduous vine
Aristolochiaceae (Birthwort Family)

Size and Habit.   Grows vigorously and climbs by twining to heights of 8 m/25 ft.

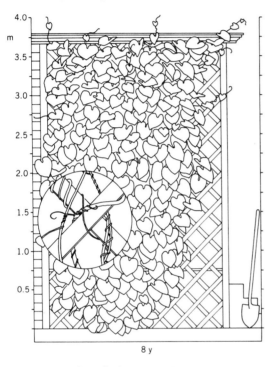

Aristolochia macrophylla.

Native Range.   East-central United States.

Useful Range.   USDA Zones 4b–7b.

Function.   Screen (with support).

Seasonal Interest.   *Flowers:* Inconspicuous but interesting pipelike greenish flowers. *Foliage:* Dark green, heart-shaped or kidney-shaped leaves to 30 cm/12 in. long and broad, giving very coarse texture.

Aristolochia macrophylla.

Problems and Maintenance.   This vine is relatively trouble-free and needs practically no maintenance.

Adaptability

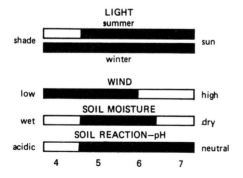

Aronia arbutifolia 5

RED CHOKEBERRY
Deciduous shrub
Rosaceae (Rose Family)

Native Range.   Most of eastern United States.

Useful Range.   USDA Zones 4b–9a.

Function.   Specimen, shrub border, naturalizing. Most useful in mass plantings, except for the cultivar 'Brilliantissima.'

Size and Habit

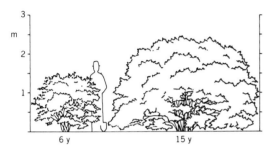

Aronia arbutifolia.

Adaptability.   This shrub is unusually versatile with respect to soil and climatic adaptation, including dry, infertile soils.

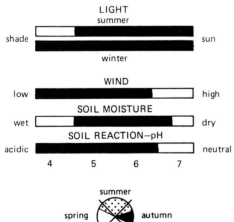

Seasonal Interest.   *Flowers:* Small, white (or pinkish), in clusters, only moderately showy, in late spring. *Foliage:* Medium or gray-green leaves, 3–5 cm/1–2 in. long, fuzzy underneath, lustrous above, turning reddish in autumn. *Fruits:* Bright red berries in clusters, showy in autumn.

Aronia arbutifolia.

Problems and Maintenance.   Chokeberries are subject to some of the problems of the rose family in general and pome fruits in particular, but less so than many others in that group and generally require little maintenance.

Cultivar.   'Brilliant' (= 'Brilliantissima') has unusually showy, shiny red berries.

Related Species

Aronia melanocarpa 3–4 (black chokeberry). This shrub is similar to *A. arbutifolia,* except that it has more upright branching, tending to form low thickets, and black berries. It is useful in Zones 3b–7b.

Aronia ×prunifolia 5 (purple chokeberry). This hybrid of *A. arbutifolia* × *A. melanocarpa* is similar to *A. arbutifolia,* but with less showy, purple berries.

Artemisia abrotanum 4

SOUTHERNWOOD, OLDMAN
WORMWOOD
Deciduous subshrub
Asteraceae (Compositae; Aster Family)

Native Range.   Southern Europe, escaped from cultivation in the United States.

Useful Range.   USDA Zones 3b–8b.

Function.   Border, mass planting (in dry or alkaline soil), special effects (foliage).

Size and Habit

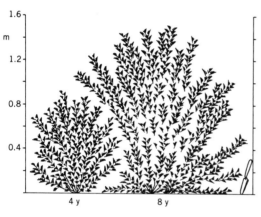

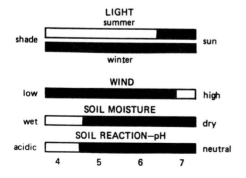

Artemisia abrotanum.

Adaptability.   This plant is unusually tolerant of dry and alkaline soils, hot summers, and salt spray.

Seasonal Interest.   *Foliage:* Finely dissected, fine-textured, grayish foliage is strongly pungent when crushed or brushed against.

Problems and Maintenance.   A relatively trouble-free plant, the top kills to the ground each winter in northern areas, returning vigorously the following growing season.

Cultivars.   'Nana' is a dwarf form that usually remains below 50 cm/20 in. high, spreading widely to 2 m/6.6 ft or more. Foliage color is not particularly good, and this cultivar is not as hardy as the species, but it is useful in Zones 4b–8b.

Related Species

Artemisia schmidtiana 3 (satin wormwood). This perennial herb from Japan has finely dissected silvery gray foliage, aromatic when crushed. The low-growing selections 'Nana' and 'Silver Mound,' remaining lower than 15 cm/6 in. and 30 cm/12 in. respectively, are functional groundcovers during the growing season, useful in Zones 3b–9a+.

Artemisia stelleriana 3 (dusty miller, beach wormwood).   This groundcover or low massing plant is grown for the white, felty, dissected foliage, coarser than that of *A. abrotanum.* Like other *Artemisia* species, it is relatively salt tolerant.

Asarum caudatum 2

BRITISH COLUMBIA WILD GINGER
Evergreen groundcover
Aristolochiaceae (Birthwort Family)

Native Range. Northwestern North America: British Columbia to California.

Useful Range. USDA Zones 6a–8a, probably also Zones 4 and 5 where snow cover is reliable, or with other protection from full winter sun and wind.

Function. Groundcover.

Size and Habit

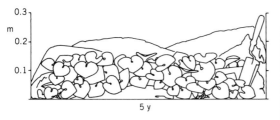

Asarum caudatum.

Adaptability. The requirement for shade is greater in the South and Midwest than in northern and mountain areas.

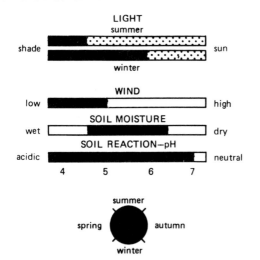

Seasonal Interest. *Flowers:* Brownish crimson, distinctive and interesting, but borne under the leaves and seldom fully visible, in late spring.

Foliage: Evergreen, lustrous, heart-shaped, 10–15 cm/4–6 in. long, providing exceptional year-round textural interest.

Problems and Maintenance. Wild gingers usually are trouble-free, given a proper site initially.

Related Species

Asarum canadense 2 (American wild ginger, Canada snakeroot). This native of northeastern North America, from New Brunswick to North Carolina and Missouri, differs from *A. caudatum* in that it is deciduous or semievergreen at best. It is useful in Zones 4a–7a and parts of warmer zones with moderate summers.

Asarum canadense.

Asarum europaeum 2 (European wild ginger). This impressive evergreen from Europe has more glossy and rounded leaves than *A. caudatum*, seldom more than 8 cm/3 in. across, making it one of the most handsome of all groundcovers, useful in Zones 5a–8b. Like *A. caudatum*, it requires protection from full sun.

Asarum shuttleworthii 2 (Shuttleworth wild ginger). This native of the southeastern United States from North Carolina to Alabama, has evergreen, elongated, heart-shaped leaves, 5–8 cm/2–3 in. long, sometimes beautifully mottled with light and dark green. Useful in Zones 6b–8b, perhaps also Zone 5, and is best in sites that are fully or at least half shaded.

Several other *Asarum* species are of considerable landscape interest and are beginning to enter commerce. These include A. *ariifolium* and A. *virginicum* from the southeastern United States as well as several species from China and Japan.

Asimina triloba 6–7

PAWPAW
Deciduous tree
Annonaceae (Custard Apple Family)

Native Range.   Eastern United States.

Useful Range.   USDA Zones 5b–8a.

Function.   Specimen, screen, mass planting, edible fruit.

Size and Habit.   Form stiffly upright and pyramidal, spreading by suckers.

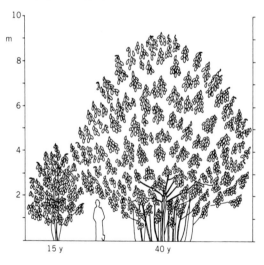

Asimina triloba.

Adaptability.   At least partial shade is needed for establishment, and after establishment in areas with hot summers.

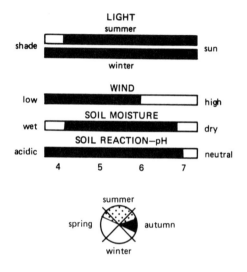

Seasonal Interest.   *Flowers:* Dark red, inconspicuous but interesting, in midspring. *Foliage:* Dark green, drooping, giving distinctive texture, turning bright yellow in autumn. *Fruits:* Green to yellow-brown, somewhat banana-like, edible, in early autumn. Two fruiting forms exist, one with palatable yellow flesh, the other with greenish white flesh of inferior flavor. At least two

Asimina triloba.

clones (cultivars or seedlings) must be present for cross-pollination and good fruiting.

Problems and Maintenance. This shrub has wide-ranging roots, making it almost impossible to transplant with bare roots. This can be overcome by planting seedlings or grafted cultivars that have been started in deep pots or tubes. Once established, it grows suckers and spreads quickly into a thicket or "pawpaw patch." Trees can be trained with a single trunk by removing suckers as they develop. As single trunked trees

continue to grow, sucker production usually slows to a minimum.

Cultivars. Several cultivars are available, but there has been little comparison for landscape use. Reportedly, some fruits may be produced from a single clone without cross-pollination; but for heavy fruit production, growers recommend planting at least two cultivars, or one with a seedling pollinator, in proximity. Most popular cultivars include 'Mary Foos Johnson,' 'Overleese,' 'Sunflower,' 'Sweet Alice,' and 'Taylor.'

Aspidistra elatior 3

ASPIDISTRA, CAST IRON PLANT
Evergreen groundcover
Liliaceae (Lily Family)

Native Range. Japan.

Useful Range. USDA Zones 8b–9a+.

Function. Groundcover, accent.

Size and Habit

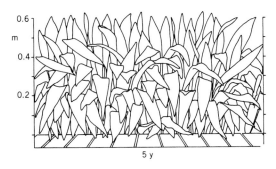

Aspidistra elatior.

Adaptability

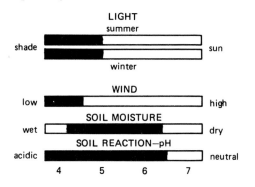

Seasonal Interest. *Foliage:* Dark green, parallel-veined, evergreen, the leaves stiff and swordlike, narrowing to a petiole at the ground. Numerous leaves make a tight mass in time.

Problems and Maintenance. In spite of its general durability, the leaves will scorch in full sun, and occasionally will be frozen back in Zones 8 and 9a, but they return rather quickly. Otherwise, this is a low-maintenance groundcover, since the tight foliage mass resists weed invasion.

Cultivars. Several cultivars with variegated leaves have been selected, mostly for indoor use in our area. 'Asaki' has a broad zone of white over much of the terminal half of each leaf. 'Cynthia Johnson' has a center stripe of lighter green. The broad leaves of 'Milky Way' (= 'Minor') are covered with white spots, and 'Ginga' is similar except that it has narrower leaves and is lower in stature. 'Variegata' has broadly striped deep green and white leaves and is more readily available as a landscape plant than the others.

Aucuba japonica 5

JAPANESE AUCUBA, JAPANESE
LAUREL
Evergreen shrub
Cornaceae (Dogwood Family)

Native Range.   Japan to Himalayas.

Useful Range.   USDA Zones 7b–9a+.

Function.   Screen, specimen, mass or foundation planting.

Size and Habit

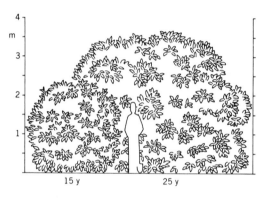

15 y   25 y

Aucuba japonica.

Adaptability.   Given reasonably moist soil and shade from full winter sun, this plant is widely adaptable, even to city conditions.

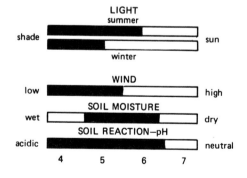

Seasonal Interest.   *Flowers:* Small, reddish brown, inconspicuous in early spring, dioecious. *Foliage:* Evergreen, dark olive green, leathery leaves, 8–18 cm/3–7 in. long and half as wide, giving a coarse texture. Some cultivars have variegated foliage. *Fruits:* Red fruits, to 1.5 cm/0.6 in. across, in clusters 3–8 cm/1–3 in. long on female plants, colorful in winter. For maximum fruiting interest, plant mostly females with an occasional male for pollination.

Problems and Maintenance.   Foliage burns in full sun, so shade should always be provided, especially in winter and especially for cultivars with variegated foliage. A leaf-spot disease is occasionally troublesome in warmer zones. Otherwise, this shrub is relatively trouble-free. Occasional pruning may be desirable to restrain height growth and maintain fullness.

Cultivars.   'Crotonifolia' is an old cultivar, similar to 'Variegata' and no longer widely available. 'Goldieana' has a large blotch of gold in the center of each leaf. 'Longifolia' (= 'Angustifolia', = 'Salicifolia') has narrow green leaves and has red fruits. 'Macrophylla' has unusually large leaves. 'Mr. Goldstrike' has large leaves, more heavily splashed with gold than those of 'Variegata.' 'Nana' is dwarf and dense, with small leaves spotted with light green. 'Picturata' (= 'Aureomaculata') has a gold blotch in the center of each dark green leaf. 'Serratifolia' has long, sharply toothed leaves and red fruits. 'Sulfur' has lighter green leaves with yellow margins. 'Variegata' (= 'Gold Dust', = 'Maculata') has blotched and spotted leaves and red fruits.

Baccharis halimifolia 5

GROUNDSEL BUSH, EASTERN
BACCHARIS

Deciduous or evergreen shrub

Asteraceae (Compositae; Aster Family)

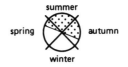

Native Range. Atlantic Coast marshes, Massa-chusetts to Texas.

Useful Range. USDA Zones 4a–9a.

Function. Specimen, mass plantings (in wet or salty sites).

Size and Habit

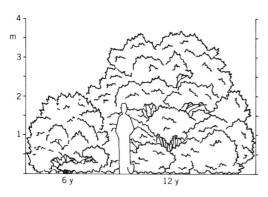

Baccharis halimifolia.

Adaptability. This loose shrub is remarkably well adapted to sites subject to salt spray as well as to wet soil, and it is used primarily for this reason but also grows well in "normal" planting sites.

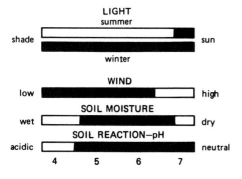

Seasonal Interest. *Flowers:* Whitish, in small heads, noticeable but not showy, in late summer. *Foliage:* Deciduous in the North to evergreen in the South, the leaves medium green, 2.5–7 cm/1–2.8 in. long, fine-textured, and making a loosely open mass. *Fruit:* Seed heads carry the whitish appearance of the flowers into autumn.

Baccharis halimifolia.

Problems and Maintenance. This shrub is rel-atively trouble-free, but pruning may occasion-ally be needed to maintain vigor and fullness.

Cultivars. 'White Caps' has very showy white seed heads.

Related Species.

There are several hundred species of Baccharis in the world, and a dozen or so are known to be cultivated, primarily in landscapes that include natural or reconstructed plant communities. Three in addition to B. halimifolia are native within our area. B. glomulifera grows wild from North Carolina to Florida, B. salicina in the south-central United States, and B. neglecta from Nebraska southwest to Texas and Mexico. Several more come from the southwestern deserts, and from southern Argentina and Chile.

Atriplex canescens 4 (four-wing saltbush). This deciduous shrub in the Chenopodiaceae (Goose-foot Family), native to western North America and Mexico, is useful at least in Zones 3b–9a, assuming selection of appropriate (nearby) seed sources. It grows, rather thinly, to 1.5 m/5 ft tall and about as wide, with narrow, grayish or whitish-green leaves. While it is not particularly colorful, it is unusually tolerant of drought, salt, wind, and cold, assuming that local or at least regional seed sources are used.

Bambusa multiplex 5–6

Synonyms: *B. Argentea, B. Glaucescens*
Evergreen Shrub

HEDGE BAMBOO

Poaceae (Gramineae; Grass Family)

Native Range.   China.

Useful Range.   USDA Zone 9a+, and protected sites in Zone 8b, but suffers some winterburn even in Zone 9a.

Function.   Hedge, screen, specimen.

Size and Habit

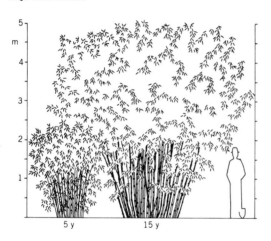

Bambusa multiplex.

Adaptability.   Protection from full winter sun and wind will reduce winterburn of foliage.

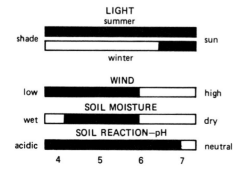

Seasonal Interest.   *Foliage:* Evergreen leaves, up to 15 cm/6 in. long, are medium green, whitened underneath. *Stems:* Green at first, becoming dull yellow when mature, to 3 cm/1.2 in. across, making a dense mass adequate for screening.

Problems and Maintenance.   Bamboos are generally free of pest problems in our area. Some may become a problem themselves by spreading aggressively, but *B. multiplex* is not one of the worst offenders.

Varieties and Cultivars.   'Alphonse Karr' has stems emerging pinkish, maturing golden yellow, with longitudinal green stripes. It grows to heights of 8–10 m/26–33 ft under ideal conditions, but usually remains lower in our area.
    'Fernleaf' has finer-textured foliage than the species type and rarely exceeds 5–6 m/16–20 ft in height.
    'Riviereorum' (Chinese goddess bamboo) is dwarf, growing to 2–3 m/6.6–10 ft under ideal conditions, often lower in our area, with arching branches and fine-textured foliage, useful only as a specimen for accent.
    'Silverstripe' has some white striped leaves, others normal yellow-green, with narrow yellow stripes on some stems, growing to 8–10 m/26–33 ft or taller under ideal growing conditions.
    'Stripestem Fernleaf' is a lower-growing selection, 2–3 m/6.6–10 ft tall, with green striped yellow stems.

Related Species

Phyllostachys aurea 6 (synonym: *Bambusa aurea;* golden or fishpole bamboo).   This Chinese species is one of the taller bamboos that are useful for screening, in this case Zones 7b–9a+. Its stems are distinctly golden yellow and of good wood quality.

Phyllostachys aureosulcata 6 (yellowgroove bamboo).   This Chinese species is similar in general effect to *P. aurea*, but it spreads more aggressively. Its dull green stems, striped yellow, are not as strong as those of *P. aurea*. Its dull green stems, striped yellow, are not as strong as those of *P. aurea*. It is useful at least in Zones 6b–9a+.

Phyllostachys bambusoides 7 (timber bamboo). This Chinese species is widely cultivated in Japan and elsewhere in eastern Asia for construction purposes. It is useful for special effect in Zones 7b–9a+.

Phyllostachys nigra 6 (black bamboo).   Another Chinese species, this is distinctive in that the stems mature to a brownish or purplish black. It is useful for special effects and screening in Zones 7b–9a+.

Pleioblastus pygmaeus 2 (synonyms: *Arundinaria pygmaea, Bambusa pygmaea, Sasa pygmaea*; pygmy bamboo).   This low, mat-forming bamboo from Japan with bright green leaves and purplish stems is useful as a groundcover, especially on wet soils, in Zones 6b–9a+. It is invasive, and it should be contained by pavement or substantial edging. The selection 'Variegata' has white-margined leaves.

Pleioblastus pygmaeus var. *distichus* 3 (synonyms: *Arundinaria disticha, Bambusa disticha, B. nana, Sasa disticha*; dwarf fernleaf bamboo).   This

Pleioblastus variegatus.

Sasa palmata.

Sasa palmata.

bamboo is slightly taller than the species type, with interesting foliage texture.

Pleioblastus simonii 6 (synonym: *Arundinaria simonii*; Simon bamboo).   This Japanese native reaches about the same size as *Bambusa multiplex*, but is somewhat less aggressive and more cold hardy, useful in Zones 6b–9a+.

Pleioblastus variegatus 3 (synonym: *Arundinaria variegata*).   This native of Japan with white-striped foliage makes an effective but rather tall groundcover. It is useful in Zones 6b–9a+.

Sasa palmata 4 (synonym: *Bambusa palmata*; palmate bamboo).   This species from Japan and Sakhalin is one of the hardiest of all bamboos, useful at least in Zones 6a–8a. It is not as functional as many, though, since it is too tall for a groundcover and not reliably tall enough for screening, and it is aggressive and difficult to control.

Sasa veitchii 3 (Kuma bamboo grass).   This fast-spreading bamboo from Japan makes an effective large-scale groundcover, but is too aggressive for many situations. With this limitation, it is useful in Zones 6b–9a+, and perhaps also Zone 6a. At the end of summer, the leaf margins dry to an ivory-buff color, leaving the leaf centers deep green and giving this bamboo a distinctive variegated effect in autumn and winter.

Berberis julianae 4

WINTERGREEN BARBERRY
Evergreen shrub
Berberidaceae (Barberry Family)

Native Range.   China.

Useful Range.   USDA Zones 6b–9a.

Function.   Border, hedge, barrier, specimen.

Size and Habit

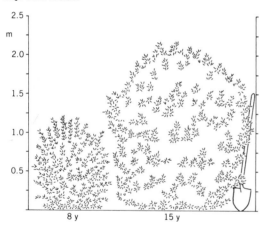

Berberis julianae.

Adaptability.   This handsome shrub grows best in full sun in Zones 7a–8a, but it will benefit from light shade and protection from wind in winter in Zone 6b and in summer in Zones 8b and 9a.

Seasonal Interest.   *Flowers:* Yellow, small but fairly showy, in midspring. *Foliage:* Evergreen, dark green, lustrous, 5–10 cm/2–4 in. long, on spiny or thorny branches. *Fruits:* Inconspicuous blue-black berries in autumn.

Problems and Maintenance.   Certain species of *Berberis* serve as alternate hosts for black stem rust of wheat, an economically serious disease. Except for the highly susceptible B. *vulgaris*, those mentioned here are listed as resistant to this disease by the U.S. Department of Agriculture. These barberries are relatively free of troubles and need for maintenance. Their thorniness makes them difficult to handle in landscape construction, and they are best avoided in children's play areas.

Cultivars.   'Compacta' remains more compact and lower than the species type, not exceeding 1.5 m/5 ft for many years.

Related Species and Hybrids

Berberis gagnepainii var. *lanceifolia* 4 (black barberry), B. *panlanensis* 4 (synonym: B. *sanguinea*; red-flowered barberry), B. *sargentiana* 4 (Sargent barberry), and B. ×*wisleyensis* 4 (synonym: B. *triacanthophora*; threespine barberry). These are all evergreen and Chinese in origin, except for B. ×*wisleyensis*, which is a hybrid of unknown Chinese parents. All of these are listed as "resistant" to black stem rust. They are similar

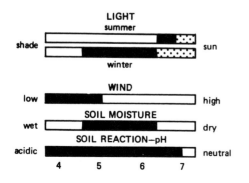

Berberis ×*wisleyensis.*

to *Berberis julianae* but are probably not quite as vigorous and cold-hardy as that species and are usually not as widely available.

Berberis ×*gladwynensis* 'William Penn' 3 (*B. julianae* × *B. verruculosa;* William Penn barberry). This handsome evergreen shrub combines the vigor of *B. julianae* with the low, moundlike habit of *B. verruculosa.* It has purple flowers in spring, yellow and purple fruits in summer and autumn, and excellent dark green foliage that turns a deep mahogany red in autumn and winter.

Berberis koreana 4

KOREAN BARBERRY
Deciduous shrub
Berberidaceae (Barberry Family)

Native Range.   Korea.

Useful Range.   USDA Zones 3b–8a.

Function.   Border, hedge, specimen. Neither full nor tall enough to be an effective visual screen.

Size and Habit

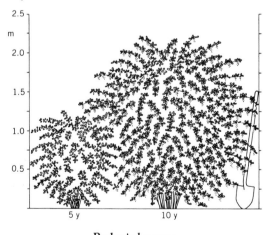

Berberis koreana.

Adaptability

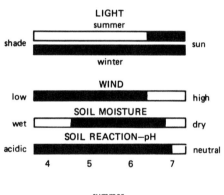

Seasonal Interest.   *Flowers:* Small, golden-yellow, in fairly showy hanging clusters, in midspring. *Foliage:* Relatively large leaves (for a barberry), rounded and finely spined on thorny branches, turning bright red in autumn. *Fruits:* Bright red berries in showy hanging clusters in autumn.

Problems and Maintenance.   This shrub is relatively trouble-free but requires occasional light pruning to maintain fullness. It should only be pruned heavily for renewal, since this destroys its form and fruiting display for a time. Use of all deciduous barberries is barred in Canada as a control measure for black stem rust of wheat.

Related Species

Berberis gilgiana 4 (wildfire barberry).   This Chinese shrub is similar to *B. koreana* in appearance and landscape function and useful in Zones 5b–8a, but not generally available.

Berberis vulgaris 5 (common barberry).   Similar to *B. koreana,* this European species, naturalized in North America, is commonly seen in many areas of eastern North America. Unlike the other species included here, it is susceptible to black stem rust of wheat, so it has been largely eradicated in wheat-growing areas and must, by law, be removed when found in Canada. It obviously should not be planted in these areas.

Berberis koreana.

Berberis ×mentorensis 4

MENTOR BARBERRY
Semievergreen shrub
Berberidaceae (Barberry Family)

Hybrid Origin.   *B. julianae* × *B. thunbergii.*

Useful Range.   USDA Zones 5b–9a.

Function.   Hedge, border, specimen.

Size and Habit

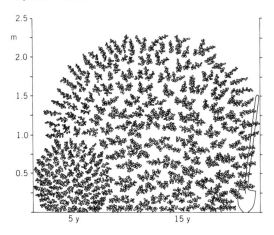

Berberis ×mentorensis.

This, with cold hardiness, makes it a valued plant in the Midwest.

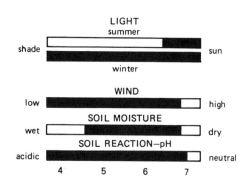

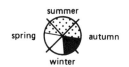

Seasonal Interest.   *Flowers:* Small, yellow, noticeable but not showy, in midspring. *Foliage:* Fine-textured, leathery, blue-green, and slightly spiny; semievergreen, finally turning red-orange before falling in early winter. *Fruits:* None.

Problems and Maintenance.   This is one of the most maintenance-free shrubs, seldom requiring more than occasional pruning, and that only where it is used as a formal hedge.

Adaptability.   This shrub is unusually well adapted to hot, dry summers, retaining good foliage character even in substantial drought.

Berberis thunbergii 4

JAPANESE BARBERRY
Deciduous shrub
Berberidaceae (Barberry Family)

Native Range. Japan.

Useful Range. USDA Zones 4b(a)–9a, depending on cultivar.

Function. Hedge, border, specimen.

Size and Habit

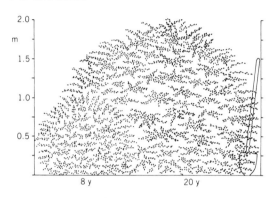

Berberis thunbergii.

Adaptability

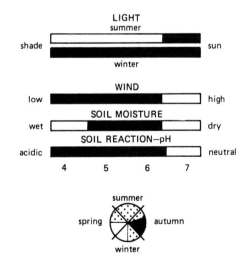

Seasonal Interest. *Flowers:* Small, yellow, interesting with expanding foliage but not showy. *Foliage:* Neatly fine-textured, bright green, turning scarlet in autumn. *Fruits:* Numerous, small, elongated red berries are noticeable with green foliage, and add striking interest as the leaves change to red and remain after leaf fall.

Problems and Maintenance. This species is relatively durable and trouble-free, requiring little maintenance in good sites. For years, *B. thunbergii* was assumed to be resistant to black stem rust of wheat (see under *B. vulgaris*); new races of this fungus have infected certain red-leaved cultivars belonging to f. *atropurpurea* (see below).

Forms and Cultivars. Clones belonging to f. *atropurpurea* differ from the species type in that their foliage turns deep red-purple in direct sun. At least one such clone, and perhaps more than one, has long been sold under the name 'Atropurpurea.' Several of these cultivars have been found susceptible to black stem rust and are now prohibited in Canada, where many of them originated, as well as in wheat and oat growing areas of the United States. This is true of some of the full-sized red-leaved cultivars, but a notable exception is 'Redbird,' which is on the U.S. Department of Agriculture's "resistant" list at this writing. That list has been amended several times in recent years and probably will be again. All of the cultivars of *B. thunbergii* listed below are considered to be "resistant" for quarantine purposes, unless stated otherwise.

'Atropurpurea' is a collective name (approximately synonymous with f. *atropurpurea*) for plants of *B. thunbergii* that have red foliage and grow to full size for the species (to about 1.5 m/5 ft tall and at least as broad). Since it almost certainly includes more than one clone, it is a questionable cultivar name, but it will be found listed as such in some plant catalogs.

'Atropurpurea Nana' (= 'Crimson Pygmy') is a fine dwarf selection that functions at 50–80 cm/20–32 in. and is broader than high.

'Aurea' has yellow-green foliage at emergence, bright yellow in early summer, dulling in late summer and falling with little other change. It is effective for color accent and becomes somewhat larger than 'Atropurpurea Nana.'

'Erecta' (sometimes called truehedge Japanese barberry) has a vertical branching habit, making it useful for narrow hedges; but if it is not kept vigorous it may not remain upright, individual branches falling into ascending or prostrate positions.

'Gold Ring' (= 'Golden Ring') is similar in size to 'Aurea,' but has red-purple leaves with narrow yellow-green margins.

'Kobold' is a low growing, dense selection no taller than 'Atropurpurea Nana,' with excellent, rich green foliage.

'Rose Glow' (= 'Rosy Glow') is similar in size to 'Aurea,' upright and compact in growth habit.

Its distinctive feature is its variegated (white, pink, rose) young foliage, eventually turning deep red-purple in full sun.

'Sparkle' has unusually glossy, leathery, rich green foliage, turning red, orange, and yellow in autumn. It is slightly more compact than the species type, but eventually reaches full height and spread for the species.

'Thornless' differs from the species type only in the absence (or near absence) of thorns.

Berberis verruculosa 3

WARTY BARBERRY
Evergreen shrub
Berberidaceae (Barberry Family)

Native Range.   China.

Useful Range.   USDA Zones 6a–9a.

Function.   Border, hedge, specimen.

Size and Habit.   Lower in relation to height than most other barberries; moundlike and compact.

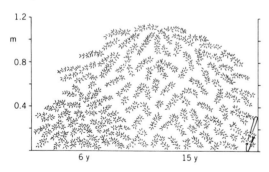

Berberis verruculosa.

Adaptability.   Best in full sun in Zones 6b–8a, it benefits from light shade and protection from wind in winter in Zone 6a and from light shade in summer in Zones 8b–9a.

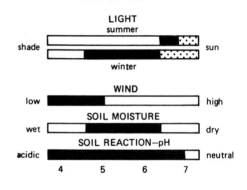

Seasonal Interest.   *Flowers:* Yellow, small but fairly showy, in midspring. *Foliage:* Evergreen, dark green and lustrous above, chalky white underneath, fine-textured and spiny on thorny branches, bronzing in winter. *Fruits:* Inconspicuous blue-black berries in autumn.

Problems and Maintenance.   Certain species of *Berberis* serve as alternate hosts for black stem rust of wheat, an economically serious disease (see Problems and Maintenance, *B. julianae*).

Related Species

All listed here are resistant to black stem rust, according to the U.S. Department of Agriculture.

Berberis buxifolia 5 (Magellan barberry). This is usually seen as the dwarf selection 'Nana,' a low, moundlike plant to only 30 cm/12 in. high, useful in Zones 6a–8a.

Berberis candidula 3 (paleleaf barberry). This is similar to *B. verruculosa* in appearance, landscape function, and hardiness, but is seldom available.

Berberis darwinii 4–5 (Darwin barberry). Like *B. buxifolia*, this handsome evergreen shrub is native to southern Chile. It performs well in mild maritime climates in Zones 7b–9a+, but its adaptability to those same zones in the southeastern United States is not well known. Where it is adapted, its dense mass of small, leathery leaves, golden to orange-yellow flowers, and dark blue fruits give it both functional and ornamental value. Several cultivars have been selected, but few or none are available in North America.

Berberis candidula.

Berberis ×*stenophylla* 5 (*B. darwinii* × *B. empetrifolia*; rosemary barberry). This handsome evergreen with very narrow leaves has several uses, depending on the cultivar selected. The tall growing species type, sometimes called 'Stenophylla,' is tall enough for screening as well as barrier use. 'Compacta' (= 'Nana Compacta') grows only to about 60 cm/2 ft tall, as do several other low forms, most not available in North America. Like its parents, *B.* ×*stenophylla* is useful in Zones 7b–9a+.

Betula lenta 7–8

SWEET BIRCH, CHERRY BIRCH
Deciduous tree
Betulaceae (Birch Family)

Native Range. Northeastern United States and southward in the Appalachian Mountains to northern Alabama.

Useful Range. USDA Zones 4a–7b.

Function. Shade tree, naturalizing.

Size and Habit

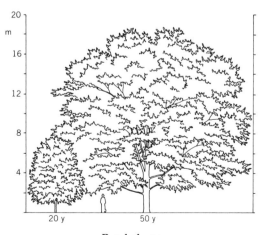

Betula lenta.

Adaptability

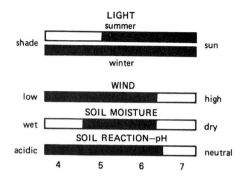

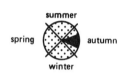

Seasonal Interest. *Foliage:* Clean, dark green, turning bright golden yellow in autumn. *Trunk and branches:* Red-brown, lustrous and lenticular, cherrylike. *Twigs:* Inner bark of young twigs has a wintergreen flavor and is a commercial source of this flavoring.

Problems and Maintenance. Two insects, the bronze birch borer and leaf miner, are potential problems, but limited experience suggests that *B. lenta* is not nearly as susceptible as the white-barked birches. It is susceptible to stem canker disease, but less so in naturalized settings or where adequate moisture is available.

Related Species

Betula alleghaniensis 7–8 (synonym: *B. lutea;* yellow birch). This tree is similar in size, form, and growth rate to *B. lenta,* and it grows wild in about the same area as well as westward in the

Betula alleghaniensis.

Great Lakes region to Minnesota. This tree is also susceptible to stem cankers and is somewhat less tolerant of heat and dry soil than *B. lenta,* although it performs better in the central Midwest than might be expected. This species differs from *B. lenta* in its amber to silvery gray, peeling bark and less spectacular yellow autumn foliage. It is not very common in landscape use, but is a good shade tree in sites in Zones 3b–6b with moderate summer temperatures and adequate moisture.

Betula nigra 8

RIVER BIRCH
Deciduous tree
Betulaceae (Birch Family)

Native Range. Eastern United States: south to Florida, north to Minnesota, west to Kansas.

Useful Range. USDA Zones 4a–9a with selection of appropriate genetic material.

Function. Shade tree, specimen, naturalizing.

Size and Habit

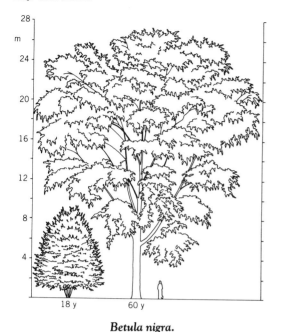

Betula nigra.

Adaptability.   This is probably the most widely adaptable of all the birches, but it occasionally shows iron chlorosis in soil of neutral and higher pH. It is far superior to other birches in the South and Midwest.

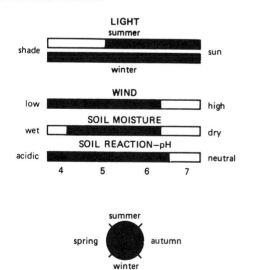

Seasonal Interest. *Foliage:* Clean, medium green foliage, turning yellowish in autumn. *Trunk and branches:* Reddish brown to pale tan bark peels and curls, giving young trunks and branches a handsome, bicolored appearance.

Problems and Maintenance. This tree is widely used and seldom troubled by bronze birch borer. Leaf miner can be a minor problem, especially in the Northeast.

Cultivars.   'Cully' Heritage®, Plant Patent No. 4409, 1979) has exceptional bark interest, is strongly exfoliating, and has paler creamy-buff bark than average for the species. Otherwise, it is as vigorous and handsome as any river birch, useful in Zones 4b–9a. 'Little King' (Fox Valley®) is a dwarf tree, to 3 m/10 ft in 10 years, and probably to at least twice that in time.

Betula nigra.

Related Species

Betula albosinensis 8 (Chinese red or paper birch). This tree from western China is similar in some respects to *B. nigra* and *B. papyrifera.* Its curling, pale pink to orange-red bark is even more striking than that of *B. nigra* and makes this tree useful as a specimen for accent and color in Zones 5b–8a. The variety *septentrionalis* is similar but somewhat taller (to 30 m/100 ft), with less colorful bark but somewhat greater cold hardiness (to Zone 5a).

Betula davurica 7 (Dahurian birch).   This uncommon tree from northeastern Asia is being used increasingly as a substitute for *B. nigra* in the coldest parts of our area (Zone 4a and colder). There is no assurance that it has much resistance to bronze birch, borer, however.

Betula papyrifera 8

PAPER BIRCH, CANOE BIRCH
Deciduous tree
Betulaceae (Birch Family)

Native Range. Northern North America: Labrador to Alaska and southward into the northern United States and in the Appalachian and Rocky Mountains.

Useful Range. USDA Zones 2b–7a with selection of appropriate genetic material, but not fully satisfactory in warmer areas than Zone 5a.

Function. Shade tree, specimen.

Size and Habit

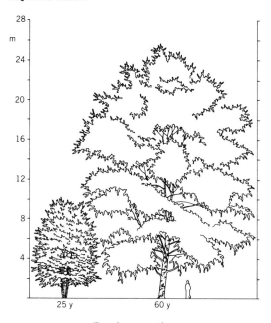

Betula papyrifera.

Adaptability. *B. papyrifera* performs best in areas having mild summers and adequate moisture.

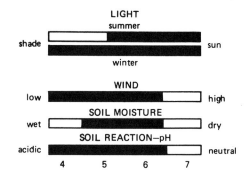

Seasonal Interest. *Foliage:* Rich green leaves, 5–10 cm/2–4 in. long, turn clear yellow before falling in autumn. *Trunk and branches:* Smooth bark, marked with horizontal lenticels, is reddish brown at first, becoming papery white on the trunk as the tree ages, striking in all seasons.

Problems and Maintenance. This handsome tree is very susceptible to bronze birch borer, especially when growing under moisture stress, which is usually the case in the Midwest and South. It is best reserved for northern, mountain, and coastal areas having cool summers, but it can be functional for short life spans in other

Betula papyrifera.

parts of its useful range with careful maintenance: irrigation and spraying for bronze birch borer. Planting on shaded north sides of buildings has been helpful in some areas, suggesting that soil temperature is a critical factor in this tree's success, although shade has also been said to discourage egg deposition by borers. In the northeastern United States and adjacent Canada, leaf miners are also troublesome, disfiguring the foliage annually unless a carefully timed spray program is adhered to.

Varieties. Several natural varieties exist over the native range, from tall trees to shrubby mountain forms, but there has not been enough interest in selecting distinctive forms to lead to the naming of cultivars, which has been done with *B. pendula*. In general, it is best to use sources as close as possible to the areas where the resulting trees will be used.

Related Species

Betula costata 8 (Korean birch).   This handsome tree with creamy white peeling bark and yellow-gold autumn foliage has received renewed interest from plant explorations in Korea in the 1980s. The limits of its hardiness are not well known, but it appears useful at least in Zones 5b–8a. Most trees seem not to be resistant to bronze birch borer, but efforts are underway to find more resistant clones.

Betula mandshurica 7 (synonym: *B. platyphylla*; Manchurian birch).   This white-barked birch is generally similar to *B. papyrifera*, and equally cold-hardy. Its most commonly used forms belong to the variety *japonica*, and the selection 'Whitespire' is to be preferred because of its demonstrated resistance to bronze birch borer, in contrast to var. *japonica* as a whole. This selection was initially propagated by seed, which raises questions about the borer-resistance of some trees now under the 'Whitespire' label. Trees are now being produced clonally from the original 'Whitespire' tree. To be sure of maximum resistance to borers, it is a good idea to specify *clonal* 'Whitespire,' to stress the difference from the 'Whitespire' seedlings that have been in circulation. This tree is useful at least in Zones 5a–7b, perhaps also Zone 4.

Betula maximowicziana 8 (monarch birch).   This vigorous Japanese tree is similar in size and landscape use to *B. papyrifera*, but has larger leaves, 8–14 cm/3–5.5 in. long, and is much less cold-hardy, only to Zone 5b or 6a, depending on genetic material. There has been much interest in this tree because of its alleged resistance to bronze birch borer, but this has not been well established and may vary among individual trees. "Hybrids" of this species from open-pollinated seeds are being sold as borer-resistant birches, but the degree of resistance in most cases is yet to be learned. Regardless of this, it is a handsome although somewhat coarse tree, with trunk bark ranging from tawny pink to creamy white.

Betula pendula 7–8 (synonyms *B. alba*, *B. verrucosa*; European white birch).   This handsome shade and specimen tree from northern Europe is widely used in our area, where it is poorly adapted. Its requirements and susceptibility to attack by borers are similar to those of *B. papyrifera*, and the species type can be considered equivalent in landscape use, even though it is smaller at maturity, seldom exceeding 20 m/66 ft in height, and slightly less cold-hardy, useful in Zones 3b–5b. This species is planted primarily for its distinctive cultivars, which include the following. 'Dalecarlica' (= 'Laciniata') is a tall tree with pendulous branches and cutleaved foliage. 'Gracilis' is also pendulous, even more finely cutleaved and much smaller in stature, to 5–6 m/16–20 ft tall and nearly as wide at maturity. 'Fastigiata' is fastigiate (narrow branch angles), with a columnar form when young, broadening to oval with age. 'Purpurea' and 'Monle' (Purple Rain™) have deep purple foliage, contrasting with the white bark in summer and yellow-orange autumn foliage in some years. 'Tristis' is a tall tree with pendulous branches and normal foliage, while 'Youngii' is a much smaller tree, so gracefully pendulous that it must be grafted on an upright seedling to keep its branches off the ground. 'Trost's Dwarf' is a truly dwarf tree, to only 2 m/6.6 ft after many years, with finely dissected foliage reminiscent of the threadleaved Japanese maples.

Betula populifolia 6–7 (gray birch).   This small tree from the northeastern United States and adjacent Canada has slender, usually multiple, trunks. Its grayish-white bark is more distinctly black-marked than that of the other white-barked species mentioned here, and its foliage is badly disfigured by leaf-miners in much of the Northeast. In spite of these problems and a tendency to be pulled over in ice storms, this tree is widely adaptable to wet and dry soils and is commonly used in clump form for accent in and near its native range, in Zones 4a–7a.

Betula utilis var. *jacquemontii* 7–8 (synonym: *B. jacquemontii*; Jacquemont birch). This handsome tree is believed to have the whitest bark of any birch, but this does not apply to all trees of var. *jacquemontii*. Furthermore, there is evidence of susceptibility to borers in this variety, so selection of white-barked, borer-resistant clones seems to be in order. The oval, sharply toothed leaves of this tree turn yellow in autumn.

Buddleia alternifolia 5

FOUNTAIN BUDDLEIA
Deciduous subshrub
Loganiaceae (Logania Family)

Native Range.   China.

Useful Range.   USDA Zones 4b–7b.

Function.   Border, specimen, cutting.

Size and Habit

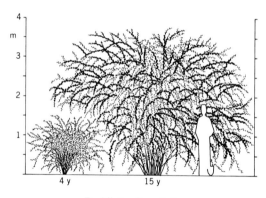

Buddleia alternifolia.

Adaptability. This graceful shrub is well adapted to poor soils but not to wet or excessively dry soils.

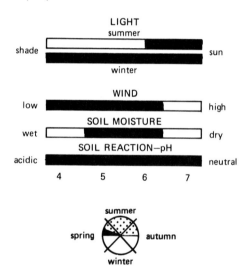

Seasonal Interest.   *Flowers:* Small lilac or lavender flowers in clusters all along the past year's stem growth, giving the appearance of long spikes, on pendulous main branches in midspring. *Foliage:* Gray-green, narrow leaves present a graceful, airy appearance.

Problems and Maintenance.   This shrub is relatively trouble-free, requiring little or no maintenance other than pruning every few years after flowering, for thinning and removal of winterkilled twig tips (in northern zones).

Cultivars.   'Argentea' has more silvery gray foliage than is typical.

Buddleia alternifolia.

Buddleia davidii.

Related Species

Buddleia davidii 4 (orange-eye butterfly bush). This plant functions as a specimen for late summer color and to attract butterflies. It is root-hardy in Zone 4 but tops kill back in most winters in Zone 6 and colder. Even when the tops are not winterkilled, best results can be obtained by cutting the tops back each spring. Plants return rapidly flowering in middle or late summer of the same season. The deliciously fragrant flowers are borne in upright or nodding spikes 10–25 cm/4–10 in. long, in late summer. Many cultivars are available, in a wide range of flower colors. A few of the most popular are listed: 'Black Knight' (very deep purple), 'Empire Blue' (bright, rich blue), 'Ile de France' (rich violet, long clusters), 'Nanho Blue' (deep blue, compact growth), 'Nanho Petite Indigo' (lilac blue, dwarf), 'Nanho Petite Plum' (reddish purple, with orange eye, dwarf), 'Pink Delight' (deep pink, very fragrant), 'Royal Red' (red-purple, large clusters), 'White Profusion' (white with yellow eye, large clusters).

Vitex agnus-castus 4–5 (chaste tree). This member of the Verbenaceae (verbena family) from southern Europe has become naturalized in parts of the South, where it grows into a large, rangy shrub, useful only for its aromatic, compound gray-green leaves and loose panicles, 10–20 cm/4–8 in. long, of fragrant violet flowers in late summer. It is useful in Zones 6a–9a+, but north of Zone 7 it usually winterkills to the ground, quickly returning to flower at a height of 1–1.5 m/3.3–5 ft the same summer, in much the same way as *Buddleia davidii.* It does, of course, require annual removal of deadwood. There are a few cultivars selected for flower color, including: 'Abbeville Blue' (deep blue), 'Alba' and 'Silver Spire' (white), 'Fletcher Pink' (lavender pink), and 'Roseum' (pink).

Vitex negundo 4–6 (Negundo chaste tree). This tall shrub, occasionally a small tree, is native to southeastern Africa and southern and eastern Asia. Its foliage is finer textured than that of *V. agnus-castus*, and its flowers are less conspicuous, but it is more cold-hardy, useful in Zones 5b–9a+ but remaining below 2 m/6.6 ft because of winterkill in Zones 5b–6b. A closely related species is *V. incisa*, once considered to be *V. negundo* var. *heterophylla* (synonym: var. *incisa*), with smaller, dissected leaflets.

Buxus sempervirens 4–5

COMMON BOX
Evergreen shrub
Buxaceae (Box Family)

Native Range.   Mediterranean region (Africa, Asia, and Europe), and Asia Minor.

Useful Range.   USDA Zones 6a–8b, some cultivars to Zone 5a.

Function.   Hedge, specimen, rock garden, edging.

Size and Habit

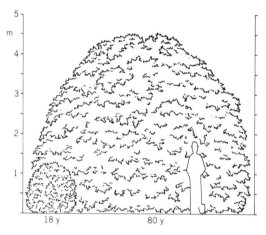

Buxus sempervirens.

Adaptability.   Some shade from winter sun is desirable at the northern extremities of the useful range of any specific cultivar (see Cultivars). This plant is very susceptible to salt damage.

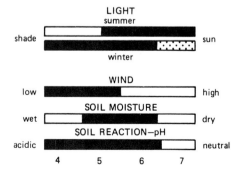

Seasonal Interest.   *Foliage:* Fine-textured, evergreen, dark green to dull bluish green, depending on cultivar.

Problems and Maintenance.   Relatively trouble-free and maintenance-free. Even light pruning is seldom necessary except when it is used as a formal hedge. Insects and mites may necessitate periodic control measures. Leaves, and especially clippings, of box are toxic to livestock, so this plant should not be used within reach of foraging animals.

Cultivars.   There are many cultivars of *B. sempervirens*, and they are often confused in commerce. For northern range extremes, a few cultivars have proven unusually cold-hardy. Some of these are 'Inglis,' 'Northern Find,' 'Northland,' 'Vardar Valley,' and 'Welleri.' Of these, 'Vardar Valley' is a low, spreading plant with blue-green foliage. The others are similar to each other, with more upright growth and darker green foliage. There are many other selections for cold-hardiness, and some of them may emerge as outstanding after broader testing.

In the milder parts of the useful range, many other cultivars can be grown, including the following: 'Argenteo-variegata,' 'Elegans,' and 'Elegantissima' have white-variegated foliage. 'Aureo-variegata' and 'Marginata' have yellow-

Buxus sempervirens, with *Iberis sempervirens.*

Buxus microphylla, hedge.

variegated foliage. 'Angustifolia' and 'Salicifolia' have narrow elongated leaves. 'Arborescens' is upright and treelike in habit, to 8 m/25 ft tall in time, but not well suited for smaller hedges or mass plantings. This is probably the species type. 'Bullata' has large, puckered leaves. 'Columnaris,' 'Conica,' 'Fastigiata,' 'Handsworthiensis,' and 'Pyramidalis' all have upright forms, but 'Graham Blandy' is the most narrowly upright of all, with height usually at least 5 to 6 times its width. 'Suffruticosa' (called English box or edging box in the South) is a dwarf selection that remains below 3–5 ft in height for many years.

Related Species and Hybrids

Buxus microphylla 3–4 (littleleaf box). This highly variable species from China, Japan, and Korea differs from *B. sempervirens* primarily in its size, but its foliage is usually paler or brighter green than those of *B. sempervirens*, in some cultivars bronzing in winter. Useful at least in Zones 6a–9a+. Several cultivars exist: 'Compacta' (= 'Kingsville Dwarf') is dwarf; 'Curly Locks' has unique texture from many tiny axillary leaf clusters; 'Green Pillow' is low and moundlike; and 'Sunnyside' is fast growing, yet cold-hardy to Zone 5b with shelter from wind.

The var. *japonica* has relatively large (1–3 cm/0.4–1.2 in. long), lustrous green to yellow-green leaves and is useful in Zones 6b–9a+. The selection 'Green Beauty' is cold-hardy at least to the Toronto area (Zone 6a) where it was selected, perhaps colder areas as well. Other cultivars include 'Morris Dwarf' (dwarf), Morris Midget' (even more dwarf), and 'Rotundifolia' (large, round leaves).

The var. *koreana* (Korean box) has small (0.6–1.5 cm/0.25–0.6 in. long), dull green leaves, usually turning purplish brown in winter. This variety includes some of the most cold-hardy cultivars of *Buxus* obtainable, useful in Zones 5a–8a, perhaps Zone 4 with protection: 'Wintergreen,' with bright green foliage that browns very little in winter, is the most popular *Buxus* cultivar in the Midwest.

The var. *sinica* (= *Buxus harlandii*; Chinese box) 3 is a low growing species from southern China and has bright green leaves, to 3 cm/1.2 in. long and conspicuously notched at the apex. This species is less cold-hardy than the other species listed here, useful in Zones 8b–9a+. The selection 'Richard' belongs here.

Sheridan Hybrids. The following interspecific hybrids (*B. microphylla* × *B. sempervirens*) were developed at Sheridan Nurseries, Etobicoke, Ontario. 'Green Gem' is a slow growing, globose form with deep green foliage. 'Green Mountain' is upright and pyramidal in form, with deep green foliage. 'Green Velvet' is vigorous, with a full, rounded shape and especially good winter color, especially useful for low hedges. 'Winter Beauty,' not a hybrid but a selection from *B. microphylla* var. *koreana*, is globe-shaped with particularly attractive bronze winter foliage color. Several other cultivars are available. Because they vary greatly in adaptation to northern and southern range extremes and because considerable confusion still exists about cultivar names in spite of great progress made by The Boxwood Society, the best guide to success is to use material propagated from plants that have been growing in the local area for some time.

Callicarpa dichotoma 4

CHINESE BEAUTYBERRY
Deciduous shrub
Verbenaceae (Vervain Family)

Native Range.   China, Korea, occasionally escaped in the United States.

Useful Range.   USDA Zones 5b–8b.

Function.   Border, specimen.

Size and Habit

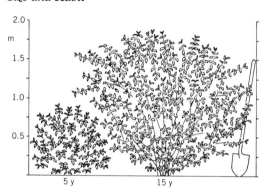

Callicarpa dichotoma.

Adaptability

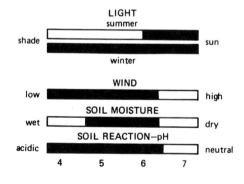

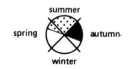

Seasonal Interest.   *Flowers:* Pale pink in middle to late summer, more or less obscured by foliage. *Foliage:* medium green, turning purplish or yellowish in late autumn. *Fruits:* Light purple berries in axillary clusters, small but striking because of their unusual color, in autumn.

Problems and Maintenance.   Because of winter dieback in some locations and years and a tendency toward rank growth, it is difficult to keep this plant in attractive form without regular pruning. When it is used in a mixed shrub border for fruiting interest, this may not be a serious problem, since it will be partly hidden by other plants. Some pruning, however, will almost certainly be needed in any case.

Callicarpa americana.

Related Species

Callicarpa americana 4–5 (American beautyberry or French mulberry).   This native of the south-central United States is similar to C. *dichotoma* except that it is slightly larger and much less cold-hardy, useful in Zones 7a–9a, perhaps also Zone 6b. The selection 'Lactea' gives an exceptional display of white fruits.

Callicarpa japonica 4 (Japanese beautyberry). This shrub is similar to C. *dichotoma* in general effect, size, and useful range, differing in having deeper purple fruits and yellow autumn foliage. The selection 'Leucocarpa' has white fruits and is more compact in form than the species type.

Callicarpa bodinieri 5.   This species from central and western China is best known for the selection 'Profusion,' which has significant flowering interest, outstanding fruit display, and long, narrow leaves that turn pink to rose-purple in autumn. Useful at least in Zones 6b–9a, perhaps also 6a.

Callistemon citrinus 5

Synonym: C. *Lanceolatus*
CRIMSON BOTTLEBRUSH
Evergreen shrub
Myrtaceae (Myrtle Family)

Native Range.   Australia.

Useful Range.   USDA Zones 9a+.

Function.   Massing, specimen (for its open branching pattern and flowering interest), partial screen.

Size and Habit

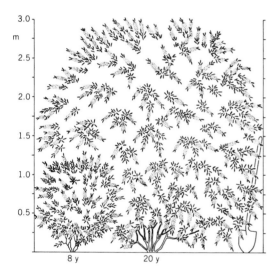

Callistemon citrinus.

Adaptability.   This plant should be grown on the dry side, in full sun or nearly so, with low soil fertility to avoid excessive growth. Good for seashore planting.

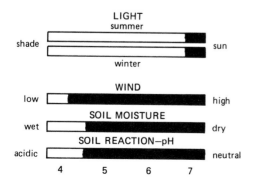

Seasonal Interest.   *Flowers:* Bright red flowers in dense spikes resembling bottlebrushes, in greatest numbers in spring, but intermittently year-round. *Foliage:* Evergreen leaves, linear or broader, to 8 cm/3 in. long, stiff and leathery.

Problems and Maintenance.   If the soil is too moist, root- and crown-attacking fungus diseases can be a problem. Maintain it on the dry side with low fertility and good air circulation. This will also promote a more compact and attractive plant form.

Cultivars.   'Jeffersii' differs from the species type only in having pink flowers. 'Splendens' has very narrow linear leaves and unusually showy deep red flowers.

Related Species.

Several other Callistemon species are in limited use in our area, most no more hardy or useful

Myrtus communis.

than *C. citrinus*. The following two species, however, show promise of greater cold hardiness as well as different flower color.

Callistemon pityoides 2–4 (synonym: *C. sieberi*; alpine bottlebrush). This shrub from higher elevations in Australia has creamy yellow flowers. It is available in very few nurseries in North America, but is worth trying in Zones 8–9.

Callistemon salignus var. *viridiflorus* 4 (synonym: *C. viridiflorus*; Tasmanian bottlebrush). This species is native to South Australia; the variety to the colder climate of Tasmania, where it grows in wet and compacted soils at elevations up to 1200 m/4000 ft. It has been successful in Oregon's Willamette Valley, where it has shown tolerance of wet soils. It remains to be seen how it will fare in the summer heat of milder climates in eastern North America, but it is worthy of initial trial in Zones 8 and 9.

Myrtus communis 4–5 (myrtle). This evergreen shrub, native to the Mediterranean region, has been used more widely in Europe than in North America, but it is useful in Zone 9a+ in our area. With dark green, aromatic leaves to 5 cm/ 2 in. long and small white flowers in late spring, it makes an elegant, compact mass when young and vigorous, and it takes on a more open, tufted habit with age. Myrtle is especially noted for growing well in hot, dry sites, but it performs better with a regular supply of moisture, remaining fuller and less leggy. Cultivars include the following.

'Compacta' is slow growing and compact with small leaves, remaining below 1 m/3.3 ft for an extended period of time. It is barely cold-hardy in Zone 9a.

'Variegata' has small, white-edged leaves and is about as slow-growing and tender as 'Compacta,' barely useful in our area.

All true myrtles are difficult to transplant unless grown in containers and should be specified as potted plants.

Calocedrus decurrens 7

Synonym: *Libocedrus decurrens*
INCENSE CEDAR
Evergreen tree
Cupressaceae (Cypress Family)

Native Range. Western United States and adjacent Mexico.

Useful Range. USDA Zones 6b–9a and Zone 6a in protected sites.

Function. Specimen, screen.

Size and Habit. In our area, this tree does not attain the full size that can be seen in its moist native habitats on the West Coast.

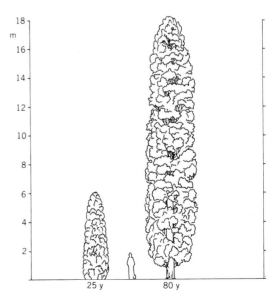

Calocedrus decurrens.

Adaptability. Regular supply of soil moisture favors maximum growth and development.

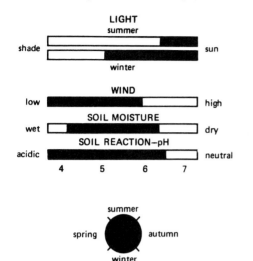

Seasonal Interest. *Foliage:* Evergreen, lustrous, dark green, scalelike, in vertical planes, pleasantly aromatic when crushed. *Trunk and branches:* Cinnamon-brown to reddish brown bark tends to shred, adding minor landscape interest to larger trees.

Problems and Maintenance. This tree is relatively trouble-free once established in a good site.

Calycanthus floridus 5

SWEETSHRUB, CAROLINA ALLSPICE

Deciduous shrub

Calycanthaceae (Calycanthus Family)

Native Range. Southern United States, coastal plain.

Useful Range. USDA Zones 5b–9a+.

Function. Specimen, border, foundation.

Size and Habit

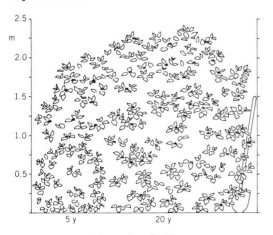

Calycanthus floridus.

Adaptability

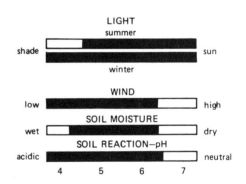

Seasonal Interest. *Flowers:* Deep red or reddish brown, pleasantly fragrant but not showy, opening with newly expanding leaves in late spring. *Foliage:* Lustrous, dark green, fragrant when crushed, turning yellowish in autumn, never striking but always clean looking.

Problems and Maintenance. This shrub is unusual in its freedom from problems and mainte-

Calycanthus floridus.

nance. It may require renewal pruning after several years to avoid a leggy appearance, but even this will seldom be needed.

Cultivars. 'Athens' and 'Margarita' are selected for yellow or chartreuse flowers, and 'Edith Wilder' is chosen for its large, fragrant flowers.

Related Species

Calycanthus fertilis 5 (mountain spicewood, sweetshrub). Similar to *C. floridus*, but native to Appalachia and much less fragrant. Useful in Zones 5b–9a.

Calycanthus mohrii 5 (Mohr sweetshrub). Similar to *C. floridus* and equivalent in landscape use.

Calycanthus chinensis 5–6 (synonym: *Sinocalycanthus chinensis*; Chinese wax shrub). This member of the Calycanthaceae, native to a few mountain slopes in eastern China, was introduced into North America in 1980 by the University of British Columbia Botanical Garden (*Arnoldia* **51**(1):18–22, 1991). The lustrous leaves of this vigorous shrub are larger than those of *Calycanthus*, up to 15 cm/6 in. long and 10 cm/4 in. wide. The unscented flowers are white, 6–10 cm/2.4–4 in. wide, with about 15 tepals (sepals and petals, collectively), nodding on short stalks. Even though this species does not appear to be in commerce at this writing, it probably will be in a very short time.

Camellia sasanqua 6

SASANQUA CAMELLIA
Evergreen shrub
Theaceae (Tea Family)

Native Range. China and Japan.

Useful Range. USDA Zones 7b–9a+.

Function. Screen, border, specimen. This plant is more useful in the landscape than *C. japonica* because it is denser yet less formal in appearance.

Size and Habit

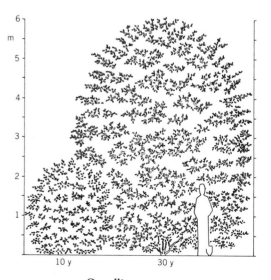

Camellia sasanqua.

Adaptability.   Camellias grow and flower best with full sun during the growing season, but they require light shade and protection from wind during winter in Zone 7 to prevent foliage scorch.

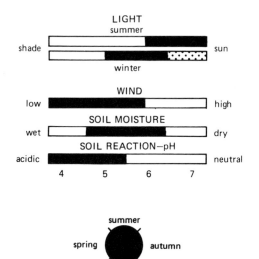

Camellia sasanqua.

Seasonal Interest. *Flowers:* Large (4–6 cm/1½–2½ in.), white or pink, single (double in a few cases), opening over a two- to three-month period in autumn. *Foliage:* Evergreen, lustrous, and dark green, of medium texture (leaves to 5 cm/2 in. long).

Problems and Maintenance.   Mulching is necessary for best performance, since camellias are shallow-rooted. Occasional irrigation may be needed during prolonged dry periods. Scale insects can be troublesome and spraying may be necessary. A twig dieback disease is also a problem in some areas.

Cultivars.   At least 200 cultivars of *C. sasanqua* and 2000 of *C. japonica* are in cultivation, but not all commercially available. In fact, only a few are usually available in a particular locality. Select cultivars for local use in consultation with local nurserymen and other specialists. Cultivars vary primarily in floral characteristics, but also in growth habit, an important consideration in selecting for functional use.

Related Species

Camellia japonica 6 (common camellia).   This species differs from *C. sasanqua* in having larger leaves and usually larger and more showy flowers, opening from late autumn until spring. Since its growth habit usually is looser and more open, *C. japonica* is not usually as functional a landscape plant as *C. sasanqua* and, in fact, is usually planted as a garden specimen or for cut flowers in much the same way as garden roses are. *C. japonica* has about the same useful range as *C. sasanqua.*

Camellia oleifera 6 (oil-bearing camellia).   This species is used in its native range in China and Vietnam primarily as a source of oilseeds, but a selection from northern China has been used at the U.S. National Arboretum as a hardy breeding parent in developing a group of cultivars that are cold-hardy beyond the useful range heretofore expected for camellias. Nine cultivars have been released: 'Polar Ice,' 'Snow Flurry,' 'Winter's Hope,' and 'Winter's Waterlily' have white flowers of different types, sizes, and flowering times; 'Winter's Dream' and 'Winter's Rose' have

Camellia japonica.

pink flowers; 'Winter's Charm' and 'Winter's Interlude' have lavender-pink flowers; and 'Winter's Star' has reddish pink flowers, some with white centers. These cultivars have thus far been cold-hardy in Zone 7a (Washington), and they are worthy of trial in Zone 6 as well.

Camellia reticulata 6 (net-veined camellia). This shrub or small tree has larger flowers than

C. japonica, to 15 cm/6 in. across, and persistent, leathery, dull green leaves. Useful in Zone 9a+, but of interest primarily as a parent of large-flowered hybrids.

Many additional species of *Camellia* exist, but only these three are much involved in cultivation in North America except occasionally as parents of useful cultivars.

Campsis radicans 1

Synonym: *Bignonia radicans*
COMMON TRUMPET CREEPER,
TRUMPETVINE
Deciduous vine
Bignoniaceae (Bignonia Family)

Native Range. East-central to south-central United States.

Useful Range. USDA Zones 4b–9a.

Function. Specimen, screen (with support).

Size and Habit. Grows very rapidly and climbs by aerial rootlets to heights of 8–10 m/26–33 ft or greater.

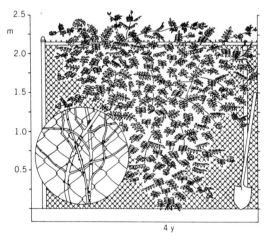

Campsis radicans.

Adaptability. Unusually widely adapted to different soil and environmental conditions but will not perform well in shade.

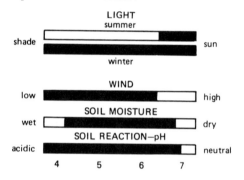

Seasonal Interest. *Flowers:* Large (5 cm/2 in.), bright red-orange or yellow, trumpet shaped, in midsummer. *Foliage:* Doubly compound, dark green, of crisp texture, unfolding late and with little autumn interest. *Fruit:* Pendent capsules, 8–12 cm/3–5 in. long, resemble those of *Asclepias* (milkweed).

Problems and Maintenance. This vine is relatively trouble-free, but its great vigor presents a problem in any but large-scale situations. It requires strong support because of its mass. Regular pruning to control size and maintain fullness close to the ground is essential when using this vine as a screen.

Cultivars. 'Crimson Trumpet' (Plant Patent No. 4119, 1977) has large, velvety deep crimson

Campsis radicans.

flowers. 'Flava' (= 'Yellow Trumpet') has golden yellow flowers.

Related Species and Hybrids

Campsis grandiflora 1 (Chinese trumpetvine). Weakly climbing but vigorous vine with very large (8 cm/3 in.), scarlet to orange-pink flowers in loose clusters in late summer. Much less cold-hardy than *C. radicans* (Zones 7b–9a+).

Campsis ×*tagliabuana* 'Madame Galen' 1 (Madame Galen trumpetvine). This vigorous hybrid (*C. grandiflora* × *C. radicans*) combines much of the hardiness of *C. radicans* with flowers about as large and showy as those of *C. grandiflora*. This is a larger-flowering substitute for *C. radicans* in Zones 5b–9a.

Bignonia capreolata 1 (crossvine). Because of recent nomenclatural revision, this close relative of *Campsis* is now named *Anistostichus capreolata*. It differs from *Campsis* in having evergreen foliage and a relatively short flowering period in spring and is less cold-hardy, useful in Zones 6b–9a+. Its flowers are similar but smaller (to 5 cm/2 in. long), reddish orange, paler inside. It has the same disadvantages as *Campsis radicans*: excessively vigorous growth and greater size than can be accommodated by small-scale landscapes. It is equally free of insect and disease problems; and it climbs by tendrils with adhesive discs, making a large evergreen mass on wall supports very quickly. The selection 'Atrosanguinea' has long, narrow leaves and dark purplish flowers.

Clytostoma callistegiodes (synonyms: *Bignonia speciosa, B. violacea*; violet or lavender trumpetvine, Argentine trumpetvine). Another relative of *Bignonia* and *Campsis* in the Bignoniaceae (bignonia family), this vigorous, high-climbing vine has large (to 8 cm/3 in. long and wide) pale lavender and purple-streaked, trumpetlike flowers, appearing in great numbers in spring. The evergreen, compound leaves terminate in tendrils and add year-round interest. This plant is inevitably sparse at the base, a consideration in its use. Useful only in the mildest climates of the South (Zone 9a+) in full sun or partial shade.

Macfadyena unguis-cati 1 (synonyms: *B. tweediana, Doxantha unguis-cati*; catclaw creeper). This vigorous, high-climbing vine from Mexico, the West Indies, and South America holds to its support by hooked tendrils, hence the common name. It has pale, evergreen leaves with two narrow leaflets and a central tendril and has large numbers of bright golden yellow funnel-shaped flowers, to 10 cm/4 in. long, in midspring. Useful in Zones 9a+, with some winter dieback in Zone 8.

Caragana arborescens 6

SIBERIAN PEATREE
Deciduous shrub
Fabaceae (Leguminosae; Pea Family)

Native Range. Manchuria and Siberia.

Useful Range. USDA Zones 2a–6b, but of questionable value in Zones 5 and 6.

Function. Shelter belt, windbreak, screen border, specimen.

Size and Habit

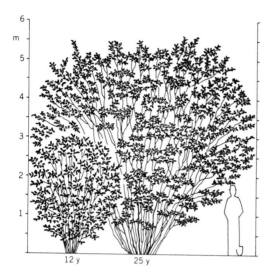

Caragana arborescens.

Adaptability. This shrub's landscape value rests primarily on its ability to withstand the extreme cold and dryness of the northern areas of the United States and Canada.

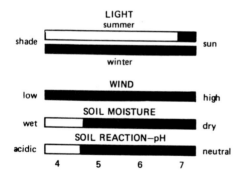

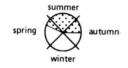

Seasonal Interest. *Flowers:* Small, yellow, and pealike in late spring or early summer. *Foliage:* Small, compound leaves make a sparse mass. *Fruits:* Small, inconspicuous pods turn brown on ripening.

Problems and Maintenance. Mites and insects frequently defoliate this plant in late summer. Even though it grows reasonably well in spite of this, its appearance is impaired. Because of this problem and its general sparseness, this shrub is seldom useful in small-scale plantings but is reserved primarily for shelter-belt planting in exposed northern areas, where it requires no maintenance.

Cultivars. 'Lorbergii' is a graceful plant, to 2.5 m/8 ft tall, with linear leaves, producing a very fine texture. It is not very widely available, but is a possibility as a textural accent in a mixed border or as a specimen.

'Nana' includes variable plants of unpredictable growth rate. Some individuals remain dwarf, below 1 m/3.3 ft, for several years. Others grow rapidly above eye level. In any case, these plants usually are more ornamental than the species type because of their greater fullness and concentration of flowers and foliage. Plants that reach heights of 2.5 m/8 ft are superior to the species type for visual screening. Further selection for desirable clones, and maintenance of their identity, may make this plant more useful in the future.

'Pendula' has a strongly weeping growth habit and usually is grafted on a standard (high on an upright seedling) and used as a specimen for accent in formal landscapes.

'Walker' is a popular hybrid of 'Lorbergii' and 'Pendula,' with the strongly weeping habit of 'Pendula' and the fine foliage texture of 'Lorbergii.'

Related Species

Caragana aurantiaca 3 (orange peashrub) and *C. pygmaea* 3 (pygmy peashrub). These low-growing, compact shrubs from Siberia and adjacent areas are useful in the same areas as *C. arborescens*, when small shrubs are needed.

Caragana frutex 5 (Russian peashrub). This shrub is intermediate in height between the dwarf species (above) and *C. arborescens* and it usually makes a denser mass than *C. arborescens*, with dark green, fine textured foliage. Its only problem is a tendency to sucker freely. 'Globosa,' selected from *C. frutex* at the Skinner Nursery, Dropmore, Manitoba, is very compact, maturing at 1 m/3.3 ft, dark green, non-suckering, and apparently mite-resistant.

Caragana microphylla 5 (littleleaved peashrub). This shrub is similar to *C. arborescens*, except in its slightly finer textured foliage and more spreading growth habit.

Colutea arborescens 5 (bladder senna). This Mediterranean shrub is similar to *Caragana arborescens* except that it is less cold-hardy and has large inflated pods. It is useful in Zones 6a–9a, and perhaps also Zone 5. Its red-marked yellow flowers appear with those of *Caragana arborescens* in late spring, then continue through midsummer. The low-growing selection 'Bullata,' 1.5 m/ 5 ft tall, is of some interest as a dwarf plant.

Halimodendron halodendron 4 (salt tree). This native of central Asia is similar to its close relative *Caragana arborescens* in general effect, except that it has lilac-purple flowers, less than 2 cm/0.8 in. across in small clusters, opening in early summer. This shrub's principal value is its ability to tolerate difficult conditions, including alkaline and even saline soils. It is useful in Zones 3a–6b but of questionable value other than for its salt tolerance.

Senna corymbosa 5 (synonym: *Cassia corymbosa*; flowery senna). This native of South America is not dense enough or permanent enough for screening, but is planted for its yellow flowers, which are showy from late summer well into autumn. It is useful in Zones 8b–9a+.

Carpinus betulus 7

EUROPEAN HORNBEAM
Deciduous tree
Betulaceae (Birch Family)

Native Range. Europe and Asia Minor.

Useful Range. USDA Zones 5a–7a.

Function. Shade and street tree, specimen, screen.

Size and Habit

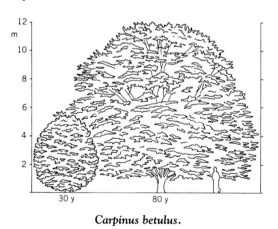

Carpinus betulus.

Adaptability

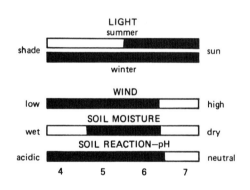

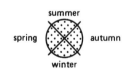

Seasonal Interest. *Foliage:* Dark green, crisply textured, remaining green late in autumn, occasionally turning yellowish before falling. *Fruits:* Pendulous clusters of small nutlets partly enclosed by green, leafy bracts, inconspicuous. *Trunk and branches:* Smooth gray bark is darker than that of beeches, otherwise similar.

Carpinus betulus 'Fastigiata.'

Problems and Maintenance. This tree is relatively trouble-free and long-lived, but may be damaged in areas subjected to frequent ice storms.

Cultivars. 'Columnaris' is narrowly oval and compact in habit, maintaining a central trunk, sometimes mistakenly sold under the name 'Fastigiata.' It is useful primarily as a specimen or large-scale screen.

'Fastigiata' (= 'Pyramidalis') is fastigiate (with narrow branching angles, broomlike), in outline oval to vase-shaped with age, not maintaining a single central trunk. Somewhat broader and more open than 'Columnaris,' it is seldom available. Seedlings of C. *betulus* show considerable variation in growth rate, branching angles, and width, and a large number of variants could be selected and named if one wanted to add to the considerable confusion that exists over the few existing cultivars.

Carpinus caroliniana 7

AMERICAN HORNBEAM, BLUE BEECH, IRONWOOD

Deciduous tree

Betulaceae (Birch Family)

Native Range.   Eastern North America.

Useful Range.   USDA Zones 3b–9a.

Function.   Shade, patio, or street tree; specimen; naturalizing.

Size and Habit

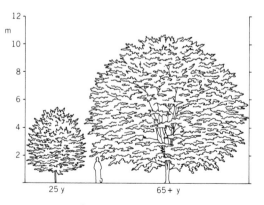

Carpinus caroliniana.

Adaptability

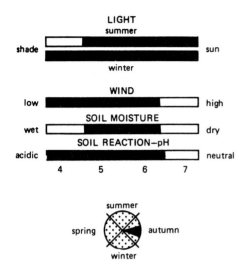

Seasonal Interest. *Foliage:* Lacy, light green in spring, turning deep green by midsummer, then to red-orange in autumn. *Fruits:* Pendulous clusters of small nutlets partly enclosed by green leafy bracts, inconspicuous. *Trunk and branches:* Sinewy appearing main branches with smooth, light gray bark add distinct winter interest.

Problems and Maintenance. This tree is relatively trouble-free and needs little maintenance, but it may be damaged in areas subjected to frequent ice storms.

Related Species

Carpinus cordata 7. This small tree from eastern Asia is very similar to C. *japonica* and functionally equivalent, but not commonly available. Both show promise as small shade trees.

Carpinus japonica 7 (Japanese hornbeam). This species is similar to C. *caroliniana* in landscape use and general appearance but differs in having somewhat larger leaves, turning dull red in autumn, and red-tinged fruiting clusters in late summer. It is also less hardy, useful in Zones 5b–8b.

Carpinus caroliniana.

Carpinus cordata.

Carya illinoinensis 8

Synonyms: *Carya pecan, Hicoria pecan*
PECAN
Deciduous tree
Juglandaceae (Walnut Family)

Native Range. Central North America from the Mississippi Basin westward to Kansas and Texas and southward to high elevations in Mexico.

Useful Range. USDA Zones 6a–9a+. For good results in Zones 6 and 7a, use only the hardiest cultivars, originating from the northern parts of the natural range.

Function. Shade tree, specimen, naturalizing, preservation of wild stands, edible nut production.

Size and Habit

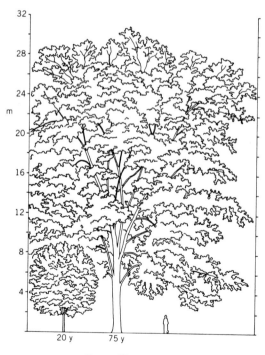

Carya illinoinensis.

Adaptability

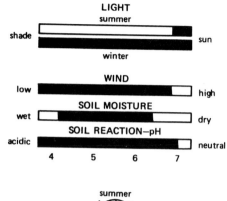

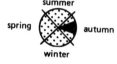

Seasonal Interest. *Foliage:* Medium green, compound leaves allow filtered sunlight to pass, and they turn clear yellow in autumn. *Fruits:* Edible nuts are highly valued, the most important commercially of any *Carya* species. Husks open on the tree and the nuts fall, leaving the husks attached to the branches for a time. *Trunk and branches:* Light gray or tan bark has landscape interest in winter sun.

Problems and Maintenance. This tree is not easily transplanted, but it is considerably less difficult than most other *Carya* species. Where nut production is secondary to use, it needs little maintenance.

Cultivars. Selections of *Carya illinoinensis* have been made for nut production and for hardiness. For landscape use, cultivars are of less specific value except for northern areas, where selection of hardy cultivars may prove the easiest way of ensuring adapted trees. Trees grown from nuts collected from wild trees in the northern parts of the range may be as well adapted as hardy cultivars, however. When nut production is of interest, follow the advice of local nut growers concerning cultivars wherever possible.

Carya ovata 8

SHAGBARK HICKORY
Deciduous tree
Juglandaceae (Walnut Family)

Native Range.   Eastern United States and parts of adjacent Canada, scattered in high elevations in Mexico.

Useful Range.   USDA Zones 4b–8b.

Function.   Shade tree, specimen, naturalizing, edible nut production.

Size and Habit

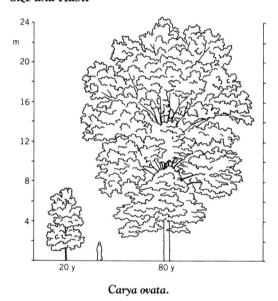

Carya ovata.

Adaptability

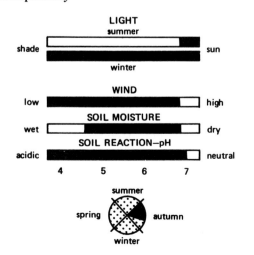

Seasonal Interest.   *Foliage:* Rich green, compound leaves turn golden-bronze in autumn. *Fruits:* Edible nuts in small husks, the sweetest and thinnest-shelled among the hickories, except the pecan (*C. illinoinensis*). *Trunks and branches:* Shaggy bark comes off in large plates, adds considerable landscape interest year-round.

Problems and Maintenance.   Hickories as a group are difficult to transplant in large sizes because they have a deep tap root and feeding roots so extensive that few can be recovered in digging. Young trees that have been root pruned regularly or container grown are less difficult to establish. Foliage and husks make considerable ground litter.

Cultivars.   Cultivars of *Carya ovata* have been selected for nut production. For landscape use, it is not necessary to use cultivars. In situations where nut production also is a consideration, consult local nut growers about suitable cultivars for the area where the trees are to be planted.

Related Species

Carya cordiformis 8 (bitternut hickory).   This large tree, to 20–30 m/66–98 ft, native to the eastern United States and adjacent Canada, has inedible nuts and less landscape character than several other *Carya* species, but it is worth preserving in site development in Zones 4b–8b.

Carya glabra 8 (pignut hickory).   This very large tree, to 30–40 m/98–131 ft tall in time, native to the eastern United States and parts of adjacent Canada, has nuts of little value, but it is better adapted to dry soil and temperature extremes than most hickories. It is useful in Zones 5b–9a+ but difficult to transplant, and it more often will be preserved in site development than planted.

Carya laciniosa 8 (shellbark hickory).   This very large tree, to 30–40 m/98–131 ft tall in time, native to east-central North America from New York to Iowa and south to Tennessee and Texas, is very similar to *C. ovata* and just as useful for planting or preservation in development in Zones 5b–8b.

Carya tomentosa 8 (mockernut hickory). Another large tree, to 20–30 m/66–98 ft, this native of the eastern United States and parts of adjacent Canada is similar in landscape effect and usefulness to *C. cordiformis*. Its usefulness is largely limited to preservation in site development in Zones 5a–9a.

Caryopteris ×*clandonensis* 3

BLUEBEARD
Deciduous subshrub
Verbenaceae (Vervain Family)

Hybrid origin. *C. incana* × *C. mongholica*.

Useful Range. USDA Zones 4a–8b. Tops are winterkilled regularly in Zones 4–6 and in some winters in Zones 7–8, but the plant returns to bloom in a single season.

Function. Specimen, border.

Size and Habit

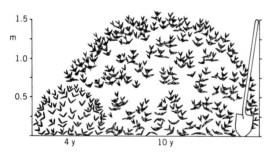

Caryopteris ×*clandonensis.*

Adaptability

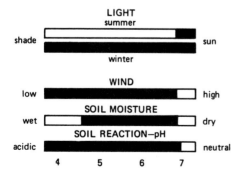

Seasonal Interest. *Flowers:* Blue, in flat, lateral clusters in late summer and into early autumn. *Foliage:* Grayish green, medium fine in texture.

Problems and Maintenance. Since the tops are often winterkilled, they should be pruned to within a few inches of the ground each spring. The plant then will return quickly to flower in the same year. Even when the tops are not winterkilled, successive seasons' growth can become straggly, so drastic spring renewal pruning is recommended even in the South to maintain plant form. Otherwise, little or no maintenance is needed.

Cultivars. Several selections have been made, and new ones probably will appear in the future. 'Blue Mist' with light blue flowers, 'Longwood Blue' with bright blue flowers, opening over a long period, and 'Azure' and 'Heavenly Blue' with deeper blue flowers, are among the most popular.

Related Species

Caryopteris incana 4 (synonym: *C. tangutica;* blue spirea, bluebeard). This shrub from China and Japan is taller and less cold-hardy than *C.* ×*clandonensis* (to Zone 7a) and largely replaced by the hybrid in landscape use.

Caryopteris mongholica 3 (Mongolian bluebeard). This shrub is unusually cold-hardy (to Zone 3b) but less showy than *C. clandonensis* and largely replaced by it in landscape use.

Castanea mollissima 7

CHINESE CHESTNUT
Deciduous tree
Fagaceae (Beech Family)

Native Range.   China and Korea.

Useful Range.   USDA Zones 5b–7b.

Function.   Shade tree, specimen, edible nut production.

Size and Habit

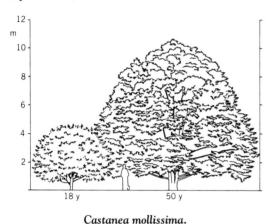

Castanea mollissima.

Adaptability

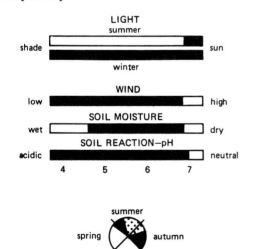

Seasonal Interest.   *Flowers:* Creamy white, cylindrical male catkins, to 12 cm/5 in. long, in late spring or early summer. *Foliage:* Leathery,

dark green, and lustrous above, soft-downy underneath, remaining green late, finally turning yellow-bronze in late autumn. *Fruits:* Edible nuts in large, sharply prickly husks, a nuisance when they litter the ground.

Problems and Maintenance.   For good nut production, it is necessary to provide for cross-pollination between two or more cultivars or seedlings and to follow a spray program as necessary. The troublesome prickly husks form whether or not pollination occurs. Otherwise, *C. mollissima* is relatively trouble-free. Even though the tree is cold-hardy in Zone 5b and perhaps in sheltered areas in Zone 5a, summers may be too cool and too short in these zones for the nuts to ripen fully.

The most serious problem of *Castanea* species is the chestnut blight disease, which eradicated the tops of virtually all wild chestnut (*C. dentata*) trees in North America during the first half of the twentieth century, leaving many live stumps. Some of these stumps continue to sprout, the new tops usually succumbing to the blight before trees reach bearing age. Genetic engineering has now developed synthetic viruses that reportedly can convert the deadly blight fungus into a more benign form. It is hoped that the converted fungus, when sprayed on infected chestnut stumps, will "breed" with the virulent form, rendering it benign. If field testing of this modified fungus should be successful, this could be a means by which *C. dentata* can return to usefulness.

Castanea mollissima.

Castanea mollissima.

Cultivars. Many hybrids of *Castanea dentata, C. mollissima,* and other *Castanea* species have been selected for nut production, timber, and landscape use by the U.S. Department of Agriculture, the Connecticut Agricultural Experiment Station at New Haven, Chestnut Hill Nursery, Alachua, FL, and the Badgersett Research Farm in Canton, MN. More than 20 disease-resistant hybrid cultivars and another 10 or more *C. mollissima* selections are commercially available at writing. When selecting trees for a specific locality, it is best consult the local Cooperative Extension Service office or a local member of the North American Nutgrowers Association.

Related Species

Castanea crenata 7 (Japanese chestnut). This blight-resistant species is being used in hybridization to obtain blight-resistant cultivars with superior nut production. It is useful in Zones 6a–7b and perhaps more widely.

Castanea dentata 8 (American chestnut). This handsome, large tree has superior nuts, timber, and landscape value, and is hardy in Zones 4b–8a, but unfortunately it has been nearly decimated by chestnut blight. A few trees growing outside the principal range of the species prior to the outbreak of this disease have managed to escape it for long periods, but they presumably would be susceptible if the disease were introduced into their locality. In spite of great public interest in finding resistant trees, no truly resistant forms have been found. *C. dentata* has been crossed with blight-resistant species (e.g., *C. crenata*) in attempts to develop superior cultivars. Evaluation is still going on.

Castanea pumila 6 (Alleghany chinquapin). This small, shrubby tree, native to the eastern and South-central United States, is useful as a specimen or for naturalizing in sandy soil in Zones 5a–9a. Its leaves are green above and whitened underneath, turning yellow in autumn.

Castanea sativa 8 (Spanish chestnut). This large tree, native to the Mediterranean region, is the source of most edible chestnuts marketed in North America. It is less hardy than *C. dentata* and *C. mollissima* (to Zone 6b) and blight-susceptible as well, so it is no better a prospect for landscape use than *C. dentata.*

Catalpa bignonioides 7

SOUTHERN CATALPA, INDIAN BEAN

Deciduous tree

Bignoniaceae (Bignonia Family)

Native Range. Southeastern United States: Mississippi to Florida, and naturalized in many areas farther north.

Useful Range. USDA Zones 5a–9a.

Function.   Shade, specimen.

Size and Habit

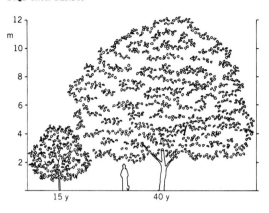

Catalpa bignonioides.

Adaptability.   One of the most widely adaptable of all trees to heat and cold, wetness and dryness, and varying light and soil conditions.

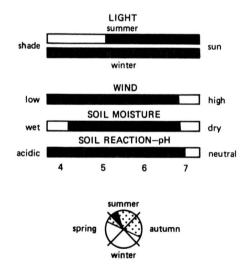

Seasonal Interest.   *Flowers:* White with brown or yellowish markings in throat, very showy in early summer. *Foliage:* Large, bright green leaves give the tree a coarse texture. *Fruits:* Long, hanging seed pods are conspicuous after the leaves have fallen, and a litter problem later.

Problems and Maintenance.   The long, leathery seed pods of this tree create a serious litter problem when they fall at different times during fall and winter. Catalpas are often infested with large worms that are valued as bait by fishermen, but they are objectionable in small-scale situa-

Catalpa speciosa.

tions and can defoliate trees when present in large numbers.

Cultivars.   'Aurea' has bright golden foliage in early summer, soon turning green but making the tree a striking landscape accent for a short time. 'Nana' is a dwarf form, usually grafted on a standard (high on an upright seedling), making a rather strong landscape accent, and grown solely for its unusual form.

Related Species

Catalpa ovata 7 (Chinese or yellow catalpa). This Chinese species is similar to C. *bignonioides* in size, with poorer form and with yellowish flowers marked orange and purple in late spring. It is useful in Zones 4b–9a.

Catalpa speciosa 8 (northern or western catalpa). This tall, rather narrow tree to 20–30 m/66–99 ft, is native from southern Indiana to Arkansas and western Tennessee and is even coarser than C. *bignonioides* because of its larger leaves and pods. Useful in large-scale, parklike plantings in Zones 4a–9a.

Chilopsis linearis 6 (desert willow).   This loose, multiple-trunked, shrubby tree in the Bignoniaceae (Bignonia Family) is native from Texas into Mexico and west to southern California. It grows to 5–10 m/16–33 ft tall and wide, with very narrow leaves (15–30 cm/6–12 in. long), purple-tinted white flowers, similar to those of *Catalpa* in clusters to 10 cm/4 in. long, and pencil-sized seed pods. Useful in Zones 7b–9a+, at least in the southwestern corner of our area (central Texas). The selection 'Burgundy' has fragrant, deep red-purple flowers.

×*Chitalpa tashkentensis* 6 (chitalpa).   This is not a true genus and species, but rather an intergeneric cross of *Catalpa bignonioides* by *Chilopsis linearis*, the shrubby, narrow-leaved "desert willow" of northern Mexico and the southwestern United States. Chitalpa is a large shrub or small tree resembling a small catalpa but with much narrower leaves (to 18 cm/7 in. long by 4.5 cm/1.8 in. wide). and large clusters of showy white or pink flowers in early summer. Little is yet known about this plant's useful range, but it may prove to be a useful small to medium tree in our area. At least two cultivars have been selected: 'Morning Cloud' has very pale pink to white flowers and an upright growth habit; 'Pink Dawn' has pale pink flowers and a more spreading growth habit.

Ceanothus ovatus 3

INLAND CEANOTHUS
Deciduous shrub
Rhamnaceae (Buckthorn Family)

Native Range.   Northeastern United States to Manitoba, Nebraska, Colorado, and Texas.

Useful Range.   USDA Zones 3b–8a.

Function.   Massing, border, foundation, specimen.

Size and Habit

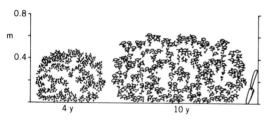

Ceanothus ovatus.

Adaptability.   This is one of the most adaptable low shrubs to temperature extremes, dryness, wind, and poor soil, in part because of its ability to fix and use atmospheric nitrogen.

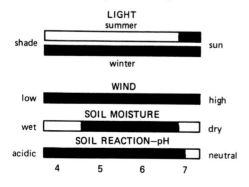

Seasonal Interest.   *Flowers:* Small, white, in flattened clusters in early summer. *Foliage:* Medium green leaves, 2.5–5 cm/1–2 in. long, neutral in effect.

Problems and Maintenance.   This shrub is trouble-free and requires no maintenance—not even pruning, since its growth habit is dense and compact, but it tends to be short-lived.

Related Species and Hybrids

Ceanothus americanus 3 (New Jersey tea).   This species is slightly taller and later flowering than *C. ovatus*, otherwise deciduous like *C. ovatus* and similar in appearance and useful range. Native from Ontario and Manitoba to Nebraska, South Carolina, and Texas.

Ceanothus ovatus.

Ceanothus ×*delilianus* 5 (French hybrid ceanothus). This hybrid of *C. americanus* by the deciduous but tender azure ceanothus (*C. coeruleus*), from Mexico, may be useful in our area in Zones 7 and 8, in areas having moderate summers, but probably is not commercially available.

Ceanothus ×*pallidus* 4. This hybrid of *C.* ×*delilianus* by *C. ovatus* is a white- or pink-flowering deciduous shrub, but has been used very little within our area. It probably is useful in Zones 6–8. Several cultivars were selected a century ago; a few of the most popular are 'Ceres,' with lilac-pink flowers, and 'Marie Simon', with pale pink flowers.

Many additional species of *Ceanothus* and their hybrids native to western North America are in landscape use on the West Coast. These are evergreen and far more handsome than the above species, but they are not cold-hardy in the northeastern and midwestern United States and are apparently poorly adapted to the southeastern states as well. They might be tried experimentally in Zones 8a–9a+.

Cedrus libani 7–8

CEDAR OF LEBANON
Evergreen tree
Pinaceae (Pine Family)

Native Range. Asia Minor.

Useful Range. USDA Zones 5b–9a. Only the var. *stenocoma* is cold-hardy in areas colder than Zone 7.

Function. Specimen, screen, massing.

Size and Habit

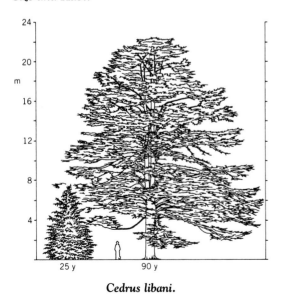

Cedrus libani.

Adaptability

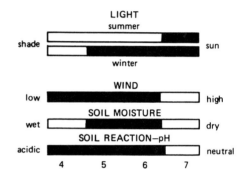

Seasonal Interest. *Foliage:* Dark green, evergreen, needlelike, solitary or in rosettes. *Cones:* Male cones numerous, small, on low branches; female cones large, to 10 cm/4 in. long, few, on short branches in top of tree, erect, requiring two years to develop, ripening purplish and then disintegrating on the tree.

Problems and Maintenance. Cedars occasionally are subject to damage by borers, especially in the South. Otherwise they are trouble-free.

Subspecies

Cedrus libani ssp. *libani* 8 (cedar-of-Lebanon). This is the typical population, long called by this

Cedrus libani

Cedrus libani ssp. *atlantica* 'Glauca.'

species name and described above. Native to Lebanon, Syria, and Turkey, ssp. *libani* also includes several dwarf and slow-growing cultivars which are useful primarily for accent or bonsai treatment. A few that are available in our area are listed here: 'Aurea-prostrata' has golden yellow foliage and irregularly prostrate form; 'Gold Tip' has yellow new foliage, turning green except for the tips after early summer; 'Nana' is a dwarf form valued for bonsai; 'Pendula' is prostrate in habit or pendulous when grafted on a standard or planted at the top of a retaining wall; 'Green Prince' is dwarf and dense, most useful for bonsai; 'Sargentii' is slow growing and spreading to slightly pendulous, remaining below 1.5 m/5 ft for many years.

Cedrus libani ssp. *atlantica* 7 (synonym: *C. atlantica*; Atlas cedar). This native of the Atlas Mountains of northwestern Africa is potentially a large tree, but seldom exceeds 18 m/60 ft in landscape use. This tree is somewhat more open and sparsely branching than ssp. *libani* and is

useful in Zones 7a–9a. The selection 'Glauca,' with strikingly blue foliage, is widely planted for accent in color and form. 'Glauca Pendula' is similar except pendulous when grafted on a standard or staked. 'Fastigiata' is similar to 'Glauca' but more narrowly pyramidal. 'Pendula' is pendulous but not generally available.

Cedrus libani ssp. *brevifolia* 7 (synonym: *C. brevifolia*; Cyprus cedar). This rare tree, once native to the mountains of Cyprus but now preserved only in cultivation, is not usually available commercially. It probably is less cold-hardy than the hardiest trees of ssp. *libani*, but otherwise the two subspecies differ very little from each other.

Cedrus libani ssp. *stenocoma* 8 (synonym: *C. libani* var. *stenocoma*). This includes a subpopulation that grows at high elevations in Turkey, and it includes several relatively cold-hardy forms that have been introduced into our area by the Arnold Arboretum, the New York Botanical Garden, and others. The vigorous and gracefully semipendulous selection 'Purdue Hardy' has persisted for at least 35 years on the Purdue University campus (hardiness zone 5b), suffering only minimal browning of needle-tips after "test" winters (minimum temperatures of −25°F. and lower) in the 1970s and showing no visible damage in equally rigorous winters in the early 1980s. It is not commercially available at writing.

Related Species

Cedrus deodara 7 (Deodar cedar). This native of central Asia is potentially a large tree but usually does not exceed 15 m/50 ft in height in most landscape use. It is picturesque, with gracefully sweeping, plumose branches. This is a popular specimen tree in Zones 7b–9a+, but the cultivars 'Kashmir' and 'Shalimar' are useful in slightly colder areas, probably to Zone 6b. Several other cultivars have been selected for form and foliage color. A few of those available in our area are listed here: 'Albispica' has creamy white new shoot tips, which fade to pale yellow by midsummer; 'Aurea' has golden new foliage, which fades to greenish yellow in summer and holds that color over the winter; 'Gold Cone' is similar to 'Aurea' but narrower in outline, occupying less space; 'Klondike' has lime-green foliage in summer, then turns golden yellow in winter; 'Pendula' (= 'Prostrata') is prostrate, growing rapidly and eventually covering large areas, or is pendulous when staked and trained or grafted on a standard; 'Prostrate Beauty' has gray-blue foliage and spreads with layering of branches, 'Pygmy' (= 'Pygmaea') is dwarf with steely blue foliage, making a small mound.

Celastrus scandens 1 and 2

AMERICAN BITTERSWEET

Deciduous vine

Celastraceae (Staff Tree Family)

Native Range.   Eastern United States and adjacent Canada, southwesterly to New Mexico.

Useful Range.   USDA Zones 3b–8b.

Function.   Screen (with strong support), specimen, large-scale groundcover.

Size and Habit.   Grows rapidly and scrambles over ground or climbs by twining to heights of 4–6 m/13–19 ft.

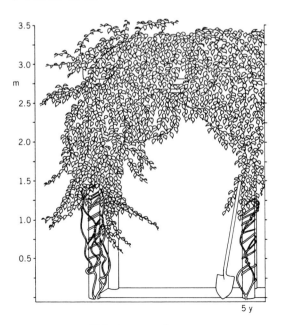

Celastrus scandens.

Adaptability

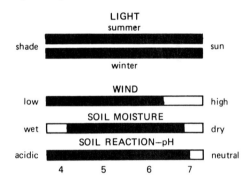

Seasonal Interest.   *Foliage:* Lustrous, bright green, turning clear yellow in autumn. *Fruits:* Deep yellow in terminal clusters with red-orange arils covering the seeds and appearing as the fruit splits, showy in autumn and well into winter. Usually dioecious; plant females with an occasional male in the same planting to ensure maximum fruiting.

Problems and Maintenance.   Generally trouble-free, but very vigorous, best in large-scale situations.

Cultivars.   'Indian Brave' and 'Indian Maiden' are staminate (male) and pistillate (female) clones, respectively. One male plant (nonfruiting) will usually provide pollen for a planting of several female plants. Plants of known sex are available without cultivar designation in some nurseries. Hermaphroditic clones (with flowers of both sexes on the same plant) may exist (as they certainly do in *Celastrus orbiculatus*), but are seldom available.

Related Species

Celastrus loeseneri 1 and 2 (Loesener bittersweet) and *C. rosthornianus* 1 and 2 (Rosthorn bittersweet). These species, both from China, are possible substitutes for *C. scandens* in Zones 4b–8b, with fruiting interest similar but in lateral rather than terminal clusters.

Celastrus orbiculatus 1 and 2 (oriental bittersweet). This species is native to China and Japan and now naturalized in many places in eastern North America, in some areas a pest. This is the most vigorous *Celastrus* species in most of our area and is high-climbing (to 10–12

m/33–40 ft). It is somewhat less cold-hardy than *C. scandens* (to Zone 5a) and bears fruits in lateral clusters. Otherwise, it is equivalent to *C. scandens* in the landscape.

Tripterygium regelii 1 and 5 (tripterygium). This native of Japan, Korea, and Manchuria forms a large, sprawling shrub growing to 2 m/6.6 ft or higher and at least as wide, but with support it will function as a loosely scrambling vine. It is effective as a visual screen and barrier where enough ground space can be given to its spread. Its small, creamy white flowers are borne in showy terminals clusters, to 20 cm/8 in. long, in midsummer, and its pale green, three-winged fruits add mild interest in autumn, but the lustrous bright green leaves, 8–15 cm/3–6 in. long, and the dense mass that they form are the most important landscape feature of this plant. It is tolerant of a wide range of soils and exposures and is useful in Zones 5b–8b and perhaps colder zones as well.

Celtis occidentalis 8

COMMON HACKBERRY
Deciduous tree
Ulmaceae (Elm Family)

Native Range. Northeastern and north-central United States and adjacent Canada.

Useful Range. USDA Zones 3b–8b.

Function. Shade, street, or avenue tree. Perhaps the best substitute in form and adaptability for the American elm in the Midwest.

Size and Habit

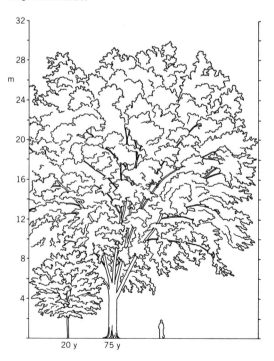

Celtis occidentalis.

Adaptability. Unusually well adapted to cold, heat, dryness, wind, and alkaline soils, therefore a valuable tree in the Midwest and plains states.

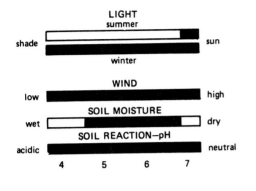

LIGHT
summer
shade — sun
winter

WIND
low — high

SOIL MOISTURE
wet — dry

SOIL REACTION–pH
acidic — neutral
4   5   6   7

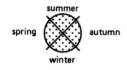

summer
spring — autumn
winter

Seasonal Interest. *Foliage:* Medium green, of medium to coarse texture, the leaves 5–12 cm/ 2–5 in. long, turning dull yellow in autumn. *Fruits:* Small, inconspicuous, purple-black berries in late summer and autumn. *Trunk and branches:* Medium gray bark, sometimes smooth to warty, sometimes vertically ridged.

Problems and Maintenance. This tree is susceptible to a witch's broom condition, caused by a mite, in which many small twigs proliferate from a single point on a branch and then die. The condition seldom damages trees seriously, but it can become unsightly. On the other hand, large numbers of witch's brooms can add winter branching interest. When this tree is selected, it should be in spite of this problem rather than with the expectation of controlling it. The same is true for nipple gall of the foliage, caused by an insect, which disfigures the leaves but usually does little permanent damage.

Cultivar. 'Prairie Pride' grows rapidly, with ruggedly compact growth habit, globose form, and lustrous, dark green, leathery leaves, which turn yellow in autumn in some years. This cultivar seems to be quite resistant to witch's broom.

Related Species

Celtis bungeana 7 (Bunge hackberry). This tree from northeastern Asia is smaller than *C. laevigata,* to 15 m/50 ft, with smooth, light gray bark and lustrous, bright green foliage. It is not susceptible to the witch's broom condition that affects most *Celtis* species and is a handsome, functional tree, useful in Zones 6a–9a, perhaps also in colder zones, but very seldom commercially available.

Celtis laevigata 8 (sugar hackberry). This slender-branched tree from the southeastern and south-central United States is slightly smaller than *C. occidentalis,* to 20–25 m/66–82 ft tall, and unusually well adapted to hot, dry climates and alkaline soils. Its light green leaves, smaller than those of *C. occidentalis,* turn dull yellow in autumn, and its light gray, smooth bark is roughened by corky, warty growths, giving mild winter interest. It is useful in Zones 6a–9a+. The selection 'All Seasons' grows rapidly, with oval form. Its fine textured foliage turns yellow in autumn and its twigs are heavier than average for the species and less likely to shed. This cultivar is unusually cold-hardy for the species, at least to Zone 5b and perhaps also Zone 5a.

Celtis sinensis 7 (Chinese hackberry). This graceful tree is notable for its smooth bark and leathery, glossy green leaves, 5–8 cm/2–3 in. across. Its fruits are slightly larger than those of *C. occidentalis* and dark orange when ripe. It is resistant to witch's broom and useful in Zones 6b–9a, but is seldom available.

Pteroceltis tatarinowii 7. This wide spreading tree in the Ulmaceae (Elm Family), from northern and central China, is similar in appearance to the closely related *Celtis* except for its shaggy, light gray bark, peeling off in long strips, which adds year-round interest and a minor litter problem. Useful in Zones 5b–8b, but seldom available.

Cephalanthus occidentalis 5

BUTTONBUSH
Deciduous shrub
Rubiaceae (Madder Family)

Native Range. Eastern North America and southwestward to Texas and California.

Useful Range. USDA Zones 4b–9a, with selection of appropriate genetic material.

Function. Shrub border, naturalizing in wet sites.

Size and Habit

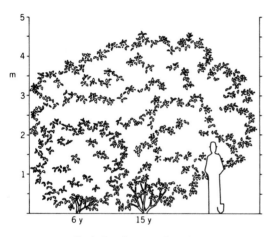

Cephalanthus occidentalis.

Adaptability. Valued for its extremely wide adaptability, this shrub is planted for its tolerance of wet soil more than for any other reason.

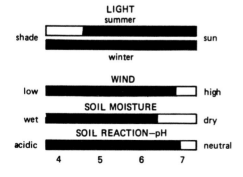

Seasonal Interest. *Flowers:* Creamy white, in globular heads 2–3 cm/1 in. across in midsummer, attractive to bees. *Foliage:* Dark green, lustrous in summer through early autumn. *Fruits:* Globular, similar to flower heads, but greenish or red tinged in early autumn, then disintegrating.

Problems and Maintenance. This shrub is coarse and short-lived and loses its form after a few years. At that point, it is best to cut it down close to the ground in spring for renewal. Otherwise it is trouble-free.

Related Species

Adina rubella 5 (glossy adina). This graceful relative of *Cephalanthus* has deep green, glossy foliage similar in texture to that of *Abelia* ×*grandiflora,* not nearly as evergreen but persisting late into autumn. The leaves, only 2.5 cm/1 in. long, are reddish bronze when young, adding more interest than the small heads of the flowers, which are whitish or tinted red-purple, appearing in middle to late summer. This shrub is probably not commercially available at present but is potentially useful in Zones 6b–9a. Winter damage tends to restrict its height to less than 1.5 m/5 ft north of Zone 7, similar to *Abelia* ×*grandiflora.*

Emmenopterys henryi 6–7. This tree in the Rubiaceae, native to central and western China, was introduced into cultivation by E. H. Wilson in 1907, but it has remained in cultivation only in a few arboreta and botanical gardens. It is reported to grow to a height of 30 m/100 ft in native habitat, but probably reaches less than half that size in cultivation in our area. Like the closely related *Pinckneya,* it owes much of its landscape interest to the showiness of its occasional enlarged and showy calyx lobes in midsummer, but in this species they are white rather than rosy-pink as in *Pinckneya.* The flowers, borne on current season's growth, are otherwise not showy, but the accompanying prominently veined leaves, similar to those of *Cephalanthus,* are an asset. Potentially useful in Zones 7a–9a, perhaps also Zone 6b.

Leptodermis oblonga 3 (Chinese leptodermis). This delicate shrub has medium green, fine-textured foliage, with individual leaves only 2 cm/0.8 in. long and small clusters of violet-purple flowers opening from midsummer to early autumn. Even though it is probably not commercially available yet, it is potentially useful as a low border shrub or for massing in Zones 6b–9a.

Pinckneya pubens 6 (fevertree, Georgia bark). This small, narrow tree with distinctive hori-zontal branching is native to the extreme southeastern United States. It is colorful in flower in midsummer because of the rosy pink calyx lobes, enlarged and petal-like, to 8 cm/3 in. long. The true petals are fused into a pale yellow, trumpet-shaped corolla about 2.5 cm/1 in. long. *Pinckneya* is soft-wooded, short-lived, and seldom commercially available, but it is highly distinctive and potentially useful in Zones 8a–9a+.

Cercidiphyllum japonicum 8

KATSURA TREE
Deciduous tree
Cercidiphyllaceae (Cercidiphyllum Family)

Native Range.   Japan and China.

Useful Range.   USDA Zones 5a–9a, but in Zones 8 and 9 it is useful only in good soil with ample moisture and in partial shade.

Function.   Shade tree, specimen. Form depends on method of training and age (see Problems and Maintenance).

Size and Habit

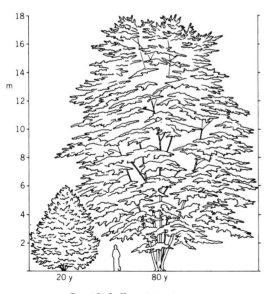

Cercidiphyllum japonicum.

Adaptability.   Best in full sun in soil with adequate moisture, except in Zones 8 and 9, where some shade is necessary.

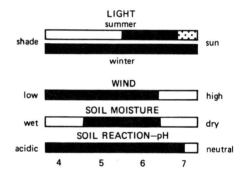

Seasonal Interest.   *Foliage:* Bright red when first unfolding in some trees, medium green and of distinctive texture in summer, the leaves rounded, 5–10 cm/2–4 in. long, turning yellowish, pink, or deep red in autumn, depending on moisture and soil fertility. *Trunk and branches:* Bark on older trees is grayish brown and slightly shaggy, adding mild year-round interest.

Problems and Maintenance.   Left alone, this tree tends to form several trunks and an interesting habit. When a single trunk is wanted, competing trunks must be removed from the young tree.

Varieties. The var. *magnificum*, from higher elevations on Japan's main island, is smaller than the species type but with larger (to 10 cm/4 in.), rounder, and more leathery leaves, which may color yellow, orange-red, or salmon pink in autumn.

The var. *sinense* from China does not differ appreciably from the Japanese species type except that it is probably considerably less cold-hardy and seldom is commercially available.

Cultivar. 'Pendulum' has long arching, strongly pendulous branches. The original tree has lived for at least three centuries at a temple on Honshu Island, Japan, and is revered as a national monument there, according to Krussman (*Manual of Cultivated Broadleaved Trees and Shrubs*, Timber Press, Beaverton, Oregon), but it has only recently become very popular in our area.

Related Species

Euptelea polyandra 7.   This rare Japanese deciduous tree is in the Trochodendraceae, a family probably more closely related to the Cercidiphyllaceae than any other, grows to 10–15 m/33–50 ft tall and not so wide, with broadly oval, coarsely toothed and sharply pointed leaves that are reddish as they unfold and bright red and yellow in autumn. The flowers, opening before the leaves in early spring, lack petals and are not showy but the clusters of red anthers add color briefly before the leaves begin to unfold. Potentially useful in Zones 6b–9a, and sheltered sites in Zone 6a, but rarely commercially available.

Tetracentron sinense 7.   This deciduous tree is in its own family, Tetracentraceae, but rather closely related to Cercidiphyllum, which it resembles in leaf and form, Euptelea, and Trochodendron. It has alternate leaves, unlike the leaves of *Cercidiphyllum*, which are predominantly opposite. Its small yellow flowers, in small pendulous spikes resembling catkins, open in early to middle summer. First brought out of China by E. H. Wilson in 1901, it is still barely in cultivation and is probably not commercially available at this writing. Potentially useful in at least Zones 8a–9a, probably also at least parts of Zone 7, and perhaps even Zone 6b.

Trochodendron aralioides 5–6.   This evergreen shrub or small tree is in the Trochodendraceae, closely related to the Cercidiphyllaceae. It is reported to reach heights of 10–20 m/33–66 ft in cloud forests of Japan, Korea, and Taiwan, where it sometimes grows as an epiphyte on *Cryptomeria*, but it grows slowly and in landscape use in our area it is more likely to reach 3–5 m/ 10–16 ft at most. Its dark green, leathery leaves, 3–8 cm/1–3 in. long and half as wide, are attached in a neat spiral arrangement, appearing as terminal whorls, and its interesting bright yellow-green flowers are arranged in a ring, developing into a radial aggregation of follicles. Useful in Zones 7a–9a+ and sheltered sites in Zone 6b, it needs protection from strong wind, especially in winter, and performs best when given at least partial shade.

Cercis canadensis 6–7

EASTERN REDBUD
Deciduous tree
Fabaceae (Leguminosae; Pea Family)

Native Range.   Eastern and south-central United States, southward into Texas.

Useful Range.   USDA Zones 5b(a)–9a+ with selection of appropriate genetic material. Hardiness in Zone 5a depends on selection from most northern wild material.

Function.   Patio tree, specimen, naturalizing.

Size and Habit. Form varies from low (to 6 m/ 20 ft), compact, and rounded in full sun to loose, open, and taller (to 12 m/40 ft) in shaded sites.

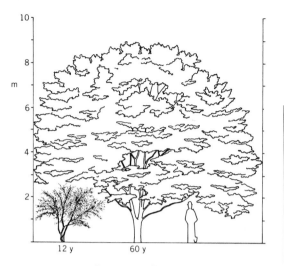

Cercis canadensis.

Adaptability. Even though the family Leguminosae includes many plants that can use atmospheric nitrogen, *Cercis* species apparently lack this ability. Nevertheless, these trees succeed in soil of relatively low fertility.

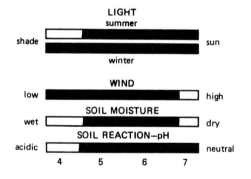

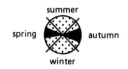

Seasonal Interest. *Flowers:* Purplish pink, clear pink or white, small clusters appearing before foliage in early to midspring, sometimes developing in large clusters directly on trunks and large branches. *Foliage:* Light green as it emerges during the last days of flowering, dark green in summer, turning bright yellow in autumn in most years. *Fruits:* Flat pods to about 8 cm/3 in. long, from late summer into winter, conspicuous when borne in large numbers after the leaves have fallen. *Trunk and branches:* Dark gray-brown bark sloughs off on trunks and branches of older trees to expose reddish inner bark.

Cercis canadensis.

Cercis canadensis.

Problems and Maintenance. Several insects can disfigure the foliage but are not usually serious problems. Stem canker and verticillium wilt occasionally can be serious. Otherwise, this tree has few problems and requires little maintenance.

Cultivars. 'Alba,' selected from the wild in Missouri, and 'Royal White' (= 'Royal'), from Illinois, have pure white flowers, those of 'Royal White' the larger of the two.

'Flame' (= 'Double Flame'), selected from the wild in Illinois, has purplish pink, semidouble flowers with as many as 20 petals and is much more vigorous than most trees of the species.

'Forest Pansy' has foliage opening bright crimson, turning to deep red purple as it matures, and then to bronze later in the summer. This cultivar makes a striking specimen in early summer, and it may retain its deep purple color throughout the summer in regions where summer nights are cool, such as the coastal Pacific Northwest, according to J. C. Raulston of North Carolina State University. It seems to be cold-hardy in USDA Zones 6b, perhaps also in Zone 6a, but probably not in Zone 5, at least in the Midwest.

'Pinkbud' and 'Wither's Pink Charm' (='Pink Charm') have clear, bright pink flowers, more versatile in combination with certain other colors than the typical purplish pink flowers of the species. 'Wither's Pink Charm' may no longer be commercially available. 'Ruby Atkinson' has soft shell-pink flowers, borne in large numbers.

'Silver Cloud,' selected by Theodore Klein in Crestwood, Kentucky, has silver-white variegated leaves but few flowers. Its hardiness is not yet well known, but J. C. Raulston has pointed out that the white-variegated foliage is most effective on vigorous plants under full sun but cool conditions.

Related Species

Cercis chinensis 6 (Chinese redbud).   This small tree from China is more shrubby than C. *canadensis,* offering little shade. It is usually planted for its bright rosy purple flowers, larger than those of C. *canadensis* and opening about two weeks later. It is useful in Zones 6b–9a+. The selection 'Alba' has white flowers but may not be commercially available. 'Avondale' has large numbers of exceptionally showy red-purple flowers.

Cercis occidentalis 6 (western or California redbud).   This thicket-forming shrub or small tree has pink to deep red-purple flowers slightly larger than those of C. *canadensis* and often deep red seed pods at maturity. It is commercially available on the West Coast and useful in Zones 7b–9a+, but it is questionable whether it will tolerate the summer heat of those zones in eastern North America.

Cercis reniformis 6 (synonym: C. *canadensis* var. *mexicana,* C. *canadensis* var. *texensis,* C. *mexicana,* C. *texensis;* Mexican or Texas redbud). Classification of *Cercis* populations in Mexico, New Mexico, and Texas is highly confused. Because of the continuity and breadth of the variation in this group, it is unclear whether any of these populations should be considered as species separate from C. *canadensis,* but C. *reniformis* is more widely accepted as such than the others. Because of all this, it is necessary to recognize that all of these names represent populations from the Southwest. Most members of this group are useful in Zones 8a–9a+, and many probably are hardy to Zone 7 as well. The following cultivars are commercially available: 'Oklahoma,' selected from the wild in Oklahoma, has glossy, leathery foliage and deep reddish flowers and is unusually cold-hardy (at least to Zone 6b). J. C. Raulston reminds us that 'Oklahoma' must be cloned (cutting-propagated, grafted, or tissue-cultured) to be true-to-type, which has been difficult, but plants grown from seeds cannot legitimately be called 'Oklahoma.' Moreover, they are inferior as landscape plants, and it is likely that they will also be less cold-hardy than the cultivar.

Cercis reniformis 'Oklahoma.'

Cercis siliquastrum 6–7 (Judas tree or Mediterranean redbud).   This native of southern Europe and adjacent Asia Minor has flowering interest similar to C. *chinensis* but is more treelike. It is probably useful only in Zones 7a–9a+, and plants are seldom available in our area.

Chaenomeles speciosa 4

Synonyms: *Chaenomeles lagenaria, Cydonia lagenaria*
FLOWERING QUINCE
Deciduous shrub
Rosaceae (Rose Family)

Native Range. China, long cultivated in Japan.

Useful Range. USDA Zones 4b–9a. May flower poorly following severe winters in Zones 4b and 5 and mild winters in Zones 8b and 9a.

Function. Specimen, border, barrier, hedge. When used as a hedge, it is best pruned informally to preserve flowering and character of form. Density and thorny branches make it an effective barrier.

Size and Habit

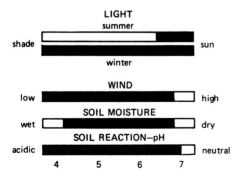

Chaenomeles speciosa.

Adaptability. This shrub is widely adapted to soil and moisture variations but performs best in full sun.

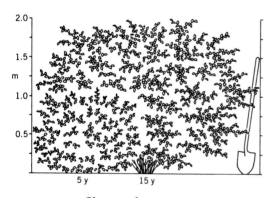

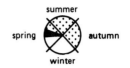

Seasonal Interest. *Flowers:* Showy, red, pink, or white, single or double, in early spring to mid-spring. *Foliage:* New foliage emerges red-bronze in late spring, then turns glossy dark green, remaining green until it falls in late autumn. *Fruits:* Applelike, pale green to yellow, interesting but not showy, useful in making preserves when fully ripe (yellow) in autumn.

Problems and Maintenance. This shrub is subject to occasional gall and mite infestations, apple scab, and fire blight, but differs in susceptibility among cultivars. It requires minimal pruning to maintain form and vigor. Overwinter rabbit damage can be severe in the North in some years and areas.

Cultivars. Well over 100 cultivars exist, but much fewer are commercially available at any one time. In practice it is best to use those that have performed well in the locality in question. A few of the most popular are listed here: 'Appleblossom' is a vigorous, medium-tall plant with pale pink flowers, red in the bud. 'Cameo' has double, apricot-pink flowers on a thornless, low-spreading plant. 'Nivalis' has white flowers on an upright and vigorous but full branching plant. 'Spitfire' is medium-tall with vivid red flowers. 'Toyonishiki' is vigorous and relatively trouble-free, with white, pink, and red flowers on the same plant. More cultivars are listed under Related Species.

Related Species and Hybrids

Chaenomeles japonica 3 (Japanese or lesser flowering quince). This species is much lower growing than *C. speciosa*, seldom exceeding 1 m/ 3.3 ft in height, and is useful for this low stature in the same zones as that species. The more popular cultivars include the following. 'Mones' (Low 'n White™) has large white flowers and remains very low. 'Minerva,' a hybrid of *C.*

japonica and *C. cathayensis,* is also low and has velvety cherry-red flowers. 'Orange Delight' has orange flowers. 'Rubra' is low, with deep red flowers. 'Moned' (Super Red™) has bright red flowers.

Chaenomeles ×*superba* 4 (hybrid Japanese flowering quince). This hybrid group is similar to its parents *(C. japonica × C. speciosa),* but intermediate in size, to 1.5 m/5 ft tall. A few of the most popular cultivars are listed here. 'Crimson Gold' has coral-red flowers. 'Jet Trail' is similar to 'Texas Scarlet' (below) except for its

soft white flowers. 'Texas Scarlet' is low and profusely flowering (cherry-red), one of the most popular cultivars in our area.

Chaenomeles ×*californica* 4 (California hybrid flowering quince). This is a mixed hybrid group involving at least three parent species (C. ×*superba* 'Corallina' × *C. cathayensis*), developed by W. B. Clarke of San Jose, California. It includes several showy cultivars, mostly less cold-hardy than those listed above but useful at least in Zones 6b–9a. 'Pink Beauty,' with rose-pink flowers, has remained very popular.

Chamaecyparis lawsoniana 3–7

LAWSON FALSE CYPRESS, PORT ORFORD CEDAR

Evergreen tree or shrub

Cupressaceae (Cypress Family)

Native Range. Northwestern United States.

Useful Range. USDA Zones 5b–8a. Hardiness north of Zone 6b depends on cultivar and selection of planting site away from afternoon sun and wind in winter.

Function. Specimen tree, screen (species type and taller cultivars), foundation (intermediate cultivars), and rock garden (dwarf cultivars).

Size and Habit

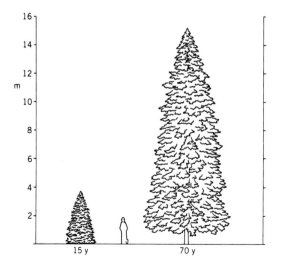

Chamaecyparis lawsoniana.

Adaptability. This species performs best in relatively moist soil and high humidity, especially in coastal areas.

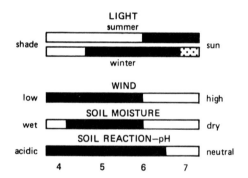

Seasonal Interest. *Foliage:* Evergreen, dense, scalelike (needlelike when juvenile) in flat sprays arranged in more-or-less vertical planes, strikingly so in some cultivars, medium green to steely blue-green, golden in certain cultivars. *Trunk and branches:* Shredding, reddish brown bark adds interest to larger specimens at all seasons.

Problems and Maintenance. This evergreen is relatively free of problems and maintenance when used in the proper climate, but in areas with hot, dry summers it is susceptible to serious mite infestations.

Chamaecyparis lawsoniana.

Cultivars. 'Allumii' (scarab false cypress) is a columnar form with steely blue-green foliage, striking in its vertical layering. It is an excellent narrow screen, reaching 2–4 m/6.6–13 ft in height fairly quickly, eventually 6–10 m/20–33 ft if left unpruned.

"Ellwoodii' (Ellwood false cypress) is upright, compact, and relatively slow-growing with soft, blue-green juvenile foliage. It reaches screening height (2 m/6.6 ft) only after 10 or more years, so it is used primarily as a specimen for accent.

'Fletcheri' (Fletcher false cypress) is similar to 'Ellwoodii' in general form and growth rate but has deep blue-green, partly juvenile foliage and an unusually interesting texture for this species.

'Forsteckensis' (Forsteck false cypress) is a dwarf, globose form, not exceeding 1 m/3.3 ft in height and spread for many years, with dense, blue-green foliage on twisted branchlets.

'Golden Showers' is compact in growth habit, with yellow-green foliage, pendulous, bright yellow branch tips, and outstanding winter color.

'Oregon Blue' has strikingly blue foliage and grows unusually fast for the species.

Many other cultivars are used on the West Coast, varying from very dwarf to full-size forms and including bright to bluish green, golden-yellow, and variegated foliage variants. Most are planted in eastern North America only by collectors.

Related Species

Chamaecyparis nootkatensis 6–8 (Alaska or Nootka false cypress). This tall tree, to 40 m/ 130 ft in native habitat from Alaska to Oregon but seldom over 15 m/49 ft in our area, is useful

Chamaecyparis nootkatenis 'Pendula.'

in Zones 5b–7b, in areas with relatively cool, moist summers. The cultivar 'Aurea' is compact and rather slower-growing, with light yellow new foliage, turning light green in summer. 'Compacta' is much slower-growing, remaining below eye level for years. 'Glauca' is similar to the species type except that it has strongly bluish foliage. 'Pendula' is a handsome accent plant with strongly pendent branchlets.

Chamaecyparis thyoides.

Chamaecyparis thyoides 5–7 (swamp or Atlantic white cedar). This tree, native from Maine to northern Florida and coastal Alabama and Mississippi, is useful, depending on geographic origin of genetic material, in Zones 5a–9a+. It is similar in general appearance to *Juniperus virginiana.* The cultivars 'Andelyensis,' an excellent, tightly columnar, semidwarf form growing slowly to 3 m/10 ft, and 'Ericoides,' a semidwarf, low-pyramidal form, growing to 1.5 m/5 ft with heathlike foliage texture, are fairly commonly used as specimens.

Chamaecyparis obtusa 3–7

HINOKI FALSE CYPRESS
Evergreen tree or shrub
Cupressaceae (Cypress Family)

Native Range.   Japan and Taiwan.

Useful Range.   USDA Zones 5a–8a.

Function.   Specimen tree, screen (species type and taller cultivars), foundation (intermediate varieties), rock garden (dwarf cultivars), and bonsai.

Size and Habit

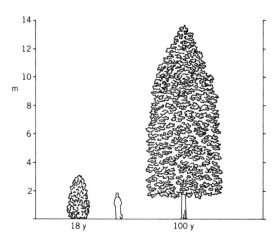

Chamaecyparis obtusa.

Adaptability.   This species performs best in relatively moist soil and high humidity but tolerates more average conditions as well.

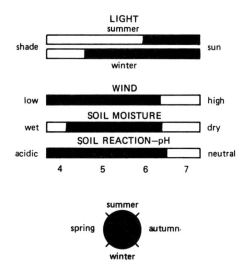

Seasonal Interest.   *Foliage:* Evergreen, glossy, dark green, scalelike leaves, white-marked underneath, give outstanding color and texture at all seasons. *Trunk and branches:* Shredding, reddish brown bark adds interest to older specimens at all seasons.

Problems and Maintenance.   This plant is relatively free of problems and maintenance when used in the proper climate, but in areas with hot, dry summers it is susceptible to mite infestations.

Cultivars.   There is a continuous range of slow-growing variants, much confused and frequently misnamed. The more common ones often can be obtained under the following cultivar names.

'Compacta' has compact branching habit, eventually reaching at least 2 m/6.6 ft in height and spread. It may even reach screening height, but too slowly to consider this a normal function.

'Nana Gracilis' is similar to 'Compacta' except that it has more obviously twisted branchlets and is somewhat more vigorous and less compact, eventually reaching at least 3 m/10 ft in height.

'Nana' is similar to 'Nana Gracilis,' but much slower-growing, varying greatly in growth rate but usually remaining below 1 m/3.3 ft for many years. The extreme dwarfs are even smaller.

Many other variants in foliage color, texture, and growth rate have been named. A few of the more common are listed here.

'Coralliformis' is a dwarf with twisted twigs (foliage), a coral-like texture, and dark green color.

'Crippsii' is slow-growing, to 3 m/10 ft or taller in time, with handsomely textured foliage that is bright golden-yellow where it is exposed to direct sun.

'Filicoides' is slow-growing, to 3 m/10 ft or taller in time, with loosely arranged, dark green, fernlike foliage giving a picturesque appearance to the plant. Useful only as a specimen, but an excellent choice for this purpose in intensive landscapes where moisture can be supplied.

'Lycopodioides' is a dwarf with tightly packed and spirally arranged foliage.

'Spiralis' is a dwarf with spirally twisted small branches.

'Tetragona' is a dwarf with tufted branches, tending to be four-sided in cross section.

'Tetragona Aurea' is similar to 'Tetragona' except that it has golden-yellow foliage in direct sun.

Chamaecyparis pisifera 3–8

SAWARA FALSE CYPRESS, RETINOSPORA

Evergreen tree or shrub

Cupressaceae (Cypress Family)

Native Range. Japan.

Useful Range. USDA Zones 5a–8a.

Function. Screen, specimen tree, rock garden (dwarf cultivars), bonsai. The species and full-sized cultivars are sometimes used as foundation plantings but soon outgrow such sites and must be replaced. Such cultivars should be grown as trees, and slow-growing forms of this and other species should be used for small-scale plantings.

Size and Habit

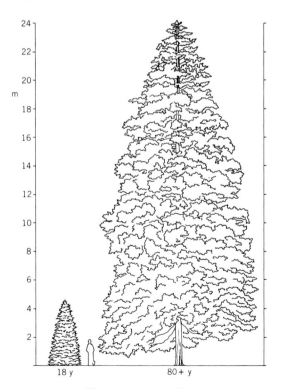

18 y   80+ y

Chamaecyparis pisifera.

Adaptability. This species of *Chamaecyparis* performs best in relatively moist soil and high humidity, but it grows well in average sites in the central Midwest.

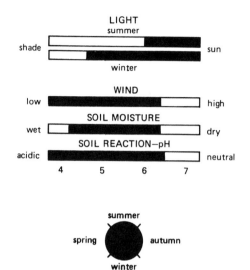

Seasonal Interest. *Foliage:* Evergreen, bright, dark or bluish green, of three distinct types (see Cultivars). *Trunk and branches:* Shredding, reddish brown bark adds interest to larger specimens at all seasons.

Problems and Maintenance. This plant is relatively free of problems and maintenance when used in the proper climate.

Cultivars. Cultivars belong to three foliage groups. Those in the "filifera" group (thread Sawara false cypress) have pendent, threadlike branches giving an unusual, fine, stringy texture. Individual leaves are scalelike and appressed tightly to the stem. Those in the "plumosa" group (plume Sawara false cypress) have foliage similar to the species type except that it is more plumose. Individual leaves are scalelike but spread away from the stem more than those of the "filifera" group. The "squarrosa" group (moss Sarawa false cypress) has soft, needlelike leaves spreading widely from the stem, giving a moss-like appearance.

Within these groups, many variants in growth rate, form, and color have been selected and named. A few of the more common are:

'Boulevard' (='Cyano-viridis') is a slow-growing, densely pyramidal form in the "squarrosa" group, with steely blue-green foliage, needle-like but soft to the touch.

'Filifera' is typical of the "filifera" group, not a dwarf but remaining below 3 m/10 ft for years.

'Filifera Aurea' is similar to 'Filifera' except for its golden-yellow foliage in full sun, especially bright as it first emerges.

'Filifera Aurea Nana' and 'Golden Mop' are dwarfs in the "filifera" group with golden-yellow foliage, remaining below 1 m/3.3 ft for 10 years or more.

'Plumosa' is typical of the "plumosa" group, growing to full size.

'Plumosa Aurea' is similar to 'Plumosa' except that the foliage on the outside of the plant exposed to direct sun is golden-yellow, especially in early summer.

'Plumosa Compressa' is a dwarf, moundlike form in the "plumosa" group, not exceeding 1 m/3.3 ft in height and spread in 10 years or more. Its upright, nearly mosslike branches are tipped with pale yellow.

'Plumosa Nana' is a dwarf, flattened and globe to pillowlike in form. It seldom exceeds 1.5 m/5 ft in height but will double that in spread after several years.

Other cultivars are available from nurseries specializing in dwarf conifers and are planted primarily by collectors.

Chimonanthus praecox 5

WINTERSWEET
Deciduous shrub
Calycanthaceae (Calycanthus Family)

Native Range. China.

Useful Range. USDA Zones 7b–9a+.

Function. Screen, border, specimen. Functions well as a screen when suckers are allowed to develop at base, but requires much space.

Size and Habit.

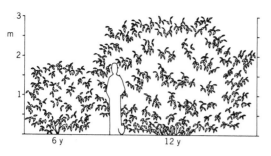

Chimonanthus praecox.

Adaptability. In areas having hot summers, this shrub performs best with at least light shade. It is widely adapted to soil conditions, including fairly wet soil.

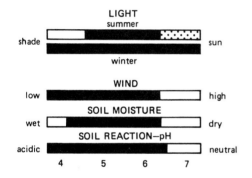

Seasonal Interest. *Flowers:* Pale yellow with deep red-brown centers, very fragrant, opening very early in spring, long before the leaves unfold, or even in warm periods in late winter. *Foliage:* Rich green, relatively coarse, the leaves 8–15 cm/3–6 in. long, making a dense mass and remaining green until frost.

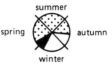

Problems and Maintenance. This shrub is virtually trouble-free, requiring no maintenance except occasional pruning to rejuvenate the plant by removing old wood.

Varieties. The var. *grandiflorus* has larger leaves and larger but less fragrant flowers.

Cultivars. 'Grandiflorus' has larger leaves and larger but less fragrant flowers, with prominent dark red centers. 'Luteus' has large, clear pale yellow flowers, opening later than the species type.

Chionanthus virginicus 6

WHITE FRINGETREE, OLD MAN'S BEARD
Deciduous shrub
Oleaceae (Olive Family)

Native Range. Southeastern and south-central United States.

Useful Range. USDA Zones 5a–9a.

Function. Specimen, border.

Size and Habit

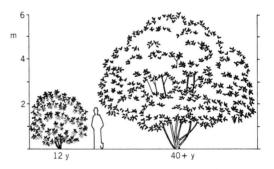

Chionanthus virginicus.

Adaptability. Performs best in reasonably moist sites in full sun.

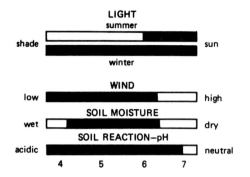

Seasonal Interest. *Flowers:* White, fringelike, dioecious, in loose clusters, 10–20 cm/4–8 in. long, the largest on male plants, very showy in late spring. *Foliage:* Coarsely textured, elliptical leaves, 8–20 cm/3–8 in. long, expanding very late in spring, turning yellow in autumn. *Fruits:* Blue-black fruits on female plants resemble small olives, to 2 cm/0.8 in. long. Male plants must be in the vicinity for pollination and fruit set.

Problems and Maintenance. Little maintenance is needed other than pruning out old branches every few years.

Cultivars. None are available, nor are plants of known sex unless they are selected when old

Chionanthus virginicus.

enough to flower, since this species is usually propagated by seeds.

Related Species

Chionanthus retusus 6 (oriental fringetree). This Asian counterpart of C. *virginicus* from China and Taiwan flowers later than C. *virginicus*

Chionanthus retusus.

Chionanthus virginicus.

Chionanthus retusus var. *serrulatus.*

and is more tolerant of calcareous soils. The species type becomes a small, ascending tree, to 6 m/20 ft, resembling a miniature American elm in form, with lightly striped bark. The var. *serrulatus* from Taiwan has a very different form, branching close to the ground and assuming a broad vase shape. It has handsome, exfoliating, cinnamon-brown bark. *C. retusus* is hardy in Zones 6a–9a, but var. *serrulatus* may not be hardy in colder areas than zones 6b or 7a.

Chionanthus retusus var. serrulatus.

Cinnamomum camphora 7

CAMPHOR TREE
Evergreen tree
Lauraceae (Laurel Family)

Native Range. China, Japan, Taiwan.

Useful Range. USDA Zone 9a+.

Function. Shade tree, specimen, screen, wind-break. Well adapted to city street use except for fruit litter.

Size and Habit

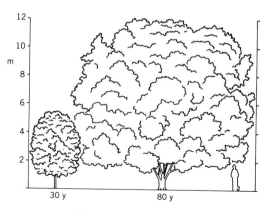

Cinnamomum camphora.

Adaptability

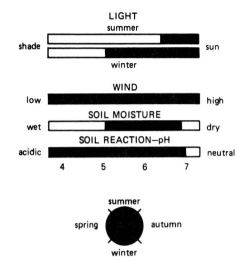

Seasonal Interest. *Flowers:* Inconspicuous, in spring. *Foliage:* Evergreen, glossy, bright to olive green, giving off a camphor odor when crushed. *Fruits:* Small, round, black fruits add minor landscape interest but litter the ground when they fall.

Problems and Maintenance. This tree is very shallow-rooted and casts dense shade, discouraging the use of turf or groundcover plants underneath it. Probably best handled in a mulched bed, but it also grows well close to paved areas when good drainage is provided. In Zone 9a, the top occasionally freezes back and pruning is necessary to remove deadwood. This has the effect of maintaining the size of the tree under 10 m/33 ft. In warmer climates, this tree reaches heights of 25–30 m/82–98 ft.

Cultivars. 'Monum' (Majestic Beauty™) is reported to grow more uniformly, with better foliage, than most trees of the species.

Related Species

Laurus nobilis 6 (laurel, sweet bay). This is the true laurel from the Mediterranean, the foliage of which was used in wreaths in early times and is the bay leaf seasoning used in cooking. Even though it forms a tree to 10 m/33 ft or taller in its native habitat, it seldom becomes more than a shrubby tree to 5 m/16 ft in the southeastern United States but is effective as a very small shade or patio tree. It is best grown in full sun in open, breezy sites on well-drained soil. Flowering and fruiting interest are insignificant compared with the crisp, olive green foliage. Useful in Zones 8a–9a+ and in protected sites in Zone 7.

Persea borbonia 6 (red bay persea). This evergreen tree in the Lauraceae (Laurel Family), native to the southeastern United States, grows to heights of 10 m/33 ft and occasionally nearly twice that in native habitat. Its flowers in middle spring are not conspicuous, but the berries that follow add landscape interest in late summer and early autumn. They are lustrous, blue-black, 1 cm/0.4 in. across, borne in loose clusters on red pedicels that remain colorful after the berries have fallen. This tree is considered difficult to establish and is seldom used. If the problem of establishment is solved by producing the tree in containers, it will be a most useful landscape tree for Zones 8a–9a+, tolerating wet soils but also performing well in soils of average moisture content.

Persea palustris 6 (swamp bay persea). This tree is similar to *P. borbonia* in just about every respect. The two species can be considered equivalent in landscape use but neither is often available. *P. palustris* may be even more tolerant of wet soil than *P. borbonia*.

Umbellularia californica 7–8 (California laurel, Oregon myrtle). This large tree is similar in general landscape effect to *Laurus nobilis* while young and, except for its dense foliage canopy, to *Persea* species, but eventually may reach heights of 20 m/66 ft or greater in good sites. This is a popular shade tree on the West Coast but probably is not commercially available in our area except from West Coast sources. No doubt some attempts have been made to use it in the southeastern United States, and it deserves further trial in Zones 8 and 9a.

Cistus ×*purpureus* 4

PURPLE ROCKROSE
Evergreen shrub
Cistaceae (Rockrose Family)

Hybrid origin.   *C. incanus* ssp. *creticus* × *C. ladanifer*.

Useful Range.   USDA Zones 7b–9a+.

Function.   Specimen, border, massing.

Size and Habit

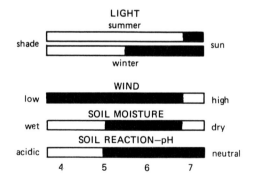

Cistus ×*purpureus.*

Adaptability.   *Cistus* species perform best on well-drained limestone soil in full sun.

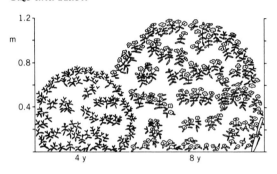

Seasonal Interest.   *Flowers:* Purple with yellow and deep red center blotches and yellow stamens, to 8 cm/3 in. in diameter, early summer and intermittently until autumn. *Foliage:* Ever-green, rather fine-textured, narrow (6–8 cm/2–3 in. long), gray-green and thickly pubescent underneath.

Problems and Maintenance.   *Cistus* species are maintenance-free once established except for occasional pruning for rejuvenation. All are considered difficult to transplant; use pot-grown plants.

Related Species and Hybrids

More than 20 species and hybrids are presently in cultivation, but few are available in our area. A few of the most common are listed here.

Cistus ×*cyprius* 5 (spotted rockrose).   Flowers 6–8 cm/2.4–3 in. across with white, purple, and yellow blotches, yellow stamens, and glandular-sticky foliage. Hybrid origin: *C. laurifolius* × *C. ladanifer*. Hardy in Zones 7b–9a+.

Cistus ×*corbariensis* 3 (synonym: *C.* ×*hybridus;* white rockrose).   This hybrid of *C. populifolius* × *C. salviifolius* has white flowers with yellow throats, resembling single roses, 3.5 cm/1.4 in. across, in early summer. It is useful in Zones 8b–9a+.

Cistus incanus 3 (synonym: *C. villosus;* hairy rockrose).   Rose to purple, yellow-centered flowers, 5 cm/2 in. across, foliage roughened and scaly-pubescent with longer gray hairs underneath. From southwestern Europe. Useful in Zones 7b–9a+. The hybrid (probably *C. incanus* ssp. *creticus* × *C. laurifolius*) 'Silver Pink' is a low

Cistus ×*glaucus.*

shrub, to 0.5 m/1.6 ft, with clear, light pink flowers and silvery gray foliage.

Cistus ladanifer 4 (laudanum, gum rockrose). White flowers, yellow in center, 8–10 cm/3–4 in. across, and glandular-sticky foliage. From the western Mediterranean. Hardy in Zone 7b–9a+.

Cistus laurifolius 4 (laurel rockrose). White flowers, yellow in center, 5–8 cm/2–3 in. across, foliage dark green and smooth above, glandular-sticky below. From the Mediterranean region. Hardy in Zones 7b–9a+; one of the hardiest species of *Cistus*. Its hybrid (with *C. monspeliensis*), *C.* ×*glaucus* 3, bears flowers in larger numbers and is useful in Zones 8a–9a+.

Cistus salviifolius 3 (sage rockrose). This rockrose has sage-green, net-veined leaves and flowers similar to those of *C.* ×*hybridus*, but larger, in late spring. Useful in Zone 8b–9a+.

Helianthemum nummularium 2 (sunrose). This low-growing relative of *Cistus* has evergreen or semievergreen leaves to 2.5 cm/1 in. long, and flowers similar to those of the rockrose except that they are only 2.5 cm/1 in. across, borne in clusters in midsummer. Useful as a groundcover in hot, dry sites, especially in full sun and high-limestone soil, in Zones 6b–9a+ and northward to Zone 6a with protection from winter sun and wind and to Zone 5a with reliable winter snow cover. Several cultivars are available, with pink, white, or different shades of yellow and orange flowers.

Cladrastis lutea 7

Synonym: *C. Kentukea*
AMERICAN YELLOWWOOD
Deciduous tree
Fabaceae (Leguminosae; Pea Family)

Native Range.   Southeastern United States, in Appalachians and as far west as Missouri and Arkansas.

Useful Range.   USDA Zones 4b–8a.

Function.   Shade tree, specimen.

Size and Habit

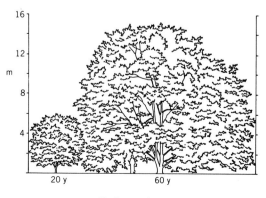

Cladrastis lutea.

Adaptability

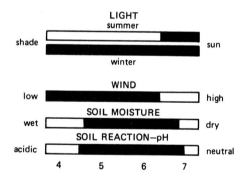

Seasonal Interest.   *Flowers:* Fragrant, white, pealike, in hanging clusters, 25–40 cm/10–16 in. long, resembling those of wisteria, in late spring. *Foliage:* Dark green, compound, casting very heavy shade and turning delicate shades of gold and orange in autumn. *Fruits:* Small, inconspicuous pods. *Trunk and branches:* Smooth, silvery gray bark, similar in color and texture to that of Asiatic magnolias and beech, maintains the tree's interest in winter.

Problems and Maintenance.   This tree is generally trouble-free but is occasionally subject to a vascular disease that originates in the narrow crotches of the main limbs where moisture can collect and eventually kills the tree. A dense canopy of large trees is less troublesome to turf grass underneath than might be expected, probably because of deep rooting, but alternatives to turf such as groundcover or mulch may still be preferable for low maintenance. Care should be taken not to break or prune branches in spring, since they will bleed sap heavily at that season, weakening the tree if excessive.

Related Species

Cladrastis platycarpa 8 (Japanese yellowwood). The Asian counterpart of *C. lutea*, this tree is similar in general landscape effect but differs in its upright clusters of flowers that are somewhat later and less showy than those of *C. lutea*. The useful range of *C. platycarpa* is not well known, but it includes at least Zones 5b–7b. It is seldom available commercially.

Maackia amurensis 7 (Amur maackia).   Similar in general form to *Cladrastis*, but slower-growing, with somewhat finer-textured compound leaves, yellowish white flowers in upright clusters in midsummer, and smooth bark of an unusual olive-brown color. Its overall usefulness is no greater than that of *Cladrastis*, and it has less

Maackia amurensis.

showy flowers and little or no autumn foliage color. It is even more drought-tolerant than *Cladrastis* and is well adapted to northern climates, with a useful range of Zones 4b–6b or perhaps wider. The related *M. chinensis*, slightly more showy in flower and probably less cold-hardy, is seldom available commercially.

Clematis armandii 1

ARMAND CLEMATIS
Evergreen vine
Ranunculaceae (Buttercup Family)

Native Range.   China.

Useful Range.   USDA Zones 7b–9a+.

Function.   Specimen, screen (with support). Like most *Clematis* species, this requires a wire or trellis support to accommodate twining petioles. Its effectiveness as a screen is limited by narrow leaves and a tendency to become leafless at the base (see Problems and Maintenance).

Size and Habit

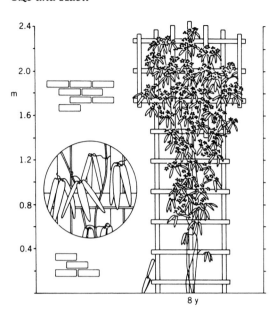

Clematis armandii.

Adaptability

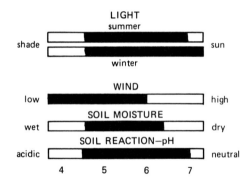

Seasonal Interest. *Flowers:* Fragrant, white, and starlike against dark green foliage, in axillary clusters in late spring. *Foliage:* Evergreen, leathery, narrow leaves make a dense mass because of their numbers. *Fruits:* Plumy styles give added interest in late summer.

Problems and Maintenance. To maintain fullness at the base of the plant and its effectiveness as a screen some top pruning may be necessary immediately after flowering, every two to three years. Aphids may be a problem in many areas but can be controlled by an appropriate spray if necessary.

Cultivars. 'Farquhariana' (= 'Apple Blossom') has light pink flowers but is less cold-hardy (Zone 9a+).

Clematis ×jackmanii 1

JACKMAN CLEMATIS
Deciduous vine
Ranunculaceae (Buttercup Family)

Hybrid origin. C. *lanuginosa* ×C. *viticella*.

Useful Range. USDA Zones 4a–8a. Certain hybrids are somewhat less cold-hardy, some only to Zone 6a.

Function. Specimen. Vining *Clematis* species and cultivars climb by twining petioles, so wire or trellis support must be provided. Most of the large-flowered types do not grow vigorously enough to function as effective screens, but C. ×*jackmanii* is more vigorous than many.

Size and Habit

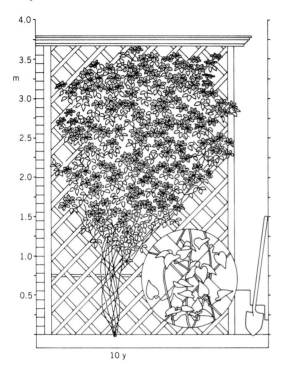

Clematis ×*jackmanii*.

Adaptability. Large-flowered *Clematis* species and cultivars require rather precise site conditions, including relatively cool soil (deep preparation of planting holes and use of a mulch, groundcover, or low shrub cover to shade the soil surface). Incorporation of lime in acidic soils is also standard practice. The less vigorous cultivars should receive partial shade in summer, especially in hot areas.

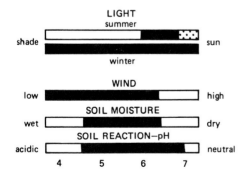

Seasonal Interest. *Flowers:* Large (to 10–15 cm/4–6 in.), with 4 rich, velvety purple (rich deep red, violet, pale blue or white in certain cultivars) sepals, on new growth in midsummer. *Foliage:* Medium green. *Fruits:* Plumy styles are fairly showy in late summer and early autumn.

Problems and Maintenance. The large-flowered *Clematis* species and cultivars commonly are winterkilled to the ground in the North. Even when this does not occur, those that flower on current season's growth, including C. ×*jackmanii* and its cultivars, should be pruned back heavily in spring to encourage low branching, vigor, and flowering.

Cultivars and Hybrids

Jackman hybrids. Cultivars selected from C. ×*jackmanii* populations and hybrids with other species are called the Jackman Hybrid Group. All flower in summer on current year's growth. Few are available at a given time or place, except from specialists. A few of the best known are listed here.

'Alba' (a selection from C. ×*jackmanii*) has large white flowers, with pale blue edges on double flowers (up to 8 sepals) from old wood, if not winterkilled; those on new growth are white with 4–6 sepals.

'Comtesse de Bouchaud' (often misspelled "Bouchard") has large, soft rose-pink flowers with 6 sepals.

'Gipsy Queen' has 6 deep purple sepals, vaguely red-striped.

'Hagley Hybrid' has cup-shaped flowers of 6 pointed sepals, shell-pink with brown stamens and borne in great numbers.

'Mme. Baron-Veillard' has large, pale lilac-pink flowers in early summer, then occasionally until autumn.

'Mme. Edouard Andre' has 4–6 velvety, deep red-purple sepals in midsummer.

'Mrs. Cholmondeley' has very large, light blue flowers in early summer and occasionally until autumn.

'Niobe' flowers have large, pointed, very dark ruby-red sepals and golden yellow stamens, and open from early summer until frost.

'Rubra' (a selection from C. ×*jackmanii*) has deep red-purple flowers in midsummer, including a few double flowers early in the season from the previous season's wood (if not winterkilled).

'Star of India' has 4-inch violet-purple flowers with red-striped sepals.

'Superba' (a selection from C. ×*jackmanii*) has unusually large deep purple flowers.

Lanuginosa hybrids. This group of hybrids is derived from the C. *lanuginosa* parent of C. ×*jackmanii*. Its members are similar to the Jackman Group except less hardy (Zones 6a–8a, colder zones in a few cases). Some of the best known are listed here.

'Elsa Spaeth' has large numbers of medium-to-large dark blue flowers in late summer.

'General Sikorsky' has lavender-blue sepals with slightly scalloped edges, and creamy yellow stamens.

'Henryi' has large flowers with 6–8 white sepals and dark brown stamens.

'Lady Caroline Neville' has 6–8 pale lilac, dark banded sepals opening in midsummer and occasionally until autumn, the earlier ones larger and often double.

'Mme Le Coultre' and 'Marie Boisselot' have large flowers with 8 pure to creamy white sepals and pale yellow stamens, opening in late spring (if not winterkilled) and again in late summer (these two cultivars are very similar and thought by some to be identical).

'Nelly Moser' has very large flowers with 8 pale lavender sepals, each marked with a red-purple midstripe, and golden brown stamens.

'Ramona' has large, pale lavender blue flowers in midsummer.

'William Kennett' has lavender flowers in early summer to midsummer; its 8 overlapping sepals have wavy margins.

Viticella hybrids. This group of hybrids, flowering on current year's growth like the Jackman and Lanuginosa hybrids, has a C. *viticella* parent. A few of the more common hybrids that are hardy northward at least to Zone 4b are listed here.

'Ascotiensis', has large sky-blue flowers in late summer.

'Ernest Markham' flowers have 6–8 overlap-

Clematis 'Ville de Lyon.'

ping, bright rose-magenta sepals and golden stamens in late summer.

'Huldine' flowers have pearly white sepals with pale violet stripes underneath, produced prolifically from midsummer to autumn.

'Lady Betty Balfour' flowers have deep velvety purple flowers with contrasting pale yellow stamens.

'Ville de Lyon' flowers have deep red-purple, rounded sepals and yellowish stamens, opening in midsummer and occasionally thereafter.

Related Species

Clematis alpina 1 (alpine clematis). This Eurasian species is notable for its bell-shaped, blue-violet flowers and low habit, climbing only a few feet. Since it flowers on previous season's wood in early spring, its floral display is vulnerable to winterkill in the North unless it can overwinter under heavy snow, as it does in its native habitat. This species and its several cultivars, with white, pink, rose, and purple flowers, are useful in Zones 6b–8a, and at least to Zone 4 with reliable snow cover.

Clematis florida 1 (cream clematis). This Chinese species with creamy white sepals and showy purple stamens, flowering in early summer on the previous season's wood, is useful in Zones 6b–9a and is best known for its hybrids: 'Belle of Woking,' with large, double, pale mauve to silvery gray flowers, and 'Duchess of Edinburgh,' with large, fragrant, double, pure white flowers, both flowering in spring on the previous season's wood.

Clematis lanuginosa 1 (Ningpo clematis).   Another Chinese native, this species has large white
to pale lilac flowers. It is little used other than as
a parent of the Lanuginosa hybrids (see Cultivars
and Hybrids).

Clematis ×*lawsoniana* 1 (Lawson clematis).
This hybrid species (*C. lanuginosa* × *C. patens*)
has large, rosy purple to pale blue flowers, noteworthy among the *C. lanuginosa* hybrids only for
the selection 'Henryi,' which has large white
flowers (brownish stamens) appearing in late
summer.

Clematis macropetala 1 (big-petal clematis).
This native of northern China and Siberia is
useful in Zones 3b–7a, perhaps also in colder
zones. It has large, bell-shaped, nodding, blue-
violet flowers, the centers filled with staminodes
(modified stamens resembling petals) of paler
color. Several cultivars have been selected, the
most popular of which is 'Markham's Pink,' with
rose-pink flowers.

Clematis occidentalis 1 (synonym: *C. verticillaris;*
mountain clematis).   This native of northeastern and north-central North America is one of
the most cold-hardy of all *Clematis* species, useful
in Zones 3a–5b and farther south at high elevations, but it seldom is available or used, even in
cold climates.

Clematis patens 1 (lilac clematis).   Like *C. florida,* this species and most of its hybrids flower on
the previous season's wood but usually somewhat
earlier than *C. florida,* in late spring. Some
members of this group often fail to flower in
northern climates because of winterkilling of
tops, including dormant flower buds, and most
are best used in Zones 6b–8a or farther south in
areas with relatively cool summers. *C. patens*
has very large, lilac-colored flowers with purple
stamens. A few of the more common hybrids are
listed here.
'Barbara Jackman' has very large flowers with

bright magenta-striped blue-purple sepals and
creamy white stamens, opening in spring from
previous season's growth (if not winterkilled),
sometimes with a lighter second flowering in
late summer.
'Bee's Jubilee' has very large flowers with 6–
8 pale mauve, overlapping sepals prominently
striped with bright red-purple.
'Doctor Ruppel' has large flowers with 6–8
deep rose-red sepals having lighter margins.
'Lasurstern' has very large flowers with deep
blue-purple sepals and creamy yellow stamens,
opening in spring from previous season's growth
(unless winterkilled), followed by a second
flowering from current season's growth in late
summer, in some years.
'Miss Bateman' has medium-sized flowers with
white sepals and contrasting red-brown stamens,
and even some fragrance, mostly opening in
spring and early summer from previous season's
growth, sometimes with a lighter flowering in
late summer.
'President' (= 'The President') has very large
flowers with 8 deep purple sepals, silvery on
the underside, and purple stamens, flowering
continuously from early to late summer and intermittently into autumn, more useful in the
North than some other members of this group.
'Wada's Primrose' (= 'Moonlight') has large
flowers with 8 or more pale yellow to creamy
white sepals and yellow stamens, opening from
early through late summer.

Clematis viticella 1 (Italian clematis).   This Eurasian species is involved in many hybrids, including the Jackman hybrids and Viticella hybrids.
The parent species has blue or purple flowers, to
5 cm/2 in. across, in middle to late summer, is
best known in the form of its hybrids, and is
adapted to use in Zones 5a–7b. The recent
selection, 'Betty Corning,' released in the early
1970s by the U.S. National Arboretum, flowers
more freely and over a longer period than typical
C. viticella.

Clematis montana 1

ANEMONE CLEMATIS
Deciduous vine
Ranunculaceae (Buttercup Family)

Native Range.   Central China to Himalayas.

Useful Range.   USDA Zones 6b–8a.

Function.   Specimen, screen. This species is more vigorous than many *Clematis* species, functioning well as a screen (to 5–6 m/16–20 ft) with good growing conditions from Zone 6b southward.

Size and Habit

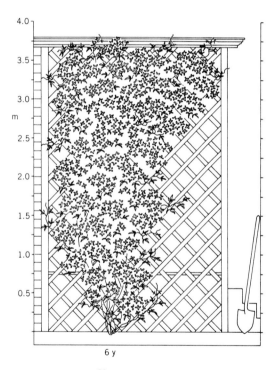

Clematis montana.

Adaptability.   This species is adaptable to the same conditions as C. ×*jackmanii* and most of the large-flowered hybrids.

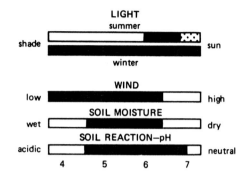

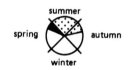

Seasonal Interest.   *Flowers:* Medium in size (about 5 cm/2 in.), white or pink, in late spring, initiated on previous season's growth. *Foliage:* Medium green. *Fruits:* Plumy styles add interest in summer and early autumn.

Problems and Maintenance.   Since flowers of C. *montana* are initiated in the previous growing season like those of C. *florida* and C. *patens* hybrids (see under C. ×*jackmanii*), the dormant flower buds must survive winter before they can flower in any number. So when plants are killed to the ground in colder climates, they may return with luxuriant vegetation but with no flowers. Because of this, the species and hybrids in this group are usually not recommended in areas colder than Zone 6a, and some are marginally useful even there.

Varieties and Cultivars.   'Alba' has whitish flowers and pale green foliage. 'Alexander' has fragrant, creamy white, fragrant flowers, larger than average for the species, with yellow stamens. 'Elizabeth' has very pale pink, fragrant flowers. The f. *grandiflora* is extremely vigorous and floriferous, with white flowers. 'Marjorie' has semi-double flowers with creamy pink sepals and salmon-pink petal-like stamens. 'Pink Perfection' is a vigorous and floriferous selection from var. *rubens* with small, deep pink flowers. The var. *rubens* is a natural population of individuals with pink to rose flowers, often with bronze-tinted new foliage, from which several clones (cultivars) have been selected. 'Tetrarose' is a tetraploid from var. *rubens*, with large mauve-pink flowers and bronzed foliage and stems. The var. *wilsonii* has large, fragrant white flowers, and is very floriferous.

Clematis montana.

Clematis tangutica 1

GOLDEN CLEMATIS
Deciduous vine
Ranunculaceae (Buttercup Family)

Native Range.   Mongolia and northern China.

Useful Range.   USDA Zones 2b–8a.

Function.   Specimen.

Size and Habit

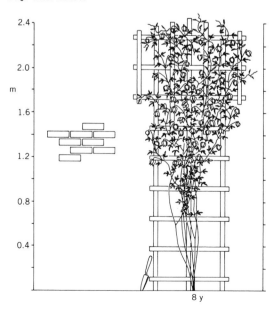

Clematis terniflora.

Adaptability.   This species is similar in requirements to most other *Clematis* species but is less tolerant of shade than most, performing best in full sun.

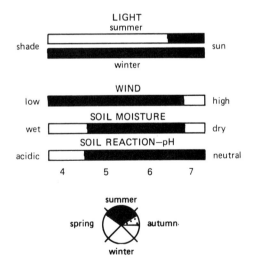

Seasonal Interest.   *Flowers:* Soft yellow, bell-shaped, with sepals spreading somewhat to 5–10 cm/2–4 in. across, flowering heavily in June, intermittently during the summer, and again heavily in late summer or early autumn. *Foliage:* Finer textured than that of many *Clematis* species, seldom full enough for effective screening. *Fruits:* Long, plumy styles add interest from midsummer through autumn along with the flowers.

Problems and Maintenance. The top kills to the ground in cold climates, but the plant returns vigorously to bloom in the same growing season.

Clematis tangutica.

Clematis terniflora 1

Synonyms: C. *maximowicziana,* C. *dioscoreifolia* var. robusta, and C. *paniculata,* as it is most commonly known in commerce. The true C. *paniculata* is an entirely different species from New Zealand.

SWEET AUTUMN CLEMATIS
Deciduous vine
Ranunculaceae (Buttercup Family)

Native Range.   Japan.

Useful Range.   USDA Zones 4a–9a.

Function.   Screen (with support), specimen. This is clearly the most effective *Clematis* species for functional use in the North, and probably the best for the South also. Since *Clematis* species climb and hold by twining petioles, they require wire or fine lattice trellis support and are especially well adapted to cover chainlink fences.

Size and Habit

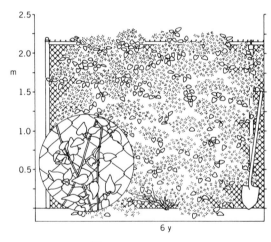

Clematis tangutica.

Adaptability.   This species is more widely tolerant of site conditions than many *Clematis* species but performs best in full sun and well-drained soil that is not too acidic.

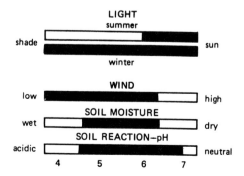

ally reaching heights of 15–20 m/50–65 ft. It has lustrous, dark green foliage, flowering interest similar to that of *C. alternifolia* except slightly later, and plated bark similar to that of *C. florida* except coarser in texture. This tree is not well known and probably is not available at present, but it is a potentially useful tree in Zones 6a–8a and perhaps colder zones as well.

Cornus amomum 5

SILKY DOGWOOD
Deciduous shrub
Cornaceae (Dogwood Family)

Native Range. Eastern and north-central United States and adjacent Canada.

Useful Range. USDA Zones 4b–9a+; one of the few shrub dogwoods that is well adapted to the far South.

Function. Naturalizing, screen, border.

Size and Habit

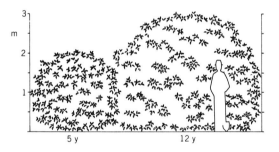

Cornus amomum.

Adaptability. Broadly adapted to soil type, acidity, and moisture conditions, as well as to considerable shade and full sun. Commonly found on old strip-mined sites in the Midwest.

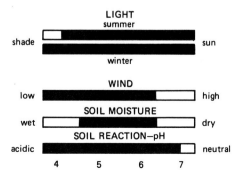

Seasonal Interest. *Flowers:* Small, yellowish white, in early summer in flattened clusters covered with silky hairs. *Foliage:* Medium green, making a fairly dense mass suitable for screening when grown in full sun, turning dull to rich red in autumn. *Fruits:* Blue berries in late summer and autumn. *Twigs:* Reddish from autumn until early spring, adding landscape color in winter, but less so than stems of *C. alba* and *C. stolonifera.*

Problems and Maintenance. This shrub occasionally may be infested with scale insects, but these can be controlled without difficulty in the few cases where it is necessary.

Related Species

Cornus obliqua 5 (synonym: *C. purpusii;* pale dogwood). This shrub is similar to *C. amomum* but is more northern in native habitat and in useful range (Zones 3b–8a). It is less useful for screening than *C. amomum* because of its more open branching, but occasionally it is used for naturalizing or preserved in its natural range.

Cornus florida 6–7

FLOWERING DOGWOOD
Deciduous tree
Cornaceae (Dogwood Family)

Native Range. Eastern United States from New England to Florida, westward to Michigan and Texas, and a small part of adjacent Ontario.

Useful Range. USDA Zones 5b–8b (5a and 9a with selection of appropriate genetic material).

Function. Specimen, patio tree, naturalizing, border accent.

Size and Habit

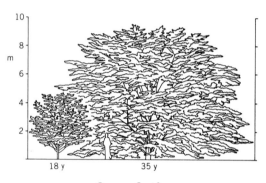

Cornus florida.

Adaptability. Performs best in full sun in the North but with some shade in the South.

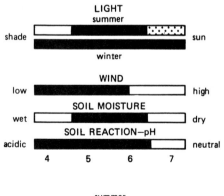

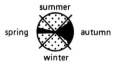

Seasonal Interest. *Flowers:* Small terminal clusters surrounded by snow white (or pink to red) bracts in midspring. *Foliage:* Medium green, not noteworthy in summer but turning deep to bright red in autumn. *Fruits:* Bright red and shiny in tight terminal clusters in autumn. *Twigs:* Smooth, gray-green, the layered branching providing quiet winter interest. *Trunks:* Coarsely plated bark on all but very young trees.

Problems and Maintenance. This tree is susceptible to borers but less so with a good maintenance program, including fertilization, and irrigation in times of severe drought. Good soil drainage is essential. Transplanting is sometimes difficult and must be done carefully, taking care not to plant too deeply. This fine tree is being devastated in some parts of its native range by an anthracnose disease that has become a serious threat during the 1980s and 1990s.

Cultivars. 'Cherokee Princess,' 'Cloud 9,' 'Spring Grove' (Plant Patent No. 8500, 1993), 'Springtime,' and others are selections for precocious flowering, large, pure white bracts and good form.

'Fragrant Cloud' is erect in growth habit, with white bracts and a gardenialike fragrance when the flowers open fully.

'Daybreak' (Cherokee Daybreak; Plant Patent No. 6320, 1988) is upright in form, with white bracts and scorch-resistant leaves with creamy white margins that turn pink (margins) and deep red in autumn.

'First Lady' has white bracts and striking pale

Cornus florida.

yellow-margined leaves, turning gold to red and maroon in autumn.

'Plena' (= 'Alba Plena,' = 'Pluribracteata') has multiple bracts, up to twice the normal number.

'Rainbow' and 'Welchii' have white bracts and tricolored (green, white, and pink) leaves and are very striking plants, but less vigorous than most other cultivars.

'Fastigiata' has a narrow form when young, broadening considerably with age.

'Nana' is very compact, with white bracts, remaining below 1 m/6.6 ft for many years.

'Pendula' has a strongly weeping growth habit and is useful only for accent.

The f. *rubra* includes all naturally occurring forms with pink or red bracts. 'Cherokee Chief' and 'Sweetwater Red' are selections from f. *rubra* for deep rose or red bracts and are of southern origin (hardy in Zones 6a–8b). 'Sunset' (Cherokee Sunset;™ Plant Patent No. 6305, 1988) is upright and spreading in form, with purplish red bracts, pink-tipped new growth, and pale yellow-margined leaves, which turn mixtures of gold, pink, bright red and maroon in autumn. 'Welch's Junior Miss' (Junior Miss™) has pink bracts, white at the tip and base, and good autumn foliage color. Its greatest value may be its adaptability to southern areas (through Zone 9) because of a low chilling requirement for breaking winter bud dormancy. This cultivar presumably would not be hardy as far north as many others.

Likewise, plants grown from extreme northern seed sources are more cold-hardy than most plants in commerce (to Zone 5a). Such plants have been grown by nurseries located near the northern extremes of the natural range.

Hybrids. See under *Cornus kousa*.

Related Species

Cornus canadensis 2 (bunchberry). This herbaceous groundcover plant, growing only to about

Cornus florida 'Welchii.'

20 cm/8 in. tall, covers large expanses of deciduous forest floor from Greenland through northern North America to northeastern Asia. In our area it grows wild as far south as the mountains of West Virginia. Its white-bracted flowers in late spring or early summer and tight clusters of red berries in late summer and autumn bear a startling resemblance to those of *C. florida*. Bunchberry is not easy to establish, and it grows best in mountain and seashore areas where summers are relatively cool and moist. It requires acidic, well-drained soil that is not excessively dry and at least partial sun. Useful, under these conditions, in Zones 2–5b, perhaps to Zone 6b or 7a in some coastal areas in the Northeast where the predominantly sandy soils would need to be supplemented with organic matter such as peat.

Cornus nuttallii 6 (Pacific dogwood). A magnificent tree, to 25 m/80 ft tall in native habitat in the Pacific Northwest, but not well adapted in the eastern half of North America. It is of interest here primarily for the cultivar 'Eddie's White Wonder,' believed to be a hybrid of C. *florida*, with as many as six large bracts surrounding flower clusters. Early trials suggest that it is hardy at least in Zones 7a–8b, but it is not yet fully proven as a landscape plant for the eastern United States.

Cornus kousa 6

JAPANESE OR CHINESE DOGWOOD
Deciduous tree
Cornaceae (Dogwood Family)

Native Range. Japan, Korea, China.

Useful Range. USDA Zones 5a–7b.

Function. Specimen, patio tree, border accent.

Size and Habit

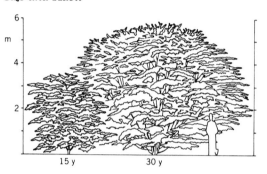

Cornus kousa.

Adaptability. Similar to *C. florida* in requirements except that it is less tolerant of shade and slightly more tolerant of heat and drought in the Midwest and Upper South.

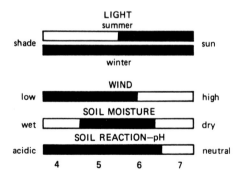

Seasonal Interest. *Flowers:* Small terminal clusters surrounded by white, pointed bracts in early summer. Bracts may become tinged with pink if the nights are very cool during flowering. *Foliage:* Medium green leaves are slightly smaller than those of *C. florida,* not noteworthy in summer but turning dull to bright red in autumn. *Fruits:* Dull red, dangling, aggregate fruits, superficially resembling oversize raspberries, add interest in late summer. For heavy fruiting, and especially for development of viable seeds, more than one individual plant or clone must be present. *Twigs:* Light gray-brown, offering less winter interest than those of *C. florida* even though they show similar horizontally layered branching. *Bark:* Gray outer bark peels away in irregularly rounded flakes, exposing the lighter colored inner bark in a bicolored pattern.

Problems and Maintenance. This tree is relatively trouble-free if planted in well-drained soil, given some protection from strong winds, and maintained well (i.e., fertilized every year or two and irrigated in times of severe drought).

Cornus kousa.

Varieties and Cultivars. The var. *angustata* is notable because it is semievergreen in Zone 7b to evergreen in Zone 9, probably useful in Zones 7b–9a+. This variety has been in North America for only a few years, so has not yet been widely tried.

The var. *chinensis* includes all plants of this species having their origin in China rather than Japan or Korea and supposedly distinguishable from the species type by somewhat larger bracts, leaves, and perhaps stature, as well as minor differences in leaf pubescence. Some have claimed greater hardiness for var. *chinensis*, but there is little clear evidence for this, and trees have been confused in commerce. It is likely that different seed sources in China, and probably Japan and Korea as well, vary in hardiness, but too small a sample of native Chinese and Korean genetic material has been introduced into North America to give any assurance that the hardiest existing material has yet been brought here.

More than 20 cultivars are available at writing. A few of the most popular are listed here.

'China Girl' is very free-flowering and starts flowering as a very young tree.

'Gold Star' has strikingly variegated leaves, with golden centers and green margins.

'Lustgarten Weeping' and 'Pendula' have strongly weeping form.

'Milky Way' is an especially free-flowering selection from var. *chinensis*, with heavy fruiting and good plant form.

'Rochester' has large white bracts and is notable for its vigor.

'Rosabella' has persistent pink bracts.

'Summer Stars' (= 'Summerstar') has rather small but abundant inflorescences. It is notable because it retains its white bracts for many weeks; they add color well into midsummer but lose much of their attractiveness by the time they fall in late summer.

Related Hybrids

Cornus ×*rutgersensis* 6 (Rutgers hybrid dogwoods). This is a group of hybrids (*C. florida* × *C. kousa*) which were introduced recently from the breeding program of Elwin Orton of Rutgers University. They have yet to be fully evaluated over a wide geographic range, but they are resistant to both dogwood borer and anthracnose and show much promise. Flowering is intermediate in timing between the parent species, generally in late spring. These hybrids are useful in Zones 6b–8b, perhaps also Zone 9a and parts of Zone 5 with careful siting.

'Rutban' (Aurora®; Plant Patent No. 7205, 1990). This selection has large, overlapping white bracts, making a nearly solid floral display of white at their peak. It is about equal in height and width.

'Rutcan' (Constellation®; Plant Patent No. 7210, 1990). This selection has narrower, well-separated white bracts, giving a lighter, billowy effect. It is somewhat taller than wide in form.

'Rutdan' (Galaxy®; Plant Patent No. 7204, 1990). This selection has rounded bracts, cupped and greenish at opening but soon becoming flat and white. It is upright in habit and full at the base.

'Rutlan' (Ruth Ellen®; Plant Patent No. 7732, 1991). This selection has rounded but not overlapping bracts, opening slightly earlier than the other cultivars in this series. It is lower and wider spreading than the others, more like *C. florida* in habit.

'Rutgan' (Stellar Pink®; Plant Patent No. 7207, 1990). This selection has rounded, slightly overlapping pale pink bracts with subtle darker pink veining. It is slightly wider than tall and is rounded in outline.

Cornus mas 6

Synonym: *.c. mascula*
CORNELIAN CHERRY
Deciduous shrub or small tree
Cornaceae (Dogwood Family)

Native Range.   Southeastern Europe and western Asia.

Useful Range.   USDA Zones 5a–8a, but flower buds are sometimes winter killed in Zone 5a.

Function.   Screen, hedge, border, specimen.

Size and Habit

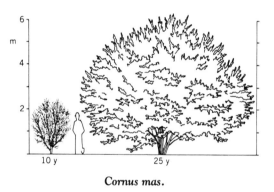

Cornus mas.

Adaptability.   One of the most widely adapted of the dogwoods but not as tolerant of wet soil as most of the shrub dogwoods.

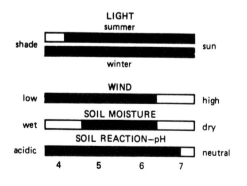

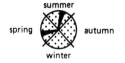

Seasonal Interest.   *Flowers:* Small, yellow, in large numbers in rounded clusters (umbels) before foliage appears in early spring, best displayed against a dark background of shadow or evergreen trees. *Foliage:* Dark green, lustrous, crisp-appearing, as handsome as that of any dogwood, making a dense mass that functions as a most effective screen. May or may not turn red in autumn, apparently depending on soil, climate, and perhaps genetic material. If it does not color well, it at least holds good green color until it falls in late autumn. *Fruits:* Bright cherry-red (rarely white or yellow; see Cultivars), resembling elongated cherries, to 1.5 cm/0.6 in. long, ripening in late summer or early autumn, edible and valued in the natural range, especially southwest Asia, for making desserts, preserves, soft drinks, and wines. *Trunk and branches:* Flaking, bicolored bark in muted gray and tan adds quiet winter interest to older plants.

Problems and Maintenance.   This is one of the most trouble-free landscape plants in good sites.

Cultivars.   'Golden Glory' is more showy in flower than average for the species and narrowly upright in form, a good choice for screening in smaller spaces. "Redstone," selected primarily for wildlife, shelterbelts, and revegetation projects by the USDA Soil Conservation Service, is being distributed as seeds and seedlings rather than cloned plants, so may not be uniform enough to qualify it for cultivar status. The

Cornus mas.

Cornus officinalis.

parent plant has developed an umbrella-shaped canopy, somewhat broader than tall, reportedly has superior foliage and vigor, and has performed well in climates of the Corn Belt (Zones 5a–7a). 'Alba,' with white fruits, 'Aurea,' with yellow foliage, 'Elegantissima,' with pink-flushed, yellow-margined leaves, and 'Xanthocarpa' (= 'Flava'), with yellow fruits, probably are not commercially available in our area.

Related Species

Cornus officinalis 6 (Japanese cornel). This Asian shrub or small tree is very similar to C. *mas* but more open in growth habit, making it less useful as a screen or hedge but more valuable as a specimen shrub or small patio tree. Its flowering interest is similar, and the bicolored, flaking winter bark is somewhat more conspicuous than that of C. *mas*.

Cornus racemosa 5

Synonym: C. *Paniculata*
GRAY DOGWOOD
Deciduous shrub
Cornaceae (Dogwood Family)

Native Range. Northeastern United States and adjacent Canada to Nebraska, southward to northern Georgia.

Useful Range. USDA Zones 3b–7b.

Function. Naturalizing, massing, screen, border.

Size and Habit

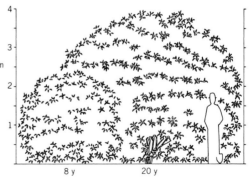

Cornus racemosa.

Adaptability. Widely adapted to difficult site conditions, including dry, gravelly soil often found at roadsides.

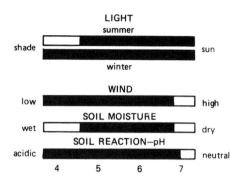

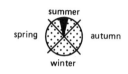

Seasonal Interest. Flowers: Small, creamy white, not as showy as some of the other shrub dogwoods, in early summer. *Foliage:* Light green, medium-fine texture, turning purplish to deep purple in autumn. *Fruits:* White berries on bright red-pedicels are colorful in midsummer but usually are taken by birds rather quickly. The red pedicels remain colorful for most of the summer. *Twigs:* Older branches gray, very young twigs red-tinged, offering subtle winter interest, most noticeable in late winter.

Problems and Maintenance. This shrub needs little maintenance in naturalized settings except to control occasional insect infestations, especially scale insects, which are troublesome in some areas. When used for massing, pruning to within a few inches of the ground every few years will promote fullness. Such drastic pruning should be done no later than the beginning of summer to allow time for new growth and acclimation in preparation for the next winter.

Cultivars. 'Cinderella' (Plant Patent No. 7766, 1992) has yellow variegated green leaves.

Related Species

Cornus asperifolia var. *drummondii* (Synonym: *C. drummondii*, roughleaf dogwood). This plant is similar to *C. racemosa* in foliage, flowering, and fruiting; but it is a coarser plant, sparser at the base, and does not form thickets as freely. It is useful for naturalizing or preserved in native stands throughout its range, from Ontario and the midwestern states to Texas in Zones 4b–8b. It is sometimes inadvertently sold as *C. racemosa.*

Related Species

Cornus stricta 5 (synonym: *C. foemina*; stiff dogwood). Like *C. racemosa*, this shrub is stiffly upright in growth habit, but it is less tolerant of dry soil and much more southern in distribution and useful range (Zones 5b–9a). Like *C. racemosa*, it is a neutral plant, useful for massing or naturalizing.

Cornus stolonifera 5

Synonym: *C. Sericea*
RED OSIER DOGWOOD
Deciduous shrub
Cornaceae (Dogwood Family)

Native Range. Newfoundland to Manitoba, south to Virginia and Nebraska, and extending westward to the Pacific Northwest and New Mexico.

Useful Range. USDA Zones 3a–8a.

Function. Screen, massing, bank cover, border, specimen. Spreads rapidly by creeping stems (stolons) into large masses.

Size and Habit

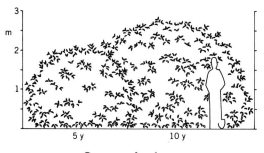

Cornus stolonifera.

Adaptability

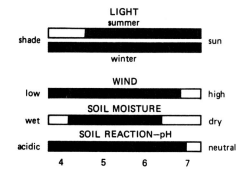

Seasonal Interest. *Flowers:* Small, white, in flattened clusters in late spring and early summer. *Foliage:* Medium green, making a dense mass suitable for screening, turning dull to rich red in autumn. *Fruits:* White to pale blue in late summer and autumn. *Twigs:* Reddish (or yellow-green) from late summer until late autumn, becoming progressively brighter red (or yellow) until early spring, then reverting to green as new growth begins.

Problems and Maintenance. This species is one of those that are susceptible to fungal twig blights, which usually can be controlled by pruning out and removing affected stems. Cutting stems back to stubs annually or every two or three years in middle to late spring can reduce

twig blight as well as maximize the intensity of winter twig color.

Cultivars and Varieties. 'Baileyi' (Synonym: *C. baileyi;* Bailey dogwood) is a selection with somewhat larger whitish fruits, leaves pubescent underneath, dark red twigs, and a nonstoloniferous habit more like that of *C. alba.*

'Cardinal' was selected at the Minnesota Landscape Arboretum for its unusually bright orange-red winter twigs.

The var. *coloradensis,* native from northwestern Canada to Colorado and New Mexico, has smaller leaves, brownish red winter twigs, and bluish white fruits. It is presumably more tolerant of dry soil, and its northern provenances represent unusually cold-hardy genetic material (Zone 2).

'Flaviramea' (= 'Aurea,' = 'Lutea'; goldentwig dogwood) differs from the species type in lacking red pigmentation, so fall foliage and winter twig color is yellow instead of red. The bright yellow winter twigs turn greenish yellow later in spring. This cultivar is useful for individual accent or massed, but when yellow-twigged and red-twigged dogwoods are mixed rather than kept in separate masses in large-scale plantings, the two colors tend to mask each other.

'Isanti', another Minnesota Landscape Arboretum introduction, forms a lower, denser mound than the species type, remaining below eye level for years.

'Kelseyi' (Kelsey dwarf dogwood) is a miniature version of *C. stolonifera,* reaching a maximum height of 0.6 m/2 ft with compact form and attractive foliage, useful as a large scale

Cornus stolonifera 'Kelseyi.'

groundcover. However, it does not flower or fruit and is disappointing in winter because the stems do not color well. It is also less cold-hardy than the species type (only to Zone 5a).

'Silver and Gold,' which originated as a genetic sport of 'Flaviramea,' has creamy white-margined leaves, which turn yellow in autumn. This selection is as beautiful in summer and autumn as it is for its yellow twig color in winter and early spring.

Related Species

Cornus rugosa 5 (synonym: *C. circinata;* round-leaved dogwood). This upright shrub is useful for naturalizing or preserving stands in its native range, from Nova Scotia to Manitoba and southward to Iowa and Pennsylvania (Zones 3a–7a). It is generally similar to *C. sericea* except that it has less colorful purplish twigs and pale bluish berries.

Coronilla varia 2

CROWN VETCH
Herbaceous groundcover
Fabaceae (Leguminosae; Pea Family)

Native Range. Europe; naturalized in northeastern North America.

Useful Range. USDA Zones 4b–9a, to Zone 3b with reliable snow cover.

Function. Large-scale groundcover, roadside bank cover.

Size and Habit

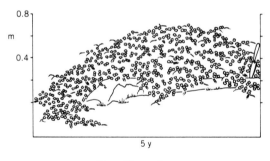

Coronilla varia.

Adaptability. Highly acidic soils should be limed at least to pH 6.0, preferably to pH 6.5.

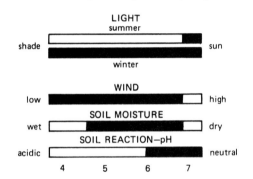

Seasonal Interest. *Flowers:* Light pink or white, individually only 1.2 cm/0.5 in. long but borne in great numbers in crown-shaped clusters to 4 cm/1.6 in. across, starting to flower in early summer and continuing intermittently until early autumn. *Foliage:* Compound leaves with many small leaflets give a vaguely fernlike appearance and form a dense mass, killing to the ground in late autumn.

Problems and Maintenance. Relatively trouble-free, crown vetch requires little or no maintenance after establishment, which usually is rapid if the soil is adequately limed before planting. Old plantings may benefit from cutting and removing the tops in spring.

Cultivars. Several cultivars have been selected for rapid establishment and vigor. 'Emerald' and 'Penngift' are perhaps the most widely available.

Related Species

Lotus corniculatus 2 (birdsfoot trefoil). This Eurasian legume with deep green leaves and golden-yellow flowers during summer and intermittently into autumn is useful in the same ways that crown vetch is. It is not as vigorous and tall-growing as crown vetch but it is more tolerant of wet and acidic soils. For best results, the soil should be limed to at least pH 6.0 if necessary. This plant is useful in Zones 3b–9a and perhaps colder zones as well.

Trifolium incarnatum 2–3 (crimson clover). This vigorous legume from southern Europe, naturalized in areas of the southern United States, is actually an annual plant, perpetuating itself by natural reseeding in the South. Even when it is used for temporary revegetation, it often persists as a large-scale groundcover. It is useful in Zones 6a–9a and farther north but with less reliable reseeding. Mowing can be done, but it must be delayed past seed ripening if the cover is to be perpetuated for another year. The spikes of crimson flowers, to 6 cm/2.4 in. long, add color from late spring to midsummer.

Corylopsis glabrescens 5

FRAGRANT WINTER HAZEL
Deciduous shrub
Hamamelidaceae (Witch Hazel Family)

Native Range. Japan.

Useful Range. USDA Zones 5b–9a.

Function. Screen, border, specimen; requires much ground space.

Size and Habit

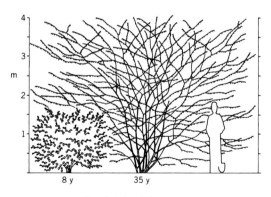

Corylopsis glabrescens.

Adaptability. Avoid dry or windy locations or sites prone to late spring frosts to protect the early flowers.

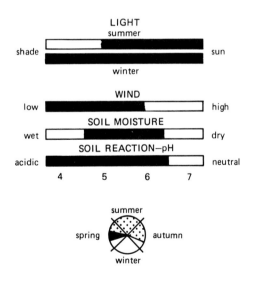

Seasonal Interest. *Flowers:* Fragrant, pale yellow, in drooping clusters, 2–4 cm/0.8–1.6 in. long, before the new foliage appears. *Foliage:* Medium or bluish green with interesting texture caused by venation and leaf shape, borne on gracefully slender branches and sometimes turning clear yellow in autumn.

Corylopsis sinensis.

Problems and Maintenance.   This shrub is relatively trouble-free in good soil and a protected location except for the susceptibility of the early flowers to late spring frosts.

Related Species

Corylopsis pauciflora 4 (buttercup winter hazel). Smaller than C. *glabrescens*, slightly less colorful in flower, and slightly less cold-hardy (Zones 6a–9a).

Corylopsis sinensis 5 (Chinese winter hazel). Similar to C. *glabrescens* but more showy in flower and slightly less cold-hardy (Zones 6a–9a). The var. *calvescens* 4 (synonym: C. *veitchiana*; Veitch winter hazel) is similar, but remains below or near eye level for years.

Corylopsis spicata 4 (spike winter hazel).   Similar in size to C. *pauciflora*, but its flowers are more showy. Brighter yellow than those of C. *sinensis*. Useful in Zones 6a–9a.

Corylus avellana 5

EUROPEAN HAZEL OR FILBERT
Deciduous shrub
Betulaceae (Birch Family)

Native Range.   Europe.

Useful Range.   USDA Zones 4b–8b.

Function.   Specimen, border accent. Nuts are edible.

Size and Habit

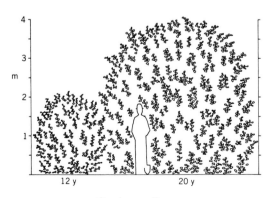

Corylus avellana.

Adaptability.   This is one of the best adapted large shrubs to poor, dry soil over a wide climatic range.

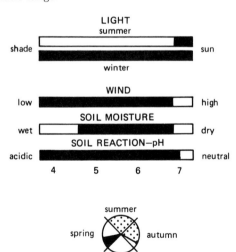

Seasonal Interest.   *Flowers:* Large, pendulous male catkins in late winter or early spring. The female flowers are inconspicuous. *Foliage:* Crisp, dark to medium green, of interesting texture. *Fruits:* Nuts with distinctive husks add quiet summer and autumn interest. *Twigs:* Of distinctive, year-round interest in the case of the culti-var 'Contorta' only (see Cultivars).

Problems and Maintenance.   Relatively trouble-free, this plant seldom requires maintenance, but rootstocks of grafted cultivars may produce root suckers that must be removed to prevent their overgrowing the cultivar scion.

Cultivars.   'Aurea' (golden hazelnut) has bright yellow foliage in spring and early summer, turning dull green by midsummer. 'Contorta' (contorted hazelnut, Harry Lauder's walking stick) has curled and contorted twigs and branches, making it a popular specimen for accent, especially in formal landscaping settings, reaching heights of about 2 m/6.6 ft. 'Pendula' (weeping hazelnut) is strongly pendulous and rounded in form, making an interesting specimen, but it is not very functional. Usually grafted on a seedling of *C. avellana*, 1–1.5 m/3.3–5 ft above ground level, the grafted plant ultimately reaches about 2 m/6.6 ft in height.

Related Species

Corylus americana 5 (American hazelnut).   This thicket-forming shrub, native to much of the eastern United States and Canada, occasionally reaches 3 m/10 ft in height but usually remains lower, especially in poor, gravelly soils in which it nevertheless grows well. Useful primarily for naturalizing in poor soil in Zones 3a–8b, and occasionally for the edible nuts.

Corylus cornuta 5 (beaked hazelnut).   Native to approximately the same range as *C. americana*, this species is generally similar to and interchangeable with it in landscape use in Zones 2b–8b.

Corylus maxima 6 (filbert).   This large shrub or small tree from southeastern Europe and adjacent Asia is valued for its edible nuts. In landscape use it is most valued for the selection 'Purpurea,' with deep purple foliage. It is useful in Zones 5b–8b.

Corylus colurna 7–8

TURKISH FILBERT
Deciduous tree
Betulaceae (Birch Family)

Native Range.   Southeastern Europe and adjacent Asia.

Useful Range.   USDA Zones 5a–8b.

Function.   Shade tree, specimen, edible nuts.

Size and Habit

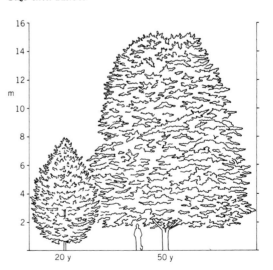

Corylus colurna.

Adaptability. This is an unusually drought-tolerant shade tree, worth planting for this and for its ease of maintenance.

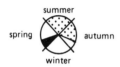

Corylus columna.

Seasonal Interest. *Flowers:* Large, pendulous male catkins in early spring or late winter. Female flowers are inconspicuous. *Foliage:* Crisp, dark to medium green, of interesting texture. *Fruits:* Nuts, with distinctive husks, are edible, but seldom form in small plantings, probably because of self-infertility. This may change as the species becomes more widely used. *Twigs and Bark:* Roughly corky, gray, mildly interesting in winter.

Problems and Maintenance. Relatively trouble-free but damaged by sapsuckers in some areas, otherwise requiring little or no attention.

Cotinus coggygria 5–6

SMOKE TREE, SMOKE BUSH
Deciduous shrub or small tree
Anacardiaceae (Cashew Family)

Native Range. Southern Europe to Himalayas and China.

Useful Range. USDA Zones 5a–7b.

Function. Specimen, border, massing. Usually not full enough for effective screening.

Size and Habit

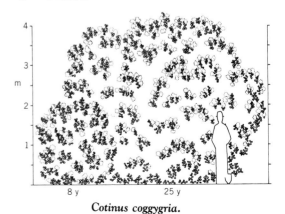

Cotinus coggygria.

Adaptability

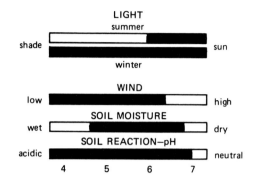

Seasonal Interest. *Flowers:* Small, individually inconspicuous but borne in loose, fuzzy panicles to 20 cm/8 in. across. *Foliage:* Leaves bluish green (except in red- and purple-leaved cultivars) and rounded, making a loose foliage mass, turning yellowish to orange in autumn in some years. *Fruits:* Small and individually inconspicuous, but by fruiting time the large loose panicles are showy because of the plumose hairs borne by sterile flowers in the cluster. The effect is to give the plant a "smoky" appearance in middle to late summer.

Problems and Maintenance. Relatively trouble-free, this plant requires little maintenance except when pruning to enhance foliage color (see Forms and Cultivars).

Cotinus coggygria.

Forms and Cultivars. The f. *purpureus* (= 'Atropurpureus') has more or less purple fruiting panicles and young leaves. Color varies among individual plants or clones, and with vigor. Included in this category are several red or purple-leaved cultivars, which tend to be somewhat less cold-hardy than the species type. A few of the most popular are listed here. 'Nordine' has purplish red foliage, turning yellow-orange in autumn, and deep rosy pink fruiting panicles, and is probably the most cold-hardy of these cultivars. 'Purple Supreme' is similar to 'Royal Purple' in appearance and is reported to be resistant to vascular wilts. 'Royal Purple' is a clone selected from f. *purpureus* for its deep purple foliage, turning red-purple in autumn, and smoky red-purple fruiting panicles. 'Velvet Cloak' has outstanding velvety rosy purple foliage, turning wine-red in autumn, and rosy red fruiting panicles, and it is unusually vigorous. Heavy pruning of these cultivars will promote vigor and intense summer foliage color while keeping the plant below eye-level, but at the expense of fruiting interest. When plants are grown from seed of f. *purpureus* or its cultivars, many variants in foliage color, from nearly green to pale reddish or purple can be obtained, but the color of the parent plant will rarely be seen in the progeny.

Related Species and Hybrids

Cotinus obovatus 7 (synonym: *C. americanus;* American smoke tree). Native to the south-central United States, this tree, to 10 m/33 ft or taller, is much less showy in fruit than *C. coggygria* but has fine bronze to red-orange fall foliage in some years. Unfortunately, it is weak-wooded, and trees may be devastated by ice storms that do only minor damage to many other trees. Useful in Zones 5b–8a, perhaps also Zone 5a.

Cotinus 'Grace', an interesting new hybrid between *C. coggygria* 'Velvet Cloak' and *C. obovatus,* is intermediate between the parents, growing to at least 6 m/20 ft tall as a vigorous, rangy shrub or small tree (with training). It has distinctive blue-green and smoky pink-bronze foliage turning deeper red-purple in autumn, and deep red fruiting panicles. It is not yet widely used or available in our area but presumably will be similar to its parents in adaptability.

Cotoneaster apiculatus 3

CRANBERRY COTONEASTER
Deciduous shrub
Rosaceae (Rose Family)

Native Range.   Western China.

Useful Range.   USDA Zones 5a–8b, but may be impractical south of Zone 7b because of insect problems.

Function.   Border (front), rock garden, groundcover (with mulch), espalier.

Size and Habit

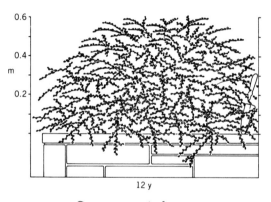

Cotoneaster apiculatus.

Adaptability.   This species is more resistant to extremes of soil and climate than most of the other low-growing cotoneasters and for this reason is favored in the Midwest.

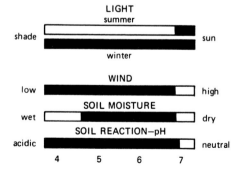

Seasonal Interest.   *Flowers:* Small, rosy pink with the unfolding leaves in late spring. *Foliage:* Lustrous, dark green, to 1.5 cm/0.6 in. long, refined in texture and pattern, turning deep reddish in autumn. *Fruits:* Bright red, larger (to 1 cm/0.4 in.) than those of other low-growing cotoneasters, in late summer and autumn.

Problems and Maintenance.   Cotoneasters in general, like other members of the pome-fruit subfamily of the rose family, are susceptible to a variety of insect pests and diseases, but this is not a serious enough problem to eliminate them as landscape plants except in the South. Some maintenance is required in some years to control lacebugs, mites, scale insects, and fire blight. *C. apiculatus* is less troubled than average among cotoneasters in the Midwest.

Cultivars.   'Blackburn' is densely compact in habit and bears larger fruits, in greater quantities, than average for the species. 'Tom Thumb' is a slow-growing dwarf selection, useful in rock gardens or small-scale, formal situations.

Cotoneaster dammeri 2

BEARBERRY COTONEASTER
Evergreen to semievergreen groundcover
Rosaceae (Rose Family)

Native Range.   Central China.

Useful Range.   USDA Zones 6a–9a+, but may be impractical in some far southern areas because of insect problems. May persist for several years in zones colder than 6a under reliable winter snow cover.

Function.   Rock garden, groundcover.

Size and Habit

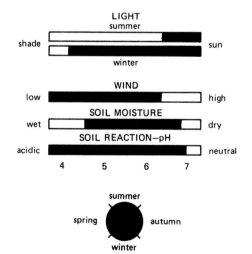

Cotoneaster dammeri.

Adaptability

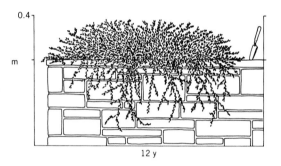

Seasonal Interest.   *Flowers:* White with deep red anthers, only 1 cm/0.4 in. across, contrasting with the dark foliage in late spring. *Foliage:*

Evergreen (Zones 8a–9a+) or semievergreen (Zones 6a–7b), lustrous medium to dark green leaves, 1.5–3 cm/0.6–1.2 in. long, in a loose branching pattern. *Fruits:* Bright red, 0.6 cm/0.25 in. across, colorful in autumn.

Cotoneaster dammeri.

Problems and Maintenance.   Like all cotoneasters, this species is susceptible to a variety of insect pests and diseases (see C. *apiculatus*, Problems and Maintenance), but it is less troubled than many other cotoneasters, one of the reasons that it is useful in the South as well as farther north.

Cultivars.   'Coral Beauty' (probably = 'Royal Beauty'), 'Lowfast,' and 'Skogsholmen' (= 'Skogsholm') show slightly greater cold hardiness than average for the species and are vigorous, covering large areas relatively quickly. 'Skogsholmen' sometimes does not fruit well, but 'Lowfast' and especially 'Coral Beauty' produce good quantities of bright red fruit. 'Lowfast' and 'Mooncreeper' are vigorous and very prostrate, rapidly forming a 10 cm/4 in. mat over the ground.

Related Species

Cotoneaster congestus 3 (Pyrenees cotoneaster). This relatively low, compact shrub has evergreen leaves smaller than those of C. *dammeri* and none of its trailing habit. It is useful primarily as a rock garden specimen in Zones 6b–9a.

Cotoneaster microphyllus 3 (little-leaved cotoneaster). This handsome low shrub with fine-textured evergreen foliage and spreading growth habit is similar to *C. congestus* but slightly more cold hardy, useful in Zones 6a–9a. The selection

'Cochleatus' is slow-growing with strongly arching branches, making a low mound of elegant foliage. The var. *thymifolius* has somewhat elongated leaves, but usually doesn't fruit very heavily.

Cotoneaster divaricatus 4

SPREADING COTONEASTER
Deciduous shrub
Rosaceae (Rose Family)

Native Range. China.

Useful Range. USDA Zones 5a–8b, but may be impractical south of Zone 7b because of insect problems: lacebugs, mites, scale insects.

Function. Border, informal hedge, massing, specimen, espalier.

Size and Habit

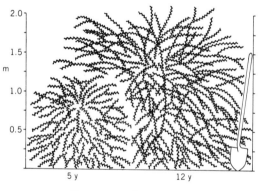

Cotoneaster divaricatus.

Adaptability. This is among the best adapted cotoneasters for the Midwest.

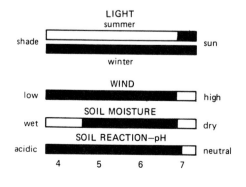

Seasonal Interest. *Flowers:* Small, pale pink, with the young leaves in late spring. *Foliage:* Lustrous, dark green, to 2 cm/0.8 in. long, spaced along stems to produce a loose but regular pattern, remaining green late but turning reddish before falling in autumn in some years. *Fruits:* Small (0.6 cm/0.25 in.), red, in late summer and autumn.

Problems and Maintenance. Like all cotoneasters, this species is susceptible to a variety of insect pests and diseases, few serious enough to eliminate it as a landscape plant except in the South and in areas where fire blight is severe. Some maintenance may be necessary in some years to control lacebugs, mites, scale insects, and fire blight, but less than for many other *Cotoneaster* species.

Related Species

Cotoneaster dielsianus 4 (Diel's cotoneaster). This close relative of *C. divaricatus*, also from

Cotoneaster divaricatus.

China, is similar in its arching branches and small leaves, but its branches are more pendulous and its fruits brighter red. It is useful in Zones 6a–8b.

Cotoneaster franchetii 5 (Franchet cotoneaster). This larger Chinese shrub has small-to-medium-small leaves like C. *dielsianus* and C. *divaricatus* and bright, red-orange fruits. It is hardy in Zones 6a–8a.

Cotoneaster horizontalis 3

ROCKSPRAY COTONEASTER
Deciduous shrub
Rosaceae (Rose Family)

Native Range. Western China.

Useful Range. USDA Zones 5b–8b, but may be impractical south of Zone 7b because of insect problems: lace bugs, mites, scale insects.

Function. Border (front), rock garden, groundcover (with mulch), espalier.

Size and Habit

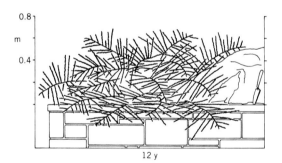

12 y

Cotoneaster horizontalis.

Adaptability

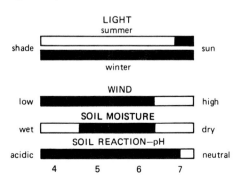

Seasonal Interest. *Flowers:* Small, pink, with the young leaves in late spring. *Foliage:* Lustrous, dark green, refined in texture and regularly spaced along stems branching in a "fishbone" pattern, remaining green late in autumn, sometimes turning reddish before falling. *Fruits:* Small (0.5 cm/0.2 in.), bright red, held tightly against the stems in late summer and autumn.

Problems and Maintenance. Like all cotoneasters, this species is susceptible to a variety of insect pests and diseases (see C. *divaricatus*, Problems and Maintenance), few serious enough to eliminate it as a landscape plant except in the South and in areas where fire blight is severe.

Varieties and Cultivars. The var. *perpusillus* is lower-growing than the species type and has smaller leaves. It is useful only as a specimen

Cotoneaster horizontalis.

Cotoneaster adpressus.

in small-scale plantings. 'Robustus' is somewhat taller and more vigorous than the species type. 'Variegatus' has white-variegated foliage, turning pink and red in autumn in some years.

Related Species

Cotoneaster adpressus 2 (creeping cotoneaster). This excellent creeping plant forms a denser mat of foliage than most low-growing cotoneasters and is slower-growing than C. *apiculatus* and C. *horizontalis*, valuable for rock gardens and other small-scale sites where adherence to modest size is important. Hardy in Zones 5b–8b. 'Little Gem' is a dwarf form of the species, comparable with C. *apiculatus* 'Tom Thumb.'

Cotoneaster nanshan 2 (synonym: C. *adpressus* var. *praecox*; Nan Shan or early creeping cotoneaster). This early-flowering cotoneaster is more vigorous, resembling C. *apiculatus*, but not as cold-hardy (to Zone 6b).

Cotoneaster lucidus 5

HEDGE COTONEASTER
Deciduous shrub
Rosaceae (Rose Family)

Native Range.   Central Asia: Altai Mountains.

Useful Range.   USDA Zones 2b–6b, possibly even colder zones.

Function.   Hedge, screen, windbreak.

Size and Habit

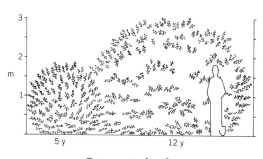

Cotoneaster lucidus.

Adaptability.   This is one of the most cold-hardy of cotoneasters and among the hardiest of all shrubs. Valued as a screen and small-scale windbreak in the northern prairies of Canada and the United States, it is adaptable farther

south but not widely used, since alternatives are more attractive.

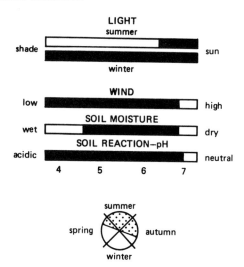

Seasonal Interest.   *Flowers:* Small, pink, in late spring and early summer. *Foliage:* Glossy leaves, 2.5–5.0 cm/1–2 in. long, turn orange before falling in autumn. *Fruits:* Small, black, and inconspicuous.

Problems and Maintenance.   This species is susceptible to the usual insect and disease problems of cotoneasters and other members of the pome-fruit subfamily of the rose family, and maintenance may be necessary in some years to control mites, scale insects, and fire blight.

Related Species

Cotoneaster acutifolius 5 (Peking cotoneaster). Similar in most respects to C. *lucidus,* but with foliage turning red-orange shortly before falling. This species and C. *lucidus* are confused in commerce, many plants of C. *lucidus* being sold as C. *acutifolius.* The two are similar in hardiness.

Cotoneaster multiflorus 5

MANY-FLOWERED COTONEASTER
Deciduous shrub
Rosaceae (Rose Family)

Native Range.   Western China.

Useful Range.   USDA Zones 4b–7a.

Function.   Border, screen, specimen, espalier.

Size and Habit

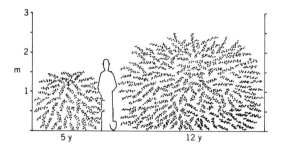

Cotoneaster multiflorus.

Adaptability

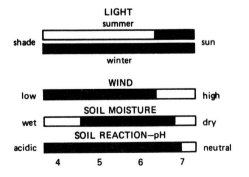

Seasonal Interest.   *Flowers:* White, small but making a great show in numbers in midspring.

Foliage: Dull green, forming a good neutral background for the flowers and fruits. Falls with little or no color change in autumn. *Fruits:* Bright red berries are fairly showy in autumn. Isolated plants may not fruit well, possibly because of a need for cross-pollination.

Problems and Maintenance.   This shrub is subject to the usual insect and disease problems of cotoneasters and other members of the pome-fruit subfamily of the rose family, but less so than many cotoneasters. Some maintenance may still be needed in some years to control fire blight, mites, and scale insects.

Varieties.   The var. *calocarpus* has larger, more showy fruits borne in great numbers and is usually used in preference to the species type.

Cotoneaster racemiflorus var. *songaricus.*

Related Species

Cotoneaster racemiflorus 5 (redbead cotoneaster). This shrub is similar in size and habit to *C. multiflorus* but with slightly smaller, dull gray-green leaves and greater cold hardiness (Zones 3b–7a). It is most commonly used in the form of the variety *songaricus* (Sungari cotoneaster), which gives a magnificent display of pink fruits in late summer and autumn.

Cotoneaster salicifolius 5

WILLOWLEAF COTONEASTER
Evergreen or semievergreen shrub
Rosaceae (Rose Family)

Native Range.   Western China.

Useful Range.   USDA Zones 6b–9a+, but hardiness in Zones 6b and 7a is restricted to the variety *floccosus*.

Function.   Informal hedge or screen, specimen, espalier.

Size and Habit.   The var. *floccosus* is illustrated.

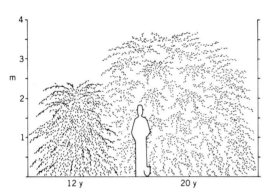

Cotoneaster salicifolius var. *floccosus*.

Adaptability

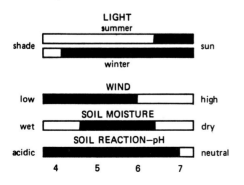

Seasonal Interest.   *Flowers:* Small, white, inconspicuous, early summer. *Foliage:* Handsome, narrow, leathery leaves, to 8 cm/3 in. long, are dark green above, whitish underneath, and evergreen (Zones 8a–9a+) to semievergreen (Zones 6b–7b), turning reddish in autumn. *Fruits:* Small but numerous and bright red, making a striking display in autumn and early winter.

Problems and Maintenance.   Subject to the usual insect and disease problems of cotoneasters, this species succeeds better in the South than most cotoneasters in spite of this. It may require maintenance in some years to control lacebug, scale, and fire blight and, since it grows rapidly and becomes large quickly, it may require pruning to keep it in scale in some situations, but a better solution is to use it only where there is ample space for it.

Varieties and Cultivars.   The var. *floccosus* has glossy foliage, woolly underneath, and is more cold hardy (Zone 6b) than the species type, but not widely available. 'Autumn Fire' (= 'Herbstfeuer') is vigorous and prostrate (to 30 cm/12 in. tall), with great quantities of bright red fruit. 'Repens,' a creeping selection from var. *floccosus*, forms a low mat but does not root down as it grows. 'Scarlet Leader', a creeping form to 25 cm/8 in. high, has reddish new growth, turning glossy dark green, and red fruits in autumn. Other selections are known in Europe but seldom available in our area.

Cotoneaster salicifolius.

Cotoneaster lacteus.

Related Species and Hybrids

Cotoneaster henryanus 5 (Henry cotoneaster). Another large shrub from China for the South (Zones 7b–9a) with semievergreen foliage, this is similar to *C. salicifolius* in general appearance but has larger leaves, 5–12 cm/2–5 in. long.

Cotoneaster lacteus 5 (synonym: *C. parneyi;* milky cotoneaster). This handsome, semievergreen shrub from China is useful in the South (Zones 7b–9a). It is distinctive for its white, downy, young leaves and stems, contrasting with the olive green color of older foliage, and for its showy red fruits that persist well into winter.

Cotoneaster ×*watereri* 6 (Waterer cotoneaster; hybrids of C. *frigidus,* C. *rugosus,* and C. *salicifolius*). This group includes many cultivars with dark green, narrow evergreen leaves and colorful fruits that are extremely showy in autumn and winter. These cultivars vary in form from strongly upright to broad procumbent, weeping, or even dwarf. The showy red, pink, golden, creamy pale yellow, apricot yellow, or pink-blushed yellow fruits are popular in Europe but are seldom, if ever, available in our area. They are useful in Zones 7b–9a.

Crataegus apiifolia 6

Synonym: *C. Marshallii*
MARSHALL OR PARSLEY HAWTHORN
Deciduous tree
Rosaceae (Rose Family)

Native Range. Southeastern and south-central United States.

Useful Range. USDA Zones 6b–9a.

Function. Specimen, patio tree.

Size and Habit

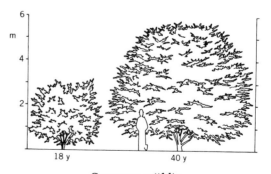

Crataegus apiifolia.

Adaptability. This species is unusual among the hawthorns for its ability to tolerate wet soil, but it performs best with good drainage.

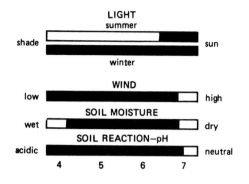

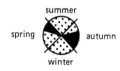

Seasonal Interest. *Flowers:* Small, white or pinkish, in numerous clusters in late spring. *Foliage:* Medium green, finely cut, giving a "parsley" appearance from which the common name is taken, turning yellowish in autumn. *Fruits:* Bright red, to 0.8 cm/0.3 in. across, colorful from middle to late autumn. *Trunks and branches:*

Flaking, gray-brown outer bark reveals red-brown inner bark that adds winter interest.

Problems and Maintenance. This species is subject to problems of hawthorns in general but is more trouble-free than most in the South.

Related Species

Crataegus aestivalis 6 and *C. ovata* 6 (both called mayhaw). These species have bright, red edible fruit, about 1 cm/0.4 in. across (to 1.5 cm/0.6 in. across in selected cultivars). They are valued for making preserves and jellies in their native ranges: *C. aestivalis* in the southeastern to south-central United States and *C. ovata* in the south-central to southwestern United States), and elsewhere in Zones 8b–9a+.

Crataegus brachyacantha 7 (blueberry hawthorn). This is a handsome tree with small white flowers that fade to orange, and waxy blue fruits, about 1 cm/0.4 in. across, that are ornamental in late summer. Native to southeastern Texas and Louisiana, and useful at least in Zones 8a–9a+.

Other *Crataegus* species native to the South may be of value locally and sometimes are worth preserving in development even when not available for planting.

Crataegus crus-galli 6

COCKSPUR HAWTHORN
Deciduous tree
Rosaceae (Rose Family)

Native Range. Northeastern North America, south to North Carolina, west to Kansas.

Useful Range. USDA Zones 4a–6b.

Function. Specimen, screen, barrier, patio (with pruning to eliminate the hazard of thorns on the lower part of the plant).

Size and Habit

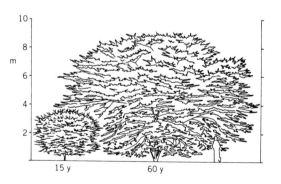

Crataegus crus-galli.

Adaptability. This tree is well adapted to environmental stresses, including urban environments, but its thorns preclude some urban uses.

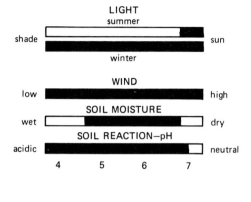

LIGHT

Seasonal Interest. *Flowers:* Small, white, in clusters in late spring. *Foliage:* Glossy, dark green leaves, 2.5–8 cm/1–3 in. long, making a dense mass and persisting with little color change until they fall in late autumn. *Fruits:* Bright red, to about 1 cm/0.4 in. across, persisting until winter (when not diseased). *Twigs and branches:* Strongly horizontal branches are conspicuous at all seasons and bear very large thorns.

Problems and Maintenance. *C. crus-galli* is moderately susceptible to infection by the cedar

Crataegus ×*lavallei.*

apple rust fungus, especially the fruits, which take on the rusty color of the fungus fruiting bodies but lose their autumn show. Plant away from native eastern red cedar (*Juniperus virginiana*) and its cultivars, which are alternate hosts of the causal fungus, or be prepared to tolerate a certain amount of disease. Transplanting problems have been encountered but do not seem serious with proper handling. Dormant trees should be planted after a few days' activation in a warm, moist atmosphere, with care to prevent drying during handling.

Cultivars. 'Cruzam' (Crusader®) and 'Inermis' are thornless selections. Both are reported to be highly resistant to rust.

Related Species

Crataegus ×*lavallei* 6 (synonym: C ×*carrierei*; Lavalle hawthorn). This hybrid (probably *C. crus-galli* × *C. pubescens* f. *stipulacea*) is stiffly upright in habit when young, later becoming ovoid in form, and usually thornless. Its dark green, lustrous leaves, to 10 cm/4 in. long, turn bronze in autumn and the large (1.5 cm/0.6 in.), orange-red fruits persist well into winter. Unfortunately, leaves and fruits are often disfigured by rust. Also, this tree is slow to become anchored after transplanting, requiring longer initial staking. It is useful in Zones 4b–7a.

Crataegus ×*prunifolia* 6 (synonym: C. *crus-galli* 'Splendens'). This hybrid, probably of *C. crus-galli* × *C. succulenta* var. *macracantha*, is not greatly different from *C. crus-galli* and can be considered interchangeable in landscape use.

Crataegus succulenta 6 (fleshy hawthorn). This wide-ranging species from the northeastern to southwestern United States is similar in landscape effect to *C. crus-galli.* The variety *macracantha* (synonym: *Crataegus macracantha*) is somewhat denser and more vigorous and is valued in the north-central United States as a hedge, screen, or specimen.

Crataegus mollis 6

DOWNY HAWTHORN
Deciduous tree
Rosaceae (Rose Family)

Native Range. Eastern and central North America: Ontario to Virginia, westward to South Dakota and Kansas.

Useful Range. USDA Zones 3a–6b.

Function. Patio tree, specimen, naturalizing. More often preserved in natural sites than planted.

Size and Habit

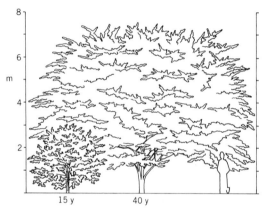

15 y   40 y

Crataegus mollis.

Adaptability

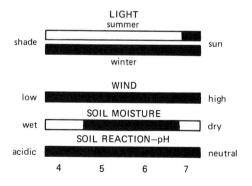

Seasonal Interest. *Flowers:* White, to 2.5 cm/1 in., not persisting for long. *Foliage:* Dull medium green, coarser than that of the better hawthorns and disfigured by rust where the disease is present, turning yellowish in autumn. *Fruits:* Bright red, to 2 cm/0.8 in., sweet and edible, falling by early autumn.

Problems and Maintenance. This species is more susceptible to cedar apple rust fungus than most hawthorns and is best used where the eastern red cedar (*Juniperus virginiana*) is not present in quantity. Aphids also can be troublesome. Transplanting difficulties have been reported but usually are not serious with proper handling (see *C. crus-galli,* Problems and Maintenance).

Related Species

Crataegus punctata 6 (dotted hawthorn). This species, native to northeastern North America, exhibits in the extreme the horizontal branching that is typical of many hawthorns, spreading in time to a width of as much as 12 m/40 ft, while reaching only half of that in height. Fruits are similar to those of *C. mollis* except duller red and with dots over their surfaces. Fruits of 'Aurea' ripen yellow instead of red, but this cultivar is seldom, if ever, available. 'Ohio Pioneer,' selected at the Ohio Agricultural Research and Development Center, is thornless.

Other *Crataegus* species native to the North may be of value locally and sometimes are worth preserving in development even when not available for planting.

Crataegus monogyna 6

SINGLESEED HAWTHORN, ENGLISH
HAWTHORN
Deciduous tree
Rosaceae (Rose Family)

Native Range. Mediterranean Region: southern Europe, North Africa, Asia Minor.

Useful Range. USDA Zones 5a–7b.

Function. Specimen, patio tree, screen,
hedge.

Size and Habit

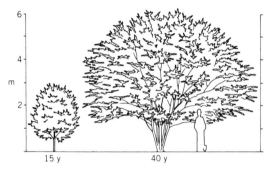

Crataegus monogyna.

Adaptability

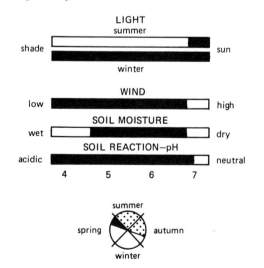

Seasonal Interest. *Flowers:* Small, white, in
clusters in very late spring. *Foliage:* Medium
green, strongly lobed and finer in texture than
most hawthorns, remaining green and falling
early in autumn. *Fruits:* Red, to about 1 cm/0.4
in. across, but not as showy as those of some
other hawthorns. *Trunk and branches:* Smooth
bark is olive green to yellow-orange, often striking in color at close range.

Problems and Maintenance. Like all hawthorns, this tree is susceptible to cedar apple rust
and is best used where the eastern red cedar
(*Juniperus virginiana*) is not present in great quantity. Aphids also can be troublesome. Transplanting difficulties have been experienced but
usually are not serious with proper handling
(see *C. crusgalli,* Problems and Maintenance).
A trunk canker disease, perhaps initiated or
aggravated by sun-scald in winter, can be a
serious problem in some areas, especially on
the columnar selection 'Stricta.' Consult local
plantsmen about the seriousness of this problem
in specific areas.

Cultivars. 'Stricta' is thornless, and narrowly
columnar when young, broadening with age to
an oval form.

Related Species

Crategus laevigata 6 (synonym *C. oxyacantha;*
English hawthorn; May tree). This native of
Europe and North Africa has been used as a
specimen, hedge, and screen for hundreds of
years in Europe; its cultivars are the most showy
in flower of all the hawthorns, and colorful again
when the bright red fruits ripen in late summer
and early autumn. The species type is useful in

Crataegus laevigata.

Crataeguis laevigata.

Zones 5a–7b but some cultivars are not reliably hardy north of Zone 6a. Unfortunately it is also more prone to disease problems and aphids than most hawthorns, and there are better choices for most landscape purposes in our area. The cultivars 'Paul's Scarlet' (= 'Paulii'), 'Plena,' and 'Rubra Plena' (= 'Rosea-plena) have, respectively, double rose, double white, and double pink flowers. 'Superba' (= 'Crimson Cloud') has large, single rose-red flowers with white centers.

Crataegus ×*mordenensis* 6 (Morden hawthorn). This is actually a group of hybrids of C. *laevigata* 'Paul's Scarlet' × C. *succulenta.* The first and best known selection is 'Toba,' a small tree (to 5 m/16 ft), with double pink flowers, darkening with age, followed by only a few red fruits and glossy, lobed leaves. This cultivar resembles C. *laevigata* 'Paul's Scarlet' and 'Rubra-plena' and is equally susceptible to fire blight but much more cold-hardy, to Zone 3b. A more recent selection of C. ×*mordenensis*, 'Snowbird,' has pure white flowers and relatively few bright crimson fruits and is even more cold-hardy than 'Toba.'

Crataegus pinnatifida 6 (Chinese hawthorn). This very hardy tree (Zones 3b–7a) from northeastern Asia has been found to grow well in North Dakota. It has lustrous, dark green, finely cut leaves, snowy white flowers in late spring, and bright red fruits to 2.5 cm/1 in. across in autumn. The var. *major* is more vigorous, with outstanding glossy dark green foliage. It is round-headed and compact in form, making an excellent specimen or patio tree with relatively few small thorns.

Crataegus phaenopyrum 6

WASHINGTON HAWTHORN
Deciduous tree
Rosaceae (Rose Family)

Native Range. Southeastern United States, west to Missouri.

Useful Range. USDA Zones 4b–8b.

Function. Specimen, patio tree, screen, hedge.

Size and Habit

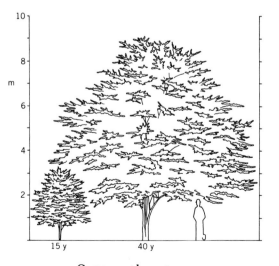

Crataegus phaenopyrum.

Adaptability

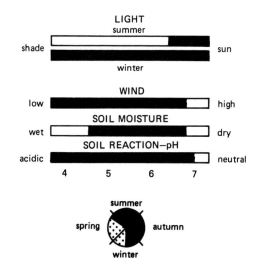

Crataegus phaenopyrum.

Seasonal Interest. *Flowers:* Small, white, in clusters in late spring or early summer. *Foliage:* Dark green, lustrous, 2.5–8 cm/1–3 in. long, turning orange-red in autumn in some locations in some years. *Fruits:* Shiny, bright red, only 0.6 cm/0.25 in. across but large numbers are borne in showy clusters in autumn and part or all of winter. *Twigs and branches:* Horizontally layered branching, but less striking than some other hawthorns.

Problems and Maintenance. This species is less susceptible to insect and disease problems than most hawthorns, only occasionally requiring control measures. Because of this and its outstanding seasonal interest, *C. phaenopyrum* is

one of the most versatile and valuable of all the hawthorns for landscape use. Transplanting difficulties have been reported but usually are not serious with proper handling (see *C. crusgalli*, Problems and Maintenance).

Cultivars. 'Fastigiata' is columnar to narrowly pyramidal in form, with smaller flowers and fruits than the species type. 'PNI 1661' (Princeton Sentry®) is also narrowly pyramidal and nearly thornless. 'Vaughn,' probably a hybrid between *C. phaenopyrum* and *C. crus-galli*, has long-lasting scarlet fruits, somewhat larger and more showy than those of *C. phaenopyrum*, in winter, and has horizontal branching similar to that of *C. crus-galli*. Its foliage usually turns bright red in autumn and its winter fruiting interest is simply outstanding, but it is difficult to handle in production because of its many large thorns, and it is more susceptible to rust than *C. phaenopyrum*.

Crataegus viridis 6–7

GREEN HAWTHORN
Deciduous tree
Rosaceae (Rose Family)

Native Range. Southeastern and south-central United States.

Useful Range. USDA Zones 5a–9a and perhaps colder zones as well.

Function. Specimen, patio tree, screen, hedge.

Size and Habit

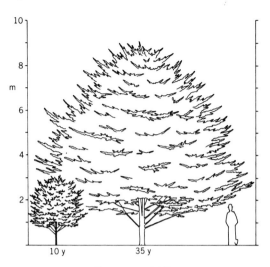

Crataegus viridis.

Adaptability. This species is unusual among hawthorns for its ability to grow well in both wet and dry sites.

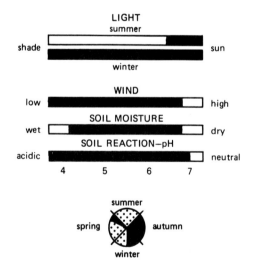

Seasonal Interest. *Flowers:* Small, white, in loose clusters in late spring. *Foliage:* Bright green, lustrous, with little autumn color change. *Fruits:* Bright orange-red but not lustrous, 0.6–0.8 cm/0.25–0.3 in. across, in clusters persisting through part or all of winter. *Trunk and branches:* Silvery gray, adding winter interest, along with

Crataegus viridis 'Winter King.'

the persistent fruits. Bark on older trunks flakes off, exposing the orange-brown inner bark in interesting patterns.

Problems and Maintenance. This species is less susceptible to insect and disease problems than most hawthorns, seldom requiring maintenance.

Cultivars. 'Winter King,' a selection for outstanding fruit size and retention, was introduced in 1955 by Simpson Orchard Co., Vincennes, Indiana. It has grown rapidly in popularity, rivaling C. *phaenopyrum* in the Midwest.

Related Hybrids

Crataegus ×*nitida* 6 (C. *crus-galli* × C. *viridis*; glossy hawthorn). This handsome hawthorn has flower, foliage, and fruiting interest similar to that of C. *viridis*, but is more compact and horizontally branching.

Cryptomeria japonica 8

CRYPTOMERIA, JAPANESE CEDAR
Evergreen tree
Taxodiaceae (Taxodium Family)

Native Range. Japan.

Useful Range. USDA Zones 6b–9a+.

Function. Specimen, screen.

Size and Habit

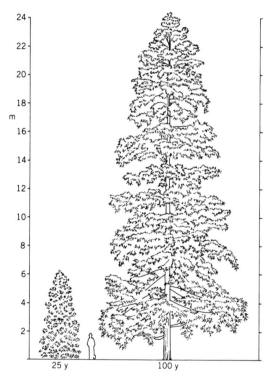

Cryptomeria japonica.

Adaptability. This tree performs best with light shade, at least in winter, in northern inland areas. In coastal areas, where this tree is at its best, exposure to full sun gives best results.

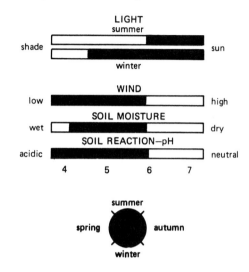

Seasonal Interest. *Foliage:* Short, glossy needles, attached spirally to long, whiplike twigs in plumy clusters, give an elegant and distinctive texture to the plant throughout the year. Foliage bronzes in winter. *Trunk:* Rich reddish-brown bark shreds in long strips like that of *Chamaecyparis* species and *Sequoiadendron.*

Problems and Maintenance. This tree and its cultivars are relatively trouble-free in most sites, but can be disfigured by a leaf blight disease during prolonged wet periods. In some plants, dead foliage clings rather than falling and must be removed manually to bring out the plant's best appearance. Windy sites in mild climates promote sweeping away of dried foliage by wind and rain.

Cultivars. More than 30 cultivars are available in our area, mostly introduced from Japan. Some have only their Japanese cultivar names; others when brought to Europe and North America have been given Latin cultivar names—a practice illegitimate since January 1, 1959. A partial list of Japanese cultivar names in *Cryptomeria* and their synonyms can be found in Krussmann's *Manual of Cultivated Conifers* (Timber Press).

Cryptomeria japonica.

The clone called 'Lobbii' is generally believed to be more elegantly sculptured and compact than most other plants of C. *japonica,* but observers of mature specimens see little difference between 'Lobbii' and many others. The distinctness of 'Lobbii' may be largely the contrast between its mature foliage and that of juvenile seedlings. Since this clone is typically propagated by grafting on seedlings, if nothing more this is a means of obtaining the mature plant character in a shorter time.

A dozen or so dwarf and semi-dwarf cultivars have become popular in our area. These are useful primarily for small-scale accent or bonsai treatment and include 'Bandai-sugi,' which has strikingly irregular growth and congested foliage, reaching a size of little more than 1 m/3.3 ft after 20 years or more, and 'Jindai-sugi,' which makes an irregular dark green mass to about 1.5 m/5 ft. Other clones are slow-growing but more regular in shape, including 'Compressa,' with dark green foliage that turns plum-purple in winter, making

a globe to about 1.5 m/5 ft, and 'Vilmoriniana,' which is even more dwarf, to only about 0.6 m/2 ft.

Foliage of some clones remains juvenile for many years, with longer, more slender needles, giving a distinctly softer, more delicate texture. 'Elegans' is one of these, with light, bright green foliage, turning a smoky purple in winter. Similar but slower growing forms include 'Elegans Compacta' and 'Elegans Nana.'

'Viminalis' has long, whiplike branches, with clusters of shorter branches at their ends, producing a dramatic effect. Others that are similar (some think identical) are 'Araucarioides,' 'Dacrydioides,' 'Lycopodioides,' and 'Selaginoides.'

'Tansu' makes a small shrub, distinctive for its twisted branching habit and exceedingly fine texture, whereas it is the needles of 'Spiralis' that are twisted around the stems, producing a distinctly ropy appearance.

'Yoshino' is a shapely, vigorous tree, to about 10 m/33 ft tall, with bright green foliage year-round and a reputation for being unusually resistant to leaf blight. It is surely one of the most functional clones of *Cryptomeria,* as a screen or specimen for accent.

Related Species

Taiwania cryptomerioides 8 (taiwania). This large, evergreen tree from the mountains of Taiwan is closely related to *Cryptomeria.* It has not been tried in much of our area but has been growing successfully for years in at least one site in Zone 9a. If it were available, this tree could be used more widely as an evergreen screen in the mildest parts of our area and southward.

Cunninghamia lanceolata 8

COMMON CHINA FIR
Evergreen tree
Taxodiaceae (Taxodium Family)

Native Range.   China.

Useful Range.   USDA Zones 7a–9a+.

Function.   Specimen, screen.

Size and Habit

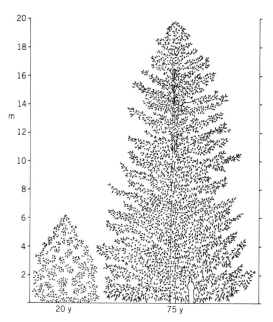

Cunninghamia lanceolata.

Cunninghamia lanceolata.

back or killed by cold, lower parts of branches regenerate many shoots that eventually replace those lost. Even trees killed nearly to the ground will regenerate sprouts from the trunk and roots.

Problems and Maintenance.   This tree is relatively trouble-free except for winter desiccation of foliage or killback of branches in northern areas and occasional mite infestation.

Adaptability.   Best in full sun except at northern edges of the useful range, where light shade, especially in winter, reduces winter desiccation.

Seasonal Interest. *Foliage:* Glossy, acicular needles are prickly to the touch and give the plant a distinctive texture. The foliage turns bronze in winter. *Trunk and branches:* The bark is fibrous and rich red-brown, similar to that of *Chamaecyparis* and *Sequoiadendron.* When cut

Araucaria araucana.

Araucaria araucana.

Cultivars. 'Glauca' has more-or-less blue-green foliage.

Related Species

Araucaria araucana 8 (monkey-puzzle tree, Chilean pine). This large, evergreen tree has sharply pointed needles on closely spaced, conspicuously whorled, ropelike branches and is useful in Zones 8a–9a+. Other *Araucaria* species, *A. bidwillii* 8 (bunya-bunya), from Australia, and *A. heterophylla* 8 (synonym: *A. excelsa*; Norfolk Island pine), are considered subtropical, although *A. bidwillii* has survived limited trial in Zone 9a.

×*Cupressocyparis leylandii* 8

CUPRESSOCYPARIS, LEYLAND CYPRESS
Evergreen tree
Cupressaceae (Cypress Family)

Hybrid origin. *Chamaecyparis nootkatensis* × *Cupressus macrocarpa.*

Useful Range. USDA Zones 7a–9a+.

Function. Screen, hedge, specimen.

Size and Habit

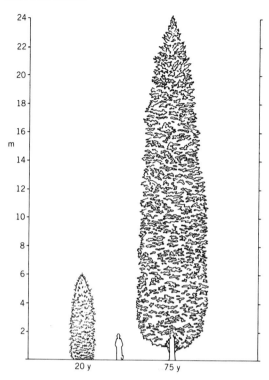

×*Cupressocyparis leylandii.*

Adaptability

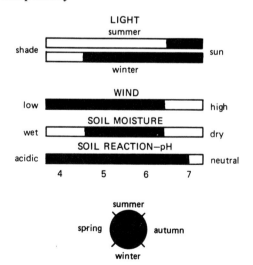

Seasonal Interest. *Foliage:* Dark green or blue-green, scalelike, resembling that of *Chamaecyparis nootkatensis.*

Problems and Maintenance. This hybrid has been relatively trouble-free to date but occasion-ally may be infested with mites. It was not widely used in North America during the first 70 years after its discovery in 1888, but it is rapidly becoming a popular choice for screening. Further growth in popularity may uncover other problems.

Cultivars. In Great Britain, several color and form variants have been selected, but such culti-vars are seldom available in North America at present. Once well known, their popularity could grow rapidly. A few of the most distinctive selections are 'Castlewellan Gold,' with yellow foliage in summer, bronzing in winter, 'Leighton Green,' which is narrowly columnar, 'Naylor's Blue,' which has blue-green foliage, and 'Silver Dust,' which is a white variegated mutant of 'Leighton Green' that was selected at the U.S. National Arboretum in 1960.

Related Species

Cupressus arizonica 7 (Arizona cypress). This more-or-less columnar tree has blue-green, scale-

Cupressus arizonica.

like foliage and reddish brown, peeling bark. It does best in full sun and very well-drained, even dry, soil and probably is not widely useful in the eastern United States but should be hardy in Zones 7b–9a.

Cupressus bakeri 7 (Modoc cypress). Large, dense shrub or small tree with blue-green, scale-like foliage and reddish brown, peeling bark. This is the hardiest *Cupressus* species (Zones 6b–9a), yet not widely used in our area.

Cupressus macrocarpa 8 (Monterey cypress). This large, long-lived tree is native to California and valued for seaside planting there. In spite of its involvement in ×*Cupressocyparis leylandii, C.*

macrocarpa itself seems poorly adapted to the eastern United States, except possibly in seashore sites, where it should be planted only experimentally in Zones 8a–9a+.

Cupressus sempervirens 7 (Italian cypress). This rather tall tree with dark-green scalelike foliage is best known in the form of the selection 'Stricta' (columnar Italian cypress), familiar in photographs of Mediterranean gardens as an extremely narrow specimen, often six to ten times as tall as it is broad. It grows well in southern coastal gardens in Zones 9a+, but it usually is short-lived because the moist climate of the southeastern United States encourages foliage diseases that can become serious.

Cycas revoluta 3–4

SAGO PALM, JAPANESE FERN PALM
Evergreen shrub
Cycadaceae (Cycad Family)

Native Range.   Southern Japan.

Useful Range.   USDA Zones 8b–9a+.

Function.   Specimen, massing, foundation.

Size and Habit

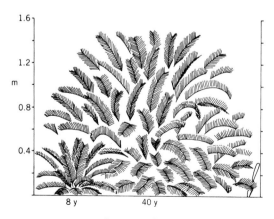

Cycas revoluta.

Adaptability.   Within its useful range, this plant is broadly tolerant of different soil conditions.

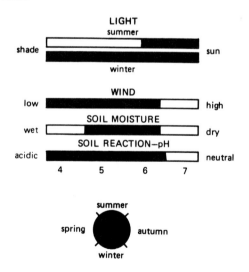

Seasonal Interest.   *Flowers and seeds:* Cycads are dioecious. The male inflorescence or strobilus (bearing spore cases) is conelike, erect in the center of the plant, and up to 0.5 m/1.6 ft long. The corresponding structures on female plants are flat and spreading, eventually bearing large numbers of orange-red seeds, 4 cm/1.6 in. across. *Foliage:* The rich, dark green, compound leaves, 0.5–1 m/1.6–3.3 ft long on young plants to 2 m/

6.6 ft on old plants, are similar to those of ferns or palms, arising fountainlike out of the center of the plant, each new set of leaves unfolding in spring.

Problems and Maintenance. This plant is practically trouble-free and requires no maintenance other than cleaning: removing dust from the leaves and any debris from the center of the plant. Foliage and seeds are reported to be poisonous to animals.

Related Species

Zamia pumila 3 (synonym: *Z. floridana*; coontie, Seminole bread). This lower growing relative of *Cycas revoluta* belongs to another family of cycads, the Zamiaceae (Zamia Family). Native to Florida, it is less cold-hardy than *Cycas revoluta* but useful in Zones 9a+. In general appearance it is similar to *Cycas* but slightly less regular, and it has smaller and less interesting male strobili and less colorful seeds.

Cyrtomium falcatum 3

HOLLY FERN
Evergreen groundcover
Polypodiaceae (Polypody Family)

Native Range.   Asia, Polynesia, South Africa.

Useful Range.   USDA Zones 8b–9a+.

Function. Groundcover, specimen. Spreads slowly, so it is particularly useful in small areas for contrast with finer-textured groundcovers.

Size and Habit

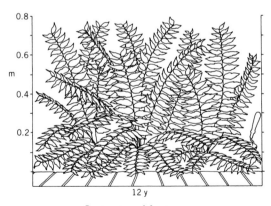
Cyrtomium falcatum.

Adaptability. Best with a reliable supply of moisture, but can tolerate occasional periods of drought.

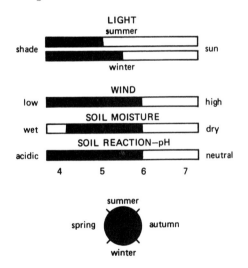

Seasonal Interest. *Foliage:* Evergreen, leathery, glossy, yellow-green to dark green, superficially resembling holly leaves.

Problems and Maintenance. Relatively trouble-free, requiring little or no maintenance once established.

Cultivars. A few named foliage variants are available commercially, including the following. 'Butterfieldii' and 'Rochfordianum' have deeply incised leaf margins. 'Rochfordianum' is the most common cultivar in landscape use. 'Compactum' is lower in stature, compact in growth.

Cytisus ×kewensis 2

KEW BROOM
Deciduous shrub
Fabaceae (Leguminosae; Pea Family)

Hybrid origin. *Cytisus ardoinii* × *C. multiflorus.*

Useful Range. USDA Zones 6b–9a+.

Function. Specimen, groundcover, rock garden.

Size and Habit

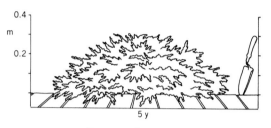

Cytisus ×*kewensis.*

Adaptability. Full sun and well-drained soil are essential to the success of *Cytisus* species. They are tolerant of wind except during winter cold extremes in the northern parts of their useful ranges, and their ability to use atmospheric nitrogen enables them to tolerate infertile soils.

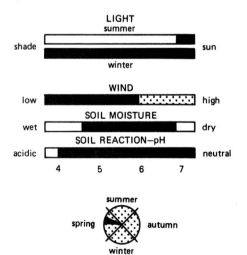

Seasonal Interest. *Flowers:* Pale yellow, pea-like, borne on ascending tips of creeping stems before the small leaves emerge in midspring. *Foliage:* Very small leaves are inconspicuous. *Twigs and branches:* Green twigs are fairly conspicuous in winter.

Problems and Maintenance. *Cytisus* species are relatively free of insect and disease problems but difficult to transplant except as container-grown plants. They may need to be pruned occasionally to remove deadwood in the North or to control the size of the plant in the South. Light pruning to remove old flowering branches will stimulate new stem growth and enhance flowering in the following year.

Related Species

Chamaecytisus albus 2 (synonym: *Cytisus albus;* Portuguese broom). A low-growing broom with paler yellow flowers than those of *Cytisus* ×*kewensis*, not to be confused with the taller white Spanish broom (*Cytisus multiflorus*), which also has been misnamed *Cytisus albus.* Useful in Zones 6a–9a+.

Chamaecytisus purpureus 3 (purple broom). This is a very distinctive species, with purple flowers at the same time as *Cytisus* ×*kewensis.* In fact the two make an excellent companion planting, since their flower colors are complementary and harmonious. Cultivars have been selected for a wider range of color: 'Albus' with white flowers, 'Atropurpureus' with deep burgundy purple flowers, 'Roseus' with pale pink flowers, and others. Useful in Zones 6a–9a+.

Cytisus ardoinii 2 (Ardoin broom). This low-growing Mediterranean broom has bright yellow flowers and very small leaves. The selection 'Cottage' has creamy yellow flowers. Useful in Zones 6b–9a+, but seldom available.

Cytisus ×*beanii* 2 (Bean's broom). This hybrid of *C. ardoinii* × *C. purgans* has deep yellow flowers and is useful in Zones 6a–9a+ but seldom available.

Cytisus decumbens 2 (prostrate broom). This Mediterranean native is one of the finest low groundcovers (0.2 m/0.7 ft) among the brooms, with brilliant yellow flowers in late spring. Useful in Zones 6a–9a+.

Cytisus procumbens 3 (ground broom). This is similar to *C. decumbens* except taller (to 0.8 m/ 2.6 ft), and it is less likely to be commercially available.

Cytisus ×*praecox* 4

WARMINSTER BROOM
Deciduous shrub
Fabaceae (Leguminosae; Pea Family)

Hybrid origin. *Cytisus multiflorus* × *C. purgans.*

Useful Range. USDA Zones 6a–9a+.

Function. Specimen, rock garden.

Size and Habit

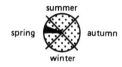

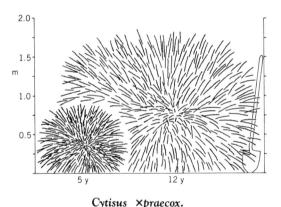

Cytisus ×praecox.

Adaptability. See C. ×*kewensis*, Adaptability.

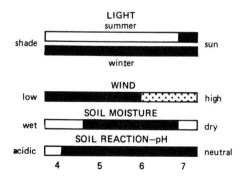

Seasonal Interest. *Flowers:* Pale yellow, pealike, with an unpleasant odor, borne on twigs before the small leaves emerge in midspring. *Foliage:* Very small leaves are inconspicuous. *Twigs and branches:* Green twigs are conspicuous in winter and evident in all seasons because of the sparse foliage.

Problems and Maintenance. See C. ×*kewensis*, Problems and Maintenance.

Cytisus ×praecox.

Cultivars. Several cultivars have been selected in Europe, but few of these are available at any given time in North America. Some of the more popular ones are listed here. 'Albus' is lower growing, to 1 m/3.3 ft in height, with white flowers. 'Allgold' is similar to the typical form but with golden yellow-flowers. 'Hollandia' has pink and red flowers. 'Luteus' is slower-growing, to 1 m/3.3 ft in height, with golden-yellow flowers. 'Zeelandica' is quite vigorous, with pale yellow, cream, and lilac-pink flowers, giving an overall appearance of pale pink.

Related Species

Cytisus multiflorus 4 (synonym: *C. albus;* white Spanish broom). This tall-growing species, to 2m/6.6 ft or occasionally taller, makes a striking display of white flowers at about the same time as its hybrid, *C.* ×*praecox* or slightly, later, and is slightly less cold-hardy, useful in Zones 6b–9a+.

Cytisus nigricans 3 (spike broom). Hardier than most brooms, useful in Zones 5a–9a, and later-flowering, with lemon-yellow flowers in terminal spikes in early summer.

Cytisus purgans 3 (Provence broom). Similar in effect to *C. nigricans,* with yellow flowers borne toward the ends of stiffly upright branches, but flowers in late spring and is less hardy, useful in Zones 6a–9a+.

Cytisus scoparius 4

SCOTCH BROOM
Deciduous shrub
Fabaceae (Leguminosae; Pea Family)

Native Range.   Central and southern Europe.

Useful Range.   USDA Zones 6b–9a+, marginally hardy in Zones 6a, the hybrids hardy northward only to Zone 7a or 7b.

Function.   Specimen, border, large-scale rock garden. Too tall to be useful as a groundcover.

Size and Habit

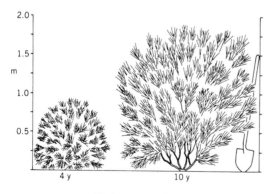

Cytisus scoparius.

Adaptability.   See C. ×*kewensis,* Adaptability.

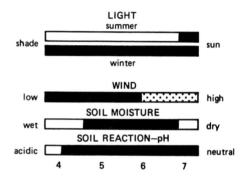

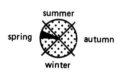

Seasonal Interest. *Flowers:* Yellow (many other colors in hybrids—see Cultivars), pealike, borne on upright stems before leaves emerge. *Foliage:* Small, relatively inconspicuous leaves. *Twigs and branches:* Green twigs are fairly conspicuous in winter and noticeable at other seasons.

Problems and Maintenance.   This shrub is relatively free of insect and disease problems but difficult to transplant except as container-grown plants. It may need pruning to remove deadwood following extreme winters in the North or for renewal in the South.

Cultivars.   More than 50 cultivars, mostly hybrids with unknown male parents, are in commerce, but very few of these are available in eastern North America. A few of the most common, and those most likely to be available at any given time, are listed here.

'Andreanus' is an upright selection with flowers yellow except for wing petals marked with deep red, the first plant of the species to be found with other than yellow flowers.

'Burkwoodii' is also upright in form with rich red-brown flowers.

'Golden Sunlight' is spreading in habit with bright golden-yellow flowers.

'Moonlight' is upright in habit with pale yellow flowers, similar in effect to *C.* ×*praecox*.

'Pink Beauty' is one of the best pink-flowered selections.

'Prostratus' is prosrate in habit, sometimes

grafted on an upright seedling, or "standard," resulting in an umbrella or weeping form.

'Red Wings' and 'San Francisco' have deep velvety red flowers. 'Stanford' has multicolored flowers with the general effect of orange from a distance.

Related Species

Argyrocytisus battandieri 6 (synonym: *Cytisus battandieri;* Morocco broom). This tall shrub, to 4 m/13 ft, is unusual among the brooms for its large, silvery, hairy leaves, to 9 cm/3.5 in. long, and golden-yellow flowers in dense, upright spikes, to 13 cm/5 in. long. Useful only in Zones 8b–9a+, and seldom available in our area.

Daphne ×*burkwoodii* 3–4

BURKWOOD DAPHNE
Semievergreen shrub
Thymelaeaceae (Mezereum Family)

Hybrid origin. *D. caucasia* ×*D. cneorum.*

Useful Range. USDA Zones 4b–7b, perhaps colder zones with reliable winter snow cover and areas with mild summers and cool soils in Zone 8.

Function. Specimen, foundation, border, rock garden.

Size and Habit

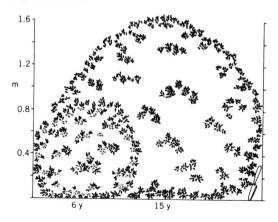

Daphne ×*burkwoodii.*

Adaptability. This plant is more easily grown than most *Daphne* species, but it must have perfect soil drainage and a relatively cool root zone, and it seems to perform best in sandy soils of low fertility but with a reasonably reliable moisture supply. It has been written that limestone soil is necessary for *Daphne* species, but this probably is not true.

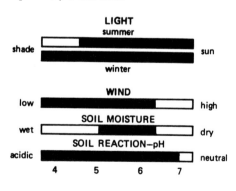

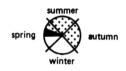

Seasonal Interest. *Flowers:* Small, white, but pink in bud, fragrant, mid to late spring. *Foliage:* Small, rounded, dull blue-green leaves offer neat texture in summer through autumn, and part of

Daphne ×*burkwoodii* 'Carol Mackie.'

winter in the South, with little color change. *Fruits:* Small red berries in early summer are poisonous to animals, including humans.

Problems and Maintenance. This shrub is difficult to transplant except as container-grown plants. *Daphne* species have been known to die suddenly and mysteriously, but at least some such cases can be explained by temporary raising of water tables during unusually wet seasons. Both foliage and fruits of *Daphne* species are strongly poisonous, so these plants should not be used where they are accessible to animals and small children.

Cultivars. 'Carol Mackie' has uniformly creamy, white-margined leaves, contrasting with the normal dark green in a strikingly crisp texture pattern. 'Somerset' is probably no better than some plants now carried in commerce simply as *D.* ×*burkwoodii,* but this clone probably is more floriferous and compact than average for the species.

Related Species

Daphne cneorum 2 (rose daphne). This low, moundlike plant from Europe has neat, fine-textured, more or less evergreen foliage and rosy pink, delightfully fragrant flowers. It has been highly popular for rock garden or groundcover use, and probably would have even greater use if it were not for its tendency to die suddenly without any explanation. Plantings have performed well for many years on light, sandy soils having perfect drainage, lending support to the idea that perfect soil aeration may be the key to longevity of *Daphne* species. It is hardy in Zones 4b–7b and in colder zones where winter snow cover is reliable. 'Alba' is a vigorous selection with white flowers. 'Eximia' has large leaves and large lilac-rose flowers. 'Ruby Glow' has deeper rose-pink flowers.

Daphne giraldii 3

GIRALDI DAPHNE
Deciduous shrub
Thymelaeaceae (Mezereum Family)

Native Range.   Northwestern China.

Useful Range.   USDA Zones 2b–7a, perhaps somewhat farther south as well.

Function.   Specimen, border, rock garden.

Size and Habit

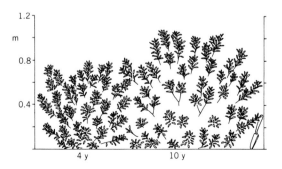

Daphne giraldii.

Adaptability.   As with other *Daphne* species, cool, perfectly drained soil of low fertility seems to give the best performance.

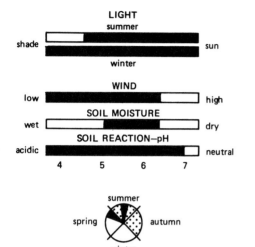

Daphne giraldii.

Seasonal Interest. *Flowers:* Small, yellow, lightly fragrant, in clusters in late spring. *Foliage:* Similar in texture to that of *D. mezereum,* whitish underneath but not conspicuously so. *Fruits:* Small, bright scarlet in midsummer, poisonous (see *Daphne* ×*burkwoodii*).

Problems and Maintenance.   This shrub seems relatively trouble-free but is not used widely enough to predict potential problems with certainty. Its cold-hardiness and yellow flowers distinguish it from other *Daphne* species. Plant parts are poisonous (see *Daphne* ×*burkwoodii*).

Related Species

Daphne alpina 2 (alpine daphne).   This dwarf plant from the European Alps is uncommon in our area but a good rock garden specimen when available. It appears as a smaller version of *D. caucasica* ssp. *altaica,* to 45 cm/18 in. tall, and is useful in Zones 5a–7a, and probably colder zones as well with snow cover.

Daphne caucasica ssp. *altaica* 4 (synonym *D. altaica;* Altai daphne).   This deciduous shrub from the Altai mountains of central Asia is similar in general effect to *D. giraldii* except for its fragrant white flowers and yellow to dark red fruits. It is useful at least in Zones 5a–7a, and probably in much colder areas as well.

Daphne mezereum 3

FEBRUARY DAPHNE

Deciduous shrub

Thymelaeaceae (Mezereum Family)

Native Range.   Europe and western Asia, naturalized in the northeastern United States.

Useful Range.   USDA Zones 3b–7b.

Function.   Border, specimen, foundation.

Size and Habit

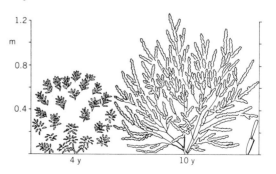

Daphne mezereum.

Adaptability. This shrub performs best in sandy soil, high in organic matter but low in fertility, with reliable moisture supply but perfect drainage. Contrary to a common belief, limestone soil is probably of no specific benefit.

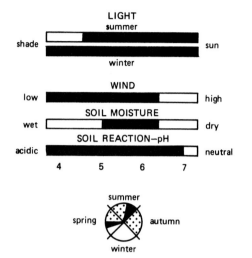

Seasonal Interest. *Flowers:* Small, fragrant, rosy purple (or creamy white), conspicuous because they appear before leaves begin to expand, in early spring. *Foliage:* Rather small (3–8 cm/ 1–3 in.), elongated leaves, rounded on the ends,

dull green and inconspicuous. *Fruits:* Bright scarlet (yellow in the white flowering cultivar), to 0.8 cm/0.3 in., borne close to the stems in late summer, and poisonous (see *Daphne* ×*burkwoodii*).

Problems and Maintenance. This shrub is relatively trouble-free but difficult to transplant except as container-grown plants. It is usually more reliable than some *Daphne* species once it is established in a suitable site. In fact, it has become naturalized in the northeastern United States. Plant parts are poisonous (see *Daphne* ×*burkwoodii*).

Cultivars. 'Alba' is identical with the species type except that it has creamy white flowers and yellow fruits.

Related Species

Daphne genkwa 3 (lilac daphne). This low shrub has fragrant, lilac-colored flowers in large clusters that superficially resemble those of lilac and appear before the new leaves in early spring. It is not widely used or available, but it is a good selection for variety and early spring color. Useful in Zones 6b–9a.

Daphne odora 3–4

WINTER DAPHNE
Evergreen shrub
Thymelaeaceae (Mezereum Family)

Native Range. China.

Useful Range. USDA Zones 7a–8b.

Function. Border, specimen, foundation.

Size and Habit

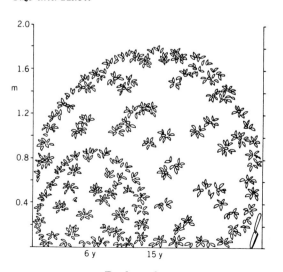

Daphne odora.

Adaptability.   Like other *Daphne* species, this shrub is best grown in perfectly drained soil of low fertility. Unlike other *Daphne* species, it grows best with at least partial shade and in soil that is never excessively dry.

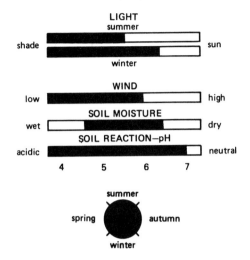

Seasonal Interest. *Flowers:* Small, highly fragrant, rosy purple outside, nearly white inside, from early through middle spring. *Foliage:* Evergreen, leathery, dark green, 5–8 cm/2–3 in. long, and narrow, making a compact, fine-textured mass year-round.

Problems and Maintenance.   This shrub reputedly is difficult to transplant and unreliable in establishment, but specialists do not fully agree on this. It apparently performs reasonably well in the South but is not long-lived. Plant parts are poisonous (see *Daphne ×burkwoodii*).

Daphne odora.

Forms and Cultivars.   Flowers of f. *alba* (synonym: 'Alba') are white. Leaves of f. *marginata* (synonym: 'Marginata') have white to yellow margins; this form includes 'Aureo Marginata' and 'Variegata,' both with yellow margins and rose or pink flowers, respectively.

Related Species

Daphne laureola 4 (spurge laurel).   This upright evergreen from southern Europe and western Asia has relatively inconspicuous yellow-green flowers in early spring, with odor varying from mildly fragrant to slightly disagreeable, followed by black fruits. It is unusually shade-tolerant, and has become naturalized in a few wooded localities in the coastal Pacific Northwest. Not widely available but useful in Zones 7b–9a.

Daphne ×mantensiana 3 (Manten's daphne). This low evergreen hybrid (*D. ×burkwoodii × D. tangutica*) is represented commercially by the selection 'Manten,' with fragrant and showy orchid-purple flowers, opening intermittently from late spring to early autumn. Its useful range is not well established but includes at least Zones 7a–8b.

Daphne ×napolitana 3 (*D. sericea×D. cneorum*). This evergreen shrub, to 0.75 m/2.5 ft tall, with fragrant, showy rosy purple flowers in late spring and intermittently in summer. Its useful range includes that of *D. sericea*, probably also Zone 7, and perhaps Zone 6b as well.

Daphne sericea 3 (synonym: *D. collina*).   This compact, rounded shrub from the eastern Mediterranean is smaller than *D. odora*, with lustrous evergreen foliage and showy clusters of rosy purple flowers in late spring. It is useful at least in Zones 8a–9a.

Daphne tangutica 3–4 (synonym, in part: *D. retusa*).   This evergreen shrub from western China has fragrant flowers, rosy purple outside and near-white inside, in spring. Populations once called *D. retusa* but now combined in *D. tangutica* are somewhat lower in habit. Adaptability is not well known, but the useful range includes at least Zones 7–8, and perhaps Zone 6b as well.

Davidia involucrata 6–7

DOVE TREE
Deciduous tree
Nyssaceae (Tupelo Family)

Native Range.   Western China.

Useful Range.   USDA Zones 6b–8b, var. *vilmoriniana* also in Zone 6a.

Function.   Specimen, border, patio tree (with pruning for form). Usually used more for its unique flowering interest than for specific function.

Size and Habit

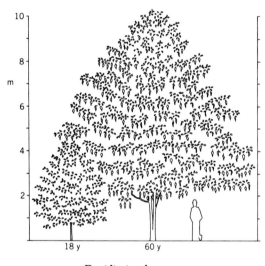

Davidia involucrata.

Adaptability

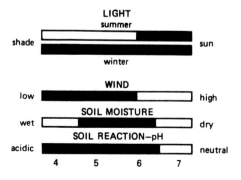

Seasonal Interest.   *Flowers:* Small, yellow, in crowded globose heads, surrounded at the base by two large, white, papery, pointed bracts, the lower 15 cm/6 in. long, the upper one much smaller, showy in late spring. Usually does not flower annually, but the creamy white bracts give it a truly unique appearance when it does. *Foliage:* Coarsely toothed, dull green, giving textural contrast. *Fruits:* Green, oval, 2–3 cm/1 in. long.

Problems and Maintenance.   This tree, although introduced in 1904 with much publicity, still is not widely enough used to suggest that all its potential problems are known. To date it has proved trouble-free except for the poorly understood unreliability of flowering, perhaps variable among different plants.

Varieties.   The var. *vilmoriniana* (synonym: *D. vilmoriniana*) differs little from the species type except in having slightly duller, smoother foliage and slightly greater cold-hardiness, at least to Zone 6a.

Deutzia gracilis 3

SLENDER DEUTZIA
Deciduous shrub
Hydrangeaceae (Hydrangea Family)

Native Range.   Japan.

Useful Range.   USDA Zones 4b–8b.

Function.   Border, low informal hedge.

Size and Habit

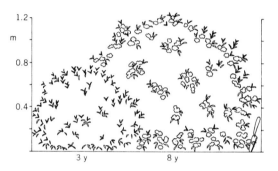

Deutzia gracilis.

Adaptability

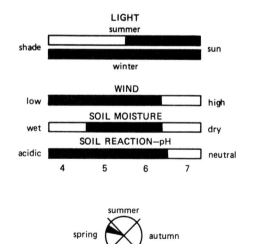

Seasonal Interest.   *Flowers:* White, in upright clusters, 5–8 cm/2–3 in. long, in late spring. *Foliage:* Dull green, somewhat finer-textured, falling in autumn without much color change.

Problems and Maintenance.   This shrub is relatively free of insect and disease problems but requires fairly regular pruning (every 2–3 years) to remove old stems and maintain plant form and vigor.

Cultivars.   'Aurea' has yellow foliage but is not one of the better yellow-leaved shrubs.

Related Species and Hybrids

Deutzia crenata 3–5.   This species is known in our area only as the dwarf form 'Nikko,' which is usually listed as, and looks like, a cultivar of *D. gracilis.* 'Nikko' grows compactly to 0.6 m/2 ft high and wide, perhaps eventually larger, with dense masses of white flowers and foliage that turns purplish in autumn. Useful at least in Zones 5a–8b, perhaps even parts of Zone 4.

Deutzia ×lemoinei 4 (Lemoine deutzia).   This hybrid (*D. parviflora* × *D. gracilis*) has showy flowers in clusters similar to but slightly later than those of *D. gracilis* in late spring and is more cold-hardy than *D. gracilis* (Zones 5a–8b). The selection 'Compacta' differs in its compact growth to a maximum height of about 1.5 m/5 ft and slightly greater cold hardiness (to Zone 4b).

Deutzia ×lemoinei.

Deutzia parviflora 4 (Mongolian deutzia).   This plant differs from *D. ×lemoinei* primarily in its flattened clusters of white flowers and slightly greater cold hardiness (Zones 4b–8a). Seldom available.

Deutzia scabra 5

FUZZY DEUTZIA
Deciduous shrub
Hydrangeaceae (Hydrangea Family)

Native Range.   China, Japan.

Useful Range.   USDA Zones 6a–8b.

Function.   Specimen, border, screen (with careful pruning in Zones 6b and southward).

Size and Habit

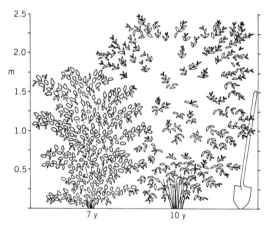

Deutzia scabra.

Adaptability

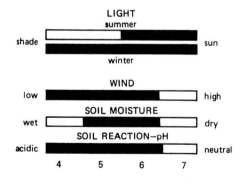

Seasonal Interest.   *Flowers:* White or pink outside, in upright clusters, 6–12 cm/2.5–5 in. long, in late spring and early summer. *Foliage:* Dull green, neutral in summer with rough pubescence and little or no autumnal color change.

Problems and Maintenance.   This shrub is relatively free of insect and disease problems but requires annual pruning in the North to maintain good form and condition, since some winter twig and branch dieback occurs regularly in Zone 6 and sometimes in Zone 7. Deutzias generally do not flower on current season's growth but initiate flower buds that become dormant before opening and must survive the winter in a dormant condition to flower the following spring or summer.

Cultivars.   'Candidissima' is late flowering (very early summer) with pure white, double flowers in large upright clusters. Because of the double-flowered condition, usually associated with sterility, petal drop is not triggered by pollination and flowers remain showy for a relatively long time. But this is still a short time in the full annual cycle, and the plant remains uninteresting for most of the year.
   'Codsall Pink' is upright in habit, with peeling, orange-brown bark and double pink flowers.
   'Pride of Rochester' is the best known cultivar of *D. scabra* with double white flowers, purple on the outside. 'Flore Pleno' and 'Plena' are similar to 'Pride of Rochester' and to each other (probably identical).

Related Species and Hybrids

Deutzia ×elegantissima 5.   This tall hybrid of *D. purpurascens × D. scabra* has rosy pink flowers and is useful in Zones 6b–8a but is usually available only as the selection 'Rosalind,' with deep carmine-red flowers.

Deutzia ×rosea 4 (rose deutzia).   This hybrid of *D. gracilis × D. purpurascens* has pink and white flowers at about the same time as its parents in late spring and is useful in Zones 6a–8b. The cultivar 'Eximia' is outstanding, with large pink flowers.

Diervilla sessilifolia 4

SOUTHERN BUSH HONEYSUCKLE
Deciduous shrub
Caprifoliaceae (Honeysuckle Family)

Native Range.   Southeastern United States.

Useful Range.   USDA Zones 4b–8a.

Function.   Large-scale groundcover, bank cover. Spreads by underground stems to make a dense mass.

Size and Habit

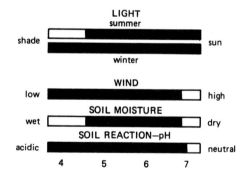

Diervilla sessilifolia.

Adaptability.   Unusually widely adapted to soils, light, and moisture conditions.

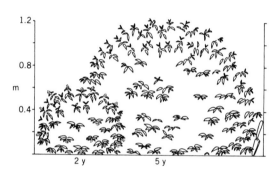

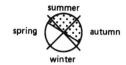

Seasonal Interest.   *Flowers:* Yellow, similar to those of the honeysuckles, in early summer; interesting but not showy. *Foliage:* Smooth, dark green, turning reddish before falling in autumn.

Problems and Maintenance.   This shrub is unusually free of insects and diseases but requires pruning every three years or so to maintain form and density. This can be accomplished most easily by drastic renewal pruning: cutting off tops a short distance above ground level in spring, allowing ample time for regrowth and acclimation before the onset of winter.

Related Species

Diervilla lonicera 3 (synonym: *D. trifida;* northern bush honeysuckle).   This shrub is very similar to *D. sessilifolia* except that it is lower in stature with smaller leaves and inflorescences, and considerably more cold-hardy. It is useful in Zones 2b–7b.

Diervilla rivularis 4.   This shrub is very similar to *D. sessilifolia* and completely interchangeable in landscape function and appearance. Seldom available for planting, it grows wild in the cooler parts of the southeastern United States.

Diospyros virginiana 7

COMMON PERSIMMON
Deciduous tree
Ebenaceae (Ebony Family)

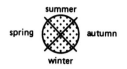

Native Range. Southeastern and south-central United States.

Useful Range. USDA Zones 5b–9a+.

Function. Shade tree, naturalizing, edible fruit. Well adapted to city use, but not as a street tree because of the fruit litter.

Size and Habit

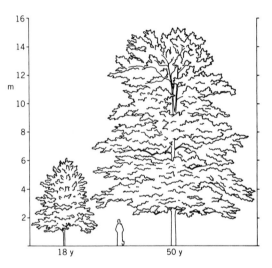

Diospyros virginiana.

Adaptability

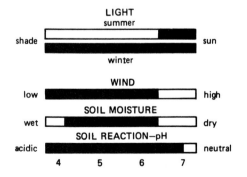

Seasonal Interest. *Flowers:* Small, whitish, inconspicuous, mostly dioecious, but sometimes with a few perfect flowers on male or female trees. *Foliage:* Dark green, making a dense canopy, turning dull yellow or orange in autumn. *Fruits:* Relatively large, to 3.5 cm/1.4 in., borne close to branches, dull green at first, then dull yellow-orange and edible when fully ripe, falling to the ground and causing a litter problem. *Trunk:* Bark is regularly fissured, exposing cracks of red-orange inner bark that is interesting at close range in all seasons.

Diospyros virginiana.

Problems and Maintenance. This tree is unusually trouble-free except for a leaf-spot disease that limits its use in the South. Maintenance consists largely of cleaning up fallen fruits in autumn. Transplanting is difficult; when possible, specify young, container-grown trees.

Cultivars. Cultivars have been selected for fruit size and quality rather than for landscape use, but most make acceptable landscape trees. Popular cultivars include the following: 'Early Golden' is very widely planted and somewhat self-fertile; but for heavy fruiting, growers recommend planting with a different cultivar or seedling for cross-pollination. 'John Rick' has long been a standard commercial cultivar, with large red-blushed fruits and excellent flavor. 'Meader'

is self-fertile, a good pollinator for other cultivars, and seedless if not pollinated—a good
choice for climates with cool summers. At least
a dozen other cultivars are available or under
trial, and some may prove equal or superior to
those listed. For landscape use, especially in
urban plantings, it would be more appropriate to
select cultivars to be nonfruiting as well as to
have outstanding foliage and form. This has not
been done, but male trees sold by nurseries as
pollinators are probably the best bet for such
areas at present.

Related Species

Diospyros kaki 7 (Japanese persimmon). Like
D. virginiana, this is a medium-height tree, to
10–15 m/33–49 ft, that functions as a good
shade tree as well as having edible fruit. The
fruits are considerably larger than those of *D.
virginiana,* to 8 cm/3 in. across, and are borne on
most plants, since the dioecious tendency is
weak in this species. Usually grown primarily for
fruit, incidentally for landscape effect, and useful
only in Zone 9a+.

Diospyros lotus 7 (date plum).   This is an Asian
counterpart of *D. virginiana* and very similar in
landscape effect but perhaps slightly less cold-
hardy. It is seldom used or available.

Bumelia lanuginosa 6 (woolly buckthorn, gum-
elastic, chittimwood).   This spiny shrub or
small tree, native to the southeastern and south-
central United States from Virginia to Missouri
and southward to Florida and Texas, is in the
Sapotaceae (Sapodilla Family), which is closely
allied to the Ebenaceae. *Bumelia* has no outstanding seasonal interest, but its rounded
leaves, 3–8 cm/1–3 in. long, dark green and
lustrous above and woolly underneath, remain
green very late into autumn. The feature that
gives it landscape value is its freedom from problems and outstanding tolerance of heat and dryness, and it finds occasional use in Zones 6b–9a
in the southwestern parts of our area.

Dirca palustris 4

L E A T H E R W O O D
Deciduous shrub
Thymelaeaceae (Mezereum Family)

Native Range. Much of eastern North
America.

Useful Range.   USDA Zones 4a–8b.

Function.   Specimen, border, naturalizing,
massing.

Size and Habit

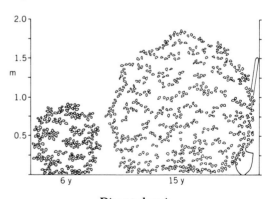

Dirca palustris.

Adaptability. Especially useful in wet soil in cold climates, but unusually wide in its adaptation to soil and climate.

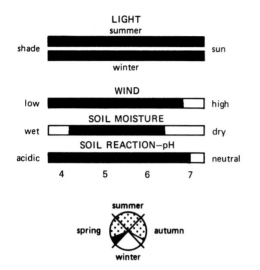

Edgeworthia papyrifera.

Seasonal Interest. *Flowers:* Small, pale yellow before foliage in early spring; not showy, but conspicuous at short range at that season. *Foliage:* Medium to light green, rounded. Inconspicuous but distinctive. *Fruits:* Small, pale green or reddish. *Twigs:* Exceptionally flexible and tough, giving rise to the common name.

Problems and Maintenance. This shrub is trouble-free once it is established, and is reported to be of little or no interest to browsing deer, but is seldom commercially available at this writing.

Related Species

Edgeworthia papyrifera 4 (paperbush). This deciduous shrub from China is similar in growth habit to *Daphne* and *Dirca,* its relatives in the Mezereum Family, except for its more open growth and ternate branching. Its fragrant yellow flowers, covered with silky hairs in bud, are borne in pendulous clusters in early spring before the new foliage emerges. The common name, paperbush, comes from the use of this plant in making fine quality paper in Japan. This is an interesting specimen for early spring flowers in parts of the Deep South (Zones 7b–9a+) where summer heat is moderate (high elevations or coastal areas).

Elaeagnus angustifolia 6

RUSSIAN OLIVE, OLEASTER
Deciduous shrub or small tree
Elaeagnaceae (Oleaster Family)

Native Range. Southern Europe to central Asia.

Useful Range. USDA Zones 3a–7b.

Function. Hedge, screen, windbreak, specimen tree.

Size and Habit

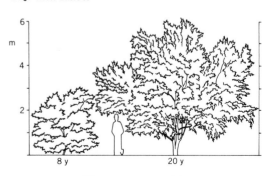

Elaeagnus angustifolia.

Adaptability. Well adapted to the cold, drought, and wind of the northern prairies of Canada and the United States, and frequently included in shelter-belt plantings there. Well adapted also to the seashore and other high-salt areas.

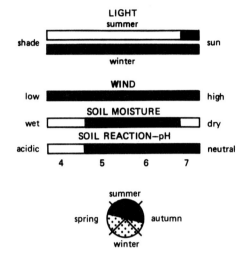

Seasonal Interest. Flowers: Small, fragrant, yellow, effective only at close range, in very late spring. *Foliage:* fine-textured and silvery gray-green as it first emerges in late spring, and it holds most of this color until late autumn. *Fruits:* Green to yellowish when ripe, covered with silvery scales. Interesting and conspicuous when borne in large numbers. *Trunk and branches:* Rich brown, shredding bark adds quiet year-round interest.

Problems and Maintenance. This shrub is fairly trouble-free except for a canker disease that occasionally kills a tree within a year after first symptoms appear. For this reason and the fact that it is prone to damage from ice storms, this plant is losing popularity in Zones 5–6. When planted in beds with plants other than turf, it will be necessary to remove root suckers occasionally.

Related Species

Elaeagnus commutata 5 (silverberry elaeagnus). This native of much of northern Canada and the Rocky Mountain region is an irregularly growing, strongly suckering shrub with the most intensely silvered foliage of all *Elaeagnus* species that can be grown in the North. It is useful for screening, with some pruning to promote fullness, or for a silvery gray accent in shrub borders in Zones 2a–6b, possibly even in Zone 1.

Elaeagnus pungens 5

THORNY ELAEAGNUS
Evergreen shrub
Elaeagnaceae (Oleaster Family)

Native Range.   Japan.

Useful Range.   USDA Zones 7a–9a+.

Function.   Hedge, screen, border.

Size and Habit

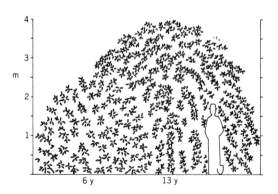

Elaeagnus pungens.

Adaptability. Unusually well adapted to soil and climatic extremes within the South, including seashore conditions.

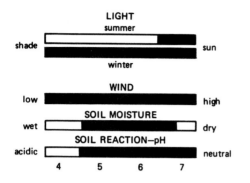

Elaeagnus pungens.

Seasonal Interest. *Flowers:* Small, fragrant, silvery white in midautumn. *Foliage:* Evergreen, dark green with a few silvery scales on the upper surface and covered with silvery and brown scales underneath, borne on spiny branches. *Fruits:* Brown, then red when fully ripe in spring, to 1.5 cm/0.6 in. with scattered silvery or brown scales.

Problems and Maintenance. This shrub is trouble-free, requiring little maintenance beyond pruning when treated as a hedge, a major reason for its great popularity in the South.

Cultivars. Several foliage and form variants have been selected. Some of the most common are listed here. 'Aurea' has golden-yellow leaf margins. 'Fruitlandii' has unusually handsome, dark green leaves and rapid, dense growth. 'Maculata' (= 'Aureo-maculata') has an irregular golden blotch in the center of each leaf. 'Variegata' has pale yellow leaf margins.

Related Species and Hybrids

Elaeagnus ×*ebbingei* 5.   This hybrid (*E. macrophylla* × *E. pungens*), originating in Holland, is similar in most respects to *E. pungens*, including its useful range, but it is not spiny and has slightly larger leaves. 'Gilt Edge' is less vigorous, reaching only 1.5–2 m/5–6 ft in height, and has bright yellow leaf margins.

Elaeagnus macrophylla 5.   This species from Japan and Korea is similar to *E. pungens* except that it has larger leaves and is not spiny, but it is seldom available.

Elaeagnus umbellata 5

AUTUMN ELAEAGNUS, AUTUMN OLIVE

Deciduous shrub

Elaeagnaceae (Oleaster Family)

Native Range.   China, Japan, Korea.

Useful Range.   USDA Zones 5a–9a.

Function.   Hedge, screen, border, naturalizing, wildlife cover.

Size and Habit

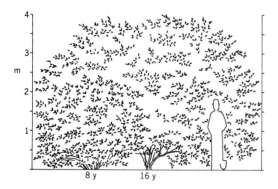

Elaeagnus umbellata.

Adaptability. Widely tolerant of soil and climatic conditions, including exposure to salt.

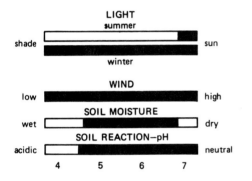

Seasonal Interest. *Flowers:* Small, fragrant, pale yellow with silvery scales in late spring. *Foliage:* Medium green, flecked with silvery scales, especially underneath. *Fruits:* Silvery brown, then red with flecks of silver when ripe in autumn, attractive to birds.

Problems and Maintenance. This shrub is trouble-free, requiring no maintenance other than pruning to develop fullness and to control size when necessary.

Cultivars. The so-called Cardinal Strain is a seedline developed by the U.S. Soil Conservation Service. It is recommended by that agency as superior to the species type for conservation use as well as for landscape interest and vigor.

Elaeagnus multiflora.

Related Species

Elaeagnus multiflora 5 (cherry elaeagnus). This shrub from China and Japan functions as a smaller version of *E. umbellata*, reaching heights of 2–3 m/6.6–10 ft, with a relatively wide-spreading habit. It is otherwise similar to *E. umbellata* except in having larger red fruits, ripening in late summer. It is somewhat less cold-hardy than *E. umbellata*, but useful in Zones 5b–9a.

Eleutherococcus sieboldianus 5

Synonyms: *Acanthopanax pentaphyllus, A. Sieboldianus*

FIVELEAF ARALIA

Deciduous shrub

Araliaceae (Aralia Family)

Native Range. Japan.

Useful Range. USDA Zones 4a–8a.

Function. Border, barrier hedge or mass, screen.

Size and Habit

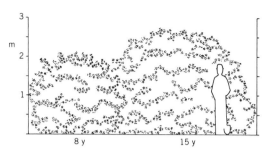

Eleutherococcus sieboldianus.

Eleutherococcus sieboldianus.

Adaptability.   Well-adapted to dry, city conditions and considerable shade.

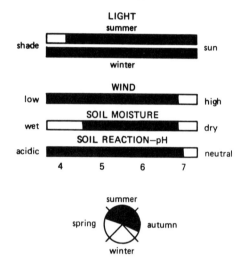

Seasonal Interest.   *Flowers:* Small, pale green, in small radial clusters (umbels), not conspicuous but interesting at close range. *Foliage:* Attrac-

tive, dark green, palmately compound leaves, the leaflets, 2.5 cm/1 in. or more in length, give a rich effect with distinctive texture when the form of the plant is properly maintained. Prickles are small and inconspicuous yet wickedly sharp, making the plant an effective barrier.

Problems and Maintenance.   Little maintenance is usually required, but pruning by selective thinning of old branches and light heading-back is necessary on almost an annual basis to maintain the form of the plant. Under poor growing conditions, where this plant nevertheless might well be used, pruning can be done less frequently. Under such conditions, the alternative of renewal pruning in spring to a few inches from the ground can be considered, but under good growing conditions this may promote excessive vigor and soft, sprawling growth.

Cultivars.   'Variegatus,' with white-margined leaves, is striking but not widely available.

Elsholtzia stauntonii 3

STAUNTON ELSHOLTZIA
Deciduous subshrub
Lamiaceae (Labiatae; Mint Family)

Native Range.   Northern China.

Useful Range.   USDA Zones 5a–7a.

Function.   Border (front).

Size and Habit

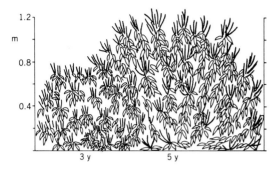

Elsholtzia stauntonii.

Adaptability

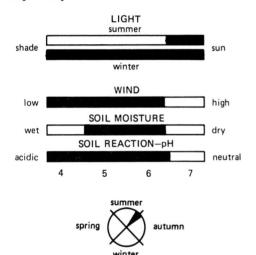

Seasonal Interest. *Flowers:* Lilac-purple, in terminal spikes in late summer and beginning of autumn. *Foliage:* Aromatic when crushed but of little other interest.

Cultivars. 'Alba' has white flowers.

Problems and Maintenance. Elsholtzia is one of many subshrubs that have the ability, when winterkilled to the ground, to return quickly and flower heavily in late summer of the same year. When this happens, it is only necessary to remove the dead stems in spring, but any live stems are best pruned away at the same time to maintain good form. Otherwise, elsholtzia is relatively free of maintenance, since it is seldom troubled by insects or diseases.

Elsholtzia stauntonii.

Related Species

Perovskia atriplicifolia 3–4 (Russian or silver sage).   This subshrub from central Asia, in the Lamiaceae like *Elsholtzia*, is regularly top-killed in winter but returns to flower by the following midsummer, functioning as a vigorous herbaceous perennial. This species in some ways is more attractive than *Elsholtzia*, as its slender white-fuzzy branches and very finely dissected silvery foliage provide fine visual texture, and its many soft blue flower-spires, 30–50 cm/12–20 in. long, providing color from midsummer to autumn. Useful at least in Zones 5b–8a. The selection 'Blue Spire' is upright and similar to the species type, but more branched and fuller.

Empetrum nigrum 2

CROWBERRY
Evergreen groundcover
Empetraceae (Crowberry Family)

Native Range.   Arctic (Asia, Europe, North America) and coastal areas and high elevations in temperate North America, southward to New York and northern California.

Useful Range. USDA Zones 2–6b (in areas having moderate summers).

Function. Groundcover, rock garden.

Size and Habit

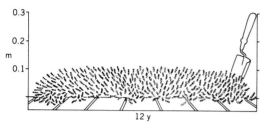

Empetrum nigrum.

Adaptability. This plant is best adapted to northern bogs and mountaintop sites where it grows wild, but it can be used equally well in rock gardens and other landscape situations if soil moisture is provided with excellent drainage.

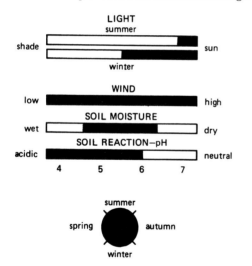

Seasonal Interest. *Flowers:* Very small, purple, inconspicuous, in midspring. *Foliage:* Evergreen, very fine-textured, needlelike, dark green, lustrous, making a thick mass that is handsome at all seasons. *Fruits:* Round, black, as wide as the needlelike leaves are long (0.5 cm/0.2 in.), not showy.

Problems and Maintenance. Given a proper site and adequate time for establishment, this plant is relatively maintenance-free. It does not compete well with weeds, so it should be heavily mulched, especially during establishment.

Related Species

Empetrum eamesii 2 (rockberry). This creeping plant from Newfoundland, Labrador and adjacent Quebec is slightly finer textured than *E. nigrum* and with red fruits, but similar enough to be interchangeable in landscape use. The ssp. *hermaphroditum* has black fruits and somewhat more compact growth. It is seldom available but useful in Zones 2–6b in areas with cool summers.

Ceratiola ericoides 4 (ceratiola, rosemary). This evergreen shrub native to the Coastal Plain of the southeastern United States has needlelike foliage similar to that of *Empetrum* and green or reddish fruits. It is useful in Zone 8b–9a+ but is seldom available for planting.

Corema conradii 2 (poverty grass, broom crowberry). This low shrub native to the northern Atlantic Coast is useful as a groundcover on sandy soil, and has evergreen, needlelike foliage with purple flowers, fairly colorful on male plants, in spring. It is useful in Zones 5b–7a, perhaps in more southern zones as well. It is seldom available for planting, but with care it can be preserved in its native habitat.

Enkianthus campanulatus 5–6

REDVEIN ENKIANTHUS
Deciduous shrub
Ericaceae (Heath Family)

Native Range. Japan.

Useful Range. USDA Zones 5b–8a.

Function. Specimen, border. Adds variety to mixed ericaceous plantings.

Size and Habit

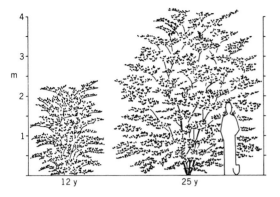

Enkianthus campanulatus.

Adaptability

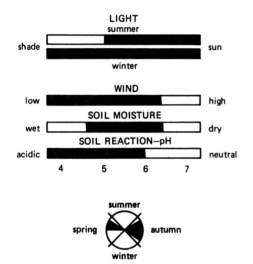

Seasonal Interest.   *Flowers:* Small, bell-shaped, yellowish with red markings, in middle to late spring. *Foliage:* Dark green with red petioles, giving distinctive color and texture, turning dull to brilliant red in autumn.

Problems and Maintenance.   Once established in proper site and soil, this plant requires little or no maintenance other than to control occasional mite infestations. Even this is seldom a problem in good soils.

Varieties and Cultivars.   'Albiflorus' has pale, nearly white flowers. The var. *palibinii* has flowers more intensely red-marked and more showy than those of the species type, and flowers later.

'Red Bells', selected for its strongly red-veined petals, is very popular.

'Red Velvet' has rose-pink flowers, exceptional red fall foliage, and an upright growth habit.

Related Species

Enkianthus perulatus 4 (white enkianthus). This is a smaller shrub, to about 2 m/6.6 ft, with pure white flowers, slightly earlier and smaller than those of *E. campanulatus* but conspicuous because of their contrast with the dark green foliage. It is slightly less cold-hardy than *E. campanulatus* but useful in Zones 6a–8b.

Elliottia racemosa 5–6 (southern plume, Georgia plume).   This large shrub or very small specimen tree, to 3 m/10 ft or occasionally taller, has clusters of lightly fragrant white flowers in midsummer. It grows best in sandy, acid soils and withstands some drought. It is seldom available as yet, but may become more widely available in the future. Useful in Zones 7b–9a, perhaps also Zones 6b–7a.

Tripetaleia paniculata 4.   This Japanese member of the Heath Family is similar to *Enkianthus perulatus* in size but resembles *Elliottia* more in habit and flowering, with white or pink tinged flowers in late summer. It probably is not commercially available, but it is a potentially useful addition to landscapes in Zones 7a–9a and perhaps also Zone 6.

Zenobia pulverulenta 4 (dusty zenobia).   Similar to *Enkianthus perulatus* in size and flowers, this

Enkianthus campanulatus.

shrub is much less regular in outline, with foliage strongly whitened by a waxy bloom. Its fragrant white flowers appear in late spring or early summer. It grows wild on the coastal plain of the southeastern United States and requires acid, well drained soil. Like *Elliottia* and *Tripetaleia*, it belongs to the Heath Family and is seldom available for planting.

Epigaea repens 2

TRAILING ARBUTUS, MAYFLOWER
Evergreen groundcover
Ericaceae (Heath Family)

Native Range.   Eastern North America, Newfoundland to northern Florida.

Useful Range.   USDA Zones 3a–8b.

Function.   Groundcover (small-scale), naturalizing.

Size and Habit

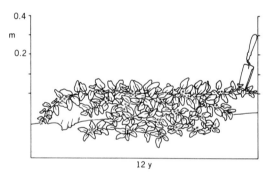

Epigaea repens.

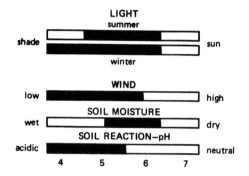

Seasonal Interest.   *Flowers:* Small, to 0.8 cm/ 0.3 in., but very fragrant, pink or white, appearing in early spring. This is the state or provincial flower of Massachusetts and Nova Scotia. *Foliage:* Evergreen, leathery, forming a loose mat on the ground.

Adaptability.   This plant requires acidic, sandy soil with good surface drainage, a light mulch, and watering to prevent excessive drying during establishment. Protect it from wind and full sun. Use only nursery-grown plants, preferably potted, to ease transplanting. There is little chance of success in moving wild plants, and it is illegal in most areas because this species is becoming endangered in the wild.

Problems and Maintenance.   This plant is trouble-free once established, but its slow growth and difficulty in establishment in any but the required site conditions has limited its use.

Related Species

Chimaphila umbellata 2 (pipsissewa, wintergreen). This creeping plant has evergreen foliage and flowering stems ascending to 25 cm/10 in. tall. Small (1.5 cm/0.6 in.) pink flowers are borne in small, flat clusters in late summer. This plant is similar in site requirements to *Epigaea repens* but is not a member of the Heath Family (Ericaceae)—rather the closely related Shinleaf Family (Pyrolaceae). It is no more difficult to establish than *Epigaea*, and useful in Zones 4b–7b, but is available in very few specialized nurseries.

Epimedium grandiflorum 2

BISHOP'S HAT, BARRENWORT
Herbaceous groundcover
Berberidaceae (Barberry Family)

Native Range. Northeastern Asia.

Useful Range. USDA Zones 3b–8a.

Function. Groundcover.

Size and Habit

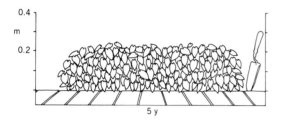

Epimedium grandiflorum.

Adaptability

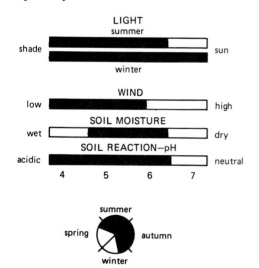

Seasonal Interest. *Flowers:* Distinctively shaped, like a Bishop's hat, 2.5–5 cm/1–2 in. across, the sepals deep red and violet, the petals white, opening in late spring. *Foliage:* Light green, heart-shaped, thin, leathery leaflets, to 8 cm/3 in. long, borne in clusters of three on wiry petioles, are red-bronze as they unfold and again in autumn, making an impressive mass of foliage.

Problems and Maintenance. *Epimedium* species are generally trouble-free and require little maintenance other than cutting off the dead foliage before new growth begins in spring.

Cultivars. Several cultivars have been selected, but those belonging to the different species are confused in commerce (see Related Species). The selection 'Violaceum' (synonym: *E. violaceum*) has more dominantly violet flower parts. 'Rose Queen' and 'White Queen' have, respectively, red and white flowers.

Related Species and Hybrids

Epimedium alpinum 2 (alpine barrenwort). This native of southern Europe has small red and yellow flowers, 1.5 cm/0.6 in. across, but otherwise is similar to *E. grandiflorum.*

Epimedium pinnatum 2 (yellow barrenwort). This central Asian plant has bright yellow flowers, about 2 cm/0.8 in. across, with red spurs.

Epimedium ×rubrum 2 (synonym: *E. alpinum* var. *rubrum;* red barrenwort). This hybrid of *E. alpinum × E. grandiflorum* has predominantly bright crimson flowers.

Epimedium ×youngianum 2 (Young's barrenwort). This hybrid of *E. grandiflorum × E. diphyllum* has relatively large, to 2.5 cm/1 in. across, white or pink flowers. The selection 'Niveum' (synonym: *E. grandiflorum* 'Niveum') has pure white flowers, and 'Roseum' has lilac-rose flowers.

Podophyllum peltatum 2 (mayapple). This distinctive groundcover plant in the Barberry Family (Berberidaceae) grows wild in the woods of most of eastern North America, from Quebec to Florida and Texas. Its uniquely lobed, umbrella-like leaves form a loose or dense canopy about 30–40 cm/12–16 in. above the ground, and the white flowers and yellowish fruits hang underneath, largely out of sight. Mayapple is more often conserved than planted, but in any case it makes a superb but transient woodland groundcover until early summer, in Zones 4a–9a.

Erica carnea 2

Synonym: *E. Herbacea*
SPRING HEATH
Evergreen groundcover
Ericaceae (Heath Family)

Native Range. Central and southern Europe.

Useful Range. USDA Zones 6b–7b, north to Zone 5a in areas having reliable snow cover for protection from winter wind, and south to Zone 8b in areas having mild summers.

Function. Rock garden, front of ericaceous border.

Size and Habit

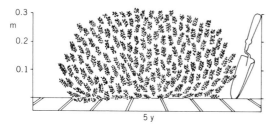

Erica carnea.

Adaptability. This plant requires a combination of well-drained but not excessively dry, acid soil, high humidity, moderate temperatures, and full sun during the growing season for best growth and flowering. Relatively few places in eastern North America can supply all of these conditions. The southern and middle Atlantic coast, southern Appalachians, and northern areas with snow cover are the regions where this plant is most likely to be successful.

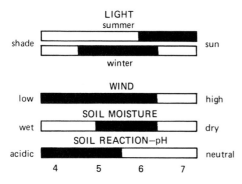

Seasonal Interest. *Flowers:* Red, pink, or white; small but numerous, in short (to 5 cm/2 in.), upright clusters in early spring, or winter in very mild climates. *Foliage:* Evergreen, needle-like, deep green, yellow in at least one cultivar.

Problems and Maintenance. Once the rather specific conditions for establishment have been met, this plant is relatively trouble-free. A light mulch should be maintained in all seasons to stabilize soil moisture.

Cultivars. 'Aurea' has golden yellow foliage, especially toward the outside of the plant, and pink flowers. 'King George' and 'Vivellii' have bright rosy red flowers over a long blooming period. 'Pink Spangles' has bicolored pink and lilac flowers, early; 'Sherwoodii,' 'Springwood Pink,' and 'Winter Beauty' have pink flowers, early. 'Springwood White' has white flowers and, like 'Springwood Pink,' is very low growing (15–30 cm/6–12 in. high).

Related Species

Erica cinerea 2 (twisted or Scotch heath). This is slightly less cold-hardy than *E. carnea*, useful in Zones 6b–7b and to 5a with snow cover. Some cultivars flower very early in summer, others continuing through midsummer. The following are among the best and most easily available: 'Atrosanguinea' and 'C. D. Eason' have deep magenta-red flowers in early and mid-summer. 'Eden Valley' has lilac-pink flowers. 'Golden Drop' has pink flowers in early summer and coppery gold foliage that turns reddish in winter. 'P. S. Patrick' has pink flowers.

Erica × darleyensis 2–3 (Darley or winter heath). This hybrid of *E. carnea* and *E. erigena* appears as a taller version of *E. carnea*, reaching heights of 0.2–0.6 m/8 in.–2 ft and taller, with similar flowering interest. Its cultivars are useful in Zones 7a–8a, usually flowering from midsummer well into autumn. A few are popular in our area: 'Arthur Johnson' and 'Mediterranean Pink' have lilac flowers and 'Mediterranean White' has white flowers, from midsummer well into autumn, and these three are very low growing (15–25 cm/6–10 in.). 'George Rendall' has pink-tipped green foliage, and 'Ghost Hills' has white-tipped green foliage. 'Silberschmelze' has deep green foliage, red-tipped in winter, and white flowers.

Erica erigena 3 (synonyms: *E. hibernica, E. mediterranea*; Irish or Mediterranean heath). This species includes cultivars growing from 20 cm–1.5 m/8 in to 5 ft in height with white to pink and red-purple flowers. These are quite tender compared with the above species (Zones 8–9 in maritime climates) and not useful in much of eastern North America.

Erica tetralix 2 (crossleaf heath, bog or bell heath). This is one of the most cold-hardy of all the heaths, useful from Zone 4b (perhaps 4a or even 3b with snow cover) to Zone 7a. Its foliage is gray-green, woolly, and flowers white, soft pink, or red. Of more than two dozen cultivars, the following are most available in our area: 'Alba Mollis' has white flowers and silvery gray foliage, about 15 cm/6 in. tall senic; 'George Fraser' has deep rose-pink flowers and gray-green foliage and is unusually vigorous (to at least 30 cm/1 ft tall) and floriferous. 'Pink Star' has deep pink flowers and gray-green foliage, to 15 cm/6 in. tall.

Erica vagans 2 (Cornish heath). This plant is similar in size and hardiness to *E. carnea* but flowers from summer through early autumn. Some of the best cultivars include 'Alba' and 'Nana,' low growing with white flowers; 'Lyonesse,' much taller (60 cm/2 ft) with pure white flowers; 'Mrs. D. F. Maxwell,' relatively tall (40 cm/1.3 ft) with long clusters of bright rose-pink flowers; and 'St. Keverne,' similar in height to 'Mrs. D. F. Maxwell' but with lighter, clear pink flowers.

The summer flowering heaths tend to be somewhat taller than is desirable for groundcover use, but they can be kept lower by annual pruning in spring. This treatment is not appropriate for spring flowering heaths, since it interferes with flowering.

In addition to the relatively small number of *Erica* species that are hardy in the cold temperate zone, there are hundreds of additional species, mostly from South Africa, that can be used in climates where minimum temperatures drop only a few degrees below freezing. Unfortunately, these large flowered *Erica* species are not adapted to our area.

Bruckenthalia spiculifolia 2 (spike heath). This dwarf shrub from the eastern Mediterranean region is similar to *Erica* in landscape use and requirements and has pink flowers in midsummer. It is seldom used in our area, and its useful range is not clearly known, but it is at least suited to Zones 6b–7b, perhaps also Zone 8 where moisture is available.

Calluna vulgaris 2 (heather). This close relative of *Erica* is native to much of Europe and naturalized in a few places in the northeastern United States. Its site requirements are very similar to those of *Erica carnea* and it is useful, given those requirements, in Zones 5b–7b, perhaps Zone 8a as well, and as far north as Zone 4b in areas with reliable snow cover. Flowers, opening in late summer or early autumn, are white, pink, reddish, or purple, and the scalelike leaves are golden-yellow, light or dark green, silvery or bronze-purple. Many cultivars are available from specialty nurseries in the United States and Canada. The following are a few of the most common. 'Alba' has white flowers and gray-green foliage. 'Alportii' has rose-red flowers and is 50 cm/20 in. tall and vigorous. 'Aurea' and 'Cuprea' have purple flowers and yellow foliage, bronzing in winter. 'Corbett's Red' has striking red flowers

Calluna vulgaris, Erica spp., as groundcovers.

in midsummer. 'County Wicklow' has double, shell pink flowers and is relatively tall growing, to 40 cm/16 in. 'H. E. Beale' has double, silvery pink flowers in long spikes and grows vigorously to 50 cm/20 in. tall. 'J. H. Hamilton' has double, bright salmon pink flowers, and is vigorous but low growing, to 25 cm/10 in. 'Mrs. Ronald Gray' has rosy pink flowers and is very low growing, to only 10 cm/4 in. tall. 'Nana' (= 'Pygmaea') has purple flowers and grows to no more than 15 cm/6 in. tall but probably is not available. 'Silver Queen' has silvery gray foliage and lilac-pink flowers in late summer, reaching a height of 30 cm/12 in. 'Spring Cream' has bright green foliage, cream-tipped in spring, followed by pink flowers in late summer, reaching a height of 45 cm/18 in. 'Spring Torch' has green foliage, brightly orange or bronze-tipped in spring, followed by pink flowers in late summer, reaching a height of 30 cm/12 in.

Daboecia cantabrica 2–3 (Irish heath).   This low evergreen shrub from maritime western Europe, with dark green needlelike foliage and purple flowers over a long period from early summer to autumn, is similar in hardiness, site require-

Calluna vulgaris 'Mrs. Ronald Gray.'

ments, and landscape effect to *Erica carnea* but has larger flowers and may grow taller, up to about 60 cm/24 in. Availability is limited, but the following cultivars are often available: 'Creeping White' is very low (15 cm/6 in.), with pure white flowers. 'Praegerae' has large, deep pink flowers, and low habit, to 30 cm/12 in. 'Wm. Buchanan Gold' has creamy white variegated, dark green foliage and showy rosy purple flowers lasting for most of the summer, growing to heights of 45–60 cm/1.5–2 ft.

Eriobotrya japonica 6

LOQUAT, JAPANESE PLUM
Evergreen shrub or small tree
Rosaceae (Rose Family)

Native Range.   China.

Useful Range.   USDA Zones 8a–9a+.

Function.   Specimen, patio tree, border, screen.

Size and Habit

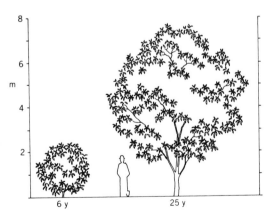

Eriobotrya japonica.

Adaptability

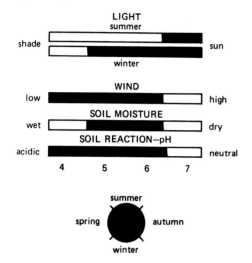

Seasonal Interest. *Flowers:* Small, fragrant, creamy white, partly hidden in large, brown, woolly clusters in late autumn and early winter. *Foliage:* Large (to 30 cm/12 in. long), evergreen, leathery, dark green leaves with woolly tan undersides and coarsely toothed margins; their coarse texture gives a tropical appearance. *Fruits:* Orange-yellow, slightly pear shaped, 3–4 cm/ 1.2–1.6 in. long, in late spring. Fruit is aromatic and edible, with a tart-sweet flavor. Fruits are seldom able to ripen north of Zone 8b or 9a.

Problems and Maintenance. This shrub is seriously affected by fire blight disease in some areas. Consult local professionals concerning its performance. Other than this it is trouble-free, given perfectly drained soil.

Cultivars. 'Gold Nugget' is a selection for dark green foliage and large, pear-shaped fruits, profusely borne. Other cultivars exist, including 'Variegata,' with white-variegated leaves, but they are seldom available in our area.

Related Species

Eriobotrya deflexa 6 (bronze loquat). This species is somewhat less cold-hardy (Zone 9a+) than *E. japonica*, with smaller leaves and fruits, and its new leaves are bronze at emergence, turning green as they mature.

Escallonia virgata 3

Synonym: *E. Philippiana*
TWIGGY ESCALLONIA
Evergreen shrub
Glossulariaceae (Currant Family)

Native Range.   Chile.

Useful Range.   USDA Zones 8b–9a+.

Function.   Foundation, border, massing.

Size and Habit

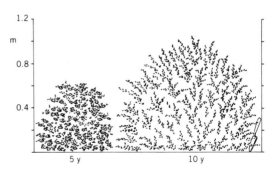

Escallonia virgata.

Adaptability. This is more tolerant of salt than most shrubs and is therefore useful in seashore situations.

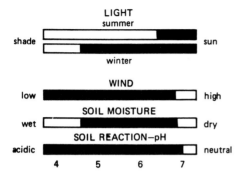

Problems and Maintenance. This shrub is relatively trouble-free where it is adapted.

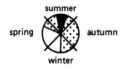

Seasonal Interest. *Flowers:* Small (1 cm/0.4 in.), white (or pink) in short clusters, in midsummer. *Foliage:* Fine-textured (leaves are about as large as flowers), leathery, semievergreen.

Cultivars. 'Gwendolyn Anley' has pink flowers and low, compact growth habit.

Related Species

The following are less cold-hardy than E. virgata, marginally hardy at best in Zone 9a, but worthy of trial there. All are evergreen.

Escallonia bifida 5 (synonyms: *E. floribunda, E. montevidensis;* Montevideo or white escallonia). This tall-growing, evergreen, fall-flowering species can be pruned into tree form.

Escallonia ×*exoniensis* 5. This hybrid of *E. rosea* × *E. rubra* is a tall evergreen shrub, but it can be kept in size group 4 with pruning. The selection 'Frades' (= 'Pink Princess') has rich pink flowers in summer and compact form. It is useful for foundation or hedge planting.

Escallonia laevis 5 (synonym: *E. organensis;* Organ Mountain escallonia). Another tall shrub, this species has bronzed green leaves and pink flowers in early summer and can be trained into a small tree form. 'Jubilee' (*E. laevis* × *E. rubra*) is a compact selection with rosy pink flowers in summer.

Escallonia ×*langleyensis* 4–5 (synonym: *E. edinensis;* Langley escallonia). This hybrid of *E. rubra* × *E. virgata* is evergreen and variable with several popular cultivars, including 'Apple Blossom,' a slow growing, compact form with pale pink flowers, 'Slieve Donard,' a shrub to 2 m/6.6 ft with white or pale pink flowers, and several other 'Donard' cultivars with pale to deep pink flowers and compact to arching growth habit. The selection 'Red Elf,' of uncertain parentage, has red flowers and a compact growth habit.

Escallonia rubra 6 (red escallonia). This species from Chile may be marginally hardy in our area or even parts of Zone 8, but is best known as a parent of *E.* ×*exoniensis.*

Eucalyptus gunnii 6–7

CIDER GUM
Evergreen tree
Myrtaceae (Myrtle Family)

Native Range. Tasmania.

Useful Range. USDA Zone 9a+.

Function. Specimen, fast (temporary) shade tree, screen, or windbreak.

Size and Habit. Trees reach heights of 30 m/ 98 ft in good sites in their native habitat but seldom exceed 20 m/66 ft in North America and 10–15 m/33–49 ft in even the mildest parts of Zone 9a.

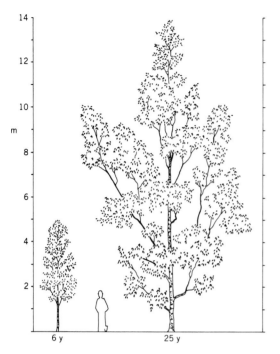

Eucalyptus gunnii.

Adaptability. *Eucalyptus* species grow best in full sun in relatively dry sites, where they tolerate conditions that would dehydrate many other trees. Too much moisture may encourage active growth in autumn, predisposing trees to freezing injury.

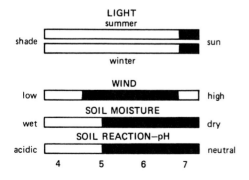

Seasonal Interest. *Flowers:* Yellow, about 1.5 cm/0.6 in. across, borne in large numbers in early autumn. *Foliage:* Evergreen, blue-green, nearly circular, to 6 cm/2.4 in. across, the loose canopy giving mottled shade. *Trunk and branches:* Smooth bark is peeling, bicolored green and white.

Problems and Maintenance. Mites and mealy bugs sometimes can be troublesome enough to require control measures. But the most serious problem of *Eucalyptus* species in our area, even Zone 9a, is freezing damage. Even though the hardier species such as *E. gunnii* perform well in comparable hardiness zones in California, they do not do as well in southeastern North America, probably because autumn weather is conducive to growth rather than acclimation for winter. Withholding fertilizer and water (when possible) in early autumn may be helpful in promoting slowed growth and acclimation, but results have been spotty at best. It is therefore not realistic to expect these trees to attain full size here or to develop without occasionally suffering freezing injury.

Related Species

Eucalyptus cinerea 6 (silverdollar tree or Argyle apple). The silvery leaves, nearly circular, with the pairs often fused across the stem, give this tree from southeastern Australia its "silverdollar" name. A small tree at best and not very functional, this species usually is used as a specimen for accent or for cutting of foliage. Its trunk is covered with fibrous, reddish brown bark but often is too weak to support a canopy of any size unless it is staked. Useful in Zone 9a+, especially in the southwestern parts of our area (Texas).

Eucalyptus citriodora 7 (lemon-scented gum). Even though this species is probably not cold hardy enough to serve as a landscape tree in our area, it is a handsome smooth-trunked tree with white bark (sometimes tinted pink or blue-gray) and white flowers in autumn. Several eucalypts are cultivated for their aromatic oils, in this instance the lemony scent of the crushed leaves.

This is possible even where trees are not fully hardy; occasionally winter-damaged trees sometimes grow back rapidly from the roots in the mildest parts of our area.

Eucalyptus globulus 7 (blue gum). This potentially huge tree from Tasmania is physically weak, surface-rooted, and excessively fast-growing, and it is frequently damaged by freezes, leaving it ungainly in form. The selection 'Compacta' is very compact and more useful. Both forms have silvery white immature leaves, turning dark blue-green, giving the tree a blue cast.

It is barely useful in Zone 9a in our area, but well adapted to the warmer parts of California, where it has become naturalized.

Eucalyptus niphophila 6 (snow gum). From high elevations in southeastern Australia, this is thought by some to be the hardiest species of *Eucalyptus* currently cultivated in North America. Even though it may be hardy in Zone 8a on the West Coast, like other *Eucalyptus* species it is subject to the problem of delayed acclimation in the moister climate of the Southeast.

Eucommia ulmoides 7

HARDY RUBBER TREE
Deciduous tree
Eucommiaceae (Eucommia Family)

Native Range.   Central China.

Useful Range.   USDA Zones 5b–8b.

Function.   Shade, street tree.

Size and Habit

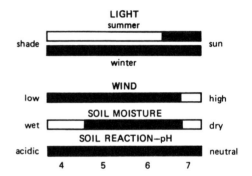

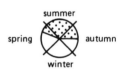

Seasonal Interest. *Foliage:* Bright green, lustrous, lightly wrinkled when mature, falling in midautumn with little color change. Leaves and

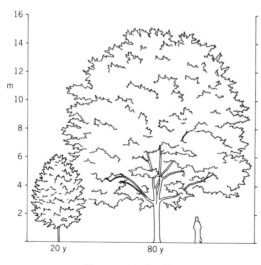

Eucommia ulmoides.

Adaptability.   This tree is well adapted to hot, dry summers. This and its freedom from insect and disease problems are the principal reasons for its use.

Eucommia ulmoides.

other parts contain latex, which appears in long strands when a leaf is carefully broken apart. *Fruits:* Small but numerous, encircled by a leathery wing, adding marginal seasonal interest to female trees in late summer and autumn.

Problems and Maintenance. This tree's freedom from insect and disease problems is one of its best features. It has a strong tendency to produce vertical "water sprouts" from main branches and may require pruning to remove them where branching pattern is an important asthetic concern. But spring pruning only increases the vigor of such sprouting in the following year, so pruning, if done at all, may be best delayed until summer. A more satisfactory solution where this is a problem may be to select a different tree.

Euonymus alatus 5

WINGED EUONYMUS, WINGED
SPINDLETREE, BURNING BUSH
Deciduous shrub
Celastraceae (Staff-tree Family)

Native Range. Northeastern Asia.

Useful Range. USDA Zones 4a–8a.

Function. Border, massing, screen, hedge, specimen.

Size and Habit

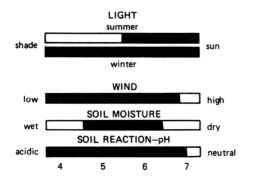

Euonymus alatus.

Adaptability

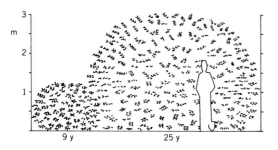

Seasonal Interest. *Foliage:* Medium green, crisp, turning scarlet to purplish red in autumn, fading to delicate shades of pink. *Fruits:* Lobed capsules opening to show scarlet arils covering seeds in autumn, toxic if eaten. *Twigs and branching:* Corky wings or ridges on twigs add interest in winter and early spring during leafing out. Branching is more-or-less horizontal, resulting in a mass as broad as it is tall.

Euonymus alatus.

Problems and Maintenance. This is one of the least susceptible *Euonymus* species to scale, but occasionally it is found infested. It is also reported to be resistant to euonymus caterpillar and otherwise is trouble-free, requiring little pruning except for restricting its size or in a formal hedge.

Cultivars. 'Compactus' is slower growing and more compact than the species type, with narrow wings that provide only marginal winter interest. The fall foliage color of this clone is intense—too intense for some landscape situations, especially when used in quantity. Even though this cultivar starts out small and compact, in time it can grow to a height of 3 m/10 ft and nearly equal spread. It is also less cold hardy than the species type, but useful in Zones 5a–8a. The search for superior compact forms has turned up other candidates, including the following: 'Nordine' is similar to 'Compactus' in growth rate and autumn foliage color, but it is more cold

hardy, fruits more heavily, and its stems are heavily winged. 'Rudy Haag' is much like 'Compactus' but grows only about half as fast. Forty-year-old plants are under 2 m/6.6 ft tall, and 25-year-old plants about 1.2 m/4 ft. 'Rudy Haag' was in production at this writing and should be commercially available soon.

Related Species

Euonymus phellomanus 6.   Like *E. alatus*, this species has large corky wings on the twigs, but the similarity ends there, since this shrub is taller and more rangy, without very striking fall foliage color but with showy, pink fruits. It is rarely seen and probably not available commercially, but potentially useful in Zones 5b–8a.

Euonymus bungeanus 6

WINTERBERRY EUONYMUS
Deciduous shrub or small tree
Celastraceae (Staff-tree Family)

Native Range.   Northern China and Manchuria.

Useful Range.   USDA Zones 4b–7b.

Function.   Specimen shrub or small patio tree, border, screen (with pruning).

Size and Habit

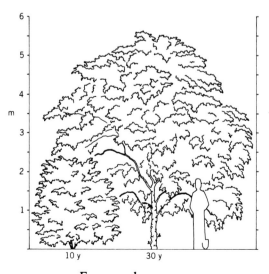

Euonymus bungeanus.

Adaptability

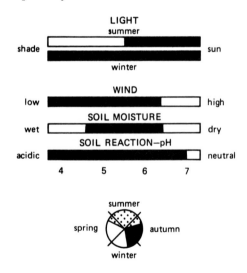

Seasonal Interest.   *Foliage:* Light green, long-petioled and relatively long and drooping leaves, to 10 cm/4 in., turning dull yellow before falling. *Fruit:* Lobed capsules turn light pink in early autumn, open in midautumn to show orange-scarlet arils, and remain persistent and colorful after leaves fall. Toxic if eaten. *Trunk and branches:* Striped with light and dark gray, especially noticeable on old specimens.

Problems and Maintenance. This shrub is not as susceptible to euonymus scale as some species, but occasionally it is found infested. Otherwise, it is relatively trouble-free but may require pruning to maintain fullness if used as a screen, and to remove suckers.

Varieties and Cultivars. 'Pendulus' has long, pendulous branches, making it useful only as a specimen. The var. *semi-persistens* has semievergreen foliage and fruits sparsely.

Euonymus europaeus 6

EUROPEAN SPINDLETREE,
EUROPEAN EUONYMUS
Deciduous shrub
Celastraceae (Staff-tree Family)

Native Range. Europe to western Asia; naturalized in the northeastern United States.

Useful Range. USDA Zones 4a–7b.

Function. Screen, border.

Size and Habit

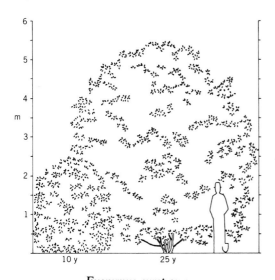

Euonymus europaeus.

Adaptability

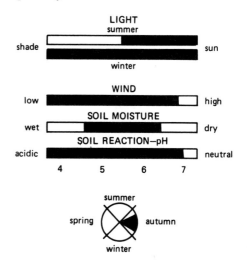

Seasonal Interest. *Foliage:* Medium to dark green leaves are relatively large (to 8 cm/3 in.) and turn dull reddish in autumn. *Fruits:* Showy, lobed capsules vary from pink to red, open to expose orange arils in midautumn. They are toxic if eaten.

Problems and Maintenance. This species is not as susceptible to scale as some *Euonymus* species but occasionally is infested. Aphids are a more common pest, causing leaf disfiguration, but the euonymus caterpillar has recently become a serious problem on plants of this and some other *Euonymus* species. Even though this problem can be reduced through biological control (*Bacillus thuringiensis*), some recommend replacing susceptible species such as *E. europaeus* and *E. atropurpureus* with *E. hamiltonianus* ssp. *sieboldianus*, which shows much resistance (see Related Species). Fruits (and other parts) of this and other *Euonymus* species have been reported to be toxic to children and animals.

Cultivars.   Several cultivars have been selected for heavy fruiting and compact growth, but few are currently available. The best known is 'Aldenhamensis,' an upright, vigorous clone with outstanding red fruits and autumn foliage. 'Red Cap' and 'Red Cascade' also have outstanding red fruiting display.

Related Species

Euonymus americanus 5 (strawberry bush).   This upright shrub, smaller and less cold-hardy (Zones 6b–9a) than *E. europaeus*, is known chiefly for its large, warty, crimson fruits, toxic if eaten. Not commonly planted, but sometimes preserved in development where native, from New York to Florida and Texas.

Euonymus atropurpureus 5 (wahoo, burning bush).   This tall shrub or very small tree suckers heavily and is not commonly planted, but it can be preserved in native stands in most of our area. The small purple flowers are inconspicuous but are a distinctive means of identification in late spring. The principal seasonal interest is the bright crimson fruits, which are toxic if eaten. Useful in Zones 3b–7b.

Euonymus hamiltonianus ssp. *sieboldianus* 6 (synonym: *E. yedoensis*; Yeddo euonymus, burning bush).   This tall shrub has a flat-topped growth habit and unusually large leaves, to 12 cm/5 in. long. Its pinkish fruits are colorful but should not be eaten, and the bright red autumn foliage is outstanding. Useful in Zones 4a–7b and reportedly resistant to euonymus caterpillar.

Euonymus hamiltonianus ssp. sieboldianus

Euonymus latifolius 6 (broadleaf euonymus). This tall shrub has large leaves, to 12 cm/5 in. long, reddish underneath and turning completely red in autumn. Its pink fruits are comparable with those of *E. hamiltonianus* ssp. *sieboldianus*, and it is useful at least in Zones 5b–7b.

Euonymus obovatus 2 (running euonymus). This excellent, deciduous groundcover is native to the northeastern and central United States and adjacent Canada and useful in Zones 4a–7b but seldom commercially available. It forms a mass quickly in sun or partial shade and will tolerate full shade. Fruits and red foliage add autumn interest in sunny sites.

Euonymus sachalinensis 6 (synonym: *E. planipes*; Sakhalin euonymus).   This tall shrub is notable for its large, angular, lanternlike fruits, large, red-scaled winter buds, and rosy purple autumn foliage. One of the earliest of all *Euonymus* species to leaf out in spring, it is little-used but worthy of wider trial. Its useful range is not well established but includes at least Zones 6a–7b.

Euonymus fortunei (1–2 and 4)

Synonym: *E. Radicans*, var. *acutus*
WINTERCREEPER
Evergreen vine, groundcover, or shrub
Celastraceae (Staff-tree Family)

Native Range.   China, Japan, Korea.

Useful Range.   USDA Zones 4b–9a, but not all cultivars are hardy in Zone 4b. Even though adaptable to the Deep South, susceptibility to scale insects and better alternative plants limit its use in Zones 8 and 9.

Function.   Groundcover, vine, foundation shrub (some cultivars). The climbing types cover chimneys, masonry walls, or tree trunks, holding by aerial rootlets (without injury to the tree).

Size and Habit. 'Coloratus' (left) and 'Sarcoxie' (right) are illustrated.

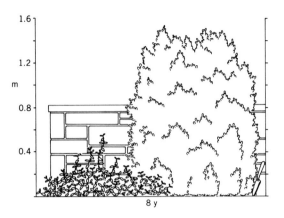

Euonymus fortunei.

Adaptability. Protection from full winter sun and wind is necessary in the northern extremes of its useful range to reduce desiccation of foliage.

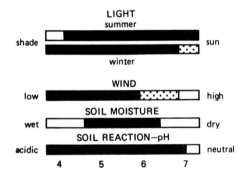

Seasonal Interest. *Flowers:* Small, pale green, inconspicuous. *Foliage:* Evergreen, leathery, variegated with white or yellow in cultivars, turning purplish in winter in at least one cultivar, 'Colorata.' *Fruits:* Light orange, opening to show the red-orange aril, showy in autumn, and toxic when eaten, but many cultivars have little or no fruiting interest.

Problems and Maintenance. This plant's only real problem, euonymus scale, is so serious in some areas that it limits its use. At best, the need for periodic spraying to control this pest should be expected. Once such maintenance is provided, this species is trouble-free and durable. Control of scale is especially important when this plant is used as a climber, since infestations above eye level may not be noticed until serious damage has been done.

Cultivars. 'Carrierei' (Carriere wintercreeper) is a loosely shrubby form to 1.5 m/5 ft or higher with support. Fruits are colorful but not consistently displayed in all areas and probably toxic if eaten. It is cold-hardy to Zone 5b.

'Coloratus' (purpleleaf wintercreeper) is a groundcover to 0.3 m/1 ft, with deep green foliage of medium texture, turning red-purple in winter, but without fruiting interest. It is cold-hardy to Zone 4b.

'Emerald Cushion' is dwarf and moundlike, eventually growing to 1 m/3.3 ft tall and twice as broad. It is cold-hardy to Zone 5a.

'Emerald Gaiety' is upright with spreading branches, to 1.5 m/5 ft tall, with white variegated foliage and no fruiting interest. It is cold-hardy to Zone 5b.

'Emerald 'n Gold' is similar to 'Emerald Gaiety' except for its yellow variegated foliage and slightly lower form. It is cold-hardy to Zone 5b.

'Emerald Pride' is erect in form, to 1.2 m/4 ft tall and nearly as broad. It is cold-hardy to Zone 5b.

'Golden Prince' (Plant Patent No. 3211, 1972) has golden-yellow variegated foliage in early summer, later turning mostly green. It is vigorous, yet remains low, perhaps not exceeding 0.8 m/2.6 ft in height. It is cold-hardy at least to Zone 5b.

'Gracilis' (= 'Argenteo-marginatus,' = 'Pictus,' = 'Tricolor') is an outstanding groundcover form with white variegated foliage sometimes tinged with pink or yellow. It is cold-hardy to Zone 5b.

'Greenlane' is a compact shrubby selection, to about 1 m/3.3 ft tall and wide, with lustrous, rich green foliage and orange fruits in autumn.

'Ivory Jade' is densely mounded, to 0.6 m/2 ft tall and 1.8 m/6 ft wide, with handsome ivory-margined leaves and no fruits.

'Longwood' is an excellent groundcover, prostrate but tending to "pile up" in the center to a

Size and Habit

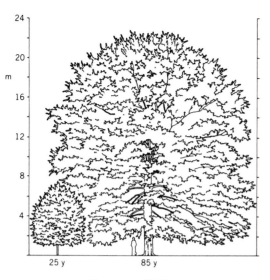

Fagus grandifolia.

Adaptability. Best performance requires a well-aerated, at least slightly acidic soil with a good moisture supply. If this is not possible, another tree should be selected. Less drought-tolerant than its European counterpart, *F. sylvatica.*

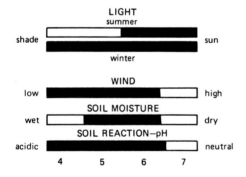

Seasonal Interest. *Foliage:* Dense, medium green, crisp and clean, turning golden bronze in autumn, then drying to a warm tan color and persisting into early winter, especially on young trees. *Fruits:* Small triangular nuts, one or two in a small burr. Although inconspicuous, they are interesting and edible. *Trunk and branches:* Smooth, light gray bark is an asset in all seasons, especially striking in winter.

Fagus grandifolia.

Problems and Maintenance. Surface roots preclude establishment of vegetative groundcovers underneath. Mulch may be used as an alternative, but unpruned trees grown in the open will be clothed in foliage to the ground, eliminating the need for any other groundcover. This tree is reputedly difficult to transplant. This is true of wildling trees, but nursery-grown trees in the hands of competent landscapers are not difficult to transplant.

Fagus sylvatica 8

EUROPEAN BEECH
Deciduous tree
Fagaceae (Beech Family)

Native Range.   Europe.

Useful Range.   USDA Zones 5a–9a. Adaptability in Zones 8 and 9 depends on adequate moisture.

Function.   Shade tree, specimen.

Size and Habit

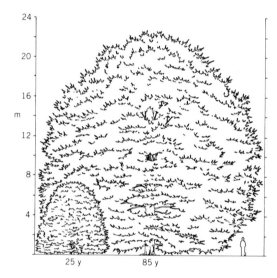

Fagus sylvatica.

Adaptability.   Best performance requires a well-aerated, at least slightly acidic soil with a good moisture supply.

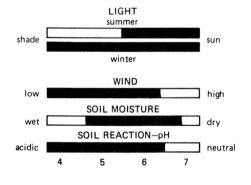

Seasonal Interest. *Foliage:* Dense, dark green—other colors in cultivars (below)—turning more-or-less bronze in autumn. *Fruits:* Small, triangular nuts in small burrs, inconspicuous but interesting. Reports that they are poisonous, although perhaps not true, should be checked out before eating. Good crops of seeds are not often produced in landscape sites outside the native range. *Trunk and branches:* Smooth gray bark is interesting in all seasons, especially winter, lending an elephantine appearance to the trunks of older trees.

Problems and Maintenance.   Surface roots preclude the use of vegetative ground covers,

***Fagus sylvatica* 'Fastigiata'**

Ficus carica.

sired. This vine will damage wood or painted surfaces if allowed to cling to them.

Cultivars. 'Minima' has smaller leaves and slower growth. 'Variegata' has white variegated foliage. More than 30 cultivars selected for outstanding fruiting are commercially available.

Related Species

Many species of *Ficus* grow from Zone 9 into the tropics but fall outside the scope of this book.

Ficus carica 5–6 (common fig). This species is the hardiest of all figs, growing as a tree in Zones 8b–9a+ and as a shrub controlled by winter killback in Zones 6b–8a. Its distinctively coarse foliage and branching give it a unique appearance but leaf and fruit litter and winter killback (in colder zones) make it an untidy plant. The edible fruits often are the primary reason for growing *F. carica*, with the landscape value considered in addition. This species performs best in full sun and tolerates dry soil.

Firmiana simplex 6–7

Synonyms: *F. Platanifolia, sterculia platanifolia*
CHINESE PARASOL TREE, PHOENIX TREE, JAPANESE VARNISH TREE
Deciduous tree
Sterculiaceae (Sterculia Family)

Native Range. China and Japan.

Useful Range. USDA Zones 7b–9a+, but marginally functional in Zone 7b and 8a.

Function. Shade tree for quick effect. Reaches full size, to 15 m/49 ft, only in Zone 9a+, but will function as a small tree, irregular in size because of periodic winter killback, in Zones 7b–8b. Reaches functional size rapidly.

Size and Habit

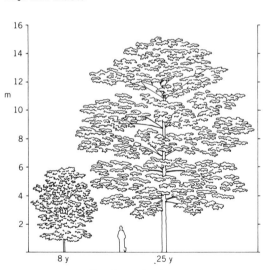

Firmiana simplex.

Adaptability. This tree is at its best in full sun and fairly moist soil, but out of strong wind, which can damage the foliage.

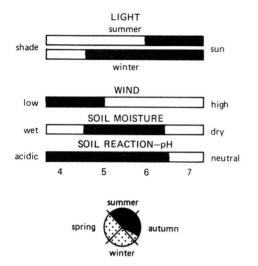

Firmiana simplex.

Seasonal Interest. *Flowers:* Small, white, in showy upright clusters, sometimes to 50 cm/ 20 in. long, in midsummer. *Foliage:* Very large leaves, to 30 cm/1 ft across, palmately lobed, reminiscent of those of *Platanus orientalis*, rusty pubescent as they emerge and begin to expand, turning bright yellow in autumn. Relatively few leaves are needed to provide dense shade. *Fruits:* Unusual greenish capsules turn brown and open when ripe. Small black seeds are borne on edges of capsule segments. Interesting but not showy. *Trunk and branches:* Smooth, lustrous, green bark adds interest at all seasons. Branches are arranged in accentuated whorls.

Problems and Maintenance. This tree is unusually free of pest problems. Pruning is necessary only to remove winterkilled parts and occasionally for rejuvenation. Otherwise, it is trouble-free and easy to grow.

Firmiana simplex.

Fontanesia phillyreoides 4–5

FONTANESIA
Deciduous shrub
Oleaceae (Olive Family)

Native Range. China.

Useful Range. USDA Zones 7b–9a+

Function. Hedge, screen (with pruning to maintain fullness).

Size and Habit

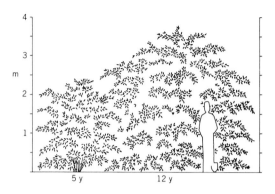

Fontanesia phillyreoides ssp. *fortunei.*

Adaptability

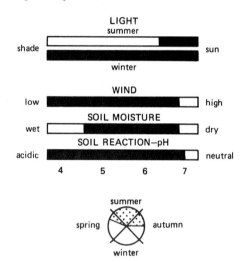

Seasonal Interest. *Flowers:* Small, greenish white, not showy. *Foliage:* Bright green, similar in general effect to that of deciduous *Ligustrum* species, falling early in autumn with little color change.

Problems and Maintenance. This shrub is relatively trouble-free and needs little maintenance other than annual pruning to maintain fullness for screening. Since there are many equally good and more colorful shrubs for this purpose, this cannot be considered a high priority landscape plant except in difficult situations where its broad adaptability serves it well.

Subspecies. *Fontanesia phillyreoides* ssp. *fortunei* 5 (synonym: *F. fortunei;* Fortune fontanesia) is looser and taller than the species type (ssp. *phillyreoides*), much more cold-hardy, useful in at least Zones 5b–8b, and of interest only because of its hardiness.

Related Species

Forestiera acuminata 5 (swamp privet).   This deciduous shrub, also in the Olive Family, is native to the southeastern United States but is seldom available for planting except in sites where it can be transplanted from the wild, which is not a good idea since this species is rare in native habitat. Its flowers have no petals, so are inconspicuous when they appear in early spring, and the plant has little seasonal interest other than the deep purple, olivelike fruits on female plants. Useful as a neutral border shrub or for naturalizing on moist to wet soils in Zones 6b–9a.

Forestiera neomexicana 5 (New Mexican privet, desert olive).   This shrub or small tree, native from elevations of 2000–2300 m/6600–7600 ft in Colorado, New Mexico, and Arizona to California, is rounded in form, to 3m/10 ft high, occasionally taller, and about the same in spread. Its small gray-green leaves (1.3–3.8 cm/0.5–1.5 in.) turn golden-yellow in autumn. Its small, yellowish flowers open before leaf-expansion in early spring, and 0.6-cm/0.25-in. blue-black fruits are borne in summer on female and monoecious plants. This plant is very tolerant of dry, saline, and alkaline soils (at least to pH 8) and is useful in the western parts of our range, in Zones 4b–7a, but is not widely available in commerce. The University of Minnesota selection 'Jemez' has better-than-average form and foliage.

Forsythia ×*intermedia* 5

SHOWY BORDER FORSYTHIA

Deciduous shrub

Oleaceae (Olive Family)

Hybrid Origin. *F. suspensa* × *F. viridissima.*

Useful Range. USDA Zones 5b–8a, and will grow successfully in Zones 4b and 5a, but the flower buds are usually winterkilled there, so flowering occurs only after very mild winters or below the snow line.

Function. Specimen, border, screen.

Size and Habit

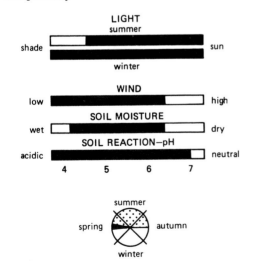

Forsythia ×*intermedia.*

Adaptability

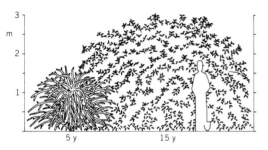

Seasonal Interest. *Flowers:* Brilliant yellow, before the foliage in early to middle spring, very showy. *Foliage:* Rich green, lustrous leaves persist well into autumn with little color change, sometimes turning yellow or purplish before falling.

Problems and Maintenance. This shrub is relatively trouble-free except for the killing of flower buds in severe winters. As with many other flowering shrubs and trees, flower buds are initiated the summer prior to flowering and thus must survive winter before opening in spring. Flower buds of most *F.* ×*intermedia* cultivars are hardy to −26° to −28°C/−15° to −19°F in midwinter and are less cold-hardy in late winter and spring, and thus they fail to flower in some winters even in Zone 5b (for hardier forsythias, see *F. ovata* and cultivars).

Cultivars. 'Arnold Dwarf', actually a hybrid between *F.* ×*intermedia* and *F. japonica*, remains below 1 m/3.3 ft for several years and makes a good large-scale groundcover in Zones 5a–8a. Unfortunately, it flowers only sparsely.

'Beatrix Farrand' has large deep yellow flowers that make a strong display, but less so than if they were held more erect on the flowering stems. The plant is also somewhat stiff and coarse.

'Karl Sax' is a polyploid, with many large flowers, but like 'Beatrix Farrand' is less graceful than some other cultivars.

'Lynwood' (= 'Lynwood Gold') is one of the most showy and graceful cultivars with bright yellow flowers held well erect and wide open.

'Spectabilis' was one of the earliest selections from *F.* ×*intermedia*, from which several other cultivars have been derived. It is still one of the most showy and satisfactory.

'Spring Glory' is also very showy, with slightly lighter yellow flowers.

'Tremonia' is densely branched and remains below 1 m/3.3 ft for some time, with strikingly dissected leaves that provide interest after flowering.

At least one cultivar with yellow-variegated leaves exists, but is not yet widely available.

Related Species

Forsythia suspensa 4–5 (weeping forsythia). This Chinese shrub, long cultivated in Japan,

Forsythia suspensa.

Forsythia suspensa.

varies in height from about 1.5 m/5 ft in the strongly pendulous form, to more than 2 m/6.6 ft in the upright var. *fortunei,* which differs little from *F.* ×*intermedia.* The flowers are also very similar in general effect and in hardiness to those of *F.* ×*intermedia* cultivars. The typical weeping form, sometimes called var. *sieboldii,* gives a strikingly different landscape effect, especially when it is planted at the tops of banks and walls, where its long branches can trail for some distance. The selection 'Aurea' has yellowish foliage in early summer but is not one of the best yellow-leaved shrubs. *F. suspensa* is generally useful in Zones 5b–8a, flowering in the majority of years.

Forsythia viridissima 'Bronxensis.'

Forsythia viridissima 5 (greenstem forsythia). This Chinese species differs from *F.* ×*intermedia* in that it is less showy in flower and has greenish stems of some interest in winter. It is about equal in hardiness to the hybrid. The variety *koreana,* from Korea, is more showy and may hold some promise for colder climates but has not been

tested thoroughly and is not widely available. The dwarf selection 'Bronxensis' remains below 0.5 m/1.6 ft in height for several years, bears fair quantities of pale yellow flowers, and has excellent summer foliage texture, making an effective groundcover.

Forsythia ovata 4

EARLY FORSYTHIA
Deciduous shrub
Oleaceae (Olive Family)

Native Range. Korea.

Useful Range. USDA Zones 5a–7a, and will grow in Zone 4, but the flower buds usually are winterkilled there, so flowering occurs only after very mild winters or below the snow line.

Function. Specimen, border.

Size and Habit

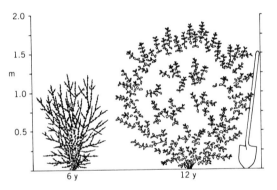

Forsythia ovata.

Adaptability

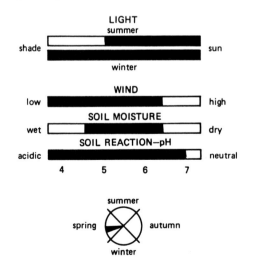

Seasonal Interest. *Flowers:* Light yellow, about half the size of those of *F.* ×*intermedia,* and somewhat earlier, displayed on stiffly upright branches. *Foliage:* Dull green, less handsome than that of *F.* ×*intermedia.*

Problems and Maintenance. Winterkilling of flower buds is the most serious problem of this species, just as it is with *F.* ×*intermedia,* but flower buds of *F. ovata* are somewhat hardier than those of *F.* ×*intermedia,* killing in midwinter at −29° to −31°C/−20° to 24°F. Occasional pruning may be necessary to maintain good form and should be done soon after flowering.

Cultivars and Hybrids. Several selections of *F. ovata* have been introduced since the late 1960s, including the following, from Iowa State University, 'Sunrise's has a compact, rounded growth habit. 'Ottawa' and 'Robusta' are unusually vigorous and upright in form, and 'Tetragold' is compact and low-growing, to about 1 m/3.3 ft, with large flowers.

Several hybrids of *F. ovata* by *F. europaea* have shown remarkable flower bud hardiness, to −34° to −38°C/−30° to −36°F. The most popular are 'Meadowlark,' 'Northern Gold,' and 'Northern Sun.' These are usefully cold-hardy through Zone 4 and perhaps also 3b. 'New Hampshire Gold,' a hybrid of *F. ovata* × *F.* ×*intermedia* 'Lynwood,' developed by Paul Joly of Cornish, New Hampshire in the 1960s, is similar in size to *F. ovata,* but broader and fuller, growing to 1.5 m/5 ft high and 1.8 m/6 ft wide. The plant is hardy to at least −37°C/−35°F, and flower buds are hardy to about −30° to −33°C/−22° to −26°F. Useful in Zones 4b–7a.

Related Species

Forsythia europaea 5 (Albanian forsythia). This little-known shrub has relatively hardy flower buds and deep yellow flowers that do not open fully enough to give a display comparable with the showier species. It is seldom if ever used except as a parent in breeding for winter-hardy cultivars (see Cultivars and Hybrids).

Forsythia giraldiana 5 (Giraldi forsythia). This native of northern China is seldom encountered but has been available commercially in the past. Like *F. europaea* and *F. ovata,* it has relatively cold-hardy flower buds, so it may be of interest in colder regions.

Forsythia mandshurica 4 (Manchurian forsythia). This species seems to have unusually cold-hardy flower buds, making it of interest in some of the coldest parts of our area. The selection 'Vermont Sun,' introduced by the University of Vermont, has flowers similar in color to those of *F. ovata* but larger and slightly earlier, and unusually large leaves. *F. mandshurica* has been under observation in Canada for several years and is useful in Zones 5a–7a and probably also in at least parts of Zone 4.

Abeliophyllum distichum 4 (Korean abelialeaf). This close relative of *Forsythia,* sometimes called white forsythia, has fragrant flowers, white or pink tinged in some years, smaller than those of *F. ovata,* about 1.5 cm/0.6 in. across, but otherwise similar, opening in early spring with or ahead of those of *F. ovata.* Its foliage is lustrous

Abeliophyllum distichum.

and dark green, turning purplish before falling in middle to late autumn. Under ideal conditions it remains full at the base, functioning as a low-maintenance facing shrub or foundation plant in Zones 4b–7b, but this does not always hold true, and flowering is uncertain in Zones 4b to 5a because of killing of flower buds in some winters.

Fothergilla major 5

Synonym: *F. monticola*
LARGE FOTHERGILLA OR WITCH-
ALDER
Deciduous shrub
Hamamelidaceae (Witch Hazel Family)

Native Range.   Northern Alabama and Georgia, southwestern North Carolina.

Useful Range.   USDA Zones 5b–9a.

Function.   Specimen, border, naturalizing.

Size and Habit

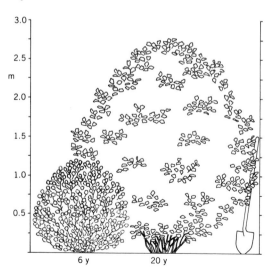

Fothergilla major.

Adaptability

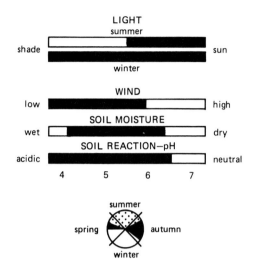

Fothergilla gardenii.

Seasonal Interest. *Flowers:* Fragrant, creamy white, in terminal, bottlebrushlike clusters to 6 cm/2.4 in. long, flowering with the new foliage in middle spring at the same time as *Cercis canadensis*. *Foliage:* Leaves resemble those of witch hazel, but are somewhat smaller, turning bright yellow in autumn, some overlaid with scarlet.

Problems and Maintenance. This is one of the most trouble-free of flowering shrubs, seldom needing pruning except to rejuvenate old plants.

Related Species

Fothergilla gardenii 3–4 (synonym, in part: *F. parviflora;* dwarf fothergilla). This shrub, na-

tive from Virginia to Florida, is smaller than *F. major* in all respects. It seldom exceeds a height of 1.5 m/5 ft and many plants, especially those coastal plain populations once called *F. parviflora,* stay below 1 m/3.3 ft. Plants of *F. gardenii* bear flower clusters about 3 cm/1.2 in. long before the leaves expand, a little earlier than those of *F. major.* Useful in Zones 5b–9a. Several cultivars have been selected: 'Blue Mist' has strongly bluish foliage and very fragrant flowers. 'Jane Platt' and 'Seaspray' are more dwarf than average, to 0.6 m/2 ft tall. 'Mt. Airy' is an excellent flowering form, with upright habit, to 1–1.5 m/3.3–5 ft tall, possibly a hybrid with *F. major,* and reported to be somewhat hardier than average for the species.

Franklinia alatamaha 6

Synonym: *Gordonia alatamaha*
FRANKLINIA, FRANKLIN TREE
Deciduous shrub or small tree
Theaceae (Tea Family)

Native Range. Originally found growing wild in southeastern Georgia by John Bartram, one of the earliest plant collectors and nurserymen in North America. He transplanted it to his Philadelphia nursery and sent plants to England. Named in honor of Benjamin Franklin, this

plant was seen in the wild for the last time in 1790 and has been preserved through cultivation.

Useful Range. USDA Zones 6b–7b. It does not perform very well in Zones 8 and 9, even though those zones include its last known native habitat.

Function. Specimen, border.

Size and Habit

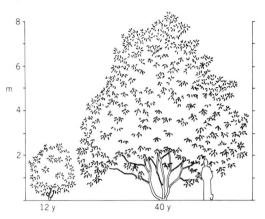

Franklinia alatamaha.

Franklinia alatamaha.

Adaptability

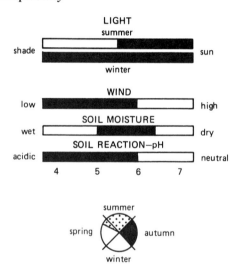

ganic, perfectly drained soil. The plant has been difficult to establish in some areas, perhaps because of the disease problem. In any case, it probably is best reserved for situations where its distinctive landscape interest is particularly desired and where good maintenance can be carried out.

Seasonal Interest. Flowers: Large, showy, white with yellow centers, resembling single white *Camellia japonica* flowers, in late summer and autumn until frost. *Foliage:* Lustrous, dark green leaves turn wine-red in autumn, making a fine background in both green and red phases for the white flowers. *Trunk and branches:* Dark and light gray striped bark adds interest.

Problems and Maintenance. The most serious problem of *Franklinia* is *Verticillium* wilt disease. The best means of protection is to plant in soil where the disease has not been active or in fumigated soil and to provide acidic, highly or-

Franklinia alatamaha.

Related Species

Gordonia lasianthus 7 (Loblolly bay gordonia). The name *Gordonia,* sometimes erroneously used in referring to *Franklinia,* is correctly applied to this plant. A handsome evergreen tree, or shrub in very poor soil, it is native to the Coastal Plain of the southeastern United States but is seldom used in landscaping. With its large (to 6 cm/2.4 in. across), fragrant, white flowers in summer, its tolerance of moist to swampy soils, and its dense mass of leathery leaves (to 15 cm/6 in. long), it appears to be an overlooked plant useful for screening in Zones 8a–9a+ and for a patio tree in Zones 8b–9a+. Limited experience suggests that it is rather difficult to transplant and slow in establishment, but the evidence for this is not complete.

Fraxinus americana 8

WHITE ASH

Deciduous tree

Oleaceae (Olive Family)

Native Range.   Eastern United States and adjacent Canada.

Useful Range.   USDA Zones 4a–9a, with selection of appropriate genetic material.

Function.   Shade, street tree.

Size and Habit

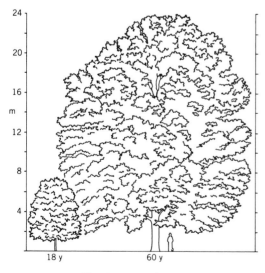

Fraxinus americana.

Adaptability.   This tree is widely adapted to different soils and environments provided full sun is available.

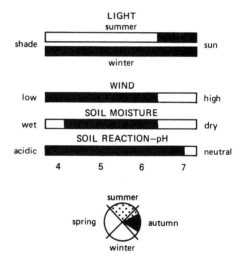

Seasonal Interest.   *Foliage:* Dark green in summer, turning yellowish in autumn with a deep or rosy purple overlay, at an early stage appearing hazy gray-purple.

Problems and Maintenance.   The litter and weed potential of fruiting trees is the greatest problem of most ashes. Fortunately, nonfruiting cultivars exist. *F. americana* is somewhat prone to storm damage, yet is a good combination of fast growth with reasonable durability.

Cultivars.   Several nonfruiting clones with colorful fall foliage have been selected since the middle 1960s.

'Autumn Applause' has good form and branching and long-lasting (for an ash) deep wine-red foliage. Useful in Zones 5a–8b, perhaps also 4b.

'Autumn Blaze' is lightly fruiting, with good oval form and purple fall foliage. Selected in the Canadian prairies, it is cold-hardy to Zone 3b, perhaps even 3a.

'Autumn Purple'® is nonfruiting and fast growing, and has good form and red-purple foliage color. This popular cultivar is useful in Zones 5a–8b, perhaps also Zone 4b.

'Rosehill,' the first *F. americana* nonfruiting cultivar to be selected, has good form and upright branching and fairly good red-purple autumn foliage in most years. Useful in Zones 5b–8b.

'Skyline' (Plant Patent No. 4756, 1981) is nonfruiting, narrower in outline than most *F. americana* clones, but broadening with age, and has deep bronze-purple to orange-red fall foliage. Useful in Zones 4b–8b.

Related Species

Fraxinus biltmoreana 7 (Biltmore ash). This species is sometimes included in *F. americana* and is similar except not as large, to 15 m/49 ft tall, and with pubescent foliage. It is native from New Jersey to Alabama and worth preserving in development there but seldom available for planting.

Fraxinus profunda 8 (synonym: *F. tomentosa*; pumpkin ash). This species is also similar to *F. americana* but with larger leaves (to 25 cm/10 in.). It is native in a spotty range from western New York to Illinois and south to Louisiana and northern Florida. It is seldom available for planting but worth preserving when possible.

Fraxinus texensis 7 (Texas ash). This native of Texas is sometimes planted near its native range in the extreme southwestern part of our area. With good yellow autumn foliage color, it is useful at least in Zones 7b–9a.

Fraxinus excelsior 8

EUROPEAN ASH
Deciduous tree
Oleaceae (Olive Family)

Native Range.   Europe and Asia Minor.

Useful Range.   USDA Zones 4b–8b. Insect problems preclude very wide use in Zones 6b–8b.

Function.   Shade, street tree.

Size and Habit

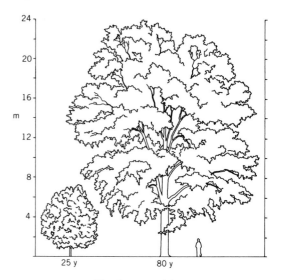

Fraxinus excelsior.

Adaptability

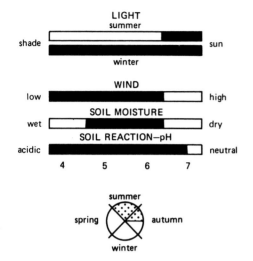

Seasonal Interest. The species type has little seasonal interest other than its dark green foliage that does not change color in autumn. Some selections have better foliage and twig color (see Cultivars).

Problems and Maintenance. The most serious problem of this tree is borers, which can kill a tree within a few years if they are not controlled. Scale insects also can be troublesome but can be controlled without difficulty in the North.

Cultivars. 'Aurea' has yellow twigs, showy in winter. 'Hessei' has simple, dark green, and lustrous leaves, and is more resistant to borers than the species type. 'Pendula' has strongly weeping branches but is not graceful compared with some other weeping trees. It is primarily a curiosity and seldom seen.

Related Species

Fraxinus holotricha 7. This tree from the Balkans is noteworthy only for the cultivar 'Moraine,' which bears very few fruits and is relatively low in stature. In many areas it is seriously affected by borers.

Fraxinus ornus 7

FLOWERING ASH
Deciduous tree
Oleaceae (Olive Family)

Native Range. Southern Europe and adjacent Asia.

Useful Range. USDA Zones 6a–8b. Some trees are hardy in Zone 5b. Usefulness in the Deep South is not well known.

Function. Shade, street tree.

Size and Habit

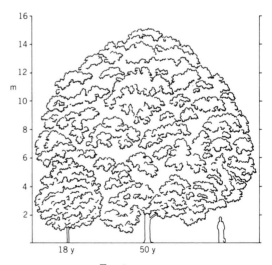

Fraxinus ornus.

Adaptability

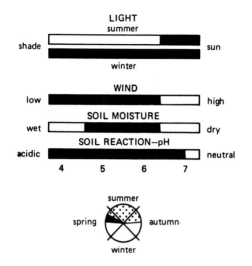

Seasonal Interest. *Flowers:* Fragrant, white, small, in dense clusters to 12 cm/5 in. long. Showy, unlike those of most ashes, in late spring. *Foliage:* Rich green leaves make a dense canopy and remain green or yellowish until they fall in autumn.

Problems and Maintenance. A popular street tree in Europe for years, *F. ornus* has not been used widely enough in eastern North America to be fully evaluated here. When it has been tried more widely, its susceptibility to scale and borers will be better known.

Related Species

Fraxinus bungeana 6 (Bunge ash). This very small, shrubby tree from northern China, to 4– 5 m/13–16 ft tall, is rare and probably not in landscape use in our area. With flowering similar to that of *F. ornus* and small in stature, it might be a useful tree for small-scale situations in Zones 5a–8b, perhaps also Zone 4.

Fraxinus cuspidata 6 (Mexican ash). Another small, shrubby tree with showy, fragrant flowers, this species is native to Mexico, southern Arizona, New Mexico, and Texas and is useful in Zones 8b–9a+, perhaps also Zone 8a.

Fraxinus mariesii 6 (Maries ash). Yet another small, shrubby tree with flowering interest similar to *F. ornus* and its relatives, this Chinese species has an added summer attraction in its purplish fruits and is useful in Zones 8a–9a, perhaps also Zone 7.

Fraxinus pennsylvanica 8

GREEN OR RED ASH
Deciduous tree
Oleaceae (Olive Family)

Native Range. Eastern United States and adjacent Canada and northern Great Plains.

Useful Range. USDA Zones 2a–9a with selection of appropriate genetic material.

Function. Shade, street tree.

Size and Habit

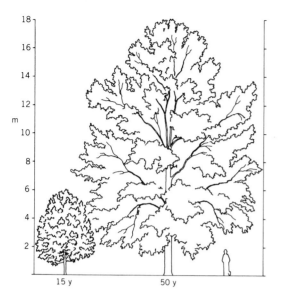

Fraxinus pennsylvanica.

Adaptability. This tree is one of the most widely occurring in the wild and most adaptable in landscape use in North America. It is especially useful in the Great Plains of the United States and Canada, where tolerance of climatic extremes determines success.

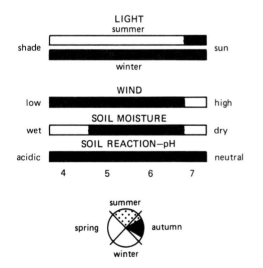

Seasonal Interest. *Foliage:* Medium to dark green in summer, turning clear yellow in autumn, falling rather early.

Problems and Maintenance. As with *F. americana*, fruit litter and weed seedlings are the principal problems of this tree. Fortunately, nonfruiting cultivars are available (see Cultivars). Both *F. americana* and *F. pennsylvanica* are far less troubled by borers than some of the European species.

Varieties and Cultivars. The var. *integerrima* (synonym: var. *lanceolata*; green ash) has narrow, lanceolate leaves with little or no pubescence and typically clear or golden yellow foliage in autumn. The species type, var. *pennsylvanica* (red ash), has broader, ovate leaflets, usually pubescent underneath, and yellow-bronze to deep reddish autumn foliage. Nonfruiting clones have been selected from both varieties, and given cultivar names. Some of the most popular are listed here.

'Bergeson' (Plant Patent No. 4904, 1982), selected in Minnesota, is cold-hardy at least to Zone 3b, probably also Zone 3a and perhaps even Zone 2. It grows rapidly with good form, somewhat loose as a young tree but filling in with age, and narrow, lustrous leaflets.

'Cimmzam' (Cimmaron®, Plant Patent No. 8077, 1992). This recent, nonfruiting red ash selection reportedly has good branching structure and foliage that turns maroon, then brick red in autumn, an unusual color for *F. pennsylvanica*. Its full range of adaptability is yet to be determined.

'Dakota Centennial' (Plant Patent applied for) is a recent nonfruiting selection made at North Dakota State University, with good structure, globose form, and rapid growth. Cold-hardy at least to Zone 3b.

'Emerald' is another nonfruiting red ash selection, from Nebraska, with lustrous foliage, heavily furrowed bark, and golden yellow autumn foliage in some years and sites. Useful in Zones 5b–8a, perhaps also 5a.

'Lednaw' (Aerial™, Plant Patent No. 7120, 1990). This recent nonfruiting selection, a genetic mutation of 'Summit,' is similar but much narrower in outline. Its full range of hardiness may or may not prove to be the same as that of 'Summit.'

'Marshall's Seedless' is the first seedless cultivar of green ash to be introduced, in 1946. Even though some of the recent selections may have better structure, this is still one of the most popular cultivars in commerce, with lustrous dark green foliage, turning clear yellow in autumn. Useful in Zones 3b–8a.

'Newport' (= 'Bailey's Select') is similar to 'Marshall's Seedless' but with better structure and presumably equally nonfruiting and cold-hardy.

'Patmore' was selected in western Alberta and introduced by Patmore Nursery in Brandon, Manitoba. It is nonfruiting and very cold-hardy, at least to Zone 3a, and has become one of the most popular green ash cultivars.

'Prairie Spire' (Plant Patent applied for) is another nonfruiting North Dakota State University selection for narrowly pyramidal to elliptical form. Cold-hardy at least to Zone 3b.

'Wandell' (Skyward™, Plant Patent applied for). This nonfruiting, rather narrow red ash selection is hardy at least to Zone 5b, with heavily furrowed bark and heavy foliage, turning bronze-red in autumn.

'Summit' is an old cultivar (1957) and still one of the most popular. Selected in Minnesota, it has good structure and upright habit, broadening with age, and fine-textured foliage, turning yellow very early in autumn, and is cold-hardy at least to Zone 3b.

'Urbanite'® (Plant Patent No. 6215, 1987) is another recent red ash selection for compact, pyramidal form, heavy foliage, and strongly furrowed bark. Useful at least in Zones 5b–8a.

Related Species

Fraxinus caroliniana 7 (water ash). This rather small tree, native from Virginia and Florida westward to Texas, is tolerant of wet soil and potentially useful in Zones 8a–9a+, but it probably is not commercially available.

Fraxinus mandshurica 8 (Manchurian ash). This uncommon species is very cold-hardy, with large leaves, sometimes mediocre fall color, and often sparse and open habit. However, the nonfruiting selection 'Mancana,' introduced in Manitoba, has a good globose form and lustrous, dark green foliage that sometimes turns a fairly good yellow in autumn. Useful at least to Zone 3a, perhaps also Zone 2b.

Fraxinus velutina 7 (velvet ash). This small tree, native to the southwestern United States and Mexico, is best known for the var. *glabra* (Modesto ash), a useful, small, shade or street tree for the dry and alkaline soils of the south-central United States and other areas in Zones 6a–9a+, but it is troubled by borers and other insects and requires a spray program.

Fraxinus quadrangulata 8

BLUE ASH
Deciduous tree
Oleaceae (Olive Family)

Native Range. Central United States, Michigan to Arkansas and Tennessee.

Useful Range. USDA Zones 4a–8a, perhaps also Zones 8b and 9a.

Function. Shade, street tree.

Size and Habit. This tree is very high-branching, making it a good avenue tree.

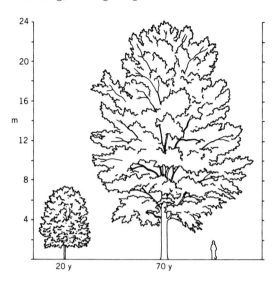

Fraxinus quadrangulata.

Adaptability. This tree is widely adapted in the central United States but not as tolerant of dry sites as *F. pennsylvanica.*

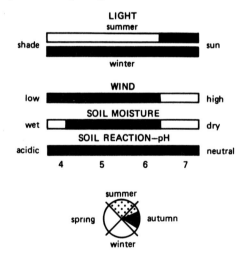

Seasonal Interest. *Foliage:* Dark green in summer, turning pale yellow or yellow-bronze in

Fraxinus quadrangulata.

autumn. *Twigs:* four-angled in cross section, sometimes slightly winged, adding minor winter interest. *Trunks and branches:* Inner bark is light orange-brown, sometimes adding winter interest.

Problems and Maintenance. Nonfruiting cultivars are not yet available and probably will not be in the future since this tree is not dioecious, but the numbers of fruit set are not as great as those of *F. americana* or *F. pennsylvanica.* The extent of pest problems is not yet well known.

Cultivars. 'Urbana' is a large, high-branching selection with distinctly orange-brown inner bark, probably not yet available commercially.

Related Species

Fraxinus nigra 8 (black ash). This large tree, native from Newfoundland to Manitoba and southward to West Virginia and Arkansas, grows wild in wet places. Its ability to grow in poorly drained soils and its hardiness make it potentially useful in Zones 3a–6b with selection of appropriate genetic material, but it is presently little used and perhaps not commercially available. 'Fallgold,' selected in Manitoba, is a nonfruiting, narrowly upright tree with outstanding golden yellow foliage, persisting well into autumn. It is cold hardy at least to Zone 3b.

Fuchsia magellanica 3–4

MAGELLAN FUCHSIA
Semievergreen subshrub
Onagraceae (Evening Primrose Family)

Native Range. Peru to southern Chile.

Useful Range. USDA Zones 7a–9a. A few cultivars may be hardy in Zone 6 in protected sites. Can be grown only in areas with relatively cool summers such as coastal and mountain areas.

Function. Specimen, border.

Size and Habit

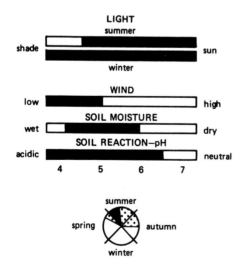

Fuchsia magellanica.

Adaptability

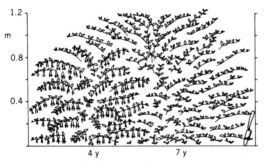

Seasonal Interest. *Flowers:* Red and purple-pink or violet, pendulous in clusters resembling small hanging lanterns, and very showy all sum-

mer. *Foliage:* Handsome and lustrous, marked with red or purple in some cultivars.

Problems and Maintenance. The top of this plant kills back to the ground in winter and should be cut off in spring before new growth starts. Since a flowering plant must be formed in only a few weeks, attention to soil fertility and moisture is crucial. Mounding with mulch material around the crown is usually recommended for winter protection.

Cultivars. Several cultivars exist, varying in habit and flower color and size. Availability is haphazard at best in eastern North America, and it is best to seek local advice on cultivars for specific areas or to stay with the species type.

Related Species

Many other species of *Fuchsia* exist, but *F. magellanica* is the only one adapted to our area. A considerable number of hybrid cultivars, probably involving *F. magellanica* as a parent, are useful in Zone 9a+ and subtropical areas on the West Coast, but they are seldom practical in our area except when used as annuals during cool seasons.

Galax urceolata 2

Synonym: G. *aphylla*

GALAX

Evergreen, herbaceous groundcover

Diapensiaceae (Diapensia Family)

Native Range. Southern Appalachian Mountains: Virginia to Georgia.

Useful Range. USDA Zones 5a–8b in cool, moist sites, and perhaps colder zones where snow cover is reliable.

Function. Naturalizing, small-scale groundcover (does not spread rapidly).

Size and Habit

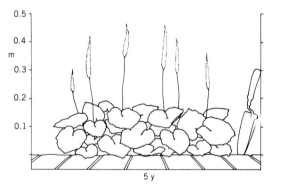

Galax urceolata.

Seasonal Interest. *Flowers:* Small, white, in vertical, taperlike clusters, 50 cm/20 in. or more long, in early summer. *Foliage:* Evergreen, lustrous leaves to 12 cm/5 in. across, heart-shaped to rounded and slightly cupped, providing unusual texture, medium green in full shade, turning reddish bronze in direct sun, in autumn.

Problems and Maintenance. Once established, galax is trouble-free and requires no maintenance except for removal of competing weeds. But establishment can be difficult and should not be attempted if the site requirements cannot be satisfied.

Related Species

Shortia galacifolia 2 (Oconee bells). This close relative of galax has a very limited natural habitat within the same range. Its foliage is similar to that of galax but its white flowers in spring are much larger, to 2.5 cm/1 in. across, borne singly on vertical stalks. This plant is even less vigorous than galax and useful only in very small-scale situations in cool, moist sites in Zones 5a–8b.

Adaptability. Requires essentially full shade in summer, and at least light shade in winter helps to keep the foliage in good condition.

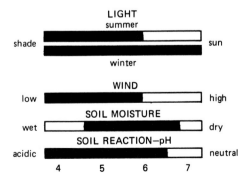

Galium odoratum 2

Synonym: *Asperula odorata*
SWEET WOODRUFF
Herbaceous groundcover
Rubiaceae (Madder Family)

Native Range. Europe, Asia, and northern Africa.

Useful Range. USDA Zones 5a–9a+.

Function. Groundcover.

Size and Habit

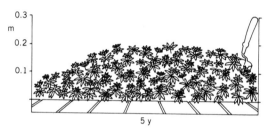

Galium odoratum.

Seasonal Interest. *Flowers:* White, only 0.5 cm/0.2 in. across, but daintily attractive against the rich green foliage in late spring. *Foliage:* Narrow leaves, 2.5 cm/1 in. long, are borne in whorls of six to eight on sticky, angular stems, rich green and fragrant, providing a dense, fine-textured mass until the tops die down in autumn.

Galium odoratum.

Adaptability. This is one of the few groundcovers that will tolerate full shade and dry soil simultaneously.

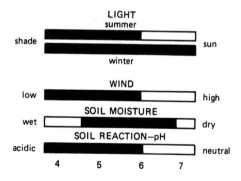

Problems and Maintenance. This ground-cover is trouble-free once established, needing only occasional weeding or sometimes to be weeded out itself to control its spread.

Related Species

Several other species of *Galium* (bedstraw) have been introduced to our area from Europe and are potential groundcovers, but most are more coarse and weedy than G. *odoratum*. G. *verum* (yellow bedstraw) is especially well adapted to dry soils but is very weedy, escaping cultivation in many areas.

Gardenia augusta 3–4

Synonym G. *jasminoides*
GARDENIA, CAPE JASMINE
Evergreen shrub
Rubiaceae (Madder Family)

Native Range.   China.

Useful Range.   USDA Zones 8b–9a+.

Function.   Specimen, massing, border, cutting.

Size and Habit.   Shrubs of this species can grow to 5–10 m/16–33 ft under ideal conditions but in our area they seldom grow much above eye level.

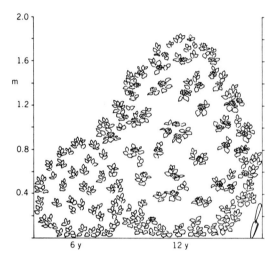

Gardenia augusta.

Adaptability.   Grows and flowers better with light shade than in full sun in areas with hot summers.

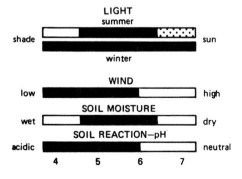

Seasonal Interest.   *Flowers:* Highly fragrant, waxy appearing, white, often double, 5–8 cm/2–3 in. across, in early summer and intermittently later in the summer. *Foliage:* Evergreen, leathery, glossy, and distinctive, with wavy margins and impressed veins.

Problems and Maintenance.   Use of this plant in southern landscapes has declined because of insect and nematode problems. Plants grafted on nematode-resistant rootstocks, or at least plants free of nematodes, should be used if available. In areas known or suspected to be nematode-infested it is essential to fumigate the soil in which gardenias are to be planted. A regular spray program will also be needed to control white fly and the resulting sooty mold as well as occasional scale and mealybug infestations.

Cultivars.   'August Beauty' is compact in habit with large, double, long-lasting white flowers (to 6.5 cm/2.5 in.), opening throughout the summer. 'Mystery' is also compact in habit, with double to semidouble white flowers. 'Radicans,' called dwarf gardenia, reaches a height of only 0.3–0.6 m/1–2 ft and has many small flowers. It is considered a choice shrub or groundcover in Zones 9a+. 'Radicans Variegata' is similar to 'Radicans' but with creamy white-margined leaves. 'Veitchii' is upright in form yet compact, with double flowers, smaller than those of 'August Beauty' and opening throughout the summer.

Gaultheria procumbens 2

CHECKERBERRY, WINTERGREEN
Evergreen groundcover
Ericaceae (Heath Family)

Native Range. Northern United States and adjacent Canada, northeasterly to Newfoundland, southerly to northern Georgia.

Useful Range. USDA Zones 3a–7a.

Function. Groundcover (small-scale), naturalizing.

Size and Habit

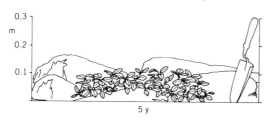

Gaultheria procumbens.

Adaptability

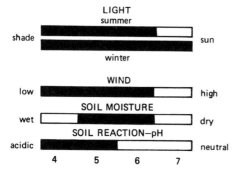

Seasonal Interest. *Flowers:* Small (to 0.7 cm/ 0.3 in.), white, bell-shaped, in late spring, partly hidden by foliage. *Foliage:* Evergreen, 2–4 cm/ 0.8–1.6 in. long, lustrous and bright green, aromatic (wintergreen flavor). *Fruits:* Small (to 1.0 cm/0.4 in.), bright red, aromatic when crushed, colorful from late summer throughout the winter.

Problems and Maintenance. Establishment is the only problem, and that is not difficult in woodland sites similar to its native habitat. Use pot-grown plants or sods and give especial attention to soil drainage.

Related Species

Gaultheria hispidula 2 (synonym: *Chiogenes hispidula;* creeping snowberry, maidenhair berry). This creeping plant, native to much of northern North America, has evergreen leaves less than half as large as those of *G. procumbens,* smaller flowers, and snow-white berries to 0.7 cm/0.3 in., adding interest in late summer and autumn. Useful only as a rock garden plant in partial shade in areas having cool summers in Zones 4a–6b.

Gaultheria shallon 3 (shallon or salal). This tall groundcover occasionally reaches heights of 1.5 m/5 ft or greater in native stands in the Pacific Northwest, has handsome evergreen foliage with leaves 5–12 cm/2–5 in. long, white or pink, bell-shaped flowers in late spring, and purple-black berries in autumn. In the past it has been largely restricted to landscapes in its native region, but it is being tried increasingly in the milder climates of the East in Zones 7 and 8. It grows well in full sun or shade in its native habitat but needs some protection from full sun in the Southeast. It should be considered experimental in eastern North America.

Gaultheria mucronata 3 (synonym: *Pernettya mucronata;* Chilean pernettya). This low shrub from the southern tip of South America has

Gaultheria shallon.

small (1–2 cm/0.4–0.8 in.), sharply pointed, lustrous evergreen leaves, very small white or pink flowers, and highly showy berries in white, pink, rosy red, or deep purple. For good fruiting, plant more than one cultivar, since cross-pollination seems to be necessary. Although not widely available commercially, this plant is potentially useful in Zones 7b–9a in areas having mild summers, but it should be considered experimental in eastern North America. Several cultivars are available.

Mitchella repens 2 (partridgeberry, squawberry). This trailing, hardy, herbaceous plant grows wild over much of eastern North America from Nova Scotia and Minnesota to Florida and Texas, even into eastern Mexico. It is not an assertive groundcover and will not persist in full sun, but in a naturalized, partially shaded woodland setting it adds small-scale interest with its small (1–2 cm/0.4–0.8 in.), dark green, white-marked, evergreen leaves and bright red fruits (to 0.8 cm/0.3 in.), which persist all winter or until eaten by wildlife. Even though it belongs to the Rubiaceae (Madder Family), its requirements are similar to such members of the Ericaceae as *Gaultheria*.

Gelsemium sempervirens 1 and 2

CAROLINA JESSAMINE
Evergreen vine or groundcover
Loganiaceae (Logania Family)

Native Range.   Southeastern United States to Central America.

Useful Range.   USDA Zones 8a–9a+.

Function.   Screen (with support), fence or bank cover, groundcover.

Size and Habit.   Climbs by twining to heights of 5–10 m/16–33 ft.

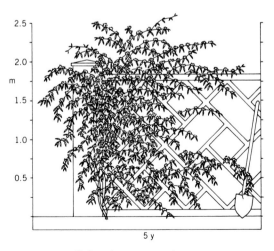

Gelsemium sempervirens.

Adaptability

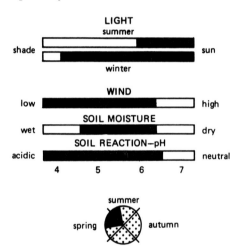

Seasonal Interest.   *Flowers:* Fragrant, bright golden-yellow, trumpetlike flowers in masses, early spring to early summer. *Foliage:* Evergreen and lustrous but usually arranged sparsely, turning purplish in winter.

Problems and Maintenance.   This vine is free of insect and disease problems. The foliage is arranged rather sparsely on wiry stems, and the plant looks ragged as a groundcover or screen unless pruned back heavily occasionally to promote fullness. Unfortunately, plants and flowers of *Gelsemium* are toxic when ingested. There are reports of children being poisoned by pulling the tubular flowers from the plant and sucking nectar from them. There are some situations where this plant clearly should be avoided, and children should be taught to avoid potentially dangerous plants at an early age.

Cultivars. 'Plena' (= 'Floraplena', = 'Pride of Augusta') has double flowers, which are retained longer than the single flowers of the species type.

Genista tinctoria 3–4

DYER'S GREENWEED, WOADWAXEN
Deciduous shrub
Fabaceae (Leguminosae; Pea Family)

Native Range. Europe, western Asia.

Useful Range. USDA Zones 3a–8a, perhaps somewhat warmer zones as well.

Function. Groundcover (on poor soils), specimen, rock garden.

Size and Habit

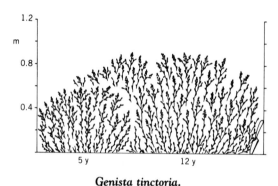

Genista tinctoria.

Adaptability. Especially valuable in poor, dry soils in full sun.

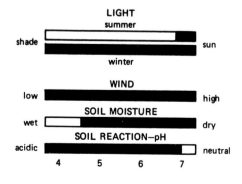

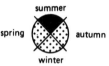

Seasonal Interest. *Flowers:* Bright yellow, pea-like, in early summer and continuing variably during the remainder of summer. *Foliage:* Narrow, bright green leaves, to 2.5 cm/1 in. long, falling without color change in autumn. *Twigs and branches:* Green, adding mild winter interest.

Problems and Maintenance. Relatively trouble-free, this plant requires little maintenance other than cutting back winterkilled stems after severe winters. *Genista* species all have the reputation of being difficult to transplant, so pot-grown plants should be specified.

Cultivars. 'Plena' has deep yellow, double flowers and compact growth, to 50 cm/16 in. tall. 'Royal Gold' is vigorous, reaching 80 cm/26 in. in height, with bright golden yellow flowers.

Related Species

Some of the following species are not widely available but are sometimes offered for sale by specialists and nurseries specializing in rare plants.

Genista aetnensis 5–6 (Mt. Etna broom). This tall shrub or small tree with slightly weeping habit is useful in Zones 8a–9a+, perhaps also sheltered sites in Zone 7. This plant is not always available, but is a unique choice for mild climates, with showy yellow flowers displayed effectively on the virtually leafless stems in midsummer.

Genista cinerea 3–4 (ashy woadwaxen). This Mediterranean shrub with leaves and twigs cov-

Genista tinctoria.

ered with grayish silky hairs is useful in Zones 7b–9a+, but seldom available in our area. In the mildest of our climates it may approach a height of 2 m/6.6 ft, with yellow flowers in upright clusters to 20 cm/8 in. long in early summer.

Genista germanica 3 (German woadwaxen). This low, more-or-less spiny shrub from central Europe is useful in Zones 5a–7b, but is not often available and not as showy as G. tinctoria in flower, with gray-woolly stems and leaf undersides.

Genista hispanica 2 (Spanish gorse or broom). This low-growing plant from southwestern Europe is one of the most showy Genista species in bloom, with bright yellow flowers in early summer. It also has many long, slender green spines that add winter interest along with the green twigs. Useful in Zones 7a–9a+, but not often available.

Genista lydia 2 (Lydia woadwaxen). The arching branches of this low spreading shrub are loaded with bright yellow flowers in summer. Useful in Zones 7a–9a+, perhaps colder zones with shelter or snow cover.

Genista pilosa 2 (silkleaf woadwaxen). This European species, like G. cinerea and G. germanica, has silky gray-green twigs and leaf undersides, but it is more cold-hardy, more shade-tolerant, and more prostrate than those species. Useful in Zones 5b–8b. The selection 'Vancouver Gold' is a superb groundcover, 5–10 cm/2–4 in. high, making a mat of gold when in flower in spring.

Genista sagittalis 2 (winged broom). This low-growing plant (0.3–0.5 m/1–1.6 ft) from Europe and western Asia has few leaves, but its broadly winged twigs give it the appearance of being evergreen, and its bright yellow flowers are like those of G. tinctoria in early summer. Useful in Zones 3a–8a, perhaps even colder zones with snow cover.

Spartium junceum 5 (Spanish broom). This tall shrub from The Mediterranean region and Canary Islands resembles Cytisus and Genista, with very small blue-green leaves and showy and fragrant yellow flowers to 2.5 cm/1 in. from late spring through summer. Useful in Zones 7b–9a+ and similar to its requirements to Cytisus and Genista except that it must be pruned more frequently to maintain good form.

Ginkgo biloba 8

GINKGO, MAIDENHAIR TREE
Deciduous tree
Ginkgoaceae (Ginkgo Family)

Native Range.   Eastern China.

Useful Range.   USDA Zones 4b–8b and possibly also warmer zones.

Function.   Shade or street tree, specimen.

Size and Habit

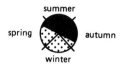

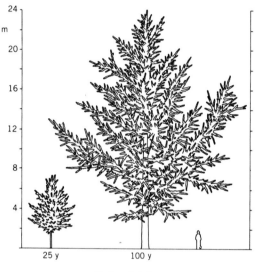

Ginkgo biloba.

Adaptability.   Especially well adapted to most city conditions.

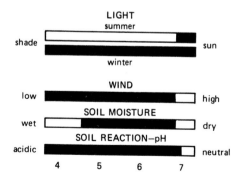

Seasonal Interest. *Foliage:* Distinctive, fan-shaped leaves turn bright yellow in autumn in some years. *Fruits:* Dioecious; the fruits (on fe-

male trees) are interesting but pose a serious problem (see Problems and Maintenance). *Twigs and branches:* Spurlike side shoots add textural interest in winter and result in a very sparse and open growth habit that gives the entire tree a distinctive winter aspect.

Problems and Maintenance.   This tree is singularly free of insect and disease problems and physically durable. Because of its neat, open branching, it seldom, if ever, requires pruning except where too little space is available for normal development. The fallen fruits constitute a serious litter problem and give off an unpleasant odor as they decay if they are not removed promptly.

Ginkgo biloba.

Ginkgo biloba.

Ginkgo biloba 'Fastigiata.'

Cultivars. Because of the fruiting problem, almost any male tree can be considered to be superior to any female tree for most sites. Trees propagated by cuttings or grafts from known male trees are usually available, and several male cultivars with other useful characteristics have been introduced. The following male cultivars are among the most popular and available.

'Autumn Gold'™ has a full, symmetrical form and outstanding golden yellow fall foliage, growing to be a tall and fairly broad tree.

'Fairmount' has an upright, pyramidal form, with dense branching and yellow autumn foliage.

'Fastigiata' (sentry ginkgo) has excellent narrowly pyramidal form (height 3 to 4 times width), but some trees sold under this name are not the original cultivar.

'Lakeview' is narrowly pyramidal but not extremely so, about twice as tall as it is wide.

'Pendula,' with weeping form, is a curiosity but not widely used or available.

'PNI 2720' (Princeton Sentry®) is about as narrow as 'Fastigiata' but more columnar than narrowly pyramidal in form.

'Saratoga' is somewhat oval in shape, with a strong central leader.

Gleditsia triacanthos 8

HONEY LOCUST
Deciduous tree
Fabaceae (Leguminosae; Pea Family)

Native Range.   Central United States.

Useful Range.   USDA Zones 4b–9a. Certain selections will also succeed in Zone 4a if properly grown (see Problems and Maintenance).

Function.   Shade or street tree.

Size and Habit.   The var. *inermis* is illustrated.

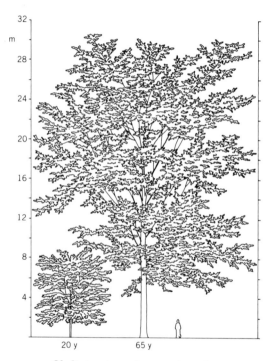

Gleditsia triacanthos var. inermis.

Adaptability.   This tree is tolerant of most city conditions.

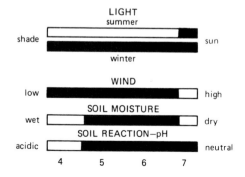

Seasonal Interest. *Foliage:* Bright to deep green, compound to doubly compound, typically with more than 100 small (less than 2.5 cm/1 in. long) leaflets on a single leaf. Leaves turn golden bronze in autumn in some but not all years. *Fruits:* Long (to 45 cm/18 in.), leathery, twisted, flat pods, absent from the better selections (see Varieties and Cultivars).

Problems and Maintenance.   Unless cultivars are used, the seed pods are a major litter problem, and unless cultivars—or at least var. *inermis*—are used, the huge, branched thorns are a hazard. Once these problems are eliminated by selection of cultivars, the greatest remaining problem is the mimosa webworm, which can damage the foliage severely in some years if not controlled. In spite of their good landscape qualities, *G. triacanthos* and its cultivars have been overused in many areas. At the northern edge of the useful range, winter hardiness can be improved by avoiding cultural practices such as heavy fertilization or late pruning and regular irrigation that promote overly vigorous growth and by maintaining sod over the feeding root system to compete for water and nutrients.

Varieties and Cultivars.   The var. *inermis* (thornless honeylocust) is thornless but not necessarily nonfruiting. Seeds from this variant generally produce thornless seedlings, which otherwise are not particularly uniform. The following cultivars are selections from var. *inermis*. They are thornless and, except as noted, nonfruiting. The most-used cultivars are listed here.

'Christie' (Halka™) is one of the most popular of the newer cultivars, with rapid, strong, and symmetrical growth, broadly ovate to rounded in outline. It is useful for street as well as lawn planting, except that it is not reliably nonfruiting. Cold-hardy to Zone 4a, perhaps also 3b.

'Impcole' (Imperial®), introduced in 1957, is still among the most popular cultivars, for its rounded vase shape, wide branching angles, and rather compact and formal outline. Cold-hardy to Zone 4a, perhaps also 3b.

'PNI 2835' (Shademaster®), introduced in 1956, has remained popular ever since, for its long, straight trunk and high vase shape. Like 'Moraine' (below), it was touted as a substitute in form (not texture) for American elm during the height of elm decline in the 1950s and 1960s, and is still a good lawn and street tree, cold-hardy to Zone 3b, and with some resistance to mimosa webworm.

'Skycole' (Skyline®), introduced in 1957, may be the most widely used cultivar in the 1990s. Its upright, pyramidal outline, strong leader, and well-spaced branches make it a very good street tree, cold-hardy to Zone 3b.

'Suncole' (Sunburst®) is a delightful lacy mass of golden foliage when leaves first unfold in early summer. Later the foliage turns green but the growing tips remain yellow for much of the summer. But for its golden foliage, it surely would not have its great popularity, because it is slow-growing, with unpredictable form, and highly susceptible to mimosa webworm.

Several other cultivars have merit, even though they are not now as widely used as the above.

'Fairview' is described as similar to 'Moraine' but stronger mechanically and growing rapidly. Cold-hardy to Zone 3b.

'Green Glory' is narrowly pyramidal to pyramidal at maturity, growing rapidly and tolerating urban conditions well. It holds its foliage longer in autumn than most honeylocusts. Cold-hardy to Zone 3b.

'Moraine' was the first cultivar to be introduced, in 1949, and had little competition for almost a decade. It is still widely used, for its graceful broad vase shape, the most elmlike honeylocust in shape and branching, without a strong central leader at maturity. It is also one of the most resistant cultivars to mimosa webworm.

'Rubylace' is as unique as Sunburst®, with ruby-red new foliage, turning to bronze and finally green. It makes a beautiful contrast to other foliage but, unfortunately, does not always grow well and usually has poor form. Cold-hardy to Zone 5b.

'Baillace' (Summerlace®) is a recent selection for light green new growth, contrasting with the dark green mature foliage in much the same way as the golden new growth of 'Suncole' (Sunburst®). It is reported to be well shaped and a strong grower.

'True-Shade'® is broadly pyramidal and fast-growing and is reported to have good structure.

'Wandell' (=Perfection honeylocust; Plant Patent No. 6709, 1989) is broadly pyramidal, with heavy, dark green foliage, and grows more rapidly than most honeylocusts.

Gymnocladus dioica 8

KENTUCKY COFFEE TREE
Deciduous tree
Fabaceae (Leguminosae; Pea Family)

Native Range. Central United States.

Useful Range. USDA Zones 4a–7b, assuming selection of appropriate genetic material.

Function. Shade tree, specimen.

Size and Habit

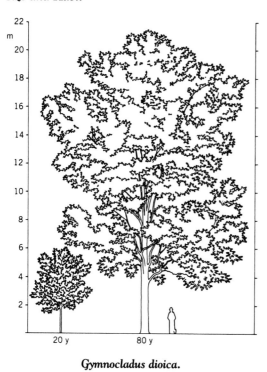

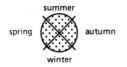

Gymnocladus dioica.

Adaptability. Unusually tolerant of soil compaction (foot traffic) and most urban conditions.

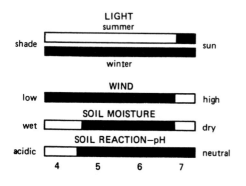

Seasonal Interest. *Foliage:* Dark green, doubly compound, individual leaves to 35 cm/14 in. long and of up to 100 leaflets, much larger (5–8 cm/2–3 in. long) than those of *Gleditsia triacanthos.* Foliage is not attractive in autumn and constitutes a litter problem when it falls. *Fruits:* Short (seldom over 15 cm/6 in. long) but thick and broad pods (on female trees only) offer seasonal interest after leaves fall in autumn, posing a litter problem later. The pulp that surrounds the seeds has been reported to be poisonous. *Trunk and branches:* covered with handsomely textured gray bark, the coarse, stubby branches offer an interesting texture in winter.

Problems and Maintenance. This tree is trouble-free, requiring little maintenance other than cleaning up litter in late autumn. Grows slowly the first few years after planting.

Varieties and Cultivars. Considerable variation exists in this wide-ranging species, and it is probably a good idea to select landscape trees from seedlings grown from local or nearby seed trees.

'Espresso' is a seedless selection with excellent elmlike form and upright branching but not narrow branching angles, growing to at least 20 m/66 ft tall and 12 m/40 ft wide.

'J. C. McDaniels' (Plant Patent pending; Prairie Titan™) is an exceptionally vigorous, pyramidal male (non-fruiting) tree on the University of Illinois campus.

Halesia tetraptera 6-7

Synonym: *H. carolina*
CAROLINA SILVERBELL
Deciduous tree
Styracaceae (Styrax Family)

Native Range. Southeastern United States.

Useful Range. USDA Zones 5a–9a.

Function. Small shade or patio tree, naturalizing.

Size and Habit

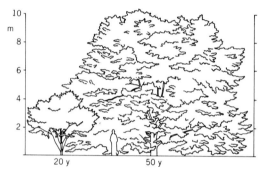

Halesia tetraptera.

Adaptability

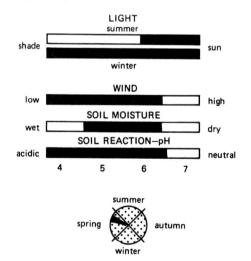

Seasonal Interest. *Flowers:* White, bellshaped, pendulous, 1–1.5 cm/0.4–0.6 in. long, in clusters of up to five in late spring. *Foliage:*

Halesia tetraptera.

Clean, dark green leaves, turning yellowish in autumn. *Fruits:* Pendulous, four-winged, green, ripening brown, 2–3.5 cm/0.8–1.4 in. long, adding quiet interest in late summer and early autumn. *Trunk and branches:* Smooth with a molded appearance, covered with subtly striped bark, whitish on dark gray, blocky and ridged on older trees.

Problems and Maintenance. Relatively trouble-free, requiring little or no maintenance.

Related Species

Halesia diptera 6–7 (two-winged silverbell). The fruits of this species have two instead of four wings, and the tree has the reputation of being somewhat less free-flowering. It is not widely available but is worth preserving in its native habitat (southeastern United States) and similar enough to *H. tetraptera* to be considered inter-

Halesia monticola.

changeable for landscape use except in Zone 5, where it may not be fully hardy.

Halesia monticola 7–8 (mountain silverbell). This is a large tree (to 20 m/66 ft and occasionally taller) with larger flowers and fruits than *H.*

tetraptera. It probably is less tolerant of the climate of the Deep South (useful in Zones 5a–8a), but otherwise similar in requirements to *H. tetraptera.* The selection 'Rosea' has pale pink flowers.

Hamamelis mollis 6

CHINESE WITCH HAZEL
Deciduous shrub
Hamamelidaceae (Witch Hazel Family)

Native Range.   Central China.

Useful Range.   USDA Zones 6a–9a, some cultivars also Zone 5b. Best in areas having mild summers in the South.

Function.   Specimen, border.

Size and Habit

Seasonal Interest.   *Flowers:* Fragrant, yellow, with narrow, ribbonlike petals in late winter or very early spring. *Foliage:* Downy, gray-green, turning rich yellow in midautumn. *Fruits:* Interesting but inconspicuous dry capsules opening explosively and discharging seeds for some distance in autumn.

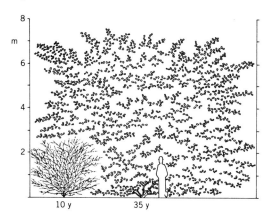

Hamamelis mollis.

Hamamelis mollis.

Adaptability

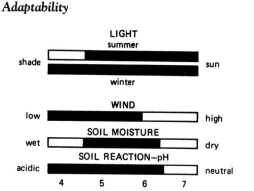

Hamamelis mollis.

Problems and Maintenance. This shrub is relatively trouble-free and requires little or no maintenance other than light selective pruning where space is limited.

Cultivars. 'Coombe Wood' has larger than average bright golden yellow flowers and wide-spreading form. 'Goldcrest' has bright golden yellow petals, deep red at their bases. 'Pallida' is a longtime favorite, with light sulfur-yellow flowers, showy even on dark days. Some specialists regard it as a hybrid (*H. ×intermedia*).

Related Species

Hamamelis ×intermedia 6 (hybrid witch hazel). This includes all hybrids between *H. japonica* and *H. mollis*, more than a dozen cultivars in all. Some of the best are listed here. 'Arnold Promise' has bright golden yellow petals, 1.5 cm/0.6 in. long, and yellow-orange fall foliage; it has long been one of the most showy yellow-flowering witch hazels but now may be outdone by one or two of those listed below. 'Diane' is probably the best red-flowering witch hazel, opening deep maroon-red and fading to orange-red, with red-purple fall foliage. 'Feuerzauber' (= 'Fire Charm,' = 'Firecracker,' = 'Magic Fire') makes an excellent display of red-orange flowers; a newly imported selection, it is reported to have excellent yellow fall foliage. 'Jelena' (= 'Copper Beauty') is an outstanding selection with coppery orange flowers and yellow-orange fall foliage. 'Orange Beauty' makes a strong flowering display with deep yellow petals with deep red bases, giving an orange effect from a distance. 'Primavera' flowers heavily with large light lemon-yellow petals, slightly reddened at their bases; it is considered superior to *H. mollis* 'Pallida' by

some observers. 'Sunburst,' a new cultivar to our area, touted as the most showy of all the witch hazels, has brilliant sulfur-yellow flowers in large clusters. 'Westerstede,' a recent import from Germany, has large yellow-orange flowers and orange-red fall foliage.

Hamamelis japonica 5 (Japanese witch hazel). This species is most notable for its involvement as a parent of the hybrid witch hazels, but a few selections have been made directly from this species as well: 'Arborea' is tall growing, and horizontal branched, with small yellow flowers, and yellow fall foliage. 'Sulphurea' and 'Zuccariniana' are also tall forms with sulfur-yellow flowers and yellow fall foliage. Also, the var. *flavopurpurascens* is sometimes available, but not greatly different from the cultivars (above). *H. japonica* and its hybrids are useful in the same range as *H. mollis*.

Hamamelis vernalis 5 (vernal witch hazel). This native of the south-central United States flowers at about the same time as the Asian species and hybrids, but has smaller flowers. Its dense growth (except in full shade) makes it more useful as a visual screen than most *Hamamelis* species. A few cultivars are available. 'Carnea', or f. *carnea*, is a name sometimes applied generically to reddish-flowering forms, but there is at least one clone with distinctly red flowers, fading to pink. 'Lombart's Weeping' is a small, weeping selection, not usually exceeding 2 m/6.6 ft in height, with red flowers. 'Sandra' is a selection primarily for superb red fall foliage display, but it also has fairly showy clear yellow flowers, opening variously from late autumn to early spring, according to different observers, and purplish emerging leaves in spring.

Hamamelis virginiana 6

COMMON WITCH HAZEL
Deciduous shrub
Hamamelidaceae (Witch Hazel Family)

Native Range. Eastern and central United States.

Useful Range. USDA Zones 4a–9a.

Function. Border, screen, naturalizing.

Size and Habit

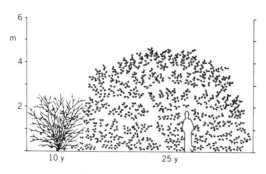

Hamamelis virginiana.

Adaptability. Grows best with at least light shade in the South and Midwest.

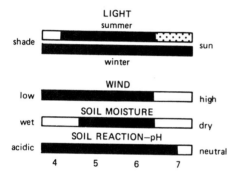

Seasonal Interest. *Flowers:* Yellow, with narrow, ribbonlike petals and light, spicy fragrance, showy in middle to late autumn, especially after the leaves have fallen. *Foliage:* Clean, bright green, turning clear yellow in early to midautumn. *Fruits:* Explosive capsules discharge seeds for some distance in autumn a year after flowering and add mild seasonal interest.

Problems and Maintenance. This plant is relatively trouble-free and requires little or no maintenance.

Forms and Cultivars. The f. *rubescens* has reddish petals but is little known. Cultivars have not been developed, but sufficient variation exists to justify selection for form and foliage quality and late flowering, since flowers are largely masked by the leaves until they fall. Hybridization with spring flowering *Hamamelis* species might accomplish this.

Hedera helix 1 and 2

ENGLISH IVY
Evergreen vine or groundcover
Araliaceae (Aralia Family)

Native Range. Europe, western Asia, North Africa.

Useful Range. USDA Zones 6a–9a+. A few cultivars are hardy northward to Zone 5a, a few tender in Zone 6.

Function. Groundcover, wall cover, vine climbing by aerial rootlets.

Size and Habit

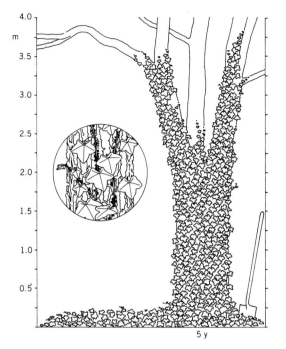

Hedera helix.

Handsome, evergreen, lobed leaves, unlobed in the mature form, 4–10 cm/1.6–4 in. long, with lighter vein markings in some cultivars. *Fruits:* Also only on the mature form, the small black berries, in round clusters about golf-ball size, are poisonous if eaten. The fact that cases of actual poisoning are not known probably attests to their lack of appeal.

Hedera helix, mature foliage.

Adaptability. Some protection from full winter sun and wind is necessary at the northern edges of the useful range (Zone 5b) to avoid winter drying of foliage.

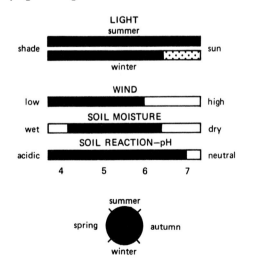

Seasonal Interest. *Flowers:* Present only on the mature (arborescent) form, in interesting but not conspicuous round clusters (umbels). *Foliage:*

Problems and Maintenance. Relatively trouble-free, but susceptible to infestation by mites in areas with hot, dry summers and by scale insects and slugs in warm, moist climates.

Cultivars. More than 100 cultivars—varying from cutleaf to curled and crinkled leaves, and white and yellow variegated forms—are available for use in our milder climates (Zones 7a–9a+). For Zone 5, only a few of these are cold-hardy enough to be useful, including the following. 'Baltica,' 'Bulgaria,' and 'Rumania' are selections from the wild in the named regions and are useful as groundcovers in areas as cold as Zone 5a, with careful attention to site, but useful as wall covers in areas only as cold as Zone 5b, again, with correct siting (northern and eastern exposures only). 'Ogallala' has proved the most cold-hardy of several strains at the Minnesota Landscape Arboretum, succeeding in Zone 4b with attention to site. 'Thorndale,' a handsome form with heavily whitened veins, is valued highly in the Midwest, performing well as a groundcover most winters in Zone 5b.

Related Species

Hedera canariensis 1 and 2 (Algerian or Canary ivy). This species is useful and usually preferred over *H. helix* from Zone 9a southward. It is marginally hardy in Zone 8. It is more vigorous than *H. helix*, with larger leaves (to 15 cm/6 in.), and makes a thick mat of vegetation to 0.5 m/1.6 ft deep. Several cultivars exist, but the most commonly used is 'Gloire de Marengo' (= 'Variegata') with white variegated leaves.

Hedera colchica 1 and 2 (Colchis or Persian ivy). This species from western Asia is notable for its large, leathery leaves, 10–25 cm/4–10 in. long. It is not as widely available as the other *Hedera*

species listed, but is useful in Zones 8a–9a+ and in protected sites in Zone 7b. 'Dentata' is a vigorous selection with large green, slightly toothed leaves, to 25 cm/10 in. long. 'Dentata Variegata' is similar except for its silvery gray and white margined leaves, as effective as those of *H. canariensis* 'Gloire de Marengo' ('Variegata') and more cold-hardy (to Zone 7, perhaps also Zone 6b). 'Sulphur Heart' (= 'Paddy's Pride') has leaves splashed and speckled sulfur yellow.

Hemerocallis fulva 3

ORANGE OR TAWNY DAYLILY
Herbaceous groundcover
Liliaceae (Lily Family)

Native Range.   Eurasia, naturalized in North America.

Useful Range.   USDA Zones 3b–9a+.

Function.   Groundcover, massing, specimen.

Size and Habit

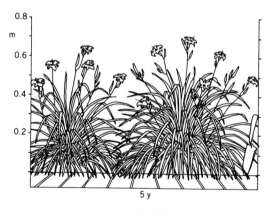

Hemerocallis fulva.

Adaptability.   Full sun is best for heaviest flowering, but as much as half shade can be tolerated if the sunny part of the day is in morning or midday.

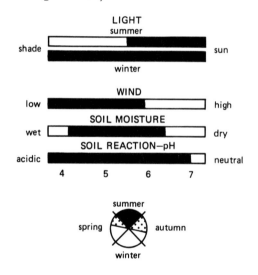

Seasonal Interest.   *Flowers:* Orange (and many other colors in hybrids), lilylike, each flower normally remaining open only for a day, very colorful for most of midsummer. *Foliage:* Medium to bright green, narrowly straplike, making a dense mass 0.5–0.7 m/1.6–2.8 ft high, dying down over winter (some hybrids, useful in mild climates, have persistent foliage).

Problems and Maintenance.   Daylilies are essentially trouble-free but may occasionally be infected with a leaf-spot disease. They require little or no maintenance once established, even

Hemerocallis fulva, as groundcover.

when tightly matted. Dividing and fertilizing old plantings undoubtedly will improve flowering, but temporarily reduces the effectiveness of groundcover plantings in resisting weed encroachment.

Species and Hybrids

Hemerocallis lilio-asphodelus 3 (synonym: *H. flava;* yellow daylily, lemon lily). This species, widely distributed across Asia, has become naturalized in our area. It differs from *H. fulva* in being somewhat less vigorous and not quite so tall and in having clear yellow flowers somewhat earlier in summer.

Several other *Hemerocallis* species have been involved in a very active breeding effort in the United States, much of the effort the work of amateur specialists, and a very large number of cultivars now exists. Many have been developed for flowering characteristics, some also for good foliage, and the effectiveness of most for massing in landscape use is not well known. In selecting cultivars, it is best to rely on local experience and availability.

Hibiscus syriacus 5

SHRUB ALTHEA, ROSE OF SHARON
Deciduous shrub
Malvaceae (Mallow Family)

Native Range.   China, India.

Useful Range.   USDA Zones 5b–9a.

Function.   Border, specimen.

Size and Habit

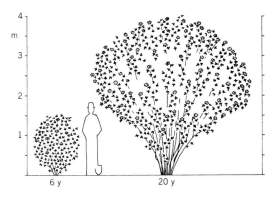

Hibiscus syriacus.

Adaptability.   This shrub is tolerant of seashore conditions.

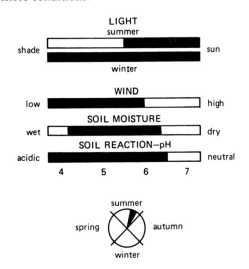

Seasonal Interest.   *Flowers:* Large (6–10 cm/ 2.4–4 in. across) and showy, single or double, white, pink, red, violet, or blue in late summer. *Foliage:* Smooth, lobed, bright green leaves are sparsely arranged on stems.

Problems and Maintenance. Stems are occasionally killed back in spring in Zones 5b–6b. Although it is necessary to remove the deadwood, this does not interfere with flowering, which occurs on new growth. In fact, heavy pruning in spring may improve flowering by increasing the general vigor and length of new growth. Regular annual pruning to enhance flowering results in a shrub functioning in size group 4 (1–1.5 m/3.3–4.9 ft) rather than the size group 5 that would otherwise be attained.

Cultivars. Two dozen or more cultivars were selected years ago, and several are still popular in spite of the keen competition offered by the newest cultivars, especially the sterile triploids bred and introduced by Donald Egolf at the U.S. National Arboretum.

Single-flowered old cultivars include the following: 'Bluebird' is unique because of its large, nearly azure-blue flowers, with small red centers, and thus remains among the most popular cultivars. 'Coelestis' has large, pale blue-violet flowers. 'William R. Smith' has very large, pure white flowers. 'Woodbridge' has large, rich pink flowers with red centers.

Double-flowered cultivars have been favored because their mostly sterile flowers precluded any problem with escaping seedlings. Most of these have no other advantage and their flowers lack the interesting character of single flowers, but several are still popular. 'Ardens' has semidouble, light orchid-purple flowers. 'Blushing Bride' has double, pale blushed-pink flowers. 'Jeanne d'Arc' has double white flowers. 'Lady Stanley' has semidouble white flowers, with petals red-marked at the base and sometimes flushing into the rest of the petal. 'Lucy' has double red flowers.

The Egolf cultivars are outstanding for the substance of their flowers and foliage, as well as their tendency to flower longer over a longer season. Since they are triploid, a condition that usually confers sterility, these single-flowered cultivars do not produce weed seedlings. 'Aphrodite' has large, crinkled rose-pink petals, red at the base. 'Diana' has very large, pure white flowers, with crinkled petals. 'Helene' has large white flowers with deep red centers with streaks forming multipointed stars. 'Minerva' flowers are very large and lavender-pink with a red center.

Related Species

Hibiscus rosa-sinensis 6 (Chinese hibiscus). This species is, practically speaking, out of our range, but it is sometimes grown with protection in Zone 9a. It is a large shrub, to 5 m/16 ft or more under good growing conditions, with large flowers, 10–20 cm/4–8 in. across, white, pink, or red, depending on the cultivar.

Hippophaë rhamnoides 6

SEA BUCKTHORN
Deciduous shrub or small tree
Elaeagnaceae (Oleaster Family)

Native Range. Europe and Asia.

Useful Range. USDA Zones 3a–7a.

Function. Specimen, border, barrier, massing.

Size and Habit

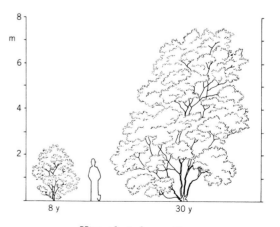

Hippophaë rhamnoides.

Adaptability. Like some other members of the Oleaster Family, this is a nitrogen-fixing species, adaptable to very poor, dry soil. It is one of the best shrubs for cold climates on dry, even somewhat alkaline soils. It grows well in seaside sites and is relatively tolerant of road salt as well.

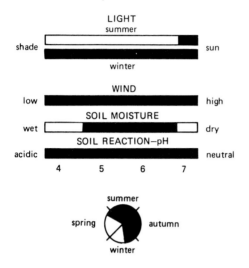

Hippophaë rhamnoides.

Hippophaë rhamnoides, as accent.

Seasonal Interest. *Flowers:* Dioecious, pale yellow, small and inconspicuous in early spring. *Foliage:* Narrow, silvery green leaves on spiny branches give distinctive color and fine texture in summer. *Fruits:* Bright yellow-orange, only 0.8 cm/0.3 in. across but borne in great numbers on female plants, very showy well into winter.

Problems and Maintenance. Establishment has sometimes been difficult, but this probably is not a serious problem if pot-grown plants are specified. Requires occasional pruning to maintain fullness, if this is desired, and to remove root suckers as they develop if a thicket-type growth is to be avoided.

Hosta plantaginea 2

Synonym: *H. subcordata*
FRAGRANT PLANTAIN LILY
Herbaceous groundcover
Liliaceae (Lily Family)

Native Range. China and Japan.

Useful Range. USDA Zones 3b–9a+.

Function. Groundcover, massing, specimen.

Size and Habit

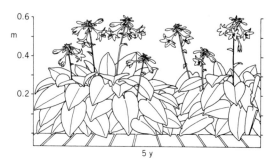

Hosta plantaginea.

Adaptability. Partial shade is best for growth, but this plant tolerates complete shade, with lessened flowering, and full sun, although growth is stronger and leaf color better in light shade, especially in the Midwest and South.

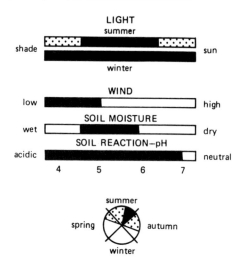

Seasonal Interest. *Flowers:* Fragrant, pure white, funnel-shaped, to 12 cm/5 in. long, in clusters on stalks to at least 60 cm/2 ft tall in late summer and early autumn, persisting longer than those of other species. *Foliage:* Bright green, the leaf blades 15–25 cm/6–10 in. long and 10–15 cm/4–6 in. broad, conspicuously parallel veined, making a solid, pleasingly coarse mass from late spring until late autumn, dying down over winter.

Problems and Maintenance. Garden slugs and leaf-spot diseases may be troublesome in very wet years. Otherwise, plantain lilies are trouble-free and require practically no maintenance.

Varieties and Hybrids. The var. *grandiflora* (= 'Grandiflora') is taller than the species (1–1.2 m/3.3–4 ft), with very large flowers, more fragrant than the species type. 'Royal Standard,' a hybrid of *H. plantaginea,* also has exceptionally fragrant flowers, but does not grow as tall (0.6 m/2 ft).

Related Species and Cultivars. The species listed below are only a few of the more common ones. All are similar to *H. plantaginea* in basic requirements and useful range, but they and their cultivars vary considerably in vigor, sun and drought tolerances, resistance to disease and pests, effectiveness of flowers, and visual character of the foliage.

Hosta fortunei 2 (Fortune plantain lily). This species is an effective groundcover to about 30 cm/12 in. high and twice as wide, with medium-sized leaves to 30 cm/12 in. long and half as wide. The selection 'Albo-marginata,' with wide white leaf margins, is very popular and 'Gloriosa,' with a thin white margin on dark green leaves, is especially effective.

Hosta lancifolia 2 (lanceleaved plantain lily). This low, spreading groundcover makes a low mass about 30 cm/12 in. high and half again as wide. The deep green leaves are lance-shaped, to 15 cm/6 in. long and only 5 cm/2 in. wide.

Hosta montana 3 (mountain plantain lily). This vigorous plant, to 80 cm/32 in. tall and half again as wide, makes a high mound of dark green leaves, to 30 cm/12 in. wide and half again as long, serving as a background for smaller plants. In early summer it bears showy white flowers well above the foliage.

Hosta sieboldiana 3 (Siebold plantain lily). This vigorous plant is similar in size to *H. montana,* but differs in having puckered blue-green leaves, giving a very bold landscape effect by its positive color and texture. Several cultivars have been introduced, one of the most popular of which is 'Elegans,' similar to the species type but even more bold in effect.

Hosta undulata 2 (wavy leaved plantain lily). This plant forms a mound 25–50 cm/10–20 in. tall and somewhat greater width. Its wavy, variegated leaves, 12–22 cm/5–9 in. long by 8–

15 cm/3–6 in. wide, are its distinctive feature, and several selections have been made, the most popular of which is 'Albo-marginata,' with white leaf margins, and 'Variegata,' with white splashes and streaks in the center of each leaf.

Hybrid Cultivars. Because of the widespread interest in hostas, and with the development of tissue culture techniques for propagating these plants, hundreds of hybrid cultivars are commercially available in eastern North America. New cultivars are still being added, and it is virtually impossible for anyone other than a serious collector to keep up with more than a small fraction of this diversity. More detailed information can be gotten from books on herbaceous perennials, and specifically on hostas, as well as from the American Hosta Society. Since most hostas are effective landscape plants, any given landscape need usually can be met by more than one cultivar, which is fortunate because choices often must be made from the rather small number of cultivars available at any specific time and place.

Hydrangea arborescens 3

SMOOTH HYDRANGEA
Deciduous shrub or subshrub
Hydrangeaceae (Hydrangea Family)

Native Range. Eastern and central United States.

Useful Range. USDA Zones 4a–9a.

Function. Border, specimen, informal low hedge.

Size and Habit. 'Grandiflora' is illustrated.

Adaptability

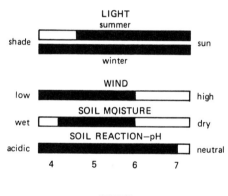

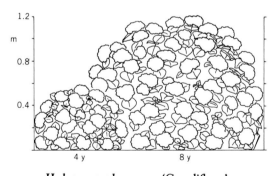

Hydrangea arborescens 'Grandiflora.'

Seasonal Interest. *Flowers:* White, in large (to 15 cm/6 in.), flat clusters, inconspicuous fertile flowers in the center and more showy sterile flowers around the margin of the clusters, or in globose clusters of sterile flowers in cultivars. Showy from early to midsummer. *Foliage:* Coarse, dark green, forming a good background for flowering but usually not attractive thereafter.

Problems and Maintenance. Relatively trouble-free, but kills to the ground in most winters in the North. Even when it does not, it is best pruned close to the ground in spring, since it returns vigorously to flower in the same year and retains a more-or-less regular, moundlike form. Plant parts are poisonous (see *Hydrangea anomala*).

Subspecies and Cultivars. The ssp. *radiata* (synonym: *H. radiata*; silverleaf hydrangea) is similar to ssp. *arborescens*, the species type, except that its leaves are white and fuzzy underneath, giving the lower surface a silvery appearance.

'Annabelle' has unusually large, globose flower clusters, to 20 cm/8 in. or more across, composed almost entirely of sterile flowers.

'Grandiflora' (hills-of-snow hydrangea) is a long-cultivated selection with sterile flowers in globose clusters, 5–15 cm/2–6 in. across.

Hydrangea macrophylla 3

BIGLEAF OR FLORIST HYDRANGEA
Deciduous shrub
Hydrangeaceae (Hydrangea Family)

Native Range.   Japan.

Useful Range.   USDA Zones 6b–9a.

Function.   Specimen, border.

Size and Habit

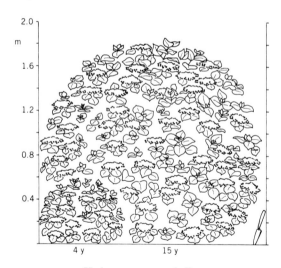

Hydrangea macrophylla.

intermediate range, some cultivars produce mauve or magenta flowers, not usually very attractive. Plant growth is usually best below about pH 6.5, leaving a rather narrow range of optimal acidity for both good growth and pink flowers.

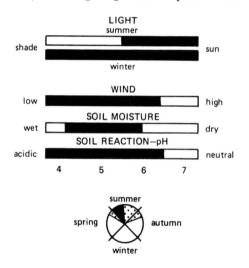

Seasonal Interest. *Flowers:* White, pink, or blue, in large clusters, those composed of fertile flowers are flattened and those of sterile flowers are globose, both very showy in summer. *Foliage:* Lustrous, bright green, somewhat leathery, falling without color change in autumn.

Adaptability. In the South, this shrub does best in relatively cool, moist sites, for instance, on the north sides of buildings. Flower color in blue and pink cultivars is controlled by the amount of soluble aluminum in the plant—in turn controlled by soil acidity. For clear blue color, soil pH should be no higher than 5.5, for clear pink color, no lower than 6.0. In the

Problems and Maintenance. Relatively trouble-free, but may require regular adjustments of soil acidity in some areas. Pruning should be done as soon as possible after flowering to allow time for new stem growth and initiation of flower buds for the next year. In no case should live stems be pruned back in spring because *H. macrophylla*, unlike *H. arborescens*, usually does not produce flowers in a single growing season. Typically, flower buds are initiated in summer, then must survive winter and receive their chilling requirement before opening the following summer. Plant parts are poisonous (see *Hydrangea anomala*).

Subspecies, Varieties, and Cultivars. The ssp. *macrophylla*, the typical subspecies, has smooth stems and leathery leaves tending to be evergreen in very mild climates. It includes the following varieties.

The var. *macrophylla*, the so-called hortensia types, with entirely sterile flowers in large, globose heads. Many cultivars have been selected from var. *macrophylla*, some not fully cold-hardy in Zone 6b. A few of the most common follow. 'All Summer Beauty' is a relatively recent selection for heavy flowering and compact growth. It usually is grown in acid soil for blue flowers, but is interesting with multicolored blooms in the transitional zone around pH 6.0. 'Blue Prince' is effective in either the blue or pink pH range. 'Domotoi' is unique in having large clusters of double flowers and useful in either the blue or pink pH ranges but usually most effective with light blue flowers in acid soil since it grows weakly in soil of higher pH. Hardy northward to Zone 6b. 'Forever Pink' is low growing, to about 0.6 m/2 ft tall, with rich pink flowers (high soil pH) and red-marked leaf-veins. 'Mandshurica' is effective in either the blue or pink pH range and is unusually cold-hardy (to Zone 6a in protected sites) but may not be available. 'Nikko Blue' is most effective in acidic soils, with deep blue flowers. 'Otaksa' is effective in either the blue or pink pH range, but more color-stable in acidic soil, with large clusters of blue flowers and compact growth habit. 'Pink Beauty' is most satisfactory in the pink pH range.

The var. *normalis*, the wild type of *H. macrophylla*, has an inflorescence of the "lacecap" type, a flattened cluster with sterile flowers only around the edge, and cultivars of this type are often associated with it, even though logic suggests that this wild type must have been the ancestor of plants with both types of inflores-

Hydrangea macrophylla var. *normalis*.

cences. Anyway, cultivars with the lacecap type of inflorescence have their own visual quality, and some think they are more graceful than the hortensia types. A few of the most common of these are listed here. 'Blue Billow' is a relatively new selection with cool blue flowers (in acidic soil) in small clusters, making a graceful low mound; also, its flower buds are more cold-hardy than those of most other cultivars, reportedly to −25°C/−13°F. 'Blue Wave' also has showy flat flower clusters, best in the blue range, in acidic soil. 'Mariesii' has large, rosy pink flowers in slightly acidic to neutral soil and has blue flowers in strongly acidic soil. 'Mariesii Variegata' is similar to 'Mariesii' except that its leaves have white margins. The blue color phase is perhaps more attractive in combination with this foliage than the pink phase.

The ssp. *serrata* (synonyms: *H. acuminata, H. serrata*; tea-of-heaven) differs from ssp. *macrophylla* in having smaller, less leathery leaves, and more hairy foliage and stems. Its flowers are typically borne in flattened, "lacecap" clusters. Specialists in this genus suggest that some cultivars of ssp. *serrata* may be misassigned to ssp. *macrophylla*, and that may be true of some of those listed above. There is no question that the selection 'Bluebird' belongs to ssp. *serrata* (or *H. serrata*, for those who maintain that this is a separate species). Cultivars so assigned have the reputation of being more compact in form and slightly more cold-hardy than most of those in ssp. *macrophylla*.

Hydrangea paniculata 6

PANICLE HYDRANGEA
Deciduous shrub
Hydrangeaceae (Hydrangea Family)

Native Range. Japan.

Useful Range. USDA Zones 4a–8a.

Function. Specimen, border.

Size and Habit. 'Grandiflora' is illustrated.

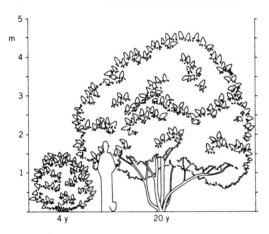

Hydrangea paniculata 'Grandiflora.'

Adaptability

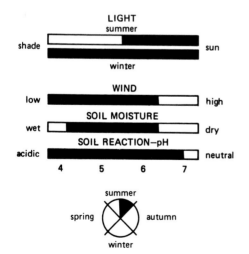

Seasonal Interest. *Flowers:* White, in large (to 25 cm/10 in. long), upright pyramidal clusters, mostly of small fertile flowers but with showy sterile flowers at the base or mostly sterile flowers in a cultivar. Clusters turn pinkish in late summer, light brown in autumn. *Foliage:* Coarse, medium green, adding little landscape interest.

Problems and Maintenance. This shrub is relatively trouble-free. Plant parts are poisonous but probably not troublesome (see *Hydrangea petiolaris*).

Cultivars. 'Grandiflora' (peegee hydrangea) has clusters of mostly sterile flowers resembling huge, pyramidal snowballs. This is by far the most common form of *H. paniculata* in landscape use. Sometimes pruned into treelike forms and called tree hydrangea, it has been widely promoted by mail-order houses and disseminated more widely than is justified by its landscape value. Individual plants occasionally assume dwarf or compact growth habit for no clear reason, then may revert to the typical vigorous growth just as mysteriously.

'Praecox' (early panicle hydrangea) flowers about 20 days earlier than the species type and has a few more sterile flowers in each cluster.

'Tardiva' (late panicle hydrangea) flowers later than the species type and its flower clusters are a little smaller, making the plant more graceful.

Hydrangea petiolaris 1 and 2

Synonym: *H. anomala ssp. petiolaris*
CLIMBING HYDRANGEA
Deciduous vine
Hydrangeaceae (Hydrangea Family)

Native Range. Japan, Taiwan.

Useful Range. USDA Zones 5a–7b. May be used in Zone 8 in relatively cool, moist sites.

Function. Wall cover, specimen, ground-cover. Vine climbing by aerial rootlets, sometimes to heights of 20–25 m/66–82 ft.

Size and Habit

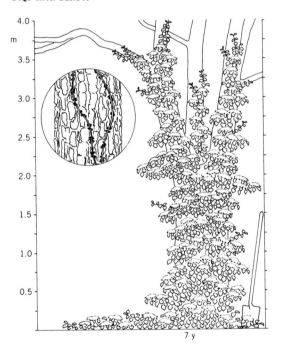

Hydrangea petiolaris.

Adaptability

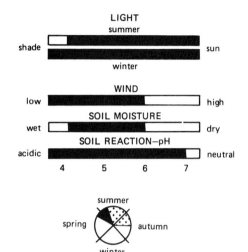

Seasonal Interest. *Flowers:* White, in large flat clusters, inconspicuous fertile flowers in the center and more showy sterile flowers around the margin of the cluster, conspicuous against the handsome foliage in late spring and early summer. *Foliage:* Dark green, lustrous, neat in appearance, the leaves, 5–10 cm/2–4 in. long, fall in autumn with little color change. *Twigs and branches:* Covered with flaky tan bark, interesting with the aerial rootlets only at very close range.

Problems and Maintenance. Relatively trouble-free and requiring almost no maintenance, although it is very slow-growing for the first few years. It can be troubled by mites occasionally, especially in dry sites or dry years, but this is not a serious problem with attention to soil and site conditions. Plant parts are poisonous but of little appeal and apparently not troublesome.

Related Species

Decumaria barbara 1 and 2 (decumaria, wood vamp). This vine, climbing by aerial rootlets, is a close relative of *Hydrangea*, native to the southeastern United States. It has much the same growth habit as *H. petiolaris* but less vigor, seldom climbing higher than 5–10 m/16–33 ft. The leaves are smaller than those of *H. petiolaris*

Decumaria barbara.

Schizophragma hydrangeoides.

but equally lustrous and handsome. It has white flowers in late spring, less showy than those of *H. petiolaris*, and grows best in fairly moist sites in partial shade in Zones 6b–9a.

Pileostegia viburnoides 1 and 2.   This vigorous vine from Southern China and Taiwan has ever-

Decumaria barbara.

green leaves, to 15 cm/6 in. long, and climbs by aerial rootlets much like the related *H. petiolaris*, to heights of 10–15 m/33–49 ft. It grows best in at least some shade and tolerates deep shade, even flowering well there. The small, white flowers appear in large clusters from midsummer through early autumn. It is useful in Zones 8a–9a+, but probably not commercially available in eastern North America.

Schizophragma hydrangeoides 1 and 2.   This Japanese species is closely related to *Hydrangea petiolaris* and sometimes confused with it, but it can be distinguished easily by two features. First, its sterile flowers, arranged on the margin of the flower clusters, have only a single large sepal (about 3 cm/1.2 in. long) rather than 4 or 5 sepals as in *H. petiolaris*. Second, its leaves are more coarsely toothed, less lustrous, and usually lighter green than those of *H. petiolaris*. The requirements of *S. hydrangeoides* are similar to those of *H. petiolaris*, but is somewhat less cold-hardy, useful in Zones 6a–7b.

Schizophragma integrifolium 1 and 2.   This species, from China, differs from *S. hydrangeoides* in having larger leaves (10–18 cm/4–7 in. long) and, especially, having creamy white marginal sepals more than twice as large (about 7 cm/2.8 in), hanging from the stems in an interesting pattern in midsummer. This plant is almost never seen in eastern North America and is only occasionally available, but it is potentially useful at least in Zones 8–9a+, perhaps also in sheltered sites in Zone 7b.

Hydrangea quercifolia 4–5

OAKLEAF HYDRANGEA
Deciduous shrub
Hydrangeaceae (Hydrangea Family)

Native Range. Southeastern United States.

Useful Range. USDA Zones 5b–9a. Tops are winterkilled frequently in Zones 5b and 6a, occasionally in Zone 6b.

Function. Border, specimen, massing, naturalizing.

Size and Habit

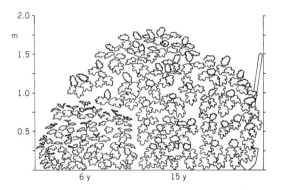

Hydrangea quercifolia.

Adaptability

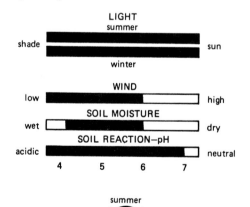

Seasonal Interest. *Flowers:* White, in upright, pyramidal clusters, to 25 cm/10 in. long, composed mostly of small, fertile flowers but with showy, sterile flowers at the base or mostly of sterile flowers in some cultivars. Clusters turn pinkish in late summer, brown in autumn. Flower buds are initiated the previous summer as in *H. macrophylla* and are often winterkilled with stems in colder zones, eliminating flowering interest for the year. *Foliage:* Coarse but handsome, oaklike leaves, to 20 cm/8 in. long, provide strong landscape interest in summer even in nonflowering years in the North and turn a rich russet-red in autumn. *Twigs and branches:* New twig growth is covered with a dense mat of short, reddish brown hairs.

Hydrangea quercifolia.

Problems and Maintenance. This shrub is relatively trouble-free. In the North, in some years, annual pruning will be necessary to remove winterkilled branches. This should be done at about the same time that new growth starts, when the extent of injury is known. Winter injury has the effect of maintaining the functional height of the shrub below eye level in northern zones. Plant parts are poisonous (see *Hydrangea petiolaris*).

Cultivars. 'Harmony' and 'Roanoke' differ from the species type in having large infleorescences, mostly composed of showy, sterile flowers, resembling huge, elongated snowballs, usu-ally heavy enough to weigh branches down, giving the plant an irregularly pendulous form. They may no longer be available. 'Snow Queen' also has large clusters (panicles) of sterile flowers held erect on the plant, making a beautiful display. 'Snowflake' also makes a fine display, with flowers that are double (extra sepals) as well as sterile, producing a distinctive effect.

Hypericum calycinum 2

AARONSBEARD ST. JOHN'S-WORT
Evergreen or semievergreen groundcover
Hypericaceae (Hypericum Family)

Native Range.   Southeastern Europe and adjacent Asia.

Useful Range.   USDA Zones 6b–9a, Zone 6a with winter protection.

Function.   Groundcover, useful for large areas, making a dense mat of foliage.

Size and Habit

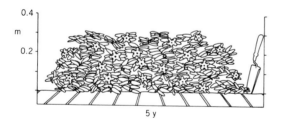

Hypericum calycinum.

Adaptability

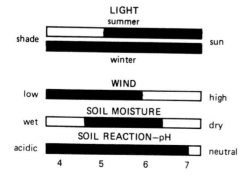

Seasonal Interest.   *Flowers:* Large (to 5–8 cm/ 2–3 in. across), bright golden yellow with prominent stamens, nearly as long as the petals, and reddish anthers, middle to late summer. *Foliage:* Handsome, rich green, rounded leaves, 5–10 cm/2–4 in. long, semievergreen in Zones 6 and 7, evergreen in the Deep South.

Problems and Maintenance.   Relatively trouble-free and requiring no maintenance other than occasional to annual pruning. (in early summer) in small-scale sites. St. John's-worts are toxic to some animals if eaten (by photosensitization), so keep plantings away from farm animals.

Hypericum calycinum.

Related Species and Hybrids

Hypericum buckleyi 2 (Buckley or Blue Ridge St. John's-wort).   This native of eastern North

America is similar to *H. calycinum* in habit and function, but deciduous, with smaller flowers (2.5 cm/1 in.) a little earlier in summer and slightly more cold-hardy. Useful in Zones 6a–8a.

Hypericum × 'Hidcote' 2–3 (Hidcote St. John's-wort). The parents of this fine hybrid are not fully known, but most people believe that one of them is *H. calycinum*. 'Hidcote' has fragrant, golden yellow flowers about 5 cm/2 in. across. In mild climates (Zones 8–9a+) it is fully evergreen and seldom suffers winter dieback, reaching a height of 1.5 m/5 ft and flowering throughout the summer. In Zones 5b–6, stems are killed back to the ground in most winters, after which new stems return rapidly and flower by middle or late summer. In the transitional Zone 7, this plant is not fully evergreen, and stems are killed back in some years, so an annual decision can be made whether or not to prune the plant back to the ground in spring.

Hypericum ×*moserianum* 2 (gold flower). This hybrid (*H. calycinum* × *H. patulum*) is intermediate in height (to 0.5 m/1.6 ft) and flower size (to 6 cm/2.4 in) between its parents and functions as a rather tall groundcover for mild climates (Zones 7a–9a+), flowering over most of the summer. Foliage of the selection 'Tricolor' is variegated, pink, creamy white, and gray-green.

Hypericum patulum 3 (goldencup St. John's-wort). This semievergreen shrub with yellow

Hypericum 'Hidcote.'

flowers, 2.5–5 cm/1–2 in. across, is useful in Zones 7a–9a, but does not flower as well as 'Hidcote' after winter killback. This species is much confused in cultivation, and its name has been misapplied to several other *Hypericum* species and cultivars, including *H. beanii*, *H.* ×*cyanthiflorum* 'Gold Cup,' *H. forrestii*, *H.* ×'Hidcote,' and *H. kouytchense*, all useful members of the genus but, except for 'Hidcote,' seldom used in our area.

Hypericum reptans 2 (creeping St. John's-wort). This fine-textured, usually mat-forming groundcover (under 0.3 m/1 ft) from the Himalayas has very small leaves (to about 2 cm/0.8 in. long) and flowers 2–3.5 cm/0.8–1.4 in. across. Useful in Zones 7a–9a, and Zone 6 with protection, but rarely seen in our area.

Hypericum prolificum 3

SHRUBBY ST. JOHN'S-WORT
Deciduous shrub
Hypericaceae (Hypericum Family)

Native Range. Eastern United states and adjacent Canada.

Useful Range. USDA Zones 4b–8b.

Function. Border, specimen, massing.

Size and Habit

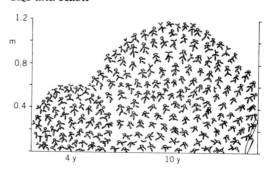

Hypericum prolificum.

Adaptability. This is one of the most widely adaptable of all *Hypericum* species.

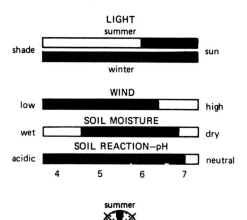

Hypericum prolificum.

Seasonal Interest. *Flowers:* Bright yellow, to 2 cm/0.8 in. across, in clusters, very colorful in midsummer. *Foliage:* The handsome, bright green leaves (3–8 cm/1.2–3 in. long and much narrower) give relatively fine texture and fall in autumn with little color change. *Twigs and branches:* Light brown peeling bark adds minor winter interest.

Problems and Maintenance. This shrub is relatively trouble-free and requires no maintenance other than removal of deadwood after severe winters in Zones 4 and 5a. Plant parts are toxic to some animals if eaten (see *Hypericum calycinum*).

Related Species

Hypericum frondosum 3 (golden St. John's-wort). This native of the southeastern United States has larger flowers (to 5 cm/2 in. across) and slightly broader leaves than *H. prolificum* and is somewhat less cold-hardy. It is useful in Zones 5b–9a, perhaps also Zone 5a. The selection 'Sunburst' is outstanding, with heavy flowering in midsummer and blue-green foliage, turning red-orange in autumn.

Hypericum kalmianum 3 (Kalm St. John's-wort). This shrub is more northern in origin than *H. prolificum*, growing wild well into Canada from the Great Lakes area. It is lower-growing and has smaller flowers, to 2.5 cm/1 in. across. Useful in Zones 4b–8b.

Iberis sempervirens 2

EVERGREEN CANDYTUFT
Evergreen groundcover
Brassicaceae (Cruciferae; Mustard Family)

Native Range. Mediterranean region: southern Europe, western Asia, North Africa.

Useful Range. USDA Zones 5a–7b.

Function. Groundcover (small-scale), rock garden.

Size and Habit

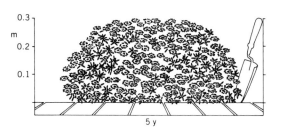

Iberis sempervirens.

Adaptability

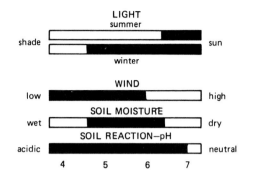

Seasonal Interest. *Flowers:* Pure white, in small rounded clusters about 2.5 cm/1 in. across, showy for two to four weeks in late spring, and again in early autumn in a few cultivars. *Foliage:* Fine textured, very dark green, evergreen, and leathery.

Problems and Maintenance. Relatively trouble-free, requiring little maintenance. Foliage may become less attractive by midsummer, but clipping after flowering to promote new growth will help to avoid this.

Cultivars. Several excellent cultivars have been selected, for dwarfness, vigor, or spring and autumn flowering.

'Alexander's White,' 'Purity,' and 'Snowflake'

are among the most popular selections, growing about 20–25 cm/8–10 in. tall, with outstanding spring flowering.

'Autumn Beauty,' 'Autumn Snow,' 'Christmas Snow,' and 'October Glory' flower in both spring and fall, growing to about 20–25 cm/8–10 in. tall.

'Compacta,' 'Kingwood Compact,' 'Little Gem,' and 'Pygmaea' are dwarf to compact in habit, growing about 10–15 cm/4–6 in. tall. They are excellent for rock gardens and as very-small-scale groundcovers, but the faster growing forms may be more practical for the usual groundcover needs.

'Snowmantle' is unusually vigorous, growing 30–38 cm/12–15 in. tall, with very showy and long-lasting flowers.

Related Species

Iberis gibraltarica 2 (Gibraltar candytuft).   This evergreen groundcover grows somewhat taller and looser than *I. sempervirens,* with pink to light rosy purple-tinted flowers in middle spring. Less cold-hardy than *I. sempervirens.* Useful in Zones 6b–9a and perhaps colder zones as well.

Iberis pruitii 2.   Another Mediterranean species, this plant from Italy has pink-tinged flowers. It is useful in Zones 7a–9a and perhaps in colder zones but it is seldom if ever available.

Iberis saxatilis 2.   Another native of southern Europe, this is similar to and often confused with *I. sempervirens* but has narrower leaves and more consistently low habit. It is useful in Zones 6b–9a and perhaps also colder zones.

Idesia polycarpa 7

IDESIA, IIGIRI TREE
Deciduous tree
Flacourtiaceae (Flacourtia Family)

Native Range.   China, southern Japan.

Useful Range.   USDA Zones 7a–9a and perhaps colder zones as well, but may not fruit well in Zone 7.

Function.   Shade or patio tree.

Size and Habit

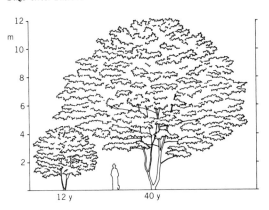

Idesia polycarpa.

Idesia polycarpa.

Adaptability

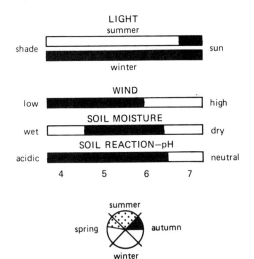

Seasonal Interest. *Flowers:* Inconspicuous but fragrant, in pendulous clusters to 25 cm/10 in. long in late spring. *Foliage:* Large, bright green leaves, 15–25 cm/6–10 in. long, vaguely resembling those of *Catalpa* but not as coarse in texture, falling in autumn with little color change. *Fruits:* Red-orange berries (on female trees), small but borne in large, pendent clusters and showy in early autumn. Some plants are dioecious, some monoecious (both male and female flowers on the same plant). Plants with at least some female flowers should be used to ensure colorful fruiting.

Problems and Maintenance. This tree has so seldom been used in the past that any problems are not yet well known, but it appears relatively trouble-free in trial plantings. Its useful range is also not accurately known, and after further trial it may be found to include more than the Zones 7b–9a indicated. It is seldom commercially available as yet.

Related Species

Stachyurus praecox 5 (early spiketail).   This rare native of Japan, in its own family but closely related to the Flacourtiaceae (Flacourtia Family), is popular in Europe but little known in North America. Its usefulness depends on questionable availability, but it has good potential for specimen use because of its pale yellow flowers in very early spring in stiffly pendulous clusters 5–8 cm/2–3 in. long, semievergreen foliage, and reddish winter twigs. It is useful in Zones 7a–9a+, but effective in flower only in areas where hard freezes are not common.

Stachyurus chinensis 5 (Chinese stachyurus or spiketail).   This rare species differs from *S. praecox* in having more gracefully pendulous flower spikes (racemes), 10–13 cm/4–5 long, and more slender, graceful branches, but it is much more tender, useful in Zone 9a+.

Ilex aquifolium 6

ENGLISH HOLLY
Evergreen shrub or small tree
Aquifoliaceae (Holly Family)

Native Range.   Asia, southern Europe, North Africa.

Useful Range.   USDA Zones 7a–9a+.

Function.   Specimen, screen, hedge.

Size and Habit.   This plant seldom attains the size in our area that it reaches in its native habitat and rarely exceeds heights of 4–6 m/13–20 ft except in mild coastal climates.

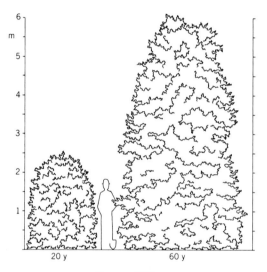

Ilex aquifolium.

Seasonal Interest.   *Flowers:* Small, white, dioecious, insignificant in the landscape. *Foliage:* Handsome, spiny and glossy, evergreen leaves. *Fruits:* Bright red berries (on females) remain colorful during fall and winter, occasionally until spring in the South. Male plants must be located nearby for pollination, except for a few parthenocarpic cultivars that set fruits (not seeds) without pollination.

Problems and Maintenance.   The most troublesome holly insects are holly leaf miners, mites, and scale insects. These are not often major problems for *I. aquifolium.*

Ilex aquifolium.

Adaptability.   Shade in summer improves performance in the South and in winter reduces foliage burn in Zone 7.

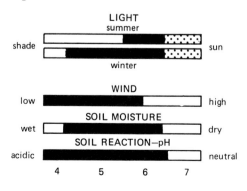

Cultivars.   Many cultivars have been selected in Europe but few are available in eastern and central North America. Those few include the following.

'Albomarginata' and 'Argenteo-marginata' have white-margined leaves. These are properly collective names rather than cultivar names, applied to more than one clone.

'Angustifolia,' with narrow leaves, is also a collective name, applied to both female and male clones.

'Aureo-marginata' has yellow-margined leaves.

'Bacciflava' and 'Fructu Luteo' have yellow berries, but may not be available in our area.

'Balkan's' is properly a collective name, since it is applied to at least two clones of different sex that grow to more than 3 m/10 ft tall. For this reason it is necessary to specify them by sex as well as cultivar. These are claimed to be the most hardy cultivars of *I. aquifolium*.

'Ferox' (hedgehog or porcupine holly). This very old male cultivar is a dwarf plant, growing to 1.5 m/5 ft in height and width, with small silvery spines on the upper leaf surfaces. 'Ferox Argentea' is similar but with creamy white-margined leaves, and the leaves of 'Ferox Aurea' are splashed with yellow.

'Monvila' (Gold Coast™; Plant Patent No. 5143, 1983) is male, with compact, rounded form, to m/6.6 ft tall. Its small dark green leaves have golden yellow margins, colorful even without fruit.

'Monler' (Sparkler™) is vigorous pyramidal in form, growing to 4 m/13 ft or more tall, with deep green leaves and shiny, bright red berries in autumn.

Related Hybrids

Ilex ×altaclerensis 'Camelliifolia' 6. This cultivar is probably the only clone of the hybrid *I. aquifolium* × *I. perado* that is available in our area, but several other cultivars are in use in Europe. This looks very much like *I. aquifolium* in size and form, but has leaves that are spineless except at the tip.

Ilex ×aquipernyi 'Brilliant' 6. This hybrid of *I. aquifolium* × *I. pernyi* becomes a pyramidal tree 5–8 m/16–26 ft tall with small, glossy, spiny leaves and large bright red berries, without the need for a male pollinator. Useful in Zones 7a–9a, perhaps 6b with further trial. Other available hybrids of this parentage include the following: 'Dorothy Lawton' has distinctive, dark green, slightly rounded leaves. 'Meschick' (Dragon Lady™; Plant Patent No. 4996, 1983) is columnar in habit. 'Patricia Varner' has dark green foliage and large numbers of red berries. 'San Jose' is upright, but broad and compact, with red fruits if pollinated by a male plant of *I. aquifolium*, *I. ×aquipernyi*, or *I. pernyi*, and cold hardy to Zone 6b, perhaps sheltered sites in Zone 6a.

Ilex × 'Joe McDaniel'. This complex hybrid (*I. ×aquipernyi* × *I. cornuta*) has glossy, dark green, spiny foliage and a compact, pyramidal form and is reported to be cold-hardy to −26°C/−15°F. A male clone, it is an effective pollinator in its group.

Ilex × 'Nellie R. Stevens' 6 (*I. aquifolium* × *I. cornuta*). This vigorous and handsome hybrid is upright and pyramidal in form, growing rapidly to 6 m/20 ft and more in height. It bears heavy crops of orange-red fruits and is useful in Zones 6b–9a.

Ilex cassine 6

DAHOON
Evergreen shrub or small tree
Aquifoliaceae (Holly Family)

Native Range.   Southeastern United States.

Useful Range.   USDA Zones 7b–9a+.

Function.   Specimen, massing, naturalizing.

Size and Habit

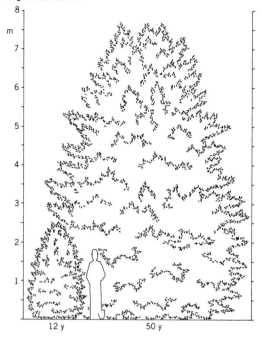

Ilex cassine.

Adaptability. This shrub is well adapted to seashore planting.

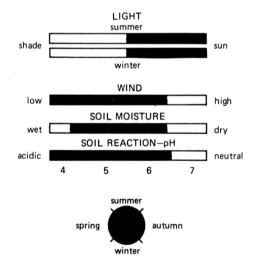

Seasonal Interest. *Flowers:* Small, white, dioecious, insignificant in the landscape. *Foliage:* Evergreen leaves, variable in length, 4–10 cm/ 1.6–4 in., and narrow, not toothed or slightly toothed at leaf apex, light to dark green, turning purplish in winter. *Fruits:* Red berries (on females) in clusters, colorful in autumn and winter.

Problems and Maintenance. Relatively trouble-free and requiring no maintenance except for pruning if greater fullness is desirable.

Varieties and Cultivars. The var. *cassine*, the typical form, has lustrous, medium-green leaves to 10 cm/4 in long, entire or with very few teeth, and small berries (0.6 cm/0.25 in.), colorful in autumn and early winter. The var. *angustifolia* has smaller and narrower leaves. 'Lowei' has narrow, dark green leaves and small yellow fruits. Other selections for yellow fruits have been made, but are seldom available.

Related Species and Hybrids

Ilex ×attenuata 6.   This hybrid group (*I. cassine*; ×*I. opaca*) is useful in Zones 7a–9a+, also Zone 6b with careful siting. It includes several narrowly conical selections with foliage intermediate between the parents. Some of the most popular are listed here.

'Eagleson' has nearly spineless foliage and is compact, growing to about 4.5 m/15 ft tall in time, with large quantities of red berries.

'Foster No. 2' (= 'Fosteri') is thus far the most widely used cultivar of *I. ×attenuata*, with spiny, dark green foliage and red berries, growing vigorously to 6 m/20 ft tall.

'Foster No. 4' is a male (nonfruiting) form, similar to 'Foster No. 2' in size and shape and used primarily as a pollinator for that and other *I. ×attenuata* cultivars.

'Savannah' has spiny, lighter green foliage and heavy crops of berries.

Related Species

Ilex myrtifolia 6 (synonym: *I. cassine* var. *myrtifolia*).   This species has very small (to 4cm/1.6 in), dark green leaves; otherwise, it is similar to *I. cassine*.

Ilex cornuta 5–6

CHINESE HOLLY
Evergreen shrub
Aquifoliaceae (Holly Family)

Native Range. Eastern China.

Useful Range. USDA Zones 7a–9a+, with selection of appropriate cultivars.

Function. Specimen, screen, massing.

Size and Habit. 'Burfordii' is illustrated.

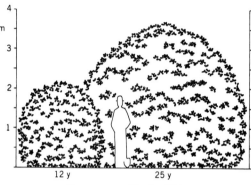

Ilex cornuta 'Burfordii.'

Adaptability. This shrub grows well in full sun to half shade, but for best fruiting (female plants) full sun is best.

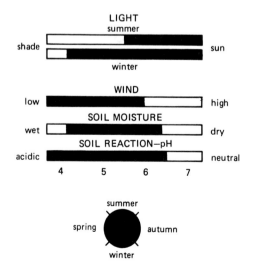

Seasonal Interest. *Flowers:* Small, white, dioecious, insignificant in the landscape. *Foliage:*

Handsome, evergreen leaves, with few large, spined lobes (or none in cultivars), easily recognized by the downturned spines at the ends of the leaves. *Fruits:* Bright red berries (on females) are colorful well into winter, occasionally until spring in the South. Through parthenocarpy, fruits appear on female plants without benefit of pollination, so it is not necessary to include males in the same planting.

Problems and Maintenance. The most serious problem is scale insects, which can be controlled with carefully timed sprays. Because of the vigor of this species, occasional pruning may be necessary to keep it within bounds. When this is the case, avoid shearing, since this removes newly formed fruits and reduces future color as well as losing the form of the plant. Prune by cutting out individual branches selectively as necessary. Soil fertility must be maintained for heavy annual fruiting.

Ilex cornuta 'Dwarf Burford.'

Cultivars. 'Avery Island' has deep green foliage and yellow berries.

'Berries Jubilee' is slow-growing, reminiscent of 'Rotunda' as it makes a dense mound 1–1.5 m/3.3–5 ft high and wide with very large, spiny, glossy green leaves, but it differs from the male 'Rotunda' in bearing very large red berries, even as a young plant.

'Burfordii' (Burford holly) is the best known of all *I. cornuta* cultivars, introduced in 1934. It is vigorous, upright and full, reaching heights of

3–5 m/10–16 ft in less than 20 years. Unlike the species type, each leaf has only a single terminal spine and a distinctly convex upper surface. This selection bears very heavy crops of red berries, and is useful in Zones 7a–9a.

'Carissa' is a dwarf male clone that grows to a height of 1 m/3.3 ft and spread of 1.5 m/5 ft only after many years.

'Dazzler' is a compact, upright shrub, to 3 m/ 10 ft, with spiny, rich glossy green foliage and an outstanding display of large red fruits.

'D'Or' is similar in size to the species type of *I. cornuta* but bears bright yellow berries, which are displayed handsomely against the dark green foliage.

'Dwarf Burford' (= 'Burfordii Compacta') is full and compact, reaching heights of 2 m/6.6 ft only after many years. It can be kept below eye level indefinitely with pruning, but this reduces the quantity of dark red fruits.

'Needlepoint' (= 'Aniset Delcambre') is similar to 'Burfordii' and 'Dwarf Burford,' but with somewhat narrower, slightly twisted leaves.

'Rotunda' is a slow-growing, compact male form with typically spiny foliage, making a dense globe or mound that remains below eye level for

Ilex cornuta 'Rotunda.'

several years, but eventually reaching a height of at least 2 m/6.6 ft. Pruning should be avoided for the sake of the character of the plant.

Related Hybrids

Ilex cornuta × *I. ciliospinosa* 5–6.   This series of cultivars was developed at the U.S. National Arboretum. These are not yet widely available but include the female clones 'Albert Close,' 'William Cowgill,' and 'Edward Goucher,' and the male clones 'Howard Dorsett' and 'Harry Gunning.'

Ilex cornuta × *I. pernyi* 5–6.   At least one clone, 'Doctor Kassab,' has resulted from this cross. This cultivar becomes densely pyramidal, 4.5–6 m/15–20 ft tall, with spiny dark green leaves and bright red berries.

Ilex cornuta 'Burfordii' ×, *I. pernyi*.   This cross has produced several cultivars, notable among them 'John T. Morris' and 'Lydia Morris,' male and female clones, respectively, introduced by the U.S. National Arboretum in 1961. Both are dense, conical plants reaching heights of 5 m/16 ft and 4 m/13 ft, respectively, in less than 25 years. Both have excellent foliage and are useful in Zones 6b–9a. 'Lydia Morris' has bright red fruits from autumn until midwinter.

Ilex cornuta 'Rotunda,' with *Pachysandra terminalis.*

Ilex crenata 3–5

JAPANESE OR BOX-LEAVED HOLLY
Evergreen shrub
Aquifoliaceae (Holly Family)

Native Range.   Japan.

Useful Range.   USDA Zones 6a–9a, with appropriate site, culture, and selection of cultivars (see Adaptability and Problems and Maintenance).

Function. Specimen, hedge, border, rock garden.

Size and Habit

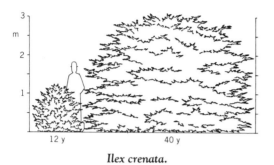

Ilex crenata.

Adaptability. This shrub is best in full sun in the North and tolerant of partial shade as well, but it performs best in partial shade in summer in Zones 8 and 9. Protection from winter wind is important in Zone 6.

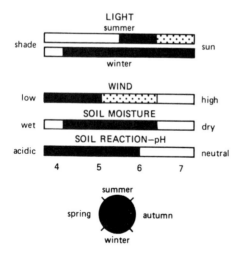

Seasonal Interest. *Flowers:* Small, white, dioecious, insignificant in the landscape. *Foliage:* Glossy, bright to deep green, leathery, evergreen leaves, to 3 cm/1.2 in. long with indefinitely toothed margins, some cultivars with convex-rounded upper surfaces. *Fruits:* Small black berries (on females), with little landscape interest.

Problems and Maintenance. Mite infestations can be troublesome, especially in areas having

hot, dry summers. Because of this and a limited tolerance of summer heat and dryness, *I. crenata* is best reserved for areas where summers are less extreme or else grown with some shade and irrigation as necessary. In poor soil, annual fertilization is helpful. The roots of most *Ilex* species are very susceptible to freezing injury. Those such as *I. crenata* that are grown in Zones 6 and 7a should be protected from root killing in severe winters by mulching, because soil temperatures as high as −5°C to −7°C (20° to 23°F) are low enough to cause damage.

Cultivars. A large number of variants exist, but most of the basic forms available can be summarized by the following cultivars.

'Allen Seay' has upright form and very dark green foliage, similar to that of 'Microphylla' in texture. It proved to be one of the most cold-hardy cultivars at Bernheim Forest after severe winters in the mid-1980s.

'Beehive' is a dwarf, formally rounded, male selection from Rutgers University, slightly wider than high, with lustrous bright green foliage.

'Compacta' has dark green, only slightly convex leaves and compact growth habit. It usually functions below 1 m/3.3 ft but will grow much taller in time.

'Convexa' (= 'Bullata,' convexleaf Japanese holly) has strongly convex upper leaf surfaces giving distinctive texture as each leaf is highlighted from any perspective. Usually functions below or slightly above 1 m/3.3 ft but will grow to at least twice that height and at least half again as wide in time. Cold-hardy to Zone 6b, 6a with protection.

'Dwarf Pagoda' is extremely dwarf, with

Ilex crenata 'Convexa.'

closely packed foliage, of value for bonsai treatment or very-small-scale sites.

'Glory' is similar to 'Convexa' in form and growth rate, but with smaller, flatter leaves, making a dense, broad mound to 1 m/3.3 ft, or more in time. This cultivar survived extreme winters at Bernheim Forest in the mid-1980s without injury, while several standard cultivars, including 'Convexa' and 'Rotundifolia,' were badly damaged.

'Golden Gem' is a compact male form with golden yellow new foliage, especially in full sun.

'Green Dragon' is a dwarf selection from Rutgers University, for dark green, clustered leaves and picturesquely twisted branches, useful for bonsai treatment or small-scale accent.

'Green Lustre' is compact female form with lustrous dark green foliage, making a broad mound to 0.8 m/2.6 ft tall and about 1 m/3.3 ft wide.

'Helleri' is moundlike and compact with very small leaves, taking many years to exceed 1 m/3.3 ft in height. Its form is twiggy and interesting, making it a choice landscape plant. It is cold-hardy to Zone 6a.

'Hetzi' is very similar to 'Convexa' except with larger leaves and faster growth, reaching a height of 1 m/3.3 ft almost as rapidly as 'Rotundifolia.' Cold-hardy to Zone 6b.

'Ivory Tower' is a slow-growing, upright form with ivory fruits.

'Latifolia' (= 'Fortunei') is a vigorous, fast-growing selection with relatively large leaves, reaching heights of 3–5 m/10–16 ft in 10 to 15 years. It is an excellent plant for hedges and massing, cold-hardy to Zone 6b.

'Microphylla' has leaves almost as small as those of 'Helleri,' but is vigorous, growing almost

Ilex crenata 'Stokesii.'

as fast as 'Latifolia.' It is stiffly upright and picturesque when left unpruned.

'Rotundifolia' is little if any different from 'Latifolia' and can be considered interchangeable in landscape use.

'Sky Pencil' is very narrowly and tightly columnar, with height: width ratio of about 5:1, making a strong vertical accent.

'Stokesii' is comparable to 'Helleri' in form and growth rate and is among the hardiest cultivars of *I. crenata*.

Related Species

Ilex sugerokii 5 (Sugeroki holly). This native of China and Japan has handsome leaves to 4 cm/1.6 in. long, red berries (on female plants), and is useful in Zones 7b–9a but not generally available.

Ilex yunnanensis 5 (Yunnan holly). This native of western China resembles *I. crenata* except in its pyramidal habit and red berries (on female plants) and is useful in Zones 6b–9a, but probably not commercially available.

Ilex decidua 6

POSSUM HAW
Deciduous shrub
Aquifoliaceae (Holly Family)

Native Range. Southeastern and south-central United States.

Useful Range. USDA Zones 5b–9a+.

Function. Border, screen, massing, hedge, naturalizing.

Size and Habit

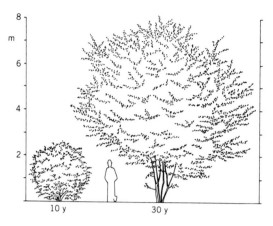

Ilex decidua.

Adaptability

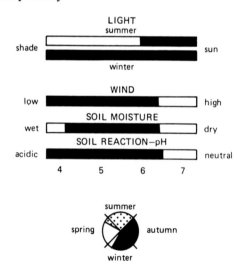

Seasonal Interest. *Flowers:* Small, white, dioecious, insignificant in the landscape. *Foliage:* Lustrous, medium green, deciduous in late autumn with little color change. *Fruits:* Red to orange-red berries (on female plants), to 0.8 cm/ 0.3 in. across, borne in great numbers on some plants and remaining colorful late, often all winter. Occasional male plants are needed for pollination and fruiting effectiveness of females. *Twigs and branches:* Light gray, contrasting well with berries.

Problems and Maintenance. This shrub is relatively trouble-free and requires little or no maintenance other than pruning for fullness when used as a hedge or for screening.

Cultivars. Several cultivars have been selected for superior form and fruiting, and at least one for use as a pollinator. 'Byers Golden' has golden yellow fruit. 'Council Fire' is rounded in form, with smaller and darker red fruits than most other cultivars and narrow leaves that persist later. 'Pocahontas' is more upright in growth, with glossy bright red fruits. 'Red Cascade' is broadly rounded in form, with quantities of large, glossy red fruits that persist throughout the winter. 'Sentry' is tall and unusually narrow in form, with red fruits. 'Warren's Red' is upright when young, rounded later, with great quantities of glossy red fruits, and silvery bark. *Pollination:* All of the above can be pollinated by the male *I. decidua* cultivar, 'Red Escort' or by any male clone of this species or *I. opaca* that flowers concurrently.

Related Species

Ilex ambigua 6 (synonym: *I. montana;* mountain holly or mountain winterberry). This is a tall, sparse shrub or small tree native to the Appalachian Mountains from Massachusetts to Alabama. Not often available, but of some landscape interest near its native habitat.

Ilex longipes 6 (synonym: *I. decidua* var. *longipes;* Georgia haw). This species differs little from *I. decidua,* except that its berries are borne on stalks to 2 cm/0.8 in. long, and it is less tolerant of wet soils. It is seldom available commercially but may be encountered and preserved in the development of wild areas.

Nemopanthus mucronatus 5 (mountain holly, catberry). This thicket-forming shrub, growing above eye level, is a close relative of the true hollies, native to the northeastern United States and adjacent Canada to Newfoundland. With dull red berries in summer, it is not of great landscape value, but it is useful in natural and naturalistic landscapes within the native range in Zones 4b–6a.

Ilex glabra 5

INKBERRY, GALLBERRY
Evergreen shrub
Aquifoliaceae (Holly Family)

Native Range.   Eastern coastal United States and northward to Nova Scotia.

Useful Range.   USDA Zones 5a–9a with selection of appropriate genetic material.

Function.   Border, hedge, massing.

Size and Habit

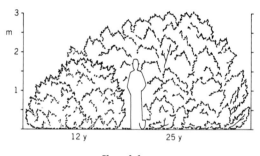

Ilex glabra.

Adaptability.   This shrub is well adapted to seashore planting and relatively tolerant of de-icing salt.

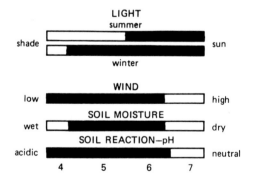

Seasonal Interest.   *Flowers:* Small, white, dioecious, insignificant in the landscape. *Foliage:* Evergreen, lustrous, flat leaves are small (2.5–5 cm/1–2 in.), not spiny, and have only a few teeth toward the apex. *Fruits:* Small black berries (on females), interesting but not a significant landscape feature except in the white variants (see Cultivars).

Problems and Maintenance.   This shrub usually is trouble-free, but mites can be a problem in dry sites. It needs pruning for fullness in hedging or screening and responds well to shearing into hedge form.

Ilex glabra.

Cultivars.   'Compacta', 'Densa', 'Green Magic,' 'Chamzin' (Nordic®, Plant Patent No. 6962, 1989), and 'Shamrock' are similarly compact forms of this species, equivalent to each other in landscape. 'Ivory Queen' and f. *leucocarpa* are selections for ivory fruits.

Ilex latifolia 6–7

LUSTERLEAF HOLLY
Evergreen shrub
Aquifoliaceae (Holly Family)

Native Range. Japan

Useful Range. USDA Zones 8a–9a+.

Function. Screen, specimen.

Size and Habit

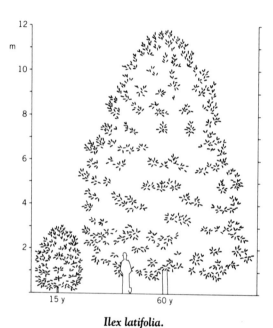

Ilex latifolia.

Adaptability. Unlike most hollies, this species requires light shade for best growth. It is less tolerant of poor, dry soil than most hollies.

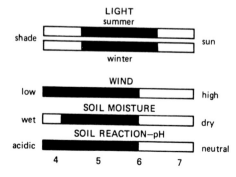

Seasonal Interest. *Flowers:* Small, white, dioecious, insignificant in the landscape. *Foliage:* Handsome, leathery leaves, 18 cm/7 in. long, finely toothed but not lobed or sharp-spined. *Fruits:* Red berries in clusters, showy in autumn, but not as striking as the fruits of some other hollies.

Ilex latifolia.

Problems and Maintenance. Scale insect infestations can be troublesome but are controlled with carefully timed sprays.

Hybrids. A few hybrids are available, including the following. 'Emily Bruner,' of uncertain parentage, may be a hybrid of *I. latifolia,* with large, glossy dark green, coarsely toothed leaves and bright red berries, growing into a very large pyramidal shrub or small tree (to 6 m/20 ft tall).

'Kurly-Koe,' believed to be a hybrid of *I. latifolia,* has very large leaves (to 25 cm/10 in. long) and red berries, eventually becoming a large, upright shrub or small tree.

'Lib's Favorite,' a hybrid of *I. latifolia* × *I. cornuta,* has large leaves and very large clusters of bright red berries.

'Mary Nell,' a hybrid of (*I. cornuta* × *I. pernyi*) × *I. latifolia,* becomes an impressive pyramidal tree to at least 4.5 m/15 ft, with dark green, spiny foliage and masses of bright red berries.

Related Species and Hybrids

Ilex fargesii 6.   This species from western China has long (6–12 cm/2.4–4.8 in.), narrow leaves with fine teeth toward the apex and fruiting interest (on females) similar to that of *I. latifolia*. It is useful in the same range as *I. latifolia*.

Ilex integra 6 (mochi tree).   This shrub or small tree from Japan, to 6 m/20 ft, has moderately large leaves (5–10 cm/2–4 in.), seldom with teeth or spines, and large red fruits (on females). It is useful in the same range as *I. latifolia*.

Ilex ×koehneana 7.   This supposed hybrid between *I. aquifolium* and *I. latifolia* becomes a large tree, eventually at least 15 m/49 ft tall, but functions in smaller size for a considerable time. Its leaves are large, leathery, and densely spiny toothed like those of *I. latifolia*.

Ilex ×meserveae 4–5

MESERVE OR BLUE HOLLY
Evergreen shrub
Aquifoliaceae (Holly Family)

Hybrid origin.   *Ilex rugosa* × *I. aquifolium*.

Useful Range.   USDA Zones 5a–8a and perhaps colder and milder zones as well with further trial.

Function.   Specimen, foundation, massing.

Size and Habit

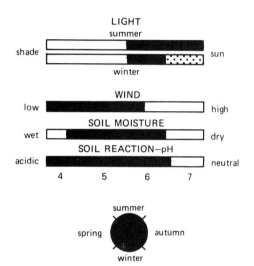

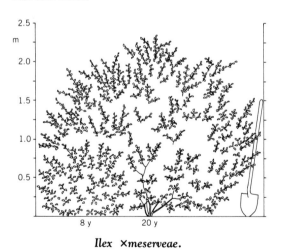

Ilex ×meserveae.

Adaptability.   Grows well in full sun to half shade in summer; but for best fruiting (female cultivars) and most compact growth, full sun is best. At the northern extremes of the useful range (not well known, but probably in Zone 5), light shade will reduce winterburn of foliage.

Seasonal Interest.   *Flowers:* Small, white, dioecious, insignificant in the landscape. *Foliage:* Spiny evergreen leaves are deep, glossy blue-green, purpling slightly in winter, borne on bluish purple stems. *Fruits:* Small, to 0.8 cm/0.3 in., bright red and shiny (on females). Because of the dioecious condition, an occasional male must be present within about 100 meters (about 300 ft) for reliable pollination.

Problems and Maintenance.   Limited experience to date shows this species to be among the most trouble-free of evergreen hollies, and little or no maintenance other than mulching should be needed. Pruning normally is not necessary.

Cultivars.   The following cultivars have been introduced, and more may follow.
'Blue Boy' and 'Blue Girl,' male and female respectively, were the first two selections to be

named (1964), both growing to about 1 m/3.3 ft, with irregular upright habit. Even though they have been superseded by newer cultivars (below), they are still quite popular in commerce.

'Blue Prince,' introduced in 1972, quickly developed a reputation as a highly effective pollinator, not just for other *I.* ×*meserveae* selections but for many other hollies as well. It also grows taller than 'Blue Boy,' to about 3.6 m/12 ft tall and 2.4 m/8 ft wide, with a broad upright shape that can easily be modified by pruning, and cold-hardiness to Zone 5b.

'Blue Princess' and 'Blue Angel' were introduced in 1973 as replacements for 'Blue Girl.' 'Blue Princess' develops about the same size and shape as 'Blue Prince,' setting fruit abundantly, and it is cold-hardy to Zone 5b. 'Blue Angel' was developed by back-crossing *I.* ×*meserveae* with *I. aquifolium* and shows the dominant influence of the more tender *I. aquifolium* in its larger leaves and reduced cold-hardiness (to Zone 7a, perhaps also 6b). It is similar to 'Blue Princess' in shape, but smaller (to 2 m/6.6 ft).

'Mesid' (Blue Maid®; Plant Patent No. 4685, 1981) and 'Mesan' (Blue Stallion®, Plant Patent No. 4804, 1982) are more recent introductions. Blue Maid® is similar to 'Blue Princess' in overall size, but has a more moundlike to pyramidal form. It is also more cold-hardy than the other Meserve hollies, reportedly to Zone 5a and perhaps even 4b. Blue Stallion® is another good pollinator and the most vigorous of the Meserve holly cultivars, to 4.5 m/15 ft tall and 3.6 m/12 ft wide, and cold-hardy to Zone 6a, perhaps also 5b.

'Mesgolg' (Golden Girl®, Plant Patent No. 7652, 1991) has the general habit of Blue Maid® but is more vigorous, as large as Blue Stallion® but with more rounded to pyramidal form, and it bears large quantities of golden yellow fruits.

Related Hybrids. At about the same time Blue Stallion® was introduced, two hybrids of *I. cornuta* × *I. rugosa* were released, with the expectation that they would prove more heat-tolerant than the Meserve hollies. While this seems to be true, these so-called China Hybrids are also proving notably more cold-hardy, to Zone 5a and perhaps Zone 4b.

'Mesdob' (China Boy® Plant Patent No. 4803, 1982) is fast-growing and vigorous, with lustrous foliage, and will pollinate China Girl®, although that may not be necessary if China Girl® proves to set fruit without pollination (parthenocarpy) as reliably as many *I. cornuta* cultivars.

'Mesog' (China Girl®; Plant Patent No. 4878, 1982). This selection has the same rounded habit as China Boy®, with great masses of bright red fruits. Its foliage is lustrous and rich green but not quite up to the standard of China Boy®. China Girl® has been suggested as a landscape substitute for yews, which may be appropriate for sunny sites, but this plant is not shade-tolerant enough to be successful in all sites where yews grow well.

Related Species

Ilex rugosa 3 (prostrate or Tsuru holly).   This species from northern Japan and Sakhalin is one of the hardiest of evergreen holly species. Plants are low and spreading with wrinkled, leathery, evergreen leaves to 5 cm/2 in. long, spineless and barely toothed. Although it is best known as the parent of *I.* ×*meserveae* and the China Hybrids, it is a useful landscape plant in its own right in Zones 4a–7a, but it is little known and seldom available at present.

Ilex rugosa.

Ilex opaca 7

AMERICAN HOLLY
Evergreen shrub or tree
Aquifoliaceae (Holly Family)

Native Range.   Eastern United States.

Useful Range.   USDA Zones 6a–9a, but the same cultivars do not grow well at both range extremes.

Function.   Specimen, screen, hedge.

Size and Habit

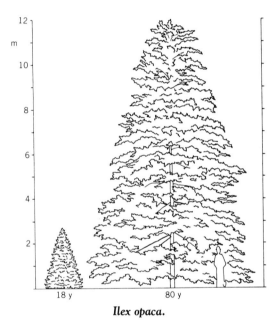

Ilex opaca.

Adaptability.   Grows well in full sun to half shade in summer, but for heavy fruiting (female plants) and most compact growth, full sun is best. At the northern extremes of the useful range light shade may reduce winterburn of foliage.

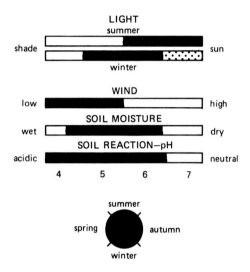

Seasonal Interest.   *Flowers:* Small, white dioecious, insignificant in the landscape. *Foliage:* Evergreen, spiny leaves are dull or lustrous, depending on cultivar. *Fruits:* Bright red berries (on females) are colorful in fall and early winter, throughout winter in certain cultivars. For best fruiting, occasional male plants should be nearby (within a few hundred feet) to serve as pollinators.

Ilex opaca.

Problems and Maintenance.   The most serious insect pest of *I. opaca,* leaf miner, can be controlled with carefully timed sprays; so can occasional scale infestations. Leaf-spot diseases are also troublesome. Some, primarily tar-spot disease in the South, are caused by fungi. Spinespot is simply damage from spines of one leaf blowing against the surface of another leaf. Purple blotch seriously disfigures foliage of some plants and is considered a physiological disorder, the cause of which is as yet unknown. It can be avoided by careful selection of cultivars.

Cultivars.   At least 300 cultivars exist in arboreta and plant collections, but probably only about 50 are available in any commercial sense. A few of those are listed here.

Cultivars selected for superior red fruiting display as well as good foliage include 'Cardinal,' 'Cave Hill No. 1,' 'Croonenberg,' (with both male and female flowers, so it may not need a male pollinator), 'Cumberland,' 'Dan Fenton,' (with dark green, glossy leaves), 'Diane' (with orange-red berries), 'Farage,' 'Greenleaf,' 'Jersey Delight' (which is exceptionally showy in fruit), 'Jersey Princess,' 'Judge Brown,' 'Klein's No. 1,' 'Merry Christmas,' 'Miss Helen' (with glossy dark red berries), 'Old Heavy Berry' (which is especially vigorous, hardy, and heavily fruiting), 'Peace,' 'Secrest,' and 'Wayside's Christmas Tree.'

The f. *xanthocarpa* includes those cultivars that have yellow berries. Cultivars selected primarily for the quantity and showiness of their yellow fruit are 'Arden' (with yellow fruit at first, gradually turning to deep red), 'Callaway,' 'Canary' (with light canary yellow berries), 'Cecil Yellow' (with golden yellow berries), 'Fallaw,' 'Fruitland,' 'Galleon Gold' (with golden yellow berries), 'Goldie,' 'Longwood Gardens' (with golden yellow berries), 'Morris Arboretum' (with saffron yellow berries), and 'Princeton Gold' (with golden yellow berries, hardy to Zone 6a and perhaps 5b).

Just about any male plant of *I. opaca* can be used as a pollinator and kept in the background if it lacks elegance itself, but a few male cultivars have been introduced which are not only good pollinators but also handsome in their own right. These include 'Jersey Knight,' 'Leatherleaf,' and 'Warrior.'

Ilex pedunculosa.

A few American holly cultivars are used for their uniqueness in size, habit, or foliage, including 'Hickman' (a male clone with rather narrow leaves, providing interesting texture), 'Maryland Dwarf' (a low, spreading form that makes a mound under 1 m/3.3 ft high and twice as wide), 'Nelson West' (an upright male clone with very narrow leaves, producing a lacy effect), and 'St. Mary' (very dwarf but fruiting heavily and sometimes used as a Christmas potted plant).

Ilex pedunculosa.

Related Species

Ilex pedunculosa 6 (longstalk holly).   This large Japanese species is densely to loosely pyramidal in habit, reaching heights of 4–6 m/13–20 ft or more, with pointed leaves, 3–7 cm/1.2–2.8 in. long, without teeth or spines. Bright red berries are borne on stalks, 2–4 cm/0.8–1.6 in. long, giving a different fruiting effect than that of other hollies. This is one of the hardiest of the evergreen hollies, useful in Zones 6a–9a and perhaps protected sites in Zone 5b.

Ilex pernyi 6

PERNY HOLLY
Evergreen shrub
Aquifoliaceae (Holly Family)

Native Range.   China.

Useful Range.   USDA Zones 7a–9a.

Function.   Specimen, border. Upright, often sparse growth gives the plant distinctive character but eliminates it for screening use.

Size and Habit

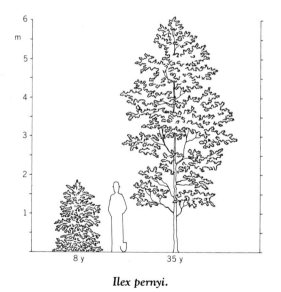

Ilex pernyi.

Adaptability.   This shrub grows well in full sun to half shade, but for best fruiting (female plants), full sun is best.

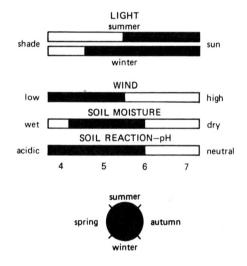

Seasonal Interest.   *Flowers:* Small, white, dioecious, insignificant in the landscape. *Foliage:* Relatively spiny, evergreen leaves borne close to the sparsely branching stems. *Fruits:* Small, bright red berries (on females) in clusters, showy in autumn and early winter. Occasional male plants must be located nearby for pollination to have a significant show of fruits.

Problems and Maintenance.   This plant is relatively trouble-free and requires little maintenance, although light pruning for shaping may be desirable in some situations.

Hybrids.   See under *Ilex aquifolium, I. ×aquipernyi,* and *I. cornuta.*

Related Variety and Species

Ilex pernyi var. *veitchii* 6 (Veitch holly). This variety differs from *I. pernyi* var. *pernyi* in having larger leaves with 9–11 spines rather than the 3–7 typical of var. *pernyi*. Although it is available, some plants sold under the name *I. pernyi* var. *veitchii* probably are not truly of this species. The form most commonly available is male.

Ilex ciliospinosa 6. Closely related to *I. pernyi*, this species is more shrubby and compact but eventually reaches heights of 4 m/13 ft and taller.

Both *I. ciliospinosa* and *I. pernyi* are better known for their hybrids with *I. aquifolium* and *I. cornuta* than for themselves.

Ilex verticillata 4–5

WINTERBERRY, BLACK ALDER
Deciduous shrub
Aquifoliaceae (Holly Family)

Native Range. Eastern North America.

Useful Range. USDA Zones 4a–9a with selection of appropriate genetic material.

Function. Border, screen, massing, stream banks (forms thickets).

Size and Habit

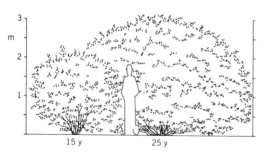

Ilex verticillata.

Adaptability

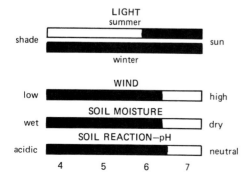

Seasonal Interest. *Flowers:* Small, white, dioecious, insignificant in the landscape. *Foliage:* Pale to rich green, turning yellowish and blackening in early autumn, then falling early. *Fruits:* Bright red and glossy, borne close to the twigs, adding striking interest (to female plants) in late autumn and early winter. Occasional males are needed for pollination and fruiting effectiveness of females. *Twigs and branches:* Dark gray or brown in winter.

Problems and Maintenance. Foliage is frequently affected by leaf spots and mildew, but it is seldom completely disfigured. Susceptibility varies considerably from plant to plant. Otherwise, this shrub is relatively trouble-free.

Cultivars and Hybrids. Many selections for colorful and long-lasting berries as well as superior foliage have been made from *I. verticillata*, and a few others have been made from hybrids of *I. serrata* × *I. verticillata*. Some of the best known are listed here, along with male cultivars that flower at the same time, so they are effective pollinators. (Information on pollination provided by Robert C. Simpson, Vincennes, Indiana.)

'Afterglow' is a low-growing selection (1–1.8 m/3.3–6 ft) with moundlike habit and large orange-red fruit. Pollinated by 'Jim Dandy.'

'Apollo' is a hybrid male (*I. serrata* × *I. verticillata*), selected by the U.S. National Arboretum as a pollinator for their hybrid introduction, 'Sparkleberry.' It also pollinates at least two other cultivars of the same hybrid parentage, 'Bonfire' and 'Harvest Red.'

'Aurantiaca' is low-growing selection (1–1.5 m/3.3–5 ft) with fruit that first turns red, then yellow-orange. Pollinated by 'Jim Dandy.'

'Bonfire' is a hybrid selection (*I. serrata* × *I. verticillata*) of large size (to 3.5–4.5 m/12–15 ft tall) with great quantities of small red fruits. Pollinated by 'Apollo,' 'Country Gentleman,' and 'Raritan Chief.'

'Cacapon' is similar to 'Afterglow' in size but more upright in form, with good foliage and abundant red fruits. Pollinated by 'Jim Dandy.'

'Christmas Cheer' is a recent selection for abundant red fruits. Pollinated by 'Jim Dandy.'

'Harvest Red' is a hybrid selection (*I. serrata* × *I. verticillata*) of medium size (2–3 m/6.6–8 ft tall and equally wide) has excellent foliage that turns deep red-purple in autumn, along with heavy crops of very persistent red berries. Pollinated by 'Apollo,' 'Jim Dandy,' and 'Raritan Chief.'

'Jim Dandy' (= 'Dwarf Male') is a low-growing male selection useful for pollinating several early flowering cultivars of northern origin, as shown in this list.

'Raritan Chief' is a hybrid male selection (*I. serrata* × *I. verticillata*), an effective pollinator for 'Bonfire,' 'Harvest Red,' and 'Sparkleberry.'

'Red Sprite' (= 'Nana') is the smallest *I. verticillata* selection (0.6–1.2 m/2–4 ft tall and wider than tall). It has rather dull foliage but bears quantities of very large fruits (to 1.3 cm/0.5 in), probably the largest of any cultivar. Pollinated by 'Apollo' and 'Jim Dandy.'

'Shaver' is a compact, upright selection (1–1.8 m/3.3–6 ft tall) with very large orange-red berries and glossy foliage. Pollinated by Jim Dandy.

'Southern Gentleman' (= 'Early Male') is a low-growing male selection (1–1.8 m/3.3–6 ft tall) useful for pollinating several late-flowering cultivars of southern origin, as shown in this list.

This and the cultivars it pollinates are probably useful northward to Zone 5a, perhaps parts of Zone 4b.

'Sparkleberry' is another hybrid (*I. serrata* × *I. verticillata*) selected at the U.S. National Arboretum. It is upright, vigorous, and spectacular in fruit, but not yet widely available. Pollinated by 'Apollo' and 'Raritan Chief.'

'Stoplight' (= 'Hopperton') is a recent, promising selection with very large, glossy deep red berries. Pollinated by Jim Dandy.

'Sunset' is a vigorous, spreading selection of medium size (2 m/6.6 ft tall) with large, persistent bright red berries. Pollinated by 'Southern Gentleman.'

'Winter Gold' is very much like 'Winter Red' (below) except that it has gold to orange-pink berries. Pollinated by 'Southern Gentleman.'

'Winter Red' is a vigorous, tall-growing selection (2–2.7 m/6.6–9 ft tall) with large, persistent, bright red berries that persist well into winter. This is probably the most popular deciduous holly cultivar at this writing. Pollinated by 'Southern Gentleman.'

Related Species

Ilex laevigata 5 (smooth winterberry).   This species differs from *I. verticillata* in having slightly larger, orange-red berries, forming in considerable numbers through parthenocarpy (without fertilization or development of seeds). It is useful in Zones 4b–7b and perhaps farther southward but seldom available commercially. The f. *herveyi* has yellow berries.

Ilex serrata 5 (Japanese winterberry or finetooth holly).   This is the Asian counterpart of *I. verticillata* and differs from that species in having slightly smaller berries that ripen earlier in autumn and sometimes are taken quickly by birds and in being less cold-hardy. It is useful in Zones 6a–9a and perhaps in somewhat colder zones. White- and yellow-fruited forms, f. *leucocarpa* and f. *xanthocarpa*, are seldom available.

Ilex vomitoria 6

YAUPON
Evergreen shrub
Aquifoliaceae (Holly Family)

Native Range.   Southern United States.

Useful Range.   USDA Zones 8b–9a+ in tree form; 7b–9a+ as a shrub.

Function.   Specimen, massing, hedge.

Size and Habit

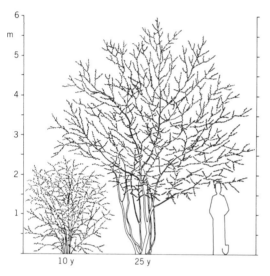

Ilex vomitoria.

Adaptability.   This species is especially well adapted to seashore planting and is better adapted to wind and hot climates than most evergreen hollies.

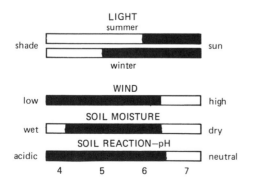

Seasonal Interest.   *Flowers:* Small, white, dioecious, insignificant in the landscape. *Foliage:* Evergreen and lustrous, medium to gray-green leaves averaging about 2.5 cm/1 in. long, arranged sparsely on the stems. *Fruits:* small (to 0.6 cm/0.25 in.) berries in clusters, borne in very large numbers (on female plants). An occasional nearby male pollinator is necessary for heavy fruiting.

Problems and Maintenance.   Leaf miner infestations occasionally can be a problem, especially to the selection 'Nana,' and mites can be troublesome in dry sites. Regular pruning is necessary when this plant is to be used as a hedge or in other situations where fullness of form is desired.

Cultivars and Forms.   'Nana' (= 'Compacta'; dwarf yaupon) is a female clone with dark green foliage and compact, moundlike form, usually remaining below 1 m/3.3 ft for many years, but sometimes becoming twice that height and very broad. Popular in the South as a low hedge or edging plant, it is useful in Zones 7b–9a+, but it is thoroughly confused in commerce with 'Schilling's Dwarf' (= 'Stokes Dwarf') and other dwarf selections. 'Schilling's Dwarf' is a male selection, similar in form to 'Nana' but some-

Ilex vomitoria '**Nana.**'

what smaller, about 0.6 m/2 ft tall and 1.2 m/4 ft wide.

The f. *pendula* (weeping yaupon) is a strongly pendulous tree form of striking habit. Several cultivars have been selected, including 'Folsom Weeping' and 'Grey's Littleleaf' (= 'Grey's Weeping'). These are useful in Zones 8b–9a+ but are questionable in colder zones except in sheltered sites.

'Pride of Houston' is similar in size and form to the species type, but superior in form, foliage, and fruiting.

Illicium anisatum 6

JAPANESE ANISE TREE
Evergreen shrub
Illiciaceae (Illicium Family)

Native Range.   Japan and southern Korea.

Useful Range.   USDA Zones 8a–9a+.

Function.   Screen, massing, specimen.

Size and Habit

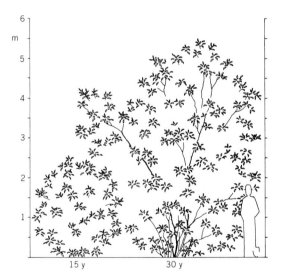

Illicium anisatum.

Adaptability

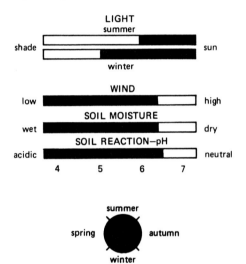

Seasonal Interest.   *Flowers:* Fragrant, white to yellow, to 4 cm/1.6 in. across in late spring. *Fruits:* Flattened terminal capsules, rarely produced in cultivation in North America. *Foliage:* Evergreen, smooth, lustrous, leathery, olive green, and dense, making the plant effective as a screen. Leaves are pleasantly aromatic when crushed and as much as 10 cm/4 in. long.

Problems and Maintenance.   This species seems to be free of trouble and requires no maintenance other than occasional pruning for shaping when desirable, but even this is seldom necessary.

Related Species

Illicium floridanum 4–5 (Florida anise tree). This shrub seldom exceeds 3 m/10 ft in height,

Illicium anisatum.

Illicium parviflorum.

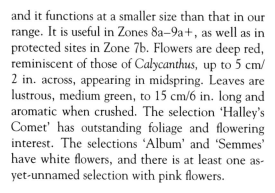

Illicium parviflorum.

and it functions at a smaller size than that in our range. It is useful in Zones 8a–9a+, as well as in protected sites in Zone 7b. Flowers are deep red, reminiscent of those of *Calycanthus*, up to 5 cm/ 2 in. across, appearing in midspring. Leaves are lustrous, medium green, to 15 cm/6 in. long and aromatic when crushed. The selection 'Halley's Comet' has outstanding foliage and flowering interest. The selections 'Album' and 'Semmes' have white flowers, and there is at least one as-yet-unnamed selection with pink flowers.

Illicium parviflorum 5 (Ocala anise).   This native of northern Florida is intermediate in size between *I. anisatum* and *I. floridanum*, with highly fragrant, creamy to yellowish starlike flowers and smooth but not shiny, flattened leaves, borne semierect at narrow angles with the stems. The interesting texture and fullness of the foliage makes this species a welcome addition to the list of evergreen shrubs for the Deep South—that is, Zones 8b–9a+.

Other species of *Illicium*, not usually available at this writing, include *I. mexicanum* 4–5 (Mexican anise tree), which is similar to *I. floridanum* but with slightly larger red flowers and perhaps less cold-hardy, and two Chinese species: *I. henryi* 5–6 (Chinese or Henry anise tree), a large shrub or small tree with pink flowers, useful in Zones 7b–9a+, and *I. lanceolata* 5–6 (lance-leaved anise tree), similar to *I. henryi* but with longer and much narrower leaves and perhaps slightly more cold-hardy (to Zone 7a).

Kadsura japonica 1 (scarlet kadsura).   This twining climber, to 4 m/13 ft, from Japan and Korea, a member of the Schisandraceae (Schisandra

Family), has leathery dark green leaves, 5–10 cm/2–4 in. long, semievergreen in Zones 7b–8 and evergreen in Zone 9a+, turning reddish in winter. Its unisexual flowers are fragrant but not showy. However, the bright scarlet fruits that follow, in clusters about 2.5 cm/1 in. across (on female plants), are very showy in autumn and early winter. At least one male plant should be included in any planting for pollination if fruiting is desired, not an easy thing to do since plants of this species are usually sold unsexed. This vigorous climber is useful for screening on fence or trellis support in Zones 7b–9a+, but seldom commercially available. The selection 'Variegatum,' with creamy yellow leaf margins, is also seldom available.

Schisandra chinensis 1 (Chinese magnolia vine). This deciduous vine from northeastern Asia was once classified in the Magnoliaceae (Magnolia Family), but now has been split off, with *Kadsura*, into the closely related Schisandraceae (Schisandra Family). It is noted for its small but fragrant, white to pale pink flowers in summer, and its autumn show of red fruits in drooping clusters to 10 cm/4 in. long, on female plants (with a male plant included in the planting for pollination). Useful in Zones 7–9a+, as well as in protected sites in Zone 6b.

Schisandra propinqua 1 (magnolia vine). This deciduous to semievergreen relative of *S. chi-* *nensis* from central China has orange flowers to 1.5 cm/0.6 in. across in summer, but its primary seasonal interest is its bright red berries, in drooping clusters to 15 cm/6 in. long on female plants in autumn. As with *S. chinensis* and *Kadsura*, occasional males must be included in the planting for pollination in order for fruits to be produced. Useful in Zones 8a–9a+, perhaps 7b in protected sites.

Indigofera kirilowii 3

KIRILOW INDIGO

Deciduous shrub or subshrub

Fabaceae (Leguminosae; Pea Family)

Native Range.　Northern China and Korea.

Useful Range.　USDA Zones 5a–7b.

Function.　Groundcover, massing.

Size and Habit

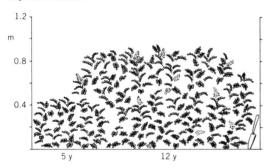

Indigofera kirilowii.

Adaptability

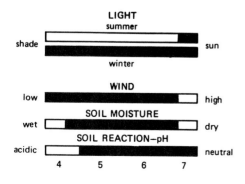

Seasonal Interest. *Flowers:* Small, purplish rose, in elongated clusters, 10–12 cm/4–5 in. long, in early summer. *Foliage:* Compound, of interesting texture.

Problems and Maintenance. Stems are winterkilled regularly in Zone 5, frequently in Zone 6, and occasionally farther south, and occasional pruning is necessary to remove dead twigs and avoid a ragged appearance. Since new growth and flowers return quickly in spring, plants can be pruned to a few inches from the ground in early spring, annually if desired. If allowed to grow unpruned in mild climates, this species may reach heights of 1 m/3.3 ft or more.

Related Species

Indigofera divaricata 3 (spreading indigo). This little-known plant from China and Japan is used in southern Louisiana as a tall, rather loose groundcover in partially shaded sites. Its regularly compound foliage provides a lacy appearance, and its flowers, in clusters similar to those of *I. kirilowii*, open intermittently during most of the growing season. Useful in Zone 9a+, this plant may be hardy in slightly colder zones as well.

Indigofera heterantha 3–5 (synonym: *I. gerardiana*; Himalayan indigo). This species from the northwestern Himalayas grows to 2.5 m/8 ft tall

Indigofera incarnata 'Alba.'

in Zones 8–9a+, but is kept lower by top-kill in cold areas—for example, 0.6–0.9 m/2–3 ft in Zone 6. It has bright green, compound leaves with many small leaflets, and rosy purple flowers in terminal clusters from midsummer through early autumn.

Indigofera decora 3 (=I. incarnata; Chinese indigo). This plant is slightly lower than *I. kirilowii* and more tender, regularly topkilling in winter, but useful in Zones 6a–8a. It is commercially available only as the white flowered form 'Alba,' flowering in midsummer.

Itea virginica 4–5

VIRGINIA SWEETSPIRE
Deciduous shrub
Glossulariaceae (Currant Family)

Native Range. Southeastern United States and north to New Jersey.

Useful Range. USDA Zones 6b–9a+.

Function. Naturalizing, border, specimen.

Size and Habit. The irregular habit of this shrub is best in naturalized situations. It remains mostly below 1 m/3.3 ft in height in northern zones and poor sites, but it can reach 3 m/10 ft in moist sites in the South.

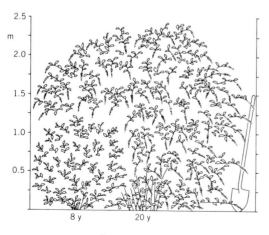

Itea virginica.

Adaptability. Performs best with at least light shade in areas having hot summers.

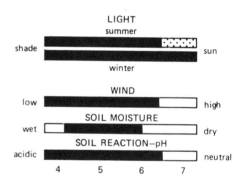

Seasonal Interest. *Flowers:* Fragrant, white, small, in upright to drooping spikes to 10–15 cm/4–6 in. long, attractive in late spring and early summer. *Foliage:* Dull green but turning bright red in autumn before falling.

Problems and Maintenance. This shrub is relatively trouble-free and requires little maintenance other than occasional pruning to maintain form when used as a specimen.

Cultivars. 'Henry's Garnet' is a popular compact selection for larger and more fragrant flowers and brilliant red autumn foliage. 'Longspire' has longer spikes of white flowers. 'Sarah Eve,' a Florida selection, has pink and white flowers and may prove to be less cold-hardy than more northern genetic material.

Related Species

Itea ilicifolia 4–5 (holly leaf sweetspire). This Chinese species, unlike *I. virginica,* is evergreen and useful only in the southern extremities of our area, perhaps no farther north than Zone 9a. As the name suggests, it has spiny toothed leaves to 8–10 cm/3–4 in. long and greenish white flowers in hanging clusters, 15–30 cm/6–12 in. long. This is a handsome landscape plant but little known and seldom commercially available in our area.

Itea japonica 5 (Japanese sweetspire). This large deciduous shrub is not greatly different from *I. virginica* in form and flowering interest, but

Itea virginica.

somewhat taller and usually with more subdued autumn foliage color. Reportedly useful in Zones 6b–9a+. The dwarf selection 'Beppu' grows to about 1 m/3.3 ft in height and has wine-red autumn foliage. It is reported as cold-hardy in Zone 6a, perhaps 5b.

Jasminum mesnyi 4

Synonym: *J. primulinum*
PRIMROSE JASMINE
Evergreen, scrambling shrub
Oleaceae (Olive Family)

Native Range. Western China.

Useful Range. USDA Zone 9a+, and Zone 8 with protection.

Function. Massing, bank cover, trailing over walls or fences, specimen.

Size and Habit. Branches trail to lengths of 2–3 m/6.6–10 ft if not pruned.

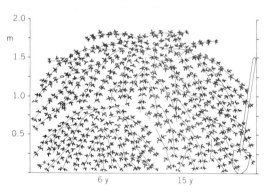

Jasminum mesnyi.

Adaptability

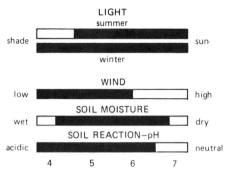

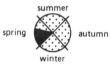

Jasminum floridum.

to the ground every year or by cutting the entire plant back in spring every four or five years.

Seasonal Interest.   *Flowers:* Soft yellow, large (to 4 cm/1.6 in. across), single to semidouble, mostly in spring but appearing occasionally at most other seasons. *Foliage:* Evergreen, trifoliolate leaflets to 8 cm/3 in. long.

Problems and Maintenance.   This plant is relatively trouble-free but requires pruning to maintain its graceful form—frequent pruning if it is to be kept in a restricted space. Shearing completely destroys its graceful landscape effect; prune by thinning out a few of the older branches

Related Species

Jasminum floridum 4 (flowering jasmine).   This species differs from *J. mesnyi* in its somewhat lower stature, greater cold-hardiness (Zones 7b–9a+), and smaller (to 1.3 cm/0.5 in.), fragrant, bright yellow flowers, borne in clusters of five and more in late spring and intermittently in summer. Like *J. mesnyi,* it is evergreen, but with finer-textured foliage, moundlike, and graceful in habit, and it may be trained as a scrambling climber over fences and walls.

Jasminum nudiflorum 4–5

WINTER JASMINE
Deciduous, scrambling shrub
Oleaceae (Olive Family)

Native Range.   China.

Useful Range.   USDA Zones 6b–9a+.

Function.   Massing, bank cover, trailing over walls or fences, specimen.

Size and Habit. Branches trail to lengths of 3–5 m/10–16 ft if not pruned.

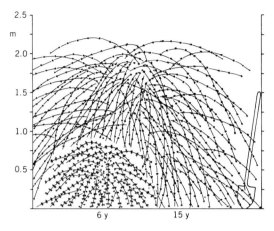

Jasminum nudiflorum.

Adaptability

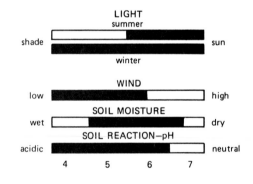

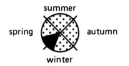

Seasonal Interest. *Flowers:* Fragrant, bright yellow, to 2.5 cm/1 in. across, in late winter on leafless stems resembling a rather sparse, early-flowering forsythia. Favored for forcing indoors. *Foliage:* Deciduous but remaining green well into autumn, trifoliolate with leaflets to 2.5 cm/1 in. long. *Twigs and branches:* Green, adding quiet winter interest even before flowering begins.

Problems and Maintenance. This plant is relatively trouble-free but requires occasional pruning to maintain its graceful form. This should be done carefully by removing a few older branches each year rather than by shearing, which destroys its graceful landscape effect. An alternative pruning method is to cut the entire top back close to the ground every few years, if the appearance of the plant deteriorates enough to make renewal necessary. This should be done in spring at or before the time new growth is beginning, to allow maximum time for regrowth before winter.

Jasminum officinale 1 and 3

COMMON JASMINE, POET'S JASMINE

Semievergreen, scrambling, vinelike shrub
Oleaceae (Olive Family)

Native Range. Iran to western China.

Useful Range. USDA Zones 7b–9a+.

Function. This procumbent, scrambling shrub has weak stems that need support at first, but it can be trained as a rambling climber to cover banks, walls, fences, and trellises.

Size and Habit.   Branches trail to lengths of 5–10 m/16–33 ft if not pruned.

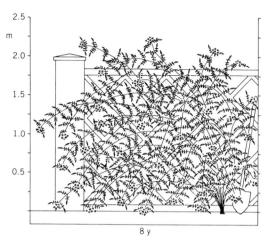

Jasminum officinale.

Adaptability

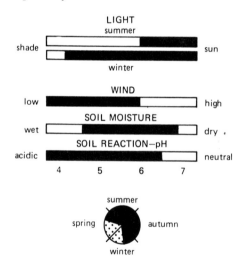

Seasonal Interest.   *Flowers:* Fragrant, white, to 2.5 cm/1 in. across, in clusters of up to 10, most showy in late spring and summer but continuing with occasional bloom well into autumn. *Foliage:* Glossy and dark green, compound with five to nine leaflets, tending to be semievergreen. *Twigs and branches:* Green, adding quiet winter interest after leaves fall.

Problems and Maintenance.   This plant is relatively trouble-free but requires occasional pruning for control of size and for thinning and shaping. Since it is a weak climber, its branches

must be tied to their support if trained on trellis or wire.

Forms and Cultivars.   'Affine' (=f. *affine*) has more and larger flowers, pink on the outside. 'Aureum' (='Aureo-variegatum') has yellow-variegated leaves. Plants of f. *grandiflorum* have larger flowers, to 4 cm/1.6 in. across, white with pink-flushed centers, and relatively stout stems, not as easily trained as the species type.

Jasminum officinale.

Related Species and Hybrids

Jasminum beesianum 1 and 3 (pink jasmine). This low deciduous shrub makes an irregular mound or scrambles weakly to 2 m/6.6 ft when support is available. It has fragrant, pink to rosy red flowers, unusual in this genus, in middle to late spring. Useful in Zones 7b–9a+, but not usually available.

Jasminum humile 1 and 4 (Italian jasmine).   In spite of its common name, this is another Chinese species of *Jasminum*, usually grown as a scrambling climber. It has nearly evergreen, fine-textured foliage and small, poorly scented yellow flowers in late spring. The selection 'Revolutum' is semievergreen, with much larger (to 2.5 cm/1 in.) and more fragrant flowers. Useful in Zones 7b–9a+.

Jasminum parkeri 2 (Parker's jasmine).   This dwarf shrub is evergreen, with yellow flowers in summer. Useful in Zones 7b–9a+.

Jasminum polyanthum 1 (pink Chinese jasmine). This vigorous scrambling and climbing or trailing plant is remarkable for the showiness of its fragrant pale pink flowers. Useful in Zone 9a+, perhaps also parts of Zone 8.

Jasminum ×*stephanense* 1 and 3 (Stephan jasmine). This hybrid combines the pink flower color (although paler) of *J. beesianum* with the scrambling habit of *J. officinale* 'Grandiflorum,' but is rank-growing and not easily trained, so it is of limited interest in its useful range of Zones 7b–9a+.

Juglans nigra 8

EASTERN BLACK WALNUT

Deciduous tree

Juglandaceae (Walnut Family)

Native Range. Eastern United States and southern Ontario.

Useful Range. USDA Zones 4b–9a, with selection of appropriate genetic material.

Function. Shade tree, naturalizing.

Size and Habit

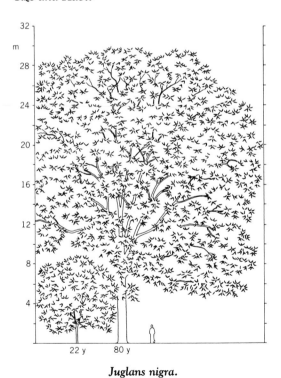

Juglans nigra.

Adaptability

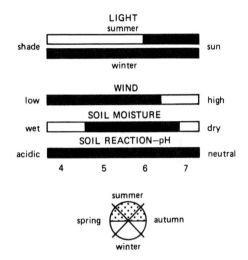

Seasonal Interest. *Flowers:* Hanging catkins (male) to 8 cm/3 in. long, add mild spring interest. *Foliage:* Coarse, compound, bright green leaves give the tree unique character in summer, and fall with little color change in autumn. *Fruits:* Large edible nuts in husks add interest in early autumn. *Trunks and branches:* Thickly ridged, dark gray-brown bark is distinctive but not a major source of landscape interest.

Problems and Maintenance. The nuts are a serious litter problem when they fall to the ground in autumn along with occasional twigs, ruling this tree out for use in street plantings or in other intensive sites. Its overall size rules it out for small properties. In short, *J. nigra* and other walnuts are best planted only in parklike or naturalized situations, but existing trees are worth preserving in development elsewhere.

For many years, *J. nigra* and other walnuts have been known to exert toxic effects on certain other plants under some conditions. There

Juglans nigra.

is still some uncertainty about the required conditions, but the toxic material, *juglone*, is thought to be formed by the oxidation of *hydrojuglone*, a material present in large amounts in walnut roots, when roots of sensitive plants come in contact with those of walnut. Sensitive plants include tomato, potato, alfalfa, blackberry, red pine, and several members of the Ericaceae (Heath Family). Lack of information on compatibility of walnut with the great bulk of other landscape plants suggests a cautious approach to the use of walnuts in mixed plantings and provides an additional reason for using them in parklike situations rather than in intensive landscapes.

Cultivars.   'Laciniata' has finely dissected foliage but is similar to the species type otherwise. It is seldom if ever commercially available at present. Many cultivars selected for superior nut quality are available from specialized nut tree nurseries.

Related Species and Hybrids

Juglans ailanthifolia 7 (synonym: *J. sieboldiana*; Japanese walnut).   This is a relatively small tree, usually growing to only about 15 m/50 ft.

Useful in Zones 5a–8b, it is otherwise subject to the same limitations as *J. nigra*. *J. ailanthifolia* var. *cordiformis* 7 (synonyms: *J. cordidormis*, *J. sieboldiana* var. *cordiformis*; heartnut) differs little from the species type as a landscape tree. A few cultivars have been selected for nut production.

Juglans cinerea 8 (butternut).   This native of the northeastern and north-central United States and adjacent Canada is generally similar to *J. nigra* but slightly more cold-hardy (Zones 3b–7a), somewhat less impressive as a shade tree, and relatively short-lived because of its susceptibility to blight and canker diseases. Seldom, if ever, is this tree planted other than for nuts, but it is worthy of preservation in development in some situations. A few cultivars have been selected for nut production.

Juglans cinerea × *J. ailanthifolia* var. *cordiformis* 8 (buartnut).   This hybrid is best known for its cold-hardiness (to Zone 4b, perhaps also 4a) coupled with good-quality nuts that are much easier to shell than butternuts or black walnuts. This is a tree that could well be tried for shade or park use in Zones 3b and 4, where the only *Juglans* species known to survive is butternut.

Juglans regia 8 (English or Persian walnut). This tree from southeastern Europe and Asia, used primarily for nut production, is potentially useful as a lawn or park shade tree, with its rugged trunk and branches covered with light tan-gray bark, bright green, compound leaves, and open branching habit. This tree poses the same litter problem as *J. nigra* and is generally useful in Zones 7a–7b, but the so-called Carpathian walnut, a seed source found in the Carpathian Mountains, is more cold-hardy, useful northward to Zone 6a and good sites in Zone 5b. Many cultivars have been selected for nut production.

Juniperus chinensis 2–7

CHINESE JUNIPER
Evergreen shrub or tree
Cupressaceae (Cypress Family)

Native Range.   China, Japan.

Useful Range.   USDA Zones 4a–9a with selection of appropriate cultivars.

Function.   Screen, specimen, massing, groundcover.

Size and Habit. Upper drawing: *J. chinensis.* Lower set of drawings: *J. chinensis* 'Keteleeri' (rear), *J.* × *media* 'Pfitzeriana' and 'Armstrongii' (left and right), and *J. sargentii* (front).

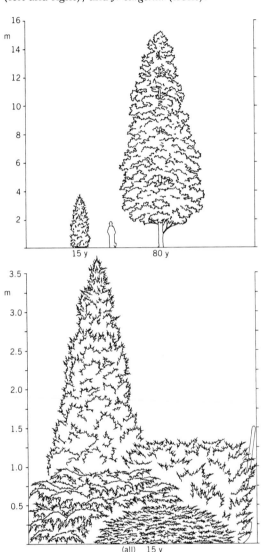

Juniperus chinensis, J. ×*media*, and *J. sargentii.*

Adaptability

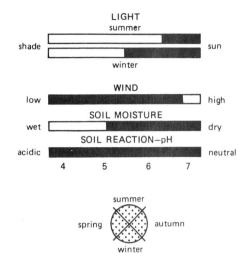

Seasonal Interest. *Foliage:* Evergreen, dull olive green to bluish green, occasionally bright green. Commonly both juvenile (needlelike) and mature (scalelike) forms are present on the same plant, but occasionally the foliage is entirely juvenile or predominantly mature. The foliage usually undergoes little or no color change in winter. *Fruits:* Relatively large (to 0.8 cm/0.3 in. across), whitish blue at first, ripening brownish in the second year, on female plants (dioecious).

Problems and Maintenance. This evergreen is relatively trouble-free in most areas at most times, but bagworms are a serious problem in some areas, and mites and *Phomopsis* twig blight (juniper blight) can be troublesome occasionally. Pruning is seldom needed except to control the size of spreading forms. It should be done by cutting back individual branches rather than by shearing so as not to destroy the form of the plant.

Cultivars. (See also "Hybrids" for cultivars once assigned to this species but now to the hybrid group *J.* ×*media.*)

'Ames,' 'Iowa,' and 'Maney' are semierect and vigorous, to 2–3 m/6.6–10 ft, selected at Iowa State University. They have dull blue-green foliage, mostly needlelike (juvenile). 'Maney' is well adapted for use in planters and is cold-hardy to Zone 3b. 'Iowa' fruits heavily in most years.

These selections may be affected by juniper blight in wet years.

'Blue Point' is upright and densely pyramidal, to 4.5 m/15 ft tall, height:width ratio about 2:1, with blue-green foliage.

'Columnaris' is a handsome, dark green, narrowly conical form, excellent for screening, reaching a height of at least 10 m/33 ft in time, with height:width ratio of 4:1.

'Fairview' (= 'Hetzii Columnaris') is upright and narrowly pyramidal, to 4.5 m/15 ft tall, height:width ratio about 5:1, with bright green, needlelike foliage.

'Hook's' (= 'Hook's No. 6) is upright, dense, and narrowly pyramidal, to 5 m/16 ft tall, height:width ratio about 5:1, foliage needlelike (juvenile), bright green.

'Kaizuka' (= 'Torulosa'; Hollywood juniper) is upright, roughly pyramidal but with spiraled, irregular branching, bright yellowish green foliage and bluish berries. It is useful as a specimen for accent in formal landscapes in Zones 6a–9a. It usually functions in the 1–2 m/3.3–6.6 ft height range but can reach at least 3–4 m/10–13 ft eventually.

'Kaizuka Variegata' (= 'Torulosa Variegata') is similar to 'Kaizuka' except for its creamy yellow variegated foliage.

'Keteleerii' is similar to female plants of the species type except that it has much denser, brighter green foliage. This makes an effective large screen, growing to heights of 3–4 m/10–13 ft with height:width ratio of about 3:1. Useful at least in Zones 4a–8a.

'Mountbatten' is dense, narrowly pyramidal, and nonfruiting, growing to 3–4 m/10–13 ft, with height:width ratio of about 4:1 and with grayish or bluish green, mostly needlelike foliage. It is useful for vertical accent or as a narrow screen in Zones 4b–8a.

'Pyramidalis' is similar to 'Stricta' with prickly, steely blue foliage, but is more narrowly columnar in form and is seldom, if ever, seen in North America.

'Robusta Green' is a compact, columnar form growing to 3 m/10 ft tall, perhaps eventually much taller, height:width ratio 2:1, with deep green, somewhat tufted foliage. Considered by some to belong to *J. virginiana*; if true, it probably would be susceptible to cedar-apple rust (see *J. virginiana*), but I have not seen it affected.

'San Jose' is a low, spreading form with a mixture of patches of both needlelike (juvenile) and scalelike (mature) leaves. It usually remains below 0.5 m/1.6 ft for many years but spreads widely.

'Spartan' is upright and densely pyramidal, to 5 m/16 ft tall, height:width ratio 3:1, foliage needlelike (juvenile), bright green.

'Stricta,' sometimes incorrectly labeled *J. excelsa* 'Stricta' or spiny Greek juniper, is mentioned here as a warning rather than a recommendation. This plant is stiffly upright, nonfruiting, with steely blue, very prickly, needlelike (juvenile) foliage. This and its tightly conical shape make it too formal a plant for most landscapes. Furthermore, after a few years the lower foliage begins to turn brown, and this progresses upward, destroying any ornamental quality that the plant might have had.

'Wintergreen' is upright and densely pyramidal, with both scalelike and needlelike leaves, to at least 6 m/20 ft tall, height:width ratio 3:1, with deep, bright green foliage that holds its color well in winter.

Hybrids. A group of cultivars once assigned to *J. chinensis* are now believed (but not proven) to be hybrids of *J. chinensis* × *J. sabina*. The collective name for these is *J.* × *media* 2–5. Some of the most popular of them are listed here.

'Armstrongii' is in effect an upright version of 'Pfitzeriana' with bright olive-green foliage. It is male, compact, and blocky in form, growing to a height and width of 1.5 m/5 ft, and more in time, and favored for plantings where horizontal space is at a premium.

'Blaauw' is densely columnar and slow-grow-

Juniperus ×*media* 'Armstrongii.'

ing, giving a formal, urnlike appearance that is difficult to assimilate into some plantings. In time it will reach a height of at least 1.5 m/5 ft, with height:width ratio about 2:1 and deep green, mostly scalelike foliage.

'Monlep' (Mint Julep™) and 'Sea Green' are very similar (perhaps identical). They are also similar to 'Pfitzeriana' and 'Pfitzeriana Compacta,' to a height of about 1.5 m/5 ft and somewhat greater spread, with gracefully arching branches.

'Pfitzeriana' is the "root" cultivar, from which many others have come as a result of genetic "sports" (mutations). This is a wide-spreading shrub, eventually to a height of 2 m/6.6 ft or more, but remaining below 1.5 m/5 ft for 10 years, and much longer with careful pruning, while spreading to 5 m/16 ft or more in time. This male (nonfruiting) form was introduced into cultivation nearly a century ago. It has gray-green to olive green foliage, mostly scalelike but with occasional patches of needlelike leaves. Useful in Zone 4a–9a+.

'Pfitzeriana Compacta' (= 'Nick's Compact')

and 'Kallay Compact' are similar to 'Pfitzeriana' except in being more compact, staying well under 1 m/3.3 ft for many years while spreading to 2–3 m/6.6–10 ft. 'Fruitlandii' is similar to 'Pfitzeriana Compacta,' but reported to have brighter green foliage.

'Pfitzeriana Aurea' is similar to 'Pfitzeriana,' but with bright golden yellow outside foliage, turning to yellowish green by autumn. It is less vigorous than 'Pfitzeriana' and may be slightly less cold-hardy, to Zone 4b. 'Old Gold,' a mutation from 'Pfitzeriana Aurea,' and 'Aurea' (Gold Coast™) are similar but more compact, remaining below 0.8 m/2.6 ft while spreading to 1.5 m/5 ft, and with bright golden yellow to bronze foliage that holds its color well into winter. 'Saybrook Gold' (Plant Patent No. 5014, 1983) reportedly has the brightest gold color of any juniper, and it holds its color year-round. 'Bakaurea' (Gold Star®) has light blue-green foliage except for soft golden yellow branch tips, producing a distinctive effect.

'Pfitzeriana Glauca' (blue Pfitzer juniper) is similar to 'Pfitzeriana' except that it has blue-green foliage, turning silvery to purplish blue in winter, and it is intermediate in growth rate between 'Pfitzeriana' and 'Pfitzeriana Compacta.' 'Angelica Blue' is reported to be even bluer and is as vigorous as 'Pfitzeriana.'

Another possible group of hybrids includes the cultivars 'Hetzii' (formerly assigned to *J. chinensis* or *J. ×media*) and 'Grey Owl' (formerly assigned to *J. virginiana*). 'Hetzii' is described as a female (fruiting) clone, and 'Grey Owl' is described as a male (nonfruiting). Otherwise, they are very difficult to tell apart except by the forms of older

Juniperus ×media 'Pfitzeriana' (front) and 'Hetzii.'

Juniperus ×media 'Pfitzeriana Aurea.'

plants or by detailed cytological examination. There is now (inconclusive) evidence that one or both of these clones may be hybrids between *J. ×media* 'Pfitzeriana' and *J. virginiana* 'Glauca.' Adding to the confusion about these cultivars, there are at least two clones in commerce sold as 'Hetzii,' including at least one male and one female.

'Hetzii' (the common female clone) is an extremely vigorous upright, spreading plant, reaching 5 m/16 ft in height and about the same in spread. At least one male clone also labeled 'Hetzii' reaches similar size. The foliage of both is very glaucous, silvery blue-green year-round. 'Hetzii' is too large for many of the sites where it has been used—for example, in plantings that eventually nearly covered the one-story homes beside which they were planted. Nevertheless, there are larger-scale sites where such large evergreen shrubs are appropriate.

'Grey Owl' (a male clone) is known to have been selected from seed of *J. virginiana* 'Glauca' growing near *J. ×media* 'Pfitzeriana.' This clone is somewhat less vigorous than *J. ×media* 'Hetzii', but grows to at least 2–3 m/6.6–10 ft tall by 3 m/10 ft wide in time.

Related Species

Juniperus davurica 2 (Dahurian juniper). This low-growing species is native to central Asia, especially Siberia. The species type may not be in cultivation in North America, but a few cultivars are listed here. 'Expansa' (synonym: *J. chinensis* 'Parsonii') is a low, stiffly spreading groundcover, reminiscent of *J. procumbens* but with bluish green foliage, both needlelike and scalelike. 'Expansa Aureospicata' and 'Expansa Aureovariegata' (synonym: *J. chinensis* 'Parsonii Variegata') are like 'Expansa' but with yellow variegated foliage.

Juniperus procumbens 2–3 (synonym: *J. chinensis* var. *procumbens*; Japanese garden juniper). This is a low, broad-spreading plant to 0.5 m/ 1.6 ft high and eventually very broad, with short-needlelike (juvenile), pale to bright green foliage and ascending branch tips. The selection 'Nana' is lower and more compact, an excellent groundcover. Both forms are useful in Zones 5a– 9a, perhaps colder zones as well. This species from Japan is known only in cultivation there,

Juniperus procumbens.

apparently extinct in the wild or a chance mutation that never became wild.

Juniperus sargentii 2–3 (synonym: *J. chinensis* var *sargentii*; Sargent juniper). This species, from the Kurile Islands, north of Japan, is also a low, broad-spreading plant to 0.5 m/1.6 ft high and eventually very broad. Its foliage is bright to deep green, usually with only needlelike leaves, which are much shorter than the juvenile leaves of other junipers, giving a distinctive texture. This is an excellent groundcover plant for sunny sites in Zones 4a–9a. Several variants are available: 'Compacta' is lower and slower growing; 'Glauca' is dark bluish green; and 'Viridis' is much lighter, brighter green.

Juniperus squamata 2–5 (singleseed juniper). This variable species from central Asia has highly glaucous, needlelike foliage, strikingly blue in the landscape. Several cultivars have been selected, including the following: 'Blue

Juniperus sargentii.

Carpet' is a groundcover form, about 0.3 m/1 foot high and spreading to at least 1.5 m/5 ft wide, originating as a mutation of 'Meyeri' (below). 'Blue Star' is a dwarf form, originating as a witch's-broom mutation on 'Meyeri,' growing to a height of about 40 cm/16 in. and a spread not much greater. 'Holger' may be a hybrid between *J. squamata* and *J.* ×*media* 'Pfitzeriana Aurea.' It makes a mass 1 m/3.3 ft high by 1.5 m/5 ft wide, eventually larger, with yellowish new growth contrasting with the gray-green older foliage. 'Meyeri' is an irregularly upright shrub, valued for its steely blue needlelike foliage, but it is difficult to use because of its positive accent and irregular form. It becomes very large, eventually to at least 2–3 m/6.6–10 ft in height and spread,

but before it reaches half that size it is usually disfigured by dead foliage that persists on its branches and is difficult to remove. Useful in Zones 5a–9a.

Microbiota decussata 2–3. This mat-forming evergreen from southeastern Siberia has the appearance of a juniper and is used in the same way as a creeping juniper. Its olive-green foliage turns a dull brown in winter, and it would not compete with the better low junipers except that it is somewhat more shade-tolerant. Once considered rare, it is now easily available. Exploration for genetically diverse material of this species might turn up clones with better winter color. Useful at least in Zones 3b–8a.

Juniperus communis 2–6

COMMON JUNIPER
Evergreen shrub
Cupressaceae (Cypress Family)

Native Range.   Northern parts of Asia, Europe, North America.

Useful Range.   USDA Zones 3a–8a with selection of appropriate cultivars.

Function.   Groundcover, specimen, rock garden.

Size and Habit

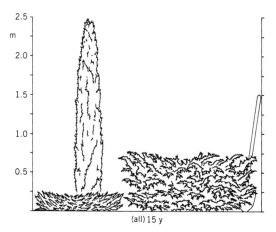

(all) 15 y

Juniperus communis: **'Hibernica' (left rear), ssp. *depressa* (right), and ssp. *alpina* (left front).**

Adaptability.   This species is relatively tolerant of salt in seashore sites and where de-icing salt is used.

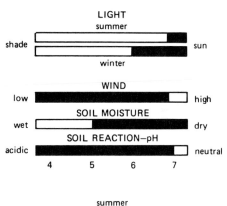

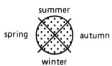

Seasonal Interest.   *Foliage:* Evergreen, sharply needlelike, dull yellowish green to deep blue-green, mostly turning brownish in winter. *Fruits:* Blue-black with a waxy bloom, to 0.6 cm/0.24 in. across, usually dioecious.

Problems and Maintenance.   Relatively trouble-free in most cases, but mites and bagworms can be troublesome. Pruning should be carried out, if at all, in the manner described for *J. chinensis.* Most individuals of this species have poor color and form and are of little landscape value, but selected cultivars and varieties are useful.

Subspecies, Varieties, and Cultivars. The ssp. *alpina* (synonyms: ssp. *nana,* var. *montana,* var. *saxatilis;* mountain juniper) includes populations of low-growing to prostrate plants originating in the mountains of Eurasia as well as on the Pacific coast of North America. This includes several handsome low-growing clones with blue-green foliage and shorter needles, sold under such names as 'Montana,' 'Saxatilis,' and others. 'Berkshire' is a dwarf, growing as a small, handsome mound, of interest for extremely small-scale sites or to collectors. Within ssp. *alpina,* populations of very low-growing plants (var. *jackii*) from the mountains of the Pacific Northwest have shown great promise as groundcovers, with very small, dark bluish green needles that produce an elegant texture. 'Gold Beach,' an equally handsome groundcover form selected in California, with lighter green foliage, probably also belongs to var. *jackii.*

The ssp. *depressa* is the spreading shrub distributed widely in old fields and pastures across northern North America, usually lower than 1 m/3.3 ft but much broader after many years. Clones with better-than-average form and color have been selected for landscape use in cold climates (Zones 3a–5a), and a few have proved useful farther south. 'Depressa Aurea' (= 'Aurea') is typical of ssp. *depressa* except that the new growth emerges bright yellow, changing to dull yellow later in the summer and then green the following year. 'Repanda' (= 'Effusa') is low-growing (to 40 cm/16 in. high and at least 1.5 m/ 5 ft wide), making a relatively fast and effective groundcover.

Several slow-growing, narrowly upright selections of *J. communis* have been made, including the following: 'Compressa' is a narrowly columnar dwarf, growing slowly to 1 m/3.3 ft. 'Gold Cone' is also dwarf and densely columnar to narrowly pyramidal, with bright golden yellow foliage. Both of these are interesting plants for small-scale accent. 'Pencil Point' is narrowly columnar in the extreme, with handsome blue-green foliage, suggesting a miniature version of *J. scopulorum* 'Skyrocket,' reaching a height of 1–1.5 m/3.3–5 ft and height:width ratio of about 10:1.

Larger narrowly upright selections have also been made: 'Hibernica' (= 'Stricta'; Irish juniper) and 'Suecica' (Swedish juniper) are vigorous, tightly columnar forms, reaching heights of 3–5 m/10–16 ft and height:width ratio of about 6:1, with good medium bluish-green foliage. 'Hibernica' has vertical branch tips, while those of 'Suecica' are nodding. Even though these cultivars are cold-hardy at least to Zone 4b, they may be broken or pulled apart by the weight of ice and snow, especially with wind, unless they are carefully tied together. They are also susceptible to scorch from winter sun and wind, especially if fully exposed to the south and west.

Related Species

Juniperus rigida 6 (needle juniper). This tall shrub or small tree from northeastern Asia has foliage very similar to that of *J. communis* but arranged loosely on drooping branches. It is seldom available for landscape use but potentially useful in Zones 5a–8a and perhaps also colder zones.

Juniperus communis 'Depressa Aurea.'

Juniperus conferta 2

SHORE JUNIPER
Evergreen groundcover
Cupressaceae (Cypress Family)

Native Range. Japan, Sakhalin.

Useful Range. USDA Zones 6a–9a+. Selections from northern extremes of the natural range may prove useful in Zone 5.

Function. Groundcover, specimen, rock garden. In appropriate sites, this is one of the fastest evergreen groundcovers to become established.

Size and Habit

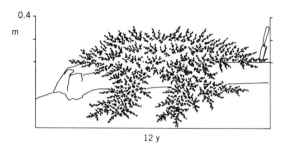

Juniperusa conferta.

Seasonal Interest. *Foliage:* Evergreen, sharply needlelike, bright green to slightly bluish, not changing appreciably in winter. *Fruits:* Black with a waxy bloom, to 1.2 cm/0.5 in. across. Dioecious.

Juniperus conferta.

Adaptability. This plant is unusually tolerant of seashore conditions and de-icing salts and is usually at its best in infertile soil.

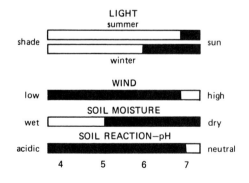

Problems and Maintenance. This groundcover is relatively trouble-free in most situations, but mites occasionally can be troublesome.

Cultivars. Only a few cultivars have been selected, including the following: 'Blue Pacific' has blue-green foliage and, if fully prostrate, remains below 15 cm/6 in. high and spreads rapidly to make a fine groundcover. 'Emerald Sea' is very much like 'Blue Pacific' but has soft-green foliage, turning yellow-green in winter. 'Luchuensis' is much slower growing, with its annual growth reportedly only about 10 cm/4 in. 'Silver Mist' has very pronounced white stomatal lines, producing a silvery bicolored effect.

Juniperus horizontalis 2

CREEPING JUNIPER
Evergreen groundcover
Cupressaceae (Cypress Family)

Native Range. Northern North America: Nova Scotia to Alaska, southward to New Jersey, Minnesota, and Montana.

Useful Range. USDA Zones 2a–9a with selection of appropriate genetic material.

Function. Groundcover, specimen, rock garden.

Size and Habit. 'Douglasii' is illustrated.

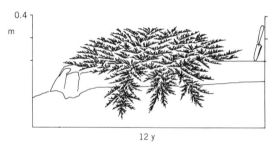

Juniperus horizontalis 'Douglasii.'

Adaptability. This species is unusually tolerant of seashore conditions and de-icing salts.

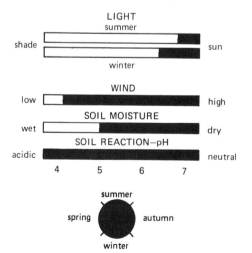

Seasonal Interest. *Foliage:* Evergreen, bluish green to soft, gray-green or rich, deep green, usually mostly scalelike at maturity with some juvenile (needlelike) foliage, but some variants are entirely or predominantly juvenile. *Fruits:* Light blue berries (on female plants), to 0.8 cm/ 0.3 in. across, add landscape interest. Dioecious.

Problems and Maintenance. Many cultivars are susceptible to *Phomopsis* twig blight (juniper blight) under environmental conditions favorable for the disease (moist weather in spring). This disease can be a serious problem, especially since it is difficult to control. The problem is somewhat localized, so selection of cultivars should be guided by local experience. Mites can be troublesome in hot, dry weather.

Juniperus horizontalis 'Douglasii.'

Cultivars. More than 30 cultivars of this species are currently in use in our area. Some of the most useful and available are listed here.

'Bar Harbor' is a creeping, nonfruiting selection from Maine, with bluish leaves, both needlelike and scalelike. It is thoroughly confused with other clones in the trade. When specifying this cultivar, one can be reasonably sure only that some creeping form of *J. horizontalis* will be supplied. Fortunately, most such forms are useful landscape plants. Useful in Zones 3a–8b.

'Blue Chip,' selected in Denmark, makes a low groundcover to 0.3 m/1 ft, with excellent blue color becoming even more striking in winter.

'Douglasii' (Waukegan juniper) is an excellent nonfruiting creeping clone of midwestern origin, with steely blue-green foliage that turns silvery purple in winter, on twig tips ascending to no more than 0.5 m/1.6 ft high but usually about half that height. This cultivar is less confused in the trade than most and seems to be less susceptible to *Phomopsis* than most cultivars of *J. horizontalis*. Useful in Zones 3a–8b.

'Emerald Isle' is low-growing, to 15 cm/6 in. high, with green foliage of frondlike texture.

'Emerald Spreader' is a matlike, spreading selection with rich green foliage, useful in Zones 4a–8b and perhaps Zone 3 as well.

'Glauca' is a creeping selection similar to 'Bar Harbor' and 'Wiltonii' but not as widely used. Useful in Zones 3b–8a.

'Hughes' grows into a low, dense mat with exceptionally blue foliage. Its distinctive texture results from straight branchlets radiating from main branches, seen in other cultivars such as 'Douglasii' and accentuated in 'Hughes.'

'Mother Lode' (Plant Patent No. 5948, 1987) is a golden yellow sport of 'Wiltonii,' very similar except for the color. The yellow turns to deep yellow-orange in fall and is tinted with plum-purple in winter.

'Plumosa' (Andorra juniper) is a nonfruiting, spreading form with branches ascending to 30–45 cm/12–18 in. Foliage is entirely short-needle-like, soft green in summer and deep silvery purple (fertile soil) to rosy plum-purple (infertile soil) in winter. Useful in Zones 4a–8b but susceptible to juniper blight.

'Plumosa Compacta' and 'Youngstown' (= 'Plumosa Youngstown') are similar to 'Plumosa' except lower-growing, staying below 25 cm/10 in. in height.

'Prince of Wales' is an excellent low, mat-forming, nonfruiting selection introduced in 1967 by the Agriculture Canada Research Station at Morden, Manitoba, and originating in Alberta. Its foliage is bright medium green with a silvery purple cast on exposed foliage in winter. Useful in Zones 2a–8a.

'Monise' (Turquoise Spreader™) is a vigorous, mat-forming groundcover, to 20–25 cm/8–10 in. high, with blue-green foliage. Useful in Zones 4a–9a.

'Webberi' is a very low, carpetlike plant with blue-green foliage.

'Wiltonii' (blue rug juniper) is an excellent dense, nonfruiting, creeping form with silvery blue foliage, so low that it assumes the form of the surface it covers, except for slight mounding at plant centers, giving it a subtly irregular surface. Originating in Maine, it is useful in Zones 3a–9a.

'Wisconsin,' selected at the University of Wisconsin, is low and carpetlike, staying below 15 cm/6 in. and spreading to 2 m/6.6 ft in time, with neat, feathery dark blue-green foliage.

Juniperus sabina 2–5

SAVIN JUNIPER
Evergreen shrub
Cupressaceae (Cypress Family)

Native Range. Southwestern Europe to Siberia.

Useful Range. USDA Zones 3b–8b with selection of appropriate cultivars. May be useful farther south as well.

Function. Groundcover, specimen, massing. The taller cultivars are not easy to use because of their vaselike form.

Size and Habit. 'Von Ehren' (rear), 'Tamariscifolia' (right), and 'Broadmoor' (left) are illustrated.

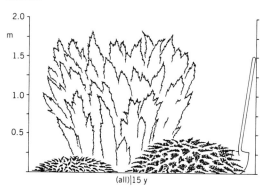

Juniperus sabina: **'Von Ehren' (rear), 'Tamariscifolia' (right), and 'Broadmoor' (left, front).**

Adaptability

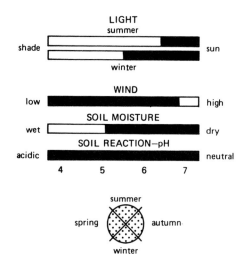

Seasonal Interest. *Foliage:* Evergreen, bright yellowish green to deep green, blue-green occasionally, usually predominantly scalelike but in some cultivars mostly needlelike with scale leaves toward the branch tips. Foliage gives off a pungent (unpleasant?) odor when crushed. *Fruits:* Blue-black with whitish, waxy bloom, inconspicuous. Dioecious.

Problems and Maintenance. *Phomopsis* twig blight can be a problem for some cultivars. Consult people with local experience when making selections. Mites can be troublesome, especially in dry climates and years.

Cultivars. A few of the most common and useful cultivars are listed here.

'Arcadia' is a low, spreading form with ascending branch tips, to about 0.5 m/1.6 ft tall, originating in the Ural Mountains of Russia. Predominantly scalelike foliage is a bright, pale green. Nonfruiting, it is useful in Zones 3b–7b, and probably more widely.

'Blue Danube' makes a horizontal mass 0.5–0.7 m/1.5–2.3 ft in high and to 1.5 m/5 ft wide, with light bluish to gray-green foliage.

'Blue Forest' has many vertical branches that rise to about 0.3 m/1 ft, resembling a miniature forest, before falling into a prostrate position. In this respect, it is similar to *J. horizontalis* 'Alpina,' which may no longer be available, but is lower and has bluer foliage.

'Broadmoor,' from the Ural Mountains, reaches a height of about 0.5 m/1.6 ft and spreads to 1.5–2 m/5–6.6 ft. The foliage is bright green and feathery, with mostly needlelike leaves. This nonfruiting selection is useful in Zones 4a–8b.

'Buffalo' is similar to 'Broadmoor' but even more dense and brighter green.

'Monna' (Calgary Carpet™), a mutation from 'Arcadia,' makes a very low carpet (13–25 cm/5–10 in.) of soft, lacy green foliage.

'Monard' (Moor-Dense™, Plant Patent No. 6656, 1989) is similar to 'Broadmoor' but denser and lower (20–30 cm/8–12 in.), spreading to 2 m/6.6 ft.

'Skandia,' another selection from the Ural Mountains, is similar to 'Arcadia,' but with mostly needlelike, blue-green foliage. Useful in Zones 3b–7b, perhaps more widely.

'Tamariscifolia' (tamarix juniper) is a hand-

Juniperus sabina **'Broadmoor.'**

some, broad-spreading plant, to about 0.6 m/2 ft high, eventually somewhat taller, with feathery blue-green foliage consisting mostly of short needlelike leaves, giving the distinctive "tamarix" texture. This nonfruiting selection is useful in Zones 4a–8b, and perhaps more widely, but is susceptible to juniper blight.

'Tamariscifolia New Blue' is similar to 'Tamariscifolia' but with bluer foliage.

'Von Ehren' is extremely vigorous and broadly vase-shaped, eventually to at least 2 m/6.6 ft high and 3 m/10 ft wide, with dark green foliage. Because of its size and shape, it is difficult to use.

Juniperus scopulorum 2–7

ROCKY MOUNTAIN JUNIPER, WESTERN RED CEDAR

Evergreen tree

Cupressaceae (Cypress Family)

Native Range. Western United States and southwestern Canada.

Useful Range. USDA Zones 3b–6b with selection of appropriate cultivars or other genetic material. May be useful in warmer zones as well.

Function. Specimen, screen, massing.

Size and Habit

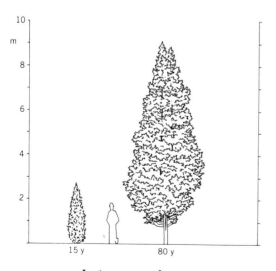

Juniperus scopulorum.

Adaptability

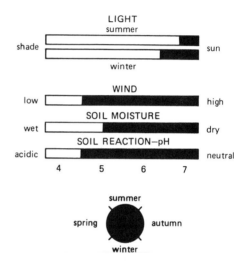

Seasonal Interest. *Foliage:* Evergreen, medium green to striking silvery blue, predominantly scalelike except in young seedlings. Little color change in winter. *Fruits:* Bright blue with whitish, waxy bloom similar in color to the foliage in silvery blue selections, to 0.6 cm/0.24 in. across or slightly larger. Dioecious.

Problems and Maintenance. In some areas, this species and its cultivars are made almost useless by a twig blight (probably *Phomopsis* blight). Its best performance seems to be in the western part of our range (western Central Plains and Great Plains), especially in the northern portions, but good specimens can be found in certain sites all the way to the Atlantic Coast. Bagworms can be a serious problem in some areas. Before selecting this species, it is advisable to inquire about local experience or to proceed on a small scale.

Cultivars. There has been considerable interest in variants of this species in the Northern Plains and Rocky Mountain areas of the United States and Canada, and at least 25 cultivars have been selected and named. A few of the most common or most widely adaptable are listed here.

'Blue Heaven' (sometimes incorrectly listed as 'Blue Haven'), is a vigorous but compact, silvery blue, pyramidal form selected in Nebraska.

'Cologreen' is vigorous and columnar to a height of 6 m/20 ft, with height:width ratio 3:1 and bright green foliage. Selected in Colorado, it is at its best west of most of our range.

'Gray Gleam' is a relatively slow-growing pyramidal form with blue-gray foliage, grayer in winter. It grows to 5 m/16 ft tall, with height:width ratio of 2:1.

'Medora' is a vigorous narrowly pyramidal clone selected by Donald Hoag of North Dakota State University from the South Dakota Badlands, to 4 m/13 ft tall, with height:width ratio 3:1 and blue-green foliage.

'Moffetii' is pyramidal and denser than most other cultivars, growing to 5 m/16 ft tall, with height:width ratio about 2:1 and silvery blue-green foliage.

'Monam' (Blue Creeper™, Plant Patent No. 5084, 1983) forms a broad mound 0.6 m/2 ft high and 2 m/6.6 ft or more in spread, with bright blue foliage, intensifying in winter.

'Monwade' (Green Ice™) is a densely pyramidal form with gray-green foliage except for the pale green, nearly vertical branch tips. Winter color reportedly is best in coldest climates.

'Moonglow' is pyramidal and very dense, to 4 m/13 ft tall, with height:width ratio 2:1 and intensely silver-blue foliage.

'Pathfinder' is a narrowly pyramidal form, growing 6 m/20 ft tall, with height: width ratio about 4:1 and blue-gray foliage.

'Platinum' is densely narrow-pyramidal and slow-growing, to 2–3 m/6.6–10 ft tall, with silvery blue foliage, a striking plant for accent.

'Skyrocket' is strikingly columnar, probably the narrowest upright juniper on the market, to 4 m/13 ft tall, with height:width ratio 6:1 to 8:1 and silvery blue foliage. This is a striking large-scale accent but somewhat susceptible to break-

Juniperus scopulorum 'Medora.'

age from heavy snow. This cultivar was once thought to belong to *J. virginiana*, but now is assigned to *J. scopulorum*.

'Sutherland' is broadly and densely pyramidal, to 5 m/16 ft tall, with silvery green foliage.

'Tolleson's Blue Weeping' is broadly pyramidal, with gracefully ascending main branches, vertically pendulous, stringlike side branches, and silvery blue-green foliage.

'Tolleson's Green Weeping' is very similar to 'Tolleson's Blue Weeping' except for its soft green foliage.

'Welchii' is slow-growing and densely and narrowly upright, to 2.5–4 m/8–13 ft tall, with silvery green new foliage, turning to brighter green with age.

'Wichita Blue' is compact and pyramidal, to 5–7 m/16–23 ft tall, with height:width ratio 2:1 to 3.1, with as bright blue foliage as any selection of *J. scopulorum*, holding well throughout the year.

Juniperus virginiana 5–8

EASTERN RED CEDAR
Evergreen shrub or tree
Cupressaceae (Cypress Family)

Native Range.   Eastern United States and adjacent southern Ontario.

Useful Range.   USDA Zones 3b–9a with selection of appropriate cultivars or other genetic material.

Function.   Specimen, screen, massing.

Size and Habit

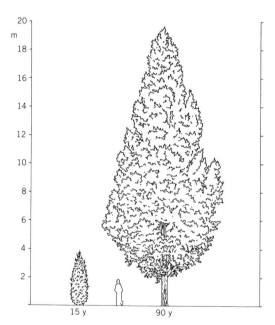

Juniperus virginiana.

Adaptability

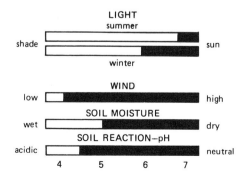

Seasonal Interest.   *Foliage:* Evergreen, deep green to silvery blue-green in a few cultivars, usually predominantly scalelike except in young seedlings, turning purplish or brownish in winter. *Fruits:* Bright blue to grayish, to 0.6 cm/0.24 in. across, colorful in some cultivars, especially in combination with bright green foliage. Dioecious.

Problems and Maintenance.   Mites can be troublesome occasionally, and bagworms are a potential problem in certain areas and must be controlled to avoid serious damage. *J. virginiana* is susceptible to *Phomopsis* blight and is also a

Juniperus virginiana.

Juniperus virginiana 'Hillspire.'

principal alternate host to the fungus that causes cedar apple rust. The fruiting bodies of this fungus can be considered either interesting or unsightly but do little harm to the tree except in cases of very heavy infections. But the disease is a serious problem of the other alternate hosts: the pome fruits such as apples and hawthorns, and selection of *J. virginiana* should be done with other susceptible species in mind. This species should at least be avoided in the vicinity of commercial apple orchards.

Cultivars. Many cultivars have been selected over the years, but probably fewer than 25 are commercially available in North America at this writing. A few of the most useful and available are listed here.

'Burkii' is broadly pyramidal, 6–7 m/20–23 ft tall, with fine-textured gray-blue foliage that turns deep purple in winter, nonfruiting, and one of the most tolerant junipers of poor soils, cold, and wind.

'Canaertii' is one of the most popular and distinctive cultivars, with an irregularly pyramidal form, to 5 m/16 ft tall, irregularly tufted foliage that remains a rich, deep green year-round, and small, bright blue fruits. It is very adaptable in most respects, but notoriously sensitive to certain spray chemicals; check tolerance before planning spray programs.

'Corcorcor' (Emerald Sentinel™, Plant Patent No. 5041, 1983) is narrowly pyramidal, to 8 m/26 ft tall, with height:width ratio 5:1 and bright green foliage.

'Glauca' is loosely and irregularly pyramidal, to 4–5 m/13–16 ft tall, with silvery gray-blue foliage, tufted somewhat in the manner of 'Canaertii.' Unlike 'Canaertii,' this cultivar is male (nonfruiting), faster growing, and not as elegant in appearance.

'Grey Owl' (see under *J.* ×*media*)

'Hillii' (= 'Dundee') is a slow-growing, pyramidal selection to 4–5 m/13–16 ft, with blue-green foliage, turning plum-purple in winter.

'Hillspire' (= 'Cupressifolia') is a narrowly pyramidal to columnar form with rich green foliage, growing to 7 m/23 ft tall, with height:width ratio 3:1 to 5:1.

'Manhattan Blue' is compactly pyramidal, to 3–4 m/10–13 ft tall, with height:width ratio about 2:1 and bluish green foliage.

'Skyrocket' (see under *J. scopulorum*)

Kalmia latifolia 5

MOUNTAIN LAUREL
Evergreen shrub
Ericaceae (Heath Family)

Native Range.   Eastern North America.

Useful Range.   USDA Zones 5a–9a with selection of appropriate genetic material.

Function.   Border, specimen, screen, naturalizing, roadside.

Size and Habit

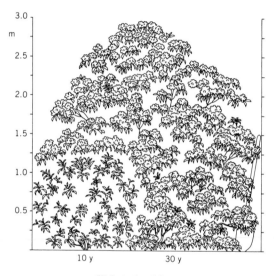

Kalmia latifolia.

Adaptability.   This shrub is tolerant of full sun or shade in summer in the North, but flowering is reduced by shade. In the South it is useful only in relatively cool sites: northern exposures with at least some shade. Light shade in winter reduces winterburn of foliage in Zone 5.

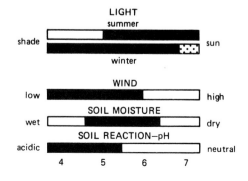

Seasonal Interest.   *Flowers:* White to deep rosy pink, to 2.5 cm/1 in. across, in showy terminal clusters in late spring to early summer. *Foliage:* Evergreen, leathery, and dark green, slightly lustrous, individual leaves to 10 cm/4 in. long.

Problems and Maintenance.   Relatively trouble-free, given a cool site and acidic soil, but subject to a controllable leaf-spot disease. Removal of flowers after they fade prevents fruiting and enhances flowering in the following year. Foliage of this and most other members of the Ericaceae is toxic to cattle, sheep, and humans.

Cultivars.   Variations in size, form, foliage, and flower color and markings have been known for many years and have been used in the *Kalmia* breeding program of Richard Jaynes of the Connecticut Agricultural Research Station at New Haven, but difficulties in commercial cutting propagation limited dissemination of superior clones. Since tissue culture propagation of this species became feasible in the early 1980s, at least 50 cultivars have become commercially available. A few of those most generally available are listed here.

Cultivars with white flowers include 'Angel,' with pure white flowers and bright green foliage; 'Snowdrift,' with white flowers having a small red center, dark green foliage, and dense, mounded growth habit; and 'Pristine,' with white flowers and compact growth habit, remaining below eye level.

Cultivars with pink buds and flowers include 'Pink Charm,' 'Pink Frost,' and the dwarf 'Tiddlywinks.'

A few cultivars with red buds opening pink are 'Heart of Fire,' with many large flowers and excellent foliage; 'Ostbo Red,' one of the earliest selections, with bright red buds opening very pale pink; 'Richard Jaynes', with red buds opening a deep, rich pink, and glossy foliage; and the vigorous 'Sarah' and 'Weston Redbud', with red buds opening deep rose pink.

'Carol' has red buds, opening white, with glossy dark green leaves and compact, low form. 'Little Linda' is even more dwarf (below 1 m/3.3 ft), with red buds opening near-white and aging to pink.

'Raspberry Glow' has maroon buds, opening to a deep raspberry pink, as close to true red as has yet been seen in this species. 'Bay State' is equally distinctive, with coral-pink flowers.

'Silver Dollar' has pink buds, opening as very large near-white flowers. 'Elf' is dwarf, with pink buds opening white. 'Minuet' is dwarf, with pink buds opening white but also with bright red band and rays.

Interest in selecting and breeding of new *K. latifolia* cultivars is still high at this writing, and new cultivars will probably continue to appear.

Kalmia polifolia 3

BOG LAUREL

Evergreen shrub

Ericaceae (Heath Family)

Native Range. Northeastern North America to Pennsylvania and Minnesota in bog habitats.

Useful Range. USDA Zones 2a–6a, perhaps in warmer zones in cool microclimates.

Function. Specimen, bog, or rock garden with ample moisture.

Size and Habit

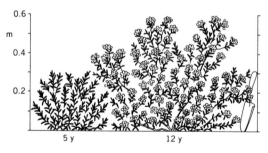

Kalmia polifolia.

Adaptability. This plant is tolerant of full sun or partial shade, but flowering is reduced by shade. Acidic and well-drained but moist soil is essential for success. Limited to relatively cool sites, even in Zone 5.

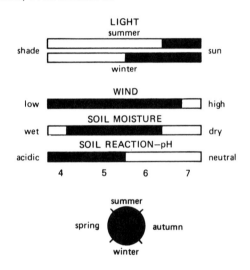

Seasonal Interest. *Flowers:* Rosy purple, to 1.5 cm/0.6 in. across, in terminal clusters in late spring or early summer. *Foliage:* Small, narrow, evergreen leaves to 3.5 cm/1.4 in. long, with edges rolled underneath, the upper side deep green to whitish, the lower side waxy and whitened. Toxic to animals.

Problems and Maintenance. This species is relatively trouble-free given a good site (cool, moist, but well-drained acidic soil). It is not commonly available but can be found in some northern nurseries.

Cultivars. Selections for white and deep reddish pink flowers have been made, but are seldom available commercially.

Related Species

Kalmia angustifolia 3 (lamb kill, sheep laurel). This small, usually straggling shrub, native to northeastern North America, has pale green, evergreen foliage and small purplish pink flowers in lateral clusters. Not a greatly valued landscape plant, it is worthy of preservation in some natural landscapes. As its name suggests, its foliage is highly toxic to sheep and cattle. Useful in Zones 2b–7b. The var. *caroliniana* (southern sheep laurel) is useful southward to Zone 8b. A few cultivars, including 'Alba' (= 'Candida'?), 'Hammonasett' (deep pink flowers) and 'Pumila' (dwarf), are sometimes available.

Kalmia cuneata 3 (white wicky). This low deciduous or evergreen shrub, to 1 m/3.3 ft tall, spreading by rhizomes, grows wild on the Coastal Plain of the Carolinas. Its white flowers, to 2 cm/0.8 in across, are borne in axillary clusters in summer. This species is seldom available for planting; it should be avoided or preserved in development, because it is rare and endemic to a very small area in the Carolinas, in Zone 8.

Kalmia hirsuta 2 (sand laurel). This very low evergreen shrub, to 0.5 m/1.6 ft, grows wild in pine savannahs and woods in the southeastern states. It is seldom used in built landscapes, but may find some use as the current interest in native plants grows. Potentially useful at least in Zones 9a+, probably somewhat colder zones as well.

Kalmiopsis leachiana 2. This compact, tufted shrub from Oregon has leathery leaves, only 1–2 cm/0.4–0.8 in. long, and terminal clusters of rosy purple flowers, opening in early summer and resembling those of *Kalmia,* but with stamens not inserted in the corolla. This is a rare shrub; specify cloned or at least nursery-grown plants. Useful for miniature gardens in Zones 7a–9a, perhaps also Zone 6b.

Andromeda polifolia 2 (bog rosemary). This evergreen, moundlike shrub, usually remaining below 0.5 m/1.6 ft, is native to northern Eurasia as well as northern North America. It is similar to *Kalmia polifolia* in landscape use, useful range and requirements, and its limited availability. Its white to pale pink flowers appear at the same time as those of *Kalmia polifolia* or slightly later, but are only half as large.

Loiseleuria procumbens 2 (alpine azalea). This low alpine shrub from northern Eurasia and North America varies from a tight mat of foliage only a few centimeters thick on mountain summits to somewhat taller in more protected sites. Its small, clear, rosy pink flowers are exquisite in early to midsummer, and its very fine textured foliage is evergreen. Its landscape usefulness is limited to rock gardens, probably only in Zones 2b–5b or in unusually cool microclimates in Zone 6.

Kalopanax septemlobus 8

Synonym: *K. pictus*
CASTOR ARALIA
Deciduous tree
Araliaceae (Aralia Family)

Native Range. China, Japan, Korea.

Useful Range. USDA Zones 5a–8a.

Function. Shade tree, specimen.

Size and Habit

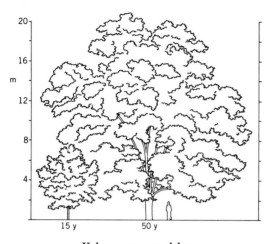

Kalopanax septemlobus

Adaptability

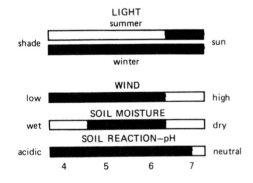

Seasonal Interest. *Flowers:* White, small, in large clusters (compound umbels), very striking in middle to late summer. *Foliage:* Individual leaves similar in shape to those of sweetgum but larger, the blades 25 cm/10 in. or more across, and petioles sometimes an additional 25 cm/10 in. or more. Deep green, forming a dense, irregular canopy in summer, turning reddish in autumn. *Fruits:* Small, shiny, black, in clusters, interesting in early autumn but usually taken quickly by birds. *Twigs and branches:* Heavy and coarse, with large terminal buds and many large and sharp prickles, even on trunks of young trees.

Problems and Maintenance. This tree is unusually trouble-free but appears stark and sparse when young, becoming round-headed in a few years. Prickles on lower trunk and branches must be removed where small children are present, but once this is done no further attention is necessary.

Varieties. The var. *maximowiczii* has more deeply lobed leaves than the species type, densely pubescent underneath.

Kerria japonica 4

K E R R I A
Deciduous shrub
Rosaceae (Rose Family)

Native Range. China.

Useful Range. USDA Zones 5b–9a.

Function. Border, specimen.

Size and Habit

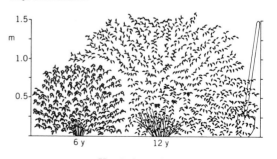

Kerria japonica.

Adaptability

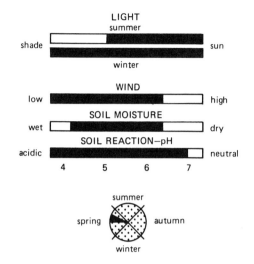

Seasonal Interest. *Flowers:* Bright yellow and showy, to 4.5 cm/1.8 in. across, in midspring. Often a few flowers will open intermittently during late summer and autumn. *Foliage:* Bright green with crisp texture; leaves long tapered and sharply toothed, to 5 cm/2 in. long, sometimes turning yellow before falling in autumn. *Twigs and branches:* Pale green, adding considerable winter interest.

Problems and Maintenance. This shrub is relatively trouble-free but needs to be thinned every few years to maintain form. This is especially true of the double-flowered cultivar.

Cultivars. 'Albaflora' has pale creamy yellow flowers. 'Golden Guinea' has single golden yellow flowers, larger than usual for this species. 'Pleniflora' has double flowers, almost globose in shape, remaining colorful longer than the single flowers of the species type and gradually turning to a deep orange-yellow. 'Variegata' (= 'Picta'), with irregularly white-edged, smaller leaves, is much daintier and slower-growing than the species type. But it is genetically unstable, often undergoing bud mutations back to the species type, which, because of their greater vigor, soon take over. 'Variegata' is best reserved for small-scale gardens where the plant is frequently inspected so that such genetic reversions can be cut out promptly.

Koelreuteria paniculata 7

GOLDEN RAIN TREE
Deciduous tree
Sapindaceae (Soapberry Family)

Native Range.   China and Korea.

Useful Range.   USDA Zones 5b–9a.

Function.   Specimen, patio tree, small shade tree.

Size and Habit

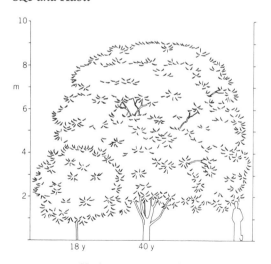

Koelreuteria paniculata.

Adaptability

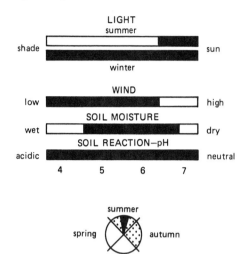

Seasonal Interest. *Flowers:* Yellow with red centers, small but borne in large, loose, upright clusters; showy in midsummer on most trees, but in late summer on some. *Foliage:* Deep green, deeply cut, compound with a few leaflets doubly compound, falling in autumn without color change. *Fruits:* Large (to 5 cm/2 in. long), papery, inflated capsules, pale yellow-green in late summer, later turning brown and persisting well into autumn.

Problems and Maintenance. This tree is trouble-free except for being weak wooded and subject to damage during ice and wind storms.

Cultivars. 'September' was selected for its late flowering, a full five weeks or more later than typical trees of this species. It did not get into commerce very quickly, but is available at this writing from at least one large mail-order nursery, and may become more widely accessible soon. Useful at least in Zones 6–9a, and probably 5b as well. Late flowering trees of this species have been observed in several places, but this probably is the first clone introduced, by J. C. McDaniel of the University of Illinois.

Related Species

Koelreuteria bipinnata 7 (golden rain tree).   This tree gives much the same landscape effect as its more cold-hardy relative, *K. paniculata*. Its papery, bladderlike pods, similar to those of *K.*

paniculata, are pink at first, drying a warm tan color, and its foliage turns yellowish before falling. Useful in Zone 9a+ and perhaps Zone 8 as well in protected sites.

Koelreuteria elegans 7 (synonym: *K. formosana;* Chinese flame tree, flamegold).   Generally similar to *K. bipinnata* and often confused with it, but less cold-hardy. It is useful in Zone 9a+ and most common south of our range in Florida.

Sapindus drummondii 7 (western soapberry, wild China tree).   This native of the south-central and southwestern United States from southern Missouri to Arizona and adjacent Mexico is drought-resistant and trouble-free, potentially useful as a street tree in Zones 6b–9a+, but little used and seldom available. It reaches heights of up to 15 m/49 ft, the trunk and branches covered with scaly bark showing reddish orange inner bark. The lustrous, medium green, compound leaves turn golden yellow before falling in midautumn. Very small, yellowish white flowers are borne in loose clusters to 25 cm/10 in. long in late spring, and the yellow, translucent fruits, to 1.5 cm/0.6 in. across, ripen in early autumn, then turn black and hang on for some time. The seeds occasionally send up weed seedlings much as the related *Koelreuteria* does.

Xanthoceras sorbifolium 6 (xanthoceras).   This small, shrubby tree, to 8 m/25 ft tall, native to China, is little used and not generally available. But it has good landscape qualities, including white flowers, yellow to red in the center, in clusters 15–25 cm/6–10 in. long in midspring, followed by hard, thick-walled fruits, 4–6 cm/ 1.6–2.4 in. across, superficially resembling those of quince. The lustrous foliage remains dark green late into autumn. It has broad soil and environmental tolerance and is useful in Zones 6b–9a.

Kolkwitzia amabilis 5

BEAUTYBUSH
Deciduous shrub
Caprifoliaceae (Honeysuckle Family)

Native Range.   Central China.

Useful Range.   USDA Zones 5a–8a.

Function.   Border, specimen.

Size and Habit

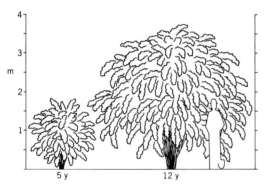

Kolkwitzia amabilis.

Adaptability

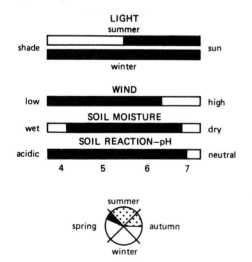

Seasonal Interest.   *Flowers:* Pale pink with yellow-orange throat, only 1.5 cm/0.6 in. long but borne in great numbers all along the arching branches, making this one of the most spectacular of flowering shrubs in late spring. *Foliage:*

Medium green, pointed leaves resemble those of the small-leaved mock oranges and turn reddish in autumn in some years. *Fruits:* Brown or pinkish and bristly, adding little to the plant's interest in summer and early autumn. *Twigs and branches:* Light tan bark peels off in large strips and patches, giving a ragged winter appearance.

Problems and Maintenance.   This shrub is relatively trouble-free but requires regular pruning (thinning by removal of large branches) to maintain the potentially graceful form. Pruning for control of size is not practical. Rather the plant should be used only where there is enough space to accommodate its height and spread. At the northern edge of its useful range (Zone 5) it suffers occasional twig kill, requiring some additional pruning to remove winterkilled branch tips.

Cultivars.   'Pink Cloud' was selected for unusually showy pink flowers. Other, unnamed selections are sometimes available.

Related Species

Dipelta floribunda 6.   This large shrub from China is closely related to *Kolkwitzia*, which it resembles, except that it grows to 5 m/16 ft tall, with larger flowers than those of *Kolkwitzia*. It is potentially useful in Zones 6b–9a, as well as in sheltered sites in Zone 6a, but is probably not available.

Heptacodium miconioides 5 (synonym: *H. jasminoides*; seven-sons plant).   This shrub in the Caprifoliaceae (Honeysuckle Family) was found by E. H. Wilson in central China and was first named from Wilson's herbarium specimen by Alfred Rehder in 1916. Living plants were not introduced into North America until seeds were collected by the Sino-American Botanical Expedition to China in 1980. Plants were then grown by the Arnold Arboretum and the species is commercially available in a few nurseries. This large shrub or very small tree (with training) grows very rapidly to at least 3–5 m/10–16 ft tall, with gracefully arching branches, distinctly trinerved (three main veins) leaves, and curling, papery, tan bark. Its creamy white 2.5-cm/1-in. flowers, in seven-flower clusters, open in late summer and are followed in autumn by fruits interesting for their deep crimson sepals, similar to those of *Abelia* but larger. Useful in Zones 6a–9a, perhaps also parts of Zone 5.

Laburnum ×watereri 6

Synonym: *L. vossii*
Deciduous tree
WATERER LABURNUM, GOLDEN CHAIN TREE
Fabaceae (Leguminosae; Pea Family)

Hybrid origin.   *L. anagyroides × L. alpinum.*

Useful Range.   USDA Zones 6a–7b and relatively cool sites in Zone 8.

Function.   Specimen, patio tree, border accent.

Size and Habit.   'Vossii' is illustrated.

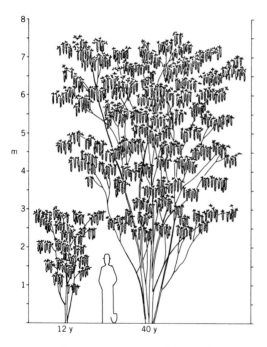

Laburnum ×watereri 'Vossii.'

Adaptability

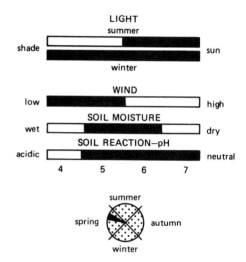

Seasonal Interest.   *Flowers:* Bright yellow, individually to 2.5 cm/1 in., in pendulous clusters, 25–50 cm/10–20 in. long, in late spring, lasting for only a week or two. *Foliage:* Bright green leaves of three leaflets, each 3–8 cm/1–3 in. long, falling without color change in autumn. *Twigs and branches:* Smooth, olive green bark is distinctive in the landscape in winter.

Problems and Maintenance.   This tree is relatively trouble-free where it is fully hardy. At the edges of its useful range it is prone to sun-scald of the bark where exposed to afternoon sun in winter. Foliage "burning" may occur in summer if used in dry or windy sites. The seeds are poisonous to both livestock and humans.

Cultivars.   'Vossii', sometimes incorrectly listed as *L. vossii*, is an extremely showy selection for its fullness and long chains of flowers.

Related Species

Laburnum alpinum 6 (Scotch laburnum).   This tree, from the mountains of southern Europe in spite of its common name, is similar to *L.* ×*watereri* except somewhat less showy in flower (chains 30–35 cm/12–14 in. long) and at least a little more cold-hardy, to Zone 5b with proper siting.

Laburnum anagyroides 6 (golden chain, bean tree). This tree is slightly more upright and less cold-hardy than *L. alpinum,* with shorter chains of flowers (20 cm/8 in. long), making it less showy than either *L. alpinum* or *L.* ×*watereri.* There is little reason for using it when the others are available, except for 'Pendula,' which is pendulous in habit, accentuated by the hanging flower clusters.

Lagerstroemia indica 3–6

CRAPE MYRTLE
Deciduous shrub or small tree
Lythraceae (Loosestrife Family)

Native Range.   China.

Useful Range.   USDA Zones 7b–9a+.

Function.   Specimen, border.

Size and Habit

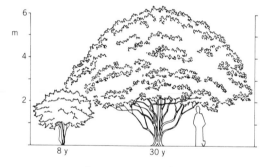

Lagerstroemia indica.

Seasonal Interest.   *Flowers:* Brilliant red, pink, lavender, or white, crinkly textured, in showy clusters of 15 cm/6 in. and larger in middle to late summer. *Foliage:* Neatly textured oval leaves are deep reddish bronze as they unfold, quickly turn rich medium green, and then turn reddish or yellowish before falling in autumn. *Trunk and branches:* Smooth, silvery gray to pinkish tan or brown, usually bicolored bark and sinewy main branches add strong winter interest.

Problems and Maintenance.   North of Zone 7b this plant will persist, but tops will frequently winterkill and must be removed each spring. Since this plant flowers on new growth, it will return and give a flowering display in late summer but will not attain full size or develop trunk and bark interest. Powdery mildew can be troublesome, especially for plants in shaded sites,

Adaptability.   Performs best in well-drained soil of good water-holding capacity rather than sandy soils that tend to dry out rapidly.

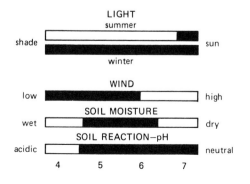

Lagerstroemia indica.

Lagerstroemia indica.

but resistant cultivars are being developed (see Cultivars). In areas where Japanese beetle has spread, this insect can cause severe damage to the flowers.

Cultivars. At least 100 cultivars are available in the United States, and many of these are of the "new generation" of cultivars that have appeared since about 1970. Many of the best of these were selected or bred by the late Donald Egolf at the U.S. National Arboretum (USNA), but other excellent new cultivars have been developed at commercial nurseries. Some of those listed are selections of *L. indica*, while others are hybrids of *L. indica* × *L. fauriei*, as noted. They are listed by size category.

Size Group 3 (dwarf, pendulous shrubs, 0.5–1 m/ 1.6–3.3 ft tall):
'Baton Rouge' (Plant Patent No. 4183, 1978) has deep red flowers.
'Bourbon Street' (Plant Patent No. 4182, 1978) has watermelon-red flowers.

'Delta Blush' (Plant Patent No. 4186, 1978) has pink flowers.
'New Orleans' (Plant Patent No. 4184, 1978) has purple flowers.
'World's Fair' (Plant Patent pending) has watermelon-red flowers and is the smallest of this group, below 0.6 m/2 ft in height.

Size Group 4 (small shrubs, 1–2 m/3.3–6.6 ft tall):
'Centennial' has bright purple flowers and mildew-resistant foliage, turning orange in autumn.
'Hope' has pink-flushed white flowers and mildew-resistant foliage.
'Monink' (Chica Pink™, Plant Patent pending) and 'Moned' (Chica Red™, Plant Patent pending) have pink and red flowers, respectively, and grow to 1 m/3.3 ft.
'Moners' (Petite Embers™), 'Monhid' (Petite Orchid™), 'Monkie' (Petite Pinkie™), 'Monum' (Petite Plum™), 'Monimp' (Petite Red Imp™), and 'Monow' (Petite Snow™) have flower colors described by their trademarked names, and grow to about 1.5 m/5 ft tall.
'Victor' has brilliant red flowers.

Size Group 5 (medium shrubs, 2–4 m/6.6–13 ft):
'Acoma' is an *L. fauriei* hybrid from the USNA, growing to at least 3 m/10 ft tall and wider, with semipendulous habit, white flowers over a long season, bright red new foliage, and red-purple autumn foliage.
'Hopi' is unusually hardy for an *L. fauriei* hybrid (Zone 7a?), growing to 3 m/10 ft tall, with pink flowers and mildew-resistant foliage, turning orange-red in autumn.
'Pecos' is an *L. fauriei* hybrid from the USNA, upright in form, growing to 2.5 m/8 ft tall, with medium pink flowers (over a long season) and mildew-resistant foliage.
'Tonto' is an *L. fauriei* hybrid from the USNA, growing to 2.5 m/8 ft tall and wider, with large clusters of bright red flowers, striking light tan mottled bark, and deep crimson autumn foliage.
'Zuni' is an unusually hardy *L. fauriei* hybrid from the USNA (Zone 7a?), growing to 2.5 m/8 ft tall and as wide, with orchid flowers over a long season and glossy, mildew-resistant foliage, turning orange-red in autumn.

'Near East' is a *L. indica* selection, growing to 2 m/6.6 ft, with very showy, soft-pink flowers.

'Seminole' is a USNA *L. indica* selection, compactly globose and growing to 2.5 m/8 ft tall, with showy pink flowers.

Size Group 6 (large shrubs or small trees, 4–8 m/ 13–26 ft):

'Apalachee' is a USNA *L. fauriei* hybrid, growing to 4.5 m/15 ft tall, with pale lavender flowers, dark green foliage, turning orange-red in autumn, and outstanding mottled cinnamon-brown bark.

'Biloxi,' another unusually hardy USNA *L. fauriei* hybrid (to Zone 7a?), grows to at least 6 m/20 ft tall, with light pink flowers, gracefully arching branches, and deep brown, mottled bark.

'Byers Wonderful White' is upright, to 6m/20 ft tall, with great masses of white flowers and mildew-resistant foliage, turning yellow in autumn.

'Carolina Beauty' is an *L. indica* selection, growing to 6 m/20 ft tall, with deep red flowers and dark green foliage, turning orange in autumn.

'Catawba,' an *L. indica* selection from the USNA, grows to 4.5 m/15 ft tall, with bright violet-purple flowers and bright orange autumn foliage.

'Choctaw' is a USNA *L. fauriei* hybrid, upright to at least 6 m/20 ft, with wide-spreading branches and bright pink flowers, mildew-resistant foliage, turning bronze-maroon in autumn, and mottled cinnamon-colored bark.

'Comanche' is a USNA *L. fauriei* hybrid, growing to 4.5 m/15 ft tall, with deep coral-pink flowers, similar to 'Watermelon Red,' mildew-resistant foliage, turning purplish red in autumn, and excellent light brown mottled bark.

'Lipan,' another *L. fauriei* cross from the USNA, grows to 4.5 m/15 ft tall, with pale lavender flowers, mildew-resistant foliage that turns yellow-bronze in autumn, and outstanding whitish-beige exfoliating bark.

'Miami' is another USNA *L. fauriei* hybrid, growing to 6 m/20 ft tall, with elongated clusters of deep coral-pink flowers, foliage that is deep red as it emerges, turning deep green, then russet in autumn, and excellent chestnut-brown bark.

'Muskogee' is a USNA *L. fauriei* selection, to 7 m/23 ft tall, with mildew-resistant foliage, light lavender flowers, and brown exfoliating bark.

'Natchez' is also a USNA *L. fauriei* hybrid, growing to 7 m/23 ft tall, with white flowers, glossy dark green foliage that turns orange-red in autumn, and superb dark brown/beige mottled bark.

'Osage,' another USNA *L. fauriei* hybrid, grows to 4.5 m/15 ft tall and somewhat wider, with clear pink flowers, mildew-resistant young leaves, bronze as they unfold and dark red in autumn, and dark brown/chestnut mottled bark.

'Potomac' is a USNA *L. indica* selection, growing to 6 m/20 ft tall, with bright coral-pink flowers (over a long season) and mildew-resistant dark green foliage.

'Regal Red' is a hardy (Zone 7a) *L. indica* selection, growing to 4.5 m/15 ft tall, with deep red flowers.

'Tuscarora,' an *L. fauriei* hybrid from the USNA, grows to 6 m/20 ft tall and wide, with deep coral-pink flowers, mildew-resistant foliage, turning orange-red in autumn, and mottled light brown bark.

'Tuskegee," another USNA *L. fauriei* hybrid, is strongly horizontal (4.5 m/15 ft tall and 6 m/ 20 ft wide), with deep rose flowers, leathery and mildew-resistant foliage, turning reddish orange in autumn, and striking exfoliating bark.

'Watermelon Red' is a selection of *L. indica* that grows to at least 6 m/20 ft tall, with deep watermelon-pink flowers. 'William Toovey' is similar but not so large (4 m/13 m tall).

'Yuma,' yet another USDA *L. fauriei* hybrid, is unusually hardy (Zone 7a?), growing to 4.5 m/15 ft tall, with long clusters of semidouble lavender flowers.

Related Species

Lagerstroemia fauriei 6 (Japanese crape myrtle). This is a counterpart species from the Ryukyu Islands of Japan, significant primarily because of its role as a parent of many of the hybrid cultivars described above, but a useful small tree in its own right. The selection 'Fantasy,' introduced by the North Carolina State University Arboretum, is a graceful tree with remarkable red exfoliating bark, useful in Zones 7b–9a+, possibly 7a as well.

Lamium maculatum 2

SPOTTED DEAD NETTLE
Herbaceous groundcover
Lamiaceae (Labiatae; Mint Family)

Native Range.   Europe.

Useful Range.   USDA Zones 5a–9a.

Function.   Groundcover.

Size and Habit

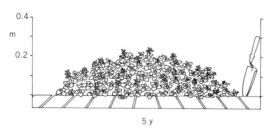

Lamium maculatum.

Adaptability.   Widely adapted to full sun or shade except that light shade or snow cover reduces winter injury in Zone 5.

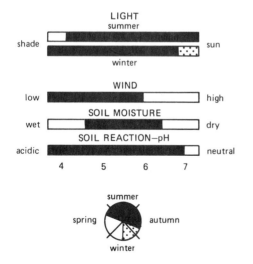

Seasonal Interest. *Flowers:* Small, purplish rose or white, in short, erect clusters from late spring to midsummer. *Foliage:* Deep sage green leaves, to 4 cm/1.6 in. long, each with a whitish stripe down the center, making a solid mat of attractive color and texture.

Problems and Maintenance. This groundcover is trouble-free and needs no maintenance other than to restrict its growth occasionally, since it can be weedy.

Cultivars. 'Album' has dark green leaves with a white midstripe and has white flowers. 'Aureum' has golden yellow leaves with a pale whitish midstripe, and white flowers.

'Beacon Silver,' 'Pink Pewter,' and 'White Nancy' have silvery white leaves with narrow green margins; 'Beacon Silver' and 'Pink Pewter' have pink flowers, and 'White Nancy' has white flowers. All three are very low (10–15 cm/4–6 in.) groundcovers, offering a bright accent in full shade, where they perform best.

'Beedham's White' has bright golden yellow foliage with a whitish midstripe and has white flowers.

'Chequers' and 'Shell Pink' have silver-marbled leaves; flower color of 'Chequers' is rose-pink, and that of 'Shell Pink' is pale pink.

Related Species

Lamium galeobdolon 2–3 (synonym: *Lamiastrum galeobdolon;* golden deadnettle, yellow archangel).   This species of *Lamium,* once given genus status, is native to southern Europe and adjacent Asia. Unlike *L. maculatum,* it has brown-marked yellow flowers, to 2 cm/0.8 in. long in midsummer. Its leaves are bright green, except in certain cultivars. This species can grow to 0.6 m/2 ft high, with trailing stems that make it a fast-covering groundcover and allow it to grow out of control rapidly if neglected. 'Herman's Pride,' a relatively new cultivar to North America, is more moundlike in habit, to less than 0.3 m/1 ft high, and not invasive like the species, with tidy silver-mottled foliage. The more common 'Variegatum' also has silver-blotched leaves and is not as invasive as the species. The few other cultivars are not widely available. Useful at least in Zones 5b–9a.

Nepeta mussinii 2 (catmint).   This native of the Caucasus region of western Asia has gray-green foliage and masses of small lavender flowers in early summer, and again in late summer or autumn if the plant is cut back after the first flowering. This effective groundcover needs a little more maintenance than *Lamium* species to keep it neat and within bounds, but it is useful in the same range as *Lamium maculatum*.

Larix decidua 8

EUROPEAN LARCH
Deciduous tree
Pinaceae (Pine Family)

Native Range.   Northern and central Europe.

Useful Range.   USDA Zones 4a–6b and possibly colder and warmer zones as well.

Function.   Specimen, massing, naturalizing.

Size and Habit

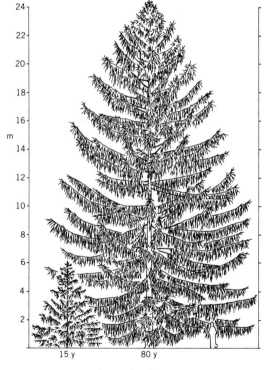

Larix decidua.

Adaptability

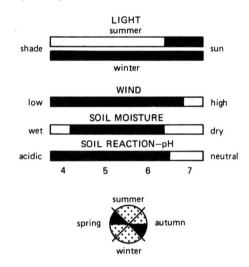

Seasonal Interest. *Foliage:* Deciduous, pale green needles, giving a lacy effect in spring, dark green later in summer, turning dull to bright yellow in late autumn before falling. *Fruits:* Cones to 3.5 cm/1.4 in. long in autumn and into winter; not adding greatly to the landscape interest of the tree. *Trunk and branches:* Branches are thickly spaced and the branchlets hang gracefully, especially noticeable in spring when accentuated by the new foliage.

Problems and Maintenance.   The larch casebearer insect occasionally can seriously disfigure trees and must be controlled except in naturalized situations. Larches drop twig and cone litter but fallen needles are scarcely noticeable.

Cultivars.   'Pendula' has gracefully weeping branches. 'Pyramidalis' is narrowly pyramidal in form, but seldom available.

Related Species

Larix laricina 8 (eastern larch or tamarack). This species is native to North America from eastern Canada and adjacent United States to Alaska and useful in Zones 2–6b. It differs from *L. decidua* in having much smaller cones, clearer yellow autumn foliage, and somewhat narrower growth habit and is especially well adapted to wet soils. 'Girard Nana' and 'Newport Beauty' are dwarf, globose forms. 'Newport Beauty' (and probably also 'Girard Nana') is a witch's-broom seedling. They are useful for small-scale accent.

Larix kaempferi 8 (synonym: *L. leptolepis*; Japanese larch). This tree differs from *L. decidua* in having heavier lateral branches more widely spaced on a massive central trunk, giving a more open growth habit. It is somewhat faster growing and is useful in Zones 4a–6b. 'Pendula' has pendulous branches, but is seldom available.

Larix kaempferi.

Lavandula angustifolia 3

Synonyms: *L. officinalis, L. spica, L. vera*
ENGLISH LAVENDER
Herbaceous groundcover or subshrub
Lamiaceae (Labiatae; Mint Family)

Native Range. Mediterranean region.

Useful Range. USDA Zones 6a–8b. Some cultivars useful in Zone 5.

Function. Groundcover, specimen, front of border, rock garden.

Size and Habit

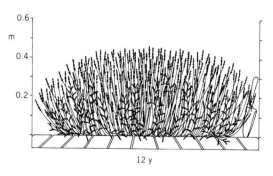

Lavandula angustifolia.

Adaptability

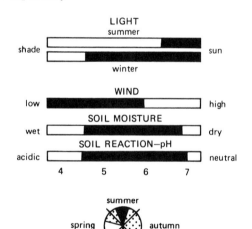

Seasonal Interest. *Flowers:* Lavender to purple, fragrant, very small, in erect spikes to 8 cm/ 3 in. long from early to late summer. *Foliage:* Very fine textured, the narrow, semievergreen leaves are grayish green and fragrant when crushed.

Problems and Maintenance. Trouble-free, requiring no maintenance other than pruning back after severe winters in the North.

Subspecies and Cultivars. *L. angustifolia* includes two subspecies, each until recently considered a species in its own right. The ssp. *pyrenaica* (synonym: *L. pyrenaica*) is little used, but ssp. *angustifolia,* the species type, is commonly used and available. Several cultivars have been selected, including those listed here. 'Alba' and 'Nana Alba' are white flowering forms, perhaps the same one. 'Hidcote,' 'Munstead,' and 'Nana' are compact forms, 30–45 cm/12–18 in. tall and more cold-hardy than average for this species, to Zone 5b, perhaps 5a with reliable snow cover.

Related Species

Conradina verticillata 2 (Cumberland mountain rosemary). This low, mound-forming shrub in the Lamiaceae (Mint Family), native to Tennessee, has small, needlelike evergreen leaves, aromatic much like rosemary *(Rosmarinus)*. Its lavender-pink flowers, 1.5 cm/0.6 in. long, are clustered in elongated series of whorls around the stems and are fairly showy. This plant is environmentally threatened; specify cutting-propagated plants, available in a few nurseries. Useful at least in Zones 7a–8b and relatively tolerant of dry sites.

Rosmarinus officinalis 2–4 (rosemary). This shrub, widely used for seasoning but with significant landscape value as well, reaches heights of 0.6–1.8 m/2–6 ft high and 1–2.4 m/3–8 ft wide, variable by cultivar, with evergreen, bright to dark green, needlelike leaves and with blue flowers in late spring. Useful in Zones 8a–9a+, some cultivars into Zone 7. The selection 'Arp' is notably more cold-hardy than others, at least to Zone 7b, growing to 0.6 m/2 ft high and at least as wide, with lighter green foliage having a lemon fragrance. 'Collingwood Ingram,' 'Huntington Carpet,' and 'Prostrata' are also low-growing selections, but 'Huntington Carpet' eventually spreads to 2–2.6 m/6.6–8 ft wide. 'Tuscan Blue' is a fine larger selection, growing to 1.8 m/6 ft tall but not as wide. All perform best in full sun.

Ledum groenlandicum 2–3

LABRADOR TEA
Evergreen groundcover
Ericaceae (Heath Family)

Native Range.   Northern North America.

Useful Range.   USDA Zones 2b–6b.

Function.   Specimen, rock garden.

Size and Habit

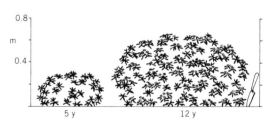

Ledum groenlandicum.

Adaptability

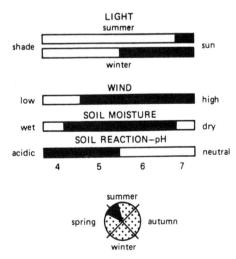

Seasonal Interest.   *Flowers:* Small, white, in flat clusters, making an interesting contrast with the foliage in late spring and early summer. *Foliage:* Evergreen, medium green and wrinkled

Ledum groenlandicum.

Ledum palustre.

on upper surfaces with dense, rusty pubescence, underneath and on stems. Leaves are about 2.5–5 cm/1–2 in. long, and narrow, almost linear.

Problems and Maintenance. Once established in a proper site, it is trouble-free and requires no maintenance other than weed control, preferably by mulching.

Cultivars. 'Compactum' is more compact than the species type, remaining well below 0.5 m/1.6 ft for many years, with wider leaves and smaller flower clusters.

Related Species

Ledum palustre 2–3 (wild rosemary). This Eurasian species differs little from *L. groenlandicum,* its North American counterpart, and can be considered interchangeable in landscape use when available.

Leiophyllum buxifolium 2 (box sandmyrtle). This low, moundlike plant from the New Jersey coastal plain to the Piedmont and mountains of the Carolinas eventually grows to about 0.5 m/1.6 ft tall and much wider, but for the first several years it remains small. It is useful in acidic, well-drained rock gardens. Probably its greatest value is that it gives the same effect as several other ericaceous plants that grow in bogs, but is more tolerant of drier soil. However, it requires ample moisture following transplanting. Since it is somewhat difficult to transplant otherwise, specify pot-grown plants. The white or pinkish flowers appear at the same time as those of *Ledum groenlandicum* with about the same effect. Useful at least in Zones 6a–8b. The var. *prostratum,* native to high elevations in the mountains of North Carolina, remains below 10 cm/4 in. in height and is probably more cold hardy, at least to Zone 5b.

Leitneria floridana 5–6

CORKWOOD
Deciduous shrub
Leitneriaceae (Corkwood Family)

Native Range. Southeastern United States from Florida to Texas and northward to Missouri.

Useful Range. USDA Zones 6a–9a+.

Function. Naturalizing in wet areas.

Size and Habit. In Zones 8 and 9 this plant eventually forms a loosely open, suckering tree to 5 m/16 ft; in colder zones it usually remains below 3 m/10 ft because of winter injury.

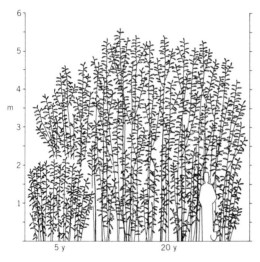

Leitneria floridana.

Adaptability

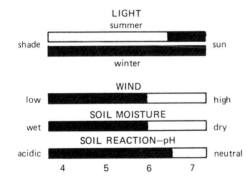

Seasonal Interest. *Foliage:* Long, rather narrow, bright green leaves, smooth with a faint silky pubescence, giving a clean, somewhat coarse texture, falling in autumn without color change.

Leitneria floridana.

Problems and Maintenance. This shrub's greatest limitation is that it is seldom commercially available. When preserved in the wild or naturalized, it is trouble-free and requires no maintenance beyond establishment, but its commercial availability is very limited.

Lespedeza bicolor 5

SHRUB BUSH CLOVER
Deciduous shrub or subshrub
Fabaceae (Leguminosae; Pea Family)

Native Range. China, Japan.

Useful Range. USDA Zones 5a–7b.

Function. Border, specimen, massing.

Size and Habit

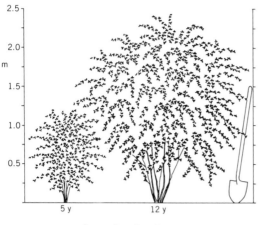

Lespedeza bicolor.

Adaptability

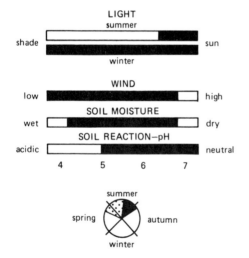

Seasonal Interest. *Flowers:* Small, rosy purple, in small to large, loose clusters in late summer and early autumn. *Foliage:* Medium- to fine-textured and airy, of three leaflets, each to 4 cm/ 1.6 in. long, upper surface dark green, lower paler gray-green.

Problems and Maintenance. This shrub is subject to winter dieback of branches, especially in Zone 5, so it requires some pruning in most years, in spring after new growth begins so that the extent of winter injury can be seen. In warmer zones, occasional pruning (thinning out of large stems and selective tip pruning) is neces-sary to maintain form. When necessary, it can be cut back to the ground and will return and flower in the same year. It is not widely available.

Related Species

Lespedeza cuneata 3 (synonym: *L. sericea;* Chinese bush clover, sericea). This low subshrub, to 1 m/3.3 ft, with wandlike, ascending branches and whitened, fine textured foliage, is useful for roadside planting in Zones 6a–9a+ and is recommended by the U.S. Soil Conservation Service for use as a roadside cover and for stabilizing stripmine spoils as well as for forage.

Lespedeza cyrtobotrya 5. This shrub has dense clusters of red-purple flowers very late in summer and into autumn. It is slightly less hardy than *L. bicolor,* Zones 6a–8a, and also not commonly available.

Lespedeza japonica 5 (sometimes called *L. thunbergii* f. *albiflora;* Japanese bush clover). This species is very similar to *L. thunbergii* but has white flowers, later than those of *L. bicolor.* Useful in Zones 6a–8a.

Lespedeza thunbergii 5 (Thunberg bush clover). This subshrub is similar to *L. japonica* except that it has rosy purple flowers. A few cultivars have been selected. 'Alba' and 'White Fountain' have white flowers. 'Gibraltar' has unusually showy, deep lavender flowers. 'Pink Fountain' has pinkish-purple flowers, upright habit, and gracefully arching branches.

Leucophyllum frutescens 4

Synonym: *L. texanum*
CENIZA, TEXAS SAGE
Semievergreen shrub
Scrophulariaceae (Figwort Family)

Native Range.   Texas to Mexico.

Useful Range.   USDA Zones 8a–9a+, perhaps slightly colder areas as well, useful primarily in the southwestern parts of our area.

Function.   Hedge, specimen.

Size and Habit

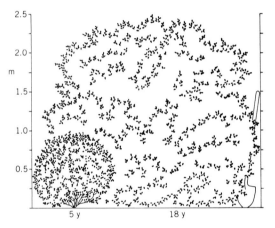

Leucophyllum frutescens.

Adaptability.   Outstanding for tolerance of high-limestone soils, drought, and heat.

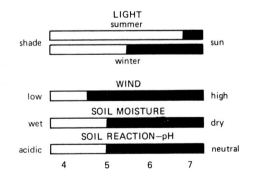

Seasonal Interest.   *Flowers:* Pink to rosy purple, funnel shaped, to 2 cm/0.8 in. across, in great numbers in summer or following rains.

Foliage: Silvery felted, to 2.5 cm/1 in. long, giving color and textural interest, nearly evergreen but becoming dingy by late winter.

Problems and Maintenance.   This shrub is trouble-free but little known and seldom available outside its native habitat, which includes the southwestern corner of our area. It may not perform well in the more humid climate of the southeastern states but is worth trying experimentally there.

Cultivars.   'Compactum' is lower growing and more compact than the species type, growing to about 1.5 m/5 ft tall and wide, with masses of pink flowers. The following introductions from Texas A&M University make good use of the variation in flowering and foliage that exists in this species. 'Green Cloud'™ grows to at least 2 m/6.6 ft tall and wide, with deep green foliage (rather than the typical blue-gray of the species type) and pink flowers. 'White Cloud'™ is also a full-sized selection, differing from the species type in having white rather than pink or purple flowers. See additional cultivars in this series under *L. candidum,* below.

Other Species and Cultivars

Leucophyllum candidum 4 (silver sage).   This is a slightly smaller version of *L. frutescens* with very silvery foliage. Two cultivars of this species are included in the Texas A&M series. 'Silver Cloud'™ is compact, growing to only about 1.5 m/5 ft tall and wide, with dense silvery gray foliage and blue-purple flowers. 'Thunder Cloud'™ is even more compact than 'Silver Cloud'™, otherwise similar, remaining below 1 m/3.3 ft in height and width.

Leucophyllum laevigatum 4 (Chihuahuan sage). This open shrub to 1.2 m/4 ft tall and 1.5 m/5 ft wide has dark green foliage and showy lavender-purple flowers. Useful in about the same range as *L. frutescens*.

Leucophyllum langmaniae 4.   The cultivar 'Rio Bravo'™, introduced by Mountain States Nursery, is a dense shrub with dark green foliage and lavender flowers, growing to about 1.5 m/5 ft tall and wide, serving as a smaller version of 'Green Cloud'™.

Leucophyllum pruinosum 4–5.   The cultivar 'Sierra Bouquet'™, introduced by Mountain States Nursery, is a large shrub, to about 2 m/6.6 ft tall and wide, with silvery gray foliage and deep purple flowers, reported to be intensely fragrant.

Leucophyllum zygophyllum 3 (blue ranger).   This is a small shrub, not exceeding 1 m/3.3 ft in height and spread, with soft silvery gray foliage and light blue flowers. This species is reported to be even more sensitive to overwatering than other *Leucophyllum* species.

Related Species

Lycium barbarum 4 (synonyms: *L. chinense, L. halimifolium;* common matrimony vine).   This large, rambling, vinelike shrub from southeastern Europe and adjacent Asia has become naturalized in some parts of our area. It is one of the few woody temperate zone members of the Solanaceae (Nightshade Family), loosely allied to the Scrophulariaceae (Figwort Family). Its spiny, arching branches make it an effective barrier, but it is potentially troublesome in the same way as *Rosa multiflora*, suckering and spreading quickly to become a weed. Its small purple flowers, beginning in early summer and continuing sporadically, give it minor added interest; and its orange-red fruits, each only up to 2 cm/0.8 in. long but borne in large numbers, add color in late summer and autumn. Its usefulness, in Zones 6a–9a, comes from its effectiveness as a barrier and its tolerance of very dry soil and salt.

Leucothoë fontanesiana 3–4

Synonyms *L. catesbaei, L. editorum*
FOUNTAIN OR DROOPING
LEUCOTHOE
Evergreen shrub
Ericaceae (Heath Family)

Native Range.   Virginia to Georgia and Tennessee.

Useful Range.   USDA Zones 5b–9a.

Function.   Border, naturalizing. Especially useful as a facing shrub in combination with rhododendrons in a border or screen.

Size and Habit

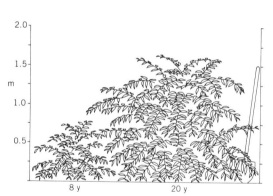

Leucothoë fontanesiana.

Adaptability. Protection from full winter sun is necessary, at least in the North, to prevent winterburn.

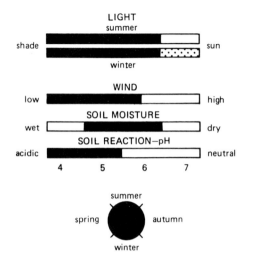

Seasonal Interest. *Flowers:* Waxy, white, in drooping spikes, 4–8 cm/1.6–3 in. long, in late spring. *Foliage:* Evergreen, leathery, dark green and sharp-pointed, arranged in double rows on the arching branches, turning deep bronze-purple when exposed to direct sun in winter.

Problems and Maintenance. This shrub is relatively trouble-free and requires little maintenance other than occasional pruning, which must be done carefully by removing older stems close to the base of the plant and letting them be replaced by suckers from the roots, since there are few lateral buds on the lower stems. The plant is toxic to animals (see *Kalmia latifolia*).

Cultivars. 'Zebonard' (Lovita™, Plant Patent No. 5229, 1984) forms a dense mound to only 0.6 m/2 ft high and 1.2 m/4 ft wide, with smaller leaves, turning deep bronze in winter sun. 'Rainbow' is a slow-growing selection with pink-tinged new growth and leaves variegated with creamy white, turning wine-red in autumn and winter when exposed to full sun for part of the day. Remains below 0.6 m/2 ft for years but eventually grows to 1 m/3.3 ft or slightly more. 'Rollisonii' is compact and graceful, to 0.9 m/3 ft high and twice as wide. 'Zeblid' (Scarletta™, Plant Patent No. 5195, 1984) has showy, bright scarlet

new growth in spring, turning dark green in summer, then deep red-purple in autumn, and matures at 0.9 m/3 ft high and 1.5 m/5 ft wide.

Related Species

Leucothoë axillaris 4 (synonym: *L. catesbaei;* coast leucothoe). This evergreen shrub is very similar to *L. fontanesiana*, easily confused with it, and interchangeable in landscape use except in Zone 5, where it is not fully hardy. The selection 'Compacta' is more compact in form, remaining below 0.6 m/2 ft for several years but eventually growing to at least 1 m/3.3 ft high and at least 1.5 m/5 ft wide.

Leucothoë keiskei 2 (Japanese leucothoe). This dwarf shrub, to 0.5 m/1.5 ft high, has small, red-tinted leaves (2.5–5 cm/1–2 in. long), turning wine-red in winter, and the largest flowers of any leucothoe, individually 1.2–2 cm/0.5–0.8 in. long, in nodding clusters 2.5–5 cm/1–2 in. long

Leucothoë fontanesiana 'Rainbow.'

Leucothoë racemosa.

in summer. It is not widely available but is growing more popular, in at least Zones 7a–9a.

Leucothoë populifolia 5 (synonym: *L. acuminata*). This rangy shrub from the far southeastern United States is less valued for landscape planting than *L. axillaris* and *L. fontanesiana* but can be preserved or naturalized to good effect in Zones 7b–9a.

Leucothoë racemosa 5 (sweetbells).   Unlike the other species of *Leucothoë* mentioned, this is a deciduous shrub, tall and rangy, with white to pinkish flowers in early summer and bright green foliage that turns red before falling in late autumn or early winter. It is useful in Zones 6a–9a for massing and screening.

Ligustrum japonicum 5–6

Synonyms: *L. texanum, and often confused with L. lucidum (see Cultivars and Related Species)*
JAPANESE PRIVET, WAX LEAF LIGUSTRUM
Evergreen shrub or small tree
Oleaceae (Olive Family)

Native Range.   Japan and Korea.

Useful Range.   USDA Zones 7b–9a+.

Function.   Hedge, screen, small specimen tree, containers.

Size and Habit

Adaptability.   This is one of the most widely adaptable broadleaved evergreens for the South.

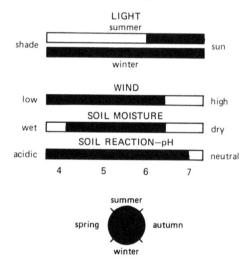

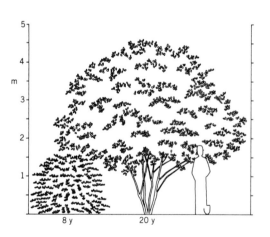

Ligustrum japonicum.

Seasonal Interest.   *Flowers:* Small, in upright clusters, fragrant as is characteristic of *Ligustrum* species, not universally considered pleasantly so; interesting but not truly showy, in late summer. *Foliage:* Deep green with a waxy luster, evergreen and leathery, elegant in color and texture, and striking in the landscape, especially in winter. *Fruits:* Small, green and ripening black, of little landscape significance.

Problems and Maintenance.   Sooty mold and accompanying aphids, white flies, and scale insects can disfigure this plant if not controlled. Nematodes also can be troublesome in some areas in Zone 9a and southward. In such areas only plants grafted on nematode-resistant rootstocks such as *L. quihoui* (see *L. vulgare,* Related

Species) should be used. Also, privets are shallow rooted plants, and others planted close to them may not compete well for water and nutrients.

Cultivars. 'Jack Frost' has leaves with creamy white marginal variegation and is upright and quite vigorous, in time reaching 2–3 m/6.6–10 m in height and slightly less in spread. 'Silver Star' also has leaves with creamy white marginal variegation, but is slower-growing, staying below eye level for at least several years.

'Recurvifolium' has rounded leaves with a wavy margin and is reported to grow to 2–3 m/6.6–10 ft tall. 'Rotundifolium' (synonyms: var. *rotundifolium*, *L. coriaceum*, and 'Suwannee River'; curlyleaf ligustrum) has rounded, curled leaves, slightly notched at the apex. This selection may eventually grow to a height of 2 m/6.6 m, but it does not reach that size fast enough to be a reliable visual screen.

'Texanum' (sometimes called *L. texanum*) is not a species but a selection for highly waxy foliage and tolerance of dry soil. It has a compact growth habit, eventually growing to 2–3 m/6.6–8 ft, and can be kept lower by careful pruning. The selection called 'Texanum Aureo-marginata' has young leaves with yellow margins, turning green as they age or in shade.

Ligustrum japonicum is a variable species with large- and small-leaved selections and treelike or shrubby forms. Some of these have been incorrectly called *L. lucidum*. For true *L. lucidum*, see Related Species.

Related Species

Ligustrum lucidum 6 (glossy privet). This tall shrub or small tree, to 8–10 m/25–33 ft but most often seen in the 5–8 m/16–25 ft range, has large, evergreen leaves, not as glossy as those of *L. japonicum* in spite of its name. It is rank growing with less landscape character than *L. japonicum*, but does produce a display of huge clusters of purple-black fruits on orange stems in autumn and holding throughout winter. The selection 'Variegatum,' not common in commerce, has white, marginally variegated leaves, but should not be confused with those *L. japonicum* cultivars that have similar variegation.

Ligustrum obtusifolium 4–5

BORDER PRIVET
Deciduous shrub
Oleaceae (Olive Family)

Native Range. Japan.

Useful Range. USDA Zones 4b–8a.

Function. Informal hedge, border, specimen.

Size and Habit. The var. *regelianum* is illustrated.

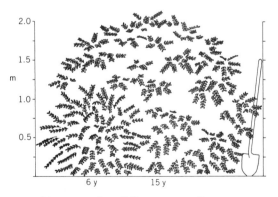

Ligustrum obtusifolium var. regelianum.

Adaptability

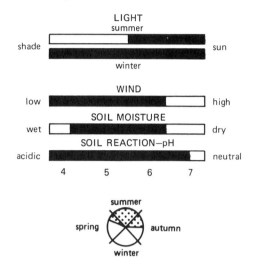

Seasonal Interest. *Flowers:* Small, white, in small clusters, fragrant but not pleasantly so to some people, in late spring. *Foliage:* Deciduous, medium green to lustrous deep green, the individual leaves about 5 cm/2 in. long, turning yellow to purplish in autumn in some locations and years. *Fruits:* Small, blue-black, adding quiet autumn interest.

Problems and Maintenance. This shrub is about as trouble-free as any privet and requires less maintenance than most deciduous privets, since pruning is seldom necessary except for renewal.

Varieties. The var. *regelianum*—or, more specifically, the *clone* usually sold as 'Regelianum' (Regel privet)—is the preferred form, with gracefully arching horizontal branching, a compact, "blocky" form at maturity, and handsome, lustrous foliage. Seedlings of 'Regelianum' are sometimes sold as the clone, and may look like this description, but usually are more open and less horizontal in branching, reaching heights of 2–3 m/6.6–10 ft. The true clone 'Regelianum' usually stays below 1.5 m/5 ft for several years and exceeds 2 m/6.6 ft only after many years. This plant makes an excellent informal (natural) hedge, but it should never be sheared as a formal hedge. This destroys its character. Light selective pruning to reduce size while preserving plant form is a possibility, but most cases where that is necessary are the result of using nonclonal material.

Related Species

Ligustrum amurense 5 (Amur River privet). This privet is usefully hardy northward to Zone 4b. It is trouble-free in northern areas except for occasional killing back in winter, has bright green to light green foliage, and is easily pruned into a formal hedge. Fertilization improves foliage color but predisposes the plant to winter injury, as does shearing later than midsummer.

Ligustrum ovalifolium 5

CALIFORNIA PRIVET
Deciduous or semievergreen shrub
Oleaceae (Olive Family)

Native Range. Japan.

Useful Range. USDA Zones 6a–9a.

Function. Hedge, screen, border.

Size and Habit

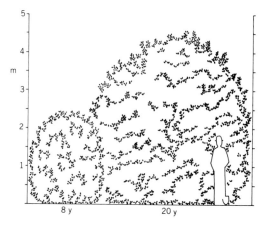

Ligustrum ovalifolium.

Adaptability

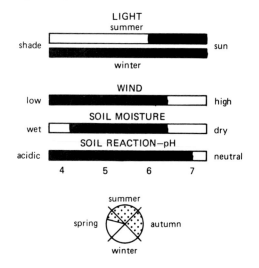

Seasonal Interest. *Flowers:* Small, white, in small upright clusters, fragrant but not pleasantly so to some people, in late spring or early summer. *Foliage:* Lustrous, bright to deep green, deciduous (North) to semievergreen (South), somewhat leathery. *Fruits:* Small, blue-black, adding quiet autumn interest.

Problems and Maintenance. This shrub is occasionally troubled with aphids and scale insects but is not nearly as susceptible to insect problems as the fully evergreen privets. In Zone 6 it can be damaged severely in occasional very cold winters, and this susceptibility to cold injury is heightened by late season pruning or overfertilization.

Cultivars. 'Aureum' (= 'Aureo-marginata') has yellow-margined leaves. Contrast between the green and yellow is enhanced by high soil fertility levels, but this predisposes the plant to winter injury in the north, so this cultivar probably should be used only from Zone 7a southward.

Ligustrum ovalifolium 'Aureum.'

Related Species

Ligustrum ×*ibolium* 5 (Ibolium privet). This hybrid (*L. ovalifolium* × *L. obtusifolium*) is very similar to *L. ovalifolium* except it is deciduous earlier and noticeably more cold-hardy. It is useful at least in Zones 5b–8b and is a good substitute for *L. ovalifolium* in Zones 5b and 6a.

Ligustrum ×*vicaryi* 5 (Vicary or golden Vicary privet). This hybrid (*L. ovalifolium* 'Aureo-marginata' × *L. vulgare*) is slower growing and somewhat broader spreading than either of its parents. Its principal feature is its foliage, which is golden yellow where exposed to full sun. It remains yellow throughout the growing season but is especially bright in early summer. This is an effective accent plant, useful in Zones 5b–8b, overused in some parts of our area, especially the Midwest. The so-called Hillside Strain, selected for use in Minnesota, is cold-hardy to Zone 4b.

Ligustrum sinense 5

CHINESE PRIVET
Deciduous or semievergreen shrub
Oleaceae (Olive Family)

Native Range.   China.

Useful Range.   USDA Zones 7a–9a+.

Function.   Screen, hedge, massing, border.

Size and Habit

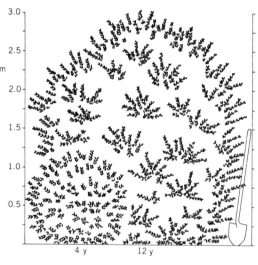

Ligustrum sinense.

Seasonal Interest.   *Flowers:* Small, white, in many large clusters, fragrant but not pleasantly so to some people. Unusually showy in flower for a privet, in early to midsummer. *Foliage:* Medium green, not distinguished except in the variegated cultivar. Tends to be semievergreen in the South. *Fruits:* Small, blue-black, adding quiet autumn interest.

Problems and Maintenance.   This shrub is fairly trouble-free but occasionally becomes infested by aphids or white flies. It can be a problem in itself, as a weed, in the Deep South, but this is less true of 'Variegatum.'

Cultivars.   'Pendulum' has somewhat pendulous branches, giving it a gracefully moundlike form. 'Variegatum' has white variegated foliage and is a most striking plant in the landscape in late spring and early summer with a shining, yellow-white appearance. In late summer and autumn it fades to a pale gray-green color. As with most variegated plants it is less vigorous than the green-leaved species type.

Adaptability

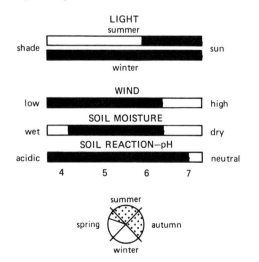

Ligustrum vulgare 4–6

COMMON PRIVET
Deciduous shrub
Oleaceae (Olive Family)

Native Range.   Europe and North Africa. Naturalized in eastern North America.

Useful Range.   USDA Zones 4b–8a with selection of appropriate cultivars.

Function.   Hedge, screen, border.

Size and Habit

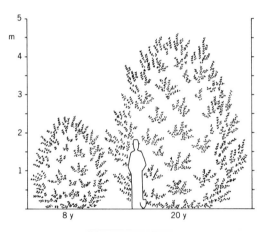

Ligustrum vulgare.

Adaptability

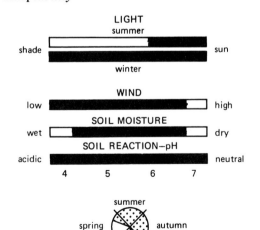

Seasonal Interest.   *Flowers:* Small, white, in upright clusters, fragrant but not pleasantly so to some people, in early summer. *Foliage:* Dark green and lustrous, holding the color well until it falls in late autumn. *Fruits:* Small, black, and shiny, holding well into winter and adding quiet interest.

Problems and Maintenance.   Relatively trouble-free in most areas but subject to a serious blight disease in some localities and to be avoided where experience dictates. As with other *Ligustrum* species, *L. vulgare* is prone to occasional severe winter dieback in the northern part of its useful range (Zones 4b and 5).

Cultivars.   'Cheyenne,' selected in the Great Plains, is notably more resistant to cold and drought than most other privets and is possibly useful as far north as Zone 4a.

'Lodense' (= 'Nanum') is a dwarf form with smaller leaves, making a dense, moundlike plant only 0.5–1 m/1.6–3.3 ft tall and one and a half to two times as broad after many year's growth. Unfortunately, it often has been grafted on understock of the species type, which frequently suckers and overgrows the dwarf plant unless the suckers are pruned out promptly. It is useful northward to Zone 5b, perhaps colder zones.

Related Species

Ligustrum quihoui 5.   This vigorous species from China differs from *L. vulgare* in its more stiffly upright form, lower ultimate height of 2–3 m/6.6–10 ft, late summer flowers, and large fruits in heavy clusters. Best known as a nematode-resistant understock for the southern evergreen privets, it is considerably better adapted to the North than is often supposed. Useful in Zones 5b–9a+ and perhaps slightly colder zones as well.

Lindera benzoin 5

Synonym: *Benzoin aestivale*
SPICEBUSH
Deciduous shrub
Lauraceae (Laurel Family)

Native Range. Northeastern North America to Florida and Texas.

Useful Range. USDA Zones 5b–9a and Zone 5a, using native plants in northeastern North America.

Function. Naturalizing, specimen.

Size and Habit

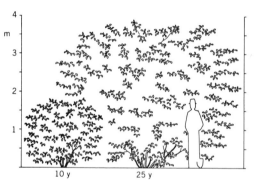

Lindera benzoin.

Adaptability

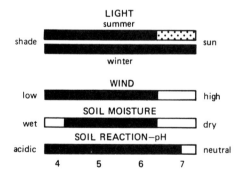

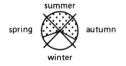

Seasonal Interest. *Flowers:* Small, fragrant, yellow, interesting but not showy, in early spring. Dioecious. *Foliage:* Clean, medium green, aromatic when crushed, turning clear yellow in autumn. *Fruits:* Shiny, bright red berries are fairly showy in autumn, especially after the leaves fall, when they persist until taken by birds.

Lindera benzoin.

Lindera obtusiloba.

Problems and Maintenance. This shrub is essentially trouble-free, given a favorable site with some shade and at least moderately moist soil. It requires little or no maintenance, especially since its primary use is in naturalized landscapes.

Related Species

Lindera melissifolia 4 (synonym: *Benzoin melissifolium;* southern spicebush). Similar to *L. benzoin* but more restricted to the South in natural distribution and lower growing, making a low thicket in wet sites. Not available for planting but useful in a few natural sites in Zones 7a–9a.

Lindera obtusiloba 6 (synonym: *Benzoin obtusilobum*). This native of China, Japan, and Korea is a large shrub or small tree with handsome, lobed leaves, gray-green in summer and golden-yellow in autumn. Flowers are yellow and appear almost as early as those of *L. benzoin,* in somewhat larger clusters but still not showy. It is potentially useful in Zones 6a–9a.

In addition to these species of *Lindera,* about a dozen more are available in at least one nursery, but none of that dozen has become "mainstreamed" commercially. Most of the ones that can be seen with any frequency have small yellow flowers in early spring and deciduous to evergreen, aromatic foliage. Leaves of several of these dry to an attractive tan by early winter and remain on the plant until spring. None of them are as cold hardy as *L. benzoin,* but several seem to have survived at least a decade or two in Zone 7b. None of these is yet widely available.

Liquidambar styraciflua 8

S W E E T   G U M
Deciduous tree
Hamamelidaceae (Witch Hazel Family)

Native Range. Southeastern, east-central and south-central United States, southern Mexico, and Central America.

Useful Range. USDA Zones 5b–9a+, with selection of appropriate genetic material.

Function. Shade, street tree, specimen.

Size and Habit

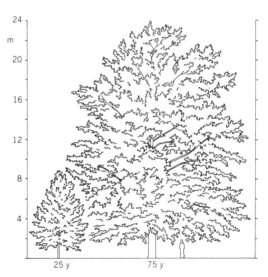

Liquidambar styraciflua.

Adaptability. Tolerates seaside sites if protected from high winds.

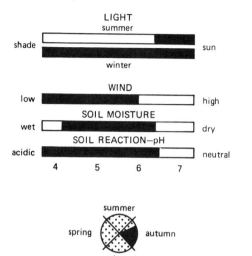

Seasonal Interest. Flowers: Small, greenish yellow, in tightly globose clusters, not striking in the landscape. *Foliage:* Star-shaped leaves emerge pale green, turn deep green, lustrous, and rather leathery in summer. Foliage turns yellow to red or bronze in autumn, sometimes displaying all of these colors, together with green, at a single time in autumn. Individuals vary greatly in time of leaf coloring. Trees of northern origin usually color early, those from the south later. *Fruits:* Globose clusters with horny projections, green at first, ripening brown, interesting as they ripen in autumn and persist into winter, releasing the seeds through openings in the fruit. *Trunk and branches:* Massive, the smaller branches covered with smooth, silvery gray bark and sometimes corky winged.

Liquidambar styraciflua.

Problems and Maintenance. This tree is relatively trouble-free and requires little maintenance. It is reputedly difficult to transplant, but this is not a major problem for experienced landscapers except with large trees. Fruits constitute a litter problem in some sites. The most important limitation relates to adaptability. It is important to select trees of northern origin (Kentucky and Virginia northward) for use in Zones 5 and 6 and probably equally important to select trees of southern origin for Zones 8b and 9.

Cultivars. 'Aurea,' 'Goduzam' (Gold Dust®), 'Gold Treasure,' and 'Variegata' all have irregularly yellow-mottled leaves and pink and deep red autumn foliage.

'Burgundy'®, 'Festival'®, and 'Palo Alto'® are selections for good summer foliage and fall color. Autumn foliage of 'Burgundy'® is deep wine red; that of 'Festival'® is shades of peach, pink, and yellow; and that of 'Palo Alto'® is a brilliant orange-red. 'Palo Alto'® was the first sweet gum cultivar to be released.

'Moraine' is a cold-hardy selection grafted from an old parent tree planted in Indianapolis. It is cold-hardy to at least −13°C/−25°F and fast-growing, with bright red autumn foliage. Other clones, unnamed as yet, from native seed sources near the northern range limit of this species in Missouri, New Jersey, and perhaps elsewhere are available. These are probably among the most cold-hardy genetic material of this species available.

'Rotundiloba' has foliage distinctly different from any other sweet gum, with small, strikingly rounded, oval lobes, much more rounded even than the lobes of *L. orientalis.* This variant was first observed by R. E. Wicker of Pinehurst, North Carolina, who sent samples to the Arnold Arboretum for identification. There it was described and named f. *rotundiloba* by Alfred Rehder (*Journal of the Arnold Arboretum,* 1931), propagated and disseminated to a few botanical institutions. In 1968, it was noticed that an old tree of this form planted on the University of North Carolina campus was a nonfruiting clone, and propagating material is now being distributed by the North Carolina State University Arboretum. The cold-hardiness of this cultivar is not yet well known, but as a native of central North Carolina it cannot be assumed to be cold-hardy north of Zone 7b. Further trial *may* show it to be hardy in Zone 7a as well.

'Ward' (Cherokee™) is an essentially non-fruiting selection by Earl Cully of Jacksonville, Illinois, scheduled for release in 1996. The original tree has produced fewer than a dozen fruits in 30 years and has withstood low temperatures to −33°C/−28°F without injury, so should be useful in Zones 5b–8b, perhaps also parts of Zone 5a.

At least two other nonfruiting forms of sweet gum have been selected and are under evaluation. One or more of these may prove to be useful farther north than Zone 7b.

Recently, several sweet gum cultivars named in England have been imported into North America, including 'Lane Roberts' and 'Worplesdon.' These may prove to be welcome additions to the list of useful cultivars for our area. It can be speculated that since they were selected in a mild maritime climate they may need less summer heat for their development, but only through trial will it be found how tolerant to cold, heat, and drought they really are.

Related Species

Liquidambar formosana 8 (Formosan sweet gum). This handsome tree from elevations up to 2000 m/6600 ft in the mountains of Taiwan resembles *L. styraciflua* but is rarely seen in our area. It is potentially useful in at least Zones 8a–9a, probably also Zone 7b, but further trial is needed to confirm its hardiness in any colder areas.

Liquidambar orientalis 6 (oriental sweet gum). This may become a larger tree in native habitat in Asia Minor, but in the few places where it is planted in our area it is a shrubby tree seldom exceeding a height of 6–8 m/20–26 ft. Potentially useful in Zones 8b–9a+, perhaps also Zone 8a, but barely commercially available at this writing.

Liriodendron tulipifera 8

TULIP TREE, YELLOW POPLAR
Deciduous tree
Magnoliaceae (Magnolia Family)

Native Range. Eastern United States and adjacent Ontario.

Useful Range. USDA Zones 5a–9a and 4b with selection of appropriate genetic material.

Function. Shade or specimen tree, street tree where enough space is available to accommodate its size and to provide the soil mass to hold enough moisture for good growth.

Size and Habit

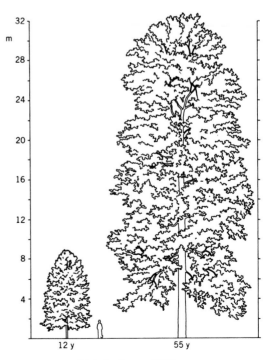

Liriodendron tulipifera.

Adaptability

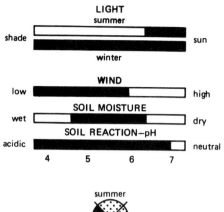

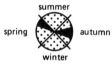

Liriodendron tulipifera.

Seasonal Interest. *Flowers:* Tulip-shaped, to 5 cm/2 in. long, borne upright, singly at the ends of twigs. Petals are pale green, deep orange at the base, showy when they open before the unfolding foliage is fully expanded in late spring. *Foliage:* Clean, medium green, turning clear yellow in late summer and autumn, moderately coarse textured. Distinctive lobed leaves are squared off at the end as though the tip had been cut off with scissors. *Fruits:* Conelike, made up of overlapping scales, the tan bottom scales persisting well into winter, adding quiet seasonal interest after the foliage has fallen. *Trunk and branches:* Gray bark, finely striped with light gray or off-white on branches and trunks of young trees, adds quiet winter interest.

Problems and Maintenance. This tree is relatively free of serious problems, but the foliage is sometimes affected by aphids and a leaf spot disease that causes early fall of older leaves. Its principal limitations relate to its size, site requirements, and geographical variation. Trees grown from seed sources in the same region usually should be specified. This is especially important at the northern and southern range extremes. Unless ample space and reasonably good soil are available, other trees should be used. Branches are somewhat prone to wind breakage; not a serious problem but reason to use other species in very windy sites.

Cultivars. 'Fastigiatum' (= 'Arnold,' = 'Pyramidale') is a fastigiate clone, reaching a height of at least 12–15 m/40–50 ft, with height:width ratio of about 4:1. 'Aureo-marginatum' (Majestic Beauty™) has deep green leaves with yellow margins.

Related Species

Liriodendron chinense 8 (Chinese tulip tree). This rare tree may have future value in the Deep South, but it is barely commercially available at present. It is smaller than *L. tulipifera*, growing only to about 15 m/60 ft tall, with smaller, more deeply lobed leaves and smaller flowers, and is useful only from about Zone 7b or 8a southward.

Liriope spicata 2

CREEPING LILYTURF OR LIRIOPE
Evergreen, herbaceous groundcover
Liliaceae (Lily Family)

Native Range. China and Vietnam.

Useful Range. USDA Zones 6a–9a+, perhaps also Zone 5b, with shelter from winter sun and wind, but not fully evergreen in Zones 5 and 6, so it loses much of its effectiveness in late winter and early spring.

Function. Groundcover on a large or small scale, edging, accent plant.

Size and Habit

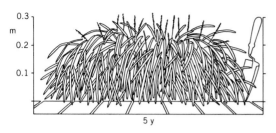

Liriope spicata.

Adaptability. Broadly adapted to light and soil conditions and relatively salt-tolerant.

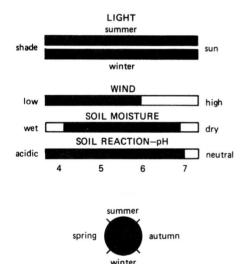

Seasonal Interest. *Flowers:* Lavender or nearly white, very small, borne tightly clustered in upright spikes to 10 cm/4 in. long in middle or late summer. *Foliage:* Evergreen leaves are medium green, narrowly straplike, 25–40 cm/10–16 in. long and 0.6 cm/0.25 in. wide. *Fruits:* Blue-black berries are round, less than 1 cm/0.4 in. across, ripening in autumn.

Problems and Maintenance. This plant is trouble-free and requires little or no maintenance once established. Thinning is seldom necessary but can be done for propagation of new plants.

Cultivars. Only a few cultivars of this species have been selected, but two of the most popular are listed here.

'Franklin Mint' is large in all its parts, looking more like *L. muscari* than *L. spicata*, but spreading like *L. spicata*, with deep green leaves and showy lavender-purple flowers, grows to 30–38 cm/12–15 in tall, and performs well in sun or shade.

'Silver Dragon' has narrow leaves with silvery white stripes and lavender flowers, and it grows to 20–30 cm/8–12 in. tall.

Related Species

Liriope muscari 2 (big blue lilyturf or liriope). This native of China and Japan is somewhat larger than *L. spicata*, usually to 30–38 cm/12–15 in. tall, with straplike leaves 30–50 cm/12–20 in. long and 1.3–1.5 cm/0.5–0.6 in. wide; it has deep violet flowers, more showy than those of *L. spicata.* Some 20 cultivars are available and most are useful in Zones 7a–9a+, as well as in Zone 6 with protection from wind and winter sun. A few of the most popular are listed here.

'Big Blue' has broad bluish green leaves and showy lilac-purple flowers.

'Christmas Tree' (='Monroe's No. 2') has broad, deep green leaves and spikes of pinkish lavender flowers, grows slowly, and does best in shade.

'Gold Banded' (='Gold Band') has broad, deep green leaves with narrow golden margins and grows to 30–45 cm/12–18 in. tall.

'Majestic' has broad, deep green leaves and lavender-blue flowers in showy, crested spikes.

'Monroe White' (='Monroe's No. 1') has dark green leaves and nicely contrasting white flowers and does best in shade.

'Royal Purple' has deep green leaves and showy, deep purple flowers.

'Silvery Sunproof' has excellent white-striped foliage (yellowish in shade) and showy lavender flowers, standing well above the foliage, and does well in sun or shade.

'Variegata' has pale yellow striped leaves and purple flowers.

Ophiopogon japonicus 2 (dwarf liriope or Mondo grass). This fine-textured, almost grasslike plant from Japan is very low, to about 15 cm/6 in. high, with very dark green, lustrous leaves 25–35 cm/10–14 in. long but only 0.3 cm/0.12 in. wide, and has small spikes of white or pale lavender flowers. Its requirements and uses are similar to those of *Liriope* species and it is useful in most of the same range as *Liriope muscari* (Zones 7b–9a+), but less cold-hardy than *L. spicata*. Only a few cultivars are available, including the following. 'Nanus' is very dwarf, usually below 8 cm/3 in. high. 'Silver Dragon' and 'Silver Mist' have white striped leaves. A closely related species, *Ophiopogon planiscapus*, is best known for the selection 'Nigrescens' (= 'Arabicus,' = 'Black Dragon,' = 'Ebony Knight'), which has purple-black foliage and small pale pink to lilac flowers, and is reported to be more cold-hardy than other cultivars.

Ophiopogon japonicus.

Lonicera alpigena 5

ALPS HONEYSUCKLE
Deciduous shrub
Caprifoliaceae (Honeysuckle Family)

Native Range. Mountains of south-central Europe.

Useful Range. USDA Zones 4b–8b.

Function. Screen, border.

Size and Habit

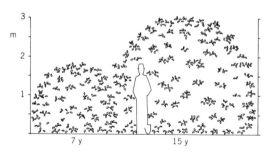

Lonicera alpigena.

Adaptability

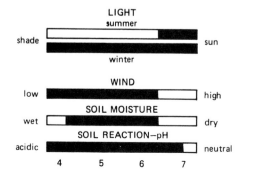

Seasonal Interest. *Flowers:* Yellowish, tinged dull red, not showy, in late spring. *Foliage:* Deep green, relatively large leaves, to 10 cm/4 in. long. *Fruits:* Bright red, hanging on slender stalks, colorful in late summer and early autumn.

Problems and Maintenance. This shrub is relatively trouble-free, requiring little maintenance other than pruning, either by annual thinning or radical renewal every five to eight years. Not as weedy as some other shrub honeysuckles; resistant to honeysuckle aphid.

Cultivars. 'Nana' is an excellent dwarf, moundlike selection, seldom exceeding 1.5 m/5 ft in height but becoming considerably wider than that. Neither this cultivar nor the species is easily available.

Lonicera fragrantissima 5

FRAGRANT HONEYSUCKLE
Semievergreen shrub
Caprifoliaceae (Honeysuckle Family)

Native Range.   China.

Useful Range.   USDA Zones 5b–9a.

Function.   Screen, hedge, specimen, border.

Size and Habit

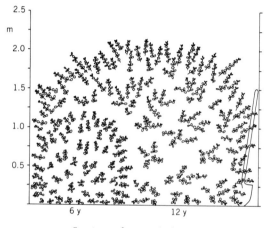

Lonicera fragrantissima.

Adaptability.   Retains foliage quality in dry soil better than most *Lonicera* species.

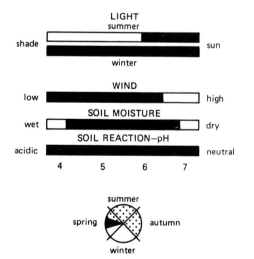

Seasonal Interest. *Flowers:* Fragrant, white, before the new foliage in early spring. *Foliage:*

Blue-green, leathery, semievergreen. *Fruits:* Red berries in early summer.

Problems and Maintenance.   Relatively trouble-free and requiring little maintenance other than annual thinning or radical renewal every 5 to 8 years. It is not as weedy as some other shrub honeysuckles but occasionally escapes cultivation in the South. Resistant to honeysuckle aphid.

Related Species and Hybrids

Lonicera caerulea 4 (blue honeysuckle).   This Eurasian species, naturalized in North America, is useful in Zones 3a–8a for massing or as a specimen. Its landscape interest is not striking, but its compact growth habit requires little pruning and its elongated, dark blue berries are edible.

Lonicera ×*purpusii* 5.   This hybrid of *L. standishii* ×*L. fragrantissima* is similar to *L. fragrantissima* with its fragrant flowers and semievergreen foliage. Its leaves are larger than those of *L. fragrantissima,* and it is useful in Zones 6a–9a and perhaps also parts of Zone 5 but seldom available.

Lonicera standishii 4 (Standish honeysuckle). This Chinese semievergreen shrub functions as a lower-growing version of the related *L. fragrantissima,* with larger leaves, to 10 cm/4 in. long, and fragrant flowers in early spring. Useful in Zones 6a–9a but seldom available.

Lonicera fragrantissima.

Leycesteria formosa 4 (Himalayan honeysuckle, flowering nutmeg). This relative of *Lonicera* from southwestern China and the Himalayas is useful for massing or as a specimen for its whitish flowers, borne in the axils of colorful red-purple bracts, in hanging clusters to 10 cm/4 in. long in late summer. Its bright green leaves give the plant an interestingly coarse texture. This shrub is seldom available but potentially useful in Zones 7b–9a+. The tops are frequently killed back in winter in Zones 7 and 8, causing new, arching branches to develop low on the plant. The best way to prune is drastic renewal: cutting the entire top down to stubs each spring.

Leycesteria formosa.

Lonicera japonica 1 and 2

JAPANESE HONEYSUCKLE
Evergreen or semievergreen vine
Caprifoliaceae (Honeysuckle Family)

Native Range. Eastern Asia, naturalized in eastern United States.

Useful Range. USDA Zones 5b–9a+, but too aggressive a weed in the South to recommend for most uses in Zones 7 through 9.

Function. Groundcover, especially on banks and rough terrain, screen (with support), cover for stone walls and fences, climbing by scrambling and twining, to 5–10 m/16–33 ft.

Size and Habit

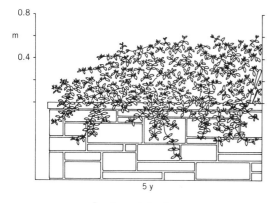

Lonicera japonica.

Adaptability. Partial shade helps to prolong retention of foliage in winter in northern areas (Zones 5 and 6).

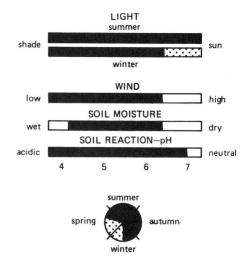

Seasonal Interest. *Flowers:* Fragrant, white, tinged with purple in some plants, turning yellowish with age, beginning in late spring and continuing intermittently through the summer. *Foliage:* Semievergreen in the North, evergreen in the South, handsome, leathery, and deep green in summer, bronzing in winter.

Problems and Maintenance. This vine is relatively trouble-free but requires pruning to restrict its growth because of its extreme vigor. In the

South this is so serious a problem that it cannot be recommended for planting (see *L. henryi* under Related Species). Like other vine honeysuckles, this is resistant to honeysuckle aphid.

Lonicera japonica.

Cultivars. 'Aureo-reticulata' has smaller leaves, net-veined in golden-yellow, and is much less vigorous than the species type, a striking variegated climber. 'Halliana' (Hall's honeysuckle) differs little from the species, but its fragrant white flowers turn clear, pale yellow only a few days after opening. This probably is the most common form found in the United States. 'Purpurea' (Hall's purple honeysuckle, Kansas purple honeysuckle) has purple-tinted foliage and flowers that are dark red-purple on the outside at first, opening white and then turning yellow. Makes a good groundcover.

Related Species

Lonicera henryi 1 and 2 (Henry honeysuckle). This handsome, semievergreen to evergreen, weakly twining vine has most of the good qualities of *L. japonica* and is not as weedy, but it is more effective as a groundcover than as a climber. Its leaves are more elongated and sharp-pointed than those of *L. japonica* and do not bronze so much in winter, and its yellowish or reddish flowers are fairly interesting in early summer. It is useful in Zones 6a–9a and perhaps also part of Zone 5.

Lonicera maackii 6

Deciduous shrub
Caprifoliaceae (Honeysuckle Family)

Native Range.   Northeastern Asia.

Useful Range.   USDA Zones 3a–8a.

Function.   Border, specimen, screen (with pruning).

Size and Habit

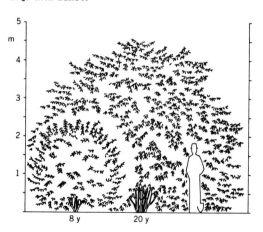

Lonicera maackii.

Adaptability

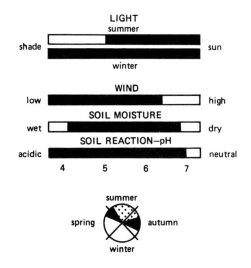

Seasonal Interest. *Flowers:* Fragrant, white, turning yellow, in late spring to early summer. *Foliage:* Lustrous, deep green, long-pointed, remaining green well into autumn, serving as a background for the late red berries as well as the flowers. *Fruits:* Bright red berries, ripening in autumn and providing strong, late autumn landscape interest.

Problems and Maintenance. This species apparently has some resistance to honeysuckle aphid and is relatively trouble-free otherwise, but it is a source of trouble itself, as a noxious weed, especially where it has escaped into natural woodlands. It has now become the most serious woody weed in many parts of the Midwest and Northeast. In such areas it should not be specified for landscape planting but rather eradicated, when that is feasible.

Selections. The f. *podocarpa* differs very little from the species. It is claimed that this variant holds its foliage and fruits later in autumn than the species type, but both types are highly variable in these respects and it unlikely that specifying either will give predictable results. The seed line called "Rem Red," introduced by the U.S. Soil Conservation Service as a wildlife plant, probably is not uniform enough for cultivar status, but a larger question is whether planting of any *L. maackii* should be encouraged in most of our area.

Lonicera morrowii 4

MORROW HONEYSUCKLE
Deciduous shrub
Caprifoliaceae (Honeysuckle Family)

Native Range. Japan; naturalized in eastern United States.

Useful Range. USDA Zones 5a–8b.

Function. Border, specimen, informal hedge.

Size and Habit

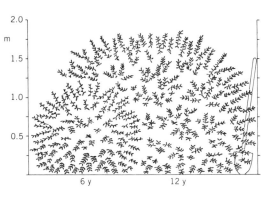

Lonicera morrowii.

Adaptability

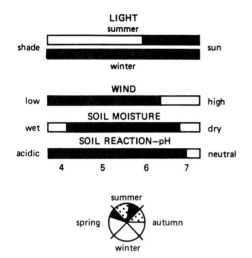

Seasonal Interest. *Flowers:* White, turning yellow, late spring. *Foliage:* Soft gray-green, downy, effectively fine textured on horizontally spreading branches. *Fruits:* Red (or golden yellow) berries in middle to late summer.

Problems and Maintenance. This shrub is relatively trouble-free and requires little pruning because of its dense, moundlike growth habit, but it can be weedy in some areas, and it is susceptible to honeysuckle aphid.

Cultivars. 'Xanthocarpa' has golden yellow to orange-yellow berries, otherwise does not differ from the species type.

Related Species

Lonicera albertii 3 (Albert honeysuckle). This honeysuckle from west-central Asia has narrow, blue-green leaves, rosy purple flowers in early summer, and deep red-purple berries in late summer. Like *L. morrowii*, it is gracefully wide-spreading, effective in the front of a shrub border or for foundation planting. It is useful in Zones 3b–8a, but most highly valued in Zones 3 and 4.

Lonicera syringantha 5 (lilac honeysuckle). This wide-spreading, moundlike shrub from northern China has fragrant, pink to rosy purple flowers in late spring and red berries in late summer, and is useful in Zones 5a–8a. The var. *wolfii* has redder flowers than the species type.

Lonicera pileata 3

PRIVET HONEYSUCKLE
Evergreen shrub
Caprifoliaceae (Honeysuckle Family)

Native Range. China.

Useful Range. USDA Zones 7b–9a+.

Function. Massing, specimen, rock garden.

Size and Habit

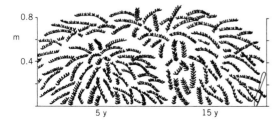

Lonicera pileata.

Adaptability. This shrub grows vigorously in moist, partly shaded sites but functions better in the landscape and requires less pruning when grown more slowly in rather dry, windy sites in full sun.

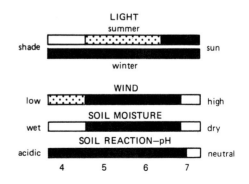

Seasonal Interest. *Flowers:* Fragrant, white, small, not showy, in middle spring. *Foliage:* Evergreen or nearly so, lustrous and dark green, the leaves 1–4 cm/0.4–1.6 in. long and two-ranked on the stem, giving an interesting texture. *Fruits:* Small, violet-purple, translucent, not showy but interesting at close range.

Problems and Maintenance. This shrub is largely trouble-free, but aphids occasionally can become a problem. It tends to accumulate dead twigs low on the plant, especially when growing vigorously, requiring occasional renewal pruning in intensive situations.

Cultivars. 'Royal Carpet' is more prostrate than the species type, reaching a height of less than 0.5 m/20 in. but spreading to at least 1.5 m/5 ft wide.

Related Species

Lonicera nitida 4 (synonym: *L. pileata* f. *yunnanensis*). This shrub is a slightly taller-growing version of *L. pileata* with more uniformly small evergreen leaves. It functions better than *L. pileata* as a small clipped hedge, and equally well as an informal garden specimen, except that it becomes taller and is more cold-hardy, useful in Zones 6a–9a. These two similar species are often confused. 'Baggesen's Gold' is a low, dense form, to 0.6, 1 m/2 ft high, with arching branches, small golden leaves in early summer, turning yellow-green later, and pale purplish blue fruits in early autumn.

Lonicera pileata.

Lonicera sempervirens 1 and 2

TRUMPET HONEYSUCKLE
Evergreen or semievergreen vine
Caprifoliaceae (Honeysuckle Family)

Native Range. Eastern United States, west to Nebraska and Texas.

Useful Range. USDA Zones 4a–9a, with selection of appropriate genetic material.

Function. Fence cover, screen (with support and pruning), groundcover, twining specimen, to 4–6 m/13–20 ft.

Size and Habit

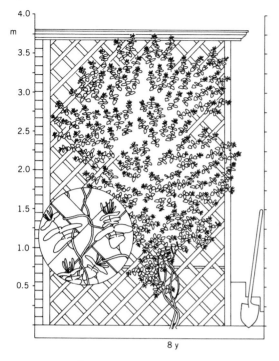

Lonicera sempervirens.

Adaptability

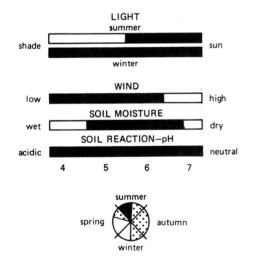

Seasonal Interest. *Flowers:* Scarlet and yellow-orange in showy clusters in summer. *Foliage:* Semievergreen or evergreen in the Deep South, bluish-green, the terminal pairs of leaves perfoliate (two opposite leaves fused into a single blade,

surrounding the stem). *Fruits:* Red berries in autumn, not particularly showy.

Problems and Maintenance. Like other vine honeysuckles, this is resistant to honeysuckle aphid, but it can be disfigured by serious green aphid infestations in certain years and localities. Density for screening usually depends on pruning to encourage filling-in of open areas.

Cultivars. 'Magnifica' is a selection for late and free flowering. 'Sulphurea' has clear sulfur-yellow flowers. 'Superba' has bright red flowers and is free-flowering. Other cultivars are listed in catalogs. Some probably are duplicate names for some of the above.

Related Species and Hybrids

Lonicera ×*brownii* 1 and 2 (Brown's honeysuckle). This hybrid of *L. sempervirens* × *L. hirsuta* differs little from *L. sempervirens* and can be used interchangeably when available. It is useful in Zones 3b–9a. 'Dropmore Scarlet' (*L. hirsuta* × *L. sempervirens*), with large numbers of red-orange flowers, is one of the finest of the vine honeysuckles, especially for cold climates. It is useful in Zones 3a–8a.

Lonicera 'Dropmore Scarlet.'

Lonicera etrusca 1 and 2 (Etruscan honeysuckle). This climbing species from the Mediterranean area is somewhat more showy than most cultivars of *L. sempervirens*, but much less cold-hardy and useful in Zones 7b–9a+. The selection 'Superba' has very showy, creamy-white flowers, turning orange with age, and tends to be less evergreen.

Lonicera flava 1 and 2 (yellow honeysuckle). Native in the southeastern United States and to Oklahoma, this weakly twining vine has showy and fragrant orange-yellow flowers and is useful in Zones 6a–9a.

Lonicera ×*heckrottii* 1 and 2 (everblooming or goldflame honeysuckle). This weakly climbing, deciduous vine of uncertain hybrid origin is one of the heaviest and longest-flowering of twining honeysuckles, and one of the most widely available. Its flowers are pink and yellow, borne in large clusters from early summer until early autumn, and it is nearly as cold-hardy as *L. sempervirens,* useful in Zones 4b–9a. Like *L. sempervirens,* it can be seriously troubled by green aphids. The selection 'Goldflame' has a deeper purplish overlay.

Lonicera ×*heckrottii.*

Lonicera hildebrandiana 1 and 2 (Hildebrand, giant or Burmese honeysuckle). This extremely vigorous evergreen twining and high-climbing vine probably is not cold-hardy in our area, but it might be tried in sheltered sites in Zone 9a, since it returns rapidly after being killed back to the ground. Mounding around the base may be helpful in winters when temperatures remain below −2° to −3°C/26 to 28°F for several hours. With large clusters of fragrant, creamy yellow-white flowers, turning to red-orange as they mature in late summer, it is by far the showiest and most vigorous of the twining honeysuckles.

Lonicera hirsuta 1 and 2 (hairy honeysuckle). This high-climbing twiner native to the northern United States and Canada is as hardy as *L. sempervirens,* but less effective as a landscape plant and seldom used or available.

Lonicera periclymenum 1 and 2 (woodbine). This long-cultivated, weakly climbing twiner from Europe and the Mediterranean area is similar to several other vining honeysuckle species. It has creamy-white to yellow flowers, rosy pink to purplish on the outside, varying by cultivar. 'Belgica,' with leathery foliage, flowers that are white at first, later turning yellow, and purple outside, is sometimes used as a substitute for *L. japonica,* as it is easier to control. 'Monul' (Berries Jubilee™) has blue-green foliage and fragrant yellow flowers in summer and fall, followed by bright red berries. 'Graham Thomas' has white flowers that turn pale to deep coppery yellow with no trace of pink or purple, lasting from early summer to a peak in early fall, and beyond that in mild autumns. 'Serotina' (late Dutch honeysuckle) has narrow, blue-green leaves and flowers that open yellow inside and deep purple outside, in late summer and autumn. 'Serotina Florida' has fragrant flowers from early summer to frost, deep red in bud, opening creamy white and yellow inside and rich red outside. These cultivars useful in Zones 5b–9a.

Lonicera tragophylla 1 and 2 (Chinese woodbine). This Chinese native has very large yellow, unscented flowers, to 8 cm/3 in. long in large clusters, and is useful in Zones 6b–9a+. The related *L.* ×*tellmanniana* (red-gold honeysuckle), a hybrid of *L. tragophylla* × *L. sempervirens,* tends to be more deciduous, with unscented but very showy deep pink-flushed yellow flowers, and is useful in Zones 6a–9a+.

Lonicera tatarica 5

TATARIAN HONEYSUCKLE
Deciduous shrub
Caprifoliaceae (Honeysuckle Family)

Native Range.   Southwestern Soviet Union to the Altai Mountains.

Useful Range.   USDA Zones 3b–8a.

Function.   Border, screen, specimen, hedge.

Size and Habit

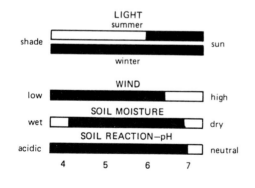

Lonicera tatarica.

Adaptability

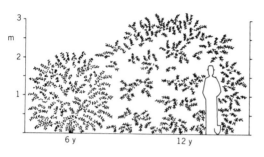

Seasonal Interest.   *Flowers:* White to pink or rose-red, in late spring. *Foliage:* Dull to lustrous, dark green, falling in autumn without color change. *Fruits:* Red (or yellow) berries in middle to late summer.

Problems and Maintenance.   Until the early 1980s, this shrub was considered to be essentially trouble-free, even though it required periodic renewal pruning to keep it in shape and had become a serious weed problem in some areas. But most *L. tatarica* cultivars turned out to be susceptible to honeysuckle aphids, which disfigured them each summer. Fortunately, several other species proved to be resistant (see *L.* ×*xylosteoides* and *L. xylosteum*, under Related Species), and work began to develop other aphid-resistant cultivars (see below).

Cultivars.   'Alba' has pure white flowers.
'Arnold Red' has deep purplish red flowers, the reddest of any cultivar but not as showy from a distance as some of the pink and rose flowering cultivars. However, it has turned out to be resistant to honeysuckle aphids and thus has become an important parent for breeding new resistant cultivars.
'Freedom' is an aphid-resistant selection that was introduced by the Minnesota Landscape Arboretum as a temporary replacement for the susceptible shrub honeysuckles soon after it became apparent that honeysuckle aphid was becoming a serious problem in the early 1980s. Now that 'Honeyrose' has been and introduced, 'Freedom' probably will take a back seat for residential landscaping, but its vigor will still make it a good choice for shelter-belt plantings.
'Honeyrose' is an aphid-resistant hybrid of 'Arnold Red' and 'Zabelii,' developed recently at the Minnesota Landscape Arboretum as a substitute for 'Zabelii,' which it resembles.
'Lutea' has pink flowers and bright yellow berries, but is seldom available in our area.
'Morden Orange' is compact, with a moderate growth rate, light pink flowers, and orange berries, and it may have some resistance to honeysuckle aphid, but it is not widely available.
'Rosea' has rosy pink flowers but is very susceptible to honeysuckle aphid.
'Zabelii' (synonym: *L. korolkowii* 'Zabelii') has deep rosy pink flowers, bluish green foliage, and full growth, especially at the base, but is very susceptible to honeysuckle aphid and thus will probably will be replaced by the newer 'Honeyrose' in areas where that insect is prevalent.

Outbreaks of honeysuckle aphid have drastically changed the shrub-honeysuckle cultivar picture. Breeding of other aphid-resistant cultivars probably will continue as many of the old standard cultivars fall into disuse.

Related Species and Hybrids

Lonicera ×*amoena* 5. This hybrid of *L. tatarica* × *L. korolkowii* is best known for the cultivar 'Arnoldiana,' which has pink-flushed, white flowers and is very similar to *L. tatarica* except for more gracefully arching branches. Useful in Zones 4b–8a.

Lonicera ×*bella* 5 (belle honeysuckle). This group of hybrids of *L. morrowii* and *L. tatarica* is very similar to *L. tatarica* in habit, with flower color ranging from white ('Albida') to yellow ('Chrysantha') and deep pink ('Atrorosea'). Since it has become apparent that these shrubs have the potential to become a weed problem and, more recently, that they are susceptible to honeysuckle aphid, they have been used much less, and only a few cultivars are still commercially available.

Lonicera ×*xylosteoides* 'Clavey's Dwarf.'

Lonicera korolkowii 5 (blueleaf honeysuckle). This distinctive shrub has blue-green foliage, sometimes almost bluish white, and rose-pink to white flowers. It is seldom available commercially, but potentially useful in Zones 5a–8a. The selection sold as *L. korolkowii* 'Zabelii' more closely resembles *L. tatarica* and is considered a cultivar of that species here.

Lonicera ×*xylosteoides* 'Clavey's Dwarf.'

Lonicera ×*xylosteoides* 5. This hybrid of *L. tatarica* × *L. xylosteum* is represented in commerce by the compact growing selection 'Clavey's Dwarf.' This excellent, dense, rounded shrub eventually will function as a screen above eye level, but since plants may require 10 years to attain that height, faster growing cultivars may be preferred for that function. In the short term, 'Clavey's Dwarf' is most commonly used for massing or foundation planting and can be kept below eye level for many years with a little pruning. It has creamy white flowers, blue-green foliage, and bright red fruits and is useful in Zones 3b–8a. 'Hedge King' is similar to 'Clavey's Dwarf' but more narrowly columnar. 'Miniglobe' is a smaller version of 'Clavey's Dwarf,' growing to about 1 m/3.3 ft in height and width. All three of these cultivars are resistant to honeysuckle aphid.

Lonicera xylosteum 5 (European fly honeysuckle). This shrub, common in the wild from Europe

Lonicera xylosteum 'Nana.'

through Asia to the Altai, has relatively inconspicuous yellowish white flowers, but shiny, beadlike, dark red berries that are displayed effectively against the deep green foliage in late summer. The dwarf selection 'Nana' (emerald mound honeysuckle) is truly dwarf, remaining below 1 m/3.3 ft in height without pruning for many years while spreading to nearly twice that distance. It is useful in Zones 3b–8a and is resistant to honeysuckle aphid.

Loropetalum chinense 5

LOROPETALUM, FRINGE FLOWER
Evergreen shrub
Hamamelidaceae (Witch Hazel Family)

Native Range.   China.

Useful Range.   USDA Zones 8a–9a+ and protected sites in Zone 7b.

Function.   Border, specimen, espalier, screen (with pruning).

Size and Habit

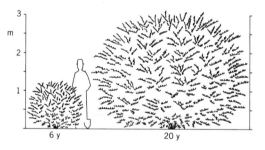

Loropetalum chinense.

Adaptability.   Performs best when protected from full sun in summer and from sun and wind in winter in Zone 8a and colder.

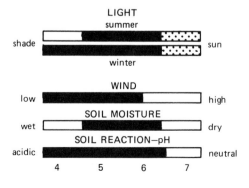

Seasonal Interest.   *Flowers:* Creamy white, with narrow petals like those of *Hamamelis* species, effective against the dark green foliage on arching branches in early to middle spring. *Foliage:* Deep green leaves, reminiscent of those of *Hamamelis* but evergreen and only about 5 cm/2 in. long.

Loropetalum chinense.

Problems and Maintenance.   This shrub is trouble-free, given a relatively cool, moist soil and at least partial shade. Foliage may suffer winter burn in the northern parts of the useful range, but the plant usually recovers quickly in the spring.

Form and Cultivars.   The f. *rubrum* includes the following selections with pink to deep rose-colored petals and usually bronzed or purplish foliage. 'Blush' has foliage with a burgundy cast and deep burgundy-rose flowers. Foliage of 'Burgundy' is also flushed burgundy-red, with bright pink flowers. 'Fire Dance' has bright rose-red flowers.

'Hillier' and 'Snow Dance' are compact forms, remaining below 1 m/3.3 ft in height, with white flowers. 'Monraz' (Razzleberri™) grows to 1.2–

1.8 high and nearly as wide and has bright red flowers, with repeat bloom, and coppery new foliage, turning olive green at maturity.

Lyonia lucida 4

FETTERBUSH
Evergreen shrub
Ericaceae (Heath Family)

Native Range.   Southeastern United States.

Useful Range.   USDA Zones 7b–9a+, with selection of appropriate genetic material.

Function.   Border, specimen, naturalizing.

Size and Habit

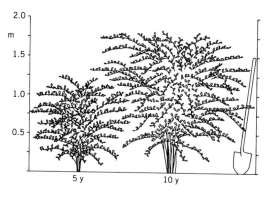

Lyonia lucida.

Adaptability

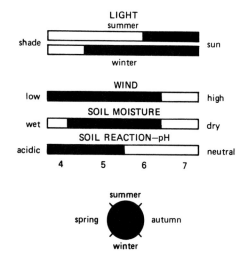

Seasonal Interest.   *Flowers:* Small, white or pink, in axillary clusters, forming leafy, wandlike flowering stems in late spring. *Foliage:* Evergreen, bright green and lustrous, 2.5–8 cm/1–3 in. long on the wandlike stems, the leaves typically smaller toward the ends of stems. *Fruits:* Inconspicuous dry capsules.

Problems and Maintenance.   Relatively troublefree and needing little or no maintenance.

Cultivars.   'Morris Minor' has small leaves, and fine texture. 'Rubra' has deep pink flowers.

Related Species

Lyonia ferruginea 5–6 (rusty fetterbush).   This large evergreen shrub or straggling small tree, ranging from 3–8 m/10–26 ft in height, is native to the southern tip of South Carolina and to the Coastal Plain of Georgia, Florida, and Alabama. It is covered with rusty scales and has small white flowers in nodding clusters. Seldom available commercially, this species is sometimes preserved in development or planted in naturalized settings in the southeastern coastal lowlands. Useful only on the edge of our area, in Zones 9a+.

Lyonia ligustrina 5 (maleberry, he-huckleberry). This deciduous shrub, native to a large part of eastern North America and correspondingly variable, is more likely to be preserved in development than planted. It has small white flowers in terminal clusters, 8–15 cm/3–6 in. long, in early summer and resembles blueberries in branching habit, but with dry capsules and purplish fall foliage. Useful, with selection of more-or-less local genetic material, in Zones 4b–9a+.

Lyonia mariana 4 (staggerbush).   This deciduous to semievergreen counterpart of *L. lucida*, native from southern New England to Florida and west to Arkansas, has large numbers of small white or pink flowers in wandlike clusters 15–20 cm/6–8 in. long in late spring or early summer, and its foliage turns reddish purple in autumn. This plant is useful primarily for naturalizing in sites with dry, sandy soil, or as preserved vegetation in natural areas.

Chamaedaphne calyculata 3 (synonym: *Cassandra calyculata*; leatherleaf or cassandra).   This low evergreen shrub functions as a lower and more northern counterpart of *L. lucida*. Native to bogs and high elevations in northern Eurasia, the U.S. Pacific Northwest, and eastern North America as far south as Georgia, it is quite variable, and selection of appropriate genetic material is probably essential to success. Useful in Zones 3a–7b and perhaps Zone 8 as well.

Maclura pomifera 7

OSAGE ORANGE, HEDGEAPPLE
Deciduous tree
Moraceae (Mulberry Family)

Native Range.   South-central United States.

Useful Range.   USDA Zones 5b–9a+.

Function.   Windbreak, barrier, hedge, shade tree.

Size and Habit

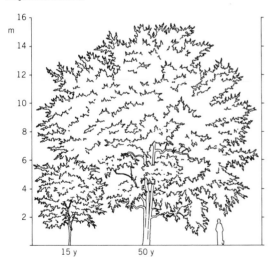

Maclura pomifera.

Adaptability.   Unusual in its broad adaptability to difficult soils and environments. Because of this, it is valued in the Central and Great Plains as a windbreak and livestock barrier hedge.

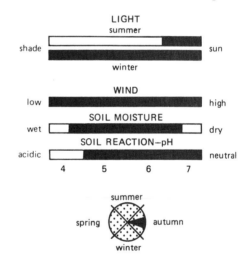

Seasonal Interest.   *Foliage:* Lustrous, bright green leaves on spiny branches, turning clear yellow in autumn. *Fruits:* Massive, compound fruits, to 13 cm/5 in. across, on female trees, at first are green and then ripen yellow-orange. *Trunk and branches:* One-year-old branches are yellow-brown; sinewy trunk has orange-brown inner bark, seen through the shredding, gray outer bark.

Problems and Maintenance.   This tree is free of serious diseases and insect problems, but fallen branches and fruits (from female trees) constitute a serious litter problem. This, the spiny branches, and a tendency for roots to grow into and clog drainage lines, prohibit the use of this tree in intensive situations.

Cultivars. 'Inermis' is free of spines, but seldom available. 'Park,' a nonspiny male (nonfruiting) selection, is available in at least one nursery.

Related Species and Hybrid

Cudrania tricuspidata 6 (Chinese silkworm tree). This small tree from China, Korea, and Japan serves as a smaller version of the closely related *Maclura.* Its smaller leaves, 3–8 cm/1–3 in. long, are used for feeding silkworms in China; its red 2.5 cm/1 in. fruits are edible; and it is at least as thorny as *Maclura,* useful as a barrier hedge in Zones 8a–9a+, perhaps also Zone 7b, but seldom available.

×*Macludrania hybrida* 6–7. This intergeneric hybrid between *Cudrania tricuspidata* and *Maclura pomifera* is a spiny tree to 8–10 m/26–33 ft tall,

with foliage similar to that of *Maclura.* It is potentially useful as a small tree or barrier hedge in Zones 6b–9a+ but is seldom, if ever, available commercially.

Maclura pomifera.

Magnolia acuminata 8

CUCUMBERTREE MAGNOLIA
Deciduous tree
Magnoliaceae (Magnolia Family)

Native Range.   East-central United States and adjacent Ontario.

Useful Range.   USDA Zones 4b–8b.

Function.   Shade tree.

Size and Habit

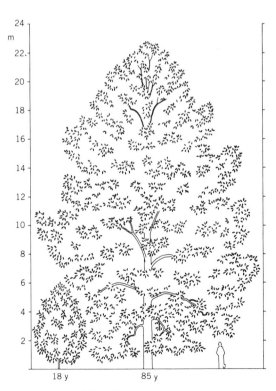

Magnolia acuminata.

Adaptability

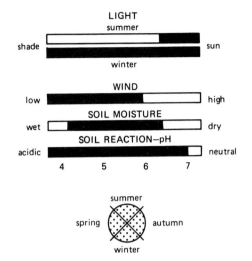

Seasonal Interest.   *Flowers:* Silvery blue-green in bud, opening greenish yellow, to 8 cm/3 in. long, six petals, loosely cup-shaped, interesting but inconspicuous, with or after the leaves in late spring. *Foliage:* Large, deep green leaves, 10–25 cm/4–10 in. long, form a dense canopy with pleasingly coarse texture, falling with little color change in early autumn. *Fruits:* Reddish, knobby, to 8 cm/3 in. long, opening by slits to expose the red-orange seeds in late summer. *Twigs and branches:* Smooth, silvery gray bark on stout branches and twigs adds landscape interest in winter.

Problems and Maintenance.   This tree is somewhat soft-wooded and prone to breakage by severe icing conditions and wind, but less so than most other magnolias, and it usually recovers quickly because of its rapid growth. Some old trees show evidence of considerable breakage in earlier years; others show none. It is not clear whether this is a genetic trait or merely results from differences in microclimate and soil fertility. Otherwise, this tree is remarkably trouble-free. Some maintenance is required in raking up the large leaves in autumn along with any fruit and branch litter. Because of brittleness and litter, *M. acuminata* is not a good choice for street planting. Because of its ultimate size, it is not an appropriate tree for small urban or suburban sites.

Varieties and Cultivars.   The var. *acuminata* is the species type, as described above.

The var. *subcordata* (synonym: M. *cordata*, M. *acuminata* var. *cordata*; yellow cucumbertree). This tree is typically smaller than the species type, usually reaching heights of 10–12 m/33–39 ft, but occasional trees become much larger in time. The clear yellow flowers are more showy than those of the species type and open slightly earlier, and thus they are less hidden by the partly expanded foliage. Useful in Zones 5a–9a. 'Butterflies' and 'Golden Glow' are selections for brighter yellow, well-shaped flowers. 'Miss Honeybee' was selected for unusually large, pale yellow flowers.

Related Hybrids

Magnolia ×*brooklynensis* 6 (Brooklyn Hybrids). These hybrids of M. *acuminata* × M. *liliiflora* combine the showy flowers of M. *liliiflora* and the cold-hardiness and later flowering of M. *acuminata*, so they are well adapted to the North, especially where late spring frosts are common.

'Evamaria' was the first of this cross to be introduced, by the Brooklyn Botanic Garden in 1970. Its 9-cm/3.5-in. flowers are purple overlaid with pale green and yellow. It is expected to reach a height of at least 6 m/20 ft and to be useful in at least Zones 5b–8b. Both 'Evamaria' and 'Woodman' are interesting curiosities, more important as parents in hybridization than as landscape plants on their own.

'Woodsman' was introduced by the late J. C. McDaniel in 1974, at the University of Illinois. Its 13-cm/5-in. flowers vary in color from outside to inside tepals (petals and sepals), ranging from green to deep purple or sometimes chocolate, and pink-white. It is expected to reach a height of at least 6 m/20 ft and to be useful in at least Zones 5b–8b. Professor McDaniel also developed a clone that he called "Ko-1," which is reported to be superior in flower color to 'Woodsman'; it is only in limited circulation at this writing.

Other M. acuminata hybrids.   Another Brooklyn Botanic Garden hybrid is 'Elizabeth' (Plant Patent No. 4145, 1977), parentage M. *denudata* × M. *acuminata*, a shrubby tree to at least 6 m/15 ft in time, with showy ivory-yellow flowers, borne prolifically from an early age. It is expected to prove useful at least in Zones 6a–8b, perhaps also Zones 5b and 9a.

Once it became apparent that M. *acuminata* is a likely parent for breeding yellow-flowered mag-nolias, crosses with M. ×*soulangiana*, M. *stellata*, and other parents were made, and other yellow-flowering hybrids, such as 'Gold Star,' 'Yellow Bird,' and 'Yellow Lantern,' began to appear. Such efforts probably will continue.

Magnolia grandiflora 8

SOUTHERN MAGNOLIA, BULL BAY
Evergreen tree
Magnoliaceae (Magnolia Family)

Native Range.   Southeastern United States.

Useful Range.   USDA Zones 7a–9a+ with se-lection of appropriate genetic material. Foliage burn occurs in some winters in Zone 7.

Function.   Shade tree, specimen.

Size and Habit

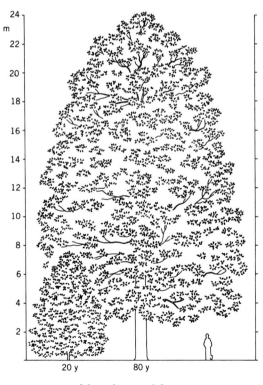

Magnolia grandiflora.

Adaptability

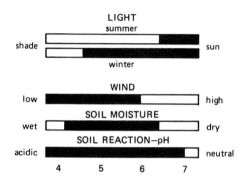

Seasonal Interest.   *Flowers:* Fragrant, white, to 15–20 cm/6–8 in. across, in late spring and intermittently through summer. *Foliage:* Ever-green, lustrous, and leathery, dark green, to 20 cm/8 in. long, varying in shape from tree to tree, the undersides varying from gray-green to rusty red. *Fruits:* Rusty red-brown, 8 cm/3 in. long, opening by slits to expose the red-orange seeds in early autumn.

Problems and Maintenance.   This tree is free of problems but requires maintenance in the form of cleaning up leaf and twig litter, and for this reason not the best choice as a street tree, although it is often used for this purpose in the South.

Cultivars.   Many cultivars have been selected and named, so local experience and availability should be considered. A few of the most widely available are listed here.
'Bracken's Brown Beauty' was selected for its

heavily brown-felted leaf undersides and compact growth habit. It is expected to reach a mature height of at least 6 m/20 ft in time. Its stems and buds have proven unusually cold-hardy in laboratory tests at the University of Georgia, but its leaves did not do as well, suggesting that it might be defoliated by winter cold that its buds and stems would still survive. Useful at least in Zones 7b–9a.

'Edith Bogue' is widely believed to be the most cold-hardy cultivar of this species, and the University of Georgia freezing tests seemed to confirm this. This cultivar reaches a height of at least 9 m/30 ft. It has narrow leaves with a light tan tomentum underneath, and has withstood the weight of wet snows better than most *M. grandiflora* cultivars. Useful in Zones 6b–9a.

'Ferruginea' is a Hillier's Nursery (England) selection, with erect, compact habit, to 6 m/20 ft tall. It has large flowers and small leaves with a red-brown tomentum underneath. Useful at least in Zones 8a–9a+.

'Goliath' is large in every way, with leaves averaging about 20 cm/8 in. across, flowers sometimes 30 cm/1 ft in diameter, and a mature stature of 12 m/40 ft. Its leaves have little tomentum underneath, and it is not known to be especially cold-hardy, probably useful in Zones 8a–9a+.

'Little Gem' is compact and narrowly upright in form, to 6–8 m/20–26 ft tall and 3–5 m wide. Its leaves are small, with rusty bronze tomentum underneath, and it flowers prolifically, with considerable rebloom. Useful at least in Zones 8a–9a+, probably also Zone 7b.

'Monlia' (Majestic Beauty™) is a full-sized tree, with very large leaves and large, fragrant flowers. Useful at least in Zones 8a–9a+.

'Poconos,' cloned from a planted tree in the Pocono Mountains of eastern Pennsylvania, probably will prove to be unusually hardy, perhaps comparable with 'Edith Bogue.' This is one to watch in Zone 6.

'Russet' is a selection for very compact, narrowly pyramidal habit, to at least 6 m/20 ft tall and 4 m/13 ft wide, outstanding for its narrow leaves with russet-red undersides. Useful at least in Zones 8a–9a+, perhaps also Zone 7.

'Saint Mary' is compact, to about 6 m/20 ft in height and width, and somewhat flattened in growth habit so it is easily trained in espalier form, but it can also be kept in pyramidal shape. It has large, fragrant, cupped flowers, borne early and profusely, and deep bronze tomentum on leaf undersides. Useful at least in Zones 7a–9a, perhaps also in Zone 6b.

'Samuel Sommer' is a broadly pyramidal tree, to 9 m/30 ft in height and width, with large leaves having a deep rusty brown tomentum underneath and exceptionally large, fragrant flowers, to 30–35 cm/12–14 in. across, with 12 tepals in three layers and unusually bright red fruits. Useful in Zones 8a–9a+, probably also in Zone 7b.

'Victoria' is a large tree with very broad leaves with little tomentum, popular in the Pacific Northwest, but a relative newcomer to our area. Probably useful in Zones 7b–9a+.

Magnolia grandiflora.

Magnolia ×*loebneri* 6–7

LOEBNER MAGNOLIA
Deciduous tree
Magnoliaceae (Magnolia Family)

Hybrid origin. *M. stellata* × *M. kobus.*

Useful Range. USDA Zones 5a–9a.

Function. Specimen, patio tree, border accent.

Size and Habit

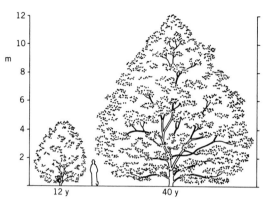

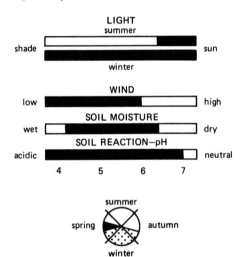

Magnolia ×*loebneri.*

Adaptability

Seasonal Interest. *Flowers:* Fragrant, white, 8–10 cm/3–4 in. across, of approximately 12 tepals (petals and petallike sepals) in early to middle spring. *Foliage:* Medium green, not a major landscape feature but forming a rather dense canopy, falling in early autumn with little color change. *Fruits:* Reddish, knobby, to 8 cm/ 3 in., seldom developing fully but opening by slits to expose a few red-orange seeds in early

autumn. *Trunk and branches:* Smooth, silvery gray bark adds winter interest.

Problems and Maintenance. This tree has few problems other than the general tendency of magnolias to be soft-wooded and somewhat prone to breakage in ice storms.

Cultivars. 'Ballerina' is a hybrid originating from seeds of M. ×*loebneri,* possibly back-crossed with M. *stellata.* Its flowers are unusual in having as many as 30 tepals (petals and petalloid sepals), and they are longer lasting than average for this group. It functions as a much larger version of M. *stellata,* to at least 6–8 m/20–26 ft tall and 5 m/16 ft wide.

'Leonard Messel,' thought to be a hybrid of M. *kobus* × M. *stellata* 'Rosea,' is outstanding for its clear pink flowers, deeper than those of its presumed M. *stellata* 'Rosea' parent. It is less vigorous than the other cultivars of M. ×*loebneri,* but makes a small, graceful tree to at least 3–5 m/10–16 ft tall and 2–3 m/6.6–10 ft wide.

'Merrill' (= 'Dr. Merrill') is the earliest cultivar of M. ×*loebneri* to be developed in North America, at the Arnold Arboretum (1939). It is a vigorous tree, to 8–10 m/26–33 ft tall and nearly as wide, with a broad pyramidal habit and white flowers, sometimes slightly pink-flushed at the centers, borne precociously and profusely.

'Spring Snow' is a more recent introduction selected by J. C. McDaniel at the University of Illinois. It is about the same size as 'Merrill,' with pure white flowers.

Related Species

Magnolia kobus 6–7 (Kobus magnolia). This species varies from a shrubby small tree, about 8 m/25 ft, to a medium-sized tree, to about 20 m/ 65 ft. Because it often does not flower appreciably until it is relatively old, this species is being replaced by the similar but more floriferous M. ×*loebneri* in many landscape situations. Nevertheless, it is a handsome tree, useful in Zones 5a–8b.

Magnolia macrophylla 7

BIGLEAF MAGNOLIA

Deciduous tree

Magnoliaceae (Magnolia Family)

Native Range.   Kentucky to Florida and Louisiana.

Useful Range.   USDA Zones 5b–9a, with selection of appropriate genetic material.

Function.   Specimen, shade, or patio tree.

Size and Habit

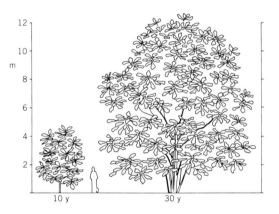

Magnolia macrophylla.

to 25–30 cm/10–12 in. across, in middle to late spring. *Foliage:* Very large, papery leaves, to 80 cm/30 in. long and 30 cm/12 in. across, auriculate (lobed at the base of the leaf blade), forming an umbrellalike canopy, and falling with little color change in autumn. *Fruits:* Reddish, knobby, to 8 cm/3 in. long, opening by slits to expose the red-orange seeds in early autumn. *Trunk and branches:* Smooth, silvery gray bark adds winter interest to the coarse, upright branches.

Magnolia macrophylla.

Adaptability

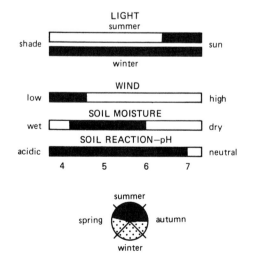

Seasonal Interest.   *Flowers:* Fragrant, creamy white, spotted or tinted red-purple at the center,

Problems and Maintenance.   The fragility of the leaves and stems is the only serious problem of this species but this is sufficient to limit its use to sites sheltered from winds that would dry and tear the leaves, and having ample soil moisture.

Related Species and Hybrids

Magnolia ashei 6 (Ashe magnolia).   This native of northwest Florida, which appears as a southern extension of M. *macrophylla* and has been classified by some botanists as M. *macrophylla* ssp. *ashei*, is much like M. *macrophylla* except smaller in all parts, growing to 6–8 m/20–26 ft tall, with leaves 30–50 cm/12–20 in. long and auriculate, and flowers to 13 cm/5 in across. Useful in Zones 6b–9a+ and available in a small number of nurseries within our area.

Magnolia fraseri 7 (Fraser magnolia).   This species, from Alabama, Georgia, and Virginia, is closely related to M. *macrophylla* but has smaller leaves, like those of M. *ashei,* and slightly smaller flowers, 20–25 cm/8–10 in. across. Useful in Zones 5b–9a, with selection of appropriate genetic material, but seldom commercially available.

Magnolia hypoleuca 7–8 (synonym: M. *obovata;* white-leaf Japanese magnolia). This is the Asian counterpart of the American large-leaved magnolias (M. *ashei,* M. *fraseri,* M. *macrophylla,* M. *pyramidata,* and M. *tripetala*) but it is potentially larger than any of these, to 20 m/66 ft or even taller in good sites, and its leaves, to 40 cm/16 in. long, are distinctly whitened underneath. Its bark is also a whiter gray than that of most other magnolias. Useful in Zones 6a–9a, perhaps also parts of Zone 5, but it is not widely available.

Magnolia pyramidata 6. This species from Alabama to Florida and Georgia is very similar to M. *fraseri,* but smaller, 6–8 m/20–26 ft tall, with leaves only 15–18 cm/6–7 in. long. It is useful in Zones 6b–9a+, but seldom commercially available.

Magnolia sieboldii ssp. *sieboldii* 6–7 (Oyama magnolia). This small Japanese tree, to 8–10 m/26–33 ft tall, has fragrant white flowers to 10 cm/4 in across, with a showy ring of crimson stamens in the center of each. Unlike the nodding flowers of ssp. *sinensis* (below) and M. *wilsonii,* those of M. *sieboldii* ssp. *sieboldii* are held more-or-less horizontally, making a colorful show over several weeks in early summer. This species is less tolerant of full sun and limestone soil than many magnolias and, unfortunately, its growth habit is somewhat awkward and open. Nevertheless, there is enough demand for it to keep it in short supply. Useful in Zones 6b–9a. The selection 'Charles Coates,' a hybrid of M. *sieboldii* × M. *tripetala,* is at least as hardy as M. *sieboldii* and, like the parent, requires partial shade. Its flowers are pleasantly fragrant.

Magnolia sieboldii ssp. *sinensis* 6 (synonym: M. *sinensis;* Chinese magnolia) is a smaller tree, 4.5–6 m/15–20 ft tall, with similar interest except that its flowers are nodding, seen best from underneath the canopy. Useful in Zones 8a–9a+, perhaps also in Zone 7b.

Magnolia ×*thompsoniana* 7 (Thompson magnolia). This handsome hybrid (M. *tripetala* × M. *virginiana*) has smaller leaves than M. *tripetala,* to about 20 cm/8 in. long, of better substance, and bears pleasantly fragrant, creamy white flowers over a relatively long period in early summer in Zones 7a–9a+. The selection 'Urbana' is outstanding in cold hardiness, useful in Zones 5b–9a.

Magnolia tripetala 7 (umbrella magnolia). This native of the southeastern and south-central United States as far north as Pennsylvania is the most cold-hardy of the large-leaved magnolias, useful in Zones 5a–9a, and protected sites in Zone 4. It is open and umbrellalike in growth habit, functioning well as a patio tree away from strong winds. Its leaves are smaller than those of M. *macrophylla,* to 50 cm/20 in. long and 25 cm/10 in. wide, and cuneate (base of the leaf blade tapered, wedgelike), and its flowers are also slightly smaller, with a mildly disagreeable odor.

Magnolia tripetala.

Magnolia tripetala.

Magnolia wilsonii 6 (Wilson magnolia). This rare species from China differs from M. *sieboldii* ssp. *sinensis* only in details, but may be somewhat less cold-hardy. The selection 'Bovee' is reported to be a superior clone. Useful in Zones 8a–9a+, perhaps also Zone 7b.

Magnolia salicifolia 7

ANISE MAGNOLIA
Deciduous tree
Magnoliaceae (Magnolia Family)

Native Range. Japan.

Useful Range. USDA Zones 5a–9a.

Function. Specimen, border accent.

Size and Habit

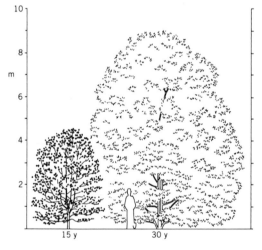

Magnolia salicifolia.

Adaptability

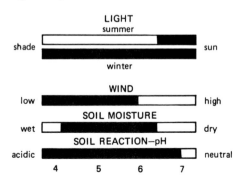

Seasonal Interest. *Flowers:* Fragrant, white or purplish at base, to 12 cm/5 in. across, with six petals, in early to middle spring. Flowers appear on relatively young trees. *Foliage:* Light green leaves about 8–10 cm/3–4 in. long and narrow, giving neater, finer foliage texture than most other magnolias and yet a fairly dense, upright foliage mass. *Fruits:* Reddish, knobby, to 7 cm/3 in. long, opening by slits to expose red-orange seeds in early autumn. *Trunk and branches:* Smooth, silvery gray bark adds winter interest.

Problems and Maintenance. This tree is relatively trouble-free and requires little maintenance. It is less prone to storm breakage than most deciduous magnolias.

Cultivars. Only a few selections have been made from this species, and they are not in wide circulation, but they are available from a few nurseries: The most common are: 'Else Frye,' with white flowers, purple at the base; 'Iufer,' with 15-cm/6-in. flowers, pure white with red-tipped stamens, a superior form; 'Jermyns,' with larger-than-typical leaves and flowers; 'Kochanakee,' a vigorous, upright form with large, fragrant white flowers; 'Miss Jack,' a vigorous, upright form with pink-flushed white flowers and strongly scented foliage; 'W. B. Clarke,' another vigorous form with large, fragrant white flowers.

Related Hybrids

Magnolia ×*kewensis* 7 (Kew magnolia). Plants in this group are traditionally considered to be hybrids of M. *kobus* × M. *salicifolia*. 'Wada's Memory' is thought to be a product of this cross, but there is still some question about this. This superb tree, about 9 m/30 ft tall and nearly as wide at maturity, is one of the most floriferous and precocious of magnolias, producing large white flowers, more than 15 cm/6 in. across, which stand erect as they open, then flag and flutter in the breeze, especially effective from a distance. The foliage emerges soon after flowering, bronze at first, then green in summer, followed in some years by good yellow fall color. This cultivar is useful in Zones 5a–9a.

Magnolia ×*proctoriana* 6 (Proctor magnolia). Plants in this group traditionally have been considered hybrids of *M. salicifolia* × *M. stellata*, but this is now disputed by some botanists, who include these plants under *M. salicifolia*. Regardless of this, plants so-called are upright and pyramidal in habit, but showier in flower than *M. salicifolia* (as narrowly named), with up to twice the number of tepals in each flower. They are similar in adaptability to *M. salicifolia*, but less commonly available.

Magnolia ×*soulangiana* 7

SAUCER MAGNOLIA
Deciduous tree
Magnoliaceae (Magnolia Family)

Hybrid Origin.   *M. denudata* × *M. liliiflora*

Useful Range.   USDA Zones 5a–9a.

Function.   Specimen, patio tree, border accent.

Size and Habit

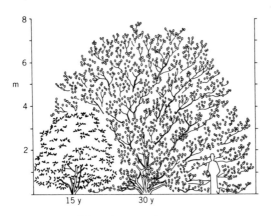

Magnolia ×soulangiana.

Adaptability

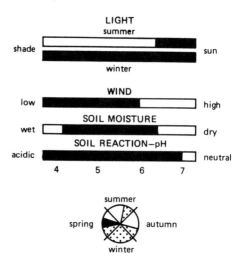

Seasonal Interest. *Flowers:* White, pink to purple, cuplike, 8–12 cm/3–5 in. long, fragrant in a few cultivars, in middle to late spring. *Foliage:* Light green, rather coarse, falling in autumn with little color change. *Fruits:* Reddish, knobby, to 8 cm/3 in., seldom developing fully but opening by slits to expose a few red-orange seeds in early autumn. *Trunk and branches:* Smooth, silvery gray bark adds winter interest.

Problems and Maintenance. This tree is relatively trouble-free and requires little maintenance. It is moderately prone to storm breakage.

Cultivars. More than a dozen cultivars are currently available in the United States and Canada, and considerably more than that number can be found in arboreta and botanic gardens. Seldom are more than a handful available in a locality, except by mail order from a few specialists, so local experience should be noted. A few of the best cultivars are listed here.

'Alba Superba' (= 'Alba') has large, white flowers, with a slight pink flush toward the center, but is seldom available.

'Alexandrina' has large, early flowers, rose-purple outside and white inside; it is an old favorite and still an outstanding cultivar.

'Brozzoni' has huge (15–20 cm/6–8 in.) white flowers, flushed with lavender-pink at the base, late, and is an excellent fast growing tree.

'Coates' is a seedling of 'Rustica Rubra,' with lighter red-purple flowers.

'Grace McDade' has huge flowers, white inside and flushed lavender-pink outside, and a loose, shrubby habit.

'Lennei,' a very old cultivar, is still very popular, with huge, deep purple flowers, white inside, late.

'Lennei Alba' is a seedling of 'Lennei,' with ivory-white flowers, heavy flowering, and late but not as late as 'Lennei.'

'Lilliputian' has small, light pink-purple flowers and is slow-growing and shrubby.

'Picture' is an introduction from the Wada nursery in Japan, with huge flowers, red-purple outside and white inside. Even though it was introduced in 1969, it has not yet become widely available in our area.

'Picture Superba,' another Wada introduction, has large milk-white flowers.

'Rustica Rubra' (= 'Rustica', = 'Rubra') has moderately large deep red-purple flowers, whitish inside.

'Speciosa' has large ivory-white flowers, very late.

'Verbanica' has moderately large flowers, clear rosy pink outside and white inside, very late. It is slow-growing and compact.

Related Species

Magnolia denudata 7 (synonyms: *M. heptapeta*, *M. conspicua*; Yulan magnolia). This long-cultivated Chinese species has fragrant, ivory-white flowers in middle spring, along with the earliest *M.* ×*soulangiana* cultivars. It becomes a very showy tree, to 10 m/33 ft in height and width under good conditions in Zones 6a–9a.

Magnolia liliiflora 5 (synonym: *M. quinquepeta*; lily magnolia). This shrubby species from China has showy purple flowers in late spring, with or following the latest *M.* ×*soulangiana* cultivars, such as 'Speciosa' and 'Verbanica.' The selection 'Nigra,' with deep purple flowers, opening two weeks later than *M.* ×*soulangiana*, is useful in Zones 5b–9a, primarily for its late flowering.

Magnolia campbellii 7 (Campbell's magnolia). This large tree, native from the Himalayas to China, has been called the "queen of magnolias" because of its stature and majestic appearance when in flower. Its tepals can be 14 cm/5.5 in. long and 6 cm/2.4 in. wide, giving flower diameters up to 25 cm/10 in., colored rose-pink, paler inside, and held vertically at the ends of branches, elegant as oval buds and remarkable as fully open cup-and-saucer flowers. Unfortunately, trees of the species type, ssp. *campbellii*, usually take at least 20–25 years to flower, trying the patience (and perhaps longevity) of those who plant them. The species type, ssp. *campbellii*, is cold-hardy to Zone 9a, perhaps also Zone 8 in the maritime climates of the Pacific Northwest, but not in the summer heat of the Southeast. The var. *alba* is a population of white-flowering trees in the wild; otherwise, it is typical of the species. It is seldom seen in cultivation, but is valued as a parent for hybridization.

Magnolia campbellii ssp. *mollicomata* 7 (downy Campbell magnolia). This subspecies occurs as a population at the eastern end of the species distribution, in China, and is distinct enough from ssp. *campbellii* to warrant subspecies status in the eyes of some botanists and horticulturists. First, and perhaps most important, trees of ssp. *mollicomata* flower at an earlier age than the species type, probably by the age of 15. The cylindrical flower buds appear delicately perched upright at upper branch tips, starting to open later than those of the species type, but then opening very rapidly. Trees of ssp. *mollicomata* also are reported as somewhat more cold hardy than ssp. *campbellii*, probably to Zone 8b and perhaps Zone 8a in favored sites. The cultivar

'Lanarth' (purple Lanarth magnolia) is unusually vigorous, growing to well over 12 m/40 ft tall in time, with unusual violet-red, cup-and-saucer-shaped flowers, fading to dark violet purple, and about 23 cm/9 in. across. This cultivar has been used as a breeding parent.

Magnolia sargentii 7 (Sargent magnolia). This probably is the largest of the Chinese magnolias, to at least 10–12 m/33–40 ft tall, the species type sometimes taller. Flowers are white, flushed mauve-pink and deeper purple on the outside, to 30 cm/12 in. across and hanging loosely. Like *M. campbellii*, it is very slow to flower, but var. *robusta*, a lower, broader shrubby tree, may flower in only 12 years. This variety may be the only form of the species in cultivation in our area, and probably the only one commercially available. Useful in about the same range as *M. campbellii*.

Magnolia sprengeri 7 (Sprenger magnolia). This Chinese native, to 15 m/49 ft tall and 10 m/33 ft wide at maturity, is one of the most showy and impressive of flowering trees, with large (20 cm/8 in. across), rosy-red to pale pink flowers, flowering as a relatively young tree (usually within its first ten years), as compared with other Chinese species such as *M. campbellii* and *M. sargentiana*, which can take twice as long. *M. sprengeri* 'Diva' is the best-known form in our area, and perhaps the only one available in North America. This cultivar is a showy tree, with rosy red flowers, probably usefully hardy at least in Zones 7a–9a, although there are isolated reports of considerably greater cold-hardiness. The cultivars 'Galaxy' and 'Spectrum,' both hybrids of *M. liliiflora* 'Nigra' × *M. sprengeri* 'Diva,' were developed at the U.S. National Arboretum. 'Galaxy' has a narrow-upright, nearly columnar habit, growing to at least 8 m/26 ft tall and 4–5 m/13–16 ft wide in time, with great quantities of light purplish pink flowers, late. 'Spectrum' has larger, darker purplish pink flowers and is more broad-oval in form. These two may prove useful in Zones 6b–9a. They are prone to bark-splitting in early winter in Zone 6a.

Related Hybrids. The hybrid 'Star Wars' (M. *liliiflora* 'Nigra' × *M. campbellii*) is reported to be vigorous and well-shaped, 5–6 m/16–20 ft tall,

with large quantities of pinkish-purple flowers, sepals spreading widely, 20–30 cm/8–12 in. across.

Magnolia × *veitchii* 7 (Veitch magnolia). This hybrid of *M. campbellii* × *M. denudata* becomes a tall tree in time, to 15 m/50 ft. It is rare in our area, but is probably useful at least in Zones 7b–9a+ and perhaps also in 7a. The few cultivars of *M.* × *veitchii* are seldom, if ever, available in our area, but one, 'Peter Veitch,' has been used in further hybridization (see Gresham Hybrids, below).

Gresham Hybrids. This group of hybrids has elicited intense interest in the milder parts of our range because it has combined the relative cold-hardiness of *M. liliiflora* (probably 'Nigra') and certain *M.* × *soulangiana* cultivars with the superb color and form of flowers of the tender *M. campbellii*, through its hybrid, *M.* × *veitchii* (probably the selection 'Rubra'). Further crosses have involved other species: *M. campbellii* and ssp. *mollicomata*, *M. sargentiana* var. *robusta*, *M. dawsoniana*, *M. sprengeri* 'Diva,' and additional *M.* × *soulangiana* cultivars. These hybrids resulted from the efforts of the late D. Todd Gresham, a California plant breeder, starting in the middle 1950s. By the time of his death in 1969 he had produced 3000 seedlings, many of which he did not live to see flower, but his breeding records and many of his seedlings were transferred to Bill Dodd, a magnolia specialist in southern Alabama, and continue to be evaluated at Bill Dodd Nursery, Magnolia Nursery, and Tom Dodd Nursery, in the same area. Selections from the Gresham seedlings continue to be named and released by Magnolia Nursery.

The use of *M. liliiflora* and *M.* × *soulangiana* apparently has conferred on some of these hybrids enough heat tolerance and cold-hardiness to make them better prospects than *M. campbellii* for parts of eastern North America. Because these hybrids have not yet fully entered commerce, their cold-hardiness is not at all well known, but some of them apparently are performing well in southern Alabama, where heat tolerance is important. Based on this experience and their parentage, it can be speculated that as a group they may be useful in Zones 7b–9a, and it seems possible that a few might prove cold-hardy to Zone 7a or even parts of Zone 6. Wherever they turn out to be useful, they promise to have a major impact. A few of the most widely available cultivars are listed here.

Hybrids of *M. liliiflora* 'Nigra' by *M.* ×*veitchii* include the following: 'Dark Raiment' has 12-cm/5-in.-long, sickle-shaped buds, opening red-purple, and very dark green foliage; 'Heaven Scent' has honey-scented, dark pink 12-cm/5-in. flowers; 'Peppermint Stick' has honey-scented white flowers, blue-violet at the base and flushed pink; 'Raspberry Ice' has lavender-pink flowers, lighter away from the center; 'Royal Crown' has very large flowers, dark red-purple outside, near-white inside.

Hybrids of *M.* ×*veitchii* by *M.* ×*soulangiana* 'Lennei Alba' include the following: 'Rouged Alabaster' has very large (30 cm/12 in.) white flowers flushed with rose pink; 'Sayonara' has 20-cm/8-in. rounded flowers, flushed pink; 'Tina Durio' is exceptionally vigorous, with very large flowers (28 cm/11 in.).

Hybrids of *M.* ×*veitchii* by *M.* ×*soulangiana* 'Rustica Rubra' include: 'Darrell Dean,' 'Todd Gresham,' and 'Joe McDaniel,' all with very large red-purple flowers, white inside.

There is at least one hybrid of *M.* ×*veitchii* 'Peter Veitch' by *M.* ×*soulangiana* 'Lennei Alba,'

Magnolia liliiflora 'Nigra.'

namely, 'Mary Nell.' This hybrid has a habit similar to that of *M.* ×*soulangiana* and has large (25 cm/10 in. across) white flowers, deeply red stained at the base and of excellent substance.

Other Gresham hybrids, recently introduced, include: 'Dark Shadow,' compact in habit, with red-purple flowers; 'Deep Purple Dream,' a small tree with the deepest red-purple flowers; '14 Karat,' with porcelain-white flowers; 'Full Eclipse,' a fast-growing columnar form with purple flowers; 'Jon Jon,' with large white tepals and red stamens; 'Moondance,' with huge white flowers, early; 'Pink Goblet' with goblet-shaped, rosy pink flowers; 'Sangreal,' with cupped purple flowers, early; and 'Winelight,' with white flowers, washed purple-pink at the base.

Magnolia stellata 5

Synonym: (See nomenclatural note under *M.* ×*loebneri* Related Species)
STAR MAGNOLIA
Deciduous tree
Magnoliaceae (Magnolia Family)

Native Range. Japan.

Useful Range. USDA Zones 5a–9a.

Function. Specimen, patio, border accent.

Size and Habit

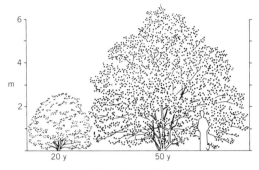

Magnolia stellata.

Adaptability

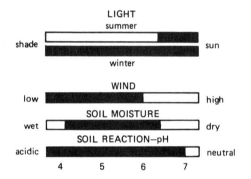

Seasonal Interest. *Flowers:* Fragrant, white (or pink), 8–10 cm/3–4 in. across of 12–18 tepals (petals and petal-like sepals) in early spring. *Foliage:* Medium green, finer textured than that of most other magnolias, forming a dense mass, falling in early autumn with little color change. *Fruits:* Reddish, knobby, to 5 cm/2 in., seldom developing fully but opening by slits to expose a few red-orange seeds in early autumn. *Twigs and branches:* Smooth, silvery gray bark adds winter interest.

Problems and Maintenance. This plant is relatively trouble-free and requires little maintenance but is soft-wooded and prone to breakage in ice storms.

Cultivars. 'Centennial' has larger flowers than typical, has been called an "improved" 'Wa-

terlily,' and is similar to that cultivar, with good form and vigor, growing to 6 m/20 ft high and wide.

'Jane Platt' is very similar to 'Rosea,' but said to have slightly lighter pink tepals.

'Rosea' has clear, pale pink flowers, fading to white after a few days, and good form and vigor, the standard for comparison for new pink flowering clones.

'Royal Star' has pink buds opening to large white flowers (12 cm/5 in. in diameter), and flowers a week or more earlier than typical, sometimes escaping late spring freezes.

'Rubra' has purplish-pink flowers, darker than the pink flowers of 'Rosea' but not as easy a color to use in the landscape.

'Waterlily' has pale pink buds, opening to fragrant white flowers, with many narrow tepals.

'Pink Stardust' has light pink flowers each with more than 40 tepals, selected by Tom Dodd, Jr. of Semmes, Alabama.

Related Hybrids. The following hybrids between *M. liliiflora* and *M. stellata* were developed by William Kosar and introduced by the U.S. National Arboretum in 1968. They are all shrubby small trees, flowering later than *M. stellata* and not so susceptible to late spring frosts.

'Ann' is erect in habit and has erect flower buds, with the earliest flowers in this group opening deep pink-purple and 10 cm/4 in. across and having a distinctive cinnamon scent.

'Betty' has the largest flowers of this group, to 20 cm/8 in. across, in early to middle spring and grows vigorously.

'Jane' is the latest of this group to flower,

Magnolia stellata.

opening in late spring and long-lasting, medium red-purple outside, white inside, 10 cm/4 in. across.

'Judy' is erect, with red-purple flowers outside, white inside. This cultivar is not as easily available as the others in this group.

'Pinkie' has large flowers, to about 15 cm/6 in. across, delicately rosy-pink inside and out, deepening toward the base, with 12 tepals, wider than those of other cultivars in this group, resembling flowers of M. *sprengeri* 'Diva.'

'Randy' is the smallest of these cultivars, to

only about 3 m/10 ft at maturity and narrow, with many-sepaled flowers like those of M. *stellata*, 12 cm/5 in. across, purple in bud and white inside. This cultivar has an open, upright habit.

'Ricki' has a vigorous, upright, full habit, to at least 4 m/13 ft at maturity, with large numbers of deep rosy-purple buds, opening a dusky light lavender-pink to almost white.

'Susan' has an excellent growth habit and flower buds held erect on the branch-tips, opening red-purple inside and out, the sepals slightly twisted.

Magnolia virginiana 6–7

Synonym: M. *glauca*

SWEET BAY

Evergreen to semievergreen tree

Magnoliaceae (Magnolia Family)

Native Range. Southeastern and eastern United States coastal areas, Massachusetts to Florida and Texas.

Useful Range. USDA Zones 5b–9a+ with selection of appropriate genetic material.

Function. Specimen tree or shrub, border.

Size and Habit

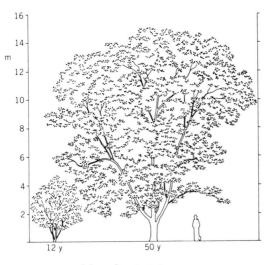

Magnolia virginiana.

Adaptability

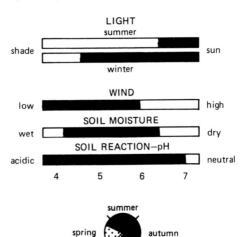

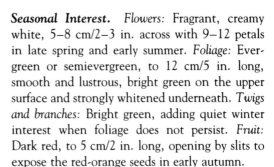

Seasonal Interest. *Flowers:* Fragrant, creamy white, 5–8 cm/2–3 in. across with 9–12 petals in late spring and early summer. *Foliage:* Evergreen or semievergreen, to 12 cm/5 in. long, smooth and lustrous, bright green on the upper surface and strongly whitened underneath. *Twigs and branches:* Bright green, adding quiet winter interest when foliage does not persist. *Fruit:* Dark red, to 5 cm/2 in. long, opening by slits to expose the red-orange seeds in early autumn.

Problems and Maintenance. This is a trouble-free plant, susceptible only to mechanical dam-

Magnolia virginiana.

age from severe ice storms, and less so than most other magnolias.

Varieties and Cultivars. The var. *australis*, occurring in the southern coastal plain, is more nearly evergreen than the species type (var. *virginiana*) and would be presumed to be less cold-hardy, but the evidence for this is not great. The selection 'Henry Hicks' has been fully hardy for many years in Zone 6a, and may be adapted to colder zones as well.

Mahonia aquifolium 3–4

OREGON HOLLY-GRAPE
Evergreen shrub
Berberidaceae (Barberry Family)

Native Range. Pacific Northwest from British Columbia to Oregon.

Useful Range. USDA Zones 5b–9a with selection of appropriate genetic material.

Function. Border, specimen, massing.

Size and Habit

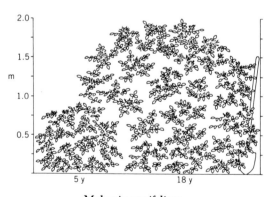

Mahonia aquifolium.

Adaptability   Grows best in at least light shade in the South.

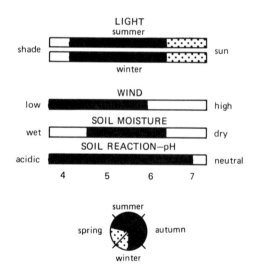

Seasonal Interest. *Flowers:* Bright yellow, in clusters to 8 cm/3 in. across in midspring. *Foliage:* Evergreen, leathery, compound with 2 to 4 pairs of spiny margined leaflets, lustrous and dark green or dull in some plants, turning purplish green in winter, often suffering winterburn in the North. *Fruits:* Blue-black with a whitish waxy bloom, resembling purple grapes, effective in summer.

Problems and Maintenance. Relatively trouble-free in good sites but highly susceptible to foliage dehydration in some winters in Zones 5b

Mahonia aquifolium.

and 6, occasionally killing back in Zone 5b. Shade from winter sun and snow cover reduce winterburn of foliage in Zone 5. Certain species of *Berberis* and *Mahonia* are susceptible to black stem rust of wheat, serving as alternate hosts to the causal fungus and thus enabling it to complete its life cycle and return to infect wheat again (see also *Berberis julianae:* Problems and Maintenance). M. *aquifolium* is highly resistant to this disease, as are M. *nervosa* and M. *repens*.

Cultivars. 'Compacta' has glossy, dark green foliage, remains under 0.5 m/1.6 ft for several years, and is more cold hardy than average for the species. Much variation exists in this species, and more cultivars probably will emerge in time.

Related Species

Mahonia nervosa 3.   This handsome, low-growing species, also from the Pacific Northwest, has larger leaves than M. *aquifolium*, with as many as nine pairs of leaflets as compared with the four pairs usually found in M. *aquifolium*. It is seldom available, and its limits of adaptability in eastern North America are not well known, but its useful range includes Zones 6b–9a.

Mahonia repens 2 (creeping mahonia).   This creeping groundcover with dull bluish green fo-liage is less handsome than M. *aquifolium* but well adapted as a groundcover on rather dry soils and similar in general adaptability to the most cold-hardy plants of M. *aquifolium* (Zones 5b–9a).

Mahonia swaseyi 3 (Texas mahonia).   This species from east-central Texas is low-growing, with compound leaves having 1 to 3 pairs of small leaflets (3 cm/1.2 in. long and 1 cm/0.4 in. wide), dull gray-green, lighter underneath, yellow flowers in spring, and red-flushed, whitish-yellow fruits in late summer. It is rare in native habitat and is susceptible to black stem rust, so it should not be planted in wheat-growing areas. Useful in Zones 8a–9a+, and probably in Zone 7b as well.

Mahonia trifoliolata 4–5 (Laredo mahonia). This species, from southern Texas and Arizona to Mexico, has trifoliolate (3-leaflet) leaves, with leaflets 6.5 cm/2.5 in. long and 3 cm/1,2 in. wide, lobed and spiny-tipped, blue-green to thickly white-glaucous. This is a striking plant, especially the var. *glauca*, which has silvery-blue foliage. Useful in the southwestern corner of our range (Texas) in Zones 8b–9a+, perhaps also in Zone 8a and even Zone 7b.

Intergeneric Hybrids

×*Mahoberberis aquisargentii* 4.   This hybrid between *Mahonia aquifolium* and *Berberis sargentiana* has glossy, deep green leaves varying widely in shape, either simple or trifoliolate. It is a vigorous upright shrub 1.5–2 m/5–6.6 ft tall and is useful in Zone 6b–9a, perhaps also in Zone 6a. This is the most presentable of the ×*Mahoberberis* hybrids and is reported to be immune to black stem rust. Probably none of these hybrids is commercially available in North America, although some of them can be found in arboretum collections.

Mahonia bealei 4

LEATHERLEAF MAHONIA
Evergreen shrub
Berberidaceae (Barberry Family)

Native Range.   China.

Useful Range.   USDA Zones 6b–9a+.

Function.   Specimen, border accent, massing; especially useful in formal, architectonic settings.

Size and Habit

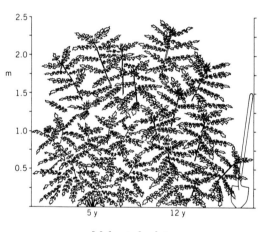

Mahonia bealei.

Adaptability.   Grows best in at least light shade in the South.

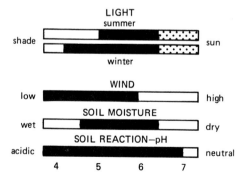

Seasonal Interest.   *Flowers:* Fragrant, pale to lemon yellow, in large (to 15 cm/6 in.) upright clusters, several radiating from one branch, early to middle spring. *Foliage:* Evergreen, leathery, to 40 cm/15 in. long, compound with up to 15 spiny margined leaflets, deep blue-green, giving striking textural effect, and remaining green in winter. *Fruits:* Blue-black with a whitish waxy bloom, elongated, in large, semipendulous clusters, striking in early summer.

Problems and Maintenance.   This shrub is trouble-free but eventually needs pruning to maintain fullness toward the base. It is susceptible to winterburn, especially in Zones 6 and 7, and should be planted in sites protected from sweeping winds.

Related Species

Mahonia fortunei 4 (Fortune or Chinese mahonia).   This evergreen shrub has finer textured foliage than other *Mahonia* species, because its leaflets are only about 1 cm/0.4 in. wide and up to 12 cm/5 in. long. Foliage emerges bright green and remains deep green in winter. Flowers and fruits are less showy than those of *M. bealei,* and the entire plant is less cold-hardy, useful in Zones 8b–9a+.

Mahonia lomariifolia 5 (Chinese or Burmese mahonia).   This striking shrub is not greatly different from *M. bealei* in general appearance but has larger leaves than any other *Mahonia* species discussed here, sometimes 50 cm/20 in. long, with more than 25 leaflets, giving a strong textural accent valued in highly architectonic landscapes. Flowering and fruiting interest is comparable with that of *M. bealei,* but *M. lomariifolia* is no more cold-hardy than *M. fortunei.*

Malus baccata 7

SIBERIAN CRABAPPLE
Deciduous tree
Rosaceae (Rose Family)

Native Range.   Northeastern Asia.

Useful Range.   USDA Zones 3a–7a.

Function.   Specimen, shade tree, screen.

Size and Habit

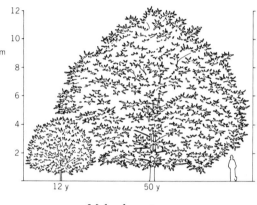

Malus baccata.

Adaptability

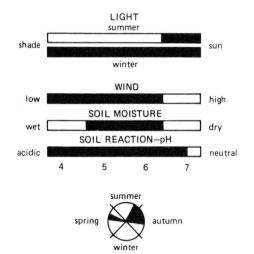

Seasonal Interest. *Flowers:* Fragrant, white, showy, to 4 cm/1.6 in. across in middle spring, borne annually. *Foliage:* Bright green and quietly attractive, except when infected by apple scab. Falls in early to midautumn without color change. *Fruit:* Red or yellow, very small, to 1 cm/0.4 in. across, borne annually and remaining on the tree after leaves have dropped until early winter. *Trunk and branches:* Bark is yellow-brown, a small but sometimes appreciable contribution to winter color.

Problems and Maintenance.   Many trees of the species type are moderately susceptible to apple scab disease. Resistant cultivars have been selected (see Varieties and Cultivars). The better *M. baccata* selections generally are resistant to the other important diseases of crabapples. Scale insects and borers can be troublesome, especially in warmer parts of the useful range, and may need to be controlled there.

Varieties and Cultivars.   'Columnaris' (columnar Siberian crabapple) is somewhat columnar when young, but eventually becomes almost as wide as it is tall (8–10 m/26–33 ft). Its white flowers are borne in good numbers annually, and its 1-cm/0.4-in. yellow and reddish fruits are persistent well into autumn. Its only disease problem is fire blight, so it should be used cautiously in areas where that disease is often severe. Cold-hardy to Zone 3a.

The var. *jackii* (= 'Jackii') (Jack flowering crabapple), from Korea, differs from the species type in its deep red fruits and resistance to apple scab as well as the other primary diseases of crabapples.

The var. *mandshurica*, native from northern Japan to Manchuria and central China, is not greatly different from the species type in size and general appearance, but is slightly earlier flowering and fruiting, with fragrant flowers. This variety has had mixed reviews on disease resistance, perhaps the reason why it is not commonly available. Some find it resistant, whereas others find it highly susceptible to scab and moderately susceptible to mildew. There may be a wide enough genetic complement in commerce to account for this, and to provide an opportunity for further selection. Reported to be unusually cold hardy, like the species type.

Hybrids of *Malus baccata*

Malus ×*adstringens* 7.   This hybrid group has resulted from crosses of M. *baccata* and M. *pumila* 'Niedzwetskyana,' the converse cross, and, in practice, open-pollinated seedlings from these hybrids. Included are the Morden Rosybloom cultivars, originated at the Canada Department of Agriculture (CDA) research station at Morden, Manitoba, and at least some of the original Rosybloom group that originated in the work of Miss Isabella Preston at the CDA Central Experimental Farm at Ottawa, although the full parentage of most of that group is not known.

Malus prunifolia.

The Rosybloom crabapples in general are very cold-hardy (useful in Zones 3a–7a) and large and spreading in habit. Their flowers are red-purple and their foliage is more-or-less purple, especially in spring. They tend to flower well only in alternate years and to be highly susceptible to apple scab, but there are important exceptions to these generalizations, as can be seen from descriptions of individual cultivars, listed under *Malus* Hybrid Cultivars. Cultivars in this group that are on that list are 'Baskatong,' 'Hopa,' 'Kelsey,' 'Makamik,' 'Radiant,' 'Red Silver,' 'Red Splendor,' 'Royalty,' 'Selkirk,' and 'Thunderchild.'

Malus ×*micromalus* 6 (midget crabapple).   This hybrid, probably M. *spectabilis* × M. *baccata*, is notable for its deep rosy pink flowers that fade very little with age and its small (1.3 cm/0.5 in.) red fruits that remain showy until midautumn and persist until early winter. The name refers to the small fruits, not the size of the tree, although it seldom exceeds 4–5 m/13–16 ft in height. Useful in Zones 4a–7b, but susceptible to fire blight.

Malus ×*robusta* 6 (cherry crabapple).   This group of vigorous and cold-hardy (to Zone 3b) hybrids of M. *baccata* × M. *prunifolia* has given rise to several useful selections, the best known of which is 'Dolgo' (see *Malus* Hybrid Cultivars).

Related Species and Their Hybrids

Malus prunifolia 6 (plumleaf or pearleaf crabapple).   This native of eastern Asia is closely related to M. *baccata*, but slightly less cold-hardy

(to Zone 4a). It is best known for its hybrids, M. ×*robusta* and M. ×*scheideckeri*. M. *prunifolia* 'Pendula' differs only in its weeping growth habit, and probably is not commercially available, but it has played a prominent role through its parentage of other pendulous cultivars (see *Weeping crabapples* under *Malus floribunda*).

Malus pumila 7 (common apple).   Although best known for commercial fruiting apples, M. *pumila* has been involved in the parentage of many flowering crabapples as well, especially as represented by the interesting but disease susceptible M. *pumila* 'Niedzwetzkyana,' a shrubby, small tree with reddish flowers, fruits, flesh of fruits, and wood of twigs. Commercial fruiting cultivars of *Malus pumila* and *Malus sylvestris* also can be functional landscape plants, used as shade trees or in allée or bosque plantings in situations where the fruits are considered an asset rather than a liability. For successful fruit production, at least a minimal spray maintenance program probably will be necessary. Consult state, provincial, or county extension service offices about local requirements and procedures.

Malus ×*purpurea* 6 (purple crabapple).   This variable group of hybrids of M. *pumila* 'Niedzwetzkyana' and M. ×*atrosanguinea* (M. *halliana* × M. *sieboldii*) is noted for early, red-purple flowers and fruits and, to varying degrees, purple foliage, fading to bronze or greenish by late summer. Most members are susceptible to apple scab. Several cultivars useful in Zones 3b–7a have been selected and named, but few are used much today. Two that are still in use are

'Lemoinei' and 'Liset' (see under *Malus* Hybrid Cultivars).

Malus spectabilis 6 (Chinese flowering crabapple). This species, not known in the wild, has very showy single, semidouble, or double pale pink flowers flowers, rosy pink in bud, but its yellowish fruits, about 2.5 cm/1 in. across, have little ornamental value. The single-flowered forms are of little landscape value, but the selections 'Albiplena,' with double white flowers, 4 cm/1.6 in. across, and 'Riversii,' with double pink flowers, 5 cm/2 in. across, have been in cultivation for many years. Today, other cultivars with showy double flowers coupled with colorful fruits, such as 'Blanche Ames,' 'Dorothea,' and 'Katherine,' are usually selected in preference to the M. spectabilis cultivars, and the latter are barely available. 'Blanche Ames' originated as an open-pollinated seedling of M. spectabilis 'Riversii' (see 'Blanche Ames' under *Malus* Hybrid Cultivars).

Malus floribunda 6

JAPANESE FLOWERING CRABAPPLE
Deciduous tree
Rosaceae (Rose Family)

Native Range.   Japan.

Useful Range.   USDA Zones 4b–8b, possibly colder zones and Zone 9a as well.

Function.   Specimen, massing, patio tree.

Size and Habit

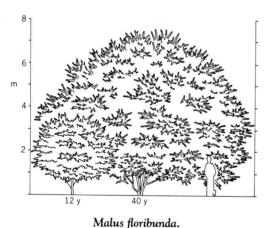

Malus floribunda.

Adaptability

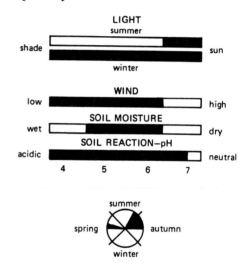

Seasonal Interest. *Flowers:* Fragrant, red in bud, opening rosy pink and fading to white, to 3–4 cm/1.2–1.6 in. across, borne in great numbers in middle spring annually. *Foliage:* Bright green, neat and attractive, falling without color change. *Fruit:* Yellow with slight red blush, only to 0.8 cm/0.3 in. across, borne annually but remaining on the tree for only a short time after leaves drop, in part because they are favored by birds.

Problems and Maintenance. This tree is fairly resistant to apple scab, rust, and mildew, and usually is not troubled with fire blight, although damage has occurred in some years. It needs little or no pruning, and the fruits are less of a litter problem than those of many crabapples. While crabapples in general cannot be considered low-maintenance plants, M. *floribunda* usually requires very little attention.

Hybrids of Malus floribunda

Malus ×*arnoldiana* 6 (Arnold crabapple). This hybrid of M. *floribunda* × M. *baccata* is a smaller tree than either parent, seldom exceeding 5 m/16 ft in height, with strongly horizontal to moundlike growth habit. Its flowers are similar to those of M. *floribunda* except slightly larger and deeper red in bud, and it is similar to M. *floribunda* in useful range and site requirements. Unfortunately, it is very susceptible to apple scab and rarely available. Hybrids of M. ×*arnoldiana* include 'Dorothea' (M. ×*arnoldiana* × M. *halliana* 'Parkmanii') and 'Van Eseltine' (probably M. ×*arnoldiana* × M. *spectabilis*). See these under *Malus* Hybrid Cultivars.

Malus ×*scheideckeri* 6 (Scheidecker crabapple). This hybrid of M. *floribunda* × M. *prunifolia* is a small tree, 4–6 m/13–19 ft tall, with slender branches, graceful when allowed to assume its natural form. Its semidouble, rosy pink flowers appear at about the same time as those of the parents, relatively early among crabapples, and its small yellow fruits are effective in early autumn. It is useful in Zones 5a–8b, but moderately susceptible to apple scab and highly susceptible to fire blight.

Weeping Crabapples. Even though *Malus floribunda* itself shows little weeping tendency, it has figured heavily, along with M. *prunifolia* 'Pendula,' in the development of several weeping crabapple cultivars. 'Exzellens Thiel' (M. *floribunda* ×M. *prunifolia* 'Pendula') is a gracefully pendulous small tree with much of the flowering interest of M. *floribunda*. It requires staking to support its trunk for a few years after planting,

Malus 'Red Jade.'

and probably is no longer available. But this cultivar was breeding parent for the next generations of weeping crabapples, including 'Oekonomierat Echtermeyer,' 'Red Jade,' and 'Seafoam' (see *Malus* Hybrid Cultivars). Newer weeping and semiweeping crabapples (parentage often not as well known) include 'Manbeck Weeper' (Ann E™), 'Blanche Ames' (semiweeping), 'Coral Cascade' (semiweeping), 'Louisa,' 'Molozam' (Molten Lava™), 'Sinai Fire,' 'Weepcanzam' (Weeping Candied Apple®; semiweeping), and 'Cascole' (White Cascade®). See these under (*Malus* Hybrid Cultivars).

Malus 'Red Jade.'

Malus hupehensis 6

Synonym: M. *theifera*
TEA CRABAPPLE
Deciduous tree
Rosaceae (Rose Family)

Native Range.   China.

Useful Range.   USDA Zones 4b–8b.

Function.   Specimen, patio tree.

Size and Habit

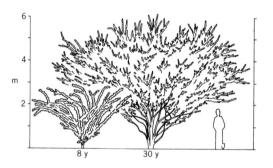

Malus hupehensis.

Adaptability

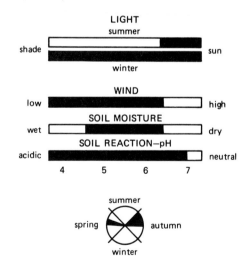

Malus hupehensis.

Malus hupehensis.

Seasonal Interest. *Flowers:* Fragrant, deep pink in bud, opening blush pink and fading to white, to 4 cm/1.6 in. across, borne in alternate years. *Foliage:* Deep green, displayed to good advantage by the picturesque, open branching habit. *Fruits:* Greenish yellow with red blush, giving significant but not outstanding interest in early autumn in alternate years. *Habit:* Open branching habit is among the most picturesque of all crabapples, with long, irregularly spreading, sparsely branching limbs.

Problems and Maintenance.   This species is resistant to most crabapple diseases but is occasionally troubled by fire blight.

Cultivars.   'Cardinal' and 'Strawberry Parfait' are selections from seedlings from open-pollinated M. *hupehensis*—that is, hybrids involving M. *hupehensis* as one parent (see *Malus* Hybrid Cultivars).

Related Species and Hybrids

The following are related to M. *hupehensis* more in landscape effect than genetically.

Malus halliana 5 (Hall flowering crabapple). This small tree (to about 4 m/13 ft), cultivated in the Far East but not known in the wild there, is gracefully spreading to vase-shaped and has relatively early, bright rose flowers.

'Parkmanii' (Parkman flowering crabapple) is the most-used cultivar of *M. halliana* (but no longer used very much), with late, semidouble,

pale pink flowers and impressive disease resistance. Its fruits are small and dull red and do not persist past early autumn, and this is one of the *least* cold-hardy flowering crabapples, only to Zone 6a or perhaps to Zone 5b.

'Katherine' is a very showy hybrid of *M. halliana* and *M. baccata* (see *Malus* Hybrid Cultivars).

Malus ioensis 6

IOWA OR PRAIRIE CRABAPPLE
Deciduous tree
Rosaceae (Rose Family)

Native Range. North-central United States.

Useful Range. USDA Zones 4a–6b.

Function. Specimen, massing, patio tree.

Size and Habit

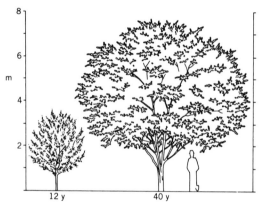

Malus ioensis.

Adaptability

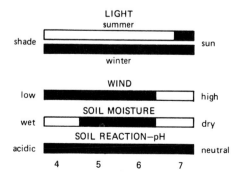

Seasonal Interest. *Flowers:* Fragrant, clear, light pink, single or double, to 4–5 cm/1.6–2 in. across in late spring after most flowering crabapples have finished flowering, borne annually. *Foliage:* Medium to light green, rather coarse. *Fruits:* Greenish and inconspicuous. *Twigs and branches:* Bark is more or less light silvery gray, adding winter interest.

Problems and Maintenance. *Malus ioensis* and the other native American crabapples, including *M. angustifolia* and *M. coronaria*, are alternate hosts for the cedar apple rust fungus and should be grown only in areas free of native American junipers, especially eastern red cedar (*Juniperus virginiana*), or where intensive spraying maintenance is available. In areas free of cedar apple rust, members of this group still have other disease problems. They are generally susceptible to apple scab and fire blight. Because of their susceptibility to disease, native American crabapples should only be used when there are compelling reasons or when preserved in natural or naturalized settings.

Cultivars and Hybrids. Several selections have been made from *M. ioensis*. All are susceptible to cedar-apple rust, but some are very useful in areas where eastern red cedar is not present.

'Plena' (Bechtel crabapple) is the original double-flowered selection of *M. ioensis*, with fragrant, double flowers to 5 cm/2 in. across and having as many as 30 petals. Because of other disease and insect problems, this is gradually being replaced by other cultivars such as 'Klehm' (= 'Klehm's Improved Bechtel'), which probably is a selection from M. *coronaria* rather than M. *ioensis*, 'Mazam' (Madonna®), and 'Prairie Rose' (see *Malus* Hybrid Cultivars).

Related Species

Malus angustifolia 6 (southern or wild sweet crabapple).   This wild tree native to the southeastern United States as far south as northern Florida is the only flowering crabapple that performs well as far south as the Gulf Coast, and it is useful in Zones 6b–9a. It is not a highly functional landscape tree there, but with its gracefully irregular form and fragrant, pale pink single flowers (to 2.5 cm/1 in.) it has distinctive charm in natural and naturalized settings. Like the more northern native American crabapples, it is susceptible to cedar apple rust, and it is often defoliated before autumn when growing in the same area as *Juniperus virginiana* or its cultivars.

Malus coronaria 6 (wild sweet crabapple).   This native of the eastern United States, from New York and Ontario to Alabama and Indiana can be considered the northeastern counterpart of M. *angustifolia* and M. *ioensis*, from which it differs very little. It is useful in Zones 5a–7a. Several selections have been made but only the following cultivars have become at all well known. 'Charlottae' has fragrant, clear pink, semidouble flowers, to 2.0–2.5 cm/0.8–1 in. across, appearing at about the same time in late

spring as those of M. *ioensis*. It is susceptible to cedar apple rust, apple scab, and fire blight.

Other, less commonly used species in the native American group include M. *glaucescens* and M. *platycarpa*. These and the hybrid groups M. ×*heterophylla* (M. *coronaria* × M. *pumila*) and M. ×*soulardii* (M. *ioensis* × M. *pumila*) all share the disease problems common to the group.

Malus ioensis.

Malus sargentii 5

SARGENT CRABAPPLE
Deciduous tree
Rosaceae (Rose Family)

Native Range.   Japan.

Useful Range.   USDA Zones 4b–8b.

Function.   Specimen, massing.

Size and Habit

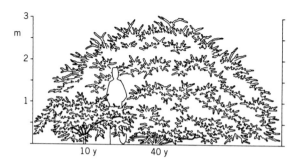

Malus sargentii.

Adaptability

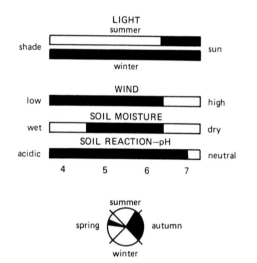

Seasonal Interest. *Flowers:* Fragrant, light pink in bud, opening pure white, no more than 2.5 cm/1 in. across, flowering heavily only in alternate years. *Foliage:* Deep green, partly lobed, neat in texture. *Fruits:* Shiny, deep red, small, about 1 cm/0.4 in. across, adding interest throughout autumn in alternate years.

Problems and Maintenance. Biennial flowering and fruiting is a limitation in any flowering crabapple and is often sufficient reason for discarding one cultivar in favor of another. M. *sargentii* has remained in favor in spite of this drawback because of its uniqueness in size, form, and function. The species and the selection 'Rosea' (see Cultivars) are highly resistant, but not immune, to apple scab and fire blight. Pruning is seldom necessary, except to remove dead, damaged, or rubbing branches.

Cultivars. 'Candymint' is slightly larger than M. *sargentii*, with pink flowers. 'Jewelberry' looks much like M. *sargentii*, but flowers and fruits annually, retains its fruits longer, and promises eventually to replace M. *sargentii* in many landscape applications. 'Mary Potter' is a hybrid, looking very much like M. *sargentii* except larger, with a picturesque horizontal branching habit. 'Pink Princess' is a very recent selection from M. *sargentii*, with rosy-pink flowers and good purple to bronze foliage. 'Rosea' is very similar to the species type except that it grows slightly larger, and its flowers are rosy red in bud before opening white. See all of these under *Malus* Hybrid Cultivars.

Malus sieboldii 6

TORINGO CRABAPPLE
Deciduous tree
Rosaceae (Rose Family)

Native Range. Japan and Korea.

Useful Range. USDA Zones 4a–8b (see Varieties).

Function. Specimen, massing, patio tree.

Size and Habit. M. ×*zumi* (synonym: M. *sieboldii* var. *zumi*) is illustrated.

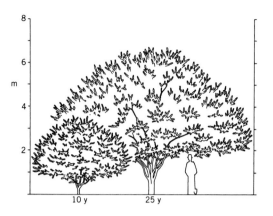

Malus ×*zumi (M. sieboldii var. zumi).*

Adaptability

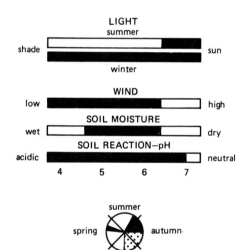

Seasonal Interest. *Flowers:* Fragrant, single, pink in bud, opening pale pink or white, 2 cm/0.8 in. across, borne annually in middle to late spring (see Varieties). *Foliage:* Medium green, variously lobed. *Fruits:* Small (0.8 cm/0.3 in. across), brownish yellow or red, borne annually.

Problems and Maintenance. This species is resistant to most diseases. Some pruning for establishment of structure may be desirable in var. *arborescens*.

Varieties. The var. *arborescens* (tree Toringo crabapple) is distinctly a tree form, to 8–10 m/25–23 ft tall and equally wide at maturity. It is valued primarily for its annual display of fragrant, small, pink to white flowers opening in late spring and for its disease resistance. Useful in Zones 5a–8a and perhaps in colder zones as well.

Related Hybrids

Malus ×*atrosanguinea* 6 (carmine crabapple). This hybrid of M. *halliana* × M. *sieboldii* is a small, shrubby tree with deep red flower buds, opening bright rose, to 3 cm/1.2 in. across, midway in the flowering season. It has little fruiting interest. It is resistant to apple scab but can be seriously affected by fire blight in some areas and is useful in Zones 5a–8b.

Malus ×*zumi* 6 (synonym: M. *sieboldii* var. *zumi*; Zumi crabapple). This hybrid of M. *baccata* var. *mandshurica* × M. *sieboldii* has large numbers of white flowers, pink in bud, borne biennially in middle spring, and small bright red fruits. The selection 'Calocarpa' holds its fruits well into winter, but this is only a biennial display. In some locations and some years, foliage turns orange before falling. 'Calocarpa' is more resistant to fire blight than average for M. ×*zumi* and is useful in Zones 4a–8a. Hybrids of M. ×*zumi* are noted for their colorful fruits, persisting into late autumn or winter. They include 'Donald Wyman,' 'Indian Magic,' 'Indian Summer,' 'Professor Sprenger,' and 'Snowdrift' (see all of these under *Malus* Hybrid Cultivars). Also in that list are 'Bob White,' 'Golden Hornet,' 'Ormiston Roy,' and 'Winter Gold,' which *may* also be M. ×*zumi* hybrids.

Malus toringoides 6

CUTLEAF CRABAPPLE
Deciduous tree
Rosaceae (Rose Family)

Native Range.   Western China.

Useful Range.   USDA Zones 4b–8a.

Function.   Specimen, massing, patio tree.

Size and Habit

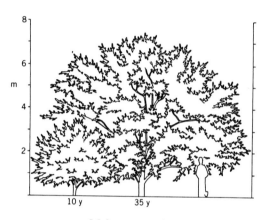

Malus toringoides.

Adaptability

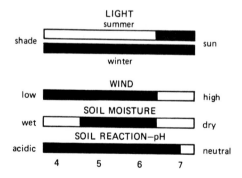

Seasonal Interest.   *Flowers:* Fragrant, white, to 2.5 cm/1 in. across, borne in quantity only in alternate years in late spring. *Foliage:* Medium green, usually lobed, making a fairly dense canopy. *Fruits:* Distinctively pear-shaped, yellow with a red blush on the sunny side, to 1.2 cm/0.5 in. long, very striking, late summer to late autumn in alternate years.

Problems and Maintenance.   This species is somewhat resistant to apple scab and rust, but highly susceptible to fire blight in some areas. The dense, twiggy growth habit tends to discourage pruning, which is hardly necessary anyway. Rarely are plants of this species on the market, but seeds are usually commercially available.

Related Species

Malus tschonoskii 7 (Tschonoski crabapple). This Japanese tree is unlike any other crabapple, primarily because of its foliage interest. Young leaves are covered with a thick felt of silvery white hairs, which gradually disappears from the upper leaf surface, remaining on the lower surface. In some locations and in some years, the leaves turn bright shades of yellow, red, and purple in autumn. The foliage interest, unhampered by apple scab, and its regularly pyramidal form give this species value as a landscape tree, but it has only minor flowering and fruiting interest and unfortunately is susceptible to fire blight. It is gradually becoming more widely available and is useful in Zones 4b–8b.

Malus Hybrid Cultivars 5–7

Most flowering crabapples specified for landscape use are cultivars, but some are species or botanical varieties. Some species have their own major headings, and others are included as "Related Species" under these headings. Botanical varie-

ties and cultivars selected from single species are also listed under the individual species. Hybrid cultivars and those of uncertain parentage, on the other hand, are included under this heading. This listing includes hybrid cultivars that are usually available, although some are much more common than others.

Cultivar names are listed first, followed by any applicable trade name. Names labeled with the registered trademark symbol ® were already registered at the time of writing. The ™ symbol indicates that trademarking of that name had been applied for. Current trademarking requires that a separate cultivar name be supplied in addition to the trade name, to serve as a generic name, as is done for any trademarked chemical. Plant patent numbers in force at this writing are also appended. Plant patents, like other patents, are in force for 17 years, but legislation under discussion at this writing, if enacted, would extend that time period to 20 years. To allow for that possibility, patent numbers assigned in 1977 or later are included in this edition.

The majority of flowering crabapples are cold-hardy in Zone 4b, but some are much hardier than that, and a few are less hardy. Only departures from 4b, insofar as they are known, are noted in this list.

"Disease-resistant" means that infections are few, do not progress very far, or do not occur. "Disease-tolerant" usually means that infections may occur, but do not cause trees to defoliate, at least until the extent of infection is great.

The following abbreviations are used to evaluate disease-resistance: A = Excellent, B = Good, C = fair, D = poor), referring to fire blight (FB), apple scab (SC), cedar-apple rust (CR), and powdery mildew (ML).

Assessing resistance of crabapples to diseases takes time. Apple scab, fire blight, and mildew are very weather-dependent. Amounts of infection can vary widely from year to year and place to place. This is fairly predictable for scab and mildew, less so for fire blight. Cultivars are often introduced as "disease-resistant" in good faith, only to be found susceptible in later years and in other localities. Because of this, it is important to be in touch with other experience in the particular locality where trees will be planted. Consult state or county Cooperative Extension Service offices, local arboretums, nurseries, or landscape installation firms.

The following list is not exhaustive, because there are at least 200 cultivars of flowering crabapples in commerce, not counting obsolete cultivars still preserved in arboreta and apple cultivars grown primarily for their fruit. Those listed are among the most widely available, or promising, or have some specific redeeming quality, except as noted.

'Adams,' introduced by Adams Nursery (Westfield, Massachusetts) in 1951, is still considered a superior cultivar, to 6–8 m/20–26 ft tall and nearly as wide, with deep pink flowers and 1.5-cm/0.6-in. red, persistent fruits, borne every year. Disease-resistance: SC-B, FB-B, CR-A, ML-B.

'Adirondack' is a recent introduction from the breeding program of Dr. Donald Egolf at the U.S. National Arboretum. It is upright and vase-shaped at maturity, to 5 m/16 ft tall and 3–3.5 m/12 ft wide, with large quantities of red buds opening to white flowers of excellent substance and borne every year, followed by pendulous, bright orange red, persistent 1.3-cm/0.5-in. fruits. Disease-resistance: SC-A, FB-A, CR-A, ML-A.

'American Beauty,' introduced by Princeton Nurseries (New Jersey) in 1968, has very large, deep rose, double flowers, purple foliage, turning bronze in summer, and few or no fruits. Remarkably showy in flower and upright in habit. It is less often used today than in the past because of its susceptibility to scab, fire blight, and cedar-apple rust.

'Amazam' (American Masterpiece®) is a recent release, expected to grow to 8 m/26 ft high and 6 m/20 ft wide, with bright red flowers, red foliage in spring and early summer and deep maroon thereafter, and persistent, pumpkin-orange, 1-cm/0.4-in. fruits.

'Baskatong' is one of the more disease-resistant of the Rosybloom Crabapples (see M. ×adstringens under M. baccata, Hybrids), developed by the Canada Department of Agriculture before 1950. It is little used now except on the Canadian and U.S. prairies, but is valued there for its size, to at least 9 m/30 ft in height and width, and its cold-hardiness, to Zone 3a. Flowers are rosy purple, fading to dull pink as they age, and

2.5 cm/1 in. reddish purple fruits add little and fall early. Disease-resistance: SC-B, FB-A, CR-A, ML-B.

'Beverly' was introduced in 1940 by Arie den Boer, whose work at the Des Moines (Iowa) Waterworks Park was the basis for his book, *Flowering Crabapples*, a classic published by the American Association of Nurserymen in 1959. This old cultivar has remained in favor because of its dense, upright habit, to 6 m/20 ft high and wide, white flowers, and orange-red fruits that persist through most of autumn. Disease-resistance: SC-A, FB-C, CR-A, ML-A.

'Blanch Ames' was selected from open-pollinated seedlings of *M. spectabilis* 'Riversii' by Dr. Karl Sax at the Arnold Arboretum, introduced in 1947, and named for Blanche Ames, the noted botanical illustrator. This tree is gracefully semiweeping, 6–8 m/20–26 ft high and 8–9 m/26–30 ft wide, with fragrant, semidouble, pink flushed white flowers, borne annually, giving the tree a billowy appearance. Its 0.8-cm/0.3-in. yellow fruits are attractive in late summer but fall by September. It is highly disease-resistant, yet not common today, perhaps because of the current emphasis on autumn and winter fruiting interest. Useful in Zones 4a–8a.

'Bob White,' introduced by the Arnold Arboretum more than a century ago and believed to be an *M. ×zumi* selection (see under *M. sieboldii*, Related Hybrids), has a dense, rounded habit and white flowers, pink in bud, but borne in quantity only in alternate years. Its yellow, 1.3-cm/0.5-in. fruits persist all winter. Disease-resistance: SC-A, FB-C, CR-A, ML-B.

'Branzam' (Brandywine®), developed at Simpson Nursery, Vincennes, Indiana, was introduced by Lake County Nursery (Perry, Ohio) in 1979. It grows to 5–6 m/16–20 ft in height and width and has large, fragrant, double rose-pink flowers, individually as showy as those of the large-flowered Oriental cherries. Its 2.5-cm/1-in. fruits ripen golden yellow and fall early, making a litter problem. Because of its *M. coronaria* or *M. ioensis* parentage, it is susceptible to cedar-apple rust, so it should not be used in the same area as *Juniperus virginiana*. It is also somewhat susceptible to scab.

'Callaway,' introduced by Callaway Gardens, Pine Mountain, Georgia, has been an excellent performer in the Deep South and is probably useful in Zones 4b–8b, possibly even Zone 9a. Identified as a seedling of *M. prunifolia* by Donald Wyman and Arie F. den Boer, this tree is pyramidal in habit, to 5 m/16 ft or taller in time. Disease-resistance: SC-C, FB-B, CR-C, ML-B.

'Camzam' (Camelot®) is one of the Round Table Series™ of genetically dwarf crabapples recently introduced by Lake County Nursery. It is rounded and compact, to 3 m/10 ft high and nearly as wide, with white/fuchsia-pink flowers, red in bud, purplish dark green foliage, and 1-cm/0.4-in. deep burgundy fruits. Reported to be disease-resistant.

'Canary,' originating as a chance seedling and introduced by Simpson Nursery, is upright and rounded in habit, to about 5 m/16 ft high and wide. It has great numbers of small white flowers and very small but effective canary-yellow fruits, persisting through midautumn, and is reported to be disease-resistant.

'Candymint' (= 'Candymint Sargent'; Plant Patent No. 6606, 1989), a Simpson Nursery introduction, is an *M. sargentii* seedling about the size of 'Mary Potter' (also an *M. sargentii* seedling), to 3 m/10 ft high and at least half again as wide, with red buds and red-edged pink petals, remaining in flower longer than most crabapples, and purplish green summer foliage. Disease-resistance: SC-A, FB-A, CR-A, ML-A.

'Canterzam' (Canterbury™), another of the Round Table Series™, is densely rounded and horizontal in habit, to 3 m/10 ft high and nearly 5 m/16 ft wide, with light pink flowers, deep pink in bud, and bright red and very persistent 0.6-cm/0.25-in. fruits. Reported to be disease-resistant.

'Cardinal' (Plant Patent No. 7174, 1990) is a recent introduction with broad, open vase shape, 5–6 m/16–20 ft tall and wide, with bright red flowers and small, deep red fruits, colorful in early autumn. This originated as a seedling of *Malus hupehensis* 'Strawberry Parfait.' It has been reported to be resistant to scab and mildew, but with any hybrid of *M. hupehensis* there must always be some question about fire blight until it has been planted in many areas and proved resistant. *Note:* Two other crabapples have been given the name 'Cardinal.' One has been renamed 'Fozam' (Foxfire™); the plant patent on the other has expired and the plant may no longer be in commerce.

'Cascole' (White Cascade®), selected by Henry Ross of Strongsville, Ohio, in 1974, is a refined weeping crabapple, to 5m/16 ft high and wide, with white flowers, bright rose in bud, bright green foliage, and 0.9-cm/0.35-in. yellow to amber fruits, effective in late summer. Disease-resistance: SC-B, FB-A, CR-A, ML-A.

'Centzam' (Centurion®), selected at Simpson Nursery and introduced by Lake County Nursery in 1979, has upright, pyramidal habit, to 7–8 m/23–26 ft tall and 5–6 m/16–20 ft wide, with rose-red flowers, red in bud, and 1.5-cm/0.6-in. cherry-red fruits that persist until early winter. It has excellent disease resistance except for slight susceptibility to scab.

'Chrishozam' (Christmas Holly), originated by the late Fr. John L. Fiala (expert on lilacs and crabapples, author of *Flowering Crabapples: The Genus Malus* (Timber Press, 1994), parish priest, and educator) and introduced by Lake County Nursery, has a compact, rounded habit, growing to 5 m/16 ft high and wide, with fragrant, pure white flowers, red in bud, and 8-cm/0.3-in. bright red fruits, persisting through autumn. Reportedly disease-resistant.

'Cinzam' (Cinderella®) is the smallest of the Round Table Series™, with upright, compact habit, to 2.4 m/8 ft tall and 1.5 m/5 ft wide, with deeply lobed foliage, white flowers, red in bud, and golden yellow, 0.6-cm/0.25-in. fruits, persistent until late autumn. Reported as disease-resistant.

'Coral Cascade' (Plant Patent No. 7142, 1990) is a recent introduction with semiweeping habit, to 5 m/16 ft high and 5–6 m/16–20 ft wide, with coral-red flower buds, opening blush-white, and 1-cm/0.4-in. deep coral fruits, persisting well into winter. Reported to be highly disease-resistant.

'Coralcole' (Coralburst®) is a very small, distinctive tree, to 3–4 m/10–13 ft tall and 2.5–3 m/8–10 ft wide, with a dense, rounded head, semidouble rose-pink flowers, and 1.3-cm/0.5-in. red-orange fruits, usually not borne in large numbers and falling by early autumn. It is susceptible to apple scab but otherwise disease-resistant. This is an appropriate tree for small-scale, formal situations where autumn interest is not important.

'David,' selected by Arie den Boer (see 'Beverly') and introduced in 1957, is still competi-

tive, growing to 6 m/20 ft high and wide, with white flowers, pink in bud, and scarlet fruits, 1.5 cm/0.5 in. across and persistent until early winter. Disease-resistance: SC-C, FB-B, CR-A, ML-A.

'Dolgo,' introduced by N. E. Hansen in South Dakota in 1917, is outstanding for its cold-hardiness (at least to Zone 3a) and the quality of its fruits for jelly-making. It is a large tree, to 12 m/40 ft tall and 9 m/30 ft wide, with masses of white flowers, pale pink in bud, and large yellow, deeply red-blushed fruits, 3 cm/1.2 in. across, falling by late summer. Disease-resistance: SC-B, FB-B, CR-A, ML-A.

'Donald Wyman,' introduced by the Arnold Arboretum in the early 1970s, is upright to rounded in habit, to 6 m/20 ft tall and 8–9 m/26–30 ft wide in time, with masses of white flowers, pink in bud, excellent dark green foliage that turns golden in autumn in some years, and 1-cm/0.4-in., bright red fruits, persisting well into midwinter, sometimes until spring. There have been isolated reports of infection by scab and fire blight, but others have found this cultivar highly disease-resistant (check local experience).

'Dorothea,' named by Donald Wyman for his daughter and introduced by the Arnold Arboretum in the late 1940s, is irregular to upright and spreading in habit, with semidouble rose-pink flowers, 5 cm/2 in. across, and bright yellow fruit, 1.5 cm/0.6 in. across. It is less available than a decade or two ago, probably because of its irregular growth habit when young, its susceptibility fire blight, or both.

'Doubloons' (Plant Patent No. 7215, 1990) a Fr. John Fiala introduction, is densely and broadly upright, to 5.5 m/18 ft high and 5 m/16 ft wide, with double white flowers and at least fairly persistent yellow fruits, about 1 cm/0.4 in. across. Reported to be disease-resistant.

'Excazam' (Excalibur™), another of the Round Table Series™, is a densely upright tree to 3 m/10 ft tall and 2.5 m/8 ft wide with white flowers, deeply lobed foliage, pale gold fruits, 6 cm/2.5 in. across, persisting through autumn. Reported to be disease-resistant.

'Flame,' a 1934 University of Minnesota introduction, is broadly oval in habit, to 8 m/26 ft high and 6 m/20 ft wide, with white flowers, pink in bud, and 19-cm/0.75-in. bright red fruits, persistent through most of autumn. Disease-resistant except for apple scab. Cold-hardy to at least Zone 3b, perhaps also Zone 3a.

'Fozam' (Foxfire™) is a recent selection with broad-spreading habit, growing to 5 m/16 ft tall and wide, with pure white flowers, dark green foliage, and unusual gold-tipped red fruits. It is described as "disease-tolerant."

'Golden Hornet,' introduced in 1948 by John Waterer & Sons Nursery (England) and thought to be a M. × zumi selection, is a large, upright tree with white flowers and outstanding golden yellow fruit, 2.8 cm/1.1 in. across, effective through autumn, at least. It was reported to be disease-free in England, but did not become as popular in North America because it proved to be highly susceptible to fire blight in many parts of our area. Presumably it is still useful in areas where fire blight is not a serious problem, such as the coastal Pacific Northwest.

'Guinzam' (Guinevere®, Plant Patent No. 7773, 1992), another of the Round Table Series™, has a rounded habit, growing to 3 m/10 ft high and wide, with mixed mauve and white flowers, very dark green foliage with a wine-red overlay, and 1-cm0.4-in. bright red fruits, persistent through autumn. It is described as "disease-resistant."

'Hamzam' (Hamlet®) is another of the Round Table Series™, growing to 3 m/10 ft high and wide, with fragrant, rosy-pink flowers, deep red in bud, green foliage with a wine-red overlay, and deep red fruit, persisting into autumn. Described as "disease-resistant."

'Hargozam' (Harvest Gold®) is upright in habit, 6 m/20 ft tall and 5 m/16 ft wide, with white flowers, pink in bud, dark green foliage and 1-cm/0.4-in. golden yellow fruits. It was thought to be disease-resistant but is showing susceptibility to scab in some area. On balance, it is probably the most reliably showy yellow fruited crabapple. It is of interest as a small street tree because of its upright habit and small fruits and is reported to be salt-tolerant.

'Henry Kohankie' has a rounded habit, to 6 m/20 ft high and wide, with white flowers, pink in bud, and large (2.5 cm/1 in.), glossy red fruits that persist all winter. Disease-resistance: SC-B, FB-B, CR-A, ML-A. This cultivar is not widely used but is one of the best for large, persistent fruits.

'Hopa,' meaning "beautiful" in the Sioux language, was introduced in 1920 as the first of the Rosyblooms (see M. × adstringens, under M. baccata, Hybrids) by the Canada Department of Agriculture. It was very popular early and has retained much of that popularity in the face of far superior newer introductions. Like other Rosybloom cultivars, it is very cold-hardy, at least to Zone 3b, but its purplish-pink flowers quickly fade to a pale, almost grayish mauve, its dull purplish red fruits are not persistent, and it is very susceptible to scab. This cultivar should be discarded as a contemporary landscape tree, in favor of newer, more disease-resistant cultivars.

'Indian Magic,' introduced by Simpson Nursery, is a upright and spreading in habit, to 5 m/16 ft in height and width, with deep purplish rose flowers and 1.2-cm/0.5-in. fruits, red at first ripening, gradually turning translucent golden-orange, and then the color of apple cider, persisting through autumn. Its deep green foliage turns golden orange in autumn in some years. Disease-resistance: SC-C, FB-B, CR-B, ML-A.

'Indian Summer,' also introduced by Simpson Nursery, is rounded in habit, growing to 5–6 m/16–20 ft in height, and slightly wider, with rosy-red flowers and bright red 1.6-cm/0.63-in. fruits, persisting well into winter, sometimes until spring. Disease-resistance: SC-B, FB-A, CR-A, ML-A. Lightly bronzed green foliage turns golden bronze in autumn in some years.

'Inglis' (White Angel®), introduced by Inglis Nursery in 1962 and reintroduced by Dugan Nursery (Ohio), is broadly globe-shaped, 6 m/20 ft high and wide, with large white flowers, glossy dark green foliage, and orange-red fruits, 1.2 cm/0.5 in. across, persisting through autumn. Disease-resistance: SC-B, FB-C, CR-C, ML-A.

'Jewelberry', another Simpson Nursery introduction, is a small, shrubby tree, reminiscent of M. sargentii except for its pink-edged white flowers, more reliably produced, and persistent bright red 1.2-cm/0.5-in. fruits, lasting until late autumn. It is as disease-resistant as M. sargentii: SC-A, FB-A, CR-A, ML-A.

'Jewelcole' (Red Jewel™), a Cole Nurseries introduction in 1972, is an upright, pyramidal tree to 5 m/16 ft tall and 3.5 m/12 ft wide, with white flowers and handsome cherry red fruits, to 1.2 cm/0.5 in., persisting until middle or late winter. Disease-resistance: SC-B, FB-C, CR-A, ML-B.

'Katherine,' a hybrid of *M. halliana* × *M. baccata* originating in the Rochester Parks System and introduced by the Arnold Arboretum in 1943, is open and vase-shaped in habit, 3–4 m/ 10–13 ft tall with double (15–24 petals) pink flowers, quickly fading to white and at least 5 cm/ 2 in. across, reminiscent of the large flowering oriental cherries. Unfortunately, this crabapple flowers well only every other year, is susceptible to scab, and has red-blushed yellow fruits that are not really conspicuous. Yet it has survived in commerce, apparently solely for its remarkable biennial show of flowers.

'Kelsey' has been applied to two different crabapples. The 'Kelsey' sold today is a Rosybloom crabapple (see *M.* ×*adstringens*, under *M. baccata*, Hybrids), introduced by the Canada Department of Agriculture Research Station at Morden, Manitoba, in honor of the Manitoba Centennial, of 1969. It is upright and rounded in habit, to 5–6 m/16–20 ft high and slightly broader, with semidouble, purplish-red flowers and deep red fruits, persisting well into winter. It is cold-hardy at least to Zone 3b, probably also Zone 3a, but susceptible to scab. The other 'Kelsey' was an open pollinated seedling of *M. floribunda*, introduced in 1934 by Kelsey-Highlands Nursery, Boxford, Massachusetts, under the name 'Snowbank,' and later changed to 'Kelsey' to honor H. P. Kelsey, an early explorer of northern Manitoba, the same person for whom the Canadian 'Kelsey' was named (information from John den Boer, in *Malus*, Vol. 6, No. 1, Summer 1992). The Massachusetts 'Kelsey' is also very ornamental in flower, with horizontal branches forming a white mound. It probably is no longer in commerce, but may be found in arboretums.

'Kibele,' originated in Springfield, Illinois before 1949, is a small tree (2.5 m/8 ft tall and wide), with rose-pink flowers, dark red in bud, lustrous purplish-red foliage, and deep purplish-red 1.2-cm/0.5-in. fruits. One of the most disease-resistant crabapples: SC-B, FB-B, CR-A, ML-A.

'Kinarzam' (King Arthur™) is the largest of the Round Table Series™, growing to nearly 4 m/13 ft high and 3 m/10 ft wide, with white flowers, pink in bud, and bright red 1.2-cm/

0.5-in. fruits, effective in autumn. Described as disease-resistant.

'Klehm' (= 'Klehm's Improved Bechtel') is usually attributed to *M. ioensis*, partly because the original Bechtel crabapple was a *M. ioensis* selection, but now is believed by several specialists to be a seedling of *M. coronaria*. Anyway, it is one of the most satisfactory American crabapple cultivars, with large, double, clear light pink flowers, but, like all the rest, is susceptible to cedar-apple rust, so it probably should not be planted in the same area as eastern red-cedar (*Juniperus virginiana*). (See also *Malus ioensis*: Problems and Maintenance.)

'Lanzam' (Lancelot™, Plant Patent No. 8056, 1992), another of the Round Table Series™, grows to 3 m/10 ft tall and 2.5 m/8 ft wide, with white flowers, red in bud, crisp green summer foliage, reported to turn gold in autumn, and 1-cm/0.4-in. golden yellow fruits, reported to persist into midwinter.

'Lemoinei,' a *Malus* ×*purpurea* selection, has been around since its introduction in 1928, and for much of that time was considered one of the best rose-red flowering crabs, but it has shown susceptibility to scab and may be replaced by newer cultivars that are similar in size, growth habit, and seasonal effects.

'Liset,' a hybrid of *Malus* ×*purpurea* 'Lemoinei' × *M. sieboldii* introduced from the Netherlands in 1952, is upright and spreading in habit and grows to only about 5 m/16 ft high and wide, with large rose flowers, red-purple foliage early, turning bronze-green by late summer, and deep red fruits, 1.2 cm/0.5 in. across, and not particularly effective in the landscape. Disease-resistance: SC-B, FB-B, CR-A, ML-C.

'Louisa,' a Polly Hill introduction, has an excellent strongly weeping habit, growing to only 5 m/16 ft tall and wide, with pure pink flowers, excellent dark green foliage, and 1-cm/ 0.4-in. yellow fruits. Disease-resistance: SC-A, FB-B, CR-B, ML-B.

'Makamik' is perhaps the best of the original Rosybloom crabapples (see *M.* ×*adstringens*, under *M. baccata*, Hybrids) and one of the showiest of all flowering crabapples in bloom, with flowers every year and eventually growing to 8 m/26 ft in height and even greater width. It is highly resistant to scab and has no other serious disease problems. Its relatively large (2 cm/0.8 in.) purplish-red fruits persist through autumn, sometimes later.

'Manbeck Weeper' (Ann E™) is a weeping crabapple, similar to 'Red Jade,' to at least 3 m/ 10 ft in height and width, with large numbers of white flowers, pink in bud, followed by glossy dark green foliage and bright red, persistent 1-cm/0.4-in. fruits. It is reported resistant to scab and fire blight.

'Mary Potter,' originated by Karl Sax at the Arnold Arboretum and introduced in 1947, is a hybrid of *Malus sargentii* 'Rosea' by *M.* ×*atrosanguinea*. It tends to breed true from open-pollinated seed by apomixis (development of an embryo without fertilization) which also occurs in the parent, *M. sargentii*. This cultivar looks like a larger edition of *M. sargentii* 'Rosea,' growing to 3–4 m/10–13 ft high and 5–6 m/16–20 ft in width, with picturesque, crooked horizontal branching and white flowers, rosy pink in bud. In a few locations it has been reported to flower well only biennially, but in many sites it flowers and fruits well almost every year. Disease-resistance: SC-B, FB-C, CR-A, ML-C.

'Mazam' (Madonna®), Plant Patent No. 6672, 1989) is a Fr. John Fiala origination, introduced by Lake County Nursery, with compact, upright habit, to 6 m/20 ft tall and 4–5 m/ 13–16 ft wide, with very large and fragrant, double white flowers that remain effective for some three weeks, bronze-green to dark green foliage, and red-blushed golden fruits that are effective past mid-autumn. This crabapple is finding use as a small street tree. It was originally reported to be disease-resistant, but apple scab has infected it in some areas.

'Molozam' (Molten Lava™) is a promising weeping crabapple originated by Fr. Fiala (see Christmas Holly™) and recently introduced by Lake County Nursery, growing to 5 m/16 ft high and nearly as wide, with white flowers, red in bud, followed by cascades of 1-cm/0.4-in. red fruits on the pendulous branches, throughout autumn. It is reported to be resistant to scab and, if that observation holds, it may be a good replacement for 'Red Jade,' which is susceptible.

'Morton' (Morning Sun™), recently released by the Morton Arboretum, originated as a yellow fruiting seedling from open-pollinated *M.* × *zumi* 'Calocarpa.' It has been observed closely

there for over 50 years and has a spreading habit, to 7.5 m/25 ft tall and 10.5 m/35 ft wide at maturity, with fragrant white flowers, bright green, disease-resistant foliage, and 1.2-cm/0.5-in. yellow fruits that turn a "pleasant rusty" color in midautumn and then persist all winter.

'Naragansett' is a recent introduction from the U.S. National Arboretum (see 'Adirondack'), with upright, spreading habit, growing to 4 m/13 ft tall and 3 m/10 ft wide in 12 years, and may grow considerably larger than that in time. It blooms annually, with pink-tinged white flowers, followed by bright orange-red fruits, which persist through autumn. Disease-resistance remains to be fully evaluated.

'Oekonomierat Echtermeyer' (= 'Echtermeyer,' = 'Pink Weeper'), introduced in 1914 by Ludwig Spaeth Nurseries in Germany, was the only red-purple flowering weeping cultivar for many years, with old trees growing to heights of 5 m/16 ft tall and somewhat greater width. It has now been largely superseded by newer weeping cultivars, in part because it is very susceptible to scab.

'Ormiston Roy,' introduced in 1954, was named by Arie F. den Boer (see 'Beverly') for W. Ormiston Roy, a Canadian landscape architect and horticulturist who had admired the tree. It is *not* 'Roy Ormiston,' as it has occasionally been called (nor Roy Orbison!). This tree is upright and spreading, eventually broad-rounded, to 7–8 m/23–26 ft tall and wide, with white flowers, rose-red in bud, borne annually and followed by 1.2-cm/0.5-in. fruits, yellow at first ripening, turning orange-yellow with a reddish blush that covers the fruits after first frost and keeps them colorful all winter. Disease-resistance: SC-A, FB-B, CR-A, ML-A.

'Parrsi' (Pink Princess™) is a recently introduced selection from *M. sargentii*, reportedly with all the good features of that species along with rose-pink flowers and purple to bronze foliage. Reported to be disease-resistant.

'Pink Beauty,' an open-pollinated seedling from a Rosybloom crabapple (see 'Baskatong'), selected at the Morden, Manitoba, Research Station and named and introduced by Simpson Nursery prior to 1958, is upright and spreading, at least 5 m/16 ft high and wide, with light pink flowers, deeper rosy pink in bud, flowering well only in alternate years, and moderately suscepti-ble to scab. It is very showy in full bloom, but seldom available.

'Pink Satin' is a recent Simpson introduction with upright, rounded habit, single clear pink flowers, green foliage, and dark red 1-cm/0.4-in., persistent fruits. Reported to be disease-resistant and, according to C. E. Hubbuch of Bernheim Forest Arboretum, not as attractive to Japanese beetles as many crabapples.

'Pink Spires,' a recent Rosybloom-type intro-duction from Saskatchewan, is narrowly oval, broadening with age, 5–6 m/16–20 ft tall and 4–5 m/13–16 ft wide, with rose-pink flowers, red-purple to bronze foliage, and deep red, 1.2-cm/0.5-in. fruits, not particularly effective. Dis-ease-resistance: SC-C, FB-C, CR-A, ML-B. Cold-hardy at least to Zone 3a.

'Prairifire' (= 'Prairie Fire'), a fairly recent introduction from the University of Illinois, is upright and rounded in habit, to 6 m/20 ft high and wide, with the most nearly true-red flowers of any crabapple, deep red-purple to reddish green foliage, and 1-cm/0.4-in. maroon fruits, persistent through autumn. It is resistant to apple scab and reportedly to the other crabapple dis-eases as well.

'Professor Sprenger,' an open-pollinated seed-ling of *M. sieboldii* found in the experimental gardens at Wageningen, Holland about 1950 and named for the director of those gardens, is a pyramidal to globose tree to 8 m/26 ft high and nearly as wide, with white flowers, persistent, 1.2-cm/0.5-in. red-orange fruits and excellent disease-resistance.

'Profusion,' a hybrid of similar parentage as 'Lemoinei' and 'Liset,' is upright and spreading, to 6 m/20 ft high and wide, with rose-red flowers, fading to rose-pink, purplish foliage turning bronze-green, and 1.2-cm/0.5-in. maroon fruits, persisting for a time. Disease-resistance: SC-C, FB-B, CR-A, ML-A.

'Radiant,' originating as an open-pollinated seedling of 'Hopa' at the University of Minne-sota, has deep rose-pink flowers, red in bud, foliage red-purple as it opens, quickly turning deep green, and bright red, 1.2-cm/0.5-in. fruit, persisting into winter. Disease-resistance: SC-D, FB-A, CR-A, ML-C.

'Ralph Shay,' selected by Prof. Ralph Shay at Purdue University and introduced by Robert C. Simpson of Simpson Nursery, is upright and rounded in habit, to about 6 m/20 ft high and wide, with masses of white flowers followed by large (3 cm/1.2 in.), brilliant red fruits that persist through winter and into spring, reducing the usual litter problem associated with large fruits. Very disease-resistant, and the fruits make excellent jellies.

'Red Barron' (sometimes misspelled 'Red Baron'), a selection from the Arnold Arboretum introduced by Simpson Nursery, is narrowly up-right to vase-shaped and compact, to 5–6 m/16–20 ft tall and 2.5–3 m/8–10 ft wide, with dark red flowers, purple foliage, fading to bronze-green, often turning golden-bronze in autumn, and persistent, glossy dark red fruits, 1.2 cm/0.5 in. across. Disease-resistance: SC-C, FB-B, CR-B, ML-A.

'Red Jade,' an open-pollinated seedling from the old weeping crabapple 'Exzellenz Thiel,' was introduced by the Brooklyn Botanic Garden in 1953 and has been the standard for weeping crabapples for many years. It has strongly weep-ing habit, to 3 m/10 ft high and wide, small white flowers followed by glossy red fruits, 1.2 cm/0.5 in. across and very effective against the jade green foliage in late summer and early au-tumn, and golden-olive, pendulous branches adding winter interest. Its disease-resistance (SC-C, FB-C, CR-A, ML-C) raises questions about its future, given the number of other good weeping crabapples now available, but thus far it remains very popular.

'Red Silver,' a Rosybloom-type crabapple (see 'Baskatong'), introduced in 1928 in South Da-kota, was a parent of 'Red Splendor' (see below) and is occasionally used in the landscape today because of its red-purple foliage, but it is very susceptible to scab and also susceptible to fire blight and cedar-apple rust and is much inferior to 'Royalty' (see below) in foliage color.

'Red Splendor,' a Rosybloom-type crabapple (see 'Baskatong'), introduced by Bergeson Nurs-eries in Minnesota in 1948, is upright and spreading in habit, to 6 m/20 ft high and wide, with rose-pink flowers, red in bud, glossy red-dish-green foliage, and bright red fruits, 1.5 cm/0.6 in across, persisting over winter, so it is never a litter problem. Disease-resistance:

SC-C, FB-C, CR-B, ML-B. Cold-hardy to at least Zone 3b.

'Robinson,' a C. M. Hobbs & Sons (Indianapolis) introduction, is very fast growing, with upright and then spreading habit, deep pink flowers, reddish-purple foliage, turning green, then yellow-orange in autumn in some years, and glossy, deep red fruits, 1 cm/0.4. in. across, persisting through autumn. Disease-resistance: SC-B, FB-A, CR-A, ML-A.

'Royal Ruby,' originated at Simpson Nursery and introduced by Cole Nurseries in the early 1970s, is fast-growing and upright in habit, to 6 m/20 ft tall and 5 m/16 ft wide, with very large (5 cm/2 in.), cupped, double red flowers and very few fruits. Unfortunately, it has proved highly susceptible to scab, and thus it is not widely used.

'Royscezam' (Royal Scepter™), a seedling from 'Mazam' (Madonna®) recently introduced by Lake County Nursery, is narrowly upright in habit, to 5.5 m/18 ft tall and 3 m/10 ft wide, with fragrant, double white and mauve flowers, red in bud, wine-red summer foliage, and orange-red fruits in autumn. Described as "disease-resistant."

'Royalty,' a Rosybloom crabapple introduced in Saskatchewan in 1962, is upright and spreading in habit, 5–6 m/16–20 ft high and wide, with by far the deepest and longest-lasting dark red-purple foliage of any widely available crabapple (but also see 'Thunderchild', below), and flowers and fruits that are of only incidental interest by comparison. Disease-resistance (SC-D, FB-C, CR-A, ML-A) makes this a questionable choice where scab and fire blight are prevalent. Cold-hardy to Zone 3a.

M. transitoria 'Schmidtcutleaf' (Golden Raindrops™), a recent release from Frank Schmidt & Son Nursery (Boring, Oregon), is upright and vase-shaped in habit, growing to 5.5 m/18 ft tall and 4 m/13 ft wide, white flowers, finely textured, cutleaved green foliage, 0.6-cm/0.25-in. yellow fruits, and golden tan bark, at least on young branches. Disease-resistance reported as SC-A, FB-B, CR-A, ML-A.

'Seafoam,' a semipendulous seedling of 'Oekonomierat Echtermeyer,' selected by A. F. den Boer (see 'Evelyn') and introduced by him in 1952, has pink-flushed white flowers, rosy-pink in bud, deeply lobed green leaves, and 1.3-cm/

0.5-in. yellow fruits, persistent through autumn. It is reported to be disease resistant but, unaccountably, has nearly disappeared from commerce.

'Selkirk,' one of the best of the Rosyblooms and a preferred substitute for 'Hopa,' introduced in Canada in 1962, is upright and spreading, rounded at maturity, growing to 6 m/20 ft high and slightly broader. It has purplish rose-pink flowers, dark green foliage, purple-tinted when it first emerges, and glossy, bright red fruits, 2 cm/0.8 in. across, persisting only to mid-autumn. Disease-resistance: SC-B, FB-B, CR-A, ML-C. Cold-hardy to Zone 3a.

'Sentinel,' another Simpson introduction, is narrowly upright to vase-shaped, to 6 m/20 ft tall and 4 m/13 ft wide, with pink-tinted white flowers, glossy dark green foliage, and bright red fruits, 1.2 cm/0.5 in. across, persisting through late autumn. Disease-resistance: SC-B, FB-B, CR-A, ML-A.

'Sirgazam' (Sir Galahad®), another of the Round Table Series™, is rounded in shape, to 3 m/10 ft tall and 2.5 m/8 ft wide, with white flowers, pink in bud, lustrous and leathery green foliage, and 1.2 cm/0.5 in., golden yellow fruits, gradually turning to red by early winter. It is described as "disease-tolerant."

'Silver Drift' is of unknown origin, resembling 'Snowdrift' except that its small red fruits persist and hold their color until the end of autumn. Described as having disease-resistant foliage.

'Silver Moon,' a distinctive Simpson introduction, is narrowly upright in habit, to 6 m/20 ft tall and 4 m/13 ft wide, late-flowering, with pink-tinted white flowers in quantity, some persisting after tree is in leaf, glossy dark green foliage, and persistent bright red fruits, 1.2 cm/0.5 in. across. Disease-resistance: SC-B, FB-B, CR-A, ML-A.

'Sinai Fire' (Plant Patent No. 7492, 1991) is a weeping crabapple, to 5 m/16 ft in height and width, with large white flowers, excellent glossy, bright green foliage, and bright red fruits, 1–1.2 cm/0.4–0.5 in across. Disease-resistance: SC-A, FB-C, CR-A, ML-C.

'Snow Magic' (Plant Patent No. 4815, 1982), introduced by Willoway Nursery (Avon, Ohio), is fast-growing, with a compact pyramidal habit and excellent branching, to 6 m/20 ft tall and wide, with masses of white flowers, pink in bud, and wine-red fruits, 0.8 cm/0.3 in across. Described as pest- and scab-resistant.

'Snowcloud,' introduced in 1969 by Princeton Nursery and a hybrid of 'Katherine' and 'Almey,' is narrowly upright, to 7 m/23 ft tall and 5 m/16 ft wide, with large, double white flowers, pink in bud, dark green foliage, and little fruiting interest. Reports on disease-resistance vary.

'Snowdrift,' introduced by Cole Nursery in 1965, is upright and spreading in habit, eventually broadly ovate and rounded, with white flowers, pink in bud, glossy green foliage, and glossy orange-red fruits, 1 cm/0.4 in. across and persistent until midautumn. Disease-resistance: SC-B, FB-D, CR-A, ML-A. This is a very popular crabapple, but probably not a good choice where fire blight is a serious problem.

'Sparkler,' introduced by the University of Minnesota in 1969, is horizontally spreading in habit, to 5 m/16 ft high and at least 6 m/20 ft wide, with bright rose-pink flowers, foliage reddish at first, turning dark green, and dark red 1-cm/0.4-in. fruits, persisting through early winter. Described as disease-resistant, but probably slightly susceptible to scab. Cold-hardy to Zone 4a, probably also Zone 3b.

'Spring Snow,' an open-pollinated seedling of 'Dolgo,' selected in Saskatchewan and introduced by Interstate Nurseries in 1966, is narrowly upright in habit, to 8 m/26 ft tall and 5–6 m/16–20 ft wide, with masses of flowers annually, but no fruits. Disease-resistance: SC-C, FB-C, CR-B, ML-A. Cold-hardy to Zone 3a. Useful in cold climates, where scab and fire blight are not prevalent and where freedom from fruit litter is important.

'Strawberry Parfait' (Plant Patent No. 4632, 1981), a hybrid of *M. hupehensis* by *M. ×atrosanguinea*, is broadly irregular to vase-shaped, similar to *M. hupehensis*, to 5–6 m/16–20 ft high and 7–8 m/23–26 ft wide, with large, fragrant light pink flowers with deeper pink margin, foliage red-purple at first, turning deep green in summer, and 1-cm/0.4-in. red-blushed yellow fruits in late summer. It remains to be seen whether this hybrid will prove susceptible to fire blight, like its *M. hupehensis* parent, but otherwise it is disease-resistant.

'Sutyzam' (Sugartyme®, Plant Patent No. 7062, 1989), selected by Prof. Milton Baron of Michigan State University and released by Lake County Nursery, is upright and oval in habit, to 5–6 m/16–20 ft tall and 5 m/16 ft wide, with masses of white flowers, pale pink in bud, green foliage, and rich red 1.2-cm/0.5-in. fruits that persist over winter. Disease-resistance: SC-B, FB-C, CR-A, ML-A.

'Sweet Perfume' is a recent introduction by Lake County Nursery, narrowly upright and rounded in habit, to at least 5.5 m/18 ft tall and 4 m/13 ft wide, with pure white flowers, pink in bud and reported to be the most fragrant of those of any crabapple grown by that nursery. Summer foliage is dark green and its golden yellow fruits are effective in autumn.

'Thunderchild,' a Rosybloom crabapple introduced by the Saskatchewan plantsman, Percy Wright, in 1978, has an upright, spreading habit, 5–6 m/16–20 ft high and wide. It is similar to 'Royalty' except that its foliage emerges green, soon turning deep red-purple, as dark as that of 'Royalty' but not as glossy. The pink flowers of 'Thunderchild' open before the green foliage unfolds, and thus are more effective than the deeper red-purple flowers of 'Royalty,' which are soon obscured by the dark foliage. 'Thunderchild' has been reported to be somewhat more resistant to fire blight than 'Royalty,' but longer and wider observation is necessary before there is any consensus on this. Cold-hardy to Zone 3a.

'Tina' is a selection from *M. sargentii* with growth habit much like the species except smaller, eventually to 2–2.5 m/6.6–8 ft in height and 2.5–3 m/8–10 ft width, and seasonal interest similar to that of *M. sargentii* 'Rosea.' It is resistant to the four principal diseases of crabapples.

'Van Eseltine,' introduced by the New York Agricultural Experiment Station at Geneva in 1938, has a narrowly vase-shaped habit, to 5–6 m/16–20 ft tall and 2–2.5 m/6.6–8 ft wide, with spectacular, 5-cm/2-in. double pink flowers followed by red-blushed yellow fruits, 1.8 cm/0.7 in. across. Disease-resistance: SC-B, FB-D, CR-B, ML-A. This tree is spectacular in flower, but best used where fire blight is not a serious problem, and then only for formal accent, because of its shape.

'Velvetcole' (Velvet Pillar™, Plant Patent No. 4758, 1981) is narrowly upright and pyramidal in habit, to 6 m/20 ft tall and 4 m/13 ft wide, with pink flowers, dull purple foliage, and 1.2 cm/0.5-in. red fruits, but flowers and fruits are sparse. Disease-resistance: SC-C, FB-C, CR-A, NL-B.

'Weepcanzam' (Weeping Candied Apple®), introduced by Lake County Nursery in 1977, is broadly horizontal to semiweeping in habit, 3–5 m/10–16 ft tall and 5 m/16 ft wide, with masses of pink flowers, red-overcast dark green foliage, 1-cm/0.4-in. cherry-red fruits, which persist through autumn and into winter. Disease-resistance: SC-C, FB-A, CR-A, ML-A.

'White Candle,' a Simpson origination introduced by Inter-State Nurseries (Iowa), is narrowly upright and columnar in habit, 5–6 m/16–20 ft tall and 2.5 m/8 ft wide, with masses of large, semidouble, pink and white flowers, and bears few fruits. Reported to be susceptible to scab and perhaps also fire blight, in areas where these diseases are severe.

'Winter Gold' is an import, first introduced in Holland in the 1940s, with rounded to vase-shaped habit (according to different reports), white flowers, red in bud, and persistent yellow fruits, 1.2 cm/0.5 in. across. Observations on disease-resistance have varied as widely as descriptions of form, suggesting that more than one clone may have been imported. This crabapple has apparently nearly disappeared from commerce in North America.

'Zumarang' was selected as an open-pollinated seedling of M. × zumi 'Calocarpa' at Willoway Nurseries (Ohio) in 1978, and more recently introduced. This tree is not yet well known, but is reported to have a pyramidal habit, white flowers, wine-red fruits, and cherrylike bark. Disease-resistance in our area is yet to be assessed.

Menispermum canadense 1 and 2

COMMON MOONSEED

Deciduous vine

Menispermaceae (Moonseed Family)

Native Range. Eastern North America: Quebec to Manitoba and south to Georgia and Arkansas.

Useful Range. USDA Zones 5a–9a+.

Function. Groundcover, screen (with support). Climbs by twining to heights of 3–4 m/10–13 ft, in Zones 5–8, kills back almost to the ground each winter, returning rapidly the following spring and summer.

Size and Habit

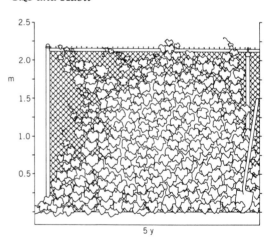

Menispermum canadense.

Adaptability

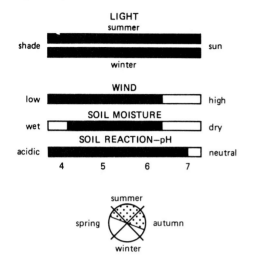

Seasonal Interest. *Foliage:* Lustrous, dark green, distinctively round-lobed, 10–20 cm/4–8 in. long, making a handsomely textured, dense mass, remaining green until the tops are killed back by hard freezes. *Fruits:* Blue-black, 0.8 cm/0.3 in. across, in clusters resembling grapes on pistillate (female) plants, adding both landscape interest and potential hazard, since they are toxic and may be taken for grapes by children.

Menispermum canadense.

Problems and Maintenance. This trouble-free vine requires no maintenance except to remove winterkilled tops and to prune back the vine when it threatens to become overly aggressive, which it commonly does. This is not a plant to be used in intensive situations.

Related Species

Cocculus carolinus 1 (Carolina moonseed). This native of the southeastern United States, also in the Menispermaceae (Moonseed Family), resembles *Menispermum canadense* generally but has smaller, rounded leaves, 5–8 cm/2–3 in. long, and red fruits (on pistillate plants), 0.8 cm/0.3 in. across, in showy clusters in late summer and autumn. Carolina moonseed climbs by twining to about the same height as common moonseed and is useful as a partial screen, with support, in Zones 7a–9a+. Like *Menispermum canadense*, it can become a weed in some areas.

Metasequoia glyptostroboides 8

DAWN REDWOOD
Deciduous tree
Taxodiaceae (Taxodium Family)

Native Range.   Western China.

Useful Range.   USDA Zones 5b–9a.

Function.   Specimen, screen (summer).

Size and Habit

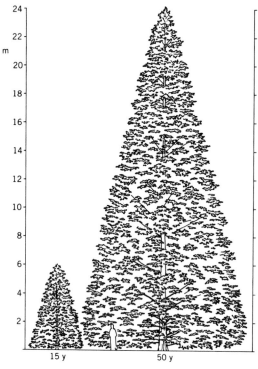

Metasequoia glyptostroboides.

Adaptability.   *Metasequoia* is notable for its ability to grow close to the edges of ponds or streams, but it will also grow well in soil of average moisture content.

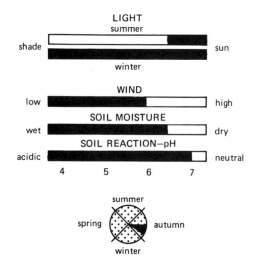

Seasonal Interest.   *Foliage:* Deciduous, needle-like, giving fine, feathery texture; lacy and light green in spring, medium green in summer, and turning delicate shades of pinkish tan to brown before falling in late autumn. *Metasequoia* can easily be distinguished from *Taxodium distichum* (common bald cypress) by the opposite arrangement of lateral branchlets and large winter buds; in *Taxodium* the arrangement is mostly alternate and the winter buds are small and inconspicuous. *Trunk and branches:* Lower branches are borne horizontally on the strong, straight, tapered, and eventually buttressed central trunk with interestingly fissured and shredded bark.

Metasequoia glyptostroboides.

Special note. One of the most interesting features of *Metasequoia glyptostroboides* is its story. Known only in the fossil record as a presumably extinct tree of North America and Asia before 1941, it was found in the wild in that year in Szechwan province, China. Seeds were received by the Arnold Arboretum of Harvard University in 1948 and quickly disseminated to other arboreta around the world. As a result, it quickly became cultivated as a landscape tree and is now readily available in most areas. In landscape function it differs little from *Taxodium distichum* (common bald cypress) except that it is slightly less cold-hardy than *Taxodium* of northern origin.

Problems and Maintenance. This tree grows well in soils that are wet to moderately moist; it should not be used in distinctly dry sites, since the foliage will be damaged by drought stress and mite infestations. Avoid planting in frost pockets, since this tree often makes late growth and is prone to early autumn freezes.

Cultivars. 'National,' a selection made at the U.S. National Arboretum, is narrow in form, growing rapidly in height. 'Sheridan Spire,' introduced by Sheridan Nurseries near Toronto, Canada, is at least as narrow as 'National' and more compactly columnar.

Metasequoia glyptostroboides.

Michelia figo 5

Synonyms: *Magnolia fuscata, Michelia fuscata*
BANANA SHRUB
Evergreen shrub
Magnoliaceae (Magnolia Family)

Native Range. China.

Useful Range. USDA Zones 8b–9a+ and protected sites in Zone 8a.

Function. Specimen, massing, screen, border.

Size and Habit

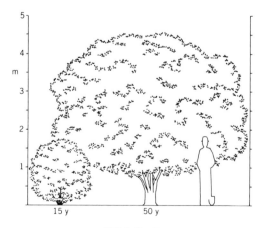

Michelia figo.

Adaptability.   Although this plant will tolerate a considerable amount of wind, for full benefit of the fragrance it is better used in sites where the air is fairly still.

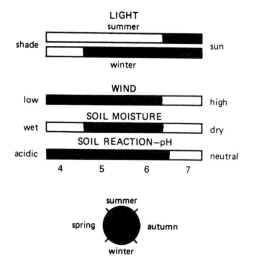

Seasonal Interest.   *Flowers:* Pale yellow with crimson margins and brown outside, from brown velvety winter buds, opening to 3.5 cm/1.4 in. across, with a strong bananalike fragrance. *Foliage:* Evergreen, neatly textured, medium green, with leaves about 4–6 cm/1.6–2.5 in. long on stems covered with a scurf of rusty colored hairs. *Fruits:* Small, brown, magnolialike pods with fleshy orange seeds are seldom seen in cultivation.

Michelia figo.

Problems and Maintenance.   This plant seems to be completely trouble-free. Its slow growth

probably has discouraged its use to some extent, but for many landscape situations this is outweighed by its permanence and freedom from maintenance.

Cultivars.   'Port Wine' has purple-pink, highly fragrant flowers. 'Stubb's Purple' is compact in growth habit, with fragrant purplish flowers.

Related Species

Michelia compressa 6–7.   This small to medium evergreen tree from Japan and Taiwan is upright in habit, eventually broadening, with glossy green leaves 10 cm/4 in. long and half as wide, and small flowers, red-marked creamy pale yellow, almost insignificant from a distance but interesting at close range. Useful in Zones 7b–9+, perhaps also Zone 7a, but not often available.

Michelia doltsopa 6–7.   This striking evergreen tree from western China and the Himalayas is strongly upright in habit, with glossy green leaves, 20–25 cm/8–10 in. long and 8–10 cm/3–4 in. wide, and fragrant and showy, pale yellow to white flowers, to 10 cm/4 in. across, with 12–16 long, narrow tepals. Once thought to be hardy only in Zones 9 and 10, recent experience suggests that this species may be useful in at least Zones 8b–9a+. The selection 'Silver Cloud' has larger, creamy-white flowers with up to 30 tepals. 'Strybing' differs in having shorter, broader tepals than the species.

Michelia × *foggii* 6.   This hybrid between M. *doltsopa* and M. *figo* is intermediate between the parents, with fragrant, creamy white or pink-edged white flowers, 8 cm/3 in. across, and probably cold hardy to Zone 8b, perhaps also Zone 7b. Several selections have been made: 'Allspice' has large flowers, with an allspice fragrance. 'Fogg #2' has red-tipped and edged white flowers, 6.4 cm/2.5 in. across. 'Fogg #3' has highly fragrant white flowers, 9.5 cm/3.7 in. across. 'Fogg #4' has fragrant white, cupped flowers, 9 cm/3.5 in. 'Jack Fogg' has large, purple-pink edged white flowers. All of these are available, but in only a few nurseries.

Morus alba 7

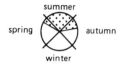

WHITE MULBERRY
Deciduous tree
Moraceae (Mulberry Family)

Native Range. China; widely naturalized in Eurasia and North America.

Useful Range. USDA Zones 5a–9a; some selections in Zone 4 as well.

Function. Small shade tree.

Size and Habit

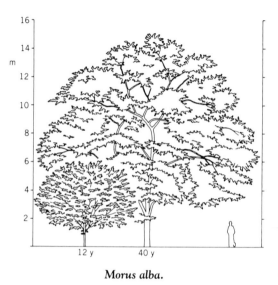

Morus alba.

Seasonal Interest. *Foliage:* Variously lobed, usually more or less lustrous and bright green, falling in early autumn with little color change. *Fruits:* Small, blackberrylike, edible, crimson, pink or white, borne on most trees and constituting a major litter problem, but some trees are dioecious (all flowers on a tree of only one sex), giving rise to nonfruiting selections. *Trunk and branches:* Bark is orange-brown, a slight but sometimes appreciable contribution to winter color.

Morus alba.

Adaptability. Unusually well adapted to the difficult climates of the Great Plains within its useful range.

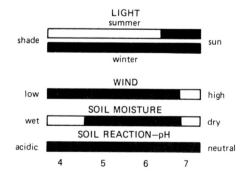

Problems and Maintenance. This tree requires little or no maintenance except for light pruning to maintain form and remove low-hanging branches. Its most serious problem is the fruit litter, which discolors pavement, and the seedlings, generated by bird-carried seeds, which appear in flower beds, alleys, and anywhere else they happen to land. Nonfruiting cultivars (below) are, of course, free of both these problems.

Cultivars. 'Fruitless,' 'Kingan,' and 'Striblingii' (= 'Mapleleaf') are nonfruiting forms, useful in more intensive landscapes than fruiting trees. 'Chaparral' and 'Pendula' are weeping forms to about 2.4–3.6 m/8–12 ft tall and eventually broader. 'Tatarica' (Russian mulberry) was selected for its unusual cold-hardiness (to Zone 4a), making it useful in much of the northern Great Plains of the United States, and for its small fruits.

Related Species

Morus australis 6 (Synonym: *M. bombycis*). This shrubby tree from eastern China, Japan, and Korea grows to about 8 m/26 ft tall and wide. Like *M. alba,* it has edible fruits. Trees of the species from seed sources in northern Japan (Hokkaido) are useful in at least Zones 5b–8b. The contorted selection 'Unryu,' the only form usually seen in our area, has not been used widely enough for its climatic limits to be known. It is cold-hardy in Zone 7b and may well prove useful to Zone 6b, perhaps even 6a. 'Unryu' is distinctive for its corkscrew-shaped twigs and branches, particularly striking in winter, when they are fully visible.

Morus rubra 7–8 (red mulberry). This native North American mulberry is generally similar to *M. alba* except that it has fairly good yellow autumn foliage color. No nonfruiting cultivars have been selected to date. Useful in Zones 4b–9a with selection of appropriate genetic material, but nursery-grown plants are seldom available.

Broussonetia papyrifera 7 (paper mulberry). This native of China and Japan is occasionally naturalized in the central and southeastern United States. Like *Morus* species, it is well adapted to difficult site conditions within its useful range of Zones 6b–9a. Its gray-green, irregularly lobed leaves make a dense canopy, and trunks of old trees are irregular and picturesque with smooth, gray bark. On the negative side, it suckers freely and is soft-wooded and drops considerable twig and fruit (female trees) litter, so it is neither durable nor a low-maintenance tree.

Myrica pensylvanica 4–5

BAYBERRY
Deciduous or semievergreen shrub
Myricaceae (Bayberry Family)

Native Range.   Eastern North America, mostly the Atlantic Coast.

Useful Range.   USDA Zones 4b–9a, with occasional winter damage in Zone 4.

Function.   Border, massing, foundation, screen (in good soil).

Size and Habit

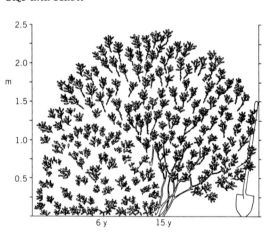

Myrica pensylvanica.

Adaptability. This shrub is unusually tolerant of seaside and roadside salt and infertile soil. All *Myrica* species are capable of fixing and using atmospheric nitrogen, and they do this most effectively in soils low in fertility.

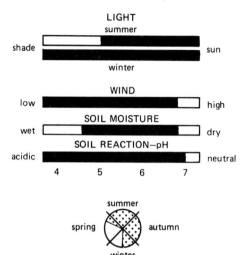

Seasonal Interest. *Foliage:* Clean, bright to dull green as summer progresses, persisting well into early winter. Strongly and pleasantly aromatic when crushed. *Fruits:* Borne only on female plants (dioecious), but male plants are needed nearby for pollination to have significant fruiting interest, a reason for using this plant in mass plantings. The gray, waxy berries, only 0.5 cm/0.2 in. across but borne in great numbers close to the twigs, add significant fall and winter interest before and after leaves drop. Fruits, like the foliage, are aromatic, and the wax covering them can be removed and added to candle wax to make bayberry candles.

Problems and Maintenance. This shrub is unusually trouble-free and requires little or no maintenance. It does not require pruning unless used as a formal hedge, and this is not an appropriate use for this plant, since shearing destroys its character. It is reputedly difficult to transplant, but this is no problem with pot-grown or even field-grown plants if properly handled.

Related Species

Myrica cerifera 6 (synonym: *M. caroliniensis*; wax myrtle).   This tall shrub or small tree is native to eastern North America, northward only to New Jersey, but far southward well into Florida and Texas. It resembles *M. pensylvanica* closely except that it is more fully evergreen and usually considerably taller. Useful in Zones 6b–9a+, it is a serviceable, low-maintenance plant for the South, especially in coastal areas, where its salt-resistance is a great asset. It is somewhat more tolerant of wet soils than *M. pensylvanica.* The var. *pumila* (synonym: *M. pusilla*) is a thicket-forming shrub to 1 m/3.3 ft tall.

Myrica gale 4 (sweet gale).   This fine-textured, thicket-forming shrub is less handsome than *M. cerifera* or *M. pensylvanica,* with small, dull, dark green leaves on upright branches. Native to edges of lakes and streams in the northern parts of both Eurasia and North America, its cold-hardiness and tolerance of wet soils are its most important qualities. It is useful in Zones 1–8a with selection of appropriate genetic material, but is seldom available in nurseries.

Comptonia peregrina 2 (synonyms: *C. asplenifolia, Myrica asplenifolia;* sweet fern).   This low, thicket-forming shrub is native from the northeastern United States and Canada to the Great Lakes area and south on the Atlantic Coast to North Carolina. Its graceful, dissected foliage is pleasantly scented, like that of the closely related *Myrica* species. It is useful primarily on sandy, infertile soils, where, like *Myrica* species, it uses atmospheric nitrogen through bacteria associated with its roots. This plant has grown rapidly in popularity for highway landscaping in the Northeast, but its commercial availability is still limited. Useful in Zones 4a–8a, it is difficult to establish unless pot-grown.

Comptonia peregrina.

Nandina domestica 3–5

NANDINA, HEAVENLY BAMBOO
Evergreen shrub
Berberidaceae (Barberry Family)

Native Range.   China and Japan.

Useful Range.   USDA Zones 7a–9a+ and sheltered sites in Zone 6b.

Function.   Specimen, border. If allowed to reach full height for screening, it becomes leggy and open.

Size and Habit

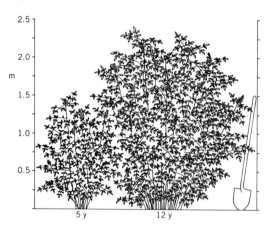

Nandina domestica.

Adaptability

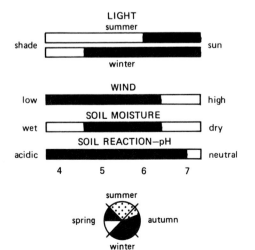

Seasonal Interest.   *Flowers:* Small, white, in loose clusters, 20–30 cm/8–12 in. long, in late spring. *Foliage:* Evergreen, doubly or triply compound with small, sharp-pointed, leathery leaflets, forming an attractive open pattern. New leaves emerge bronze to red in spring, and foliage turns dull red-purple to bright red in autumn in full sun. *Fruits:* Bright red berries, to 0.8 cm/0.3 in., in large clusters add striking landscape color in autumn and throughout winter. *Branches:* Little-branched canes give the superficial appearance of a bamboo (hence the common name), and contribute to the leggy growth habit (see Problems and Maintenance).

Nandina domestica.

Problems and Maintenance.   This shrub has a rank, open growth habit and requires regular pruning (annual removal of older canes) to maintain good form. With pruning, it functions in size group 4 instead of the 5 indicated. Mildew can be a problem with some plants, especially in humid coastal areas.

Cultivars.   'Alba' with white fruits, and little or no red winter foliage color, is distinctive in winter but not widely available.

'Lutea' has whitish yellow fruits and is seldom available.

'Moyers Red' is a full-sized cultivar, to 2 m/6.6 ft tall, with broad leaflets, pinkish flowers early, large red fruits, coloring early, and showy red foliage in winter, even in warm climates.

'Umpqua Chief' grows to 1.5–2 m/5–6.6 ft tall, with bright red fruits and narrow leaflets, red-spotted in autumn and turning bright red in winter.

'Royal Princess is similar in size to 'Umpqua Chief,' but finer-textured, with narrower leaflets that turn bright red in winter.

'Compacta' grows vigorously but stays full, growing only to 1–1.5 m/3.3–5 ft tall, with still narrower leaflets than the above cultivars.

'Umpqua Princess' has still finer textured, delicately fernlike foliage, with a much more open look than 'Compacta,' growing to about 1 m/3.3 ft tall, with little winter coloration.

'San Gabriel' also has finely textured, airy foliage, delicately apricot-colored in spring, turning green in summer, and then bright crimson in autumn. Not yet widely available.

'Nana,' 'Nana Compacta,' and 'Nana Purpurea' are confused in commerce and often used synonymously for at least two clones, one with wide leaflets, purplish in summer and deeper red-purple in winter, and not spreading much, the other with narrower leaflets, green in summer, red in winter, and spreading rapidly. Both grow to about 30 cm/12 in. high.

'Firepower,' 'Harbour Dwarf,' and 'Wood's Dwarf' all are densely compact, growing to approximately 45–60 cm/1.5–2 ft in height and width. 'Firepower' has red-tinged green foliage in summer, turning brilliant red in winter. New growth of 'Harbour Dwarf' is pinkish bronze, turning green in summer, and then bronze-red in winter. 'Wood's Dwarf' has light green summer foliage, turning bright red-orange in winter. These dwarf cultivars may prove only semievergreen in severe winters in Zones 6b and 7a.

Nandina domestica 'Compacta.'

Nerium oleander 6

OLEANDER

Evergreen shrub

Apocynaceae (Dogbane Family)

Native Range.   Mediterranean region to Japan.

Useful Range.   USDA Zone 9a+. A few cultivars can be used in Zone 8 in protected sites, functioning in size group 4 or 5.

Function.   Screen, hedge, border, massing, specimen: permanent or in containers.

Size and Habit

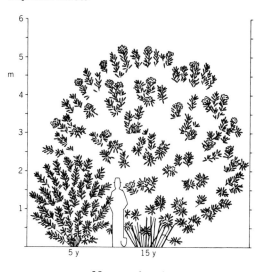

Nerium oleander.

Adaptability. Widely adaptable to strong sun and wind, dry soil, and salt spray in seashore sites.

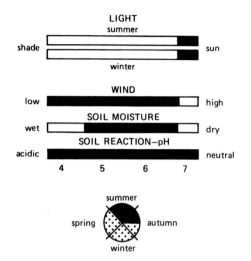

Seasonal Interest. *Flowers:* Fragrant, single or double, 3–5 cm/1–2 in. across, white, pink, red, or yellow, in early summer and continuing to a lesser extent into late summer and autumn. *Foliage:* Evergreen, dark green, long (10–15 cm/4–6 in.) and narrow (2–4 cm/0.8–1.6 in.), smooth. *Fruits:* Elongated green pods to about 15 cm/6 in., not adding significant landscape interest.

Problems and Maintenance. All parts of this plant are poisonous to humans, and even smoke from burning wood can cause serious irritation, so prunings should be disposed of in ways other than burning. Otherwise, this plant is trouble-free. Winter hardiness can be maximized by withholding fertilizer and water in late summer so that growth slows and hardening takes place in autumn. This is especially important in Zone 8.

Cultivars. 'Hardy Pink,' 'Hardy Red,' 'Hardy White,' 'Isle of Capri,' and 'Sister Agnes' are full-sized selections, growing 4–5 m/13–16 ft tall, with single flowers that are bright red, salmon-pink, white, pale yellow, and white, respectively. 'Calypso' is also a full-sized clone, with single, cherry-red flowers, and is reported to be more cold-hardy than 'Hardy Pink' and 'Hardy Red,' possibly to Zone 8a in protected sites. 'Mrs. George Roeding' is also a full-sized clone, with double salmon-pink flowers.

Monrovia Nursery's North African series: 'Monal' (Algiers™), 'Monca' (Casablanca™), and 'Monta' (Tangier™) are intermediate in size, to 2.5–3 m/8–10 ft tall, with single flowers that are deep red, white, and soft pink, respectively. 'Monvis' (Ruby Lace™, Plant Patent No. 5866, 1987) is also intermediate in size, with showy clusters of very large ruby-red flowers having fringed petals.

The Los Angeles State and County Arboretum has introduced two lower-growing cultivars (to 2 m/6.6 ft tall and wide): 'Petite Pink,' with single, pearly shell-pink flowers, and 'Petite Salmon,' with single, bright salmon-pink flowers.

Nyssa sylvatica 8

TUPELO, SOUR GUM, BLACK GUM, PEPPERIDGE
Deciduous tree
Nyssaceae (Tupelo Family)

Native Range. Eastern North America.

Useful Range. USDA Zones 5a–9a+ with selection of appropriate genetic material.

Function. Shade tree, specimen, massing.

Size and Habit

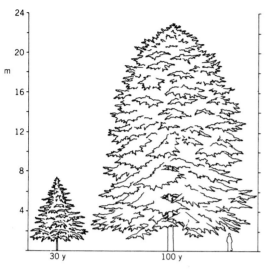

Nyssa sylvatica.

Adaptability. One of the best shade trees for swampy sites, but grows well with average soil moisture as well. Relatively tolerant of seashore conditions except where exposed to strong winds.

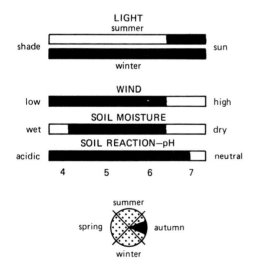

Seasonal Interest. *Foliage:* Glossy, bright to deep green, medium-fine texture, with leaves to 10 cm/4 in. long and half as wide, turning yellow-orange to blazing scarlet in autumn. *Fruits:* Small, blue-black, in clusters or pairs, ripening in autumn but inconspicuous in the landscape. Trees are mostly dioecious. *Twigs and branches:* Silvery gray bark adds winter interest along with the distinctly horizontal branching.

Problems and Maintenance. This tree is generally trouble-free and requires little maintenance but is relatively difficult to transplant, so it should be specified in relatively small sizes, preferably in containers.

Varieties. The var. *biflora* grows wild in the southern part of the range and otherwise differs only in botanical details. The more important distinction that should be made in landscape use is that trees for extreme northern areas should be of northern origin and those for the Deep South should be of southern origin.

Related Species

Nyssa aquatica 8 (water tupelo, cotton gum). This tree is native to the southeastern United States and northward in the Mississippi Basin to southern Illinois and on the Atlantic Coast to Virginia. It can be considered equivalent to *N. sylvatica* for wet soil sites in full sun in the South, but is seldom available except by accident when the two species are confused. Useful in Zones 7a–9a+, possibly also parts of Zone 6.

Nyssa ogeche 7–8 (Ogeechee lime, plum, or tupelo.). This tree, native from southern South Carolina to northern Florida, matures and bears fruit when only 2–3 m (6–10 ft) tall in poor sites, and when 20 m/66 ft tall in the best sites, where it grows at a rate of at least 0.5–0.8 m/16–26 in. yearly. This tree is seldom cultivated and not normally commercially available. It gets its name from its red, edible fruits. 2–4 cm/0.8–1.6 in. across. It grows wild in Zones 8b–9a and is potentially useful there (and perhaps farther north) as a landscape tree for moist sites.

Nyssa sinensis 7 (Chinese tupelo). This upright but eventually wide-spreading tree from central China is similar in general appearance to *N. sylvatica* but has slightly larger leaves and fruits. It is just as spectacular in autumn foliage color as *N. sylvatica*, but not nearly as cold-hardy; it is useful in Zones 7b–9a+, perhaps also Zone 7a.

Orixa japonica 5

JAPANESE ORIXA
Deciduous shrub
Rutaceae (Rue Family)

Native Range. Japan.

Useful Range. USDA Zones 5b–8b, perhaps 5a and 9a as well.

Function. Screen, specimen, border. Occasional winter dieback limits its use as a screen in Zones 5 and 6.

Seasonal Interest. *Foliage:* Glossy, bright green, oval leaves, to 10 cm/4 in. long, are slightly puckered, giving a distinctive texture. They are strongly aromatic when crushed, and they fall with little or no color change in mid-autumn.

Problems and Maintenance. This shrub is relatively trouble-free and requires no maintenance except occasional pruning to remove dead twigs and maintain form. Availability is limited.

Size and Habit

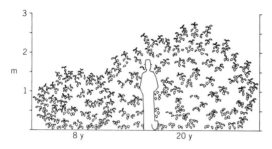

Orixa japonica.

Orixa japonica.

Adaptability

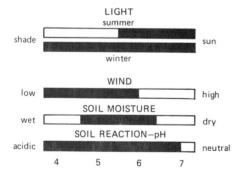

Cultivar. 'Variegata,' with leaves tinted silvery gray, shading to a white margin, was selected by Robert de Belder, Kalmthout, Belgium; it is described in European references, but probably not yet in North America.

Osmanthus fragrans 5–6

SWEET OLIVE, TEA OLIVE
Evergreen shrub or tree
Oleaceae (Olive Family)

Native Range.   Eastern Asia.

Useful Range.   USDA Zones 8b–9a+.

Function.   Border, specimen tree. Functional height varies from about 3 m/10 ft in Zone 8b to 8–10 m/26–33 ft in warmer zones, after some time.

Size and Habit

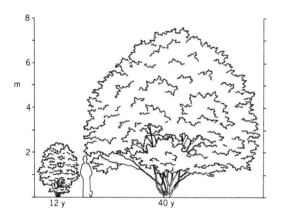

Osmanthus fragrans.

Adaptability

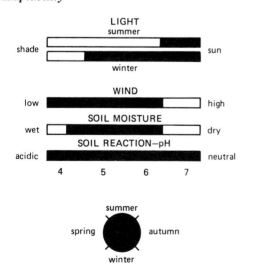

Seasonal Interest.   *Flowers:* Very small, white, highly fragrant, year-round but most heavily in spring and autumn. *Foliage:* Evergreen, leathery. to 10 cm/4 in. long. *Fruit:* Small, blue-black, seldom seen and not adding significant landscape interest when they do develop.

Problems and Maintenance.   This plant is trouble-free, requiring little maintenance when properly used in a formal shrub border or as a specimen. It does not respond well to pruning, so it should not be used as a hedge or screen.

Cultivars and Forms.   The forma *aurantiaca* has fragrant orange flowers. Selections from this form include 'Apricot Gold' and 'Butter Yellow' (which names describe their flower color), 'Live Oak Gold,' which has golden yellow flowers and excellent dark green foliage, and 'Orange Supreme,' a superior orange-flowering clone.

Related Species

Osmanthus americanus 5–6 (devilwood osmanthus).   This native of the southeastern United States becomes a small tree, to 8–10 m/26–33 ft, from Zone 8b southward, but functions as a large shrub to one third that height as far north as Zone 6b. Its very small flowers are fragrant in early spring, but less so than O. *fragrans*. Its blue-black fruits, to 1.3 cm/0.5 in. long, are more conspicuous than those of O. *fragrans*. Otherwise, except for the difference in cold-hardiness, the two species are functionally similar.

Osmanthus fragrans.

Osmanthus heterophyllus 5

Synonym: *O. ilicifolius*
HOLLY OSMANTHUS
Evergreen shrub
Oleaceae (Olive Family)

Native Range. Japan.

Useful Range. USDA Zones 7b–9a+.

Function. Hedge, screen, specimen.

Size and Habit

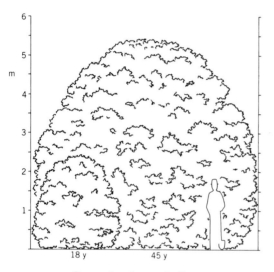

Osmanthus heterophyllus.

Seasonal Interest. *Flowers:* Very small, white or yellowish, fragrant, in middle to late summer. *Foliage:* Evergreen, dark green, leathery, mostly toothed and spiny tipped, resembling holly leaves but easily distinguished by the opposite arrangement (hollies have alternate leaves). Degree of toothing varies greatly from leaf to leaf on the same plant. *Fruits:* Blue-black, to 1.5 cm/0.6 in. long, adding significant landscape interest only at close range in autumn.

Problems and Maintenance. This shrub is trouble-free and requires little or no maintenance except when pruned as a formal hedge.

Osmanthus heterophyllus.

Adaptability

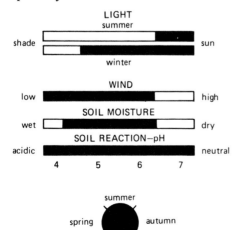

Cultivars. Several form and foliage variants have been selected, including the following. 'Aureus' has yellow leaf margins, but probably is no longer available in North America. 'Goshiki' is compact, to 3 m/10 ft tall, with pink new leaves, unfolding as creamy-white, yellow and bronze variegated, dark green spiny leaves. 'Gulftide' has small, glossy dark green, very "hollylike" leaves and an upright and densely compact habit, to 2 m/6.6 ft tall. 'Purpureus' (= 'Purpurascens') has deep red-purple young stems and some flushing of the leaves. 'Rotundifolius' is slow-growing, 1.5–2 m/5–6.6 ft tall, with nearly round, slightly crinkled leaves, to 4 cm/1.6 in. long, with few teeth. 'Variegatus' is a dwarf selection, 1–1.5 m/3.3–5 ft tall, with creamy-white leaf margins.

Related Species

Osmanthus decorus 5 (synonyms: *Phillyrea decora, P. vilmoriniana;* lanceleaf osmanthus or phillyrea). This large, evergreen shrub with glossy, leathery, lance-shaped leaves to 12 cm/5 in. long is useful for background and screening in Zones 8b–9a+, but it has been used very little in the southeastern United States and probably is available only from West Coast sources, if at all. It bears clusters of small white flowers in late spring and red fruits that ripen black in late summer and early autumn, but the handsome foliage is its most important landscape feature.

Osmanthus ×fortunei.

Osmanthus delavayi 4 (synonym: *Siphonosmanthus delavayi;* Delavay osmanthus). This compact, fine-textured shrub has leaves less than 2.5 cm/1 in. long, more-or-less holly-toothed, and fragrant white flowers, larger than those of other *Osmanthus* species listed here, in small clusters in early spring (and sometimes with scattered flowering in late autumn). This plant is not widely available but deserves greater use in Zones 8b–9a+ and possibly in sheltered sites in colder zones.

Osmanthus ×fortunei 6 (Fortune osmanthus). This hybrid of *O. heterophyllus* × *O. fragrans* has generally shallowly toothed, spiny tipped leaves, and very fragrant flowers in midsummer to autumn. It is nearly as cold-hardy as *O. heterophyllus,* useful in Zones 7b–9a+. In form, it is dense and compact, almost as broad as tall, and functions in size group 5 for several years before growing into size group 6, where it can be trained into a small tree form if desired.

Ostrya virginiana 7–8

HOP HORNBEAM, IRONWOOD
Deciduous tree
Betulaceae (Birch Family)

Native Range.   Eastern North America.

Useful Range.   USDA Zones 3b–9a with selection of appropriate genetic material.

Function.   Shade tree, specimen, naturalizing.

Size and Habit

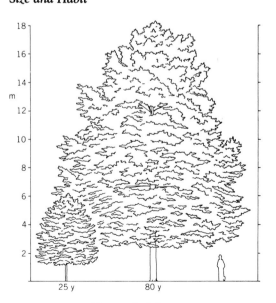

Ostrya virginiana.

Adaptability.   This tree is unusually intolerant of salt so should not be used in roadside plantings in the North.

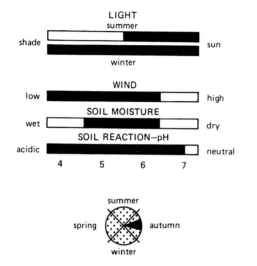

Seasonal Interest.   *Foliage:* Medium to dark green, finely toothed, similar to those of birch and elm, making a rather dense canopy, turning yellow before falling in midautumn. *Fruits:* Small, inflated pods in tight, hanging clusters, to 6 cm/2.4 in. long, resembling fruits of the hop vine, hence the name hop hornbeam, quietly interesting in midsummer to early autumn in South and North, respectively. *Trunk:* Finely shredded bark and "muscled" conformation of the trunk add quiet interest in all seasons.

Problems and Maintenance.   This is one of the most trouble-free of all deciduous trees, requiring little or no maintenance. As the name ironwood suggests, this is one of the most hard-wooded of temperate zone trees, seldom injured by wind or ice storms. But this strength is the result of a slow growth rate, which has kept the tree from being widely and easily available. It also has the reputation of being difficult to transplant, so it should be nursery-grown and moved in small sizes. Container-grown trees should be specified if they are available. In spite of these problems, this is a high-quality tree that deserves greater landscape use for its permanence and low maintenance.

Related Species

Ostrya carpinifolia 7 (European hop hornbeam). This Eurasian counterpart of *O. virginiana* differs little from *O. virginiana* but is considerably less cold-hardy to Zone 5b, perhaps also Zone 5a. It is not often available in North America, and usually there is not much incentive to use it in place of *O. virginiana*.

Oxydendrum arboreum 7–8

SOURWOOD, SORREL TREE
Deciduous tree
Ericaceae (Heath Family)

Native Range.   Eastern United States.

Useful Range.   USDA Zones 5b–9a.

Function.   Specimen, patio tree, naturalizing.

Size and Habit

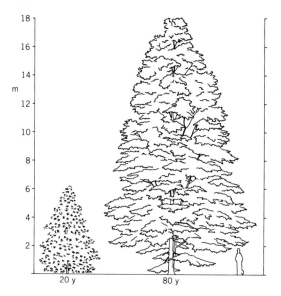

Oxydendrum arboreum.

Adaptability

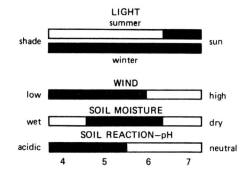

Seasonal Interest. *Flowers:* Small, white, resembling lilies of the valley, in gracefully nodding clusters 10–25 cm/4–10 in. long, in middle to late summer. *Foliage:* Lustrous and leathery, pale to deep green, turning rich maroon to scarlet in autumn and persisting late. *Fruits:* Small capsules carry the flower cluster interest into autumn.

Problems and Maintenance. This tree is trouble-free and requires little or no maintenance if planted in well-drained, acidic soil. It is sometimes considered difficult to transplant, but this is only true in large sizes. Specify relatively small sizes, preferably container-grown, and transplant in the spring. Like other members of the heath family, *Oxydendrum* has a fibrous root system that is easily dug and handled when the tree is young. Very light pruning occasionally may be needed to maintain good form, but generally the less pruning the better. Even though this tree is ordinarily hardy northward to Zone 5b, trees recently planted can be damaged in exposed sites even in Zone 6.

Pachysandra terminalis 2

JAPANESE SPURGE
Evergreen groundcover
Buxaceae (Box Family)

Native Range. Japan.

Useful Range. USDA Zones 5a–7b.

Function. Groundcover.

Size and Habit

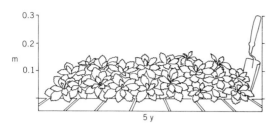

Pachysandra terminalis.

Pachysandra terminalis.

Adaptability.   Not only tolerates but requires shade from full sun for satisfactory performance. Will tolerate half sun in the North, but not in the South.

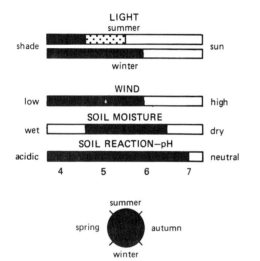

Seasonal Interest.   *Flowers:* Small, white, in short spikes, not showy, in spring. *Foliage:* Lustrous and dark green, forming a dense, evergreen groundcover.

Problems and Maintenance.   This groundcover is relatively trouble-free once established in a proper site. Because of its dense foliage canopy, this is one of the most effective groundcovers in resisting encroachment of weeds, so little maintenance is required once the canopy is established. A light mulch will reduce the need for weed control during establishment.

Cultivars.   'Green Carpet' has unusually dark green, glossy foliage and is lower growing than the species type. 'Green Sheen' has glossy green, almost waxy foliage. 'Cutleaf' and 'Kingwood' have more deeply toothed and cut leaves, giving a finer foliage texture. 'Silveredge' and 'Variegata' have irregularly variegated creamy-white leaf margins and are somewhat lower and slower growing than the species type.

Related Species

Pachysandra procumbens 2 (Alleghany pachysandra).   This native of the southern Appalachian Mountains is deciduous to semievergreen, with dull green but interesting leaves. It is less vigorous than *P. terminalis* and less versatile as a groundcover but excellent in a naturalized woodland setting, with spikes of white or pinkish purple flowers, more showy than those of *P. terminalis,* appearing before the new leaves in middle to late spring. Useful in Zones 5a–7b.

Paeonia suffruticosa 4

TREE PEONY
Deciduous subshrub
Ranunculaceae (Buttercup Family)

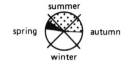

Native Range.   China to Bhutan and long cultivated in much of eastern Asia.

Useful Range.   USDA Zones 6a–7b, protected sites in the milder parts of Zone 5, and cool sites in Zone 8.

Function.   Specimen, border.

Size and Habit

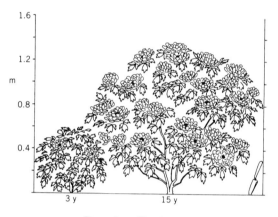

Paeonia suffruticosa.

Adaptability.   Exposure to full sun for a major part of the day, preferably morning, is necessary for good flowering, but partial shade during the hottest part of the day is desirable except in coastal areas that have hazy, mild summers. In winter, protection from full sun will reduce dehydration of the stems in areas where that is a problem. Soil drainage must be perfect for best results.

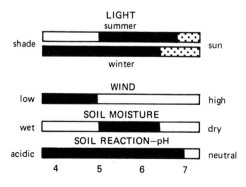

Seasonal Interest.   *Flowers:* White, yellow, bronze, pink, rose, or rich red, double or single, with bright yellow stamens in the center, 10–30 cm/4–12 in. across, spectacular in bloom. *Foliage:* Dull blue-green and distinctive in texture, but deciduous early and not a major landscape feature.

Problems and Maintenance.   Like many other plants that have been bred for extreme showiness (e.g., hybrid tea roses), tree peonies have several insect problems and should be watched carefully during the growing season. When pest control is necessary, instructions can be obtained through county, state, or provincial extension service offices.

Cultivars.   Several hundred cultivars have been developed in China and Japan, and at least 80 are now available in the United States. Since few are available in a specific time and place, they must be selected for availability above all else. Most cultivars are hybrids of *P. suffruticosa* with other tree peony species, *P. delavayi* and/or *P. lutea* (see Related Species).

Related Species and Hybrids

Paeonia delavayi 4 (Delavay tree peony).   This subshrub has relatively small (8 cm/3 in.), dark red flowers and is best known as a parent of hybrids. Like *P. suffruticosa*, it is from China and it is comparable in hardiness.

Paeonia lutea 4 (yellow tree peony).   This plant is not greatly different from other tree peony species except in having yellow flowers, about 5 cm/2 in. across. Like *P. delavayi*, it is best known through its parentage of hybrids with *P. suffruticosa*, and it, too, is from China and comparable in hardiness to other tree peonies.

Herbaceous peonies.   Hundreds of cultivars of herbaceous peonies are in cultivation. Most are selections or hybrids of *P. lactiflora*, with flower colors ranging from white to pink and red. The Saunders Hybrids and those that have followed have made use of additional parent species having yellow flowers, thereby broadening the range of flower color to yellow, bronze, and peachy tones. Herbaceous peonies are usually thought of as decorative, but they also have architectural uses, primarily as low dividers between subareas or for massing. Because there are so many cultivars, it is a good idea to select them on the basis of their availability at a particular time and place.

Parkinsonia aculeata 6

JERUSALEM THORN, MEXICAN OR GREEN PALO VERDE
Deciduous tree
Fabaceae (Leguminosae; Pea Family)

Native Range.   Tropical America.

Useful Range.   USDA Zone 9a+.

Function.   Shade, patio, or specimen tree, barrier hedge.

Size and Habit

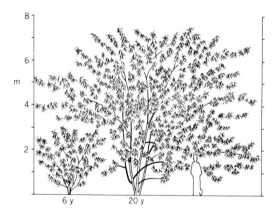

Parkinsonia aculeata.

Adaptability.   Resistant to salt spray in seashore sites.

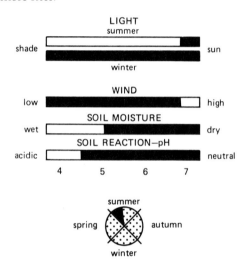

Seasonal Interest. *Flowers:* Fragrant, bright yellow, about 2.5 cm/1 in. across, borne in great numbers in loose clusters in early summer in Zone 9a, and later as well in warmer climates. *Foliage:* Long, whiplike, compound leaves, to 30 cm/12 in. or longer with up to 50 tiny leaflets, giving very light, filtered shade until they fall in autumn. *Twigs and branches:* Loose and open branching with many thorns, to 2.5 cm/1 in. long, borne on twigs and branches that remain smooth and green year-round.

Problems and Maintenance.   This tree is at its best south and west of our area, and smaller branches occasionally will be winterkilled in Zone 9a. Nevertheless, it is usefully hardy there. The sharp thorns can be troublesome when people come in contact with branches, so lower limbs will need to be pruned away or cleaned of thorns in patio situations. *Parkinsonia* is a short-lived tree at best, in our area sometimes dying suddenly following temporary flooding or excessive wetting of the soil. Plant in sites with maximum soil drainage. Because of the rapid growth rate of this species, dead trees can be replaced fairly quickly.

Related Species

Parkinsonia florida 6 (synonym: *Cercidium floridum;* blue palo verde). This small tree differs little from *P. aculeata* in landscape use and is less common than *P. aculeata* in the southwestern parts of our area (Louisiana and East Texas), but is very common in the drier climates of the Far Southwest.

Parrotia persica 6–7

PERSIAN PARROTIA
Deciduous tree or large shrub
Hamamelidaceae (Witch Hazel Family)

Native Range. Iran.

Useful Range. USDA Zones 6a–9a, and Zone 5b in protected sites.

Function. Specimen, shade tree.

Size and Habit

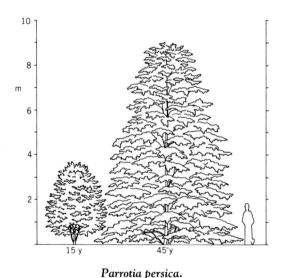

Parrotia persica.

Adaptability

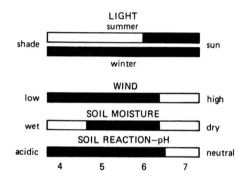

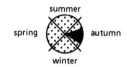

Seasonal Interest. Flowers: Small, inconspicuous except when the stamens first emerge ruby-red, adding color at close range very early in spring. *Foliage:* Medium bright green, lustrous, providing interesting medium texture, similar to foliage of the witch hazels but more handsome, turning to bright yellow, orange, and scarlet in autumn, when in full sun. *Trunk and branches:* Bark on trunks and main branches of older trees flakes off, leaving a handsomely mottled pattern of gray and off-white.

Problems and Maintenance. This plant is relatively free of problems and requires little maintenance beyond initial pruning to establish form. This involves a decision, however: whether to gradually remove lower branches to expose the interesting bark year-round and allow the tree to serve in a patio situation, or to allow the lower

Parrotia persica.

Disanthus cercidifolius.

branches to remain and the tree to attain its greatest gracefulness. In this case, the ground surface beneath should be mulched and turfgrass limited to the outer periphery, where it can be cut without trimming under the tree. This tree deserves much wider use, but is not yet widely available.

Cultivars. 'Pendula' is a strongly and gracefully weeping clone, making a dense mound of foliage to 2–3 m/6.6–10 ft high and at least as wide, with outstanding autumn foliage color. The bark is interesting in winter, and in summer as well when it is visible through the foliage canopy.

Related Species

Disanthus cercidifolius 5.   This member of the witch hazel family is a graceful, tall shrub with heart-shaped leaves strongly resembling those of *Cercis* species. Deep blue-green and leathery, they turn deep red in autumn with orange overtones. Seldom available commercially, it may become better known in the future. It is potentially useful in Zones 7a–9a in semishaded sites with at least moderately acid, well-drained soil with a good supply of moisture.

Distylium racemosum 5–6.   This large evergreen shrub in the Hamamelidaceae (Witch-hazel Family) grows slowly to 25 m/83 ft in its native habitat in southern Japan, but probably will not exceed one-third that size in cultivation in North America. Its flowers lack petals but are briefly colorful when they first open in late winter or early spring because of their red anthers, much like the closely related but deciduous *Parrotia*. Useful in Zones 8a–9a+, perhaps also Zone 7b.

Parrotiopsis jacquemontiana 6.   This small tree is closely related to and resembles *Parrotia* except that it flowers in late spring and its inconspicuous flowers are surrounded by showy whitish bracts to 5 cm/2 in. across, giving a little of the effect of *Davidia* (dove tree). Foliage is similar to that of the witch hazels and turns yellow in autumn. This tree, like *Disanthus*, deserves much wider trial, but it is seldom commercially available at present. It is potentially useful in Zones 7a–9a+.

Sycopsis sinensis 6.   This large evergreen shrub or small tree grows to 6 m/20 ft tall, with leathery, elliptical leaves to 12 cm/5 in. long. Its flowers lack petals but have fairly conspicuous red-tinted golden stamens, opening very early in spring, about the same time as those of the closely related *Parrotia*. Potentially useful in Zones 8b–9a, perhaps also Zone 8a, but seldom available.

Parthenocissus quinquefolia 1 and 2

Synonym: *ampelopsis quinquefolia*
VIRGINIA CREEPER, WOODBINE
Deciduous vine
Vitaceae (Grape Family)

Native Range. Eastern United States and adjacent Canada.

Useful Range. USDA Zones 3b–9a+.

Function. Cover for walls and fences, rambling large-scale groundcover.

Size and Habit. Climbing vine, holding by branched tendrils, many with adhesive discs, older stems also holding by aerial rootlets, and climbing to heights of at least 15 m/50 ft on tree trunks and masonry walls.

Adaptability

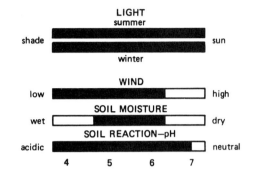

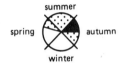

Seasonal Interest. *Flowers:* Inconspicuous, in early summer. *Foliage:* Deep green, dull to lustrous, palmately compound, with five leaflets to 10 cm/4 in. long, giving an interesting, coarse texture, turning brilliant red in sun in early autumn. *Fruits:* Small, blue-black with a whitish, waxy bloom, resembling wild grapes, in loose clusters on mature, high-climbing plants, fairly conspicuous after the leaves have fallen in autumn.

Problems and Maintenance. This vine is relatively trouble-free and usually requires no maintenance other than pruning to control growth in small-scale situations.

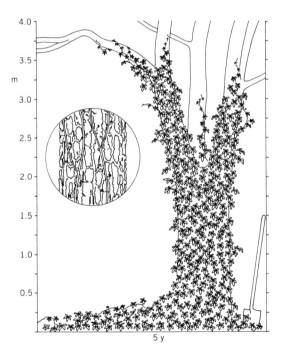

Parthenocissus quinquefolia.

Parthenocissus quinquefolia.

Cultivars. 'Engelmannii' has somewhat smaller leaflets than the species type, giving a more refined texture, especially appropriate to smaller-scale use.

Related Species

Parthenocissus henryana 1 and 2 (silvervein creeper). This weakly climbing vine is used for its striking foliage. Leaves are about 10 cm/4 in. or less across, bright red as they open, dark green and leathery in summer with white-marked veins, and finally bright red again before falling. The white vein markings, which only develop well in the shade, make it a striking specimen, but too open in growth habit to function as a solid groundcover or wall cover. It is much less cold-hardy than *P. quinquefolia*, useful only in Zones 8b–9a+.

Parthenocissus inserta 1 and 2. This vine is very similar to *P. quinquefolia* in general appearance and range, differing in that its tendrils do not bear adhesive discs and so it is not effective in holding to masonry. When a vine is needed for this purpose, care should be taken to obtain *P. quinquefolia*, not *P. inserta*. Otherwise the two are equivalent as landscape plants.

Parthenocissus tricuspidata 1 (synonym: *Ampelopsis tricuspidata*; Boston ivy). This neatly textured, deciduous vine, with three-lobed leaves similar to those of some grapes, is not useful as a groundcover but is one of the most satisfactory vines for covering masonry walls, holding by branched tendrils with adhesive discs and climbing to heights of 15 m/50 ft and more. The foliage turns orange-red in autumn and the fruits, similar to those of *P. quinquefolia*, add interest

Parthenocissus tricuspidata.

after the leaves fall. This plant is trouble-free, well adapted to most city conditions, and useful in Zones 4b–8b. When used as a wall cover, some maintenance is required to keep it from covering windows.

Several selections have been made: 'Beverley Brook' has small leaves, about half the size of those of the species type. 'Green Showers' and 'Green Spring' have large, glossy leaves, to 25 cm/10 in. across. 'Lowii' has very small leaves, about 2.5 cm/1 in. across, especially appropriate for very small-scale situations. 'Purpurea' has reddish-purple foliage through summer, becoming more reddish in autumn, but may not be available in North America. 'Robusta' is a vigorous selection with average-sized leaves (10–20 cm/4–8 in. across) having long petioles and turning red-orange in autumn. 'Veitchii' is a juvenile form (no flowers or fruits), with small leaves (5–8 cm/2–3 in. across), unlobed but with a few large teeth, or trifoliolate. Not all plants sold as this cultivar are true-to-name.

Passiflora caerulea 1 and 2

BLUECROWN PASSIONFLOWER
Semievergreen to evergreen vine
Passifloraceae (Passionflower Family)

Native Range. Southern Brazil and Argentina.

Useful Range. USDA Zones 8a–9a+, perhaps also Zone 7b.

Function. Specimen, groundcover, screen (with support). Climbs by tendrils to heights of 5–10 m/16–33 ft, but kills back to the ground in severe winters in Zone 8 and colder.

Size and Habit

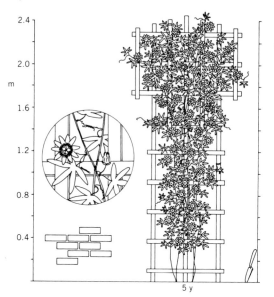

Passiflora caerulea.

Adaptability

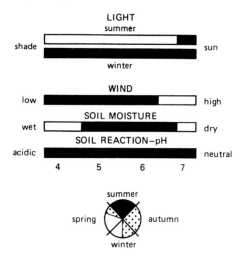

Seasonal Interest. *Flowers:* Lightly fragrant, blue, pale pink, and white, complex in structure and remarkably radially symmetrical, to 10 cm/4 in. across, opening during most of the summer. *Foliage:* Distinctive, five-lobed leaves are medium green, semievergreen in Zone 8, fully evergreen farther south.

Problems and Maintenance. This is one of the most trouble-free *Passiflora* species, seldom requiring any maintenance other than pruning for restraint when it begins to grow out of bounds and to remove the dead tops after severe winters. Nematodes can be troublesome in the Deep South.

Cultivars. 'Constance Elliott' has pure white flowers. 'Grandiflora' has unusually large flowers, to 15 cm/6 in. across.

Related Species

Passiflora incarnata 1 (maypop, wild passionflower). Native to the southeastern United States and northward to Missouri and Virginia, this vine has purple-marked, pinkish white flowers to 5 cm/2 in. across, opening from midsummer to early autumn, and edible yellow fruits, about the size of apricots. It is useful as a screen (with support) in Zones 7b–9a+ and sheltered sites in Zone 7a, but does not make a dense groundcover.

Passiflora lutea 1 (yellow passionflower). Native to the southeastern United States, northward to Pennsylvania and westward to Texas, this is the most cold-hardy of the *Passiflora* species, useful in Zones 7a–9a+ and sheltered sites in Zone 6b, but its greenish yellow flowers, only 2 cm/0.8 in. across, are not nearly as showy as those of other passionflowers, and it finds little landscape use.

Paulownia tomentosa 7

EMPRESS TREE

Deciduous tree

Scrophulariaceae (Figwort Family); some authors place it in the Bignoniaceae (Bignonia Family)

Native Range. China; escaped to the wild in east-central United States.

Useful Range. USDA Zones 6b–9a+.

Function. Specimen, shade tree.

Size and Habit

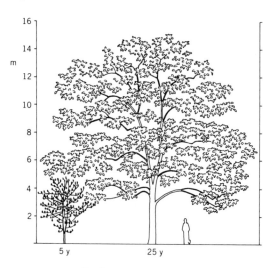

Paulownia tomentosa.

Adaptability

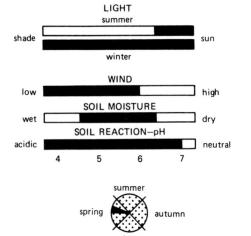

Seasonal Interest. *Flowers:* Fragrant, pale violet-purple, tubular, individually 5 cm/2 in. long, borne in loosely pyramidal clusters of 10 or more, making this one of the showiest flowering trees of the temperate zone. *Foliage:* Deep green, downy, heart-shaped, to 25 cm/10 in. long (and even larger on vigorous young trees), giving an unusually coarse textural effect, falling without color change. *Fruits:* Rounded capsules to 4 cm/1.6 in. across, pale green, ripening brown in early autumn and breaking open to release large numbers of small seeds, the opened capsules then persisting well into winter. *Winter buds:* Flower buds form in summer and are conspicuous on the tree all winter, rounded and covered with rusty pubescence, 0.5 cm/0.2 in. across and expanding to twice that size before opening in spring.

Problems and Maintenance. Unfortunately, this spectacular, fast-growing tree is soft-wooded, short-lived, and weedy, in mild climates rivaling *Ailanthus* as a source of weed seedlings. In the North (Zones 5 and 6) the tree will persist but be killed back severely in winter, sometimes to the ground. Following this drastic pruning by winter cold, plants recover rapidly, often producing stems 2–4 m/7–13 ft tall during the following growing season. Such growth is exceptionally soft, even for this tree, and even more prone to damage the next winter. Since flower buds form one year and open the next, winterkilling of the stems eliminates flowering interest. Considering all of this, *Paulownia* should be considered a high maintenance tree and questionable as a functional tree.

Paxistima canbyi 2

Synonym: *Pachistima canbyi*
CANBY PAXISTIMA
Evergreen groundcover
Celastraceae (Staff-tree Family)

Native Range. Eastern United States: central Appalachian Mountains.

Useful Range. USDA Zones 4a–7b, only in cool microclimates in Zone 7, and with snow cover or other protection in Zone 4.

Function. Groundcover, specimen, rock garden.

Size and Habit

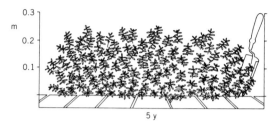

Paxistima canbyi.

Adaptability. Grows well in full sun to half shade in the North, but needs at least light shade for good performance in Zone 7. Foliage may winterburn in full sun in the North. Often referred to as an acid-soil plant, actually it also grows well in nearly neutral soils, provided they are well drained.

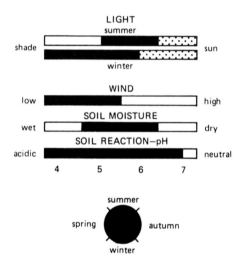

Seasonal Interest. *Foliage:* Very small leaves, to 2.5 cm/1 in., are evergreen, leathery, toothed, and dark green, making a very effective, fine-textured, year-round groundcover that bronzes when it is exposed to winter sun. *Flowers and fruits:* Inconspicuous.

Problems and Maintenance. This groundcover usually is relatively trouble-free but is occasionally subject to infestations of euonymus scale insects. Once established in a good site, it requires little maintenance, but old plantings may become ragged with a mass of leafless stems underneath. If they are otherwise in good condition, they can be rejuvenated by pruning back heavily and fertilizing the soil lightly in spring.

Paxistima canbyi.

Cultivars. 'Compacta' is compact and low, excellent for small-scale plantings.

Related Species

Paxistima myrtifolia 3 (Synonym: *P. myrsinites;* Oregon paxistima). This low shrub, native from British Columbia to New Mexico, is very similar to its eastern relative in general appearance but so little cultivated that its performance in eastern North America is not well known. It may be useful in Zones 6b–8b, but probably is never available in our area.

Phellodendron amurense 7–8

AMUR CORKTREE
Deciduous tree
Rutaceae (Rue Family)

Native Range. Northern China and Manchuria.

Useful Range. USDA Zones 4b–7b, also Zone 3 if appropriate genetic material is available, and possibly Zone 8a as well.

Function. Shade tree, specimen.

Size and Habit

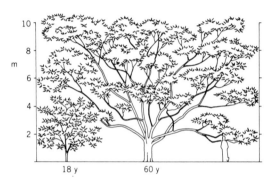

Phellodendron amurense.

Adaptability

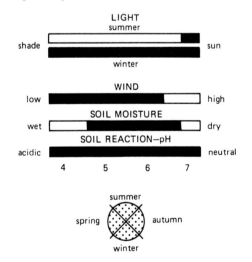

Seasonal Interest. *Flowers:* Inconspicuous, dioecious. *Foliage:* Dark green, compound, with a turpentine odor when crushed, forming an effective canopy of mottled shade, in some locations and years turning yellow before falling early and suddenly in autumn. *Fruits:* Small, black, and aromatic when crushed. *Trunk and branches:* Bark on trunks and main limbs of older trees is corky and heavily furrowed. Branching is picturesque and open, with few massive side branches, adding landscape interest in all seasons.

Problems and Maintenance. This tree is trouble-free, requiring almost no maintenance. Dropping fruits and foliage constitute a minor litter problem in some situations.

Cultivars. 'Macho'® and 'PNI 4551' (Shademaster®) are vigorous male selections, free from fruit litter.

Related Species

Phellodendron sachalinense 8 (Sakhalin corktree). This close relative of *P. amurense* differs very little but tends to have less corky bark, and so

Phellodendron amurense.

less winter interest. The two species may be confused in commerce, and both are variable in height and bark character. Except for degree of bark interest, they can be considered to be equivalent for most landscape use.

Other species of *Phellodendron* exist, all from eastern Asia, but they are seldom, if ever, available and are usually considered to be inferior in landscape use to the two listed above.

Philadelphus coronarius 5

SWEET MOCKORANGE
Deciduous shrub
Hydrangeaceae (Hydrangea Family)

Native Range.   Southwestern Europe.

Useful Range.   USDA Zones 4a–7b.

Function.   Border, screen, specimen. Functional as a visual screen only in full sun and with some pruning.

Size and Habit

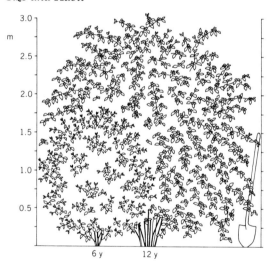

Philadelphus coronarius.

Adaptability

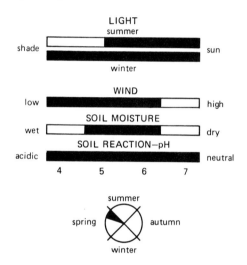

Seasonal Interest.   *Flowers:* Fragrant, white, single, about 3 cm/1.2 in. across, in late spring. *Foliage:* Deep green leaves, 6–8 cm/2.3–3.2 in. long, widely spaced on wiry stems, giving rather coarse texture, usually making a rather loose mass.

Problems and Maintenance.   This shrub is essentially trouble-free but requires occasional careful pruning to maintain fullness.

Cultivars.   'Aureus' has bright yellow new foliage, which fades during the growing season to green. Plants are less vigorous than the species but eventually reach heights of close to 2 m/6.6 ft. Flowering is not profuse, the primary landscape color coming from the yellow foliage in late spring and early summer.

Related Species

Philadelphus inodorus 5 (scentless mockorange). This native of the southern Appalachian Mountains is unusual for its unscented flowers, but also for having better than average form in the landscape. The species type and its varieties all are more-or-less moundlike in form with foliage and flowers right down to the base of the plant. The species type and var. *grandiflorus* (synonym: *P. grandiflorus*; bigleaf scentless mockorange) are tall, broadly moundlike shrubs to 3 m/10 ft, and somewhat broader than tall at maturity. Var. *laxus* (synonym: *P. laxus*; drooping mockorange) has drooping branches, as the name suggests, and seldom exceeds 2 m/6.6 ft in height, but may be 3 m/10 ft wide. *P. inodorus* and its varieties are useful in Zones 5b–9a and perhaps in Zone 5a as well.

Philadelphus lewisii 4–5 (Lewis mockorange). This variable species is native to western North America from Alberta and British Columbia to northern California, and includes several populations that have sometimes been considered to be separate species: *P. columbianus*, *P. gordonianus*, and *P. californicus*, now *P. lewisii* ssp. *californicus*. The northern forms are of special interest since they include individuals with unusual cold-hardiness, useful in the northwestern parts of our area. The best known example is *P. lewisii* 'Waterton,' selected in Alberta and useful northward at least to Zone 3b and probably to Zone 2. This cultivar is compact in growth yet reaches heights of about 2 m/6.6 ft under good conditions. Its flowers are displayed well but are unscented like those of the species.

Philadelphus purpurascens 5–6 (purplecup mockorange). This native of China is one of the largest of mockoranges, to 4 m/13 ft tall under good conditions, spreading widely with arching branches. The fragrant flowers are borne in purple, cuplike calyces and are displayed very effectively since they are not covered by the relatively small (to about 2–3 cm/1 in. long) leaves. Useful in Zones 5b–8a, but seldom available. Except for the purple calyces, *P. purpurascens* has little advantage over *P. coronarius* or any of the other scented, large-growing mockoranges.

Philadelphus schrenkii 5 (Schrenk mockorange). This hardy shrub from Korea and Manchuria is well adapted to the northern plains of our area: useful in Zones 3a–7a, perhaps even in Zone 2. The var. *jackii* may be somewhat less cold-hardy but is useful in Zone 3b, and it is one of the earliest of all mockoranges to flower, as much as two weeks earlier than *P. ×lemoinei* and *P. ×virginalis*.

Philadelphus ×splendens 5.   This hybrid of *P. inodorus* var. *grandiflorus*, probably by *P. lewisii*, has large flowers, to 5 cm/2 in. across but only slightly fragrant, and excellent moundlike form, to 2.5 m/8 ft tall and greater in width, branching well to the ground. Useful in Zones 5b–8a and perhaps colder zones as well.

Several other species of *Philadelphus* exist in collections but add little to the range of characteristics offered by those mentioned and are seldom, if ever, commercially available. In fact, several of those listed will be found difficult to obtain, since large mockoranges are, at best, limited in function and seasonal interest.

Carpenteria californica 4 (tree anemone).   This evergreen shrub in the Philadelphaceae (Mockorange Family), native to central California, grows to 1–2 m/3.3–6.6 ft high and wide, with a rounded habit, handsome lustrous leaves, and 5–10 cm/2–4 in. white flowers with golden yellow stamens, similar to those of *Philadelphus*, opening in early and middle summer. Useful in Zones 8a–9a+, perhaps also Zone 7b, in California, but little tried in the higher humidity of eastern North America.

Philadelphus ×lemoinei 4

LEMOINE MOCKORANGE
Deciduous shrub
Hydrangeaceae (Hydrangea Family)

Hybrid origin.   P. microphyllus × P. coronarius.

Useful Range.   USDA Zones 4b–8a, but some cultivars are cold-hardy only to Zone 5.

Function.   Border, specimen (those selections having good form).

Size and Habit

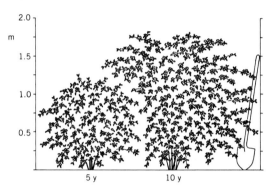

Philadelphus ×lemoinei.

Adaptability

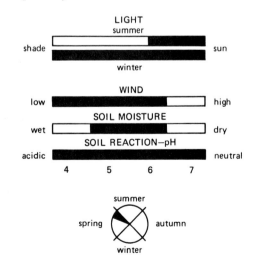

Seasonal Interest.   *Flowers:* Fragrant, white, single to double, 2.5–5.5 cm/1.0–2.2 in. across, from late spring to very early summer. *Foliage:* Deep green, leaves are variable, 1.5–4 cm/0.6–1.6 in. long, but usually small, the most consistent difference between P. ×lemoinei and P. ×virginalis cultivars.

Problems and Maintenance.   This shrub is relatively trouble-free but mostly requires pruning to maintain form, and some cultivars have poor form in spite of pruning. Prune in spring or after flowering has ended in early summer by removing a few older branches at or near ground level and cutting tips of other branches back to encourage branching. Do not prune later than early summer, since this encourages rank growth and reduces winter hardiness.

Cultivars.   Many cultivars have been selected over the years. A few of the best and most popular are listed here. Most of these are useful in Zones 5a–8a, and perhaps also Zone 4b, with shelter.
  'Avalanche' is an old, upright selection, with very fragrant flowers, to 1.5 m/5 ft tall.
  'Enchantment' is compact and full, to 2.5 m/8 ft tall, with very fragrant, double, pure white flowers.
  'Lemoinei,' the type of this hybrid group, is a spreading shrub with very fragrant, pure white flowers.
  'Mont Blanc' has unusually good, moundlike form, growing to a little over 1 m/3.3 ft high, and fragrant, single white flowers.
  'Silver Showers' is a gracefully arching and unusually free flowering form, growing to 1.5–2 m/5–6.6 ft tall and wide, with fragrant white flowers.

Related Species and Hybrids

Philadelphus microphyllus 4 (little-leaved mockorange).   This small, sparse shrub, native to the southern United States and Mexico, is notable only as an important parent of many smaller-growing hybrid mockoranges. In itself, it has little landscape usefulness and probably is not available commercially, but does have fragrant white flowers and could be used in Zones 6a–9a+.

Philadelphus ×*virginalis* 4–5 (virginal mock-orange). This group of hybrids of *P.* ×*lemoinei* by an unknown parent, possibly *P. nivalis*, includes some of the showiest mockorange cultivars, but mostly with poor form, along with an occasional one with good form as well as showy flowers. These cultivars are generally useful in Zones 4b–8a; some may also be cold-hardy in Zone 4a. Only a few of the better cultivars are included here: 'Bouquet Blanc,' usually associated with *P.* ×*virginalis* but so different as to cause speculation about its true origin, has outstanding landscape form and is one of the few mockoranges that are very useful as functional landscape plants. This one is moundlike and useful for massing, but at best it is barely tall enough to function as a visual screen. Useful in Zones 4b–8a (see Other Hybrids).

'Galahad' is a semi-dwarf shrub, to just under 1.5 m/5 ft tall and wide, with compact habit and fragrant, single white flowers.

'Glacier' is a semi-dwarf shrub, to 1.5 m/5 ft tall and nearly as broad, with good, symmetrical form and fragrant, double white flowers, 3 cm/1.2 in. across.

'Minnesota Snowflake' is a vigorous selection with upright, leggy form and very large, fragrant, double flowers, to 5 cm/2 in. across, useful in Zones 4b–8a and possibly 4a as well.

'Natchez' is a fairly well-branched shrub to 2–2.5 m/6.6–8 ft tall and nearly as broad, with fragrant, single white flowers, 5 cm/2 in. across.

'Virginal' is the first *P.* ×*virginalis* hybrid cultivar selected. It is similar to 'Natchez' in size, with fragrant, semi-double flowers, 5 cm/2 in.

across, but has a rather leggy shape and is usually too sparse to make an effective screen. It is still fairly popular, but seems destined to be replaced by cultivars with better form.

Other Hybrids

'Belle Etoile,' believed to be a hybrid of *P.* ×*lemoinei* by *P. coulteri*, a small Mexican shrub, grows to 1.5–2 m/5–6.6 ft tall, with very fragrant white flowers with purple centers, to 8 cm/3 in. across.

'Buckley's Quill' is an excellent semi-dwarf shrub from the Canada Department of Agriculture in Ottawa, grows to nearly 1.5 m/5 ft tall and nearly as wide, with large clusters of fragrant double flowers with quill-shaped petals.

'Bouquet Blanc' (a selection from *P.* ×*cymosus*, which itself is of unknown parentage) is a compact shrub, 1.5–2 m/5–6.6 ft tall, with very fragrant, double white flowers in large clusters.

'Miniature Snowflake,' a dwarf mockorange introduced by Bailey Nurseries (Minnesota), is upright but grows to only 1 m/3.3 ft tall and only 0.6 m/2 ft wide, with very fragrant, double white flowers.

'Snowbelle,' a semi-dwarf selection introduced by the Canada Department of Agriculture, grows to 1.2 m/4 ft tall, has large clusters of very fragrant, cupped white flowers, each with a central cluster of smaller, irregular petals.

'Snowgoose,' another Canadian introduction, is semi-dwarf, to 1.5 m/5 ft tall but less than 1 m/3.3 ft wide, with fragrant, pure white, double flowers.

Phlox subulata 2

MOSS PINK, MOUNTAIN PINK
Semievergreen herbaceous groundcover
Polemoniaceae (Phlox Family)

Native Range. Eastern United States from New York to Michigan and southward to North Carolina.

Useful Range. USDA Zones 3b–8a, and to a limited extent in Zone 8b.

Function. Groundcover, rock garden.

Size and Habit

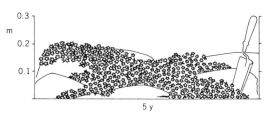

Phlox subulata.

Adaptability

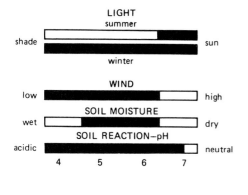

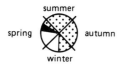

Seasonal Interest. *Flowers:* Bright magenta, pale violet, lavender, blue, pink, or white, to 2 cm/0.8 in. across, borne in such great numbers that they form a solid carpet of bloom on the ground in midspring. The magenta colors are so strong that they can be overpowering and fail to harmonize with other colors. Use strong colors on a small scale or at a distance, with careful attention to companion flower colors. *Foliage:* Bright green, sharp, needlelike leaves are less than 2.5 cm/1 in. long, remaining green well into the winter but suffering winterburn and deteriorating in late winter, especially in the North.

Problems and Maintenance. This plant occasionally is subject to several diseases, but these are seldom serious enough to require control. Some maintenance is required, however, primarily to renovate old plantings that eventually develop dead spots at the centers of old plants. Need for replanting can be forestalled for years by cutting back the tops after flowering to force vigorous new growth.

Cultivars. Many selections have been made for superior foliage and form, vigor, and flower colors from white to blue, lavender, pink, rose, and red. A few of the most popular are: 'Apple Blossom,' with pale pink flowers; 'Blue Hills' and 'Emerald Blue,' with bright lavender-blue flowers; 'Crimson Beauty,' with deep rose-red flowers; 'Emerald Pink,' with bright pink flowers; 'Maiden's Blush,' pink-flushed white with red center; 'Red Wings,' with deep rose flowers and darker red center; 'Scarlet Flame,' with bright scarlet flowers; and 'White Delight,' with large, pure white flowers. At any one time and place, the choice will be limited, so selection will depend on availability.

Related Species

Phlox nivalis 2 (trailing phlox). This plant has a more southerly native range than *P. subulata*, from Virginia to Alabama and Florida, and may be better adapted to landscape use in the Deep South. It is so similar in appearance to *P. subulata* that the two are often confused. The selections 'Azurea' and 'Camla' are outstanding, with pale blue and salmon pink flowers, respectively. Both are useful in Zones 5b–8b, perhaps colder zones, and probably Zone 9a.

Photinia ×*fraseri* 6

FRASER PHOTINIA
Evergreen shrub
Rosaceae (Rose Family)

Hybrid origin. *P. serratifolia* × *P. glabra*.

Useful Range. USDA Zones 8a–9a+ and protected sites in Zone 7b.

Function. Screen, specimen, border, hedge, massing.

Size and Habit

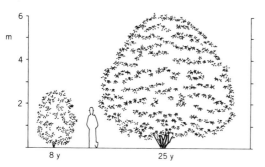

Photinia ×fraseri.

Adaptability. Full sun and good air circulation help to control severity of leaf diseases, and root rot diseases are less troublesome in exceptionally well-drained soil.

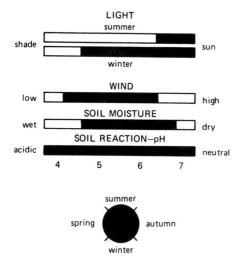

Seasonal Interest. *Flowers:* Small, white, in flat clusters about 10–15 cm/4–6 in. across in late spring. *Foliage:* New foliage and stems emerge glossy and orange to bronze-red in spring, turn green as they mature, and remain deep green and lustrous until leaves fall in spring or summer of the following year. Leaves are large, to 10–12 cm/4–5 in., giving a coarse texture year-round.

Problems and Maintenance. *P. ×fraseri* is intermediate between its parents in susceptibility to disease (see *P. serratifolia*, Problems and Maintenance). It is more seriously troubled by root rot and leaf spot diseases than *P. serratifolia*, less

so than *P. glabra.* And it is less troubled by mildew than *P. serratifolia.* All photinias should be planted in perfectly drained sites with good air circulation. Annual pruning stimulates vigor and maximum development of the flame-red color of the new shoots. This is routinely done in hedges, but must be done more selectively where some of the form of the plant is to be retained. Irrigation may be needed in some sites during drought periods, but water should be withheld in autumn to promote hardening.

Cultivars. 'Monstock' (Indian Princess™, Plant Patent No. 5237, 1984) is dense and slow-growing, probably remaining below 2 m/6.6 ft for years. 'Red Robin,' a New Zealand selection, is also compact in growth, and very colorful in spring, when the new growth is brighter red than typical plants of *P. ×fraseri.*

Related Species

Photinia davidiana 6 (synonym: *Stranvaesia davidiana*). This wide-spreading evergreen shrub grows loosely to 6–8 m/20–26 ft tall and wide, with showy scarlet fruits to 0.8 cm/0.3 in. across, produced in quantity, colorful in autumn, and persisting later in mild winters. Useful in Zones 7b–9a, but not often available.

Photinia glabra 5 (Japanese or red leaf photinia). This large shrub is frequently used in the South for color accent, alone or in borders or hedges. Like *P. ×fraseri*, its chief seasonal interest is the bright red, newly emerging foliage in middle to late spring. Flowering interest is less significant than in *P. ×fraseri* or *P. serratifolia*, since the

Photinia villosa f. *maximowicziana.*

clusters are only about half as large, and fruiting is seldom as prominent as in *P. serratifolia.* It is slightly less cold-hardy than *P.* ×*fraseri* and *P. serratifolia,* but useful in Zones 8a–9a+. As with the other two species, close attention to soil drainage is crucial to the success of this species. In fact, root rot disease is so serious a problem that *P.* ×*fraseri* is increasingly being substituted for *P. glabra.*

Photinia villosa 6 (oriental photinia).   This tall deciduous shrub or small tree from China, Japan, and Korea is too open to function as a screen, but its bright red berries and foliage add substantial autumn interest. Fire blight can be a serious problem in some areas. Otherwise, this plant is useful in Zones 6a–8a. The f. *maximowicziana* from Korea is somewhat more cold-hardy, to Zone 5b, but probably is not available.

Photinia serratifolia 6

Synonym: *P. serrulata*
CHINESE PHOTINIA
Evergreen shrub or small tree
Rosaceae (Rose Family)

Native Range.   China.

Useful Range.   USDA Zones 7b–9a+.

Function.   Screen, specimen, border, patio tree (with pruning).

Size and Habit

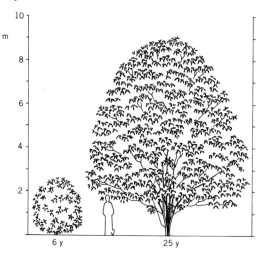

Photinia serratifolia.

Adaptability.   Full sun and good air circulation help to control the severity of leaf diseases. Root rot diseases are less troublesome in well-drained soil.

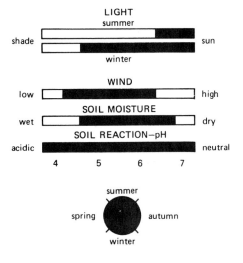

Seasonal Interest.   *Flowers:* Small, white, in flat clusters to 10–15 cm/4–6 in. across in middle to late spring. *Foliage:* New foliage emerges glossy reddish or bronze in spring, turns green as it matures, and remains deep green and lustrous until spring or summer of the following year, when it falls, often reddening first. Leaves are leathery, to 15–18 cm/6–7 in. long, sharply and finely toothed, giving a relatively coarse texture year-round.

Problems and Maintenance.   *P. serratifolia* has the usual problems of evergreen photinias in general. Fire blight and a leaf-spot disease are highly destructive in some areas, and mildew can be serious in shaded sites with little air movement or in humid coastal areas. Observe local experience when selecting this plant. In good sites, plants are often trouble-free for many years. Pruning will eventually be needed to promote vigor and is sometimes done routinely to maintain high vigor and maximum bronzing of the new foliage. Water should be withheld in autumn to promote hardening.

Cultivars. 'Aculeata' (red-twig Chinese photinia) has more sharply and deeply toothed leaves, new twigs that are very red, and a more compact growth habit, reaching an ultimate height of little over 3 m/10 ft, less than half that of the species type.

Photinia serratifolia.

Physocarpus opulifolius 4–5

EASTERN NINEBARK
Deciduous shrub
Rosaceae (Rose Family)

Native Range. Northeastern and north-central United States and adjacent Canada.

Useful Range. USDA Zones 3a–6b with selection of appropriate genetic material.

Function. Border, massing, hedge, bank cover (dwarf variety).

Size and Habit

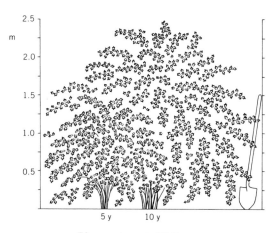

Physocarpus opulifolius.

Adaptability. This is one of the most broadly adaptable shrubs to different soil conditions.

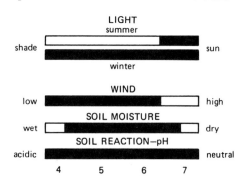

Seasonal Interest. *Flowers:* White or off-white, small, in clusters to 5 cm/2 in. across, adding significant color very early in summer. *Foliage:* Deep to olive green (or yellowish in a cultivar) on wiry branches. Texture is somewhat coarse, even though leaves are seldom much over 5 cm/2 in. long, falling without much color change, occasionally turning reddish first. *Fruits:* Small dried pods, fused, two to five together, almost insignificant in autumn, but briefly reddish in late summer. *Twigs and branches:* Shredding bark adds slight winter interest.

Problems and Maintenance. This shrub is more trouble-free than most members of the rose family but requires regular pruning to maintain any gracefulness of form. More often than not, it is encountered as a rather ragged specimen for lack of pruning.

Varieties and Cultivars. The var. *intermedius* (synonym: *P. intermedius*) is a low-growing, more compact form, seldom exceeding 1.5 m/5 ft and easily kept below 1 m/3.3 ft with radical renewal pruning (cutting back to short stubs in spring or early summer) every three to five years. Primary function is as a large-scale groundcover, especially for banks, where it tolerates a wide range of soil moisture. The foliage is finer textured than in the species type, giving a much neater effect.

'Dart's Gold' is compact and rounded in habit, 1–1.5 m/3.3–5 ft tall and broad, with bright yellow foliage all summer.

'Luteus' (= 'Aureus') differs from the species type only in its yellow to bronze new foliage, which fades to nearly green by midsummer. It is as coarse as the species type, yet well-pruned

Physocarpus opulifolius var. *intermedius.*

plants with their arching branches make striking specimens as the new foliage emerges.

'Nanus' is as dwarf as var. *intermedius*, originally distinguished from that variety only by its fuzzy fruits and small differences in foliage and form. It may be no more than a form of this variety, and occasional plants sold as the cultivar probably are not distinguishable from var. *intermedius.*

'Nugget,' introduced by South Dakota State University, has dense, compact habit, to 1.5–1.8 m/5–6 ft tall and wide, with fine-textured foliage, emerging golden yellow, bronzing slightly before turning lime-green in summer.

Picea abies 3–8

Synonym *P. excelsa*
N O R W A Y S P R U C E
Evergreen tree or shrub
Pinaceae (Pine Family)

Native Range. Northern and central Europe.

Useful Range. USDA Zones 3a–8a.

Function. Screen, specimen, hedge, corner and foundation planting (dwarf cultivars).

Size and Habit

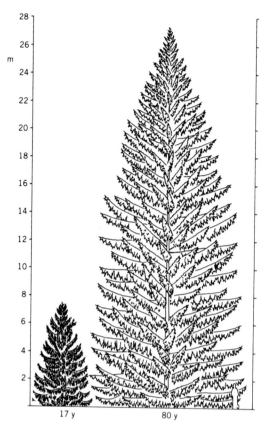

Picea abies.

Adaptability

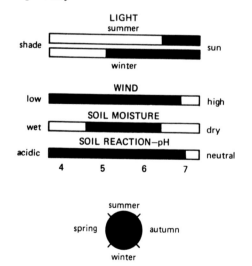

Seasonal Interest. *Foliage:* Evergreen, needle-like, lustrous, and deep green, no more than 2.5

cm/1 in. long, usually shorter, not harsh to the touch, on pendulous branchlets hanging from the ascending main branches. *Cones:* Large, to 15 cm/6 in. long, cylindrical, light brown, with many thin scales, pendulous from upper branches of mature trees.

Problems and Maintenance. This tree is relatively trouble-free, but mites can be troublesome in hot, dry sites, and insect infestation occasionally can require spraying. Pruning is seldom if ever necessary except for hedges. The greatest single limitation of the species type is its ultimate size; frequently it is planted where too little space is available. It is ironic that the greatest limitation to commercial acceptance of the dwarf cultivars is their slow growth.

Cultivars. Several full-sized selections varying in form, foliage color, or branching are known. Most are curiosities or collector's items rather than functional plants. A few of the more easily available ones are listed here.

'Columnaris' is a narrowly columnar selection, useful for screening where ground space is limited.

'Cupressina' is somewhat smaller, to at least 10 m/33 ft in time, more broadly columnar than 'Columnaris' or pyramidal.

'Inversa' is a weeping form to 10 m/33 ft tall, with some branches weeping vertically close to the trunk and others erect and eventually contorted, becoming quite irregular and picturesque, a striking specimen but not especially functional.

'Pendula' is not a single cultivar, but a collective name for several weeping clones. Some of the clones that bear this name are more interesting than others.

'Pyramidata' is tall, with fastigiate branching and narrowly columnar form, useful for a tall screen where ground space is at a premium. This clone may be offered as 'Pyramidalis.'

'Viminalis' grows to at least 20 m/66 ft tall, with main branches like those of the species type and ropelike, vertically pendulous branchlets that give a sparse, open look and eliminate screening as a function of this admittedly interesting tree.

'Virgata,' meaning wandlike, does more than justice to this extremely irregular, sparsely branching form with ropy, snakelike, sometimes intertwining branches. Plants under this name may represent more than one clone, because some are distinctly treelike while others are shrubby.

There are at least 50 dwarf and slow-growing cultivars of *P. abies* in cultivation, many of them similar to each other. The following few are relatively distinctive, useful, and available.

'Clanbrassiliana' is a true dwarf, rounded-pyramidal in form, remaining under 1 m/3.3 ft high and half again as wide for many years, and growing at 2–5 cm/0.8–2 in. annually.

'Gregoryana' is cushionlike and very dwarf, remaining below 0.5 m/1.6 ft for many years, its branches growing only about 2 cm/0.8 in. annually. It is useful as a rock garden plant or in very-small-scale sites.

'Little Gem' is similar to 'Nidiformis' in shape, but slower growing, to 2–3 cm/1 in. annually.

'Maxwellii' is dwarf and cushionlike, to 1 m/3.3 ft high only after many years, growing at 2.5 cm/1 in. annually, with radially arranged, sharp-pointed needles that give a prickly texture.

Picea glauca 'Conica.'

'Nidiformis' (nest spruce) is the most commonly available dwarf cultivar of *P. abies*, with compact horizontal branching, in the shape of a bird's nest, remaining under 1 m/3.3 ft for a decade or two, but eventually approaching 1 m/6.6 ft in height and nearly twice as wide, growing at 2.5–5 cm/1–2 in. annually.

'Remontii' is broadly and fairly regularly conical to rounded, dwarf, growing at about 5 cm/2 in. annually, to at least 1 m/3.3 ft in height in 20 years or so, and eventually reaching 2 m/6.6 ft in height and width.

'Repens' is one of the most distinctive and useful cultivars, with light blue-green foliage and twigs arching outward and downward to face the ground and form a symmetrical, pillowlike mound. It remains under 0.5 m/1.6 ft for at least 15 years while spreading to 1.5 m/5 ft wide, but eventually becomes larger, so it should be considered slow-growing rather than dwarf.

In addition to these, many other cultivars are commercially available, and it is a good idea to check local sources before specifying.

Related Species

Picea asperata 8 (dragon spruce).   This Chinese spruce is similar in general appearances to *P. abies* except that it has foliage prickly to the touch and grows more slowly in our area. It is seldom available but useful in Zones 6a–8a when it can be found.

Picea breweriana 8 (Brewer's spruce).   This majestic native of only a few locales in southwestern Oregon and adjacent California is similar in overall shape to *P. abies*, but more striking for its whiplike, pendulous branchlets, to at least 2 m/6.6 ft long, which give the tree a most graceful appearance. It is probably useful in Zones 6b–8b, but has not been much planted in eastern North America.

Picea glauca 8 (white spruce).   This native North American spruce is similar in general appearance to *P. abies*, but it has much smaller cones, to no more than 5 cm/2 in. long, and usually lighter blue-green foliage. Although it can be substituted for *P. abies* in Zones 2a–7a, and sometimes is, it is slightly less handsome in most sites. The juvenile dwarf, *P. glauca* 'Conica' (dwarf Alberta spruce), is useful for formal effect with tightly conical form and tightly packed, slender needles. Since it grows at a rate of only 3–5 cm/1.2–2 in. per year, it is likely to be expensive, but even small specimens have the desired formal character. Because of the fine-textured juvenile needles, it is more susceptible to winter dehydration than most spruces and is most useful in Zones 5b–7a. The selections 'Arneson Blue' and 'Sander's Blue' are very much like 'Conica' except that they have more bluish-green foliage. Another form of *P. glauca,* once called *P. glauca* var. *densata,* but now reduced to cultivar status as 'Densata' (Black Hills spruce), is rather densely conical, growing much faster than 'Conica' but only half as fast as the species type. It has thick needles, is better adapted to the northern plains than most evergreens, and is widely used in shelter-belt plantings.

Picea mariana 7–8 (black spruce). This North American tree is native from Labrador to Alaska, southward to the northern states, and in the Appalachian Mountains to Virginia. It is often found in bog habitats and, predictably, grows well in wet landscape sites in the North, but is at best a thin, small tree with little landscape function. A few dwarf cultivars (e.g., 'Beissneri' and 'Doumetii') exist and are useful in small scale situations. Useful, with these limitations, in Zones 1b–6b.

Picea rubens 8 (red spruce). This species is native to the northeastern United States and adjacent Canada, from Newfoundland to the North Carolina mountains. It is not a very useful or handsome landscape plant outside the immediate environs of its native habitat and seldom if ever is available commercially. Care should be taken to preserve native stands, however, especially the fragile "Krummholz" or low, shrubby, or cushion forms assumed in mountaintop tree-line climates in the Appalachians.

Picea omorika 8

SERBIAN SPRUCE
Evergreen tree
Pinaceae (Pine Family)

Native Range. Southeastern Europe.

Useful Range. USDA Zones 4b–8a.

Function. Screen, specimen. Requires less space than most spruces because of its narrow habit.

Size and Habit. Most branches are so strongly pendulous that the form of the tree is held to narrowly pyramidal or almost columnar in older trees.

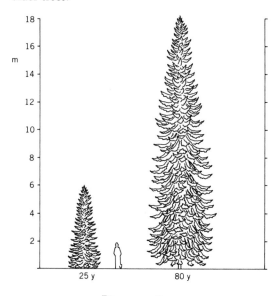

Picea omorika.

Adaptability

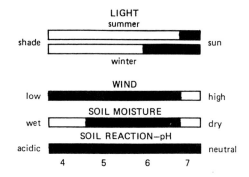

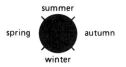

Seasonal Interest. *Foliage:* Evergreen, needle-like, flattened, and sharp-pointed, lustrous, deep green underneath, the upper surface whitened, giving a bicolored appearance. *Cones:* Lustrous, purple, about 5 cm/2 in. long, not an important landscape feature.

Problems and Maintenance. This tree is relatively trouble-free and requires essentially no maintenance other than occasional spraying for mites in warm climates. Foliage winterburns in exposed sites in Zones 4b and 5a in some years.

Cultivars. 'Nana' is a handsome, bright, green-white bicolored true dwarf, densely pyramidal to globose, remaining below 0.5 m/1.6 ft for 15–20 years but probably reaching 1.5 m/5 ft or taller in time. "Pendula" is not a single cultivar, but a collective name for several clones that show a stronger weeping tendency than even that of the species type, but may differ considerably from each other.

Picea orientalis 8

ORIENTAL SPRUCE
Evergreen tree
Pinaceae (Pine Family)

Native Range. Southeastern Europe and Asia Minor.

Useful Range. USDA Zones 5b–8a.

Function. Screen, specimen, hedge.

Size and Habit

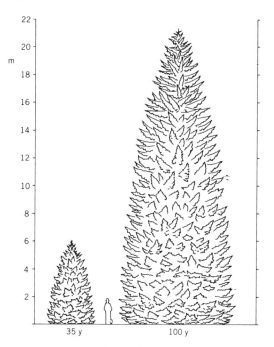

Picea orientalis.

Adaptability

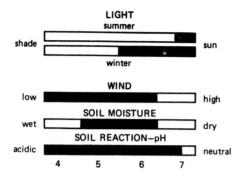

Seasonal Interest. *Foliage:* Evergreen, needle-like, lustrous, and dark green, short and blunt, less than 1 cm/0.4 in. long, on gracefully pendulous branches. *Cones:* Colorful, red-purple as they begin to develop in spring, later turning brown and growing to 6–9 cm/2.4–3.6 in. long.

Problems and Maintenance. This tree is relatively trouble-free and probably superior to *P. abies* in the South (Zones 6b–8a) even with its slower growth. It is not yet widely used or available in most nurseries.

Cultivars. 'Aurea' (= 'Aureospicata') is an upright tree form with ivory-yellow new growth, turning dark green by early summer.

'Aurea Compacta' is compact in growth, 5–8 cm/2–3 in. annually, with yellow foliage in direct sun year-round.

'Compacta' (= Echinoformis') is dwarf and broadly conical in habit, growing to 2 m/6.6 ft in height and width in time.

'Gowdy' is narrower than the species, providing vertical accent, with branches that sweep the ground and short, glossy dark green needles.

'Nigra Compacta' is slow-growing, with compact habit, very wide when young, eventually becoming more upright, with short, dark green needles.

'Skylands' is moderately slow-growing, especially while young, with bright yellow foliage in sun, holding this color year-round.

Picea pungens 8

COLORADO SPRUCE
Evergreen tree
Pinaceae (Pine Family)

Native Range. Rocky Mountains of the western United States and northern Mexico.

Useful Range. USDA Zones 3a–7b.

Function. Screen, specimen.

Size and Habit

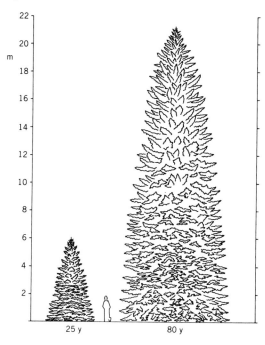

Picea pungens.

Adaptability

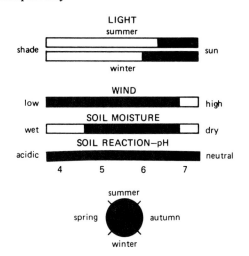

Seasonal Interest. *Foliage:* Evergreen, needle-like, with thick, sharp pointed needles to 3 cm/ 1.2 in. long, spreading radially around the twigs, dull green to striking silvery blue, with all intermediates. *Cones:* Cylindrical, light brown, 6–10 cm/2.4–4 in. long, with many thin scales, not a striking landscape feature.

Problems and Maintenance. Insect and mite infestations occasionally can be serious problems if not controlled, since the formal symmetry of the tree can be destroyed.

Forms and Cultivars. The f. *glauca* includes all trees having a heavy, white and waxy (glaucous) coating over their needles, giving them a more-or-less blue appearance. Such individuals vary widely in color and are not easily or clearly separated from the species type. Seed propagation of f. *glauca,* or any of the blue cultivars, below, yields seedlings ranging from the green of the species type to a wide range of blue and blue-green shades, but few seedlings equal the intensity of blue of the parent. When strikingly blue forms are required for accent, it is necessary to specify vegetatively propagated plants of one of the blue cultivars, even at the somewhat greater cost entailed by grafting or cutting propagation and subsequent nursery care.

'Bakeri' is a full-sized tree with silvery blue needles, darker than those of 'Moerheim.'

'Glauca Globosa' (= 'Globosa') is a more-or-less dwarfed selection with an informally globose outline and distinctly glaucous foliage, reaching a height of about 1 m/3.3 ft and greater spread after 20 to 30 years.

'Glauca Pendula' is strongly pendulous and contorted and is as graceful as this species is capable of being, but highly irregular and eye-catching, eventually reaching a height of at least 2 m/6.6 ft.

'Hoopsii' is one of the most intensely silvery blue forms, growing relatively rapidly for this species.

'Hunnewelliana' is densely pyramidal and slow-growing, with foliage blue-green as it first expands, turning silvery blue later. Plants usually remain below 3 m/10 ft for 20–30 years. This cultivar is not very commonly available.

'Koster,' with silvery white foliage and striking, stiffly formal outline, is one of the most commonly available cultivars.

'Mission Blue' is another full-size clone, fast-growing and similar in appearance to 'Koster'.

'Moerheim' is one of the most popular cultivars, with dense and relatively narrow growth habit and strikingly silvery blue foliage.

'Montgomery' (= 'R. H. Montgomery') is a very slow-growing (6 cm/2.4 in. annually) broadly conical selection, reaching a height of 2 m/6.6 ft and equal or greater width only after many years. Its intensely silvery-blue foliage makes it a striking accent plant.

'Thume' is one of the larger compact forms, with gray-blue foliage, comparable in growth rate to 'Hunnewelliana' but not as blue.

Blue Colorado spruce cultivars are frequently misused by planting them in quantity rather than for specific landscape accent. For screens and other mass plantings, there are better choices.

Related Species

Picea engelmannii 8 (Engelmann spruce). This tree from the Rocky Mountain region is similar to the closely related *P. pungens*, but its bluer forms are slightly softer and less positive in appearance. Useful in Zones 3a–7b and possibly in Zone 2, but seldom available commercially in eastern North America.

Pieris floribunda 4

MOUNTAIN ANDROMEDA
Evergreen shrub
Ericaceae (Heath Family)

Native Range. Virginia to Georgia.

Useful Range. USDA Zones 5a–7b, sites with reliable snow cover in Zone 4, and sites with mild, moist summers in Zone 8.

Function. Border, specimen, massing.

Size and Habit

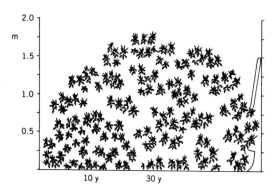

Pieris floribunda.

Adaptability. Needs protection from full winter sun in the North (Zones 4–5). For best growth, the soil must be acidic and extremely well drained yet not excessively dry.

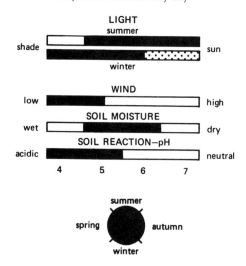

Seasonal Interest. *Flowers:* Waxy white, resembling those of lily of the valley, in semierect clusters 5–10 cm/2–4 in. long in early to middle spring. *Foliage:* Evergreen, lustrous, leathery, and deep green, making a loose mass of interesting texture. *Fruits:* Small, round capsules, green in summer, ripening dull brown, not a significant landscape feature. Moreover, if allowed to develop, they repress formation of flower buds for the following year.

Problems and Maintenance. This plant is relatively trouble-free in good sites, but a stem-rot disease has become a serious problem in some areas, especially where soil drainage and air circulation are not perfect. In northern areas, foliage can be damaged if plants are exposed to sweeping winds and full sun in winter. Pruning is necessary to remove deadwood and occasionally for light shaping of the plant. Removal of old flower heads immediately after flowering, called dead-heading, promotes formation of new flower buds for the following year.

Cultivars and Hybrids. 'Millstream' is low-growing and compact, with good annual flowering, even when fruits and seeds are allowed to develop. In 15 years, plants can be expected to grow to a height of 0.5 m/1.6 ft and a width of 1–1.5 m/3.3–5 ft, under good conditions.

'Brouwer's Beauty' is a hybrid of *P. floribunda* and *P. japonica*, growing to about 1.5 m/5 ft tall and at least as broad, under good conditions, with fairly showy red-purple winter flower buds, opening as horizontally arching clusters of white flowers. Probably useful at least in Zones 5b–8a, perhaps also Zone 5a in protected sites or with heavy snow cover.

'Karenoma' is another hybrid of the same parentage as 'Brouwer's Beauty,' with red winter flower buds, opening to white flowers in upright panicles, and bronze-red new foliage. Probably useful in Zones 5b–8a, perhaps also Zone 5a in protected sites.

Related Species

Pieris phillyreifolia 1 and 3.   This native vine or shrub of swamps and other wetlands of Alabama, Florida, and Georgia has been reintroduced into cultivation and is commercially available. It can be a climber in native habitat, moving up tree trunks with its stems virtually imbedded in the bark, but functions as a small shrub in landscape use. In spite of its wet native habitats, it will also grow well in acid soils of normal moisture given proper care. It is useful in Zone 9a+, and perhaps in Zone 8 as well.

Pieris japonica 4–5

JAPANESE ANDROMEDA
Evergreen shrub
Ericaceae (Heath Family)

Native Range.   Japan.

Useful Range.   USDA Zones 6a–8a, protected sites in Zone 5, and moist, cool sites in Zones 8b–9a+.

Function.   Border, specimen, screen (under ideal growing conditions).

Size and Habit

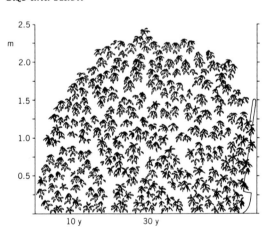

Pieris japonica.

Adaptability.   Needs protection from full winter sun in the North (Zones 5–6).

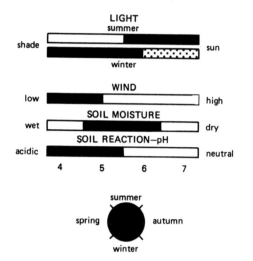

Seasonal Interest.   Flowers: Dormant flower buds are more or less reddish, adding additional winter color. The flowers open waxy white, resembling those of lily of the valley, in pendulous clusters up to 12 cm/5 in. long, displayed effectively against the dark green foliage in early spring. *Foliage:* Evergreen foliage first emerges glossy red, bronze, or yellow-green, then turns deep green and lustrous for the remainder of the year. *Fruits:* Small, round capsules, green in summer, ripening dull brown, not a significant feature in the landscape. If allowed to develop, they may interfere with formation of flower buds for the following year.

Problems and Maintenance.   The most serious problem of this shrub in northern areas is dehydration by winter sun and wind. Sites should be selected carefully to avoid exposure to sweeping winds and strongest sun. Damaged plants may be invaded by secondary disease organisms. The greatest limitation is moisture in the South, where irrigation is needed regularly. Insects such as lace bugs and mites can be troublesome at times, but are less so in sites with adequate moisture. Pruning is necessary to remove deadwood and occasionally for light shaping of the plant. Removal of old flower heads immediately after color fades (dead-heading) allows formation of new flower buds for the following year.

Cultivars and Hybrids.   More than 40 cultivars have been selected and named, and selection of new forms continues. A few of the best and most available are listed here.

'Dorothy Wyckoff' has dark red winter flower buds that turn lighter red as they swell in early spring and then clear pink to white as they open. The foliage is dark green, taking on a reddish bronze color in winter.

'Flamingo' is a heavy bloomer with deep rose-red flowers.

'Flaming Silver,' originating as a genetic sport of the hybrid, 'Forest Flame,' is similar except for its white-margined foliage and somewhat slower growth. Useful in Zones 7b–9a, probably also Zone 7a.

'Forest Flame' is a hybrid of *P. japonica* and *P. formosa* var. *forrestii* 'Wakehurst' (see Related Species). Growing to about 2 m/6.6 ft high and wide, it is notable because its new foliage emerges bright orange-red, then reverts to green through pink and whitish stages. It also has large flower clusters and excellent form and is useful in Zones 7a–9a, and Zone 6b with careful siting.

'Grayswood,' introduced by Brookside Gardens, is vigorous, forming a large mound, with bronze new growth, and is free-flowering, with unusually long clusters of white flowers. Useful range probably as for the species.

'Mountain Fire' is a compact form, to 1.2–1.8 m/4–6 ft high and broad, with the reddest new foliage of any *P. japonica* selection, rivaling 'Forest Flame,' and flowering heavily as well. Useful range as for the species.

'Pygmaea' is dwarf in habit, growing to 1.2–1.5 m/4–5 ft high and somewhat wider in time, with small, narrow, glossy leaves giving a very

Pieris japonica.

fine, feathery foliage texture. It seldom flowers well but is useful for its size and foliage effect in the same range as the species.

'Scarlet O'Hara' is a full-sized selection with red new foliage and red-speckled creamy white flowers. Useful range as for the species.

'Snowdrift' is probably a selection from the Taiwan population of the species, once called *P. taiwanensis* but now included under *P. japonica.* This cultivar grows to 1.5–1.8 m/5–6 ft tall and 1.2–1.5 m/4–5 ft wide, with large and very showy pure-white flowers. Useful at least in Zones 7a–9a, perhaps also Zone 6b.

'Temple Bells,' a selection from the Ryukyu Islands, grows to 1.5–1.8 m/5–6 ft tall and wide, with horizontal branching, light green new foliage that soon turns apricot, bronze, then dark red-bronze, and finally green in summer, and large white flowers. Useful at least in Zones 7a–9a, perhaps also Zone 6b.

'Valley Rose,' originating in the breeding program of Dr. Robert L. Ticknor at the Willamette Valley Research Station of Oregon State University, has an excellent mounded habit and dark rose winter flower buds, opening light pink. Useful range probably as for the species.

'Valley Valentine,' another Ticknor introduction, has compact, mounded habit, to 1.5 m/5 ft high and wide, with the brightest red flowers of any *P. japonica* cultivar. Useful range /as for the species.

'Variegata' is notable for its white-margined leaves, somewhat smaller than those of the species type, and is somewhat slower growing but by no means dwarf, eventually growing to 1.5–2 m/

Pieris japonica 'Variegata.'

5–6.6 ft tall and broad. Useful range as for the species.

'White Cascade,' a full-sized selection, flowers heavily, with long pendulous clusters of long-lasting white flowers, sometimes remaining colorful for four to five weeks. Useful range as for the species.

Related Species

Pieris formosa var. *forrestii* 5 (synonym: *P. forrestii;* Chinese or Forrest pieris). This handsome plant from China and the Himalayas has large, lightly fragrant white flowers, in pendulous clusters to 15 cm/6 in. long, and bright red new foliage. The selection 'Wakehurst' has broader leaves, even brighter red in the immature stage than the species type, and is useful in Zone 8 (perhaps also 7b) and relatively cool, moist sites in Zone 9a+.

Pinus aristata 4–6

BRISTLECONE PINE
Evergreen shrub or small tree
Pinaceae (Pine Family)

Native Range. High mountains of the south-western United States.

Useful Range. USDA Zones 4a–7a, probably Zone 3 as well.

Function. Specimen for accent.

Size and Habit

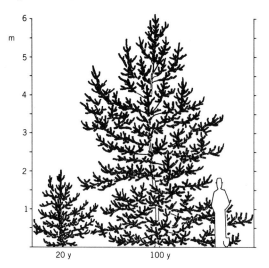

Pinus aristata.

Adaptability

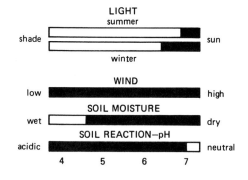

Seasonal Interest. *Foliage:* Evergreen and persisting for several years, dark green, the needles in fascicles of five, packed tightly on sparsely branching stems, giving an irregular, picturesque form. White resin dots on needles are normal but may be confused with scale insects.

Problems and Maintenance. Slow growth is this plant's most serious limitation in landscape use, yet it is also the greatest source of landscape value. Trees are very long-lived and remain in scale in landscape situations for a great many years. Wild trees on west-facing slopes of the White Mountains of California are known to be at least 4000 years old and are thought by some to be the oldest living trees on earth, surpassing even the sequoias.

Cultivars. A few dwarf and prostrate selections have been made, but they are seldom available.

Pinus banksiana 8

JACK PINE
Evergreen tree
Pinaceae (Pine Family)

Native Range. Far northern and northeastern North America.

Useful Range. USDA Zones 2a–6a.

Function. Massing or large-scale screening on dry sites.

Size and Habit

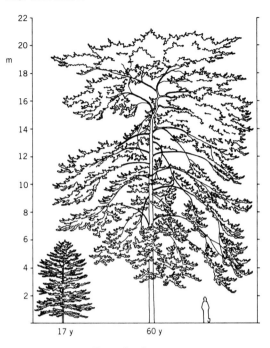

Pinus banksiana.

Adaptability

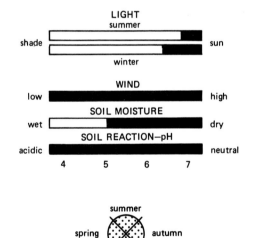

Seasonal Interest. *Foliage:* Evergreen, medium green to yellow-green needles are short (averaging 2.5–3.5 cm/1–1.4 in. long), in fascicles of two, arranged sparsely and persisting for only 2–4 years. Foliage usually is fuller and more handsome in the northern parts of the useful range than in the southern parts, but even there turns yellowish in winter. *Cones:* Lustrous, yellow-brown, 2.5–5 cm/1–2 in. long, persisting on the tree for several years but adding little to its landscape interest.

Problems and Maintenance. This tree is relatively trouble-free and requires little maintenance. Needle-fall is so light that it provides little mulch, so weed encroachment may be a problem. But in the large-scale dry sites where this tree is most useful, weed growth is not strong enough to be very competitive or objectionable visually.

Cultivars. Several selections have been made for dwarfness, from witch's-broom seedlings, but they are not widely available. Some are low, moundlike forms, useful in small-scale plantings in very cold climates. Availability of other selections for fastigiate growth habit and varying foliage color is similarly limited. 'Uncle Fogey,' a contorted semidwarf weeping form, is an interesting accent plant for cold climates.

Related Species

Pinus contorta 6–8 (shore pine).   This native of the Pacific Northwest from Alaska to California and eastward to Colorado exists in two principal types:

The var. *contorta,* the species type from Pacific coastal areas, is an interesting, contorted, low-growing tree that reaches heights of 4–8 m/13–26 ft. It is valued on the West Coast, especially in Japanese gardens, where it seems appropriate in spite of its North American origin. It has been used very little in the eastern United States and may not be adapted to the climate of any of our area.

The var. *latifolia* (lodgepole pine), the mountain counterpart, grows wild farther inland, is a much larger tree, to 20 m/65 ft or sometimes more than 30 m/98 ft, and is relatively narrow in outline. Even though it is not commonly used in eastern North America and may be less useful than native species, it is at least reasonably well adapted here in Zones 5b–8a.

Pinus bungeana 6–7

LACEBARK PINE
Evergreen tree
Pinaceae (Pine Family)

Native Range.   Northern China.

Useful Range.   USDA Zones 5a–9a. Limited to areas with moderate summer temperatures in Zones 8 and 9.

Size and Habit.   Grows slowly and remains shrubby for many years.

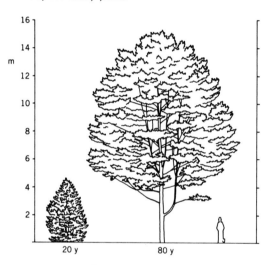

Pinus bungeana.

Adaptability

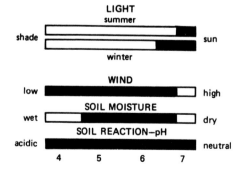

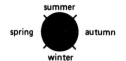

Seasonal Interest.   Foliage: Evergreen, medium green needles, 5–10 cm/2–4 in. long, in fascicles of three, persistent for only 3–4 years and seldom dense enough to make an effective visual screen. *Trunk and branches:* Bark is smooth, and on branches more than about 5–10 cm/2–4 in. across it flakes off in large, irregular, rounded patches, giving a gray, green, and off-white tricolored effect.

Pinus bungeana.

Problems and Maintenance.   Bark interest, the primary reason for using this tree, seldom becomes significant until the tree is at least 10–15 years old, and the tree has little interest as a specimen until that time. Careful pruning to expose the bark more fully may be desirable. Otherwise, the tree is relatively free of maintenance and troubles.

Related Species

Pinus edulis 6–7 (pinyon or nut pine).   This native of the southwestern United States, from

Wyoming and Texas to California, has been considered in the past to be a variety of *P. cembroides*. It is especially valued as a landscape plant in the southwestern edges of our area in Zones 5a–8a (Kansas to Texas), as well as for its edible seeds.

Pinus cembra 6–8

SWISS STONE PINE
Evergreen tree
Pinaceae (Pine Family)

Native Range. Central Europe to northern Asia.

Useful Range. USDA Zones 3b–6b and high elevations (with moderate summers) in Zone 7 with selection of appropriate genetic material.

Function. Specimen, screen (in time).

Size and Habit

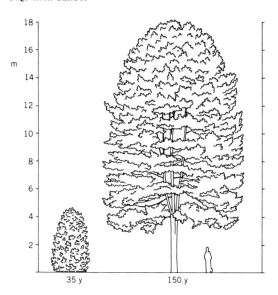

Pinus cembra.

Adaptability

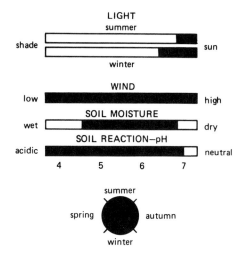

Seasonal Interest. *Foliage:* Evergreen, dense, with needles in fascicles of five, usually 5–10 cm/2–4 in. long, occasionally longer, retained for four to five years, dark green with whitened stomatal lines evident.

Problems and Maintenance. This tree is relatively trouble-free and requires little or no maintenance. Its principal limitation is its slow

Pinus cembra.

growth, and it is most useful in small-scale landscapes.

Cultivars. Several selections have been made for form, foliage color, or dwarfness. These are primarily of interest to collectors, but work equally well for accent in small-scale landscapes. Among the most popular and available are: 'Compacta Glauca' (= 'Compact'?), with even more compact growth than the species type; 'Nana,' a tightly pyramidal dwarf; and 'Pygmaea,' a dwarf, beehive-shaped form that remains under 1.5 m/5 ft for years.

Pinus pumila.

Subspecies and Related Species

Pinus cembra ssp. *sibirica* 8 (synonym: *P. sibirica;* Siberian pine). This tree from Siberia and adjacent Russia is faster growing than the species type, ssp. *cembra,* becoming 30–40 m/98–131 ft tall under ideal conditions. It is useful in the North, in at least Zones 2b–5b, but is seldom commercially available.

Pinus koraiensis 8 (Korean pine). This 5-needled pine from Korea resembles *P. strobus* but with somewhat more layered branching when young and slightly larger needles, spreading more widely. This tree is gaining recognition as one of the most beautiful and useful pines for northern climates (at least Zones 4a–7b) and is becoming more easily available. A few color variants are marginally available, and primarily of interest to collectors.

Pinus pumila 4–5 (dwarf stone pine). This spreading shrub is usually seen below 1.5 m/5 ft,

Pinus pumila.

but in time can reach 2–3 m/6.6–10 ft in height, with even greater spread. Native to northeastern Siberia and Japan, it has been in cultivation in our area for many years but still is not widely available. Useful in Zones 4a–7a, perhaps also Zone 3.

Pinus densiflora 7–8

JAPANESE RED PINE
Evergreen tree
Pinaceae (Pine Family)

Native Range. Japan.

Useful Range. USDA Zones 5b–7b, and northward to Zone 4b with careful selection of genetic material.

Function. Specimen, massing.

Size and Habit

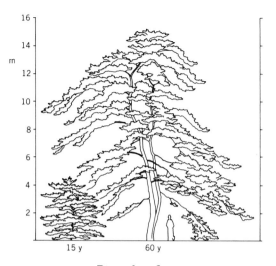

Pinus densiflora

Adaptability

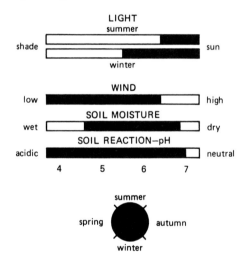

Seasonal Interest. *Foliage:* Evergreen, usually rather sparse, bright bluish to olive green with slender needles, mostly 8–10 cm/3–4 in. long, occasionally longer, in fascicles of two, persisting for three years. *Cones:* Yellow-brown, to 5 cm/2 in. long, persisting on the tree for two or three years. *Trunk and branches:* Bark on large branches and trunks is distinctly orange-red, adding interest at all seasons. This and the picturesque growth habit are the distinctive reasons for using this species.

Problems and Maintenance. This tree usually is trouble-free and requires little maintenance. Growth is relatively slow for a pine, but not slow enough to discourage its use.

Cultivars. 'Oculus-draconis' (dragon's eye pine) is unusual for its variegated needles, each with two yellow bands. It is useful primarily as a striking specimen while young and is slower growing than the species type. Useful in Zones 6a–7b.

'Pendula' (weeping Japanese red pine) is a vigorous, strongly weeping form with very long needles, an impressive accent plant.

'Umbraculifera' (Tanyosho pine) has many branches in a vase shaped arrangement and a foliage canopy more flattened even than the species type and umbrella like. The striking branching is accentuated by the orange-red bark. Slower growing than the species type, but ultimately reaches heights of 3–4 m/10–13 ft in Zones 5b–7b.

Pinus densiflora 'Umbraculifera.'

Several dwarf cultivars are available to a limited extent and are of interest to collectors.

Related Species

Pinus thunbergii 6–7 (synonym: *P. thunbergiana*; Japanese black pine). This picturesque tree, occasionally growing to 20 m/66 ft or taller in native habitat in Japan and Korea, seldom exceeds 10 m/33 ft in landscape use in our area. Its irregular, open form gives it distinctive character, and its tolerance of salt spray and wind makes it especially useful in coastal sites in Zones

6a–9a, but it does not do well in poorly drained soil or in sites that are periodically flooded. Many variants in form, color, and dwarfness have been selected, but few are commercially available. 'Monina' (Majestic Beauty™, Plant Patent No. 5078, 1983) is dense and compact, with dark foliage, remaining green year-round, and reportedly tolerant of air pollution. 'Oculus-draconis' has banded needle variegation similar to that of *P. densiflora* 'Oculus-draconis' but is seldom available. 'Thunderhead' is dwarf and densely compact, with dark green mature needles that serve as background for the white candles (immature shoots), a striking effect.

Pinus flexilis 8

LIMBER PINE
Evergreen tree
Pinaceae (Pine Family)

Native Range. Mountains of western United States and adjacent Canada.

Useful Range. USDA Zones 4b–7b with selection of appropriate genetic material.

Function. Specimen, screen.

Size and Habit

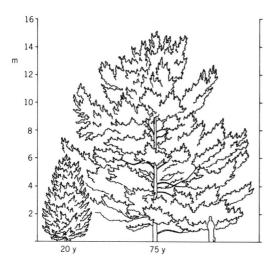

Pinus flexilis.

Adaptability. Better adapted to dry soil and windy sites than the related *P. strobus.*

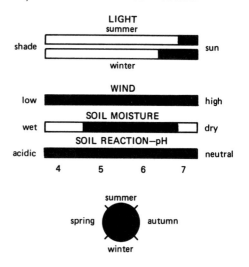

Seasonal Interest. *Foliage:* Evergreen, blue-green, fine-textured but making a dense mass, with slender needles, 3.5–8 cm/1.4–3 in. long, in fascicles of five, persisting for five years. Foliage of some trees is twisted, giving texture similar to that of *Pinus parviflora* 'Glauca.' *Cones:* Light brown and lustrous, to 15 cm/6 in. long. *Trunk and branches:* Branches are very flexible, covered with dark greenish gray bark; trunk bark is roughened, dark gray.

Problems and Maintenance. This tree is trouble-free and requires little or no maintenance but is rather slow-growing. It is noticeably less susceptible to winterburn and salt injury than most other five-needled pines.

Cultivars. 'Glauca Pendula' is semipendulous, vigorously spreading over the ground unless

Pinus flexilis.

it is shrubby to prostrate at high elevations, occasionally has found its way into landscape use in Zones 4a–7a, but it is much less likely to be available in our area than the related *P. flexilis*. It receives its name from its distinctly whitened bark.

Pinus strobiformis 8 (southwestern white pine). This species, native to an area stretching from southern Colorado to central Mexico, is a southern counterpart of *P. flexilis*, growing to more than 25 m/83 ft tall. Trees of this species have succeeded in southwestern Michigan. However, because of the wide north–south range of this species, it is probably important to use genetic material from as close as possible to the latitude where it will be planted. Assuming this is done, the useful range for this species probably includes at least parts of Zones 5b–9a. At least some trees of this species have tightly clustered needles that provide an elegant texture similar to that of *P. parviflora* 'Glauca.'

grafted on a standard, with good blue color. 'Glenmore' is highly glaucous, silvery blue in color, and pyramidal, selected and used in Colorado but not common farther east. 'Vanderwolf's Pyramid' is a dense but vigorous form, growing to at least 5 m/16 ft tall, with excellent blue-green foliage.

Related Species

Pinus albicaulis 6 (white bark pine).   This native of the mountains of the Pacific Northwest, where

Pinus mugo 4–8

Synonym: *P. montana*
MUGHO OR MOUNTAIN PINE
Evergreen shrub
Pinaceae (Pine Family)

Native Range.   Mountains of southern Europe.

Useful Range.   USDA Zones 3a–7b.

Function.   Foundation, massing, specimen, border.

Size and Habit.   Growth rate and height are highly variable, even when plants of the dwarf variety are specified (see Varieties and Cultivars).

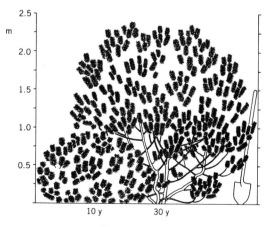

Pinus mugo.

Adaptability

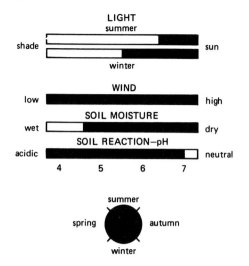

Seasonal Interest. *Foliage:* Evergreen, dense, with thick, dark green needles, 3–8 cm/1.2–3.2 in. long, in fascicles of two, persisting for four years or longer in some plants. *Cones:* Dull brown, to 6 cm/2.4 in. long.

Problems and Maintenance. This shrub is often trouble-free, requiring little maintenance, but insects (pine shoot moth, mugho pine scale) occasionally are troublesome in some areas. Fol-

low local experience. Growth is usually rather slow, but this is seldom as much a problem as the overly fast, rank growth of seedlings that were expected to remain low and compact.

Subspecies and Cultivars

P. mugo ssp. *mugo* 4–6. This is the more-or-less shrubby species type of mugho pine, with ascending branches and growing to 1–5 m/3.3–16 ft tall. Within this range, seedlings vary widely in growth rate and compactness. When plants that will remain low are needed, it is best at least to specify var. *mugo* or var. *pumilio*, questionable categories that usually include seedlings from relatively compact parents, not growing over 1.5–2 m/5–6.6 ft tall. If uniformity is important, it is much better to specify cloned dwarf cultivars such as 'Aurea,' 'Hessei,' 'Prostrata,' or 'Valley Cushion.' Somewhat larger forms, still not growing taller than 1.5–2 m/5–6.6 ft, are 'Enci,' 'Gnome,' and 'Mops.'

P. mugo ssp. *uncinata* 7–8 (synonyms: *P. mugo* var. *rostrata, P. uncinata*). This is similar to ssp. *mugo* in foliage characteristics and adaptation but not in function, since this is an upright tree to 20 m/66 ft tall. This tree is seldom available except as seeds and has little advantage over many other pines.

Pinus nigra 8

BLACK PINE
Evergreen tree
Pinaceae (Pine Family)

Native Range. Central and southern Europe and adjacent Asia.

Useful Range. USDA Zones 4a–8a with selection of appropriate genetic material.

Function. Specimen, screen, windbreak.

Size and Habit

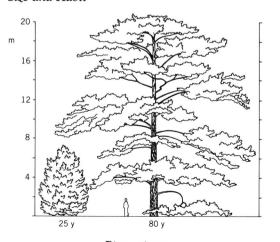

Pinus nigra.

Adaptability. Tolerates city situations better than most other pines.

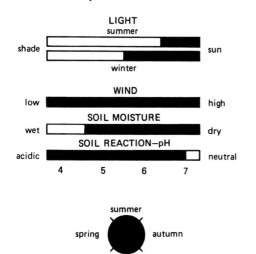

Seasonal Interest. *Foliage:* Evergreen, dense, with thick, dark green needles, 8–15 cm/3–5 in. long, in fascicles of two, persistent for three years. *Cones:* Shiny, yellow-brown, to 8 cm/3 in. long, persisting for two years. *Trunk:* Bark of large trees is coarsely marked with irregular plates, deep gray-brown and almost white.

Problems and Maintenance. This tree has serious disease problems in some areas, especially a twig blight *(Diplodia)*, and it can be severely damaged by sapsuckers. It may require spraying as well as removal of cone and twig litter. Its use as a screen is limited to the first decade or two of its life, since its lower branches usually remain no longer than this. Top pruning may lengthen this period somewhat.

Subspecies and Varieties

Several subspecies and varieties have been described over this species' wide range in southern Europe. The ssp. *nigra* (synonym: *P. nigra* var. *austriaca;* Austrian pine) is the typical form of the species, and the one ordinarily encountered in landscape use in North America.

Pinus palustris 8

LONGLEAF PINE
Evergreen tree
Pinaceae (Pine Family)

Native Range. Southeastern United States.

Useful Range. USDA Zones 7b–9a+.

Function. Specimen, massing, shade tree.

Size and Habit

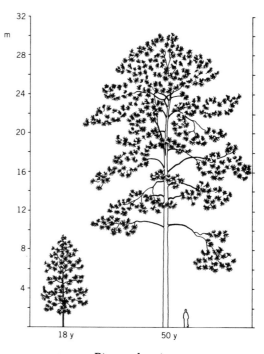

Pinus palustris.

Adaptability

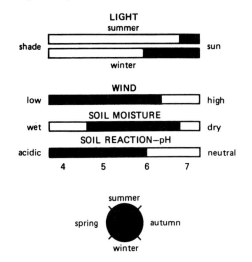

Seasonal Interest. *Foliage:* Evergreen with bright green needles, 20–40 cm/8–16 in. long, usually in fascicles of three, in "tufts" of many fascicles giving an open, picturesque appearance. *Cones:* Large, 15–30 cm/6–12 in. long, add interest but considerable litter. *Trunk:* Orange-brown, plated bark adds interest to large trees.

Problems and Maintenance. This tree is generally trouble-free, but in the colder parts of its useful range occasional snow and ice can break branches and destroy the form of the tree. Slow growth during the first three years can be discouraging, but an extensive root system is formed during this period, and later growth is rapid. Cones cause a modest litter problem.

Related Species

Pinus elliottii 8 (slash pine). This native of the southeastern Coastal Plain differs from *P. palustris* in having somewhat shorter needles (15–25 cm/6–10 in.) in fascicles of two and three, with less "tufting." Like *P. palustris*, it is a tall, upright tree, to 30 m/98 ft. It is useful in Zones 8b–9a+ and performs best in those areas where it is native: coastal Mississippi to southern South Carolina.

Pinus glabra 8 (spruce pine). This tree is native to much of the same area as *P. elliottii* and *P. palustris*. It, too, is a tall tree, but differs in being a little slower growing and more tolerant of wet soils, but does not grow well in coastal sites. Its foliage is finer textured than that of the other species, with slender, twisted needles to 8 cm/3 in. long, mostly in fascicles of two. In spite of its slender needles, it produces a dense mass of foliage, effective for screening.

Pinus ponderosa 8

PONDEROSA OR WESTERN YELLOW PINE
Evergreen tree
Pinaceae (Pine Family)

Native Range. Western United States and adjacent Canada and Mexico.

Useful Range. USDA Zones 3b–8a with selection of appropriate genetic material.

Function. Specimen, screen, windbreak.

Size and Habit

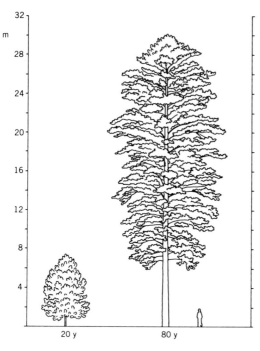

Pinus ponderosa.

Adaptability. Frequently does not perform as well in eastern North America as pines that are native here, but worth trying in problem areas, especially in the Central Plains.

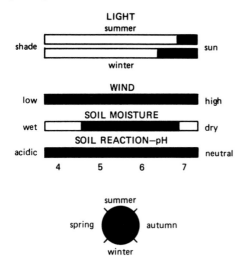

Seasonal Interest. *Foliage:* Evergreen with deep green needles, 10–25 cm/4–10 in., in fascicles of two and three, persisting for three years. *Cones:* Reddish or yellowish brown and lustrous with curved spines (umbos) on the outside of the scales, 8–15 cm/3–6 in. long. *Trunk:* Yellow-brown to cinnamon-brown bark is irregularly and lightly fissured on older trees.

Problems and Maintenance. This tree is relatively trouble-free and requires little or no maintenance, but a disease of the needle fascicles occasionally can be troublesome, especially in humid areas. Cones constitute a minor litter problem, and this is one of the most difficult pines to transplant.

Related Species

Pinus jeffreyi 8 (Jeffrey pine). This species from high elevations in California and adjacent Nevada and Oregon is very similar to *P. ponderosa* and functionally equivalent, but it is much less likely to be commercially available.

Pinus resinosa 8

RED PINE, NORWAY PINE (so-called in spite of its native origin)

Evergreen tree

Pinaceae (Pine Family)

Native Range.   North-central and northeastern United States and adjacent Canada.

Useful Range.   USDA Zones 3a–6b.

Function.   Screen, specimen, windbreak.

Size and Habit

Adaptability

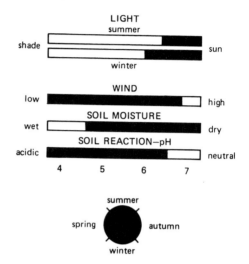

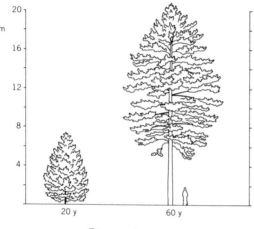

Pinus resinosa.

Seasonal Interest.   *Foliage:* Medium to yellow-green with soft texture and slender needles, 12–18 cm/5–7 in. long, in fascicles of two, sometimes persisting for four years. *Cones:* Brown, about 5 cm/2 in. long, ripening the first year, persisting for two to three years, but not adding significant interest. *Trunk and branches:* Inner bark is reddish brown.

Problems and Maintenance.   This tree is relatively trouble-free and requires little or no maintenance other than removal of cone litter.

Varieties.   No varieties and very few cultivars are known, although occasionally columnar or globose forms can be found. This species is notable among the pines for its low variability.

Pinus strobus 8

EASTERN WHITE PINE

Evergreen tree

Pinaceae (Pine Family)

Native Range.   North-central and northeastern United States, and adjacent Canada, and southward in the Appalachian Mountains to Georgia.

Useful Range.   USDA Zones 3a–9a with selection of appropriate genetic material.

Function.   Specimen, shade tree, screen, hedge.

Size and Habit

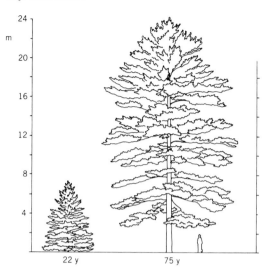

Pinus strobus.

Adaptability. Grows best in good soil of moderate moisture content. Not a good choice for roadsides, urban plantings, very dry or windswept areas (see Problems and Maintenance), or for planting in heavy soils.

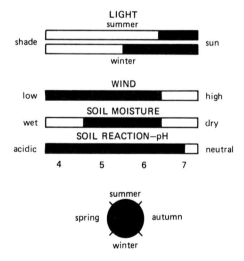

Seasonal Interest. *Foliage:* Evergreen, soft, blue-green, fine textured with very slender needles, 5–12 cm/2–5 in. long, persisting for three years. *Cones:* Dull brown, cylindrical, 8–20 cm/3–8 in. long, persisting for two years or longer. *Trunk and branches:* Bark on branches is smooth, olive green to gray; trunk bark is smoother than that of most pines, dark gray.

Problems and Maintenance. This is one of the most satisfactory and trouble-free evergreen trees in most of our area, except for urban centers. White pine blister rust is a serious disease that has been eliminated largely from the native range by the elimination of its alternate host, certain species of *Ribes* (currants). Foliage is subject to winter desiccation. Recently transplanted trees are especially sensitive but usually recover after establishment. This tree is very sensitive to road salt and ocean salt spray.

Cultivars. Nearly 100 cultivars are commercially available, but most of these are offered by very few specialists. The following are among the most popular and generally available:

'Blue Shag' is a dwarf, mounding form, to 1–1.5 m/3.3–5 ft tall and 2 m/6.6 ft across in time, with short, bluish needles.

'Fastigiata' is a full-sized tree, nearly columnar when young but broadening with age to become narrowly pyramidal and eventually oval in shape.

'Golden Candles' is an upright tree, distinctive for its golden new growth, which doesn't fade completely for several months.

'Horsford Dwarf' is truly dwarf, forming a

Pinus strobus 'Fastigiata.'

tight mound with long needles, making an excellent specimen for accent.

"Nana" is not a single cultivar, since the name has been applied to several clones, most probably or perhaps all originating as witch's-broom seedlings. Plants so labeled are usually dwarf, remaining below 1 m/3.3 ft in height and somewhat greater spread for many years. Other clones of this type are sold under cultivar names such as 'Brevifolia,' 'Globosa,' 'Pygmaea,' and 'Umbraculifera.'

'Pendula' is a graceful, strongly pendulous plant that reaches heights of at least 3 m/10 ft in 20 years or so. This clone sometimes grows in one direction, until its center of gravity is quite some distance from the trunk. This can be avoided by careful early pruning.

'White Mountain' is upright and pyramidal in shape, with strongly silvery-blue foliage, a very striking tree.

Related Species

Pinus ayacahuite 8 (Mexican white pine).   This native of the mountains of Mexico can be a very large tree in its native habitat (to 30–40 m/99–132 ft) but is no larger than *P. monticola, P. strobus,* or *P. wallichiana* in landscape use. Useful in Zones 6a–9a, with selection of appropriate genetic material, but not widely available.

Pinus lambertiana 8 (sugar pine).   This handsome tree reaches heights of more than 60 m/200 ft in its native habitat in California and is notable for its huge cones, to 50 cm/20 in. long. Seldom used or available in eastern North America, it probably could be used in areas protected from strong wind in Zones 6b–8a.

Pinus monticola 8 (western white pine).   This close relative of *P. strobus* from the Pacific Northwest is somewhat denser in growth habit but not distinctive enough to justify selecting it over the native *P. strobus* in eastern North America. It is potentially useful in Zones 5a–6b and perhaps farther south as well, but it is seldom available at present.

Pinus sylvestris 7–8

SCOTS PINE
Evergreen tree
Pinaceae (Pine Family)

Native Range.   Europe through Siberia.

Useful Range.   USDA Zones 3a–8b with selection of appropriate genetic material.

Function.   Specimen, massing, screen (when young).

Size and Habit

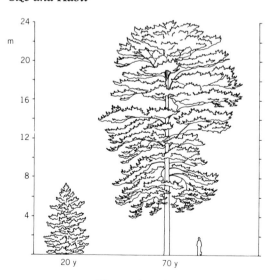

Pinus sylvestris.

Adaptability. Grows best in reasonably fertile soil but tolerates relatively infertile soil as well as wet or dry sites.

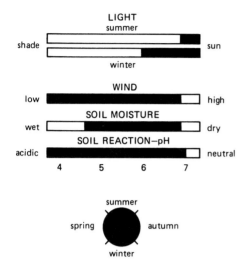

Seasonal Interest. *Foliage:* Evergreen, blue-green to yellow-green, with flattened and twisted needles, 2.5–8 cm/1–3 in. long, in fascicles of two, persisting for three years. *Cones:* Yellowish brown, 2.5–8 cm/1–3 in. long, falling at maturity. *Trunk and branches:* Inner bark is bright orange-tan, adding year-round interest to mature trees.

Problems and Maintenance. This tree is subject to a twig blight disease (*Diplodia*) that can be a serious problem if not controlled, especially in humid climates. Pruning is needed to control size and maintain fullness in screen plantings. Otherwise, screens become open and nonfunctional with age.

Cultivars. More than 50 cultivars are in commerce, but many of those are not at all common. A few of the most useful and available are listed here.

'Beuvronensis' (often misspelled "Beauvronensis") is densely but irregularly broad-globose, remaining below 0.5 m/1.6 ft for at least 20 years, with blue-green foliage.

'Compressa' (= 'Nana Compressa'?) is a dwarf but is upright in habit, with very short needles tightly appressed to the stems, growing slowly with clustered needles.

'Fastigiata' is tall and narrowly pyramidal, with height/width ratio about 5:1, holding this nearly columnar form much longer than *P. strobus* 'Fastigiata.'

'Globosa Viridis' is upright and broadly pyramidal, but dwarf, with rich, deep green foliage that holds its color in winter.

'Hillside Creeper' is a creeping form, to about 0.5 m/1.6 ft high and spreading vigorously, with blue-green foliage, turning a good yellow-green in winter.

'Nana' (= 'Glauca Nana') is flattened-globose in form and semi-dwarf, growing to about 1 m/3.3 ft in 10 years, with deep blue-green foliage. Old plants can reach 2–3 m/6.6–10 ft in height and twice that in spread. Plants labeled 'Nana' may actually be 'Watereri.'

'Watereri' is broadly ovate to globose in shape, growing slowly but eventually exceeding 3–4 m/10–13 ft in height and twice that in spread, with silvery blue-green foliage.

Some of the available cultivars and seed lines are sold primarily for Christmas tree production, but they may also yield superior landscape forms.

Related Species

Pinus brutia 8 (Turkish or Calabrian pine). This native of a large area from Greece and Turkey to Lebanon and the Black Sea coast is of little interest in our area except for its ssp. *eldarica* (Eldar or Afghan pine) which, because of its extreme drought resistance, is of great interest in New Mexico and other parts of the southwestern United States, potentially including the southwestern extremes of our area (central Texas). Useful at least in Zones 7b–9a, perhaps also Zone 7a.

Pinus halepensis 7 (Aleppo pine). This open-branched Mediterranean species has been widely planted in southern Europe and may have promise for seashore sites in our Gulf Coast area.

Pinus heldreichii 8 (Balkan pine). This native of the western Balkan Peninsula, Greece, and southeastern Italy is not often used or available in our area, but its var. *leucodermis* (synonym: *P. leucodermis;* Bosnian pine) is much-planted in Europe because of its densely branched form, glossy dark green, stiff and sharp-pointed needles, and whitened twigs with a "snakeskin" look after the needles fall. Useful in Zones 5b–8b, with selection of appropriate genetic material.

Pinus pinaster 7–8 (cluster pine). This tree from southwestern Europe and Morocco is well adapted to the sandy soils and salt spray of seashore sites but needs further trial in Zones 7b– 9a before its adaptability to our area is known. It is reputedly difficult to transplant, but this presumably can be overcome by the use of container-grown plants of small size.

Pinus taeda 8

LOBLOLLY PINE
Evergreen tree
Pinaceae (Pine Family)

Native Range.   Southeastern to south-central United States.

Useful Range.   USDA Zones 7b–9a.

Function.   Specimen, massing, shade tree, fast but temporary screen.

Size and Habit

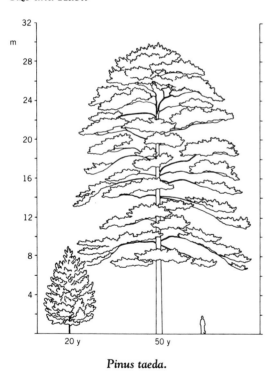

Pinus taeda.

Adaptability.   Tolerates very poor soil and exposed sites.

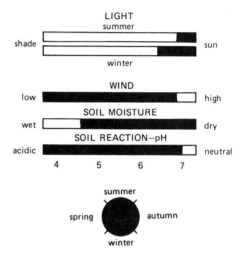

Seasonal Interest. *Foliage:* Evergreen with bright green needles, 15–25 cm/6–10 in. long, in fascicles of three. *Cones:* Light brown, shiny, 6–10 cm/2.4–4 in. long, adding minor landscape interest. *Trunk:* Handsome, reddish brown bark is fissured into heavy scaly plates, interesting in all seasons.

Problems and Maintenance.   This is among the most durable and trouble-free of the southern pines in landscape use. Borers occasionally are troublesome, usually when trees have been damaged by pruning or other breakage in spring and summer. *P. taeda* is difficult to transplant in larger sizes, so specify young seedlings or container-grown trees. Growth is so rapid that trees quickly attain functional size even when starting as young seedlings.

Cultivars.   Plants of 'Nana' originated some three decades ago as seedlings from a genetic witch's broom. After 30 years at North Carolina

State University, these trees had grown to a height of about 5 m/16 ft, with a soft, billowy, irregularly globose head, some 3–4 m/10–13 ft across. Groups of seedlings such as this are usually too variable to be given a single cultivar name, but these individual trees do not vary much in form or character, so using one cultivar name for them may be appropriate. Grafted plants from these parent plants have been available, at least temporarily. These dwarfs are a handsome and distinctive addition to the list of conifers for the South (Zones 7b–9a).

Related Species

Pinus echinata 8 (shortleaf pine). This is one of the most northerly ranging of the southern pines, growing wild from New Jersey, Ohio, and Illinois to Texas, and recognizable from a distance by the presence of young branches growing from the trunk inside the main canopy. As this tendency suggests, it recovers better from pruning than most other pines. Useful for shade, massing, or naturalizing in Zones 6a–9a, but is seldom available for planting.

Pinus virginiana 7

VIRGINIA PINE, SCRUB PINE
Evergreen tree
Pinaceae (Pine Family)

Native Range.   East-central United States from New Jersey to Alabama.

Useful Range.   USDA Zones 5b–9a.

Function.   Massing, naturalizing, large-scale screening, roadside bank planting.

Size and Habit

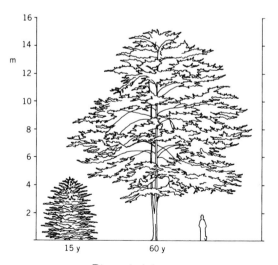

Pinus virginiana.

Adaptability.   Especially useful on poor, dry soils.

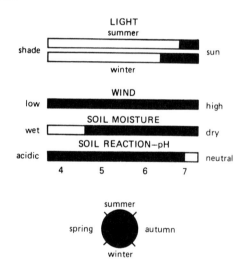

Seasonal Interest.   *Foliage:* Evergreen, twisted needles, 5–8 cm/2–3 in. long, in fascicles of two, persisting for three to four years, deep green in summer but yellowing in winter. *Cones:* Lustrous, reddish brown, to 5 cm/2 in. long, maturing in the second year but persisting longer.

Problems and Maintenance.   This tree is relatively trouble-free and requires little maintenance other than spraying if insect infestations become heavy.

Pinus virginiana.

Pinus virginiana.

Related Species

Pinus pungens 7 (Table Mountain pine or hickory pine). This tree is closely related to P. *virginiana* and similar in general appearance, but differing in its sharp, prickly needles and thorny cone-scales. It is rarely planted as a landscape tree, but is useful at least in the region of its native range, from New Jersey to Georgia, primarily in the mountains (Zones 6b–7b, and probably extending at least to Zone 6a and Zone 8b).

Pinus rigida 7–8 (pitch pine). This native of the east-central United States from Maine to the southern Appalachian Mountains is useful on very poor, dry soils in Zones 4b–7a. Usually it is less attractive for this purpose than P. *virginiana* or P. *banksiana*, but it can become picturesque with age.

Pinus wallichiana 8

Synonyms: P. *excelsa,* P. *griffithii*
HIMALAYAN OR BHUTAN PINE
Evergreen tree
Pinaceae (Pine Family)

Native Range. Himalayas westward to Afghanistan.

Useful Range. USDA Zones 5b–9a with selection of appropriate genetic material.

Function. Specimen, shade tree, screen.

Size and Habit.   Resembles a more massive edition of *Pinus strobus* and so needs plenty of space.

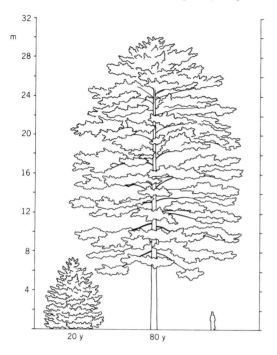

Pinus wallichiana.

Adaptability.   Foliage is very sensitive to winter windburn in Zones 5 and 6.

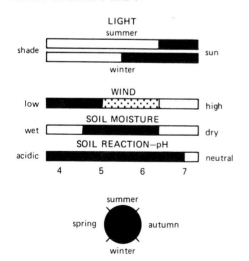

Seasonal Interest. *Foliage:* Evergreen, soft blue-green, fine-textured, with very slender needles, 10–20 cm/4–8 in. long, drooping and giving distinctive texture. *Cones:* Cylindrical, 15–25 cm/6–10 in. long, ripening yellow-brown and pendulous, adding interest because of their size. *Trunk and branches:* Bark on branches is smooth, olive green to gray; trunk bark is roughened, dark gray.

Problems and Maintenance.   Young trees may need protection from winter wind until they have been established for several years. Even older trees will not tolerate extreme exposures in colder zones.

Cultivars.   Few selections have been made from this species, and even fewer are available. 'Densa' has a dense conical habit and shorter needles than the species type. 'Glauca' is like the species type but with conspicuously blue needles. 'Nana' is truly dwarf, broadly globose in form, with typically long, silvery blue needles, a very distinctive small plant. 'Zebrina,' a nearly full-sized tree with gold-banded needles, is probably the best-known variant of this species.

Related Species

Pinus armandii 8 (Chinese white pine).   This variable tree usually is picturesque and irregular in form, smaller than *P. wallichiana*, yet wide-spreading in relation to its height (15–20 m/60–80 ft). It is seldom available commercially at present but is potentially useful in Zones 5a–9a.

Pinus parviflora 7–8 (Japanese white pine). This picturesque, rather slow-growing tree has very short needles, seldom longer than 6 cm/2.4 in., with conspicuous whitened stomatal lines.

Pinus wallichiana.

Its branching habit is usually strongly tiered or layered, providing strong horizontal line. The selection 'Adcock's Dwarf' is extremely dwarf, with gray-green needles less than 2.5 cm/1 in. long, crowded together at the twig tips, making an irregularly dense mound that remains below 75 cm/30 in. but greater spread. 'Glauca' is slower growing than the species type, to about 10 m/33 ft tall after many years, with more distinctly whitened blue-green needles, clumping together to give an interesting textural effect. 'Templehof' is a vigorous tree form with a very heavy trunk. Several other selections have been made, but few are available in our area.

Pinus peuce 7 (Macedonian pine).   This native of the Balkans is little used and seldom available but potentially useful in Zones 5a–9a. Compact and slower growing than most of the white pines, yet not as slow as *P. cembra.* It can be maintained as an effective screen for many years, since it retains its lower branches longer than most pines. It is apparently resistant to white pine blister rust.

Pistacia chinensis 8

CHINESE PISTACHIO OR PISTACHE
Deciduous tree
Anacardiaceae (Cashew Family)

Native Range.   China.

Useful Range.   USDA Zones 7b–9a+; individual trees reportedly are hardy northward to Zone 6b.

Function.   Shade tree, rootstock for edible pistachio nut tree, *P. vera.*

Size and Habit

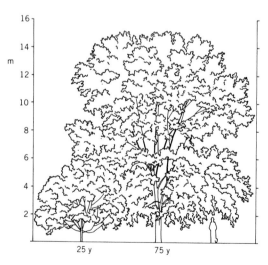

25 y   75 y

Pistacia chinensis.

Adaptability.   One of the most widely adaptable of all shade trees within its useful range. Much more resistant to wind than its relatives the *Rhus* species, and relatively salt tolerant and resistant to extreme heat and drought.

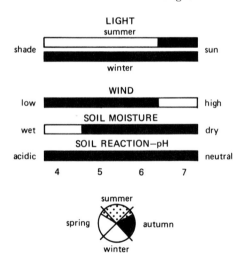

Seasonal Interest.   *Flowers:* Small and inconspicuous, dioecious. *Foliage:* Rich green, compound leaves with narrow leaflets 5–8 cm/2–3 in. long turn red to golden-orange in autumn virtually every year. *Fruits:* Red, later purple, round, 0.5 cm/0.2 in. across in showy clusters 15–20 cm/6–8 in. long in autumn on female trees.

Problems and Maintenance. This tree is essentially trouble-free, requires little or no maintenance, and is unusually free of insects and diseases.

Cultivars. Few cultivars are yet available, but the increasing popularity of this tree in the South and lower Mississippi Basin along with variation in form, hardiness, and the desirability of heavily fruiting forms suggests that more cultivars may be selected in the future.

Pistacia chinensis.

Pittosporum tobira 4–5

JAPANESE PITTOSPORUM
Evergreen shrub
Pittosporaceae (Pittosporum Family)

Native Range. China and Japan.

Useful Range. USDA Zones 8b–9a+ and in sheltered sites in Zone 8a.

Function. Screen, massing, specimen, foundation.

Size and Habit

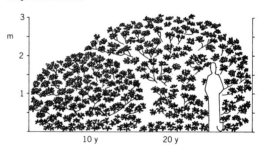

Pittosporum tobira.

Adaptability. Tolerates seaside wind and salt spray.

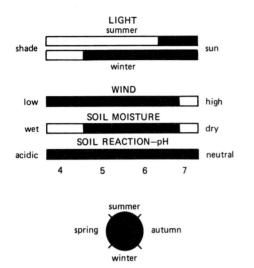

Pittosporum tobira 'Variegata.'

Seasonal Interest. *Flowers:* White to pale yellow, very fragrant, individually 1.3 cm/0.5 in. across, in clusters to 8 cm/3 in. across, in midspring. *Foliage:* Evergreen, bright to deep green, rounded leaves to 10 cm/4 in. long in full shade, but more commonly half that length, giving rather fine texture. *Fruits:* Capsules, developing in summer, are not conspicuous but in some years add autumn interest as red seeds are exposed. *Branching:* Sympodial branching, as in most azaleas and flowering dogwood, accentuates the broad-spreading growth habit.

Problems and Maintenance. This shrub is usually trouble-free, but occasionally is subject to disease and insect problems, the most serious of which are aphids and scale insects, which must be controlled early to prevent serious damage.

Cultivars. 'Variegata' has gray-green foliage, variegated creamy white. It is a striking specimen plant, considerably slower growing than the species type, and seldom exceeding heights of about 1.5 m/5 ft, so it is not suitable for screening.

'Wheeler's Dwarf' is compact in growth, remaining below 0.5 m/1.6 ft for several years, and can be kept below 0.8 m/2.6 ft indefinitely with occasional pruning. The deep green leaves are about as large as those of the species type, packed into a dense mass of distinctive texture. This handsome and useful dwarf plant is popular for foundation planting and massing in Zones 8a–

Pittosporum tobira 'Variegata.'

9a+ and may prove adapted to sheltered sites in Zone 7b.

Related Species. Many other species of *Pittosporum* are known, primarily from Australia, New Zealand, and southeastern Asia, and a few are used as landscape plants in California. *P. tobira* is the only one in general use in the eastern United States.

Pittosporum tobira 'Wheeler's Dwarf.'

Platanus occidentalis 8

SYCAMORE, AMERICAN PLANETREE
Deciduous tree
Platanaceae (Planetree Family)

Native Range.   Eastern North America.

Useful Range.   USDA Zones 5a–9a and to Zone 4b with selection of northern seed sources.

Function.   Shade tree, street tree, specimen.

Size and Habit

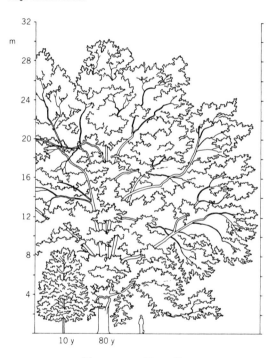

Platanus occidentalis.

Adaptability.   This tree is one of the most tolerant to city conditions.

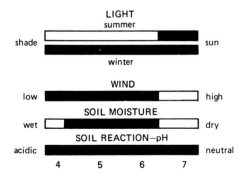

Seasonal Interest. *Foliage:* Medium green, lobed, adding coarse texture in summer, turning brown before falling in autumn. *Fruits:* Globose heads, green, ripening tan, about 2.5 cm/1 in. across, pendulous on long stalks, adding quiet interest in autumn and early winter. *Trunk and branches:* Smooth bark exfoliates in large flakes, exposing patterns of creamy white inner bark with contrasting areas of gray and brown, providing striking interest during the leafless season and mild interest the rest of the year.

Problems and Maintenance.   Anthracnose is a serious disease of this tree, causing twig blight and occasionally cankers, sometimes weakening trees but seldom killing them. The seriousness of the disease in any year depends to a great extent on weather conditions. Cool, moist weather following leaf emergence favors the disease. Minimum control consists of cleaning up and burning of leaf and twig litter in autumn. When necessary, appropriate spraying will further reduce the incidence and extent of the disease. The tendency of this species to litter the ground with leaves, twigs, bark, and fruits makes it far from an ideal street tree. But its tolerance of difficult city conditions has resulted in its widespread use for this purpose, and it is admittedly functional where there is enough space for it, in spite of its disadvantages, especially in the Midwest.

Varieties.   There are no commercially available selections of this species, but the general rule for selection of seed source applies: When possible, use trees grown from seed parents native to the region in question.

Related Species

Platanus ×*acerifolia* 8 (synonyms: *P.* ×*hispanica*, *P.* ×*hybrida*; London planetree).   This hybrid (*P. occidentalis* × *P. orientalis*) has been planted widely as a street and shade tree in Europe and in its useful range in eastern and central North

Platanus orientalis.

Platanus orientalis.

America (Zones 6a–9a). Most members of this hybrid population are intermediate between the American parent (*P. occidentalis*), which is cold-hardy to Zone 5a but susceptible to anthracnose, and the Eurasian parent (*P. orientalis*), which is resistant to anthracnose but less cold-hardy (to Zone 6b or 7a). Individual clones within the hybrid population vary in both hardiness and disease-resistance, as would be expected.

Over the nearly 300 years this hybrid has been known, some trees have been propagated by seeds from open-pollinated trees of the hybrid population. In North America, nearby trees of native sycamore (*P. occidentalis*) have often served as pollen parents, so succeeding generations of seed-produced plants have gradually changed in their parentage, so that most so-called London planetrees today are probably more than half *P. occidentalis* and less than half *P. orientalis* in their genetic makeup, and thus show less resistance to anthracnose and greater cold-hardiness than first-generation hybrids. Because of this, Dr. Frank Santamour, geneticist at the U.S. National Arboretum, set out about 1970 to re-create a first-generation hybrid by crossing *P. occidentalis* of known native origin in Maryland by *P. orientalis* of authentic Turkish origin. Two decades later, two selections from these crosses, 'Columbia' and 'Liberty,' were introduced into commerce. These selections grow rapidly and have good form and foliage. Leaves of 'Columbia' are deeply lobed, more like those of *P. orientalis* than *P. occidentalis*. Foliage of 'Liberty' is more similar to the foliage of *P. occidentalis*. Both cultivars have shown good disease-resistance in their early years, but they have

Platanus orientalis.

not yet been tested long enough and widely enough to fully establish their disease-resistance and cold-hardiness. Dr. George Ware, geneticist at the Morton Arboretum, has made similar crosses, but using a *P. occidentalis* parent from northern Illinois. Hybrids from this northern pollen parent may prove more cold-hardy than previous ones, but these hybrids, too, will need to be tested further before their northern limits will be known.

Unfortunately, the picture is still clouded by the gradual spread of cankerstain, another serious disease that is potentially lethal for *P. orientalis* and *P.* ×*acerifolia,* but apparently less so for *P. occidentalis.* It remains to be seen which *Platanus* species or hybrids will prove to be most useful for different parts of eastern North America in the long run, but at this writing the selection 'Bloodgood,' introduced in 1900, is still the most widely used cultivar in our area. It is fast-growing, broadly and openly pyramidal in form, reportedly resistant to anthracnose but susceptible to cankerstain disease (see below), and useful at least in Zones 6a–9a, perhaps also Zone 5b.

Platanus orientalis 8 (oriental planetree). This native of southeastern Europe and adjacent Asia is a common street tree in European cities, often kept in scale by pollarding. It does not grow as tall as the other *Platanus* species mentioned, reaching heights of about 25 m/82 ft, but is wide-spreading when left unpruned. In the past, *P. orientalis* has been relatively resistant to disease, but cankerstain disease now raises questions about its future, and it is considerably less cold-hardy than *P. occidentalis,* with a useful range of Zones 7a–9a, and perhaps protected sites in Zone 6b.

Podocarpus macrophyllus 5–7

Synonym: *P. chinensis*
YEW (OR BIGLEAF) PODOCARPUS
Evergreen tree or shrub
Podocarpaceae (Podocarpus Family)

Native Range. Japan.

Useful Range. USDA Zones 8b–9a+ and sheltered sites in Zones 7b and 8a.

Function. Specimen, hedge, screen.

Size and Habit. Size is limited by climate; this plant remains in size group 5 in Zones 7b and 8a, but reaches size group 7 in Zone 9a.

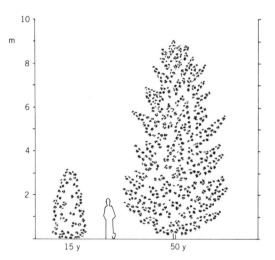

Podocarpus macrophyllus.

Adaptability.   Partial shade from full summer sun is beneficial, especially in the Deep South. In Zones 7b and 8a, protection from full sun and wind in winter reduces leaf scorch.

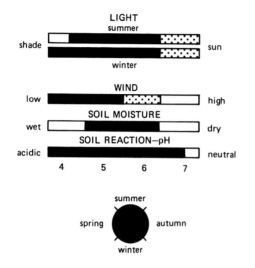

Seasonal Interest.   *Foliage:* Evergreen, broad-needlelike, to 10 cm/4 in. long and 0.8 cm/0.8 in. broad, glossy dark green on upper surface, light green underneath, handsome in all seasons. *Fruits:* Greenish to purple, on female plants, inconspicuous.

Problems and Maintenance.   This plant is relatively trouble-free and requires little or no maintenance. Light pruning may be necessary in the Deep South to restrict size in some sites. This should be done by removing individual branch tips, not by shearing, except when used as a formal hedge. Scale insects may occasionally be troublesome in warm areas.

Varieties and Cultivars.   The var. *angustifolius* has narrow leaves and growth habit, but is seldom available. 'Maki' is a shrubby plant, growing slowly to 2–3 m/6.6–10 ft tall but in time reaching twice that size. Dense and erect, this selection is commonly used in foundation plantings around large buildings.

Related Species

Podocarpus nivalis 3 (alpine totara).   This low, densely shrubby evergreen from the mountains of southern New Zealand resembles a dwarf yew, with needles to 1.8 cm/0.7 in. long, making a useful groundcover or specimen plant in parts of Zones 8a–9a+ having mild summers.

Polygonum aubertii 1

CHINA OR SILVER FLEECEVINE, SILVERLACE VINE

Deciduous vine

Polygonaceae (Buckwheat Family)

Native Range.   Western China.

Useful Range.   USDA Zones 4b–8b and to Zone 3b where snow cover is reliable.

Function.   Screen (with support), specimen; vine growing rapidly and climbing by twining to heights of 5–10 m/16–33 ft, but not effective as a screen near the ground without training.

Size and Habit

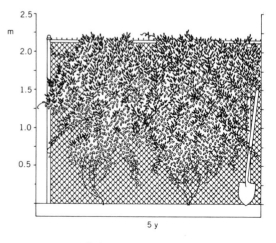

Polygonum aubertii.

Adaptability

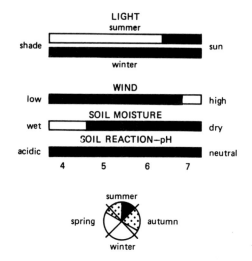

Polygonum cuspidatum var. *compactum.*

Seasonal Interest.   *Flowers:* Greenish white at first, then white or sometimes pinkish at maturity in late summer; small but numerous, making a solid mass of bloom over the upper parts of the plant. *Foliage:* Reddish as it unfolds, quickly turning bright green, falling without color change in autumn.

Problems and Maintenance.   Japanese beetles can be troublesome in areas within the range of this insect. In northern areas, vines may kill to the ground during winter but return vigorously during the following summer. When used as a visual screen (e.g., on a chainlink fence) coverage near ground level depends on the vine reaching the top of its support and falling back to the ground as it continues to grow. For this reason, low coverage may never be complete in Zones

4 and 5, and other species may be preferred for screening.

Related Species

Polygonum cuspidatum 3–5 (Japanese knotweed, Mexican bamboo).   This clump-forming plant to 2 m/6.6 ft or more tall spreads vigorously by underground stems and is extremely difficult to eradicate, so it should be used and contained very carefully. In most instances, better plants can be found, but few plants are as effective in stabilizing soil on steep banks. This plant kills to the ground at the first hard freeze in autumn, looks unsightly until the dead stalks are removed, then returns with seemingly redoubled vigor during the next growing season. It is useful in Zones 4b–9a.

The var. *compactum* (synonym: *P. reynoutria*) grows in much the same manner as the species type, but usually to heights of 0.2–1 m/0.7–3.3 ft. It has reddish flowers, is slightly less difficult to control, and is just as effective in slope stabilization. There is considerable variation in the height and vigor of this variety, leading to the use of (usually unnamed) clones in some areas.

Antigonon leptopus 1 (coralvine, mountain rose, rosa de montana, confederate vine).   This Mexican member of the Polygonaceae makes a vigorous screen with support and pruning, climbing loosely by tendrils to heights of 5–10 m/16–33 ft, and higher well south of our area. It is unusual in its tolerance of hot, dry climates and poor, dry soils, and it produces masses of bright coral-pink flowers in midsummer. This otherwise trouble-free vine usually freezes back in winter in Zone 8b, where it reaches its northern limit,

Polygonum aubertii.

and requires annual pruning for renewal, usually done by cutting back close to the ground after the first frost, then adding a winter mulch. From the southern extremes of our area (Zone 9a) to the tropics, severe pruning is necessary to control size and promote vigor, but this practice delays flowering if overdone. The selection 'Album,' with white flowers, is seldom available. 'Baja Red' has deeper rose-colored flowers.

Poncirus trifoliata 6

TRIFOLIATE ORANGE, HARDY ORANGE

Deciduous shrub

Rutaceae (Rue Family)

Native Range.   Northern China and Korea.

Useful Range.   USDA Zones 6b–9a+, and Zone 6a in sheltered sites.

Function.   Specimen, barrier, hedge, rootstock for citrus fruits.

Size and Habit

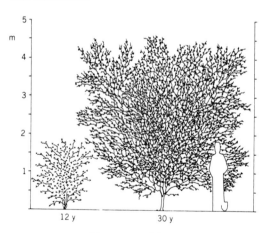

Poncirus trifoliata.

Adaptability.   Best in full sun, and grows well in hot, dry sites.

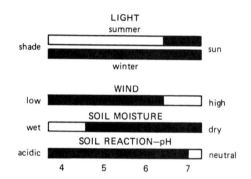

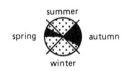

Seasonal Interest.   *Flowers:* Fragrant, white, similar to those of *Citrus* species, 3–5 cm/1.2–2 in. across. *Foliage:* Compound leaves with three leaflets and winged petiole. Not dense enough in mass to function as a visual screen, falling in midautumn with little or no color change. *Fruits:* Yellow-orange, globose, to about 5 cm/2 in.

Poncirus trifoliata.

across, resembling small oranges, fragrant but not edible, ripening in early autumn. *Twigs and branches:* Heavy, angled, deep green twigs and smaller branches bear sharp, rugged thorns.

Problems and Maintenance. This plant is relatively trouble-free and requires little maintenance other than pruning for use as a hedge or to keep the thorny branches out of contact with people. The heavy, thorny branches make this plant a highly effective barrier, but it can be troublesome in intensive situations, especially where children are present. Its relative cold-hardiness and nematode resistance, which make

it a valuable understock for citrus, also expand its uses as a landscape plant.

Related Species

Choisya ternata 5 (Mexican orange).   This evergreen shrub from Mexico with foliage mass denser than that of *Poncirus* reaches heights of 2–3 m/6.6–10 ft, occasionally taller. It is useful for barrier plantings in hot, dry sites in Zones 8b–9a+ and in protected sites in Zones 7b and 8a, with fragrant white flowers, to 3 cm/1.2 in. across, borne in showy clusters in late spring. The dark blue fruits, to 1.5 cm/0.6 in. across, are not showy.

Populus alba 8

WHITE POPLAR
Deciduous tree
Salicaceae (Willow Family)

Native Range.   Central Europe to central Asia.

Useful Range.   USDA Zones 4a–9a.

Function.   Specimen, shade tree, screen.

Size and Habit

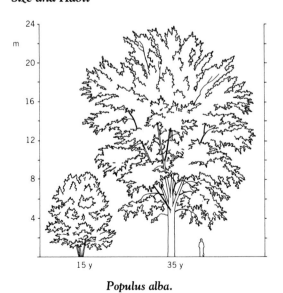

Populus alba.

Adaptability

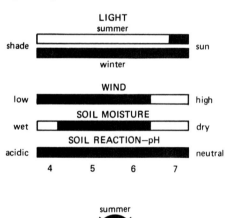

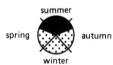

Seasonal Interest. *Foliage:* Three-lobed, maplelike leaves are lustrous and deep green above and white and felty underneath, giving a striking glitter effect as they are tumbled over by even light breezes. In autumn, the green is dulled, sometimes giving way to a reddish or russet color before they fall in midautumn. *Trunk and branches:* Whitish gray-green bark is interesting at all seasons.

Problems and Maintenance. Poplars as a group are soft-wooded, short-lived, and prone to storm breakage, usually aggravated by their

Populus alba 'Pyramidalis.'

susceptibility to serious stem and trunk canker diseases. They quickly send roots into moist areas, frequently clogging drainage lines and disrupting pavement. In fact, they are prohibited in many places by city ordinances. *Populus alba* is not as prone to serious diseases as many other poplars, and for this reason usually is longer-lived, yet it has enough problems to justify caution in planting it. On the other side of the ledge, this and other poplars are extremely fast-growing and handsome as young trees. *P. alba* is certainly one of the most satisfactory of this group.

Cultivars. 'Nivea' has unusually thick, white pubescence underneath the leaves and is especially striking in summer but becomes unsightly where large amounts of dust or soot are present. 'Pyramidalis' (synonym: 'Bolleana'; Bolleana poplar) is fastigiate and columnar in outline when young, later narrowly pyramidal. It is a more durable alternative to the lombardy poplar, *P. nigra* 'Italica.'

Hybrids

Populus ×*canescens* 8 (gray poplar). This is a natural hybrid (*P. alba* × *P. tremula*) occurring from central Europe to Iran, represented in our area by the selection 'Tower,' introduced by the Morden Research Station of Agriculture Canada in Manitoba. It is seedless, fast-growing, narrowly pyramidal in form, and reportedly disease-resistant, useful at least in Zones 3a–6b, perhaps farther south.

Populus balsamifera 8

Synonym: *P. tacamahaca*
BALSAM POPLAR, TACAMAHAC
Deciduous tree
Salicaceae (Willow Family)

Native Range. Northern North America.

Useful Range. USDA Zones 2–5; will grow in southern zones also, but not as a useful landscape tree.

Function. Shade tree.

Size and Habit

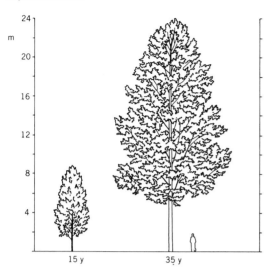

Populus balsamifera.

Adaptability

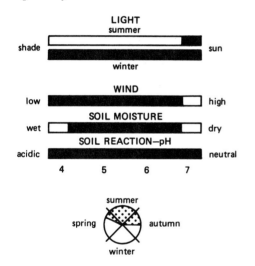

Seasonal Interest. *Foliage:* Bright green with brownish pubescence giving a "brassy" appearance and medium-coarse texture, falling in mid-autumn with little color change.

Problems and Maintenance. This tree is subject to the problems of poplars in general in warm climates, but a fairly satisfactory large shade tree in its natural range in the Far North. It is usually not available elsewhere.

Related Species and Hybrids

Populus ×acuminata 7 (lanceleaf cottonwood). This hybrid of *P. angustifolia* × *P. deltoides* has glossy dark green, narrowly oval, long-pointed leaves, to 10 cm/4 in. long, turning yellow in autumn. It is useful in the same range as *P. angustifolia.*

Populus angustifolia 7 (synonym: *P. balsamifera* var. *angustifolia;* narrow-leaved cottonwood). This narrow tree from the Great Plains and eastern Rocky Mountain region to high elevations in Mexico has potential as a landscape tree throughout the Northern Plains (Zone 3a–5b), with selection of locally or regionally adapted genetic material. It has narrow leaves to 10 cm/4 in. long, smooth bark, and orange branches.

Populus ×jackii 8 (Jack poplar). This hybrid of *P. balsamifera* × *P. deltoides* is a large tree much like *P. balsamifera* in appearance and function. The selection 'Gileadensis' (balm-of-Gilead) has large leaves (to 15 cm/6 in. long), with the undersides made very "brassy" in appearance by a heavy coating of resin, which emits a distinctive odor under some weather conditions, giving rise to its name, but it is seldom, if ever, available except from the wild. The selection 'Northwest,' however, is available commercially.

Populus maximowiczii 8 (Japanese poplar). This tree is one of the most disease-resistant of all poplars, growing to about the same size as *P. balsamifera,* with handsome dark green foliage and light green bark. Useful in Zones 4a–5b, perhaps also colder areas.

Populus simonii 7 (Simon poplar). This little-used native of northern China is similar in appearance to *P. angustifolia.* The selection 'Pendula' is strongly pendulous in habit, and 'Fastigiata' is narrowly pyramidal. They are potentially useful in Zones 3a–6b, but not widely available.

Populus trichocarpa 8 (western balsam poplar, black cottonwood). This large, western North American tree is potentially useful in the Northern Plains (Zones 2–4) and perhaps elsewhere, but it is probably not in use or available in our area.

Populus deltoides 8

COTTONWOOD
Deciduous tree
Salicaceae (Willow Family)

Native Range.   Eastern United States and adjacent Canada.

Useful Range.   USDA Zones 3a–9a.

Function.   Shade tree.

Size and Habit

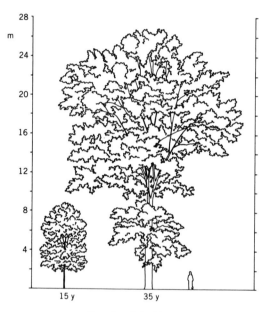

Populus deltoides.

Adaptability

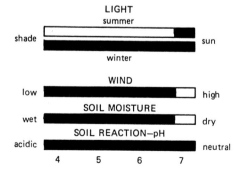

Seasonal Interest.   *Foliage:* Lustrous, bright to deep green leaves, to 12 cm/5 in. long and broad, giving a rather coarse texture. *Fruits:* Catkins on female trees bear many seeds surrounded by silky or cottony hairs. Their release in late spring gives rise to the common name, cottonwood. Fruits and seeds of other *Populus* species are much the same but not so noticeably "cottony."

Problems and Maintenance.   Cottonwood is subject to the problems of poplars in general (see *P. alba*) but longer-lived than most. It is primarily of value as a massive shade tree in the far North (Zones 3–4) and is fairly effective in this role, but it drops a considerable amount of branch and leaf litter, and female trees also release seeds that germinate as fast-growing weed seedlings.

Cultivars.   'Mighty Moe,' a recent introduction of the University of Nebraska, is male (nonfruiting, cottonless) and is expected to be disease-resistant, thus probably long-lived. 'Siouxland,' a male selection introduced by South Dakota State University, is fast-growing, with a rounded head at maturity, and has large, dark green leaves and is reported to be at least somewhat disease-resistant.

Subspecies.   The species type, ssp. *deltoides* (synonyms: *P. angulata*, *P. candicans*; eastern cottonwood), native to the greater part of the eastern United States, westward to the beginning of the Great Plains, and ssp. *monilifera* (synonym: *P. deltoides* var. *occidentalis*; plains cottonwood), which is distributed through the Great Plains from Texas to Alberta differ in botanical details, as do northern and southern populations of both subspecies, but their landscape usefulness is similar. The plains cottonwood may, on the average, be more tolerant of dry climates, and northern populations are undoubtedly more cold-hardy than southern populations. A third subspecies, *wislizenii*, is native to Colorado and New Mexico, outside our area.

Related Species and Hybrids

Populus ×*berolinensis* 7–8 (Berlin poplar).   This hybrid (*P. laurifolia* × *P. nigra* 'Italica') is narrowly pyramidal to oval, not as narrow as 'Italica.' It is potentially useful in Zones 3a–9a, but seldom if ever available in our area.

   Populus ×*canadensis* 8 (Canada poplar). This group of extremely vigorous hybrids of *P. deltoides* × *P. nigra* includes several cultivars. In general, they are weak-wooded and tend to clog drains, disrupt pavement even more rapidly than many other poplars, and be short-lived, but they are certainly among the fastest-growing of trees and may be useful for temporary shade in Zones 3a–9a, to be replaced by slower trees that are more durable and trouble-free. Cultivars are more-or-less narrowly pyramidal with glossy, deep green foliage and smooth, gray-green bark and include

'Eugenei' (Carolina poplar), a nonfruiting clone, 'Nor'easter', a sterile female clone with rounded head, rapid growth, and disease-resistance superior to that of 'Robusta' and 'Siouxland,' and several others, at the University of Nebraska. 'Robusta' is a popular seedless clone with broad-oval shape, introduced by the University of Minnesota, not to be confused with a narrowly pyramidal clone introduced in France as 'Robusta' a century ago and now widely planted in Europe (according to Krüssman).

Populus nigra 8 (black poplar).   This large Eurasian tree is best known in our area as the narrowly columnar form 'Italica' (Lombardy poplar), commonly planted for its striking vertical effect. Its most appropriate use is as a temporary screen or windbreak in Zones 3a–9a. Unfortunately, in this role it is seldom removed soon enough and becomes large, devastated by canker disease, and costly to remove. The selection 'Afghanica' (= 'Thevestina'; Theves poplar) is reportedly more resistant to canker disease and longer-lived than 'Italica,' with whitened bark.

Populus tremuloides 6–8

QUAKING OR TREMBLING ASPEN
Deciduous tree
Salicaceae (Willow Family)

Native Range.   Northern North America.

Useful Range.   USDA Zones 2b–6b, but so short-lived that it is barely useful in zones warmer than 5b.

Function.   Naturalizing, massing.

Size and Habit

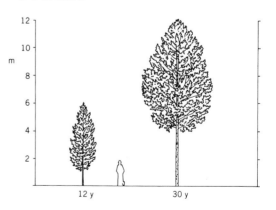

Populus tremuloides.

Adaptability

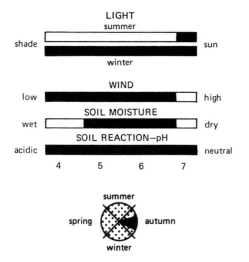

Seasonal Interest. *Foliage:* Casts light, mottled shade. Leaves are small, 3–8 cm/1.2–3 in. long, the upper surface dull or deep green, whitened underneath, giving a glittering, bicolored effect as they are turned over by even slight wind, because of the flattened petioles typical of all *Populus* species. Foliage turns clear, bright yellow in autumn. *Trunk and branches:* Smooth, pale gray-green bark becomes almost white with age, adding significant year round interest.

Problems and Maintenance. Like other *Populus* species, *P. tremuloides* is weak-wooded, disease-susceptible, and short-lived, and thus it is best used in naturalized plantings. Unlike many poplars, *P. tremuloides* and its close relatives

(see Related Species) are not easily propagated by cuttings.

Cultivars. 'Pendula,' with weeping branches, probably is not commercially available. *P. tremuloides* is one of the widest ranging of all trees, suggesting that much genetic variation exists, but few selections have been made, probably because of the difficulty of propagating them as well as the minor importance of this species as a landscape tree in most heavily populated areas. Most plants used are seedlings, and selection of nearby seed sources probably is a useful precaution, as with other wide ranging species.

Related Species

Populus grandidentata 6–7 (bigtooth aspen). This tree has larger leaves than *P. tremuloides*, to 8–10 cm/3–4 in. long, coarsely toothed, and giving less of the mobile effect of those of *P. tremuloides*. This species is more tolerant of warm sites and moist and heavy soils than *P. tremuloides*, has similar bark interest, and is equally short-lived. It is useful in Zones 4a–7a.

Populus tremula 6–8 (European aspen). This tree is the European counterpart of *P. tremuloides*. It is almost never used in our area but is noteworthy for the narrowly columnar cultivar 'Erecta,' which is being tested in Canada and the United States and thus far seems to be more trouble-free and durable than other narrow poplars. Weeping and purple-leaved cultivars are available in Europe, but probably not in North America.

Potentilla fruticosa 3

SHRUBBY CINQUEFOIL
Deciduous shrub
Rosaceae (Rose Family)

Native Range. Northern North America and Eurasia.

Useful Range. USDA Zones 2b–7b and good sites in Zone 8.

Function. Border, massing.

Size and Habit

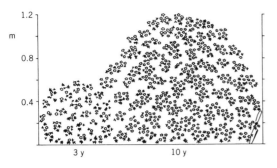

Potentilla fruticosa.

Adaptability. One of the most widely tolerant of all shrubs to soil extremes and to seashore or de-icing salts. Planting in sites with good air circulation helps control mildew disease.

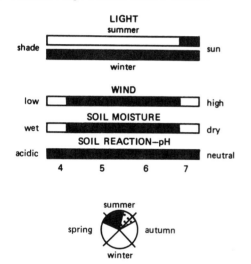

Seasonal Interest. *Flowers:* Yellow, red-or-ange, or white, to 2–3 cm/0.8–1.2 in. across, showy in early summer and continuing intermit-tently until fall. *Foliage:* Bright to gray-green, fine textured, hairy, compound leaves, falling in autumn with little or no color change. *Fruits:* Inconspicuous dry capsules.

Problems and Maintenance. Leaf-spot dis-eases, mildew, and chewing insects occasionally are troublesome. Pruning is seldom necessary, but older plants that have become ragged can be renewed by pruning close to the ground in spring.

Varieties. The var. *arbuscula* (= 'Arbuscula'), from China and the Himalayas, has bright yellow flowers on ascending or creeping branches, to 0l.6 m/2 ft high.

The var. *davurica* (= P. davurica, = 'Davur-ica'), from China and central to eastern Siberia, has white to pale yellow branches, to 0.5 m/1.6 ft high.

The var. *mandshurica* (= 'Manchu'), from Manchuria, is low-growing (0.45 m/1.5 ft) with white flowers.

Cultivars. More than 40 cultivars are currently in use in North America. A few of the more common are listed here.

'Abbotswood,' with large, pure-white flowers and outstanding blue-green foliage, may still be the best white-flowered cultivar. 'Snowbird' and 'Snowflake' are promising newer cultivars with excellent green foliage and a mixture of single and double white flowers. 'Mount Everest,' still popular in spite of its mediocre yellow-green foliage, has large white flowers. 'McKay's White,' a genetic sport of 'Katherine Dykes,' has creamy white flowers and a mounded growth habit.

'Primrose Beauty' has large, pale yellow flow-ers over a long season and its silvery foliage remains attractive in autumn. 'Katherine Dykes' has an arching habit and soft-yellow flowers, somewhat darker than those of 'Primrose Beauty' and especially effective in late season.

'Moonlight' (= 'Maanelys') has medium yel-low flowers, slightly darker than those of 'Katherine Dykes,' and an erect habit similar to that of 'Jackman.' 'Longacre' is low and spreading in habit, with large sulfur yellow flowers. The

Potentilla fruticosa.

newer 'Yellow Gem'® is also low and spreading, but with bright yellow ruffled flowers, red young twigs, and hairy gray foliage. Another newer selection, 'Yellowbird,' has a mixture of single and semidouble yellow flowers, good foliage, and a rounded habit.

Many cultivars have golden-yellow flowers. Some of the best and most widely used in our area are listed here. 'Coronation Triumph' is early and long-flowering. 'Goldstar' is low-growing, with very large flowers (to 5 cm/2 in.) 'Goldfinger' has large and extremely showy flowers. 'Jackman' has smaller numbers of large flowers and excellent dark green foliage. 'Elizabeth' (= 'Arbuscula', = 'Sutter's Gold') has bright yellow flowers over a long season and large, mounded form. 'Gold Drop' (= 'Farreri') is an old favorite that is being superseded by other cultivars such as those above as well as the floriferous 'Dakota Sunrise,' and 'Klondyke,' which has dark yellow flowers with reflexed petals and upright habit. 'Parvifolia' (= P. parvifolia, = P. fruticosa var. parvifolia) differs in its fine-textured, silky foliage.

For many years, the search has been on for a red-flowered shrubby Potentilla. The closest approach thus far probably is 'Red Ace,' which has light red to reddish-orange flowers in areas with cool summers, but may be disappointing elsewhere. 'Tangerine' has lightly orange-tinted flowers in cool and shady sites, but not the orange that the name suggests. Several more-or-less pink-flowered cultivars have been selected recently. Thus far, most of them lose much or all of their pink color in heat, emerging a soft yellow. 'Daydawn,' a genetic sport of 'Tangerine,' has pink-tinged creamy white flowers. 'Pink Queen' and 'Blink' (Princess®; Plant Patent No. 5106, 1983) have soft pink-flushed flowers, reportedly

Potentilla tridentata.

fading less in heat than some of the others. 'Royal Flush' is similar but dwarf.

Related Species

Potentilla tridentata 2 (wineleaf cinquefoil). This woody native of eastern North America from Labrador and Manitoba to eastern Tennessee has small white flowers and lustrous, leathery, evergreen, compound leaves, each with three notched leaflets, turning wine-red in winter. In well-drained, acidic soil and in full sun it forms a solid mass of foliage and serves as a handsome, small-scale groundcover. Useful in Zones 3a–7b and perhaps also in coastal sites in Zone 8.

Several low-growing herbaceous *Potentilla* species are useful as groundcovers during the growing season, with strong displays of yellow flowers in spring or early summer. A few of the most common species are *P. cinerea* 2 (synonym: *P. tommasiniana*; rusty cinquefoil), *P. crantzii* 2, and *P. neumanniana* (synonym: *P. verna*). These species are useful in Zones 4b–6b, *P. cinerea* to colder zones as well, and *P. crantzii* southward to Zone 7b.

Prinsepia sinensis 4–5

CHERRY PRINSEPIA
Deciduous shrub
Rosaceae (Rose Family)

Native Range. Manchuria.

Useful Range. USDA Zones 2b–6b, perhaps farther south as well.

Function. Barrier hedge, screen, massing, specimen.

Size and Habit

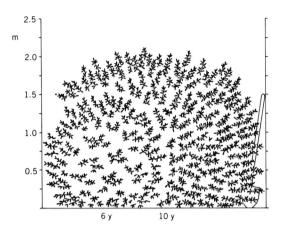

Prinsepia sinensis.

Adaptability.   Well-adapted to wind, cold, and heavy, neutral soils of the Northern Plains.

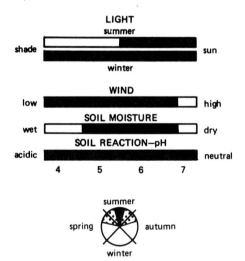

Seasonal Interest.   *Flowers:* Yellow, small, and inconspicuous, in small clusters in midspring. *Foliage:* Bright green leaves, to 8 cm/3 in. long, unfolding very early and remaining green until heavy frosts in autumn. *Fruits:* Red to red-purple, resembling small cherries, to 1.5 cm/0.6 in. across, showy against the green foliage in midsummer. *Branches:* Gracefully arching with many small, sharp spines; bark on older branches peels, adding slight winter interest.

Problems and Maintenance.   This shrub is occasionally troubled by insects and diseases but seldom seriously so in the North. It is easily pruned as an informal hedge and may require severe renewal pruning after several years of growth. This is best done when growth begins in spring, especially in the far North.

Prinsepia sinensis.

Related Species

Prinsepia uniflora 4 (hedge prinsepia).   This native of northern China resembles *P. sinensis* in growth habit but has narrower leaves and finer foliage texture. It is not tall enough or dense enough to function as a visual screen but is about as effective a barrier as *P. sinensis*. Useful in Zones 4a–6b and perhaps farther south as well, but rarely available commercially.

Oemleria cerasiformis 5 (synonym: *Osmaronia cerasiformis;* Indian plum, oso berry).   This tall shrub from the coastal Pacific Northwest is used in naturalizing in that region. Growing to 2–3 m/6.6–10 ft in cultivation, with a graceful, willowy growth habit, it is valued for its early, lightly fragrant white flowers in nodding clusters of 6 to 12, opening before the new foliage from late winter through spring. Its foliage remains a rather bright green all summer, and its stone fruits, like small pink-blushed yellow cherries (about 1.2 cm/0.5 in. long) when immature in late summer are often taken by birds before they ripen to the black stage. But it is the flowers that are the real landscape interest, lighting up dark woodland edges during dark days in early spring. This shrub may be useful in parts of eastern North America having mild summers, even though it has not often been tried here. Useful at least in Zones 7b–9a, but probably not commercially available in our area.

Prunus americana 5

AMERICAN PLUM
Deciduous shrubby tree
Rosaceae (Rose Family)

Native Range. Eastern North America to Utah and New Mexico.

Useful Range. USDA Zones 3b–9a, perhaps Zone 3a as well with selection of northern genetic material.

Function. Naturalizing, border, edible fruits.

Size and Habit

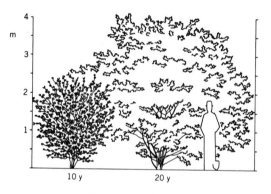

Prunus americana.

Adaptability

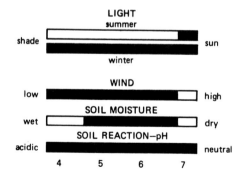

Seasonal Interest. *Flowers:* White, fairly showy for a short period in midspring. *Foliage:*

Medium green, not distinctive or particularly ornamental, changing to yellow or orange before falling in early autumn. *Fruits:* Red or yellowish with a minimal blush, about 2.5 cm/1 in. across, in late summer; sometimes used to make excellent preserves and jellies.

Problems and Maintenance. This tree is subject to several disease problems, usually is not long-lived, and tends to form thickets. It is best restricted to naturalized areas to reduce the need for intensive maintenance.

Cultivars. Several cultivars selected for good fruiting are in commerce but are not widely available.

Related Species

Prunus alleghaniensis 5 (Alleghany plum). This small, thicket-forming tree from the northeastern United States resembles *P. americana* but has smaller, dark purple fruits. It is seldom planted but worth preserving in natural and naturalized landscapes. Useful in native habitat in Zones 5b–6b.

Prunus angustifolia 5 (Chickasaw plum). This small tree from the southeastern United States also forms thickets and is useful in much the same way as *P. alleghaniensis*. It is useful in Zones 6a–9a.

Prunus maritima 4 (beach plum). This straggling shrub or very small tree, usually remaining below 2 m/6.6 ft in height, is valued near its native habitat on the Atlantic Coast from Maine to Delaware for its salt tolerance, flowering interest, and edible fruits, much like those of *P. americana* but slightly smaller. Useful in Zones 4b–7a and perhaps farther south in coastal areas.

Prunus mexicana 6 (Mexican or big-tree plum). This tree does not form thickets like the other plums listed and is native from the Mississippi Basin of Kentucky to Oklahoma and into Mexico. Relatively drought-resistant, it is seldom used in landscape planting but may be preserved in natural and naturalized areas. The fruits are valued locally for preserves. Useful (and native) in Zones 7a–9a.

Prunus nigra 5–6 (Canada plum). This native of eastern Canada and adjacent United States is very similar in general effect and usefulness to *P. americana* but is probably significantly more cold-hardy and useful in Zones 3a–6b and perhaps Zone 7 as well. The selection 'Princess Kay' is upright in habit, with double white flowers and red fruits.

Prunus avium 6–8

MAZZARD CHERRY, SWEET CHERRY
Deciduous tree
Rosaceae (Rose Family)

Native Range. Eurasia.

Useful Range. USDA Zones 6a–8b in sites near bodies of water or otherwise protected from temperature extremes for effective flowering and fruiting; tree will grow well without fruiting in Zone 5 as well.

Function. Shade tree, specimen, edible fruits.

Size and Habit

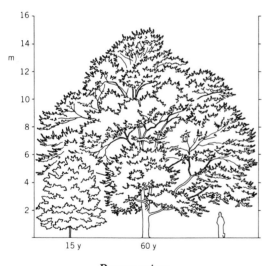

Prunus avium.

Adaptability

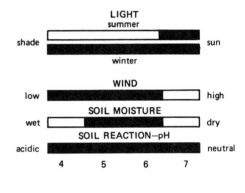

Seasonal Interest. *Flowers:* White, single or double, 2.5–3.5 cm/1–1.4 in. across, in clusters in midspring. *Foliage:* Medium green, not distinctive or particularly ornamental and not changing color before falling in autumn. *Fruits:* Very deep red and sweet at maturity. Commercial sweet cherries belong to this species. For fruit production, more than one cultivar or clone usually is needed for cross-pollination. *Trunk and branches:* Typical "cherry" bark, deep red-brown with horizontal lenticels, but not nearly as striking as that of some other cherry species.

Problems and Maintenance. Stone fruits are subject to a variety of insect and disease problems and require at least a minimal spray program for best results, even when used as landscape trees. Consistent production of good-quality fruits requires a more detailed spray schedule and a moderate climate free of severe temperature fluctuations, since flower buds are susceptible to freezes in winter and early spring. For most landscape purposes there are better and more trouble-free *Prunus* species, and this species probably should only be used where the edible fruits are also desired, except for the cultivars below.

Cultivars. 'Plena' has double flowers. Since extra petals are derived by modification of functional organs, this cultivar is sterile. As a result, the flowers are considerably longer lasting, barring freezes, than single flowers of the species type and there are, of course, no fruits.

'Scanlon' is a smaller, double-flowered selection, remaining below 6 m/20 ft in height.

Many cultivars have been selected for outstanding commercial fruit production. For more information on cultivars and other aspects of fruit production, consult the nearest county, state, or provincial extension service office.

Related Species

Prunus cerasus 6–7 (sour cherry). This small Eurasian tree is the parent species of commercial sour cherry cultivars. Although it is reasonably effective as a small shade tree, there are better choices for most situations where edible fruit production is not a concern, and in many situations the presence of fruit can cause problems with litter and birds. It is more shade tolerant than most cherry species yet requires at least partial sun for effective flowering and fruiting, and it is useful in Zones 5a–8b.

Prunus fruticosa 4 (ground cherry). This spreading Eurasian shrub, usually to 1 m/3.3 ft high, but occasionally to twice that, has white flowers, 1.5 cm/0.6 in. across, in small clusters, glossy dark green leaves, and dark red fruits to 1 cm/ 0.4 in. across. It is seldom available, but of interest in cold climates, useful at least in Zones 4b–6b, perhaps also colder zones.

Prunus besseyi 3

WESTERN SAND CHERRY
Deciduous shrub
Rosaceae (Rose Family)

Native Range. Northern Great Plains of the United States and Canada.

Useful Range. USDA Zones 3a–6a; can be grown somewhat farther south but is not particularly useful there.

Function. Massing, edible fruits.

Size and Habit

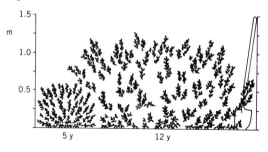

Prunus besseyi.

Adaptability

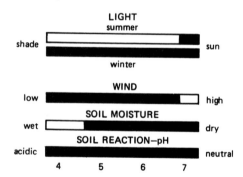

Seasonal Interest. *Flowers:* Small, white, adding minor landscape interest in middle to late spring. *Foliage:* Gray-green leaves are whitish underneath, 2.5–5 cm/1–2 in. long. *Fruits:* Deep purple, nearly black, 1.5 cm/0.6 in. across, borne in great numbers in native habitat, valued locally as edible fruits.

Problems and Maintenance. Brown rot disease may be troublesome in moist years and must be controlled to avoid serious damage. In relatively dry areas where this plant finds its greatest value, the disease may not often be severe.

Selections. "Hansen bush cherries" are selected seed strains from superior parent plants but are much more variable than vegetatively propagated cultivars would be. Occasional plants of *P. besseyi* have whitish or yellowish fruits and such selections have been made but not distributed widely.

Related Species

Prunus pumila 4 (sand cherry). This native of the Great Lakes region is similar to *P. besseyi* in appearance and function, but less prostrate and a little more shrubby. It is seldom available commercially.

Prunus caroliniana 6–7

CAROLINA LAURELCHERRY, CHERRY LAUREL

Evergreen tree

Rosaceae (Rose Family)

Native Range. Southeastern United States.

Useful Range. USDA Zones 7b–9a+ and limited use as a shrub in Zone 7a.

Function. Garden or patio tree, screen, hedge.

Size and Habit

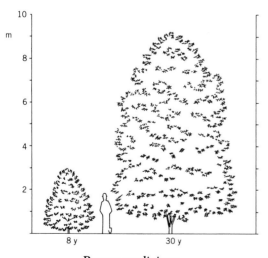

Prunus caroliniana.

Adaptability. Unusually sensitive to poorly drained soil but tolerant of salt in seashore situations.

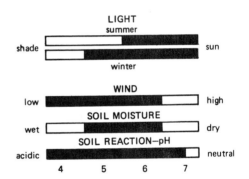

Seasonal Interest. *Flowers:* Very small, white, in racemes to 2.5 cm/1 in. long in midspring. *Foliage:* Evergreen, lustrous, leathery leaves, 5–10 cm/2–4 in. long, pointed. *Fruits:* Blue-black, shiny, cherrylike, 0.8 cm/0.3 in. across, in autumn, adding minor landscape interest until eaten by birds.

Problems and Maintenance. This plant has fewer problems than most *Prunus* species but is susceptible to white fly infestations in the Deep South and occasionally is attacked by borers. It requires pruning for maximum fullness as a visual screen but only for removing damaged wood when it is left to assume a small tree form. It is rather susceptible to physical breakage, especially from occasional ice and heavy snow in the northern parts of its useful range.

Prunus caroliniana.

Prunus cerasifera 6

CHERRY PLUM, MYROBALAN PLUM
Deciduous tree
Rosaceae (Rose Family)

Native Range. Southeastern Europe to central Asia.

Useful Range. USDA Zones 4b–9a with selection of appropriate cultivars.

Function. Specimen, patio tree, border accent.

Size and Habit

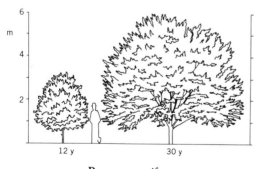

Prunus cerasifera.

Adaptability. Tolerates light shade, but the purple-leaved cultivars need full sun for best development of foliage color.

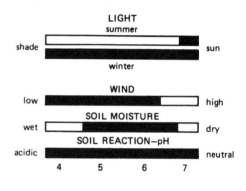

Seasonal Interest. *Flowers:* Pale to deep pink, small (1.8 cm/0.7 in. across) but numerous, showy in spring except for cultivars with deep pink flowers masked by emerging foliage. *Foliage:* Medium green in the seldom-used species type, cultivars vivid maroon-purple, fading to bronze-purple by late summer, variable depending on cultivar. *Fruits:* Maroon-purple plums are hardly noticeable among the leaves but are useful for jellies.

Problems and Maintenance. The better purple-leaved cultivars, at least, seem to be less troubled by insects and diseases in the Midwest, where they are most popular, than most plums and most other *Prunus* species. They require little maintenance other than occasional pest control.

Prunus cerasifera 'Atropurpurea.'

Cultivars. 'Atropurpurea' (= 'Pissardii') was the first selection for red-purple foliage, before 1880, and has been largely overshadowed by newer cultivars with more intense and long-lasting foliage color, but it is still useful in Zones 5a–9a.

'Hollywood' (= 'Trailblazer') is distinctive because its foliage first emerges green, then quickly turns purple, much like that of *P. virginiana* 'Schubert,' but it is not as commonly used in our area as 'Newport,' 'Thundercloud,' and 'Frankthrees' (Mt. St. Helens®) and is reportedly not as cold-hardy (Zone 6b–9a).

'Frankthrees' (Mt. St. Helens®; Plant Patent No. 4987, 1983) originated as a genetic sport on 'Newport,' selected for its greater vigor, stronger branching habit, and more intense and long-lasting foliage color, which gradually turns bright crimson in autumn in some years. Useful in Zones 4a–8b, probably as cold-hardy as 'Newport.'

'Newport,' long considered the most cold-hardy purple-leaved plum, was introduced by the University of Minnesota in the 1920s and is useful in the Northern Plains and elsewhere in Zones 4a–7b, with reddish purple foliage and pink flowers. This is probably a hybrid involving *P. americana*, *P. cerasifera* 'Atropurpurea,' and *P. salicina*.

'Nigra' is similar to 'Newport' in general ap-

pearance, but is probably less cold-hardy and not widely used.

'Pendula' is a broadly weeping green-leaved form, with pink flowers, probably useful in Zones 4b–9a but not widely used or available.

'Thundercloud,' since its introduction in 1937 has been one of the best and most widely used cultivars, with regularly broad-oval form and outstanding deep purple foliage color, holding well through the summer. Useful at least in Zones 5b–9a, probably also Zone 5a.

'Vesuvius' (= 'Krauter's Vesuvius'), selected by Luther Burbank in 1929, is similar to 'Thundercloud' but slightly smaller and more upright, with globose form and deep red-purple to black-purple foliage. Its light pink flowers seldom appear. It is useful at least in Zones 5b–9a.

Related Species

Prunus ×*blireiana* 6 (blireiana plum).   This hybrid of *P. cerasifera* 'Atropurpurea' × *P. mume* is similar in general effect to the other purple-leaved plums, but has wider leaves and semidouble, pink flowers. It is not as well adapted to the extreme North but is useful in Zones 6a–9a.

Prunus ×*cistena* 5 (purple-leaved sand cherry). This hybrid of *P. pumila* × *P. cerasifera* 'Atropurpurea' is distinctly shrubby rather than a tree (see exception below), usually reaching a height of 2 m/6.6 ft or a little more. Its white flowers contrast nicely with the deep red-purple immature new foliage. This hybrid is more cold-hardy than *P. cerasifera* cultivars, useful in Zones 3b–8a; there is occasional winter dieback in Zones 3b and 4a, which is not a serious problem since this plant needs occasional renewal pruning to maintain form and foliage color. The selection 'Schmidtcis' (Big Cis™; Plant Patent No. 5003, 1983) is much more vigorous, reported to grow twice as fast as other clones to a height of 4 m/ 13 ft, making it useful as a very small tree, larger than other *P.* ×*cistena* clones but smaller than *P. cerasifera*.

Prunus domestica 6–7 (garden plum).   This Eurasian species includes the blue or purple fruited commercial plum cultivars. Except for the fruit, it probably will not find much value in landscape planting. It is useful in Zones 5a–8b as a landscape tree, but for information on region and site for commercial fruit production as well as cultivars, consult county, state, or provincial extension service offices.

Prunus salicina 6–7 (Japanese plum).   This native of China includes the so-called Japanese or Oriental red plum cultivars grown commercially primarily on the West Coast, the south Atlantic coast, and the lower Mississippi Basin. This species is useful in Zones 6b–9a but, as with *P. domestica,* there is little reason for including it in landscaping plantings other than for fruit production.

Prunus glandulosa 4

D W A R F   F L O W E R I N G   A L M O N D ,
A L M O N D   C H E R R Y
Deciduous shrub
Rosaceae (Rose Family)

Native Range.   China and Japan.

Useful Range.   USDA Zones 4b–9a+.

Function.   Specimen, border, massing.

Size and Habit

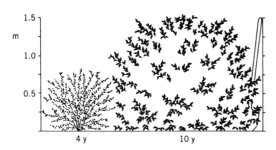

Prunus glandulosa.

Adaptability

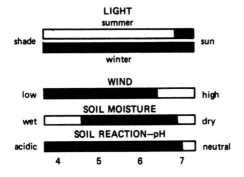

Seasonal Interest.   *Flowers:* Very showy, white or pink, single or double, to 1.5 cm/0.6 in. across, borne in large numbers in midspring just as leaves are beginning to unfold. *Foliage:* Medium green, lustrous but not especially interesting, falling without color change. *Fruits:* Small (to 1.2 cm/0.5 in. across) red cherries in summer. Not developed in double-flowered cultivars.

Problems and Maintenance.   This shrub is occasionally subject to several insect and disease problems, but its principal problems are borers in the South and mice in the North. When damaged, it can be pruned to the ground in spring or early summer and will return but will not flower for a year.

Cultivars.   'Alba Plena' (= 'Alboplena') has double white flowers. 'Sinensis' (= 'Rosea Plena', with double pink flowers, is the clone usually supplied when only *P. glandulosa* is specified; it is also sold under the name 'Rosea,' which properly applies to the single pink form, which is not widely available.

Related Species

Prunus tenella 4 (dwarf Russian almond).   This low shrub is of value for its extreme cold-hardiness, to Zone 3a. Its flowering interest is similar to that of the single-flowered forms of *P. glandulosa,* but it produces many root suckers, making it difficult to contain. The selection 'Fire Hill' is similar except that it has brighter pink flowers, a more upright habit, a lesser tendency to sucker, and excellent orange autumn foliage color.

Prunus triloba 5–6 (flowering almond). This tall shrub from China is striking in bloom in early spring, with large, double, pink or white flowers up to 2.5 cm/1 in. across. But, like the other members of this group, it is not very interesting in other seasons. It is susceptible to several insect and disease problems common to the stone fruits, and to rabbit damage as well,

making it a questionable selection where little maintenance will be provided. The selection 'Multiplex,' with bright pink, double flowers, is most commonly seen; f. *simplex* is the single-flowered wild form, found after the species type had been described as the double-flowered form. Whether 'Multiplex' or only the species is specified, the double-flowered form usually will be supplied. To obtain the single form, specify var. *simplex*, but this is rarely available. Useful in Zones 4a–9a and sheltered sites in Zone 3b.

Prunus laurocerasus 4–6

CHERRY LAUREL, ENGLISH LAUREL

Evergreen shrub

Rosaceae (Rose Family)

Native Range.   Southeastern Europe and adjacent Asia.

Useful Range.   USDA Zones 7a–9a+ and protected sites in Zone 6 with selection of appropriate cultivars (see Cultivars).

Function.   Massing, border, hedge, screen.

Size and Habit

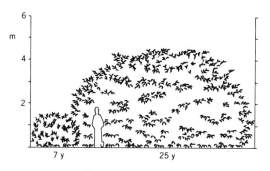

Prunus laurocerasus.

Adaptability.   In northern areas, protection from full winter sun and wind is necessary to reduce leaf scorch. Even though this plant grows best with average soil moisture, allowing soil to become drier in late summer and autumn reduces the tendency to grow late and enables the plant to harden properly for winter.

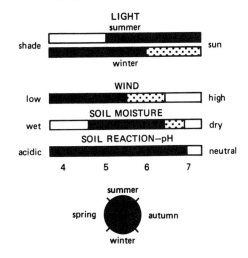

Seasonal Interest.   *Flowers:* Small, white, in racemes 5–12 cm/2–5 in. long, in midspring. *Foliage:* Evergreen, lustrous and leathery, bright to deep green, to 15 cm/6 in. long and 4–8 cm/1.6–3.2 in. wide, variable with cultivar. *Fruits:* Green, 0.8 cm/0.3 in. across, ripening purple-black in autumn.

Problems and Maintenance. This species is relatively trouble-free as *Prunus* species go, but is subject to a blight caused by the brown rot fungus that infects many stone fruits and may be infested by white flies and occasionally borers. Pruning may be necessary to control size unless ample space is provided for this wide-ranging plant, but it responds well to pruning, even shearing.

Prunus laurocerasus.

Cultivars. Even though 25 or more cultivars are used in Europe, only three are seen in our area with any frequency.

'Otto Luyken' is the smallest of these, re-maining below 1 m/3.3 ft at maturity and spreading horizontally to twice that, with lustrous medium-green leaves, 8–10 cm/3–4 in. long and 2.5 cm/1 in. wide. It is one of the hardier cultivars, surviving mild winters in Zone 6a but fully hardy only in Zones 6b–9a+.

'Schipkaensis' is probably the most cold-hardy cultivar of this species, growing in a vase shape to 1 m/3 ft high and twice as wide in 8–10 years, and to 2 m/6.6 ft high after many years, with lustrous, deep green leaves, 10–12 cm/4–5 in. long and 4–5 cm/1.5–2 in. wide. Useful in Zones 6a–9a, at least in sheltered sites.

'Zabeliana' is horizontal in habit but vigorous, growing to 1.5 m/5 ft high and twice as wide in 8–10 years, with handsome, glossy leaves, 10–15 cm/4–6 in. long but only 2–3 cm/1 in. wide. Useful in Zones 7a–9a+, and possibly in sheltered sites in somewhat colder zones.

Related Species

Prunus lusitanica 5–6 (Portuguese laurel). This native of Spain and Portugal is generally similar in appearance and landscape function to *P. laurocerasus* but is more easily trained into tree form and has larger flower clusters, to 25 cm/10 in. long. Useful in Zones 7b–9a+.

Prunus maackii 7

AMUR CHOKECHERRY
Deciduous tree
Rosaceae (Rose Family)

Native Range. Korea and Manchuria.

Useful Range. USDA Zones 3b–7a and possibly farther south.

Function. Specimen, border, small shade tree.

Size and Habit

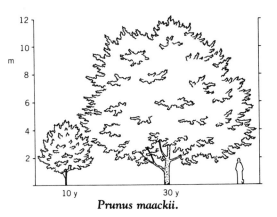

Prunus maackii.

Adaptability

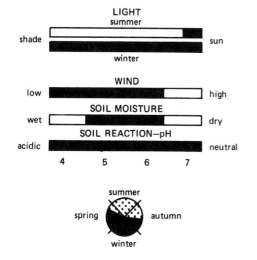

LIGHT
summer

shade | | sun

winter

WIND

low | | high

SOIL MOISTURE

wet | | dry

SOIL REACTION—pH

acidic | | neutral

4   5   6   7

summer

spring | | autumn

winter

Seasonal Interest. *Flowers:* Small, white, in racemes to 8 cm/3 in. long in middle to late spring. *Foliage:* Medium to bright green, dense but not distinctive, appearing early and falling early with little color change. *Fruits:* Black, inconspicuous. *Trunk and branches:* The bright amber to coppery orange bark curls as it peels off, lending striking winter interest.

Prunus maackii.

Problems and Maintenance. This tree is relatively trouble-free for a cherry in the far North, but more subject to disease and insect problems when used in Zones 6 and 7. It may assume either a single or multiple trunked form and may need initial pruning to ensure that the desired form is taken, but it is relatively free of maintenance thereafter.

Related Species

Prunus padus 7 (European bird cherry). This Eurasian tree (Europe through northern Asia to Japan) has fragrant white flowers in upright to drooping racemes 10–15 cm/4–6 in. long in middle spring after the leaves have expanded, giving mature trees a distinctive, billowy appearance at this season. The small black cherries are inconspicuous in midsummer, the foliage is not distinctive either in summer or autumn, and the tree has little or no winter interest. Useful in Zones 3b–7b and perhaps farther south as well, but highly susceptible to black knot disease. The var. *commutata* is about three weeks earlier than the species type in flowering and leafing out, with somewhat larger flower clusters, to 15 cm/6 in. long. The selection 'Watereri' is unusually showy, with almond-scented flowers in pendulous clusters to 20 cm/8 in. long, but may no longer be available in our area.

Prunus pensylvanica 7 (pin cherry, wild red cherry). This native of much of North America from Newfoundland to British Columbia and southward to Colorado and high elevations in North Carolina usually is rather short-lived, and so it is best used in naturalizing or temporary plantings. It is one of the first woody species to return to disturbed sites on poor soil, so there should be increasing use for this purpose (e.g., revegetating road cuts). It is a handsome tree with shiny, mahogany-red bark, small, shiny red cherries in late summer, and bright, yellow-orange to red fall foliage. Useful in Zones 3a–7a and perhaps farther south as well.

Prunus virginiana 6 (chokecherry). This shrub or small tree native to much of North America from Newfoundland to Saskatchewan and southward to Kansas and North Carolina has little landscape character and is so susceptible to the eastern tent caterpillar that it has been partially eradicated in parts of the northeastern United States to reduce caterpillar infestations. Its tendency to sucker heavily completes the case for eliminating the species type from planting lists. Its fruits are astringent but not bitter and have been used to make preserves and wine. The purple-leaved selection 'Schubert' (= 'Canada Red') is a useful small tree. Its leaves unfold green, turn deep red-purple as they mature, and change little before they fall in early autumn. The suckering habit of this species can be overcome by grafting on a non-suckering rootstock such as *P. padus*. This species and cultivar are useful in Zones 2b–7a, but are not at their best in Zones 6 and 7.

Prunus persica 6

PEACH
Deciduous tree
Rosaceae (Rose Family)

Native Range.   China.

Useful Range.   USDA Zones 6a–9a.

Function.   Patio tree, edible fruits.

Size and Habit

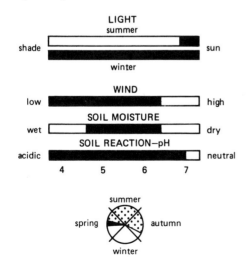

Prunus persica.

Adaptability

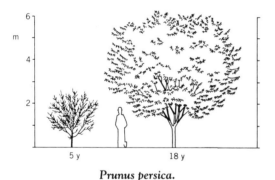

Seasonal Interest. *Flowers:* Pink to red or white, single or double, 2.5–3.5 cm/1–1.4 in. or more across in midspring. *Foliage:* Lustrous, somewhat leathery leaves are long (to 15 cm/6 in.), down-curving, and pointed, giving striking textural effect until they fall with little color change in late autumn. *Fruits:* Aside from their obvious edible value, the yellow-red fruits have some small landscape value. But when edible fruits are not wanted, they may be more a liability than an asset in the landscape, since they litter the ground. Double-flowered cultivars do not bear fruit.

Problems and Maintenance.   Peaches are subject to a wide array of insect and disease problems, the most serious of which is borers, which can kill trees in a short time. Peaches, whether for fruit or as an ornamental flowering tree, should be avoided unless a maintenance program is provided, at least for protection against borers. In addition, peach trees and flower buds frequently suffer freezing damage in winter or early spring in much of the useful range and probably are best planted only in the South and in northern areas that are considered suitable for commercial peach production.

Cultivars.   A few single-flowering, but mostly double-flowering, ornamental selections have been made, along with a few selections for red or purple foliage and dwarf habit. A list of all selections without regard for possible duplication would be very long, and only a few cultivars are available at any one time or place. Some of the more common cultivars are listed here to illustrate the variety that exists, not to recommend these over others. Select cultivars according to general type, availability, and known performance in the locality in question.

'Alba' has single, white flowers.

'Alboplena' and 'Iceberg' have double, white flowers.

'Atropurpurea' has deep red-purple leaves, changing to bronze, then green during the growing season.

'Bonanza' and 'Flory Dwarf' are dwarf fruiting cultivars used primarily as curiosities or specimens for accent rather than as functional landscape plants.

'Cardinal,' 'Early Double Red,' 'Late Double Red,' and 'Rubroplena' have double red flowers.

'Peppermint Stick' and 'Versicolor' have double flowers variegated respectively in red-white and pink-white.

'Pink Charming' and 'Roseoplena' have double, pink flowers.

'Rubra' has single, red flowers.

Related Species

Prunus armeniaca 7 (apricot). Although primarily used for fruit production, this tree from western Asia is also occasionally used as a landscape tree. In fact, it is more reliable in northern areas as a landscape tree than for fruiting, since flower buds open so early in spring that they frequently are frozen, preventing fruit set. In southern areas, brown rot disease may be very difficult to control. It is useful in Zones 5b–9a with reservations, but the Japanese apricot *(P. mume)* usually is preferred in the South.

Prunus dulcis 6 (synonym: *P. amygdalus*; almond). Several double-flowered cultivars of this species have been selected for landscape use, but they are not as commonly used or available in our area as the flowering peach cultivars and are less cold-hardy, useful in Zones 7a–9a.

Prunus mandshurica 5–6 (Manchurian apricot, bush apricot). This species is valued for its cold-hardiness in Zones 3b to 5b. It is usually used for its fruit but also has landscape value when its pinkish flowers open.

Prunus mume 6–7 (Japanese apricot). Well over 200 ornamental cultivars have been selected in Japan, often with almond-scented, single and double, white, pink, rose, and red flowers, opening in early spring. Only a few of these have found their way into commerce in North America. Some of the most popular are listed here.

'Alboplena' (= 'Alba Plena') has double white flowers, early.

'Bonita' has semidouble rose-red flowers.

'Dawn' has large, double, ruffled shell pink flowers, slightly later than most other cultivars.

'Matsubara Red' has dark red, double, lightly clove-scented flowers.

'Peggy Clarke' has very showy double rose-pink flowers, enclosed in red calyces and with long golden stamens in the center.

'Rosemary Clarke' has double white flowers, enclosed in red calyces, earlier than average.

'Rose Bud' has large, semidouble soft pink flowers.

'W. B. Clarke' develops a weeping form with age, and has pale pink, double flowers.

Prunus sargentii 7–8

SARGENT CHERRY
Deciduous tree
Rosaceae (Rose Family)

Native Range. Japan, Korea, Sakhalin.

Useful Range. USDA Zones 5a–9a, and will grow without reliable flowering in Zone 4b.

Function. Shade tree, specimen.

Size and Habit

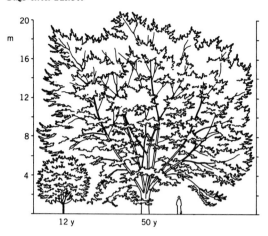

Prunus sargentii.

Adaptability

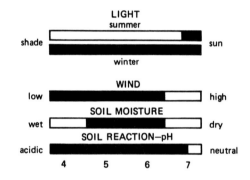

Seasonal Interest. *Flowers:* Single, rose-pink, to 4 cm/1.6 in. across, borne in large numbers before the foliage in midspring. *Foliage:* Reddish as it unfolds, turning deep green in summer and orange-red in autumn. One of the few *Prunus* species with reliable autumn color. *Fruits:* Small, purple-black cherries, inconspicuous. *Trunk and branches:* Bark is deep red-brown and lustrous with prominent horizontal lenticels, handsome in winter.

Problems and Maintenance. This is one of the most trouble-free of the flowering cherries, yet it is occasionally subject to some insect and disease problems, and it sometimes is short-lived. Pruning is seldom if ever necessary, provided enough space is given to this fairly large tree.

Cultivars. 'Columnaris' is distinctly narrower than the species type, with more upright branching. It is not truly columnar but narrowly oval in outline.

Prunus serotina 8

BLACK, RUM, OR WILD CHERRY
Deciduous tree
Rosaceae (Rose Family)

Native Range. Eastern United States and adjacent Canada.

Useful Range. USDA Zones 3b–9a.

Function. Shade tree, naturalizing.

Size and Habit

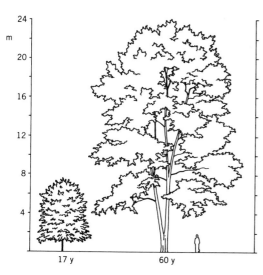

Prunus serotina.

Adaptability

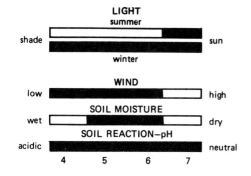

Seasonal Interest. *Flowers:* Small, white, lightly fragrant, in drooping clusters about 12 cm/5 in. long in late spring. *Foliage:* Deep green, slightly leathery leaves, 5–12 cm/2–5 in. long, turning yellowish or orange in autumn in northern areas. *Fruits:* Small cherries, to 1 cm/0.4 in. across, red in midsummer, then ripening black in late summer, slightly bitter but used for wines and preserves. *Trunk and branches:* Lenticular bark, cracking and curling back, adds quiet winter interest.

Problems and Maintenance. This is one of the more trouble-free of the cherries, usually not seriously enough affected by insects and diseases to require corrective spraying, especially in naturalized or parklike situations where this tree is at its best, but it may be seriously damaged by the eastern tent caterpillar and black knot in some areas. The wood is somewhat brittle and susceptible to breakage in ice storms.

Prunus serrulata 6

ORIENTAL CHERRY, JAPANESE FLOWERING CHERRY
Deciduous tree
Rosaceae (Rose Family)

Native Range. China, Japan, Korea.

Useful Range. USDA Zones 6b–8b, some cultivars hardy northward to Zone 6a.

Function. Specimen, patio tree, massing.

Size and Habit.   Becomes a large tree, occasionally to 20 m/66 ft in its native range but seldom exceeds 6–8 m/20–26 ft in landscape use in our area, since it tends to be short-lived. The Sato-zakura Hybrid 'Sekiyama' is illustrated.

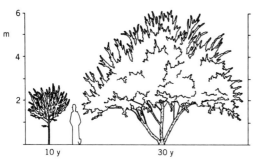

Prunus serrulata 'Sekiyama.'

Adaptability

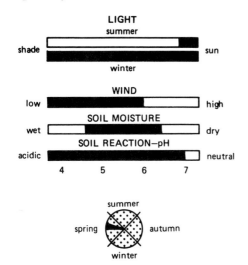

Seasonal Interest.   *Flowers:* White or pink, single or double, in certain cultivars fragrant, 4–6 cm/1.6–2.4 in. across in clusters of three to five, extremely showy in midspring. *Foliage:* Leaves are briefly bronze as they unfold, then deep green until they fall in midautumn, rather coarse in texture. *Fruits:* Small, black, inconspicuous. *Trunks and branches:* Bark is deep red-brown, lustrous, with prominent horizontal lenticels, handsome in winter, but not as striking as that of some of the other cherries (e.g., *P. serrula*).

Problems and Maintenance.   Like other cherries, this species and its hybrids are affected by many diseases and insects, but most occur only occasionally. For good performance of flowering cherries, it is best to follow a careful maintenance program consisting of necessary spraying and removal and destruction of affected parts. Otherwise, pruning is seldom necessary and should be avoided, since it is easy to disfigure these trees by excessive pruning. Several cultivars of this species can be carriers of serious cherry virus diseases without showing symptoms themselves. Trees of this species are seldom long-lived.

Varieties and Hybrids.   The cultivars once called Serrulata Hybrids have been reclassified in a major revision of the taxonomy of the oriental cherries by Roland M. Jefferson and others at the U.S. National Arboretum. Since the species name *P. serrulata* was first applied to a showy double-flowered form, wild trees of this species cannot be considered to be the taxonomic "type," so specialists have retained the name *P. serrulata* var. *spontanea* (synonym: *P. jamasakura;* Japanese mountain cherry) for the wild population that is believed to be involved in the Sato-zakura Group of hybrid cherries (see below).

Sato-zakura Group.   This is a collective name for the cultivars once called Serrulata Hybrids, believed to be derived from *P. serrulata* var. *spontanea* and various other species. There are many cultivars in this group, but only a few are commercially available in North America. Some of those are listed here:

'Amanogawa' (= 'Erecta') is narrowly fastigiate as a young tree, to about 6 m/20 ft tall, but may broaden considerably with age, with fragrant, translucent pale pink to white, semidouble flowers, nearly 5 cm/2 in. across, in large clusters.

'Caespitosa' (= 'Takasago'), a selection from *P.* × *sieboldii* (*P. speciosa* × *P. apetala*), has a rounded growth habit, with bright, light pink semidouble flowers, to 4.5 cm/1.8 in. across. This cultivar is probably equal to 'Sekiyama' in cold-hardiness, but is much less common.

'Fugenzo' (= 'Beni-fugen,' = 'James H. Veitch,' = 'Kofugen') is a broad-spreading form with unscented, very double, pink flowers, to 6 cm/2.4 in. across.

'Royal Burgundy' (Plant Patent No. 6520,

1989) is similar to 'Sekiyama' in growth habit, with deeper pink flowers and red-purple foliage that turns red-orange in autumn.

'Sekiyama' (= 'Kanzan,' = 'Kwanzan') is by far the most common cultivar of this group in North America. With unscented, very double, pink flowers, to 6 cm/2.4 in. across, borne in large clusters, and a stiffly upright, vase-shaped growth habit, it lacks the delicacy usually associated with Japanese cherries. For outright showiness, though, it is most impressive, and it is among the most cold-hardy in this group, to Zone 6a and protected sites in Zone 5b.

'Shiro-fugen' (= 'Albo-rosea') is fast-growing and wide-spreading, with unscented double white flowers to 6 cm/2.4 in. across, rosy pink in bud, together with the coppery immature foliage.

'Shirotae' (= 'Kojima,' = 'Mt. Fuji') has fragrant, pure white, semidouble to double flowers, to 6 cm/2.4 in. across, and wide-spreading, flat-topped growth habit. One of the most handsome of the oriental cherries, this cultivar performs better in the southern parts of our area than in the North.

'Shogetsu' is wide-spreading and flat-topped with age, with very double, translucent pale pink flowers, opening late in the season and fading to white.

'Taihaku' (= 'Tai Kaku'), translated "great white cherry," is a large tree, growing to 10–12 m/33–36 ft in height and width, with a broad vase-shaped habit, with red-bronze new leaves, becoming green and very large, to 20 cm/8 in. long and 12 cm/4.7 in. wide, at maturity, then turning gold in autumn. Flowers are single, cupped, to 6 cm/2.4 in. across, pale pink in bud and opening pure white.

'Ukon' (= f. *grandiflora*, = 'Mangetsu,' = f. *viridiflora*) is distinctive for its semidouble, greenish yellow flowers, to 4.5 cm/1.8 in. across, with red-bronze new foliage and an upright-spreading growth habit.

Prunus subhirtella 6

HIGAN CHERRY
Deciduous tree
Rosaceae (Rose Family)

Native Range. Japan

Useful Range. USDA Zones 6a–8b and some cultivars in Zones 5b, or 9a.

Function. Specimen, patio tree.

Size and Habit

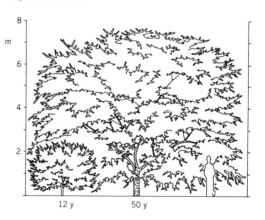

Prunus subhirtella.

Adaptability

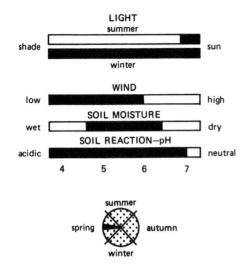

Seasonal Interest. *Flowers:* Pale to deep pink, single or double, about 2.5 cm/1 in. across, giving a loose, airy effect in early to middle spring. *Foliage:* Deep green, falling in autumn with little color change. *Fruits:* Small, black, inconspicuous. *Trunks and branches:* Bark is deep red-brown with prominent horizontal lenticels, distinctive but not offering the strong winter interest of some other flowering cherries.

Problems and Maintenance. This species is not as seriously affected by diseases and insects as some other Asian cherries, but for good performance, it is best to follow a careful maintenance program (see *P. serrulata*).

Prunus subhirtella 'Pendula.'

Varieties, Cultivars, and Hybrids. The var. *ascendens* is a large, upright tree with white flowers; it is seldom, if ever, available for landscape use.

'Autumnalis' (= 'Jugatsu Sakura') differs little from the species type except that it is smaller (to 5–6 m/16–20 ft tall), with a rounded growth habit, and some of its flowers open during warm periods in autumn.

'Pendula' (= 'Ito Sakura,' = 'Shidare Higan') is the name used for the common weeping cherries, widely used in Zones 5b–8b and among the most graceful of all flowering trees. Since these trees are quite variable in vigor and flower color and include some double-flowered trees, this probably should not be considered a cultivar, but rather a form (f. *pendula*), as has been done in the past, especially since there are also clones with cultivar names such as 'Pendula Alba,' 'Pendula Plena Rosea,' and 'Snofozam' (see below).

'Pendula Plena Rosea' (= 'Sendai Ito Sakura') is a weeping form with double pink flowers.

'Rosea' is an upright, oval to rounded form, growing to 8 m/25 ft tall and wide, with deep, bright pink flowers.

'Rosy Cloud' (Plant Patent No. 4540, 1980) is an upright form, growing to 6–8 m/20–26 ft tall, with long-lasting (for a cherry), bright pink, double flowers.

'Snofozam' (Snow Fountains®), 'Wayside White Weeper,' and 'White Fountain' are vigorous white flowered weeping cherries, growing to 2.5–3.5 ft/8–11 ft, and reported to have golden-orange foliage color. There may be some duplication of names in this group.

'Whitcomb' has an open, broad globe shape, growing to 10 m/3.3 ft tall and wide, with single pink flowers.

The following are hybrids involving *P. subhirtella:*

'Hally Jolivette' 5 (*P. subhirtella* × *P.* ×*yedoensis*) is a small, shrubby tree to 2–4 m/6.6–13 ft tall, upright and loosely graceful in flower, outstanding because its semidouble, pink and white flowers open gradually over about three weeks, lasting longer than those of most flowering cherries. It is useful in Zones 5b–8b and protected sites in Zone 5a.

'Pandora' (*P. subhirtella* 'Rosea' × *P.* ×*yedoensis*) is shrubby with upright branches to 6 m/20 ft tall and half as wide, with great quantities of single pink bicolored flowers. Introduced in England in the 1930s, it may not be commercially available in North America.

'Accolade' (*P. subhirtella* × *P. sargentii*) is a vigorous upright tree to 6–9 m/20–30 ft tall, with semidouble pink flowers, probably cold-hardy to Zone 5a, considering its parentage.

Related Species and Additional Hybrids

Prunus campanulata 6 (Taiwan cherry). This small tree from Japan and Taiwan is outstanding in bloom very early in spring, with white to bright pink bell-shaped flowers, 2.5 cm/1 in. across, borne in nodding clusters. This flowering interest alone is enough to justify its use in Zones 8a–9a+, and perhaps Zone 7b. The hybrid 'Okame' (*P. campanulata* × *P. incisa*), introduced by the Morris Arboretum from England in 1946, is a graceful, upright small tree, narrowly oval at first, broadening in old age, to 7 m/23 ft tall and nearly as wide, with long-lasting, bright rose-pink flowers, starting very early in spring and, at least in some years, by golden to red-orange autumn foliage. Useful in Zones 6b–9a, perhaps also sheltered sites in Zone 6a.

Prunus incisa 5–6 (Fuji cherry). This shrubby, eventually round-headed tree from the mountains of Japan, to 4–8 m/13–26 ft tall, is very showy in early spring, but only briefly, since its white to rose flowers drop their petals rather quickly. Useful in Zones 6a–9a, but rarely available.

Prunus nipponica 5–6 (Japanese alpine or Nippon cherry). This shrubby small tree makes a showy display of single, white or pink flowers in early to middle spring, but its yellow to orange autumn foliage is a more distinctive feature. Useful in Zones 6a–8b, but seldom available.

Prunus serrula 6 (paperbark cherry). The principal landscape feature of this uncommon tree from western China is its lustrous, deep red bark, handsomely marked with large horizontal lenticels. Its small white flowers are only of incidental interest and, unfortunately, it is susceptible to some of the most destructive virus diseases. When virus-free trees are available, it is worth using for its remarkable bark interest, in Zones 6a–8a, and perhaps sheltered sites in Zone 5b.

Prunus ×*yedoensis* 6 (Yoshino cherry, Potomac cherry). This and the Sato-zakura group are the predominant cherries in the famous planting of Japanese cherries in the Tidal Basin area of Washington, D.C. The Yoshino cherry does not have a wild form, and its origin has long been unclear, but specialists now consider it to be a hybrid between *P.* ×*subhirtella* and another Japanese cherry, *P. speciosa* (Oshima cherry). *P.* ×*yedoensis* is one of the most showy of all flowering cherries in bloom, with many fragrant single flowers, about 3 cm/1.2 in. across, opening white, soon turning pink. It is not particularly long-lived here, seldom exceeding 8 m/26 ft in height, with somewhat greater spread, but it grows larger in Japan. The selection 'Afterglow' (Plant Patent No. 5730, 1986) is typical of *P.* ×*yedoensis* except that it has rich pink flowers that do not fade, and is reported to be more cold hardy (Zone 6a?). 'Akebono' (translation: 'Daybreak') is an older selection, magnificent in bloom, with soft-pink flowers, translucent in overall effect. 'Shidare Yoshino' (synonyms: var. *perpendens*, 'Pendula') is a strongly pendulous form with white flowers. It is very effective but seldom available.

Prunus serrula.

Prunus tomentosa 5

NANKING OR MANCHU CHERRY
Deciduous shrub
Rosaceae (Rose Family)

Native Range.   Northeastern Asia to the Himalayas.

Useful Range.   USDA Zones 3a–6b, but may suffer serious injury in some years in Zones 5 and 6 from spring freezes following premature activity during warm periods in late winter.

Function.   Screen, hedge, border, specimen.

Size and Habit

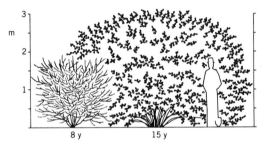

Prunus tomentosa.

Adaptability.   One of the best adapted shrubs to the Northern Plains, tolerating extreme cold and considerable wind and dryness.

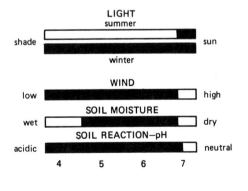

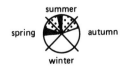

Seasonal Interest.   *Flowers:* Small but numerous, white or pinkish, in early to middle spring.

Foliage: Dull, deep green leaves are hairy and wrinkled, giving distinctive texture but no great seasonal interest. *Fruits:* Red cherries are tart but edible in much the same way as those of sour cherry (*P. cerasus*), in pies and preserves. They tend to be borne in large numbers in alternate years when more than one plant (seedling) is present for cross-pollination. Isolated plants do not always fruit well.

Prunus tomentosa.

Problems and Maintenance.   This shrub is subject to damage by rodents and to many of the diseases and insects of cherries in general, but this does not rule it out in low-maintenance situations, at least in the far North (Zones 3 and 4).

Cultivars.   Selections for outstanding flowering and fruiting have been made but are not widely available. One such selection is 'Geneva.' The white-fruited form 'Leucocarpa' is seldom available.

Related Species

Prunus japonica 4 (Chinese or Japanese bush cherry, Korean cherry).   This hardy shrub from northeastern Asia serves as a smaller edition of *P. tomentosa* in the landscape, with comparable fruiting value, without which it would have little landscape value. It is useful in about the same range as *P. tomentosa* but is seldom available.

Pseudocydonia sinensis 6

Synonym: *Cydonia sinensis*
CHINESE QUINCE
Deciduous shrub or small tree
Rosaceae (Rose Family)

Native Range.   China.

Useful Range.   USDA Zones 6b–9a.

Function.   Specimen or patio tree. Grown primarily for bark interest.

Size and Habit

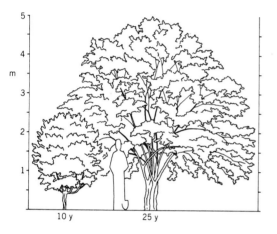

Pseudosinensis sinensis.

Adaptability.   This plant is widely adapted to soil and moisture variations but grows best in full sun or light shade.

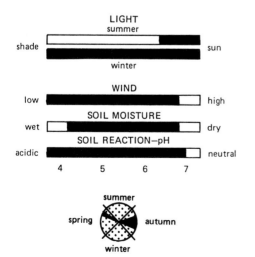

Seasonal Interest.   *Flowers:* Pale pink in late spring, partly obscured by the leaves and not showy. *Foliage:* Gray-green, rather sparse, turning red in autumn. *Fruits:* Large, aromatic, yellow when ripe, useful for preserves. *Trunk and branches:* Multicolored flaking bark and sinewy form of trunk and main branches of old specimens add landscape interest year-round.

Pseudocydonia sinensis.

Problems and Maintenance.   This plant is subject to occasional mite infestation and fire blight in some areas, and it needs minimal pruning to maintain form.

Related Species

Cydonia oblonga 6 (quince).   This central Asian tree is the quince from which preserves are made commercially, seldom used solely for its landscape character. Its form and flowering are less impressive than those of several other small trees, and it has several insect and disease problems. It is useful in Zones 6a–9a.

Pseudolarix amabilis 8

Synonyms: *P. kaempferi, Chrysolarix amabilis*
GOLDEN LARCH
Deciduous tree
Pinaceae (Pine Family)

Native Range.   Eastern China.

Useful Range.   USDA Zones 6a–7b, perhaps sheltered sites in Zone 5, also Zone 8 in moist sites with moderate summer temperatures.

Function.   Specimen, screen.

Size and Habit

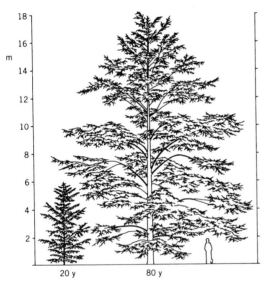

Pseudolarix amabilis.

Seasonal Interest.   *Foliage:* New leaves, flattened needles, to 6 cm/2.4 in. long and 0.3 cm/0.12 in. broad, emerge a delicate light green in middle to late spring, turn a soft medium green in summer, and then, briefly, yellow to russet-gold before falling in middle to late autumn. *Cones:* Yellow-green, ripening red-brown, 5–8 cm/2–3 in. long, borne erect on the upper surfaces of main branches of older trees, composed of fleshy scales that disintegrate on the tree in midautumn. *Branching:* Horizontally spreading to gracefully descending main branches and somewhat pendulous side branches add interest at all seasons.

Pseudolarix amabilis.

Problems and Maintenance.   This is one of the most trouble-free of all trees given proper site and soil conditions. It seldom requires even pruning provided it has ample space in which to grow and assume its graceful form.

Adaptability

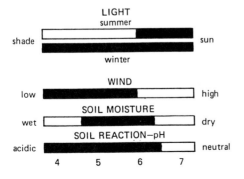

Pseudotsuga menziesii 8

Synonyms: *P. Douglasii, P. taxifolia*
DOUGLAS FIR
Evergreen tree
Pinaceae (Pine Family)

Native Range.   Western United States and adjacent Canada and Mexico.

Useful Range.   USDA Zones 3b–6b with selection of appropriate genetic material, and Zone 7, perhaps even Zone 8, in areas with moderate summer temperatures.

Function.   Screen, specimen.

Size and Habit

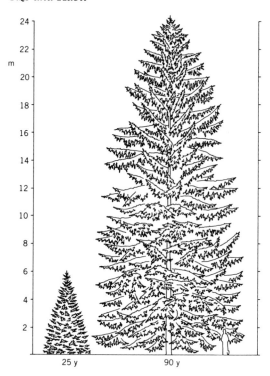

Pseudotsuga menziesii.

Adaptability.   Trees from Rocky Mountain seed sources probably tolerate wind and high soil pH better than Pacific Coast types.

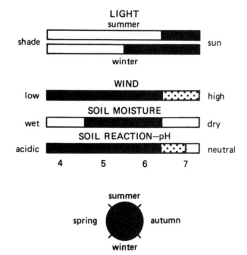

Seasonal Interest. *Foliage:* Deep green or slightly blue-green needles, 2–3 cm/0.8–1.2 in. long and slightly flattened, form a dense mass, handsome in all seasons. *Cones:* Medium brown, 5–10 cm/2–4 in. long, with distinctive forked bracts protruding from between scales.

Problems and Maintenance.   Several diseases and insects can be troublesome, but not enough to require control measures except in occasional cases of severe outbreaks. Maintenance requirements are much the same as for spruces (*Picea* species).

Subspecies and Cultivars. The ssp. *glauca* (blue or Colorado Douglas fir), native to the Rocky Mountains, is slower growing than the coastal-growing species type, ssp. *menziesii,* with a heavier waxy layer on the needles, thus more bluish-green and more tolerant of cold and wind than the coastal form. This is the form usually used in our area. At least 50 selections have been made for form, color, and dwarfness, but few of these are available commercially in North America.

'Fastigiata' is a vigorous selection for narrowly conical form, with height at least four times its width, useful for vertical accent.

'Fletcheri' is a dwarf form with blue-green foliage and a flat-globose form, to 1–2 m/3.3–6.6 ft high and twice as wide, in time.

'Glauca Pendula' has glaucous, blue-green foliage and weeping branches. Probably more than one clone is sold under this name.

'Globosa' and 'Pumila' are dwarf forms, slow-growing, with rounded to pillowlike form.

'Pendula' is actually a collective name for several different weeping forms. It is usually necessary to hand-select plants to be sure of their form and growth rate.

Related Species

Pseudotsuga japonica 8 (Japanese Douglas fir), *P. sinensis* 8 (Chinese Douglas fir), and *P. wilsoniana*

8 (Taiwan Douglas fir).   These species, native to eastern Asia, can be found in arboreta but are seldom, if ever, commercially available in our area.

Pseudotsuga macrocarpa 7–8 (California Douglas fir, bigcone spruce).   This species resembles *P. menziesii* except for its much larger cones (to 15 cm/6 in. long). It is native to southern California, little known outside that area, and probably not adapted in our area.

Ptelea trifoliata 6

WAFER ASH, HOP TREE
Deciduous shrub or small tree
Rutaceae (Rue Family)

Native Range.   New York to Minnesota, south to Florida and Texas.

Useful Range.   USDA Zones 4a–9a, with selection of appropriate genetic material.

Function.   Border, patio tree, naturalizing.

Size and Habit

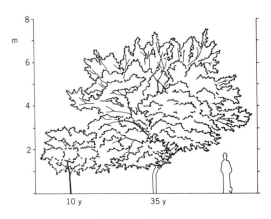

Ptelea trifoliata.

Adaptability

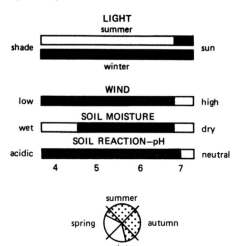

Seasonal Interest.   *Flowers:* Male and female flowers occur on the same tree, small, greenish white, inconspicuous. *Foliage:* Bright to deep green, trifoliate leaves are aromatic when crushed, fall without color change in midautumn. *Fruits:* Thin, waferlike, winged fruits, to 2.5 cm/1 in. across, are pale yellowish green, adding quiet interest from late summer through autumn and into winter in some areas.

Problems and Maintenance. This is one of the most trouble-free small trees, some compensation for its lack of striking seasonal interest, but occasionally it is infected with a leaf-spot disease, especially in warm, moist climates. It may require initial training when used in tree form, but needs little maintenance thereafter except to control occasional insect infestations.

Related Species. Several additional species occur as large shrubs or small trees in the southeastern and southwestern United States and adjacent Mexico. Of these, probably only *P. polyadenia* 5 (dwarf wafer ash) is commercially available (and barely so). Useful in Zones 7a–9a, perhaps also Zone 6.

Ptelea trifoliata.

Pterocarya ×rehderiana 8

REHDER WINGNUT
Deciduous tree
Juglandaceae (Walnut Family)

Hybrid Origin. *P. fraxinifolia × P. stenoptera*

Useful Range. USDA Zones 6b–9a, and probably some sites in Zone 6a, but little-tried.

Function. Shade tree and street tree, but only where sufficient space is available.

Size and Habit

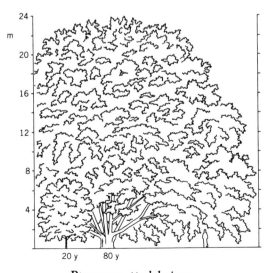

Pterocarya ×rehderiana.

Adaptability

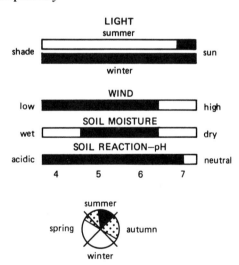

Seasonal Interest. *Flowers:* Male and female catkins occur on the same tree and are inconspicuous. *Foliage:* Rich, deep green, compound leaves, 20–40cm/8–16 in. long, of 11–19 leaflets, attached to a lightly or partially winged rachis (midrib), remaining deep green until they fall in late autumn. *Fruits:* Winged nutlets, borne in pendulous chains to 40 cm/16 in. long, add light green contrast to the deep green foliage in summer.

Problems and Maintenance. This tree seems to be generally trouble-free, but it is so infrequently used that there has been little opportunity to observe potential disease problems. Pruning is necessary only to remove any damaged wood and for size control in situations where space limitations should have deterred planting.

Pterocarya ×rehderiana.

Related Species

Pterocarya fraxinifolia 8 (Caucasian wingnut). This species, native from the Caucasus to Iran, can be distinguished from *P. ×rehderiana* and *P. stenoptera* by its completely unwinged leaf-rachis. It is at least as cold-hardy as the hybrid and is useful in Zones 6a–9a, but is little-tried and seldom, if ever, available.

Pterocarya stenoptera 8 (Chinese wingnut). This Chinese counterpart of *P. fraxinifolia* differs very little from that species except that it is less cold-hardy, and with each leaf-rachis distinctly winged. Useful in Zones 7a–9a, but hardly ever available.

Platycarya strobilacea 7 (cluster-walnut). This distinctive and graceful small to medium-sized tree from China, also in the Juglandaceae, is even less common than *Pterocarya* in North America. It gives the effect of a small walnut tree, with compound leaves, 15–30 cm/12 in. long, with 7–15 toothed leaflets. The male catkins, terminal on the new growth, add quiet interest in late summer. Female catkins, on the same tree, are smaller. It is potentially useful at least in Zones 6b–8a and sheltered sites in Zone 6a, but is not presently available.

Pterostyrax hispida 7

EPAULETTE TREE
Deciduous tree
Styracaceae (Styrax Family)

Native Range.   Japan.

Useful Range.   USDA Zones 6a–9a+.

Function.   Specimen, patio tree.

Size and Habit

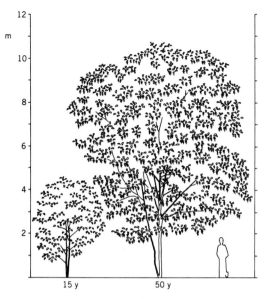

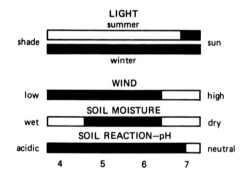

Pterostyrax hispida.

Adaptability

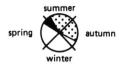

Seasonal Interest. *Flowers:* Fragrant, creamy white, in pendulous, fringelike panicles, to 20 cm/8 in. long, in late spring. *Foliage:* Light green leaves give a rather coarse effect and fall with little color change in midautumn. *Fruits:* Small dry fruits are bristly and hang on after leaves fall but add little additional landscape interest.

Problems and Maintenance. This tree seems to be relatively trouble-free but is so little used that there has not been much opportunity to observe potential disease and insect problems. Pruning is not necessary other than to remove dead and damaged wood and to remove "suckers" arising from the rootstock. It is seldom available commercially, but it is a distinctive tree that might be used more widely, especially in the South.

Related Species

Pterostyrax corymbosa 6 (shrubby epaulette tree). This shrubby species is smaller than *P. hispida* but can be trained into a very small tree, to 3–5 m/10–16 ft. Its flower clusters are somewhat smaller (to about 10–12 cm/4–5 in. long), and it may be slightly less cold-hardy, but it does not produce as much "sucker" growth. It is useful at least in Zones 7b–9a+ but is less likely to be available than *P. hispida.*

Pueraria lobata 1 and 3

Synonym: *P. Thunbergiana*
K U D Z U   V I N E
Deciduous vine
Fabaceae (Leguminosae; Pea Family)

Native Range. China and Japan.

Useful Range. USDA Zones 6b–9a+, killing back to the ground and returning from the roots in most winters in Zones 6b–7b and frequently in Zone 8.

Function. Screen (with support), twining loosely, climbing to heights of 15 m/50 ft in mild climates; large-scale groundcover for erosion control. Since it grows extremely rapidly, it has attracted some interest in revegetation of stripmined areas.

Size and Habit

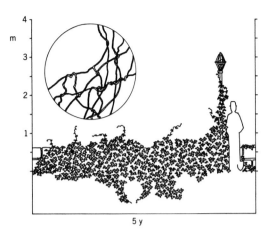

Pueraria lobata.

Adaptability

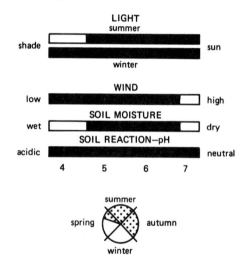

Seasonal Interest.   *Flowers:* Violet-purple, pea-like, in upright clusters to 25 cm/10 in. long in late summer in zones where winter dieback is not complete. *Foliage:* Compound, with three leaflets, the largest (central) to 18 cm/7 in. long, medium to light green and hairy, borne on coarse, heavy, loosely twining stems.

Problems and Maintenance.   Trouble-free but itself a problem because of its rampant growth, Kudzu vine should be planted, if at all, only in large-scale situations where other plants will not function as well, and where it is not likely to escape. In some areas of the South, this plant has covered acres of land, climbing over utility poles and lines, trees, and anything else standing in its way.

Pueraria lobata.

Punica granatum 4–6

POMEGRANATE
Deciduous shrub
Punicaceae (Pomegranate Family)

Native Range.   Southeastern Europe to the Himalayas.

Useful Range.   USDA Zones 7b–9a+.

Function.   Hedge, specimen, border.

Size and Habit

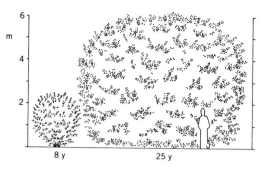

Punica granatum.

Adaptability. This is one of the most successful shrubs in hot, dry sites and calcareous soils, but not in poorly drained soils.

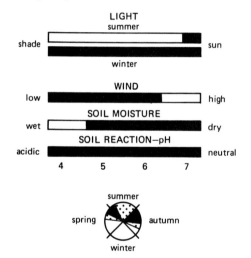

Seasonal Interest. *Flowers:* Scarlet, yellow, or white, single or double, to 3 cm/1.2 in. across from late spring to early summer. *Foliage:* Deciduous but glossy and somewhat leathery leaves, reddish as they unfold, then bright green, 2.5–8 cm/1–3 in. long, borne on stiff, somewhat spiny branches, falling in autumn with little color change. *Fruits:* Domelike, deep yellow, burnished red-orange, scarlet, or purplish red, 5–8 cm/2–3 in. across, rather dry, with tart, edible, red seeds, the whole fruit colorful in autumn.

Problems and Maintenance. One of the most trouble-free shrubs, pomegranate requires practically no care other than occasional pruning for shaping if it is to be used as an informal hedge.

Cultivars. 'Alba Plena' (= 'Multiplex') has creamy white, double flowers, but no fruits.

'California Sunset' (= 'Mme. Legrelle') is a large shrub, to at least 3 m/10 ft tall and wide, with semidouble flowers, coral-pink with creamy white petal margins.

'Chico' is low-growing, usually to only 2 m/ 6.6 ft tall and wide, with double, bright red-orange flowers over the entire summer, but no fruit.

'Flavescens' has single yellow flowers, but is seldom available commercially.

'Nana' is a dwarf, to 1–3 m/3.3–6.6 ft tall and wide, with considerably smaller leaves, flowers, and fruits than the species type and other cultivars. This is a very popular and useful plant because its size works well in small-scale situations.

'Nochi Shibara,' introduced by Brookside Gardens, Wheaton, Maryland, is similar in size and form to 'California Sunset,' but with fully double, deep orange-red flowers.

'Toyosho,' another Brookside introduction, is similar to 'Nochi Shibara' in overall appearance, but with light apricot, fully double flowers.

'Wonderful' is a full-sized plant selected for outstanding fruit production. Many other cultivars selected for fruit quality are in use on the Gulf Coast as well as the West Coast.

Pyracantha coccinea 3–5

SCARLET FIRETHORN
Semievergreen or evergreen shrub
Rosaceae (Rose Family)

Native Range. Southern Europe and western Asia.

Useful Range. USDA Zones 6a–9a and a few cultivars in Zone 5 as well.

Function. Border, wall shrub (espalier), foundation, hedge.

Size and Habit. Most cultivars remain below eye level in the North but grow taller in the South, some to 4 m/13 ft or taller if given espalier training.

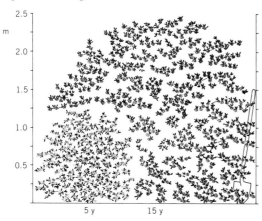

Pyracantha coccinea.

Adaptability. Planting in sites with good air circulation helps to control diseases in the South, but strong winds, especially in winter, should be avoided in the northern extremes of its useful range.

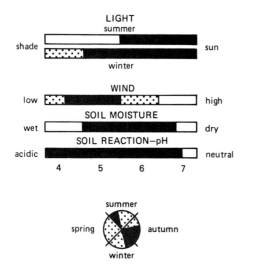

Seasonal Interest. *Flowers:* Small, white, in clusters, effective against the new foliage in early summer. *Foliage:* Rich green leaves are variable in size and shape, up to 4 cm/1.6 in. long and rather narrow, semievergreen in the North (Zones 6 and 7), evergreen in the South (Zones 8 and 9). *Fruits:* Bright orange, red-orange, or yellow, about 0.6 cm/0.25 in. across, borne in large numbers in good sites and showy from early autumn into early winter, depending on cultivar. *Branching:* Stiffly irregular branching pattern is interesting and lends well to training in a vertical plane (espalier), especially against a south-facing wall.

Problems and Maintenance. Several insects and diseases occasionally are troublesome but can be controlled. The most consistent problems are fire blight, difficult to control when weather conditions are favorable, and scab, which can disfigure fruits during prolonged moist periods, especially in sites with poor air circulation. Cultivars vary in their resistance to these diseases. Aphids, lace bugs, mites, and scale insects are occasionally troublesome.

Cultivars and Hybrids. Many cultivars are in use. Some of the most widely used are listed here.

'Fiery Cascade,' a recent introduction from the breeding program of Elwin Orton at Rutgers University, makes a tall mound, to 2.4 m/8 ft tall and 2.8 m/9 ft wide, with cascading branches covered with glossy dark green foliage and heavy crops of berries, orange in late summer, turning bright red in autumn. It is highly resistant to apple scab and fire blight and is useful in Zones 6b–9a and perhaps also Zone 6a.

'Golden Charmer,' a hybrid of *P. coccinea* × *P. rogersiana* from Holland, is narrowly upright, to 2.4 m/8 ft tall, with golden yellow fruits. It is resistant to apple scab and useful in Zones 6b–9a, perhaps also Zone 6a.

'Kasan' is compact in growth, but eventually to at least 2 m/6.6 ft tall and wide, with orange berries, and is one of the most cold-hardy of all cultivars, useful in Zones 5b–9a, and sheltered sites in Zone 5a, but its berries are susceptible to apple scab.

'Lalandei' is one of the oldest and widely used cultivars in northern landscapes, growing to 2–3 m/6.6–10 ft tall, with orange berries similar to those of 'Kasan.' It is useful in Zones 5b–9a, but its berries are susceptible to apple scab.

'Lalandei Thornless' is similar to 'Lalandei' except that it is less thorny, useful in public areas where people may brush against it, but not widely available.

'Lowboy' is much lower growing than the above cultivars, to 0.75–0.9 m/2.5–3 ft tall and at least twice as wide, with orange berries, useful for bank planting and as a large-scale groundcover in Zones 7a–9a+ and protected sites in Zone 6.

'Monrovia' (='Lalandei Monrovia') is a vigorous, upright plant, to 2.4–3 m/8–10 ft tall, with bright orange berries, useful at least in Zones 7a–9a+ and protected sites in Zone 6b.

'Orange Charmer,' a hybrid of *P. coccinea* × *P. rogersiana* from Holland, is similar to 'Golden Charmer' in habit, foliage, disease-resistance, and hardiness, but has larger, deep orange berries.

'Orange Glow,' another import from Holland, believed to be a hybrid of *P. coccinea* × *P. crenatoserrata*, has a loosely branching, narrowly upright growth habit and deep orange to orange-red fruits. It is resistant to scab and useful in Zones 7a–9a+, perhaps also parts of Zone 6.

'Rutgers,' another recent introduction from Rutgers University, is a low-growing form, to 0.8–0.9 m/2.5–3 ft tall and twice that in spread. It is free of apple scab and fire blight, useful in Zones 6b–9a, and to be preferred over 'Lowboy.'

'Wyatt' is another selection for vigorous, upright growth, 2–3 m/6.6–10 ft tall and wide, with orange berries, useful in Zones 6a–9a.

Pyracantha koidzumii 5

Synonym: *P. Formosana*
FORMOSA FIRETHORN
Evergreen shrub
Rosaceae (Rose Family)

Native Range. Taiwan.

Useful Range. USDA Zones 7b–9a+.

Function. Screen, wall shrub (espalier), hedge, specimen.

Size and Habit

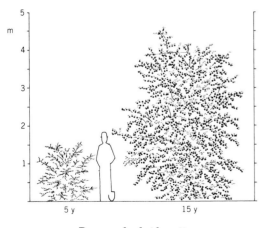

Pyracantha koidzumii.

Adaptability. Planting in breezy sites helps control diseases by reducing air stagnation.

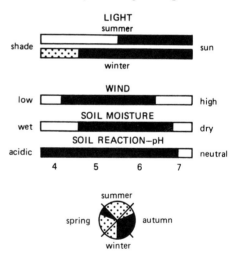

Seasonal Interest. *Flowers:* Small, white, in clusters, effective against the deep green foliage in late spring. *Foliage:* Rich, deep green leaves are similar to those of *P. coccinea* except more distinctly rounded on the end, evergreen except when occasionally winterburned in the northern extremes of its useful range. *Fruits:* Orange-red to deep red, about 0.6 cm/0.25 in. across, borne in very large numbers in good sites, and showy from early autumn well into winter.

Problems and Maintenance.   Troubles are generally similar to those of *P. coccinea* and other *Pyracantha* species. Fire blight is the most serious problem, although less so than on *P. coccinea*. It can be partly controlled by removing and burning new infections as soon as they appear, but it is difficult to control fully during severe outbreaks. Selection of resistant cultivars is a more satisfactory solution. Scab frequently disfigures the fruits, especially in sites with poor air circulation and in wet seasons.

Cultivars.   Most of the cultivars involving this species are hybrids with other species, but a few selections have been made directly from *P. koidzumii*, including the following popular cultivars.

'Rosedale' has long arching branches, with excellent dark green foliage and bright red berries, especially valuable for espalier training.

'Santa Cruz' is low to prostrate, to 0.9 m/3 ft high and at least 1.2 m/4 ft wide, with great masses of red berries in late summer, autumn, and later.

'Victory' is vigorous and upright in habit, to 2.4–3 m/8–10 ft tall and not so wide, with many clusters of red berries, coloring late in the season and lasting throughout winter.

Hybrid Cultivars.   Some of the more widely used hybrids involving *P. koidzumii* are listed below. Several are from the breeding program of Donald Egolf at the U.S. National Arboretum.

'Apache,' a National Arboretum introduction in 1987, is a complex hybrid involving 'Orange Glow' and *P. koidzumii* selections 'Rosedale' and 'Victory.' It is very compact, to 1.5 m/5 ft tall and 2 m/6.6 ft wide, with bright red berries that persist throughout winter; it also has nearly evergreen foliage (in Zone 7b) and is highly resistant to both apple scab and fire blight. Useful in Zones 7a–9a+, possibly also in Zone 6b.

'Government Red,' a selection of uncertain parentage, has large, handsome leaves and red berries, useful in Zones 7a–9a+. Once very popular, it is being superseded by other hybrids.

'Mohave,' another National Arboretum introduction, in 1963, is a hybrid of *P. coccinea* 'Wyatt' and *P. koidzumii*. This vigorous hybrid grows to at least 3 m/10 ft high, in time, with bright red-orange berries and is highly resistant

to both apple scab and fire blight. Useful at least in Zones 7a–9a+, perhaps also protected sites in Zone 6.

'Navaho,' another National Arboretum introduction, is a complex second-generation hybrid involving *P. angustifolia* and 'Watereri' (*P. atalantoides* × *P. rogersiana*). This plant is compact in habit, to 2 m/6.6 ft tall and 2.5 m/8 ft wide, with quantities of berries, orange in late summer, turning orange-red in autumn, and useful at least in Zones 7a–9a, perhaps also sheltered sites in Zone 6.

'Pueblo,' another National Arboretum hybrid, of *P. coccinea* var. *pauciflora* by *P. koidzumii* 'Belli,' forms a mound to at least 2–2.5 m/6.6–8 ft high and nearly twice as wide, with nearly evergreen foliage and orange-red fruits that remain colorful into early winter. It is resistant to apple scab and fire blight and useful in Zones 7b–9a+, perhaps also Zone 7a but probably semievergreen there.

'Monelf' (Red Elf™) is a dwarf form, making a dense mound to 0.6 m/2 ft high and wide, with bright red berries. Useful in Zones 7b–9a+, perhaps also Zone 7a.

'Ruby Mound' makes a compact mound to 1–1.2 m/3.3–4 ft high and 1.2–1.8 m/4–6 ft wide, with bright red fruits. Resistant to apple scab and useful in at least Zones 7b–9a.

'San Jose,' a wide-spreading hybrid selection, probably *P. crenatoserrata* × *P. koidzumii*, has bright red berries. Useful in Zones 7b–9a+.

'Shawnee,' another National Arboretum introduction, is an open-pollinated hybrid of 'San Jose,' densely globe-shaped, to about 1 m/3.3 ft tall and wide, with glossy, clear yellow to pale orange berries. It is resistant to fire blight and apple scab and is useful at least in Zone 7b–9a+.

'Teton,' yet another National Arboretum introduction, hybrid of 'Orange Glow' by *P. rogersiana* 'Flava,' has striking vertical growth habit, to 4 m/13 ft tall and only 2.5–3 m/8–10 ft in spread, even narrower while young, and bright orange berries. It is one of the most resistant cultivars to fire blight and is useful in Zones 6b–9a+.

Related Species

Pyracantha angustifolia 5 (narrow-leaved firethorn).   This native of southwestern China differs from *P. koidzumii* primarily in its narrow leaves, usually bristle-tipped or notched, and slightly larger red-orange fruits, persistent through most of the winter. Useful at least in Zone 6b–9a, perhaps also Zone 6a. A few cultivars have been selected.

'Gnozam' (Gnome®) is a densely branching plant that does not exceed a height 1 m/3.3 ft for several years and matures at less than 2 m/6.6 ft. It is significantly more cold-hardy than the species type and is useful at least in Zones 5b–9a, perhaps also Zone 5a. This cultivar has performed well at Purdue University (Zone 5b) since 1982, with top-damage in a few severe winters, and has shown little disease during that time.

'Harlequin' (= 'Variegata') is notable for its creamy-white-variegated leaves, which take on a pink winter color in some areas, and red berries. This may be a hybrid rather than simply a selection of *P. angustifolia,* and it is somewhat less hardy than the species but it is useful in Zones 8a–9a+ and perhaps in protected sites in Zone 7b.

'Monom' (Yukon Belle™) is a compact selection, growing to 2–2.4 m/6.6–8 ft tall and wide, with orange berries, and reported to be one of the most cold-hardy firethorns, useful at least in Zones 5b–9a, perhaps also Zone 5a.

Pyracantha atalantoides 5–6 (synonym: *P. gibbsii;* Gibbs firethorn). The red fruits of this tall-growing (5–6 m/16–20 ft) native of China persist longer than those of *P. koidzumii,* sometimes throughout the entire winter. Useful in Zones 7b–9a+. The selection 'Aurea' has golden yellow berries.

Pyracantha crenatoserrata 5 (synonyms: *P. fortuneana, P. yunnanensis;* Chinese firethorn). This native of western China has remotely sawtoothed leaves and is very vigorous and heavy-fruiting, with red berries. The selection 'Graberi' is vigorous and upright in form, to 3–4 m/10–13 ft tall and 2.4–3 m/8–10 ft wide, with huge clusters of large red berries, and is useful in Zones 7b–9a+, perhaps also Zone 7a.

Pyracantha crenulata 6 (Nepal firethorn).   This large-growing plant, to 5–6 m/16–20 ft tall is of interest primarily as a parent of hybrids; a few cultivars have been selected, but they are not often available.

Pyracantha rogersiana 5 (synonym: *P. crenulata* var. *rogersiana;* Rogers firethorn).   The leaves of this native of southwestern China are fully evergreen and among the smallest of any firethorn, fully exposing the showy red-orange berries. The selection 'Flava' has yellow berries. Useful in Zones 8a–9a+, probably also Zone 7b.

Pyrus calleryana 7

CALLERY PEAR
Deciduous tree
Rosaceae (Rose Family)

Native Range.   China.

Useful Range.   USDA Zones 5a–9a.

Function.   Small shade, street, or patio tree.

Size and Habit.   'Bradford' is illustrated.

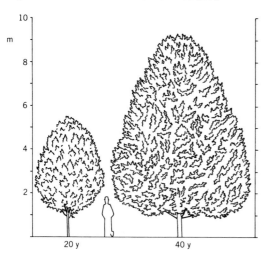

Pyrus calleryana 'Bradford.'

Adaptability

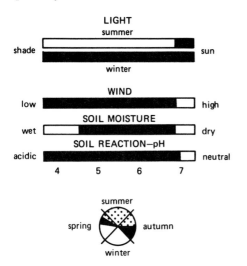

Seasonal Interest.   *Flowers:* White, in clusters, beginning in midspring before the foliage. *Foliage:* Lustrous and leathery, unfolding pale green, turning deep green when fully expanded, then mahogany-red and sometimes finally bright orange-red in late autumn after foliage of many other trees has fallen. *Fruits:* Round, brown, only about 1 cm/0.4 in. across, insignificant either as litter or landscape interest.

Problems and Maintenance.   Of all the pear species, *P. calleryana* is one of the most resistant to fire blight; the more widely planted cultivars show little or no evidence of infection. Cultivars

vary in branching habit. Those with closely spaced branches and narrow branching angles, including 'Bradford,' lose their shape because of branch spreading and breakage after 20–30 years, and they need to be replaced fairly soon after that. This deterioration can be delayed by pruning young trees to avoid close spacing of branches on the trunk, to eliminate the narrowest branch angles, and to preserve the dominance of the central trunk.

Cultivars.   'Aristocrat,' selected by William T. Straw in Kentucky and introduced by the Cole Nursery Co. of Circleville, OH in 1974, is the most vigorous cultivar of this species to date. A 20-year-old tree at Purdue University has reached a height of at least 12 m/40 ft and width of 8 m/26 ft, while holding its shape well. This clone is much looser branching than 'Bradford,' with more upright growth habit, and its flowers open a week or two later, making them somewhat less susceptible than those of 'Bradford' to late spring freezes. Its dark green, lustrous and leathery leaves are similar to those of 'Bradford' except somewhat larger and more pointed and have strikingly crinkled edges. They do not color as reliably as those of 'Bradford' and some of the newer cultivars, but their red-orange autumn color is far from insignificant. 'Aristocrat' is essentially thornless and is useful at least in Zones 5a–8a. It bears more fruits than most other cultivars, but their small size keeps them from being a serious litter problem.

'Autumn Blaze' (Plant Patent 4591, 1980), introduced by M. N. Westwood of Oregon State University, has wide branching angles, which lessen the need for corrective pruning. In autumn its foliage turns brilliant red, two to three weeks earlier than that of 'Bradford,' and falls earlier as well, signaling earlier acclimation to winter cold. In comparison, 'Autumn Blaze' is reported to be the most cold-hardy of the Callery pear selections, useful in at least Zones 5a–8a and perhaps also in Zone 4b. It is broadly pyramidal in form but, when top-pruned as a young tree, assumes a lower, irregularly rounded shape, eventually to 10 m/33 ft tall and 7 m/23 ft wide.

'Bradford,' introduced in 1963 but released for testing several years earlier by the U.S. Dept. of Agriculture Plant Introduction Station at Glenn Dale, Maryland, is symmetrically oval and dense in habit, well-suited to formal street or garden planting. It is also thornless and nearly free of fruits, at least when not grown near other clones of this species. Its foliage is retained late and colors late, but reliably, mahogany-red at first and bright scarlet by late autumn in many years, long after most other deciduous foliage has fallen. Its dense branching and narrow branching angles lead to weakness and loss of shape after 20–30 years unless it is carefully pruned as described above to improve its structure. This selection is sometimes thought of as a small to medium-small tree, and so it remains for a few years, but the oldest known trees of this cultivar have exceeded 13 m/43 ft in both height and width. It is usefully hardy in Zones 5b–8b, and perhaps some sites in Zone 5a.

'Capital,' selected at the U.S. Plant Introduction Station at Glenn Dale, Maryland, and introduced by the National Arboretum in 1981, has a narrowly pyramidal form, to at least 10 m/33 ft tall and 3–4 m/10–13 ft wide, with a strong central leader and heavy lateral branches that soon curve upward, nearly paralleling the trunk. This structure as a young tree bodes well for its durability at maturity, but only time will tell. Conflicting reports suggest that this tree may be susceptible to fire blight in some areas. Useful at least in Zones 5b–8b.

'Chanticleer' (= 'Cleveland Select'), introduced by Edward H. Scanlon of Olmstead Falls, Ohio, in 1965, is narrowly pyramidal in shape, to 12 m/40 ft tall and 5 m/16 ft wide, not unlike 'Capital,' and is an outstanding cultivar in all respects: thornless, resistant to fire blight, and with greater structural durability than 'Bradford.' It has outstanding gold-red to plum-colored autumn foliage, some three weeks earlier than that of 'Bradford,' suggesting that it may begin winter acclimation earlier as well. Its narrow form makes it a good choice where lateral space is at a premium, and it is useful in Zones 5a–8a, perhaps also Zone 4b.

'Rancho,' another Scanlon introduction in 1965, is similar to 'Chanticleer' in general appearance, but less fully branched and at least a week earlier to color in autumn. This is another good selection for small spaces and is useful at least in Zones 5a–8b and perhaps also in Zone 4b, but is not as widely used or available as some of the other cultivars.

'Redspire' was introduced by Princeton Nurseries in 1975. This widely used cultivar, a seedling of 'Bradford,' is reported to be somewhat hardier, with larger flower clusters. It is narrowly oval in form, to 10 m/33 ft tall and 8 ft/26 ft wide, with stronger branching structure than 'Bradford,' seldom needing any pruning. It is useful in Zones 5a–8a, with foliage coloring a little earlier than that of 'Bradford' but, according to some reports, not as well in northern zones.

'Stone Hill' is believed by some to be the same clone as 'Chanticleer.' Others list it separately and refer to a more orange autumn leaf color. Whether it is identical or not, at least it is very similar.

'Trinity' (Plant Patent No. 4530, 1980) was introduced by Handy Nursery Co. of Oregon and is globose to oval in form, similar in form to 'Bradford' but somewhat smaller, to 9 m/30 ft tall and 8 m/26 ft wide, with slightly toothed leaves that reliably turn orange-red in autumn, and few fruits. Useful at least in Zones 5b–8b, perhaps also Zone 5a.

'Whitehouse,' another U.S. National Arboretum introduction, in 1977, originated as an open-pollinated seedling of 'Bradford.' It is narrowly pyramidal in form, to 9 m/30 ft tall and 6 m/20 ft wide, with a strong central leader, with leaves coloring early and persisting late. Useful at least in Zones 5b–8b.

The Northern Series™ of *P. calleryana* cultivars, recently introduced by Lake County Nursery, includes a variety of shapes: 'Bursnozam' (Burgundy Snow™), 'Cleprizam' (Cleveland Pride®), and 'Gladzam' (Gladiator™) are pyramidal in habit, with a height:width ratio of about 1.5. 'Mepozam' (Metropolitan™) is broadly pyramidal, nearly equal in height and width; 'Fronzam' (Frontier™) and 'Valzam' (Valiant™) are narrowly upright, nearly twice as tall as they are wide. While they have been selected in part for cold-hardiness, it will be some time before they are widely tested. 'Fronzam' (Frontier™) is described as the hardiest of this group.

Related Species

Pyrus fauriei 6 (synonym: *P. calleryana* var. *fauriei* or 'Fauriei'; Korean Callery pear).   This round-headed tree, to 5–6 m/16–20 ft tall and at least as wide, is smaller than most trees of *P. calleryana*, but sometimes very broad with age. Its white flowers are very showy and autumn foliage color quite good in some trees. Useful in Zones 5a–8a.

Pyrus regelii 6 (Regel pear).   This shrubby tree, 6–9 m/20–30 ft tall, from western Asia, has small gray-green leaves, variously cut into lobes, sometimes deeply, and white or sometimes pinkish flowers. Probably not available and of little value except for the selection 'Bailwing' (Angel Wings®), with deeply cut, lacy foliage and pinkish-white flowers. Probably useful in Zones 6a–8a, perhaps also parts of Zone 5.

Pyrus salicifolia 5–6 (willowleaf pear).   This semi-weeping to weeping small, shrubby tree from southeastern Europe and western Asia has narrow leaves, 3–9 cm/1.2–3.5 cm long, covered with a whitish down, most striking in early summer. Its white flowers are not conspicuous among the silvery gray leaves, and the few green fruits that form add little landscape interest. This species is useful at least in Zones 5b–8a, but is quite susceptible to fire blight. 'Pendula' was selected for its more strongly weeping habit. 'Silfrozam' (Silver Frost®) is similar.

Pyrus ussuriensis 7 (Ussuri pear).   This tree from northeastern Asia (Manchuria and eastern Siberia) is the only *Pyrus* species found fully cold-hardy at the Agriculture Canada research station at Morden, Manitoba. Like *P. calleryana*, it has considerable resistance to fire blight. Its fruits, while larger than those of *P. calleryana*, are only 4 cm/1.6 in. across, more acceptable for a landscape tree than those of most pear species. Because of its extreme hardiness, it has a place as a flowering and shade tree in the far northern parts of our area. Useful at least in Zones 3b–6b. 'Mordak' (Prairie Gem®), a North Dakota State University introduction, is smaller than the species type, 6–7 m/20–23 ft tall and 5–6 m/16–20 ft wide, with white flowers and leathery, deep green leaves, turning golden-yellow in autumn.

Quercus acuta 7

JAPANESE EVERGREEN OAK
Evergreen tree
Fagaceae (Beech Family)

Native Range.   China, Japan, Korea.

Useful Range.   USDA Zones 8b–9a+, and at least certain sites in Zone 8a.

Function.   Small shade tree, specimen, screen.

Size and Habit

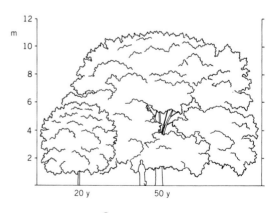

Quercus acuta.

Adaptability

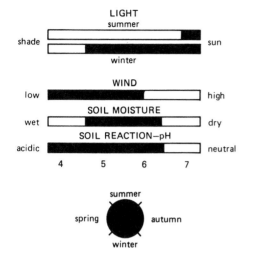

LIGHT

summer

shade | sun

winter

WIND

low | high

SOIL MOISTURE

wet | dry

SOIL REACTION—pH

acidic | neutral

4   5   6   7

spring — summer — autumn — winter

Seasonal Interest. *Flowers:* Small and inconspicuous. *Foliage:* Evergreen, leathery, olive green, gray-green underneath, 10–12 cm/4–5 in. long, not lobed or toothed, but with wavy margins, making a dense canopy year-round. *Fruits:* Small acorns add little landscape interest or litter.

Problems and Maintenance. There is reason to suspect that several diseases and insects of oaks in general affect this species under some conditions, but experience is so limited that such problems have not been evaluated adequately. Experience to date has been favorable. *Q. acuta* is not yet widely available.

Related Species

Quercus glauca 7 (blue Japanese oak). This tree from China, Japan, and Taiwan is similar to *Q. acuta* in general appearance, but with more bluish-green leaves, clearly toothed above the middle. It can grow to 15 m/50 ft in height in its native habitat, but in cultivation is more likely to be seen as a smaller, round-headed, shrubby tree, useful in Zones 8b–9a+ and protected sites in Zone 8a.

Quercus myrsinifolia 7 (Japanese live oak). This evergreen tree from China and Japan is often confused with *Q. acuta* and *Q. glauca*, but differs in its more subtly toothed leaves, along most of the margin. These three species differ little in landscape usage and tolerances, which is fortunate since none of them is very widely available. When there is a choice, *Q. myrsinifolia* grows slightly larger than the other two, eventually to 20 m/66 ft in height, and may be slightly more cold-hardy, probably to Zone 7b.

Quercus glauca.

Quercus acuta.

Quercus glauca.

Quercus salicina 7 (willow-leaved Japanese oak). This evergreen tree from Japan has much narrower leaves than the species mentioned above, usually untoothed, the young leaves conspicuously silvery white-hairy underneath. It is re- ported to be the most cold-hardy of the evergreen Japanese oaks, but has been so little used that this remains to be seen. It has been confused in commerce with a similar oak, *Q. bambusaefolia,* as well as other evergreen oaks.

Quercus acutissima 7

SAWTOOTH OAK
Deciduous tree
Fagaceae (Beech Family)

Native Range.   China, Japan, and Korea.

Useful Range.   USDA Zones 6a–9a, possibly also Zone 5 with selection of hardy genetic material. Trees of undetermined geographic origin have survived in Zone 5b for up to 15 years, only to be devastated by occasional severe winters.

Function.   Shade tree, specimen.

Size and Habit

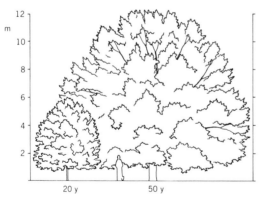

Quercus acutissima.

Adaptability

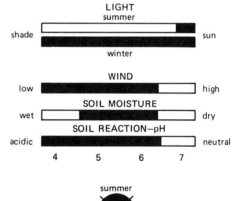

Seasonal Interest.   *Flowers:* Small and inconspicuous. *Foliage:* Toothed leaves, resembling those of chestnut, pale green as they unfold, expanding and remaining deep green and lustrous well into autumn, then drying light brown and persisting, sometimes until midwinter. *Fruits:* Small acorns add little landscape interest or litter, except for heavy-fruiting selections (see below).

Problems and Maintenance.   Disease and pest problems are relatively minor, requiring attention only in intensive situations or where outbreaks are severe. Pruning is needed only for removal of any deadwood.

Cultivars.   'Gobbler' is a seed strain selected by the U.S. Soil Conservation Service for its rapid growth (reported as 12 m/40 ft in 15 years) and cold-hardiness to an extreme minimum temperature of −29°C/−20°F (roughly equivalent to average annual minimum temperature −21°C/

−5°F to −24°C/−10°F, or USDA Zone 6a). It was selected primarily to attract wildlife, with large crops of acorns, reportedly to 5.7 kg/125 lbs per tree at maturity.

Related Species

Quercus cerris 8 (Turkey oak).   This large, Eurasian tree has relatively small leaves, 5–12 cm/2–5 in. long, with small, bristle-tipped lobes, themselves toothed. Useful in Zones 7a–9a, perhaps also Zone 6a with selection of hardy genetic material, but not widely available for use in our area.

Quercus chenii 7 (Chen or Chinese chestnut oak).   This uncommon oak from central China is closely related to *Q. acutissima* and differs little except that trees from some seed sources may prove somewhat more cold-hardy than material of *Q. acutissima* presently in North America, to Zone 5b, perhaps even 5a.

Quercus variabilis 8 (oriental oak or Chinese cork oak).   This tree, native to the same region as *Q. acutissima* and closely related to it, has chestnutlike foliage and corky bark, of minor landscape interest. It is useful in about the same

Quercus cerris.

range as *Q. acutissima* and functions as a larger version of that species but is less likely to be commercially available.

Quercus alba 8

WHITE OAK
Deciduous tree
Fagaceae (Beech Family)

Native Range.   Eastern United States from Maine and Minnesota southward to Florida and Texas.

Useful Range.   USDA Zones 4b–9a.

Function.   Shade tree, specimen, naturalizing.

Size and Habit

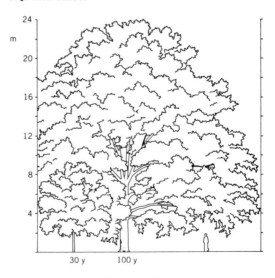

Quercus alba.

Adaptability

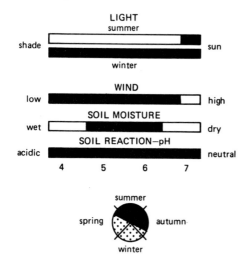

Seasonal Interest. *Flowers:* Small, pale green-ish yellow catkins are interesting along with newly expanding leaves in spring. *Foliage:* Dull, deep green leaves with rounded lobes turn pur-plish in middle to late autumn before falling. *Fruits:* Relatively small acorns are borne in great numbers in some years but add little landscape interest and pose a litter problem. *Trunks and branches:* Rugged framework of massive branches and light colored, slightly shaggy bark make this a majestic and interesting tree in all seasons.

Problems and Maintenance. Disease and pest problems are minor, requiring attention only when severe outbreaks occur. *Q. alba* is resistant to oak wilt, a serious disease in the Midwest. Pruning is needed only for removal of any dead-wood. The most serious limitation to acceptance is its slow growth, but this can be hastened somewhat by early attention to fertilization and irrigation during prolonged drought, and it is compensated for by the tree's longevity. Even when not planted, *Q. alba* should receive high priority for protection during site development, since it is highly sensitive to disturbance.

Related Hybrids. Trees from acorns of hybrid oaks are unpredictable in character because pollen parents are seldom known and may even change from year to year, but some such seedlings are promising as landscape plants and are available from a few specialists. Grafted trees are sometimes available, and experimentation with cutting and tissue-culture propagation offers the likelihood of more routine cloning at some point. Ken Asmus of Kalamazoo, Michigan, Earl Cully Jacksonville, Illinois, Guy Sternberg of Petersburg, Illinois, and others are actively work-ing with oak hybrids for reforestation and land-scape use. A few natural hybrids of *Q. alba* with closely related species are known but available to only a limited extent, and then usually as open-pollinated seeds or seedlings. Hybrids with landscape potential, according to oak specialist Guy Sternberg, include the following:

Quercus ×*bebbiana* 8 (*Q. alba* × *Q. macrocarpa*). This vigorous hybrid is intermediate between the parents in appearance and is more tolerant of cold (to Zone 3b) and calcareous soils than *Q. alba.* One clone selected by Guy Sternberg and identified as No. 190, but not yet named at this writing, shows extreme vigor, with multiple growth flushes resulting in an early growth rate of 1.5 m/5 ft annually.

Quercus ×*deamii* 8 (originally believed by Deam to be *Q. muehlenbergii* × *Q. alba,* now thought by some specialists to be a hybrid of *Q. mac-rocarpa* × *Q. muehlenbergii*). This is more adaptable than *Q. alba* to difficult site condi-tions, including heavy calcareous soils. Useful range is probably similar to that of the parents: Zones 5a–8b, perhaps also Zone 4b.

Quercus ×*jackiana* 8 (*Q. bicolor* × *Q. alba*). This is intermediate between the parents in ap-pearance, very vigorous, well adapted to heavy or compacted soils, and easier to transplant than *Q. alba.* Probably useful, based on the parentage, in Zones 4b–8b, perhaps also Zone 4a.

Quercus ×*saulii* 8 (*Q prinus* × *Q. alba*). This is intermediate between the parents, with hybrid vigor. One clone selected by Guy Sternberg and identified as No. 168, but as yet unnamed, is very vigorous, with long-lasting burgundy au-tumn foliage. Probably useful in Zones 5a–9a, perhaps also Zone 4b.

Quercus ×*schuettei* 8 (synonym: *Q.* ×*hillii;* par-entage *Q. bicolor* × *Q. macrocarpa*). This is intermediate between the parents and tolerant of compacted or wet soil, with handsome corky, ridged bark, showing reddish-brown inner bark, and picturesque form. Probably useful at least in Zones 4a–8b.

Related Species

Quercus austrina 7–8 (bluff oak) and *Q. sinuata* var. *sinuata* 7–8 (synonym: *Q. durandii;* Durand or bluff oak).   These deciduous natives of the Coastal Plain and Piedmont in the southeastern and south-central states appear as smaller versions of *Q. alba,* useful in Zones 8a–9a+, probably also Zone 7 when nearby native material is used.

Quercus chapmanii 5–6 (Chapman oak).   This evergreen to semievergreen shrub or small tree, native to the Coastal Plain from South Carolina to much of Florida, is useful in Zones 9a+ and perhaps parts of Zone 8, but is seldom available.

Quercus gambelii 5–6 (Gambel or Rocky Mountain white oak).   This deciduous shrub or small tree, occasionally larger in its native habitats in the Rocky Mountains, is unusually tolerant of dryness. With selection of appropriate ecotypes, it is useful in Zones 4a–6b in its native region, but seldom available elsewhere.

Quercus garryana 8 (Oregon white oak).   This large tree, to 15–25 m/50–82 ft tall at maturity, resembles *Quercus alba* and, if useful in our area, probably would fill the same landscape niche, but it has not been widely tried here. Since trees in the coldest parts of its native range seldom, if ever, experience temperatures as low as −18°C/0°F, there has not been much incentive to try it here as an alternative to other white oaks or for hybridization (but see *Q. turbinella* hybrids, under *Q. virginiana*).

Quercus lobata 8 (California white oak, valley oak).   This stately tree, like *Q. garryana,* is an unlikely candidate for usefulness in our area, but limited trials in Michigan suggest that it may be more cold-hardy than would be expected.

Quercus falcata 8

SOUTHERN RED OAK, SPANISH OAK

Deciduous tree

Fagaceae (Beech Family)

Native Range.   Southern and south-central United States.

Useful Range.   USDA Zones 6b–9a.

Function.   Shade tree, specimen, naturalizing.

Size and Habit

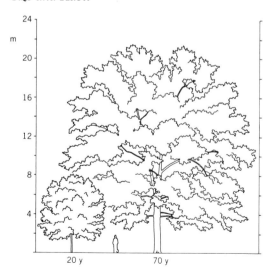

Quercus falcata.

Adaptability

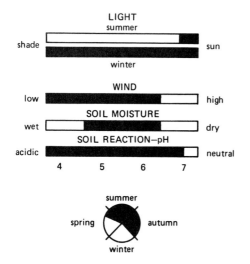

Seasonal Interest. *Flowers:* Yellow-green catkins add interest to newly expanding foliage in middle spring. *Foliage:* Deeply cut leaves with narrow, bristle-tipped lobes, often curved (falcate), lustrous, deep green, not forming a dense mass of foliage but allowing light penetration, turning orange-russet to red-orange in autumn. *Fruits:* Small acorns add little landscape interest or litter.

Problems and Maintenance. Problems such as oak galls are minor, requiring attention only when severe outbreaks occur. Pruning is seldom needed, only for removing any deadwood. Transplanting is easier than for *Q. alba* or *Q. coccinea,* for example, and this species should receive high priority for preservation during site development.

Related Species

Quercus laevis 6 (turkey oak). This small deciduous tree, native to sandy sites on the southeastern Coastal Plain, is very tolerant of dry sites and has showy red autumn foliage. Useful in Zones 8a–9a+, perhaps also Zone 7b.

Quercus pagoda 8 (synonym: *Q. falcata* var. *pagodifolia;* cherrybark or swamp Spanish oak). This species differs from *Q. falcata* in having more evenly lobed leaves and bark vaguely resembling that of *Prunus serotina* (black cherry). It is more tolerant of wet soil than *Q. falcata* and most other oaks, and useful at least in Zones 6b–9a. The naturally occurring hybrid (in the southeastern United States) *Quercus* ×*ludoviciana* 8 (*Q. pagoda* × *P. phellos*) is intermediate between its parents, with leaves varying from coarsely toothed to irregularly lobed, and may have landscape potential with selection and commercial cloning of superior individuals.

Quercus imbricaria 8

SHINGLE OAK
Deciduous tree
Fagaceae (Beech Family)

Native Range. East-central United States from Pennsylvania to Nebraska and south to Georgia and Arkansas.

Useful Range. USDA Zones 5a–9a and perhaps certain sites in Zone 4b with selection of hardiest genetic material.

Function. Shade tree, specimen, naturalizing, screen (as a hedge).

Size and Habit

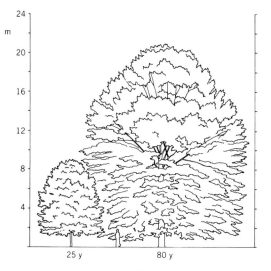

Quercus imbricaria.

Adaptability. This tree is more tolerant of calcareous, neutral, or slightly alkaline soil than *Q. palustris*, which it resembles in form and function (although not in foliage character).

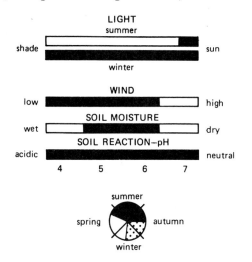

Seasonal Interest. *Flowers:* Pale yellow-green catkins add interest to newly expanding foliage in middle spring. *Foliage:* Leaves are neither lobed nor toothed, but dark green and leathery, 8–16 cm/3–6 in. long and 2.5–4 cm/1–1.6 in. wide, drying a warm tan color in late autumn and usually persisting past midwinter. *Fruits:* Small acorns add little landscape interest or litter.

Problems and Maintenance. Problems such as oak galls are minor, requiring attention only when severe outbreaks occur. Pruning is needed only for removing any deadwood and gradually removing lower branches when necessary to allow access underneath. Since foliage falls gradually in late winter, there is a slight, continuing litter problem.

Quercus imbricaria.

Hybrids. At least two natural hybrids of this species are known, but not available commercially except possibly as acorns (see precautionary note under *Quercus alba* hybrids). *Quercus* ×*leana* 8 (*Q. imbricaria* × *Q. velutina*) resembles *Q. imbricaria* more than *Q. velutina*, with variable leaves, entirely with a wavy margin or having 3 to 7 distinct but shallow bristle-tipped lobes.

Related Species

Quercus hemisphaerica 8 (laurel oak). This name is both the correct name for this upland species and an invalid name for another laurel oak, *Q. laurifolia*. The principal difference between the two is that *Q. laurifolia* is more tolerant of wet soil, but the usefulness of that fact is diminished by the confusion in names.

Quercus incana 6 (blue-jack oak, upland willow oak). This small deciduous to semievergreen tree, native to the southeastern states, has entire leaves 5–10 cm/2–4 in. long, 2.5 cm/1 in. wide, white-tomentose when young but only on the undersides at maturity. Useful in Zones 7b–9a+, but not widely available.

Quercus laurifolia 8 (synonym: *Q. hemisphaerica*; swamp laurel oak). This semievergreen native of the southeastern United States is widely used as a fast-growing shade tree, but it is weak-wooded and shorter-lived than most other oaks. Useful in Zones 8a–9a+, and some sites in Zone 7b.

Quercus macrocarpa 8

BUR OAK, MOSSYCUP OAK
Deciduous tree
Fagaceae (Beech Family)

Native Range. Northeastern North America from Nova Scotia to Manitoba and southward to Texas.

Useful Range. USDA Zones 3a–9a with selection of appropriate genetic material.

Function. Shade tree, specimen.

Size and Habit

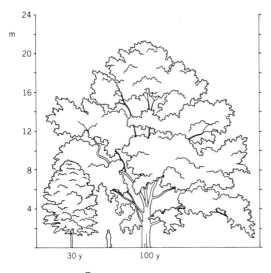

Quercus macrocarpa.

Adaptability. This is one of few trees that are well adapted to the Northern Plains. It is and was native to the prairies and is able to tolerate periodic fires, presumably because of its heavy bark.

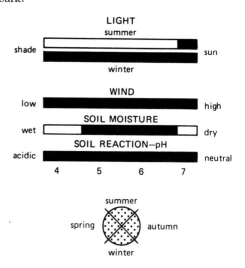

Seasonal Interest. *Flowers:* Small, pale yellowish catkins add minor interest along with newly expanding leaves of the same color. *Foliage:* Deeply round-lobed leaves turn deep green and leathery when fully expanded, grayish underneath with a felt of fine hairs, falling in autumn without color change. *Fruits:* The large acorns, to 3.5 cm/1.4 in., are about half covered by the heavy cup. *Trunks and branches:* The bark is unusually thick, heavily furrowed on the trunk, and irregularly ridged on the branches, giving the framework a massive appearance in winter.

Problems and Maintenance. Problems, most commonly oak galls, are minor, requiring atten-

Quercus macrocarpa.

Quercus bicolor.

tion only when severe outbreaks occur. Pruning is seldom necessary. Principal limitation to use is slow growth and difficulty in transplanting.

Hybrids. At least three natural hybrids of this species are known, but not available commercially except possibly as open-pollinated acorns. See *Q. alba* hybrids, *Q. muehlenbergii* hybrids, *Q. robur* hybrids, and *Q. turbinella* hybrids under *Q. virginiana.*

Related Species

Quercus bicolor 8 (swamp white oak).   This tree has much of the character of *Q. alba* and *Q. macrocarpa,* but is more tolerant of wet soil and is useful in Zones 4a–8b. Hybrids: See hybrids of *Q. alba* (above) and *Q. robur.*

Quercus liaotungensis 8.   This species from northeastern Asia is promising for use in our colder zones, potentially useful at least in Zones 3a–5b. At this writing it is under test in eastern North America but not generally available.

Quercus lyrata 8 (overcup oak, swamp post oak). This close relative of *Q. macrocarpa,* native to the southeastern states and northward to New Jersey and Missouri, functions as a large shade tree with large acorns, to 2.5 cm/1 in. long, usually almost completely covered by the cup, hence the common name. It seldom is planted but is worthy of greater use and certainly is worth preserving in site development. It has the reputation of being more tolerant of wet soil than either *Q. macrocarpa* or *Q. stellata,* yet usually grows wild in well-drained sites. Useful in Zones 6a–9a with selection of appropriate genetic material.

Quercus margarettiae 5–6 (synonym: *Q. stellata* var. *margaretta;* sand post oak).   This shrubby small tree is native to sandy sites in about the same range as *Q. stellata* but only as far north as Virginia. It differs from *Q. stellata* in its lower, stoloniferous habit and less distinctly lobed leaves. Useful at least in Zones 7a–9a.

Quercus mongolica 7–8 (Mongolian oak).   This rare tree has been used experimentally in Minnesota and Manitoba and promises to be a very cold-hardy, small shade tree for the northern plains, somewhat resembling a smaller edition of *Q. macrocarpa* but with foliage more similar to that of *Q. prinus* or *Q. muehlenbergii.* It may take a number of years for this tree to become available commercially in any quantity, but it is presumably potentially useful in Zones 3a–5b and perhaps in warmer areas as well.

Quercus stellata 7–8 (post oak). This wide-ranging tree from Massachusetts and Florida west to Nebraska and Texas is seldom planted but worthy of preservation in site development. Foliage is dark green, forming a densely rounded canopy. Useful in Zones 6a–9a. A few natural hybrids of Q. *stellata* are known, including Q. ×*bernardiensis* (Q. *prinus* × Q. *stellata*), Q. ×*fernowii* (Q. *alba* × Q. *stellata*), Q. ×*guadalupensis* (Q. *macrocarpa* × Q. *stellata*), and Q. ×macnabiana (Q. *sinuata* var. *sinuata* × Q. *stellata*), but probably none of these is in cultivation, much less in commerce. See also hybrids of Q. *turbinella* under Q. *virginiana*.

Quercus nigra 8

Synonym: *Q. aquatica*
WATER OAK
Semievergreen tree
Fagaceae (Beech Family)

Native Range.   Southeastern United States.

Useful Range.   USDA Zones 6b–9a+.

Function.   Shade and street tree, specimen.

Size and Habit

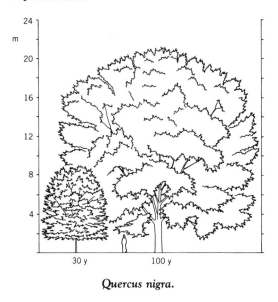

Quercus nigra.

Adaptability.   Even though tolerant of wet or poorly drained soils, Q. *nigra* does best on well-drained soils in landscape situations.

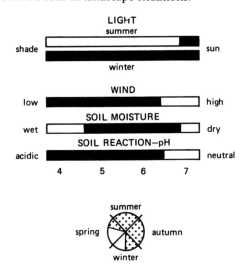

Seasonal Interest.   *Flowers:* Small, pale yellowish green catkins add minor landscape interest along with newly expanding foliage. *Foliage:* Pale green at first, then deep to olive green, leaves varying in shape from unlobed to remotely three-lobed to occasionally strongly lobed, persisting well into winter in the Deep South before falling with little color change. *Fruits:* Small acorns add little seasonal interest and minimal litter.

Problems and Maintenance.   This tree is subject to several disease and insect problems including galls, leaf spots, scale insects, and borers. Mistletoe infestations sometimes are severe enough to damage host trees of Q. *nigra*. This species is softer-wooded and more prone to storm damage than most oaks, perhaps a by-product of its rapid growth. All things considered, it is not as maintenance-free as its wide use suggests. Therefore, other species such as *Q. ilex, Q. imbricaria, Q. phellos* and *Q. virginiana* should be considered as possible alternative street trees in the Deep South.

Related Species

Quercus arkansana 6 (Arkansas oak). This small deciduous tree is very similar to *Q. marilandica* except in having more pubescent young shoots. It is also less likely to be available and somewhat less cold-hardy, but is useful in Zones 7a–9a, perhaps also Zone 6.

Quercus marilandica 6–7 (blackjack oak). This relatively small tree, usually not over 8–10 m/ 26–33 ft tall, is irregularly and narrowly upright. Its leaves are irregularly club-shaped in outline, giving rise to its common name. Native to the southeastern states, it is worth preserving in development, and is difficult to transplant unless container-grown. It has burnt-orange autumn foliage and tolerates very poor, dry soils, but is a more attractive tree in better soils. Useful in Zones 5b–9a. A few natural hybrids of *Q. marilandica* are known but are seldom, if ever, available. *Quercus ×bushii* 6 (*Q. marilandica* × *Q. velutina*) is more similar to *Q. marilandica* than to *Q. velutina* in size and foliage, and is as tolerant of dry soil as the parents. See also *Q. ilicifolia* and *Q. phellos* hybrids.

Quercus palustris 8

PIN OAK
Deciduous tree
Fagaceae (Beech Family)

Native Range. Northeastern to central United States.

Useful Range. USDA Zones 5a–8b and some sites in Zones 4b–9a.

Function. Shade tree, specimen.

Size and Habit

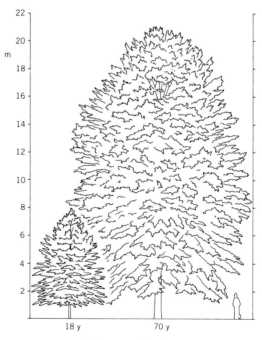

Quercus palustris.

Adaptability. *Q. palustris* is strikingly intolerant of neutral or calcareous soils, developing chlorosis (foliar yellowing) because of insufficient iron uptake.

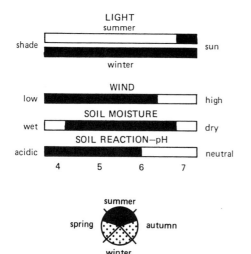

Seasonal Interest. *Flowers:* Pale yellow-green catkins add interest to newly expanding foliage in midspring. *Foliage:* Leaves are about 10 cm/4 in. long, deeply incised, with narrow, bristled lobes, giving a rather fine texture. They are yellow-green as they expand, then deep green and lustrous in proper soil, yellowing or bronzing slightly before drying a warm tan color in late autumn, some of the leaves usually persisting into winter. *Fruits:* Small acorns add little seasonal interest but may produce considerable litter in heavy fruiting years. *Trunk and branches:* Striking form with drooping to ascending branches and often mastlike trunk add interest even in winter.

Problems and Maintenance. Most insect and disease problems are not serious, and this is one of the easiest oaks to transplant. The greatest maintenance problem is that of correcting iron chlorosis in trees planted on calcareous soil. This usually can be done with some success through foliar sprays of soluble iron, but it requires repeated applications over the years. A better solution is to substitute other trees when soil conditions are not favorable for pin oak. Other oaks with more or less similar branching and general functional effect include *Q. imbricaria* and *Q. phellos.* These differ in foliage character but, like the pin oak, do not form a dense canopy that interferes with turfgrass growth underneath.

Hybrids. Several natural hybrids are known but are seldom, if ever, commercially available. *Quercus* ×*exacta* 8 *(Q. imbricaria* × *Q. palustris)* is intermediate between the parents, with regularly spaced teeth. *Quercus* ×*richteri* 8 *(Q. palustris* × *Q. rubra)* looks much like *Q. palustris* in form, but with leaves similar to those of *Q. coccinea,* and is potentially useful in Zones 4b–8b. *Quercus* ×*schochiana* 8 *(Q. palustris* × *Q. phellos)* is intermediate between the parents, with narrow, irregularly lobed leaves.

Related Species

Quercus coccinea 8 (scarlet oak). This fine tree, native to much of our area, would be far more commonly used if it were not considered very difficult to transplant. Nevertheless, some landscape nurserymen and contractors are moving scarlet oaks successfully. *Q. coccinea* resembles *Q. rubra* in general growth habit and *Q. palustris* in foliage texture and is more reliably colorful in autumn, with maroon to brilliant scarlet foliage. It grows best in somewhat acidic soil but is not as sensitive to limestone as *Q. palustris.* Useful

Quercus coccinea.

in Zones 5a–9a with selection of appropriate genetic material.

Quercus ellipsoidalis 8 (northern pin oak).   This northern counterpart of *Q. palustris,* native from the northern lake states to Manitoba, resembles *Q. palustris* and extends the useful range of this form northward to Zone 3b. Presumably the two species can be used interchangeably in Zones 5–6. *Q. palustris* is the preferred species in Zones 7 and 8 and probably will be used in preference to *Q. ellipsoidalis* in most areas because it is more widely available and easier to transplant.

Quercus georgiana 4–5 (Georgia or Stone Mountain oak).   This very small, shrubby tree, native to dry, gravelly sites, has foliage that resembles

that of *Q. palustris* and turns scarlet-orange in autumn. Based on its native occurrence it may, like *Q. palustris,* require acidic soil to grow well. Because of its scarcity, wild populations should be preserved.

Quercus ilicifolia 4–6 (bear oak).   This scrubby deciduous shrub or small tree native from New England to the mountains of Virginia is probably of little landscape value itself, but is involved in several natural hybrids, some of which may have landscape potential. *Q.* ×*brittonii* 6 (*Q. ilicifolia* × *Q. marilandica*), *Q.* ×*fernaldii* 6–7 (*Q. ilicifolia* × *Q. rubra*), *Q.* ×*giffordii* 6–7 (*Q. ilicifolia* × *Q. phellos*), *Q.* ×*rehderi* 6–7 (*Q. ilicifolia* × *Q. velutina*), and *Q.* ×*robbinsii* 6–7 (*Q. coccinea* × *Q. ilicifolia*) are intermediate between their

Quercus phellos 7–8

WILLOW OAK
Deciduous tree
Fagaceae (Beech Family)

Native Range.   Eastern and central United States.

Useful Range.   USDA Zones 6a–9a.

Function.   Shade and street tree, naturalizing.

Size and Habit

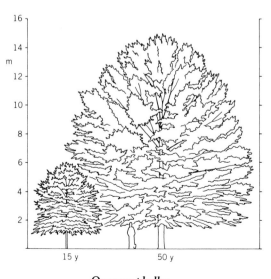

Quercus phellos.

Adaptability

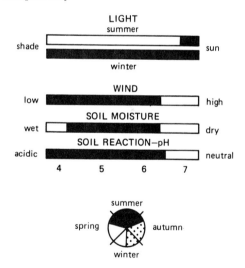

Seasonal Interest.   *Flowers:* Pale yellow-green catkins add interest in midspring along with the newly expanding leaves. *Foliage:* Leaves are very narrow, almost willowlike, 5–10 cm/2–4 in. long and seldom over 1 cm/0.4 in. wide, yellow-green as they emerge in spring, then remaining bright green through summer, turning dull yellow to reddish in midautumn and persisting well into winter in the Deep South. *Fruits:* Small acorns add little landscape interest or litter. *Trunk and branches:* Form is reminiscent of the pin oak, making the tree mildly interesting even while not in leaf.

Problems and Maintenance. Most insect and disease problems are not serious, and this is one of the easiest oaks to transplant. Maintenance is minimal, but the pendulous lower branches, like those of the pin oak, may have to be removed in small-scale situations to accommodate pedestrian traffic. This changes the landscape character of the tree and should be done carefully to avoid disfiguring it.

Hybrids. Several natural hybrids are known, but are seldom commercially available, except possibly as acorns (see cautionary note under *Q. alba* hybrids). *Quercus* ×*rudkinii* 7 (*Q. marilandica* × *Q. phellos*) has highly variable leaves, some entire, others with a few shallow lobes. Unlike most hybrids, it apparently comes more-or-less true from seeds. See also hybrids of *Q. ilicifolia*, *Q. pagoda*, *Q. palustris*, *Q. rubra*, and *Q. shumardii*.

Quercus prinus 8

Synonym: *Q. montana*
CHESTNUT OAK
Deciduous tree
Fagaceae (Beech Family)

Native Range. Eastern United States from Maine to Alabama.

Useful Range. USDA Zones 5a–9a.

Function. Shade tree, specimen, naturalizing.

Size and Habit

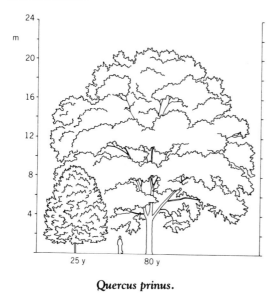

Quercus prinus.

Adaptability. This is one of the best oaks for use on dry soils.

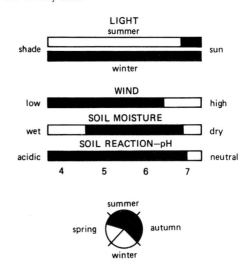

Seasonal Interest. *Flowers:* Pale green catkins add interest in midspring along with newly expanding foliage. *Foliage:* Leaves, 12–17 cm/5–7 in. long, shallowly round-lobed or round-toothed, vaguely resembling those of chestnuts, pale green as they unfold, turning and remaining dark green through summer and early autumn, then turning red-orange to golden brown before falling. *Fruits:* Relatively large acorns add only slight seasonal interest in early autumn and can pose a mild litter problem in some years. *Trunk and branches:* Bark is dark gray-brown and heavily ridged, adding slight additional interest.

Quercus prinus.

Problems and Maintenance. Most disease and insect problems are not usually serious and seldom require attention except in small-scale situations. This tree is more likely to be encountered as a subject for potential preservation in site development than it is to be planted. It is somewhat difficult to transplant and not widely available commercially.

Hybrids. Several natural hybrids are known but seldom, if ever, available. See hybrids of *Q. alba*, *Q. robur*, and *Q. stellata.*

Related Species

Quercus aliena 8 (oriental white oak). This native of China, Japan, and Korea resembles *Q. prinus* except that its leaves are white-downy underneath and its acorns are borne on short stalks. Uncommon in cultivation and rarely available commercially, but potentially useful in Zones 6a–9a.

Quercus dentata 8 (Japanese emperor oak). This tree from Japan, Korea, and Manchuria grows to 25 m/82 ft tall and is notable for its very large leaves, to 20–30 cm/8–12 in. long and nearly as wide. It is potentially useful at least in Zones 6b–9a, probably also Zone 6a, and perhaps colder with selection of Manchurian genetic material. The selection 'Pinnatifida' has finely divided, almost threadlike leaves, making a slow-growing but interesting specimen. Neither the cultivar nor the species is widely available. The hybrid *Q.* ×*vilmoriniana* 7–8 (*Q. dentata* × *Q. petraea*), found in Europe, is a fast-growing tree with large leaves, probably useful in Zones 6b–9a, perhaps also Zone 6a.

Quercus michauxii 8 (synonym: *Q. prinus*, but not to be confused with true *Q. prinus*, chestnut oak; basket oak, swamp chestnut oak). This native of central and southern parts of the eastern United States from Delaware to Missouri and Texas with foliage similar to that of chestnut oak is little used as a landscape tree and seldom available. Nevertheless, it is a beautiful, round-headed shade tree when grown in the open and should receive high priority for preservation in site development. When planted, it performs best in fairly moist soil and will tolerate occasionally wet soil. Useful in Zones 6b–9a. At least one natural hybrid is known; see *Q. alba* hybrids.

Quercus muehlenbergii 8 (Chinquapin oak, yellow chestnut oak). This native of much of the United States from the Northeast to the Midwest and as far southwest as Texas and New Mexico is seldom available for planting but definitely worth preserving in site development. It has foliage much like that of *Q. prinus* and is as

Quercus muehlenbergii.

adaptable to dry soil as that species but with a more narrow, vase-shaped growth habit. This species is more tolerant of neutral, calcareous soils than most oaks but is less desirable than several others where soils are acidic. Useful in Zones 5a–8b and perhaps 9a with selection of appropriate genetic material. One natural hybrid is known, but probably is not in cultivation; see *Q. alba* hybrids.

Quercus prinoides 4–5 (dwarf chinquapin oak). This spreading shrub, to 2 m/6.6 ft tall, or occasionally small tree to 4 m/13 ft, is seldom planted, but may be of interest in site development. Native over a wide range, from Maine to Alabama and Minnesota to Texas, it is potentially useful in Zones 4a–8b, with selection of nearby native material, but seldom available commercially.

Quercus robur 7–8

ENGLISH OAK
Deciduous tree
Fagaceae (Beech Family)

Native Range. Europe, northern Africa, and western Asia.

Useful Range. USDA Zones 5b–9a with selection of appropriate genetic material (see Problems and Maintenance).

Function. Shade tree, specimen.

Size and Habit

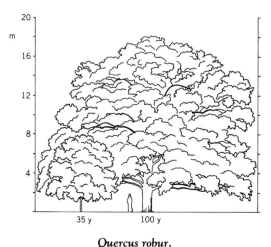

Quercus robur.

Adaptability

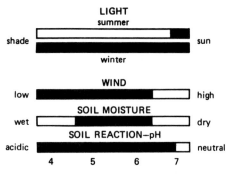

Seasonal Interest. *Flowers:* Small, pale yellowish green catkins add minor landscape interest along with newly expanding leaves. *Foliage:* Leaves are small, 5–12 cm/2–5 in. long, evenly round-lobed, giving uniform texture. They unfold pale green, turning to olive green or deep green in summer, and remain deep green long into autumn, finally drying a light brown color and persisting well into winter. *Fruits:* Elongated acorns, about 1–1.5 cm/0.4–0.6 in. across and 1.5–2.5 cm/0.6–1 in. long, hanging singly or in groups of as many as five on one long pendulous stalk, adding slight landscape interest in late summer and early autumn.

Problems and Maintenance. Disease and insect problems are not usually serious, but powdery mildew disfigures the foliage in warm, humid climates. Cold hardiness is precarious and probably depends on selection of genetically hardy stock, which is not available except through local experience. *Q. robur* seems to be a good example of imperfect adaptation, since mature trees in Zones 5 and 6 have been known to be killed outright by an occasional severe winter. And it appears that this species is not particularly well adapted to the hot, dry summers of our Zones 7, 8 and 9, even though it thrives in such zones in Europe. Best adaptation is to coastal areas and sites located on the east sides of the Great Lakes in Zones 6a–8b.

Cultivars. 'Fastigiata,' with columnar to narrowly pyramidal growth habit, is a good choice where vertical accent is needed, with a greater degree of permanence than can be expected from columnar poplars. Since this form comes approximately true-to-type from seed, there are several clones of it in cultivation under this name. One such clone is sold as 'Fastigiata' under the trademark name Skyrocket™. Another clone is 'Wandell' (Plant Patent applied for). Both are reported to be resistant to mildew. A less-narrow pyramidal selection, 'Pyramich' (Skymaster™ oak), has a height:width ratio of about 2:1, with a strong central leader and broad crotch angles. 'Michround' (Westminster Globe™ oak) is broadly spreading and symmetrical.

Several other cultivars are occasionally available: 'Argenteomarginata' has white leaf margins. 'Argenteovariegata' (= 'Variegata') has white-variegated, red-flushed leaves and twigs lined with red and white. 'Atropurpurea' (= 'Purpurea') has purple new foliage, soon turning brownish. 'Concordia' is striking in spring as its new leaves emerge bright yellow, turning greenish-yellow by the time they have expanded fully and fully green within a few more weeks. 'Filicifolia' has deeply cut leaves and grows slowly into a specimen for accent. 'Nigra' has deep purple foliage throughout the growing season. Several other cultivars are in commerce in Europe.

Hybrids. Several natural hybrids of *Q. robur* with other European species are known, but most of them do not hold much promise for our area. However, hybrids of *Q. robur* with some of the North American white oaks are promising new shade and accent trees for our area, offering greater cold hardiness than *Q. robur*.

'Crimschmidt' (Crimson Spire™) is a fastigiate hybrid of *Q. robur* × *Q. alba,* with dark green, mildew-resistant foliage that turns reddish in autumn.

Two clones selected from the hybrid: *Q. robur* 'Fastigiata' × *Q. bicolor* by Earl Cully of Jacksonville, Illinois, are promising. 'Long' (Plant Patent applied for; Regal Prince™) is upright-oval in shape with a height:width ratio of about 2:1 and leaves strongly silvered underneath. It is expected to be introduced in 1997. The other clone is as narrow as *Q. robur* 'Fastigiata,' with a height:width ratio of 3.5:1, and has handsome, mildew-resistant foliage, but probably will not be available for a few more years. Both clones are more cold-hardy than *Q. robur,* at least to USDA Zone 5a, perhaps also parts of Zone 4.

Another Cully hybrid (*Q. robur* × *Q. macrocarpa*) with densely pyramidal form, a strong central leader, and handsome mildew-resistant and tatter-resistant foliage shows greatly increased hardiness and vigor over *Q. robur* and is expected to be cold-hardy at least to Zone 4a or 3b.

Q. × *sargentii* (*Q. prinus* × *Q. robur*) is very similar to *Q. prinus,* with leaves more coarsely toothed than lobed but slightly lobed at the base, as with *Q. robur.*

Related Species

Quercus frainetto 8 (Hungarian oak). This majestic, fast-growing shade tree from the Balkans and southern Italy reaches heights of 30 m/100 ft in native habitat, with a neatly oval head and regularly lobed and incised, lustrous dark green leaves. Useful in Zones 6b–8b, perhaps also Zone 6a. The selection 'Schmidt' (Forest Green®) has excellent foliage and form.

Quercus haas 8 (Haas oak). This tree from Asia Minor is closely related to *Q. robur,* but with larger leaves. It is reported to be more resistant to mildew, but may be less cold-hardy than *Q. robur.* Probably useful at least in Zones 6b–9a but seldom, if ever, commercially available.

Quercus petraea 8 (Durmast oak). The strong, mastlike trunk of this stately tree has made it an important timber tree in its native habitat in northern and eastern Europe, and it has potential as a shade tree in parts of our area. It can reach a height of 40 m/132 ft in European forests, but probably will remain below 25–30 m/82–100 ft in landscape use here. It is highly variable in growth rate and perhaps in hardiness as well, but with selection of appropriate genetic material it should be useful at least in Zones 6a–8b. It is seldom commercially available, but can be found in arboretums in our area.

Quercus rubra 8

Synonyms: *Q. borealis, Q. borealis var. maxima*
NORTHERN RED OAK
Deciduous tree
Fagaceae (Beech Family)

Native Range.   Eastern North America from Nova Scotia to Minnesota, Kansas, and Georgia.

Useful Range.   USDA Zones 3b–8b with selection of appropriate genetic material.

Function.   Shade and street tree, naturalizing.

Size and Habit

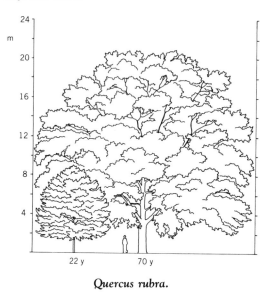

22 y   70 y

Quercus rubra.

Adaptability.   *Q. rubra* is one of the best oaks for city street planting, out-performing many other tree species in relatively small soil volumes.

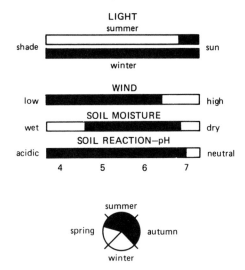

Seasonal Interest.   *Flowers:* Pale yellow-green catkins add interest along with newly expanding foliage in midspring. *Foliage:* Relatively large leaves, 12–20 cm/5–8 in. long with broad, bristle-tipped lobes, pale green as they unfold, then a rich, deep lustrous green in summer, turning deep to bright red in midautumn. *Fruits:* Rather large acorns are borne in great quantities in some years. They add little landscape interest and pose a litter problem.

Problems and Maintenance.   Most disease and insect problems are minor, but one, oak-wilt disease, has proved lethal to trees of *Q. rubra* and other species in the red oak group in certain parts of the Midwest. It was thought at one time that this disease might become more widespread, and this may yet happen, but its spread has so far been moderate where measures have been taken to reduce it, including prompt removal and destruction of infested trees, control of insects that can serve as vectors, and delaying pruning until summer to reduce spreading on pruning tools during the most active season for the disease, when the tree growth is also most active. In areas where oak-wilt has not developed, *Q. rubra* remains a popular and serviceable shade and street tree. Transplanting *Q. rubra* is not difficult when compared with many other oaks.

Hybrids. Several natural hybrids are known but seldom available. Selection of outstanding clones would make useful and fast-growing shade trees, once they were commercially cloned. See the information on hybrid oaks under *Q. alba* hybrids. It remains to be seen what landscape value the *Q. rubra* hybrids may have, but some of them are listed here: *Quercus* ×*benderi* 8 (*Q. coccinea* × *Q. rubra*) is an absolutely majestic tree with age, resembling *Q. rubra* but somewhat faster-growing, and probably useful in Zones 4b–8b. *Quercus* × *hawkinsiae* 8 (*Q. rubra* × *Q. velutina*) is intermediate between the parents and might be a useful shade tree for sandy soils in Zones 4a–8b. *Quercus* ×*heterophylla* 8 (*Q. phellos* × *Q. rubra*) is very fast-growing and similar to *Q. rubra* except with much narrower leaves, ranging from entire to shallowly lobed and bristled and turning red or bronze in autumn. Potentially useful in Zones 5a–8b. *Quercus* ×*runcinata* 8 (*Q. imbricaria* × *Q. rubra*) has symmetrical leaves with 7 to 9 bristle-pointed lobes, often falcate (curved or sickle-shaped), like those of *Q. falcata,* and is probably useful in Zones 4b–8b.

Related Species

Quercus velutina 8 (black oak).   This native of much of our area is seldom available commercially, probably because it is considered difficult to transplant. It is among the most susceptible species to oak-wilt disease but is worth preserving in site development. It is often untidy in appearance because it holds dead branches for a long time, but it performs somewhat better than *Q. rubra* in dry, sandy soils. Its glossy, dark green foliage is handsome in summer and turns red in autumn. Useful in Zones 4b–8b, with selection of appropriate genetic material.

Quercus shumardii 8

SHUMARD OAK
Deciduous tree
Fagaceae (Beech Family)

Native Range.   Southeastern and south-central United States: North Carolina and Florida west-ward to Texas and Kansas, northward to Michigan.

Useful Range.   USDA Zones 6a–9a.

Function.   Shade tree, specimen, naturalizing.

Size and Habit

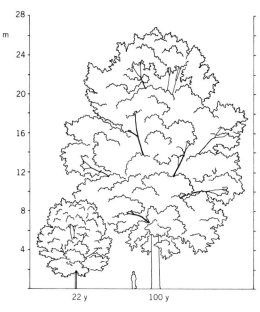

Quercus shumardii.

Adaptability

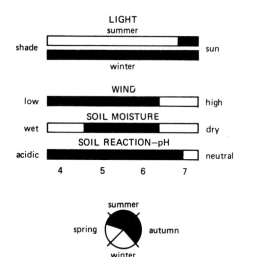

Seasonal Interest. *Flowers:* Pale yellow-green catkins add substantial interest along with newly expanding foliage in midspring. *Foliage:* Relatively large leaves, 8–18 cm/3–7 in. long with wide-spreading, bristle-tipped lobes, pale green as they unfold, then deep, glossy green in summer, turning bright red in midautumn. *Fruits:* Medium-sized acorns provide little landscape interest and only a minor litter problem.

Problems and Maintenance. Disease and insect problems are minor, making this one of the more trouble-free oaks, although it remains to be seen whether oak-wilt disease will become serious in this species. *Q. shumardii* is about as easy to transplant as *Q. palustris* and *Q. rubra,* considerably easier than *Q. coccinea* and *Q. velutina.*

Varieties and Hybrids

Quercus ×*mutabilis* 8 (*Q. palustris* × *Q. shumardii* var. *schneckii*) is intermediate between the parents, with variable foliage. The variety *schneckii* is of interest only as the parent of this hybrid and as a minor variant of the species. Other varieties have been named, but most have either been given species status (*Q. nuttallii* and *Q. texana*) or not accepted.

Related Species

Quercus buckleyi 6–7 (synonyms: *Q. shumardii* var. *texana, Q. texana;* Texas red oak). This tree functions as a small-scale version of *Q. shumardii,* growing to about 10 m/33 ft tall and with smaller leaves. It is native to Oklahoma and central Texas, growing in calcareous soils, so is tolerant of such soils in landscape sites. Useful at least in Zones 7a–9a, probably also parts of Zone 6, and easily available in the southwestern corner of our area, where it is of greatest interest.

Quercus texana 8 (synonym: *Q. nuttallii;* Nuttall oak). This large tree is native to moist sites in the lower Mississippi River basin from southern Missouri to Alabama, Arkansas, Louisiana, and Mississippi. Similar to *Q. palustris* in appearance and native habitat sites, it is a very useful deciduous oak nearly to the Gulf Coast. Useful at least in Zones 6a–9a.

Quercus virginiana 8

LIVE OAK

Evergreen tree

Fagaceae (Beech Family)

Native Range. Southeastern United States and Mexico.

Useful Range. USDA Zones 8b–9a+, and without full development in Zones 7b and 8a (see Problems and Maintenance).

Function. Shade tree, specimen (where plenty of space is available).

Size and Habit

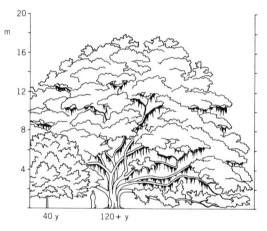

Quercus virginiana.

Adaptability

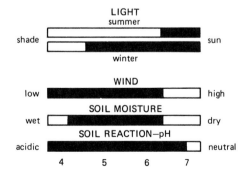

Seasonal Interest. *Flowers:* Yellow-green catkins add substantial interest in early to middle spring, just as new leaves begin to emerge. *Fo-*

liage: Evergreen in Zones 8 and 9, but not always fully evergreen in Zone 7; unlobed new leaves emerge pale yellow-green in midspring and change to lustrous dark green when they fully expand to 5–10 cm/2–4 in. long. Old leaves begin to yellow and fall as new leaves expand and mature. *Fruits:* Acorns, about 2.5 cm/1 in. long, borne in clusters of one to five on long stalks, add minor landscape interest in late summer and autumn. *Trunk and branches:* Massive horizontal limbs give old trees a uniquely majestic character. In most sites in Zones 8b–9a+, limbs are draped with large quantities of the epiphytic Spanish moss. Full development is reliable only from Zone 8b southward, where ice storm damage is negligible (see Problems and Maintenance).

Problems and Maintenance. Live oak, like longleaf pine, generally tolerates cold extremes northward to Zone 7b but occasionally is severely damaged by ice storms in Zones 7b and 8a. The northern limits of its useful range depend on whether full development is necessary to fulfill the intended function. Most insect and disease problems usually are not serious enough to require attention, but stem cankers can occasionally be really troublesome, and stress-related dieback can occur on old specimens in dry years, with dry soil or with limited soil volume. Pruning is seldom needed other than to remove deadwood or as an adjunct to transplanting, which is not especially difficult if care is used, even for fairly large specimens.

Cultivars and Hybrids. Considerable variation exists in size, growth rate, and form in different habitat sites, offering opportunities for selection of distinct forms, but few such selections have been made. 'Grandview Gold' is a selection for golden yellow foliage. Even though few other cultivars have been selected, much variation in size, growth rate, and form exists in different habitats. An unnamed hybrid of *Q. virginiana* by

Q. ×vilmoriniana (see under *Q. dentata*) has proved fully evergreen in southern Michigan (Zone 5b) over a small number of years and may prove hardy at least to Zone 6a, perhaps also parts of Zone 5.

Related Species

Quercus ilex 7 (Holm oak, holly oak). This native of southern Europe has long been a favorite shade tree in much of Europe but has not been much used in the southeastern United States, presumably because of the hot, dry summers. In areas with sufficiently mild, moist summers, it probably would be useful in Zone 9a, probably also in Zone 8. Further trial is justifiable on the chance that this excellent evergreen tree might be adaptable to our area. Its leaves, with lustrous, dark green upper surfaces and white-felted undersides, are only 2.5–8 cm/1–3 in. long and remotely toothed, and its growth habit is rounded, not exceeding 15–18 m/50–60 ft in height and less than that in spread for many years.

Quercus myrtifolia 5–6 (myrtle oak). This ever-green shrub to small tree, native to the Coastal

Quercus ilex.

Plain from South Carolina to Florida and Mississippi, is a handsome evergreen tree to 6–8 m/20–26 ft tall, with leaves similar to those of *Q. virginiana* except shorter and more strongly veined. It is tolerant of dry soil and salt spray, but notably intolerant of poorly drained soils. Useful in Zone 9a+, but not often available, except in or near its native range.

Quercus suber 7 (cork oak). The bark of this tree is the source of commercial cork, and plantings have been made in the southeastern United States for this purpose. *Q. suber*, a Mediterranean native, has grown at least reasonably well in the southeastern United States as far north as Maryland. This tree is comparable in size to *Q. ilex*, the evergreen leaves are similar in size to those of *Q. virginiana*, and the heavy corky bark is a landscape asset as well. Useful in Zones 7b–9a+.

Quercus turbinella 5–6 (shrub live oak). This shrubby, small evergreen tree, native to much of the southwestern United States, to 4–5 m/13–16 ft tall, may be a useful landscape plant for dry sites in Zones 5b–8b, but in most of eastern North America it probably should be used only in sandy or otherwise well-drained soil. Several crosses with other species exist. The *Q. garryana* × *Q. turbinella* hybrid (garrynella oak) developed by Ken Asmuth in southern Michigan grows rapidly to at least 15 m/50 ft in height, with small holly-like leaves, and may prove useful at least to Zones 6b–9a, perhaps also Zone 6a. A *Q. macrocarpa* × *Q. turbinella* hybrid (burlive oak) shows promise for very dry sites in Zones 6a–8b, perhaps also Zone 5, growing slowly to 6–9 m/20–30 ft. Hybrids with *Q. robur* and *Q. stellata* also exist and may prove to be useful for dry, calcareous soils in our area.

Mexican evergreen oaks. Currently, there is much interest in native Mexican oaks with landscape potential north of the border as well as in Mexico. Nurseries and arboretums in the southwestern corner of our range (Arkansas, Louisiana, eastern Oklahoma, and central to northeastern Texas) have been active in plant exploration, evaluation, and introduction of little-known species as well as some that have been in limited cultivation for some time. A few of those most likely to be available at this writing are included here.

Quercus canbyi 5–6 (Canby oak). This broad-spreading and open-branching semievergreen to evergreen tree has striking, dark green foliage resembling that of *Q. palustris* and is reported to be one of the most cold-hardy of the Mexican oaks, referring to genetic material from high elevations. Useful at least in Zones 8b–9a+, and possibly colder zones as well.

Quercus glaucoides 7 (synonym: *Q. laceyi*; Lacey oak). This deciduous tree, to 15 m/45 ft tall, is native from south-central Texas to northeastern Mexico. Its gray-green leaves, 5–12 cm/2–5 in. long, with 4–6 rounded lobes, give the tree a hazy look from a distance. Useful in Zones 8a–9a+, probably also Zone 7b, assuming that trees of Texas origin are used.

Quercus graciliformis 5–6 (Chisos oak). This semievergreen tree, to 4–8 m/13–26 ft tall, is similar in foliage and general appearance to *Q. canbyi*, but more upright and dense, with slender, graceful branches and narrow, leathery leaves having 7–9 bristle-pointed lobes, or few to none in var. *parvilobata*. It is probably useful at least in Zones 8b–9a+, possibly colder zones as well.

Quercus gravesii 6–7 (Graves oak). This deciduous oak from high elevations in Mexico resembles *Q. texana* in foliage and general appearance, growing to 12 m/40 ft in sheltered sites. Like *Q. texana*, *Q. gravesii* is lumped by some specialists into *Q. shumardii*. Its cold hardiness is not well known, but probably includes at least Zones 8a–9a+.

Quercus grisea 6–7 (gray oak). This evergreen shrub or small tree, growing to 4–6 m/13–20 ft at elevations to 2400 m/7800 ft in northern Mexico, has a dense crown and blue-green leaves with heavy silvery-gray pubescence underneath. Its hardiness in our area is not well known, but high-elevation seeds may be worth trying at least in Zones 8a–9a+ and perhaps colder areas.

Quercus hypoleucoides 5–6 (silverleaf oak). This graceful semievergreen shrubby tree, to 2–4 m/6.6–13 ft tall, occasionally reaching 6–9m/

20–30 ft in good sites, is native to elevations of 1200–2400 m/4000–8000 ft in extreme western Texas, Arizona, New Mexico, and Mexico. Its narrow, essentially entire, willow-like leaves, 5–10 cm/2–4 in. long, emerge covered with silvery gray tomentum, which disappears from the upper surfaces at maturity but is retained underneath. Useful at least in Zones 8b–9a+, perhaps also Zone 8a.

Quercus polymorpha 7–8 (Monterrey or Mexican white oak). This majestic evergreen tree, to 20 m/66 ft tall, is native from a limited area in southern Texas through Mexico to Guatemala. With large, leathery, gray-green leaves, it is in use in southern Texas. Useful in Zones 8b–9a+, perhaps also parts of Zone 8a.

Quercus pungens 5–6 (sandpaper oak). This shrubby, small evergreen to semievergreen tree from southwestern Texas and adjacent New Mexico, southern Arizona, and Mexico, gets its common name from the clusters of hard hairs that give a "sandpapery" feel to its dark green upper leaf surfaces. The lower surfaces of the coarsely and sharply toothed leaves retain a soft, silvery pubescence. Useful in Zones 8b–9a+, perhaps some sites in Zone 8a. The var. *vaseyana* (synonym: *Q. vaseyana*; Vasey oak) is usually a shrub to 1.5 m/5 ft high, forming large thickets, occasionally a small tree to 6 m/20 ft tall in good sites, with glossy, hollylike semievergreen leaves that turn purple in winter. Useful in Zones 8a–9a+, perhaps also Zone 7b.

Quercus rysophylla 6–7 (loquat oak). This fast-growing evergreen tree has large, olive-green, strongly textured leaves resembling somewhat those of loquat (*Eriobotrya japonica*). It is native to the mountains of northeastern Mexico and is useful in Zones 9a+, perhaps also parts of Zone 8.

Rhamnus frangula 6

ALDER BUCKTHORN
Deciduous shrub
Rhamnaceae (Buckthorn Family)

Native Range. Europe, western Asia, North Africa, naturalized in the eastern United States.

Useful Range. USDA Zones 4b–8a.

Function. Hedge, screen, border.

Size and Habit. 'Columnaris' is illustrated.

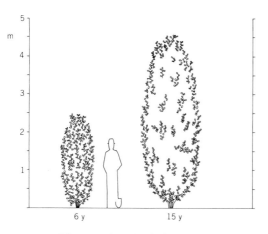

Rhamnus fragula **'Columnaris.'**

Adaptability

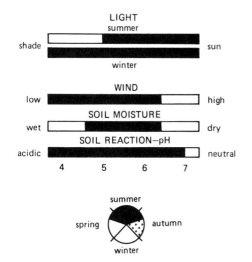

Seasonal Interest. *Flowers:* Very small, whitish yellow, inconspicuous. *Foliage:* Lustrous, rich deep green, pale green underneath, 3–8 cm/1–3 in. long, neatly textured, turning yellowish before falling in late autumn. *Fruits:* Red in midsummer, soon turning purplish black, about 0.6 cm/0.24 in. across, persisting into autumn. *Branches:* Dark gray bark marked with small white lenticels, inconspicuous but interesting at close range.

Problems and Maintenance. *R. frangula* is usually considered relatively trouble-free, but at least in some parts of the Midwest leaf-spot disease, possibly complicated by a twig blight, reduces the effectiveness of the narrow cultivar 'Columnaris' as a visual screen. Pruning may be necessary under some conditions to promote sufficient fullness for screening. Also, the tendency of this species to spread spontaneously by seed propagation makes it a potential weed in some areas. *Rhamnus* species are prohibited in many areas where oats are grown, especially in Canada (see Related Species, *R. catharticus*).

Cultivars. 'Asplenifolia' is a relatively slow-growing form with very fine-textured, almost fernlike foliage. Leaves are about as long as those of the species type, but usually less than 0.5 cm/ 0.2 in. wide with wavy margins. This makes a fine specimen for accent against architectural material: stone, stucco, gravel mulch, and so forth, in formal and small-scale landscape situations, although plants probably will reach a height and spread of at least 2 m/6.6 ft in time. This specimen plant presently is seldom available

Rhamnus frangula **'Asplenifolia.'**

but is worth introducing more generally into landscape use in the northern parts of our area.

'Columnaris' (tallhedge buckthorn) is by far the most common buckthorn in landscape use, valued for its narrowly upright growth habit and used primarily as a visual screen where lateral space is limited. Because of an apparent disease problem (see Problems and Maintenance), it is difficult to maintain foliage density toward the bottom of the plant, and lower facing plants or opaque fences must be used in combination for full visual screening. It is useful in Zones 4b–8a.

Related Species

Rhamnus carolinianus 6 (Carolina buckthorn, Indian cherry).   This large shrub or small tree is native over much of the eastern United States, north to New York and Nebraska and south to Florida and Texas. It is seldom if ever available commercially but worth preserving as a native plant in some situations. Its rather narrow leaves, to 15 cm/6 in. long and usually less than 2.5 cm/1 in. wide, are lustrous and bright green and its fruits are slightly larger and more colorful in the red stage than those of *R. frangula.* It is useful primarily for naturalizing in Zones 6b–9a, and in some sites in Zones 5b and 6a where native plants exist and can be used or preserved.

Rhamnus catharticus 6 (common buckthorn). This rather trouble-free, large, Eurasian shrub or small tree, like *R. frangula,* has become naturalized in the northeastern United States. It has very dark green leaves with prominent curved veins, dark gray bark, and black fruit borne in great numbers, but it has little other seasonal interest and is used primarily for hedges and informal screens (with some pruning to promote fullness). Since it is the alternate host to the crown rust disease of oats, it should be avoided or eradicated in areas where oats are grown. This and other *Rhamnus* species are prohibited by quarantine laws from many areas where oats are grown, especially in Canada. Moreover, *R. cathartica* is fully as likely to escape cultivation and become a weed as *R. frangula.* Useful, when these limitations do not prohibit it, in Zones 3b–6b.

Rhamnus dahuricus 6 (Dahurian buckthorn). This large shrub or small tree from north-central and northeastern Asia has light olive green leaves, to 10 cm/4 in. long, and form and fruiting similar to that of *R. cathartica.* It is unusually cold-hardy, useful in Zones 3a–6b, but seldom commercially available.

Rhamnus pallasii 4.   This native of western Asia has dark green leaves only about 2.5 cm/1 in. long and less than half as wide and is extremely cold-hardy, useful in Zones 3a–6b, but planted only experimentally in the Northern Plains, where it could become a popular, medium-sized shrub if it were more widely available.

More than 100 additional species are known, but are probably not useful and certainly not available in our area. A few are evergreen shrubs or trees, including *R. alaternus* 4–6, from the Mediterranean and Caucasus, and *R. croceus* 4, from Arizona, California, and Baja California, but these are probably not useful in eastern North America.

Rhaphiolepis indica 3–4

INDIAN RHAPHIOLEPIS, INDIAN HAWTHORN
Evergreen shrub
Rosaceae (Rose Family)

Native Range.   Southern China.

Useful Range.   USDA Zones 8a–9a+, and sheltered sites in Zone 7b.

Function.   Specimen, border, massing. Effective for accent against architectural materials.

Size and Habit

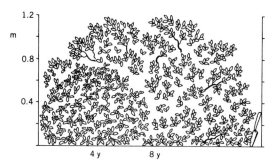

Rhaphiolepis indica.

Adaptability. Tolerates coastal salt spray and wind.

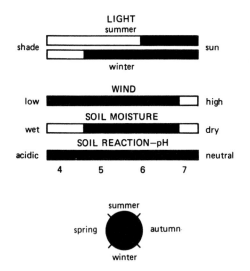

Seasonal Interest. *Flowers:* Fragrant, white, pink, or rose, to 2 cm/0.8 in. across, in loose clusters to 8 cm/3 in. across in middle spring, with or just before the new foliage. *Foliage:* Evergreen, deep green, and stiff, leathery leaves, about 5 cm/2 in. long, loosely arranged and turning purplish in full sun in winter. *Fruits:* Blue-black, about 1 cm/0.4 in. across, interesting but not showy in autumn. *Branching:* Twisting irregularly and picturesquely, giving a mildly striking accent.

Problems and Maintenance. Nematodes can be a problem in some areas. When this happens, it is necessary to fumigate and replant with nematode-free stock or other nematode-resistant species. Scale insects and a twig blight occasion-

ally are troublesome but not major problems. Pruning is not necessary and should be avoided, except for removal of deadwood, so as not to interfere with the natural character of the plant.

Cultivars. At least 20 cultivars are commercially available, to 0.8–1.5 m/2.6–5 ft in height and width, with pale pink to deep rose or white flowers. There is some confusion among cultivars and duplicate-naming in some cases, and several are roughly co-equivalent in landscape use. A few of the most common are listed here.

'Alba' is really a collective name for several white-flowered clones.

'Ballerina' grows to 0.9 m/3 ft in height and width, with soft pink flowers borne in large numbers in spring and lightly in summer.

'Jack Evans' is a vigorous selection, to 1.2 m/ 4 ft high and wide, with leathery foliage and large clusters of pink flowers in early spring.

'Monant' (White Enchantress™) forms a broad mound, 0.9/3 ft high and 1.5 m/5 ft wide, with glossy foliage and white flowers over a long season in spring to early summer.

'Moness' (Enchantress™) is similar to 'Monant' except that it has rose-pink flowers.

'Monme' (Springtime™) is vigorous, loosely branched, and graceful, to 1.5–1.8 m/5–6 ft tall and wide, with leathery, bronzed green foliage and deep pink flowers in spring.

'Monrey' (Spring Rapture™, Plant Patent No. 5215, 1984) is a low plant, about 1 m/3.3 ft high and wide, with intensely rose-pink flowers from early spring to early summer.

'Monto' (Indian Princess™, Plant Patent No. 5862, 1987) is broadly mound-forming, to 0.9 m/3 ft high and 1.5 m/5 ft wide, with large, bright green leaves and pale pink flowers in spring, fading to white.

'Pink Lady' is similar or identical to 'Monme' (Springtime™).

'Pinkie' is similar or identical to 'Moness' (Enchantress™).

'Snow White' is a medium-sized shrub, to 1.2 m/4 ft high and wide, with dark green foliage and quantities of white flowers in spring.

Related Species and Hybrids

Rhaphiolepis ×*delacourii* 3–5 (hybrid rhaphiolepis or Indian currant).   This hybrid group (*R. indica* × *R. umbellata*) includes a few cultivars that display the full range of size found in the parents. 'Belle' is vigorous and tall, with deep pink flowers. 'Montic' (Majestic Beauty™) is a vigorous large shrub, to at least 3 m/10 ft high and 2 m/6.6 ft wide, with large, deep green leaves and large clusters of pale pink flowers. Several other cultivars are notably smaller: 'Clara' and 'Peggy' have white flowers; 'Elizabeth is fast-growing, to 1.5 m/5 ft in height and width, with pink flowers; 'Janice is more compact, with bright pink flowers in spring and into summer; 'Pink Charm' is a low-growing form with deep rose-pink flowers.

Rhaphiolepis umbellata.

Rhaphiolepis umbellata 4–5 (synonyms: *R. japonica, R. ovata*; Yedda hawthorn).   This native of Japan and Korea differs little from the Chinese *R. indica* except in size. It is more vigorously upright and can become sparse at the base in time, needing smaller facing shrubs for basal cover in border plantings. It has gradually become less popular than *R. indica*, except for its dwarf selections. Its leaves are slightly broader than those of *R. indica*, and its flowers are white and fragrant. Useful in Zones 8a–9a+. 'Minor' grows compactly to only 0.9–1.2 m/3–4 ft high and wide, with white flowers in early spring.

Rhododendron calendulaceum 5

FLAME AZALEA
Deciduous shrub
Ericaceae (Heath Family)

Native Range.   Mountains of eastern United States from Pennsylvania to Georgia.

Useful Range.   USDA Zones 5a–8b.

Function.   Specimen, border, naturalizing.

Size and Habit

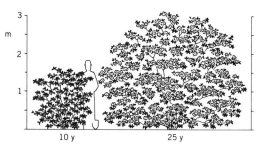

Rhododendron calendulaceum.

Adaptability.   Light shade in summer is beneficial in the South and Midwest, especially to reduce fading in red-flowered cultivars. Shade provided by tall pine trees in the South is near-optimal.

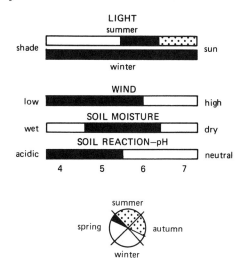

Seasonal Interest.   *Flowers:* Yellow through orange to scarlet, not fragrant, to 5 cm/2 in. across, in very showy clusters with the immature

Rhododendron calendulaceum.

foliage very late in spring. *Foliage:* Deep green, slightly lustrous, displayed to good effect by the tiered branching pattern, falling in autumn with little color change. *Fruits:* Dried capsules, inconspicuous.

Problems and Maintenance. Several diseases and insects occasionally damage the foliage of *R. calendulaceum*, but these are minor and occasional problems. Pruning is not necessary and should be avoided, since the form of most azaleas is more likely to be destroyed than improved by pruning. Where space is limited, there are many other smaller-growing azaleas that can be used in preference to large types such as *R. calendulaceum*.

Cultivars. Even though many cultivars are hybrids of *R. calendulaceum*, few selections have been made directly from the wild species. Those that have been (e.g., f. *aurantium* and 'Croceum') have been more or less replaced by hardy hybrid cultivars and probably are no longer available.

Hybrids

Ghent Hybrids (R. ×gandavense). This large hybrid group has resulted from crosses among members of older hybrid groups: the Mortier Hybrids, involving *R. calendulaceum*, *R. luteum* (synonym: *R. flavum,*) and *R. periclymenoides* (synonym: *R. nudiflorum*); the Ornatum Hybrids, involving *R. flammeum* (synonym: *R. speciosum*), *R. luteum*, *R. periclymenoides* and *R. viscosum*; and the Viscosepalum Hybrids, which involved *R. flammeum*, *R. molle* and *R. viscosum*.

Most cultivars included in the Ghent Hybrids are useful in Zones 6b–7b. Many are cold-hardy northward to Zone 5b as well. Only a few seem to be heat-tolerant enough for Zone 8. More than 300 cultivars have been selected, but most have been replaced by Knap Hill hybrids and other more recently developed hybrids. A few of those most likely to be available still are included here.

'Beaute Celeste' (= 'Cardinal') has fragrant, small, single, orange-red flowers.

'Charlemagne' has large, single, dull-orange flowers.

'Daviesii' has very large (to 5.5 cm/2.2 in. across), single, pale yellow flowers, opening late and finally fading to white. It is one of the most cold-hardy cultivars in this group, and at the same time is heat-tolerant well into Zone 8.

'Fanny' (= 'Pucella' or 'Pucelle') is also unusually cold-hardy, with very large single purplish pink flowers, opening late.

'Flamboyant' has large flowers, red-orange and yellow, very showy and late-flowering in this group.

'Gloria Mundi' is unusually cold-hardy with very large, single, bright orange flowers, slightly frilled.

'Ignaeum Novum' has very large, single, orange and red-orange flowers and unusual cold hardiness in this group.

'Minerva' has very large, red flowers, opening late.

'Narcissiflorum' has fragrant, double, yellow flowers, opening late and remaining colorful for a relatively long period of time. It is unusually cold-hardy and heat-tolerant to Zone 8 as well.

'Pallas' has very large, single, orange-red flowers with a yellow-orange blotch and is unusually cold-hardy.

'Unique' has large, single, yellow-orange flowers that open late. It is unusually cold-hardy.

Knap Hill Hybrids. This is another large, complex hybrid group, made up of four subgroups: the original Knap Hill Hybrids, the Slocock (or Goldsworth) Hybrids, the Exbury Hybrids, and the Ilam Hybrids. The Ilam Hybrids have been developed in New Zealand, the others in England. They have been produced by crossing members of the Ghent and Molle Hybrid groups, and their parents, and in some cases *R. occiden-*

tale, the western azalea. Because of their large flowers (5–8 cm/2–3 in. across) in large clusters (up to 20 to 30 flowers in a cluster) and hardiness generally comparable with that of the Ghent Hybrids, cultivars in this group have been accepted increasingly since their introduction following World War II and now probably constitute the most important group of deciduous azaleas for the northern parts of our area, excepting the very coldest regions (Zones 3 and 4). Frequently, seedlings from Knap Hill Hybrids are offered for sale with the expected variation in color and other characteristics. Even though the quality of such progeny is variable, most of them are very acceptable landscape plants. A few of the more popular cultivars in this large hybrid group are listed here. Selection should not be limited to these, and should be based on local performance and availability.

'Annabella' (Exbury) has vivid orange-yellow flowers.

'Avocet' (Knap Hill) has white flowers, tinged pink.

'Berryrose' (Exbury) has fragrant rose-red flowers, orange-blotched.

'Brazil' (Exbury) has brilliant deep orange flowers.

'Buzzard' (Knap Hill) has fragrant, pale yellow flowers, pink-tinged.

'Cannon's Double' (Exbury) has double, frilled, pale yellowish white flowers with pink lobes.

'Cecile' (Exbury) has salmon-pink flowers, with a salmon blotch.

'Evening Glow' (Knap Hill) has pale pink flowers, tinged pale yellow, with yellow throat.

'Gibraltar' (Exbury) has bright orange flowers.

'Golden Eagle' (Knap Hill) also has bright orange flowers.

'Harvest Moon' (Slocock) has frilled, bright yellow petals and a deeper yellow blotch.

'Homebush' (Knap Hill) has bright purplish-red, semidouble flowers.

'Hotspur' (Exbury) has red-orange flowers.

'Klondyke' (Exbury) has golden yellow flowers with an orange blotch.

'Old Gold' (Exbury) has pale orange-yellow flowers with a pink tinge.

'Orangeade' (Knap Hill) has orange flowers.

'Pink Ruffles' (Exbury) has pink flowers with an orange blotch.

'Redder Yet' (Knap Hill, Leach) has purplish red, brown-spotted petals.

'Rocket' (Exbury) has vivid orange-yellow flowers with a yellow blotch.

'Satan' (Slocock) has brilliant scarlet flowers.

'Scarlet Pimpernel' (Exbury) has bright red flowers.

'Seville' (Slocock) has bright orange flowers.

'Strawberry Ice' (Exbury) has yellow-pink flowers with a deeper yellow-pink overlay and orange-yellow blotch.

'Whitethroat' (Knap Hill) has large, double pure white flowers.

Ilam Hybrids. This group of hybrids was developed by the late Edgar Stead of Ilam, near Christchurch, New Zealand, combining some of the Knap Hill Hybrids with some of that group's original parents: *R. calendulaceum, R. molle,* and *R. viscosum.* J. S. Yeates, of Palmerston North, New Zealand, David Leach, of Madison, Ohio, and others continued breeding with Mr. Stead's lines, and at least 50 cultivars have now been released and are gradually becoming available. 'Brickdust' has unusually large reddish flowers. 'Ilam Carmen' has large, gold-marked, salmon-pink flowers. 'Ilam Giant' has large yellow flowers with a darker blotch. 'Maori' is unusually vigorous, with 25 cm/10 in. clusters of sparkling orange flowers. 'Red Letter' (= 'Melford Red Letter') has bright orange-red flowers. 'Spring Salvo' has large, deep red-orange flowers, with bright orange blotch, in clusters to 18 cm/7 in. across, and excellent foliage. 'Yellow Beauty' has brilliant yellow-orange flowers with frilled petal-edges.

Chinquapin Hill Hybrids. These hybrids were developed by the late Augustus "Gus" Elmer, Jr. of Pass Christian, Mississippi, to infuse heat-tolerance into some of the Exbury azaleas by crossing them with *R. austrinum.* They have proved useful in at least Zones 7a–9a, but at this writing are not generally available, except perhaps locally on the Gulf Coast.

Girard Deciduous Azalea Hybrids. Peter Girard, Sr., of Geneva, Ohio, developed many deciduous azalea cultivars (as well as evergreen azaleas and rhododendrons). In this breeding program, mostly involving Knap Hill azaleas as parents, his objectives included mildew-resistance, cold- and heat-tolerance, ease of propagation, and large and often double (hose-in-hose) flowers. Many are widely available and are usually sold with the Girard name attached. A few of the most popular are listed here. All of these are cold-hardy at least to Zone 6b, most somewhat hardier, as noted. 'Crimson Tide' has double, red flowers in compact clusters and is cold-hardy to Zone 6a. 'Mount Saint Helens' has large, fragrant flowers, yellowish pink with a large bright red-orange blotch, and is cold-hardy to Zone 5b. 'Pink Delight' (Girard Pink Delight®) has bright pink, fragrant double (hose-in-hose) flowers in large, compact clusters, cold-hardy to Zone 5b. 'Red Pom Pom' (Girard Red Pom Pom®) has fragrant, double red flowers in compact clusters and has a compact growth habit, and it is mildew-resistant. 'Salmon Delight' has large flowers, bright rose flushed with yellow, in large clusters and apparently is resistant to mildew and cold-hardy to Zone 5b. 'Yellow Pom Pom' has fragrant, double yellow flowers in large clusters and is compact in growth, apparently mildew-resistant, and cold-hardy to Zone 5b.

Related Species

Rhododendron austrinum 5 (synonym: *Azalea austrina*; Florida flame azalea). This southern counterpart of *R. calendulaceum*, native to northern Florida and adjacent Alabama and Georgia, has clusters of fragrant, golden yellow flowers in midspring (late March and early April in Zone 9a), and is useful in Zones 7a–9a+ and sheltered sites in Zone 6b.

Rhododendron flammeum 5 (synonyms: *Azalea flammea*, *A. speciosa*, *R. speciosum*; Oconee aza-

lea). This native of Georgia and South Carolina has clusters of unscented flowers, red-orange to yellow and pink, in middle to late spring. Useful in Zones 7b–8b, as well as in sheltered sites in Zone 7a.

Rhododendron luteum 5 (synonym: *Azalea lutea*, *A. pontica*, *R. flavum*; sweet or Pontic azalea). This Eurasian species with fragrant yellow flowers is seldom grown in our area but is important because of its inclusion in the Ghent and Knap Hill hybrids.

Rhododendron occidentale 4–5 (western azalea). The only azalea native west of the Rocky Mountains, this deciduous shrub is upright in form, growing from 1.5 m/5 ft to at least 3 m/10 ft tall; it has blue-green leaves that turn yellow to scarlet or crimson in autumn, as well as fragrant flowers in combinations of white and yellow to orange, pink, and red. It has a useful range of Zones 7b–9a on the West Coast, but is not sufficiently heat-tolerant for most of the parts of our area where it is cold hardy. A few selections have been made on the West Coast, including 'Leonard Frisbie,' with orange-yellow blotched light red flowers, to 9 cm/3.5 in. across, and reportedly cold hardy to Zone 6b, and 'Stagecoach Frills,' with pale pink, frilled flowers. *R. occidentale* is of greatest interest in our area as a parent of some of the Knap Hill Hybrids. It has been used in breeding programs in the Pacific Northwest and Europe; it has also been used with *R. prunifolium*, by Fred Galle in the recent Galle hybrids, which show greater heat-tolerance and will probably be valuable additions to southern landscapes.

Rhododendron carolinianum 4

CAROLINA RHODODENDRON
Evergreen shrub
Ericaceae (Heath Family)

Native Range. Southern Appalachians: North Carolina.

Useful Range. USDA Zones 5b–7b, areas with moderate summer temperatures in Zone 8, and protected sites in Zone 5a.

Function. Border, specimen, foundation.

Size and Habit

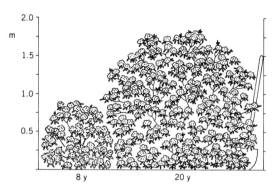

Rhododendron carolinianum.

Adaptability. Shade from full summer sun is necessary in Zones 7 and 8 except in areas where summer heat is tempered by high elevation or proximity to large bodies of water. This plant will tolerate full shade but will neither grow nor flower well. Protection from winter sun and wind is advisable, especially in Zones 5 and 6.

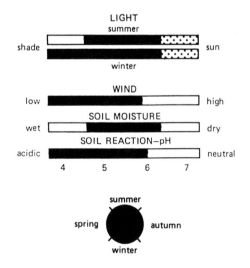

Seasonal Interest. *Flowers:* Pale pink to rosy purple (or white in a variety), to 4 cm/1.6 in. across, in terminal, rounded clusters of up to 10 flowers in the better horticultural forms, in middle to late spring. *Foliage:* Evergreen, leathery leaves are deep green with brownish scales underneath, 5–8 cm/2–3 in. long and about 2.5 cm/1 in. wide, curling tightly under drought or cold stress.

Problems and Maintenance. Relatively free of maintenance, but several pests and diseases occasionally become troublesome, so a minimal pest control program is necessary. Most common problems in northern areas are physiological and relate to improper soil preparation and/or site (see *Rhododendron catawbiense*), but *R. carolinianum* seems to be more tolerant of environmental stresses than most rhododendrons. For maximum flowering year after year, it is necessary to remove faded flower clusters to prevent fruit and seed development and the drain that this imposes on flowering in the following year.

Varieties and Cultivars. The var. *album* has pure white flowers, slightly larger than those of the species type, and can be reproduced true to type by seed propagation. It is considered a highly choice rhododendron. Selections for clear pink color have been made but seldom named or maintained in the nursery trade.

Hybrids. 'Carolina Rose,' a cross between a rhododendron (*R. carolinianum*) and an azalea (*R. prinophyllum*), is low and compact, to 1 m/ 3.3 ft tall, with an abundance of small deep pink flowers. Reportedly useful in Zones 7a–8b, but probably also at least in part of Zone 6 and perhaps still colder zones.

Rhododendron ×'Laetevirens' 4 (*R. carolinianum* × *R. ferrugineum*; Wilson rhododendron). This shrub is used more for its compact, moundlike habit and bright green foliage than for its small, rosy-pink flowers, which are not borne in large numbers and open so late that they are partly covered by the new foliage. Useful in Zones 6b–8b.

Rhododendron × P.J.M. Hybrids 4 (P.J.M. hybrid rhododendrons). This is not a cultivar, but a grex—that is, a group of hybrids of the same parentage, in this case *R. dauricum* var. *sempervirens* × *R. carolinianum*. These plants are often specified and sold simply as P.J.M. hybrids, since they are fairly consistent in their compact, rounded growth habit (1.5 m/5 ft high and 1.2– 1.5 m/4–5 ft wide) and neatly textured foliage, which turns more-or-less mahogany purple in winter. Yet there are significant clonal differences in growth rate, foliage size and color, and flower color (pale lavender-pink to deep mauve). The name "P.J.M." refers to Peter J. Mezitt, founder of Weston Nurseries, in Massachusetts, who made the cross. His son, Edmund V. Mezitt, selected and named several cultivars from this population: 'Elite' has deep pink-lavender flowers in midspring, has deep mahogany-red winter foliage, and is one of the latest-flowering and most vigorous of this group; 'Regal' has bright lavender-pink flowers, at the peak flowering time of this group, with the latest *Forsythia* cultivars, in early to middle spring; 'Victor' is slower-growing, with smaller leaves, and is among the earliest of this group to bloom, with pink-lavender flowers, and deep mahogany foliage early in winter. These hybrids are useful in Zones 5a–7b; some clones, such as 'Regal,' are hardy to Zone 4b.

Other *R. carolinianum* hybrids are listed under *R. ferrugineum* and under the main heading, Rhododendron cultivars.

Related Species

Rhododendron chapmanii 4 (Chapman rhododendron).   This native of northwestern Florida is notably more heat-resistant than *R. carolinianum* or, for that matter, most other rhododendrons. It is similar to *R. carolinianum,* so it can be considered a counterpart for the Deep South. Useful in Zones 8a–9a+, perhaps also in Zone 7 in protected areas. An endangered species, *R. chapmanii* should not be collected from the wild but rather should be grown from seeds or cultivated material.

Rhododendron davidsonianum 4–5 (Davidson rhododendron).   This native of western China can reach heights close to 3 m/10 ft in cultivation, with glossy dark green leaves only 2.5–6.4 m/1–2.5 in. long; it also has pink flowers, 4.5 cm/1.75 in. across. Top-rated by specialists, this species is unfortunately too tender to be useful in most of our area. Some of its hybrids are more useful (see Rhododendron cultivars).

Rhododendron keiskei 2–5 (Keisuke rhododendron).   This Japanese species is distinctive as the most cold-hardy of the yellow flowering *Rhododendron* species. If it were not for this, it probably would receive little attention, since its flowers have poor substance and its growth habit is loose and straggling. Its size varies widely with

elevation, and the selection 'Yaku Fairy' is an interesting prostrate form, useful in Zones 7a–7b, perhaps also 6b, and areas in Zone 8 with moderate summers. Several useful hybrids of this species are available, some with yellow flowers (see Rhododendron cultivars).

Rhododendron minus 5–6 (Piedmont rhododendron).   This close relative of *R. carolinianum* becomes a larger plant, frequently to 2–3 m/6.6–10 ft in height and spread, sometimes twice that in native habitat. Its flowers range from clear pink to rose-purple and occasionally white, in clusters of 10 to 30. Some specialists have included both *R. carolinianum* and *R. chapmanii* under *R. minus*, but this taxonomic decision has not yet been widely enough accepted in our area to warrant its inclusion here. Note that the population here called *R. carolinianum* may sometimes be found under *R. minus*, and *R. chapmanii* under *R. minus* var. *chapmanii*. *R. minus* as used here in the narrow sense is useful in Zones 6a–8b, perhaps also Zone 9a. The selection 'Chattahoochee Twilight' has peach-colored flowers.

Rhododendron racemosum 2–4.   This highly variable species from high elevations in western China ranges from 0.4–2 m/1.3–6.6 ft, and occasionally taller. All forms have small, very attractive leaves, 2–5 cm/0.8–3 in. long, and flowers, at least 2.5 cm/1 in. across, varying from white through shades of pink to deep rose. Flowers of some clones are borne laterally on long, wandlike stems in early to middle spring. In other clones they form a dense surface mass, covering most of the foliage. Useful in Zones 7a–8b, where summers are moderate, some selections perhaps to Zone 6b. A few selections have been made, including the following: 'Donna Totten' is presumed to be a hybrid of *R. racemosum* and an unknown parent, growing to about 1.2 m/4 ft tall, with pink, ivory-tinged flowers. 'Forrest' is dwarf with pink flowers, but seldom available. 'Pride of Split Rock' (= 'Split Rock') is either a selection of *R. racemosum* or a hybrid of unknown pollen parent, growing to 0.9 m/3 ft high and half again as wide, with bright pink flowers and beautiful mahogany-red autumn foliage. 'White Lace' is a form of the species, growing to about 1.2 m/4 ft high, with pure white flowers.

Rhododendron catawbiense 5

CATAWBA RHODODENDRON
Evergreen shrub
Ericaceae (Heath Family)

Native Range.   Southern Appalachians: Virginia to Georgia.

Useful Range.   USDA Zones 4a–7b, areas having moderate summer temperature in Zone 8, and protected sites in Zone 3b. Note that the Catawbiense hybrids are considerably less cold-hardy than the species type.

Function.   Border, screen, specimen, naturalizing.

Size and Habit

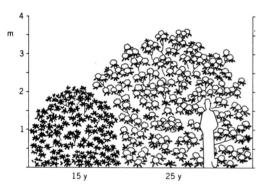

Rhododendron catawbiense.

Adaptability.   Shade from full summer sun is necessary in Zones 7 and 8, the Midwest, and other areas having hot summers. Plants tolerate full shade but do not flower well. Protection from winter sun and wind is advisable in Zones 3b, 4, and 5.

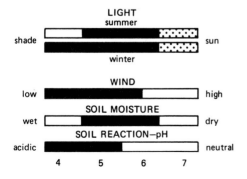

Seasonal Interest.   *Flowers:* Lilac-purple (white in a variety), 6 cm/2.4 in. across, as many as 20 packed in tight, rounded, terminal clusters up to 15 cm/6 in. across, opening in late spring but before new leaves emerge. *Foliage:* Evergreen, leathery, dark green, 8–15 cm/3–6 in. long, forming a dense mass in plants that are growing well.

Problems and Maintenance.   The most common cause of failure of newly planted rhododendrons is insufficient soil aeration. This can happen when the soil is not adequately prepared for planting, or when rhododendrons are planted too deeply. It is important to plant high enough so that after the soil settles, the plant is no deeper than before. Several insects and mites can be troublesome, but most are only occasionally serious and easily controlled. Lacewing fly can be a problem for some cultivars, and black vine and strawberry weevils and borers can be lethal if not controlled promptly.

Nematodes can be a serious problem in the Deep South. Several diseases also can affect rhododendrons, and some of these can pose serious problems. The most destructive include twig blight, dieback, and wilt diseases. When rhododendrons are to be used in quantity, a thorough plant protection program should be available.

Rhododendron catawbiense.

In many areas, plants more often show symptoms of physiological disorders than of pathogenic diseases. These include leaf scorch from winter sun and sweeping winds and chlorosis (leaf yellowing) or dieback from improper soil conditions. To prevent or reduce incidence of these problems, it is necessary to give careful attention to selection of soil and site. Protection from full sun on south and west sides of plantings and from winter wind from the north and west will go a long way to avoid leaf scorch, but remember that some sun or open sky above the plantings is necessary for full flowering.

If soils are not sufficiently acidic—below pH 5.5 or 6.0—acidification with sulfur, acid peat moss, and acid-residue fertilizer may help, as will foliar applications of ferrous sulfate or chelated iron. But in soils containing free limestone, such adjustments will be so transient as to be virtually useless. In such cases, the use of rhododendrons and their relatives may require building raised planting beds with acid-residue organic soil materials such as wood or bark chips or peat moss, alone or in combination. In areas having "problem" soils for such plants, more information can be obtained from state universities or county, state, or provincial extension service offices.

For best flowering year after year, flower clusters should be removed as soon as they fade to prevent fruit and seed development and interference of these processes with formation of flower buds for the next year. This may not be practical on large plants.

Varieties. The var. *album* is a naturally occurring population within the species of plants with white flowers, delicately tinted with a trace of pink when they first open. This variety is among the finest of rhododendrons for landscape use, with excellent form and foliage as well as flowers and cold hardiness equal to the species type, but it is even more important as a parent of hardy cultivars.

Cultivars. The list below includes selections made from *R. catawbiense* where the pollen parent is either of the same species or unknown. In addition to these, descriptions of hybrid cultivars with *R. catawbiense* as only one parent can be found under the major heading Rhododendron

cultivars. Both lists are only samplings of the cultivars that are commercially available, but they include most of the best and most easily available. Some of those that show the greatest cold-hardiness have also shown good heat-tolerance as well, but successful use of these plants south of Zone 7b is limited to areas with relatively moderate summers and requires careful maintenance, especially irrigation when necessary.

'Album Elegans' is valued for its white flowers, very late in spring, and is useful in Zones 6a–7b.

'America' has the purest red flowers available for relatively cold climates (Zones 6a–7b), but is structurally weak.

'Boursault' (= 'Catawbiense Boursault') is valued for its lilac-colored flowers and is useful in Zones 5b–7b.

'Catawbiense Album' has white flowers in late spring and is useful in Zones 5b–7b. It should not be confused with the less-commonly available *R. catawbiense* var. *album*, a naturally occurring population that is superior in both cold-hardiness (at least to Zone 4b) and landscape character.

'Charles Dickens' is a very good red-flowering form, except that it is reportedly difficult to propagate and slow-growing, which is not a liability except in production. Useful in Zones 5b–7b.

'English Roseum' is a popular rose-flowered selection, even though it is considered inferior to 'Roseum Elegans' by many specialists. Useful in Zones 5b–7b.

'Mrs. Charles S. Sargent' is one of the finest of all rhododendrons for colder climates, with excellent form and deep reddish-rose flowers. Useful in Zones 5b–7b.

'Nova Zembla' is generally considered the best red-flowering Catawba hybrid for colder climates, but is slightly less cold-hardy than 'America' and 'Charles Dickens,' useful in Zones 6a–7b.

'Purpureum Grandiflorum' is probably the best purple-flowering rhododendron for colder climates, to Zone 6a, but far inferior to the more tender Ponticum Hybrid, 'Purple Splendour' (see Rhododendron cultivars).

'Roseum Elegans' (= 'Pink Roseum') is an extremely popular flowering hybrid with good form and lavender-pink flowers, useful in Zones 5b–7b. Unfortunately, this name has been applied to more than this one superior clone.

Related Species and Hybrids

Rhododendron arboreum 7 (tree rhododendron). This truly treelike native of the Himalayas is most impressive for its size and for its large clusters of white to purplish-red or bright crimson flowers, opening very early in spring where it is hardy, which includes hardly any of our area, but Zones 8b–9a in areas with relatively mild summers. Hybrids have been made with *R. catawbiense* and a few other species, and a few of them are useful in Zone 7a, perhaps Zone 6b. None of these hybrids is comparable with *R. arboreum* in size and majesty, however.

Rhododendron decorum 6 (sweetshell rhododendron). This native of western China is not widely available, and useful only in coastal areas and high elevations in Zones 7b–8b, but it is more likely to be encountered in the form of hybrids than as the species type (see Rhododendron cultivars). Its large, fragrant, pink or white flowers are impressive, and this species is believed to be a principal parent of the Dexter Hybrids (see below).

Dexter Hybrids. The efforts of C. O. Dexter of Sandwich, Massachusetts, in hybridizing the relatively tender Chinese species to produce hybrids hardy enough for his locality (borderline of Zones 6b–7a) has attracted much interest, and some of the resulting hybrids perform well in colder zones. Many of his unnamed seedlings were grown by others, and some were eventually introduced. A few of the best-known Dexter hybrids are 'Dexter's Giant Red,' 'Dexter's Spice,' and 'Mrs. W. R. Coe,' all useful to Zone 7a; and 'Merley Cream,' 'Scintillation,' and 'Todmorden,' all useful to Zone 6b and perhaps sheltered sites in Zone 6a (see *R. fortunei* and Rhododendron cultivars).

Rhododendron dichroanthum 4 (orange-flowered rhododendron). This native of high elevations in southern China is densely compact in habit, to about 1.5 m/5 ft high and slightly wider, with rather small leaves, 4–10 cm/1.6–4 in. long, the undersides covered with a silky coating of white hairs. It has rather small clusters of pendulous, bell-shaped flowers, at least 5 cm/2 in. across, orange or varying from buff to shades of pink. This species is valued as a breeding parent for orange flower color. It is nearly useless in our area, since it is cold-hardy only to Zone 8b, but some of its hybrids are useful in Zone 6b (see 'Bangkok,' 'Hindustan,' and 'Monaco' under Rhododendron cultivars).

Rhododendron fortunei 5 (Fortune rhododendron). This native of eastern China is a magnificent landscape plant in itself in Zones 6b–7a and milder, with fragrant pink to white flowers, to 10 cm/4 in. across, and leaves 10–20 cm/4–8 in. long. It is not widely available as the species, but its parentage is present in many hybrids. Rhododendron breeders in Europe and our Pacific Northwest have use *R. fortunei* as a primary breeding parent. C. O. Dexter apparently made selections from *R. fortunei* as well as deliberate hybrids, but many Dexter selections are of uncertain parentage (see Rhododendron cultivars). A few of the more popular *R. fortunei* selections are listed here.

'Ben Moseley' is probably a hybrid of *R. fortunei* by an unknown pollen parent, to 1.5 m/5 ft tall, and one of the hardiest Dexter rhododendrons, useful in Zones 6a–8a, with large, light lilac-pink flowers, deeper purplish pink on the margins, opening in midspring.

'Betty Hume' is probably a hybrid of *R. fortunei* by an unknown pollen parent, to 1.5 m/5 ft tall, with fragrant, ruffled pink flowers to 10 cm/4 in. across, opening in middle to late spring. Useful in Zones 7a–8b and milder.

'Brown Eyes' is probably a hybrid of *R. fortunei* by an unknown pollen parent, growing vigorously to 1.8 m/6 ft high, with a superb show of rose-pink flowers, with brown centers, opening in midspring. Useful at least in Zone 6b, probably also Zone 6a.

'Josephine Everitt' is probably a hybrid of *R. fortunei* by an unknown pollen parent, crossed by C. O. Dexter and raised by the late John C. Wister of Swarthmore, Pennsylvania. It is compact in habit, to 1.2 m/4 ft tall, with large, fragrant, bicolored clear pink flowers, opening in middle to late spring. Useful in Zones 7a–8b, probably also Zone 6b.

Rhododendron griffithianum 6 (Griffith rhododendron).   This Himalayan species is best known for its huge flowers, 12–15 cm/5–6 in. across, and occasionally even larger, white or pale pink, with light yellow centers. Because of its huge flowers, this species has been used in breeding some of the finest rhododendron hybrids in the world, such as the Loder hybrids (see *R.* ×*loderi*, below), but the species itself is useful hardly anywhere in our area. Even most of its hardiest hybrids are cold-hardy in only a few wind-protected sites with very mild winters and moderate summers, such as the southern Atlantic Coast. The selection 'Mars,' an open-pollinated seedling from *R. griffithianum*, is an exception, however, as it is useful in Zones 6b–8b, and perhaps some sites in Zone 6a. 'Mars' has true, deep red, waxy, broadly bell-shaped flowers with white stamens, in densely rounded clusters. The selections 'Vulcan' and 'Vulcan's Flame,' hybrid of 'Mars' × *R. griersonianum*, are similar to 'Mars' in most respects and are cold-hardy to Zone 7b and perhaps parts of Zone 7a (see Rhododendron cultivars).

R. ×*loderi* 5 (*R. griffithianum* × *R. fortunei*; Loder hybrids).   Members of this hybrid group have been considered among the most beautiful of all rhododendrons ever since this cross was first made at the beginning of the twentieth century. These large, treelike shrubs, 2–3 m/6.6–10 ft and more in height and spread, bear fragrant, white to pale yellow or pink flowers, nearly as large as those of *R. griffithianum*. They are usefully hardy only in maritime climates and protected from strong winds, in Zones 8a–8b, perhaps also protected sites in Zone 7. A few of the best and most easily available cultivars are as follows: 'King George,' with highly fragrant 15-cm/6-in. flowers, opening pale pink and fading to white, is said to be the best white-flowered Loder hybrid; 'Pink Diamond' has fragrant, pale shell-pink flowers and is otherwise similar to 'King George'; 'Sir Edmund' has blush-pink flowers; and 'Venus' has exceptionally fragrant, soft-pink flowers. Root systems of the Loder hybrids are not easily adaptable to less-than-ideal soil conditions, and these hybrids often perform

better when grafted on adaptable rootstocks such as *R. ponticum* than on their own roots, especially in soil that is not very acidic (pH 5.5–6.5).

Rhododendron ponticum 5 (Pontic rhododendron).   This relative of *R. catawbiense* from southern Europe and adjacent Asia is extremely vigorous and is commonly used for screening in Europe. Its flower color, similar to that of *R. catawbiense*, has the same limitation for use in combination with other colors, especially reds and pinks, but the plant could be used more than it is at present in the southeastern United States as a functional screening plant. Useful in Zones 7 and 8. Because of its vigor and adaptability, *R. ponticum* has become a popular rootstock for rhododendrons that are not as adaptable to less-than-ideal sites, including marginal acidity, to at least pH 6. Several cultivars exist. A few of the most common or promising are listed here:
'Anah Kruschke' is a hybrid of 'Purple Splendour' back-crossed with *R. ponticum*, growing to 1.8 m/6 ft in height and width, with deep red-purple flowers to 8 cm/3 in. across, in middle to late spring, dense, dark green foliage, and considerable heat-tolerance, useful in Zones 6b–8b.
'Blue Jay' is a *R. ponticum* seedling of uncertain pollen parentage, growing to 1.5 m/5 ft high and wide, with 8-cm/3-in. lavender-blue flowers, with purple blotch and edges, in middle to late spring, dense, glossy green foliage, and considerable sun- and heat-tolerance. Useful in Zones 7a–8b.
'Chionoides' is a *R. ponticum* seedling of unknown pollen parentage, growing to 1.2 m/4 ft, with broad, dense habit, narrow leaves, yellow-centered white flowers in dome-shaped trusses in middle to late spring, and considerable sun-tolerance. Useful in Zones 7a–8b.
'Minnetonka,' an *R. ponticum* seedling of unknown pollen parentage, growing to 0.8 m/2.6 ft high and somewhat wider, with orange to yellow-spotted lavender-pink flowers, is significantly more cold-hardy than most *R. ponticum* hybrids, useful in Zones 5b–8b.
'Purple Splendour' is an *R. ponticum* seedling of unknown pollen parentage, growing to 1.5 m/5 ft high, with large, ruffled flowers, considered to be the best deep-purple-flowering rhododen-

dron for moderate climates in our area, to Zone 7a. It is compact in habit, flowering in middle to late spring, with dark green foliage and tolerance of full sun or shade. Useful in Zones 7a–8b.

'Variegatum' is an *R. ponticum* selection from Ireland, growing to 1.2 m/4 ft tall, with upright habit, white-margined leaves, and purple flowers in late spring. Useful in Zones 7a–8b. Several hybrids of *R. ponticum* with other species are available (see Rhododendron cultivars).

Rhododendron thomsonii 4–5 (Thomson rhododendron).   This native of eastern Himalayas is one of the most handsome of all rhododendron species, with an upright mounded growth habit, to 2–3 m/6.6–10 feet tall and wider in time, smooth blue-green, elliptical, rounded leaves, 4–10 cm/1.6–4 in. long, and deep red, bell-shaped flowers, to 8 cm/3 in. long, in early to middle spring. Useful in Zones 7b–8b, where summers are moderate, so probably not at its best anywhere in our range. It has been used in breeding for red flower color.

Rhododendron wardii 5 (Ward's rhododendron). This native of southern China and eastern Tibet, named for the famous plant explorer, F. King-don-Ward, is one of the finest rhododendron species, similar to the closely related *R. thomsonii* in habit and foliage size and shape, but the bluish young foliage of *R. wardii* turns a lustrous deep green as it matures, and its flowers are a striking yellow. At best, it is as tender as *R. thomsonii*, perhaps even more so, but some of its hybrids are cold-hardy at least to Zone 6b (see 'Golden Gala,' 'Hong Kong,' and 'Vinecrest,' under Rhododendron cultivars).

Rhododendron williamsianum 4.   This native of Szechuan province in central China is densely compact in habit, making a perfect mound to 1.5 m/5 ft tall and somewhat broader, with bright green, rounded leaves, to 1.5–4.5 cm/0.6–1.8 long and nearly as wide, which are interesting for their bronze to deep brown color as they unfold. The bell-shaped pink flowers, 5.6 cm/2.2 in. long, in nodding clusters of 2 or 3, open in early to middle spring. This species is not much less tender than *R. thomsonii* and *R. wardii*, useful in Zone 8, and perhaps Zone 7b, but some of its hybrids are at least slightly more cold-hardy (see 'Hallelujah' and 'Oudijk's Sensation' under Rhododendron cultivars).

Rhododendron cumberlandense 3–5

Synonyms: *R. bakeri*
CUMBERLAND AZALEA
Deciduous shrub
Ericaceae (Heath Family)

Native Range. Appalachian Plateau, West Virginia to Alabama.

Useful Range. USDA Zones 6a–8b, probably also some sites in Zone 5b with selection of appropriate genetic material.

Function. Specimen, border, naturalizing.

Size and Habit. Height varies widely among seedlings, from about 1 m/3.3 ft or less to nearly 3 m/10 ft.

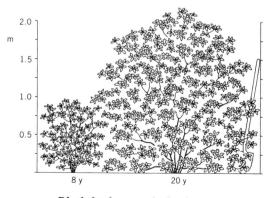

Rhododendron cumberlandense.

Adaptability. Light shade in summer is beneficial in the South and Midwest, especially to reduce fading in red-flowered cultivars. Shade provided by tall pine trees in the South is near-optimal.

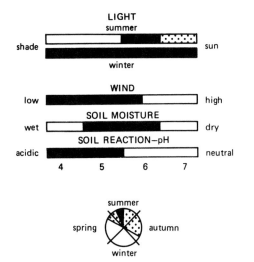

Seasonal Interest. *Flowers:* Red, orange-red, and occasionally to near-yellow, in early summer, usually at least two weeks later than *R. calendulaceum.* Flowers are about 4 cm/1.6 in. across but are borne in large clusters, striking against the fully developed background foliage. *Foliage:* Medium green, falling in autumn with little color change.

Problems and Maintenance. This species is very similar to *R. calendulaceum* except that it is diploid, whereas (R. calendulaceum is tetraploid, and it seems to be equally free of serious problems. It is still not widely planted, so more will be known about its culture in time.

Cultivars. The best-known selection from this species, 'Camp's Red,' has deep, rich red flowers, often paler at lower elevations, grows to about 2 m/6.6 ft tall, and is easily propagated by cuttings.

'Alhambra' (Gable) has bright red-orange flowers and is reportedly heat-tolerant and mildew-resistant.

'Cheulah' (Cherokee-Holsomback) has bright red flowers with orange blotch and is useful at least in Zones 7b–9a, perhaps in colder zones as well.

'Sizzler' has vivid yellowish pink to red-orange flowers and compact growth habit, about 1.2–

1.5 m/4–5 ft tall, but is reportedly difficult to propagate.

'Sunlight' has deeper red-orange flowers, grows to 2 m/6.6 ft tall, and may be cold hardy only to Zone 6b.

Hybrids. Hybrids of *R. cumberlandense* with *R. arborescens* and *R. viscosum* typically flower in early to middle summer, considerably later than most other hybrids, and reach heights of 2–3 m/6.6–8 ft and widths of 1.2–1.8 m/4–6 ft. A few of the most popular and promising are included here.

Cherokee (Holsomback) Series. 'Altanuwa' (*R. cumberlandense* × *R. viscosum*), with yellowish-pink flowers, and 'Tagu' (*R. cumberlandense* × *R. viscosum*), with pink-blushed, light orange flowers, are useful at least in Zones 7b–9a, perhaps in colder zones as well.

Leach North American Azalea Hybrids. These are hybrids of *R. cumberlandense* × *R. arborescens:* 'Chamois,' with bright yellow flowers, and 'Coloratura,' with orange and purplish-red flowers, are useful at least in Zones 6a–8b, and 'Cream Puff' and 'Pink Puff,' with bright yellow and yellowish pink flowers, respectively, are useful at least in Zones 6b–8b.

Carlson Postscript Azaleas. Many of these late-flowering selections developed by Robert Carlson of South Salem, New York, are hybrids of *R. cumberlandense* × *R. arborescens,* offer a flower color range of cream, coral, pink, and yellow, and are available as seedlings. A few clones have been selected but have not yet been propagated commercially.

Weston (Mezitt) hybrids. 'Cotton Candy,' with fragrant, bright pink flowers, 'Parade,' with fragrant, medium-red flowers, and 'Pink and Sweet,' with fragrant, purplish-pink flowers, are useful at least in Zones 5b–8b.

Related Species

Nomenclatural note: There is disagreement about the status of *R. cumberlandense* (synonym: *R. bakeri*). Some specialists lump this population with *R. calendulaceum* rather than recognize it as a separate species. In either case it is a separate population occurring at higher elevations in the Appalachians than *R. calendulaceum* as narrowly defined.

Rhododendron prunifolium 5 (plumleaf azalea). This native of southwestern Georgia and Alabama resembles *R. cumberlandense* except in its stature, to 4–5 m/13–16 ft tall in sites with ample moisture. It has forms with bright red flowers as well as intermediates to yellow that flower in midsummer and are useful in Zones 6b–9a. The Leach selection, 'S. D. Coleman', has deep reddish-orange flowers and a broad growth habit, to 1.5 m/5 ft high and 2 m/6.6 ft wide. Hybrids are known with *R. arborescens, R. calendulaceum, R. cumberlandense, R. molle, R.*

prinophyllum, and *R. viscosum.* The Cherokee hybrid 'July Joy' (R. cumberlandense × R. *prunifolium),* selected by Olin Holsomback in northwestern Georgia, has deep pink flowers with a light yellow blotch, and is useful at least in Zones 7b–9a. Fred Galle, author of the standard reference work *Azaleas* (Timber Press, Portland, Oregon, 1987), has produced a group of heat-tolerant hybrid seedlings of R. prunifolium × R. *occidentale,* with a color range from yellow to pink, unnamed at this writing.

Rhododendron ferrugineum 3

ROCK RHODODENDRON, ALPINE ROSE

Evergreen shrub

Ericaceae (Heath Family)

Native Range. Central Europe, in the Alps.

Useful Range. USDA Zones 5b–6b and protected sites in Zone 5a and perhaps Zone 4, but only in areas having moderate summer temperatures: high elevations and coastal environments.

Function. Rock garden, foundation, massing.

Size and Habit

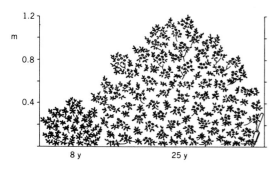

Rhododendron ferrugineum.

Adaptability. At least partial sun is necessary for best growth and flowering, but in winter, light shade and protection from extreme winds may be beneficial. This species and its close relatives (see Related Species) are more tolerant of calcareous soils than most rhododendrons.

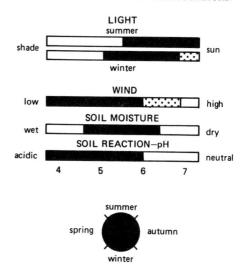

Seasonal Interest. *Flowers:* Pale to rosy pink or white, 1.5 cm/0.6 in. across, in clusters of 6 to 12, in midsummer. *Foliage:* Evergreen, lustrous, deep green, smooth but with rusty scales, the leaves to 4 cm/1.6 in. long and about 1 cm/0.4 in. wide.

Problems and Maintenance. This species is relatively trouble-free in sites meeting its environmental requirements, especially relatively even temperatures, but these conditions prevail in few parts of our area, mainly high elevations and maritime climates in the northeastern United States and the Canadian maritime provinces.

Cultivars. 'Album' has white flowers, outstanding against the lustrous, dark green foliage. 'Atrococcineum' has deep rose flowers. Neither of these is often available.

Related Species

Rhododendron fastigiatum 2.   This native of western China is, in its best forms, the most dwarf of the blue-flowering, scaly-leaved rhododendrons. Many plants of this species are fastigiate and upright, to nearly 1 m/3.3 ft tall, and spreading at the top. The better forms are moundlike or even matlike, to only 25–50 cm/10–20 in. tall, much more satisfactory for rock garden or small-scale use. Flowers are often lavender to mauve, 2.5 cm/1 in. across, opening in midspring; selections have been made for bluer flowers and blue-green foliage, but these may not yet be available in our area. Useful in Zones 6a–8a where summers are moderate: at high elevations and in coastal environments. Two hybrids of *R. fastigiatum*, 'Purple Gem' and 'Ramapo', are more popular than the species (see Rhododendron cultivars).

Rhododendron hirsutum 3 (garland rhododendron, hairy alpine rose).   This native of high elevations in central to eastern Europe is very similar to *R. ferrugineum* and virtually interchangeable in landscape use, differing only in having slightly shorter leaves with hairs on the margins and in other minor details. The f. *albiflorum* has white flowers. Useful in the same areas as *R. ferrugineum*.

Rhododendron impeditum 3.   This dwarf rhododendron from very high elevations in western China forms a tight, cushionlike mass (40–45 cm/1.6–1.8 in. high in full sun) of fine-textured blue-green foliage, with individual leaves only 1 cm/0.4 in. long and pale lavender-blue flowers to 1.5 cm/0.6 in. long, opening in midspring. Useful primarily as a rock garden plant in Zones 6a–7a, where summer temperatures are moderate: high elevations and coastal environments.

Rhododendron lapponicum 2 (Lapland rhododendron).   This very dwarf plant, remaining below 10 cm/4 in. in native habitat in the circumpolar arctic and on a few temperate zone mountaintops, in our area the summit of Mt. Washington in New Hampshire, can grow to 20–40 cm/8–16 in. high in landscape use. Its evergreen leaves, 1–2 cm/0.4–0.8 in. long, form a background for the purplish mauve flowers (1.5 cm/0.6 in. across), opening in early summer. Useful in alpine gardens in Zones 3–6 (and colder) where summer temperatures are moderate and moisture is available. The hybrid of uncertain pollen parentage, 'Barto Alpine' grows densely upright to 0.8 m/3 ft, has orchid-rose flowers all along the stems in early to middle spring and is reported to be useful in Zones 7a–8a, perhaps also colder zones.

Rhododendron micranthum 4 (Manchurian rhododendron).   This native of northeastern Asia is distinctive for its tiny (0.6 cm/0.25 in.) white flowers, in many-flowered clusters to 5 cm/2 in. across, opening very late in spring, and dark green, evergreen leaves, 2–4 cm/0.8–1.6 in. long. This plant looks more like an oversize *Ledum* than a rhododendron. Its hardiness and durability make a place for it in northern landscapes (Zones 4a–6b), but it is not often commercially available.

Rhododendron polycladum 3 (synonym: *R. scintillans*).   This handsome dwarf, like *R. impeditum* and *R. russatum*, comes from the mountains of western China. Its tiny, scaly leaves are only 0.8–1.5 cm/0.3–0.6 in. long, and its sparkling lavender to blue-purple flowers, 2 cm/0.8 in.

Rhododendron micranthum.

across, open in midspring. Useful at least in Zones 7b–8b protected sites in Zone 7a, and perhaps parts of Zone 6.

Rhododendron russatum 3.   This close relative of *R. impeditum* and *R. lapponicum*, from southwestern China, is one of the most striking of this group in flower. Some forms of this species grow to 1.2 m/4 ft high, while others reach only half that height, with densely scaly rusty-green leaves to 2–4 cm/0.8 1.6 in. long and vivid blue-purple flowers, to 2.5 cm/1 in. across in small terminal clusters, opening in midspring. Useful as a rock garden or small accent plant in Zones 6a–7b, in areas with moderate summers: high elevations and coastal environments. The selection 'Night Editor' grows to 0.9–1.2 m/3–4 ft high, with larger, twisted and rolled leaves and brilliant purple flowers.

Rhododendron indicum 3–4

Synonyms: *R. macranthum*
INDIAN OR MACRANTHA AZALEA
Evergreen shrub
Ericaceae (Heath Family)

Native Range.   Southern Japan.

Useful Range.   USDA Zones 6b–9a.

Function.   Specimen, border, naturalizing.

Size and Habit

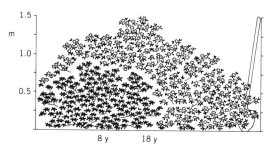

Rhododendron indicum.

Adaptability.   Light shade in summer is beneficial, especially to reduce fading of red-flowered cultivars. Light shade in winter reduces leaf scorch in northern parts of the useful range (Zones 6 and 7).

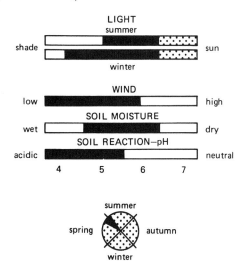

Seasonal Interest.   *Flowers:* Rose-red to scarlet, 5–6.5 cm/2–2.6 in. across, very showy in very late spring or early summer against the deep green foliage. *Foliage:* Evergreen or nearly evergreen leaves, 2.5–3.5 cm/1–1.4 in. long, deep green and slightly lustrous. Those that are first to emerge fall in autumn, and those opening in summer usually remain until new growth begins in spring.

Problems and Maintenance.   Several diseases and insects may damage foliage and flowers of azaleas, but these are seldom serious problems.

Control may be needed for infestations of mites and scale insects, and soil treatments may be needed occasionally for soil-borne diseases such as rhododendron wilt and nematodes. Pruning is seldom necessary or desirable.

Cultivars.   Most cultivars involving this species are hybrids with other species (see Hybrids) but a few selections have been made directly from the species, including the following:

'Balsaminiflorum' has fully double orange-red flowers, to 4 cm/1.6 in. across.

'Flame Creeper' is low-growing, with orange-red flowers.

'Iveryanum' has single flowers to 8 cm/3 in. across, varying from white with rose flecking to solid rose, and a low, spreading growth habit.

'J. T. Lovett' has single orange-red flowers, to 6.5 cm/2.6 in. across, and a low, dense growth habit.

'Macrantha' is a synonym for *I. indicum,* sometimes used loosely for the orange-flowered clone 'Macrantha Orange,' and occasionally for the pink-flowered clone 'Macrantha Pink' and the salmon-pink-flowered clone 'Macrantha Salmon.'

Hybrids

Belgian Indian Hybrids.   With large flowers (to 8 cm/3 in. across) in midspring, these cultivars are mostly hybrids involving *R. indicum, R. simsii, R. mucronatum,* and *R. Phoeniceum* to a lesser degree. *R. simsii* is the major contributing species. They were selected in Belgium for greenhouse forcing and are relatively tender, but some cultivars have been found useful in Zones 8b and 9a. Few are commercially available in our area.

Rutherford Hybrids.   These hybrids were developed in Rutherford, New Jersey, as greenhouse forcing cultivars from parentage not greatly different from that of the Belgian Indian hybrids—primarily *R. indicum, R. mucronatum, R. Phoeniceum,* and *R. simsii,* but other minor influences as well, including the Kurume hybrids (see *R. obtusum*). They were never intended as landscape plants, but rather as houseplants, and some are cold-hardy only in Zones 9a+. A few, however, have proved useful in Zones 7b–9a+: 'Dor-

othy Gish' has large, double (hose-in-hose), reddish-orange flowers. 'Pink Ruffles' has large, semidouble (hose-in-hose), deep pink flowers. 'Red Ruffles,' a genetic sport of 'Pink Ruffles,' has similar, but strong red flowers.

Southern Indian Hybrids.   This group originated from the importation of Belgian hybrid cultivars to the southeastern United States with subsequent spontaneous and deliberate selection and hybridization. The word Indian as the name of both hybrid groups is a misnomer, since none of the species involved are from India, and the so-called Indian azalea *(R. indicum)* is not the major contributor to the hybrid cultivars. Over the years, a considerable number of new cultivars have been selected in the South. They range in height from 2 to 3 m/6.6 to 10 ft, depending on parentage, and mostly flower in midspring. A few are listed here.

'Duc de Rohan' has single flowers to 6 cm/2.4 in. across, deep yellowish pink with a red blotch, and a spreading growth habit, showing a strong influence of *R. indicum.*

'Elegans Superbum' (= 'Pride of Mobile,' = 'Watermelon Pink') has single, light rosy pink flowers, to 6 cm/2.4 in. across, and upright growth habit.

'Fielder's White' has frilled single white flowers, to 7 cm/2.8 in. across, with a faint greenish yellow blotch and spreading growth habit.

'Formosa' has large, deep purplish-red flowers, with tall, upright growth habit.

'George Lindley Taber' has white flowers, flushed purplish pink with a deeper blotch, to 9 cm/3.5 in. across, with a tall, upright growth habit.

'Helen' has large, deep purple flowers and is large in stature.

'Jennifer' is a seedling from 'Elegans Superbum,' with upright growth habit and deeper pink (red) flowers than the parent.

'Judge Solomon,' a genetic sport of 'Formosa,' has 6-cm/2.6-in., deep purple-red flowers with a darker blotch, and tall, upright growth habit.

'Kate Arendall' has large white, hose-in-hose flowers.

'Mrs. G. G. Gerbing,' a genetic sport of 'George Lindley Taber,' has white flowers, 9 cm/3.5 in. across and upright growth habit.

'President Claeys' (= 'President Clay') has strong red flowers, with a darker blotch, to 5.7 cm/2.2 in. across, and tall, upright growth habit.

'Red Formosa,' a genetic sport of 'Formosa,' differs from that cultivar only in its more intensely purplish flower color.

'Rosea' has deep rose, semidouble flowers and lower habit, 1.5–2 m/5–6.6 ft high and wide.

'Southern Charm,' a genetic sport of 'Formosa,' is similar to 'Elegans Superba.'

'Watermelon Red' is similar to 'Elegans Superbum' but with deeper pink (red) flowers.

'White Grandeur' has large, double white flowers.

Cultivars in this group are generally useful in Zone 9a, many are also cold-hardy in Zone 8b, and a few can be used in protected sites in Zone 8a. Base selection on local experience and availability of cultivars.

Glenn Dale Hybrids.   This large group of evergreen azaleas, more than 400 in all, was developed at the U.S. National Arboretum in a very large breeding program carried out in the 1930s and 1940s. The objective of this program was to develop cultivars suitable for the Middle Atlantic region. Parent material included *R. indicum, R. kaempferi, R. mucronatum, R. obtusum, R. Phoeniceum, R. simsii, R. yedoense* var. *poukhanense,* the Indian and Kaempferi Hybrids, and several superior individual cultivars. Many of the resulting clones have become standard cultivars in the Middle Atlantic area and elsewhere in Zones 7a–8b. Because of the great variety of parent material, individual cultivars vary considerably in cold-hardiness as well as adaptability to the southern extremes of our area. In selecting cultivars, consider local experience and availability. Only a small sampling of the more popular cultivars is presented here:

'Ambrosia' has deep yellowish-pink flowers, aging light orange-yellow, 4.4–5 cm/1.7–2 in. across, in small clusters in midspring, and upright habit, to 2.4 m/8 ft tall.

'Aphrodite' has large numbers of pale rose-pink flowers in midspring, dark green foliage, and broad-spreading habit. It reaches more than 1 m/3.3 ft in height.

'Buccaneer' has brilliant red flowers, 5 cm/2 in. across, in midspring, but they fade in full sun, so partial shade is important for this and many other red cultivars to perform well. Growth habit is spreading but developing in height to 1.5 m/5 ft.

'Copperman' has brilliant orange-red flowers, to 8 cm/3 in. across, in late spring, and a dense, spreading growth habit, reaching a height of more than 1 m/3.3 ft.

'Dayspring' has 4.4–5-cm/1.7–2-in. flowers with white centers shading to light purplish-pink margins, in small clusters in middle to late spring, and broad-spreading habit, to 1.8 m/6 ft tall.

'Fashion' has orange-red flowers, 5 cm/2 in. across, in middle to late spring and an erect to arching growth habit, eventually to nearly 2 m/6.6 ft.

'Festive' has white flowers striped dull rose, to 6 cm/2.4 in. across, in early spring and an erect to arching growth habit, eventually to nearly 2 m/6.6 ft tall.

'Gaiety' has rose-pink flowers, to 8 cm/3 in. across, in late spring and an erect to broad-spreading growth habit and narrow, dark green leaves, to 1.5 m/5 ft tall.

'Geisha' has white flowers, blotched yellow-green and striped and dotted reddish-purple, 3.8–5 cm/1.5–2 in. across, in midspring, and spreading habit, to 1.8 m/6 ft high.

'Glacier' has shining white flowers, to 8 cm/3 in. across, in midspring, unusually lustrous, dark green foliage, and an erect to spreading growth habit, to 1.5 m/5 ft tall.

'Glamour' has bright rose-red flowers, to 8 cm/3 in. across, in middle to late spring, narrow, dark green leaves, and an erect to broad-spreading growth habit, to 1.5 m/5 ft tall.

'Greeting' has coral-rose flowers, to 5 cm/2 in. across, in midspring, dark green leaves, and an erect to broad-spreading growth habit, to more than 1 m/3.3 ft tall.

'Helen Close' has white flowers with a yellow blotch that fades to white, 6–8 cm/2.4–3 in. across in small clusters, in middle to late spring, and dense, twiggy habit, to 1.2 m/4 ft tall.

'Martha Hitchcock,' a Satsuki azalea, has white, red-purple margined flowers, to 8 cm/3 in. across, medium green leaves, and a broad-spreading growth habit, to about 1 m/3.3 ft tall.

'Refrain' has double (hose-in-hose) flowers with white margins grading to rosy pink centers, with a few purplish-pink stripes and dots, 4.4–5 cm/1.7–2 in. across, in midspring, upright and spreading, to 2 m/6.6 ft high.

'Sagittarius' has bright orange-pink flowers, white at the base, with a darker blotch, in late spring, and dense, broad-spreading growth habit, under 1 m/3.3 ft high.

'Treasure' has flowers pale pink in bud, opening nearly white, 9–11 cm/3.6–4.4 in. across, in midspring. It functions as an "improved" version of *R. mucronatum*, wide-spreading and vigorous, eventually reaching a height of 1.5 m/5 ft.

'Zulu' has bright purplish-red flowers with purple blotch, 8–9 cm/3–3.5 in. across, in midspring, and broad-spreading habit, to 1.5 m/5 ft high.

Satsuki Azaleas. This group takes its name from the Japanese word for fifth month. As the name implies, these cultivars are late-flowering—about as late as *R. indicum*, the common parent, in late spring or early summer. Some cultivars usually included here may be simply forms of *R. indicum*, and those mentioned earlier (see *R. indicum*, Cultivars) are sometimes included in this group.

The terms Satsuki Hybrids or Chugai Hybrids usually are meant to apply to a specific group of hybrids involving *R. indicum*, *R. simsii*, and the Belgian Hybrids, developed in Japan and carrying Japanese cultivar names. More than 50 cultivars of this group were imported by the U.S. Plant Introduction Station in the late 1930s and distributed for evaluation during the following 25 years. These are low-growing, large-flowering forms, rather unstable with respect to flower color, often with striped or flecked petals (chimeras) and with flowers of different colors on the same plant, opening in late spring. These have proved useful in Zones 7b–9a and some in sheltered sites in Zone 7a, but most have not yet become available commercially. A few of the most popular are listed below:

'Beni Kirishima' has very double flowers, bright red-orange with a darker blotch, 5 cm/2 in. across, with low, spreading growth habit.

'Chinsai' has 4–5-cm/1.6–2-in. flowers, variable in color, from primarily white to primarily deep pink with many intermediates, and in petal shape, some very narrow, with low, spreading habit.

'Chinzan' has vivid, slightly purplish-pink flowers, 4–5 cm/1.6–2 in. across, and small

elliptical leaves and is quite dwarf, valued for bonsai treatment.

'Getsutoku' has large wavy petals, varying from white to pastel salmon pink and brighter pink in stripes and shadings, and low, spreading growth habit.

'Gumpo' (= 'White Gumpo') has ruffled white flowers, 6–8 cm/2.4–3 in. across, with occasional small flecks of purplish pink, and spreading, compact growth habit, a favorite landscape plant among this group.

'Gunbi' (= 'Gunrei') has frilled white flowers, 6–8 cm/2.4–3 in. across, with variable purplish-red flecks and stripes, and low, spreading growth habit.

'Higasa' has very large, wavy petals, purplish pink with red-purple blotch, the flower to 11 cm/4.3 in. across, and low, spreading growth habit.

'Pink Gumpo' is a selection from 'Gumpo,' similar except with dominant color of light pink instead of white.

'Red Gumpo' is another selection from 'Gumpo,' similar except with dominant color of deeper rose pink.

'Shira Fuji' is a dwarf, distinctive for its small deep green leaves with creamy white marginal variegation, as well as its variable flowers, 4–5 cm/1.6–2 in. across, with white or deep reddish purple petals as well as many striped or sectorial intermediates. Useful for bonsai or very-small-scale gardens.

'Wakaebisu' (= 'Wakebisu') has deep yellowish pink double (hose-in-hose) flowers, 5–6 cm/2–2.4 in. across, with deeper pink dots in the center, and low, spreading growth habit, one of the most popular cultivars in this group (not to be confused with the Kurume hybrid of the same name.)

Robin Hill Hybrids. For 40 years, Robert Gartwell of Robin Hill Nursery in northeastern New Jersey carried out a program of hybridizing azaleas of the Satsuki type, eventually naming at least 65 cultivars, perhaps half of which can still be found in a few specialty nurseries. These hybrids are low and moundlike, some more dwarf than others, with large flowers. The handful listed here are more easily available than most of the others.

'Betty Anne Voss' is relatively vigorous, growing to 0.6–1 m/2–3.3 ft high and nearly twice as wide in time, with dark green foliage and double (hose-in-hose) orchid-pink flowers, 8 cm/3 in. across, in middle to late spring. Useful in Zones 6b–9a.

'Conversation Piece' grows more slowly, to 0.5 m/1.6 ft high and wider, with purplish-pink and white, sectored and spotted flowers, to 8.8 cm/3.5 in., with wavy, lighter pink margins, opening in middle to late spring, and useful in Zones 7a–9a.

'Hilda Niblett' grows slowly to 0.3–0.4 m/1–1.3 ft tall and at least twice as wide, with pink and white flowers, 8.2 cm/3.2 in. across, with very wavy edges, splashed with deeper rose-pink, and is useful in Zones 7a–9a.

'Nancy of Robin Hill' grows slowly to 0.4–0.5 m/1.3–2 ft high and wider, with variable pink-white semidouble to double (hose-in-hose) flowers, 8.8 cm/3.5 in. across, useful in Zones 7a–9a.

'Sir Robert' is very dense and compact, to about the same dimensions as 'Nancy of Robin Hill,' with highly variable pink and white flowers, 8.8 cm/3.5 in. across, opening from midspring over a long period. Useful in Zones 6b–9a+.

Related Species and Hybrids

Rhododendron 'Mucronatum' 4 (synonyms: *R. mucronatum* or *R. ledifolium* var. *album*; snow azalea). This handsome white-flowered azalea from Japan has been the source of much nomenclatural confusion. First, it is still occasionally offered for sale under the synonymous (not legitimate) names listed above, or as the incorrect cultivar names 'Indica Alba' or 'Ledifolia Alba.' Second, its common name allows it to be confused with the Kurume azalea 'Snow' (see under *R. obtusum*). A third source of confusion is the similarity of the name of the Korean rhododendron, *R. mucronulatum.*

As if this nomenclatural confusion were not enough, there is also a taxonomic problem: This plant was once given the species name *R. mucronatum*, even though it has never been observed as a wild population. Cultivated in Japan for centuries, its origin is uncertain, so specialists now treat it simply as a cultivar: 'Mucronatum.' This may now stabilize the problem, provided that nomenclatural specialists ignore the fact that, according to the international rules of nomenclature, Latinized cultivar names given after 1958 are not acceptable! 'Mucronatum' is an excellent selection for Zones 7a–9a+, with single, pure white flowers, to 8 cm/3 in. across, against the excellent dark green foliage in middle to late spring. Related cultivars include 'Delaware Valley White,' which is similar but reported to be somewhat more cold-hardy (to Zone 6b), the hybrid 'Fielder's White' (see *Southern Indian Hybrids*, under *R. indicum*), and 'Gulf Pride,' a genetic sport of 'Mucronatum' with pale purple flowers.

Rhododendron 'Phoeniceum' (synonyms: 'Phoenicia,' *R. phoeniceum*, *R. pulchrum* var. *phoeniceum*). This is another long-cultivated (in China) form that is not known to exist in the wild and that, like 'Mucronatum,' has been relegated to cultivar status. This plant grows to 2 m/6.6 in height and width, with deep red-purple flowers. Some specialists believe 'Phoeniceum' may be a form or hybrid of *R. scabrum*.

Rhododendron scabrum 4–5. This large, loose-growing evergreen azalea from southern Japan has large leaves and rose-red to scarlet flowers, to 10 cm/4 in. across. It is believed to be a parent of 'Mucronatum,' 'Phoeniceum,' and several of the Southern Indian hybrids and is potentially useful in Zones 7a–9a+ but seldom, if ever, available as the species.

Rhododendron simsii 5 (Sims azalea). This common, wild species of China and Taiwan has more or less red flowers and at least superficially resembles a taller, looser-growing edition of *R. indicum*. In spite of the fact that it is a colorful and potentially useful landscape plant itself in Zones 7b–9a, it is hardly known in our area other than as the probable major parent of the Indian hybrid azaleas.

Rhododendron japonicum 4

JAPANESE AZALEA
Deciduous shrub
Ericaceae (Heath Family)

Native Range.   Japan.

Useful Range.   USDA Zones 4b–8b.

Function.   Specimen, border.

Size and Habit

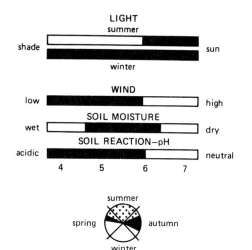

Rhododendron japonicum.

Adaptability.   At least certain cultivars of *R. japonicum* and *R. ×kosterianum* (see Hybrids) do not require as strongly acid soil as many other azaleas.

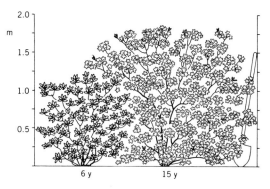

Seasonal Interest.   *Flowers:* Yellow through orange to red, 5–8 cm/2–3 in. across, in late spring with the first expansion of foliage, with an odor that is not particularly pleasant. *Foliage:* Pale to medium green, hairy and rather coarse, turning reddish in autumn in sunny sites, in some areas and years.

Problems and Maintenance.   Several diseases and insects occasionally cause minor damage, but *R. japonicum* and its hybrids usually are about as trouble-free as any azaleas. Pruning is seldom needed but can be used for renewal of old plants by pruning back a few main branches annually.

Cultivars.   Cultivars involving *R. japonicum* mostly belong to the Molle hybrids (see Hybrids), but this species is variable in both flower color and hardiness. The red-flowered forms from the northern parts of its natural range in Japan tend to be more cold-hardy than the more southern yellow-flowered forms, but this correlation is not perfect, and individual, yellow-flowered plants may be as hardy as most red-flowered plants.

Hybrids

Molle Hybrids (R. ×kosterianum).   These are hybrids of *R. japonicum* and *R. molle* (Chinese azalea). The more common cultivars tend toward the greater cold-hardiness of *R. japonicum* and are useful in Zones 5b–8b, some cultivars to Zone 5a, and others in this group are tender because of their *R. molle* parentage. The Molle hybrids are used less than in the past, since they have not been very competitive with the Knap Hill hybrids, except in parts of the South, where some of them have shown superior heat-tolerance. Currently, seedling plants are more often offered for sale than cloned cultivars, although a few cultivars are still available, including: 'Apple Blossom,' with light salmon-pink flowers (not to be confused with the Kurume hybrid of the same name); 'Dr. M. Oosthoek,' with blazing red-orange flowers; 'Hamlet,' with salmon-orange flowers marked with dark red-orange blotch; 'Koster's Brilliant Red,' with bright orange-red

Rhododendron ×*kosterianum.*

flowers; 'Lemonora,' with pink-tinged yellow flowers; and 'Saturnus,' with large, red-orange flowers.

Northern Lights Hybrids.   This group of hybrids was developed at the University of Minnesota; it started with a cross between *R.* ×*kosterianum* and *R. prinophyllum,* and additional crosses involved *R. atlanticum, R. canadense,* and perhaps others. These hybrids are exceptional for their cold hardiness, with flower buds hardy to temperatures as low as −37° to −43°C/−35° to −45°F, most opening in late spring. The resulting useful range for these cultivars is at least Zones 4b–6b and probably parts of Zone 7. Some cultivars are also hardy to Zone 3b.

'Golden Lights' is upright and rounded, to 1.5 m/5 ft tall and 1.2 m/4 ft wide, with golden-yellow flowers and dark green, mildew-resistant foliage, turning red-bronze in autumn. Useful in Zones 4b–7a.

'Northern Hi-lights' is rounded in habit to 1.2 m/4 ft high and 1.4 m/4.6 ft wide, with yellow-blotched creamy white flowers and deep green foliage with little autumn color change. Useful in Zones 4b–7a.

'Orchid Lights' is a dwarf shrub to 0.6–0.9 m/ 2–3 ft high and wide, with lilac flowers, a week or so before most of these cultivars, in middle to late spring. Useful in Zones 3b–6b.

'Rosy Lights' grows to 1.5/5 ft high and 1.8 m/6 ft wide, with fragrant, deep rosy pink flowers. Useful in Zones 3b–6b.

'Spicy Lights' grows to 1.5 m/5 ft high and 1.2 m/4 ft wide, with apricot-orange flowers in late spring and deep green leaves, not changing color in autumn. Useful in Zones 5a–6b.

'White Lights' grows to 1.5–1.8 m/5–6 ft high and wide, with pale pink flower buds, fading to white, with dark green foliage, turning bronze-purple autumn. Useful in Zones 4a–6b.

Viscosepalum Hybrids.   This group of hybrids of *R. molle* × *R. viscosum,* was developed in the 1800s in Europe. Few cultivars have survived the intervening 150 years, but at least two remain. 'Altaclerense' has fragrant, orange-blotched white flowers (not to be confused with the plant sold as 'Altaclarense,' which has orange-blotched *yellow* flowers and is seldom available today). 'Daviesii' has large, fragrant ivory flowers and upright growth habit. Viscosepalum hybrids, when available, are probably useful in Zones 6a–9a, possibly also Zone 5b.

Related Species

Rhododendron molle 4 (synonym: *R. sinense;* Chinese azalea).   This native of China with yellow flowers to 5–6 cm/2–2.4 in. across is distinctly less cold-hardy than *R. japonicum* and probably exists in landscape use in our area only in the form of remaining plants of a few Molle hybrids. Useful, if it were available, in Zones 7a–9a.

Rhododendron kiusianum 3

JAPONICUM
KYUSHU AZALEA
Semievergreen or deciduous shrub
Ericaceae (Heath Family)

Native Range. High elevations, Kyushu, Japan.

Useful Range. USDA Zones 7a–8b, a few hybrids also in Zone 6.

Function. Specimen, border, foundation, naturalizing.

Size and Habit. 'Hinodegiri' (Kurume) is illustrated.

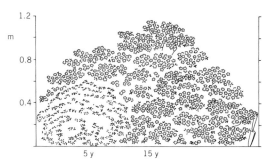

Rhododendron 'Hinodegiri' (Kurume).

Adaptability. Light shade in summer is beneficial in the South and in other areas having very hot summers for good growth and to reduce fading in red-flowered cultivars. Light shade in winter reduces leaf scorch in northern parts of the useful range (Zones 6 and 7).

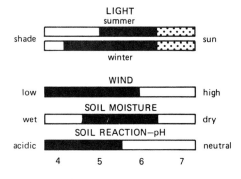

Seasonal Interest. Flowers: Purple, red, pink, or white, 2–3.5 cm/0.8–1.4 in. across, in clusters of 2–3, very showy in midspring with the partly expanded foliage. *Foliage:* Lustrous, semievergreen leaves, 1–2.5 cm/0.4–1 in. long. The "summer leaves" that develop after flowering are usually retained through most or all of winter, the last of them falling as new leaves and flowers emerge in spring.

Problems and Maintenance. Problems include mites, scale insects, and several other diseases and insects. Most do not cause severe or permanent damage, but control measures are occasionally needed, especially in warmer zones. Pruning seldom is necessary or desirable. Bark splitting at the soil line can occur in late autumn when plants have not hardened properly. To minimize this, avoid overwatering or fertilizing in late summer and early autumn.

Cultivars. More than 50 cultivars have been introduced into the United States from Japan, mostly by the U.S. National Arboretum, but very few are commercially available. A few of the most popular are listed here: 'Benichidori' has bright salmon-orange flowers; 'Benisuzumi' has small, reddish orange flowers and red, semievergreen winter foliage; 'Betty Muir' has bright pink flowers and dark green foliage; 'Komo Kulshan' is an award-winning American selection, with clear rose-pink flowers, lighter in the center and 2.5 cm/1 in. across; 'White Moon' is a selection for white flowers, very striking in bloom.

Hybrids. R. ×*obtusum* (synonym: R. *obtusum*). These hybrids of R. *kaempferi*, R. *kiusianum*, and perhaps other species are not widely different from the Kurume azaleas, but have smaller leaves and are slightly more cold-hardy. 'Amoenum' has double, deep magenta flowers and small semievergreen leaves, and it is useful in Zones 6b–8b and sheltered sites in Zone 6a. 'Amoenum

Coccineum' is similar, but with deeper red flow-ers. The Amoenum hybrids, a small group of cultivars of uncertain parentage other than 'Amoenum,' are not commonly available.

Kurume Hybrids.   The parentage of this group is not fully known, but is believed to include at least *R. kaempferi, R. kiusianum,* and *R. ×obtu-sum.* Since the first of this group was developed in Japan two to three centuries ago, hundreds of cultivars have been introduced, but only a few of those are commercially available. Most of these are rather low-growing plants, to 1–1.5 m/ 3.3–5 ft high, and wider, but a few grow larger, eventually to at least 2 m/6.6 ft. They have fine-textured, lustrous evergreen foliage, in some cultivars turning a rich mahogany-red in winter sun. These are among the best azaleas for year-round landscape effectiveness and are useful in the same range as *R. ×obtusum.* A few of the most commonly available cultivars are listed here.

'Appleblossom' (= 'Ho o') has pink-tinged white flowers with rose-pink blotch and a few red stripes (not to be confused with the Molle hybrid of the same name.)

'Blaauw's Pink' (= 'Glory'?) has salmon to rose-pink flowers and is reported to be more cold-hardy than most Kurume azaleas, at least to Zone 6a.

'Brandywine' is a hybrid of 'Snow' (see be-low), with large (6 cm/2.4 in.) yellowish pink flowers and broad-spreading habit.

'Brilliant' has strong rose-pink flowers with darker petal margins.

'Christmas Cheer' (= 'Ima-shojo,' = 'Fasci-nation') has bright red flowers, to 3 cm/1.2 in. across, and a spreading but compact growth habit. It is cold-hardy to sheltered sites in Zone 6b.

'Coral Bells' has single, bright, shell-pink flowers, usually less than 3 cm/1.2 in. across, and low, spreading growth habit.

'Hershey's Orange' is of unknown parentage but similar to the Kurume azaleas, so it is listed here. It has bright orange-red, double (hose-in-hose) flowers, 3.8 cm/1.5 in. across, and is cold-hardy to Zone 6b.

'Hershey's Red' (= 'Hershey's Bright Red') is similar to 'Hershey's Orange,' but with bright red flowers.

Rhododendron **'Coral Bells.'**

'Hino-crimson' is similar to 'Hinode Giri' ex-cept in having slightly deeper red flowers and slightly smaller leaves.

'Hinode Giri' has ruby-red flowers, to 4 cm/ 1.5 in. across, compact growth, and excellent foliage. Although this is a very good selection, cold-hardy to Zone 6b, it has been overused at the expense of the variety of colors that can be obtained from other good Kurume cultivars.

'Mother's Day' has large (to 5 cm/2 in. across), double (hose-in-hose) bright rosy-red flowers with darker spots. This is a popular hy-brid of a Belgian Indian hybrid, 'Professeur Wolt-ers,' crossed with 'Hinode Giri,' and is cold-hardy to Zone 7b, possibly Zone 7a.

'Pink Pearl' has double, deep salmon-pink flowers. Technically it probably is not a Kurume azalea, but it is similar in form and function.

'Sherwood Red' has single, orange-red flow-ers, more than 4 cm/1/6 in. across, and a low, compact growth habit. It is cold-hardy to Zone 6b.

'Snow' has single, white flowers, more than 4 cm/1.6 in. across, and vigorous upright growth, eventually to 2 m/6.6 ft tall in good sites. The impressive flowers unfortunately remain on the plant after they have turned brown. Not to be confused with the so-called "snow azalea," *R.* 'Mucronatum' (see under *R. indicum,* Related Species and Hybrids).

Kaempferi Hybrids (Malvaticum Hybrids).   These are mostly hybrids of 'Malvaticum,' a seedling of unknown origin but perhaps involving *R. mucronatum* and *R. kaempferi* (see Related Spe-cies). These are of special interest in Zone 6a and sheltered sites in Zone 5b, just outside the useful range of the Kurume azaleas. They are vigorous, upright plants, sometimes to 2 m/6.6 ft tall. A few of the most common cultivars are listed here. 'Alice' has salmon-pink flowers with a deeper blotch. 'Blue Danube' has deep red-purple flowers, spotted deeper red. 'Carmen' has deep rose-red flowers, to 6 cm/2.4 in. across. 'Fedora' has deep violet-rose flowers, to 5 cm/2 in. across. 'Fireball' has bright pink flowers. 'Oberon' has soft light pink flowers. 'Othello' has vivid red flowers, similar in color to those of 'Hinode Giri' (Kurume) but larger, to 5 cm/2 in. across, and an upright growth habit.

Related Species

Rhododendron kaempferi 5 (synonym: *R. obtusum* var. *kaempferi*; torch azalea). This native of northern Japan is deciduous. It is taller and rangier than *R. kiusianum* and distinctly more cold-hardy, useful in Zones 6a–9a, protected sites in Zone 5b, and possibly even colder zones if hardiest genetic material can be obtained. Flowers are red to salmon-red to deep salmon-rose, 3–5 cm/1.2–2 in. across. It is a valuable landscape plant in its own right as well as a parent of the Kaempferi and Kurume hybrids discussed here and the Gable hybrids (see *R. ye-doense*).

Rhododendron nakaharai 2. This prostrate shrub from Taiwan, only occasionally exceeding 0.5 m/1.6 ft in height, has glossy evergreen leaves, only 1.6–2.4 cm/0.5–0.75 in. long and red to orange-red or pink flowers (to 5 cm/1.5 in.). A few selections have been made, including 'Minipink,' with pink flowers, and 'Mt. Seven Star,' with red-orange flowers. The species and these cultivars are handsome dwarfs, probably useful at least in Zones 6b–9a, but not yet widely available.

Rhododendron maximum 6

ROSEBAY RHODODENDRON
Evergreen shrub
Ericaceae (Heath Family)

Native Range. Northeastern United States and adjacent Canada, southward in the Appalachian Mountains to Alabama.

Useful Range. USDA Zones 5a–6b, protected sites in Zone 4, and areas having moderate summer temperatures in Zone 7 with selection of appropriate genetic material.

Function. Naturalizing, border (background), screen, specimen.

Size and Habit

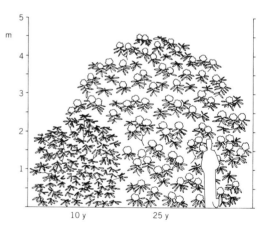

Rhododendron maximum.

Adaptability.   Shade from full summer sun is necessary in Zones 6 and 7, but flowering may be reduced in full shade. Protection from winter sun and wind is advisable in all zones.

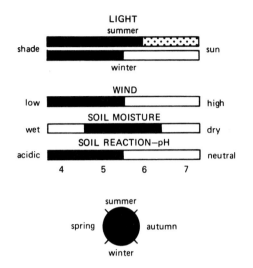

Seasonal Interest.   *Flowers:* Rose-pink, pink-margined, or white, to 4 cm/1.6 in. across, in large trusses of up to 25 or more flowers under ideal conditions, in early summer to midsummer, partly obscured by the new foliage in southern areas. *Foliage:* Leaves are evergreen, leathery, smooth or with a light rusty undersurface, 10–20 cm/4–8 in. long and 5 cm/2 in. wide, providing a coarse texture.

Problems and Maintenance.   This species is subject to the usual number of insects and diseases that trouble rhododendrons in general, but few are serious enough to require regular maintenance, especially in properly situated naturalized plantings. Leaf-scorch can be a serious problem in all zones if a protected site is not provided at the beginning. Availability is limited outside the natural range.

Varieties and Cultivars.   The var. *leachii*, from West Virginia, is much more compact in growth than the species type, with smaller leaves having deeply waved margins. It is seldom available.

'Clement Bowers' is a vigorous but compact selection from *R. maximum,* growing to about 2 m/6.6 ft or more in height in time, perhaps a hybrid of unknown pollen parent, with rosy pink flowers and excellent dark green foliage, but it is not widely available.

'Lady Clementine Mitford' is a *R. maximum* hybrid of unknown pollen parent, growing to at least 1.5 m/5 ft tall, having peach-pink flowers with small yellow centers, much less cold-hardy than its *R. maximum* parent, perhaps only to Zone 7b. This, too, is not widely available.

'Marchioness of Lansdowne' is an *R. maximum* hybrid of unknown pollen parent, growing to about 1.5 m/5 ft tall with a loosely spreading habit and soft violet-rose flowers, each with a very dark purple blotch, useful in Zones 6b–7b, and areas with moderate summers in Zone 8.

'Maxecat' is a Joseph Gable hybrid of *R. maximum* × *R. catawbiense,* with somewhat loose but symmetrical growth habit, to 2 m/6.6 ft tall, and pink flowers, opening late. Useful at least in Zones 5a–6b, perhaps protected sites in Zone 4, and areas with moderate summers in Zone 7.

'Midsummer' is an *R. maximum* hybrid of unknown pollen parent, with a somewhat open habit, to at least 1.5 m/5 ft tall, and rosy pink flowers in compact clusters, opening in early summer. Useful in Zones 6b–7b and areas with moderate summers in Zone 8.

'Pride's Pink' and 'Roseum,' selections of *R. maximum* for soft-pink flowers, are as hardy as the species type.

Rhododendron mucronulatum 4

KOREAN RHODODENDRON
Deciduous shrub
Ericaceae (Heath Family)

Native Range.   Northeastern Asia, including northern Japan.

Useful Range.   USDA Zones 5a–7b, sheltered sites in Zone 4b, and areas in Zone 8 having moderate summer temperatures.

Function.   Border, specimen.

Size and Habit

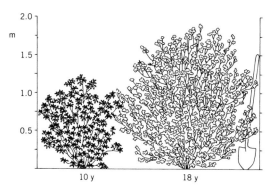

Rhododendron mucronulatum.

Adaptability. Shade from full summer sun is beneficial in areas having very hot summers. The plant will tolerate full shade but will not flower well or remain full.

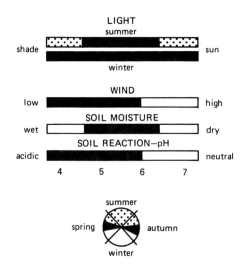

Seasonal Interest. *Flowers:* Light rosy purple (or pink), to 4 cm/1.6 in. across, in clusters of three to six at tips of branches, very showy, before the leaves emerge in early to middle spring. *Foliage:* Deciduous but leathery, about 6 cm/2.4 in. long, turning yellow to pink-bronze, or sometimes red, in autumn before falling.

Problems and Maintenance. This plant is subject to several disease and pest problems, but these are not as likely to be serious as on the evergreen rhododendrons. The deciduous character of this plant allows infected or infested foliage to be removed easily from the area annually if necessary. The tendency of flower buds to expand and open during favorable weather in early spring makes them susceptible to late spring freezes.

Cultivars. Several cultivars have been selected for flower color: 'Album' has white flowers.

'Cornell Pink' has clear, bright pink flowers, with little or none of the magenta color that makes the species type difficult to use with other colors in the red-orange to deep gold part of the spectrum.

'Crater's Edge' is a dwarf form with reddish purple flowers and red fall foliage, reported to be less cold-hardy than the species type, but this may not be accurate.

'Mahogany Red' has a compact growth habit, large, dark green leaves and deep purplish red flowers, and is reportedly less cold-hardy than the species type, but useful at least to Zone 6b.

'Mayflower' is a compact selection, to 1.5 m/ 5 ft, with deep pink flowers, later than those of other selections.

'Pink Panther' has bright pink flowers and compact habit and is cold-hardy at least to Zone 6b, perhaps also 6a.

'Radiant Pink' has bright pink flowers and upright habit.

Related Species

Rhododendron dauricum 4 (Dahurian rhododendron). This highly variable species includes both deciduous or semievergreen and evergreen forms. The deciduous forms may be confused with *R. mucronulatum*, growing to as much as 2 m/6.6 ft in height, but are inferior to *R. mucronulatum* as landscape plants. The more-or-less evergreen var. *sempervirens* is of special interest for its involvement in the P.J.M. Hybrids (see under *R. carolinianum*) and is represented by several other hybrids, as well as the white-flowering selection 'Arctic Pearl.' A few of the other hybrids are listed here.

'April Gem,' is a complex hybrid by Gustav Mehlquist of the University of Connecticut, involving *R. dauricum*, *R. carolinianum* var. *album*, and *R. mucronulatum* 'Cornell Pink,' is a compact, upright evergreen, 1 m/3.3 ft tall and 0.6 m/2 ft wide, with slightly fragrant double white flowers in early to middle spring. Useful in Zones 5b–7b, and perhaps parts of Zone 8.

'April Reign,' a Mehlquist hybrid involving the same parents as 'April Gem,' but in different proportions, is compact and upright, about the same size as 'April Gem,' but with slightly fragrant double pink flowers with lighter centers. It is similar to 'April Gem' in flowering time and cold-hardiness.

'April Rose,' a Mehlquist hybrid involving parentage similar to 'April Reign' but not identical, is similar to that cultivar in growth habit and hardiness, but with slightly fragrant double rose-red flowers in midspring.

'April Snow,' a complex hybrid by Ed Mezitt, involving *R. dauricum, R. carolinianum* var. *album*, and *R. mucronulatum* 'Cornell Pink,' grows to about 1 m/3.3 ft high and wide, with double white flowers, and is useful in Zones 6b–7b, probably also Zone 6a.

'April White' originated from the same cross as 'April Gem' and is similar to that cultivar except in having semidouble flowers and bright yellow autumn foliage.

Rhododendron prinophyllum 5

Synonyms: *R. roseum*
ROSESHELL AZALEA
Deciduous shrub
Ericaceae (Heath Family)

Native Range. Northeastern United States and adjacent Canada, southwesterly to Arkansas.

Useful Range. USDA Zones 3b–6b.

Function. Border, specimen, naturalizing.

Size and Habit

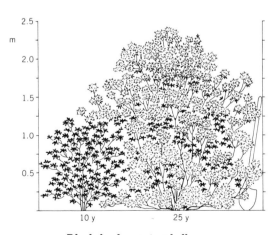

Rhododendron prinophyllum.

Adaptability

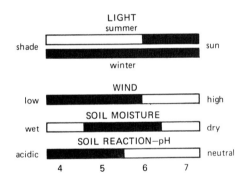

Seasonal Interest. *Flowers:* Highly fragrant, bright, clear pink, 4 cm/1.6 in. across, in clusters to 7.5 cm/3 in. across very late in spring. *Foliage:* Hairy, dull blue-green leaves are sparsely arranged, offering minor summer interest, and fall without color change in autumn.

Problems and Maintenance. This azalea is relatively trouble-free and requires little or no maintenance, although insects and mites that damage azaleas occasionally may be troublesome. Pruning is not necessary except for renewal of old plants and should not be done without good reason.

Cultivars. 'Marie Hoffman' is a Ludwig Hoffman selection for very large, fragrant, bright pink flowers and unusually heavy foliage, believed to be a tetraploid.

Hybrids

Northern Lights Hybrids.   See *R. japonicum*, Hybrids.

Related Species

Rhododendron canescens 5 (Florida pinxter or Piedmont azalea).   This handsome deciduous shrub is common and ranges widely in the southeastern United States from North Carolina to Florida and Texas. Its fragrant flowers are white with a pink tube and, like *R. prinophyllum*, with prominent extended stamens, opening in midspring before the new foliage has expanded. It is reported to be more shade-tolerant than *R. prinophyllum*, and is useful in Zones 6b–9a+. 'Phlox Pink' (= 'Varnadoe's Phlox Pink') has bright pink flowers. 'Varnadoe's Snow' has white flowers. The Galle selection 'White Flakes' has highly fragrant, light pink-tipped, double white flowers (20+ petals).

Rhododendron periclymenoides 4–5 (synonym: *R. nudiflorum*; pinxterbloom).   This common de-

Rhododendron canescens.

ciduous shrub, widely occurring in the Appalachians from Massachusetts to North Carolina and Tennessee, is similar to *R. canescens* and *R. prinophyllum* except not as large, with whitish to light pink flowers. Unlike *R. prinophyllum*, it forms thickets and has little fragrance, but it is more shade-tolerant. Useful in Zones 5b–9a, but probably should be considered of secondary value to *R. canescens* in the South and *R. prinophyllum* in the North, except when naturalizing or planting in shade.

Rhododendron schlippenbachii 5

ROYAL AZALEA
Deciduous shrub
Ericaceae (Heath Family)

Native Range.   Japan, Korea, Manchuria.

Useful Range.   USDA Zones 5b–8b and protected sites in Zone 5a.

Function.   Specimen, massing, border.

Size and Habit

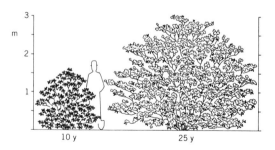

Rhododendron schlippenbachii.

Adaptability

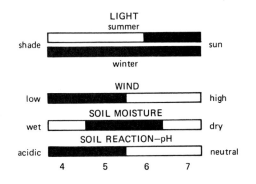

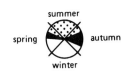

Rhododendron schlippenbachii.

Seasonal Interest. *Flowers:* Fragrant, delicately tinted, pale to rosy pink, 6–8 cm/2.4–3 in. across, before the foliage, making an extraordinary show in midspring. *Foliage:* Broad, rounded leaves give distinctive texture and turn yellow to orange-red before falling in autumn.

Problems and Maintenance. Foliage is sometimes affected by a leaf-spot disease and mites, but these usually are not serious. Flower buds are tender in Zone 5; for best flowering there, protect plants from strong winter winds as well as

frost pockets. Northern exposures may be helpful in delaying flower bud activity in spring until threat of severe cold is past.

Related Species

Rhododendron reticulatum 4–5 (rose azalea). This large deciduous shrub ranges in height from 6–8 m/20–26 ft (in gorges) to only 1 m/3.3 ft in mountaintop or northern habitats in Japan, but usually is a medium-size shrub in cultivation in our area. It is noteworthy when not in flower for its clusters of 2–3 leaves at branch tips. Its purple flowers, 4–5 cm/1.6–2 in. across, appear before the leaves, usually in pairs. Useful in Zones 6b–8a, perhaps more widely. The var. *albiflorum* has white flowers.

Rhododendron smirnowii 5

SMIRNOW RHODODENDRON
Evergreen shrub
Ericaceae (Heath Family)

Native Range. Western Asia: Caucasus Mountains.

Useful Range. USDA Zones 5b–7b, areas with moderate summer temperatures in Zone 8, and protected sites in Zone 5b, perhaps also Zone 5a.

Function. Border, specimen, foundation.

Size and Habit

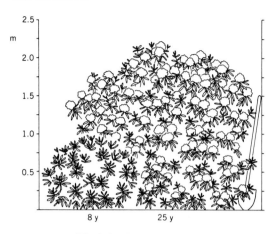

Rhododendron smirnowii.

Adaptability. Shade from full summer sun is necessary for good performance in Zones 7 and 8, the Midwest, and other areas having hot summers. Plants tolerate full shade but do not flower well. Protection from full winter sun is necessary in Zones 4 and 5.

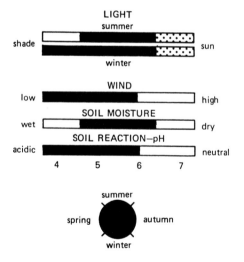

Seasonal Interest. *Flowers:* Pale to rosy lavender-pink, 6 cm/2.4 in. across, as many as a dozen packed together in clusters to 15 cm/6 in. across, opening in middle to late spring, before or with those of *R. catawbiense. Foliage:* Evergreen, leathery, 8–15 cm/3–6 in. long and rather narrow, dark green and lustrous on upper surfaces, heavily felted underneath, pure white at first, later rusty brown. Even the upper surfaces of

newly emerging leaves are felted, and traces of white sometimes remain as leaves mature.

Problems and Maintenance. Many of the insects and diseases that trouble *R. catawbiense* also affect *R. smirnowii,* but insects that feed on the undersides of leaves (e.g., lace bug) are inhibited by the heavy mat of hairs, which also help to make leaves less susceptible to damage from desiccation and rapid temperature changes. Nevertheless, attention to both site and soil is essential for good performance (see *R. catawbiense*).

Rhododendron smirnowii.

Varieties and Cultivars. Varieties of *R. smirnowii* are not known, perhaps because of the limited native habitat of this species. Nevertheless, plants in commerce under this name are highly variable because of inadvertent hybridization. While hybridization has diluted some of the desirable features of *R. smirnowii* (e.g., compact growth, heavy felting of foliage, and relatively clear pink flowers), it may also produce superior individuals differing from the species type in advantageous ways. Examination of known and speculative hybrids has produced a few useful hybrid cultivars and may produce more.

Related Species

Rhododendron brachycarpum 4–5. This relative of *R. smirnowii* from Japan and Korea is variable, with yellow-white to pink flowers and broad, elliptical leaves that are thinly felted underneath. Like *R. smirnowii,* this is one of the most cold-hardy *Rhododendron* species, useful in Zones 6a–7b but seldom commercially available.

Rhododendron caucasicum 3 (Caucasian rhododendron). This low, compact plant with yellowish white or pink-tinged flowers, and leaves 5–10 cm/2–4 in. long and rusty–felted underneath, probably is not in landscape use, but it is a parent of several fine hybrids such as the *R. catawbiense* hybrid 'Boule de Neige' and the *R. caucasicum* hybrids 'Cunningham's White' and 'Goldsworth Yellow.' See *Rhododendron* Cultivars. Useful at least in Zones 6a–7b.

Rhododendron degronianum 4.   This Japanese relative of the three above species is notable for its variable habit. Of greatest interest are some broadly compact, symmetrically moundlike forms with red-brown felted leaf undersides and pink flowers. These are not widely available, but are potentially useful in Zones 6b–7b and protected sites in Zone 6a.

Rhododendron griersonianum 5 (Grierson rhododendron). This native of western China reaches a height of 2.4 m/8 ft in cultivation, with large leaves, 9–18 cm/3.5–7 in. long, distinctively pointed, and buff-woolly underneath. It is useful on the West Coast but not in our area, except for a few of its hybrids (see Rhododendron cultivars).

Rhododendron yakushimanum 3 (Yakushima rhododendron).   This close relative of *R. degronianum* has been included in that species by some specialists, as *R. degronianum* ssp. *yakushimanum*. It is treated here as a separate species in part to avoid confusion between the two species in hybrid pedigrees. *R. yakushimanum* is a smaller and more elegant version of *R. degronianum*, growing to about 1.2 m/4 ft high and half again as wide, with truly elegant dark green leaves, to 8 cm/3 in. long, with very heavy buff felting underneath. The same tomentum appears on the upper surfaces of immature leaves, gradually disappearing as the leaf expands, except sometimes leaving a light dusting on the otherwise lustrous upper surface. Flowers, to 4.6 cm/1.8 in. across, in clusters of 10, range from rose to clear pink and white, opening in midspring. Several selections from this species have been made; a few are listed here.

'Koichiro Wada' (= "F.C.C. form") is the clone that was awarded a First Class Certificate

Rhododendron yakushimanum.

at the Royal Horticultural Society's Chelsea Flower Show in 1947 and greatly stimulated interest in using it as a parent of hybrids. This clone has abundant deep rose-red flower buds that open a delicate pink and fade to pure white, and its superb foliage is as much of an attraction as the flowers. This clone has been used widely in breeding, but still is not widely available itself.

'Mist Maiden,' a David Leach introduction, actually is probably a hybrid, of unknown origin but believed by some to involve *R. smirnowii*. It is somewhat faster-growing than the species type, yet compact, remaining below 1 m/3.3 ft, with 6.4-cm/2.5-in. flowers in clusters of about 15, deep pink in bud, opening apple-blossom pink, then fading to white. Useful in Zones 6a–7b and parts of Zone 8.

'Yaku Angel' is a low form, to 0.75 m/2.5 ft high and twice as wide, with purplish-pink flower buds opening white with light brown spotting, in clusters of about 15. This selection by Harold Greer of Eugene, Oregon is useful in Zones 6b–7b and in Zone 8 where summers are moderate.

Hybrids.   Over the last few decades, this species has grown in popularity among rhododendron breeders for its outstanding traits and small stature. A few of the most commonly available hybrids are described under the main heading, Rhododendron cultivars.

Rhododendron vaseyi 5

PINKSHELL AZALEA
Deciduous shrub
Ericaceae (Heath Family)

Native Range.   Mountains of North Carolina.

Useful Range.   USDA Zones 5a–8b.

Function.   Border, naturalizing, massing, specimen, screen (in good sites).

Size and Habit

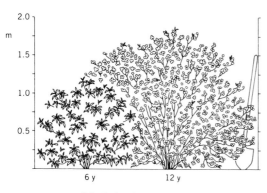

Rhododendron vaseyi.

Adaptability.   Tolerance of wet soils does not extend to heavy clay soils, but this species is a good choice for pond and stream bank sites in lighter soils.

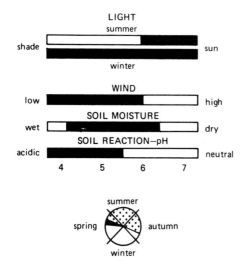

Seasonal Interest.   *Flowers:* Fragrant, light pink, two-lipped, to at least 2.5 cm/1 in. long, in clusters before the new foliage in middle to late spring. *Foliage:* Smooth leaves, to at least 10 cm/4 in. long, bright green but turning light red before falling in autumn, differing from most azalea leaves in smoothness and texture.

Problems and Maintenance.   This shrub is relatively trouble-free and requires little maintenance, although minor insect and mite problems may arise occasionally. Usually does not need to be pruned except for rejuvenation of very old plantings, and even this is not necessary in naturalized plantings in good, moist sites. An endangered species, *R. vaseyi* should not be collected from the wild.

Forms and Cultivars.   The var. *album* has white flowers, and 'White Find' is a clone selected from var. *album*, for pure white flowers.

Related Species

Rhododendron canadense 3 (rhodora).   This native of moist to wet sites in northeastern North America from Newfoundland and Labrador to northern Pennsylvania has two-lipped, rosy-purple flowers, to 2 cm/0.8 in. long, and dull blue-green foliage. 'Albiflorum' (= 'Album') has white flowers. Not as showy in flower as most azaleas, *R. canadense* is useful primarily in naturalized plantings, especially in the Far North. Useful in Zones 3a–5b, probably also Zone 2, and cool, moist sites in Zone 6.

Rhododendron vaseyi.

Rhododendron viscosum 5

SWAMP AZALEA
Deciduous shrub
Ericaceae (Heath Family)

Native Range.   Eastern United States, Maine
to Georgia and Alabama.

Useful Range.   USDA Zones 4b–9a, with selection of appropriate genetic material.

Function.   Border, naturalizing.

Size and Habit

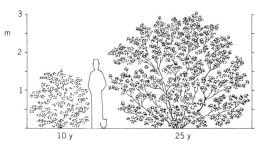

Rhododendron viscosum.

Adaptability.   Tolerance of wet soil gives this
plant added usefulness but does not make it
suitable for wet clay soils. In the wild, it occurs
in swamps on hummocks. In wet soils in landscape sites, it should be planted in shallow planting holes or in artificial hummocks or mounds of
organic material such as wood chips or peat
moss, or a combination of these.

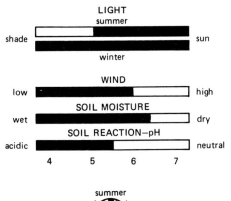

Rhododendron viscosum.

Seasonal Interest.   *Flowers:* Highly fragrant,
white or pink-flushed, to 2.5 cm/1 in. long,
opening from early summer to midsummer. *Foliage:* Bright green, sparse, turning dull orange
before falling in autumn.

Problems and Maintenance.   This shrub is relatively trouble-free and requires little maintenance, comparable with *R. prinophyllum* in this
respect. Pruning is neither necessary nor desirable in naturalized situations, but in more formal
landscapes the strong tendency to form thickets
may make occasional pruning necessary.

Cultivars and Hybrids.   'Arpege,' a hybrid (*R.
viscosum* × 'Koster's Brilliant Red') from Felix
and Dyjkhuis of Boskoop, The Netherlands, has
fragrant, bright golden yellow flowers, 4.3 cm/
1.7 in. across, with pink-flushed tubes. Cold-
hardy at least in Zones 6b–8b, perhaps also
Zone 6a.
  'Betty Cummins' has bright pink flowers.
  'Delaware Blue', a Polly Hill selection, has
heavily glaucous, blue-green foliage and pure
white flowers, pale pink in bud.
  'Pink Mist' has pink flowers that do not fade
rapidly.
  For other *R. viscosum* hybrids, see Cherokee
azaleas under *R. calendulaceum* Hybrids, *R. cumberlandense* Hybrids, and Viscosepalum Hybrids
under *R. japonicum.*

Related Species

Rhododendron alabamense 3–4 (Alabama azalea).
This rare deciduous shrub species is a low,

thicket-forming shrub, found on rather dry soils in northern Alabama and adjacent Georgia. It has deliciously fragrant white flowers, sometimes with yellow centers, and is useful in Zones 7a–9a, probably also Zone 6b. This species is now available in several nurseries. Because of its rarity, seedlings of this species should never be dug from the wild; there is no need for that, anyway, since it is easily propagated by cuttings and seed.

Rhododendron arborescens 5 (sweet or smooth azalea).   This mountain counterpart of *R. viscosum* grows wild in the Appalachians from Pennsylvania to northern Alabama and is useful in Zones 5a–9a. Its flowers are fragrant like those of *R. viscosum*, and its glossy, bright green foliage turns red in autumn. It is less tolerant of wet soil than *R. viscosum;* and it flowers later, after the leaves are fully expanded in early summer. 'Rubescens' has rosy pink flowers, but is not widely available even though it has been around for several decades. 'White Lightning' is a selection for highly fragrant white flowers. *R. arborescens* has been used widely as a parent in breeding hardy and fragrant hybrids. See Carlson Postscript Azaleas, Leach North American Azalea Hybrids, and Weston Hybrids, all under *R. cumberlandense,* hybrids.

Rhododendron atlanticum 2–3 (Atlantic or coast azalea).   This native of the Atlantic Coast from Delaware to South Carolina tolerates dry soil better than either *R. arborescens* or *R. viscosum,* but is less shade-tolerant. As a low, thicket-forming shrub, its primary usefulness is for naturalizing in its native area, but it can be used in Zones 6a–9a. Its flowers are similar to those of *R. arborescens* and *R. viscosum* and are equally fragrant, opening somewhat earlier.

Rhododendron oblongifolium 4–5 (Texas azalea). This native of Arkansas, Louisiana, Oklahoma, and Texas is very similar to *R. serrulatum* and *R. viscosum,* extending the usefulness of this complex of species westward. It is available in a few nurseries, but not widely planted outside its native range. Potentially useful in Zones 7a–9a.

Rhododendron serrulatum 6 (hammocksweet azalea).   This shrub is so similar to *R. viscosum* that specialists have combined it with that species, so both populations will now be officially *R. viscosum.* The useful range for this population, regardless of what it is called, will continue to be Zones 7–9a+, and, as usual in dealing with species that exist over major climatic gradients, attention will need to be given to the origin of commercial selections.

Rhododendron yedoense 4

YODOGAWA AZALEA
Deciduous shrub
Ericaceae (Heath Family)

Native Range.   This species is a cultivated form that, according to the International Code of Botanical Nomenclature, must be assigned the species name. The wild type, var. *poukhanense,* is native to Korea.

Useful Range.   USDA Zones 5b–8b and sheltered sites in Zone 5a.

Function.   Specimen, border, massing, foundation.

Size and Habit.   The var. *poukhanense* is illustrated.

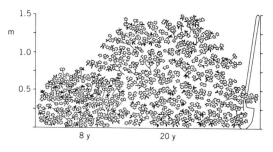

Rhododendron yedoense var. poukhanense.

Adaptability. Light shade in summer is beneficial in the South and other areas having very
hot summers for best performance.

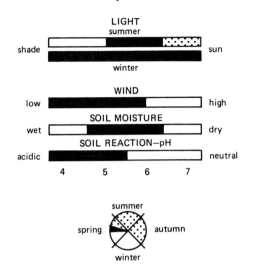

Seasonal Interest. *Flowers:* Rosy lavender,
double (single in var. *poukhanense*), to 5 cm/2
in. across, in middle to late spring. *Foliage:*
Medium green, slightly silky, remaining green
late, then turning purplish before falling in late
autumn.

Problems and Maintenance. Disease and insect problems, mostly not serious, are much
the same as for *R. obtusum.* Pruning is neither
necessary nor desirable. Bark splitting and resulting death of the plant can occur in late
autumn if plants have not hardened adequately.
To reduce the chances of this happening, avoid
overwatering and fertilization in late summer
and early autumn.

Varieties. The var. *poukhanense* (synonym: *R.
poukhanense;* Korean azalea) is the wild type of
this species. Ordinarily the wild type would be
considered the species type, but in this case the
garden form with double flowers was described
before Western botanists were aware of the single-flowered wild type. According to the International Code of Botanical Nomenclature, the
first-named type becomes the species type. The
var. *poukhanense* is an excellent landscape plant
in itself, freely bearing purplish lavender flowers
and making a low, mounded mass of foliage and
bloom. It is at least as cold-hardy as the Yodo-

gawa azalea and at least reasonably successful in
good sites in Zone 5a. Moreover, it has been
used as a parent in breeding many hardy hybrids,
including most of the Gable Hybrids and a few of
the hardier Glenn Dale Hybrids (see *R. indicum*).

Hybrids

Gable Evergreen Azalea Hybrids. These varied
hybrids mostly originated in the breeding program of Joseph B. Gable, Stewartstown, Pennsylvania, but were eventually named and introduced by others. Most of them grow to 1.5–2.0
m/5–6.6 ft tall, a few are taller. Most have *R.
yedoense* var. *poukhanense* and *R. kaempferi,* or
both, in their parentage and owe their cold-
hardiness to those parents. Other parents include
R. indicum, 'Mucronatum,' and some of the Kurume hybrids. Most of these hybrids are useful in
Zones 6a–8b, some also to Zone 5b, but a few
are probably limited to Zone 6b or milder, so it is
important to select them by individual cultivar,
relying on local experience and availability.
Some of the most popular cultivars are listed
here.

'Boudoir' has medium (4 cm/1.6 in.), single
violet-rose flowers with a deeper blotch.

'Cameo' has medium, double (hose-in-hose)
light pink flowers.

'Campfire' has medium to large (4.5 cm/1.8
in.), double (hose-in-hose) red flowers.

'Caroline Gable' has medium to large, single
bright red flowers with a darker blotch.

'Elizabeth Gable' has very large (6.4 cm/2.5
in.), frilled, single bright red flowers with a
deeper blotch.

'Herbert' has medium to large, frilled, double
(hose-in hose), bright red-purple flowers with
darker blotch, and a low, spreading growth
habit.

'Lorna' has medium, fully double, light purplish-pink flowers.

'Louise Gable' has very large, semidouble
deep purplish-pink flowers with darker blotch.

'Polaris' has very large (5.8 cm/2.3 in.), double (hose-in-hose) white flowers with faint
green throat.

'Purple Splendor' is similar to 'Herbert' in
flowering and growth habit.

'Robert Lee' has very large, ruffled single
white flowers, and a low, spreading growth habit.

'Rosebud' is similar to 'Lorna,' with fully double but deeper purplish-pink flowers.

'Rose Greeley' has very large, double (hose-in-hose), fragrant white flowers and a low, dense growth habit.

'Stewartstonian' has large, single, bright red flowers and wine-red winter foliage and is among the most cold-hardy of this group, at least to Zone 6a and sheltered sites in Zone 5b.

Great Lakes Hybrids.   This is an informal collective name for cultivars developed by a few hybridizers located east of Cleveland, Ohio, near the shore of Lake Erie. It includes the *Girard Evergreen Azalea Hybrids,* developed by Peter Girard, Sr. of Geneva, Ohio, and the *Shammarello Azalea Hybrids,* introduced by Anthony M. "Tony" Shammarello of Euclid, Ohio. More-or-less similar are the *Pride Hybrids,* developed by Orlando Pride of Butler Pennsylvania, and the *Stanton Hybrids,* developed by Ernest Stanton of Grosse Isle, Michigan. A few of the most popular cultivars from this group are listed here.

'Border Gem' (Girard Border Gem®) is dense and dwarf in habit, with very small leaves and 2.5–3.8 cm/1–1.5 in. rosy pink flowers that open to cover the plant.

'Cascade' (Shammarello) has medium (4 cm/1.6 in.) white flowers, probably cold-hardy to Zone 6a.

'Chiara' (Girard Chiara®) is semidwarf, probably to at least 1 m/3.3 ft in a decade, with very large (2.5–3.8 cm/1–1.5 in.), double (hose-in-hose), ruffled, deep purplish pink flowers with reddish orange blotch, hardy to Zone 6b.

'Clara Marie' (Girard Clara Marie®) has very large (6.4 cm/2.5 in.), frilled white flowers, cold-hardy at least to Zone 7a, probably also Zone 6b.

'Edith Pride' (Pride) is tall-growing (to 2 m/6.6 ft) with red-orange flowers, hardy to Zone 6b, probably also Zone 6a.

'Elsie Lee' (Shammarello) has very large, semidouble, light red-purple flowers, and is slow-growing, to 1–1.5 m/3.3–5 ft high, and probably hardy to Zone 6a.

'Girard's Crimson' (Girard Crimson®) is dwarf, to 50–75 cm/20–30 in. in a decade, with very large purplish red flowers with bright red blotch, hardy at least to Zone 7b, perhaps also Zone 7a, or even 6b.

'Harry Scanlon' (Pride) is tall-growing (to 2 m/6.6 ft) with light pink flowers, hardy to Zone 6b, probably also Zone 6a.

'Helen Curtis' (Shammarello) is semidwarf, probably to only 50 cm/20 in a decade, with very large pure white semidouble flowers with frilled petals, hardy at least to Zone 6b, probably also Zone 6a.

'Hino-red' (Shammarello) is a hybrid between the Kurume azalea 'Hino-crimson' and *R. yedoense* var. *poukhanense,* compact and spreading in habit, probably not exceeding 50 cm/20 in. in height and twice that in spread in a decade, and hardy to Zone 6b and probably Zone 6a.

'Hot Shot' (Girard Hot Shot®) is semidwarf, to less than 1 m/3.3 ft in a decade, with large, fiery deep orange-red flowers, spotted dark red, hardy to Zone 6b.

'Lake Erie' (Stanton) is low-spreading in habit, to about 75 cm/30 in. high and somewhat wider in a decade, with 5 cm/2 in. deep pink flowers and red-orange blotch, hardy to Zone 6b, perhaps also Zone 6a. 'Lake Michigan,' 'Lake Ontario,' and 'Lake Superior' have more purplish pink flowers.

'National Beauty' (Girard National Beauty®) is semidwarf in habit, probably not exceeding 0.8 m/2.6 ft in height and twice that in width in a decade, with large deep, ruffled flowers, and lustrous foliage, reddening in autumn and winter. Hardy at least to Zone 7a, probably also Zone 6b.

'Pride's Pink' is upright and spreading in habit, probably to about 1.5–2 m/5–6.6 ft in a decade, with large pink flowers, hardy at least to Zone 6b, probably also Zone 6a.

'Red-red' (Shammarello) is semidwarf and spreading in habit, to 0.6 m/2 ft high and 1 m/3.3 ft wide in a decade, with medium (5 cm/2 in.) brilliant red flowers, hardy at least to Zone 6b, perhaps also to Zone 6a.

'Thor' (Pride) is a strong growing plant, eventually to 2 m/6.6 ft tall, with large reddish purple flowers, and is hardy at least to Zone 6b, probably also Zone 6a.

'Wintergreen' (Shammarello) is semidwarf and low-spreading, remaining under 50 cm/20 in. in height but spreading to twice that in a decade.

RHODODENDRON HYBRID CULTIVARS

Azalea Cultivars 2–5

'Alhambra' (Gable): see *R. cumberlandense.*

'Alice': see Kaempferi Hybrids.

'Altaclarense': see note under 'Altaclerense,' in text.

'Altaclerense': see Viscosepalum Hybrids.

'Altanuwa' (Holsomback): see hybrids of *R. cumberlandense.*

'Ambrosia': see Glenn Dale Hybrids.

'Amoenum': see *R. ×obtusum*, under *R. kiusianum* Hybrids.

'Amoenum Coccineum': see under *R. ×obtusum.*

'Aphrodite': see Glenn Dale Hybrids.

'Apple Blossom': see Molle Hybrids.

'Appleblossom': see Kurume Hybrids.

'Annabella' (Exbury): see Knap Hill Hybrids.

'Arpege': see *R. viscosum.*

'Avocet' (Knap Hill): see Knap Hill Hybrids.

'Balsaminiflorum': see *R. indicum.*

'Beau Celeste': see Ghent Hybrids.

'Benichidore': see *R. kiusianum.*

'Beni Kirishima': see Satsuki Azaleas.

'Benisuzume': see *R. kiusianum.*

'Berryrose' (Exbury): see Knap Hill Hybrids.

'Betty Ann Voss': see Robin Hill Hybrids.

'Betty Cummins': see *R. viscosum.*

'Betty Muir': see *R. kiusianum.*

'Blaauw's Pink': see Kurume Hybrids.

'Blue Danube': see Kaempferi Hybrids.

'Border Gem' (Girard): see Great Lakes Hybrids.

'Boudoir': see Gable Evergreen Azalea Hybrids.

'Brandywine' see Kurume Hybrids.

'Brazil' (Exbury): see Knap Hill Hybrids.

'Brickdust' (Ilam): see Ilam Hybrids.

'Brilliant" see Kurume Hybrids.

'Buccaneer': see Glenn Dale Hybrids.

'Buzzard' (Knap Hill): see Knap Hill Hybrids.

'Cameo': see Gable Evergreen Azalea Hybrids.

'Campfire': see Gable Evergreen Azalea Hybrids.

'Camp's Red': see *R. cumberlandense.*

'Cannon's Double' (Exbury): see Knap Hill Hybrids.

'Cardinal': see 'Beau Celeste.'

'Carmen': see Kaempferi Hybrids.

'Caroline': see Gable Evergreen Azalea Hybrids.

'Cascade' (Shammarello): see Great Lakes Hybrids.

'Cecile' (Exbury): see Knap Hill Hybrids.

'Chamois' (Leach): see hybrids of *R. cumberlandense.*

'Charlemagne': see Ghent Hybrids.

'Cheulah' (Holsomback): see *R. cumberlandense.*

'Chiara' (Girard): see Great Lakes Hybrids.

'Chinsai' see Satsuki Azaleas.

'Chinzan': see Satsuki Azaleas.

'Christmas Cheer': see Kurume Hybrids.

'Clara Marie' (Girard): see Great Lakes Hybrids.

'Coloratura' (Leach): see hybrids of *R. cumberlandense.*

'Conversation Piece': see Robin Hill Hybrids.

'Copperman': see Glenn Dale Hybrids.

'Coral Bells': see Kurume Hybrids.

'Cotton Candy' (Mezitt): see hybrids of *R. cumberlandense.*

'Cream Puff' (Leach): see hybrids of *R. cumberlandense.*

'Crimson Tide' (Girard): see Girard Deciduous Azalea Hybrids.

'Daviesii': see Viscosepalum Hybrids.

'Dayspring': see Glenn Dale Hybrids.

'Delaware Blue': see *R. viscosum.*

'Delaware Valley White': see under 'Mucronatum'.

'Dorothy Gish': see Rutherford Hybrids.

'Dr. M. Oosthoek': see Molle Hybrids.

'Duc de Rohan': see Southern Indian Hybrids.

'Edith Pride' (Pride): see Great Lakes Hybrids.

'Elegans Superbum': see Southern Indian Hybrids.

'Elizabeth Gable': see Gable Evergreen Azalea Hybrids.

'Elsie Lee' (Shammarello): see Great Lakes Hybrids.

'Evening Glow' (Knap Hill): see Knap Hill Hybrids.

'Fanny': see Ghent Hybrids.

'Fashion': see Glenn Dale Hybrids.

'Fedora': see Kaempferi Hybrids.

'Festive': see Glenn Dale Hybrids.

'Fielder's White': see Southern Indian Hybrids.

'Fireball': see Kaempferi Hybrids.

'Flamboyant': see Ghent Hybrids.

'Flame Creeper': see *R. indicum*.

'Formosa': see Southern Indian Hybrids.

'Gaiety': see Glenn Dale Hybrids.

'Geisha': see Glenn Dale Hybrids.

'George Lindley Taber': see Southern Indian Hybrids.

'Getsutoku': see Satsuki Azaleas.

'Gibraltar' (Exbury): see Knap Hill Hybrids.

'Girard's Crimson': see Great Lakes Hybrids.

'Glacier': see Glenn Dale Hybrids.

'Glamour': see Glenn Dale Hybrids.

'Gloria Mundi': see Ghent Hybrids.

'Golden Eagle' (Knap Hill): see Knap Hill Hybrids.

'Golden Lights': see Northern Lights Hybrids.

'Greeting': see Glenn Dale Hybrids.

'Gulfpride': see under 'Mucronatum'.

'Gumpo': see Satsuki Azaleas.

'Gunbi': see Satsuki Azaleas.

'Gunrei': see 'Gunbi'.

'Hamlet': see Molle Hybrids.

'Harry Scanlon' (Pride): see Great Lakes Hybrids.

'Harvest Moon' (Slocock): see Knap Hill Hybrids.

'Helen': see Southern Indian Hybrids.

'Helen Close': see Glenn Dale Hybrids.

'Helen Curtis' (Shammarello): see Great Lakes Hybrids.

'Herbert': Gable Evergreen Azalea Hybrids.

'Hershey's Orange': see Kurume Hybrids.

'Hershey's Red': see Kurume Hybrids.

'Higasa': see Satsuki Azaleas.

'Hilda Niblett': see Robin Hill Hybrids.

'Hino Crimson': see Kurume Hybrids.

'Hinode Giri': see Kurume Hybrids.

'Hino-red' (Shammarello): see Great Lakes Hybrids.

'Homebush' (Knap Hill): see Knap Hill Hybrids.

'Hotshot' (Girard): see Great Lakes Hybrids.

'Hotspur' (Exbury): see Knap Hill Hybrids.

'Ignaeum Novum': see Ghent Hybrids.

'Ilam Carmen' (Ilam): see Ilam Hybrids.

'Ilam Giant' (Ilam): see Ilam Hybrids.

'Indica Alba': see 'Mucronatum'.

'Iveryanum': see *R. indicum*.

'J. T. Lovett': see *R. indicum*.

'Jennifer': see Southern Indian Hybrids.

'Judge Solomon': see Southern Indian Hybrids.

'July Joy' (Holsomback): see *R. prunifolium*.

'Kate Arendall': see Southern Indian Hybrids.

'Klondyke' (Exbury): see Knap Hill Hybrids.

'Komo Kulshan': see *R. kiusianum*.

'Koster's Brilliant Red': see Molle Hybrids.

'Lake Erie' (Stanton): see Great Lakes Hybrids.

'Lake Michigan' (Stanton): see Great Lakes Hybrids.

'Lake Ontario' (Stanton): see Great Lakes Hybrids.

'Lake Superior' (Stanton): see Great Lakes Hybrids.

'Ledifolia Alba': see 'Mucronatum.'

'Lemonora': see Molle Hybrids.

'Leonard Frisbie': see *R. occidentale*.

'Lorna': see Gable Evergreen Azalea Hybrids.

'Louise Gable': see Gable Evergreen Azalea Hybrids.

'Macrantha': see *R. indicum.*

'Macrantha Orange': see *R. indicum.*

'Macrantha Pink': see *R. indicum.*

'Macrantha Salmon': see *R. indicum.*

'Maori' (Ilam): see Ilam Hybrids.

'Marie Hoffman': see *R. prinophyllum.*

'Martha Hitchcock': see Glenn Dale Hybrids.

'Melford Red Letter': see 'Red Letter'.

'Minerva': see Ghent Hybrids.

'Minipink': see *R. nakaharai.*

'Mother's Day': see Kurume Hybrids.

'Mount Saint Helens' (Girard): see Girard Deciduous Azalea Hybrids.

'Mrs. G. G. Gerbing': see Southern Indian Hybrids.

'Mt. Seven Star': see *R. nakaharai.*

'Mucronatum': see under *R. indicum*; Related Species.

'Nancy of Robin Hill': see Robin Hill Hybrids.

'Narcissiflorum': see Ghent Hybrids.

'National Beauty' (Girard): see Great Lakes Hybrids.

'Northern Hi-lights': see Northern Lights Hybrids.,

'Oberon': see Kaempferi Hybrids.

'Old Gold' (Exbury): see Knap Hill Hybrids.

'Orangeade' (Knap Hill): see Knap Hill Hybrids.

'Orchid Lights': see Northern Lights Hybrids.

'Othello': see Kaempferi Hybrids.

'Pallas': see Ghent Hybrids.

'Parade' (Mezitt): see hybrids of *R. cumberlandense.*

'Phlox Pink': see *R. canescens.*

'Phoeniceum': see under *R. indicum*: Related Species.

'Pink and Sweet' (Mezitt): see hybrids of *R. cumberlandense.*

'Pink Delight' (Girard): see Girard Deciduous Azalea Hybrids.

'Pink Gumpo': see Satsuki Azaleas.

'Pink Mist': see *R. viscosum.*

'Pink Pearl': see Kurume Hybrids.

'Pink Puff' (Leach): see hybrids of *R. cumberlandense.*

'Pink Ruffles' (Exbury): see Knap Hill Hybrids.

'Pink Ruffles': see Rutherford Hybrids.

'Polaris': see Gable Evergreen Azalea Hybrids.

'President Claeys': see Southern Indian Hybrids.

'President Clay': see 'President Claeys'.

'Pride of Mobile': see 'Elegans Superbum.'

'Pride's Pink': see Great Lakes Hybrids.

'Pucella' and 'Pucelle': see 'Fanny'.

'Purple Splendor': see Gable Evergreen Azalea Hybrids.

'Red Formosa': see Southern Indian Hybrids.

'Red Gumpo': see Satsuki Azaleas.

'Red Letter' (Ilam): see Ilam Hybrids.

'Red Pom Pom' (Girard): see Girard Deciduous Azalea Hybrids.

'Red-red' (Shammarello): see Great Lakes Hybrids.

'Red Ruffles': see Rutherford Hybrids.

'Redder Yet' (Knap Hill: Leach): see Knap Hill Hybrids.

'Refrain': see Glenn Dale Hybrids.

'Robert Lee': see Gable Evergreen Azalea Hybrids.

'Rocket' (Exbury): see Knap Hill Hybrids.

'Rose Greeley': see Gable Evergreen Azalea Hybrids.

'Rosea': see Southern Indian Hybrids.

'Rosebud': see Gable Evergreen Azalea Hybrids.

'Rosy Lights': see Northern Lights Hybrids.

'Rubescens': see *R. arborescens.*

'S. D. Coleman' (Leach): see *R. prunifolium.*

'Sagittarius': see Glenn Dale Hybrids.

'Salmon Delight' (Girard): see Girard Deciduous Azalea Hybrids.

'Satan' (Slocock): see Knap Hill Hybrids.

'Saturnus': see Molle Hybrids.

'Scarlet Pimpernel' (Exbury): see Knap Hill Hybrids.

'Seville' (Slocock): see Knap Hill Hybrids.

'Sherwood Red'; see Kurume Hybrids.

'Shira Fuji': see Satsuki Azaleas.

'Sir Robert': see Robin Hill Hybrids.

'Sizzler': see *R. cumberlandense.*

'Snow': see Kurume Hybrids.

'Southern Charm': see Southern Indian Hybrids.

'Spicy Lights': see Northern Lights Hybrids.

'Spring Salvo' (Ilam): see Ilam Hybrids.

'Stagecoach Frills': see *R. occidentale.*

'Stewartstonian': see Gable Evergreen Azalea Hybrids.

'Strawberry Ice' (Exbury): see Knap Hill Hybrids.

'Sunlight': see *R. cumberlandense.*

'Tagu' (Holsomback): see hybrids of *R. cumberlandense.*

'Thor' (Pride): see Great Lakes Hybrids.

'Treasure': see Glenn Dale Hybrids.

'Unique': see Ghent Hybrids.

'Varnadoe's Phlox Pink': see 'Phlox Pink'.

'Varnadoe's Snow': see *R. canescens.*

'Wakaebisu': see Satsuki Azaleas.

'Watermelon Pink': see 'Elegans Superbum.'

'Watermelon Red': see Southern Indian Hybrids.

'White Find': see *R. vaseyi.*

'White Flakes': see *R. canescens.*

'White Grandeur': see Southern Indian Hybrids.

'White Lightning': see *R. arborescens.*

'White Lights': see Northern Lights Hybrids.

'White Moon': see *R. kiusianum.*

'Whitethroat' (Knap Hill): see Knap Hill Hybrids.

'Wintergreen' (Shammarello): see Great Lakes Hybrids.

'Yellow Beauty' (Ilam): see Ilam Hybrids.

'Yellow Pom Pom' (Girard): see Girard Deciduous Azalea Hybrids.

'Zulu': see Glenn Dale Hybrids.

Rhododendron Cultivars 2–5

Cultivars that are selections from a single species and hybrids of unknown pollen parent are listed below, but described under the species (seed parent) as noted. Those that are known to involve more than a single species are mostly described as listed below, but may be described under the primary species if part of a grex or other group.

The American Rhododendron Society (ARS) has assigned cold-hardiness designations H-1 through H-7. These designations correspond approximately to the USDA Plant Hardiness Zones that are used throughout this book, and this correspondence is given in the chart below. Since ARS ratings are based on extreme minimum temperature and USDA ratings on average annual minimum temperature, the assumption has been made that expected extreme minimum temperatures are approximately 8.3°C/15°F lower than corresponding average annual minimum temperatures, which is at best an approximation. Since ARS ratings of H-6 and H-7 relate to milder climates than are included in the scope of this book, they are omitted in the table.

ARS

Rating	Extreme °F	Temperature °C	Corresponding USDA Hardiness Zones
1	−25	−31.7	5b–8a and sheltered sites in 5a
2	−20	−28.9	6a–8a and sheltered sites in 5b
	−15	−26.1	6b–8b and sheltered sites in 6a
3	−10	−23.3	7a–8b and sheltered sites in 6b
	−5	−20.6	7b–8b and sheltered sites in 7a
4	0	−17.8	8a–8b and sheltered sites in 7b
	+5	−15.0	8b–9a and sheltered sites in 8a
5	+10	−12.2	9a and sheltered sites in 8b

Note also that when hardiness zone *ranges* are specified, the *higher* range number is related to heat-tolerance, and that may vary among cultivars in a single group.

Note that cultivars listed in a given zone are also cold-hardy in zones with higher numbers; for example, plants rated as hardy in Zone 5a are also cold-hardy in Zone 5b and higher-numbered zones.

Cultivars Useful in ARS H-1 (Zones 5b–8a)

'Album' (selection of *R. ferrugineum;* see under that species).

'Album' (selection of *R. mucronulatum;* see under that species).

'Anna H. Hall' (*R. catawbiense* × *R. yakushimanum,* crossed by David G. Leach) is densely compact, under 1 m/3.3 ft in height and somewhat broader, with leaves buff-felted underneath and 5 cm/2 in. white to pale pink flowers in clusters of up to 15, in early to middle spring. Probably also hardy in Zone 5a.

'April Gem': see under *R. dauricum.*

'April Reign': see under *R. dauricum.*

'April Rose': see under *R. dauricum.*

'April White': see under *R. dauricum.*

'Arctic Pearl': selection of *R. dauricum;* see under that species.

'Atrococcineum': see under *R. ferrugineum.*

'Balta' (a P.J.M. Hybrid × *R. carolinianum* var. *album,* crossed by Ed Mezitt, Weston Nurseries) is densely compact, like a P.J.M. Hybrid, but slower-growing, to 1 m/3.3 ft high and slightly broader, with small leaves and 3.8-cm/ 1.5-in. white to pale pink flowers in large clusters, in early to middle spring. Probably also hardy in Zone 5a and protected sites in Zone 4b.

'Boule de Neige' (*R. caucasicum* × an unnamed Catawbiense Hybrid, crossed in France in the 1870s) is compact in habit, to 1–1.5 m/ 3.3–5 ft high and wider, with 5.6 cm/2.2 in. flowers in compact clusters of up to 15, in midspring. Susceptible to lacewing fly.

'Boursault' (= 'Catawbiense Boursault): see under *R. catawbiense.*

'Calsap' (*R. catawbiense* var. *album* 'Catalga' × 'Sappho,' a hybrid of unknown parentage but possibly involving *R. maximum)* is compact, to 1.5 m/5 ft tall and wide, with 7.6 cm/3 in. white

flowers having wavy petals and a small, deep maroon blotch, in clusters of about 20, in middle to late spring. Possibly also hardy in Zone 5a.

'Catawbiense Album': see under *R. catawbiense.*

'Charles Dickens': see under *R. catawbiense.*

'Clement Bowers': selection of *R. maximum;* see under that species.

'Cornell Pink': selection of *R. mucronulatum;* see under that species.

'Elite': see under *R. carolinianum.*

'Mars': see under *R. griffithianum.*

'Maxecat' is a hybrid of *R. maximum* × *R. catawbiense* with good form and pink flowers in clusters of 25, probably also hardy in Zone 5a and protected sites in Zone 4.

'Minnetonka': see under *R. ponticum.*

'Mrs. Charles S. Sargent': see under *R. catawbiense.*

'Nepal' (*R. catawbiense* var. *album* × a hybrid of *R. wightii* × *R. fortunei,* crossed by David Leach) is full, compactly rounded, to at least 2 m/6.6 ft tall and wide, with large, glossy, veined leaves, 14–20 cm/5.5–8 in. long, and large, pink-flushed white flowers, in clusters of 15, in midspring.

"P.J.M. Hybrids": see under *R. carolinianum.*

'Pride's Pink': see under *R. maximum.*

'Ramapo' (*R. fastigiatum* × *R. carolinianum,* crossed by Guy Nearing) is a dwarf rhododendron, to 0.6 m/2 ft tall, with nearly circular 2.5 cm/1 in. leaves, dusty blue as they unfold, turning a metallic blue-green in winter, and small but abundant bright pinkish-violet flowers, in early to middle spring.

'Regal': see under *R. carolinianum.*

'Roseum': selection of *R. maximum;* see under that species.

'Roseum Elegans': see under *R. catawbiense.*

'Russell Harmon' is a hybrid of *R. maximum* and *R. catawbiense,* similar to 'Maxecat' except with magenta flowers.

'Victor': see under *R. carolinianum.*

'Wally' (= 'Vallya'), an Ed Mezitt hybrid (*R. caroliniana* var. *alba* × *R. mucronulatum* 'Cornell Pink'), is semievergreen, growing to at least 1.5 m/5 ft high and nearly as wide, with soft-pink flowers in early spring, followed by dark green leaves that turn orange-red to yellow in autumn. Useful in Zones 5b–7b, probably also Zone 5a.

'Windbeam', a *R. carolinianum* hybrid involving *R. racemosum* and an unknown parent, is somewhat straggly when young, later developing a more compact, rounded shape, to 1.2 m/4 ft high and wide, with small, aromatic leaves and small, red-spotted, soft-pink flowers all along the wandlike stems, in early to middle spring. White or apricot-flowered forms of this cultivar have been reported, suggesting that it may be genetically unstable for flower color.

Cultivars Useful in the Colder Half of ARS H-2 (Zones 6a–8a)

'Aglo,' an Ed Mezitt hybrid of R. carolinianum by a pink-flowering selection of R. mucronulatum, this plant is not very different from 'Olga' (see below).

'Album Elegans': see under R. catawbiense.

'America': see under R. catawbiense.

'Bangkok' is a hybrid of R. catawbiense var. album with three tender species, including R. dichroanthum and R. griffithianum, yet surprisingly cold-hardy to Zone 6a, with good form and foliage and strong coral-pink flowers with soft orange-yellow centers.

'Ben Moseley': see under R. fortunei.

'Besse Howells' (hybrid involving R. catawbiense, R. caucasicum, and an unknown parent, crossed by Anthony M. Shammarello of South Euclid, Ohio) is compact, to 1.2 m/4 ft tall, with dark green leaves and ruffled, 6.4-cm/2.5-in. burgundy-red flowers, with red blotch, in early to middle spring.

'Brown Eyes': see R. fortunei.

'Chattahoochee Twilight': selection of R. minus; see under that species.

'Edmond Amateis' (R. catawbiense var. album by an unnamed seedling from a cross by C. O. Dexter of Sandwich, Massachusetts; crossed by Edmond Amateis, named by Leach) is broadly upright, to nearly 2 m/6.6 ft tall and wide, with dense, heavily textured foliage and 9-cm/3.5-in. pure white flowers with dark red blotch, in clusters of 13, in midspring.

'English Roseum': see under R. catawbiense.

'Golden Gala' (hybrid of R. catawbiense, along with R. wardii and R. yakushimanum, crossed by Leach) is broadly compact with heavy, glossy olive-green leaves and ivory to yellowish-white, broadly funnel-shaped flowers, 6.4 cm/2.5 in. across, opening in middle to late spring.

'Henry's Red' (hybrid of a red-flowering R.

catawbiense seedling by an unknown pollinator, selected by Ed Mezitt) is upright and spreading in habit, 1–1.5 m/3.3–5 ft, with deep red, 5-cm/2-in. flowers, nearly black-red in the center, in middle to late spring.

'Hindustan' is a large plant, to 2 m/6.6 ft tall and wide, with 8-cm/3-in. orange flowers in large domed trusses, useful in Zones 6a–7b, and areas with moderate summers in Zone 8.

'Hong Kong,' a Leach hybrid involving R. catawbiense var. album, R. campylocarpum, R. fortunei ssp. discolor, and R. wardii, is a very vigorous plant to at least 2.4 m/8 ft tall, and wider, with glossy yellow-green leaves and large, soft primrose-yellow flowers, with small red blotch in center, in flattened symmetrical clusters of 13, in early to middle spring.

'Jericho,' a Leach hybrid of R. keiskii and R. carolinianum, is a low plant, to 1 m/3.3 ft high and 1.5 m/5 ft wide in time, with flowers in clusters of 6, light yellow-green in bud and opening paler still, in midspring.

'Laurie' (R. carolinianum × a P.J.M. Hybrid, crossed by Ed Mezitt) is gracefully compact, to at least 1 m/3.3 ft in time, with small dark green leaves that bronze in winter, and 4.5-cm/1.8-in. pale pink to white, partly semidouble flowers in clusters of up to 33, in early to middle spring.

'Lodestar' (R. catawbiense var. album × 'Belle Heller,' another Catawbiense Hybrid, crossed by Leach) is a medium-sized shrub, to 1.5 m/5 ft, with pale lilac flowers, opening in middle to late spring and gradually fading to white.

'Mist Maiden': see under R. yakushimanum.

'Molly Fordham' ('Balta' × R. carolinianum, crossed at Weston Nurseries) is densely compact, to 1.2 m/4 ft high and at least as wide, with excellent foliage that remains glossy green in winter, unlike most cultivars of similar parentage, and small but abundant nearly white to faintly pink flowers, in early to middle spring.

'Monaco' is a large shrub, to 2 m/6.6 ft tall and wide, with red flower buds opening to 8.2 cm/3.2 in. across, with strong olive yellow-blotched and spotted yellow petals with reddish backs. Useful in Zones 6a–7b.

'Nova Zembla': see under R. catawbiense.

'Olga Mezitt' is, in effect, a pink-flowering version of the P.J.M. Hybrids, even though its parentage is different (probably R. carolinianum × R. minus), compact in form, to 1 m/3.3 ft high and wider, flowering in early to middle spring.

'Party Pink,' a much-honored Leach hybrid involving *R. catawbiense* var. *album, R. caucasicum R. griffithianum,* and an unknown complement, is compact in habit, to 1.5 m/5 ft high and wide, with rich green foliage and 7.6-cm/3-in. flowers, lighter, purplish-pink and lighter toward the center, with a subtle golden-bronze flare, opening in globose clusters of 18 in midspring.

'Purple Gem' (*R. carolinianum* × *R. fastigiatum,* crossed by Joseph Gable) is similar to 'Ramapo' (see previous list) but not quite as dwarfed or cold-hardy, with handsome blue new foliage and small but abundant light purple flowers (brighter purple in a variant) in early to middle spring.

'Purpureum Grandiflorum': see under *R. catawbiense.*

'Rio' (hybrid between two Dexter hybrids of unknown parentage, crossed by Leach) is broadly compact, to 1 m/3.3 ft high and considerably broader, with glossy yellowish green leaves, and openly funnel-shaped, 8.2-cm/3.2-in. flowers, salmon-pink grading to a yellow throat, in clusters of 16, in midspring.

'Summer Summit' (*R. maximum* × an unnamed hybrid of *R. auriculatum* and *R. fortunei* ssp. *discolor,* crossed by Leach) is a large mound-forming plant (the influence of *R. maximum),* to at least 3 m/10 ft tall, with large leaves, holding on the plant for three years and making a very dense foliage mass, and 6.4-cm/2.5-in. flowers in clusters of 14, pink-flushed at first, then fading to white with dark olive-yellow spotting, opening in very late spring and early summer.

'Trinidad' (complex hybrid involving *R. catawbiense* and var. *album, R. dichroanthum* ssp. *scyphocalyx, R. fortunei* ssp. *discolor, R. campylocarpum, R. kyawii,* and *R. maximum*) is densely compact, to 1.2 m/4 ft high and broader, with dark green leaves, remaining on the plant for 3 years, and large (2.75 in./7 cm) flowers with deep cherry-red edges and ivory to light yellow centers, in clusters of 14, opening in middle to late spring.

'Weston's Pink Diamond,' an Ed Mezitt cross between a P.J.M. Hybrid and *R. mucronulatum* 'Cornell Pink,' is an upright shrub, to at least 1.5 m/5 ft tall, with glossy yellow-green foliage,

most turning red-orange to yellow and falling during the winter, but some persisting, mahogany-purple, until late winter, and purplish-pink flowers with silvery white centers, in globose clusters of 8 to 12, in early spring. May exceed its reported cold-hardiness to Zone 6a.

Cultivars Useful in the Milder Half of ARS H2 (Zones 6b–8b)

'Anah Kruschke': see under *R. ponticum.*

'April Snow': see under *R. dauricum.*

'Baden-baden' (= 'Essex Scarlet,' a hybrid of *R. forrestii* and an unknown parent; crossed by Dietrich Hobbie in Oldenburg, Germany) is a vigorous but compact plant, to 0.6 m/2 ft high and 1.2–1.5 m/4–5 ft wide, with glossy dark green, 5-cm/2-in., oval leaves and deep cherry-red, waxy, bell-shaped flowers, 5 cm/2 in. across, opening in midspring.

'Bali,' a Leach hybrid of *R. catawbiense* var. *album* by an unnamed hybrid involving *R. dichroanthum, R. fortunei* ssp. *discolor,* and *R. neriiflorum* is a compact, rounded plant, to 1.5–2 m/5–6.6 ft tall and wider, with a fine display of soft pink, 7-cm/2.7-in. flowers with creamy pale yellow centers, in clusters of 14 to 17, in middle to late spring.

'Blue Peter,' believed to be an *R. ponticum* hybrid of unknown pollen parent, is a moundlike shrub to 1.4 m/4.6 ft high and wider, with dark green foliage and light lavender-blue flowers with purple flares and frilled petal edges, in compact, pyramidal clusters of about 15, in midspring.

'Coral Velvet' is an *R. yakushimanum* hybrid of unknown pollen parent, growing to 0.75 m/2.5 ft high, with 5-cm/2-in. flowers, opening coral pink in early to middle spring, then fading to pale salmon.

'Crater's Edge': see under *R. mucronulatum.*

'Crete,' a hybrid of *R. smirnowii* × *R. yakushimanum,* is a large plant, to at least 2 m/6.6 ft tall and broader, with a dense mass of heavily felted (beneath) leaves and deep magenta flower buds that open to a pale purple and fading to white, in midspring.

'Cunningham's White,' a hybrid of *R. caucasicum* × *R. ponticum* var. *album,* grows to 1.2 m/4 ft high and at wide, 'with dense, dark green foliage, heavily felted underneath, and white flowers in middle to late spring.

'Doc' is a hybrid of *R. yakushimanum* by a hybrid of unknown origin, growing to 0.9 m/3 ft tall, with rose-pink flowers, 3.8 cm/1.5 in. across, in midspring.

'Dora Amateis,' a hybrid of *R. carolinianum* × *R. ciliatum*, is a fine semidwarf plant to 1 m/3.3 ft high and twice as wide, with dense, dark green, aromatic foliage and masses of 5 cm/2 in. white flowers, in clusters of 4–5, in early to middle spring.

'Golden Gala,' a hybrid of *R. catawbiense* and var. *album*, *R. wardii*, and *R. yakushimanum*, grows compactly to 1 m/3.3 ft high and wider, with glossy olive-green foliage and strong ivory (nearly yellow) flowers, to 6.4 cm/2.5 in. across, in clusters of 14, opening in middle to late spring.

'Hallelujah,' a hybrid involving *R. fortunei*, *R. griffithianum*, *R. williamsianum*, and some unknown parentage, is somewhat more cold-hardy than this parentage suggests, and a low shrub to 1.2 m/4 ft high, with heavily textured leaves and rose-red flowers of good substance, opening in midspring.

'Holden,' a Shammarello hybrid of 'Cunningham's White' by a red-flowered *R. catawbiense* hybrid, compact in habit, to 1.2 m/4 ft high and wider, with rose-red flowers, opening in early to middle spring.

'Janet Blair,' a Dexter hybrid of unknown parentage, is densely compact, to 1.8 m/6 ft high and greater width, with dark green foliage and frilled light pink flowers with paler centers, opening in middle to late spring.

'Ken Janeck' is a compact selection of the species, to 0.9 m/3 ft tall and twice as wide, with excellent dark green foliage, heavily felted underneath, and 6.4 cm/2.5 in. bright fuchsia-pink flowers, in clusters of about 15 in midspring.

'Koichiro Wada': selection of *R. yakushimanum*; see under that species.

'Laetevirens': see under *R. carolinianum*.

'Mahogany Red': see under *R. mucronulatum*.

'Marchioness of Lansdowne': see under *R. maximum*.

'Mars': see under *R. griffithianum*.

'Mary Fleming,' hybrid of *R. racemosum* × *R. keiskei*, is a well-shaped plant to 1 m/3.3 ft high and at least as wide, with narrow, bright green, pointed leaves, bronzing lightly in winter, and abundant yellow flowers, edged and streaked with pink, giving an overall impression of peachy salmon, opening in early spring.

'Mayflower': selection of *R. mucronulatum*; see under that species.

'Merley Cream,' an unusually cold-hardy Dexter hybrid of unknown parentage, grows to 1.5 m/5 ft, with light cream flowers, with greenish blotch, opening in midspring.

'Midsummer': selection of *R. maximum*; see under that species.

'Olin O. Dobbs,' a hybrid of 'Mars' by 'Purple Splendour,' is compact in growth habit, like 'Mars,' to 1.2 m/4 ft high, with very heavy and waxy deep reddish purple 6.4-cm/2.5-in. flowers, in domed clusters of 12–15, opening in midspring.

'Parker's Pink' originated as a Dexter seedling of unknown parentage, possibly with a contribution from *R. fortunei*. It is one of the most cold-hardy Dexter rhododendrons, with large (8.8 cm/3.5 in.) strong bright pink flowers with red spotting and white centers, opening in middle to late spring.

'Pride of Split Rock': see under *R. racemosum*.

'Radiant Pink': selection of *R. mucronulatum*; see under that species.

'Scarlet Wonder,' a hybrid of 'Essex Scarlet' (a cultivar of uncertain parentage and seldom used other than as a breeding parent) by *R. forrestii*, is a compact, vigorous plant, growing to 0.6 m/2 ft high while spreading to twice that, with bell-shaped, wavy-edged bright red flowers, opening in midspring.

'Scintillation' is an unusually cold-hardy Dexter hybrid, of unknown parentage, growing to 1.5 m/5 ft high and wider, with distinctively waxy and shiny foliage, and pastel pink flowers with golden bronze centers, in large trusses of 15, opening in midspring.

'Sumatra,' a Leach hybrid involving *R. catawbiense*, *R. forrestii* 'Repens,' *R. ponticum*, and a sizable unknown complement, grows to about 0.6 m/2 ft high and more than twice as wide, with dense yellow-green foliage and cardinal-red, 6.5-cm/2.6-in. flowers, in clusters of 8–10, opening in midspring.

'Vinecrest,' a Canadian hybrid involving *R. wardii*, *R. catawbiense*, and *R. fortunei*, is a compact plant, growing to about 1 m/3.3 ft high and wide, with olive-green foliage and peach-colored flower buds that open light greenish yellow in clusters of 12, in midspring.

'Yaku Angel': selection of *R. yakushimanum;* see under that species.

'Yaku Dutchess' is a hybrid of 'King Tut' (a Catawbiense hybrid) by *R. yakushimanum* 'Koichiro Wada,' created by Tony Shammarello and growing to 1.2 m/4 ft tall, with red flower buds, opening to deep pink 5.6-cm/2.2-in. flowers in midspring, fading to a paler pink.

'Yaku Prince,' a Shammarello selection of the same parentage as 'Yaku Dutchess,' is upright and rounded, to 0.9 m/3 ft tall and at least as wide, with narrow olive green leaves showing orange-yellow felting underneath, and 6.4 cm/ 2.5 in. purplish-pink flowers with lighter centers, in clusters of about 14, opening in midspring.

'Yaku Princess,' another Shammarello selection of the same parentage as 'Yaku Dutchess' and 'Yaku Prince,' has somewhat longer leaves and apple-blossom pink flowers and a pinker blotch, fading to light pink, in clusters of about 15, opening in midspring.

'Yaku Queen' is yet another Shammarello introduction, from the same parentage as the three other "Yaku" hybrids listed just above, with pale pink flowers, fading to white, in clusters of about 15, opening in midspring.

Cultivars Useful in the Colder Half of ARS H-3 (Zones 7a–8b)

'Barto Alpine': see under *R. lapponicum.*

'Blue Jay': see *R. ponticum.*

'Carolina Rose': see under *R. carolinianum.*

'Chesapeake,' a G. G. Nearing hybrid of *R. pubescens* by *R. keiskei,* growing to 0.9 m/3 ft high, with small leaves and apricot flowers, fading to white, opening in early to middle spring.

'Chionoides': see under *R. ponticum.*

'Donna Totten': see under *R. racemosum.*

'Forrest': see under *R. racemosum.*

'Grumpy' is an *R. yakushimanum* hybrid of unknown pollen parent, growing to 0.9 m/3 ft tall and broader than tall, and creamy flowers, tinged pink, in midspring.

'Hoppy' is an *R. yakushimanum* hybrid with input from unknown sources, growing to 0.9 m/

3 ft tall, with green-speckled white flowers in large globose clusters, in midspring.

'Josephine Everitt': see under *R. fortunei.*

'Oudijke's Sensation,' a hybrid involving *R. fastigiatum* and two closely related species, *R. augustinii* and *R. intricatum,* is similar to 'Blue Diamond' (see below), but with small violet flowers, and reported to be slightly more cold hardy.

'Patty Bee,' hybrid of *R. keiskei* 'Yaku Fairy' and *R. fletcherianum,* is well-branched, growing to 1.5 m/5 ft high, and somewhat wider, with 5 cm/2 in. yellow flowers in clusters of 6, opening in early to middle spring.

'Pink Panther': selection of *R. mucronulatum;* see under that species.

'Pride of Split Rock': see under *R. racemosum.*

'Purple Splendour': see under *R. ponticum.*

'Todmorden,' a Dexter hybrid released by the Scott Foundation, Swarthmore College, grows to 1.5 m/5 ft high and wide, with large flowers, deep purplish pink on the margins shading to much lighter centers, fading to white, in midspring.

'Variegatum': selection of *R. ponticum;* see under that species.

'White Lace': selection of *R. racemosum;* see under that species.

'Yaku Angel': selection of *R. yakushimanum;* see under that species.

'Yaku Fairy': selection of *R. keiskei;* see under that species.

'Yaku Sunrise,' a hybrid of 'Vulcan's Flame' and *R. yakushimanum* 'Koichiro Wada,' is low-growing, to 0.6 m/2 ft tall and 0.9 m/3 ft wide, with 0.7-cm/2.75-in. open bell-shaped rose flowers with darker edges, in compact clusters of about ten.

Cultivars Useful in the Milder Half of ARS H-3 (USDA Zones 7b–8b)

'Betty Hume': see under *R. fortunei.*

'Blue Diamond,' a hybrid involving *R. fastigiatum* and two closely related species, *R. augustinii* and *R. intricatum,* grows to about 1 m/3.3 ft high and wide, with large numbers of small, bright blue flowers all along the stems, opening in early to middle spring.

'Dexter's Giant Red,' a hybrid of unknown

parentage, grows to 2 m/6.6 ft high and wide, with large leaves and flowers to 10 cm/4 in. across, orange-red at first, fading to reddish pink, with dark red blotch, in clusters of up to 15, opening in late spring.

'Dexter's Spice,' a hybrid of unknown parentage, grows to 2 m/6.6 ft high, with good habit and glossy foliage and very large (10–13 cm/4–5 in.), fragrant, wavy-edged white flowers in clusters of seven, opening in midspring.

'Donna Totten': see under *R. racemosum*.

'Forrest': see under *R. racemosum*.

'Gartendirektor Rieger,' a hybrid of *R. williamsianum, R. campylocarpum, R. catawbiense, R. griffithianum*, and an unknown parent, has the unusual leaves of *R. williamsianum* and is vigorous but lower, to 1 m/3.3 ft high, with quantities of creamy white flowers, with red dot, opening in early to middle spring.

'Grace Seabrook,' a hybrid of *R. strigillosum, R. griffithianum*, and an unknown parent, is compact and spreading, to 1.5 m/5 ft wide and broader, with very large dark green leaves and bright red flowers with deeper red centers, 7.6 cm/3 in. across, in tight clusters, opening in early to middle spring.

'Halfdan Lem,' a mixed hybrid of *R. fortunei, R. griffithianum*, and an unknown parent, grows vigorously to at least 1.5 m/5 ft high, with deep green 20 cm/8 in. leaves and bright red flowers, 8.9 cm/3.5 in. across, in clusters of 13, opening in midspring.

'Lady Clementine Mitford': see under *R. maximum*.

'Mrs. W. R. Coe' is either a selection of *R. fortunei* or a hybrid of that species by an unknown pollen parent, growing vigorously to 1.8 m/6 ft high, with large (10 cm/4 in.) bright pink flowers, with crimson centers, opening in middle to late spring. Useful in Zones 7b–8b and probably also Zone 7a.

'Night Editor': selection of *R. russatum*; see under that species.

'Old Copper,' a Van Veen hybrid between 'Vulcan' and a hybrid of *R. dichroanthum × R. griersonianum*, growing upright to 1.5 m/5 ft, with long, dark green leaves and large, bell-shaped flowers of a unique copper color, in large trusses, very late in the blooming season. Notably heat-resistant.

'Pink Cherub,' a hybrid of *R. yakushimanum* and 'Doncaster,' is a cultivar of unknown parentage, growing to 0.7 m/2.3 ft tall and twice as wide, with white flowers, flushed light red-purple. Useful in Zones 7b and Zone 8 where summers are moderate.

'Princess Anne' (= 'Golden Fleece'), a hybrid of *R. hanceanum × R. keiskei*, is a very compact plant, to only 0.6 m/2 ft high and wider, with good foliage, bronzing in winter in cooler climates, and large numbers of yellow, bell-shaped 7-cm/2.8-in. flowers with a slight green cast, in clusters of 8, opening in early to middle spring.

'Shamrock,' an R. L. Ticknor hybrid between dwarf forms of *R. keiskei* and *R. hanceanum*, grows to only 0.5 m/1.6 in. high but more than twice as wide, with bright green foliage and 2.5-cm/1-in., funnel-shaped chartreuse flowers with yellow spotting, in clusters of about 8, opening in early to middle spring, in time for St. Patrick's Day.

'Taurus,' a hybrid of the same parentage as 'Grace Seabrook,' is vigorous and full in habit, to 2 m/6.6 ft tall, with deep green, pointed leaves and 9-cm/3.5-in. red bell-shaped flowers, opening in early to middle spring.

'Treasure,' a hybrid of *R. forrestii × R. williamsianum*, is a rounded shrub to 0.6 m/2 ft high and wider, with rounded dark green leaves, bronzed when young, and nodding, bell-shaped deep rose flowers, 5 cm/2 in. across, opening in early to middle spring.

'Unique,' a hybrid of *R. campylocarpum* and an unknown pollen parent, grows compactly to 1.2 m/4 ft high and slightly wider, with rich green oblong leaves and bright pink flower buds, opening a buttery cream color, flushed with pink at first, in large clusters that cover the plant in early to middle spring.

'Vivacious,' a Roy Forster cross of 'America' × 'Doctor Ross,' a complex hybrid involving *R. arboreum, R. griersonianum, R. griffithianum*, and at least two unknown parents, is rounded in habit, to 1.2 m/4 ft high and wider, with medium green leaves and 6.4-cm/2.5-in. medium cardinal red flowers, in globose clusters of 10 or more, opening in middle to late spring.

'Vulcan' and 'Vulcan's Flame': see under *R. griffithianum*.

'White Lace': see under *R. racemosum*.

Cultivars Useful in the Colder Half of ARS H-4 (Zones 8a–8b)

'Bridal Bouquet' is a selection of unknown origin, thought by some specialists to be a hybrid of *R. yakushimanum* because of its growth habit, even though its leaves are not felted. It grows to 0.9 m/3 ft tall and has yellow flowers with a peach-colored edging, opening in midspring.

'Cream Crest,' a hybrid of *R. ciliatum*, *R. moupinense*, and *R. rupicola* var. *chryseum*, grows compactly to about 1 m/3.3 ft high, with sun-tolerant foliage and bright creamy yellow, cup-shaped, 2.5 cm/1 in. flowers.

'Elizabeth,' a hybrid of *R. forrestii* × *R. griersonianum*, grows compactly to 1 m/3.3 ft high, and wider, with dark green foliage and bright red, bell-shaped, 9-cm/3.5-in. flowers, in clusters of 6–8, opening in early to middle spring.

'Golden Star,' a hybrid of *R. fortunei* × *R. wardii*, grows to 1.5 m/5 ft high and wide, with elliptical leaves and 7.6-cm/3-in. soft yellow flowers, in clusters of 7, opening in midspring.

'King George': selection from *R. ×loderi*; see under *R. griffithianum*.

'Loder's White' is a hybrid of questionable parentage; *R. griffithianum* as one parent is well-accepted, but there is disagreement whether *R. arboreum* or *R. maximum* is also involved. Its hardiness, only to Zone 8a, does not suggest much input from the hardy *R. maximum*. This plant grows compactly to 1.5 m/5 ft, with large leaves and slightly fragrant pink-edged white flowers, fading to white, opening in midspring. It is notably heat-resistant.

'Mardi Gras,' a hybrid of *R. yakushimanum* 'Koichiro Wada' × 'Vanessa,' a mixed hybrid of *R. griersonianum*, *R. fortunei*, and *R. souliei*, grows to 0.76 m/2.5 ft high, and wider, with heavily reddish brown-felted, dark green foliage, and pale pink flowers, fading to white, with deeper pink margins and outsides of the flowers, in globose clusters of 11–12, opening in early to middle spring.

'Pink Diamond': selection from *R. ×loderi*; see under *R. griffithianum*.

'Sir Edmund': selection from *R. ×loderi*; see under *R. griffithianum*.

'Venus': selection from *R. ×loderi*, see under *R. griffithianum*.

'Virginia Richards', a complex hybrid involving *R. campylocarpum*, *R. catawbiense*, *R. griersonianum*, *R. griffithianum*, *R. neriiflorum*, *R. wardii*, and an unknown complement, grows compactly to 1.2 m/4 ft high, with dark, glossy leaves and very large flowers (11.5 cm/4.5 in.), in clusters of 12, opening light yellow in midspring with a pink blush and crimson blotch, fading to a paler yellow, with an overall effect of apricot or peach.

Cultivars More Tender Than the Above

Some rhododendron cultivars are cold-hardy only in the mildest parts of Zone 8b or even Zones 9 or 10. In our area, climates this mild in winter are usually too hot for rhododendrons in summer. Before specifying rhododendron cultivars for use along the Gulf and southern Atlantic coasts, it is best to observe local experience and consult local rhododendron specialists. The cultivars in this list are a fraction of the number that are available in our area, and many others may be equally useful, if available. New cultivars appear regularly, and some of them will be improvements over old ones. Likewise, availability is constantly changing.

Rhodotypos scandens 4

Synonyms: *R. kerrioides, R. tetrapetala*
JETBEAD
Deciduous shrub
Rosaceae (Rose Family)

Native Range.   China and Japan.

Useful Range.   USDA Zones 5a–8a and areas in Zone 8b having moderate summers.

Function.   Border, massing, foundation.

Size and Habit

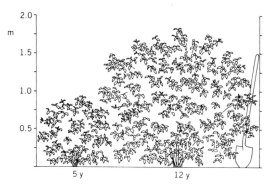

Rhodotypos scandens.

Adaptability

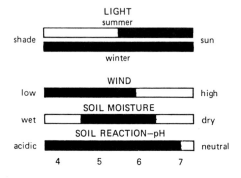

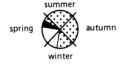

Seasonal Interest.   *Flowers:* Single, white, 3 cm/1.2 in. across, moderately showy in combination with the handsome foliage. *Foliage:* Dark green, prominently veined and sharply toothed leaves, 5–8 cm/2–3 in. long, provide distinctively crisp texture and fall in autumn with little color change. *Fruits:* Shiny, black, beadlike fruits, 0.5 cm/0.2 in. across, produced in clusters usually of four at the twig ends, persist after the leaves fall and through much of the winter, adding quiet interest during part of the leafless season.

Problems and Maintenance.   A twig-blight disease occasionally becomes troublesome but can be controlled by pruning off and burning infected stems. Otherwise pruning is necessary only to promote vigor and fullness in older plants, and overall need for maintenance is minimal.

Related Species

Neviusia alabamensis 4 (snow-wreath). This close relative of *Rhodotypos*, native to Alabama, is planted occasionally in the mid-South for its display of masses of white flowers with many stamens, giving a feathery appearance about the same time as the flowering of *Rhodotypos*. It has little other seasonal interest but is a good neutral plant for the shrub border or naturalizing in Zones 6b–8b.

Neviusia alabamensis.

Rhus aromatica 4–5

FRAGRANT SUMAC
Deciduous shrub
Anacardiaceae (Cashew Family)

Native Range.   Eastern United States and adjacent Canada.

Useful Range.   USDA Zones 3b–9a.

Function.   Border, massing, foundation, large-scale groundcover (low forms).

Size and Habit

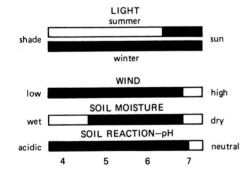

Rhus aromatica.

Adaptability

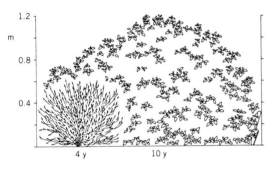

Seasonal Interest.   *Flowers:* Small, pale yellow, in terminal clusters 0.5–2 cm/0.2–0.8 in. long, not showy but fairly conspicuous because they appear before the leaves unfold in early to middle spring. *Foliage:* Softly hairy, trifoliate leaves, aromatic when crushed, with leaflets 2.5–8 cm/ 1–3 in. long, soft green as they unfold, then lustrous deep green in summer, turning orange to scarlet in autumn, at least in some forms in light soils. *Fruits:* Red, rounded, and hairy, about 0.6 cm/0.25 in. across, adding quiet interest in late summer.

Problems and Maintenance.   Leaf spot and mildew can be minor problems, but generally this plant is trouble-free. Pruning is necessary every few years for renewal and maintenance of vigor.

Rhus aromatica.

Varieties and Cultivars.   Var. *serotina,* ranging naturally from Indiana to Texas, differs from the species type in flowering later and in its height, frequently to almost 2 m/6.6 ft. It does not seem to color as reliably in autumn as the lower species type, but holds its deep green foliage rather late. The species type is usually preferred in landscape use, since its lower stature, to about 1 m/3.3 ft, is frequently more useful, except for the uncertainty of finding it. The following selections help to solve that problem.

'Green Globe' is upright and rounded, to 1.5 m/5 ft high and wide, but perhaps no longer available.

'Gro-low' is a low, spreading form that remains below 0.6 m/2 ft for years and is an excellent large-scale groundcover.

Related Species

Rhus trilobata 4–5 (ill-scented sumac, skunk-bush). This shrub, native from Illinois westward to California, is seldom intentionally planted but sometimes inadvertently offered as *R. aromatica*. Although it is essentially interchangeable with *R. aromatica*, it is usually more stiffly upright and not as functional as a groundcover. This plant is useful in the same zones as *R. aromatica* but is seldom available in our area.

Rhus aromatica.

Toxicodendron radicans 1–2 (synonym: *Rhus radicans*; poison ivy) and *Toxicodendron pubescens* 2–3 (synonym: *Rhus toxicodendron*; poison oak), both with three-leaflet leaves, are poisonous to touch, strongly so to many persons. In spite of their fine red-orange autumn foliage color, they obviously should be avoided.

Rhus copallina 5–6

SHINING SUMAC
Deciduous shrub
Anacardiaceae (Cashew Family)

Native Range. Eastern United States and parts of adjacent Canada: Maine to Florida and westward to Ontario, Minnesota, and Texas.

Useful Range. USDA Zones 4b–9a.

Function. Border, specimen, large-scale massing.

Size and Habit

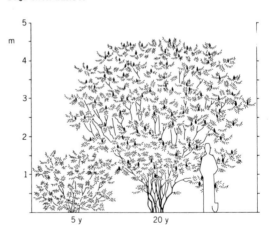

Rhus copallina.

Adaptability

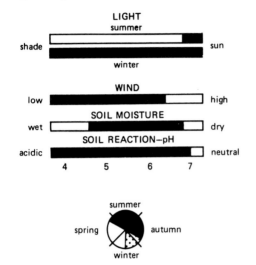

Seasonal Interest. *Flowers:* Pale yellowish green in dense, erect, terminal clusters to 15 cm/ 6 in. long, fairly conspicuous against the dark green foliage in late summer. Dioecious. *Foliage:* Glossy, dark green, pinnately compound with 9–12 leaflets, each up to 10 cm/4 in. long, more striking in summer than that of most *Rhus* species, with a distinctive winged rachis (leaf midrib), turning bright scarlet in autumn. *Fruits:* Crimson, fuzzy, in compact clusters to at least 10 cm/4 in. long, on pistillate (female) plants only, colorful in autumn and into winter.

Problems and Maintenance. Diseases and physical damage to the weak wood make this plant relatively short-lived, but this is not a serious problem in large-scale and naturalized plantings where root suckers tend to renew the tops. Maintenance requirements are similar to those of *R. typhina.*

Related Species

Rhus chinensis 6 (Chinese sumac). This plant in time becomes treelike, with creamy white flowers in upright clusters to 25 cm/10 in. long in middle to late summer and orange-red foliage and fruiting clusters in autumn. Useful in Zones 6a–9a.

Toxicodendron vernix 6 (synonym: *Rhus vernix*; poison sumac). This native of swamps from New England to Florida and westward to Minnesota and Louisiana is as poisonous to the touch as it is handsome, and so it must be avoided rather than planted.

Rhus copallina.

Rhus typhina 6

STAGHORN SUMAC
Deciduous shrub
Anacardiaceae (Cashew Family)

Native Range. Eastern United States and parts of adjacent Canada, Quebec to Georgia and westward to Iowa.

Useful Range. USDA Zones 3b–8a.

Function. Border, specimen, large-scale massing.

Size and Habit

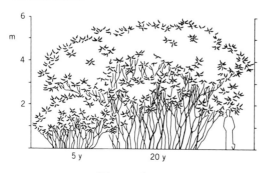

Rhus typhina.

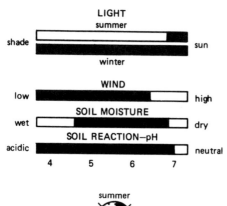

Rhus typhina, pistillate inflorescence.

Adaptability

Rhus typhina, staminate inflorescence.

Seasonal Interest. *Flowers:* Greenish in dense, erect, terminal clusters to 20 cm/8 in. long, not very conspicuous because of their color. Dioecious. *Foliage:* Medium green, velvety and hairy when young, pinnately compound with 11–31 leaflets, each up to 10 cm/4 in. long, producing strikingly coarse texture in the landscape and turning to brilliant shades of orange and red in autumn. *Fruits:* Crimson, fuzzy, in erect, clublike clusters to 15 cm/6 in. long on pistillate (female) plants only, colorful from late summer into early winter. *Twigs:* velvety and hairy twigs add mild winter interest. Those bearing the staminate (male) flower clusters after the flowers are gone resemble velvety antlers, giving the plant its common name.

Problems and Maintenance. Stem cankers and branch dieback cause this plant to be rela-

Rhus typhina.

tively short-lived. This is usually compensated for in large-scale and naturalized plantings by the tendency to produce new tops by suckering. But *R. typhina, R. copallina,* and *R. glabra* as well should be used in intensive situations only if careful maintenance is provided, particularly pruning to remove deadwood and to select some root suckers for renewal and eliminating others.

Cultivars. 'Dissecta' has finely dissected, fern-like leaves and is valued as a specimen for accent in highly architectonic planting situations. It tends to be ineffective when planted with many other plant materials but is striking against wall and window surfaces with gravel mulch.

Related Species

Rhus glabra 6 (smooth sumac).   This relative of *R. typhina* ranges even more widely, from Maine to Florida and westward to British Columbia and Texas. It differs little from *R. typhina* in general appearance but has smooth twigs and brighter red fruits. It is useful in much the same ways as *R. typhina* in a slightly larger part of our area: Zones 3a–9a. The cutleaved selection 'Laciniata' gives a similar effect as *R. typhina* 'Dissecta,' but it is less likely to be available in our area and is highly susceptible to mildew in some areas.

Ribes alpinum 5

ALPINE CURRANT
Deciduous shrub
Glossulariaceae (Currant Family)

Native Range.   Europe.

Useful Range.   USDA Zones 3b–7b.

Function.   Hedge, massing, border.

Size and Habit

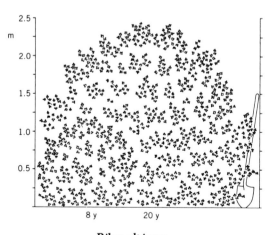

Ribes alpinum.

Adaptability. Even though growth is most compact and suitable for hedging in full sun, the plant will perform relatively well in considerable shade.

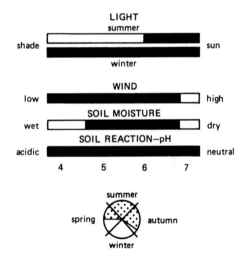

Seasonal Interest. *Flowers:* Greenish yellow, small and not showy, in midspring with the emerging leaves. Dioecious. *Foliage:* Lobed leaves, 2.5–5 cm/1–2 in. long, pale green as they emerge in midspring, turning deep green in summer and falling without color change in autumn. *Fruits:* Scarlet, small, in late summer, on pistillate (female) plants in the presence of staminate plants—an infrequent occurrence since plants in commerce usually are propagated by cuttings and therefore are clonal and of a single sex.

Problems and Maintenance. Several diseases can be minor problems, but *R. alpinum* is much less troubled by disease than most *Ribes* species (currants and gooseberries). The most serious concern when members of this genus are planted is white pine blister rust, for which many currants and gooseberries are alternate hosts and are quarantined from eastern white pine *(Pinus strobus)* habitat areas by federal regulation. *R. alpinum*, even though immune to the disease, is under quarantine and cannot be planted legally in white pine areas. Many of the western and southern parts of our area are outside the range of white pine, and *R. alpinum* does well in such areas having hot dry summers, except that mite infestations are more likely to be severe.

Cultivars. 'Green Mound' is semidwarf but faster growing than 'Pumilum', with glossy, bright green foliage, growing to 1–1.2 m/3.3–4 ft high and wide.

'Pumilum' (dwarf alpine currant) is very compact and slow growing, but reaches 1 m/3.3 ft in height and width in time, slightly taller in shade.

Related Species

Ribes aureum 4 (golden currant). This western North American counterpart of the clove currant *(R. odoratum)* is so similar that it is interchangeable in landscape use in Zones 3b–7b, and *R. aureum* is also hardy in Zone 3a.

Ribes odoratum 4 (clove currant, buffalo currant). This species, native to the Great Plains region of the United States from South Dakota to Texas, bears golden yellow flowers with a delicious clove fragrance. The plant is susceptible to premature defoliation by leaf-spot diseases and has minimal landscape character, but it might be included in a mixed shrub border for the spring flowering interest outside white pine areas. Useful in Zones 3b–7b.

Ribes sanguineum 5 (red-flowering currant). This native of the Coast Ranges of the Pacific Northwest is the most ornamental species of *Ribes* in bloom, with red to pink or white flowers. It is probably cold-hardy to Zone 6b, but may not be well adapted to the eastern United States, judging from the fact that is very seldom seen. Cultivars include 'Claremont,' a California selection with deep shell-pink flowers; 'Elk River Red,' tall-growing, with rich red flowers; 'King Edward VII', lower growing, very showy with rose-red flowers; and 'White Icicle,' with pure white flowers, a University of British Columbia Botanical Garden introduction.

Many other species of *Ribes* exist, several of them native to North America, but most have little landscape value in our area.

Robinia hispida 4

ROSE ACACIA
Deciduous shrub
Fabaceae (Leguminosae; Pea Family)

Native Range. Southeastern United States.

Useful Range. USDA Zones 4b–9a.

Function. Thickets: naturalizing or massing, specimen (with maintenance).

Size and Habit

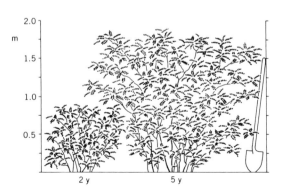

Robinia hispida.

Adaptability

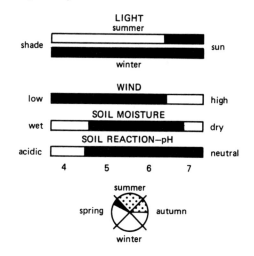

Seasonal Interest.
Flowers: Rose to lavender-pink, in showy, pendulous clusters, to 8 cm/3 in. long, in late spring. *Foliage:* pinnately compound leaves with 7–13 leaflets, each to 3.5 cm/1.4 in. long, falling in midautumn without color change. *Fruits:* Bristle-covered pods add minor interest in late summer to early autumn, seldom contain viable seeds. *Twigs and branches:* Young twigs usually are densely bristled like the pods, except in var. *fertilis* (below).

Problems and Maintenance.
The strong tendency of this shrub to sucker and form thickets makes it an ideal plant for slope stabilization, but it is difficult to keep in bounds in other landscape situations, where its use must be accompanied by a careful program to remove unwanted root suckers.

Varieties and Hybrids.
The var. *fertilis* differs from the species type in that its stems are sparsely bristled or not at all (pods are bristled), and its leaflets are somewhat narrower. Otherwise it is interchangeable with the species type.

Robinia pseudoacacia 8

BLACK LOCUST
Deciduous tree
Fabaceae (Leguminosae; Pea Family)

Native Range. East-central United States from Pennsylvania to Georgia and westward to Iowa and Oklahoma. Naturalized over most of the rest of our area, as well as in Europe.

Useful Range. USDA Zones 4b–9a and some sites in Zone 4a.

Function. Shade tree, specimen, naturalizing.

Size and Habit

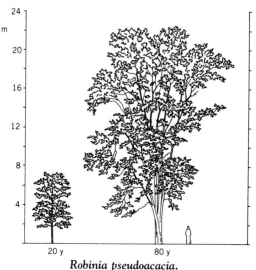

Robinia pseudoacacia.

Adaptability. Grows well in infertile soils because of its ability to assimilate atmospheric nitrogen with the help of bacteria in its roots.

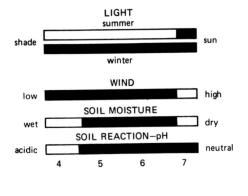

Seasonal Interest. *Flowers:* Creamy white, very fragrant, in pendulous clusters 10–20 cm/ 4–8 in. long, very late in spring. *Foliage:* Very dark green, compound with rounded leaflets only 2.5–5 cm/1–2 in. long, casting mottled shade and falling in autumn without color change. *Trunk and branches:* Heavy, gray, ropy bark adds mild but distinctive year-round interest.

Problems and Maintenance. Trunk borers are a serious problem that must be controlled by carefully timed spraying to prevent serious and permanent damage, even though infested trees often grow vigorously for some time before becoming seriously weakened. Wood rotting organisms may complicate the situation by invading the borer tunnels and hastening the decline of the tree. A leaf miner insect sometimes disfigures the foliage and the tree produces root suckers, but these are minor problems in comparison with borers.

Cultivars. 'Frisia' is a remarkable color accent as its new foliage unfolds bright yellow and holds its color through the growing season. It is upright and open in habit, not as large as the species type, a more dependable alternative to *Gleditsia triacanthos* 'Sunburst,' useful at least in Zones 5b–9a, perhaps colder areas as well.

'Umbraculifera' (umbrella black locust) has a densely globose head while young, gradually assuming a more umbrellalike shape with age, growing to only about 5 m/16 ft tall, and probably never flowering. Useful at least in Zones 5a–9a.

Related Hybrids and Species

Robinia ×ambigua 6–7. This hybrid of *R. pseudoacacia* × *R. viscosa* includes the selection 'Purple Robe,' which grows to 10–12 m/33–40 ft tall, with a compact, rounded head and rosy purple flowers very late in spring. Useful in Zones 4b–9a. The selection 'Idaho' (= 'Idahoensis') is very similar to 'Purple Robe' with flowers as showy as the best of *R. pseudoacacia* except rosy purplish pink, showy very late in spring. This cultivar is a popular small to medium-sized tree in the Great Plains and Rocky Mountains, in Zones 4b–9a, and may be assigned to *R. ×margarettiae*.

Robinia × margarettiae 5–6. This hybrid of *R. hispida* × *R. pseudoacacia* is treelike, to 5 m/16 ft tall, with strongly bristled twigs and bright rosy-purple flowers in showy, pendulous clusters to 15–20 cm/6–8 in. long. In humid climates, it grows rapidly and is open and weak-wooded and, like *R. hispida*, is somewhat invasive unless grafted on a nonsuckering rootstock such as *R. pseudoacacia*. Useful in Zones 4b–9a, but seldom available.

Robinia viscosa 7 (clammy locust). This native of the southern Appalachian Mountains, naturalized elsewhere in the southeastern United States as well, has pink flowers and is usually encountered in landscape use in the form of the hybrid *R. ×ambigua*. It is useful in Zones 4b–9a.

Rosa ×*centifolia* 4

CABBAGE ROSE
Deciduous shrub
Rosaceae (Rose Family)

Hybrid Origin.   Parentage is believed to include *R. gallica, R. moschata, R. canina, R. damascena,* and perhaps others.

Useful Range.   USDA Zones 5b–9a.

Function.   Specimen, border.

Size and Habit

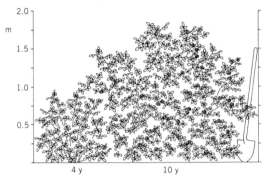

Rosa ×*centifolia.*

Adaptability

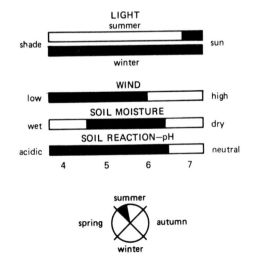

Seasonal Interest.   *Flowers:* Fragrant, very double, nodding because of their weight, 4–8 cm/1.5–3 in. across, in early summer with little or no rebloom. *Foliage:* Compound, medium green, adding only minor summer interest, falling in autumn with little color change. *Fruits:* Rose hips are borne sparsely and add little interest.

Problems and Maintenance.   Roses in general require minimal to considerable maintenance because of their susceptibility to a variety of disease and pest problems, including black spot, mildew, crown gall, cankers, rose chafer, Japanese beetle (within the range of this insect), leaf hoppers, scale insects, mites, and others. Those that are considered to be functional landscape plants require less maintenance than the so-called garden roses that are grown primarily for flowers rather than function. *R.* ×*centifolia* and its hybrids have been grown as garden subjects for centuries. For this use they have been superseded by better flowering Hybrid Tea and Floribunda cultivars, their principal usefulness today stemming from their functional value and historical interest. They surpass the modern garden roses functionally, but they do not compare well with some of the other species roses in this respect or in breadth of seasonal interest or freedom from troubles.

Cultivars.   Because of a revival of interest in "antique" roses, a greater number of older rose cultivars are available than were a decade or two ago. Only a few are "landscape roses" in the sense that they function as screens, dividers, or in other architectural ways, and not all are resistant to insects and diseases. Probably not more than a dozen *R.* ×*centifolia* cultivars are available at any one time; a few of the best known are listed here: 'Cristata' (crested moss rose) has flowers surrounded by a conspicuous green fringe of sepals. 'Muscosa' (moss rose) is distinctive for its "mossy-surfaced" flower stalks and receptacles. 'Muscosa Alba' has white flowers. These three cultivars seldom grow higher than 1 m/3.3 ft., and have a single season of bloom, but that can last for up to two months under optimal conditions.

Related Species

Rosa ×*alba* 4 (cottage rose).   This hybrid group of uncertain origin but believed to have involved

R. canina and *R. damascena* includes several cultivars with fragrant flowers, usually double and pink, in spite of the implication of the species name, but including a few good white selections such as 'Madame Legras de St. Germain,' with double white flowers. Members of this group are useful in Zones 5a–9a.

Rose canina 5 (dog rose).   This native of Europe has been widely used as an understock for other rose cultivars and has some interest and usefulness of its own. It will function as an informal hedge, dense enough for screening under ideal growing conditions, with fragrant, single, pink or white flowers, about 4 cm/1.6 in. across, in early summer and ornamental red fruits later in summer. Useful in Zones 5a–9a and as a somewhat lower shrub (to about 1 m/3.3 ft), owing to winter injury, in Zone 4.

Rosa ×*damascena* 4 (damask rose).   This hybrid of *R. gallica* and *R. moschata* has been cultivated in Europe and Asia Minor for centuries. It has fragrant, double, pink to red flowers, as large as those of *R.* ×*centifolia,* and is adapted to Zones 6a–9a, but its landscape usefulness is limited. The var. *semperflorens* (four seasons rose) differs only in having a second flowering season in late summer or autumn. 'Versicolor' (York and Lancaster rose) has flowers varying from white to pink through different degrees of striping and blotching, and was designated as a symbol of unity of the red and white rose factions at the end of the War of the Roses in the fifteenth century.

Rosa gallica 3 (French rose).   This long-cultivated native of central and southern Europe and western Asia suckers freely, forming thickets. It has limited usefulness as a landscape plant but was an important forerunner of the Hybrid Perpetual roses from which modern garden roses were developed. With single or double, pink to red-purple flowers to 7 cm/2.8 in. across in early summer followed by brick-red fruits, *R. gallica* can be used where its thicket-forming growth is

appropriate, in Zones 5a–9a and some cultivars also in Zone 4. The ancient selection, 'Officinalis' (apothecary's rose, red rose of Lancaster) has very fragrant, semidouble, rosy pink flowers, borne singly or in clusters in early summer. 'Rosa Mundi' (= 'Versicolor'), a genetic sport of 'Officinalis' (not to be confused with *R.* ×*damascena* 'Versicolor'), has white striped, crimson flowers and remains well below 0.5 m/1.6 ft, making a fairly effective groundcover.

Rosa glauca 4–5 (synonym: *R. rubrifolia*; redleaf rose).   This native of the mountains of central Europe is valued for its bluish-green foliage, overlaid with dark red, its fragrant, small pink flowers, and its extreme cold-hardiness. It can be used for massing or for variety in a shrub border in Zones 2b–8a.

Rosa moschata 3 (musk rose).   This native of southern Europe, noted for the musky fragrance of its flowers, has little value as a landscape plant and is not very cold-hardy, useful in Zones 7a–9a and colder areas only with protection. It is a parent of many of the decorative roses, including the Hybrid Musk roses, some of which are reasonably functional but only slightly more cold-hardy than *R. moschata.*

Rosa rubiginosa 4 (synonym: *R. eglanteria*; sweetbrier rose).   This European native is widely grown there, as a climber or informal hedge. It is as well known for the apple-like fragrance of its foliage as for its bright pink flowers, in early summer, followed by red-orange fruits. Hybrids with pink, copper, red, and yellow flowers exist, most useful in Zones 5b–9a.

Rose villosa 4 (synonym: *R. pomifera*; apple rose). Another native of Europe and adjacent Asia, *R. villosa* functions much the same as *R. canina*, with single, pink flowers in early summer followed by unusually large (2.5 cm/1 in. across), red, pear-shaped hips (fruits). The f. *duplex* has semidouble flowers. It is useful in Zones 4b–9a.

Rosa laevigata 1 and 5

CHEROKEE ROSE
Evergreen or semievergreen shrub
Rosaceae (Rose Family)

Native Range. China; naturalized in the southern parts of our area from Florida to Texas.

Useful Range. USDA Zones 8a–9a+.

Function. Large-scale massing or barrier, climbing specimen, naturalizing.

Size and Habit. High-climbing, to 6 m/19 ft or more, or piling up in masses to 2–3 m/7–10 ft tall with a greater spread.

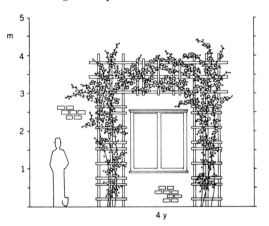

Rosa laevigata.

Adaptability

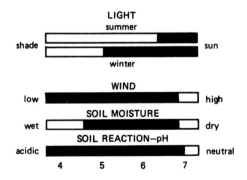

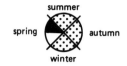

Seasonal Interest. *Flowers:* Fragrant, single, white, to 8 cm/3 in. across, showy in middle to late spring. *Foliage:* Semievergreen to evergreen, deep green and lustrous with medium texture, making an attractive but loose mass. *Fruits:* Orange-red, pear-shaped and bristly, to 4 cm/1.6 in. across, interesting in autumn and much of winter.

Problems and Maintenance. This plant is unusually free of troubles for a rose, but its vigor can be excessive in all but large-scale planting sites. Allow plenty of room, or pruning maintenance will be excessive.

Cultivars. Red- and pink-flowering selections are occasionally available but do not grow strongly and apparently are in little demand.

Related Species

Rosa bracteata 1 and 5 (Macartney rose). Like *R. laevigata*, this species originated in China and has become naturalized in the southern states. These two species are similarly wide-scrambling with arching branches, but *R. bracteata* has apple-scented flowers on first opening, blooming lightly after the first flush of flowering until frost, has finer-textured foliage than *R. laevigata*, and responds better to shearing. This species is useful in Zones 8a–9a+, perhaps in somewhat colder zones as well, but has become a serious weed problem, in parts of the South even more so than *R. multiflora*. The *R. bracteata* hybrid 'Mermaid,' with delicately buff-yellow flowers to 10 cm/4 in. across, is similar in size to *R. bracteata* and a superb plant for large-scale use. It is somewhat more cold-tolerant than *R. bracteata* and *R. laevigata*, useful to Zone 7 and perhaps colder zones as well with protection.

Rosa multiflora 5

JAPANESE OR MULTIFLORA ROSE
Deciduous shrub
Rosaceae (Rose Family)

Native Range.   Japan and Korea.

Useful Range.   USDA Zones 5b–9a.

Function.   Large-scale barrier hedge, specimen, wildlife cover.

Size and Habit

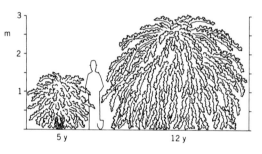

Rosa multiflora.

Adaptability

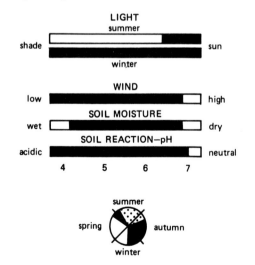

Seasonal Interest. *Flowers:* White, about 2 cm/0.8 in. across, in large clusters, fragrant and very showy in late spring or early summer, but without repeated flowering later in summer. *Foliage:* Lustrous, remaining deep green well into autumn before falling. *Fruits:* Bright red, individually no more than 0.6 cm/0.25 in. across, but borne in large numbers in clusters; colorful from early autumn to midwinter or later.

Rosa multiflora.

Problems and Maintenance.   This is one of the most vigorous and trouble-free of all roses. Underestimation of its size and vigor and resulting misuse have given *R. multiflora* a bad reputation. Because of its ultimate height of 4 m/13 ft or more and even greater spread, it should be used *only* in large-scale situations. *Note:* Legislation has been passed in some states making it illegal to plant this species, since in some areas it has escaped cultivation and has become a serious weed problem. Check with local authorities before specifying this plant.

Varieties and Cultivars.   The var. *cathayensis*, with single rosy pink flowers to 4 cm/1.6 in., in flattened clusters, is known but probably not available in our area.

'Grevillei' (= 'Platyphylla'; seven sisters rose) has single, multicolored flowers, from white to pink or deep rose-purple, fading individually within the same flower cluster.

'Nana' is a dwarf with fragrant, single flowers, ivory to pale pink, probably not available in our area.

R. multiflora is an important parent of modern garden roses, and was a common understock in the past, but is being replaced by own-root roses, propagated by cuttings or tissue culture.

Related Species

Rosa roxburghii 5 (chestnut or Roxburgh rose). This Chinese native is like no other shrub rose, with peeling, gray-tan bark that adds year-round interest, and clear, light lavender-pink flowers that open in early summer. Two forms are in cultivation. The species type, var. *roxburghii*, bears great quantities of double flowers, reblooms lightly, has few fruits, and is less vigorous and more tender than the single flowering type, useful in Zones 7a–9a. The wild type, named var. *normalis* after the double type had been named, does not flower heavily but is vigorous and useful in Zones 6b–9a. Fruits of both are reddish, to 4 cm/1.6 in. across, and very prickly, adding distinctive interest in autumn. Both forms are only occasionally available.

Rosa setigera 5 (prairie rose). This native of North America, from Ontario to Nebraska and southward to Florida and Texas, requires about as much space as *R. multiflora* but is different in growth habit, with very long canes arching out irregularly or climbing by scrambling where support is available. Although its form can be kept more regular by pruning, it is difficult to contain for long, so it is probably best to reserve this plant for large-scale, informal situations. Flowers, about 5 cm/2 in. across, open rose, fading to pale pink. Flowering is later than that of most roses, in early summer to midsummer, and some clones do not flower well at all. The red fruits, scarcely larger than those of *R. multiflora*, add moderate but unreliable interest in autumn. The foliage is not as handsome during summer as that of *R. multiflora*, but turns reddish orange before falling in autumn. Useful in Zones 4b–9a.

Rosa rugosa 4

RUGOSA ROSE
Deciduous shrub
Rosaceae (Rose Family)

Native Range. Japan, Korea, northern China; naturalized in some localities in the northeastern United States.

Useful Range. USDA Zones 3a–7b with selection of appropriate genetic material.

Function. Massing, specimen, border, informal hedge.

Size and Habit

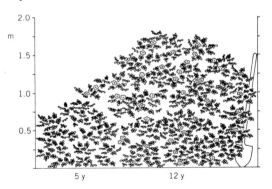

Rosa rugosa.

Adaptability. Grows best in exposed sites with full sun, except in Zone 3. It is not as tolerant of limestone soils as some other roses, but it is notably tolerant of salt, whether at the seashore or near winter-salted walks.

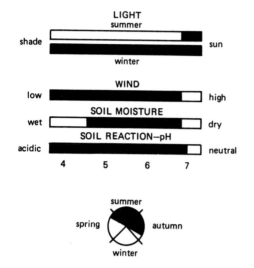

Seasonal Interest. *Flowers:* Rose-pink with a purplish cast to white, fragrant, single or double, to 8 cm/3 in. across, in late spring or early summer and continuing intermittently during the summer. *Foliage:* Deep green, leathery, and wrinkled, producing an outstanding textural effect, turning golden orange in late autumn in some years. *Fruits:* Very large, edible, orange-red hips, to 2.5 cm/1 in. across and showy in late summer and autumn; can be used for making tea and preserves, and are a very rich source of vitamin C (ascorbic acid). *Twigs and branches:* Heavy and very thorny.

Problems and Maintenance. R. rugosa is unusually trouble-free for a rose and usually needs pruning only to remove an occasional borer-infested cane or to give it a little more uniform shape in an informal hedge.

Cultivars and Hybrids. Many selections for cold climates have been made, and availability varies locally. See Rugosa Hybrids and Explorer Series, under Rose cultivars.

Related Species

Rosa acicularis 3 (circumpolar rose, prickly wild rose) and *Rosa arkansana* 3 (Arkansas rose, prairie wild rose). Low growing, very hardy species native to the prairie states and provinces. *R. acicularis* also grows wild eastward to the maritime provinces, northwestward to Alaska, and southwestward to New Mexico, and *R. arkansana* eastward to New York and westward to Alberta and Texas. Neither species is in itself much used in landscaping, but both are parents of hardy rose cultivars useful in the Northern Plains. *R. acicularis* is involved in the parentage of some of the Rugosa Hybrids, and *R. arkansana* is the dominant parent of the Parkland roses (see under Rose cultivars).

Rosa blanda 4 (meadow rose, smooth wild rose, Labrador rose). This native of the northern parts of our area from Newfoundland to Manitoba and southward to Pennsylvania and Missouri is mostly thornless, with red stems and fragrant, single, pink flowers, 5–8 cm/2–3 in. across, in late spring or early summer, and red fruits, about 1 cm/0.4 in. across, in autumn. Its rangy habit and limited flowering season make it of marginal landscape interest, but its extreme cold-hardiness makes it useful for naturalizing in the far northern parts of our area, and there has been some interest in it as a hybrid parent. It is useful in Zones 3a–6b and perhaps colder zones with selection of locally native genetic material.

Rosa woodsii 4 (western wild rose, mountain rose). This wide-ranging species from western North America: Saskatchewan to British Columbia and southward to Kansas, Colorado, and Utah, has pink to purplish pink or occasionally white flowers, opening from early to late summer. It is a useful native shrub in the Great Plains region, at least in Zones 3a–5b, with selection of local genetic material.

Rosa rugosa.

Rosa virginiana 4

VIRGINIA ROSE
Deciduous shrub
Rosaceae (Rose Family)

Native Range. Eastern North America: Newfoundland southward to Alabama and westward to Missouri.

Useful Range. USDA Zones 5a–7b, northward to Zone 4 with selection of appropriate genetic material, and southward to Zone 8 in areas having moderate summer temperatures.

Function. Massing, border.

Size and Habit

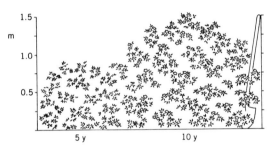

Rosa virginiana.

Adaptability

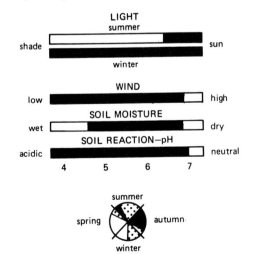

Seasonal Interest. *Flowers:* Light purplish pink, single, to 6 cm/2.4 in. across, moderately showy in early summer. *Foliage:* Deep green, glossy and clean, remaining attractive through-

out summer and turning orange-red before falling in autumn. *Fruits:* Bright red, to 1.5 cm/0.6 in. across, ripening in early autumn and remaining colorful well into winter. *Twigs:* Reddish, from early autumn through winter, adding significant interest in combination with the red fruits.

Problems and Maintenance. *R. virginiana* is less subject to disease and insect problems than most roses, and requires little or no maintenance in naturalized settings. When massed in human-made landscapes, renewal pruning will be needed every few years to keep the planting from taking on a ragged look.

Cultivars. 'Alba,' with white flowers, and 'Plena,' with double purple-pink flowers, add variety but may not be available commercially.

Related Species

Rosa carolina 3 (Carolina rose, American wild rose, pasture rose). This native of eastern North America from Nova Scotia to Minnesota and southward to Florida and Texas functions as a lower growing version of *R. virginiana* that suckers more freely, forming thickets. Less functional than *R. virginiana* except for covering areas of ground rapidly, and with less handsome foliage, it is still a useful plant for naturalizing and large-scale massing in Zones 5a–8b with selection of locally native genetic material.

Rosa nitida 3 (shining or bristly-hedge rose). This low-growing (no more than 0.5 m/1.6 ft tall) native of northeastern North America (Newfoundland to New England) has very glossy foliage that reddens in autumn and single, bright, rosy red flowers, 5 cm/2 in. across, in early summer. Useful for massing or as a specimen in Zones 4a–6b and perhaps farther south in areas with moderate summer temperatures.

Rosa palustris 4 (swamp rose). Native to upland as well as swampy areas in eastern North America from Nova Scotia to Minnesota and southward to Florida and Mississippi, this species differs little from *R. virginiana*, with somewhat inferior foliage, but it is to be preferred, when available, for wet soils. It is more likely to be available for preservation in sites being developed than for planting elsewhere, but it can be used in Zones 4b–8b with selection of appropriate genetic material, preferably locally native stock.

Rosa wichuraiana 1 and 2

MEMORIAL ROSE
Semievergreen climber or groundcover
Rosaceae (Rose Family)

Native Range. Eastern China, Japan, Korea, Taiwan.

Useful Range. USDA Zones 5b–9a.

Function. Large-scale groundcover, cover for highway slopes and other banks. Can also be trained as a climber.

Size and Habit

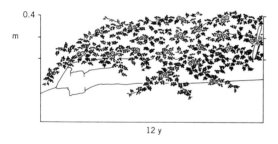

Rosa wichuraiana.

Adaptability

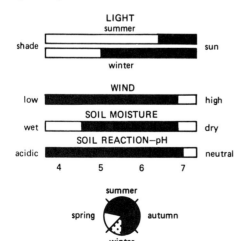

Seasonal Interest. *Flowers:* Fragrant, single, white, 5 cm/2 in. across, in midsummer. *Foliage:* Lustrous to glossy, rich deep green, persisting well into winter or longer with snow cover, making a dense mass quickly. *Fruits:* Red, 1 cm/0.4 in. across, moderately colorful in autumn.

Problems and Maintenance. This species is vigorous and relatively trouble-free, but it occasionally may need protection from mites and insects. When planted in restricted areas, this trailing shrub will need frequent pruning to keep it in bounds. It is best reserved for larger-scale situations.

Cultivars and Hybrids. 'Curiosity' (variegated Memorial rose) has irregularly white-variegated foliage and single white flowers. 'Hiawatha' has single, bright red flowers with white centers. 'Poterifolia' has a more refined, compact growth habit and single white flowers with yellow stamens. *R. wichuraiana* has been an important parent in breeding of many of the Rambler roses, which have been largely displaced by the large-flowered climbing roses. More than a dozen cultivars are still available, but not widely so, including: 'Alberic Barbier,' with white flowers; 'Camaraieux,' with mauve flowers; 'Dorothy Perkins,' an old favorite with light pink flowers; and 'May Queen,' with medium-pink flowers.

Related Species

Rosa banksiae 1 (Lady Banks rose). This vigorous, high-climbing rose from China will reach heights of 6 m/19 ft and greater in the Deep South. It is spectacular in late spring, with great masses of more or less fragrant, single or double, creamy white or yellow flowers, fine-textured evergreen foliage, and few or no prickles. Single-flowered forms probably are not commercially available, but two double-flowered forms are grown. Flowers of the double white form, var. *banksiae* (synonym: var. albo-plena), the species type, are more fragrant than those of the double yellow form, 'Lutea,' but both are extremely shade-tolerant and sometimes are encouraged to grow into tree canopies. When trained against walls or buildings, they need wire or trellis support for climbing and can be difficult to keep within bounds. Annual pruning following flowering is necessary, and an additional pruning or two may be necessary during summer, especially when space for its rambling is limited. Useful in Zones 8a–9a+.

Rosa chinensis 3 (China rose).   This low shrub with semievergreen foliage and pink flowers is an important parent of the Hybrid Perpetual and Hybrid Tea roses as well as the Polyanthas, Floribundas, and Grandifloras. It was the introduction of *R. chinensis* to existing hybrid lines in Europe in the eighteenth century and *R. odorata* soon afterward, that gave rise to most modern decorative hybrid roses. But the contribution of this species to the development of functional landscape roses—as contrasted with decorative roses—has been minimal except in the Deep South, where the climate is more amenable to hybrids with substantial *R. chinensis* parentage than elsewhere in our area. A few such hybrids are functional landscape plants for informal hedging, massing, and training on vertical surfaces. Selection of cultivars should be based on hardiness, vigor, freedom from disease and, of course, availability.

Rosa odorata 3 (tea rose).   This semievergreen, trailing or climbing plant is the key forerunner of Hybrid Tea roses, important more for their decorative than functional effect. Like *R. chinensis*, this species is Chinese in origin, tender north of about Zone 7b, and seldom, if ever, used in the species form.

Rosa xanthina f. *hugonis* 4–5

Synonym: *R. hugonis*
FATHER HUGO ROSE
Deciduous shrub
Rosaceae (Rose Family)

Native Range.   Central China.

Useful Range.   USDA Zones 5a–8a.

Function.   Border, specimen, informal hedge. Not dense enough to make an effective screen.

Size and Habit

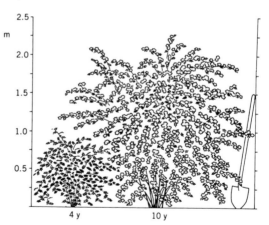

Rosa xanthina f. *hugonis*.

Adaptability

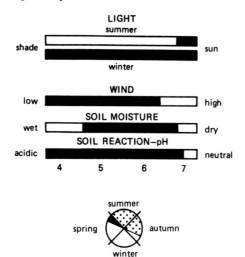

Seasonal Interest. *Flowers:* Single, lightly fragrant, bright butter yellow, to 5 cm/2 in., borne in large numbers on gracefully arching, prickly branches in late spring. *Foliage:* Compound, bluish green, and fine-textured because of the small leaflets, only 1–2 cm/0.4–0.8 in. long, falling in midautumn without color change. *Fruits:* Very dark red, only 1.5 cm/0.6 in. across, inconspicuous.

Problems and Maintenance. This species is more trouble-free than most roses but occasionally may need spraying to control insects. Renewal pruning is necessary periodically to maintain good form.

Related Forms, Species, and Hybrids

Rosa xanthina f. *spontanea* 5. This is the wild type of the species, with single yellow flowers slightly smaller than those of f. *hugonis*, another case in which the wild species was named later than the garden form and thus did not become the species type.

Rosa xanthina f. *xanthina* 5 (Manchu rose). This is the first-named species type, similar to the wild type except for its double and semidouble flowers. It is less widely used than f. *hugonis*, but is a graceful shrub with fine-textured foliage and golden-yellow flowers, useful at least in Zones 6a–8a.

Rosa foetida 5 (Austrian brier rose). This native of western Asia has deep yellow flowers, to 7 cm/2.8 in. across, with an unpleasant odor which, along with its extreme susceptibility to black spot, has limited the popularity of this otherwise appealing species. This plant does not have as fine foliage texture as that of R. *xanthina* f. *hugonis*, and it is a little larger. Two selections are popular: 'Bicolor' (= 'Austrian Copper') has single, bicolored, red and yellow flowers; and 'Persiana' (Persian yellow rose) has smaller but double yellow flowers. Both are useful in Zones 3a–8b. R. *foetida* has also been used as the parent of hybrids, one of which is listed below.

Rosa × *harisonii* 5 (Harison's yellow rose). This hybrid of R. *foetida* and R. *spinosissima* has semidouble, bright lemon-yellow flowers, to 5 cm/2 in. across, in late spring to early summer. Its foliage is fine-textured but less so than that of R. *xanthina* f. *hugonis*, and it is useful in Zones 4a–8a.

Rosa primula 4 (primrose rose). This central Asian species has pale yellow flowers, to 4 cm/1.6 in. across, in middle to late spring, and its aromatic foliage adds interest in summer. Useful in the same zones as R. *xanthina* f. *hugonis*.

Rosa spinosissima 3 (synonym: R. *pimpinellifolia*; Scotch rose, Burnett rose). This low-growing, suckering shrub, to 1 m/3.3 ft, has foliage as fine-textured as that of R. *xanthina* f. *hugonis* and somewhat smaller flowers, usually 2.5–5 cm/1–2 in. across, ranging from pink to white or yellow, in late spring. Native to Europe and western Asia, R. *spinosissima* has been widely cultivated in Europe and colonial America in a variety of forms and is variably hardy, generally useful in Zones 5a–8a, some cultivars to Zone 4. Although its cultivars are useful for massing or for seasonal color in shrub borders, they are perhaps less useful today than some of the lower-growing native roses such as R. *arkansana*, R. *carolina*, and R. *nitida* and other low shrubs with more year-round interest. The var. *altaica* (Altai rose) is an exceptionally cold-hardy population from the Altai Mountains of central Asia that has been used in breeding cold-hardy garden roses for the Northern Plains of Canada and the United States. See Manitoba Hybrids and Parkland Roses, under Rose cultivars, below.

Rose Cultivars 1–5

The cultivars listed below constitute only a fraction of the hundreds of roses that are currently available. They are a sampling some of the most functional landscape roses, which are also decorative. Most are hybrids, many of complex or uncertain origin, but a few are selections from a single species.

Rugosa Hybrids.   These range from selections of R. *rugosa* to hybrids with Hybrid Tea roses and others. They are generally cold hardy at least to Zone 4b—some to Zone 3a. Those listed are commercially available, unless specified otherwise, and among the most popular. See also the Ottawa Hybrids, below.

'Agnes,' a hybrid of R. *rugosa* × R. *foetida* 'Persiana,' has fragrant, double, pale yellow flowers to 8 cm/3 in. across. It grows to 1.5–1.8 m/5–6 ft high and wide, with an open, leggy habit, and is very susceptible to black spot disease.

'Alba' has single white flowers and orange hips (fruits) and is about as hardy as the species, growing to 1–1.2 m/3.3–4 ft high, with a leggy habit.

'Albo-plena' has fragrant, double white flowers, dark green foliage, and a dense, moundlike habit, to 1.2 m/4 ft high and wider. Its only limitation is its lack of fruits, and perhaps availability.

'Belle Poitevine' has lightly fragrant, semidouble, light purplish pink flowers, to 8 cm/3 in. across, and a compact growth habit, to 1–1.2 m/3.3–4 ft high and wide. It has little fruiting interest, but yellow-orange fall foliage, and is highly resistant to black spot disease.

'Blanc Double de Coubert' differs little from 'Albo-plena,' but is somewhat taller (1.2–1.8 m/4–6 ft), and cold-hardy at least to Zone 5a, perhaps also Zone 4.

'Dart's Dash' is similar to 'Hansa' except not quite so tall and leggy, growing to about 1.2 m/4 ft reportedly with a more continuous pattern of rebloom. It showed little or no disease in limited early trials and is probably cold-hardy at least to Zone 5a, probably also parts of Zone 4.

'F. J. Grootendorst' has small flowers, deep pink with fringed petals, with good repeat bloom in summer, growing to 1.2 m/4 ft high and wide.

This is a very popular hybrid, but lacks fruiting interest and is highly susceptible to black spot. Hardy to Zone 4b.

'Frau Dagmar Hastrup' (= 'Frau Dagmar Hartopp'), an open-pollinated seedling of R. *rugosa*, is arguably the best of the Rugosa Hybrids, with large numbers of fragrant, single light pink flowers with showy yellow stamens, followed by very large red hips that remain colorful from midsummer to late autumn. Its habit is low and densely mounded, 1–1.2 m/3.3–4 ft high, and wider, with dark green foliage that turns yellow-orange in autumn and is highly resistant to black spot and mildew. Cold-hardy at least to Zone 5a.

'Grootendorst Supreme' is similar to 'F. J. Grootendorst' with double crimson flowers, but not as vigorous.

'Hansa' has fragrant, semidouble, deep purplish-red flowers, with good intermittent bloom all summer, and a somewhat leggy habit, growing to 1.5–1.8 m/5–6 ft high, with glossy dark green foliage that is resistant to black spot and turns yellow-orange in autumn. This cultivar is useful, and very popular, in Zones 3a–7b.

'Max Graf,' a trailing hybrid (probably R. *rugosa* × R. *wichuraiana*) to only about 0.5 m/1.6 ft high, is useful as a large-scale groundcover in Zones 4b–7b. Its pinkish-white flowers are neither fragrant nor very showy, and there is little rebloom in late summer.

'Sir Thomas Lipton' has fragrant, double white flowers and no fruiting interest. It is very popular, but has problems: Its brown spent flowers are retained on the plant and become unsightly; it is moderately susceptible to black spot; its growth habit is upright and open; and it is not as hardy as the others mentioned here, probably only to Zone 5b.

'Schneezwerg' (translation: 'Snowdwarf') is mounded and dense in habit, but hardly dwarf, growing to 1.2–1.5 m/4–5 ft high and wide. It has large numbers of small, semidouble white flowers with showy yellow stamens, followed quickly by small but showy orange-red hips. It is moderately susceptible to black spot, and hardy to Zone 5a.

'Therese Bugnet,' a hybrid of unknown origin, has large and very fragrant, double medium-pink flowers, and few, if any, hips. Its blue-green foliage is slightly susceptible to black spot, and it turns yellow-orange in autumn. It grows to 1.5–1.8 m/5–6 ft high, with shiny red stems that add color in winter, but are susceptible to rose stem girdler. Winter-hardy at least in Zone 5a.

Manitoba Hybrids (see also Parkland Hybrids). Frank L. Skinner of Dropmore, Manitoba, was involved in breeding roses, as well as many other plants, from early in the twentieth century; and a succession of rose breeders at the Agriculture Canada Research Station at Morden, Manitoba, were involved in breeding of roses for the Canadian Prairies beginning a half-century ago. The Morden program, started by H. F. Harp and continued by William Godfrey, resulted in the Prairie Series of hardy cultivars, of which *R. rugosa, R. spinosissima* var. *altaica,* and others, were parents. These were introduced in Canada and to a limited extent in the United States. The most popular of these, 'Prairie Dawn,' is still available in a small number of nurseries in both countries. This is a disease-resistant shrub to 1.5 m/5 ft high, with upright branching, glossy dark green foliage and glowing pink, semidouble flowers, opening in early summer, and intermittently until frost. Another selection, 'Prairie Princess,' remarkably resistant to black spot, is probably not commercially available, but has been used as a parent in more recent breeding efforts at the Morden station (see Parkland Hybrids, below).

Parkland Hybrids. About 1960, the Morden rose breeding program was taken over by Henry H. Marshall, and he was joined in the 1980s by Lynn M. Collicutt, who continued this breeding program into the 1990s. Over this time, at least a dozen cultivars have been released, four of which are widely circulated. These cultivars are especially valued in Zones 3 and 4, but also useful in Zones 5 and 6. Most kill back to the snow-line in the most severe winters in Zones 3 and 4, but return vigorously the following spring and flower on new wood. They must be propagated on their own roots (by cuttings or tissue culture); otherwise it may be the rootstock that returns in spring. Moreover, many common rootstocks, such as *R. multiflora,* are not cold-hardy enough to survive in Zones 3 and 4.

'Adelaide Hoodless' is a vigorous shrub, 0.6–1 m/2–3.3 ft high and wide, with slightly fragrant, semidouble, bright red flowers, about 6.4 cm/2.5 in. across, in clusters of up to 25 from early summer until frost. Useful at least in Zones 3b–6b.

'Cuthbert Grant' is a vigorous shrub to 1 m/3.3 ft high and wide, with dark red, double flowers, to 10 cm/4 in. across, resembling Hybrid Tea roses, in clusters of 3 to 6, and excellent foliage. This was designated the official "Centennial Rose" for the Canadian Centennial in 1967. Useful at least in Zones 3b–6b.

'Morden Amorette' is a low-growing plant, under 0.5 m/1.6 ft high, with large, double carmine rose flowers blooming continuously from June through the growing season.

'Morden Blush' (Plant Patent No. 8054, 1992) is similar to 'Adelaide Hoodless' in size and hardiness, but with pale pink to ivory white, Hybrid Tea-type flowers, 8 cm/3 in. across, from early summer to frost—the longest bloom period of any Parkland rose. Unfortunately, it is very susceptible to black spot.

'Morden Centennial' is similar to 'Cuthbert Grant' in size and hardiness, but with rosy pink flowers, 10 cm/4 in. across, in clusters up to 15. Susceptible to black spot.

'Morden Fireglow' (Plant Patent No. 8060, 1992) grows to 0.6–0.7 m/2–2.3 ft high, with small clusters of double scarlet flowers, from early summer to frost. Useful at least in Zones 3b–6b.

'Morden Ruby' is similar to 'Adelaide Hoodless' in size and hardiness, but with clusters of fully double ruby-red flowers, from early summer to frost.

'Prairie Joy,' released in 1990, is a vigorous but very dense, rounded shrub, 1–1.5 m/3.3–5 ft high and wide, suitable for hedging, with fully double, medium-pink flowers, 7 cm/2.8 in. across, borne singly or in clusters of up to 6, for 4 to 6 weeks in early summer and then intermittently until frost. This cultivar is highly resistant to black spot, mildew, and rust, and useful at least in Zones 3b–6b.

'Winnipeg Parks,' released in 1990, is a low, dense shrub, useful for landscape bedding (groundcover) use, growing to only 0.5–0.7 m/1.6–2.3 ft high and wide, with slightly fragrant double flowers, medium red as they unfold and fading to a dark pink-red. Disease-resistance is good for mildew and rust and fair to good for black spot. Useful at least in Zones 3b–6b.

Explorer Series. The rose-breeding program at the Ottawa Research Station of Agriculture Canada was begun in the 1920s by Isabella Preston, who was famous for developing the Preston Hybrid lilacs (see under *Syringa villosa*) and the early Rosybloom crabapples (see under *Malus* cultivars) and who also introduced at least 20 hardy roses, few (if any) of which are still in use. After a hiatus following Miss Preston's retirement, the program was reactivated by Felicitas Svejda, with special emphasis on disease-resistance, long flowering period, and, of course, cold-hardiness. The first cultivar released, 'Martin Frobisher,' a large *R. rugosa* hybrid with pale pink flowers, quickly became popular. That and those that followed were named after Canadian explorers and are called the Explorer Series. Early cultivars in this group were Rugosa Hybrids, but later another important parent was introduced: an open-pollinated seedling of 'Max Graf' (see Rugosa Hybrids), raised by Wilhelm Kordes, the famous German breeder of hardy roses. This plant, called *Rosa ×kordesii*, became a parent of the climbing members of the Explorer Series, which can be left on the trellis over the winter without injury in Zone 5a, perhaps also Zone 4. The first Kordes hybrid in the Explorer series was 'John Cabot,' a red-flowered climber that quickly became popular in cold climates. It was followed by 'William Baffin,' an extremely cold-hardy climbing rose with deep pink flowers, in early summer and intermittently thereafter. Other climbers in this series are 'Henry Kelsey' and 'John Davis'; see below).

In 1986, after Dr. Svejda's retirement, this program was transferred from the Ottawa Research Station to the Agriculture Canada Research Station at L'Assomption, near Montreal, Quebec, where it is being continued by the team of Ian S. Ogilvie and Neville P. Arnold. The cultivars listed here are available in the United States, although not yet widely at this writing, and are more widely circulated in Canada.

'Alexander Mackenzie' (= 'A. Mackenzie'), a shrub to 1.5–1.8 m/5–6 ft tall with good resistance to mildew and black spot, has fragrant red flowers, in clusters of 6 to 12, similar to those of the Floribunda roses, but this cultivar is more cold-hardy than the Floribundas.

'Champlain' is a shrubby Floribunda-type rose to 0.9 m/3 ft high, with double, medium-red flowers with darker petal tips, about 6 cm/2.4 in. across, and lustrous, dark yellow green foliage. It is resistant to black spot, but somewhat susceptible to mildew.

'Charles Albanel,' a Rugosa hybrid, is a groundcover-type rose, growing to only about 0.5 m/1.6 ft high, with very fragrant, semidouble red-purple flowers and fine-textured foliage. It is resistant to black spot and mildew, but susceptible to rose stem girdler, and not very vigorous.

'David Thompson,' a Rugosa hybrid ('Schneezwerg' × 'Frau Dagmar Hastrup'), has fragrant, semidouble to double pink flowers, few (if any) fruits, and fine-textured foliage that is resistant to black spot and mildew, but it is not very vigorous and it retains its brown spent flowers.

'Henry Hudson' is a low-growing shrub, to 0.6–0.9 m/2–3 ft high, with pink buds, opening to pink-tinged white, semidouble flowers, 6.4 cm/2.5 in. across, which are retained after browning, and minor fruiting interest. This cultivar is hardy at least to Zone 5a, but weak-growing and susceptible to rose stem girdler.

'Henry Kelsey' is a trailing rose, to 0.6 m/2 ft as a groundcover, but to 2–2.5 m/6.6–8 ft when trained on a trellis or pillar. It has fragrant semidouble flowers, 8 cm/3 in. across, from early summer intermittently until frost, and is resistant to black spot and mildew.

'Jens Munk' is a Rugosa hybrid rose, to 1.2–1.8 m/4–6 ft high and wide, with fragrant, semidouble pink flowers, 6.4–7 cm/2.5–2.8 in. across, from early summer to frost. It is resistant to black spot and mildew and is cold-hardy at least to Zone 5a, but it retains its spent flowers and is susceptible to rose stem girdler.

'John Davis' is a trailing rose, to 0.6 m/2 ft as a groundcover, but to 2–2.5 m/6.6–8 ft high when trained on a trellis or pillar. It has very fragrant double flowers, pink with yellow petal bases, to at least 8 cm/3 in. across, borne in clusters of about 17, in early summer and intermittently thereafter. It is resistant to black spot and mildew and is cold-hardy at least to Zone 4b.

'John Franklin' is a shrubby rose, to 0.9 m/3 ft high, with fragrant red flowers, to 6 cm/2.4 in. across, in clusters of 30, from June through the growing season, and glossy, leathery, dark olive-green foliage, which is resistant to black spot and mildew.

'J. P. Connell' (technically not in the Explorer series, since it is not named after an explorer) is a vigorous, thornless upright shrub, to 1–1.5 m/3.3–5 ft high and nearly as wide, with very double yellow flowers, the outside petals fading to creamy white, and dark yellow-green foliage, resistant to mildew but not to black spot.

'Louis Jolliet' is a trailing rose, to 0.6 m/2 ft high as a groundcover, but to 1.2–1.9 m/4–6 ft high when trained on a trellis or pillar, with double pink flowers, to 7 cm/2.7 in. across, in clusters of 3 to 10, and dark green, glossy, leathery foliage, resistant to black spot and mildew.

Meidiland® Roses. These hybrids have become very popular since their introduction to North America in the 1980s. They are generally low plants, useful for groundcover, hedging, or in mixed borders; they require little maintenance, and most are relatively cold-hardy. Since they are propagated on their own roots, with a mulch for protection, they can be used in zones where their canes die back in winter, and they are replaced the following spring.

'Meicoublan' (Plant Patent No. 6088, 1988; White Meidiland®), grows to 0.6 m/2 ft high and 1.8 m/6 ft wide, with large (10 cm/4 in.) double white flowers and lush foliage that holds weeds down. Useful at least in Zones 5b–9a, and at least to Zone 4b if mulched, but with some cane dieback.

'Meidomonac' (Plant Patent No. 5105, 1983; Bonica®) is an upright shrub, to 1.5 m/5 ft high and wide, with clusters of very double, 6.4-cm/2.5-in. pastel pink flowers, throughout the growing season, followed or accompanied by orange-red fruits lasting into winter. Useful in about the same zones as 'Meicoublan.'

'Meiflopan' (Plant Patent No. 6891, 1989; Alba Meidiland®) grows to 0.8 m/2.5 ft high and 1.8 m/6 ft wide, with 2.5-cm/1-in., lightly fragrant, double white flowers in large clusters throughout the growing season. Useful in about the same zones as 'Meicoublan.'

'Meigekanu' (Plant Patent No. 6384, 1988; Sevillana®) is an upright shrub to 1.2 m/4 ft high and nearly as wide, with large clusters of double, fiery red flowers through the growing season, followed by bright red fruiting interest

until winter. Useful at least in Zones 6b–9a, probably also Zone 6a, and at least in Zone 5b, mulched, with cane dieback.

'Meikrotal' (Plant Patent No. 6087, 1988; Scarlet Meidiland®) forms a large mound, 0.9 m/3 ft high and 1.8 m/6 ft wide, with large clusters of 2.5-cm/1-in. double scarlet flowers and lush foliage, throughout the growing season. Useful in about the same zones as 'Meicoublan.'

'Meineble' (Plant Patent No. 7116, 1990; Red Meidiland®) is a low, mounding groundcover form, to 0.5 m/1.6 ft high and 1.5 m/5 ft wide, with clusters of single red flowers with white centers and yellow stamens, throughout the growing season. Useful in about the same zones as 'Meicoublan.'

'Meiplatin' (Plant Patent No. 6807, 1989; Pearl Meidiland®) grows to 0.8 m/2.5 in. high and 1.8 m/6 ft wide, with many shell-pink buds opening into nearly white, double, 6.4-cm/2.5-in. flowers. Useful in about the same zones as 'Meicoublan.'

English Roses. This relatively new group of roses, from David Austin of Albrighton, England, resulted from crosses of Floribundas and old garden roses. Their 8- to 12 cm/3- to 5-in. flowers are exquisite and borne throughout the growing season; they have excellent, disease-resistant foliage; and their shrubby habit makes them functional as well. More than a dozen have been released at this writing. They are expected to be useful in Zones 5b–9a, but longer trial may call for an adjustment of this estimate. A few of the best known in our area are listed here. Additional cultivars are being introduced into North America and probably will become available soon.

'Ausboard' (Plant Patent No. 6620, 1988; Gertrude Jekyll®) grows to 1.2–1.5 m/4–5 ft high and wide, with highly fragrant, glowing deep pink, fully double flowers, 10 cm/4 in. across.

'Ausblush' (Heritage®) grows compactly to 1.2 m/4 ft high and wide, with highly fragrant, fully double and cupped, shell-pink flowers.

'Auscot' (Plant Patent No. 7215, 1990; Abraham Darby®) is a climbing rose to 3m/10 ft high, with highly fragrant, very large, fully double flowers, apricot flushed with pink and yellow. It may also be kept as a large shrub to 2–3 m/5–8 ft high, with pruning, but it is most effective when trained as a climber.

'Ausleap' (Plant Patent No. 8153, 1993; Sweet Juliet®) grows vigorously to 1.5–1.8 m/5–6 ft high and nearly as wide, with fragrant, fully double, medium to pale apricot flowers.

'Ausmary' (Mary Rose®) has a neat, compact growth habit, to 1.2 m/4 ft high and wide, with large, fragrant, flattened, double rose-pink flowers.

'Ausmas' (Graham Thomas®) grows to 1.2 m/4 ft tall, and twice that when trained as a climber, with apricot flower buds, opening a rich yellow.

'Auslo' (Plant Patent No. 7212, 1990; Othello®) grows vigorously to 1.5 m/5 ft high and wide, with fragrant, fully double, deep crimson to burgundy flowers.

'Fair Bianca'™ is vigorous and erect in habit, with large, fully double, pure white, satin-like flowers.

Other Climbing Roses. 'Alchymist' is a large plant, to 2.4 m/8 ft tall as a shrub, or 3.6 m/12 ft when treated as a pillar or climbing rose, with fragrant, 10-cm/4-in. double flowers, borne profusely for a long period in early summer, but not reblooming, and glossy, bronzing, disease-resistant foliage. Useful in Zones 5b, probably also Zone 4 with snow cover or mulch, if on its own roots.

'Blaze Improved' is an improved mutant of the long-standing climbing rose, 'Blaze,' growing to 2.4–3 m/8–10 ft high with support, with large quantities of 6.4- to 8-cm/2.5- to 3-in. semidouble, bright red flowers, in early summer and intermittently thereafter. Useful in Zones 5a–9a, perhaps also parts of Zone 4, with overwinter protection.

'Don Juan' is a climbing or pillar rose, growing to 2.4–3 m/8–10 ft tall with support, with very fragrant 10- to 12-cm/4- to 5-in. dark red flowers of Hybrid Tea type, intermittently during the summer. Useful at least in Zones 5b–9a.

'Dortmund' is a climbing or pillar rose, to 2.4–3.0 m/8–10 ft, or can be used as a shrub to 1.8 m/6 ft high and wide. It is quite disease-resistant and has moderately fragrant, single strawberry-red flowers with white centers and yellow stamens, followed by large orange hips, and is probably useful at least in Zones 5b–9a,

probably also colder zones. This is one of many hardy shrub roses developed by Wilhelm Kordes in Germany, only a few of which have fully entered commerce in North America.

'Eden' (= 'Eden Climber,' = 'Meiviolin'; Plant Patent No. 6892, 1989) is a fine climbing rose from Meilland in Lyon, France, growing to 2.4 m/8 ft high with support, with lightly fragrant, 8-cm/3-in. double, cupped flowers, creamy white and suffused with shell pink. It is disease-resistant and probably useful in Zones 5b–9a, but needs further trial in our zones.

'Golden Showers' is a climbing pillar rose, growing to about 2.4 m/8 ft tall, with bright golden yellow flowers of the Hybrid Tea type, opening to 13 cm/5 in. across throughout the growing season. It is fine for cutting as well as display, but may not be cold-hardy north of Zone 6a or 6b. Further trial will determine this.

'Joseph's Coat' can be used as a climber to 2–2.4 m/6.6–8 m tall, or as a free-standing shrub to 1.5 m/5 ft, with red to orange buds opening to slightly fragrant, double, 7.5- to 10-cm/3- to 4-in. flowers, with a mixture of colors from red to bright yellow. It is reportedly disease-resistant but may not be hardy north of Zone 7.

'New Dawn' is an outstanding, vigorous climber, to 4–5 m/13–16 ft tall with adequate support, with great masses of fragrant, fully double, apple blossom-pink flowers, from early summer intermittently until fall, and dark green, glossy, disease-resistant foliage. Useful at least in Zones 5b–9a.

'White Dawn' is a vigorous climber to at least 3–4 m/10–13 ft with outstanding, disease-resistant foliage and lightly fragrant, 5- to 8-cm/2- to 3-in. very double, white, gardenia-like flowers, from early summer through the growing. Useful at least in Zones 5b–9a.

Other Shrub and Groundcover Roses. 'Betty Prior' is a Floribunda rose, growing to 1.2 m/4 ft high and at least that wide, with a profusion of fragrant, deep-pink single flowers, to 5–8 cm/2–3 in. across, throughout the growing season. Disease-resistant and useful at least in Zones 5b–9a, probably also Zone 5a.

'Buchi' (Plant Patent No. 4225, 1978; Carefree Beauty®) grows upright to 1.8 m/6 ft high and 1.2 m/4 ft wide, useful as an informal hedge or for massing, with semidouble, 10 cm/4 in., coral-pink flowers, continually during the summer, followed by orange-red hips. It is exceptionally maintenance-free and useful in Zones 5a–9a, probably also parts of Zone 4.

'Meipetac' (Plant Patent No. 7783, 1992; Carefree Wonder®) grows to 1.2 m/4 ft high and nearly as wide, a smaller version of Carefree Beauty® with large numbers of semidouble, bright deep pink flowers, 12 cm/4.5 in. across, intermittently during the summer. Like Carefree Beauty,® it requires little or no maintenance and is useful in the same areas.

'Nearly Wild' is a Brownell Sub-Zero® rose, introduced about a half-century ago but enjoying a resurgence of popularity. This is a Floribunda type, growing to 0.6–0.9 m/2–3 ft high and spreading to make a neat and effective groundcover. Its large single flowers are light pink with white centers, opening from early summer until frost, and it is reported to be disease-resistant and cold-hardy at least to Zone 5a, perhaps also parts of Zone 4.

'Noatraum' (Plant Patent No. 7282, 1990; Flower Carpet™) without pruning grows 0.6–0.8 m/2–2.6 ft high and about 1 m/3.3 ft wide, with a great abundance of semidouble, deep rose-pink flowers, over a very long season. It is reported to be highly resistant to black spot and mildew and is amenable to occasional shearing. It is marketed as a low-maintenance landscape plant, suitable for massing or groundcover use, and is potentially useful in at least Zones 5a–9a, probably also Zone 4 with consistent snow cover.

'Sea Foam,' a low-growing Polyantha rose, spreading to 2.5–3.5 m/8–12 ft wide while remaining below 0.5 m/1.6 ft, has large clusters of slightly fragrant, double, creamy white flowers, intermittently through the growing season, and glossy dark green, disease-resistant foliage. Can be used as a large-scale groundcover or trained as a climber or pillar rose. Useful at least in Zones 5b–9a, probably also Zone 5a.

'The Fairy' is another low-growing Polyantha rose, to 0.8–1 m/2.6–3.3 ft high and not much wider, with great quantities of small, double pink flowers through the growing season, and glossy green foliage, but little or no fruiting interest. Disease-resistant and useful at least in Zones 5a–9a, probably also parts of Zone 4.

'Twoadvance' (Plant Patent No. 7978, 1992; All That Jazz®) grows to 1.5 m/5 ft high and nearly as wide, with large, semidouble, coral-salmon flowers, from early summer to frost, and handsome foliage.

Rubus odoratus 4

FLOWERING RASPBERRY, THIMBLEBERRY

Deciduous shrub

Rosaceae (Rose Family)

Native Range. Eastern North America: Nova Scotia to Michigan, south to Georgia.

Useful Range. USDA Zones 4a–7b in areas meeting site requirements (see Adaptability).

Function. Shaded border, naturalizing.

Size and Habit

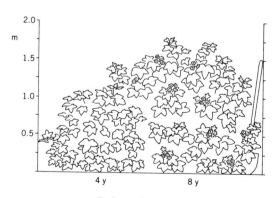

Rubus odoratus.

Adaptability. Planting sites are limited by the need for partial shade, moist (but not wet) soil, and moderate summer temperatures.

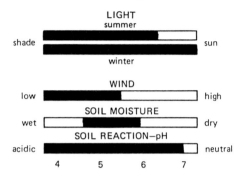

Rubus odoratus.

Seasonal Interest. *Flowers:* Fragrant, rose-purple or occasionally whitish, to 5 cm/2 in. across, borne in small clusters from early to midsummer, not in large numbers but displayed effectively against the coarse foliage. *Foliage:* Medium green, mapleleaf-shaped, 10–20 cm/4–8 in. across, occasionally larger, giving a striking, coarse texture, falling in early autumn with little or no color change. *Fruits:* Flattened red raspberries, borne in small numbers in late summer, inedible.

Problems and Maintenance. This shrub is trouble-free and requires little or no maintenance in naturalized sites, where it performs best.

Related Species

Rubus deliciosus 5 (boulder or Rocky Mountain flowering raspberry). This western relative of *R. odoratus* has white flowers, coarse foliage tex-

ture, and arching stems. It is attractive in flower in late spring, and it is of greatest interest in the northwestern parts of our area, useful in Zones 4a–7b.

Rubus hispidus 2 (swamp dewberry, running blackberry). This native of eastern North America from Nova Scotia to Minnesota and south to Georga is a reasonably good groundcover for wet soils, with prickly, trailing stems and glossy, nearly evergreen foliage. The fruits are red, then ripen black, and are very sour. Useful in Zones 4b–7b.

Rubus parviflorus 4 (thimbleberry, white-flowering raspberry). This close relative of *R. odoratus* is very similar in landscape effect but has slightly smaller leaves and white flowers. Useful in Zones 4b–7a.

Rubus tricolor 2 (Himalayan bramble). This semievergreen to evergreen creeper from western China with dark green, almost iridescent, irregularly toothed leaves to 10 cm/4 in. long, makes a handsome groundcover in at least Zones 7b–9a in the Pacific Northwest but is seldom, if ever, seen in our area. It might not succeed in these zones in our area, but might be tried.

Ruscus aculeatus 3

BUTCHERSBROOM
Evergreen shrub
Liliaceae (Lily Family)

Native Range.   Europe and adjacent Asia.

Useful Range.   USDA Zones 7b–9a+.

Function.   Border, specimen, informal hedge.

Size and Habit

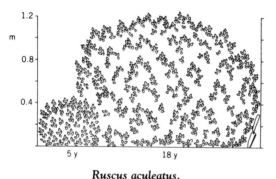

Ruscus aculeatus.

Adaptability.   Tolerates full sun to complete shade but performs best with some sun during the growing season. Tolerates wind except in colder areas, where winter wind can cause dehydration.

Seasonal Interest.   *Flowers:* Inconspicuous, dioecious. *Foliage and stems:* Bristly with small, triangular-pointed cladodes (leaflike protrusions from the stems), year-round. Stems are rigid, forming a good barrier. *Fruits:* Bright red, to 1.5 cm/0.6 in. across, in late autumn and winter on pistillate (female) plants in the presence of staminate (male) plants for pollination. Showy when borne in large numbers, but they seldom are.

Problems and Maintenance.   This plant is relatively trouble-free, rarely requiring maintenance of any kind.

Related Species

Ruscus hypoglossum 2 (low butchersbroom). This is similar to *R. aculeatus* except that it grows only 20–30 cm/8–12 in. high, with short, horizontally arching branches.

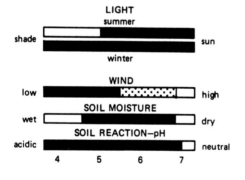

Salix alba 8

WHITE WILLOW
Deciduous tree
Salicaceae (Willow Family)

Native Range.   Europe, northern Africa, western to central Asia.

Useful Range.   USDA Zones 3a–9a with selection of appropriate genetic material.

Function.   Specimen, screen (with pruning).

Size and Habit

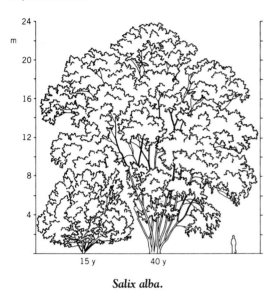

Salix alba.

Adaptability

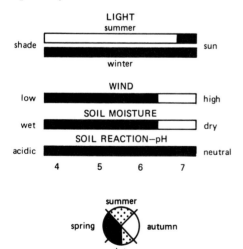

Seasonal Interest.   *Flowers:* Yellowish catkins add interest in early spring along with yellow twigs. *Foliage:* Narrow, olive-green leaves, 5–10 cm/2–4 in. long, whitish underneath, fall without color change in midautumn. *Twigs and branches:* Smooth, yellowish bark turns bright yellow in late winter and early spring.

Problems and Maintenance.   Willows in general are weak-wooded, prone to a variety of insect and disease problems, and short-lived, especially in warmer climates. They send fast-growing roots into drainage and septic lines, causing serious problems, and therefore they should be planted well away from underground lines unless underground barriers can be constructed, and they should be used in the knowledge that they probably will not be long-lived. Finally, they should be limited to situations where littering by broken twigs and branches can be tolerated. *Salix alba* has all these limitations but is more durable than some other *Salix* species. Its value in landscape use is mostly limited to the varieties listed below.

Cultivars and Varieties.   'Britzensis' (= 'var. *chermesina;* red-stem willow) has bright red-orange twigs when young and vigorous. This color mostly disappears on older, slower-growing trees, but can be restored by heavy pruning to stimulate new shoot growth. This cultivar is sometimes maintained as a shrub, 1–2 m/3.3–6.6 ft tall, by such pruning, and is used in hedges or borders primarily for this twig color in late winter and early spring.

The var. *sericea* (synonym: var. *argentea;* Siberian white willow) has whitened, silky foliage, giving some of the same effect as *Elaeagnus angustifolia* in the landscape, except for the size difference.

The var. *tristis* (synonym *S. vitellina* 'Pendula'; golden weeping willow) is the most commonly used variety of *S. alba* and is probably the most widely used of all the weeping willows because of its bright yellow pendent branches and cold-hardiness, to Zone 4a.

The var. *vitellina* (golden willow) differs from the species type only in having brighter yellow twigs and narrower leaves.

Related Species

Salix exigua 6 (coyote willow).   This small tree is native to much of western North America and useful in the northern and western Central Plains for summer color accent. The form in commerce, at least, has silvery white foliage and a graceful, semipendulous growth habit. It tends to sucker heavily, but this can be eliminated by grafting on nonsuckering rootstocks, such as *S. alba* var. *vitellina*, which has been done with some plants offered for sale by nurseries in the northern plains of the United States and Canada. It is useful in Zones 3a–7a with selection of appropriate genetic material.

Salix arenaria 2–3

Synonyms: *S. repens var. argentea and var. nitida*
CREEPING WILLOW
Deciduous shrub
Salicaceae (Willow Family)

Native Range.   Europe and Asia.

Useful Range.   USDA Zones 4b–9a and to Zone 3b with snow cover and selection of appropriate genetic material.

Function.   Specimen, groundcover, massing.

Size and Habit.   Growth habit varies from creeping and mat-forming to ascending.

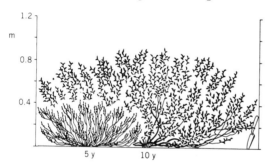

Salix arenaria.

Adaptability

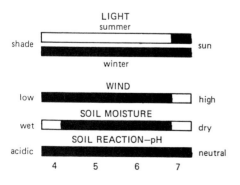

Seasonal Interest.   *Foliage:* Gray-green on upper surfaces, densely silky and white on lower surfaces, both surfaces in var. *argentea*, variable in size from 1.5–3.5 cm/0.6–1.4 in. long and in shape from narrow to elliptical, falling in autumn without color change.

Problems and Maintenance.   *S. arenaria* is subject to the limitations of willows in general (see *S. alba*), but periodic drastic pruning, useful for retaining mass when used as a large-scale groundcover, also helps control diseases by removing infected parts.

Related Species

Salix rosmarinifolia 4 (synonym: *S. repens* var. *angustifolia* and var. *rosmarinifolia*; rosemary-leaved willow). This ascending shrub from central and eastern Europe has linear leaves with a deep green and leathery upper surface and white, silky lower surface. It is useful as a specimen for accent and more effective in architectonic situations than with a variety of plant material, much like *Rhamnus frangula* 'Asplenifolia' in general effect but more useful in wet sites. Useful in Zones 4b–9a.

Salix babylonica 7

BABYLON WEEPING WILLOW
Deciduous tree
Salicaceae (Willow Family)

Native Range. Origin obscure, but cultivated in the Middle East for centuries.

Useful Range. USDA Zones 7a–9a+. May persist for a few years in Zone 6, then be winterkilled to the ground.

Function. Specimen.

Size and Habit

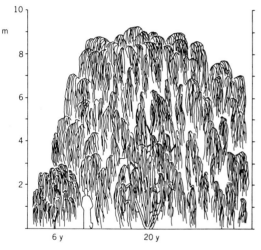

Salix babylonica.

Adaptability

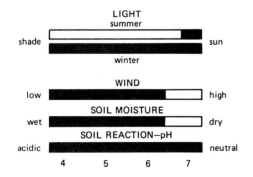

Seasonal Interest. *Flowers:* Delicate green catkins add strong interest to newly emerging foliage in spring. *Foliage:* Pale green and delicate on emergence, then olive green during summer and falling in autumn without color change. Leaves are narrow, only 1–1.5 cm/0.4–0.6 in. wide and 8–15 cm/3–6 in. long, producing a distinctive texture. *Twigs and branches:* Smooth olive to gray-green bark adds minor interest during the leafless season.

Problems and Maintenance. *S. babylonica* has all the limitations of the willows in general (see *S. alba*) and lacks the cold hardiness of most of the other *Salix* species discussed here. Some confusion about its hardiness results from the tendency of some people to call all weeping willows by this name. The true *S. babylonica* is a beautiful tree with probably the most strongly pendulous form of all the weeping willows, but it lacks the golden twig color and cold hardiness of *S. alba* var. *tristis*.

Cultivar. 'Crispa' has leaves folded longitudinally and curled into a ring, giving a distinctive texture. It is most useful as a specimen where it can be appreciated at close range.

Related Species

Salix matsudana 7 (Hangkow or Peking willow). This native of northern China resembles *S. babylonica* in foliage and twig color, but is not pendulous. It is useful in Zones 5a–9a and is usually seen as the selection 'Tortuosa' (corkscrew willow), which has spirally twisted twigs and branches and is a fairly popular large shrub or small to medium tree for accent, but usually deteriorates with age. 'Golden Curls' is probably a hybrid, of uncertain origin but perhaps involving *S. alba*. It is a small weeping tree, to 6–9 m/20–30 ft tall, with golden-yellow, corkscrew-twisted branches and curly leaves, also turning yellow in autumn. 'Scarcuzam' (Scarlet Curls®)

is similar to 'Golden Curls,' but its smaller twigs redden in winter. 'Snake' is a small pyramidal tree, to about 4–6 m/13–20 ft tall, occasionally taller, with twigs and branches highly contorted, more so than those of *S. matsudana* 'Tortuosa.' There is some confusion as to whether 'Snake' belongs to *S. alba* or *S. matsudana* or is a hybrid. 'Umbraculifera' (= 'Globosa') is a symmetrically rounded tree to 6–10 m/20–33 ft high and nearly as wide, more tolerant than most willows of dryness and heat.

Salix ×*pendulina* 7 (synonym: *S.* ×*blanda;* Wisconsin weeping willow). This probably is a hybrid of *S. babylonica* × *S. fragilis*. The form usually called Wisconsin weeping willow resembles *S. babylonica* somewhat but is considerably less pendulous and is more subject to breakage than many other willows; a variant, 'Niobe,' is still planted. Another form of *S.* ×*pendulina,* 'Elegantissima' (Thurlow willow), is more strongly pendulous. These are useful in Zones 5a–9a when available.

Salix ×*sepulcralis* 8.   This uncommon hybrid, of *S. alba* var. *tristis* × *S. babylonica,* represents a compromise between its parents, with the cold hardiness of *S. alba* var. *tristis* and much of the strongly weeping form of *S. babylonica*. Its yellow winter twigs are as colorful as many plants of *S. alba,* but less so than var. *tristis* or var. *vitellina.* Useful in Zones 5a–9a, and probably also Zone 4b.

Salix caprea 5–6

EUROPEAN PUSSY WILLOW, GOAT WILLOW
Deciduous shrub or small tree
Salicaceae (Willow Family)

Native Range.   Europe and western Asia.

Useful Range.   USDA Zones 3b–9a, but fails to attain full size in Zones 3 and 4 because of topkilling in winter.

Function.   Specimen, border.

Size and Habit

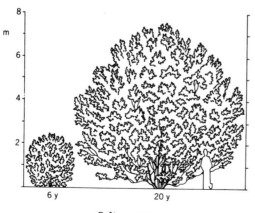

Salix caprea.

Adaptability

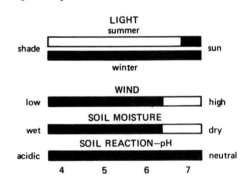

Seasonal Interest. *Flowers:* Dioecious, with silky catkins (pussy willows), to 3.5 cm/1.4 in. long and oval in shape, long before leafing out— one of the first signs of early spring. Staminate (male) catkins turn yellow with pollen to continue the interest for another week or two. *Foliage:* Pale green at emergence, turning very dark green and becoming slightly wrinkled, finally falling in autumn with little or no color change.

Twigs: Smooth and lustrous, brown in winter with large, smooth, reddish winter buds.

Problems and Maintenance. This species is subject to the problems of willows in general (see *S. alba*), but less so when pruned drastically every year or two to promote vigor and heavy flowering, if the prunings are removed and burned. This reduces overwintering insect populations and inoculum for future disease infections. The problem of roots in drainage lines remains in spite of cultural treatment. Winterkilling of tops occurs in occasional winters in Zones 3 and 4 but is less serious when annual renewal pruning is practiced.

Cultivars. 'Pendula' makes a very small tree, to 2–4 m/6.6–13 ft tall and similar in width, when grafted on a 1.2- to 1.5-m/4- to 5-ft standard, with a pronounced but stiff weeping habit, not unlike that of weeping mulberry. It is primarily useful for accent in a Japanese or other formal garden. Other pendulous cultivars available include 'Kilmarnock' and 'Weeping Sally,' but there may be some duplication in these names. 'Variegata' has creamy-white variegated foliage, adding summer interest, but is not often available.

Related Species

Salix chaenomeloides 5–6 (Japanese pussy willow). This Japanese counterpart of *S. caprea* is little-known in cultivation, but a good garden plant. It is similar in size to *S. caprea*, 4–8 m/13–26 ft tall and 3–4 m/10–13 ft wide, with catkins as large as those of *S. caprea*, silvery and sometimes with a pinkish cast. Useful in Zones 5b–9a, probably also Zone 5a.

Salix discolor 6 (pussy willow). This is the North American native counterpart of *S. caprea*, growing wild in about the northern half of our area. Its somewhat smaller silky catkins are equally valued for cutting for indoor decoration, and the plant is slightly more cold-hardy, useful in Zones 3a–9a. For maximum early spring display and attractive foliage and growth habit, *S. caprea* is the logical choice, but for long lasting spring display combined with extreme cold-hardiness and, of course, for naturalizing, *S. discolor* is preferred.

Salix gracistyla 5 (rosegold pussy willow). This compact shrub is useful in smaller spaces than would accommodate *S. caprea*. Its 3-cm/1.2-in. catkins are shaded with light red by the anthers, which later turn yellow with pollen. Its narrow leaves unfold a soft blue-gray, then turn deep blue-green, and finally yellow in autumn. Useful in Zones 6a–8b, perhaps also Zone 5b. The var. *melanostachys* (synonym: *S. melanostachys*; black pussy willow) has purplish-black winter stems, purplish black bracts that make the catkins look black, and the same anther color progression as in the species types. Only male plants of this so-called variety are known.

Salix udensis 6 (synonym: *S. sachalinensis*; Sakhalin willow). This native of Japan and Sakhalin is represented in landscape use exclusively by the unusual form 'Sekka' (Japanese fantail willow), which has stem tips contorted into fanlike claws by fasciation (fusion) of stems. This form is used exclusively as a specimen for accent, and it is better in formal, architectonic situations than in the middle of a lot of other vegetation. It has significantly showy, silky catkins in early spring on reddish brown stems and is useful in Zones 5a–9a.

Salix pentandra 7

LAUREL WILLOW, BAY WILLOW
Deciduous tree
Salicaceae (Willow Family)

Native Range.   Europe and adjacent Asia.

Useful Range.   USDA Zones 3a–9a.

Function.   Shade tree, screen, or windbreak.

Size and Habit

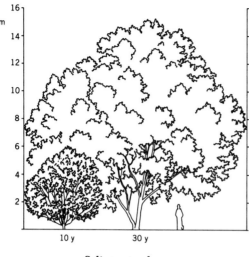

Salix pentandra.

Adaptability

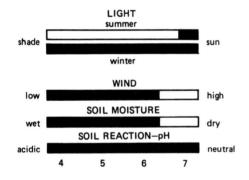

Seasonal Interest.   *Flowers:* Golden yellow catkins, 2.5–5 cm/1–2 in. long, add quiet but significant interest in spring. *Foliage:* Leaves are glossy, deep green, and broader than those of most willows, 5–12 cm/2–5 in. long and 2.5–8 cm/1–3 in. wide, making a dense, handsome foliage canopy. Leaves begin to fall in midautumn with little color change.

Problems and Maintenance.   *S. pentandra* is subject to the problems of willows in general (see *S. alba*) but is less troubled by insects and diseases than some willows and can function satisfactorily as a handsome shade tree, fast-growing but not long-lived, seldom reaching an age of 40 to 50 years. Some spraying and pruning usually is needed, so this is not a tree for street use or for parks having minimal maintenance budgets.

Hybrids and Related Species

Salix ×'Prairie Cascade'.   This hybrid derives its weeping habit and golden twigs from *S. alba*, probably var. *tristis*, and its glossy, deep green, leathery leaves from *S. pentandra*. Released by the Morden Research Station of Agriculture Canada in the early 1980s, this handsome tree is becoming popular in Zones 3a–6b, and is probably useful farther south as well.

Salix fragilis 8 (brittle willow, crack willow). This large tree, native to Europe and western Asia and naturalized on river banks in the northeastern United States and adjacent Canada, has little to recommend it as a landscape plant other than its tolerance of wet soil and salt. Better willows usually are more widely available, but this species can be used in Zones 3b–9a.

Salix nigra 7 (black willow).   This is the native "riverbank" willow in much of our area from New Brunswick to Ontario and southward to Florida and northern Mexico. There is little rationale for planting this species in formal or small-scale landscapes, but it may be planted or a subject for preservation in natural or naturalized sites. Useful in Zones 3b–9a+.

Salix purpurea 5

PURPLE OSIER, BASKET WILLOW
Deciduous shrub
Salicaceae (Willow Family)

Native Range. Europe and North Africa to central Asia and Japan.

Useful Range. USDA Zones 3b–9a.

Function. Hedge (formal or informal), specimen.

Size and Habit

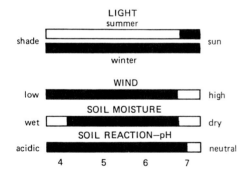

Salix purpurea.

Adaptability. More tolerant of wind than most willows because of its resilient branches, but less tolerant of wet and calcareous soils.

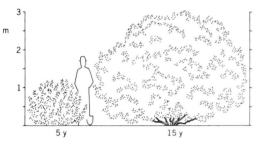

Seasonal Interest. *Flowers:* Catkins are insignificant. *Foliage:* Dull green to blue-green leaves are narrow, 5–10 cm/2–4 in. long, whitened underneath, and fall in autumn without color change. *Twigs and branches:* Slender and resilient, purplish when young, used in basket weaving.

Problems and Maintenance. *S. purpurea* is subject to the problems of willows in general, compounded by slightly different site requirements than most willows. Periodic drastic pruning with removal and burning of prunings may help to control diseases and is useful when maintaining the plant as a compact hedge.

Cultivars. 'Gracilis' (probably = 'Nana;' dwarf arctic willow) is a smaller, slender-twigged form with very narrow, blue-green leaves. This selection is planted in preference to the species type, usually as a formal or informal hedge. Useful in the same zones as the species type and perhaps also in Zone 3a. 'Pendula' has long, slender, pendulous branches, and makes an attractive accent plant to 1.5–1.8 m/5–6 ft in height and width when grafted on a 1.2-m/4-ft standard, or a mound 0.5–0.9 m/1.6–3 ft on its own.

Sambucus canadensis 5

AMERICAN ELDERBERRY
Deciduous shrub
Caprifoliaceae (Honeysuckle Family)

Native Range. Eastern North America: Nova Scotia to Manitoba and southward to Florida and Texas.

Useful Range. USDA Zones 3a–9a.

Function. Specimen, border, screen (with careful maintenance), edible fruits.

Size and Habit

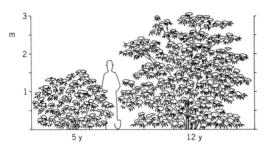

Sambucus canadensis.

Adaptability

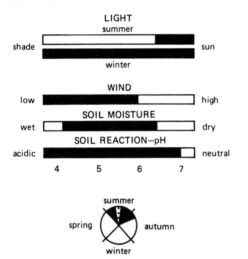

Seasonal Interest. *Flowers:* Tiny, creamy white, in large flattened clusters, to 25 cm/10 in. across, very early in summer. *Foliage:* Medium gray-green, compound leaves, serving as a neutral background for the flowers and fruits, falling soon after or with the berries in early autumn with little or no color change. *Fruits:* Shiny and purple-black when ripe in late summer, less than 0.5 cm/0.2 in. across but borne in large flattened clusters, often weighing branches down with their collective weight, valued for making preserves and wines.

Problems and Maintenance. This shrub is trouble-free but requires pruning to keep it in good form. The long branches are weak and tend to be pulled out of their usual position by the weight of large crops of fruits. Renewal pruning annually or at least biennially is necessary to maintain form and to remove any broken or winter-injured branches.

Sambucus canadensis.

Cultivars. 'Acutiloba' has dissected foliage. 'Argenteo Marginata' has white-margined leaves, but probably is not available in our area. 'Aurea' has golden-yellow foliage all summer, and red fruits. 'Maxima' has very large flower clusters, more than 30 cm/12 in. across, and rose-purple flower stalks, fairly showy after the flowers have dropped. 'Adams,' 'Kent,' 'Nova,' and 'York' are among the most popular cultivars selected primarily for heavy fruiting and fruit quality.

Related Species

Sambucus nigra 6 (European elderberry). This is the European counterpart of *S. canadensis*, with edible black fruits. It is a rangy plant that tends to go wild in many areas, and is at best no improvement on the native *S. canadensis* as a landscape plant except for its cultivars. More than 20 are available in Europe, but few in our area. The following can sometimes be found here. 'Albovariegata' has white-speckled foliage. 'Aurea' has golden-yellow to lime-green leaves, and red-flushed petioles. 'Marginata' has leaf margins gold at first, fading to pale yellow and eventually ivory. 'Purpurea' has bronze-purple foliage, with pale green flecks. Useful in Zones 4a–9a.

Sambucus pubens 5 (American red elderberry). This native of much of our area from New

Brunswick to Minnesota, southward to Georgia, and westward to Colorado grows wild in partly shaded sites and tolerates more shade in landscape sites than *S. canadensis*. Its yellowish white flowers in late spring and red fruits in midsummer are borne in pyramidal clusters, smaller than those of *S. canadensis*. Best adapted to moist sites, *S. pubens* is useful in Zones 4a–7b.

Sambucus racemosa 5 (European red elderberry). Several superior forms of this European counterpart of *S. pubens* have been selected and are valued for their summer interest in the northern parts of our area. 'Aurea' has yellowish foliage in early summer, later fading to green. 'Dropmore' has finely dissected, fernlike foliage and a dwarf growth habit. 'Laciniata' has coarsely dissected foliage. 'Plumosa Aurea' has striking, deeply and finely cut, gold foliage throughout the summer; new foliage is briefly red. 'Redman' is compact but eventually large-growing with deeply dissected leaves and showy, bright red fruits. 'Sutherland Golden' has golden foliage. These cultivars are generally useful in Zones 3a–7b. Even though some winter dieback may occur in Zones 3 and 4, the pruning required to maintain form removes any deadwood and recovery is rapid.

Sambucus pubens.

Sambucus racemosa 'Sutherland Golden.'

Santolina chamaecyparissus 3

LAVENDER COTTON

Evergreen shrub or subshrub

Asteraceae (Compositae; Aster Family)

Native Range. Southern Europe and North Africa.

Useful Range. USDA Zones 7b–9a+, and as an annual, sometimes surviving winter, in Zones 5b–7a.

Function. Small-scale groundcover, border, formal edging, or low hedge.

Size and Habit

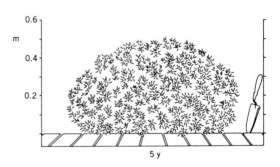

Santolina chamaecyparissus.

Adaptability.   Broadly adapted to soils and exposures, but best in full sun in well-drained, even dry, soil.

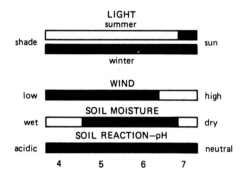

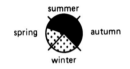

Seasonal Interest.   *Flowers:* Bright yellow, in rounded heads, 1–2 cm/0.4–0.8 in. across, in middle to late summer, but do not develop when plants are clipped as a formal edging or hedge. *Foliage:* Small leaves, 1–4 cm/0.4–1.6 in. long and finely divided, comparable in general texture to a juniper, strongly silvery gray with felty hairs, turning duller green from late autumn to midspring, aromatic when crushed.

Santolina chamaecyparissus.

Problems and Maintenance.   This plant is unusually free of insect and disease problems but requires frequent to occasional renewal pruning to maintain good form. Replacement of some plants annually may be necessary in Zones 6b–7a, but complete annual replacement is the simplest practice in Zones 5b and 6a. Even in Zones 7–9, plants are not long-lived and may need to be replaced after only a few years.

Related Species

Santolina rosmarinifolia 3 (synonyms: *S. virens, S. viridis;* green lavender cotton).   This is similar to *S. chamaecyparissus,* but has bright to deep green foliage.

Santolina pinnata 4 (Italian lavender cotton). This tall-growing species is little known in our area except in the form of ssp. *neapolitana,* which grows to 0.75 m/2.5 ft, with heavily tomentose, silvered foliage and bright yellow flowers. 'Edward Bowles,' a selection from ssp. *neapolitana,* grows only to about 0.35 m/12 in. tall, and has primrose-yellow flowers.

Sapium sebiferum 7

CHINESE TALLOW TREE
Deciduous tree
Euphorbiaceae (Spurge Family)

Native Range.   China, Japan; naturalized in a few areas in the Deep South.

Useful Range.   USDA Zones 8b–9a+.

Function.   Shade tree for quick effect.

Size and Habit

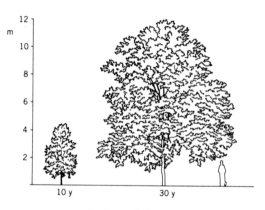

Sapium sebiferum.

Adaptability.   Unusually tolerant of widely differing soils.

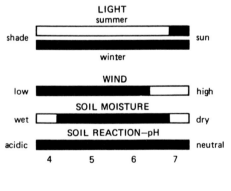

Seasonal Interest.   *Flowers:* Very small, yellowish, staminate (male) and pistillate (female) to-

gether in catkin-like terminal clusters, to 10 cm/4 in. long, in spring. *Foliage:* Pale to yellowish green, 3–8 cm/1–3 in. long, with long, slender petioles that allow leaf blades to flutter in the wind like those of poplars, turning bright red or yellow before falling in late autumn. *Fruits:* Capsules, to 1.5 cm/0.6 in. across, open to disclose white, waxy coated seeds, usually in clusters of three, which persist well into winter, adding interest after leaf fall.

Problems and Maintenance.   This tree is unusually free of insect and disease problems but is usually not long-lived. Flower and fruit litter limit its value as a tree for street or patio planting, for which it is otherwise well suited. Pruning is necessary only for initial shaping and removal of any deadwood, but should be done during the dormant season. When used as a lawn tree, the foliage canopy allows enough light for turf growth underneath, but surface roots can still interfere. A tendency to become naturalized is a problem in a few areas in the Deep South.

Related Species.   The following additional members of the Euphorbiaceae (Spurge Family) are not commonly encountered in landscape use in our area but are useful under certain conditions.

Aleurites fordii 6 (tung oil tree).   This native of south-central Asia is cultivated primarily for the oil from its seeds, but occasionally it is used as a small shade tree. It is fast growing, with leaves to 12 cm/5 in. long and broad, mostly lobed, turning red-orange before falling in late autumn. Flowers, appearing as the leaves expand in spring, are pale orange to pinkish white in showy clusters, and the smooth, rounded fruits, green at first, turning red and finally almost black, are about the size of small apples, 5–8 cm/2–3 in. across. It is useful as a shade tree in Zones 8b–9a+, but fruit is seldom produced north of Zone 9.

Croton alabamense 5 (Alabama croton).   This rangy, thicket-forming shrub, rare in the wild, is even more rarely propagated for landscape use. But with its deep green, rounded leaves, silvery whitened by a mat of fine hairs, it has distinct possibilities for human made landscapes. Not to be confused with the tropical croton of florists, *Codiaeum variegatum*, it is useful in Zones 7b–8b and perhaps elsewhere.

Daphniphyllum humile 4.   This evergreen shrub, growing to 1–2 m/3.3–6.6 ft tall and at least as wide. Its leaves are 5–12 cm/2–5 in. long and its flowers, like those of *D. macropodum* (below), are so small as to have negligible landscape interest. This shrub can be used for massing or a large-scale groundcover, probably in Zones 9a+, but possibly 8b.

Daphniphyllum macropodum 6.   This handsome, large, evergreen shrub from Japan and Korea, variously placed in the Euphorbiaceae or separated as the Daphniphyllaceae, is little known in landscape use in North America. But it has performed well in limited trials in Zone 9a and may be useful in Zone 8 as well. Foliage is dark green, forming a dense mass of lustrous, leathery leaves, each 10–20 cm/4–8 in. long, giving a texture similar to that of *Rhododendron maximum* or *Prunus laurocerasus*, yet distinctive because of the red petioles (leaf stalks) and young twigs. The small, pale green flowers in clusters only about 2.5 cm/1 in. long in late spring and the black fruits, only about 1 cm/0.4 in. long, add minor additional seasonal interest. The handsome selection 'Variegatum,' with creamy white variegated leaves, probably is not available in North America and has been found in England to be less cold-hardy than the species type.

Securinega suffruticosa 4.   This rather ungainly shrub with long, wandlike branches from northeastern Asia has been planted in the northern parts of our area but is not very useful, versatile, or colorful. Still, its bright green rounded leaves, to 3–6 cm/1.2–2.4 in. long, may add interest to the border. Since it frequently kills to the ground in winter in the areas where is is most likely to be used, Zones 3b–6b, spring pruning is necessary.

Securinega suffruticosa.

Sarcococca ruscifolia 4

FRAGRANT SARCOCOCCA, SWEET BOX

Evergreen shrub

Buxaceae (Boxwood Family)

Native Range.   China.

Useful Range.   USDA Zones 7b–9a and protected sites in Zone 7a.

Function.   Massing, shaded border, or foundation.

Size and Habit

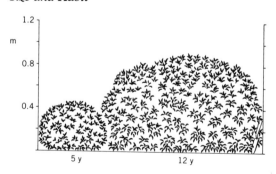

Sarcococca ruscifolia.

Adaptability

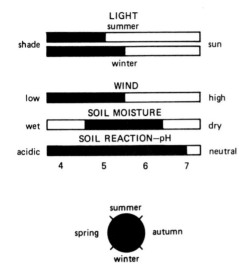

Seasonal Interest. *Flowers:* Fragrant, whitish, in small clusters in autumn, not showy but adding seasonal interest. *Foliage:* Evergreen, lustrous, stiff-leathery, sharply pointed, 3–5 cm/ 1.2–2 in. long, making a handsome, dense mass. *Fruits:* Deep red, rounded, about 0.6 cm/0.25 in. across, in small clusters in autumn and early winter.

Problems and Maintenance. This plant is apparently trouble-free given the proper site, but it is so little used in our area to date that its problems may not yet be fully known. Attention to site requirements, especially shade, is critical.

Related Species

Sarcococca confusa 4. This species has been confused with *S. ruscifolia,* from which it differs

in its greater height and its black fruits. Except for these differences, the two can be considered interchangeable for use in Zones 7b–9a.

Sarcococca hookeriana 3–4 (Hooker sarcococca or sweet box). This close relative of *S. ruscifolia* differs little but has slightly larger and less sharply pointed leaves and black fruits. It is best known for the variety *humilis* (synonym: *S. humilis;* dwarf sarcococca), which seldom exceeds 0.5 m/1.6 ft in height while making a dense mass of foliage. This form has proven useful in the Middle Atlantic and southeastern states as an excellent groundcover where some mass is needed. Its black fruits are less interesting than those of *S. ruscifolia.* It is useful in Zones 6b–9a and sheltered sites in Zone 6a, perhaps also in Zone 5b.

Sarcococca hookeriana var. *humilis.*

Sassafras albidum 7–8

SASSAFRAS
Deciduous tree
Lauraceae (Laurel Family)

Native Range. Northeastern United States, southern Ontario, and southward to Florida and Texas.

Useful Range. USDA Zones 5b–9a.

Function. Shade tree, specimen, massing, naturalizing.

Size and Habit

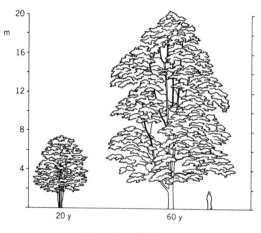

Sassafras albidum.

Adaptability

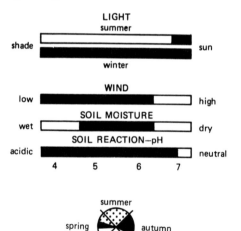

Seasonal Interest. *Flowers:* Small, yellow, in small clusters to 5 cm/2 in. long, before and at the beginning of leaf emergence, mostly dioecious. *Foliage:* Medium green, unlobed, two-lobed (mittenlike), or three-lobed, all three forms commonly found on the same tree, turning brilliant gold, orange, or orange-red in most sites and most years before falling in middle to late autumn. *Fruits:* Blue-black, on pistillate (female) plants, to 1 cm/0.4 in. long, interesting in combination with the bright red stalks and receptacles, which remain colorful for some time after fruits have been taken by birds in early autumn. *Twigs and Branches:* Horizontal branching creates an interesting pattern of greenish twigs, terminated in winter by large dormant buds, from which the next year's flowers will emerge.

Problems and Maintenance. Sassafras is subject to a variety of insect and disease problems. Most are not serious enough to require corrective action, but borers and bagworms can seriously weaken trees if not controlled. Pruning is necessary only for removal of deadwood. This tree produces root suckers, which can result in a thicket, but are easily controlled by mowing when trees are surrounded by turf. Availability is limited by difficulties in propagation and transplanting. Specifying young, container-grown plants will improve chances of successful transplanting.

Saxifraga stolonifera 2

Synonym: *S. sarmentosa*
STRAWBERRY BEGONIA,
STRAWBERRY GERANIUM
Herbaceous, evergreen or semievergreen groundcover
Saxifragaceae (Saxifrage Family)

Native Range.   Eastern Asia.

Useful Range.   USDA Zones 7a–9a+ but fully evergreen only in Zone 9a+.

Function.   Groundcover, specimen.

Size and Habit

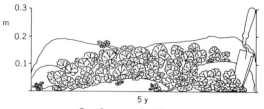

Saxifraga stolonifera.

Adaptability. Useful only in areas that remain relatively cool in summer, in shade, and with a fairly reliable supply of moisture.

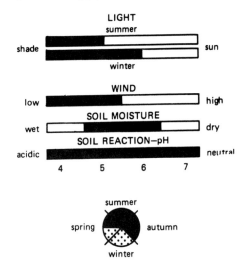

Seasonal Interest. *Flowers:* Small, white, in loose, upright clusters, 25–50 cm/10–20 in. tall, in midsummer. *Foliage:* Deep green with lighter veins, making a dense, fast-growing, highly decorative mat to 15 cm/6 in. or more deep. Foliage is the primary landscape feature of this plant, remaining evergreen or nearly so in the Deep South. Like strawberry, stolons (runners) are produced, terminating with new plantlets, enabling this plant to spread rapidly.

Problems and Maintenance. This plant is relatively free of serious problems, but slugs can be troublesome in the sites where it is at its best.

Related Species

Tiarella cordifolia 2 (foamflower). This member of the Saxifragaceae is native to the Appalachian Mountains, southward to Alabama and northward to Nova Scotia, and makes an excellent groundcover for shaded or partly shaded sites with a fairly moist soil. The deep green, lobed, and toothed leaves, vaguely maple-shaped, form a mat of interesting texture, and the delicate white flowers, arranged loosely on erect racemes to 30 cm/12 in. tall, provide added interest in midspring. Useful in Zones 5a–7b and in cool sites in Zone 8. The selection, var. *collina* 'Wherryi' (synonyms: *T. macrophylla, T. wherryi;* Wherry foamflower) is very similar to the species type, var. *cordifolia,* except that it does not spread by runners and has longer, usually more showy flower spikes. It is preferable to var. *cordifolia* in small gardens, but var. *cordifolia* may be more effective in naturalizing.

Sciadopitys verticillata 6–7

JAPANESE UMBRELLA PINE

Evergreen tree

Taxodiaceae (Taxodium Family)

Native Range. Japan.

Useful Range. USDA Zones 6b–7b, protected sites in Zone 6a, and areas in Zone 8 having moderate summers.

Function. Specimen, screen (in time).

Size and Habit

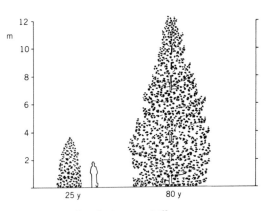

Sciadopitys verticillata.

Adaptability. Protection from full sun and wind in winter is beneficial in Zone 6, especially in the Midwest.

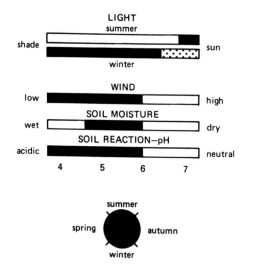

Seasonal Interest. *Foliage:* Large, fleshy needles, to 0.3 cm/0.12 in. thick and 10–12 cm/4–5 in. long, dark green and glossy on upper surface, pale underneath, arranged on the stout stems in whorls of 20 to 30, like spokes radiating from the hub of a wheel, giving a distinctive texture as well as growth habit. *Cones:* To 10–12 cm/4–5 in. long, not borne until trees are relatively old.

Problems and Maintenance. This tree is relatively free of serious problems and requires little or no maintenance in a proper site. The greatest limitation is its very slow growth, making this a plant primarily for the collector of unusual species. But it is handsome and distinctive given time to develop.

Cultivars. 'Wintergreen' was selected by Sidney Waxman of the University of Connecticut for its exceptionally glossy, bright green foliage color, especially in winter.

Sedum acre 2

GOLDMOSS STONECROP
Herbaceous, evergreen groundcover
Crassulaceae (Orpine Family)

Native Range. Europe, North Africa, and western Asia.

Useful Range. USDA Zones 4a–9a+.

Function. Groundcover, rock garden.

Size and Habit

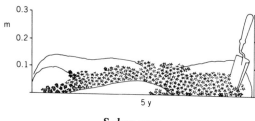

Sedum acre.

Adaptability. Although *Sedum* species are remarkably tolerant of poor, dry soil and other adverse site factors, they must have full sun and very well-drained soil for best results.

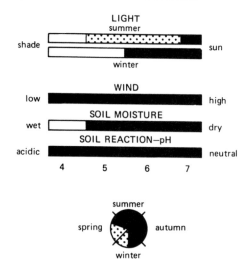

Seasonal Interest. *Flowers:* Bright yellow, making a solid mass of golden yellow in early summer. *Foliage:* Bright green year-round but in cold climates becoming dull green from midwinter until new growth begins in spring. Leaves are succulent, vaguely triangular, 0.5 cm/0.2 in. or less long. *Fruits:* Dry capsules are unattractive but can be removed for maximum effect, on a small scale.

Problems and Maintenance. *Sedum* species are unusually trouble-free and require no maintenance except for removal of plants that have exceeded the limits of the planting. Many species produce unwanted seedlings in nearby areas, but they are shallow-rooted and easily removed.

Cultivars. 'Aureum,' with bright green, yellow tipped foliage, is not widely available. 'Minor' (= 'Minus') is smaller in all respects, a logical selection for very small areas.

Related Species

Sedum species are useful groundcover plants, in at least Zones 4a–9a+ unless specified otherwise. A few of the best and most popular are listed here.

Sedum album 2 (white stonecrop). This native of the Mediterranean Region has succulent, teardrop-shaped leaves and white flowers in early summer on stalks 8–20 cm/3–8 in. tall. The selection 'Coral Carpet' has coral-pink foliage and pale pink flowers.

Sedum dasyphyllum 2. This is a cushion-forming plant, to 3–12 cm/1–5 in. high, with very small blue-gray leaves, pink-tinted stems, and white, pink-streaked flowers. The selection 'Riffense' has silver-gray leaves and pink flowers.

Sedum floriferum 2 'Weihenstephaner Gold' (sometimes sold as *S. acre* or a cultivar of *S. kamtschaticum*). This is a low form to 10–15 cm/4–6 in. high, with a brilliant show of golden yellow flowers, turning orange-gold with age, followed by red seed heads.

Sedum kamtschaticum 2. This vigorous groundcover has bright green, spatulate (obovate) leaves, 2–4 cm/0.8–1.6 in. long, and bright yellow flowers. The selection 'Variegatum' has creamy white-edged leaves and deep yellow

flowers from middle to late summer, and is slightly less vigorous than the green-leaved form.

S. middendorffianum 2. This groundcover, from eastern Siberia, Manchuria, and Mongolia, is similar to *S. kamtschaticum*, but a bit more refined in growth habit, with narrow spatulate leaves, to 4 cm/1.4 in. long, spiraled around the stems, and bright yellow flowers in middle to late summer.

Sedum reflexum 2 (synonym: *S. rupestre*). This native of western Europe grows a bit taller than *S. acre*, with nearly linear leaves to 1.5 cm/0.6 in. long. Golden yellow flowers are borne on stalks 15–25 cm/6–10 in. long, in late spring and early summer.

Sedum reflexum.

Sedum sexangulare.

Sedum sexangulare 2. This native of southeastern Europe and adjacent Asia has dark green leaves, 0.6 cm/0.25 in. long, arranged in six longitudinal, spiralled rows. Its yellow flowers appear in early summer. It can be invasive.

Sedum spathulifolium 2.   This clump-forming native of the West Coast grows to 10–15 cm/4–6 in. high and has spathulate, blue-green leaves, to less than 2 cm/0.8 in. long, and yellow flowers in early summer. It is probably significantly less cold hardy than most of the others listed, perhaps only to Zone 6b. Several selections have been made, including 'Capa Blanca' (= 'Cape Blanco'), a fine low, spreading form, and 'Purpureum,' with purple leaves.

Sedum spurium.

Sedum spurium 2 (two-row stonecrop).   This mat-forming plant from the Caucasus Mountains has deep olive-green leaves. Its pink flowers open in midsummer and quickly fade to near-white, except in the red-flowering cultivars. 'Coccineum' has medium-red flowers. 'Dragon's Blood' has dark red flowers, fading somewhat with time but remaining red, and its foliage turns red, in full sun, as it matures and through winter. 'Elizabeth,' 'Fuldaglut,' and 'Red Carpet' have pink flowers and red-purple foliage throughout the year. 'Variegatum' (= 'Tricolor') is much less vigorous, with leaves variegated creamy white and pink.

Sedum ternatum 2.   This creeping native of woodlands in eastern North America is not vigorous enough to make a strong groundcover, but makes a cushion of rounded leaves, with many small white flowers, with reddish stamens, in early summer, useful in small-scale gardens, especially where native species are required. The improved selection 'White Waters' is available in a few nurseries.

Nomenclatural note.   Several species once assigned to the genus *Sedum* have now been moved to the genus *Hylotelephium*. These are taller growing species, with foliage mass from 25–75 cm/10–30 in. high. During the 1980s, there was a major resurgence of interest in this group, especially for planting in combination with ornamental grasses and in other low-maintenance landscapes. A few of the most popular members of this group are listed here:

Hylotelephium sieboldii 2 (synonym: *Sedum sieboldii*).   This Japanese native has fleshy leaves, glaucous to purplish and more-or-less circular, to 2.5 cm/1 in. across, arranged in a most attractive and distinctive pattern, spaced along arching, radiating stems, and clusters of pale pink flowers in early autumn. Useful at least in Zones 5b–9a, perhaps somewhat colder zones as well. The selection 'Mediovariegatum' has a creamy white stripe in the center of each leaf. 'Variegatum' has glaucous blue leaves, irregularly marked with creamy white.

Hylotelephium spectabile 3 (synonym: *Sedum spectabile*).   This native of China and Korea develops a foliage mass to 0.3–0.7 m/1–2.3 ft high, and similar width, with glaucous, fleshy leaves, 4–10 cm/1.6–4 in. long and half as wide, and large clusters of pink to dull red flowers, from midsummer to early autumn, and in some cases still attractive when dried on the plant. Useful at least in Zones 5a–9a, perhaps colder zones as well. 'Brilliant' has clusters of carmine-red flowers in early autumn. 'Carmen' has clusters of bright pink flowers in early autumn. 'Indian Chief' has pale green foliage, and clusters of bright coppery-red flowers in autumn. 'Meteor' has gray-green foliage, and clusters of deep rose flowers in early autumn. 'Variegatum' has white-variegated green foliage, and pink flowers in early autumn.

Hylotelephium telephium 3 (synonym: *Sedum telephium*; live-forever).   This species from Europe and western Asia grows to 0.6 m/2 ft high, develops a foliage mass of about 2.5–7.5 cm/1–3 in. long, and half as wide, and clusters of red-purple flowers in late summer. Several selections for red-purple or bronze foliage have been made from ssp. *maximum* (synonym: *Sedum maximum*).

'Atropurpureum' has leathery, deep red-purple leaves, which retain their color through the growing season and later, and its large clusters of rose-tinted creamy flowers open in late summer or early autumn.

'Mohrchen' (probably a hybrid involving S. telephium ssp. maximum; burgundy sedum) is similar in form to 'Autumn Joy' (below) and has deep burgundy foliage like that of 'Atropurpureum,' turning ruby-red in autumn, with deep-pink flowers in late summer and early autumn.

Hylotelephium hybrids 2–3. Several hybrids exist within this genus; the following are among the most common:

'Autumn Joy' (= 'Herbstfreude' *H*; *telephium* × *H. spectabile*) grows to a foliage mass of 0.5–0.6 m/1.6–2 ft, with large clusters of rosy salmon-red flowers, aging to coppery bronze, and then a warm reddish-brown in winter, and is the most popular cultivar of all in our area.

'Ruby Glow' (= 'Rosy Glow'; probably *H. sieboldii* × *H. spectabilis* 'Atropurpureum') grows to 25 cm/10 in. high, with arching, radiating stems, red-edged, purplish-gray leaves, and rosy-red flowers in autumn.

'Vera Jameson' (probably *H. telephium* ssp. *maximum* 'Atropurpureum' or 'Honeysong' × 'Ruby Glow') has the arching growth habit of 'Ruby Glow' and deep purple foliage like that of 'Honeysong,' with dusty-pink flowers in autumn.

Sempervivum tectorum 2 (hens-and-chickens, house leeks). This European plant has been long-cultivated in many forms, all with tight rosettes of fleshy leaves that multiply until they fill in all available surface space, making a very effective groundcover for small areas in full sun and well-drained soil, or hardly any soil at all provided they do not remain wet. In addition to the many variants of S. *tectorum*, there are many additional species, although most are not very widely used. One type or another is useful almost anywhere in our area, at least northward to Zone 3b and southward to Zone 9a+.

Sequoiadendron giganteum 8

Synonym: *Sequoia gigantea*
GIANT SEQUOIA, BIG TREE, GIANT REDWOOD
Evergreen tree
Taxodiaceae (Taxodium Family)

Native Range. California.

Useful Range. USDA Zones 7a–9a+ and maritime and otherwise protected sites in Zone 6b.

Function. Specimen, large-scale screen.

Size and Habit

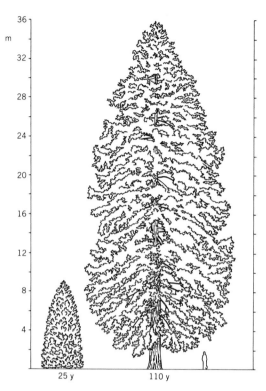

Sequoiadendron giganteum.

Adaptability. Some protection from winter sun and wind is necessary to prevent winter burn, at least in Zone 6.

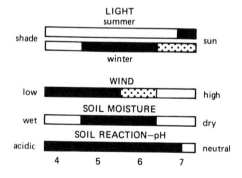

Seasonal Interest. *Foliage:* Evergreen, bluish green to olive-green needles, to 1.8 cm/0.7 in. long, resembling those of *Cryptomeria* in their spiraled arrangement on more-or-less whiplike to plumy branches. *Trunk:* Covered with thick, heavily furrowed red-brown bark.

Problems and Maintenance. A needle blight can be controlled by spraying, and a canker disease that may become troublesome is more difficult to control. The most common problems in experimental plantings in our area have been insufficient atmospheric moisture and winter burn of foliage. Pruning is not necessary.

Cultivars. 'Pendula,' a weeping selection, and 'Pygmaea,' a slow-growing variant, are curiosities and seldom available.

Related Species

Sequoia sempervirens 8 (synonym: *Sequoiadendron sempervirens;* coastal redwood). This tree can exceed *Sequoiadendron giganteum* in height, but it is more slender in growth habit. Native to coastal areas in northern California and even less well adapted to our area than *Sequoiadendron.* If at all useful in our area (and probably not), only in those places with closest to maritime climates in Zones 7a–9a.

Serenoa repens 3–4

SAW PALMETTO
Evergreen shrub
Arecaceae (Palmae; Palm Family)

Native Range. Coastal areas of the southeastern United States: South Carolina to Florida and Texas.

Useful Range. USDA Zones 8b–9a+.

Function. Groundcover, barrier, massing, specimen.

Size and Habit

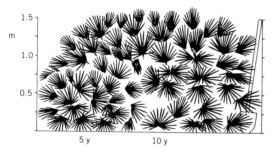

Serenoa repens.

Adaptability. Widely tolerant of soil moisture conditions, but size will vary with moisture supply, from 0.5 m/1.6 ft on dry sites to about 1.0 m/3.3 ft, occasionally 2 m/6.6 ft, on wet sites.

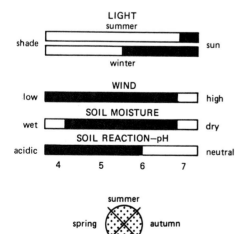

Seasonal Interest. *Flowers:* Fragrant, creamy white, but small, borne sparsely in a loose inflorescence among the leaves, adding minor interest in spring. *Foliage:* Olive to blue-green, evergreen, fanlike leaves 0.5 m/1.6 ft or more across, with saw-toothed margins on leaf stalks. Texture is too coarse for small-scale situations. *Fruits:* Small black fruits add almost negligible interest in late summer and autumn.

Problems and Maintenance. This plant is relatively trouble-free and normally requires no maintenance other than occasional weeding and removal of dead leaves.

Related Species

Sabal minor 3–4 (dwarf palmetto). This plant is similar in general effect to *Serenoa repens* and native to much the same area of the southeastern United States from North Carolina to Florida and Texas and northward to southeastern Arkansas. Slightly more cold-hardy than *Serenoa, Sabal minor* is useful in Zones 8a–9a+ and in very small size in Zone 7b.

Sabal palmetto 6–7 (cabbage palmetto). This native of Florida and the Atlantic coast to South Carolina, is the state tree of those two states. It grows to 10 m/33 ft tall, eventually taller, and nearly half that in width, making a fine shade, specimen, street, or patio tree. It is salt-tolerant and reported to be easily transplanted in June or July. Useful in Zones 9a+ and perhaps protected sites in Zone 8b.

Rhapidophyllum hystrix 3 (needle palm, blue palmetto). This clump-forming plant is similar in general effect to *Serenoa repens* except for the more distinctly blue-green color and sharp, needlelike leaf sheaths. It grows wild in moist sites from South Carolina to Florida and Mississippi and is useful in both moist and average sites in Zones 8a–9a+ and perhaps also in Zone 7b. The leaf sheaths are a potential hazard to small children, and this should be considered when using this plant.

Shepherdia argentea 5–6

BUFFALO BERRY, SILVER BUFFALO
BERRY
Deciduous shrub
Elaeagnaceae (Oleaster Family)

Native Range. North American plains: Manitoba to Kansas and Nevada.

Useful Range. USDA Zones 2b–6b.

Function. Windbreak, barrier hedge, specimen.

Size and Habit

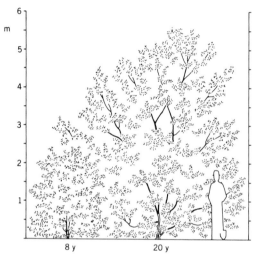

Shepherdia argentea.

Adaptability. Unusually well adapted to dry, alkaline soils. Tolerates infertile soil, in part because of its ability to fix and assimilate atmospheric nitrogen.

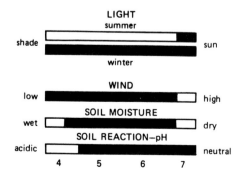

Seasonal Interest. *Flowers:* Small and yellowish, inconspicuous, in midspring. Dioecious. *Foliage:* Fine-textured and silvery like that of the related *Elaeagnus angustifolia*, with narrow leaves 2–6 cm/0.8–2.4 in. long, falling without color change in autumn. *Fruits:* Red to orange-red, to 0.6 cm/0.25 in. long, with silver flecks, sour but edible in preserves, on pistillate (female) plants only, in the presence of staminate (male) plants.

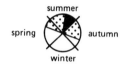

Problems and Maintenance. Leaf-spot and rust diseases are too minor to require control. Root suckers are produced and must eventually be pruned off or dug out if this plant is to be contained within a limited area. Brittle wood makes this plant susceptible to breakage under heavy snow.

Cultivars. 'Xanthocarpa' has yellow fruits.

Related Species

Shepherdia canadensis 5 (russet buffalo berry). This native of a wider range in North America from Newfoundland to Alaska and southward to Ohio, New Mexico, and Oregon is less silvery in appearance than *S. argentea* and smaller in stature but otherwise similar. Useful in Zones 2b–6b but probably not commercially available.

Shepherdia canadensis.

Shepherdia rotundifolia 4 (roundleaf buffaloberry). This somewhat spiny evergreen shrub from the Grand Canyon Plateau in northern Arizona and southern Utah is a potentially valuable landscape plant in dry climates in the southwestern extremes of our area (southeastern Kansas, Oklahoma, Texas) and perhaps somewhat farther north in the Great Plains. This handsome shrub exhibits a variety of adaptations to arid climates, including a compact, rounded growth habit and thick leaves, curled to nearly enclose the stomate-bearing undersurfaces, with a reflecting and insulating felt of silvery-white stellate hairs on both surfaces. It may be commercially available only as seed at present, but is worthy of trial in dry climates in Zones 6a–9a, perhaps also Zone 5.

Skimmia japonica 2–3

JAPANESE SKIMMIA

Evergreen shrub

Rutaceae (Rue Family)

Native Range.   Japan.

Useful Range.   USDA Zones 7b–8b and sheltered sites in Zone 7a. Best in areas having moderate summer temperatures.

Function.   Specimen,   foundation,   border, massing.

Size and Habit

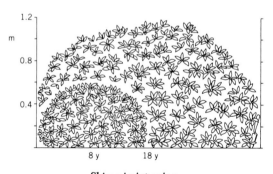

Skimmia japonica.

Adaptability

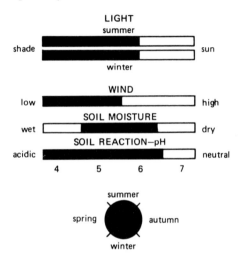

Seasonal Interest.   *Flowers:* Small, creamy white, in clusters 5–8 cm/2–3 in. long, borne terminally in middle to late spring. Dioecious. *Foliage:* Evergreen with rich, deep green color and rather coarse texture, the individual leaves 8–12 cm/3–5 in. long. *Fruits:* Bright red berries, 0.8 cm/0.3 in. across, in clusters to 8 cm/3 in. across, on pistillate (female) plants, in the presence of staminate (male) plants for pollination, ripening in autumn and persisting all winter.

Problems and Maintenance.   This plant is unusually trouble-free given a proper site with at least reasonably moist, organic soil, probably never needing to be pruned.

Cultivars.   'Rubella' is a male selection (so useful as a pollinator) with red upper leaves in winter and flowers red in the bud, then creamy white, in looser clusters than in the species type. 'Teufel's Female' and 'Teufel's Male' are compact selections, similar except for sex and with slightly smaller leaves. Plants are sometimes sold under names such as 'Dwarf Female' and 'Dwarf Male,' but such names probably have been applied to different clones. Many other cultivars are available in England, but apparently few of them have reached North America.

Subspecies.   The ssp. *reevesiana* (synonyms: *S. fortunei, S. reevesiana;* Reeves skimmia), from China, differs from the species type, ssp. *japonica,* in being lower in growth habit, with finer textured foliage, and hermaphroditic (all plants flowering and capable of pollinating). Useful in

areas with relatively mild summers in Zones 8a–9a, and perhaps also parts of Zone 7.

Skimmia japonica.

Smilax smallii 1

Synonym: *S. lanceolata*
FLORIDA OR SOUTHERN SMILAX,
LANCELEAF GREENBRIER
Evergreen vine
Smilacaceae (Smilax Family)

Native Range.   Southeastern United States, Mexico to Central America.

Useful Range.   USDA Zones 7b–9a+.

Function.   Specimen, screen (with support and pruning), climbing rapidly by tendrils to heights of 10 m/33 ft.

Size and Habit

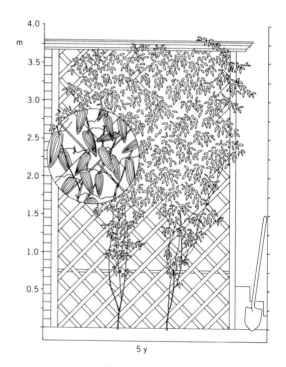

Smilax smallii.

Adaptability. One of the most widely adaptable evergreen vines within its useful range.

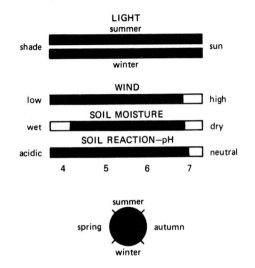

Seasonal Interest. *Flowers:* Pale green to whitish yellow, small and inconspicuous, dioecious. *Foliage:* Evergreen, lustrous, smooth and deep green, arranged rather sparsely on angled, prickly branches, eventually forming a dense mass. Individual leaves 5–8 cm/2–3 in. long and half as wide. *Fruits:* Dark red, 5–8 cm/2–3 in. across, in autumn, not borne in conspicuous numbers.

Problems and Maintenance. This vine is unusually free of insect and disease problems. It can become weedy and rank if not controlled, but control is not very difficult in spite of its tendency to spread by underground stems.

Related Species

Smilax laurifolia 1 (laurel-leaved greenbrier). This prickly plant grows wild in much the same area as the closely related *S. smallii* and is often confused with it. The two are roughly equivalent in the landscape, although *S. laurifolia* has black fruits. Useful in Zones 7a–9a+ and perhaps also in Zone 6.

Smilax megalantha 1 (coral greenbrier). This spiny evergreen native of China has very large leaves, to 12 cm/5 in. or more in length, and showy, coral-red fruits, to 2 cm/0.8 in. across, in autumn. It is useful in Zones 8a–9a+, but may not be available in North America.

Several deciduous *Smilax* species are native to our area but have little landscape value.

Sophora japonica 8

JAPANESE PAGODA TREE, CHINESE SCHOLAR TREE

Deciduous tree

Fabaceae (Leguminosae; Pea Family)

Native Range. China and Korea.

Useful Range. USDA Zones 6a–9a and Zone 5 with selection of appropriate genetic material.

Function. Shade tree, specimen.

Size and Habit

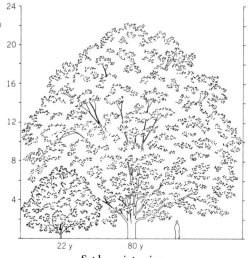

Sophora japonica.

Adaptability

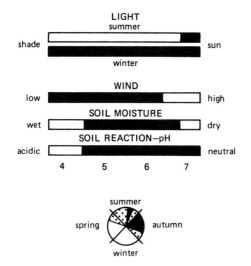

Seasonal Interest. *Flowers:* Pale yellow to creamy white, in loose clusters, 15–30 cm/6–12 in. long, in late summer, striking against the dark green foliage. *Foliage:* Compound, almost as fine-textured as that of *Gleditsia triacanthos,* bright green in early summer, turning dark green as growth ceases in midsummer and flowering begins, falling without color change in late autumn. *Fruits:* Bright yellow-green, lustrous seed pods, 5–8 cm/2–3 in. long, constricted between the seeds to resemble a string of beads, adding significant interest in autumn. *Twigs and Branches:* Smooth, olive-green, adding minor winter interest.

Problems and Maintenance. This tree is relatively trouble-free in Zones 6–9, but affected by twig blight and stem canker diseases, apparently associated with winter injury, in Zone 5. Pruning is seldom necessary except for removal of deadwood.

Cultivars. 'Pendula' is a strongly weeping form, useful only for positive accent but interesting for the form and green twigs. It grows little in height beyond the graft union, usually 1–1.5 m/3.3–5 ft from the ground, reaching 3 m/10 ft only after many years.

'PNI 5625' (Regent® scholartree), selected for rapid growth, excellent dark green foliage, and profuse flowering, develops into a broad oval tree, resistant to leaf-chewing insects and well adapted to urban conditions.

'Princeton Upright' (Plant Patent No. 5524, 1985) is upright in growth habit, and narrower than tall, useful where lateral space is limited.

Related Species

Sophora affinis 6 (coralbean). This small tree from Arkansas and eastern Texas is sometimes used in its native habitat and adjacent Louisiana as a small specimen tree with pink tinged white flowers in early summer. Useful in Zones 8b–9a+.

Sophora davidii 5 (synonym: *S. viciifolia;* vetch-leaf sophora). This large shrub from China occasionally is used for its pale blue-violet flowers, in clusters to 10 cm/4 in. long, in early summer. It is rather leggy, but is valued for its ability to grow well in hot, dry situations. Useful in Zones 6a–9a.

Sophora secundiflora 6–7 (mescal bean, frijolito, Texas mountain laurel). This small tree is native from central and western Texas to New Mexico and adjacent Mexico, only occasionally growing to more than 8 m/26 ft tall. It is valued for its 3- to 5-cm/1- to 2- in. clusters of showy and highly fragrant violet-blue flowers in early to middle spring, as well as for its glossy blue-green foliage, slightly coarser than that of *S. japonica.* Its bright red seeds, borne in 20-cm/8-in. pods, are poisonous to humans and other animals. Useful in Zones 8a–9a+, probably also Zone 7b.

Sesbania punicea 5 (synonym: *Daubentonia punicea;* rattle box). This large, wide-spreading shrub from Argentina has become naturalized in places along the Gulf Coast and occasionally is used as a landscape specimen. It is not very functional, except perhaps as a very small patio tree, but is valued for its hanging clusters of bright orange-red flowers during most of the summer. Seeds become detached and rattle in the angled pods when shaken in autumn and winter, suggesting the common name. Useful in Zone 9a+.

Sorbaria sorbifolia 4

Synonym: *Spiraea sorbifolia*
URAL FALSE SPIREA
Deciduous shrub
Rosaceae (Rose Family)

Native Range.   Northern and eastern Asia.

Useful Range.   USDA Zones 3a–8b.

Function.   Massing, specimen.

Size and Habit

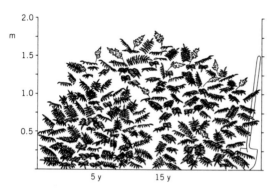

Sorbaria sorbifolia.

Adaptability

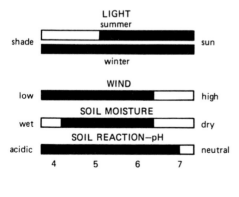

Seasonal Interest.   *Flowers:* Small, white, in fuzzy terminal panicles, 15–25 cm/6–10 in. long, showy in early summer to midsummer. *Foliage:* Medium green, compound leaves, to 50 cm/20 in. or more in length, with many sharply toothed leaflets, each 5–10 cm/2–4 in. long, falling in autumn without color change.

Problems and Maintenance.   This shrub is relatively trouble-free other than occasional mite infestations and requires little maintenance except pruning for confinement. It spreads rapidly underground and can take over a considerable area if not deliberately limited by root and top pruning. In any case, it is not a plant for small-scale situations. Occasional drastic renewal pruning may be needed to maintain form.

Related Species

Sorbaria kirilowii 5–6 (synonyms: *S. arborea, S. assurgens;* Kirilow false spirea).   This treelike shrub, native from central China to Tibet, is similar in general effect to *S. tomentosa,* but somewhat more cold-hardy, useful in Zones 6a–8b.

Sorbaria tomentosa var. *angustifolia* 5 (synonyms: *S. aitchisonii, S. angustifolia;* Kashmir false spirea).   This large shrub from Pakistan, to 3–5 m/10–16 ft tall, differs from *S. sorbifolia* in its greater stature, larger flower clusters, and reddish one-year-old stems. It is less likely to spread by suckering, usually remaining a tall, somewhat leggy shrub, and it is less cold-hardy than *S. sorbifolia,* to Zone 6a or Zone 8a, depending on climate of origin over its wide range.

Holodiscus discolor 6 (oceanspray).   This close relative of *Sorbaria* from the Pacific Northwest functions as a taller edition of *Sorbaria* without the strong tendency to become weedy, but it is also less cold-hardy. It is useful in Zones 6b–8b and perhaps slightly colder zones, depending on geographic origin, and it is striking with its large flower clusters in early summer to midsummer.

Sorbus alnifolia 8

KOREAN MOUNTAIN ASH
Deciduous tree
Rosaceae (Rose Family)

Native Range.   China, Japan, and Korea.

Useful Range.   USDA Zones 4b–7b, perhaps also colder zones with selection of appropriate genetic material.

Function.   Specimen, shade tree.

Size and Habit

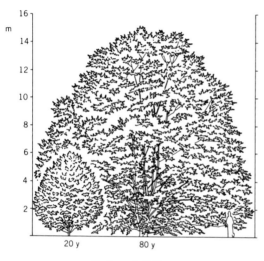

Sorbus alnifolia.

Adaptability

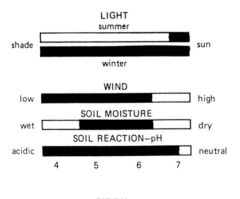

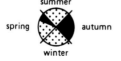

Seasonal Interest.   *Flowers:* Small, white, in loose clusters, 5–8 cm/2–3 in. across, effective against the rich green foliage in late spring. *Foliage:* Rich green, turning dark green in late summer, with a crisp texture resembling that of *Alnus, Betula,* or *Carpinus,* the simple, toothed leaves, to 5–10 cm/2–4 in. long, turning golden orange before falling in midautumn. *Fruits:* Red-orange berries, to 0.8 cm/0.3 in. across, in loose clusters covering essentially the entire tree, persisting for a time after leaf drop, colorful against the silvery gray twigs and branches. *Trunks and branches:* Smooth, silvery gray bark of large branches resembles that of *Fagus* or *Cladrastis,* adding winter interest.

Sorbus alnifolia.

Problems and Maintenance.   *S. alnifolia* has a few insect and disease problems like most other members of the Rosaceae, but the most serious pest of *Sorbus* species, borers, does not seem to be a problem with this species, perhaps in part because it is harder-wooded than most other mountain ashes. Unfortunately, *S. alnifolia* is susceptible to fire blight, a serious problem in areas where outbreaks of this disease tend to be severe.

Cultivars.   Trees of *S. alnifolia* vary widely in form; a few narrow variants have been selected but are not widely available. 'Redbird' is columnar in form, growing to 7–9 m/23–30 ft tall and about half as wide, with an abundance of translucent red fruits, and golden-yellow autumn foliage.

Sorbus alnifolia.

Related Species

Sorbus folgneri 6 (Folgner mountain ash).   This native of China is smaller in stature than *S. alnifolia*, with leaves white-felted underneath and equally colorful in autumn, with somewhat larger fruits. A graceful, small tree, useful in Zones 6a–7b and perhaps also in Zone 5 but little tried and seldom available. The selection 'Lemon Drop' has shiny yellow fruits.

Sorbus aria 7

WHITE BEAM MOUNTAIN ASH
Deciduous tree
Rosaceae (Rose Family)

Native Range.   Europe.

Useful Range.   USDA Zones 6a–7b, probably also Zone 5.

Function.   Shade tree, specimen. Used widely as a street tree in Europe but not recommended as such in our area because of the borer problem.

Size and Habit

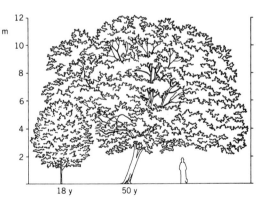

Sorbus aria.

Adaptability

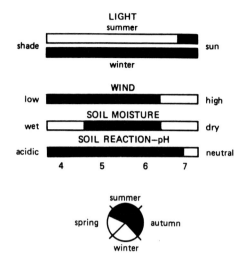

LIGHT
summer

shade   sun

winter

WIND

low   high

SOIL MOISTURE

wet   dry

SOIL REACTION–pH

acidic   neutral

4   5   6   7

summer

spring   autumn

winter

Seasonal Interest. *Flowers:* Small, white, in flattened terminal clusters, 5–8 cm/2–3 in. across, in late spring. *Foliage:* Deep green, the simple, toothed leaves, 5–12 cm/2–5 in. long, covered underneath with white, felty pubescence, giving an interesting bicolored effect in the wind and when viewed from underneath, turning reddish before falling in late autumn. *Fruits:* Bright orange-red, 1.2 cm/0.5 in. across, showy in late summer to early autumn.

Problems and Maintenance. Like most other *Sorbus* species, *S. aria* is subject to a variety of minor insects and diseases and one major problem: borers. Because of this, it should be specified only where an adequate maintenance program is available, and this rules it out for street plantings in much of our area.

Cultivars. Several selections have been made in Europe, but they are seldom if ever available in our area. The most likely to be found are 'Aurea,' with yellow foliage, and 'Majestica' (= 'Decaisneana'), with larger-than-typical fruits and large leaves, very white underneath.

Related Species

Sorbus intermedia 6–7. (Swedish whitebeam). This round-headed tree from northern Europe looks like a smaller edition of *S. aria*, with lobed leaves, with a few distinct leaflets, and gray-white-felted underneath, and probably is a hy-

brid. It is more widely used in Canada than in the United States, but has performed well in the hot and cold climates of the U.S. Midwest. Useful at least in Zones 6a–8a, and probably at least parts of Zone 5.

Sorbus torminalis 7 (wild service tree). This handsome tree from Europe and the Mediterranean is rounded in growth habit, with strongly lobed leaves having little or no pubescence but rather waxy, bright green in spring and summer, turning dull to bright red in autumn. Useful in Zones 6b–9a and at least parts of Zone 6a, but seldom commercially available in our area except as seeds.

Sorbus aria.

Sorbus aucuparia 7

EUROPEAN MOUNTAIN ASH
Deciduous tree
Rosaceae (Rose Family)

Native Range.   Northern Europe and Asia.

Useful Range.   USDA Zones 3b–7b with selection of appropriate genetic material.

Function.   Specimen, shade tree.

Size and Habit

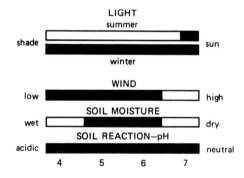

Sorbus aucuparia.

Adaptability

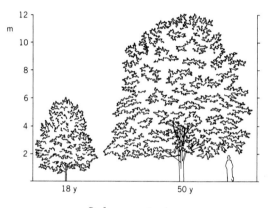

Seasonal Interest.   *Flowers:* Small, white, in large, flattened, terminal clusters, to 8–12 cm/3–5 in. across, in late spring. *Foliage:* Dull green, compound, with about a dozen small, toothed leaflets, giving a rather fine texture, in some years turning reddish before falling in late au-

tumn. *Fruits:* Bright orange to red, individually 0.8 cm/0.3 in. across, in large clusters, very colorful from late summer until middle or late autumn.

Problems and Maintenance.   Even though this is the most commonly used species of *Sorbus* in our area, it is no freer of problems than the others mentioned and less so than some. Borers are the big problem, and fire blight also can be destructive in geographic areas where outbreaks of this disease frequently are severe. Sun-scald can damage unwrapped trunks of newly planted trees in Zones 3 and 4. *S. aucuparia* and other species (see Related Species and Hybrids) should be used in street planting or other public or large-scale use only where an adequate maintenance program will be followed.

Cultivars.   Several variants have been selected. None are common in our area, but a few of those most likely to be encountered are listed here.

'Asplenifolia' (cutleaf European mountain ash) has dissected leaflets and correspondingly finer texture than the species type.

'Blackhawk' is a columnar tree to 10–12 m/33–40 ft tall and only half as wide, with large orange fruits and heavy, dark green foliage, relatively well adapted to Midwest climates.

'Fastigiata' (upright European mountain ash) has narrow branching angles and upright growth habit.

'Michred' (Cardinal Royal™), introduced by Michigan State University, is vigorous and upright, nearly as narrow as 'Blackhawk', to 9–11 m/30–36 ft tall and 5–6 m/16–20 ft wide, and very symmetrical, with rich green leaves, silvered underneath, and large quantities of bright red fruits—one of the most showy mountain ashes in fruit.

'Pendula' (weeping European mountain ash) has pendulous branches and is a curiosity more than a functional tree. It is seldom available.

'Rossica' is another columnar selection, compact and symmetrical, growing to about the same size as 'Black Hawk', but with bright red fruits.

'Variegata', with yellow-variegated leaves, and 'Xanthocarpa', with orange-yellow fruits, are not widely available, if at all, in eastern North America.

Related Species and Hybrids

Sorbus americana 7 (synonym: *Pyrus americana;* American mountain ash).   This North American counterpart of *S. aucuparia*, growing wild from Newfoundland to Manitoba and southward to high elevations in North Carolina, is very similar to that species in landscape appearance, function, and limitations. There is some evidence that *S. americana* may be slightly less tolerant of hot summers than *S. aucuparia*, but this probably varies within each species. When availability is considered, *S. americana* usually comes off in second place, but it is useful in Zones 2b–6b and farther south at high elevations near or in the natural range.

Sorbus americana.

Sorbus amurensis 7 (Amur mountain ash).   This species differs little from *S. aucuparia* in appearance, and is not widely available, but probably useful in the same areas as that species.

Sorbus ×*arnoldiana* 6–7 (Arnold mountain ash). This hybrid of *S. discolor* × *S. aucuparia* is notable for its clear pink fruits, striking in early autumn against the deep green foliage. It is available in very few nurseries but useful in Zones 3b–7b.

Sorbus decora 7 (synonym: *S. americana* var. *decora;* showy mountain ash).   This close relative of *S. americana* grows wild in the northern parts of the range of that species and differs in landscape effect only in that its fruits are larger, to 1 cm/0.4 in. across. It is useful in Zones 3a–6b. The selection 'Nana' is compact in growth and narrow in outline, at least in its early years.

Sorbus decora 'Nana.'

Sorbus discolor 6–7 (snowberry mountain ash). This native of northern China, useful in Zones 3a–7b, is not widely available but distinctive for its snow-white fruits, about the same size as those of *S. aucuparia.*

Sorbus hupehensis 6 (Hupeh mountain ash). This native of central and western China grows to 6–8 m/20–26 ft high, with an oval to globose form, and creamy-white to coral-red fruits, and foliage of great substance. The selection 'Bailfire' (Coral Fire®) has bright coral-red fruits, as well as red petioles, twig-bark, and autumn foliage. Probably useful in Zones 3a–7b.

Sorbus × *hybrida* 6–7 (hybrid mountain ash). This vigorous tree with partly lobed and partly compound leaves was originally found in Finland and is thought to be a hybrid between *S. aucuparia* and either *S. intermedia* or *S. rupicola*, a shrub growing to 2 m/6.6 ft tall in southern Scandinavia. It is reportedly tetraploid, reproducing by apomixis (embryos derived from only the seed-bearing parent) and a slightly more vigorous alternative to *S. aucuparia*, probably equally susceptible to borers but useful in Zones 3b–7b.

Sorbus ×*meinichii* 6–7 (Meinich mountain ash). This tree from southern Norway is presumed to be, like *S.* × *thuringiaca*, a hybrid of *S. aria* and *S. aucuparia*, but it reportedly a tetraploid and reproduces apomictically (embryos derived from only the seed-bearing parent), in effect reproducing as a clone.

Sorbus pohuashanensis 6–7 (Chinese mountain ash). This small tree from northern China serves as a slightly smaller version of *S. aucuparia*, with outstanding flowering, autumn foliage, and fruiting interest. It is not widely available in our area but is potentially useful at least in Zones 5a–7b, perhaps also Zone 4. The selection 'Chinese Lace' has deeply toothed leaves, which give a lacy appearance to the canopy.

Sorbus scopulina 6 (Rocky Mountain mountain ash). This shrubby small tree from western North America is occasionally used as a landscape plant in the western fringes of our area, but usually other species are selected in preference to it east of the Rocky Mountains. Useful in Zones 3a–6b.

Sorbus ×*thuringiaca* 6–7. This hybrid of *S. aria* and *S. aucuparia* is very similar to *S.* ×*hybrida*. The narrowly pyramidal selection 'Fastigiata' is commercially available in Canada but perhaps not in the United States. Useful in about the same areas as *S.* ×*hybrida*.

Sorbus tianshanica 5–6 (Turkestan mountain ash). This compact tree from central Asia serves as a still smaller (than *S. pohuashanensis*) version of *S. aucuparia*, potentially useful in the same areas as *S. aucuparia*, with yellow-orange autumn foliage and orange-red fruits. It is in commerce in our area as the selection 'Dwarfcrown' (Plant Patent No. 4157, 1977; Red Cascade™).

Sorbus vilmorinii 5–6 (Vilmorin mountain ash). This graceful shrub or small tree, to 4–6 m/13–20 ft tall, is small enough in all its parts to give a dainty, graceful appearance, and it is especially colorful in autumn, with pink-flushed white fruits and red-purple autumn foliage. Useful at least in Zones 6b–8a, perhaps somewhat colder zones as well.

Spiraea ×*billiardii* 4

BILLIARD SPIREA
Deciduous shrub
Rosaceae (Rose Family)

Hybrid Origin.   *S. douglasii* × *S. salicifolia*.

Useful Range.   USDA Zones 4a–9a.

Function. Massing, bank cover, border. Quickly forms large thickets, so must be confined in borders.

Size and Habit

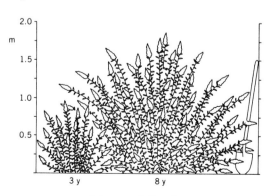

Spiraea ×*billiardii*.

Adaptability. Performs best in open, sunny areas with good air circulation.

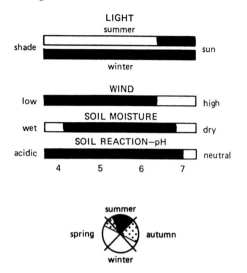

Seasonal Interest. *Flowers:* Bright rose-pink in elongated terminal clusters, 10–20 cm/4–8 in. long, early summer to midsummer and until late summer in some selections. *Foliage:* Medium to light green, whitish gray underneath, arranged sparsely on the long, stiffly arching branches. General appearance is rather coarse.

Problems and Maintenance. Powdery mildew can be troublesome in areas with poor air circulation, and aphids frequently disfigure the foliage. Drastic renewal pruning is needed every two to four years to prevent this plant from becoming a tangled mass. This usually is done easily because the stems remain fairly slender, but it constitutes a maintenance expense.

Related Species

Spiraea alba 4 (meadowsweet, meadow spirea). This thicket-forming shrub native to much of the eastern United States is similar in effect to S. ×*billiardii* but has white flowers and is a little more coarse and irregular in growth habit. Useful in Zones 3b–9a.

Spiraea douglasii 5 (Douglas spirea). This native of the Pacific Northwest is a parent of S. ×*billiardii* and very similar in general appearance and function, with deep rose flowers, beginning to open slightly later than those of S. ×*billiardii*. Useful in Zones 3b–8b with selection of appropriate genetic material. The ssp. *menziesii* is similar but somewhat smaller, to 1–1.5 m/3.3–5 ft high, native to the Pacific Northwest and ranging northward to Alaska, and useful in Zones 3a–8a with selection of appropriate genetic material.

Spiraea douglasii spp. *menziesii.*

Spiraea latifolia 4 (meadowsweet). This close relative of S. *alba* is similar, with white flowers and thicket-forming habit, but is native to somewhat more northern areas from Newfoundland to the Dakotas. Useful in Zones 3b–9a.

Spiraea tomentosa 3 (hardhack, steeplebush). This common weed of poor pastures in the northern parts of eastern North America seldom exceeds 0.5 m/1.6 ft in height on poor soils and has little value as a landscape species except in natural or naturalized situations, but it can be used for its upright clusters of rosy pink flowers and rusty-tomentose stems and leaf undersides in a shrub border, where it will occasionally reach 1 m/3.3 ft in height in good soil. Useful in Zones 3b–8a.

Spiraea japonica 3

Synonym: *S.* ×*bumalda* (in part)
JAPANESE SPIREA
Deciduous shrub
Rosaceae (Rose Family)

Native Range. Japan and China.

Useful Range. USDA Zones 4a–9a and parts of Zone 3 with some winter dieback.

Function. Massing, border, foundation.

Size and Habit

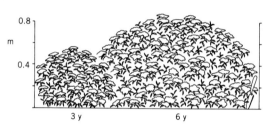

Spiraea japonica.

Adaptability

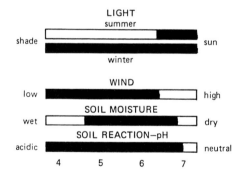

Seasonal Interest. *Flowers:* Bright crimson to rosy pink or white in flat clusters, 8–12 m/3–5 in. across, in early summer and occasionally thereafter. *Foliage:* Leaves of some cultivars emerge purplish or bronze, turning medium green as they expand, with occasional white or pale yellow streaks, making a fairly compact mass

of medium texture. Those of some cultivars, in some years, turn orange or crimson before falling.

Problems and Maintenance. This shrub is relatively trouble-free, although several insects occasionally cause minor problems. More sensitive to calcareous (high pH) soils than most spireas, and lime chlorosis occurs on some of the heavier midwestern soils.

Spiraea japonica.

Varieties and Cultivars. The var. *fortunei* (synonym: *S. dolchica*), from eastern and central China, is a moundlike shrub, usually to 1.5–2 m/5–6.6 ft high and wider, with sharply and deeply toothed leaves and pink flowers in large clusters. Useful in Zones 6a–9a, perhaps parts of Zone 5 as well.

'Albiflora' (synonym: *S. albiflora*; white Japanese spirea) has rich green foliage and white flowers.

'Alpina' is a dwarf selection, only 0.3 m/1 ft tall, with smaller leaves, making a dense mass, and soft rose-pink flowers from early summer through midsummer, useful in rock gardens and other small-scale situations. Useful at least in Zones 5a–9a.

'Anthony Waterer' is probably the oldest cultivar currently in use in North America, and still one of the most common, with a maximum height of 0.6 m/2 ft and dull rosy-pink flowers in clusters to 12–15 cm/5–6 in. across, in early summer and intermittently thereafter. Cold-hardy at least to Zone 4b.

'Atrosanguinea' (Mikado spirea), 'Dart's Red,' and 'Coccinea' are similar to 'Anthony Waterer' except that they have brighter rose-red flowers, later fading to pink. The differences among these three are so small that they are essentially interchangeable in landscape use.

'Bullata' (synonym: *Spiraea bullata*; crispleaf spirea) is a small plant, seldom taller than 0.3–0.4 m/1–1.5 ft, but wider, with dark green, leathery, crinkled leaves. Its flowers are more-or-less typical of *S. japonica*, but it is the foliage quality that makes this plant distinctive. This is not as widely available as other cultivars of this species and not as cold-hardy, but useful in Zones 6b–9a+ and sheltered sites (or with reliable snow cover) in Zones 5b and 6a.

'Crispa' is notable for its deeply cut and twisted leaf margins, giving it significant summer foliage interest. Otherwise, it is similar to 'Anthony Waterer' except that it is slower to develop to functional size and has somewhat brighter rose-pink flowers.

'Flaming Mound' is a Canadian selection, similar to 'Goldflame,' probably not yet available in the United States at this writing.

'Froebelii' is a larger version of 'Anthony Waterer', growing to nearly 1 m/3.3 ft. It is among the most cold-hardy selections of *S. japonica*, to Zone 3b.

'Gold Mound' is a compact selection from Canada, growing only to 0.5–0.6 m/1.5–2 ft high, with bronze-red new foliage, soon turning golden yellow and holding that color through the growing season, and pink flowers in early summer.

'Goldflame' is similar to 'Anthony Waterer' except slightly more compact and with bright gold, red-tipped new foliage in spring and early summer, pink flowers, and coppery orange autumn foliage. It is very striking in appearance at times, dingy brown-orange at others.

'Lisp' (Plant Patent No. 7537, 1991; Golden Princess™) is similar to 'Goldflame,' but reportedly holds its golden color better in summer heat.

'Little Princess' is densely compact, to 0.5–0.6 m/1.5–2 ft high and wider, with fine-textured light green foliage that turns deep red in autumn, and pink flowers in early summer and intermittently thereafter.

'Monhub' (Plant Patent No. 5834, 1986; Limemound™) forms a mound to 0.9 m/3 ft high and nearly twice as wide, with reddish-tinged lemon-yellow new foliage, maturing lime-green, pink flowers in early summer, and orange-red foliage in autumn.

'Norman' is larger than 'Little Princess,' to 0.9 m/3 ft high and wide, with stronger pink flowers and raspberry-purple to red autumn foliage.

'Shibori' (= 'Shirobana') forms a mound of upright branches to 0.6–0.9 m/2–3 ft high, distinctive for its heavy production of rose, pink, and white flowers.

Related Species

Spiraea betulifolia 3.   This white-flowered relative of *S. japonica* from northeastern Asia is not as well known as its hybrid, 'Rosabella,' with pink flowers, developed by F. L. Skinner of Dropmore, Manitoba. This cultivar is useful as a replacement for *S. japonica* in Zone 3, perhaps also Zone 2b.

Spiraea fritschiana 4 (Fritsch spirea). This broadly mound-forming shrub from eastern China and Korea is closely related to *S. betulifolia*, but has larger leaves, 3–8 cm/1–3 in. long, large clusters of white flowers in late spring, and red and gold autumn foliage. It is useful at least in Zones 5a–8a, perhaps also Zone 4.

Spiraea prunifolia 5

BRIDALWREATH SPIREA

Deciduous shrub

Rosaceae (Rose Family)

Native Range.   China, Korea, Taiwan.

Useful Range.   USDA Zones 5a–9a+.

Function.   Border, specimen, informal hedge.

Size and Habit

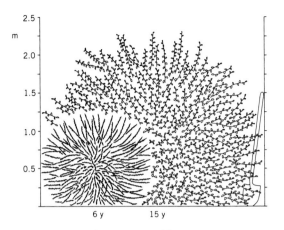

2.5
m
2.0
1.5
1.0
0.5

6 y   15 y

Spiraea prunifolia.

Adaptability

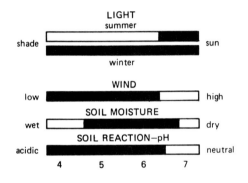

LIGHT
summer
shade   sun
winter

WIND
low   high

SOIL MOISTURE
wet   dry

SOIL REACTION–pH
acidic   neutral
4   5   6   7

summer
spring   autumn
winter

Seasonal Interest.   *Flowers:* Pure white, very double, 0.8–1.2 cm/0.3–0.5 in. across, borne in large numbers on the slender, gracefully arching branches in middle to late spring before leaves have expanded. *Foliage:* Deep green, glossy leaves are 2.5–5 cm/1–2 in. long, giving the best landscape interest of any spirea and turning bright orange-red in autumn in most years.

Problems and Maintenance.   This shrub is subject to the troubles of spireas in general, but seldom seriously except for aphids, which occasionally disfigure the excellent foliage. Pruning is needed only to remove any deadwood and for renewal of old plants. Shearing should never be done, since this destroys the gracefulness of the plant.

Spiraea prunifolia.

Forms and Cultivars.   'Plena,' the double-flowered form, is actually the species type, since it was the first form given the name *S. prunifolia,* even though it is a horticultural form. Because of this, it is technically redundant to use the cultivar designation 'Plena,' yet this is the most common way this form is listed by nurseries, and it should cause no confusion.

f. *simpliciflora,* the single-flowered wild type, is seldom encountered in landscape use, nor is it commercially available. The flowers are less showy and not as long-lasting as the double flowers of the species, accounting for the low level of interest in this form.

Spiraea thunbergii 4

THUNBERG SPIREA
Deciduous shrub
Rosaceae (Rose Family)

Native Range.   China, Japan.

Useful Range.   USDA Zones 4b–9a+.

Function.   Border, specimen, informal hedge.

Size and Habit

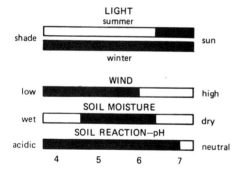

Spiraea thunbergii.

Adaptability

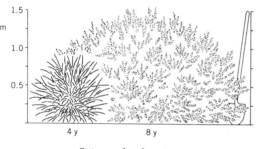

Seasonal Interest.   *Flowers:* White, only about 0.8 cm/0.3 in. across but borne in large numbers in loose clusters, showy because they open just as the leaves are beginning to expand in early to midspring. *Foliage:* Bright green, very fine-textured, with narrow leaves averaging about 2.5 cm/1 in. long, giving a loose, billowy appearance to the slender branches and turning yellow-orange in some years before falling in autumn.

Problems and Maintenance.   This species is subject to the troubles of spireas in general but is seldom affected seriously except by aphids, which cause leaf curling. Pruning is needed only to remove any deadwood and for renewal of old plants. Shearing destroys the graceful character of this plant and should be avoided. Renewal pruning should be done as described under *S. ×vanhouttei*, Problems and Maintenance.

Related Hybrids

Spiraea ×arguta 4 (garland spirea).   This hybrid of *S. thunbergii*, probably with *S. ×multiflora* (itself a hybrid of two Eurasian species: *S. crenata* and *S. hypericifolia*), is slightly more cold hardy than *S. thunbergii*, with medium-green foliage that seldom colors in autumn and is not quite so finely textured as that of *S. thunbergii*. The selection 'Compacta' remains below 1.5 m/5 ft for years in full sun and is cold-hardy to Zone 3b.

Spiraea ×cinerea 4 (ashy spirea).   This hybrid of *S. hypericifolia* by *S. cana* (from former Yugoslavia) is represented in commerce by the selection 'Grefsheim,' a very graceful shrub growing to 1.2–1.5 m/4–5 ft high and wide, flowering on gracefully arching branches, about two weeks earlier than the flowers of *S. ×vanhouttei*, followed by soft green foliage. Useful at least in Zones 4b–8b.

Spiraea ×*vanhouttei* 4

VANHOUTTE SPIREA,
BRIDALWREATH
Deciduous shrub
Rosaceae (Rose Family)

Hybrid Origin.   *S. cantoniensis* × *S. trilobata.*

Useful Range.   USDA Zones 3b–8b.

Function.   Specimen, border, massing, informal hedge.

Size and Habit

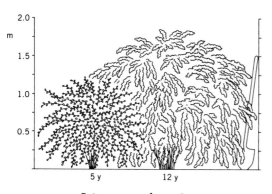

Spiraea ×*vanhouttei.*

Adaptability

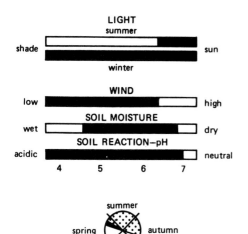

Seasonal Interest.   *Flowers:* White, about 0.8 cm/0.3 in. across, in dense flat clusters, to 4 cm/1.6 in. across, showy in late spring against the foliage on gracefully arching branches. *Foliage:* Deep, dull blue-green to dark green, with small leaves that are individually distinctive but not making a very dense or interesting foliage mass, often falling in autumn without color change but occasionally turning a delicate, dull red-orange first.

Problems and Maintenance.   There is a long list of insects and diseases that can affect *Spiraea* species, including *S.* ×*vanhouttei,* but few are commonly troublesome. Aphids frequently disfigure the foliage in summer, and powdery mildew can do the same in later summer with high humidity and poor air circulation, but these problems cause little or no permanent damage. Pruning usually is necessary only for renewal of very old plants or removal of any deadwood and should be avoided when not necessary so as not to interfere with the natural gracefulness of the shrub. When pruning is needed, never use hedge shears but thin by cutting out part (or all in drastic renewal) of the older stems to a few inches from the ground, and then selectively tip prune if necessary to promote fullness. Prune spring-flowering spireas immediately after flowering so as not to reduce bloom for that year. Summer flowering species that flower on new growth are best pruned in spring before plants have made much new growth. Drastic renewal pruning of any spirea by cutting the entire plant top to the ground should be done in early summer to allow plenty of time for regrowth and acclimation for the following winter.

Cultivars.   'Compacta' has more compact growth and reaches a height of only about 1.5 m/5 ft at maturity but is only occasionally available. 'Renaissance' was selected in the early 1990s at Bailey Nurseries, St. Paul, Minnesota, for its more disease-resistant foliage. It is increasing in popularity.

Related Species

Spiraea cantoniensis 5 (synonym: *Spiraea reevesiana;* Reeves spirea).   This parent of *S.* ×*vanhouttei* from China and Japan is used in preference to the hybrid in the Deep South, where it is semievergreen and tolerates extreme heat better. In areas where both species can be grown (Zones 7 and 8), *S. cantoniensis* has a somewhat better growth habit and drops its spent flowers more quickly. It is useful in Zones 7a–9a+, leaving *S. ×vanhouttei* as the preferred species only in Zones 3b–6b, where *S. cantoniensis* is not cold-hardy. The selection 'Lanceata' (= 'Flore Pleno') has double, pure white flowers and slightly smaller leaves than the species type.

Spiraea nipponica 5 (Nippon spirea).   This stiffly upright shrub with outward-arching branches has white flowers against the excellent, dark blue-green foliage in late spring. The var. *tosaensis*

(= 'Snowmound') is more compact than the species, growing to only 1–1.2 m/3.3–4 ft high and wide. 'Halward's Silver' is dwarfer still, remaining below 0.9 m/3 ft high, but spreading to the same width as 'Snowmound.' Useful in Zones 4b–8b.

Spiraea trilobata 4 (threelobe spirea).   This cold-hardy parent of *S. ×vanhouttei*, native to central and northeastern Asia, functions as a smaller version of *S. ×vanhouttei*, not exceeding 1.5 m/ 5 ft in height. The selections 'Fairy Queen' and 'Swan Lake' are even smaller, remaining below 1 m/3.3 ft. Useful at least in Zones 3b–8a, but particularly valuable in the Far North.

Spiraea veitchii 5

VEITCH SPIREA
Deciduous shrub
Rosaceae (Rose Family)

Native Range.   China.

Useful Range.   USDA Zones 6a–9a+, possibly also Zone 5.

Function.   Specimen, border.

Size and Habit

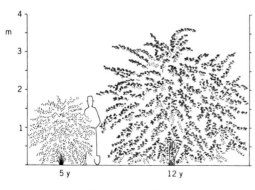

Spiraea veitchii.

Adaptability

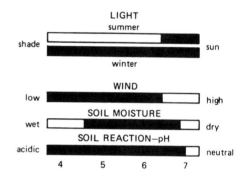

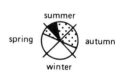

Seasonal Interest.   *Flowers:* White, in dense, flattened clusters, 3–6 cm/1.2–2.4 in. across, borne in large numbers on long, gracefully arching branches in early summer. *Foliage:* Medium green, somewhat whitened underneath, falling in autumn with little or no color change.

Problems and Maintenance.   This large shrub, handsome in flower, is subject to most of the limitations of spireas in general, but its only serious drawbacks are its availability and its size. In recent decades, demand for smaller shrubs has eclipsed this and the two related species, below, but any one of the three may be substituted for the others in Zones 6a–8b.

Related Species

Spiraea henryi 5 (Henry spirea).   Also native to China, this shrub is not as tall or showy as *S. veitchii,* yet similar in general effect and more cold-hardy. Useful in Zones 5a–8b, perhaps also parts of Zone 4, but seldom available.

Spiraea wilsonii 5 (Wilson spirea).   Another Chinese native, this species is similar in flowering effect to *S. veitchii* and intermediate in size and time of flowering between that species and *S.* ×*vanhouttei.* Useful in Zones 6a–9a, but seldom available.

Staphylea trifolia 6

AMERICAN BLADDERNUT
Deciduous shrub or small tree
Staphyleaceae (Bladdernut Family)

Native Range.   Northeastern United States and adjacent Canada, southward to Georgia and westward to Minnesota.

Useful Range.   USDA Zones 4a–7a and sheltered sites in Zone 3b.

Function.   Border, specimen, naturalized.

Size and Habit

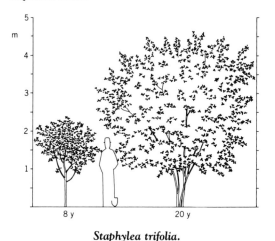

Staphylea trifolia.

Adaptability

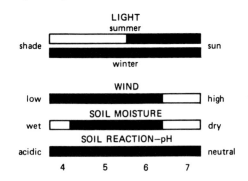

Seasonal Interest.   *Flowers:* Creamy or greenish white, lightly fragrant, individually about 0.8 cm/0.3 in. long, in nodding clusters about 4 cm/1.6 in. long, in middle to late spring. *Foliage:* Bright green leaves with three leaflets, arranged sparsely on stiff twigs, falling in midautumn with little or no color change. *Fruits:* Inflated pods, usually 3–4 cm/1.2–1.6 in. long and three-lobed, at first greenish white, ripening light brown.

Problems and Maintenance.   This species is relatively free of serious problems, although a twig-blight disease occasionally can be troublesome. Availability is very limited, since demand for this plant is restricted to situations where its peculiar fruiting interest and relative freedom

Staphylea trifolia.

from maintenance compensate for its lack of striking seasonal color.

Related Species

Staphylea bumalda 5 (Japanese bladdernut). Except for its size, to 2 m/6.6 ft tall, and slightly more showy and fragrant flowers, this species differs little from *S. trifolia*. Seldom available, but it is useful in Zones 5b–7b, perhaps also in colder zones.

Staphylea colchica 6 (Caucasian bladdernut). The flowers of this shrub are much more showy than those of *S. trifolia*, the leaves mostly have five leaflets, and the inflated fruits are larger, 5–8 cm/2–3 in. long. Less cold-hardy than the

American species but useful at least in Zones 6a–8a.

Staphylea holocarpa 6 (Chinese bladdernut). This, the tallest species of *Staphylea*, eventually reaches heights of 8 m/26 ft and can function as a patio tree in Zones 6a–8a. Its flowers are about as showy as those of *S. colchica*, but earlier, before the leaves have expanded, and the var. *rosea*, with pink flowers, is of special interest, although as yet seldom available.

Staphylea pinnata 6 (European bladdernut.) One of the most showy bladdernuts in bloom, with flower clusters 5–12 cm/2–5 in. long. This species has been used in landscape planting in Europe, where it is native, for centuries, but it is seldom available in our area, even though it is useful in Zones 5b–7b.

Euscaphis japonica 5. This large shrub or very small tree from China and Japan, in the Staphyleaceae (Bladdernut Family), is similar to *Staphylea* in habit, growing to 3–4 m/10–13 ft tall, with compound leaves composed of 7–11 leaflets, each 5–8 cm/2–3 in. long. Flowers are small and yellowish green, opening in late spring in clusters 5–12 cm/2–5 in. across, followed by very small rosy-pink fruits, opening in late summer to reveal steely blue-black seeds. Potentially useful in Zones 8a–9a, probably also Zone 7b, but seldom available.

Stephanandra incisa 3–5

CUTLEAF STEPHANANDRA
Deciduous shrub
Rosaceae (Rose Family)

Native Range.   Japan and Korea.

Useful Range.   USDA Zones 5a–8b.

Function.   Border, specimen, massing.

Size and Habit

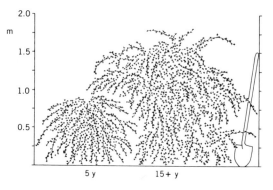

Stephanandra incisa.

Adaptability. Tolerant of considerable shade, but looks best when exposed to some direct sun.

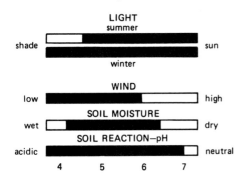

Sephanandra incisa 'Crispa.'

Stephanandra incisa 'Crispa.'

Seasonal Interest. *Flowers:* Pale greenish yellow, individually only about 0.5 cm/0.2 in. across, borne in loose terminal clusters about 2.5–5 cm/1–2 in. across, adding some interest in late spring or early summer. *Foliage:* Lobed, fine-textured, and bright green, loosely spaced on the slender, red, arching and zigzag branches, turning reddish before falling in autumn on branches exposed to full sun.

Problems and Maintenance. This shrub is seldom seriously troubled by insects and diseases, but twigs winterkill to varying degrees in the North, making at least minimal pruning a necessity. Pruning should be done selectively, removing deadwood and thinning old plants lightly. Shearing destroys the character of the plant and should be avoided.

Cultivars. 'Crispa' is much more compact in growth habit with strongly arching branches, not usually exceeding a height of 1 m/3.3 ft when planted in full sun. More useful for massing or as a tall groundcover than the species type, and more commonly available.

Related Species

Stephanandra tanakae 4 (Tanaka stephanandra). This Japanese shrub has larger leaves, more vig-

orous and coarser growth habit, and usually more brightly colored autumn foliage: yellow, orange, or scarlet. It is rarely used or available, and its useful range is not accurately known but includes at least Zones 6a–8b.

Neillia sinensis 4 (Chinese neillia). This gracefully arching shrub appears intermediate in growth habit and foliage character between its close relatives, *Physocarpus* and *Stephanandra*, but with character of its own in its bright green, lightly incised leaves, zigzag stems, and small, nodding pink flowers in late spring or early summer. Seldom available commercially but useful in Zones 6a–8b and possibly Zone 5 as well, with site requirements similar to *Stephanandra*. Several other *Neillia* species are included in institutional collections, but these are even rarer than *N. sinensis*.

Stewartia ovata 6

MOUNTAIN STEWARTIA
Deciduous shrub or small tree
Theaceae (Tea Family)

Native Range.   Southern Appalachian Mountains: Kentucky to Georgia.

Useful Range.   USDA Zones 7a–8b, perhaps also sheltered sites in Zone 6b.

Function.   Specimen, border, patio tree.

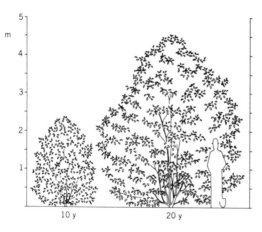

Stewartia ovata.

Adaptability.   Partial shade from summer sun is desirable for best performance and flowering, especially in areas having hot summers. Requires unusually good soil drainage.

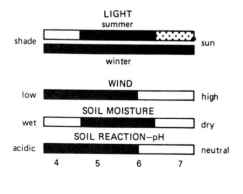

Seasonal Interest.   *Flowers:* White with yellow stamens in the center, 5–8 cm/2–3 in. across, resembling single white camellias, borne singly along the stems and opening a few at a time from middle to late summer. *Foliage:* Light green and rather coarse, serving as an effective background for the showy flowers but not very interesting in itself until autumn, when in some years it turns orange or scarlet before falling in midautumn. *Trunk and branches:* Brownish gray bark is finely fissured and rough, sometimes exposing the green inner bark but lacking the smooth, sculpted, multicolored and flaking character of the oriental stewartias.

Stewartia ovata.

Problems and Maintenance.   This plant has been relatively troublefree but it has been used so little that it has not been fully evaluated for disease problems. It is considered difficult to propagate, one reason why it has not been used more, but the principal reason may be its lack of bark interest. It is seldom commercially available except in a very small number of nurseries specializing in native plants of the southeastern states.

Varieties.   The var. *grandiflora* (showy mountain stewartia) has larger flowers than the species type, to 8–10 cm/3–4 in. across, with wavy-edged white petals and purple stamens, and is more cold-hardy, useful in Zones 6a–8b, and slightly more easily available than the species type.

Related Species

Stewartia malacodendron 6 (Synonym: *S. virginica;* Virginia stewartia or silky camellia). This shrubby tree from the southeastern states grows to 5 m/16 ft tall, with flowers similar to those of *S. ovata* var. *grandiflora,* opening slightly earlier.

Unlike *S. ovata,* it eventually develops flaking bicolored brown and tan bark that can be nearly as interesting as that of the Asian species. It is less cold hardy than *S. ovata,* useful in Zones 7b–9a.

Stewartia pseudocamellia 7

JAPANESE STEWARTIA
Deciduous tree
Theaceae (Tea Family)

Native Range.   Japan.

Useful Range.   USDA Zones 6a–8b, perhaps also 5b.

Function.   Specimen tree, massing.

Size and Habit

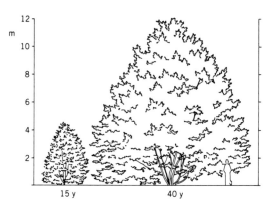

Stewartia pseudocamellia.

Adaptability.   Partial shade from summer sun is desirable for best performance and flowering, especially in areas having hot summers. Requires unusually good soil drainage.

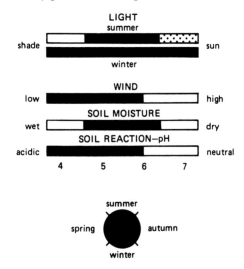

Seasonal Interest.   *Flowers:* White, with yellow-orange stamens in the center, 5–6 cm/2–2.4 in. across, resembling single white camellias, opening a few at a time from middle to late summer. *Foliage:* Rich green and of medium texture, serving as an effective background for the flowers and turning deep red-purple before falling in autumn. *Trunk and branches:* Smooth bark gives a molded or sculpted look to trunk and branches, the reddish brown outer bark peeling away in irregularly rounded flakes to expose lighter brown underneath, giving a striking, multicolored pattern, effective in all seasons.

Problems and Maintenance.   This plant is relatively trouble-free, provided that an appropriate site is used.

Cultivars. 'Cascade' is a low-branching, semi-pendulous selection that grows to only 3–5 m/ 10–16 ft high, but is barely commercially available at this writing. 'Korean Splendor': see *S. koreana*, below.

Related Species

Stewartia koreana 6–7 (Korean stewartia). This outstanding tree grows to 6–10 m/20–33 ft tall, with larger flowers than *S. pseudocamellia*, to 7–7.5 cm/2.8–3 in. across, brighter golden to red-orange autumn foliage, and bark interest equal to that of *S. pseudocamellia*. There is considerable doubt that this should be given species rank; specialists have also classified it as *S. pseudocamellia* var. *koreana*, as a deciduous var. *koreana* of the evergreen Chinese species, *S. ptero-petiolata*, or simply as a cultivar: *S. pseudocamellia* 'Korean Splendor'. Under whichever name, it is increasing in popularity and availability, and is useful in Zones 6a–8b and probably also sheltered sites in Zone 5b. The Polly Hill selection 'Ballet' grows to at least 6–9 m/20–30 ft high, with a gracefully arching habit and unusually large flowers, to 8–9 cm/3.5 in. across.

Stewartia monadelpha 7 (Hime-syara stewartia). This tree from China grows to 10–15 m/33–49 ft tall, or even taller in native habitat, with smaller flowers than the other species, to 2.5–3.5 cm/1–1.4 in. across, and rather smooth, subtly bicolored reddish brown bark that provides outstanding winter interest. It is not as widely available as *S. pseudocamellia*, but more so than the American species, and is useful in Zones 6a–8b.

Stewartia rostrata 6–7 (beaked stewartia). This Japanese tree grows to 7–10 m/23–30 ft tall,

Stewartia koreana (S. pseudocamellia 'Korean Splendor').

Stewartia koreana (S. pseudocamellia 'Korean Splendor.').

serving as a smaller version of *S. monadelpha* with larger flowers, to 5 cm/2 in. across. Seldom available but potentially useful in Zones 6b–8b.

Stewartia sinensis 6–7 (Chinese stewartia). This seldom-used Chinese species is very similar to *S. rostrata* and potentially useful in Zones 6b–8b, but is seldom available in our area.

Styrax japonicum 6

JAPANESE SNOWBELL
Deciduous tree
Styracaceae (Styrax Family)

Native Range. China, Japan.

Useful Range. USDA Zones 6b–8b, sheltered sites in Zone 6a, and areas in Zone 9a having moderate summers.

Function. Specimen, patio tree (where lateral space is available).

Size and Habit

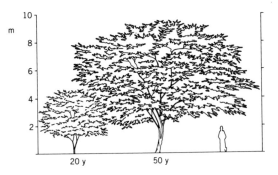

Styrax japonicum.

Adaptability

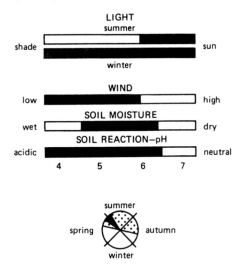

Seasonal Interest. *Flowers:* White, slightly fragrant, vaguely bell-shaped but with spreading petals, to 2 cm/0.8 in. across in small clusters to 5 cm/2 in. long, gracefully pendulous below the branches. *Foliage:* Deep green and lustrous, 3–8 cm/1–3 in. long and half as wide, giving a rather fine texture and forming a canopy above the branches, not covering the flowers hanging below, turning yellow or dull red in some years. *Fruit:* Dry, rounded capsules dangling beneath the branches are distinctive but not conspicuous. *Trunk and branches:* Bark is dark gray and fairly smooth; sometimes trunks and main limbs are sinewy.

Problems and Maintenance. *S. japonicum* is usually trouble-free and requires little mainte-

nance. Light pruning may help establish the tree's growth habit but is neither necessary nor desirable thereafter except to remove any deadwood.

Cultivars. 'Carillon' (= 'Pendula') is moderately pendulous in habit, with white flowers. 'Fargesii' is unusually vigorous and has a strongly tree-form habit, but is not often available. 'Kusan' is smaller than the species, to 3–4 m/10–13 ft high, and rounded in habit, with large white flowers. 'Pink Chimes,' a Brookside Gardens introduction, has a semipendulous habit and small, clear pink flowers. 'Rosea' has pink flowers.

Styrax japonicum.

Styrax japonicum.

Related Species

Styrax americanum 5 (American snowbell). This large shrub is native to the southeastern United States from Virginia to Florida and Louisiana. Occasionally it is used in human-made landscapes in Zones 6b–9a but is more likely to be encountered as a subject for preservation or naturalization in and near its native habitat. Its flowering interest is similar to that of *S. japonicum*.

Styrax grandifolium 6 (bigleaf snowbell). This large shrub or small tree, native to the southeastern United States from Virginia to Florida, has fragrant flowers. Like *S. americanum*, it is more likely to be available for preservation than for planting, but it is useful for either, when available, in Zones 7b–9a.

Styrax obassia 6 (fragrant snowbell). This large shrub or small tree from Japan has the largest leaves of any *Styrax* species mentioned here, to as much as 20 cm/8 in. long and frequently 10 cm/4 in. or more across. In fact, the heavy foliage partly obscures the fragrant flowers, in pendulous racemes 10–20 cm/4–8 in. long, which are nevertheless as showy as those of *S. japonicum*. This is a handsome, small tree, more upright in growth habit than *S. japonicum*, and useful in Zones 6b–8b, and good sites in Zone 6a.

Sinojackia rehderiana 6. This small tree from China closely resembles the *Styrax* species in foliage and flowers, but its flowers open earlier in spring. Potentially useful in at least Zones 7b–9a+, but seldom available.

Symphoricarpos ×*chenaultii* 3

CHENAULT CORALBERRY
Deciduous shrub
Caprifoliaceae (Honeysuckle Family)

Hybrid Origin.   Probably *S. microphyllus* × *S. orbiculatus*.

Useful Range.   USDA Zones 5a–8b.

Function.   Border, massing, large-scale groundcover.

Size and Habit

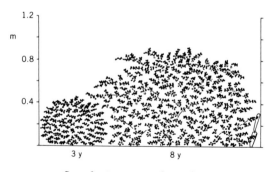

Sumphoricarpos ×*chenaultii*.

Adaptability

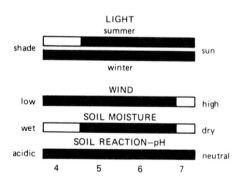

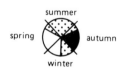

Seasonal Interest.   *Flowers*: Pink, small, and inconspicuous, in late summer. *Foliage*: Dull green, fine textured, not distinctive except in the selection 'Hancock' (see Cultivars), turning dull yellow briefly in some years before falling in early to middle autumn. *Fruits*: Berrylike, coral-red, 0.6 cm/0.25 in. across, some whitened on the side away from the sun, in terminal clusters to 4 cm/1.6 in. long, showy in autumn and persistent well into winter.

Problems and Maintenance. Several diseases occasionally may infect foliage, fruits, and stems, requiring the removal of infected material and protection with fungicidal sprays. Drastic renewal pruning, needed every few years to keep this plant in good condition, furnishes an opportunity to remove and burn any infected parts along with the rest of the tops. Protective sprays can be applied at this time if symptoms of disease have been observed.

Cultivars. 'Hancock' is an outstanding dwarf selection, reaching heights of about 0.5 m/1.6 ft with better foliage than average for the species. An excellent, large-scale groundcover, slightly less cold-hardy than the Zone 5a limit given for *S. ×chenaultii* generally, but at least to Zone 5b. It can be invasive in good soil.

Related Species and Hybrids

Symphoricarpos albus 3–4 (synonym: *S. racemosus*; snowberry). The species type, var. *albus* (eastern snowberry), native to much of eastern North America, grows to about 1 m/3.3 ft high, with whitish fruits in middle to late summer. The var. *laevigatus* (synonym: *S. rivularis*; western snowberry), native to much of western North America, has larger, more showy fruit and grows to a height of at least 1.5 m/5 ft. Both varieties have inconspicuous pale pink flowers and are planted primarily for their white fruits in autumn, in Zones 4a–8b, with selection of appropriate (nearby origin) genetic material.

Symphoricarpos ×doorenbosii 4 (*S. albus* var. *laevigatus* × *S. ×chenaultii*; Doorenbos coralberry). This vigorous hybrid has large, variously pink-flushed white fruits and good dark green foliage. The selection 'Magic Berry' is spreading in habit, to 1.2–1.5 m/4–5 ft high, with conspicuous lilac-pink fruits in autumn. 'Mother of Pearl' is more compact and semipendulous, to 1.5 m/5 ft high with white fruits marbled with pale pink. 'White Hedge' is upright in habit, to 1.8 m/6 ft high and 1.2 m/4 ft wide, with large numbers of white fruits in upright clusters.

Symphoricarpos orbiculatus 3 (coralberry; Indian currant). This parent of *S. ×chenaultii*, native to much of eastern North America from New York to South Dakota and southward to Florida and Mexico, is predictably variable in response to climate. With selection of appropriate (nearby origin) genetic material, it is a useful, large-scale groundcover with coral-red fruits, about 0.5 cm/0.2 in. across, in autumn and early winter in Zones 3b–9a, but it is most useful in Zones 3b–6b. The selections 'Albovariegatus,' with white leaf-margins, and 'Aureovariegata,' with small, yellow-margined leaves, are seldom, if ever, available in our area.

Symplocos paniculata 6

ASIATIC SWEETLEAF,
SAPPHIREBERRY
Deciduous shrub or small tree
Symplocaceae (Sweetleaf Family)

Native Range. China, Himalayas, Japan, Korea.

Useful Range. USDA Zones 6a–8b.

Function. Screen, specimen, large border.

Size and Habit

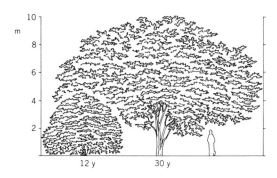

Symplocos paniculata.

Adaptability

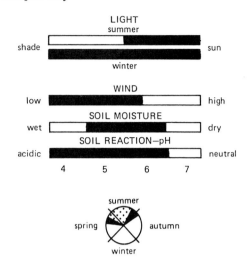

Symplocos paniculata.

Seasonal Interest. *Flowers:* Fragrant, creamy white, to only 1 cm/0.4 in. across, in panicles 4–8 cm/1.6–3 in. long, fairly showy in midspring. *Foliage:* Bright green and crisp-appearing in early summer, turning dull green and coarse-appearing later, falling with little other color change in midautumn. *Fruits:* Bright blue, individually 0.8 cm/0.3 in. across, borne in large numbers and showy, but usually taken rather quickly by birds.

Problems and Maintenance. Minor leaf-spot diseases and insect infestations are seldom serious enough to require control. Pruning is needed only for removal of any deadwood or for gradual renewal of old plants. This species is reported to be self-incompatible. To the extent that this is true, for pollination and heavy fruiting it is necessary to plant more than one plant, of seedling origin, since cloned plants are genetically identical and incompatible with each other as well as within each plant.

Related Species

Symplocos tinctoria 6 (common sweetleaf, horse sugar). This seldom-planted native of the southeastern United States from Delaware to Florida and Louisiana is of interest primarily as a subject for preservation in natural and naturalized landscapes. It forms a large shrub or small tree with semievergreen foliage, almost fully evergreen in the Deep South. Its primary landscape interest lies in its yellow flowers, borne in clusters to 5 cm/2 in. across before the new leaves emerge in midspring. Fruits are not conspicuous, and the plant form is loose and not highly functional. Useful in Zones 7b–9a+.

Syringa ×chinensis 6

Synonym: *S. rothomagensis*
CHINESE LILAC
Deciduous shrub
Oleaceae (Olive Family)

Hybrid Origin. *S. ×persica × S. vulgaris.*

Useful Range. USDA Zones 4a–8b.

Function. Specimen, border, screen, informal hedge.

Size and Habit

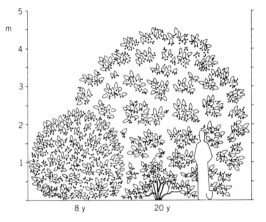

Syringa ×*chinensis.*

Adaptability

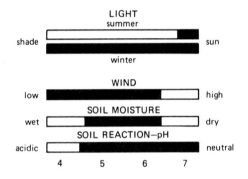

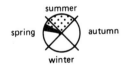

Seasonal Interest. *Flowers:* Lavender to red-purple, in rather loose, mostly erect panicles, 10–20 cm/4–8 in. long, larger in some selections under ideal conditions, very showy in late spring. *Foliage:* Medium to bright green, similar to those of *S. vulgaris* but only about 6 cm/2.5 in. long and 2 cm/0.8 in. wide, making a dense mass effective for screening but otherwise not adding distinctive interest, falling in autumn without color change.

Problems and Maintenance. Several diseases and insects can be troublesome, including bor-ers, leaf miners, scale insects, and leaf and twig blights. Powdery mildew is a perennial problem in some areas where it disfigures the foliage in late summer but does little permanent damage. Pruning is necessary for renewal of older plants. Since this species does not sucker freely, it is easier to maintain in form than its parent, *S. vulgaris.* Most lilacs are not low-maintenance plants.

Cultivars. 'Alba' has white flowers. 'Lavender Lady' has pinkish lavender flowers and is not only very free-blooming but performs well in climates where little or no winter chilling occurs, to at least Zone 9a (it may be somewhat less hardy in Zones 4 and 5). 'Saugeana' (= 'Red Rothomagensis,' = 'Rubra') is also very free-blooming, with reddish-lilac flowers.

Related Species

Syringa ×*laciniata* 4 (synonyms: *S.* ×*persica* var. *laciniata;* cutleaf lilac). This graceful, foun-tainlike hybrid (*S. protolaciniata* × *S. vulgaris*) has strongly arching branches and fine foliage texture brought about by the deeply dissected leaves. It makes an interesting addition to the shrub border because of its distinctive foliage effect and pale lavender flowers and is useful in Zones 5a–9a.

Syringa ×*persica* 4 (Persian lilac). This hybrid, perhaps of *S.* ×*laciniata* by *S. vulgaris,* is as graceful as *S. laciniata* although not cutleaved, with foliage of finer texture than that of *S.* ×*chinensis.* Most plants sold under the name "Persian lilac" probably are actually *S.* ×*chi-nensis.* True *S.* ×*persica* is neither tall enough nor dense enough to serve as a visual screen. Mostly with lavender to rosy lavender flowers, but the selection 'Alba' has pure white flowers. Useful in Zones 4b–9a.

Syringa protolaciniata 3–4 (Afghan lilac). This graceful small shrub from western China and central Asia has very finely cut foliage. 'Kabul' was selected in Afghanistan and is used in that region, but probably neither the species nor the cultivar is available in North America.

Syringa meyeri 4

Synonyms: *S. microphylla* 'Minor,' *S. palibiniana*
MEYER LILAC
Deciduous shrub
Oleaceae (Olive Family)

Native Range.   Northern China.

Useful Range.   USDA Zones 4a–7b.

Function.   Specimen, border, foundation.

Size and Habit

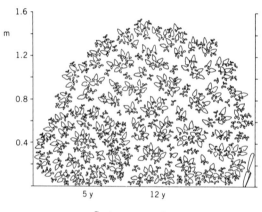

Syringa meyeri.

Adaptability

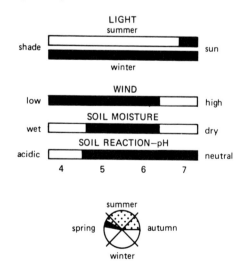

Seasonal Interest.   *Flowers:* Pale purple flowers with little fragrance in erect panicles to 8 cm/3 in. long in late spring, beginning when plants are no more than 30 cm/12 in. tall. *Foliage:* Rich green, lustrous, compact, and neatly textured, the leaves 2.5–4 cm/1–1.6 in. long with wavy margins, falling in autumn with little color change.

Problems and Maintenance.   Several diseases and insects can be troublesome (see *Syringa* ×*chinensis*) but are not often serious problems. Pruning is seldom needed for any purpose, making this one of the most maintenance-free of all lilacs.

Cultivars.   'Palibin,' probably the only commercially available selection of this species, has excellent foliage and compact growth habit, and probably differs little from the rest of the species, growing to at least 1.2–1.5 m/4–5 ft high and wide in time.

Related Species

Syringa microphylla 4 (littleleaf lilac).   This Chinese species has leaves as small as those of the closely related *S. meyeri*, but with less handsome foliage and less precocious in flowering. The selection 'Superba,' however, is outstanding: a loosely graceful plant approaching screening height with bright deep-pink flowers in spring and again in late summer, and light olive-green foliage, useful in Zones 5a–7b.

Syringa patula 5 (synonyms: *S. palibiniana*, *S. velutina*; Korean lilac).   This shrub from China and Korea has dark green, pubescent foliage of medium texture with leaves to 10 cm/4 in. long and pale purple flowers in panicles to 12 cm/5 in. long. The selection 'Miss Kim' is compact and dense with unusually handsome foliage, turning dull red-purple in autumn, and eventually becomes nearly as tall as the species type. Useful in Zones 3a–7b.

Syringa pubescens 4.   This Chinese shrub is intermediate in size, foliage, flowers, and landscape effect between *S. meyeri* and *S. patula*, but with conspicuously fragrant flowers. Useful in Zones 4a–7b.

Syringa reticulata 6–7

Synonym: *S. amurensis var. japonica*
JAPANESE TREE LILAC
Deciduous tree
Oleaceae (Olive Family)

Native Range. Japan, Manchuria, northern China.

Useful Range. USDA Zones 3a–7b with selection of appropriate genetic material.

Function. Small street tree (in cool climates), patio tree, border.

Size and Habit

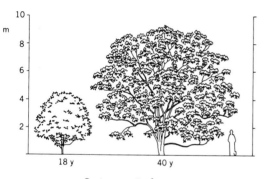

Syringa reticulata.

Adaptability

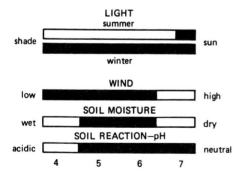

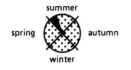

Seasonal Interest. *Flowers:* Creamy white in loose pyramidal clusters, 15–30 cm/6–12 in. long, with odor resembling that of *Ligustrum* flowers, early in summer but after flowering of *S. villosa* and its related species. *Foliage:* Dark green leaves, 8–15 cm/3–6 in. long and broadly heart-shaped like those of *S. vulgaris*, giving a rather coarse texture and sometimes turning dull yellow before falling in early to middle autumn. *Fruits:* Capsules, 1–2 cm/0.4–0.8 in. long, in loose clusters, turning yellowish in late summer. *Trunk and branches:* Bark is purplish brown and somewhat cherrylike with prominent horizontal lenticels, adding quiet winter interest.

Problems and Maintenance. This species is subject to the troubles of lilacs in general, especially borers and scale insects, and especially in warmer climates. Relatively trouble-free in Zones 3b–5b and areas of Zones 6 and 7 having mild summers. Pruning is needed only for initial training when it is used as a tree and for remov-

Syringa pekinensis.

ing any deadwood. As with *S. vulgaris*, flowering tends to be in alternate years unless spent flower clusters are removed to prevent fruit and seed set, which competes with flower bud initiation for the following year.

Varieties and Cultivars. The description above refers to var. *reticulata*, the species type. The var. *mandshurica* (synonym: *S. amurensis*; Amur lilac, Manchurian tree lilac) from northern China and Manchuria is a smaller, shrubby tree, to 4–6 m/13–20 ft tall, more cold-hardy than var. *reticulata*, at least to Zone 2b, but less useful as a tree where both forms are hardy.

'Ivory Silk' is a popular selection from Sheridan Nursery, Toronto, Canada, for symmetrical upright habit, to 6–8 m/20–26 ft tall, and good flowering when young.

'Summer Snow,' from Schictel's Nursery, Buffalo, New York, is symmetrically rounded and compact, to 5–6 m/16–20 ft tall, flowering heavily.

Related Species

Syringa pekinensis 6 (Peking lilac).   This large, rangy shrub or small tree has flowering interest similar to that of *S. reticulata* but usually is less showy. It is more irregular in form, with much narrower leaves, and usually remains below 5 m/16 ft in height, yet old trees in good soil at the Morton Arboretum near Chicago have grown to twice that height. One clone from this planting is under evaluation in the Chicagoland Grows program, and may be released as 'Morton' (China Snow™). Bark of certain trees, including 'Morton', is strongly curling, amber in color, adding winter interest. Useful in Zones 4a–7a, perhaps also Zone 3, but seldom available at this writing.

Syringa villosa 5

LATE LILAC
Deciduous shrub
Oleaceae (Olive Family)

Native Range.   Northern China.

Useful Range.   USDA Zones 3a–7b.

Function.   Screen, specimen, border.

Size and Habit

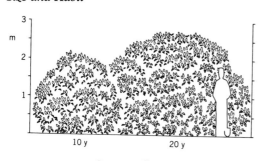

Syringa villosa.

Adaptability

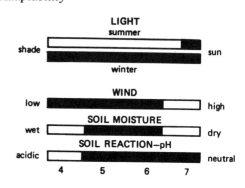

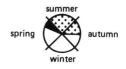

Seasonal Interest.   *Flowers:* Barely fragrant, pale rosy purple to white, in dense, erect panicles, 8–15 cm/3–6 in. long, very late in spring after *S. vulgaris* has finished flowering. *Foliage:* Dark green, paler underneath, with leaves to 15

Syringa villosa.

cm/6 in. long, making a rather coarse but dense mass, sometimes turning dull yellow before falling in midautumn.

Problems and Maintenance. This species is subject to most of the problems of lilacs in general (see *S.* ×*chinensis*). Scale insects are especially troublesome in this species and its close relatives (see Related Species and Hybrids, below). Little pruning is necessary, since the normal form of this plant is dense and it does not sucker.

Cultivars. Few, if any, selections have been made directly from *S. villosa*, but this species frequently has been a parent of hybrid selections (see Related Species and Hybrids).

Related Species and Hybrids

Syringa ×*henryi* 5 (Henry lilac).   This hybrid of *S. josikaea* and *S. villosa* is represented in commerce by the selection 'Lutece,' which has rosy violet flowers.

Syringa ×*josiflexa* 5.   This group of hybrids of *S. josikaea* and *S. reflexa* includes several good cultivars, including 'Anna Amhof' and 'Summer White,' with pure white flowers; 'Guinevere,' with magenta flowers; and 'Royalty,' with lilac-purple flowers.

'Minuet,' a complex hybrid involving *S. josikaea*, *S. reflexa*, and *S. villosa*, is more compact and slower growing than most late lilac hybrids, with little or no suckering or need for pruning and with light purple flowers. This cross (*S.* ×*josiflexa* 'Redwine' by *S.* ×*prestoniae* 'Donald Wyman') was made by the late W. A. Cumming of the Morden Research Station. It is useful in Zones 3a–7b, perhaps also Zone 2.

'Miss Canada,' another complex hybrid by Cumming (*S.* ×*josiflexa* 'Redwine' by *S.* ×*prestoniae* 'Hiawatha'), was released in 1967 in recognition of the Canadian centennial. It has rich magenta-pink flowers and is useful at least in Zones 3a–7b.

Syringa josikaea 5 (Hungarian lilac).   This native of southeastern Europe is similar in general

Syringa ×*swegiflexa.*

effect to S. *villosa,* but more upright and leggy in growth habit. Useful in Zones 2b–7b.

Syringa ×*prestoniae* 5 (Preston hybrid lilacs). The original group of hybrids of S. *reflexa* and S. *villosa* was developed by Isabella Preston, plant breeder at the Canada Department of Agriculture Research station at Ottawa at about the same time as the S. ×*josiflexa* group, and additional cultivars were introduced by the University of New Hampshire. They are similar to S. *villosa* but with a greater range of flower color. Most are fast-growing shrubs, useful in Zones 2b–7b. Those most widely available include the following: 'Agnes Smith' is an excellent white-flowered selection from the University of New Hampshire. 'Coral,' 'James Macfarlane' and 'Isabella' have light to bright pink flowers. Among these, 'James Macfarlane' flowers very heavily, with paler, yellow-green foliage, and 'Isabella' has good form and very large flower clusters (see also 'Miss Canada', perhaps the best, under S. *josiflexa*). 'Donald Wyman' and 'Nellie Bean' are outstanding purple-flowering selections. 'Hiawatha' is an excellent selection with magenta flowers. 'Nocturne' has bluish lilac flowers, deeper purple in bud.

Syringa reflexa 5 (nodding lilac).   This Chinese species, flowering with the rest of the late lilac group, is unusual for its long, narrow, nodding to pendulous clusters of pink flowers. Useful at least in Zones 5a–7b, it is not widely available except in the form of many excellent hybrids.

Syringa ×*swegiflexa* 5.   This hybrid of S. *reflexa* × S. *sweginzowii* combines the nodding flowering character of S. *reflexa* and some of the fragrance and airy gracefulness of S. *sweginzowii* and is useful in Zones 5b–7b but is not widely available.

Syringa sweginzowii 5.   This graceful, open shrub from northwest China has smaller leaves than most of the late-flowering lilacs, yet not as small as those of S. *meyeri* or S. *microphylla,* and has fragrant, rosy lilac flowers in showy clusters to 20 cm/8 in. long. It is useful in Zones 5b–7b, but available only from nurseries specializing in unusual lilacs.

Syringa vulgaris 6

COMMON AND FRENCH HYBRID LILACS

Deciduous shrub

Oleaceae (Olive Family)

Native Range.   Southeastern Europe; naturalized in many parts of the Northern Hemisphere, including much of North America.

Useful Range.   USDA Zones 3b–7b, some selections in Zone 3a.

Function.   Border, specimen, informal hedge, screen (with attention to pruning).

Size and Habit

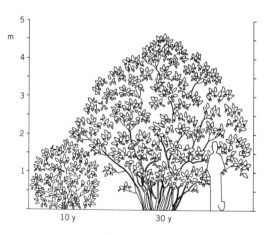

Syringa vulgaris.

Adaptability

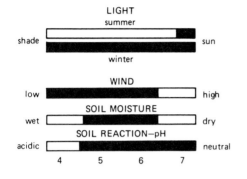

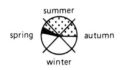

Seasonal Interest. *Flowers:* Highly fragrant, lavender, pink, purple, bluish, white, and many intermediate colors, in more or less erect clusters 10–20 cm/4–8 in. long, very showy in late spring. *Foliage:* Bright green, smooth, and distinctively heart-shaped, giving a medium texture, falling in autumn with little or no color change.

Problems and Maintenance. Several insects and diseases can be troublesome (see *Syringa* ×*chinensis*). Powdery mildew disfigures the foliage annually in areas that are typically warm and humid in late summer. Borers and scale insects may do permanent damage if not controlled. For best flowering, dried up flower clusters should be removed promptly to prevent seed development, which competes with initiation of flower buds for the next year. Failure to do this results in full flowering only in alternate years in some cultivars. Suckers form freely on most cultivars and a decision must be made as to whether they are to be removed annually. This practice is common where hybrid lilacs are being grown primarily as showy specimens, but it may be neither necessary nor desirable when lilacs are being used for large-scale visual screening, since the suckers may contribute to basal fullness of the foliage mass. Otherwise careful renewal pruning is necessary to prevent "legginess."

Cultivars. Hundreds of cultivars of *S. vulgaris* have been selected. Many of the earlier ones were developed in France, leading to the use of the name "French Hybrids" to refer to this group. But many cultivars have originated in other European countries, as well as Canada, Russia, and the United States. Most cultivars differ more in flowering characteristics (color, size, doubleness) than in functionality, but some are unique or at least distinctive. Those listed here are among the most widely used and available, distinctive in appearance or function, among the best in their flowering class, or several of these. They are arranged according to the (John) Wister color classes.

Color Class I (White)

f. *alba* (= 'Alba') is a collective name for all lilacs with single white flowers, so not all plants so designated are the same.

'Angel White' and 'Avalanche' are superior modern introductions with single white flowers. 'Angel White' reportedly flowers well without winter chilling, making it useful farther south than most lilacs. 'Slater's Elegance' is also excellent, with unusually large, single white flowers. These three are commercially available, but not widely so.

'Edith Cavell" is superb among double white-flowered selections, closely followed by 'Miss Ellen Willmot.' These two originated in the famous Lemoine Nursery in France in the early twentieth century. 'Mme. Lemoine' is older still, but still very popular.

'Emery Mae Norweb' is an excellent recent selection by the late Fr. John Fiala, a premier lilac breeder and author of the book, *Lilacs: The Genus Syringa* (Timber Press, Portland, Oregon). It has deep, creamy buds, opening white.

'Glacier' is another recent Fiala selection, with double white flowers.

'Krasavitsy Moskva' (see Miscellaneous category, below).

'Primrose' (see Miscellaneous category, below).

'Rochester,' introduced by the Rochester (New York) Parks Department, is an outstanding plant with showy upright clusters of semidouble, white flowers of great substance. It is slow-growing, perhaps the reason for its limited availability, but worthy of greater use.

Color Class II (Violet)

'Agincourt Beauty,' the first cultivar introduced by the Canadian lilac breeder, Leonard Slater, has extremely large, single, deep violet-purple flowers. Like his white-flowered introduction, 'Slater's Elegance,' after 20 years it is slowly becoming commercially available.

'Flower City' is an outstanding recent introduction of the Rochester, New York, Parks Department and the work of the prominent hybridizer, Richard Fenicchia. It has very showy deep violet flowers with silver-tinted petal-backs, a most promising lilac but not yet widely known.

'Marechal Lannes' is a Lemoine hybrid from the early twentieth century, still highly regarded and popular for its double, medium violet-purple flowers.

'Zulu,' a very showy Havemeyer origination from the 1950s, has large, single, medium-violet flowers.

Color Class III (Blue)

'Ami Schott' is a Lemoine introduction with showy, double medium blue flowers, popular after more than a half-century.

'Blue Danube' and 'Blue Delft' (see Miscellaneous category, below) are Fiala introductions from the 1980s, both with single blue flowers. 'Blue Danube' according to Fr. Fiala, had the bluest flowers of any *S. vulgaris* selection at its release in 1986. Another Fiala introduction, 'Wedgewood Blue,' has pendulous clusters of single, Wedgewood blue flowers, unfolding from pink buds. These cultivars will no doubt become very popular as they are better known.

'Monore' (Blue Skies™; Plant Patent No. 6877, 1989) has light lavender-blue flowers and is reported to flower well without winter chilling.

'Olivier de Serres' is a Lemoine hybrid from the early twentieth century, with large, double, medium to dark blue flowers, still available, but not widely so.

'President Grevy' is a more-than-century-old Lemoine hybrid, with large clusters of double blue flowers, still very popular and still one of the best blues.

'President Lincoln,' long considered one of the bluest single lilacs, is vigorous to a fault, with early leafy growth that partly obscures the flowers, and a tall, often leggy growth habit; yet it remains very popular.

Color Class IV (Lilac)

'Alphonse Lavallee' is a century-old Lemoine hybrid, with double bluish-lilac flowers, still popular but not as showy as some of the newer, larger-flowered cultivars.

'Leon Gambetta,' 'Le Notre,' 'Michel Buchner,' and 'Victor Lemoine,' also Lemoine hybrids, are very showy, double lilac-flowering selections, still excellent and available.

'Mollie Ann,' named by Fr. Fiala after his sister and released in the 1980s, blooms heavily, with large single lilac-colored flowers. Not yet widely known, but likely to become very popular in time.

'Sesquicentennial,' a Rochester Parks (Fenicchia) introduction, has very showy single flowers, an outstanding lilac. Introduced more than 20 years ago, it is just beginning to be known.

Color Class V (Pink)

'Belle de Nancy' and 'Lucie Baltet' are century-old Lemoine hybrids with double lilac-pink flowers, still very impressive and popular.

'Katherine Havemeyer,' 'Madame Antoine Buchner,' and 'Montaigne,' which are Lemoine hybrids from the early twentieth century with double, lavender-pink flowers in large clusters, are still very popular. Flowers of 'Montaigne' are pale pink.

'General Sherman' (see Miscellaneous category, below).

'Krasavitsa Moskvy' (see Miscellaneous category, below).

'Macrostachya' is a century-old selection for single, pale pink flowers in long clusters.

Color Class VI (Magenta)

'Congo' is a century-old Lemoine hybrid with bright, deep red flowers; it has remained very popular, one of the best single red-purples. 'Mrs. Edward A. Harding' and 'Paul Thirion,' later Lemoine hybrids, are double, deep red selections.

Color Class VII (Purple)

'Adelaide Dunbar,' a selection made by John Dunbar, an early lilac hybridizer in Rochester, New York, has double purple flowers and has remained popular.

'Andenken an Ludwig Spaeth' (= 'Ludwig Spaeth'), a century-old hybrid from the Spaeth Nursery in Germany, has striking deep red-purple single flowers. It is still available and always impressive even though more recent selections may be better in some respects.

'Charles Joly,' a century-old selection with double, deep red-purple flowers in rather small upright clusters, is more popular than seems warranted, considering the alternatives.

'Charles X' is a much older selection than 'Charles Joly,' with deep purple flowers. It is of historical interest and still surprisingly popular.

'Monge' is a Lemoine hybrid from the early twentieth century with single, deep red-purple flowers. It is deservedly still very popular, one of the most showy of this group in bloom.

'Mrs. W. E. Marshall' is a Havemeyer selection from the 1920s, with small but extremely dark red-purple flowers, nearly black. It is still fairly popular as a novelty.

'Sarah Sands' is a Havemeyer selection from the 1940s, with single, deep purple flowers, one of the best in this group.

Miscellaneous (Other Colors, Not Easily Classified)

'Albert F. Holden' is a recent Fiala selection with deep purple flowers, silvery on the backs of the petals, not yet well known, but distinctive.

'Blue Delft,' a Fiala introduction, has single flowers, deep blue in bud and opening to light and dark blue striped flowers, as yet not well known but promising.

'General Sherman,' a Dunbar selection from the early twentieth century, is unique for its large single, pearly pale pink flowers, which turn pearly white as they age.

'Krasavitsa Moskvy' (translation: 'Pride of Moscow'), a superb product of a cross involving 'Belle de Nancy' by the noted Russian hybridizer, Leonid Kolesnikov, and introduced here in the 1970s, has pearly pink flower buds, opening double, as light pink as can be imagined, with a silvery tinge.

'Primrose,' introduced by the Marse family of the Netherlands in the late 1940s, has unique flower color, starting out primrose yellow and fading to still paler yellow. It appears to be somewhat unstable genetically, since individual plants have slightly different colors, but special-

ists also attribute this to environmental conditions.

'Professor Robert B. Clark,' a recent Fiala introduction, has very large, semidouble flowers, pale pink in bud and opening white-pearled, still paler pink. It is not yet widely known but is one of many superb Fiala lilacs that promise to become very popular.

'Sensation,' a D. E. Marse (Netherlands) selection from the 1930s, has deep red-purple flowers with clear white petal margins, absolutely unique among lilacs. This selection, and later 'Primrose,' resulted from mutations apparently stimulated by hot water treatment during forcing for sale in the Dutch floral markets.

'Silver King,' hybridized by A. H. Lemke of Wausau, Wisconsin, and released after his death in the 1950s, has single, whitish lavender-blue flowers with silvered petal-backs, very showy and distinctive among lilacs, but available in only a few nurseries.

Related Species and Hybrids

Syringa ×*hyacinthiflora* 6.   This group of hybrids between *S. oblata* and *S. vulgaris* has become very popular in colder parts of Canada and elsewhere because of the work of Frank L. Skinner, eminent nurseryman and plant breeder in Dropmore, Manitoba, who introduced many fine cultivars in this group. Meanwhile, W. B. Clarke of the Clarke Nursery in San Jose, California, another eminent plant breeder, was introducing excellent lilacs in the *S.* ×*hyacinthiflora* group for use in California, emphasizing the remarkable range of climatic adaptability that is possible in this group. However, it is not likely that cultivars bred and evaluated in Manitoba (USDA Zone 3a) would be the best choices for San Jose (Zone 8a), and vice versa. The overall useful range for *S.* ×*hyacinthifolia* in eastern and central North America is Zones 3a–7b, perhaps also Zone 2 and 8. Skinner and Clarke each introduced some 20 cultivars, many of which are among the finest lilac cultivars today. A few of the best and most-used are listed here.

Color Class I (white).   'The Bride,' 'Sister Justena,' and 'Mount Baker,' with single flowers, and 'Gertrude Leslie', with double flowers, all from Skinner in the 1950s, are outstanding in this category.

Color Class II (violet). 'Pocahontas' (Skinner) is outstanding among all lilacs in this class, with single, deep violet-purple flowers. 'Mood Indigo' (Clarke) is also notable, but not so well known in our area.

Color Class III (blue). 'Charles Nordine' and 'Doctor Chadwick' (Skinner) and 'Spring Dawn' (Clarke) are fine hybrids, with lavender-blue flowers, but are not as blue as the better *S. vulgaris* selections. 'Laurentian' (Skinner) also has lavender-tinted blue flowers, but bluer than the others in this group.

Color Class IV (lilac). 'Assessippi' (Skinner) is a well-shaped, functional plant, tall but seldom "leggy"; it is very showy with very early and fragrant, single pale lavender flowers. 'Excel' and 'Nokomis' (Skinner) have single lilac to lavender flowers.

Color Class V (pink). 'Maiden's Blush' is an excellent Skinner hybrid from the 1960s with single, pale to medium pink flowers, an excellent "true pink." 'Bountiful,' 'Esther Staley,' and 'Pink Cloud' (Clarke) are also outstanding in this class. 'Bountiful' is upright in habit, with soft lavender-pink flowers; 'Esther Staley' has bright lavender pink flowers and is the most widely available of this class. Also outstanding is 'Daphne Pink' (Skinner), with showy purplish-pink flowers.

Color Class VI (magenta). 'Esther Staley' and 'Pink Cloud' fall between this and the previous class (see above). 'Sunset' (Clarke) is another fine choice in this class, with reddish purple flowers, one of the reddest *Syringa* cultivars.

Color Class VII (purple). 'Pocahontas' (Skinner) is by far the most popular hybrid in this class, with large, single deep purple flowers. 'Purple Gem' and 'Purple Glory' (Clarke) have single, medium-purple flowers. 'Purple Splendor' (Clarke) and 'Tom Taylor' (Skinner) are fine double purple-flowering hybrids. 'Swarthmore' (Skinner) has double, light purple flowers.

Syringa oblata 5–6 (early lilac). This close relative of *S. vulgaris* from China and Korea is best known in commerce in the form of var. *dilatata* (synonym: *S. dilatata*; Korean early lilac), a shrub ranging from 2 to 3 m/6.6–10 ft high, lower and more graceful than the species type, with fragrant pale to deep lilac-colored flowers and rather leathery, deep green leaves that turn to shades of red-purple, overlying yellow, in autumn. This variety was the parent of all or most of the *S.* ×*hyacinthiflora* hybrids.

The species type, var. *oblata* (synonym, in part: var. *giraldii*), is a tall shrub or multiple-trunked tree to 4 m/13 ft tall, seldom in commerce, but represented in living collections.

The var. *alba* is distinctive for its white flowers, otherwise quite variable. The selection 'Frank Meyer' is much more ornamental than most plants of var. *alba* and is of interest to plant breeders trying to obtain better pink-flowered hybrids.

Seed from an unusual population of *S. oblata*, brought back from Korea by the late Donald Egolf of the U.S. Arboretum in 1979, have resulted in highly vigorous plants, very full at the base, with moderately fragrant purple flowers and huge leathery leaves, to about 15 cm/6 in. long and 10 cm/4 in. wide, turning black-purple to red-purple in autumn. This population, tentatively called var. *donaldii*, in honor of Dr. Egolf, had been incorporated into his lilac breeding program by the time of his death.

Tamarix ramossimia 5

Synonyms: *T. odessana, T. pentandra*
FIVE-STAMEN OR ODESSA
TAMARISK
Deciduous shrub
Tamaricaceae (Tamarisk Family)

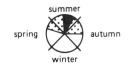

Native Range.   Southeastern Europe to central Asia.

Useful Range.   USDA Zones 4a–9a+ with selection of appropriate genetic material. Some forms are less cold-hardy.

Function.   Specimen, border.

Size and Habit.   Ultimate height is variable, from 2 m/6.6 ft to more than 5 m/16 ft if left unpruned, but when pruned to retain good form, height will seldom exceed 3–4 m/10–13 ft.

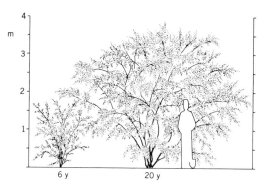

Tamarix ramosissima.

Adaptability.   Relatively salt-tolerant at seashore or near salted walks.

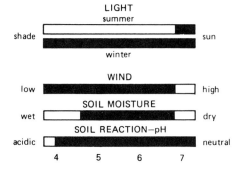

Seasonal Interest.   *Flowers:* Light to rosy pink, very small but borne in large, fluffy clusters, highly showy in midsummer and continuing with less color until late summer. *Foliage:* Bright to bluish green, very fine-textured with tiny, scale-like leaves, turning duller or yellowish before falling in autumn.

Problems and Maintenance.   Stem cankers occasionally can be troublesome and can be controlled by removing and destroying infected branches. Drastic renewal pruning is necessary every few years to retain good landscape form and to keep in useful size. Burning of pruned tops will reduce future disease problems by removing inoculum.

Cultivars.   'Summer Glow' (= 'Rubra'), the most common cultivar in commerce in our area, is vigorous and hardy, with deep pink flowers and silvery blue-green foliage. Other selections are sometimes available, and mostly similar to (or synonymous with) the above.

Related Species

Tamarix hispida 4 (Kashgar tamarix).   This native from western Asia to Manchuria, serves as a smaller edition of *T. ramosissima,* with silvery foliage and pink flowers in midsummer. Useful in the same areas as *T. ramosissima,* but seldom available.

Tamarix parviflora 5 (small-flowered tamarisk). This southern European species differs from the other *Tamarix* species listed in that it flowers in spring from flower buds initiated the previous summer. Because of this, winterkilling of tops in extreme winters in Zones 5 and 6 can eliminate most of the potential flowering interest for a year afterward. This also means that pruning should be carried out after flowering, in contrast to other *Tamarix* species, which are best pruned earlier in spring. Useful in Zones 5b–9a+ and sheltered sites in Zone 5a.

Taxodium distichum 8

BALD CYPRESS
Deciduous tree
Taxodiaceae (Taxodium Family)

Native Range. Southeastern United States and northward to Delaware and Indiana in coastal areas and river basins.

Useful Range. USDA Zones 5a–9a+, perhaps also Zone 4 with selection of appropriate genetic material.

Function. Specimen, massing, naturalizing, street tree in some areas.

Size and Habit

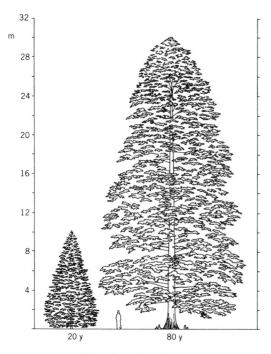

Taxodium distichum.

Adaptability

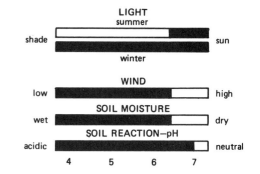

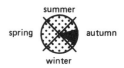

Seasonal Interest. *Foliage:* Deciduous, flattened, soft, needlelike, giving fine, billowy texture, light green in spring, soft green in summer, and turning a warm russet brown before falling in late autumn. *Trunk and branches:* Lower branches are borne horizontally on a strong, straight, tapered central trunk. Bark texture adds winter interest along with buttressing of the bases of older trunks and upward-protruding "knees," especially in wet sites.

Problems and Maintenance. Twig blight and wood-rot diseases occasionally can be problems in weakened trees, but ordinarily *T. distichum* is free of any major problems that would limit its

Taxodium distichum.

use. Its broad adaptability from the swamps of its native habitat to soils of average moisture content does not extend to very dry soils, where it can be damaged by drought, setting the stage for other problems. Pruning is not needed except to remove any deadwood, but when necessary it should be carried out after the leaves emerge so that deadwood can be seen clearly.

Cultivars. 'Mickelson' (Shawnee Brave®), selected by Earl Cully of Jacksonville, Illinois in the 1970s, is much narrower than the species type, thus useful in smaller spaces. Useful in Zones 5b–8b. Another Cully selection, as yet unnamed, is very broad, with a height:width ratio of 1.3:1 after 18 years. It is expected to be released in 1997.

The var. *nutans* (synonym: *T. ascendens*; pond cypress), native to the Gulf Coast portion of the species range and northward to Virginia, has smaller, scalelike leaves, giving the foliage a more stringy texture, and is much narrower in form than the species type. Useful in Zones 6a–9a+, and at least parts of Zone 5.

Taxus cuspidata 4–6

JAPANESE YEW
Evergreen tree or shrub
Taxaceae (Yew Family)

Native Range. Japan, Korea, Manchuria.

Useful Range. USDA Zones 4b–7b.

Function. Screen, hedge, foundation, specimen, border.

Size and Habit. 'Capitata' (left), 'Densa' (right front), and 'Thayerae' (right rear) are illustrated.

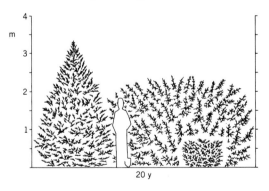

Taxus cuspidata cvs. **'Capitata' (left), 'Densa' (right front), and 'Thayerae' (right rear).**

Adaptability. Tolerant of a wide range of sun or shade in most situations, but light shade is necessary for best results in areas having hot, dry summers, and protection from full sun and wind in winter is desirable in Zone 5 to prevent drying of foliage. Newly planted yews are notoriously sensitive to poorly drained soil (often caused by planting too deeply), but well established plants are slightly more tolerant of wet soils.

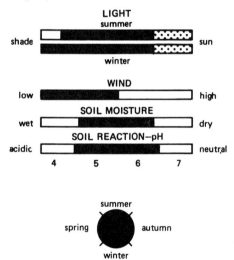

Seasonal Interest. *Flowers:* Dioecious and inconspicuous. The staminate (male) flowers discharge pollen in large quantities in late spring. *Foliage:* Rich, deep green, making a dense mass very effective in screening. Needles are flattened and more succulent than those of most other needle evergreens, clustered thickly on lighter green twigs. Those of the better cultivars retain their color well in winter and persist for several years. *Fruits:* Scarlet, round, and fleshy arils, 1.2 cm/0.5 in. across, on pistillate (female) plants, enclosing the black seeds. Interesting and sometimes conspicuous in quantity, but secondary in interest to the foliage.

Problems and Maintenance. The most common problems of yews result from unfavorable site conditions, especially poor soil drainage. The best solution to such problems is prevention, either by improving drainage during site construction or by selecting alternate species. In addition, diseases can occasionally be troublesome, but insect and mite problems are more common, the most serious being black vine weevil. Instructions for control of this and other insects can be obtained from state, provincial, or county extension service offices.

Most parts of the yew plant are poisonous to warm-blooded animals. Most cases of death by poisoning have resulted from livestock eating hedge clippings, which apparently become more toxic as they dry following removal from the plant. The red aril (fleshy part of the fruit) is not poisonous but the black seed within is highly toxic.

Cultivars. Many of the selections described here and under *Taxus* ×*media* cultivars are included among those considered the best by the late Professor L. C. Chadwick of Ohio State University, a pioneer in landscape horticulture education who assembled the most comprehensive collection of *Taxus* species and cultivars in North America, still being maintained and added to at the Ohio Research and Development Center at Wooster. Others included are either very prominent in commerce or of more recent origin, or both.

'Adams' is a vigorous, well-shaped clone, columnar for a few years, but branching at about 45 degrees and growing to 3–5 m/10–16 ft tall and somewhat wider in time. It responds well to shearing, so can be held in smaller size for hedging. Cold-hardy at least to Zone 5a, but not widely available.

'Capitata' is a name given to all upright, pyramidal, seed-propagated plants of *T. cuspidata*. While it is obviously not taxonomically correct to assign a cultivar name to the wild species, this name is now so well entrenched that it is necessary to specify it to be sure the tree form will be furnished. After seeds of *T. cuspidata* were first germinated in North America, probably in the 1870s, the name 'Capi-

tata' was given to the upright, treeform seedlings that resulted, to distinguish them from the wide-spreading plants (cutting-propagated from lower branches) that had been in North American nurseries since the 1850s.

'Densa,' a pistillate (fruiting) clone, is one of the finest low, slow-growing selections, remaining below 0.8 m/2.6 ft for many years, and below 1.5 m/5 ft almost indefinitely, while spreading to at least twice that. Its slow growth has held it back in commerce and it is marginally available at best, but it is still notable because it remains in functional size with little or no pruning for many years. Cold-hardy at least to Zone 5a, it should not be confused with 'Densiformis' (see under *T.* ×*media*).

'Greenwave,' like 'Densa,' is an excellent low form with dark green foliage on gracefully arching branches, making a dense mound. Cold-hardy at least to Zone 5a, probably also parts of Zone 4, and faster growing and more widely available than 'Densa.'

'Intermedia' is very similar in appearance and function to 'Nana' (below) as a young plant, but starts growing earlier and eventually becomes considerably larger than 'Nana,' an excellent selection, cold-hardy in Zone 5a.

'Nana' (also incorrectly called 'Brevifolia'), usually referred to as "dwarf Japanese yew," is actually faster growing than 'Densa,' but slower and more compact and "blocky" in shape than most Japanese yews. It is cold-hardy at least to Zone 5a and usually readily available.

'Thayerae' (also incorrectly called 'Andersoni') is an excellent, very wide-spreading, fast-growing pistillate (fruiting) cultivar, with narrow, curved needles. It can be held to 1 m/3.3 ft in height with pruning; otherwise, it will eventually attain almost twice that height and much greater spread. Cold-hardy in Zone 5a.

Several other cultivars are commercially available. Some are probably as good as the above for specific purposes, but perhaps not as widely available. As with other plants, attention should be given to local availability and experience. See also cultivars of *T.* ×*media*.

Related Species and Hybrids

Taxus canadensis 3–4 (Canada yew). This loosely spreading native of northeastern North

America grows wild in Zones 3a–6b, yet has winter hardiness problems in cultivation in exposed sites throughout much of this range. It should be protected from full sun in both summer and winter in most areas. Usually cultivars of *T. cuspidata* will outperform this species in landscape use, but it has value for naturalizing.

Taxus floridana 5 (Florida yew).   This native of northern Florida generally resembles *T. cuspidata* except for its sparseness and very narrow needles. Its landscape value comes from its tolerance of more southern climates than the other yews. It is useful, primarily for naturalizing or as an object of preservation, in Zones 8 and 9, but seldom available for planting.

Taxus ×*hunnewelliana* 5 (Hunnewell yew). This hybrid of *T. cuspidata* × *T. canadensis* is intermediate in form and foliage between the parents. It has a spreading habit and intermediate growth rate and turns reddish brown in winter, an objectionable color to some. Useful in Zones 4a–7a but should be protected from full sun and wind in winter in Zone 4.

Cephalotaxus fortunei 5 (Chinese or Fortune plum-yew).   This native of China is closely related to *Taxus* in the family Cephalotaxaceae, but has green to purplish fruits, 2.5 cm/1 in.

across, and larger needles. It functions much as a loose-growing, spreading yew, usually at least as wide as tall, with rich green foliage. It is useful in Zones 7b–9a+, but only in those coastal areas that have mild summer temperatures, which eliminates it as a landscape plant from most of our area.

Cephalotaxus harringtonia 4 (Japanese plum-yew). This somewhat slower-growing counterpart of *C. fortunei* is similar in its effect and limitations except that it is useful in somewhat colder areas in Zones 6a–9a+.

Torreya nucifera 5–7 (Japanese torreya).   This close relative of *Taxus* becomes a full-size tree in its native Japan, but seldom is seen as more than a tall shrub in our area. Its sharp-pointed needles are easily distinguished from the superficially similar, blunter ones of *Cephalotaxus* and have a citruslike aroma when crushed. This plant is not widely used, but it is a useful evergreen shrub or small tree in Zones 6b–9a+ and sheltered spots in Zone 6a.

Torreya taxifolia 5 (Florida torreya, stinking cedar).   This shrubby plant is seldom planted except near its natural range in northern and central Florida, but it is available for naturalizing and preservation there.

Taxus ×*media* 4–6

ANGLO-JAPANESE OR INTERMEDIATE YEW
Evergreen shrub
Taxaceae (Yew Family)

Hybrid Origin.   *T. cuspidata* × *T. baccata.*

Useful Range.   USDA Zones 5a–7b, and areas in Zone 8 having mild summers.

Function.   Hedge, screen, foundation, specimen, border.

Size and Habit.   'Hicksii' (left), 'Wardii' (center), and 'Brownii' (right rear) are illustrated.

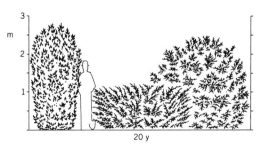

Taxus ×*media* cvs. 'Hicksii' (left), 'Wardii' (center), and 'Brownii' (right rear).

Adaptability.   Partial shade in summer is beneficial in the South and Midwest. Protection from winter sun and wind is desirable for best results in Zone 5. Poorly drained soils are troublesome in new plantings, especially when planted too deeply, but established plants are slightly more tolerant of wet soils.

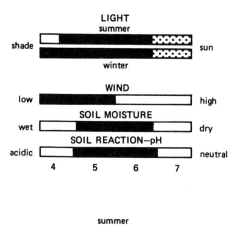

Seasonal Interest.   *Flowers:* Dioecious and inconspicuous. Staminate (male) flowers discharge pollen in large quantities in late spring. *Foliage:* Rich, deep green, making a dense mass that is very effective in screening. Flattened needles, more succulent than those of most other needle evergreens, are tightly clustered on the lighter green twigs. Those of the better cultivars retain their color well into winter. *Fruits:* Scarlet, round, and fleshy, 1.2 cm/0.5 in. across, on pistillate (female) plants, enclosing the black seeds. Interesting and conspicuous in quantity but secondary in interest to the foliage.

Problems and Maintenance.   The most common problems of yews result from unfavorable site conditions, but diseases and insects also can be troublesome (see *T. cuspidata,* Problems and Maintenance). Most parts of yew plants are poisonous to warm-blooded animals (see *T. cuspidata,* Problems and Maintenance).

Cultivars.   Many of the following are on L. C. Chadwick's "best" list; others are included for their current popularity or promise (see note under *T. cuspidata* cultivars).

Spreading, Pyramidal, Globose

'Brownii' is an excellent broad-pyramidal to globose staminate (nonfruiting) form with dark green foliage, remaining below 2 m/6.6 ft high for many years but eventually becoming at least 3 m/10 ft high and half again as wide. Unusually cold-hardy for *T. ×media* (to Zone 4b), 'Brownii' is classified as a selection of *T. cuspidata* by some specialists.

'Dark Green Spreader' is a popular spreading yew with excellent dark green foliage, remaining below 1 m/3.3 ft in height for many years while spreading to 1.5–2 m/5–6.6 ft wide, but eventually exceeding these dimensions if not pruned. Cold-hardy to Zone 4b, possibly also Zone 4a.

'Densiformis' is fairly fast-growing, yet compact, with growth habit intermediate between 'Brownii' and 'Dark Green Spreader,' but less cold-hardy (to Zone 5a) and having inferior winter color.

'Runyan' is a compact, more-or-less globose, staminate (nonfruiting) selection, somewhat faster growing than *T. cuspidata* 'Nana,' reaching a mature height of 3 m/10 ft high and 5 m/16 ft after 25 years. It is relatively cold-hardy and resistant to snow breakage and is fairly widely available.

'Taunton' is similar to 'Wardii' in form and nearly as compact, staying below 1 m/3.3 ft high for 20 years or more and eventually reaching 1.5–2 m/5–6.6 ft high and at least twice as wide. It is noted for its resistance to "winter-burn," and cold-hardiness, to Zone 4b and perhaps colder.

'Wardii' is a pistillate (fruiting) form, even lower growing than 'Taunton,' under 0.8 m/2.6 ft for 10–15 years and under 1.5 m/5 ft for many years, while spreading to at least three times its height. Its short, lustrous, dark green needles provide neat texture. Useful in Zone 5a and perhaps slightly colder zones.

Broad Columnar

'Hatfieldii' is a popular staminate (nonfruiting) selection, symmetrically columnar when young, with dark green foliage but becoming broad-pyramidal with age. It is one of the less cold hardy selections of *T. ×media,* useful to Zone 6a and protected sites in Zone 5b.

'Hicksii' is an extremely popular pistillate (fruiting) selection with narrow-pyramidal habit when young, broadening further with age, cold-hardy to Zone 5b and protected sites in Zone 5a.

'Stovekenii' is one of the best broad-columnar forms, holding to a height:width ratio of nearly 2.0 after 25 years, and more cold-hardy than either 'Hatfieldii' or 'Hicksii,' to Zone 5a and protected sites in Zone 4b. Until recently it had nearly disappeared from commerce, but now it is attracting new interest.

Narrowly Columnar

In the 1930s, John Vermeulen of Neshanic Station, New Jersey, selected a group of narrowly columnar seedlings and named several. L. C. Chadwick included on his "best" list the selection 'Flushing,' which maintains a height:width ratio of about 4.0 for several years. Other superior clones with narrowly columnar form are 'Grandifolia,' 'Sentinalis,' and 'Viridis.' These are useful for strong vertical accent in formal landscapes. None is widely available, but most can be found in a few nurseries, and for most purposes they are interchangeable.

Many other good cultivars are available. See also cultivars of *T. cuspidata,* and consider local experience and availability.

Related Species

Taxus baccata 3–6 (English yew).   Although this species from Europe and adjacent Africa and Asia can attain heights of more than 15 m/50 ft in cool climates in its native habitat, seldom does it reach half that height in our area. Since it is less cold-hardy than *T. canadensis, T. cuspidata,* or its hybrid *T. ×media* without gaining correspondingly in heat tolerance, it is generally less useful in our area than these, typically only in Zones 6b–7b and those parts of Zone 8a with mild summers, with exceptions noted below. A few cultivars are of interest in our area, and are listed here:

'Adpressa' (boxleaf yew) is a distinctive pistillate (fruiting) clone that dates back to the middle nineteenth century. It would seem different enough from other yews to justify a separate species or varietal designation if it were known to exist as a population in the wild, but it is not. It is dense and compact, remaining below 1.5 m/

Taxus baccata.

5 ft for 20–25 years, with a more-or-less globose shape, and has dark green, abruptly pointed needles, broad but barely 1.2 cm/0.5 in. long, arranged in a flat spray, on branches with slightly nodding tips. Very old plants in Europe have reached heights of at least 3 m/10 ft and similar width. Probably cold-hardy to Zone 6a and protected sites in Zone 5b (see also 'Adpressa Fowles,' below), but available in very few nurseries in our area.

'Adpressa Aurea' is similar to 'Adpressa,' but has golden yellow young shoots and is somewhat less vigorous and perhaps not as cold-hardy.

'Adpressa Fowle' is a variant of 'Adpressa' with slightly finer texture and greater cold-hardiness, to Zone 6a. With further trial, perhaps it will be found to be cold-hardy in parts of Zone 5, which probably make it the most cold-hardy form of *T. baccata,* but it is available in only a few nurseries at this writing.

'Dovastoniana' is a vigorous selection with semiweeping branches that has reached massive proportions in the climate of Newport, Rhode Island, ideally suited to yews, and has performed well in Zone 6a at the Ohio Agricultural Research and Development Center at Wooster.

'Fastigiata' (= 'Hibernica,' = 'Stricta'; Irish yew) is the strikingly columnar form so commonly seen in old churchyards in the British Isles. It appears to be somewhat more cold-hardy than many plants of *T. baccata,* performing fairly well in Cave Hill Cemetery, Louisville, Kentucky in Zone 6b, or perhaps effectively 7a because of the microclimatic effect of the surrounding city.

'Repandens' is a low, broad-spreading form

Taxus baccata 'Repandens.'

with feathery, dark green foliage not exceeding a height of 1 m/3.3 ft for 10–20 years while spreading to 2–3 times that distance. Unpruned plants under good conditions can reach heights of 2 m/6.6 ft but can easily be kept below eye level by pruning when desired. This is one of the most cold-hardy selections of *T. baccata*, to Zone 6a and sites sheltered from wind and full winter sun in Zone 5b.

Taxus brevifolia 5–6 (western yew). This native of the Pacific Northwest, from British Columbia to northern California and western Montana, resembles *T. baccata*, but is neither very successful nor available in eastern North America. In native habitat, it has been put at some risk because of harvesting for the chemical taxol, a promising cancer drug that was found in this species. It has now been found that some cultivated clones of *T. cuspidata* and *T.* ×*media* also contain commercially useful amounts of taxol, and screening of clones continues.

Ternstroemia gymnanthera 6

Synonyms: *T. japonica, Cleyera japonica*
JAPANESE TERNSTROEMIA
Evergreen shrub or small tree
Theaceae (Tea Family)

Native Range.   Japan to Malaysia and India.

Useful Range.   USDA Zones 8a–9a+, perhaps also Zone 7b.

Function.   Specimen shrub or small tree, screen.

Size and Habit

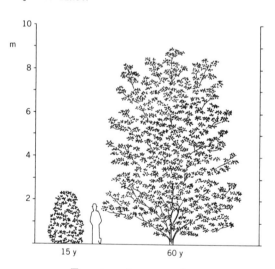

Ternstroemia gymnanthera.

Adaptability. Very intolerant of poorly drained soils.

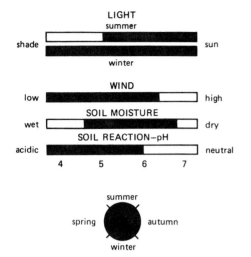

LIGHT
summer

shade ▭▬ sun
winter

WIND
low ▬▭ high

SOIL MOISTURE
wet ▭▬ dry

SOIL REACTION—pH
acidic ▭▬ neutral
4   5   6   7

summer
spring ● autumn
winter

Seasonal Interest. *Flowers:* Whitish yellow and fragrant, about 1.5 cm/0.6 in. across, in late spring. *Foliage:* Handsome, evergreen, lustrous, and leathery, leaves to 15 cm/6 in. long and one third as wide, dark green and turning deep wine red in winter. *Fruits:* Round to elongated, to 2 cm/0.8 in. long, turning from green to reddish as they ripen in early autumn but not giving major landscape interest.

Problems and Maintenance. This plant is relatively trouble-free, except for a minor leaf-spot disease, if given a good site. Occasional pruning may be needed to maintain density of the lower part of the plant for screening or for size control in small-scale situations. Often, it is sold as

Cleyera japonica, the name for another plant (see Related Species).

Cultivars. 'Burgundy' has unusually rich burgundy-red foliage in winter. 'Goldenleaf' has bright golden yellow winter foliage color. 'Grimes' (= 'Variegata') has pale yellow leaf margins. 'Ryokojo' is beautifully variegated, with creamy white leaf margins and gray-marbled centers, rose-tinted throughout.

Related Species

Cleyera japonica 5 (synonyms: *C. ochnacea, Eurya ochnacea;* Japanese cleyera). Like the closely related *Ternstroemia,* this plant is native to eastern Asia. The two are similar enough to have become thoroughly confused in the landscape industry. They differ in that the leaves of *Cleyera* are not clustered toward the twig tips like those of *Ternstroemia* but are evenly spaced along the stem, and in other botanical details. Except for the size difference and the fact that *Cleyera* is more spreading in its branching habit, they can be considered to be roughly equivalent as landscape plants. Variegated selections have been made but are probably not commercially available.

Eurya japonica 4–5 (Japanese eurya). This close relative of *Ternstroemia,* also from eastern Asia, has handsome evergreen leaves to 6 cm/2.4 in. long, dark green and rounded or notched at the apices, turning more-or-less mahogany-red in winter sun. The selection 'Winter Wine' has superior form and rich, wine-red foliage in winter. The small greenish-white flowers and black

Ternstroemia gymnanthera.

Cleyera japonica.

Eurya emarginata.

Eurya emarginata var. *microphylla.*

fruits are inconspicuous. Useful at least in Zones 8b–9a+, but not always available.

Eurya emarginata 3–4.   This evergreen shrub, also from eastern Asia, is smaller and looser in habit than *E. japonica* and is seldom seen other

than as the var. *microphylla*, which bears leaves only 1 cm/0.4 in. long and wide and has distinctive branching, reminiscent of that of *Cotoneaster horizontalis*. The useful range for this plant is not well known because it has been used so little, but includes at least Zones 9a+.

Tetradium daniellii 6–7

Synonyms: *Evodia daniellii, E. henryi,*
E. hupehensis
E V O D I A
Deciduous tree
Rutaceae (Rue Family)

Native Range.   Korea and northern China.

Useful Range.   USDA Zones 5b–8a.

Function.   Specimen, patio tree.

Size and Habit

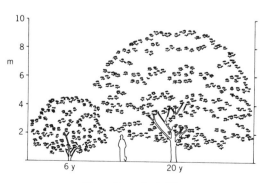

Tetradium daniellii.

Adaptability

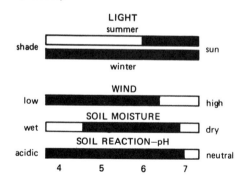

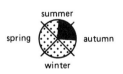

Seasonal Interest.   *Flowers:* Small, whitish, in large, flat clusters in late summer. This tree is greatly favored by beekeepers for its nectar and late flowering. *Foliage:* Medium dark green, compound leaves, showing off flowers and fruits to advantage. *Fruits:* Pinkish to dull red, opening

Tetradium daniellii.

in autumn to disclose small, shiny black berries. *Trunk and branches:* Smooth, light gray bark adds mild winter interest.

Problems and Maintenance. This species is relatively trouble-free as a young tree but relatively short-lived. Its weak wood is subject to damage from high winds and heavy ice and snow.

Related Species

Zanthoxylum americanum 6 (northern prickly ash, toothache tree).   This thicket-forming shrub or small tree will seldom be deliberately planted, but it is encountered as a wild species in site development through much of our area from Quebec to North Dakota and southward to Florida and Oklahoma. Its suckering habit and small but wicked thorns make it effective as a barrier, but other, equally effective shrubs can be controlled more easily and are more pleasing visually. Its useful range includes Zones 4a–9a.

Zanthoxylum clava-herculis 6 (southern prickly ash, Hercules' club).   This more southern counterpart of *Z. americanum* is native from coastal Virginia to Florida and Texas. It is no more useful as a landscape plant than the northern species but could be used, if there were reason, in Zones 8a–9a+.

Zanthoxylum schinifolium 6.   This large shrub or small tree from northeastern Asia is limited in its usefulness by the same characteristics as *Z. americanum*, but it has much more handsome, glossy, dark green foliage. If any species of prickly ash is to be planted deliberately, this exotic species might well be first choice. It is potentially useful in Zones 6a–9a.

Teucrium chamaedrys 2

GERMANDER
Evergreen groundcover
Lamiaceae (Labiatae; Mint Family)

Native Range.   Europe and southwestern Asia.

Useful Range.   USDA Zones 6a–8a, areas in Zone 8b and 9a having moderate summers, and perhaps colder zones in sites with reliable snow cover.

Function.   Groundcover, front of border, low hedge.

Size and Habit

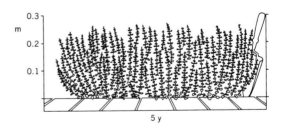

Teucrium chamaedrys.

Adaptability

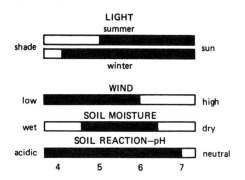

Teucrium chamaedrys.

Seasonal Interest. *Flowers:* Rosy purple, individually to 1.5 cm/0.6 in. across, in fairly showy upright spikes in late summer. *Foliage:* Deep green, glossy, semievergreen leaves, less than 2.5 cm/1 in. long and narrow, form an elegantly fine-textured foliage mass that eventually deteriorates in middle and late winter except under constant snow cover.

Problems and Maintenance. The few diseases and insects that can be troublesome are seldom seriously so, and this plant requires little maintenance other than an occasional shearing in spring to control height and for renewal and removal of deadwood.

Cultivars. 'Prostratum' is lower growing than the species type, to no more than 20 cm/8 in. tall, and is otherwise little different from the species type.

Thuja occidentalis 3–7

AMERICAN OR EASTERN ARBORVITAE, EASTERN WHITE CEDAR

Evergreen tree or shrub

Cupressaceae (Cypress Family)

Native Range. Northeastern North America: Nova Scotia to Manitoba and southward to North Carolina and Illinois.

Useful Range. USDA Zones 3b–7b, with selection of appropriate genetic material.

Function. Screen, hedge, massing, specimen.

Size and Habit

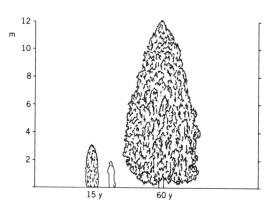

Thuja occidentalis.

Adaptability. Protection from full winter sun in Zones 3 and 4 reduces foliage scorch.

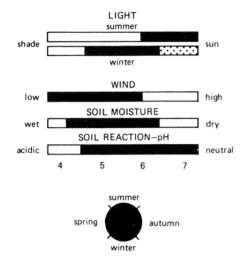

Seasonal Interest. *Foliage:* Evergreen, dark green and lustrous to dull blue-green or golden, with scalelike, mature foliage (except in an occasional dwarf cultivar). *Cones:* Small, greenish, turning brown as they ripen, providing little interest.

Problems and Maintenance. This plant is subject to several diseases and insect pests. A few of them such as bagworms, mites, scale insects, and leaf miners require control when infestations occur. Pruning is rarely necessary except for hedges and for repairing winter damage. Cultivars lacking strong leading trunks are prone to damage from heavy snow and ice, and scorch of foliage from fast freezing caused by intermittent bright sun and shadow can be disfiguring in Zones 3 and 4.

Cultivars. Many cultivars have been selected for growth rate and habit, foliage color and texture, and special features. A few of the most commonly used are listed here.

'Brandon' is an unusually cold-hardy form selected for the Canadian prairies and valued as well in the northern prairies of the United States and elsewhere. It grows to 4–6 m/13–20 ft tall but only 1–2 m/3.3–6.6 ft wide, with a compact, narrowly conical form and bright green foliage. Useful for screening and accent in Zones 3b–7b, perhaps also Zone 3a in northern and eastern exposures.

'Douglasii Pyramidalis' is a tall columnar selection, growing to 10–15 m/33–50 ft tall in time while spreading to only 2.5–4 m/8–13 ft, with rich green, frondlike foliage. Useful in Zones 4a–7a, perhaps also Zone 3b. This may be confused in commerce with 'Pyramidalis,' which is narrowly pyramidal but not as narrow as 'Douglasii Pyramidalis.' Both are useful selections for relatively narrow form.

'Ellwangeriana' is a dwarf, broad-pyramidal form with mostly juvenile (soft, needlelike) foliage, cold-hardy to Zone 5a but susceptible to winterburn in Zone 5 and not very widely available.

'Ellwangeriana Aurea' is similar to 'Ellwangeriana' except that it has golden yellow foliage, where exposed to direct sun, and turns golden-bronze in winter.

'Ericoides' is a dwarf, moundlike form while young, later forming several growing points and eventually reaching a height and spread of at least 2 m (6.6 ft), with juvenile foliage, soft green in summer and bronzing in winter, cold-hardy to Zone 4b but experiencing some foliage "burn" in Zones 4 and 5. 'Hetz Junior' is similar in foliage effect but lower and wider spreading and reported to be somewhat more cold-hardy than 'Ericoides.'

'Globosa,' 'Little Giant,' and 'Woodwardii' are globose forms of moderate growth rate, remaining below eye level for 10–15 years but reaching heights of 2–3 m/6.6–10 ft after many years. All three are readily available and are useful for formal effect in Zones 4a–7a, perhaps Zone 3b in sheltered sites.

'Hetz Midget' and 'Little Gem' (= 'Pumila') are dwarf globose forms with normal mature (scalelike) leaves, very dense and growing only about 5 cm/2 in. annually but eventually reaching a height of at least 1 m/3.3 ft, and twice that in width. Cold-hardy at least to Zone 4a, and interchangeable (identical?) in landscape use. Fairly widely available under one name or the other.

'Hetz Wintergreen' (= 'Wintergreen') is narrow and spirelike, to 6 m/20 ft tall and 1.5–2 m/5–6.6 ft wide, with good winter color, cold-hardy at least to Zone 4a.

'Holmstrup' is a slow-growing, narrowly pyramidal plant, growing to 1.5–2 m/5–6.6 ft tall and 0.6–0.8 m/2–2.6 ft wide, with bright green foliage, which holds its color well in winter. Cold-hardy at least to Zone 4b, and easily available.

'Lutea' (='Aurea,'='George Peabody') is tall-growing, eventually to 10 m/33 ft, with narrowly conical form and golden-yellow young foliage, contrasting with yellow-green older foliage. An impressive golden selection, cold-hardy to Zone 3b.

'Nigra' is similar to the species type but with full and unusually dark green foliage, cold-hardy at least to Zone 4a.

'Rheingold' is a very popular dwarf, globose when young but broadening with age and developing several upright, pyramidal branches. Its foliage is mostly juvenile (soft, needlelike), golden to bronze, developing some scalelike leaves with age. Cold-hardy at least to Zone 5a, but the thin needles are susceptible to winter drying if not protected from strong winds and afternoon sun.

'Smaragd' (translation: 'Emerald') is a symmetrically pyramidal plant with excellent bright green foliage that holds its color well in winter. It was selected in Denmark nearly 50 years ago but has not been in North America that long. Useful at least in Zones 4b–7a and perhaps also in somewhat colder zones.

'Techny' is a vigorous, full, pyramidal form with very dark green foliage, slightly darker even than that of 'Nigra.' It is one of the best selections for screening, at least in Zones 4a–7a.

'Wareana' (='Robusta') has large, scalelike, dull blue-green leaves, making a heavy foliage mass. It is very effective as a screen and probably the most drought-tolerant cultivar of *T. occidentalis*. Cold-hardy to Zone 3b and widely available.

Many other cultivars exist; consider local availability.

Related Species

Thuja koraiensis 5 (Korean arborvitae). This broad- to upright-pyramidal shrub or small tree is little known in landscape use in our area and probably is not commercially available, but it has looked promising in test plantings. The broad, scalelike leaves are similar to those of *T. occidentalis* except that they are distinctly white-marked on the undersides of branches. Probably useful in Zones 5a–7b and perhaps more widely with selection of appropriate genetic material.

Thuja plicata 7–8 (giant arborvitae; western red cedar). This native of the Pacific Northwest from Montana to Alaska and northern California is a huge timber tree in its native habitat and may reach heights of 20–30 m/66–100 ft with time in our area, but it also makes an excellent screening shrub, more trouble-free in many areas than *T. occidentalis* and much less likely to be browsed by deer (apparently it is distasteful to them). Presumably there is considerable variation in climatic adaptability in this species, with trees of far-inland origin being more adaptable to our colder zones than trees of Pacific coastal origin. One form of *T. plicata*, apparently 'Elegantissima,' is proving useful as a windbreak at an exposed site in central Indiana and has survived without winter injury in Zone 4a in Vermont. This clone has golden yellow branch tips in early summer and a tendency to bronze in full winter sun. 'Atrovirens' has unusually dark green

Thuja plicata.

foliage color, holding well into winter. With selection of appropriate genetic material, the useful range of this species should extend at least through Zones 4a–7a. A few other variants for foliage color and slower growth are occasionally available, but not widely so.

Thuja standishii 6–7 (Japanese arborvitae). This spreading pyramidal tree is more graceful than other arborvitae species. Its foliage remains green in winter but is no better than that of the best selections of *T. occidentalis* and *T. plicata.* Leaves are white-marked underneath, much like those of *T. koraiensis,* and the papery-thin reddish brown outer bark peels away in narrow strips. Useful in Zones 6a–7b, perhaps also Zone 8.

Platycladus orientalis 4–7 (synonyms: *Biota orientalis, Thuja orientalis;* oriental arborvitae). This native of China and Korea is still sold by many nurseries as *Thuja orientalis.* In its colorful forms it is all-too-common in landscape use in our area. The tree form is symmetrical and somewhat more open because of its small, scalelike leaves and slender branches often turned vertically. The color variants are even more formally symmetrical, the twisted branches arranged densely and forming strikingly vertical planes. Frequently sold as low-cost plants in garden centers, they are too positive for most landscape situations and often are killed or severely damaged in winter in many areas where they are sold. Useful in Zones 6b–9a, but frequently offered for sale in areas as cold as Zone 5a. Many cultivars have been selected. A few of the most common are listed here.

"Aurea" is not a cultivar, but a collective name for many clones with yellow foliage.

'Aurea Nana' is a dwarf, tightly oval to globose in form, growing to 0.5–0.8 m/1.6–2.6 ft tall, with branches in more-or-less parallel, strikingly vertical planes, yellow-green foliage in early summer, fading to light green, and turning yellow-brown in winter.

'Bakeri' is compact and pyramidal in form, larger than 'Aurea Nana,' to 1.2–1.9 m/4–6 ft tall, with pale green foliage, notably tolerant of heat and drought, useful in Zones 7a–9a+.

'Blue Cone' is compact and pyramidal, to 2–2.4 m/6.6–8 ft tall, with flat, vertical branches and bluish green foliage.

'Bonita' is semidwarf and broadly pyramidal, to about 1 m/3.3 ft tall, with lustrous, light green, golden-tipped foliage.

'Conspicua' (= 'Berckmans,' = 'Berckmans Golden Biota') is compact and columnar to narrowly pyramidal, 1.5–2 m/5–6.6 ft tall and 0.6–0.8 m/2–2.6 ft wide, with light green foliage, yellow at the branch tips. This clone is sometimes mistakenly sold under the name 'Aurea Nana'; also, both 'Conspicua' and 'Aurea Nana' are sometimes sold under the name 'Berckmans.'

'Elegantissima' is compact and narrowly pyramidal, eventually to 3–4 m/10–13 ft tall, with foliage golden-tipped in spring, and greenish yellow in summer.

'Westmont' is slow-growing and compact, to 1 m/3.3 ft tall and 0.7 m/2.3 ft wide, with gold-tipped dark green foliage, from late spring through autumn.

Thujopsis dolobrata 5 (false or Hiba arborvitae). This native of Japan is adapted only to small portions of our area with mild, moist climates. A large tree in native habitat, it functions as a loose-growing, shrubby tree, probably to no more than 4–5 m/13–16 ft tall, under our best conditions, with glossy, bright green leaves, similar to those of *Thuja* but larger and white-marked underneath. Useful in Zones 6b–9a. 'Nana' is slower-growing, forming a low mound. 'Nana Variegata' forms a low mound of white-variegated foliage. 'Variegata' is also white-variegated, but not very strikingly, and is not dwarf.

Tilia americana 8

BASSWOOD, AMERICAN LINDEN
Deciduous tree
Tiliaceae (Linden Family)

Native Range. Northeastern and central United States and adjacent Canada: New Brunswick westward to North Dakota and southward to Virginia and northeastern Texas.

Useful Range. USDA Zones 3a–7a, in areas with mild summers.

Function. Shade or avenue tree, naturalizing.

Size and Habit

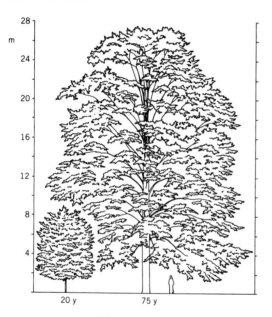

Tilia americana.

Seasonal Interest. Flowers: Highly fragrant and attractive to bees, light yellow, individually 1.5 cm/0.6 in. across, in loose, drooping clusters attached to large, pale greenish yellow, leaflike bracts, conspicuous in early summer. *Foliage:* Coarse, medium green, with broad, heart-shaped leaves 10–20 cm/4–8 in. long, turning dull green or occasionally yellowish before falling in midautumn. *Fruits:* Whitish yellow, round, nutlike, 0.5–0.8 cm/0.2–0.3 in. across, interesting in late summer.

Problems and Maintenance. Lindens in general are not well adapted to high heat and drought stress. There are exceptions, but *T. americana* is not one of them; it performs best in Zones 3a–5a and in areas with moderate sum-

Adaptability

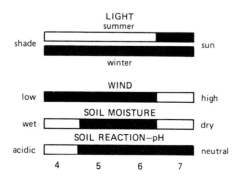

Tilia americana.

mers in Zones 6–8a. Also, mites and a variety of insects including aphids, beetles, borers, leaf miners, and scale insects are potentially troublesome. For fully adequate performance, a spray program eventually will be needed. Lindens are also susceptible to several diseases, usually not serious but occasionally requiring corrective treatment. Pruning is necessary only for early training and removal of deadwood and basal sprouts. *T. americana* has a strong tendency to produce basal sprouts and is coarser in appearance than many other *Tilia* species but finds special value in naturalized plantings.

Cultivars.   Several selections gave been made for fast growth and good form. The most common are listed here.

'American Sentry' is a selection from McKay Nursery, Waterloo, Wisconsin, for symmetrical habit and uniform branching, and light gray bark on young branches.

'Boulevard' is a recent Bailey Nurseries (Minnesota) selection for fast growth and dense foliage, with a narrowly pyramidal habit, becoming about half as wide as it is tall, otherwise similar to the species type.

'Douglas' is a vigorous, upright-growing clone, recently selected by Roy Klehm of Klehm's Nurseries, from a local population in northern Illinois, not yet widely available at this writing.

'Fastigiata' has narrower branching and more narrowly pyramidal form than typical for the species, but is seldom available.

'Lincoln' is an upright form with neatly compact growth, recently selected by Roy Klehm from a northern Illinois population, not yet widely available.

'Rosehill' is a selection for good foliage and form, pyramidal when young, rounding with age. Availability is limited.

'Wandell' (Legend™; Plant Patent applied for) was selected for its vigor, broad-pyramidal form, excellent foliage, somewhat finer texture than typical, and deep orange winter buds and is reported to be less susceptible to Japanese beetles and other chewing insects than typical for the species.

Tilia cordata 8

LITTLELEAF LINDEN
Deciduous tree
Tiliaceae (Linden Family)

Native Range.   Europe.

Useful Range.   USDA Zones 3b–8a in areas with mild summers.

Function.   Shade or street tree.

Size and Habit

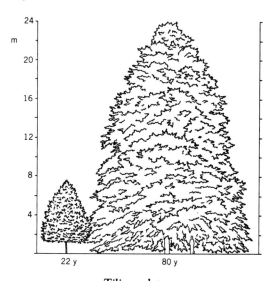

Tilia cordata.

Adaptability. *T. cordata* and other European lindens (see Related Species) are well adapted to urban planting.

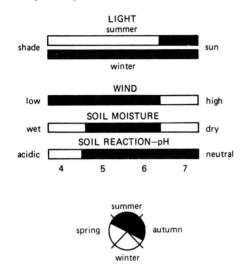

Seasonal Interest. *Flowers:* Highly fragrant and attractive to bees, light yellow, individually small but borne in loose, drooping clusters attached to large, pale greenish yellow, leaflike bracts, contrasting with the deep green leaves in early summer. *Foliage:* Medium to deep green, light green underneath, only 3–6 cm/1.2–2.4 in. long, producing a dense canopy of neat texture, falling after midautumn with little color change. *Fruits:* Whitish yellow, round, nutlike, 0.5–0.8 cm/0.2–0.3 in. across, interesting in late summer.

Problems and Maintenance. This species is susceptible to a variety of leaf-chewing insects, aphids, mites, and scale insects, but most are not

Tilia cordata.

serious enough to warrant control measures. An important exception is Japanese beetles, which can completely defoliate trees by midsummer. This damage seems to be most severe in areas recently invaded by Japanese beetles, and susceptibility varies somewhat by cultivar. Pruning is needed only for removing any deadwood, and basal sprouting is minimal in this species.

Cultivars. 'Bailey' (Shamrock™) is a recent introduction from Bailey's Nurseries with broadly pyramidal form, somewhat like that of 'PNI 6025' (Greenspire®), but somewhat looser and more vigorous, growing to 15 m/50 ft tall and 12 m/40 ft wide.

'Chancole' (Chancellor®) is narrowly symmetrical in form, growing to 15–20 m/50–66 ft tall and 6–9 m/20–30 ft wide, especially useful for street planting. Selected at the former Cole Nurseries, Circleville, Ohio, in the 1960s, it has not become as popular as might be expected considering its useful habit, but it is still fairly readily available.

'Corzam' (Corinthian®), a recent introduction from Lake County Nursery, is narrowly symmetrical, comparable to 'Chancole' but more compactly pyramidal, giving a rather formal effect.

'Glenleven,' a Canadian introduction (Sheridan Nursery, Etobicoke, Ontario), sometimes listed as a *T. cordata* selection but probably a hybrid of *T. cordata* by *T. americana* (*T. ×flavescens*), is broad-columnar in form, to 15–20 m/50–66 ft tall and 10–15 m/33–50 ft wide, with foliage intermediate between that of the parents, not as formal in outline and texture as 'PNI 6025' (Greenspire®). It is widely available and very cold-hardy.

'Olympic,' a J. Frank Schmidt Nursery introduction, is wider-spreading than other cultivars of *T. cordata*, to 12–15 m/40–50 ft tall and 9–12 m/30–40 ft wide, fast-growing, and less formal than most other cultivars.

'PNI 6025' (Greenspire®), for most of its 35 years in commerce, has been the most popular cultivar of *T. cordata* and has also been the standard by which newer introductions have been evaluated, with a strong central trunk, neatly pyramidal growth habit, and excellent dark green foliage. Unfortunately, it is highly susceptible to defoliation by Japanese beetles.

'Prestige' (Plant Patent No. 6734, 1989) was originally distributed as a numbered clone by the former Cole Nurseries in central Ohio, later selected from city plantings in Green Bay, Wisconsin, by Tim Lang, City Forester there, and propagated and named by Willet N. Wandell of Discov-Tree Research and Development Ltd., Oquawka, Illinois. It is fast to develop a crown and is broader-spreading than most *T. cordata* selections, impressive to date but not yet widely available.

'Rancho' is an old selection by Edward Scanlon of Olmstead Falls, Ohio, upright and vigorous, with small leaves and somewhat broader than 'PNI 6025' (Greenspire®). It is no longer widely available, but its partial resistance to Japanese beetles may lead to greater use, especially in areas being infested for the first time.

'Redmond' is a popular selection of uncertain parentage. Once thought to be a clone from *T. ×euchlora*, and more recently treated as a selection of *T. americana*, it has now been assigned to another hybrid group, *T. ×flavescens* (*T. cordata* × *T. americana*). This hardy cultivar has proved very useful in the Central Plains because of its rapid growth, leathery foliage, deep red winter twigs, and impressive drought-tolerance. It is useful throughout the useful ranges of its parents and is farther west than either parent, at least in Zones 3b–8a.

'Ronald' (Norlin™, Plant Patent No. 8239, 1993) is a very cold-hardy *T. cordata* hybrid selected by Wilbert Ronald of Portage la Prairie, Manitoba, in Zone 3a. It is fast-growing and resistant to sunscald, not yet widely available but promising.

Related Species and Hybrids

Tilia dasystyla 8 (Caucasian linden).   This native of southwestern Europe and adjacent Asia, with rather coarse foliage, is little-used and seldom available in our area, but known through its parentage of the following hybrid.

Tilia ×euchlora 8 (Crimean linden).   This hybrid, probably *T. cordata* × *T. dasystyla*, is valued for street and lawn planting, growing somewhat faster than *T. cordata*. 'Laurelhurst' is a superior selection, vigorous and broadly pyramidal but compact, with glossy, dark green leaves. Useful at least in Zones 5a–8a.

Tilia ×europaea 8 (common or hybrid European linden).   This hybrid of *T. cordata* × *T. platyphyllos* is widely planted in Europe, but usually considered inferior to its parents in our area because of its heavy basal sprouting. Nevertheless, it is a useful street or lawn tree where maintenance is available in Zones 3b–8a.

Tilia mongolica 6–7 (Mongolian linden).   The chief advantages of this species from northern China and Mongolia are its hardiness and small size, usually 6–10 m/20–33 ft in height or even less in dry sites. Its leaves are nearly as small as those of *T. cordata*, triangular and birchlike in outline, and its bark is rough and flaking. Even though this tree is not yet widely available, it may become so as it is better known, because it is a useful small tree in Zones 3a–6a.

Tilia platyphyllos 8 (bigleaf linden).   In spite of its common name, the leaves of this European native are considerably smaller than those of *T. americana* with only a moderately coarse texture. This is a serviceable tree valued in the northern states and adjacent Canada. It develops basal sprouts but not nearly in the same numbers as *T. ×europaea*. Useful in Zones 3b–7a.

Tilia tomentosa 8

SILVER LINDEN
Deciduous tree
Tiliaceae (Linden Family)

Native Range.   Southeastern Europe and adjacent Asia.

Useful Range.   USDA Zones 5a–8a, in areas with mild summers.

Function.   Shade or avenue tree.

Size and Habit

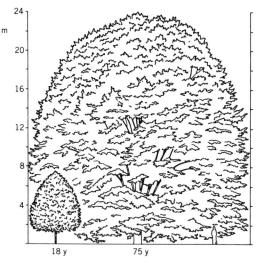

Tilia tomentosa.

Adaptability.   Full foliage interest is seen best in sites exposed to at least minimal breezes.

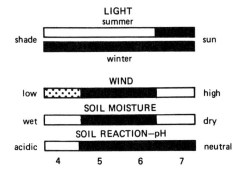

Seasonal Interest.   *Flowers:* Highly fragrant, attractive but according to some sources injurious to bees, light yellow, borne in clusters attached to pale greenish yellow, leaflike bracts. *Foliage:* Deep green, strikingly whitened underneath with silky hairs, 5–10 cm/2–4 in. long, giving medium texture and a bicolored effect when the leaves are turned over by the wind. *Fruits:* Whitish yellow, round, nutlike, 0.5–0.8 cm/0.2–0.3 in. across, interesting in late summer in clusters with the attached leafy bracts.

Problems and Maintenance.   This tree is only occasionally troubled with the wide range of insect and disease problems that can affect lindens in general (see *T. americana,* Problems and Maintenance), especially Japanese beetles, since these are inhibited by the heavy white tomentum that gives this tree its summer beauty. Incidentally, that beauty can be dulled in areas with substantial solid air pollution, which can turn the leaf undersides grayish by midsummer. Recovery from transplanting is slower than for most lindens, and newly planted trees may need to be staked for up to three years or until there is considerable new top growth.

Cultivars.   Selecting superior cultivars of this beautiful tree may seem like "gilding the lily," but a few such selections have been made.'

Tilia tomentosa.

'PNI 6051' (Green Mountain®) was selected for fast growth, a symmetrical domed crown, and good yellow autumn foliage color.

'Sashazam' (Satin Shadow™), a recent Lake County Nursery introduction, is reported to be resistant to disease and Japanese beetles.

'Wandell' (Sterling Silver®; Plant Patent No. 6511, 1989), was selected for its heavy, leathery leaves and is reportedly disease-resistant and unusually tolerant of dry sites.

Related Species

Tilia heterophylla 8 (white or beetree basswood). His native of the eastern United States from West Virginia to Indiana and southward to Florida and Alabama has leaves intermediate in size between *T. americana* and *T. tomentosa*, with a thick mat of white or brownish hairs underneath, giving it some of the foliage interest of *T. tomentosa* but not its symmetry and neat texture. It is seldom available commercially but can be preserved or naturalized in Zones 6a–9a, perhaps also Zone 5b.

Tilia petiolaris 8 (pendent silver linden). This graceful tree from southeastern Europe and adjacent Asia resembles *T. tomentosa* except for its pendulous growth habit. It is not known in native communities in that area and is given only cultivar status (*T. tomentosa* 'Petiolaris') by some specialists. Because some variation does occur, the species designation will be retained here. This tree is limited to large-scale sites because of its size, to at least 25 m/82 ft tall and 15 m/50 ft wide; since its visual effectiveness depends on retaining its full branch-spread to the ground, lower branches should not be removed to accommodate too small a site. Useful at least in Zones 6a–9a, probably also Zone 5b.

Trachelospermum asiaticum 1 and 2

Synonym: *Rhynchospermum asiaticum*
YELLOW STAR JASMINE
Evergreen vine or groundcover
Apocynaceae (Dogbane Family)

Native Range. Japan, Korea.

Useful Range. USDA Zones 8a–9a+ and sheltered sites in Zone 7 as a groundcover.

Function. Groundcover, specimen vine, or screen (with support), climbing by twining to heights of 3–5 m/10–16 ft.

Size and Habit

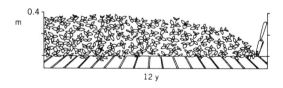

Trachelospermum asiaticum.

Adaptability. Grows best in light shade in parts of our area with very hot summers.

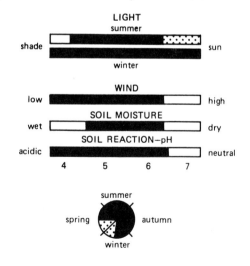

Seasonal Interest. *Flowers:* Fragrant, yellowish white, in loose terminal clusters, but they do not develop in significant numbers in groundcover use. *Foliage:* Evergreen, leathery, pointed leaves are 2.5–5 cm/1–2 in. long, borne on wiry stems, the overall effect as a groundcover similar to that of the related *Vinca minor*. Foliage turns dark red-purple in winter from Zone 8a northward. By late winter, foliage may be less attractive, but new growth in spring covers the old foliage.

Problems and Maintenance. Scale insects, white fly, and mites can be troublesome occasionally and require spraying. This can be done after shearing off the tops of groundcover plantings in spring, a practice which, if done every third year or so, keeps the groundcover low and neat in appearance.

Cultivars. The dwarf selection 'Asia Minor' has very small, glossy leaves, and there is at least one white-variegated form, not widely available.

Related Species

Trachelospermum jasminoides 1 and 2 (synonym: *Rhynchospermum jasminoides*; Confederate jasmine, Chinese star jasmine). This evergreen vine from China is popular in the far southern parts of our area, used primarily as a specimen or screening vine, climbing to heights of 3–6 m/ 10–20 ft, although it is effective as a groundcover as well. It has heavier and larger leaves than *T. asiaticum*, 5–8 cm/2–3 in. long, light green as they first emerge, then turning deep green, and waxy looking, very fragrant white flowers resembling small pinwheels because of the way the petals are twisted. Useful in Zone 9a+ and perhaps some sheltered areas in

Trachelospermum asiaticum.

Zone 8. The selection 'Madison' is reported to be slightly more cold-hardy, to Zone 7b. 'Variegatum' has white-variegated foliage, sometimes suffused with pink in full sun and cool weather.

Periploca graeca 1 (Grecian silkvine). This deciduous, high-twining climber, a member of the Milkweed Family from southeastern Europe and adjacent Asia, is effective as a visual screen (with support) to heights of 8–10 m/26–33 ft from late spring until very late autumn, since its foliage persists and remains dark green until nearly winter. Neither the unpleasant smelling flowers nor the fruits provide significant landscape interest, but for a dense foliage mass for screening, this climber is one of the best. It can be rampant and weedy if not controlled, but it is useful in Zones 6a–8a in relatively dry sites in full sun.

Trachycarpus fortunei 6

Synonyms: *T. excelsus, Chamaerops excelsa, C. fortunei*
WINDMILL PALM
Evergreen tree
Arecaceae (Palmae; Palm Family)

Native Range.   Burma, China.

Useful Range.   USDA Zones 8b–9a+.

Function.   Street tree, specimen.

Size and Habit

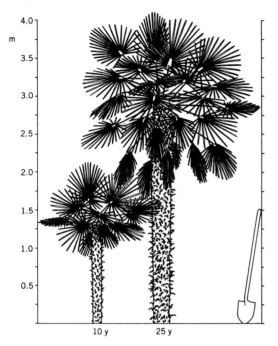

Trachycarpus fortunei.

Adaptability.   Relatively tolerant of salt in seashore sites.

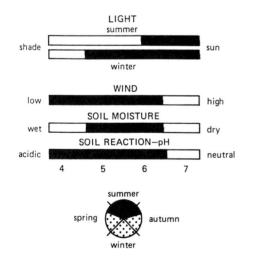

Seasonal Interest. *Flowers:* Small, yellow, among the leaves in hanging clusters, to 0.5 m/ 1.6 ft long in late spring and continuing during summer. *Foliage:* Dark green, fanlike, with segments radiating nearly in a complete circle, sometimes to 1 m/3.3 ft across, the leaflets turn-

ing duller and drooping with age but persisting year-round. *Fruits:* Bluish, more-or-less rounded, individually about 1 cm/0.4 in. across, fairly conspicuous, in large clusters. *Trunks:* Slender, very straight, covered with a conspicuous "fabric" of hairlike black fiber from old leaf sheaths.

Problems and Maintenance.   The most serious pest problem is scale insects, which at some point will need to be controlled with carefully timed sprays. Pruning is necessary only to remove dead leaves that otherwise would be unsightly.

Related Species

Brahea armata 6–7 (synonym: *Erythrea armata;* Mexican blue palm, blue rock palm).   This native of northwestern Mexico grows to 15 m/50 ft tall in zones where it is fully hardy, with a very thick trunk, to nearly 0.5 m/1.6 ft in diameter and ringed with leaf-scars. Its waxy, blue-gray, fan-shaped leaf blades, 1–1.5 m/3.3–5 ft across, with segments divided about half their length, are borne on 1–1.5 m/3.3–5 ft stalks. Its small yellow flowers and yellow-brown fruits are carried in inflorescences to 4 m/13 ft long, arching outward well past the foliage. This palm can withstand temperatures as low as −5°C/23°F without injury, and it is useful in Zones 9a+ and protected sites in Zone 8b.

Butia capitata 5–6 (synonyms: *Butia australis,* sometimes sold as *Cocos australis;* Brazilian butia palm).   This native of Brazil and other parts of South America makes a good small specimen tree, 2–6 m/6.6–20 ft tall, for Zone 9a and sheltered sites in Zone 8b. Its bluish, pinnately compound leaves, 1–1.5 m/3.3–5 ft long, are ascending at the base but arch gracefully back downward, giving a distinctive form. The flowers, red or yellow, are borne in dense clusters within very large orange bracts, to 1 m/3.3 ft long and nearly as wide, in spring and summer. Fruits are edible, datelike, yellowish, about 2.5 cm/1 in. long, borne in huge clusters. Trunks are very wide, especially toward the base, heavily roughened with persistent leaf bases.

Chamaerops humilis 5–6 (Mediterranean fan palm).   The species type, native from Portugal to Morocco, is single-trunked and may reach a height of 6 m/20 ft where it is fully hardy. The selection 'Nana,' much more common in landscape use, is low and massive, with multiple trunks, spreading slowly to 2–3 m/6.6–10 ft in height and 3–5 m/10–16 ft in width; its stiff bluish-green fans, to 0.8 m/2.6 ft across, are nearly circular. The leaf stalks have rows of sharp spines, and sheaths that eventually disintegrate into networks of fibers, giving trunks a rough, hairy surface. This palm can withstand temperatures of −8°C/18°F, making it useful in Zones 8b–9a+.

Phoenix canariensis 7 (Canary Island date palm). This native of the Canary Islands reaches heights of 15 m/50 ft and greater on fertile soils in Zone 9b, where it is used as an avenue tree. It functions as a smaller tree for specimen use, in the mildest parts of Zone 9a but occasionally suffers winter damage. It has long, pinnately compound leaves, ascending when young but later becoming pendulous, and a massive, light brown trunk, commonly 0.5 m/1.6 ft and greater in diameter. Since the leaves commonly reach 3 m/10 ft in length, young plants occupy a large area of ground until such time as the trunk has become tall enough to lift remaining leaves about head level. This palm is dioecious but seldom sets fruit in our area. Dead leaves and inflorescences must be removed by pruning, or they give the tree a ragged appearance.

Washingtonia filifera 7 (cotton palm, California Washingtonia). This robust fan palm from southern California, southwestern Arizona, and Mexico grows from 12–15 m/40–50 ft tall with trunk diameter to 0.6–0.8 m/2–2.6 ft, where it is fully hardy. Its leaf stalks are 1.5–2 m/5–6.6 ft long, and the blades another 1.5–2 m/5–6.6 ft. As the leaves die, they remain attached for some time, forming a grayish "skirt" or "beard" that covers at least the upper part of the trunk. When the dead leaves finally fall or are removed, the smooth ringed trunks become more visible. This palm is usefully hardy at least in Zones 8a–9a+ in the Southwest and is commonly used there. It has not been used as much in the same zones in our area, where climates are more humid, but is worthy of trial in the Southeast, at least in Zones 8b–9a+.

Washingtonia robusta 8 (Mexican fan palm). In spite of its name, this palm appears less "robust," except in height, than *W. filifera*. Rather it is a tall tree, to 23–25 m/76–82 ft, with a relatively slender, tapered trunk, to 0.25–0.3 m/0.8–1 ft wide, the upper parts covered with a "skirt" or "beard" of dead leaves, eventually falling to expose the roughened gray-brown trunk. Its marginally toothed leaf-stalks are about 1 m/3.3 ft long and the leaf-blades add another 1 m/3.3 ft. Useful in nearly the same zones as *W. filifera*, but slightly less cold-hardy.

Tsuga canadensis 3–8

CANADA HEMLOCK
Evergreen tree or shrub
Pinaceae (Pine Family)

Native Range. Eastern North America from Nova Scotia to Minnesota and Illinois and southward in the Appalachian Mountains to northern Alabama.

Useful Range. USDA Zones 3a–8a with selection of appropriate genetic material; best in areas with cool summers.

Function. Screen, specimen, one of the finest of all evergreens for formal or informal hedges.

Size and Habit

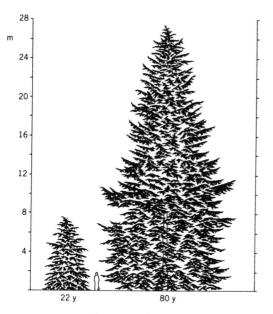

Tsuga canadensis.

Adaptability. Windswept sites and dry soils should be avoided, since the foliage, especially of newly planted trees, is very susceptible to desiccation in winter and during dry periods in summer. Light shade during summer is beneficial in the South and Midwest.

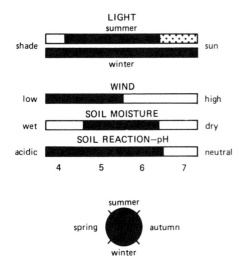

Seasonal Interest. *Foliage:* Evergreen, individual needles flattened, light green when new, then lustrous dark green and whitened on the lower surfaces, the longest only 1.7 cm/0.7 in. long, arranged mostly in a plane on twigs, giving a flat, feathery appearance to the branches. *Cones:* Light brown, 1.5–2 cm/0.6–0.8 in. long, frequently borne in large numbers, adding quiet but significant interest at close range.

Problems and Maintenance. Hemlocks are subject to a wide variety of insect and disease problems, one of which is very serious: an insect called woolly adelgid *(Adelges tsugae).* Woolly adelgid first appeared in eastern Virginia in 1961 and by 1986 had spread from there northward through eastern Maryland, Delaware, New Jersey, southeastern Pennsylvania, and New York and into southern Connecticut. By 1996 it had spread to central Virginia, farther into Pennsylvania and New York, and through Connecticut into Massachusetts, at a rate of 30 miles each year. If it continues to spread at this rate it will soon threaten most of the species population. Infestations usually kill hemlock trees in one to four years.

In landscape use, the situation is not quite so grim, because the saturation spraying that is the only control for woolly adelgid at present is practical on a small scale. Research is underway to find natural predators in Japan, where the insect is believed to have originated, so far without success. Until greater control of the adelgid is possible, planting of *Tsuga canadensis* should be guided by the proximity of the insects and the feasibility of controlling them in limited areas.

Other species of *Tsuga* vary in their susceptibility to woolly adelgid. Carolina hemlock *(T. caroliniana)* is reported to be about as susceptible as *T. canadensis,* but the western species *T. heterophylla* and *T. mertensia* (see Related Species, below) are so resistant that earlier infestations in the Pacific Northwest never really proliferated, and there is now greater interest in these species for eastern North America than in the past. When heavily infested trees of these western species are found, they are usually already under stress. The Asian *T. diversifolia* is also quite resistant to infestation.

Research on woolly adelgid continues and new long-range solutions may emerge before the two eastern species are decimated. In the short run, other *Tsuga* species will continue to draw interest.

Cultivars. Many variants selected from the wild have been given cultivar names. In an intensive study at Cornell University in 1939, John C. Swartley reduced all the variants then known into 20 classes distinct enough to justify cultivar names, showing that there had been much duplication in naming variants. Considerable confusion in names still exists, and the best way to obtain a specific form is to hand-select plants in a nursery. In recent years, many additional selections have been made, some of which extend the degree of variation previously recognized in this species. Many of the more than 150 cultivars currently available from nurseries are so slow-growing that they are primarily of interest to collectors or bonsai fanciers, but most of these are also useful in small-scale landscapes. The small sampling listed here includes many of the best and most popular for landscape use.

'Albospicata' is a compact form, not exceeding 3 m/10 ft for many years, with creamy-white-tipped foliage, especially in summer. Best in at least light shade.

'Bennett' is a dwarf, mound-forming plant, growing to 0.6–1 m/2–3.3 ft high and 1–1.5 m/3.3–5 ft wide, with a shape reminiscent of *Picea abies* 'Nidiformis.'

'Brandley' is slow-growing and densely but asymmetrically pyramidal with outstanding dark green color, reaching a height of at least 1 m/3.3 ft after about 20 years.

'Cappy's Choice' is compact and low-growing, reaching 0.6 m/2 ft in height only after many years, while spreading to 2.5–3 m/8–10 ft. Its foliage is light green touched with gold.

'Cole' (= 'Cole's Prostrate') is a fully prostrate selection, not exceeding 20 cm/8 in. high for many years, but spreading widely, eventually to a meter or two, 3.3–6.6 ft, useful in rock gardens but outgrows small spaces in time.

'Everitt's Golden' is upright and pyramidal, to 1.5–2 m/5–6.6 ft tall and less in width, with layered branching and golden-yellow new foliage, holding much of the color year-round.

'Gentsch White' (= 'Gentsch White Tip,' = 'Variegata') is globose to moundlike with silvery white new foliage, growing to 1–1.5 m/3.3–5 ft high and wide in time.

'Jeddeloh' is a semipendulous dwarf, forming a mound eventually to 1–1.5 m/3.3–5 ft high and slightly wider, with a conical depression in

Tsuga canadensis 'Pendula.'

the top, a very popular cultivar in Germany and becoming popular in our area.

'Minuta' is an extremely dwarf form, perhaps the most dwarf of all *Tsuga* cultivars, irregularly globose and growing only 1–1.5 cm/0.4–0.6 in. annually, remaining under 0.6 m/2 ft in height for several decades. This is a curiosity and a collector's item, but even so dwarf a plant is useful in very-small-scale landscapes. Surprisingly, it is reported to come true from seed.

'Pendula' (= 'Sargentii'; Sargent weeping hemlock) is a weeping form with contorted branches. It is one of the most striking specimen evergreens, but it is not particularly functional. Old specimens have reached heights of 2 m/6.6 ft and greater while spreading to more than twice that distance. This form shows a strong tendency to reproduce fairly true from seeds.

'Pomfret' is densely pyramidal in form and slow-growing, yet eventually grows tall enough to serve as a low-maintenance screen, when time is no object, or to function as a specimen. It is not widely available.

'Rugg's Washington Dwarf' is a dwarf with irregularly globose to moundlike shape, growing only about 5 cm/2 in. annually, with yellow-bronze foliage in early spring.

Related Species

Tsuga caroliniana 8 (Carolina hemlock). This native of the southern Appalachian Mountains from Virginia to Georgia differs from *T. canadensis* in having more open, less feathery branching habit, needles radiating irregularly from the twigs, and more interesting cones, opening widely when mature. Reputedly more

Tsuga caroliniana.

tolerant of city conditions than *T. canadensis*, this tree makes an equally effective hedge or screen. Useful in Zones 5b–7b, areas with cool summers in Zone 8a, and perhaps sheltered sites in Zone 5a.

Tsuga diversifolia 6–7 (Japanese hemlock). This compact, low-growing tree from Japan has unusually striking foliage with short needles radiating in all directions from the twigs and showing the whitened undersides to good advantage. Use-

ful as a small, often shrubby tree that will not exceed 10 m/33 ft for many years in our area, even though it can grow much larger in Japan. Useful in Zones 5b–7b, areas with cool summers in Zone 8a, and perhaps also in Zone 5a, but as yet seldom commercially available.

Tsuga heterophylla 8 (western hemlock). This large tree, native to two regions in the Pacific Northwest: at elevations below 600 m/2000 ft along the Pacific coast from Oregon to southeastern Alaska, and in a separate range in the Rocky Mountain region of Idaho and British Columbia, mainly at elevations of 1500–1800 m/5000–6000 ft. This species has not been much used in our area, except in arboretum collections, but there is growing interest in it in our area because of its resistance to woolly adelgid. It may be worthwhile to try a variety of seed origins, probably with emphasis on the southern parts of the interior, high-elevation range. Plants are already in cultivation in our area in at least Zones 6a–7b.

Tsuga mertensia 8 (mountain hemlock). This species grows wild from central California through the Cascade Range of Oregon and Washington and the coastal mountains from British Columbia to southeastern Alaska. As with *T. heterophylla*, there is also a separate portion of the range farther inland, in Idaho and British Columbia. It also shares the mountain hemlock's resistance to attack by woolly adelgids. This species is probably not limited in our area by cold-hardiness, but may be by summer heat and dryness. It is already growing in arboretums, and by collectors and a few nurserymen, at least in Zones 5a–7b, and a few selections have been made for special color and form.

Ulmus americana 8

AMERICAN ELM, WHITE ELM

Deciduous tree

Ulmaceae (Elm Family)

Native Range. Eastern North America: Newfoundland to Alberta and southward to Florida and Texas.

Useful Range. USDA Zones 2b–9a+.

Function. Shade or avenue tree, specimen. One of the most effective of all trees for a high canopy of shade.

Size and Habit

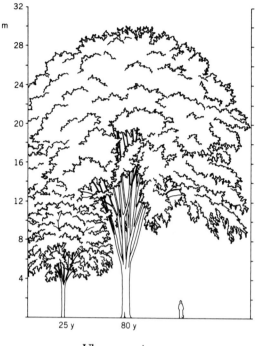

Ulmus americana.

Adaptability

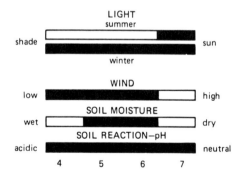

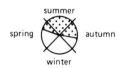

Seasonal Interest. *Flowers:* Very small but opening in large numbers before the leaves unfold, giving the tree a misty, pale yellow color. *Foliage:* Deep green and lustrous leaves, 8–15 cm/3–6 in. long, turn golden yellow before falling in autumn in some years and locations, especially in the northeastern and north-central parts of our area. *Fruits:* Small and inconspicuous, mostly concealed by the foliage.

Problems and Maintenance. The most serious problems of this species are Dutch elm disease, caused by the fungus *Ceratocystis ulmi* and transmitted by a few species of elm leaf beetle, and elm yellows (also called phloem necrosis), a lethal disease caused by mycoplasmalike organisms that affect the North American species of *Ulmus* but not the Asian and European species, which are fully tolerant (immune) to elm yellows. However, those species vary widely in their susceptibility to Dutch elm disease. Elms are among the large number of trees that are occasionally infected by the *Verticillium* fungus, which causes a serious wilt disease that is usually lethal. These diseases, individually or sometimes together, have all but eliminated *U. americana* from many areas of the northeastern and north-central states, and they continue to move into new areas. The spread has been arrested, at least temporarily, in some urban and suburban areas, through a careful program of sanitation, pruning, and spraying to control the elm leaf beetle, which is responsible for the spread of the fungus that causes Dutch elm disease. The cost of these diseases, whether in removal of infected trees or in preventive programs, is substantial, so they should be taken into consideration when specifying further planting of *U. americana* and other susceptible elms, until the long-term success of recently introduced "resistant" cultivars is assured.

Concern over the possible demise of this useful and sometimes majestic tree has brought eulogies, and it is often forgotten that the American elm was displaying other unfortunate qualities long before the appearance of Dutch elm disease. It is troubled by a wide range of lesser diseases and insects and seldom can be counted on, even in the absence of Dutch elm disease, to perform well without maintenance. It forms large buttress roots that cause serious problems when planted close to sidewalks, and it is susceptible to storm breakage, but not as much as its notoriously softwooded relative, the Siberian elm (*U. pumila*).

Several other tree species have been suggested as substitutes for *U. americana* in form, including silver maple *(Acer saccharinum)*, hackberries *(Celtis* species), some ashes *(Fraxinus* species), thornless honeylocust *(Gleditsia triacanthos* var. *inermis,* Kentucky coffee tree *(Gymnocladus dioica),* Japanese zelkova *(Zelkova serrata),* more disease-resistant elm species, and hybrids of other elm species.

Cultivars and Varieties. Several more-or-less resistant clones of *U. americana* have been selected in recent years, and a few are entering commerce at this writing. Resistance to diseases and insects is a matter of degree, unlike immunity, which is absolute, so different clones often exhibit different levels of resistance. Immunity to Dutch elm disease is not known in *U. americana* and it may be another decade or more before the degree of resistance of the new "resistant" clones is known.

"American Liberty Elms" are a mixture of six *U. americana* clones selected for resistance to Dutch elm disease by Dr. Eugene Smalley, a plant pathologist at the University of Wisconsin. These are being distributed throughout the United States by the Elm Research Institute of Harrisville, New Hampshire, in cooperation with the Boy Scouts of America, but they are not yet available from commercial nurseries. As they are planted more widely, their resistance to Dutch elm disease will become better known. They are reported to be susceptible to elm yellows (phloem necrosis).

'Delaware' (= 'Delaware II'), selected by Curtis May, U.S. Department of Agriculture, Morristown, New Jersey, from seedlings grown from seeds of native trees in North Dakota, and introduced by Princeton Nurseries, is broadly vase-shaped, growing rapidly to 20–25 m/66–82 ft tall and wide. It has been found to be highly resistant to Dutch elm disease, but not to elm yellows (phloem necrosis), and is useful in at least Zones 3b–8b, probably also Zone 3a.

'Patmore' (= 'Brandon,' = 'Patmore Ascending'), a selection from native trees at Brandon, Manitoba, is narrowly ascending and very cold-hardy, growing to about 15 m/50 ft tall as a common street tree in Edmonton, Alberta (Zone 3a) and elsewhere. While it is probably not resistant to Dutch elm disease, it is nevertheless useful in the provinces of Alberta and British Columbia, parts of Washington state, and other areas to which Dutch elm disease has not yet

spread. *A word of caution:* Clones of northern origin (in this case about 50° north latitude) may not be adapted to the combinations of temperature and photoperiod (daylength) that occur at more southern latitudes, and vice versa. Northern clones such as 'Patmore' probably should be planted only in small quantities south of about 40° North latitude (e.g., Columbus, Ohio; Indianapolis; Pittsburgh), until they have proved themselves.

'Princeton' was selected in 1922 by William Flemer, Sr. of Princeton Nurseries for its foliage, outstanding vase-shape, and fast growth. Much later it was found to be highly resistant to inoculation with the Dutch elm disease fungus and somewhat resistant to elm leaf beetle. It is useful at least in Zones 3b–8b.

'Washington' was selected from a tree growing on the National Mall in Washington, D.C., by H. V. Wester, a plant pathologist with the U.S. National Parks Service. It has the typical landscape character of *U. americana,* with glossy, deep green foliage and some resistance to Dutch elm disease. It has been found to be triploid (American elm is normally tetraploid), evidence that it probably is a hybrid involving a second, diploid species of *Ulmus. Nomenclatural note:* According to the International Code of Botanical Nomenclature, this clone should have a new cultivar name, since the name 'Washington' was earlier assigned to clonal propagations from the historic Washington elm in Cambridge, Massachusetts.

The var. *floridana* grows naturally in the extreme southeastern parts of the natural range of *U. americana* and is sometimes used as a landscape tree in that area (Zones 8b–9a+) but is not likely to be available elsewhere.

Hybrids. Since *U. americana* is usually tetraploid, it is not normally cross-compatible with other *Ulmus* species, which are diploid (except for occasional triploid hybrids), but hybrids among the diploid species exist, some with notable disease-resistance. Earlier hybrids among European species are very different from American elm in form, and some have little other than their disease-resistance to recommend them as shade trees. Some of the more recent hybrids, especially those involving Asian species, are finding greater acceptance. A few of the more common ones are described here.

'Cathedral' (Plant Patent No. 8683, 1994), a recent introduction from the elm breeding program of Dr. Eugene Smalley at the University of Wisconsin, is believed to be a hybrid of *U. japonica* and *U. pumila.* It is broadly vase-shaped, similar in form to broader trees of *U. americana,* eventually growing to 20 m/66 ft tall and wide, and is reported to be resistant to Dutch elm disease and highly tolerant of Verticillium wilt. If it should prove to be otherwise trouble-free, it would have good prospects as a substitute for American elm in Zones 5a–8b and probably parts of Zone 4.

'Danada' is a new selection from Dr. George Ware of the Morton Arboretum, an open-pollinated hybrid of 'Morton' (Accolade™, see below), probably by *U. wilsoniana.* With a good vase-shape and attractive red new foliage, its prospects as an American elm substitute should be very good if it continues to show high disease-resistance. It develops good form as a young tree with minimal pruning, and is potentially useful at least in Zones 5a–8b, but is not yet commercially available.

'Frontier,' a recently introduced hybrid of *U. carpinifolia* and *U. parvifolia* from the U.S.D.A. Shade Tree Laboratory at the National Arboretum, grows rapidly to 15 m/50 ft tall and 10–12 m/33–40 ft wide, upright-pyramidal when young, later developing a more vaselike shape, with distinctive reddish-purple autumn foliage color. It is reported to be highly resistant to Dutch elm disease, moderately resistant to elm leaf beetles, and tolerant of elm yellows (phloem necrosis). Useful at least in Zones 6a–9a, perhaps also parts of Zone 5.

'Groenveld,' selected in Holland from populations of *U.* ×*hollandica* (see Related Species and Hybrids, below), grows rapidly to 20 m/66 ft tall and 12–14 m/40–46 ft wide. It has been very resistant to European strains of the Dutch elm disease fungus, but not to the aggressive American strain. Because of that and its loosely columnar form, it has not been widely used as an American elm substitute in our area, but it is better than other *U.* ×*hollandica* selections. Useful in Zones 6a–9a, and perhaps also Zone 5b.

'Homestead,' a complex hybrid involving *U. pumila* and *U.* ×*hollandica,* grows to 18 m/60 ft tall and 13 m/43 ft wide, oval to pyramidal at first, eventually developing more arching

branches. It is reported to be resistant to Dutch elm disease and elm yellows (phloem necrosis), but is very susceptible to elm leaf beetle and Japanese beetle and is not a good prospect for resistance to storm injury. It is potentially useful in Zones 5a–8b, but there are now better choices.

'Lincoln' (Plant Patent No. 5015, 1983) may be the only named hybrid of *U. rubra,* probably by *U. pumila,* although there are many unnamed spontaneous hybrids of that parentage scattered around the Midwest. This selection grows to about 15 m/50 ft tall and 10–12 m/33–40 ft wide, with horizontal branching and a strong central leader, at least while young. It is reported to be resistant to Dutch elm disease and is potentially useful in at least Zones 4b–8b.

'Morton' (Accolade™) is a spontaneous hybrid, probably of *U. japonica* and *U. wilsoniana* parentage, rather recently discovered as an old tree growing in the Morton Arboretum. It has glossy, deep green foliage and is gracefully vase-shaped, much like American elm, but it requires careful pruning in the nursery to develop the best structure. It is useful at least in Zones 6a–8b, probably also parts of Zone 5b. It is reported in early trials to be cold-hardy in Zone 5a when grafted on *U. pumila* rootstocks, but not on its own roots.

'New Horizon' (Plant Patent No. 8684, 1994) is a hybrid of *U. japonica* and *U. pumila* from the University of Wisconsin elm breeding program. It is reported to be highly resistant to Dutch elm disease and leaf miners, tolerant of Verticillium wilt, and potentially useful at least in Zones 4a–8a.

'Pioneer,' a hybrid involving *U. glabra* and *U. carpinifolia,* is highly resistant to Dutch elm disease, but not to elm leaf beetles, and is broadly pyramidal in form while young, eventually more arching but not an acceptable substitute for *U. americana.* It is useful in at least Zones 5b–8b, but there are usually better choices.

'Regal,' another Smalley (Wisconsin) selection, is a complex hybrid involving *U. carpinifolia,* *U.* ×*hollandica,* and *U. pumila,* with narrowly oval, open form, eventually growing to 20 m/66 ft tall and 10–12 m/33–40 ft wide, not making as broad a canopy as *U. americana.* It has a strong central leader, unusual among hybrid elms, and wide crotch angles, suggesting that it may prove resistant to storm injury. It has considerable resistance to Dutch elm disease and Verticillium wilt. At this writing, it has been held back by difficulties in propagation; when they have been overcome, this may prove to be a very useful cultivar in at least Zones 5a–8b, probably also parts of Zone 4.

'Sapporo Autumn Gold,' an early University of Wisconsin introduction, probably a hybrid of *U. pumila* and *U. japonica,* is highly resistant to Dutch elm disease and tolerant of Verticillium wilt. It has a vase-shaped crown, but a "brushy" branching habit and narrow crotch angles, and has been largely superseded by better cultivars.

'Urban' (= 'Delaware No. 1') is a U.S. Department of Agriculture hybrid involving *U. carpinifolia, U. ×hollandica,* and *U. pumila,* upright and pyramidal, with a strong central trunk, growing to 18 m/60 ft tall and 13 m/43 ft wide. It is reported to be highly resistant to Dutch elm disease and elm yellows (phloem necrosis), but is somewhat susceptible to elm leaf beetles, and in some areas has commonly developed cankers following trunk injuries. Useful in Zones 4a–8b.

'Vanguard' is a Morton Arboretum selection from open pollinated seed of *U. japonica* received from the Agriculture Canada Research Station at Morden, Manitoba. The pollen parent is believed to be *U. pumila,* and the hybrid is promising but not yet available.

Related Species

Ulmus alata 7 (winged elm, wahoo elm). This small tree, usually 10–15 m/33–49 ft tall, is native to the southeastern states from Virginia to Illinois and southward to Florida and Texas. It is seldom available in nurseries, but collected trees are sometimes available in the natural range, and it is worth preserving in development, even though it is susceptible to Dutch elm disease. The winged twigs provide easy identification but add little landscape interest. Useful in Zones 6b–9a.

Ulmus carpinifolia 8 (smooth-leaved elm). This native of Europe and adjacent Africa and Asia has been cultivated for a long time and many distinctive forms have been selected and named in Europe, but few are available in our area.

Ulmus carpinifolia.

'Umbraculifera' (globe elm) is very compact and globose in shape, remaining below 6 m/20 ft for years. 'Variegata' differs from the species type in having irregularly white-variegated leaves, which make an interesting contrast with green foliage, but it is seldom used or available in our area. *Ulmus carpinifolia* and its cultivars are generally useful in Zones 5b–9a.

Ulmus glabra 8 (Scotch or Wych elm). This native of Europe and adjacent Africa and Asia, like *U. carpinifolia,* has long been cultivated, and many cultivars have been selected. This species has not been very widely used in our area, and since it is susceptible to Dutch elm disease and many lesser pests as well, it probably will not find much use in the future. Useful in Zones 4b–9a. The selection 'Camperdownii' (Camperdown elm) is strikingly pendulous, usually grafted on a 1.5-m/5-ft standard, forming a broad mound to 3 m/10 ft high, with branches hanging to the ground. Very popular in the first half of the twentieth century, it is still commercially available but no longer widely used.

Ulmus glabra 'Camperdownii.'

Ulmus glabra 'Camperdownii.'

Ulmus ×*hollandica* 8 (Holland elm).   Members of this hybrid group (*U. glabra* × *U. carpinifolia*) were among the first disease-resistant elms to be selected. They are more widely used in Europe than in our area, and they are not similar enough in form to *U. americana* to be considered substitutes. Potentially useful in Zones 5b–9a, and some cultivars to Zone 5a.

Ulmus japonica 8 (synonym: *U. davidiana* var. *japonica;* Japanese elm).   This large tree from Japan with narrow form and a strong central leader is being used extensively as a source of resistance to Dutch elm disease for breeding hybrid elm trees at the Morton Arboretum and elsewhere (see Hybrids, above). The species type itself is potentially useful at least in Zones 4a–9a. The clone 'Discovery,' selected by Wilbert Ronald of Portage la Prairie, Manitoba, in Zone 3a, has proved exceptionally cold-hardy and is scheduled to reach the commercial market in 1996.

Ulmus laevis 8 (Russian elm, European white elm).   This native of central Europe to western Asia is a large tree similar to *U. americana.* It has been planted only experimentally in our area with no evidence to date of significant resistance to Dutch elm disease. It probably is not available commercially, although potentially useful in Zones 5a–9a and perhaps also colder zones.

Ulmus procera 8 (synonym: *U. campestris;* English elm).   This large tree from Europe is widely planted there and in the United States, especially in cities, where it seems unusually well adapted. Even though it is not considered highly resistant to Dutch elm disease, many plantings have thus far escaped and remain in good condition, but the form of this tree does not resemble that of *U. americana,* so it cannot be considered a landscape substitute for that species. Useful in Zones 6a–9a.

Ulmus pumila 7–8 (Siberian elm).   This native of eastern Siberia and northern China to Central Asia unfortunately is often called Chinese elm, confusing it with the much superior, "true" Chinese elm, *U. parvifolia. U. pumila* has its place in the western extremities of our area on the dry plains, where its cold- and drought-hardiness enables it to succeed where few other trees can. However, it is commonly planted in much of the rest of our area where many better alternatives are available. Its good qualities are high resistance to Dutch elm disease and fast growth. Its liabilities are that it is softwooded and storm prone, extremely susceptible to leaf beetles, which can nearly defoliate trees by midsummer, and tends to give rise to many weed seedlings. Moreover, it has hardly any seasonal interest. Yet from Manitoba through the Dakotas, Nebraska, Kansas, and Oklahoma to Texas and westward, it is admittedly a useful tree, and several cultivars of superior form and foliage have been selected; including 'Coolshade' and 'Dropmore.' Useful, with selection of appropriate genetic material, in Zones 2b–9a.

Ulmus rubra 8 (synonym: *U. fulva;* red or slippery elm).   This American native has a range only slightly less extensive than that of *U. americana* and differs primarily in its coarser texture and less striking form. Since it has not demonstrated high resistance to Dutch elm disease and is otherwise considered somewhat inferior in the landscape industry, it seldom is available, but it is potentially useful in Zones 4b–9a.

·*Ulmus thomasii* 8 (rock elm).   This native of northeastern North America from Quebec to Nebraska and southward to Tennessee has poor growth habit for use as a shade tree and is seldom, if ever, planted. It may be worth preserving in development in some sites in Zones 4b–7b.

Ulmus wilsoniana 7–8 (Wilson elm).   This little-known species from western China grows to 25 m/83 ft tall, upright in form, with gracefully arching branches, strongly reminiscent of American elm but branching lower, with reddish new growth expanding into lustrous, dark green leaves, and whitish, finely plated bark. It is useful at least in Zones 5b–7b, and probably somewhat more widely. 'Prospector,' recently introduced by the U.S. Department of Agriculture, is a seedling selection of *U. wilsoniana* from a seedlot of unknown origin. It is reported to be resistant to Dutch elm disease and elm leaf beetles, and because of its Asian origin it is expected to be tolerant of the elm yellows organism. *U. wilsoniana* is an important parent of new hybrids (see Hybrids, above).

Ulmus parvifolia 7–8

CHINESE OR LACEBARK ELM
Deciduous or semievergreen tree
Ulmaceae (Elm Family)

Native Range.   China, Japan, Korea.

Useful Range.   USDA Zones 5b–9a and sheltered areas in Zone 5a.

Function.   Shade tree, specimen.

Size and Habit

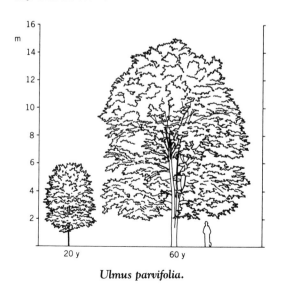

Ulmus parvifolia.

Adaptability

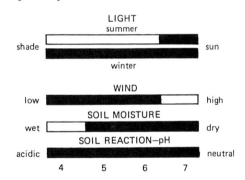

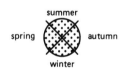

Seasonal Interest.   *Flowers:* Small and inconspicuous, opening in late summer. *Foliage:* Leathery, deep green leaves are small and tidy, 2.5–5 cm/1–2 in. long, remaining green until late autumn in the North, then turning purplish briefly before falling, but persisting and remaining green well into winter in Zone 9a. *Fruits:* Bright green, waferlike, individually about 1 cm/0.4 in. long, in clusters in early autumn, adding minor autumn interest. *Trunk and branches:* Bark of young trunks and main branches of some trees peels off in rounded patches, tan and brown, in much the same way as that of *Platanus occidentalis* except that the patches are much smaller and the mottled effect produced is finer-textured and more refined in appearance.

Problems and Maintenance. This species is resistant (although not immune) to Dutch elm disease and not as seriously affected by other disease and insect problems (such as leaf beetles) as some of the other elms, but it still needs maintenance to keep it in good condition. It is somewhat prone to breakage by ice and wind, but no more so than *U. americana* and considerably less so than *U. pumila.* Pruning is needed for initial training and for removing any dead or damaged branches thereafter.

Cultivars.   Several cultivars have been selected for growth habit, foliage character, superior bark interest, fast growth, and slow growth since dwarf forms are valued highly for bonsai treatment and compact forms for small-scale landscape use in mild climates. A few of the more popular or promising are described here.

'Aross Central Park' (Plant Patent No. 6983, 1989), named in memory of Arthur Vining Ross, originated as a tree planted in New York's Central Park more than a century ago, now 18 m/60 ft tall and at least as wide. Young plants cloned by David Karnosky, the introducer, have grown at a rate of about 0.75 m/2.5 ft annually. It has small, lustrous, deep green leaves and moderate bark interest and is useful at least in Zones 6b–8b, probably also Zone 9a.

'D. B. Cole' is a compact form (height growth 0.4 m/1.3 ft annually) with a dense head and outstanding bark interest. Probably useful in Zones 6b–9a, perhaps also colder zones.

'Drake' is a fast-growing, gracefully semipendulous tree, eventually growing to 8–10 m/26–33 ft high and 12 m/40 ft wide, with nearly evergreen foliage and fine bark interest. This selection is popular in the sun belt, probably useful in Zones 7b–9a+, perhaps also sheltered sites in Zone 7a.

'Dynasty' is a full-sized tree from the elm breeding program of Frank Santamour at the U.S. National Arboretum, from seed parents originating in Japan or Korea, with vase-shaped habit, growing moderately fast to 15–20 m/50–66 ft tall and nearly as wide. Useful in Zones 6a–9a and probably at least parts of Zone 5.

'Emer I' (= 'Emerald Isle,' Plant Patent No. 7551, 1991, Athena®) is a tree selected on the University of Georgia campus. It has broadly globose form and a very low head, growing to 9 m/30 ft tall and 16 m/54 ft wide at maturity (the size of the parent tree, estimated to be 70–75 years old). It has glossy, dark green foliage and outstanding bark interest, and is easily propagated by cuttings (but note that it is patented). Useful as a lawn tree in Zones 7a–9a+, perhaps also parts of Zone 6, but not yet widely available.

'Emer II' (= 'Emerald Vase', Plant Patent No. 7552, 1991, Allee®) is another selection from the University of Georgia campus, vase-shaped and growing to 21 m/70 ft tall and 18 m/59 ft wide at maturity (the size of the parent tree, estimated to be 80–90 years old). Like 'Emer I,' it has good foliage and bark interest, and it is presumably useful in about the same range but is not yet widely available.

'Frosty' is a shrubby, low-growing tree, notable for its subtly white-marked leaf margins; it is useful for bonsai or as a very small landscape tree. Useful at least in Zones 6b–9a.

'King's Choice' (Plant Patent No. 5554, 1985) is a full-sized, fast-growing selection made by Ben King of Hampstead, Maryland, with oval form, large, deep green leaves, to 6.4 cm/2.5 in. long, turning yellowish in autumn, and moderate bark interest as a young tree. Useful in Zones 6b–9a, probably also Zone 6a.

'Ohio' is a recent selection for vase-shaped habit, with moderately fast growth to 18 m/60 ft tall and 15 m/50 ft wide; it has high resistance to most of the diseases of elms. Probably useful in Zones 6a–9a, perhaps also parts of Zone 5.

'Prairie Shade' is a selection by Carl Whitcomb of Stillwater, Oklahoma, for good form, fast growth (1.3 m/4.3 ft annually), disease-resistance, small leaves, and ease of propagation by cuttings. Not yet widely available but probably useful in Zones 5b–9a.

'Sempervirens' is a collective name for evergreen trees, often seed-propagated, that may be closely related but vary considerably in growth habit and thus cannot be considered a single cultivar. Most are large, rounded trees, eventually to 12–15 m/40–50 ft tall and 15–18 m/50–

60 ft wide, with handsome, leathery leaves that are usually evergreen in mild winters, but may drop following unusually cold periods. Useful at least in Zones 7b–9a+.

'True Green' is nearly fully evergreen and round-headed, with small leaves. It is probably less cold-hardy than the other cultivars listed here, perhaps only Zones 9a+, so it is not useful in much of our area.

Miniature forms, most often used for bonsai treatment, include 'Hokkaido' (princess elm), said to be the smallest of all, in effect a "natural bonsai" reaching only 30 cm/12 in. high in 20 years, with tiny leaves and fine bark interest, and 'Seiju,' a mutation of 'Hokkaido,' faster growing but still dwarf, with larger leaves and rough-corky bark.

Related Species

Ulmus crassifolia 7–8 (cedar elm).   This small to large tree, generally similar to U. *parvifolia* but native from Mississippi to Texas and Mexico, is an important landscape tree in the southwestern corner of our area, which coincides with the eastern part of its natural range. On good sites in this area (Zones 7b–9a), it will reach heights of 20–25 m/66–82 ft in time, although its form may be quite variable. It is often seen more in the 10 to 15-m/33 to 49-ft size range. Like U. *parvifolia*, it flowers in late summer, is less troubled by leaf beetles and other problems than most elms, and seems to have some resistance to Dutch elm disease. Some trees have winged twigs reminiscent of those of U. *alata*. Most trees used in the past have been collected from the wild, but there is increasing interest in nursery production, so availability may increase. Spontaneous hybrids with U. *parvifolia* have been found in the natural range of U. *crassifolia*. Since both parents show resistance to Dutch elm disease, hybrids may also turn out to be useful landscape trees, but no introduction of such hybrids is known by the author at this writing.

Vaccinium angustifolium 2–3

LOWBUSH BLUEBERRY
Deciduous groundcover
Ericaceae (Heath Family)

Native Range.   Northeastern North America: Newfoundland to Saskatchewan and south to Illinois and Virginia.

Useful Range.   USDA Zones 2a–6b with selection of appropriate genetic material.

Function.   Groundcover, especially for naturalizing, edible fruits.

Size and Habit

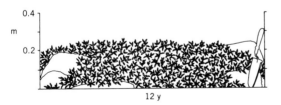

Vaccinium angustifolium.

Adaptability.   Once the requirement for acidic, well-drained soil has been met, this is one of the most widely adaptable groundcovers to sun or shade and to dry soil.

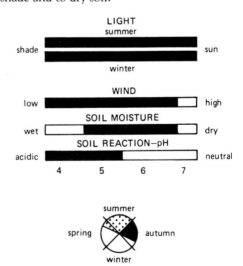

Seasonal Interest.   *Flowers:* Greenish white, bell-shaped, less than 0.8 cm/0.3 in. long and not very conspicuous. *Foliage:* Lustrous, bright green, 0.8–3.5 cm/0.3–1.4 in. long, making an irregular, rather fine-textured mass, turning bright scarlet before falling in late autumn. *Fruits:* Small, edible blueberries, ripening in late summer, adding only slight additional landscape interest.

Problems and Maintenance.   This plant is subject to several insect and disease problems, but they are rarely serious enough to require spraying. Yellowing of young foliage, caused by iron deficiency, is common in soils that are not sufficiently acidic, this is, not below about pH 5.5. Renewal pruning by mowing or burning (seldom

feasible in landscape situations) will keep this plant a low, vigorous groundcover.

Varieties and Cultivars.   Var. *laevifolium* occurs in the southern parts of the natural range, overlapping with the range of the species type. The variety grows taller than the species type, to 0.6 m/2 ft, and has larger leaves, 1.5–3.5 cm/0.6–1.4 in. long, and may not be fully cold-hardy in Zones 2 and 3. Var. *laevifolium* is the form of *V. angustifolium* that exists in large stands at low elevations in Maine, and its fruits are harvested commercially.

'Leucocarpum' has white berries but is seldom used or commercially available.

Vaccinium corymbosum 5

HIGHBUSH BLUEBERRY
Deciduous shrub
Ericaceae (Heath Family)

Native Range.   Eastern North America: Maine to Minnesota and southward to Florida and Louisiana on suitable soils.

Useful Range.   USDA Zones 4b–9a with selection of appropriate genetic material.

Function.   Border, specimen, screen, naturalizing, edible fruits.

Size and Habit

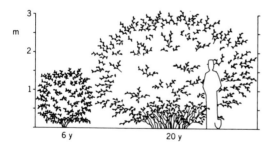

Vaccinium corymbosum.

Adaptability.   Tolerant of shade in landscape use but requires close to full sun for best fruit production.

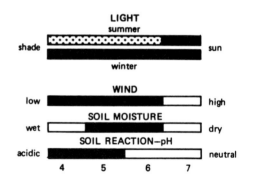

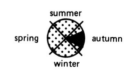

Seasonal Interest.   *Flowers:* White or pinkish, bell-shaped, mostly less than 1 cm/0.4 in. long, adding minor landscape interest along with the unfolding leaves in late spring. *Foliage:* Lustrous, bright to deep green, 3–8 cm/1.2–3 in. long, making a rather open to fairly dense mass, turning orange and scarlet, and falling in late autumn. *Fruits:* Medium to large, edible blueberries, to 1 cm/0.4 in. or larger in cultivars, ripening from middle to late summer. *Twigs and*

Vaccinium corymbosum.

branches: Twigs of vigorous plants turn red in winter, adding significant landscape interest.

Problems and Maintenance. Several insects and diseases can be troublesome, and spraying is sometimes necessary, even in landscape plantings. A careful spray program should be followed when fruit production is the primary reason for growing this shrub. Details can be obtained from county and state or provincial extension service offices. Iron chlorosis (leaf yellowing) is common in soils that are not sufficiently acidic. When soil acidification is not feasible and chlorosis is not extreme, it may be corrected by the use of chelated iron and/or foliage sprays. This information also is available from extension service offices. Regular pruning as carried out in commercial fruit production reduces the number of branches to increase fruit size, whereas pruning for use as a visual screen does just the opposite. For dual-purpose use, pruning should be limited to any that is necessary to increase fullness for screening. Even though the berries may be smaller than commercial blueberries, their total production will be considerable. Since the fullness required for effective screening can be obtained only in vigorously growing plants, this function is only attainable in sites where soil conditions are close to ideal.

Cultivars. Many cultivars have been developed for berry production. Recommended cultivars vary regionally, and information for specific areas can be obtained from extension service offices. Relative effectiveness of fruiting cultivars for landscape use has not been completely determined; suggestions probably can be obtained from local blueberry growers and extension specialists.

Related Species

Vaccinium arboreum 6 (tree huckleberry, sparkleberry, farkleberry). This tall shrub or small tree grows to 6–8 m/20–26 ft tall under ideal conditions in the southern parts of its natural range, which extends from Virginia and southern Illinois southward to Florida and Texas. Its small evergreen leaves, 2.5–5 cm/1–2 in. long, form a foliage mass a little sparse for effective screening unless thickened by pruning, but the plant's principal landscape usefulness is for naturalizing (or preservation) or as a small, multiple-stemmed tree with handsomely "molded" trunks and branches covered with close cinnamon-brown bark. Seldom used or available, but a landscape plant worthy of greater attention in Zones 7a–9a+ with selection of appropriate genetic material. Its fruits are not edible.

Vaccinium ashei 4–6 (rabbiteye blueberry). This variable species, native to the southeastern states, is an important parent of fruiting cultivars for the Deep South because of its low winter-chilling requirement. It is grown more in the form of such cultivars than as the wild type. Most cultivars grow to less than 2 m/6.6 ft in height. Their small, often rosy pink flowers are somewhat more showy in spring than those of *V. corymbosum*, and their foliage is not greatly different except that it is semievergreen, usually turning scarlet before falling in early winter. Useful in Zones 8a–9a+.

Vaccinium vitis-idaea 2

COWBERRY, MOUNTAIN
CRANBERRY, LINGONBERRY
Evergreen groundcover
Ericaceae (Heath Family)

Native Range. Circumpolar: northern Asia, Europe, and North America as far south as Massachusetts and British Columbia.

Useful Range. USDA Zones 2–6b with selection of appropriate genetic material (see Subspecies), possibly also Zone 7.

Function. Small-scale groundcover, specimen, rock garden.

Size and Habit

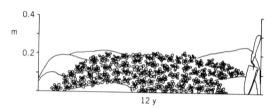

0.4
m
0.2

12 y

Vaccinium vitis-idaea.

Adaptability

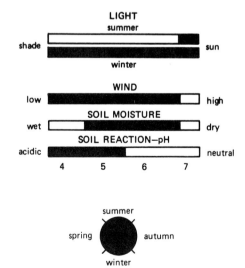

LIGHT
summer
shade   sun
winter

WIND
low   high

SOIL MOISTURE
wet   dry

SOIL REACTION–pH
acidic   neutral
4   5   6   7

summer
spring   autumn
winter

Seasonal Interest. *Flowers:* White to pinkish, only 0.6 cm/0.25 in. long but adding significant interest at close range, where this plant is most effective, in late spring and early summer. *Fo-*

liage: Evergreen and leathery, dark green and lustrous, the convex leaf surfaces enhancing the luster, only 1–3 cm/0.4–1.2 in. long, producing an elegantly fine-textured mass. *Fruits:* deep red, to 1 cm/0.4 in. across, conspicuous in late summer and early autumn when borne in significant numbers.

Problems and Maintenance. This plant is relatively trouble-free when growing in a good soil and site. It never needs pruning other than to remove any dead stems.

Subspecies and Cultivars. The ssp. *vitis-idaea* (synonym: var. *majus*; cowberry or lingonberry) is the primarily Eurasian and lowland North American form of the species, growing to heights of 30 cm/12 in. with leaves as much as 2.5–3 cm/1–1.2 in. long. Useful at least in Zones 5a–6b, perhaps also Zone 4 and areas with mild summers in Zone 7.

The ssp. *minus* (mountain cranberry or lingonberry) is the alpine form of this species, from arctic and subarctic North America, with southern limits at high elevations in New England. This form is extremely cold-hardy but is poorly adapted to areas with hot, dry summers and probably should be limited to use in Zones 3a–5b, in areas with mild summers. It is most useful in small-scale situations, where it is one of the very finest evergreen groundcovers. Its lustrous, convex leaves, no more than 1.5 cm/0.6 in. long, form a dense mat, 10–20 cm/4–8 in. thick and several feet wide, small pink or

Vaccinium vitis-idaea ssp. *minus*.

white flowers and bright red, edible fruits, 0.8–1 cm/0.3–0.4 in. across.

'Koralle' is an award-winning form of ssp. *vitis-idaea*, selected for free-fruiting and vigorous growth.

'Red Pearl' is another selection for superior fruiting, maturing earlier than 'Koralle,' and growing to 30–45 cm/12–18 in. high.

'Splendor' is a fast-growing University of Wisconsin selection, growing to 20–40 cm/8–16 in. high; it has outstanding fruit size and quality, as well as resistance to phytophthora root rot.

Related Species

Vaccinium crassifolium 2 (creeping blueberry). This evergreen native of the coastal plain and Piedmont, from Virginia to Georgia, forms a mat 12–20 cm/5–8 in. high and spreading indefinitely, making an excellent groundcover in acidic soil. It is similar in effect to *Gaylussacia brachycera*, with leathery, deep green leaves, 0.5–2 cm/0.2–0.8 in. long and at least half as wide, bell-shaped, rosy red to pale pink flowers, 0.4 cm/0.15 in. across, and small, black or dark blue fruits that are juicy and attractive to wildlife. Useful in Zones 7b–9a, probably also Zone 7a and parts of Zone 6. Two groundcover forms have been selected at North Carolina State University: 'Bloodstone' has relatively large, lustrous and leathery leaves, to 2 cm/0.8 in. long and 1.3 cm/0.5 in. wide, and reminiscent of the leaves of *Vinca minor*. Leaves of 'Wells Delight' are narrower, to only 1.0 cm/0.4 in. wide, bronze as they first unfold, then turning glossy dark green, followed by dark blue berries.

Vaccinium darrowii 2–3 (synonym: *V. myrsinites* var. *glaucum;* Darrow evergreen blueberry). This more-or-less upright shrub, to 20–80 cm/8–32 in. high, with glaucous, blue-green, evergreen leaves, 1.5–2.5 cm/0.6–1 in. long, small white flowers, and blue-black berries. Useful in at least Zones 7b–9a.

Vaccinium macrocarpon 2 (large cranberry). This creeping plant, native to northern North America, forms a low mat, to 20 cm/8 in. high

and spreading to 1 m/3.3 ft in landscape use, with small (1–2 cm/0.4–0.8 in long), narrow evergreen leaves, whitened underneath. Useful in acidic soil, in at least Zones 3a–6b.

Vaccinium oxycoccos 2 (small or European cranberry). This cranberry, native to northern North America, Europe, and Asia, is less vigorous than *V. macrocarpon,* with leaves and berries only about half as large; otherwise, it is similar but perhaps less useful as a landscape plant.

Vaccinium ovatum 3–5 (evergreen huckleberry). This evergreen shrub, native from coastal central California to British Columbia, grows to heights from 1 m/3.3 ft in full sun to 4 m/13 ft in shaded sites. Its lustrous, dark green, leathery elliptical leaves, to 1.2–3 cm/0.5–1.2 in. long, are its principal landscape feature, and its cut branches are the "huckleberry" used as florist's greens. Flowers are small and pinkish white, followed by small blackish fruits that are used in making preserves and syrups. Useful in Zones 7b–9a+ but only in climates moderated year-round, which does not include much of our area.

Vaccinium parvifolium 4–5 (red huckleberry). This deciduous native of the coastal ranges from northern California to Alaska is a fine-textured, "airy" shrub, with gracefully arching, wiry branches, light green in winter, followed by small, thin, light green leaves that hold their color even in late summer. The small bright red berries add significant color in summer. This shrub has seldom been used in eastern North America, but might be tried experimentally in Zones 6a–9a, in relatively cool sites with acidic soil, reliable moisture supply, and partial shade.

Gaylussacia brachycera 2 (box huckleberry). This blueberry relative, native to the central Appalachian mountains from Pennsylvania to Tennessee, is an effective evergreen groundcover for acidic soils, 30–50 cm/12–20 in. high, with dark green leaves about the same size as those of *V. vitis-idaea* var. *majus.* Useful in Zones 6a–7a, perhaps farther south as well, but not widely available.

Viburnum ×burkwoodii 5

BURKWOOD VIBURNUM
Semievergreen shrub
Caprifoliaceae (Honeysuckle Family)

Hybrid Origin. *V. carlesii* × *V. utile.*

Useful Range. USDA Zones 5b–8b, perhaps also Zone 9a.

Function. Border, specimen. Tall but not dense enough to function as a screen.

Size and Habit

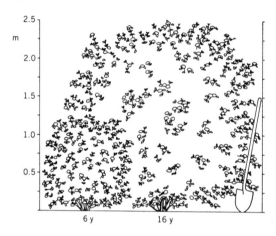

Viburnum ×burkwoodii.

Adaptability

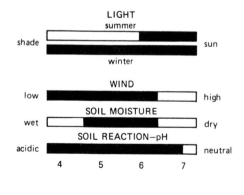

Seasonal Interest. *Flowers:* Fragrant (clovelike), pink in bud, opening white, in rounded clusters (cymes) about 6 cm/2.4 in. across as the foliage is unfolding in midspring. *Foliage:* Lustrous, dark green leaves, 3–8 cm/1.2–3 in. long, semievergreen, turning yellowish to winered before falling in early winter. *Fruits:* Red berries ripen black in early autumn but seldom are borne in large numbers.

Problems and Maintenance. Several diseases and insects can be troublesome occasionally, but not enough to justify a regular program of control. *V.* ×*burkwoodii* usually is sold on its own roots, since it can be propagated easily by cuttings, avoiding the rootstock problems that grafted plants are subject to (see *V. carlesii,* Problems and Maintenance).

Cultivars and Hybrids. The original or "type" clone, described above, is in commerce under the name *V.* ×*burkwoodii.* A sister seedling, named 'Park Farm,' with pure white flowers, probably is not available in our area. Several other clones have been given cultivar names. The most common are included here.

'Anne Russell' and 'Fulbrook' are old cultivars introduced in the 1950s in England. 'Anne Russell' flowers very early, 'Fulbrook' two weeks later. These have not been widely used in our area, and they are not widely available now.

'Chenault' has slightly more compact habit and slightly larger, less glossy leaves, flowering a week or two earlier than the type clone, and is slightly less cold-hardy.

'Chesapeake,' a Donald Egolf selection from the U.S. National Arboretum, is a complex hybrid of *V.* ×*carlcephalum* 'Cayuga' by *V. utilis,* growing to 2 m/6.6 ft tall and half again as wide, with lustrous, dark green, elliptical leaves that turn dull red-orange in autumn and persist well into winter in mild climates. Its flower clusters are intermediate between those of *V. carlesii* and *V.* ×*carlcephalum* and are fragrant. Its overall effect is of a mounding plant comparable in height to *V. carlesii* but broader, and it is more showy in flower. It is probably useful in Zones 6a–8b, and perhaps some sites in Zone 5b.

'Conoy,' another Egolf hybrid, is actually a backcross of V. ×*burkwoodii* with its tender evergreen parent, V. *utile*. It has a compact, spreading habit, growing to only 1.5 m/5 ft high but 2.4 m/8 ft wide, with fully evergreen foliage in milder climates, bronzing slightly in cold winters. Useful at least in Zones 6b–9a, perhaps also Zone 6a.

'Eskimo' is a complex hybrid resulting from self-pollinating a sister seedling of 'Chesapeake' (see parentage under that cultivar). The resulting plant is popular for its size, to 1.2–1.5 m/4–5 ft tall and 1.5 m/5 ft wide, and large flower clusters, to 8 cm/3 in. across, each densely packed with 2-cm/0.75-in. flowers, and for its leathery, glossy dark green foliage, persisting through autumn. It is useful in Zones 6b–8b, perhaps also Zone 6a.

'Mohawk' is a hybrid of V. ×*burkwoodii* back-crossed with V. *carlesii* by Egolf at the National Arboretum. It differs from V. ×*burkwoodii* in having somewhat larger leaves and bright, deep rose-red buds that are colorful for several weeks before they open. It is highly resistant to leafspot and powdery mildew diseases and may be slightly more cold-hardy than V. ×*burkwoodii*.

Related Species

Viburnum utile 4 (Honan viburnum). This parent of V. ×*burkwoodii* differs from the hybrid in being lower and more open in growth habit, with smaller but fully evergreen leaves. Even though the glossy, dark green foliage is very beautiful, the plant is less functional because of its sparseness and lesser cold-hardiness. It is useful in Zones 7b–9a+ and perhaps also in Zone 7a.

Viburnum carlesii 4

KOREAN SPICE VIBURNUM
Deciduous shrub
Caprifoliaceae (Honeysuckle Family)

Native Range.   Korea.

Useful Range.   USDA Zones 4b–8a.

Function.   Specimen, border, foundation.

Size and Habit

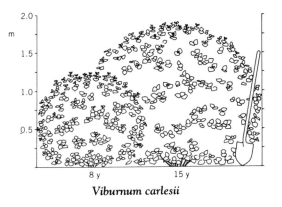

Viburnum carlesii

Adaptability

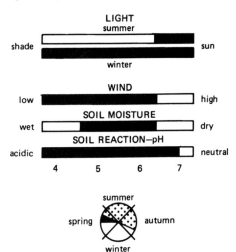

Seasonal Interest. *Flowers:* Very fragrant (clovelike), pink in bud, opening white, in rounded clusters (cymes) 5–8 cm/2–3 in. across with the unfolding foliage in midspring. *Foliage:* Gray-green, slightly lustrous to velvety, 5–10 cm/2–4 in. long and nearly as broad, turning dull reddish in some years before falling in autumn. *Fruits*: Rounded, elongated to 1 cm/0.4 in., dull red in late summer, ripening black in early autumn but seldom showy.

Problems and Maintenance. Several diseases and insects can be troublesome occasionally, but seldom are serious enough to justify control. In the past, *V. carlesii* was grafted on *V. lantana*, which, because of its greater vigor, often would overgrow the *V. carlesii* until the entire plant would appear to have been transformed into *V. lantana*. Modern cutting propagation techniques have been more successful with this species, and seedlings and cutting-grown plants on their own roots are usually available.

Cultivars. 'Aurora' is a superior selection from England, with nearly red flower buds, opening pure white and very fragrant, and downy dull green foliage, forming a mound to 1.9 m/6 ft high and wider, but it is not yet widely available.

'Compactum' is a widely used compact form, remaining below 1.5 m/5 ft high for many years, with smaller leaves and inflorescences.

Related Species and Hybrids

Viburnum bitchiuense 5 (Bitchiu viburnum). This native of Bitchiu province in Japan, and Korea is somewhat taller and looser than *V. carlesii*, with more slender and fragrant but slightly smaller flower clusters. It is seldom available commercially but potentially useful in the same Zones as *V. carlesii*, perhaps colder zones as well.

Viburnum carlesii 'Compactum.'

Viburnum × *carlcephalum* 5 (fragrant snowball). This hybrid of *V. carlesii* and *V. macrocephalum* f. *keteleeri* is taller and has larger, denser flower clusters than *V. carlesii*, but retains much of the cold-hardiness and fragrance of *V. carlesii*. The selection 'Cayuga,' released by the National Arboretum, is a hybrid of *V. carlesii* back-crossed with *V.* ×*carlcephalum*, growing to about 2 m/6.6 ft tall, with flower clusters slightly smaller than those of *V.* ×*carlcephalum* but plentiful. It is about as cold-hardy as *V. carlesii* and is more resistant to powdery mildew and leaf-spot diseases.

Viburnum ×*juddii* 5 (Judd viburnum). This hybrid of *V. carlesii* and *V. bitchiuense* is intermediate between its parents, slightly taller and looser than *V. carlesii*, but more easily propagated by cuttings and probably superior as a landscape plant.

Viburnum macrocephalum 5 (Chinese snowball). The species type, f. *macrocephalum* (= 'Sterile'), is notable for its enlarged sterile flowers, each more than 2.5 cm/1 in. across, in huge, dense clusters, at least 12–15 cm/5–6 in. across, and semievergreen foliage, another example (see also *V. plicatum*) in which the species name was first assigned to the sterile garden form. The wild type, f. *keteleeri*, from China, has enlarged sterile flowers only around the margin of the flattened flower cluster and is not widely available. Both forms can function as visual screens only with careful pruning, since they tend to be open in habit. Useful in Zones 6b–8b.

Viburnum carlesii 'Compactum.'

Viburnum dentatum 6

Synonyms: *V. Pubescens, V. recognitum, V. scabrellum*

ARROWWOOD

Deciduous shrub

Caprifoliaceae (Honeysuckle Family)

Native Range. Eastern North America: New Brunswick to Minnesota, southward to Georgia.

Useful Range. USDA Zones 4a–9a with selection of appropriate genetic material (see Varieties).

Function. Border, screen, naturalizing.

Size and Habit

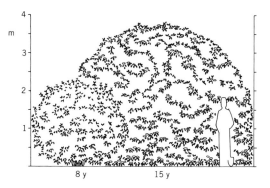

Viburnum dentatum.

Adaptability

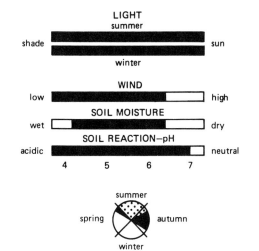

Seasonal Interest. *Flowers:* Creamy white, individually only 0.6 cm/0.25 in. across, in flattened clusters to 8 cm/3 in. across, conspicuous in late spring. *Foliage:* Dark green, usually lustrous, coarsely toothed and with prominent veins, making a handsome neutral mass, then turning bright red in some sites before falling in late autumn. *Fruits:* Blue-black, only 0.6 cm/0.25 in. across, in flattened clusters, adding mild landscape interest in early autumn.

Problems and Maintenance. This is one of the most trouble-free of the viburnums, requiring little maintenance other than spraying to control occasional insect outbreaks. Pruning may be necessary occasionally for thinning and renewal because of the tendency to produce large numbers of basal shoots, but not in naturalized plantings.

Varieties and Cultivars. This is a variable species, in leaf size, shape, and toothing, which causes considerable confusion.

The var. *deamii* (synonym: var. *indianense;* Deam arrowwood) grows wild from southern Ohio to Missouri and has rounded leaves with many sharp teeth.

The var. *dentatum* (synonyms: *V. dentatum* var. *pubescens, V. pubescens;* downy arrowwood) is the species type, growing wild from New Jersey to Florida and Texas.

The var. *lucidum* (synonym: *V. recognitum*) is the northern population, growing from New Brunswick and New York to Ohio and northern Georgia, with smooth, rounded leaves with sharp teeth.

The var. *scabrellum* (synonym: *V. scabrellum;* rough arrowwood) grows naturally from the southeastern states to Florida and Texas and extends the useful range of this species southward.

The var. *venosum,* limited to the sandy soils of coastal Massachusetts and New Jersey, has rather small leaves, toothed but nearly circular in outline, with a thick, mealy (stellate) pubescence. It is probably not in landscape use except locally in its native range, but it is worth preserving in development.

The following cultivars have been introduced

by Synnestvedt Nurseries of Round Lake, Illinois, as part of the Chicagoland Grows® program.

'Morton' (Northern Burgundy®) grows to 2–3 m/6.6–10 ft tall and nearly as wide with a rounded to moundlike growth habit and lustrous green leaves that turn a deep burgundy in early autumn. Flowers open very late in spring and the fruits that follow ripen blue-black in very late summer.

'Ralph Senior' (Autumn Jazz®) grows to 3–4.5 m/10–15 ft tall and 2–3 m/6.6–10 ft wide with an upright growth habit and glossy, bright green foliage that turns red in midautumn. Flowers open in midspring followed by blue-black fruits beginning in early autumn. This clone is reported to be more tolerant of wet soil than the other two.

'Synnestvedt' (Chicago Lustre®) grows to 2.4–3.6 m/8–12 ft tall and 2–3 m/6.6–10 ft wide with a rounded growth habit and glossy deep green foliage that turns bright orange-red, in autumn, about three weeks later than most plants of *V. dentatum.* Creamy white flowers open in early summer, about a week later than on 'Ralph Senior' and three weeks later than on 'Morton,' followed by metallic blue fruits in early autumn. This selection is reported to be less tolerant of wet soil than the other two. It may be somewhat less cold-hardy, but is useful at least in Zones 5b–9a.

Related Species

Viburnum acerifolium 4 (mapleleaf viburnum, dockmackie).   This shrub with leaves of the same general shape as *V. trilobum* is of landscape interest for its ability to tolerate rather dense shade. In fact, it does not grow well in full sun. Seasonal interest is minimal with small clusters of yellow-white flowers in late spring and purplish autumn foliage. It is native in much of eastern North America from New Brunswick to Manitoba and southward to North Carolina and is useful in Zones 3b–9a.

Viburnum acerifolium.

Viburnum acerifolium.

Viburnum molle 5 (Kentucky arrowwood).   This native of the midwestern United States from Indiana and Kentucky to Missouri differs from *V. dentatum* in its light-colored, flaking bark and is an equivalent landscape plant useful near its native range, at least in Zones 5a–9a.

Viburnum rafinesquianum 4 (Rafinesque arrowwood).   This shrub is native to a wide area of eastern North America from Quebec to Manitoba and southward to Georgia and Illinois. It differs little from *V. dentatum* except that it does not grow as tall, reaching heights of about 2 m/6.6 ft and making it a questionable choice for screening. Useful in Zones 3b–8a, but rarely commercially available.

Viburnum dilatatum 5

LINDEN VIBURNUM
Deciduous shrub
Caprifoliaceae (Honeysuckle Family)

Native Range.   Japan.

Useful Range.   USDA Zones 5b–8b.

Function.   Border, screen, specimen.

Size and Habit

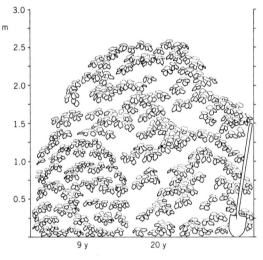

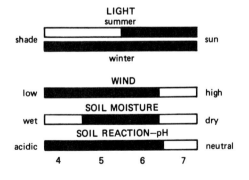

Viburnum dilatatum.

Adaptability

Seasonal Interest.   *Flowers:* White, small but numerous, in flattened clusters 8–12 cm/3–5 in. across, showy in the late spring with sporadic flowering continuing in late summer in some years. *Foliage:* Medium to deep green, usually lustrous, irregularly toothed and varying greatly in shape on the same plant, from nearly round and lindenlike to elongated and troughlike, especially on vigorous shoots, generally 5–12 cm/2–5 in. long, making a neutral and irregular but dense foliage mass, usually turning deep reddish before falling in middle to late autumn. *Fruits:* Bright red, individually only 0.8 cm/0.3 in. across but borne in clusters to 12 cm/5 in. across, showy for a long period in early until late autumn.

Viburnum dilatatum.

Problems and Maintenance.   This species is relatively trouble-free most of the time, although several insects occasionally can cause damage. Borers, the most serious, may need to be controlled. Pruning usually is not necessary except to remove any dead or weak branches or to control size if planted in too small an area.

Cultivars.   Some, perhaps all *V. dilatatum* clones tend to be self-unfruitful; that is, pollen from one clone will not readily fertilize female flowers of the same clone, so cross-pollination is needed for maximum fruit set. It is best to include more than one cultivar in any landscape planting, or else one cultivar plus a few different seedlings of the species.

'Catskill' is a U.S. National Arboretum

(Egolf) introduction selected for compact, wide-spreading growth habit and small leaves that color well in autumn. The original plant grew to 1.5 m/5 ft high and 2.5 m/8 ft wide in 15 years. The rounded leaves turn yellow, orange, and red in autumn and the dark red fruits persist through autumn and well into winter in mild climates.

'Erie' is an outstanding full-sized selection by the late Donald Egolf, compact in habit yet growing to at least 2.5 m/8 ft tall and about as wide, with relatively large leaves and large clusters of creamy white flowers in late spring, followed by large clusters of bright red fruits, coloring in early autumn and remaining colorful until late autumn. In spite of occasional reports to the contrary, this clone is largely self-unfruitful, so it needs a different pollinating clone for heavy fruiting.

'Iroquois' is another full-sized Egolf selection, with a dense, globose habit, growing to at least 2.5 m/8 ft tall and somewhat wider, making it a good selection for visual screening. It flowers heavily, at the same time as 'Catskill,' and was introduced by Dr. Egolf with 'Catskill' as two cross-pollinating clones. Its fruits are unusually large, profuse, and persistent.

'Oneida,' yet another Egolf introduction, is actually a hybrid of V. dilatatum × V. lobophyllum, a closely related, larger species from China. This hybrid is more upright and wide-spreading in form than V. dilatatum selections, growing to more than 3.3 m/11 ft tall and 3 m/10 ft wide, and somewhat more open in habit than V. dilatatum. It is unusual because of its flowering pattern: After its primary flowering in spring, it partially reblooms in much the same way as some V.

×rhytidophylloides cultivars, so that reblooming flowers appear in late summer, concurrently with fruits from earlier flowers—an interesting, even if not earth-shaking, effect.

The forma xanthocarpum differs from the species type only in having yellow fruits. A recent selection from this form, 'Michael Dodge,' found growing at Winterthur, Delaware, has unusually large yellow fruits, striking in contrast with the red autumn foliage. It is not yet widely available, but may be soon.

Related Species

Viburnum setigerum 5 (synonym: *V. theiferum*; tea viburnum). This distinctive, open, vase-shaped shrub from China is one of the most impressive of all viburnums in fruit, with bright orange-red berries, 0.8 cm/0.3 in., in clusters to 5 cm/2 in. across from early through middle autumn. The starkly vase-shaped form of this plant limits its usefulness, and it is most effective planted in the rear of the shrub border so that its leggy base is covered by other plants while its branches arch out bearing the display of fruits. The small white flowers are among the latest to open of all the viburnums, in very late spring, and the distinctively arrowhead-shaped leaves usually undergo little or no color change before falling in late autumn. Useful in Zones 6a–8b and in some years in Zone 5b, but occasionally winterkilling to the ground there. The forma *aurantiacum*, with fruit ripening yellow-orange, may be available only as seeds at present, but can be found in many arboretum plantings.

Viburnum wrightii 5 (Wright viburnum). Some specialists believe that this is the finest of all viburnums for autumn color, with crimson foliage and brilliant scarlet fruits. The better clones are at least equal to V. dilatatum and V. setigerum. Many plants sold as V. wrightii turn out to be V. dilatatum, but some nurseries are careful to offer the true V. wrightii, which differs from V. dilatatum in having glabrous (nonhairy) stems and leaves and deeper red autumn foliage color. Not all clones are equally impressive in fruiting display, but the best are spectacular over a long period in autumn. Useful in Zones 6a–8b and with mixed success in Zone 5b as well.

Viburnum setigerum.

Viburnum farreri 5

Synonym: *V. fragrans*
FRAGRANT VIBURNUM
Deciduous shrub
Caprifoliaceae (Honeysuckle Family)

Native Range. Northern China.

Useful Range. USDA Zones 5a–8a.

Function. Border, specimen, screen.

Size and Habit

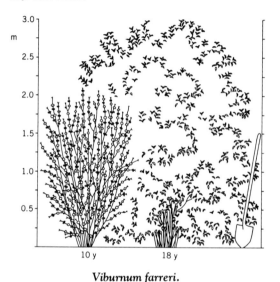

Viburnum farreri.

Adaptability

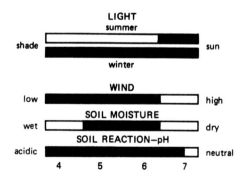

Seasonal Interest. *Flowers:* Highly fragrant, pink or white, in clusters 2.5–5 cm/1–2 in. across, small but effective because they precede the foliage in early spring, a few opening in late autumn in some sites and some years. *Foliage:* Medium green, the leaves, 5–7 cm/2–2.8 in. long and rather narrow, with red petioles on the pink-flowered species type, making a fairly dense, irregular mass of medium texture, turning reddish before falling in midautumn.

Problems and Maintenance. This shrub usually is trouble-free, although insect problems occasionally can develop. Annual pruning may be necessary to maintain fullness of form for use as a screen, but removal of deadwood and thinning every second or third year should be sufficient otherwise. Prune as soon as possible after flowering. Flower buds often open during warm periods in late winter, then are killed when freezing temperatures return. In warm, moist weather, flowers sometimes open partly or fully in autumn, to be frozen soon afterward by normal freezes or left more susceptible to winter cold. This plant is most effective in flower year after year where temperature fluctuations are modulated by closeness to bodies of water.

Cultivars. 'Album' has pure white flowers and green leaf petioles. 'Nanum' is dwarf in growth habit, remaining below 0.5 m/1.6 ft for several years and probably not exceeding 1.0 m/3.3 ft after many years.

Related Species and Hybrid

Viburnum ×*bodnantense 5* (Bodnant viburnum). This hybrid of *V. farreri* × *V. grandiflorum* functions as a large, vigorous, and more floriferous version of *V. farreri*, with larger clusters of rose-red flower buds, opening rosy pink and fading to pale pink, from late autumn to very early spring. Useful in Zones 6b–9a+ and protected sites in Zone 6a, but the flower buds are subject to winterkilling in some years in Zones 6 and 7. It is known in our area in the form of 'Dawn,' as described above, and 'Pink Dawn,' with similar flower color but reported to fade less.

Viburnum grandiflorum 5. This Himalayan shrub is not known in landscape use in our area and may not be adapted climatically, but it is stiffly upright in form and bears masses of rosy pink flowers in late winter or early spring. It probably is useful only in Zones 8 and 9, if at all in our area. The selection 'Snow White,' greatly appreciated in the climate of England, has white flowers.

Viburnum lantana 6

WAYFARING TREE
Deciduous shrub
Caprifoliaceae (Honeysuckle Family)

Native Range.   Europe and western Asia.

Useful Range.   USDA Zones 4a–7b, some selections to Zone 3b.

Function.   Border, screen, hedge, massing, specimen.

Size and Habit

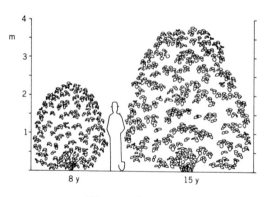

Viburnum lantana.

Adaptability.   This is more tolerant of dry soils than most viburnums.

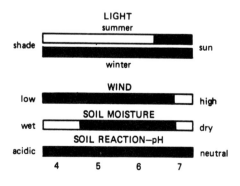

Seasonal Interest.   *Flowers:* White, small, in nearly flat clusters 5–10 cm/2–4 in. across, fairly showy in late spring. *Foliage:* Dark gray-green leaves have a wrinkled, leathery appearance, 5–12 cm/2–5 in. long and nearly as broad, with whitish, scurfy pubescence underneath, remaining dark green or turning dull reddish before falling in late autumn. *Fruits:* Berries turn from green to red to blue-black, sometimes with all stages of ripeness appearing in the same cluster, colorful in late summer, then drying and persisting, raisinlike, until taken by birds in early to late autumn.

Problems and Maintenance.   This is one of the most trouble-free of all viburnums, only occasionally troubled by a leaf spot disease and chewing insects. It tends to grow suckers from the root system but not in such great numbers that it is a problem in most landscape situations.

Viburnum lantana.

Cultivars. 'Aureum' has golden young foliage, turning to dull yellowish green as the summer progresses, but is seldom commercially available. 'Mohican' is a vigorous but dense National Arboretum selection, growing to 2 m/6.6 ft tall and 2.5 m/8 ft wide, notable for its resistance to leaf spot and its abundance of long-lasting fruits, which remain in the orange-red phase for up to a month before turning black.

Related Species

Viburnum lantanoides 5 (synonym: *V. alnifolium;* hobblebush). This native of northeastern North America from New Brunswick to northern Michigan and southward in the Appalachian Mountains to North Carolina must be planted in at least partly shaded, moist sites to grow well. Its form is rather leggy and open, but in natural areas it makes a fine display in open woodlands in middle to late spring with its showy flowers, the outermost sterile and nearly 2.5 cm/1 in. across, borne in flat clusters 8–12 cm/3–5 in. across. The rounded leaves, 10–20 cm/4–8 in. long, provide interestingly coarse texture and turn deep red in autumn. Fruiting interest is similar to that of *V. lantana.* Useful primarily for naturalizing in Zones 3b–6b in areas having relatively cool summers.

Viburnum burejaeticum 5 (Manchurian viburnum). This uncommon species, perhaps not yet available commercially, has performed well in Minnesota and Manitoba, where it functions in much the same way as *V. lantana* but has smaller leaves, 4–10 cm/1.6–4 in. long and half as broad, and smaller but abundant flower clusters in middle to late spring. Fruits are similar in seasonal effect to those of *V. lantana* but are borne in smaller clusters. One of the most distinctive features of this species is the speed with which it starts growth in spring, often producing 10–15 cm/4–6 in. of stem growth before some other species have fully opened buds. Useful in Zones 3b–6b and perhaps also Zone 7.

Viburnum odoratissimum 5–6

SWEET VIBURNUM
Evergreen shrub
Caprifoliaceae (Honeysuckle Family)

Native Range.   Japan to the Himalayas.

Useful Range.   USDA Zone 9a+ and sheltered sites in Zone 8.

Function.   Screen, border, specimen, small patio tree.

Size and Habit

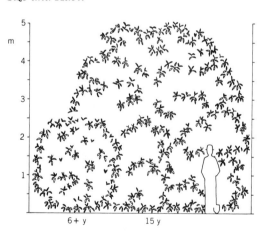

Viburnum odoratissimum.

Adaptability. Protection from full winter sun and wind is necessary in Zone 8 to reduce leaf scorch.

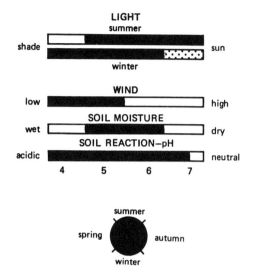

Seasonal Interest. *Flowers:* Fragrant, white, in pyramidal clusters to 10 cm/4 in. high and nearly as wide, in midspring. *Foliage:* Evergreen, bright green, lustrous to glossy, elliptical, to 15 cm/6 in. long, giving an outstanding, year-round, coarse textural effect. *Fruits:* Red, then ripening black in late summer.

Problems and Maintenance. In the colder parts of the useful range (Zone 8), winters-corch of foliage is the most common problem, but other problems such as scale insects occasionally require corrective measures. As with all evergreen viburnums, selection of site to minimize exposure to wind is essential for best results. Pruning is needed only to repair damage or restrain growth where space is inadequate.

Cultivars. 'Awabuki' (synonyms: var. *awabukii*, *V. awabukii*) is the so-called "leatherleaf form" of this species that has been popular in the Deep South for many years, with unusually large and glossy, dark green leaves and greater cold-hardiness, at least to Zone 8a. 'Nanum' is a dwarf shrub, remaining below 1 m/3.3 ft in height. It is seldom, if ever, commercially available.

Related Species and Hybrids

Viburnum japonicum 4–5 (synonym: *V. macrophyllum*; Japanese viburnum). This native of Japan is frequently confused with *V. odoratissimum*. It differs from that species primarily in its lower stature, usually under 2 m/6.6 ft, and lustrous foliage, but not as glossy as that of *V. odoratissimum* 'Awabuki.' *V. japonicum* is also more cold hardy than *V. odoratissimum,* useful in Zones 7b–9a+. This species is not widely available, but has been used by Donald Egolf at the National Arboretum as a parent of at least the following two hybrids.

'Chippewa' (*V. japonicum* × *V. dilatatum* 'Catskill'), is a densely branched semievergreen shrub, growing to 2.5 m/8 ft high and 3 m/10 ft wide in 17 years, with large, lustrous, deep green leaves that turn deep maroon to bright red in late autumn, creamy white flowers in large, lacy flattened clusters, followed by quantities of fruits that ripen dark red in late summer and persist through autumn.

'Huron' (*V. lobophyllum* × *V. japonicum*) is a densely branched, semievergreen shrub, growing to 2.2 m/7.3 ft tall and 2.8 m/9.2 ft wide in 17 years, with an overall appearance similar to that of 'Chippewa.' The parentage of 'Chippewa' and 'Huron' suggests that these hybrids are useful in at least Zones 7b–9a, perhaps also Zones 7a and 6b, but deciduous there rather than semievergreen.

Viburnum propinquum 4 (evergreen viburnum). This low-growing shrub from central and western China grows compactly to about 1.2 m/4 ft high and wide, with lustrous, dark green leaves to 6–9 cm/2.4–3.5 in. long and 2–3 cm/0.8–1.2 in wide, reminiscent of those of *Sarcococca* or *Vinca,* and more impressive than the small whitish-green flowers and small blue-black fruits. This fine evergreen massing or hedging plant is seldom available, but worth trying in Zones 7b–9a+, perhaps also Zone 7a.

Viburnum opulus 5

EUROPEAN CRANBERRYBUSH
Deciduous shrub
Caprifoliaceae (Honeysuckle Family)

Native Range.   Europe, northern Asia, and northern Africa.

Useful Range.   USDA Zones 3b–8b.

Function.   Border, screen, specimen.

Size and Habit

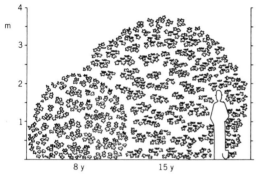

Viburnum opulus.

Adaptability

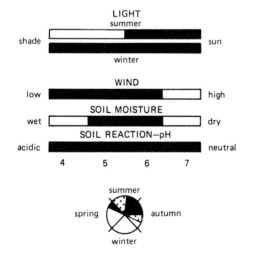

Seasonal Interest.   *Flowers:* White, the fertile flowers small, surrounded by a ring of sterile flowers, each nearly 2 cm/0.8 in. across, in flattened clusters, 8–10 cm/3–4 in. across, or a globose cluster entirely of showy sterile flowers in 'Roseum' (see Cultivars). In either case, showy against the new foliage in late spring. *Foliage:* Deep green leaves are maplelike in outline, 5–12 cm/2–5 in. long and nearly as broad, providing distinctive texture and remaining green until they fall in middle to late autumn. *Fruits:* Scarlet when ripe, to 1 cm/0.4 in. across, in showy clusters about 8 cm/3 in. across, effective in late summer and until midautumn.

Viburnum opulus.

Problems and Maintenance.   This shrub has few troubles, but frequently is infested with aphids, especially the form 'Roseum' (see Cultivars). Gradual renewal pruning, removing about one-third of the oldest branches each year, is necessary with older plants to maintain fullness, but little other maintenance is needed.

Cultivars.   'Aureum' has dull yellowish foliage, is not very attractive, and lacks vigor.

'Compactum' is compact in form, remaining below 1.5 m/5 ft for several years, and flowers and fruits well. This is an attractive and useful selection but slightly less cold-hardy than the species type. Useful northward to Zone 4a.

'Leonard's Dwarf' is a densely compact selection, reported to be only slightly less compact than 'Compactum,' remaining below 1.8 m/6 ft tall and wide. It is not widely available.

'Nanum' is a dwarf, remaining below 0.5 m/ 1.6 ft for several years and below 1 m/3.3 ft for

Viburnum opulus 'Nanum.'

Viburnum sargentii 'Susquehanna.'

many years. It does not bear appreciable numbers of flowers or fruits, but its foliage texture gives it much character. Unfortunately, a leaf-spot disease disfigures the foliage in some areas. Useful northward to Zone 4a.

'Notcutt' is slightly more vigorous than the species type with somewhat larger fruits but is not significantly different for most landscape usage.

'Roseum' (synonym: 'Sterile'; European snowball) has globose clusters of all-sterile flowers. Lack of fruiting interest and high susceptibility to aphids, which disfigure the foliage, greatly limit the usefulness of this form.

'Xanthocarpum' differs from the species type in that its fruits remain clear yellow as they ripen, effective against the dark green foliage.

Related Species

Viburnum edule 2–4 (squashberry, mooseberry). This close relative of *V. opulus* and *V. trilobum* is native to higher elevations from Labrador and Nova Scotia to Manitoba, Alaska, and southward to Pennsylvania and Colorado, also northeastern Asia. It is a shrub to 2 m/6.6 ft tall at its lower elevations, but becomes smaller with increasing elevation and thinner soils, remaining under 0.3 m/1 ft high toward the summit of Mt. Washington, New Hampshire in protected sites at 1500–1800 m/5000–6000 ft elevation. The yellow fruits, turning orange to red late, are valued for making preserves, but this plant is rarely seen in human-made landscapes and is probably not commercially available in our area.

Viburnum sargentii 5 (Sargent cranberrybush). This species from northeastern Asia is very simi-

lar to *V. opulus*; in fact, it has been included in that species by some specialists, as *V. opulus* var. *sargentii*. It differs in minute details and has been reported by some observers to be less cold-hardy than *V. opulus*, but it is useful at least in Zones 5a–8b, and at least certain selections are fully hardy in Zone 4b as well. The selection 'Flavum' has golden yellow fruits, slightly more showy than those of *V. opulus* 'Xanthocarpum.' Two selections have been made at the U.S. National Arboretum: 'Onondaga' has fine-textured, dark red new foliage that maintains a tinge of red-purple when mature and a compact growth habit, remaining below 2 m/6.6 ft for many years; 'Susquehanna,' on the other hand, is extremely vigorous, with very heavy, corky branches and leathery leaves giving a coarse texture and making a very large, upright mound, quickly reaching heights of at least 3 m/10 ft with an equal spread.

Viburnum trilobum 5 (synonym: *V. opulus* var. *americanum*; American cranberrybush). This northern North American species is very similar to *V. opulus*, treated by some specialists as a subpopulation of that species: *V. opulus* var. *americanum*. By whatever classification, it differs from European cranberrybush in three ways. It may be slightly more cold-hardy, at least to Zone 2b; its foliage frequently develops rather attractive reddish fall coloration; and its fruits are useful for making preserves if one does not object to the musky odor of the cooking berries. Several cultivars have been selected:

'Andrews' and 'Wentworth' are full-sized clones selected for heavy production of edible fruits.

'Alfredo' is a compact form, to 1.5–1.8 m/5–6 ft tall and wide, flowering and fruiting sparsely.

'Compactum' (= 'Bailey Compact') also grows to 1.5–1.8 m/5–6 ft tall and wide, with distinctly upright branches that are subject to deformation and injury from heavy snow, flowering and fruiting only sparsely. 'Hahs' is another compact form, to 1.8–2.4 m/6–8 ft high and wide, with dark green foliage turning deep red in autumn, flowering and fruiting heavily. 'Garry Pink' has slightly pink-tinged flowers, but probably is not available. 'Phillips' was selected at the University of New Hampshire for its fruit quality and freedom from musky flavor and odor in the cooking process. It is reported to make preserves equal in quality to those from red currants. 'Spring Red' is an upright form with reddish new foliage, turning green in summer, then orangered in autumn, with little flowering or fruiting, but not widely available.

Viburnum plicatum 5

Synonym: *V. tomentosum*
JAPANESE SNOWBALL OR DOUBLEFILE VIBURNUM (see forms, below)
Deciduous shrub
Caprifoliaceae (Honeysuckle Family)

Native Range.   China and Japan.

Useful Range.   USDA Zones 5b–8a with selection of appropriate cultivars (see Forms and Cultivars) and relatively cool, moist sites in Zone 8b.

Function.   Border, specimen, screen (with careful pruning).

Size and Habit.   *F. tomentosum* is illustrated.

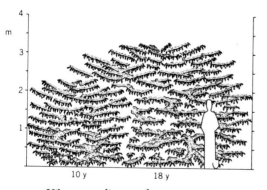

Viburnum plicatum f. *tomentosum.*

Adaptability.   This is one of the least drought-tolerant of the viburnums.

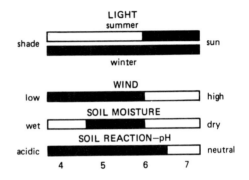

Seasonal Interest.   *Flowers:* White; in f. *tomentosum* a central cluster of small, fertile flowers is surrounded by a ring of sterile flowers, each about 3 cm/1.2 in. across. The resulting flattened clusters, 5–10 cm/2–4 in. across, are borne in leaf axils in conspicuous double rows, hence the name doublefile viburnum; in f. *plicatum*, sterile florets are crowded into globose clusters 5–8 cm/2–3 in. across. *Foliage:* Medium to deep green toothed leaves, 5–10 cm/2–4 in. long, are covered with brownish, scurfy pubescence, the prominent veins providing strong textural interest, and turn velvety dull red in autumn. *Fruits:* Borne only on plants of f. *tomentosum* and its cultivars; red for a few weeks in late summer before turning blue-black, when they are usually

Viburnum plicatum f. *plicatum*.

taken quickly by birds; small but effective in flat clusters, especially in the red stage, when they accentuate the horizontal branching.

Problems and Maintenance.   This shrub is relatively trouble-free most of the time except for its sensitivity to summer drought, but several insects occasionally can be troublesome. Borers are the worst offenders and must be controlled promptly to prevent serious damage. Pruning is seldom necessary and should be minimized so as not to detract from the gracefully horizontal branching habit, but gradual renewal of old plants by removing a few of the oldest branches annually helps to maintain the plant's character and prevent it from becoming excessively leggy.

Forms and Cultivars.   The forma *plicatum* (synonym: *V. tomentosum* var. *sterile*; Japanese snowball) is the species type—that is, the form to which the species name was first correctly assigned. With its snowball-type flower clusters hanging somewhat unevenly because of their weight, this form lacks the strong horizontally layered growth habit of f. *tomentosum*, and it has no fruiting interest since all its flowers are sterile. Also, it is significantly less cold-hardy than f. *tomentosum*, only to Zone 6a. A few selections have been made, including the following.

'Grandiflorum,' with larger flowers and clusters, is even less cold-hardy, probably only to Zone 6b or 7a.

'Newzam' (= 'Nana Newport,' Newport®) is a dwarf selection of f. *plicatum*, growing very compactly to about 1.2 m/4 ft high and 1.5 m/5 ft wide, and is useful for massing. Its small "snowball" flower clusters are usually partly hid-

den by the new foliage and there are, of course, no fruits.

The forma *tomentosum* (synonym: *V. tomentosum*; doublefile viburnum) is the wild form of the species, with mostly fertile flowers. Biology would lead us to consider this the species type, but the rule of priority in naming plants does not. Several superior or distinctive cultivars have been introduced, including the following.

'Lanarth' is compact in form, even more strongly horizontally layered than average for f. *tomentosum*, with light green foliage, growing to 2 m/6.6 ft high and somewhat wider, and flowering and fruiting profusely. It is seldom commercially available in the United States, but may be easier to find in Canada. Useful in Zones 5b–8a, and sheltered sites in Zone 5a.

'Mariesii' is perhaps the finest of the older cultivars, growing to 2–3 m/6.6–10 ft tall and at least as wide, with dark green foliage, large, showy white flowers, and usually heavy fruiting, which perhaps could be improved by providing at least one additional clone for cross-pollination. Useful at least in Zones 5b–8a.

'Roseum' (= 'Pink Beauty'?) is an old selection with pale pink flowers, deeper in some locations and years and nearly white in others, but the plant is not vigorous and is cold-hardy only to Zone 6a.

'Shasta,' a superb National Arboretum (Egolf) introduction in the late 1970s, is a hybrid of 'Mariesii' and a choice clone of f. *tomentosum* growing in the Cornell Plantations. It is a broadly compact shrub, growing at least to 2 m/ 6.6 ft high and 3.5 m/11.5 ft wide, with large flowers in clusters 9–14 cm/3.5–5.5 in. across,

Viburnum plicatum 'Lanarth.'

followed by large clusters of fruits, red and showy in August, later turning black. Useful in Zones 5b–8a.

'Shoshoni,' a more recent Egolf introduction (1986) and a seedling from 'Shasta,' is very similar to its parent except that is much lower growing, to 1.2 m/4 ft high and twice as wide after 17 years, a valuable addition to the list of small-scale landscape plants, flowering and fruiting profusely. Useful in Zones 5b–8a.

'Summer Snowflake,' introduced in the 1980s by the University of British Columbia Botanical Garden, is distinctive for its repeated flowering from late spring through summer. It is upright in habit, but only to about 2 m/6.6 ft tall and wide. Its low vigor has limited its usefulness in much of our area, but is acceptable in our Pacific Northwest, as in adjacent British Columbia. It is potentially useful in Zones 6b–8a, and perhaps Zone 6a, but that is not fully clear.

'Watanabe' is very similar to 'Summer Snowflake.'

Viburnum prunifolium 6

BLACK HAW
Deciduous shrub or small tree
Caprifoliaceae (Honeysuckle Family)

Native Range. Eastern United States, Connecticut to Wisconsin and southward to Florida and Texas.

Useful Range. USDA Zones 3b–9a.

Function. Border, screen, small specimen tree (with some training).

Size and Habit

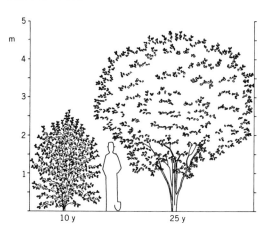

Viburnum prunifolium.

Adaptability

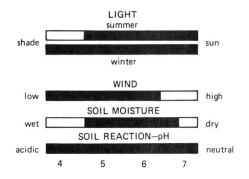

Seasonal Interest. *Flowers:* White, small but numerous, in clusters 5–10 cm/2–4 in. across, usually fairly showy in late spring. *Foliage:* Medium to dark green, lustrous and somewhat leathery, finely toothed, 3–8 cm/1.2–3 in. long, turning deep purple to scarlet before falling in middle to late autumn. *Fruits:* Pale green to yellow-green in late summer, progressing through pink, then ripening blue-black in early to middle autumn, about 1 cm/0.4 in. long, adding interest to the colorful autumn foliage.

Problems and Maintenance. This plant is usually fairly trouble-free but occasionally subject to insect problems. Scale insects and borers can be serious enough to require control measures.

Viburnum prunifolium.

Viburnum cassinoides.

***Viburnum prunifolium* trained as a tree.**

Pruning is seldom necessary except to remove deadwood unless this plant is to be used as a small tree, in which case initial training and the removal of occasional sucker shoots is needed.

Cultivars. Much variation exists in this species, and a few superior clones have been selected, but none are yet generally available. Clones are known in which the fruit color holds for several weeks in the pink-red stage before ripening. One such clone can be found at Bernheim Forest Arboretum, Clermont, Kentucky, but has not yet been introduced.

Related Species

Viburnum cassinoides 4 (withe-rod, Appalachian tea). This native of northeastern North America from Newfoundland to Manitoba and southward to high elevations in North Carolina functions as a smaller, shrubby counterpart of *V. prunifolium*, with more slender, willowy branches. It flowers later than *V. prunifolium*, in

early to middle summer, and has comparable autumn foliage and fruiting interest. It is more tolerant of wet soil but less tolerant of calcareous soil than most viburnums and is useful in Zones 3b–6b with selection of appropriate genetic material, and areas with mild summers in Zone 7.

Viburnum lentago 6 (nannyberry). This large shrub, occasionally more than 8 m/26 ft tall, is generally similar to *V. prunifolium* and sometimes

Viburnum lentago.

confused with it, but it can be recognized easily by its wavy margined leaf petioles, more arching branches, later flowering, and greater tendency to form root suckers than *V. prunifolium*. Because of this suckering habit, it is less practical for training into tree form, even though it grows tall enough in time. It is also much more susceptible to powdery mildew than *V. prunifolium*. Naturally wide-ranging, from Hudson Bay southward to Georgia and Mississippi, *V. lentago* is useful in Zones 2–7b with selection of appropriate genetic material. Individual clones with outstanding deep red autumn foliage and prolonged red stage in fruit coloration have been noted, but there are apparently no named selections.

Viburnum rufidulum.

Viburnum nudum 5 (smooth withe-rod). This is the southern counterpart of *V. cassinoides*, native from Connecticut to Kentucky and southward to Florida and Louisiana. Generally similar in appearance to *V. cassinoides* except larger in stature, flowers, and foliage. Useful in Zones 6a–9a+, perhaps some sites in Zone 5. 'Winterthur' is a superior selection of *V. nudum*, growing to 2.5–8 m/8–10 ft tall, with excellent foliage, turning wine-red in autumn, and 10-cm/4-in. clusters of creamy-white flowers, followed by fruits that progress slowly from pale green to pinkish-red and then deep blue, all colors appearing simultaneously for a few weeks.

Viburnum rufidulum 6 (southern black haw). The southern counterpart of *V. prunifolium*, this very large shrub, sometimes to more than 8 m/26 ft tall and wide-spreading, resembles *V. prunifolium* except in having larger, broader, and more leathery leaves, larger flower clusters. Native from Virginia to southern Illinois and Missouri, and southward to Florida and Texas. Cold-hardiness varies widely with seed source, but northern selections are cold-hardy to Zones 5b, perhaps also parts of Zone 5a, and surprisingly tolerant of dry conditions. 'Royal Guard' was one of a half dozen superior seedlings selected at the former Cole Nurseries of Circleville, Ohio, grown from seed native to Missouri by William Heard of Des Moines, Iowa. This cultivar, introduced by Ned Rader of Amanda, Ohio, is rather compact and narrowly upright, growing to at least 3 m/10 ft tall and 1.5 m/5 ft wide, with very glossy deep green foliage that turns deep red-purple in early autumn and remains colorful for about a month before dropping. This selection is useful in at least Zones 5b–9a. Another clone of Missouri origin, 'Morton,' has been in the Morton Arboretum collection for many years and is now being evaluated by the Chicagoland Grows® program, so it may soon be available.

Viburnum rhytidophyllum 5

LEATHERLEAF VIBURNUM
Evergreen shrub
Caprifoliaceae (Honeysuckle Family)

Native Range. Central and Western China.

Useful Range. USDA Zones 6b–8a, protected sites in Zone 6a, and areas with mild summers in Zone 8b.

Function. Border, specimen.

Size and Habit

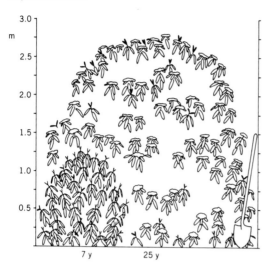

Viburnum rhytidophyllum.

Adaptability. Protection from full sun in summer is beneficial in the South and Midwest. Protection from full sun and wind in winter reduces leaf scorch, a serious problem in the colder parts of the useful range.

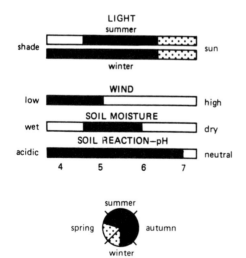

Seasonal Interest. *Flowers:* Creamy-white, small but numerous in flattened clusters, 10–20 cm/4–8 in. across, showy with the handsome foliage in late spring. *Foliage:* Evergreen in Zones 7 and 8, wrinkled and leathery leaves, 8–18 cm/3–7 in. long and 3–5 cm/1.2–2 in. wide, lustrous and dark green on the upper surface, with a heavy layer of felty pubescence turning the lower surface whitish or rusty brown. *Fruits:* Red,

ripening black, 0.8 cm/0.3 in. across in clusters 10–15 cm/4–6 in. across, effective in late summer and into early autumn.

Problems and Maintenance. Winter leaf scorch is the most common problem, making the plant less than fully evergreen in some winters in Zone 6. Borers and scale insects occasionally may require corrective action. Nothing is more important to the success of this plant than careful selection of planting sites to minimize exposure to wind.

Cultivars. Little attention has been given to selection of superior forms of this species, but considerable variation may exist in China that has not yet been seen in North America. One selection for flowers that are pink in bud, 'Roseum,' also is somewhat slower-growing but probably not presently commercially available.

Related Species and Hybrids

Viburnum buddleifolium 4 (buddleia viburnum). This deciduous native of China has soft-tomentose leaves similar to those of *V.* ×*rhytidophylloides* and can function as a lower version of that species in landscape use, but it is seldom seen in commerce. Useful, when available, in Zone 6a–8a.

Viburnum ×*pragense* 5 (Prague viburnum). This evergreen hybrid of *V. rhytidophyllum* and *V. utile* originated in the Prague (Czechoslovakia) city nursery in the 1950s. It is a vigorous, upright shrub to 2.5 m/8 ft tall, with leaves like those of *V.* ×*rhytidophylloides* but smaller, 5–10 cm/2–4 in. long and less than half as wide, with slender, gracefully open branching habit. Useful in Zones 7a–9a and protected sites in Zone 6.

Viburnum rhytidophyllum.

Viburnum ×*rhytidocarpum* 5.   This hybrid of *V. rhytidophyllum* × *V. buddleifolium* is similar in general effect to *V.* ×*rhytidophylloides* and may be confused with that species in commerce. It is useful in Zones 6a–8a.

Viburnum ×*rhytidophylloides* 5 (lantanaphyllum or hybrid leatherleaf viburnum).   This hybrid of *V. rhytidophyllum* × *V. lantana* has come into wide use in the Midwest. Even though it is not fully evergreen, it holds its foliage throughout autumn and until the first severe cold of winter, until then having much of the character of *V. rhytidophyllum*. But it is more cold-hardy and more vigorous, at least in the central states, than *V. rhytidophyllum* and more effective for screening during the growing season. Useful in Zones 5b–8a and possibly areas of Zone 8b with mild winters. The selection 'Willowwood' is outstanding in form, flowering, and fruiting, with substantial flowering in early autumn as well as spring, and so is 'Alleghany,' a hybrid of *V.*

Viburnum ×*rhytidophylloides* 'Willowood.'

rhytidophyllum and *V. lantana* 'Mohican' with typically leathery, semievergreen leaves, creamy yellow-white flowers in spring and again in early autumn, and bright red fruits, ripening black, showy from midsummer through autumn. Both mature at a little over 3 m/10 ft high and wide, serving as excellent screening plants.

Viburnum sieboldii 6

SIEBOLD VIBURNUM
Deciduous shrub
Caprifoliaceae (Honeysuckle Family)

Native Range.   Japan.

Useful Range.   USDA Zones 5b–8a.

Function.   Specimen, screen, border.

Size and Habit

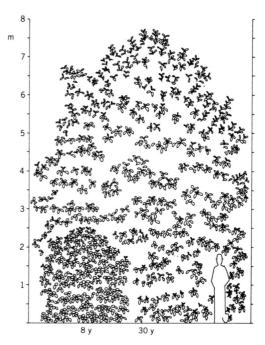

Viburnum sieboldii.

Adaptability

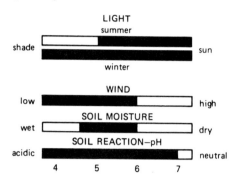

Viburnum sieboldii.

Seasonal Interest. *Flowers:* Creamy white, small but borne in rounded clusters to 10 cm/4 in. across in late spring. *Foliage:* Bright to deep green leaves, 6–12 cm/2.5–5 in. long, are lustrous and leathery, giving much of the character of large-leaved evergreen species such as V. *odoratissimum* in summer and early autumn but falling before the onset of winter. *Fruits:* Berries turn red, then blue-black, in middle to late summer, then dropping or taken by birds. The red stalks persist into autumn.

Problems and Maintenance. This is one of the most trouble-free of the viburnums, but insects sometimes can be a minor problem. Pruning is seldom if ever needed except for renewal of old plants. The outstanding foliage gives off a musky "green pepper" odor when crushed, a feature apparently objectionable to a few people.

Cultivars. Considering the variation that exists in this species and its value as a landscape plant, there has been little selection of superior forms. One such form, 'Seneca,' has been selected at the U.S. National Arboretum for its heavy flowering and especially for its fruits, which persist for as long as three months in the red stage, providing outstanding landscape interest in summer and early autumn. A second selection, made by Robert Tomayer of Wavecrest Nursery, in Michigan, is under evaluation in the Chicagoland Grows® program at this writing.

Viburnum suspensum 4–5

SANDANKWA VIBURNUM
Evergreen shrub
Caprifoliaceae (Honeysuckle Family)

Native Range. Islands of southern Japan.

Useful Range. USDA Zones 8b–9a+.

Function. Specimen, border, foundation, hedge, screen (with maximum vigor in Zone 9a+).

Size and Habit

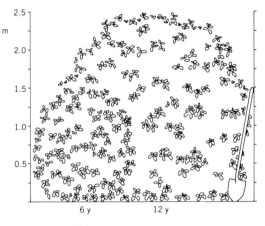

Viburnum suspensum.

Adaptability. Performs best with light shade during summer and benefits from protection from full sun and wind in winter, especially at the northern edge of its useful range.

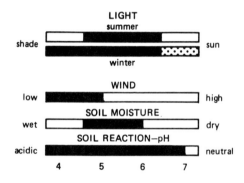

Seasonal Interest. *Flowers:* Somewhat fragrant, white or pink-tinted, in dense clusters to 4 cm/1.6 in. across in early summer. *Foliage:* Evergreen, pale to bright green, lustrous and rather leathery, 5–10 cm/2–4 in. long, making a dense mass. *Fruits:* Small, in small clusters, inconspicuous until they ripen bright red in early autumn.

Problems and Maintenance. Winter injury at the limits of its useful range is the only serious problem of this excellent shrub. Pruning is needed only to repair any winter damage or when training as a hedge.

Viburnum suspensum.

Viburnum tinus 5

LAURUSTINUS VIBURNUM
Evergreen shrub
Caprifoliaceae (Honeysuckle Family)

Native Range. Mediterranean Region.

Useful Range. USDA Zones 8a–9a with proper cultural treatment (see Problems and Maintenance).

Function. Screen, border, hedge, specimen, foundation.

Size and Habit

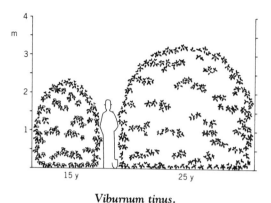

Viburnum tinus.

Adaptability

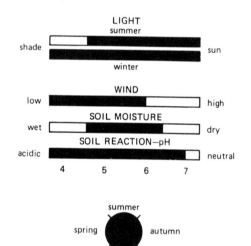

Seasonal Interest.   *Flowers:* White or pinkish, slightly fragrant, in clusters 5–8 cm/2–3 in. across in early spring, or winter in mildest areas. *Foliage:* Evergreen, dark green, and finer-textured than other evergreen viburnums, the leaves mostly under 8 cm/3 in. long. Larger leaves are a sign of excessive vigor (see Problems and Maintenance). *Fruits:* Dark blue, ripening black in late summer, fairly conspicuous, in small clusters.

Problems and Maintenance.   This versatile shrub is relatively free of problems and requires little maintenance, but it can be troubled by mites. Its most persistent problem is failure to harden sufficiently to withstand the first hard freezes of autumn because of excessive vigor. To

avoid this, late summer irrigation, fertilization, and pruning should be avoided. Pruning is seldom needed, except when this shrub is used as a hedge. Then a single shearing in early summer is sufficient, and informal hedges will not need to be pruned more than once every few years. Planting in full sun and perfectly drained soil will also reduce the likelihood of late-season growth.

Cultivars.   'Compactum' and 'Eve Price' are dense and slow-growing, to 1.5–2 m/5–6.6 ft high and wide, with leaves smaller than the species type, making them ideal for smaller hedges but less useful for screening because of the time required to reach functional size. 'Eve Price' also has pink flowers but is not widely available.

'Lucidum' has larger leaves and flower clusters than the species type, and is more tender, useful in Zones 8b–9a+. 'Robustum' is a full-sized plant, growing to 2–4 m/6.6–13 ft high and wide, with rounded leaves larger than those of the species type, and pink-flushed flowers.

'Variegatum' has yellow variegated foliage but is seldom if ever available. It is useful, when it can be found, in Zones 8b–9a+ and is best shaded from full sun.

Related Species

Viburnum davidii 3 (David viburnum).   This excellent evergreen viburnum from China remains below 1 m/3.3 ft in height after many years, forming a low, broad mound. Its deeply creased leaves, mostly 8–12 cm/3–5 in. long and elliptical, give elegant textural accent in all seasons, and its clusters of white flowers in early summer

Viburnum davidii.

are followed by bright blue fruits in late summer through autumn, at least on some plants. This shrub has been little used in our area but should be useful in Zones 7b–9a in sites protected from both summer and winter extremes and with a reliable moisture supply.

Vinca minor 2

MYRTLE, COMMON PERIWINKLE
Evergreen groundcover
Apocynaceae (Dogbane Family)

Native Range.   Europe and western Asia.

Useful Range.   USDA Zones 4b–7b, perhaps also Zone 8 in areas with moderate summers.

Function.   Groundcover.

Size and Habit

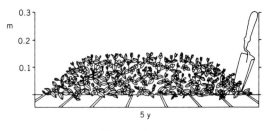

Vinca minor.

Adaptability.   Performance is improved by protection from winter sun and wind in Zones 4 and 5 and from full summer sun in the Midwest and South.

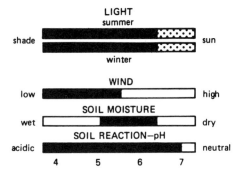

Seasonal Interest.   *Flowers:* Blue, purple, or white, in early spring, handsome against the dark green foliage. *Foliage:* Evergreen, lustrous and leathery, deep green, neatly textured, the leaves elliptical, 2–4 cm/0.8–1.6 in. long, making a dense mass.

Problems and Maintenance.   Except for one problem, a stem-dieback disease, *V. minor* is usually free of problems and requires little or no maintenance once established. Establishment may be slow, however, and a mulch to conserve moisture and control weed growth during this period may make the difference between success and failure. The stem-dieback disease is troublesome in dense masses of established plants, usually during prolonged wet periods. Avoiding excessive vigor and thinning thick masses slightly (strange as that seems for a ground cover) to allow better air circulation during damp spells may help to prevent infections.

Cultivars.   Several cultivars have been selected for flower or leaf color, as well as growth habit. A few of the more distinctive or widely used are listed here.

Vinca minor.

Vinca minor 'Argenteo-variegata.'

Vinca major.

'Alba' has dark green foliage and white flow-ers. 'Argenteo-variegata' has white-variegated leaves, mostly on the margins.

'Atropurpurea' (probably = 'Burgundy') has deep rose-purple flowers.

'Aureola' has creamy-yellow variegated leaves, along the veins rather than margins.

'Azurea,' with light blue flowers, is distinctive but not often available.

'Azurea Plena' has double, deep blue flowers.

'Bowles' (= 'Bowles's Variety,' and very simi-lar to 'La Grave') is a vigorous selection with deep blue flowers, differing from most other clones in its tendency to form dense clumps with a minimum of trailing, and for this reason is best planted closer than other cultivars.

'Emily Joy' has deep green foliage and large white flowers, but is not widely available.

'Gertrude Jekyll' (= 'Miss Jekyll,' = 'Miss Jek-yll's White') has deep slightly bluish-green fo-liage and white flowers and is vigorous, covering ground more quickly than many clones.

'Golden Bowles' is similar to 'Bowles' but with yellow-variegated foliage.

'PNI 6526' (Shademaster®) is a vigorous se-lection that is reported to be especially shade-tolerant and has purple flowers.

'Ralph Shugert' (Plant Patent No. 6960, 1989) has rich green leaves, silvery-white varie-gated along the margins, and intensely blue flowers appearing in spring and again later in the growing season.

'Rosea' has rather small leaves and violet-pink flowers but is not often available.

'Rubra' has purplish-rose flowers but is sel-dom available.

'Sterling Silver' has large, deep green leaves,

Vinca major 'Variegata.'

speckled with pale green and creamy-white var-iegated along the margins.

'Variegata' (= 'Aureo-variegata') has yellow variegated foliage. White-variegated clones are sometimes also listed by this name, causing con-fusion.

Related Species

Vinca major 2 (bigleaf periwinkle). This more vigorous but less cold-hardy relative of *V. minor* from southern Europe is useful in Zones 8a–9a+ but may suffer occasional winter injury in Zone 8a. It completely replaces *V. minor* in the South. Although it is less tidy and fine-textured than *V. minor*, it is faster-growing and easier to establish and can be supplemented with *Trachelospermum asiaticum* when finer texture is desired in the Deep South. The selection 'Variegata' has leaves with creamy white margins. It is used as a sum-mer annual in the North and occasionally as a groundcover in Zones 8b–9a+.

Viola sororia 2

Synonyms: *V. papilionacea, V. priceana*
COMMON OR WOOLY BLUE VIOLET
Herbaceous groundcover
Violaceae (Violet Family)

Native Range.   Eastern North America.

Useful Range.   USDA Zones 3b–8a.

Function.   Groundcover, naturalizing.

Size and Habit

Viola sororia.

Adaptability.   Other species of *Viola* differ in site requirements (see Related Species).

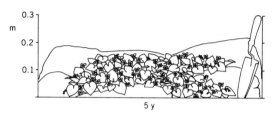

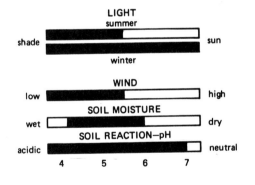

Seasonal Interest.   *Flowers:* Small but showy, usually deep rich blue, but light, grayish blue, or white in some forms, in middle to late spring. *Foliage:* Deep, rich green, broad, making an attractive, dense mass. Leaves die at the onset of winter and new leaves appear in midspring.

Problems and Maintenance.   Once established in a site with ample moisture and protection from full sun, maintenance is practically nil, but this plant can become invasive in some areas. It is probably not available from the usual commercial sources but may be available from existing wild or naturalized stands.

Varieties.   The nonhairy form of *V. sororia* sometimes is called *V. papilionacea*. It does not differ in landscape character from the species type. Another form, the confederate violet, is sometimes called *V. priceana*. Its flowers are two-toned: whitish with blue-violet veining. Many other local variations exist but are not important from a landscape viewpoint.

Related Species.   More than 50 species of *Viola* are cultivated as landscape or garden plants in North America. Most perform best in partial shade and moist soil, but some are at their best in full sun and sandy soil, and some require wet sites. Several are potentially effective groundcovers, at least in local areas. Since few are available from the usual commercial sources, the best approach may be to use native species that are known to perform well in the locality in question. An exception to this is *Viola odorata* (sweet or garden violet) and its forms. This native of Europe and the Mediterranean Region has long been cultivated in gardens and as a florist crop. Its blue-purple flowers are fragrant, and double-flowered forms exist, but primarily for florist use. It is useful in Zones 6a–9a+.

Vitis coignetiae 1

GLORYVINE
Deciduous vine
Vitaceae (Grape Family)

Native Range. Japan.

Useful Range. USDA Zones 5b–9a.

Function. Specimen, shade, or screen (with support). Grows extremely rapidly, scrambling over ground or climbing by tendrils to heights of 15 m/49 ft or more.

Size and Habit

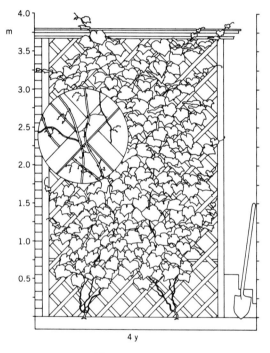

Vitis coignetiae.

Adaptability

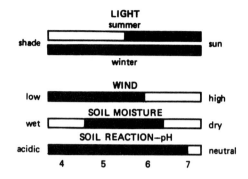

Seasonal Interest. *Flowers:* Small and inconspicuous in early summer. *Foliage:* Leaves, up to 25 cm/10 in. across, are barely lobed, dull and roughened with prominent veins, make an impressive, coarse foliage mass, and turn bright red before falling in autumn. *Fruits:* Purplish black, 0.8 cm/0.3 in. across, not edible, ripening in early autumn.

Problems and Maintenance. This vine is relatively trouble-free, although mildew and chewing insects, including Japanese beetles, occasionally may disfigure the foliage. Pruning will be needed in all but very large-scale situations, since the growth rate of this vine is exceeded

Vitis coignetiae.

only by *Pueraria lobata*. It should be avoided when space is limited. Grapes in general are rather coarse vines, useful only in highly informal or naturalized settings or where they are also desired for their fruit. *V. coignetiae* probably has more seasonal interest than any other species but lacks edible fruit.

Related Species

Vitis amurensis 1 (Amur grape).   This native of Manchuria and adjacent Siberia is somewhat less vigorous and more cold-hardy than its Japanese counterpart, *V. coignetiae*. Even though its foliage is not as handsome in summer and a more subdued red-purple in autumn, this vine is a reasonably effective substitute for *V. coignetiae* in Zones 5a–8a, perhaps also Zone 4, but it is seldom commercially available.

Vitis labrusca 1 (fox grape).   This native of the northeastern United States and southward to Georgia grows vigorously, making a dense, handsome foliage mass useful for screening on fence support and overhead enclosure of arbors and similar structures. It is the primary parent of most of the commercial grape cultivars used in northeastern North America, and itself has edible fruit that is made into preserves. Useful in Zones 5a–7b but available mostly as commercial

fruiting cultivars that function much the same as the species.

Vitis riparia 1 (frost or riverbank grape).   This high-climbing grape, native from the Canadian Maritime Provinces to Manitoba and Texas, climbs well up into tall trees in the wild. It can be used for screening (with support) but is not as effective as *V. labrusca,* where that species can be grown. The advantage of *V. riparia* is its cold hardiness, and it is useful in Zones 3b–6b but usually available only by propagating from the wild.

Vitis rotundifolia 1 (Muscadine or scuppernong grape).   This vigorous, high-climbing native of the southeastern and south-central United States and Mexico is of greatest value for its fruits, useful for preserves and other processed products, but it may also be planted as dual-purpose landscape plants (such as for supported screens) in Zones 7b–9a. This species and its cultivars tend to be more dioecious (flowers of only one sex on an individual plant) than some other species, so an occasional staminate (male) plant should be included for pollination unless newer cultivars, bearing staminate as well as pistillate flowers, are used. In any case, when grapes are being grown for their fruit, cultural instructions can be obtained from local, state, or provincial extension service offices.

Waldsteinia fragarioides 2

BARREN STRAWBERRY
Herbaceous groundcover
Rosaceae (Rose Family)

Native Range. Northeastern and central United States and adjacent Canada: New Brunswick to Minnesota and southward to Georgia and Missouri.

Useful Range.   USDA Zones 4a–7b.

Function.   Groundcover.

Size and Habit

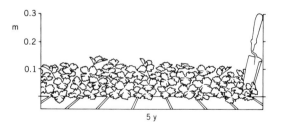

Waldsteinia fragarioides.

Adaptability

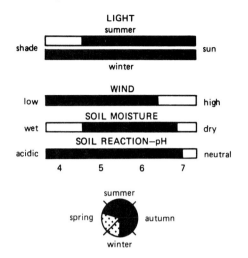

Waldsteinia fragarioides.

Seasonal Interest. *Flowers:* Bright yellow, about 1.2 cm/0.5 in. across, in fairly showy clusters in late spring. *Foliage:* Deep green and lustrous, similar to that of strawberries, evergreen and bronzing in winter but becoming dull in late winter and early spring. *Fruits:* Small and few, with little landscape significance.

Problems and Maintenance. This groundcover is usually trouble-free and requires little or no maintenance once established. In good sites it forms a thick mat, resisting weed encroachment.

Related Species

Waldsteinia ternata 2 (barren strawberry). This Asian counterpart of *W. fragarioides*, from China and Japan, has smaller leaves, giving a finer-textured effect, and slightly smaller flowers. Otherwise, the two species are interchangeable in landscape use and, in fact, are sometimes misidentified in commerce. Useful in about the same range as *W. fragarioides*.

Duchesnea indica 2 (Indian strawberry, mock-strawberry). This native of India, naturalized in the eastern United States, is similar in general

effect to *Waldsteinia*, with small yellow flowers and strawberrylike foliage and fruits. The leaves are not as fully evergreen as those of *Waldsteinia* but remain handsome and lustrous into early winter. Useful in Zones 5b–9a+ and northward at least to Zone 5a, perhaps also Zone 4 in areas having reliable snow cover.

Fragaria ×*ananassa* 2 (cultivated strawberry). This hybrid group involving *F. chiloensis*, the beach strawberry that grows wild on the western coasts of the Americas from Alaska to southern Chile, and *F. virginiana* (see below) can be used as an effective groundcover with the added advantage of the edible fruit. Specific maintenance requirements for good fruiting can be obtained from local and state or provincial extension offices. Unlike *Waldsteinia*, strawberries are not evergreen, but they are adaptable to much of our area in Zones 5a–8a and colder areas where snow cover is reliable.

Fragaria virginiana 2 (Virginia or wild strawberry). This native of much of eastern North America from Newfoundland to Georgia and westward to Alberta and Oklahoma is useful as a natural or naturalized groundcover, although it is not as vigorous or aggressive as the other species mentioned here. The fruits are delicious but so small that picking them can be tedious. Useful in Zones 3a–7b.

Weigela florida 5

Synonym: *W. rosea*
OLD-FASHIONED WEIGELA
Deciduous shrub
Caprifoliaceae (Honeysuckle Family)

Native Range.   Northern China and Korea.

Useful Range.   USDA Zones 5b–9a, some cultivars in colder zones.

Function.   Border, specimen, screen (taller selections in Zones 6–9a).

Size and Habit

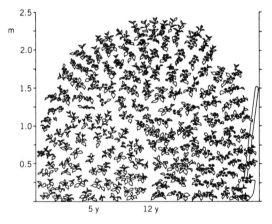

Weigela florida.

Adaptability

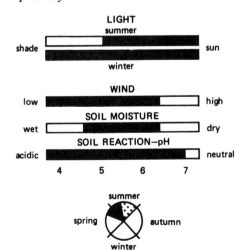

Seasonal Interest.   *Flowers:* Rosy pink to deep rosy red or white, funnel-shaped, about 3 cm/1.2 in. long, borne singly or in small clusters in late spring or early summer, continuing spasmodically through the summer in some cultivars. *Foliage:* Medium green leaves, 5–10 cm/2–4 in. long, give medium texture and no autumn interest, falling without color change.

Problems and Maintenance.   Pest problems are few and minor, and little maintenance is required. Gradual thinning every year or two is required to maintain good form. In Zones 4b–6a, and perhaps farther south, plants may be killed back severely in occasional winters and will need corrective pruning.

Varieties, Cultivars, and Hybrids.   The var. *venusta,* from Korea, has smaller leaves and lower stature (1.5–2 m/5–6.6 ft) than the species type and rosy flowers. It generally is considered to be somewhat more cold-hardy than the species but is not as widely used in cold climates as some of the cultivars listed.

Many cultivars of *Weigela* have been named. Most are hybrids of *W. florida,* with *W. floribunda, W. praecox,* and probably other species as well. In most cases, parentage is unknown or at best confused. Most of the large, pink-flowering selections are not superior to *W. florida* as landscape plants, so only a few of the more distinctive cultivars are listed here:

'Alba,' 'Bristol Snowflake,' and 'Candida' bear white flowers. Of these, only 'Bristol Snowflake' is commonly available. This selection has light green foliage and compact growth, somewhat slower growing and lower at maturity than 'Bristol Ruby.'

'Bristol Ruby' and 'Vanicekii' (= 'Newport Red') have bright crimson flowers in early summer and intermittent and sparse flowering later in the summer (from flower buds initiated in the same season). Both are usefully hardy to Zone 5a; they may be killed back in occasional severe winters, but return to light flowering during the following middle to late summer. Both begin to flower freely when less than 1 m/3.3 ft tall and remain below 2 m/6.6 ft for many years.

'Centennial,' an introduction by the Canada Department of Agriculture Research Station at Morden, Manitoba in the Canadian Centennial Year of 1967, is distinctive for its unusual cold-hardiness, to Zone 3b, and has rosy red flowers and compact growth, reaching heights of 2.5 m/8 ft.

'Dropmore Pink' is an unusually cold-hardy selection made by the late F. L. Skinner of Dropmore, Manitoba. It has mauve-pink flowers and is comparable to 'Centennial' in cold-hardiness.

'Eva Rathke' has deep red flowers, somewhat less showy than those of 'Bristol Ruby' and 'Vanicekii,' and a weaker tendency toward late summer flowering. It also grows somewhat taller than those cultivars.

'Eva Supreme' is a very compact plant, growing to 0.6–0.9 m/2–3 ft high and somewhat wider, with crimson flowers opening in early summer and intermittently to late summer.

'Evita' is very similar (identical?) to 'Eva Supreme' in its compact growth and crimson flowers, opening in early summer and intermittently thereafter.

'Foliis Purpuriis' has purplish foliage in early summer, turning green later, and pink flowers. Its best feature is its low stature, remaining below 1.5 m/5 ft for many years.

'Java Red' is compact and mounded in habit, growing to about 1.2–1.5 m/4–5 ft high and 1.5–2 m/5–6.6 ft wide, with deep green foliage, with a red-purple overlay, and red buds opening deep pink, contrasting with the darker foliage.

'Pink Princess,' introduced by Prof. Jack Weigle of Iowa State University in the 1970s, and of uncertain parentage but perhaps involving W. praecox, is compact and moundlike in habit, growing to 1.5 m/5 ft high and 2 m/6.6 ft wide, with bright pink flowers opening at least a week earlier than most other cultivars, later fading to a paler pink. Repeat flowering is usually very light. Useful in Zones 5a–9a, perhaps also Zone 4b.

'Red Prince,' another Iowa State (Weigle) introduction, in the 1980s, grows to 2 m/6.6 ft tall and 1.5 m/5 ft wide and has large, bright crimson flowers, probably the reddest of any weigela, opening in early summer, with a substantial second bloom from flower buds initiated in the same growing season. It is reported to be

the most cold hardy of the full-size red-flowering weigelas, at least to Zone 4b.

'Variegata' is a compact form, growing to 1.2–1.5 m/4–5 ft high and somewhat wider, with leaves edged in light yellow to creamy white, and light pink to white flowers, early. Useful in Zones 5b–9a.

The Dance Series. These five *Weigela* cultivars, developed by Felicitas Svejda of the Agriculture Canada Research Station in Ottawa, have filled a need for cultivars hardy enough for that location (USDA Hardiness Zone 4b) and colder areas to the north and west.

'Minuet,' a hybrid involving 'Dropmore Pink' and another hardy parent, was the first of the Dance Series to be released. It grows compactly to about 0.75 m/2.5 ft tall and wide, with purple-tinted green foliage and yellow-throated purplish-red flowers, opening in early summer and intermittently in flower for at least a month in summer. It has survived in southern Saskatchewan (USDA Hardiness Zone 3a), so can be considered usefully hardy at least to Zone 3b, and it is now popular both in Canada and the United States.

'Rumba,' a sister seedling of 'Minuet,' grows compactly to about 1 m/3.3 ft high and 1.2 m wide. It is slightly more cold-hardy than 'Minuet,' to Zone 3a, with dark red flowers, first opening in early summer and continuing, at least lightly, for about 2 months. It is available in nurseries on both sides of the border.

'Samba,' a hybrid between 'Rumba' and 'Eva Rathke' released in 1986, grows vigorously but compactly to make a mound 0.8–1 m/2.6–3.3 ft high and wide, with yellow-throated red flowers. Preliminary tests showed this cultivar to be about or nearly as cold-hardy as 'Rumba,' but it may not yet be available commercially, at least in the United States.

'Tango' and 'Polka,' introduced in 1988, were derived from 'Minuet,' 'Rumba,' and other hardy clones. 'Tango' grows to 0.6 m/2 ft high and 0.8 m/2.6 ft wide, with purple leaves and red flowers. 'Polka' is larger, to 1–1.2 m/3.3–4 ft high and 1.2–1.5 m/4–5 ft wide, and has dark green foliage and pink flowers. 'Tango' flowers in Ottawa for most of the month of June, and 'Polka' is in flower about two-thirds of the time during June, July, and August. Both sustain only light dieback there, making them usefully hardy in at least Zone 4b. Neither is yet widely available in the United States.

Related Species

Weigela floribunda 5 (crimson weigela). This Japanese shrub differs little from *W. florida* except that its deeper reddish brown flowers are usually less showy. It is somewhat less cold-hardy than *W. florida,* useful in Zones 6a–9a, and less likely to be commercially available.

Weigela middendorffiana 4 (yellow or Middendorff weigela). This native of northern China, Man-churia, and Japan, has greenish yellow flowers and good form. At least in its northern native forms it is unusually cold-hardy, probably useful in Zones 4a–7a, but it does not perform well in hot, dry summers. This rare species probably is not commercially available, although plants of *Diervilla* have been sold under this name. True *W. middendorffiana* holds promise for northern climates and might well be reintroduced.

Weigela praecox 4 (early weigela). This native of Korea is similar to *W. florida* but flowers as much as two weeks earlier and does not become as tall. It is useful in the same range as *W. florida* and perhaps slightly colder zones as well.

Wisteria floribunda 1

Synonym: *W. multijuga*
JAPANESE WISTERIA
Deciduous vine
Fabaceae (Leguminosae; Pea Family)

Native Range.　Japan.

Useful Range.　USDA Zones 5b–9a+.

Function.　Specimen, screen (with support). Grows rapidly, once established, climbing by twining to heights of 8–10 m/26–33 ft or greater.

Size and Habit

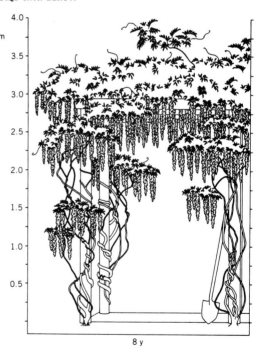

Wisteria floribunda.

Adaptability

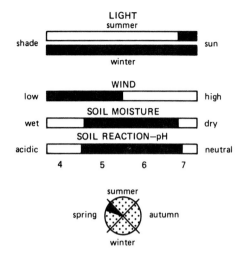

Seasonal Interest. *Flowers:* Fragrant, bluish violet to reddish violet, pink, or white, individually about 2 cm/0.8 in. long, borne in large numbers in pendent clusters 20–50 cm/8–20 in. long, longer in some cultivars, in late spring, sometimes continuing with shorter clusters into summer. *Foliage:* Rich green, compound leaves form a dense mass, remaining green until middle to late autumn, when they fall without color change. *Trunks:* Old specimens frequently develop picturesquely sinuous trunks with smooth gray bark, adding interest at close range.

Problems and Maintenance. Relatively trouble-free, wisteria vines require little maintenance once they are established and flowering well. But establishment is sometimes difficult, and pot-grown plants should be specified to minimize difficulty in transplanting. Established plants of many cultivars often do not flower for another five to ten years or even longer. Methods most commonly used to promote earlier flowering include root pruning and withholding irrigation and fertilization, except with phosphate fertilizers, but the results seem to be uncertain at best. Seedling plants may require longer to flower well than cultivars, since the latter in most cases have been selected for relatively early flowering and sometimes have been grafted onto seedling rootstocks, the scions coming from parent plants of flowering age. In the colder parts of the useful range, flower buds may be killed in some winters, greatly reducing landscape value. Wisterias in general may succeed in establishment and growth in colder areas than indicated, but may flower so seldom that they have little landscape value.

Cultivars. Not much more than a dozen cultivars are in commerce in North America, some of the most common of which are listed here.

'Alba' has moderately fragrant white or sometimes very pale lavender, flowers in clusters to 25–35 cm/10–14 long.

'Issai' has bluish flowers in clusters to 60–80 cm/24–32 in. long. The fact that this clone climbs in a clockwise direction has given rise to speculation that it may be a hybrid of *W. sinensis*, which climbs in this way, even though its flowers are more typical of those of *W. floribunda.* There are also known hybrids of these two species, collectively called *W.* ×*formosa.*

'Issai Perfect' has white flowers in clusters to at least 35 cm/14 in. long.

'Longissima Alba' has fragrant white flowers in clusters to 35 cm/14 in. long

'Macrobotrys' (= 'Longissima,' = 'Multijuga') has lavender-blue flowers in clusters 45–90 cm/18–36 in. long.

'Rosea' has fragrant, pink flowers in clusters to 45 cm/18 in. long.

'Royal Purple' has deep violet flowers in clusters to 30 cm/12 in. long.

Additional cultivars, from Japan and elsewhere, are regularly being added to the list of available plants. Some are in limited use in our area already, and others probably will be in the future.

Related Species and Hybrids

Wisteria frutescens 1 (American wisteria). This native of the southeastern United States from Virginia to Florida and Texas is useful for naturalizing but is not as effective for accent as the Asian species because its flower clusters are mostly less than 10 cm/4 in. long and are borne intermittently during the summer. Useful in Zones 6b–9a+. The selection 'Nivea,' with white flowers, has not usually been available, but is in production in at least one wholesale nursery at this writing.

Wisteria macrostachya 1 (Kentucky wisteria). Like *W. frutescens*, this species flowers after the foliage is well developed in early summer, but its violet flowers are borne in clusters as large as those of *W. sinensis*, and so it is showy, extending the season of bloom for wisterias by two to four weeks or more. Native from Kentucky and Tennessee to southern Illinois, Missouri, and Texas, this plant is useful in Zones 5a–9a, perhaps also Zone 4b. The selection 'Clara Mack' has white flowers, in longer clusters than typical for this species, to at least 35 cm/14 in., and opening a little later than typical for the species.

Wisteria sinensis 1 (Chinese wisteria). Perhaps the most common wisteria in landscape plantings in our area, this Chinese species differs from *W. floribunda* in several respects. It has a narrower range of flower color: lilac-pink to blue-violet and white. Its flowers tend to be borne in smaller clusters, mostly 15–30 cm/6–12 in. long and more dense than those of most *W. floribunda* cultivars. Moreover, *W. sinensis* is somewhat less cold-hardy than *W. floribunda*, useful in Zones 6a–9a+. A few of the more common cultivars are listed here.

'Alba' has white flowers; otherwise, it is like the species type.

'Amethyst' has fragrant rosy purple flowers.

'Aunt Dee' has slightly fragrant, light purple flowers in clusters to 30 cm/12 in. long.

'Black Dragon' (translation of: 'Kokkuryu Fuji') has very dark purple, semidouble flowers.

'Blue' is an old selection, long-popular in the Deep South, with lavender-blue flowers and great vigor.

'Caroline' has fragrant, deep blue-purple flowers.

'Cooke's Special' has large clusters of fragrant, blue-purple flowers and is highly vigorous.

'Jako' has fragrant white flowers in clusters that are longer than typical, and it is superior to 'Alba' for landscape effect.

'Rosea' is an old selection with pink flowers in longer clusters than typical.

'Sierra Madre' has fragrant, blue-violet flowers, borne in large numbers.

Wisteria venusta 1 (silky wisteria). This close relative of *W. sinensis* has fragrant white flowers in the forms in which it has been most cultivated. The selection 'Plena' has double white flowers, and 'Violacea' has lavender-violet flowers. This species differs little from *W. sinensis* in landscape use except that it flowers later, with *W. macrostachya*.

Xanthorhiza simplicissima 2–3

Synonym: *X. apiifolia*
YELLOWROOT
Deciduous groundcover
Ranunculaceae (Buttercup Family)

Native Range. Eastern United States: New York to Alabama and Florida.

Useful Range. USDA Zones 5b–9a+.

Function. Massing, groundcover.

Size and Habit

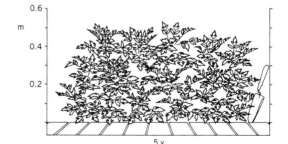

Xanthorhiza simplicissima.

Adaptability

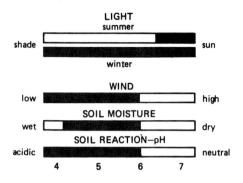

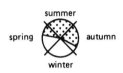

Xanthorhiza simplicissima.

Seasonal Interest. *Flowers:* Tiny, brownish crimson, borne in large numbers in loose clusters, lending a reddish cast to the plant in middle to late spring before new leaves unfold. *Foliage:* Compound, medium-green leaves give medium-fine texture similar to that of *Aegopodium podag-*

raria and turn dull yellow-orange before falling in autumn.

Problems and Maintenance. Relatively trouble-free, given the required site conditions, *Xanthorhiza* makes such a dense foliage mass once established that weed growth is minimal. Since it spreads vigorously, it can become a weed itself unless restrained by buildings, pavement, or steel edging.

Yucca filamentosa 3

ADAM'S NEEDLE
Evergreen shrub or groundcover
Agavaceae (Agave Family)

Native Range. Southeastern United States: South Carolina to Florida and Mississippi, naturalized farther northward.

Useful Range. USDA Zones 5b–9a and protected sites in Zone 5a.

Function. Specimen or massing, especially in situations where architectural and paving materials predominate.

Size and Habit

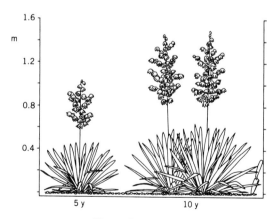

Yucca filamentosa.

Adaptability

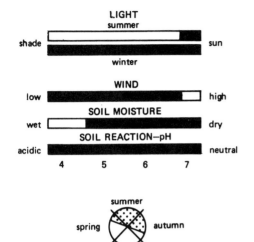

Seasonal Interest. *Flowers:* Creamy white, 5–8 cm/2–3 in. across, nodding, borne in large, upright clusters, often 1 m/3.3 ft tall, giving striking landscape accent in early summer. *Foliage:* Evergreen, stiff, gray-green, swordlike leaves, to 0.6 m/2 ft long and 5 cm/2 in. wide with curly fibers on the margins, forming a rosette with little or no stem growth in height. *Fruits:* Seed pods, about 5 cm/2 in. long, add little landscape interest and become untidy in appearance.

Problems and Maintenance. This plant is relatively trouble-free and requires little maintenance other than weed control and removal of dead leaves and flowerstalks. Stone or sand mulches are effective for weed control and visually compatible with the character of this plant. The leaves are sufficiently sharp-pointed to be dangerous in areas frequented by small children. The fruiting stalks become untidy and are best removed following flowering.

Cultivars. Several cultivars have been selected, primarily for leaf color (a few of the following may be selections of *Y. filifera* rather than *Y. filamentosa*).

'Bright Edge' has dark blue-green leaves with broad, rich yellow edges. 'Gold Edge' is similar.

'Color Guard' has a band of ivory to creamy yellow stripes in the center of each dark blue-green leaf.

'Concava Variegata' is low and compact; the short leaves are edged with creamy white, and they are tinged with pink in winter.

'Golden Sword' has soft-green leaf-margins, with a band of yellow stripes running down the center of each leaf.

'Ivory Tower' is a vigorous selection with very large, branched flower stalks, to 1.5–1.9 m/5–6 ft tall, a spectacular accent plant while in bloom in early summer.

Related Species

Yucca aloifolia 4–5 (Spanish bayonet, aloe yucca). Unlike the other *Yucca* species mentioned here, this native of the Deep South and Mexico makes considerable stem growth, forming trunks 2–4 m/6.6–13 ft tall, or taller south of our area. Foliage and flowering interest is not greatly different from that of *Y. filamentosa,* although the leaves are even sharper-pointed than those of *Y. filamentosa* and thus are potentially dangerous in some situations. Useful in Zones 8a–9a+ for positive accent. The selection 'Marginata' has yellow leaf margins.

Yucca filifera 3 (synonym: *Y. flaccida;* weakleaf yucca). This plant is similar to *Y. filamentosa,* native to about the same area, and often substituted in landscape use, but its leaves are less rigid, the outer ones bending back to the ground. Useful in Zones 5b–9a+. The selection 'Ivory Tower' has unusually large flower clusters, to 1.5 m/5 ft tall, with erect flowers, and is superior for accent at flowering time in early summer.

Yucca glauca 3 (Great Plains yucca, soapweed). This native of western North America from South Dakota to New Mexico has strongly bluish

Yucca glauca.

leaves, about as long as those of *Y. filamentosa* but only about 1 cm/0.4 in. wide. It is useful as a specimen in Zones 4b–7b but not as appropriate for large-scale massing as other *Yucca* species.

Yucca gloriosa 4–5 (Spanish dagger, moundlily yucca).   Like *Y. aloifolia*, this species is native to the southeastern states and makes considerable stem growth, sometimes reaching heights of 2–4 m/6.6–13 ft but often multiple-trunked and remaining lower. Useful for accent and massing in Zones 8a–9a+, some forms northward into Zone 7.

Agave americana 4 (century plant).   This native of Mexico is useful for accent in dry sites in Zone 9a+ and makes a striking specimen with succulent gray leaves 1 m/3.3 ft and more in length and up to 25 cm/10 in. wide. Plants grow in rosette form, sometimes for many years without flowering. When flowering does occur it is most dramatic, since the inflorescence towers far over the vegetative plant. Following flowering the original plant dies and usually is replaced by one or more sucker shoots.

Zelkova serrata 8

JAPANESE ZELKOVA
Deciduous tree
Ulmaceae (Elm Family)

Native Range.   Japan.

Useful Range.   USDA Zones 6a–9a, perhaps also Zone 5b with selection of most cold-hardy genetic material.

Function.   Shade tree.

Size and Habit

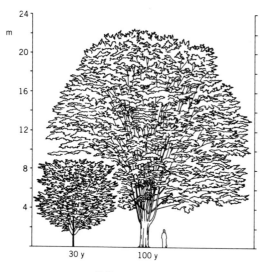

Zelkova serrata.

Adaptability

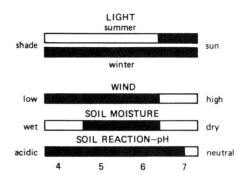

Seasonal Interest.   *Foliage:* Pale green on emergence, turning a rich, deep green in summer, then russet-yellow before falling in autumn. *Trunk and branches:* Bark on large trees peels off in patches to expose the orange-brown inner bark.

Problems and Maintenance.   Usually free of serious problems, this elm relative has been found resistant (although apparently not immune) to Dutch elm disease and has been recommended as a substitute for the American elm in

Zelkova serrata.

some areas. When considering it for this role, it is important to remember the differences in cold hardiness, ultimate size, and growth rate between the two species.

Cultivars. Only a few cultivars have been selected from this species. All of those listed are excellent substitutes in form, but not necessarily for growth rate and ultimate size, for American elm.

'Halka' (Plant Patent No. 5687, 1986) is probably the fastest-growing cultivar now available, to 15 m/50 ft in height in 30 years and eventually to 18–21 m/60–70 ft tall and 12–14 m/40–46 ft wide, with an upright vase-shape and medium green foliage that turns yellow in autumn. Probably cold-hardy to Zone 5b.

'Illinois Hardy' is a recent selection, a clone that survived a particularly harsh winter in northern Illinois, presumably making it cold-hardy to Zone 5b and perhaps some sites in Zone 5a, where it will no doubt be tried. Not yet widely available.

'PNI 6960' (Green Vase'®; Plant Patent No. 5080, 1983) is an upright, vase-shaped tree, growing vigorously to 15 m/50 ft in height in 30 years and eventually to at least 18–21 m/60–70 ft tall and 15 m/50 ft wide, with medium-green foliage that turns golden-orange in autumn. Cold-hardy to Zone 6a, probably also Zone 5b.

'PNI 6957' ('Village Green'®) is the first selection made in North America, introduced by Princeton Nurseries in the middle 1960s. It is strongly vase-shaped, growing to 12 m/40 ft in height in 30 years and eventually to at least 15–18 m/50–60 ft tall and nearly as wide, with dark green foliage that turns rusty-red in autumn. Even though new cultivars have been introduced, it remains popular. Cold-hardy at least to Zone 6a.

Related Species

Zelkova carpinifolia 8 (Caucasian zelkova). This large, graceful tree from the Caucasus makes a majestic shade tree in Europe. It is similar to *Z. serrata* in ultimate size and habit and seems fully as likely a substitute for the form of American elm, but is somewhat less cold-hardy, useful in Zones 7a–9a and perhaps also Zone 6b with selection of the most cold-hardy material. Older trees have peeling bark at least as colorful as that of *Z. serrata.* This species has been reported to be more susceptible to Dutch elm disease than *Z. serrata,* but further testing is needed.

Zelkova sinica 7 (Chinese zelkova). This tree has attracted interest in the Midwest because of its presumed cold-hardiness, but it probably is little more cold-hardy than the hardiest material of *Z. serrata.* Since it also lacks the elegant form of *Z. serrata,* it probably is of little interest as a substitute for the American elm, even though it may be a useful landscape tree in Zones 6a–9a and perhaps parts of Zone 5b as well.

Hemiptelea davidii 6 (David hemiptelea). This shrubby small tree from northeastern Asia, if it should become available commercially, would be useful in Zones 5a–8a at least, as a small specimen tree or hedge plant. Its foliage is similar to that of some of the small-leaved elms, but it has little other landscape interest.

Ziziphus jujuba 6

COMMON JUJUBE, CHINESE DATE
Deciduous shrub or small tree
Rhamnaceae (Buckthorn Family)

Native Range.   Southeastern Europe through Asia to China; naturalized in some parts of the southeastern United States.

Useful Range.   USDA Zones 6b–9a+.

Function.   Small specimen tree, edible fruits.

Size and Habit

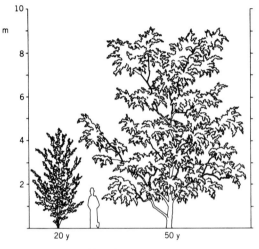

Ziziphus jujuba.

Adaptability.   This tree is unusually widely tolerant of soil conditions, including alkaline soils, but not tolerant of wet soils.

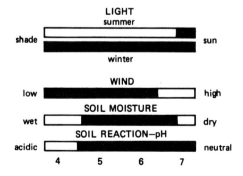

Seasonal Interest.   *Flowers:* Greenish yellow, very small and not showy, before the leaves in midspring. *Foliage:* Olive-green leaves, mostly not more than 5 cm/2 in. long and only half as wide, sparsely arranged on the spiny branches. *Fruits:* Dull green, then red, and ripening very dark red-brown in late summer, up to 2.5 cm/1 in. long, resembling dates, edible as preserves or dried.

Problems and Maintenance.   This plant is essentially trouble-free and requires little or no maintenance. Pruning is seldom necessary other than for initial training.

Varieties and Cultivars.   The var. *inermis* is free of spines, an important consideration when the fruits are to be harvested. Several cultivars have been selected for outstanding fruit production, especially in Asia, but these are seldom commercially available in our area.

Related Species

The following additional members of the Rhamnaceae are not commonly encountered in landscape use but could become more important than they are at present.

Hovenia dulcis 7 (Japanese raisin tree).   This native of China (cultivated widely in Japan) is a graceful, trouble-free, small to medium-size tree,

Ziziphus jujuba.

Hovenia dulcis.

Paliurus spina-christi.

useful in Zones 6b–7b and perhaps warmer zones as well. The flowers, opening during summer, are not showy, but the reddish stalks are interesting and allegedly edible. The fruits are not colorful but come to resemble raisins as they ripen in early autumn.

Paliurus spina-christi 6 (synonym: *P. aculeatus;* Christ thorn, Jerusalem thorn).   This exceed-ingly spiny large shrub or small tree from southern Europe and Asia has bright green leaves, about 2.5 cm/1 in. long, too loosely arranged to be effective for screening, but the thorns and dense growth make it a good choice for a barrier hedge. The small, greenish yellow flowers are fairly showy when they appear in large numbers in late spring along with the expanding leaves. It is useful in Zones 7b–9a+.

Lists *of* Plants
by Categories

Size

1. Vines, Climbers (Mostly Size Group 1)
2. Groundcovers (Size Group 2)
3. Dwarf Shrubs and Tall Groundcovers (Size Group 3)
4. Small Shrubs (Size Group 4)
5. Medium Shrubs (Size Group 5)
6. Large Shrubs and Small Trees (Size Group 6)
7. Medium Trees (Size Group 7)
8. Large Trees (Size Group 8)

Shape

9. Plants with Columnar or Narrowly Pyramidal Shape
10. Plants with Pendulous or Umbrellalike Habit
11. Plants with Contorted Habit
12. Plants with Horizontally Layered Branching
13. Cutback Shrubs, Subshrubs, and Herbaceous Perennials
14. Facing Shrubs, Branching to the Ground
15. Habit Unusually Graceful or Otherwise Distinctive

Function

16. Small- to Medium-Scale Screens: Shrubs and Vines
17. Large-Scale Screens, and Windbreaks: Large Shrubs and Trees
18. Street and Avenue Trees

Adaptation

19. Plants for Cold Climates
20. Plants for Warm Climates
21. Plants That Require Full Sun in Summer, in at Least Parts of Their Useful Ranges
22. Plants That Require Shade in Summer, in at Least Parts of Their Useful Ranges
23. Plants That Require Shade in Winter, in at Least Parts of Their Useful Ranges
24. Plants That Tolerate Full Shade in Summer, in at Least Parts of Their Useful Ranges
25. Plants That Tolerate Strong Winds, in at Least Parts of Their Useful Ranges
26. Plants that Tolerate Little Wind, in at least parts of Their Useful Ranges
27. Plants That Tolerate Wet Soil
28. Plants That Tolerate Dry Soil
29. Plants That Require Distinctly Acidic Soil (pH 6.0 or Lower)
30. Plants That Tolerate Neutral or Alkaline Soil (pH 7.0 or Higher)
31. Plants That Tolerate Salt (Seaside or Roadside)
32. Plants with Serious Insect or Disease Problems (Partial List)

Seasonal Interest

33. Plants with Fragrant Flowers or Foliage
34. Plants Flowering in Late Winter to Early Spring
35. Plants Flowering in Midsummer to Autumn
36. Plants with Colorful or Variegated Foliage in Summer
37. Plants with Colorful Foliage in Autumn or Winter
38. Plants with Fine-Textured Foliage
39. Plants with Coarse-Textured Foliage
40. Plants with Otherwise Distinctive Foliage
41. Plants with Colorful or Interesting Fruits in Fall or Winter
42. Plants with Colorful or Interesting Fruits in Summer or Early Autumn
43. Plants with Otherwise Distinctive Fruits or Cones
44. Plants with Edible Fruits or Nuts
45. Plants with Colorful or Otherwise Interesting Twigs in Winter or Year-Round
46. Plants with Twigs (or Foliage) Prickly, Spiny, or Thorny
47. Plants with Interesting Bark Color or Texture

Size

1. Vines, Climbers (Mostly Size Group 1)

Holding and Climbing by Scrambling

Celastrus spp. 1 & 2
Jasminum spp. 1 & 3–4 (several)
Lycium barbarum 4
Rosa banksiae 1
Rosa bracteata 1
Rosa laevigata 1 & 5
Rosa setigera 5
Rosa wichuraiana 1 & 2
Rosa (Climbing Roses) 1 & 5
Rosa (English Roses, some) 1 & 5
Rosa (Ramblers) 1 & 5
Tripterygium regelii 1 & 5

Holding and Climbing by Twining

Actinidia spp. 1
Akebia spp. 1 & 2
Aristolochia macrophylla 1
Celastrus spp. 1 & 2
Clematis spp. & cvs. 1 (twining petioles, not stems)
Cocculus carolinus 1
Gelsemium sempervirens 1
Holboellia coriacea 1
Kadsura japonica 1
Lonicera spp. 1 & 2 (climbing species)
Menispermum canadense 1 & 2
Periploca graeca 1
Polygonum aubertii 1
Pueraria lobata 1 & 3
Schisandra spp. 1
Stauntonia hexaphylla 1
Trachelospermum spp. 1

Holding and Climbing by Holdfasts (Aerial Rootlets)

Campsis spp. & cvs. 1
Decumaria barbara 1
Euonymus fortunei cvs. 1 & 2
Ficus pumila 1
Hedera spp. 1 & 2
Hydrangea petiolaris 1 & 2
Pieris phillyreifolia 1 & 3
Pileostegia viburnoides 1 & 2
Schizophragma spp. 1 & 2

Holding and Climbing by Tendrils, with or Without Adhesive Discs

Ampelopsis spp. 1
Antigonon leptopus 1
Bignonia capreolata 1
Clytostoma callistegioides 2
Macfadyena unguis-cati 1
Parthenocissus spp. 1 & 2
Passiflora spp. 1 & 2
Smilax spp. 1
Vitis spp. 1
Wisteria spp. 1

2. Groundcovers to 0.5 m Tall (Size Group 2)

Aegopodium podagraria
Ajuga spp.
Akebia spp.
Andromeda polifolia
Arctostaphylos uva-ursi
Ardisia japonica
Asarum spp.
Bruckenthalia spiculifolia
Callistemon pityoides
Calluna vulgaris
Cassiope umbellata
Celastrus spp.
Chamaecytisus spp.
Comptonia peregrina
Conradina verticillata
Convallaria majalis
Corema conradii
Cornus canadensis
Coronilla varia
Cotoneaster adpressus
Cotoneaster dammeri
Cytisus spp. (part)
Daboecia cantabrica

Daphne alpina
Daphne cneorum
Decumaria barbara
Empetrum spp.
Epigaea repens
Epimedium spp.
Erica spp. (most)
Euonymus fortunei (part)
Euonymus obovatus
Fragaria spp.
Galax urceolata
Galium spp.
Gaultheria hispidula
Gaultheria procumbens
Gaylussacia brachycera
Gelsemium sempervirens
Genista spp. (part)
Hedera spp.
Helianthemum nummularium
Hosta spp. (part)
Hydrangea petiolaris
Hylotelephium sieboldii
Hypericum spp. (part)
Iberis spp.
Jasminum parkeri
Juniperus spp. (part)
Kalmia hirsuta
Kalmiopsis leachiana
Lamium galeobdolon
Lamium maculatum
Ledum spp. (part)
Leiophyllum buxifolium
Leucothoë keiskei
Liriope spp.
Loiseleuria procumbens
Lonicera spp. (part)
Lotus corniculatus
Mahonia repens
Menispermum canadense
Microbiota decussata
Mitchella repens
Nepeta mussinii
Ophiopogon japonicus
Pachysandra spp.
Parthenocissus spp. (most)
Passiflora caerulea
Paxistima canbyi
Phlox spp.
Pileostegia viburnoides
Pleioblastus pygmaeus
Podophyllum peltatum

Potentilla spp. (part)
Rhododendron lapponicum
Rhododendron nakaharai
Rhododendron racemosum
Rosa wichuraiana
Rosmarinus officinalis (part)
Rubus hispidus
Ruscus hypoglossum
Salix repens
Saxifraga stolonifera
Schizophragma spp.
Sedum spp.
Sempervivum tectorum
Shortia galacifolia
Teucrium chamaedrys
Tiarella cordifolia
Trachelospermum spp.
Vaccinium spp. (part)
Viburnum edule
Vinca spp.
Viola spp.
Waldsteinia spp.
Xanthorhiza simplicissima

3. Dwarf Shrubs and Tall Groundcovers, 0.5–1 m Tall (Size Group 3)

Amorpha canescens
Amorpha nana
Ardisia spp. (part)
Aronia melanocarpa (part)
Artemisia spp. (part)
Aspidistra elatior
Berberis candidula
Berberis ×gladwynensis
Berberis thunbergii (part)
Berberis verruculosa
Buxus microphylla
Callistemon pityoides
Caragana aurantiaca
Caragana pygmaea
Caryopteris spp. (part)
Ceanothus spp. (part)
Chaenomeles japonica
Chamaecyparis cvs. (part)
Chamaedaphne calyculata
Cistus spp. (part)
Cornus hessei
Cotoneaster spp. (part)
Cycas revoluta
Cyrtomium falcatum

Cytisus spp. (part)
Daboecia cantabrica
Danaë racemosa
Daphne spp. (part)
Deutzia gracilis
Diervilla lonicera
Elsholtzia stauntonii
Erica spp. (part)
Escallonia virgata
Euonymus nanus
Eurya emarginata (part)
Fothergilla gardenii
Fuchsia magellanica (part)
Gardenia augusta
Gaultheria spp. (part)
Genista spp. (part)
Hemerocallis spp.
Hosta spp. & cvs. (part)
Hydrangea arborescens
Hydrangea macrophylla
Hylotelephium spp. & cvs. (part)
Hypericum spp. (part)
Ilex crenata (part)
Ilex rugosa
Indigofera spp.
Jasminum spp. (part)
Juniperus spp. (part)
Kalmia spp. (part)
Lagerstroemia indica (part)
Lavandula angustifolia
Ledum spp. (part)
Leptodermis oblonga
Lespedeza cuneata
Leucophyllum zygophyllum
Lonicera albertii
Lonicera pileata
×Mahoberberis aquicandidula
Mahonia spp. (part)
Microbiota decussata
Nandina cvs. (part)
Paeonia lactiflora
Paxistima myrtifolia
Perovskia atriplicifolia
Picea abies cvs. (part)
Pieris phillyreifolia
Pleioblastus spp. (part)
Podocarpus nivalis
Polygonum cuspidatum (part)
Potentilla spp. (part)
Prunus besseyi
Prunus pumila

Pueraria lobata
Pyracantha coccinea (part)
Rhaphiolepis indica
Rhapidophyllum hystrix
Rhododendron spp. & cvs. (part)
Rosa spp. (part)
Rosmarinus officinalis (part)
Rubus laciniatus
Ruscus aculeatus
Sabal minor
Salix repens
Santolina spp.
Sarcococca hookeriana (part)
Sasa veitchii
Serenoa repens
Skimmia spp.
Spiraea spp. (part)
Stephanandra incisa (part)
Symphoricarpos spp. (part)
Taxus cvs. (part)
Thuja occidentalis cvs. (part)
Trifolium incarnatum
Tsuga canadensis cvs. (part)
Vaccinium spp. (part)
Viburnum davidii
Viburnum edule
Yucca spp.
Zamia pumila

4. Small Shrubs, 1–2 m Tall (Size Group 4)

Deciduous, Semievergreen, or Herbaceous

Abelia ×grandiflora (part)
Abeliophyllum distichum
Aesculus sylvatica
Amelanchier spp. (part)
Aronia melanocarpa
Artemisia abrotanum
Atriplex canescens
Berberis spp. (part)
Buddleia davidii
Callicarpa spp.
Calycanthus spp.
Caryopteris incana
Ceanothus ×pallidus
Diervilla spp. (part)
Dirca palustris
Edgeworthia papyrifera
Enkianthus perulatus
Forsythia spp. (part)

Fothergilla gardenii
Fuchsia magellanica
Genista cinerea
Halimodendron halodendron
Hydrangea quercifolia
Hypericum hookerianum
Iberis spp.
Itea spp. (part)
Jasminum spp. (part)
Juniperus chinensis (part)
Juniperus communis (part)
Juniperus conferta
Juniperus horizontalis
Juniperus sabina (part)
Juniperus squamata (part)
Kerria japonica
Lagerstroemia indica (part)
Leycesteria formosa
Ligustrum obtusifolium (part)
Ligustrum vulgare (part)
Lindera melissifolia
Lonicera spp. (part)
Lycium barbarum
Myrica spp. (part)
Neillia sinensis
Neviusia alabamensis
Paeonia spp. (part)
Perovskia atriplicifolia
Philadelphus spp. (part)
Physocarpus opulifolius (part)
Polygonum cuspidatum (part)
Prinsepia uniflora
Prunus fruticosa
Prunus glandulosa
Prunus japonica
Prunus maritima
Prunus tenella
Pyracantha coccinea (part)
Quercus georgiana
Quercus ilicifolia
Quercus prinoides
Rhamnus pallasii
Rhododendron spp.
Rhodotypos scandens
Rhus aromatica (part)
Rhus trilobata (part)
Ribes spp. (part)
Robinia spp. (part)
Rosa spp. (part)
Salix rosmarinifolia
Securinega suffruticosa

Sorbaria sorbifolia
Spiraea spp. (part)
Stephanandra spp. (part)
Symphoricarpos albus
Symphoricarpos ×doorenbosii
Syringa spp. (part)
Tamarix hispida
Tripetaleia paniculata
Vaccinium parvifolium
Viburnum edule
Viburnum spp. (part)
Vitex spp. (part)
Weigela spp. (part)

Evergreen

Agave americana
Arctostaphylos patula
Ardisia spp. (part)
Berberis spp. (part)
Buxus spp. (part)
Callistemon spp. (part)
Carpenteria californica
Cephalotaxus harringtonia
Ceratiola ericoides
Chamaecyparis cvs. (part)
Chamaedaphne calyculata
Cistus spp. (part)
Cycas revoluta
Daphne spp. (part)
Daphniphyllum humile
Escallonia ×langleyensis
Euonymus fortunei (part)
Eurya spp. (part)
×Fatshedera lizei
Fatsia japonica
Gardenia augusta
Illicium mexicanum
Itea spp. (part)
Jasminum spp. (part)
Juniperus spp. (part)
Leucophyllum frutescens
Leucothoë spp. (part)
Lyonia spp. (part)
×Mahoberberis spp. (part)
Mahonia spp. (part)
Myrtus communis
Nandina domestica (part)
Osmanthus delavayi
Picea abies cvs. (part)
Pieris spp. (part)
Pinus aristata (part)

Pinus mugo (part)
Pinus pumila (part)
Pittosporum tobira
Platycladus orientalis cvs. (part)
Prunus laurocerasus (part)
Rhamnus alaternus
Rhamnus croceus
Rhaphiolepis spp. (part)
Rhododendron spp. (part)
Rosmarinifolia officinalis
Sabal minor (part)
Sarcococca spp.
Sasa palmata
Serenoa repens (part)
Shepherdia rotundifolia
Taxus spp. and cvs. (part)
Thuja spp. and cvs. (part)
Tsuga canadensis cvs. (part)
Vaccinium ovatum
Viburnum propinquum
Yucca spp. (part)
Zenobia pulverulenta

5. Medium Shrubs, 2–4 m Tall (Size Group 5)

Deciduous or Semievergreen

Abelia ×grandiflora (part)
Adina rubella
Aesculus parviflora
Aesculus splendens
Amelanchier spp. (part)
Aronia spp. (part)
Baccharis halimifolia
Berberis spp. (part)
Buddleia alternifolia
Callicarpa bodinieri
Calycanthus spp. (part)
Caragana spp. (part)
Cephalanthus occidentalis
Chimonanthus praecox
Clerodendrum trichotomum
Clethra alnifolia
Cliftonia monophylla
Colutea arborescens
Cornus spp. (part)
Corylopsis spp. (part)
Corylus spp. (part)
Cotoneaster spp. (part)
Decaisnea fargesii
Deutzia spp. (part)

Disanthus cercidifolius
Elaeagnus spp. (part)
Eleutherococcus sieboldianus
Elliottia racemosa
Enkianthus campanulatus
Euonymus spp. (part)
Euscaphis japonica
Exochorda macrantha
Ficus carica
Fontanesia spp. (part)
Forestiera neo-mexicana
Forsythia spp. (part)
Fothergilla major
Hamamelis vernalis
Heptacodium miconioides
Hibiscus syriacus
Hydrangea quercifolia (part)
Ilex verticillata
Itea virginica
Jasminum nudiflorum
Juniperus spp. (part)
Kolkwitzia amabilis
Lagerstroemia indica
Leitneria floridana
Lespedeza spp. (part)
Leucophyllum frutescens
Leucothoë racemosa
Ligustrum spp. (part)
Lindera benzoin
Lonicera spp. (part)
Lycium barbarum
Magnolia spp. (part)
Malus spp. (part)
Myrica pensylvanica
Myrtus communis
Nemopanthus mucronatus
Oemleria cerasiformis
Orixa japonica
Philadelphus spp. (part)
Physocarpus opulifolius
Polygonum cuspidatum
Prinsepia sinensis
Prunus spp. (part)
Ptelea polyadenia
Pyracantha spp. (part)
Pyrus salicifolia
Quercus spp. (part)
Rhododendron spp. (part)
Rhus spp. (part)
Ribes spp. (part)
Robinia ×margarettiae

Rosa spp. & cvs. (part)
Rubus deliciosus
Salix spp. (part)
Sambucus spp. (part)
Senna corymbosa
Sesbania punicea
Shepherdia spp. (part)
Sophora davidii
Sorbaria spp. (part)
Sorbus vilmorinii
Spartium junceum
Spiraea spp. (part)
Stachyurus spp.
Staphylea bumalda
Stephanandra incisa
Styrax americanum
Syringa spp. (part)
Tamarix spp. (part)
Tripterygium regelii
Vaccinium parvifolium
Viburnum spp. (part)
Vitex spp. (part)
Weigela spp. (part)

Evergreen

Arctostaphylos manzanita
Aucuba japonica
Bambusa multiplex
Callistemon citrinus
Ceanothus ×delilianus
Cephalotaxus fortunei
Chamaecyparis cvs. (part)
Chamaerops humilis
Choisya ternata
Cistus ×cyprius
Cleyera japonica
Croton alabamense
Distylium racemosum
Elaeagnus spp. (part)
Escallonia spp. (part)
Euonymus japonicus
Eurya japonica
Fatsia japonica
Ilex spp. (part)
Illicium spp. (part)
Kalmia latifolia
Leucophyllum spp. & cvs
Leucothoë populifolia
Ligustrum spp. (part)
Loropetalum chinense
Lyonia spp. (part)

Mahonia spp. (part)
Michelia figo
Nandina domestica
Osmanthus spp. (part)
Photinia glabra
Picea abies cvs. (part)
Pieris spp. (part)
Pinus aristata
Pinus mugo
Pinus pumila
Pittosporum tobira
Platycladus orientalis cvs. (part)
Podocarpus macrophyllus (part)
Prunus spp. (part)
Quercus spp. (part)
Rhaphiolepis spp. (part)
Rhododendron spp. (part)
Rosa spp. (part)
Taxus spp. and cvs. (part)
Tetrapanax papyrifer
Thuja spp. (part)
Thujopsis dolobrata
Torreya spp. (part)
Trochodendron aralioides
Tsuga canadensis (part)
Vaccinium ovatum
Viburnum spp. (part)
Yucca spp. (part)

6. Large Shrubs and Small Trees, 4–8 m Tall (Size Group 6)

Deciduous or Semievergreen

Acer spp. (part)
Aesculus spp. (part)
Albizia julibrissin
Aleurites fordii
Alnus spp. (part)
Amelanchier spp. (part)
Amorpha fruticosa
Aralia spp.
Argyrocytisus battandieri
Asimina triloba
Betula populifolia
Bumelia lanuginosa
Calycanthus chinensis
Caragana arborescens
Castanea pumila
Cercis spp.
Chilopsis linearis
Chionanthus spp.

×Chitalpa tashkentensis
Clerodendrum trichotomum
Clethra spp. (part)
Cornus spp. & hybrids (part)
Corylus maxima
Cotinus coggygria
Cotoneaster spp. (part)
Crataegus spp. (most)
Cudrania tricuspidata
Cydonia oblonga
Cyrilla racemiflora
Davidia involucrata
Dipelta floribunda
Dipteronia sinensis
Elaeagnus angustifolia
Elliottia racemosa
Emmenopteris henryi
Enkianthus campanulatus
Euonymus spp. (part)
Exochorda spp. (part)
Ficus carica
Firmiana simplex
Forestiera acuminata
Franklinia alatamaha
Fraxinus spp. (part)
Halesia tetraptera
Hamamelis spp. (most)
Hemiptelea davidii
Hippophaë rhamnoides
Holodiscus discolor
Hovenia dulcis
Hydrangea paniculata
Ilex decidua
Laburnum spp.
Lagerstroemia spp. & cvs.
Leitneria floridana
Ligustrum vulgare
Lindera obtusiloba
Lonicera maackii
×Macludrania hybrida
Magnolia spp. (part)
Malus spp. and cvs. (most)
Melia azedarach
Paliurus spina-christi
Parkinsonia spp.
Parrotia persica
Parrotiopsis jacquemontiana
Philadelphus purpurascens
Photinia villosa
Pinckneya pubens
Poncirus trifoliata

Populus spp. (part)
Prunus spp. (part)
Pseudocydonia sinensis
Ptelea trifoliata
Pterostyrax spp. (part)
Punica granatum
Pyrus spp.
Quercus spp.
Rhamnus spp. (most)
Rhus spp. (part)
Robinia ×margarettiae
Salix spp. (part)
Sambucus nigra
Shepherdia spp.
Sinojackia rehderiana
Sophora affinis
Sorbus spp. (part)
Staphylea spp. (most)
Stewartia spp. (part)
Styrax spp. (most)
Symplocos spp.
Syringa spp. (part)
Tetradium daniellii
Tilia mongolica
Toona sinensis
Vaccinium spp. (part)
Viburnum spp. (part)
Vitex negundo
Xanthoceras sorbifolium
Zanthoxylum spp.
Ziziphus jujuba

Evergreen

Bambusa multiplex
Brahea armata
Butia capitata
Callistemon citrinus
Camellia spp.
Chamaecyparis cvs. (part)
Chamaerops humilis
Daphniphyllum macropodum
Distylium racemosum
Eriobotrya spp.
Escallonia rubra
Eucalyptus spp. (part)
Feijoa sellowiana
Hibiscus rosa-sinensis
Ilex spp. (part)
Illicium spp. (part)
Juniperus spp. (part)
Laurus nobilis

Ligustrum spp. (part)
Lyonia ferruginea
Michelia spp. (part)
Myrica cerifera
Nerium oleander
Osmanthus spp. (part)
Persea spp. (part)
Photinia spp. (part)
Phyllostachys spp. (part)
Picea abies cvs. (part)
Pinus spp. (part)
Platycladus orientalis cvs.
Pleioblastus simonii
Podocarpus macrophyllus
Prunus spp. (part)
Pyracantha spp. (part)
Quercus spp.
Rhododendron spp. (part)
Sabal palmetto
Sciadopitys verticillata
Sophora secundiflora
Sycopsis sinensis
Taxus spp. (part)
Ternstroemia gymnanthera
Thuja spp. (part)
Torreya nucifera
Trachycarpus fortunei
Trochodendron aralioides
Tsuga spp. and cvs. (part)

7. Medium Trees, 8–16 m Tall (Size Group 7)

Deciduous or Semievergreen

Acer spp. (part)
Aesculus glabra
Ailanthus altissima
Alnus spp. (most)
Amelanchier arborea
Aralia spp.
Asimina triloba
Betula spp. (part)
Broussonetia papyrifera
Carpinus spp.
Castanea spp. (part)
Catalpa spp. (part)
Celtis bungeana
Cercis canadensis
Cladrastis lutea
Cornus spp. (part)
Corylus colurna

Cotinus obovatus
Crataegus spp. (part)
Davidia involucrata
Diospyros spp.
Emmenopteris henryi
Eucommia ulmoides
Euptelea polyandra
Firmiana simplex
Fraxinus spp. (part)
Halesia spp. (part)
Idesia polycarpa
Juglans ailanthifolia
Koelreuteria spp.
Maackia spp.
×Macludrania hybrida
Maclura pomifera
Magnolia spp. (part)
Malus spp. (part)
Morus spp.
Nyssa spp.
Ostrya spp.
Oxydendrum arboreum
Parrotia persica
Paulownia tomentosa
Phellodendron amurense
Picrasma ailanthifolia
Platycarya strobilacea
Populus spp. (part)
Prunus spp. (part)
Pteroceltis tatarinowii
Pterostyrax spp. (part)
Pyrus spp.
Quercus spp. (part)
Robinia spp. (part)
Salix spp. (part)
Sapindus drummondii
Sapium sebiferum
Sassafras albidum
Sorbus spp. (part)
Stewartia spp. (part)
Syringa reticulata
Tetracentron sinensis
Tetradium daniellii
Toona sinensis
Ulmus spp. (part)
Zelkova sinica

Evergreen

Abies koreana
Brahea armata
Calocedrus decurrens

Cedrus spp.
Chamaecyparis spp. (part)
Cinnamomum camphora
Cupressus spp. (most)
Eucalyptus spp. (part)
Gordonia lasianthus
Ilex spp. (part)
Juniperus spp. (part)
Michelia spp. (part)
Persea palustris
Phoenix canariensis
Phyllostachys bambusoides
Picea mariana
Pinus spp. (part)
Platycladus orientalis cvs.
Podocarpus macrophyllus
Prunus caroliniana
Pseudotsuga macrocarpa
Quercus spp. (part)
Rhododendron arboreum
Sabal palmetto
Sciadopitys verticillata
Sophora secundiflora
Thuja spp. (part)
Torreya nucifera
Tsuga spp. (part)
Umbellularia californica
Washingtonia filifera

8. Large Trees, 16 m and Taller (Size Group 8)

Deciduous or Semievergreen

Acer spp. (part)
Aesculus spp. (part)
Ailanthus altissima
Betula spp. (part)
Carya spp.
Castanea spp. (part)
Catalpa speciosa
Celtis spp. (most)
Cercidiphyllum japonicum
Cladrastis platycarpa
Cornus coreana
Corylus colurna
Fagus spp.
Fraxinus spp. (part)
Ginkgo biloba
Gleditsia triacanthos
Gymnocladus dioica

Halesia monticola
Juglans spp.
Juniperus virginiana
Kalopanax septemlobus
Keteleeria spp.
Larix spp.
Liquidambar spp.
Liriodendron spp.
Magnolia spp. (part)
Metasequoia glyptostroboides
Morus spp.
Nyssa spp.
Ostrya virginiana
Oxydendrum arboreum
Phellodendron spp.
Pistacia chinensis
Platanus spp.
Populus spp. (part)
Prunus spp. (few)
Pseudolarix amabilis
Pterocarya spp.
Quercus spp. (part)
Robinia pseudoacacia
Salix spp. (part)
Sassafras albidum
Sophora japonica
Sorbus alnifolia
Taxodium distichum
Tilia spp. (most)
Ulmus spp. (most)
Zelkova spp. (most)

Evergreen

Abies spp. (most)
Araucaria spp.
Chamaecyparis spp. (part)
Cryptomeria japonica
Cunninghamia lanceolata
×Cupressocyparis leylandii
Cupressus macrocarpa
Picea spp. (most)
Pinus spp. (part)
Pseudotsuga menziesii
Quercus virginiana
Sequoia sempervirens
Sequoiadendron giganteum
Taiwania cryptomerioides
Thuja plicata
Tsuga spp. (part)
Umbellularia californica
Washingtonia robusta

SHAPE

9. Plants with Columnar or Narrowly Pyramidal Shape

Acer platanoides cvs. 8
Acer rubrum cvs. 8
Acer saccharum cvs. 8
Calocedrus decurrens 7
Carpinus betulus 'Fastigiata' 7
Chamaecyparis cvs. 3–8
Crataegus monogyna 'Stricta' 6
Crataegus phaenopyrum cvs. 6
Cryptomeria japonica 8
×Cupressocyparis leylandii 8
Eucalyptus spp. (part) 8
Fagus sylvatica 'Fastigiata' 8
Ginkgo biloba cvs. 8
Juniperus cvs. 6–8
Larix decidua 'Pyramidalis' 8
Liriodendron tulipifera 'Fastigiatum' 8
Malus baccata 'Columnaris' 7
Malus cultivars 6:
   'Red Barron'
   'Sentinel'
   'Silver Moon'
   'Snowcloud'
   'Velvetcole'
   'White Candle'
Metasequoia glyptostroboides cvs. 8
Picea abies 'Columnaris' 8
Picea abies 'Pyramidata' 8
Picea omorika 8
Pinus strobus 'Fastigiata' 8
Pinus sylvestris 'Fastigiata' 8
Podocarpus macrophyllus 5–7
Populus alba 'Pyramidalis' 8
Populus balsamifera 8
Populus ×berolinensis 7–8
Populus ×canescens 'Tower' 8
Populus nigra 'Afghanica' 8
Populus nigra 'Italica' 8
Populus simonii 'Fastigiata' 7
Populus tremula 'Erecta' 6–8
Prunus sargentii 'Columnaris' 7–8
Pseudotsuga menziesii 8
Pyrus calleryana cvs. 7 (few)
Quercus robur 'Fastigiata' 7–8
Quercus robur 'Wandell' 7–8
Quercus 'Pyramich' 7–8
Quercus robur × Q. bicolor cvs. 7–8

Quercus robur × Q. macrocarpa cvs. 7–8
Rhamnus frangula 'Columnaris' 6
Taxodium distichum var. nutans 8
Taxus ×media 'Flushing' 6
Taxus ×media 'Grandifolia' 6
Taxus ×media 'Sentinalis' 6
Taxus ×media 'Viridis' 6
Thuja occidentalis 'Douglasii Pyramidalis' 7
Thuja occidentalis 'Pyramidalis' 7
Thuja occidentalis 'Lutea' 7

10. Plants with Pendulous or Umbrella-like Habit

Acer saccharinum cvs. 8
Caragana arborescens 'Pendula' 4–5
Cedrus deodara 'Pendula' 2–6
Cedrus libani 'Pendula' 2–5
Cedrus libani ssp. atlantica 'Glauca Pendula' 2–5
Cercidiphyllum japonicum 'Pendula' 5–6
Chamaecyparis nootkatensis 'Pendula' 6
Corylus avellana 'Pendula' 5
Euonymus bungeanus 'Pendulus' 5
Fagus sylvatica 'Pendula' 7
Forsythia suspensa var. sieboldii 2–4
Genista aetnensis 6
Ginkgo biloba 'Pendula' 7
Ilex vomitoria f. pendula 6
Juniperus rigida 6
Juniperus scopulorum cvs. 6 (part)
Larix decidua 'Pendula' 7
Malus cvs. 5–6:
   'Blanche Ames'
   'Cascole'
   'Louisa'
   'Manbeck Weeper'
   'Molozam'
   'Oekonomierat Echtermeyer'
   'Red Jade'
   'Seafoam'
   'Sinai Fire'
   'Weepcanzam'
Morus alba 'Pendula' 5
Picea abies cvs. 8
Picea breweriana 8
Picea pungens 'Pendula' 5–6
Pinus banksiana 'Uncle Fogey' 4–5
Pinus densiflora 'Umbraculifera' 6
Pinus strobus 'Pendula' 6
Populus simonii 'Pendula' 7
Prunus subhirtella cvs. 6 (part)

Prunus ×yedoense 'Shidare Yoshino' 6
Salix alba 'Tristis' 7
Salix babylonica 7
Salix exigua 6
Salix ×pendulina 7
Salix ×sepulcralis 7
Sophora japonica 'Pendula' 5

11. Plants with Contorted Habit

Corylus avellana 'Contorta' 4
Morus australis 'Unryu' 6
Picea abies 'Inversa' 7
Pinus banksiana 'Uncle Fogey'
Salix matsudana 'Tortuosa'
Salix matsudana 'Snake'
Salix udensis 'Sekka'

12. Plants with Horizontally Layered Branching

Abies homolepis 8
Abies koreana 7
Acer davidii 7
Aesculus parviflora 5
Cornus alternifolia 6
Cornus controversa 7
Cornus florida 6–7
Cornus kousa 6
Corylopsis spp. 4–5
Crataegus apiifolia 6
Crataegus crus-galli 6
Crataegus ×nitida 6
Crataegus phaenopyrum 6
Crataegus ×prunifolia 6
Crataegus punctata 6
Crataegus × 'Vaughn' 6
Crataegus viridis 'Winter King' 7
Euonymus alatus 5
Firmiana simplex 6–7
Ligustrum obtusifolium 'Regelianum' 4
Nyssa sinensis 7
Nyssa sylvatica 8
Prunus laurocerasus 4–6
Sassafras albidum 7–8

13. Cutback Shrubs, Subshrubs, and Herbaceous Perennials

Abelia ×grandiflora 4–5
Adina rubella 4–5

Aegopodium podagraria 2
Ajuga species 2
Amorpha canescens 3
Artemisia spp. 3–4
Baccharis halimifolia 5
Buddleia davidii 4
Caryopteris spp. & hybrids 3–4
Chimaphila umbellata 2
Clerodendrum trichotomum 5–6
Convallaria majalis 2
Coronilla varia 2
Elsholtzia stauntonii 3
Epimedium spp. 2
Hemerocallis spp. & cvs. 3
Hosta spp. & cvs. 2–3
Hydrangea arborescens 3
Hydrangea quercifolia 4–5
Indigofera spp. 3
Lamium spp. 2
Lavandula angustifolia 2
Ledum spp. 2–3
Leiophyllum buxifolium 2
Leycesteria formosa 4
Lotus corniculatus 2
Menispermum canadensis 1 & 2
Paeonia spp. & cvs. 3–4
Phlox spp. 2
Podophyllum peltatum 2
Polygonum aubertii 1
Rosmarinus officinalis 2–4
Securinega suffruticosa 4
Teucrium chamaedrys 2
Trifolium incarnatum 2
Vitex agnus-castus 4–5

14. Facing Shrubs, Branching to the Ground

Abelia ×grandifolia 4–5
Abies koreana 'Prostrate Beauty' 3–4
Aesculus parviflora 5
Aspidistra elatior 3
Aucuba japonica 4
Callicarpa dichotoma 4
Callicarpa japonica 4
Cistus spp. & hybrids 3–5
Comptonia peregrina 2
Cotoneaster adpressus 2
Cotoneaster apiculatus 3
Cotoneaster congestus 3
Cotoneaster dammeri 2

Cotoneaster horizontalis 2
Cotoneaster microphyllus 3
Cycas revoluta 3–4
Chamaecytisus albus 2
Chamaecytisus purpureus 3
Cyrtomium falcatum 3
Cytisus ardoinii 2
Cytisus ×beanii 2
Cytisus decumbens 2
Cytisus ×kewensis 2
Daphne alpina 2
Daphne ×burkwoodii 3
Daphne cneorum 2
Daphne ×mantensiana 3
Daphne napolitana 3
Daphne odora 3–4
Diervilla spp. 3–4
Epimedium spp. 2
Escallonia virgata 3
Escallonia × 'Red Elf' 3
Eurya emarginata 3–4
Fatsia japonica 4–5
Feijoa sellowiana 6
Hylotelephium spp. & hybrids 2–3
Hypericum calycinum 2
Hypericum frondosum 3
Hypericum × 'Hidcote' 2–3
Hypericum ×moserianum 2
Hypericum prolificum 3
Iberis sempervirens 2
Juniperus communis ssp. alpina 2
Juniperus conferta 2
Juniperus sabina cvs. 2–5 (few)
Juniperus scopulorum 'Monam' 3
Kerria japonica 4
Leucothoë fontanesiana 3–4
Leucothoë keiskei 2
Liriope spp. & cvs. 2
Lonicera alpigena 'Nana' 4
Lonicera xylosteum 'Nana' 3
Mahonia spp. 3–5
Rhaphiolepis indica 3–4
Rhododendron cvs. 2–4 (many)
Rhododendron fastigiatum 2
Rhododendron ferrugineum 3
Rhododendron (Glenn Dale Hybrids) 3–4
Rhododendron hirsutum 3
Rhododendron impeditum 3
Rhododendron indicum cvs. 3–4
Rhododendron kiusianum & hybrids 3
Rhododendron (Kurume Hybrids) 3–4

Rhododendron lapponicum 2
Rhododendron nakaharai cvs. 2
Rhododendron polycladum 3
Rhododendron (Robin Hill Hybrids) 3–4
Rhododendron russatum 3
Rhododendron (Satsuki Azaleas) 3
Rhododendron yakushimanum & hybrids 2–4
Rosa spp. & hybrids 2–4 (some)
Santolina spp. 3–4
Sarcococca spp. 3–4
Skimmia japonica 2–3
Spiraea betulifolia 3
Spiraea japonica cvs. 3
Stephanandra incisa 'Crispa' 3
Symphoricarpos spp. 3–4
Syringa meyeri 'Palibin' 3–4
Taxus baccata 'Repandens' 3–4
Taxus cuspidata 'Densa' 3–4
Taxus ×media 'Taunton' 3–4
Taxus ×media 'Wardii' 3–4
Zamia pumilum 3

15. Habit Unusually Graceful or Otherwise Distinctive

Acer griseum 6
Acer palmatum 6
Aesculus parviflora 5
Albizia julibrissin 6
Amelanchier spp. & hybrids 4–7 (some)
Araucaria spp. 8
Argyrocytisus battandieri 6
Asimina triloba 6–7
Bambusa multiplex 5–6
Buddleia alternifolia 5
Cedrus spp. 7–8
Cercidiphyllum japonicum 8
Cinnamomum camphora 7
Cornus alternifolia 6
Cornus florida 6–7
Cornus kousa 6
Cornus controversa 7
Corylopsis spp. 4–5
Cycas revoluta 3–4
Cyrtomium falcatum 3
Cytisus spp. 2–4
Davidia involucrata 6–7
Dirca palustris 4
Enkianthus spp. 4–6
Eucalyptus spp. 6–8
Firmiana simplex 6–7

Hippophae rhamnoides 6
Idesia polycarpa 7
Kolkwitzia amabilis 5
Leitneria floridana 5–6
Mahonia bealei 4
Mahonia lomariifolia 5
Malus hupehensis 6
Malus 'Strawberry Parfait' 6
Metasequoia glyptostroboides 8
Nandina domestica 3–5
Nerium oleander 6
Parkinsonia spp. 6
Parrotia persica 6–7
Phellodendron amurense 7–8
Phyllostachys spp. 6–7
Picea abies cvs. 8
Picea glauca 'Conica' 4–6
Picea orientalis 8
Pinus aristata 4–6
Pinus armandii 8
Pinus densiflora 7–8
Pinus koreana 8
Pinus palustris 8
Pinus parvifolia 8
Pinus strobus 8
Pinus taeda 8
Pinus wallichiana 8
Pseudolarix amabilis 8
Pyracantha spp. & hybrids 3–5
Pyrus calleryana 'Bradford'
Pyrus calleryana 'Chanticleer'
Quercus alba
Quercus coccinea 8
Quercus ellipsoidalis 8
Quercus frainetto 8
Quercus imbricaria 8
Quercus muehlenbergii 8
Quercus palustris 8
Quercus petraea 8
Quercus phellos 7–8
Quercus polymorpha 7–8
Quercus shumardii 8
Quercus virginiana 8
Sabal spp. 3–7
Sasa spp. 3–4
Sequoiadendron giganteum 8
Serenoa spp. 3–4
Shepherdia rotundifolia 4
Taxodium distichum 8
Trochodendron aralioides 5–6
Zamia pumila 3

FUNCTION

16. Small- to Medium-Scale Screens: Shrubs and Vines

Deciduous, Semievergreen, or Herbaceous

Acer tataricum 6
Actinidia spp. 1
Aesculus parviflora 5
Akebia spp. 1
Ampelopsis spp. 1
Aristolochia macrophylla 1
Calycanthus chinensis 5–6
Calycanthus fertilis 5
Campsis spp. 1
Celastrus spp. 1
Chimonanthus praecox 5
Clematis montana 1
Clematis terniflora 1
Clematis vitalba 1
Clerodendrum trichotomum 5–6
Clethra alnifolia 5
Cornus alba 5
Cornus amomum 5
Cornus mas 6
Cornus obliqua 5
Cornus racemosa 5
Cornus sanguinea 5
Cornus stolonifera 5
Corylopsis glabrescens 5
Corylopsis sinensis 5
Cotoneaster spp. & hybrids 5 (part)
Deutzia scabra 5
Elaeagnus multiflora 5
Elaeagnus umbellata 5
Eleutherococcus sieboldianus 5
Enkianthus campanulatus 5–6
Euonymus alatus
Euonymus kiautschovicus
Exochorda spp. 5–6
Fontanesia spp. 5
Forsythia ×intermedia 5
Forsythia suspensa 4–5
Fothergilla major 5
Franklinia alatamaha 6
Hamamelis vernalis 5
Hydrangea petiolaris 1 & 2
Hydrangea quercifolia 4–5
Leucothoë racemosa 5
Ligustrum spp. & hybrids (part)
Lonicera spp. & hybrids 5 (part)

Menispermum canadense 1
Myrica pensylvanica 4–5
Orixa japonica 5
Parthenocissus quinquefolia 1
Philadelphus spp. & hybrids 5–6 (part)
Polygonum aubertii 1
Prinsepia sinensis 5
Prunus tomentosa 5
Pueraria lobata 1
Punica granatum 6
Pyracantha koidzumii & hybrids 5 (part)
Pyrus salicifolia 5–6
Rhamnus davurica 6
Rhododendron vaseyi 5
Rosa multiflora 5
Rosa setigera 5
Sambucus spp. 5–6
Schisandra spp. 1
Shepherdia spp. 5–6 (part)
Sorbaria spp. 5 (part)
Symplocos paniculata 6
Syringa spp. & hybrids 5–6 (part)
Viburnum spp. & hybrids 5–6 (part)
Vitis spp. 1
Wisteria spp. 1

Evergreen

Arctostaphylos manzanita 5
Arundinaria simonii 6
Aucuba japonica 5
Bambusa multiplex 5–6
Berberis 4–5 (evergreen spp.)
Bignonia capreolata 1
Callistemon citrinus 5–6
Camellia sasanqua 6
Chamaecyparis spp. and cvs. 5–6
Clematis armandii 1
Distylium racemosum 5–6
Elaeagnus ×ebbingei 5
Elaeagnus macrophylla 5
Elaeagnus pungens 5
Euonymus japonicus 5
Holboellia coriacea 1
Ilex aquifolium 6
Ilex ×aquipernyi 6
Ilex bioritensis 6
Ilex cassine 6
Ilex ciliospinosa 6
Ilex cornuta 5–6
Ilex glabra 6
Ilex sugerokii 5

Illicium spp. 5–6 (part)
Kadsura japonica 1
Kalmia latifolia 5
Leucothoë populifolia 5
Ligustrum japonicum 5–6
Loropetalum chinense 5
Michelia figo 5
Myrica cerifera 6
Nerium oleander 6
Osmanthus spp. 5–6
Passiflora caerulea 1
Phillyrea decora 5
Photinia spp. 5–6
Pieris forrestii 5
Pinus cembra 6–8
Pittosporum tobira 5
Platycladus orientalis 4–7
Podocarpus macrophyllus 5–7
Prunus caroliniana 6–7
Prunus laurocerasus 4–6
Quercus acuta 7
Quercus glauca 7
Rhododendron arboreum 7
Rhododendron catawbiense 5
Rhododendron decorum 6
Rhododendron fortunei 5
Rhododendron maximum 6
Rhododendron schlippenbachii 5
Rhododendron smirnowii 5
Rhododendron wardii 5
Sciadopitys verticillata 6–7
Stauntonia hexaphylla 1
Taxus spp. and cvs. 5–6
Ternstroemia gymnanthera 6
Thuja spp. and cvs. 5–6
Thujopsis dolobrata 5
Torreya spp. 5–7
Tsuga canadensis cvs. 5–6
Viburnum japonicum 5
Viburnum odoratissimum 5–6
Viburnum rhytidophyllum 5
Viburnum tinus 5

17. Large-Scale Screens and Windbreaks: Large Shrubs and Trees

Deciduous, Semievergreen, or Herbaceous

Acer campestre 7
Alnus spp. 6–7
Caragana arborescens 6
Carpinus betulus 7

Crataegus crus-galli 7
Crataegus laevigata 6
Crataegus ×lavallei 6
Crataegus phaenopyrum 6
Crataegus viridis 7
Elaeagnus angustifolia 6
Euonymus europaeus 6
Euonymus hamiltonianus 6
Euonymus latifolius 6
Euonymus sachalinensis 6
Hamamelis virginiana 6
Ilex decidua 6
Maclura pomifera 7
Metasequoia glyptostroboides 8
Populus spp., hybrids, & cvs. 7–8
Prunus padus 7
Quercus robur 7–8
Salix alba 8
Salix pentandra 7
Syringa reticulata 6–7
Taxodium distichum 8

Evergreen

Abies spp. 7–8
Araucaria spp. 8
Calocedrus decurrens 7
Cedrus libani 8
Chamaecyparis spp. 6–8
Cinnamomum camphora 7
Cryptomeria japonica 8
Cunninghamia lanceolata 8
×Cupressocyparis leylandii 8
Cupressus spp. 7–8
Daphniphyllum macropodum 6
Distylium racemosum 5–6
Eucalyptus spp. 6–7
Feijoa sellowiana 6
Ilex ×altaclrensis 7
Ilex ×attenuata 6
Ilex cornuta 5–6
Ilex integra 6
Ilex ×koehneana 7
Ilex latifolia 6
Ilex opaca 7
Ilex pedunculosa 6
Juniperus chinensis 6–7
Juniperus scopulorum 7
Juniperus virginiana 6–8
Keteleeria spp. 8
Ligustrum lucidum 6
Michelia spp. 5–6 (part)

Phyllostachys spp. 6–7
Picea spp. 7–8
Pinus spp. 7–8 (most)
Platycladus orientalis cvs 4–7 (part)
Prunus caroliniana 6–7
Pseudotsuga spp. 7–8
Quercus ilex 7
Sequoia sempervirens 8
Sequoiadendron giganteum 8
Sycopsis sinensis 6
Thuja spp. 7–8
Tsuga spp. 6–8

18. Street and Avenue Trees

Small Trees

Acer buergerianum 6
Acer mandshuricum 6
Acer tataricum 6
Acer truncatum 6
Cercis canadensis 6–7
Cornus florida 6–7
Cornus mas 6
Crataegus apiifolia 6
Crataegus laevigata 6
Crataegus ×lavallei 6
Crataegus nitida 6
Crataegus phaenopyrum 6
Crataegus ×prunifolia 6
Fraxinus cuspidata 6
Fraxinus mariesii 6
Halesia tetraptera 6–7
Ligustrum japonicum 5–6
Malus tschonoskii 6
Pinus thunbergii 6–7
Prunus caroliniana 6–7
Prunus serrulata 6
Prunus subhirtella 6
Sabal palmetto 6–7
Sophora secundiflora 6–7
Syringa reticulata 6–7
Tilia mongolica 6
Viburnum prunifolium 6
Viburnum rudifulum 6

Medium Trees

Acer campestre 7
Acer maximowicziana 7
Acer mono 7
Carpinus betulus 7
Carpinus caroliniana 7

Carpinus cordata 7
Carpinus japonica 7
Celtis bungeana 7
Cinnamomum camphora 7
Crataegus crus-galli 7
Crataegus viridis 7
Eucommia ulmoides 7
Fraxinus biltmoreana 7
Fraxinus ornus 7
Fraxinus texensis 7
Fraxinus velutina 7
Halesia tetraptera 7
Halesia diptera 7
Koelreuteria spp. 7
Morus spp. 7–8
Ostrya spp. 7–8
Pinus densiflora 7–8
Pinus virginiana 7
Platycarya strobilacea 7
Prunus sargentii 7–8
Pyrus calleryana 7
Quercus mongolica 7–8
Sapindus drummondii 7
Ulmus alata 7
Ulmus crassifolia 7–8
Washingtonia filifera
Zelkova sinica 7

Large Trees

Acer platanoides 8
Acer pseudoplatanus 8
Acer rubrum 8
Acer saccharum 8
Celtis laevigata 8
Celtis occidentalis 8
Cercidiphyllum japonicum 8
Fraxinus americana 8
Fraxinus pennsylvanica 8
Fraxinus quadrangulata 8
Ginkgo biloba 8
Gleditsia triacanthos 8
Halesia monticola 8
Liquidambar spp. 8
Liriodendron spp. 8
Magnolia acuminata 8
Magnolia grandiflora 8
Phellodendron spp. 7–8
Pinus armandii 8
Pinus elliottii 8
Pinus flexilis 8
Pinus koraiensis 8

Pinus nigra 8
Pinus strobus 8
Pinus taeda 8
Pinus wallichiana 8
Platanus spp. 8
Pterocarya spp. 8
Quercus bicolor 8
Quercus cerris 8
Quercus coccinea 8
Quercus ellipsoidalis 8
Quercus falcata 8
Quercus imbricaria 8
Quercus lyrata 8
Quercus macrocarpa 8
Quercus michauxii 8
Quercus muehlenbergii 8
Quercus nigra 8
Quercus nuttallii 8
Quercus pagoda 8
Quercus palustris 8
Quercus phellos 8
Quercus prinus 8
Quercus rubra 8
Quercus shumardii 8
Quercus virginiana 8
Sophora japonica 8
Tilia spp. 8
Ulmus americana 8
Ulmus carpinifolia 8
Ulmus procera 8
Washingtonia robusta 8
Zelkova carpinifolia 8
Zelkova serrata 8

ADAPTATION

19. Plants for Cold Climates

Adapted to Hardiness Zone 3b or Colder

Abies balsamea 8
Abies veitchii 8
Acer tatarica ssp. ginnala 6
Acer negundo 7
Acer rubrum 8
Acer saccharinum 8
Acer spicatum 6
Aegopodium podagraria 2
Aesculus glabra 7
Ajuga spp. 2
Alnus incana 6–7

Alnus rugosa 6
Amelanchier arborea 6–7
Amelanchier laevis
Amelanchier ×grandiflora
Amorpha spp. 3–6
Ampelopsis spp. 1
Andromeda polifolia 2
Arctostaphylos uva-ursi 2
Aronia melanocarpa 3–4
Artemisia abrotanum 4
Atriplex canescens 4
Betula alleghaniensis 7–8
Betula papyrifera 8
Betula pendula 7–8
Caragana spp. 3–6
Carpinus caroliniana 7
Caryopteris mongholica 3
Cassiope tetragona 2
Ceanothus americanus 3
Celastrus scandens 1 & 2
Celtis occidentalis 8
Chamaedaphne calyculata 3–4
Chimaphila umbellata 2
Clematis macropetala 1
Clematis occidentalis 1
Clematis tangutica 1
Clematis virginiana 1
Convallaria majalis 2
Cornus alba 5
Cornus canadensis 2
Cornus obliqua 5
Cornus racemosa 5
Cornus rugosa 5
Cornus stolonifera 5
Coronilla varia 2
Corylus americana 5
Corylus cornuta 5
Cotoneaster acutifolius 5
Cotoneaster lucidus 5
Cotoneaster racemiflorus 5
Crataegus mollis 6
Crataegus ×mordenensis 6
Crataegus pinnatifida 6
Crataegus ×prunifolia 6
Crataegus punctata 6
Daphne giraldii 3
Daphne mezereum 3
Diervilla lonicera 3
Elaeagnus angustifolia 6
Elaeagnus commutata 5
Empetrum spp. 2

Epigaea repens 2
Epimedium spp. 2
Euonymus atropurpureus 6
Euonymus nanus 3
Fragaria virginiana 2
Fraxinus americana 8
Fraxinus mandshurica 8
Fraxinus nigra 8
Fraxinus pennsylvanica 8
Gaultheria procumbens 2
Genista sagittalis 3
Genista tinctoria 3
Halimodendron halodendron 4
Hemerocallis spp. 3
Hippophaë rhamnoides 6
Hosta spp. 2–3
Juniperus communis cvs. 2–6
Juniperus horizontalis cvs. 2
Juniperus sabina cvs. 2–5
Juniperus scopulorum cvs. 7
Juniperus virginiana cvs. 5–8
Kalmia angustifolia 3
Kalmia polifolia 3
Larix laricina 8
Ledum spp. 2–3
Loiseleuria procumbens 2
Lonicera albertii 3
Lonicera caerulea 4
Lonicera maackii 6
Lonicera tatarica 5
Lonicera ×xylosteoides 5
Lonicera xylosteum 5
Lotus corniculatus 2
Malus ×adstringens 7
Malus baccata 7
Malus pumila 7
Malus ×purpurea 6
Malus ×robusta 6
Microbiota decussata 2
Myrica gale 4
Ostrya virginiana 7–8
Paeonia lactiflora cvs. 3
Parthenocissus inserta 1 & 2
Parthenocissus quinquefolia 1 & 2
Philadelphus lewisii 4–5
Philadelphus schrenkii 5
Phlox subulata 2
Physocarpus opulifolius 4–5
Picea abies 3–8
Picea engelmanii 8
Picea glauca 8

Picea mariana 7–8
Picea pungens 8
Picea rubens 8
Pinus banksiana 8
Pinus cembra 6–8
Pinus mugo 4–8
Pinus resinosa 8
Pinus sibirica 8
Pinus strobus 8
Pinus sylvestris 7–8
Populus angustifolia 7
Populus balsamifera 8 & hybrids
Populus ×berolinensis 7–8
Populus ×canadensis 8
Populus deltoides 8
Populus nigra 8
Populus tremula 6–8
Populus tremuloides 6–8
Populus trichocarpa 8
Potentilla davurica 3
Potentilla ×friedrichsenii 3
Potentilla fruticosa 3–4
Potentilla grandiflora 3
Potentilla parviflora 3
Potentilla tridentata 2
Prinsepia sinensis 5
Prunus besseyi 3
Prunus ×cistena 5
Prunus japonica 4
Prunus maackii 7
Prunus mandshurica 5–6
Prunus nigra 5–6
Prunus padus 7
Prunus pensylvanica 7
Prunus pumila 4
Prunus serotina 8
Prunus tenella 4
Prunus tomentosa 5
Prunus virginiana 6
Pyrus ussuriensis 7
Quercus bicolor 8
Quercus ellipsoidalis 8
Quercus macrocarpa 8
Quercus mongolica 7–8
Quercus rubra 8
Rhamnus cathartica 6
Rhamnus davurica 6
Rhamnus pallasii 4
Rhododendron canadense 6
Rhododendron lapponicum 2
Rhododendron prinophyllum 5

Rhus aromatica 4–5
Rhus glabra 6
Rhus trilobata 4–5
Rhus typhina 6
Ribes spp. 4–5
Rosa acicularis 3
Rosa arkansana 3
Rosa blanda 4
Rosa foetida 5
Rosa glauca 4–5
Rosa rugosa 4
Salix alba 8
Salix arenaria 2–3
Salix caprea 5–6
Salix discolor 6
Salix exigua 6
Salix fragilis 7
Salix nigra 7
Salix pentandra 7
Salix purpurea 5
Sambucus racemosa 5
Securinega suffruticosa 4
Sempervivum tectorum 2
Shepherdia spp. 5–6
Sorbaria sorbifolia 4
Sorbus americana 7
Sorbus ×arnoldiana 7
Sorbus aucuparia 7
Sorbus decora 7
Sorbus discolor 7
Sorbus ×hybrida 7
Sorbus scopulina 6
Sorbus ×thuringiaca 7
Sorbus tianshanica 6
Spiraea alba 4
Spiraea ×arguta 4
Spiraea betulifolia 3
Spiraea douglasii 5
Spiraea latifolia 4
Spiraea menziesii 4
Spiraea tomentosa 3
Spiraea trilobata 4
Spiraea ×vanhouttei 4
Staphylea trifolia 6
Symphoricarpos albus 3
Symphoricarpos orbiculatus 3
Syringa ×henryi 5
Syringa ×hyacinthiflora 6
Syringa ×josiflexa 5
Syringa josikaea 5
Syringa meyeri 4

Syringa microphylla 4
Syringa patula 5
Syringa ×prestoniae 5
Syringa pubescens 4
Syringa reticulata 6–7
Syringa villosa 5
Syringa vulgaris 6
Taxus canadensis 3–4
Thuja occidentalis 3–7
Tilia americana 8
Tilia cordata 8
Tilia ×europaea 8
Tilia ×flavescens 8
Tilia mongolica 6–7
Tilia platyphyllos 8
Ulmus americana 8
Ulmus pumila 7–8
Vaccinium angustifolium 2–3
Vaccinium macrocarpon 2
Vaccinium oxycoccus 2
Vaccinium vitis-idaea 2
Viburnum acerifolium 4
Viburnum burejaeticum 5
Viburnum cassinoides 4
Viburnum edule 2–4
Viburnum lantana 6
Viburnum lantanoides 5
Viburnum lentago 6
Viburnum opulus 5
Viburnum prunifolium 6
Viburnum rafinesquianum 4
Viburnum trilobum 5
Viola sororia 2
Vitis riparia 1

Adapted to Hardiness Zone 4b, but Not Zone 3b

Abeliophyllum distichum 4
Abies concolor 8
Abies koreana 7
Acer mandshuricum 6
Acer pensylvanicum 7
Acer platanoides 8
Acer pseudo-sieboldianum 6
Acer tataricum 6
Acer truncatum 6
Actinidia arguta 1
Actinidia kolomikta 1
Actinidia polygama 1
Aesculus hippocastanum 8
Akebia spp. 1 & 2

Alnus glutinosa 7
Amelanchier alnifolia 4–5
Amelanchier canadensis 5–6
Amelanchier laevis 6
Amelanchier ×lamarckii 6
Amelanchier spicata 3–4
Amelanchier stolonifera 4
Aralia elata 6–7
Aristolochia macrophylla 1
Aronia arbutifolia 5
Aronia prunifolia 5
Asarum canadense 2
Baccharis halimifolia 5
Berberis thunbergii 4
Berberis vulgaris 5
Betula lenta 7–8
Betula nigra 8
Betula populifolia 6–7
Buddleia alternifolia 5
Calycanthus spp. 4–5
Campsis radicans 1
Carya cordiformis 8
Caryopteris ×clandonensis 3
Catalpa spp. 7–8
Ceanothus ovatus 3
Cephalanthus occidentalis 5
Chaenomeles japonica 3
Chaenomeles speciosa 4
Cladrastis lutea 7
Clematis apiifolia 1
Clematis ×jackmanii 1
Clematis ×jouiniana 1
Clematis terniflora 1
Clematis texensis 1
Clematis vitalba 1
Clethra alnifolia 5
Comptonia peregrina 2
Cornus alternifolia 6
Cornus amomum 5
Cornus drummondii 5–6
Cornus sanguinea 5
Corylus avellana 5
Cotoneaster multiflorus 5
Crataegus crus-galli 6
Crataegus ×lavallei 6
Crataegus ×nitida 6
Crataegus phaenopyrum 6
Crataegus succulenta 6
Daphne ×burkwoodii 3
Daphe cneorum 2
Deutzia parviflora 4

Diervilla rivularis 4
Diervilla sessilifolia 4
Dirca palustris 4
Eleutherococcus sieboldianus 5
Euonymus alatus 5
Euonymus bungeanus 6
Euonymus europaeus 6
Euonymus hamiltonianus 6
Euonymus obovatus 2
Fagus grandifolia 8
Fontanesia fortunei 5
Fraxinus excelsior 8
Fraxinus holotricha 7
Fraxinus quadrangulata 8
Gaultheria hispidula 2
Gleditsia triacanthos 8
Gymnocladus dioicus 8
Hamamelis virginiana 6
Hydrangea arborescens 3
Hydrangea paniculata 6
Hypericum kalmianum 3
Hypericum prolificum 3
Ilex laevigata 5
Ilex rugosa 3
Ilex verticillata 5
Juglans cinerea 8
Juniperus spp. & cvs. 2–8 (part)
Kerria japonica 4
Larix decidua 8
Larix kaempferi 8
Ligustrum amurense 5
Ligustrum obtusifolium 4–5
Ligustrum vulgare 4–6
Lonicera ×amoena 5
Lonicera ×bella 5
Lonicera ×brownii 1 & 2
Lonicera ×heckrottii 1 & 2
Lonicera hirsuta 1 & 2
Lonicera sempervirens 1 & 2
Maackia amurensis 7
Magnolia acuminata 8
Magnolia tripetala 7
Malus ×arnoldiana 6
Malus floribunda 6
Malus hupehensis 6
Malus ioensis 6
Malus ×magdeburgensis 6
Malus ×micromalus 6
Malus ×prunifolia 6
Malus sargentii 5
Malus sieboldii 6

Malus toringoides 6
Malus tschonoskii 6
Mitchella repens 2
Morus spp. 7–8
Myrica pensylvanica 4–5
Nemopanthus mucronatus 5
Parthenocissus tricuspidata 1
Paxistima canbyi 2
Phellodendron spp. 7–8
Philadelphus coronarius 5
Philadelphus ×lemoinei 4 (most)
Philadelphus ×virginalis 4–5 (most)
Phlox divaricata 2
Picea omorika 8
Pinus albicaulis 6
Pinus aristata 4–6
Pinus flexilis 8
Pinus koraiensis 8
Pinus nigra 8
Pinus pumila 4–5
Pinus rigida 7–8
Podophyllum peltatum 2
Polygonum spp. 1 & 3–5
Populus alba 8
Populus grandidentata 6–7
Populus maximowiczii 8
Potentilla cinerea 2
Potentilla crantzii 2
Prinsepia uniflora 4
Prunus americana 5
Prunus cerasifera 6
Prunus fruticosa 4
Prunus glandulosa 4
Prunus maritima 4
Prunus triloba 5–6
Ptelea trifoliata 6
Quercus alba 8
Quercus gambelii 5–6
Quercus velutina 8
Rhamnus frangula 6
Rhododendron catawbiense 5
Rhododendron japonicum 4
Rhododendron maximum 6
Rhododendron micranthum 4
Rhododendron viscosum 5
Rhus copallina 5–6
Robinia ×ambigua 7
Robinia hispida 4
Robinia ×margarettiae 5–6
Robinia pseudoacacia 8
Robinia viscosa 5

Rosa canina 5
Rosa ×harisonii 4
Rosa xanthina f. hugonis 5
Rosa nitida 3
Rosa palustris 4
Rosa primula 4
Rosa setigera 5
Rosa villosa 4
Rubus deliciosus 5
Rubus hispidus 2
Rubus odoratus 5
Salix repens 2–3
Salix rosmarinifolia 4
Salix ×sepulcralis 8
Sambucus canadensis 5
Sambucus nigra 6
Sambucus pubens 5
Sedum spp. 2
Sorbus alnifolia 8
Spiraea albiflora 4
Spiraea ×billiardii 4
Spiraea ×cinerea 4
Spiraea henryi 5
Spiraea nipponica 5
Spiraea thunbergii 4
Symphoricarpos rivularis 4
Syringa ×chinensis 6
Syringa oblata 5
Syringa pekinensis 6
Syringa ×persica 4
Syringa reflexa 5
Syringa ×swegiflexa 5
Taxus cuspidata 4–6
Taxus ×hunnewelliana 5
Thuja plicata 7–8
Tilia dasystyla 8
Tilia ×euchlora 8
Tsuga canadensis 3–8
Ulmus glabra 8
Ulmus rubra 8
Ulmus thomasii 8
Vaccinium corymbosum 5
Viburnum bitchiuense 5
Viburnum ×carlcephalum 5
Viburnum carlesii 4
Viburnum dentatum 6
Viburnum ×juddii 5
Viburnum lantana 6
Viburnum sargentii 5
Vinca minor 2
Waldsteinia spp. 2

Weigela florida 5
Weigela middendorffiana 4
Weigela praecox 4
Yucca glauca 3
Zanthoxylum americanum 6

20. Plants for Warm Climates

Adapted to Hardiness Zone 9a or Warmer

Abelia ×grandiflora 4–5
Abies firma 8
Acer barbatum 7
Acer davidii 7
Acer palmatum 6
Acer rubrum 8
Acer saccharinum 8
Actinidia deliciosa 1
Adina rubella 5
Aegopodium podagraria 2
Aeculus californica 6
Aesculus parviflora 5
Aesculus pavia 6
Aesculus splendens 5
Agave americana 4
Ailanthus altissima 7–8
Ajuga spp. 2
Akebia spp. 1 & 2
Albizia julibrissin 6
Aleurites fordii 6
Alnus rugosa 6
Amorpha spp. 3–6
Ampelopsis spp. 1
Antigonon leptopus 1
Aralia spp. 6–7
Araucaria spp. 8
Arctostaphylos manzanita 5
Ardisia spp. 2–4
Argyrocytisus battandieri 6
Aronia arbutifolia 5
Aronia prunifolia 5
Artemisia schmidtiana 2
Aspidistra elatior 3
Aucuba japonica 5
Baccharis halimifolia 5
Bambusa multiplex 5–6
Berberis candidula 3
Berberis darwinii 4–5
Berberis gagnepainii 4
Berberis julianae 4
Berberis ×mentorensis 4
Berberis ×stenophylla 4

Berberis thunbergii 4
Berberis verruculosa 3
Berberis vulgaris 5
Betula nigra 8
Bignonia capreolata 1
Brahea armata 6–7
Broussonetia papyrifera 7
Bumelia lanuginosa 6
Butia capitata 6
Buxus spp. 3–4
Callicarpa americana 4
Callistemon spp. 2–6
Calocedrus decurrens 7
Calycanthus spp. 4–6
Camellia spp. 6
Campsis spp. 1
Carpenteria californica 4
Carya glabra 8
Carya illinoinensis 8
Carya tomentosa 8
Caryopteris incana 4
Cassia corymbosa 5
Castanea pumila 6
Catalpa spp. 7–8
Ceanothus spp. & hybrids 4–5 (evergreen)
Cedrus spp. 7
Celtis bungeana 7
Celtis laevigata 8
Cephalanthus occidentalis 5
Cephalotaxus spp. 4–5
Ceratiola ericoides 4
Cercidiphyllum japonicum 8
Cercis spp. 6–7
Chaenomeles spp. 3–4
Chamaecyparis thyoides 5–7
Chamaecytisus spp. 2–3
Chamaerops humilis 5–6
Chilopsis linearis 6
Chimonanthus praecox 5
Chionanthus spp. 6
×Chitalpa tashkentensis 6
Choisya ternata 5
Cinnamomum camphora 7
Cistus spp. 3–5
Clematis apiifolia 1
Clematis armandii 1
Clematis delavayi 1
Clematis flammula 1
Clematis ×jouiniana 1
Clematis terniflora 1
Clematis vitalba 1

Clethra spp. 5–6
Cleyera japonica 5
Cliftonia monophylla 5
Clytostoma callistegioides 1
Cocculus carolinus 1
Cornus amomum 5
Cornus florida 6–7 (few cvs.)
Cornus stricta 5
Coronilla varia 2
Corylopsis spp. 4–5
Cotoneaster congestus 3
Cotoneaster dammeri 2
Cotoneaster henryanus 5
Cotoneaster lacteus 5
Cotoneaster microphyllus 3
Cotoneaster salicifolius 5
Cotoneaster ×watereri 6
Crataegus aestivalis 6
Crataegus apiifolia 6
Crataegus brachyacantha 7
Crataegus ovata 6
Crataegus viridis 7
Cryptomeria japonica 8
Cudrania tricuspidata 6
Cunninghamia lanceolata 8
×Cupressocyparis leylandii 8
Cupressus spp. 7–8
Cycas revoluta 3–4
Cyrilla racemiflora 6
Cyrtomium falcatum 3
Cytisus spp. 2–4
Daphne genkwa 3
Daphne sericea 3
Daphniphyllum spp. 4 & 6
Decaisnea fargesii 5
Decumaria barbara 1 & 2
Diospyros spp. 7
Dipelta floribunda 6
Dipteronia sinensis 6
Disanthus cercidifolius 5
Distylium racemosum 5–6
Duchesnea indica 2
Edgeworthia papyrifera 4
Elaeagnus ×ebbingei 5
Elaeagnus macrophylla 5
Elaeagnus multiflora 5
Elaeagnus pungens 5
Elaeagnus umbellata 5
Elliottia racemosa 5–6
Emmenopteris henryi 6–7
Erica spp. 2–3

Eriobotrya spp. 6
Escallonia spp. 3–6
Eucalyptus spp. 6–7
Euonymus americanus 5
Euonymus japonicus 5
Euonymus kiautschovicus 5
Euptelea polyandra 7
Eurya spp. 3–5
Exochorda spp. 5–6
Fagus spp. 8
×Fatshedera lizei 4
Fatsia japonica 4–5
Feijoa sellowiana 6
Ficus carica 5–6
Ficus pumila 1
Firmiana simplex 6–7
Fontanesia phillyreoides 5
Fothergilla spp. 3–5
Fraxinus americana 8
Fraxinus biltmoreana 7
Fraxinus caroliniana 7
Fraxinus cuspidata 6
Fraxinus mariesii 6
Fraxinus pennsylvanica 8
Fraxinus profunda 8
Fraxinus texensis 7
Fraxinus velutina 7
Fuchsia magellanica 3–4
Galium odoratum 2
Gardenia augusta 4
Gaultheria mucronata 3
Gelsemium sempervirens 1 & 2
Genista aetnensis 5–6
Genista cinerea 3–4
Genista hispanica 2
Genista lydia 2
Gleditsia triacanthos 8
Gordonia lasianthus 7
Halesia diptera 6–7
Halesia tetraptera 6–7
Hamamelis ×intermedia 6
Hamamelis japonica 6
Hamamelis mollis 6
Hamamelis vernalis 5
Hamamelis virginiana 6
Hedera canariensis 1 & 2
Hedera colchica 1 & 2
Hedera helix 1 & 2
Helianthemum nummularium 2
Hemerocallis spp. & cvs. 3
Heptacodium miconioides 5

Hibiscus rosa-sinensis 6
Hibiscus syriacus 5
Holboellia coriacea 1
Hosta spp. 2–3
Hydrangea arborescens 3
Hydrangea macrophylla 3
Hydrangea quercifolia 4–5
Hypericum spp. 2–4 (part)
Iberis gibraltarica 3
Iberis pruitii 2
Iberis saxatilis 2
Idesia polycarpa 7
Ilex spp. 3–6
Illicium spp. 4–6
Indigofera divaricata 3
Itea spp. 4–5
Jasminum spp. 1 & 2–5
Juglans nigra 8
Juniperus chinensis 2–7
Juniperus conferta 2
Juniperus horizontalis 2
Juniperus ×media 2–5
Juniperus procumbens 2–3
Juniperus sargentii 2–3
Juniperus virginiana 5–8
Kadsura japonica 1
Kalmia spp. 2–5 (part)
Kalmiopsis leachiana 2
Kerria japonica 4
Keteleeria spp. 8
Koelreuteria spp. 7
Lagerstroemia spp. & cvs 3–6
Lamium galeobdolon 2
Laurus nobilis 6
Leitneria floridana 5–6
Leptodermis oblonga 3
Lespedeza cuneata 3
Leucophyllum spp. 3–5
Leucothoë spp. 2–5
Leycesteria formosa 4
Ligustrum japonicum 5–6
Ligustrum lucidum 6
Ligustrum ovalifolium 5
Ligustrum quihoui 5
Ligustrum sinense 5
Lindera spp. 4–6
Liquidambar spp. 8
Liriodendron spp. 8
Liriope spp. 2
Lonicera ×brownii 1 & 2
Lonicera etrusca 1 & 2

Lonicera flava 1 & 2
Lonicera fragrantissima 5
Lonicera henryi 1 & 2
Lonicera ×heckrottii 1 & 2
Lonicera hildebrandiana 1 & 2
Lonicera hirsuta 1 & 2
Lonicera japonica 1 & 2
Lonicera nitida 4
Lonicera periclymenum 1 & 2
Lonicera pileata 3
Lonicera ×purpusii 5
Lonicera sempervirens 1 & 2
Lonicera standishii 4
Lonicera ×tellmanniana 1 & 2
Lonicera tragophylla 1 & 2
Loropetalum chinense 5
Lotus corniculatus 2
Lycium barbarum 5
Lyonia spp. 4–6
Macfadyena unguis-cati 1
Maclura pomifera 7
Magnolia spp. & hybrids 5–8 (most)
×Mahoberberis spp. 3–4
Mahonia spp. 2–5
Malus angustifolia 6
Malus cvs. 5–7 (few)
Melia azedarach 6
Menispermum canadense 1 & 2
Metasequoia glyptostroboides 8
Michelia spp. 5–7
Mitchella repens 2
Morus spp. 7–8
Myrica cerifera 6
Myrica pensylvanica 4–5
Myrtus communis 4–5
Nandina domestica 3–5
Nepeta mussinii 2
Nerium oleander 6
Nyssa spp. 7–8
Ophiopogon japonicus 2
Orixa japonica 5
Osmanthus spp. 4–6
Ostrya spp. 7–8
Oxydendrum arboreum 7–8
Paliurus spina-christi 6
Parkinsonia spp. 6
Parrotia persica 6–7
Parrotiopsis jacquemontiana 6
Parthenocissus henryana 1 & 2
Parthenocissus inserta 1 & 2
Parthenocissus quinquefolia 1 & 2

Passiflora spp. 1 & 2
Paulownia tomentosa 7
Persea spp. 6–7
Philadelphus inodorus 5
Phoenix canariensis 7
Photinia ×fraseri 6
Photinia glabra 5
Photinia serratifolia 6
Phyllostachys spp. 6–7
Picrasma ailanthifolia 6
Pieris forrestii 5
Pieris japonica 4–5
Pieris phillyreifolia 1 & 3
Pileostegia viburnoides 1 & 2
Pinckneya pubens 6
Pinus armandii 8
Pinus brutia 8
Pinus bungeana 6–7
Pinus echinata 8
Pinus elliottii 8
Pinus glabra 8
Pinus halepensis 7
Pinus palustris 8
Pinus parviflora 7–8
Pinus peuce 7
Pinus pinaster 7–8
Pinus taeda 8
Pinus thunbergii 6–7
Pinus virginiana 7
Pinus wallichiana 8
Pistacia chinensis 8
Pittosporum tobira 5
Platanus spp. 8
Pleioblastus spp. 2–6
Podocarpus macrophyllus 5–7
Podophyllum peltatum 2
Polygonum cuspidatum 3–5
Poncirus trifoliata 6
Populus alba 8
Populus ×berolinensis 7–8
Populus ×canadensis 8
Populus deltoides 8
Populus nigra 8
Prunus angustifolia 5
Prunus armeniaca 7
Prunus ×blireiana 6
Prunus campanulata 6
Prunus caroliana 6–7
Prunus cerasifera 6
Prunus dulcis 6
Prunus glandulosa 4

Prunus incisa 5–6
Prunus laurocerasus 4–6
Prunus lusitanica 5–6
Prunus mexicana 6
Prunus mume 6–7
Prunus persica 6
Prunus salicina 6–7
Prunus sargentii 7–8
Prunus serotina 8
Prunus triloba 5–6
Prunus yedoensis 6
Pseudocydonia sinensis 6
Ptelea spp. 6
Pterocarya spp. 8
Pteroceltis tatarinowii 7
Pterostyrax spp. 6–7
Pueraria lobata 1 & 3
Punica granatum 6
Pyracantha spp. 3–6
Pyrus calleryana 7
Quercus spp. 4–8 (most)
Rhamnus caroliniana 6
Rhaphiolepis spp. 3–4
Rhapidophyllum hystrix 3
Rhododendron spp. & hybrids 2–7 (many)
Rhus spp. 4–6 (most)
Robinia spp. 4 & 7–8
Rohdea japonica 3
Rosa ×alba 4
Rosa banksiae 1
Rosa bracteata 1 & 5
Rosa canina 5
Rosa ×centifolia 4
Rosa chinensis 3
Rosa ×damascena 4
Rosa gallica 3
Rosa laevigata 1 & 5
Rosa moschata 3
Rosa multiflora 5
Rosa odorata 3
Rosa roxburghii 5
Rosa rubiginosa 4
Rosa setigera 5
Rosa villosa 4
Rosa wichuraiana 1 & 2
Rosmarinus officinalis 2–4
Ruscus spp. 2–3
Sabal minor 3–4
Sabal palmetto 6–7
Salix spp. 2–8 (most)

Sambucus canadensis 5
Sambucus nigra 6
Santolina spp. 3
Sapindus drummondii 7
Sapium sebiferum 7
Sarcococca spp. 3–4
Sasa veitchii 3
Sassafras albidum 7–8
Saxifraga stolonifera 2
Schisandra spp. 1
Schizophragma integrifolium 1 & 2
Sedum spp. 2
Sempervivum tectorum 2
Senna corymbosa 5
Sequoia sempervirens 8
Sequoiadendron giganteum 8
Serenoa repens 3–4
Sesbania punicea 5
Skimmia japonica 2–3
Smilax spp. 1
Sophora spp. 5–8
Spartium junceum 5
Spiraea alba 4
Spiraea albiflora 3
Spiraea ×billiardii 4
Spiraea bullata 3
Spiraea cantoniensis 5
Spiraea japonica 3
Spiraea latifolia 4
Spiraea prunifolia 5
Spiraea thunbergii 4
Spiraea veitchii 5
Spiraea wilsonii 5
Stachyurus spp. 5
Stauntonia hexaphylla 1
Stewartia malacodendron 6
Styrax americanum 5
Styrax grandifolium 6
Sycopsis sinensis 6
Symplocos tinctoria 6
Syringa laciniata 4
Taiwania cryptomerioides 8
Tamarix spp. 4–5
Taxodium distichum 8
Taxus floridana 5
Ternstroemia gymnanthera 6
Tetracentron chinense 7
Tetrapanax papyrifer 5
Teucrium chamaedrys 2
Thujopsis dolobrata 5

Tilia heterophylla 8
Tilia petiolaris 8
Tilia tomentosa 8
Torreya spp. 5–7
Trachelospermum spp. 1 & 2
Trachycarpus fortunei 6
Trifolium incarnatum 3
Tripetaleia paniculata 4
Trochodendron aralioides 5–6
Ulmus spp. 7–8 (most)
Umbellularia californica 7–8
Vaccinium arboreum 6
Vaccinium ashei 4–6
Vaccinium corymbosum 5
Viburnum ×bodnantense 5
Viburnum ×burkwoodii 5
Viburnum davidii 3
Viburnum dentatum 6
Viburnum grandiflorum 5
Viburnum japonicum 5
Viburnum molle 5
Viburnum nudum 5
Viburnum odoratissimum 5–6
Viburnum ×pragense 5
Viburnum propinquum 4
Viburnum prunifolium 6
Viburnum rufidulum 6
Viburnum suspensum 4
Viburnum tinus 5
Viburnum utile 4
Vinca major 2
Viola odorata 2
Vitex spp. 4–6
Vitis coignetiae 1
Vitis rotundifolia 1
Washingtonia filifera 7
Washingtonia robusta 8
Weigela floribunda 5
Weigela florida 5
Weigela praecox 4
Wisteria spp. 1
Xanthoceras sorbifolium 6
Xanthorhiza simplicissima 2
Yucca spp. 3–5 (most)
Zamia pumila 3
Zanthoxylum spp. 6
Zelkova spp. 7–8
Zenobia pulverulenta 4
Ziziphus jujuba 6

Adapted to Hardiness Zone 8a, but Not Zone 9a

Abies cephalonica 8
Abies pinsapo 8
Acer buergerianum 6
Acer campestre 7
Acer circinatum 6
Acer diabolicum 6
Acer japonicum 6
Acer negundo 7
Acer rufinerve 7
Actinidia arguta 1
Actinidia kolomikta 1
Actinidia polygama 1
Aesculus ×carnea 8
Aesculus flava 8
Aesculus glabra 7
Aesculus hippocastanum 8
Alnus glutinosa 7
Amelanchier alnifolia 4–5
Amelanchier arborea 6–7
Amelanchier ×grandiflora 6
Amelanchier laevis 6
Amelanchier spicata 3–4
Amelanchier stolonifera 4
Artemisia spp. 3–5
Asarum spp. 2
Asimina triloba 6–7
Berberis buxifolia 5
Berberis gilgiana 4
Berberis koreana 4
Betula albo-sinensis 8
Callicarpa dichotoma 4
Callicarpa japonica 4
Carpinus cordata 7
Carpinus japonica 7
Carya cordiformis 8
Carya laciniosa 8
Carya ovata 8
Caryopteris ×clandonensis 3
Celastrus spp. 1 & 2
Celtis occidentalis 8
Chamaecyparis lawsoniana 3–7
Chamaecyparis obtusa 3–7
Chamaecyparis pisifera 3–8
Cladrastis lutea 7
Clematis alpina 1
Clematis drummondii 1

Clematis florida 1
Clematis lanuginosa 1
Clematis ×lawsoniana 1
Clematis montana 1
Clematis patens 1
Clematis texensis 1
Clematis viorna 1
Clerodendrum spp. 4–6
Comptonia peregrina 2
Conradina verticillata 2
Cornus alba 5
Cornus controversa 7
Cornus coreana 7–8
Cornus drummondii 5–6
Cornus hessei 3
Cornus mas 6
Cornus obliqua 5
Cornus officinalis 6
Cornus sanguinea 5
Cornus stolonifera 5
Corylus americana 5
Corylus avellana 5
Corylus colurna 7–8
Corylus cornuta 5
Corylus maxima 6
Cotoneaster adpressus 2
Cotoneaster apiculatus 3
Cotoneaster dielsianus 4
Cotoneaster franchetii 5
Cotoneaster horizontalis 3
Crataegus ×nitida 6
Crataegus phaenopyrum 6
Croton alabamense 5
Daphne ×mantensiana 3
Daphne odora 3–4
Davidia involucrata 6–7
Deutzia spp. 3–5
Diervilla rivularis 4
Diervilla sessilifolia 4
Dirca palustris 4
Enkianthus spp. 4–6
Epigaea repens 2
Erica cinerea 2
Erica ×darleyensis 2
Erica erigena 3
Eucommia ulmoides 7
Euonymus alatus 5
Fontanesia phillyreifolia ssp. fortunei 5
Forsythia ×intermedia 5
Forsythia suspensa 4–5
Forsythia viridissima 5

Fragaria ×ananassa 2
Fraxinus bungeana 6
Fraxinus excelsior 8
Fraxinus holotricha 7
Fraxinus ornus 7
Fraxinus quadrangulata 8
Galax urceolata 2
Genista pilosa 2
Genista sagittalis 3
Genista tinctoria 3
Ginkgo biloba 8
Halesia monticola 8
Hemiptelea davidii 6
Holodiscus discolor 6
Hydrangea paniculata 6
Hydrangea petiolaris 1 & 2
Hypericum buckleyi 2
Hypericum kalmianum 3
Hypericum prolificum 3
Indigofera decora 3
Juglans ailanthifolia 7
Juniperus communis 2–6
Juniperus rigida 6
Juniperus sabina 2–5
Juniperus squamata 2–5
Kalmia spp. 2–5 (part)
Kalopanax septemlobus 8
Kolkwitzia amabilis 5
Lavandula angustifolia 3
Leiophyllum buxifolium 2
Lespedeza cyrtobotrya 5
Lespedeza japonica 5
Lespedeza thunbergii 5
Ligustrum amurense 5
Ligustrum ×ibolium 5
Ligustrum obtusifolium 4–5
Ligustrum ×vicaryi 5
Ligustrum vulgare 4–6
Lonicera albertii 3
Lonicera alpigena 5
Lonicera ×amoena 5
Lonicera ×bella 5
Lonicera korolkowii 5
Lonicera maackii 6
Lonicera syringantha 5
Lonicera tatarica 5
Lonicera ×xylosteoides 5
Lonicera xylosteum 5
Magnolia acuminata 8
Magnolia ×brooklynensis 7
Malus cvs. 5–7 (part)

Malus floribunda 6
Malus halliana 5
Malus hupehensis 6
Malus sargentii 5
Malus ×scheideckeri 6
Malus sieboldii 6
Malus spectabilis 6
Malus toringoides 6
Malus tschonoskii 6
Microbiota decussata 2–3
Myrica gale 4
Neillia sinensis 4
Neviusia alabamensis 4
Orixa japonica 5
Parthenocissus tricuspidata 1
Paxistima myrsinites 3
Periploca graeca 1
Perovskia atriplicifolia 3–4
Philadelphus purpurascens 5–6
Philadelphus ×splendens 5
Philadelphus ×virginalis 4–5
Phlox spp. 2
Photinia villosa 6
Picea asperata 8
Picea omorika 8
Picea orientalis 8
Pieris floribunda 4
Pinus contorta 6–8
Pinus edulis 7
Pinus heldreichii 8 and var. leucoderme 8
Pinus jeffreyi 8
Pinus lambertiana 8
Pinus nigra 8
Pinus ponderosa 8
Pinus sylvestris 7–8
Platycarya strobilacea 7
Platycladus orientalis 4–7
Polygonum aubertii 1
Potentilla davurica 3
Potentilla ×friedrichsenii 3
Potentilla fruticosa 3–4
Potentilla grandiflora 3
Potentilla parviflora 3
Potentilla tridentata 2
Prunus avium 6–8
Prunus cerasus 6–7
Prunus ×cistena 5
Prunus domestica 6–7
Prunus × 'Hally Jolivette' 5–6
Prunus nipponica 6
Prunus serrula 6

Prunus serrulata 6
Prunus subhirtella 6
Prunus yedoensis 6
Pseudolarix amabilis 8
Pyrus regelii 6
Pyrus salicifolia 5–6
Quercus bicolor 8
Quercus ellipsoidalis 8
Quercus frainetto 8
Quercus macrocarpa 8
Quercus muehlenbergii 8
Quercus palustris 8
Quercus petraea 8
Quercus prinoides 4–5
Quercus rubra 8
Quercus turbinella 5–6
Quercus velutina 8
Rhamnus frangula 6
Rhododendron arboreum 7
Rhododendron calendulaceum 5
Rhododendron cumberlandense 3–5
Rhododendron fastigiatum 2
Rhododendron flammeum 5
Rhododendron japonicum 4
Rhododendron ×kosterianum 4
Rhododendron ×loderi 5
Rhododendron minus 5–6
Rhododendron periclymenoides 4
Rhododendron polycladum 3
Rhododendron ponticum 5
Rhododendrom racemosum 2–4
Rhododendron reticulatum 4–5
Rhododendron schlippenbachii 5
Rhododendron thomsonii 4–5
Rhododendron vaseyi 5
Rhododendron wardii 4–5
Rhododendron williamsianum 4
Rhododendron yakushimanum 3
Rhododendron yedoense 4
Rhodotypos scandens 4
Rhus typhina 6
Rosa carolina 3
Rosa foetida 5
Rosa ×harisonii 4
Rosa palustris 4
Rosa primula 4
Rosa rubrifolia 4–5
Rosa spinosissima 3
Rosa xanthina f. hugonis 4–5
Sasa palmata 4
Sciadopitys verticillata 6–7

Shortia galacifolia 2
Skimmia japonica 2–3
Sorbaria spp. 4–5
Spiraea betulifolia 3
Spiraea douglasii 5
Spiraea henryi 5
Spiraea nipponica 5
Spiraea tomentosa 3
Spiraea trilobata 4
Spiraea ×vanhouttei 4
Staphylea colchica 6
Staphylea holocarpa 6
Stephanandra spp. 3–5
Stewartia spp. 6–7 (most)
Styrax japonicum 6
Styrax obassia 6
Symplocos paniculata 6
Syringa ×chinensis 6
Syringa ×persica 4
Taxus baccata 3–6
Taxus ×media 4–6
Tetradium daniellii 6–7
Tiarella cordifolia 2
Tilia americana 8
Tilia cordata 8
Tilia dasystyla 8
Tilia ×euchlora 8
Tilia ×europaea 8
Tilia mongolica 6–7
Tilia platyphyllos 8
Tripterygium regelii 1 & 5
Tsuga spp. 3–8
Viburnum buddleifolium 4
Viburnum ×carlcephalum 5
Viburnum carlesii 4
Viburnum dilatatum 5
Viburnum farreri 5
Viburnum ×juddii 5
Viburnum macrocephalum 5
Viburnum opulus 5
Viburnum plicatum 5
Viburnum rafinesquianum 4
Viburnum ×rhytidocarpum 5
Viburnum ×rhytidophylloides 5
Viburnum rhytidophyllum 5
Viburnum sargentii 5
Viburnum setigerum 5
Viburnum sieboldii 6
Viburnum trilobum 5
Viburnum wrightii 5
Vinca minor 2

Viola sororia 2
Vitis amurensis 1

21. Plants That Require Full Sun in Summer, in at Least Parts of Their Useful Ranges

Abies lasiocarpa 8
Aesculus glabra 7
Ailanthus altissima 7–8
Albizia julibrissin 6
Aleurites fordii 6
Amorpha spp. 3 & 6
Antigonon leptopus 1
Argyrocytisus battandieri 6
Atriplex canescens 4
Baccharis halimifolia 5
Bumelia lanuginosa 6
Callistemon ssp. 2–5
Caragana spp. 3–6
Carya spp. 8
Caryopteris spp. 3–4
Castanea spp. 6–8
Ceanothus spp. 3
Celtis spp. 7–8
Ceratiola ericoides 4
Chamaecytisus spp. 2–3
Chilopsis linearis 6
×Chitalpa tashkentensis 6
Cinnamomum camphora 7
Cistus spp. 3–5
Colutea arborescens 5
Corema conradii 2
Coronilla varia 2
Corylus spp. 5–8
Cotoneaster spp. 2–6 (most)
Crataegus spp. 5–7 (most)
Cytisus spp. 2–4 & 6
Elaeagnus spp. 5–6 (deciduous spp.)
Empetrum spp. 2
Eucalyptus spp. 6–7
Forestiera spp. 5
Fraxinus mandshurica 8
Fraxinus pennsylvanica 8
Fraxinus texensis 7
Fraxinus velutina 7
Genista spp. 2–6
Ginkgo biloba 8
Gleditsia triacanthos 8
Gymnocladus dioica 8
Helianthemum nummularium 2

Hippophaë rhamnoides 6
Hylotelephium spp. & cvs. 3
Idesia polycarpa 7
Indigofera spp. 3–5
Juniperus spp. 2–7 (most)
Lagerstroemia spp. & cvs. 5–6
Laurus nobilis 6
Ledum spp. 2–3
Leiophyllum buxifolium 2
Leucophyllum spp. & cvs. 3–5
Loiseleuria procumbens 2
Lotus corniculatus 2
Lycium barbarum 5
Maackia spp. 7
Macfadyena unguis-cati 1
Malus angustifolia 6
Malus coronaria 6
Malus glaucescens 5
Malus ×heterophylla 6
Malus ioensis 6
Malus platycarpa 6
Malus ×soulardii 6
Melia azedarach 6
Myrtus communis 4–5
Nerium oleander 6
Paliurus spina-christi 6
Parkinsonia spp. 6
Passiflora spp. 1 & 2
Perovskia atriplicifolia 3–4
Persea spp. 6–7
Phellodendron spp. 7–8
Picea spp. 8 (most)
Picrasma quassioides 6
Pinus spp. 4–8 (most)
Populus spp. 6–8
Potentilla spp. 2–3
Prunus spp. 3–8 (deciduous spp.)
Ptelea sp. 5–6
Pterocarya spp. 8
Pterostyrax spp. 6–7
Punica granatum 6
Pyrus spp. 5–7
Quercus spp. 7–8
Rhus spp. 4–6 (most)
Robinia ×ambigua 7
Robinia ×margarettiae 6–7
Rosmarinus officinalis 2–4
Robinia pseudoacacia 8
Robinia viscosa 7
Rosa spp. 3–5 (deciduous spp.)
Sabal spp. 3–7

Salix spp. 2–8
Santolina spp. 3
Sapium sebiferum 7
Sassafras albidum 7–8
Sciadopitys verticillata 6–7
Securinega suffruticosa 4
Sedum spp. 2
Senna corymbosa 5
Sequoiadendron giganteum 8
Serenoa repens 3–4
Sesbania punicea 5
Shepherdia spp. 5–6
Sophora spp. 5–8
Sorbus spp. 6–8
Syringa spp. 4–7
Tamarix spp. 4–5
Trifolium incarnatum 3
Umbellularia californica 7–8
Vaccinium vitis-idaea 2
Wisteria spp. 1
Yucca spp. 3–5
Ziziphus jujuba 6

22. Plants That Require Partial Shade in Summer, in at Least Parts of Their Useful Ranges

Abies homolepis 8
Acer davidii 7
Acer pensylvanicum 7
Acer spicatum 6
Ajuga spp. 2
Ardisia spp. 2–4
Asarum spp. 2
Aspidistra elatior 3
Berberis spp. 3–5 (evergreen spp.)
Cephalotaxus spp. 4–5
Chimaphila umbellata 2
Chimonanthus praecox 5
Clematis alpina 1
Clematis armandii 1
Clematis delavayi 1
Clematis florida 1
Clematis lanuginosa 1
Clematis ×lawsoniana 1
Clematis macropetala 1
Clematis montana 1
Clematis occidentalis 1
Clematis patens 1
Clematis viticella 1
Convallaria majalis 2

Cornus alternifolia 6
Cornus florida 6–7
Cornus nuttallii 6
Cyrtomium falcatum 3
Daphne spp. 3–4 (evergreen spp.)
Daphniphyllum spp. 4–6
Epigaea repens 2
Epimedium spp. 2
Euonymus japonicus 5
×Fatshedera lizei 4
Fatsia japonica 4–5
Galax urceolata 2
Galium odoratum 2
Gardenia augusta 4
Gaultheria spp. 2–3
Hamamelis virginiana 6
Hosta spp. 2–3
Ilex ×altaclarensis 7
Ilex aquifolium 6
Ilex ×aquipernyi 6
Ilex crenata 3–5
Ilex fargesii 6
Ilex integra 6
Ilex ×koehneana 7
Ilex latifolia 6
Ilex sugerokii 5
Ilex yunnanensis 5
Indigofera divaricata 3
Itea spp. 4–5
Lamium spp. 2
Leucothoe spp. 2–5
Lindera spp. 4–6
Loropetalum chinense 5
Mahonia spp. 2–5 (part)
Mitchella repens 2
Pachysandra spp. 2
Paeonia spp. 4
Paxistima spp. 2–3
Pieris spp. 1 & 4–5
Pileostegia viburnoides 1 & 2
Podocarpus spp. 3 & 5–7
Podophyllum peltatum 2
Rhododendron spp. & cvs. 2–7 (most)
Rubus odoratus 5
Sarcococca spp. 4
Saxifraga stolonifera 2
Shortia galacifolia 2
Skimmia spp. 3
Stewartia spp. 6–7
Taxus spp. 3–6
Tiarella cordifolia 2

Torreya spp. 5–7
Trachelospermum spp. 1 & 2
Tsuga spp. 3–8
Viburnum acerifolium 4
Viburnum lantanoides 5
Vinca spp. 2
Viola spp. 2

23. Plants That Require Shade in Winter, in at Least Parts of Their Useful Ranges

Arctostaphylos spp. 2 & 5
Ardisia spp. 2–4
Asarum spp. 2
Aspidistra elatior 3
Berberis spp. 3–5 (evergreen spp.)
Bruckenthalia spiculifolia 2
Buxus spp. 3–4
Calluna vulgaris 2
Camellia spp. 6
Cephalotaxus spp. 4–5
Chamaecyparis lawsoniana 3–7
Chimaphila umbellata 2
Cyrtomium falcatum 3
Daboecia cantabrica 2–3
Daphne spp. 3–4 (evergreen)
Daphniphyllum spp. 4–6
Leucothoë spp. 4–5 (evergreen spp.)
Loropetalum chinense 5
×Mahoberberis spp. 3–4
Epigaea repens 2
Erica spp. 2–3
Euonymus fortunei 1 & 2–4
×Fatshedera lizei 4
Fatsia japonica 4–5
Galax urceolata 2
Gardenia augusta 4
Gaultheria spp. 2–3
Gaylussacia brachycera 2
Hedera spp. 1 & 2
Ilex ×altaclrensis 7
Ilex aquifolium 6
Ilex ×aquipernyi 6
Ilex fargesii 6
Ilex integra 6
Ilex ×koehneana 7
Ilex latifolia 6
Ilex ×meserveae 4
Ilex opaca 6
Ilex pedunculosa 6

Ilex rugosa 3
Kalmia latifolia 5
Lamium spp. 2
Mahonia spp. 2–5 (part)
Pachysandra spp. 2
Paeonia spp. 4
Paxistima spp. 2–3
Pieris spp. 1 & 4–5
Pileostegia viburnoides 1 & 2
Platycladus orientalis 4–7
Podocarpus macrophyllus 5–7
Prunus laurocerasus 4–6
Prunus lusitanica 5–6
Rhododendron spp. & cvs. 2–7 (most)
Sarcococca spp. 4
Saxifraga stolonifera 2
Sciadopitys verticillata 6–7
Sequoia sempervirens 8
Sequoiadendron giganteum 8
Shortia galacifolia 2
Skimmia spp. 3
Taxus spp. 3–6
Tetrapanax papyrifer 5
Thuja spp. 3–8
Thujopsis dolobrata 5
Tiarella cordifolia 2
Torreya spp. 5–7
Viburnum davidii 3
Viburnum japonicum 5
Viburnum odoratissimum 5–6
Viburnum rhytidophyllum 5
Viburnum suspensum 4
Vinca spp. 2

24. Plants That Tolerate Full Shade in Summer, in at Least Parts of Their Useful Ranges

Acer circinatum 6
Acer pensylvanicum 7
Actinidia arguta 1
Akebia spp. 1 & 2
Asarum spp. 2
Asimina triloba 6–7
Aspidistra elatior 3
Bambusa multiplex 5–6
Celastrus spp. 1 & 2
Cephalotaxus spp. 4–5
Cornus amomum 5
Cornus drummondii 5–6
Cornus mas 6

Cornus obliqua 5
Cornus officinalis 6
Cyrtomium falcatum 3
Daphne spp. 3–4 (evergreen spp.)
Daphniphyllum spp. 4–6
Decumaria barbara 1 & 2
Eleutherococcus sieboldianus 5
Epimedium spp. 2
Euonymus fortunei 1 & 2–4
Euonymus obovatus 2
×Fatshedera lizei 4
Fatsia japonica 4–5
Ficus spp. 1 & 5–6
Galax urceolata 2
Gaylussacia brachycera 2
Hamamelis virginiana 6
Hydrangea petiolaris 1 & 2
Hydrangea quercifolia 4–5
Itea spp. 4–5
Liriope spp. 2
Lonicera henryi 1 & 2
Lonicera japonica 1 & 2
Loropetalum chinense 5
Menispermum canadense 1 & 2
Nepeta mussinii 2
Ophiopogon japonicus 2
Pachysandra spp. 2
Parthenocissus spp. 1 & 2
Phyllostachys spp. 6–7
Pileostegia viburnoides 1 & 2
Pleioblastus spp. 2–3 & 6
Podocarpus macrophyllus 5–7
Podophyllum peltatum 2
Sarcococca spp. 4
Sasa spp. 3–4
Saxifraga stolonifera 2
Schizophragma hydrangeoides 1 & 2
Shortia galacifolia 2
Skimmia spp. 3
Smilax spp. 1
Taxus spp. 3–6
Tetrapanax papyrifer 5
Tiarella cordifolia 2
Torreya spp. 5–7
Trachelospermum spp. 1 & 2
Trochodendron aralioides 5–6
Tsuga spp. 3–8
Vaccinium spp. 2–6 (most)
Viburnum acerifolium 4
Viburnum lantanoides 5
Viburnum dentatum 6

Viburnum molle 5
Viburnum rafinesquianum 4
Vinca spp. 2
Viola spp. 2

25. Plants That Tolerate Strong Winds, in at Least Parts of Their Useful Ranges

Abies concolor 8
Abies koreana 7
Abies lasiocarpa 8
Acer mandshuricum 6
Acer maximowiczianum 7
Acer negundo 8
Acer tataricum ssp. ginnala 6
Aegopodium podagraria 2
Aesculus glabra 7
Amorpha spp. 3 & 6
Antigonon leptopus 1
Arctostaphylos spp. 2–4
Artemisia spp. 3–5
Atriplex canescens 4
Brahea armata 6–7
Bumelia lanuginosa 6
Callistemon spp. 5–6
Caragana spp. 3–6
Cassiope tetragona 2
Castanea spp. 6–8
Catalpa spp. 7–8
Ceanothus spp. 3
Celtis spp. 7–8
Cephalanthus occidentalis 5
Ceratiola ericoides 4
Cercis spp. 6–7
Chaenomeles spp. 3–4
Chamaerops humilis 5–6
Chilopsis linearis 6
×Chitalpa tashkentensis 6
Cinnamomum camphora 7
Cistus spp. 3–5
Clematis tangutica 1
Clematis texensis 1
Comptonia peregrina 2
Corema conradii 2
Cornus alba 5
Cornus alternifolia 6
Cornus hessei 3
Cornus racemosa 5
Cornus rugosa 5
Cornus sanguinea 5
Cornus stolonifera 5

Cornus stricta 5
Coronilla varia 2
Corylus spp. 5–8
Cotoneaster acutifolius 5
Cotoneaster apiculatus 3
Cotoneaster divaricatus 4
Cotoneaster lucidus 5
Crataegus spp. 5–7 (most)
Cudrania tricuspidata 6
Cydonia oblonga 6
Diervilla spp. 3–4
Dirca palustris 4
Elaeagnus spp. 5–6
Eleutherococcus sieboldianus 5
Empetrum spp. 2
Escallonia spp. 3–6
Eucalyptus spp. 6–7
Eucommia ulmoides 7
Euonymus alatus 5
Euonymus atropurpureus 6
Euonymus europaeus 6
Euonymus hamiltonianus 6
Euonymus latifolius 6
Euonymus nanus 3
Euonymus phellomanus 6
Euonymus sachalinensis 6
Fontanesia phillyreoides ssp. fortunei 5
Forestiera spp. 5
Fraxinus pennsylvanica 8
Fraxinus texensis 7
Fraxinus velutina 7
Genista spp. 2–6
Ginkgo biloba 8
Gleditsia triacanthos 8
Gymnocladus dioica 8
Helianthemum nummularium 2
Hippophaë rhamnoides 6
Hylotelephium spp. 3
Indigofera spp. 3
Juniperus spp. 2–7
Kalmia polifolia 3
Larix spp. 8
Ledum spp. 2–3
Leiophyllum buxifolium 2
Lespedeza spp. 3 & 5
Leucophyllum frutescens 5
Ligustrum amurense 5
Ligustrum quihoui 5
Ligustrum vulgare 4–6
Loiseleuria procumbens 2
Lonicera albertii 3

Lonicera nitida 4
Lonicera pileata 3
Lotus corniculatus 2
Lycium barbarum 5
×Macludrania hybrida 6–7
Maclura pomifera 7
Microbiota decussata 2–3
Morus spp. 7–8
Myrica spp. 4–7
Myrtus communis 4–5
Nerium oleander 6
Parkinsonia spp. 6
Perovskia atriplicifolia 3–4
Persea spp. 6–7
Picea abies 3–8
Picea engelmannii 8
Picea glauca 8
Picea mariana 7–8
Picea pungens 8
Picea rubens 8
Pinus albicaulis 6
Pinus aristata 4–6
Pinus banksiana 8
Pinus bungeana 6–7
Pinus cembra 6–8
Pinus contorta 6–8
Pinus echinata 8
Pinus edulis 7
Pinus flexilis 8
Pinus halepensis 7
Pinus jeffreyi 8
Pinus mugo 4–6
Pinus nigra 8
Pinus pinaster 7–8
Pinus ponderosa 8
Pinus resinosa 8
Pinus rigida 7–8
Pinus sibirica 8
Pinus sylvestris 8
Pinus taeda 8
Pinus virginiana 7
Pittosporum tobira 5
Polygonum spp. 1 & 3–5
Populus spp. 6–8 (most)
Potentilla spp. 2–3
Prinsepia spp. 4–5
Prunus alleghaniensis 5
Prunus americana 5
Prunus angustifolia 5
Prunus besseyi 3
Prunus cerasifera 6

Prunus ×cistena 5
Prunus japonica 4
Prunus maritima 4
Prunus mexicana 6
Prunus nigra 5–6
Prunus pensylvanica 7
Prunus pumila 4
Prunus tomentosa 5
Pseudocydonia sinensis 6
Pseudotsuga spp. 7–8 (part)
Ptelea spp. 5–6
Pueraria lobata 1 & 3
Pyrus spp. 5–7 (most)
Quercus alba 8
Quercus austrina 7–8
Quercus bicolor 8
Quercus ellipsoidalis 8
Quercus falcata 8
Quercus gambelii 5–6
Quercus georgiana 4–5
Quercus laevis 6
Quercus macrocarpa 8
Quercus mongolica 7–8
Quercus muehlenbergii 8
Quercus pagoda 8
Quercus palustris 8
Quercus rubra 8
Quercus stellata 7–8
Quercus velutina 8
Rhaphiolepis spp. 3–4
Rhus aromatica 4–5
Ribes spp. 4–5
Robinia ×ambigua 7
Robinia pseudoacacia 8
Robinia viscosa 7
Rosa bracteata 1 & 5
Rosa carolina 3
Rosa laevigata 1 & 5
Rosa multiflora 5
Rosa nitida 3
Rosa odorata 3
Rosa palustris 4
Rosa roxburghii 5
Rosa rugosa 4
Rosa setigera 5
Rosa virginiana 4
Rosa wichuraiana 1 & 2
Sabal spp. 3–7
Salix exigua 6
Salix purpurea 5
Salix repens 2–3

Salix rosmarinifolia 4
Sedum spp. 2
Sempervivum tectorum 2
Serenoa repens 3–4
Shepherdia spp. 5–6
Smilax spp. 1
Symphoricarpos spp. 3–4
Tamarix spp. 4–5
Trifolium incarnatum 3
Umbellularia californica 7–8
Vaccinium spp. 2–6 (most)
Washingtonia filifera 7
Washingtonia robusta 8
Yucca spp. 3–5

26. Plants That Tolerate Little Wind, in at Least Parts of Their Useful Ranges

Acer circinatum 6
Acer davidii 7
Acer japonicum 6
Acer palmatum 6
Acer pseudo-sieboldianum 6
Arctostaphylos spp. 2 & 5
Ardisia spp. 2–4
Argyrocytisus battandieri 6
Aristolochia macrophylla 1
Asarum spp. 2
Asimina triloba 6–7
Aspidistra elatior 3
Aucuba japonica 5
Bambusa multiplex 5–6
Berberis spp. 3–5 (evergreen spp.)
Buxus spp. 3–4
Calocedrus decurrens 7
Camellia spp. 6
Carpenteria californica 4
Cephalotaxus spp. 4–5
Chamaecyparis lawsoniana 3–7
Chamaecytisus spp. 2–3
Chimaphila umbellata 2
Clerodendrum spp. 4–6
Cornus florida 6–7
Cornus kousa 6
Cornus ×rutgersensis 6
Corylopsis spp. 4–5
Cotoneaster lacteus 5
Cotoneaster salicifolius 5
Cotoneaster ×watereri 6
Cryptomeria japonica 8
Cyrtomium falcatum 3

Cytisus spp. 2–4
Danaë racemosa 3
Daphne spp. 3–4 (evergreen spp.)
Daphniphyllum macropodum 6
Davidia involucrata 6–7
Decumaria barbara 1 & 2
Dipteronia sinensis 6
Emmenopteris henryi 6–7
Epigaea repens 2
Epimedium spp. 2
Euptelea polyandra 7
×Fatshedera lizei 4
Fatsia japonica 4–5
Ficus spp. 1 & 5–6
Firmiana simplex 6–7
Franklinia alatamaha 6
Fuchsia magellanica 3–4
Galax urceolata 2
Hemerocallis spp. 3
Hibiscus spp. 5–6
Hosta spp. 2–3
Hydrangea spp. 3–6 (most)
Ilex spp. 3–7 (most evergreen spp.)
Laburnum spp. 6
Leucothoë spp. 4–5
Magnolia acuminata 8
Magnolia ashei 6
Magnolia campbellii 7
Magnolia fraseri 7
Magnolia hypoleuca 7–8
Magnolia macrophylla 7
Magnolia pyramidata 6
Magnolia sargentiana 7
Magnolia sieboldii 6
Magnolia tripetala 7
Magnolia ×veitchii 7
Magnolia wilsonii 6
×Mahoberberis spp. 3–4
Mahonia spp. 3–5
Oxydendrum arboreum 7–8
Pachysandra spp. 2
Paeonia spp. 4
Pieris spp. 1 & 3–5
Pinus strobus 8
Pinus wallichiana 8
Pleioblastus spp. 2–3 & 6
Podocarpus macrophyllus 3 & 5–7
Podophyllum peltatum 2
Prunus campanulata 6
Prunus laurocerasus 4–6
Prunus lusitanica 5–6

Prunus serrulata 6
Prunus subhirtella 6
Pseudolarix amabilis 8
Pyracantha spp. & cvs 3–5 (part)
Quercus acuta 7
Quercus glauca 7
Quercus myrsinifolia 7
Quercus salicina 7
Rhododendron spp. 3–7 (most)
Rubus odoratus 5
Ruscus aculeatus 3
Sarcococca spp. 4
Sasa spp. 3–4
Saxifraga stolonifera 2
Schizophragma spp. 1 & 2
Sciadopitys verticillata 6–7
Sequoia sempervirens 8
Sequoiadendron giganteum 8
Shortia galacifolia 2
Skimmia spp. 3
Stephanandra spp. 4
Stewartia spp. 6–7
Symplocos spp. 6
Taiwania cryptomerioides 8
Taxus spp. 3–6
Tetracentron sinense 7
Tetrapanax papyrifer 5
Teucrium chamaedrys 2
Thuja spp. 3–8
Thujopsis dolobrata 5
Tiarella cordifolia 2
Toona sinensis 6–7
Torreya spp. 5–7
Trochodendron aralioides 5–6
Tsuga spp. 3–8
Viburnum acerifolium 4
Viburnum lantanoides 5
Viburnum davidii 3
Viburnum japonicum 5
Viburnum odoratissimum 5–6
Viburnum plicatum 5
Viburnum rhytidophyllum 5
Viburnum sieboldii 6
Viburnum suspensum 4
Viburnum tinus 5
Viburnum utile 4
Vinca spp. 2
Viola spp. 2
Vitis spp. 1
Wisteria spp. 1
Xanthorhiza simplicissima 2

27. Plants That Tolerate Wet Soil

Acer pensylvanicum 7
Acer rubrum 8
Acer saccharinum 8
Aegopodium podagraria 2
Aleurites fordii 6
Alnus spp. 6–7
Asimina triloba 6–7
Aspidistra elatior 3
Bambusa multiplex 5–6
Betula nigra 8
Bignonia capreolata 1
Callistemon salignus var. viridiflorus 4
Calocedrus decurrens 7
Calycanthus spp. 4–5
Campsis spp. 1
Carya illinoinensis 8
Catalpa spp. 7–8
Celastrus spp. 1 & 2
Cephalanthus occidentalis 5
Chaenomeles spp. 3–4
Chamaecyparis spp. 3–8
Chimonanthus praecox 5
Chionanthus spp. 6
Clethra spp. 5–6
Cliftonia monophylla 5
Cocculus carolina 1
Convallaria majalis 2
Cornus alba 5
Cornus stolonifera 5
Cryptomeria japonica 8
Cudrania tricuspidata 6
Cydonia oblonga 6
Cyrilla racemiflora 6
Cyrtomium falcatum 3
Decumaria barbara 1 & 2
Diospyros spp. 7
Dirca palustris 4
Forestiera acuminata 5
Forsythia spp. 4–5 (most)
Fothergilla spp. 3–5
Fraxinus americana 8
Fraxinus biltmoreana 7
Fraxinus caroliniana 7
Fraxinus nigra 8
Fraxinus profunda 8
Fraxinus quadrangulata 8
Fuchsia magellanica 3–4
Hemerocallis spp. 3
Hibiscus spp. 5–6

Holodiscus discolor 6
Hydrangea spp. 1 & 2–6
Ilex spp. 3–7
Illicium spp. 4–6
Indigofera spp. 3
Itea spp. 4–5
Jasminum floridum 4
Jasminum mesnyi 4
Kalmia angustifolia 3
Kalmia polifolia 3
Kerria japonica 4
Kolkwitzia amabilis 5
Larix spp. 8
Ledum spp. 2–3
Leitneria floridana 5–6
Lespedeza spp. 3 & 5
Ligustrum spp. 4–6
Lindera spp. 4–6
Liquidambar spp. 8
Liriope spp. 2
Lonicera spp. 1 & 2–6
Lyonia spp. 4–6
×Macludrania hybrida 6–7
Maclura pomifera 7
Magnolia spp. 5–8
Menispermum canadense 1 & 2
Metasequoia glyptostroboides 8
Neillia sinensis 4
Nyssa spp. 8
Osmanthus spp. 4–6
Phyllostachys spp. 6–7
Physocarpus opulifolius 4–5
Picea mariana 7–8
Pinus glabra 8
Pleioblastus spp. 2–3 & 6
Platanus spp. 8
Populus spp. 6–8 (most)
Potentilla spp. 2–4 (most)
Pseudocydonia sinensis 6
Quercus bicolor 8
Quercus ellipsoidalis 8
Quercus lyrata 8
Quercus laurifolia 8
Quercus nigra 8
Quercus nuttallii 8
Quercus pagoda 8
Quercus palustris 8
Quercus phellos 7–8
Quercus virginiana 7
Rhododendron atlanticum 3
Rhododendron canadense 3

Rhododendron serrulatum 6
Rhododendron vaseyi 5
Rhododendron viscosum 5
Rosa carolina 3
Rosa multiflora 5
Rosa palustris 4
Rubus hispidus 4
Sabal spp. 3–7
Salix spp. 2–8
Sambucus spp. 5–6
Sapium sebiferum 7
Sasa spp. 3–4
Shepherdia spp. 5–6
Smilax spp. 1
Sorbaria spp. 4–5
Staphylea spp. 6
Stephanandra spp. 4
Taiwania cryptomerioides 8
Taxodium distichum 8
Thuja spp. 3–8
Thujopsis dolobrata 5
Vaccinium macrocarpon 2
Vaccinium oxycoccus 2
Viburnum cassinoides 4
Viburnum dentatum 6
Viburnum lentago 6
Viburnum molle 5
Viola spp. 2
Xanthorhiza simplicissima 2

28. *Plants That Tolerate Dry Soil*

Acer maximowiczianum 7
Acer negundo 7
Acer saccharinum 8
Acer tataricum and ssp. ginnala 6
Aegopodium podagraria 2
Aesculus glabra 7
Agave americana 4
Ailanthus altissima 7–8
Albizia julibrissin 6
Amorpha spp. 3 & 6
Antigonon leptopus 1
Arctostaphylos uva-ursi 2
Argyrocytisus battandieri 6
Artemisia spp. 3–5
Asimina triloba 6–7
Atriplex canescens 4
Baccharis halimifolia 5
Berberis gilgiana 4
Berberis koreana 4

Berberis ×mentorensis 4
Berberis vulgaris 5
Bignonia capreolata 1
Brahea armata 6–7
Callistemon citrinus 5–6
Campsis spp. 1
Caragana spp. 3–6
Caryopteris spp. 3–4
Castanea spp. 6–8
Catalpa spp. 7–8
Ceanothus spp. 3–5
Celastrus spp. 1 & 2
Celtis spp. 7–8
Cercis spp. 6–7
Chamaecytisus spp. 2–3
Chaenomeles spp. 3–4
Chilopsis linearis 6
×Chitalpa tashkentensis 6
Choisya ternata 5
Cinnamomum camphora 7
Cistus spp. 3–5
Cladrastis spp. 7–8
Clematis tangutica 1
Clematis texensis 1
Clerodendrum spp. 4–6
Cleyera japonica 5
Comptonia peregrina 2
Cornus racemosa 5
Coronilla varia 2
Corylus spp. 5–8
Cotinus spp. 6–7
Cotoneaster spp. 2–6 (most)
Crataegus spp. 5–7
Cudrania tricuspidata 6
Cydonia oblonga 6
Cyrilla racemiflora 6
Cytisus spp. 2–6
Diervilla spp. 3–4
Elaeagnus spp. 5–6
Elsholtzia stauntonii 3
Escallonia spp. 3–6
Eucalyptus spp. 6–7
Eucommia ulmoides 7
Eurya spp. 3–5
Evodia spp. 6–7
Fagus sylvatica 8
Ficus spp. 1 & 5–6
Fontanesia spp. 5
Forestiera neo-mexicana 5
Fraxinus cuspidata 6
Fraxinus pennsylvanica 8

Fraxinus texensis 7
Fraxinus velutina 7
Galium spp. 2
Genista spp. 2–6
Ginkgo biloba 8
Gleditsia triacanthos 8
Gymnocladus dioica 8
Helianthemum nummularium 2
Hippophaë rhamnoides 6
Hylotelephium spp. & cvs. 3
Hypericum kalmianum 3
Hypericum prolificum 3
Indigofera spp. 3–5
Jasminum spp. 1 & 3–5
Juglans spp. 7–8
Juniperus spp. 2–8
Koelreuteria spp. 7
Kolkwitzia amabilis 5
Laurus nobilis 6
Lavandula angustifolia 3
Ledum spp. 2–3
Leiophyllum buxifolium 2
Lespedeza spp. 3 & 5
Leucophyllum frutescens 5
Liriope spp. 2
Lonicera spp. 1 & 2–6
Lotus corniculatus 2
Lycium barbarum 5
Maackia spp. 7
×Macludrania hybrida 6–7
Maclura pomifera 7
Melia azedarach 6
Microbiota decussata 2–3
Morus spp. 7–8
Myrica spp. 4–7
Myrtus communis 4–5
Paliurus spina-christi 6
Parkinsonia spp. 6
Passiflora spp. 1 & 2
Perovskia atriplicifolia 3–4
Persea spp. 6–7
Phellodendron spp. 7–8
Photinia spp. 5–6
Physocarpus opulifolius 4–5
Picea engelmannii 8
Picea pungens 8
Picrasma ailanthifolia 6
Pinus spp. 4–8 (most)
Pistacia chinensis 8
Pittosporum tobira 5
Polygonum spp. 1 & 3–5

Poncirus trifoliata 6
Populus angustifolia 7
Populus balsamifera 8
Populus trichocarpa 8
Prinsepia spp. 4–5
Prunus alleghaniensis 5
Prunus americana 5
Prunus angustifolia 5
Prunus besseyi 3
Prunus ×blireiana 6
Prunus cerasifera 6
Prunus ×cistena 5
Prunus glandulosa 4
Prunus japonica 4
Prunus maritima 4
Prunus mexicana 6
Prunus nigra 5–6
Prunus pensylvanica 7
Prunus pumila 4
Prunus tenella 4
Prunus tomentosa 5
Prunus triloba 5–6
Pseudocydonia sinensis 6
Ptelea trifoliata 6
Pueraria lobata 1 & 3
Punica granatum 6
Pyracantha spp. 4–6
Pyrus spp. 7
Quercus austrina 7–8
Quercus gambellii 5–6
Quercus glaucoides 7
Quercus grisea 6–7
Quercus hypoleucoides 5–6
Quercus ilicifolia 4–6
Quercus laevis 6
Quercus macrocarpa 8
Quercus marilandica 6–7
Quercus mongolica 7–8
Quercus muehlenbergii 8
Quercus polymorpha 7–8
Quercus prinus 8
Quercus rubra 8
Quercus stellata 7–8
Quercus turbinella 5–6
Quercus velutina 8
Rhaphiolepis spp. 3–4
Rhus spp. 4–6
Ribes spp. 4–5
Robinia spp. 4 & 7–8
Rosa spp. 1 & 2–5 (most)
Ruscus spp. 2–3

Sabal spp. 3–7
Santolina spp. 3
Sapindus drummondii 7
Sapium sebiferum 7
Sedum spp. 2
Sempervivum tectorum 2
Serenoa repens 3–4
Sesbania punicea 5
Shepherdia spp. 4–6
Smilax spp. 1
Sophora spp. 5–6 & 8
Spiraea spp. 3–5
Symphoricarpos spp. 3–4
Tamarix spp. 4–5
Ternstroemia gymnanthera 6
Toona sinensis 6–7
Trifolium incarnatum 3
Umbellularia californica 7–8
Vaccinium spp. 2–6 (most)
Waldsteinia fragarioides 2
Washingtonia spp. 7–8
Wisteria spp. 1
Xanthoceras sorbifolium 6
Yucca spp. 3–5
Zanthoxylum spp. 6
Ziziphus jujuba 6

29. Plants That Require Distinctly Acidic Soil (pH 6.0 or Lower)

Andromeda polifolia 2
Calluna vulgaris 2
Cassiope tetragona 2
Clethra spp. 5–6
Cleyera japonica 5
Cliftonia monophylla 5
Cocculus carolinus 1
Colutea arborescens 5
Cornus spp. 3–7 (part)
Coronilla varia 2
Corema conradii 2
Cornus canadensis 2
Corylopsis spp. 4–5
Cryptomeria japonica 8
Cunninghamia lanceolata 8
Cyrilla racemiflora 6
Daboecia cantabrica 3
Elliottia racemosa 5–6
Empetrum spp. 2
Enkianthus spp. 4–6
Epigaea repens 2

Erica spp. 2–3
Eurya spp. 3–5
Fothergilla spp. 3–5
Franklinia alatamaha 6
Galax urceolata 2
Gardenia jasminoides 4
Gaultheria spp. 2–3
Gaylussacia brachycera 2
Gordonia lasianthus 7
Hydrangea macrophylla 3 (for blue flowers)
Idesia polycarpa 7
Ilex spp. 3–7 (most)
Kalmia spp. 2–3, 5
Ledum spp. 2–3
Leiophyllum buxifolium 2
Leitneria floridana 5–6
Leucothoë spp. 3–5
Loiseleuria procumbens 2
Lyonia spp. 4–6
Michelia spp. 5–7
Mitchella repens 2
Oxydendrum arboreum 7–8
Phoenix canariensis 7
Pieris spp. 1 & 3–5
Pinus elliottii 8
Pinus palustris 8
Potentilla tridentata 2
Pseudolarix amabilis 8
Quercus coccinea 8
Quercus georgiana 6
Quercus palustris 8
Quercus phellos 8
Rhododendron spp. 2–7
Sabal minor 3–4
Sciadopitys verticillata 6–7
Serenoa repens 3–4
Shortia galacifolia 2
Stachyurus praecox 5
Stewartia spp. 6–7
Taiwania cryptomerioides 8
Ternstroemia gymnanthera 6
Tripetaleia paniculata 4
Vaccinium spp. 2–6
Xanthorhiza simplicissima 2
Zenobia pulverulenta 4

30. *Plants That Tolerate Neutral or Alkaline Soil (pH 7.0 or Higher)*

Abeliophyllum distichum 4
Abies concolor 8

Abies lasiocarpa 8
Abies nordmanniana 8
Abies procera 8
Acer spp. 5–8 (most)
Actinidia spp. 1
Aegopodium podagraria 2
Aesculus ×carnea 8
Aesculus glabra 7
Aesculus parviflora 5
Agave americana 4
Ailanthus altissima 7–8
Ajuga spp. & cvs. 2
Akebia spp. 1 & 2
Albizia julibrissin 6
Aleurites fordii 6
Alnus spp. 6–7
Amelanchier spp. 3–7
Amorpha spp. 3 & 6
Ampelopsis spp. 1
Antigonon leptopus 1
Aralia spp. 6–7
Argyrocytisus battandieri 6
Aristolochia macrophylla 1
Artemisia spp. 3–5
Asimina triloba 6–7
Atriplex canescens 4
Baccharis halimifolia 5
Bambusa multiplex 5–6
Berberis spp. 3–5 (most)
Bignonia capreolata 1
Brahea armata 6–7
Buddleia alternifolia 5
Callistemon citrinus 5–6
Campsis spp. 1
Caragana spp. 3–6
Carya spp. 8
Caryopteris spp. 3–4
Castanea spp. 6–8
Catalpa spp. 7–8
Ceanothus spp. 3–5
Celastrus scandens 1 & 2
Celtis spp. 7–8
Cephalanthus occidentalis 5
Cercidiphyllum japonicum 8
Cercis spp. 6–7
Chaenomeles spp. 3–4
Chamaecytisus spp. 2–3
Chionanthus spp. 6
Choisya ternata 5
Cinnamomum camphora 7
Cistus spp. 3–5

Cladrastis spp. 7–8
Clematis spp. 1
Cocculus carolinus 1
Colutea arborescens 5
Convallaria majalis 2
Cornus spp. 3–7 (most)
Coronilla varia 2
Corylopsis spp. 4–5
Corylus spp. 5–8
Cotinus spp. 6–7
Cotoneaster spp. 2–6
Crataegus spp. 5–7
×Cupressocyparis leylandii 8
Cupressus spp. 7–8
Cytisus spp. 2–4
Daphne spp. 2–4
Decumaria barbara 1 & 2
Diervilla spp. 3–4
Diospyros spp. 7
Dirca palustris 4
Edgeworthia papyrifera 4
Elaeagnus spp. 5–6
Eleutherococcus sieboldianus 5
Escallonia spp. 3–5
Eucalyptus spp. 6–7
Eucommia ulmoides 7
Euonymus spp. 1 & 2–6
Exochorda spp. 5–6
Fatsia japonica 4–5
Feijoa sellowiana 6
Ficus spp. 1 & 5–6
Fontanesia spp. 5
Forestiera spp. 5–6
Forsythia spp. 4–5
Fothergilla spp. 3–5
Fraxinus spp. 6–8
Gelsemium sempervirens 1 & 2
Genista spp. 2–6
Ginkgo biloba 8
Gleditsia triacanthos 8
Gymnocladus dioica 8
Halimodendron halodendron 4
Hamamelis vernalis 5
Hamamelis virginiana 6
Hedera spp. 1 & 2
Helianthemum nummularium 2
Hemerocallis spp. & cvs. 3
Hemiptelea davidii 6
Hippophaë rhamnoides 6
Holodiscus discolor 6
Hosta spp. 2–3

Hovenia dulcis 6
Hydrangea spp. 1 & 2–6 (most)
Hylotelephium spp. & cvs. 3
Hypericum spp. 2–3
Iberis spp. 2
Ilex cornuta 5–6
Ilex decidua 6
Ilex glabra 5
Ilex ×meserveae 4–5
Ilex pernyi 6
Ilex vomitoria 3–6
Indigofera spp. 3
Juglans spp. 7–8
Juniperus spp. 2–8
Kalopanax septemlobus 8
Kerria japonica 4
Koelreuteria spp. 7
Kolkwitzia amabilis 5
Laburnum spp. 6
Lagerstroemia indica 6
Lamium galeobdolon 2
Lamium maculatum 2
Laurus nobilis 6
Lavandula angustifolia 3
Leitneria floridana 5–6
Leptodermis oblonga 3
Lespedeza spp. 3 & 5
Leucophyllum spp. 5
Leycesteria formosa 4
Ligustrum spp. 4–6 (deciduous spp.)
Lindera spp. 4–6
Liquidambar styraciflua 8
Liriodendron spp. 8
Liriope spp. 2
Lonicera spp. 1 & 2–6
Lotus corniculatus 2
Lycium barbarum 5
Maackia spp. 7
Maclura pomifera 7
Magnolia spp. 5–8
×Mahoberberis spp. 3–4
Mahonia spp. 2–5
Malus spp. 5–7
Melia azedarach 6
Menispermum canadense 1 & 2
Metasequoia glyptostroboides 8
Michelia figo 5
Microbiota decussata 2–3
Morus spp. 7–8
Myrica spp. 4–6
Myrtus communis 4–5

Neillia sinensis 4
Nerium oleander 6
Nyssa sylvatica 8
Orixa japonica 5
Osmanthus spp. 4–6
Ostrya spp. 7–8
Pachysandra spp. 2
Paeonia spp. 3–4
Paliurus spina-christi 6
Parkinsonia aculeata 6
Parthenocissus spp. 1 & 2
Passiflora spp. 1 & 2
Paulownia tomentosa 7
Paxistima spp. 2–3
Perovskia atriplicifolia 3–4
Persea spp. 6–7
Phellodendron spp. 7–8
Philadelphus spp. 4–5
Phlox spp. 2
Photinia spp. 5–6
Phyllostachys spp. 6–7
Physocarpus opulifolius 4–5
Picea spp. 3–8
Picrasma quassioides 6
Pinus spp. 4–8 (most)
Pistacia chinensis 8
Pittosporum tobira 5
Platanus spp. 8
Platycarya strobilacea 7
Pleioblastus spp. 2–3 & 6
Podocarpus macrophyllus 5–7
Polygonum spp. 1 & 3–5
Poncirus trifoliata 6
Populus spp. 6–8
Potentilla spp. 2–4 (most)
Prinsepia spp. 4–5
Prunus spp. 4–8
Pseudocydonia sinensis 6
Pseudotsuga spp. 7–8
Ptelea spp. 6
Pterocarya spp. 8
Pterostyrax spp. 6–7
Pueraria lobata 1 & 3
Punica granatum 4–6
Pyracantha spp. 3–6
Pyrus spp. 5–7
Quercus spp. 7–8 (most)
Rhamnus spp. 4 & 6
Rhaphiolepis spp. 3–4
Rhodotypos scandens 4
Rhus spp. 4–6

Ribes spp. 4–5
Robinia spp. 4 & 7–8
Rosa spp. 1 & 2–5 (most)
Rosmarinus officinalis 2–4
Ruscus aculeatus 3
Salix spp. 2–8
Sambucus spp. 5–6
Santolina spp. 3
Sapindus drummondii 7
Sapium sebiferum 7
Sarcococca spp. 4
Sasa spp. 3–4
Sassafras albidum 7–8
Saxifraga stolonifera 2
Securinega suffruticosa 4
Sedum spp. 2
Sempervivum tectorum 2
Senna corymbosa 5
Sequoia sempervirens 8
Sequoiadendron giganteum 8
Sesbania punicea 5
Shepherdia spp. 5–6
Smilax spp. 1
Sophora spp. 5–6 & 8
Sorbaria spp. 4–5
Sorbus spp. 6–8
Spiraea ×arguta 4
Spiraea ×billiardii 4
Spiraea cantoniensis 5
Spiraea henryi 5
Spiraea japonica 3
Spiraea nipponica 5
Spiraea thunbergii 4
Spiraea trilobata 4
Spiraea ×vanhouttei 4
Spiraea veitchii 5
Spiraea wilsonii 5
Staphylea spp. 6
Stephanandra spp. 4
Symphoricarpos spp. 3–4
Syringa spp. 4–7
Tamarix spp. 4–5
Taxodium spp. 8
Ternstroemia gymnanthera 6
Tetradium daniellii 6–7
Teucrium chamaedrys 2
Thuja spp. 3–8
Tiarella cordifolia 2
Tilia spp. 6–8
Toona sinensis 6–7
Trifolium incarnatum 3

Ulmus spp. 7–8
Umbellularia californica 7–8
Viburnum spp. 3–6
Vinca spp. 2
Viola spp. 2
Vitis spp. 1
Waldsteinia spp. 2
Washingtonia spp. 7–8
Weigela spp. 4–5
Wisteria spp. 1
Xanthoceras sorbifolium 6
Yucca spp. 3–5
Zanthoxylum spp. 6
Zelkova spp. 7–8
Ziziphus jujuba 6

31. Plants That Tolerate Salt (Seaside or Roadside)

Acer ginnala 6
Acer negundo 7
Acer platanoides 8
Acer pseudoplatanus 8
Aesculus spp. 5–8
Agave americana 4
Ailanthus altissima 7–8
Amelanchier spp. 3–7
Antigonon leptopus 1
Araucaria spp. 8
Arctostaphylos spp. 2 & 5
Argyrocytisus battandieri 6
Aronia spp. 3–5
Artemisia spp. 3–5
Atriplex canescens 4
Baccharis halimifolia 5
Bambusa multiplex 5–6
Bignonia capreolata 1
Bumelia lanuginosa 6
Buxus harlandii 4
Buxus microphylla 3
Callistemon spp. 2–6
Calluna vulgaris 2
Celastrus spp. 1 & 2
Celtis spp. 7–8
Chamaecyparis spp. 3–8
Chamaecytisus spp. 2–3
Chilopsis linearis 6
×Chitalpa tashkentensis 6
Cinnamomum camphora 7
Cistus spp. 3–5
Clematis terniflora 1

Clematis vitalba 1
Cocculus carolinus 1
Coronilla varia 2
Comptonia peregrina 2
Cotoneaster spp. 2–6
Crataegus spp. 5–7 (some)
Cryptomeria japonica 8
×Cupressocyparis leylandii 8
Cupressus spp. 7–8
Cycas revoluta 3–4
Cytisus spp. 2–4
Daboecia cantabrica 3
Elaeagnus spp. 5–6
Empetrum spp. 2
Erica spp. 2–3
Eriobotrya spp. 6
Escallonia spp. 3–5
Eucalyptus spp. 6–7
Euonymus spp. 1 & 2–6
Eurya spp. 3–5
×Fatshedera lizei 4
Fatsia japonica 4–5
Feijoa sellowiana 6
Ficus spp. 1 & 5–6
Forestiera neo-mexicana 5
Galium odoratum 2
Gardenia augusta 4
Gaultheria mucronata 3
Gelsemium sempervirens 1 & 2
Halimodendron halodendron 4
Hedera spp. 1 & 2
Hemerocallis spp. 3
Hibiscus spp. 5–6
Hippophaë rhamnoides 6
Hydrangea spp. 1 & 2–6
Hypericum spp. 2–4
Iberis spp. 2
Ilex ×attenuata 6
Ilex cassine 6
Ilex crenata 3–5
Ilex decidua 6
Ilex glabra 6
Ilex opaca 7
Ilex vomitoria 6
Illicium spp. 5–6
Jasminum spp. 1 & 3–5
Juniperus spp. 2–8 (most)
Lavandula angustifolia 3
Leiophyllum buxifolium 2
Lespedeza spp. 3 & 5
Leucophyllum frutescens 5

Ligustrum spp 4–6
Liquidambar spp. 8
Liriope spp. 2
Lonicera spp. 1 & 2–6 (most)
Lotus corniculatus 2
Lycium barbarum 5
Lyonia spp. 4–6
Magnolia grandiflora 8
Magnolia virginiana 6–7
Michelia figo 5
Morus spp 7–8
Myrica spp. 4–7
Myrtus communis 4–5
Nerium oleander 6
Nyssa spp. 7–8
Ophiopogon japonicus 2
Parkinsonia spp. 6
Passiflora spp. 1 & 2
Phoenix canariensis 7
Photinia spp. 5–6
Picea pungens 8
Pinus contorta 6–8
Pinus echinata 8
Pinus elliottii 8
Pinus halepensis 7
Pinus mugo 4–6
Pinus nigra 8
Pinus palustris 8
Pinus pinaster 7–8
Pinus rigida 7–8
Pinus sylvestris 6–7
Pinus thunbergii 6–7
Pistacia chinensis 8
Pittosporum tobira 5
Platanus spp. 8
Podocarpus macrophyllus 5–7
Potentilla spp. 2–3
Prunus caroliniana 6–7
Prunus maritima 4
Prunus serotina 8
Punica granatum 4–6
Pyracantha spp. & cvs. 3–6
Quercus ilex 7
Quercus marilandica 7
Quercus myrtifolia 5–6
Quercus nigra 8
Quercus virginiana 7
Rhamnus spp. 4–6
Rhaphiolepis spp. 3–4
Rhapidophyllum hystrix 3
Rhus spp. 4–6

Robinia spp. 4–8
Rosa spp. 1 & 2–5 (most)
Ruscus spp. 2–3
Sabal spp. 3–7
Salix repens 2–3
Salix rosmarinifolia 4
Sambucus spp. 5–6
Sapium sebiferum 7
Schizophragma hydrangeoides 1 & 2
Sciadopitys verticillata 6–7
Sedum spp. 2
Sempervivum tectorum 2
Senna corymbosa 5
Serenoa repens 3–4
Sesbania punicea 5
Shepherdia spp. 4–6
Smilax spp. 1
Spiraea spp. 3–5
Syringa spp. 4–7
Taiwania cryptomerioides 8
Tamarix spp. 4–5
Taxodium distichum 8
Taxus spp. 3–6
Ternstroemia gymnanthera 6
Ulmus crassifolia 7–8
Ulmus parvifolia 7–8
Ulmus pumila 7–8
Umbellularia californica 7–8
Vaccinium spp. 2–6
Viburnum cassinoides 4
Viburnum dentatum 6
Viburnum japonicum 5
Viburnum odoratissimum 5–6
Viburnum suspensum 4
Viburnum tinus 5
Vinca major 2
Viola spp. 2
Vitex spp. 4–6
Yucca spp. 3–5
Zamia pumila 3

32. Plants with Serious Insect or Disease Problems (Partial List)

Albizia julibrissin 6
Ampelopsis brevipedunculata 1
Antigonon leptopus 1
Berberis spp. 3–5 (part)
Betula spp. 7–8 (most white-barked spp.)
Castanea spp. 8 (part)
Cornus spp. 5–7 (part)

Crataegus laevigata 6
Crataegus monogyna 6
Eriobotrya japonica 6
Euonymus spp. 1 & 2–5 (evergreen spp.)
Franklinia alatamaha 6
Fraxinus spp. 6–8 (esp. European spp.)
Gardenia augusta 2–4
Lonicera spp. 4–5 (shrub spp., in part)
Malus spp. & cvs. 5–7 (part)
Photinia spp. 5–6 (part)
Pinus nigra 8
Pinus sylvestris 8 (part)
Platanus occidentalis 8
Populus spp. (part)
Prunus spp. & hybrids 4–7 (part)
Pyracantha spp. & cvs. (part)
Rhamnus spp. 6 (part)
Ribes spp. (part)
Robinia spp. 6–8 (part)
Rosa spp. & cvs. 3–5 (part)
Salix spp. 2–8 (part)
Sorbus spp. 6–8 (part)
Tsuga spp. 6–8 (part)
Ulmus spp. 7–8 (part)

SEASONAL INTEREST

33. *Plants with Fragrant Flowers or Foliage*

Abelia ×grandiflora 4–5
Acer tataricum ssp. ginnala 6
Actinidia arguta 1
Buddleia davidii cvs. 4
Calycanthus floridus 4–5, esp. 'Edith Wilder'
Choisya ternata 5
Clematis armandii 1
Clematis terniflora 1
Clethra alnifolia 5
Cliftonia monophylla 5
Clerodendrum spp. 4–6
Comptonia peregrina 2
Conradina verticillata 2
Elsholtzia stauntonii 3
Fothergilla spp. 3–5
Gardenia augusta 3–4
Gaultheria procumbens 2
Idesia polycarpa 7
Illicium spp. 4–6
Jasminum spp. 1 & 2–4

Lavandula angustifolia 2
Lindera benzoin 5
Lonicera flava 1 & 2
Lonicera fragrantissima 5
Lonicera hildenbrandiana 1 & 2
Lonicera japonica 1 & 2
Lonicera periclymenum var. serotina 1 & 2
Lonicera ×purpusii 5
Lonicera standishii 4
Lonicera syringantha 5
Magnolia denudata 7
Magnolia grandiflora 8
Magnolia ×loebneri 6–7
Magnolia macrophylla 7
Magnolia salicifolia and hybrids 7
Magnolia ×soulangiana (part) 7
Magnolia stellata and hybrids 5
Magnolia virginiana 6–7
Malus cultivars 5–6:
　'Blanche Ames'
　'Branzam'
　'Chrishozam'
　'Hamzam'
　'Klehm'
　'Mazam'
　'Morton'
　'Royscezam'
　'Strawberry Parfait'
　'Sweet Perfume'
Michelia spp. & cvs. 5–7
Myrica spp. 4–6
Osmanthus spp. (most) 4–6
Passiflora caerulea 1 & 2
Paulownia tomentosa 7
Philadelphus coronarius 5
Philadelphus ×lemoinei cvs. 4
Philadelphus microphyllus 4
Philadelphus purpurascens 5–6
Philadelphus schrenkii 5
Philadelphus ×virginalis (part) 4–5
Pittosporum tobira 4–5
Poncirus trifoliata 6
Rosa spp. & cvs. (many) 2–4
Rosmarinus officinalis 2–4
Sarcococca spp. 3–4
Spartium junceum 5
Sophora secundiflora 6–7
Staphylea spp. 5–6
Styrax obassia 6
Syringa spp. & cvs. 4–7 (esp. S. vulgaris)
Teucrium chamaedrys 2

34. Plants Flowering in Late Winter to Early Spring

Abeliophyllum distichum 4
Acer diabolicum 6
Acer negundo 7
Acer platanoides 8
Acer rubrum 8
Acer saccharinum 8
Acer saccharum 8
Alnus spp. 6–8
Argyrocytisus battandieri 6
Betula spp. 6–8
Camellia spp. & cvs. 6
Carpinus spp. 7
Carya spp. 8
Cercis spp. 6–7
Chaenomeles spp. & cvs. 3–4
Chamaecytisus spp. 2–3
Chimonanthus praecox 5
Cliftonia monophylla 5
Corylopsis spp. 4–5
Corylus spp. 5–8
Cytisus spp. 2–4
Daphne genkwa 3
Daphne mezereum 3
Dirca palustris 4
Distylium racemosum 5–6
Erica carnea 2
Fagus spp. 8
Forsythia spp. & cvs. 3–5
Hamamelis spp. & hybrids 5–6 (except H. virginiana)
Lindera spp. 4–6
Lonicera fragrantissima 5
Lonicera ×purpusii 5
Lonicera standishii 4
Magnolia denudata 7
Magnolia kobus 6–7
Magnolia ×loebneri cvs. 6–7
Magnolia ×kewensis cvs. 7
Magnolia ×proctoriana 6
Magnolia salicifolia 7
Magnolia ×soulangiana 7
Magnolia stellata 5
Oemleria cerasiformis 5
Osmanthus americanus 5–6
Osmanthus delavayi 4
Osmanthus fragrans 5–6
Ostrya spp. 7–8
Parrotia persica 6–7

Paulownia tomentosa 7
Phlox spp. 2
Pieris spp. 4–5
Poncirus trifoliata 6
Prunus armeniaca 7
Prunus mandshurica 5–6
Prunus mume 6–7
Prunus sargentii 7–8
Prunus subhirtella 6
Prunus tomentosa 5
Pyrus calleryana 7
Quercus spp. 6–8 (most)
Rhododendron dauricum & hybrids 4
Rhododendron mucronulatum & hybrids 4
Salix spp. 5–8 (most)
Sassafras albidum 7–8
Sophora secundiflora 6–7
Spiraea ×arguta 4
Spiraea ×cinerea 4
Spiraea thunbergii 4
Stachyurus spp. 5
Sycopsis sinensis 6
Symplocos tinctoria 6
Viburnum farreri 5

35. Plants Flowering in Midsummer to Autumn

Abelia ×grandiflora 4–5
Adina rubella 5
Aesculus parviflora 5
Albizia julibrissin 6
Amorpha canescens 3
Antigonon leptopus 1
Aralia spp. 6–7
Baccharis halimifolia 5
Buddleia davidii 4
Campsis spp. 1
Caryopteris spp. 3–4
Cephalanthus occidentalis 5
Cistus spp. & hybrids 3–4
Clematis ×jackmanii 1
Clematis hybrids 1 (large-flowering, most)
Clematis tangutica 1
Clematis terniflora 1
Clematis texensis 1
Clematis viorna 1
Clerodendrum spp. 4–6
Clethra alnifolia 5
Coronilla varia 2

Elsholtzia stauntonii 3
Emmenopterys henryi 6–7
Escallonia spp. 3–6
Eucalyptus spp. 6–7
Euscaphis japonica 5
Firmiana simplex 6–7
Franklinia alatamaha 6
Fuchsia magellanica 3–4
Gardenia augusta 'August Beauty' 4
Genista spp. 2–6 (part)
Hamamelis virginiana 6
Hemerocallis spp. & cvs. 3
Helianthemum nummularium 2
Heptacodium miconioides 5
Hibiscus syriacus 5
Hibiscus rosa-sinensis 6
Hosta spp. & cvs. 2–3
Hydrangea arborescens 3
Hydrangea macrophylla 3 (part)
Hydrangea paniculata 5–6
Hydrangea quercifolia 4–5 (part)
Hylotelephium spp. & hybrids 2–3
Hypericum spp. & cvs. 2–3
Indigofera spp. 3
Itea virginica 4–5
Kalopanax septemlobus 8
Koelreuteria spp. 7
Lagerstroemia cvs. 3–6
Lavandula angustifolia 2
Leycesteria formosa 4
Lonicera ×brownii 1 & 2
Lonicera etrusca 1 & 2
Lonicera periclymenum 1 & 2
Lonicera sempervirens 1 & 2
Lonicera tragophylla 1 & 2
Lotus corniculatus 2
Maackia amurensis 7
Nerium oleander 6
Oxydendrum arboreum 7–8
Passiflora spp. 1 & 2
Persea spp. 6
Pileostegia viburnoides 1 & 2
Pinckneya pubens 6
Polygonum aubertii 1
Potentilla fruticosa 3
Platycarya strobilacea 7
Pueraria lobata 1 & 2
Rhododendron arborescens & hybrids 5
Rhododendron cumberlandense & hybrids 3–5
Rhododendron prunifolium & hybrids 5
Rhododendron viscosum 5

Rosa rugosa & hybrids 3–4 (part)
Rosa setigera 5
Rosa wichuraiana 1 & 2
Rubus odoratus 4
Santolina spp. 3–4
Sarcococca spp. 3–4
Saxifraga stolonifera 2
Schisandra spp. 1
Schizophragma spp. 1 & 2
Sedum spp. & cvs. 2
Senna corymbosa 5
Sesbania punicea 5
Sophora japonica 8
Spartium junceum 5
Spiraea alba 4
Spiraea ×billiardii 4
Spiraea douglasii 5
Spiraea latifolia 4
Toona sinensis 6
Trifolium incarnatum 2–3
Tripetaleia paniculata 4
Stewartia spp. 6–7
Tamarix ramosissima 5
Tetradium daniellii 6–7
Teucrium chamaedrys 2

36. Plants with Colored or Variegated Foliage in Summer

Abelia × grandiflora 'Francis Mason' 4
Abies concolor cvs. 8
Abies koreana 7
Abies lasiocarpa ssp. arizonica 6
Abies pinsapo 'Glauca' 8
Acer japonicum cvs. 6
Acer negundo 'Flamingo' 6
Acer negundo 'Variegatum' 6
Acer palmatum cvs. 6
Acer platanoides cvs. 8
Acer pseudoplatanus cvs. 8
Actinidia kolomikta 1 (part)
Aegopodium podagraria 'Variegatum' 2
Ajuga cvs. 2
Artemisia spp. 3–4
Aucuba japonica cvs. 5
Bambusa multiplex cvs. 5–6
Berberis thunbergii cvs. 4
Buddleia alternifolia 'Argentea' 5
Buxus sempervirens cvs. 4–5 (few)
Calluna vulgaris cvs. 2
Chamaecyparis cvs. 3–8

Cornus alba cvs. 5
Cornus alternifolia cvs. 6
Cornus florida cvs. 6
Cornus kousa cvs. 6
Cornus mas 'Elegantissima' 6
Cornus stolonifera cvs. 5
Corylus avellana 'Aurea' 5
Corylus maxima 'Purpurea' 6
Cotinus coggygria cvs. 6
Croton alabamense 5
Elaeagnus spp. & cvs. 5 (few)
Eleutherococcus sieboldianus 5
Erica spp. (some) & cvs. 2
Eucalyptus spp. 6–7
Euonymus fortunei 1–2 & 4
Euonymus japonicus 5
Fagus sylvatica cvs. 8
Feijoa sellowiana 6
Fuchsia magellanica cvs. 3–4
Gardenia augusta 'Radicans Variegata' 3
Gleditsia triacanthos 'Suncole' 7
Gleditsia triacanthos 'Rubylace' 6
Hedera cvs. 1 & 2
Hippophae rhamnoides 6
Hosta spp. & cvs. 2–3
Hylotelephium spp. & cvs. 2–3
Juniperus spp. & cvs. (many) 2–8
Kerria japonica and 'Variegata' 4
Leucophyllum spp. 3–5
Leucothoe fontanesiana 'Rainbow' 4
Ligustrum japonicum 'Jack Frost' 5
Ligustrum japonicum 'Silver Star' 5
Ligustrum ovalifolium 'Aureum' 5
Ligustrum sinense 'Variegatum' 4
Ligustrum ×vicaryi 5
Liquidambar styraciflua cvs. 7–8
Liriodendron tulipifera 'Aureo-marginata' 7
Liriope spp. & cvs. 2
Loropetalum chinense f. rubrum & cvs. 5
Mahonia trifoliolata var. glauca 4
Malus × cvs. 6
Myrtus communis 'Variegata' 4
Ophiopogon japonicus cvs. 2
Osmanthus heterophyllus cvs. 5
Pachysandra terminalis 'Variegata' 2
Parthenocissus henryana 1 & 2
Parthenocissus tricuspidata 'Purpurea' 2
Phyllostachys spp. 6–7
Pleioblastus variegatus 3
Photinia ×fraseri 6
Photinia glabra 5

Photinia serratifolia 6
Physocarpus opulifolius cvs. 4–5
Picea abies cvs. 3–8
Picea omorika 8
Picea pungens cvs. 8
Pieris japonica cvs. 5
Pieris formosa var. forrestii 5
Pinus densiflora 'Oculus-draconis' 6
Pittosporum tobira 'Variegata'
Platycladus orientalis cvs. 4–7
Populus alba 'Nivea' 8
Prunus ×blireiana 6
Prunus cerasifera cvs. 6
Prunus ×cistena 5
Prunus virginiana 'Schubert' 6
Pyrus salicifolia 5
Quercus robur cvs. 7–8
Quercus virginiana 'Grandview Gold' 8
Salix alba var. sericea 7
Salix arenaria 2–3
Salix exigua 6
Salix purpurea 5
Salix rosmarinifolia 4
Sambucus cvs. 5
Santolina spp. 3–4
Sasa veitchii 3
Sedum spp. 2
Shepherdia spp. 4–6
Sorbus aria 7
Sorbus intermedia 6–7
Tamarix spp. 4–5
Ternstroemia gymnanthera cvs. 6
Thuja occidentalis cvs. 3–7
Thujopsis dolobrata cvs. 5
Toona sinensis 'Flamingo' 6
Zenobia puverulenta 4

37. Plants with Colorful Foliage in Autumn or Winter

Acer buergerianum 7
Acer circinatum 6
Acer davidii 7
Acer griseum 6
Acer japonicum 6
Acer maximowiczianum 7
Acer palmatum 6
Acer pensylvanicum 7
Acer pseudo-sieboldianum 6
Acer rubrum 8
Acer rufinerve 7

Acer saccharum 8
Acer tataricum & ssp. ginnala 6
Acer truncatum 6
Aesculus glabra 7
Aesculus × 'Autumn Splendor' 7
Aleurites fordii 6
Amelanchier spp. 6–7 (most)
Berberis ×gladwynensis 'William Penn' 3
Berberis ×mentorensis 4
Berberis thunbergii cvs. 4
Berberis verruculosa 3
Betula spp. (most) 6–8
Carpinus caroliniana 7
Carya spp. 8
Castanea spp. 6–8
Celastrus spp. 1 & 2
Cercidiphyllum japonicum 8
Cercis canadensis 6
Chionanthus virginicus 6
Cladrastis lutea 7
Clethra alnifolia 5
Cornus alba 5
Cornus amomum 5
Cornus florida 6–7
Cornus kousa 6
Cotinus spp. 6–8
Disanthus cercidifolius 5
Enkianthus campanulatus 5–6
Euonymus alatus 5
Euptelea polyandra 7
Fagus grandifolia 8
Fothergilla spp. 3–5
Franklinia alatamaha 6
Fraxinus americana 8
Fraxinus pennsylvanica 8
Fraxinus texensis 7
Galax urceolata 2
Ginkgo biloba 8
Gleditsia triacanthos 8
Hamamelis spp. & cvs. 5–6 (part)
Hydrangea quercifolia 4–5
Hypericum frondosum 'Sunburst' 3
Itea virginica 4–5
Lagerstroemia cultivars 3–6
Larix spp. 8
Leucothoe fontanesiana 3–4
Leucothoe keiskei 2
Leucothoe racemosa 5
Lindera spp. 5
Liquidambar styraciflua 8
Liriodendron tulipifera 8

Maclura pomifera 7
Mahonia aquifolium 3–4
Malus cultivars 6:
    'Indian Magic'
    'Lanzam'
    'Red Barron'
    'Robinson'
Metasequoia glyptostroboides 8
Morus rubra 7–8
Nandina domestica cvs. 3–5
Nyssa sylvatica 8
Ostrya virginiana 7–8
Oxydendrum arboreum 7–8
Parrotia persica 6–7
Parrotiopsis jacquemontiana 6
Parthenocissus spp. 1 & 2
Pistachia chinensis 8
Potentilla tridentata 2
Prunus pensylvanica 7
Prunus sargentii 7–8
Pseudolarix amabilis 8
Pyrus calleryana cvs. (most) 7
Pyrus fauriei 6
Pyrus ussuriensis 7
Quercus alba 8
Quercus coccinea
Quercus falcata 8
Quercus laevis 6
Quercus pagoda 8
Quercus prinus 8
Quercus rubra 8
Quercus shumardii 8
Quercus velutina 8
Rhododendron japonicum 4
Rhododendron ×kosterianum 4
Rhododendron (Kurume hybrid azaleas) 3–4
    (part)
Rhododendron mucronulatum 4
Rhododendron schlippenbachii 5
Rhus spp. (most) 4–6
Rosa rugosa & hybrids 3–4
Rosa setigera 5
Rosa virginiana 4
Rosa cvs. 2–5 (few)
Salix matsudana 'Golden Curls' 6
Sapium sebiferum 7
Sassafras albidum 7–8
Skimmia japonica 'Rubella' 3
Sorbus alnifolia 8
Spiraea fritschiana 4
Spiraea japonica (some) 3

Spiraea prunifolia 5
Stephanandra tanakae 4
Stewartia spp. (most) 6–7
Taxodium distichum 8
Ternstroemia gymnanthera 6

38. Plants with Fine-Textured Foliage

Buxus spp. 3–5
Acer palmatum cvs. 6 (part)
Acer platanoides cvs. 8
Acer saccharum cvs. 8
Akebia spp. 1 & 2
Albizia julibrissin 6
Alnus glutinosa cvs. 7
Bruckenthalia spiculifolia 2
Calluna vulgaris 2
Calocedrus decurrens 7
Caragana arborescens 'Lorbergii' 5
Ceratiola ericoides 4
Chamaecyparis spp. 3–8
Comptonia peregrina 2
Conradina verticillata 2
Corema conradii 2
Crataegus apiifolia 6
Cryptomeria japonica 8
×Cupressocyparis leylandii 8
Cupressus sp. 7–8
Cytisus spp. 2–4
Daphne spp. 2–4
Empetrum spp. 2
Erica spp. 2–3
Escallonia spp. 3–6
Feijoa sellowiana 6
Ficus pumila 1
Galium odoratum 2
Genista spp. 2–6
Gleditsia triacanthos 8
Hippophae rhamnoides 6
Iberis sempervirens 2
Ilex crenata cvs. 3–5
Ilex glabra cvs. 4–5
Ilex vomitoria cvs. 3–6
Ilex yunnanensis 5
Juglans nigra 'Laciniata' 8
Juniperus spp. 2–8
Larix spp. 8
Lavandula angustifolia 3
Ledum spp. 2–3
Leiophyllum buxifolium 2
Lespedeza spp. 5

Malus transitoria 'Schmidtcutleaf' 6
Metasequoia glyptostroboides 8
Microbiota decussata 2
Parkinsonia spp. 6
Paxistima canbyi 2
Phlox spp. 2
Picea spp. & cvs. 3–8
Pinus spp. 8
Platycladus orientalis 4–7
Potentilla fruticosa 3
Pseudolarix amabilis 8
Pseudotsuga menziesii 8
Pyrus regelii 'Bailwing' 6
Quercus phellos 7–8
Rhamnus frangula 'Asplenifolia' 5
Rhus glabra 'Laciniata' 5
Rhus typhina 'Dissecta' 5
Rosa spinosissima 3
Rosa xanthina f. hugonis 4–5
Rosa cvs. (few) 2–5
Salix arenaria 2–3
Salix exigua 6
Salix purpurea 5
Salix rosmarinifolia 4
Santolina spp. 3–4
Saxifraga stolonifera 2
Sedum spp. 2
Sequoiadendron giganteum 8
Sequoia sempervirens 8
Spartium junceum 5
Sophora japonica 8
Stephanandra incisa 4–5
Syringa laciniata 4
Syringa ×persica 4
Tamarix spp. 4–5
Taxodium distichum 8
Teucrium chamaedrys 2
Thuja spp. & cvs. 3–7
Thujopsis dolobrata 5

39. Plants with Coarse-Textured Foliage

Acer pensylvanicum 7
Aesculus spp. 5–8
Ailanthus altissima 8
Aralia spp. 6–7
Aristolochia macrophylla 1
Asimina triloba 6–7
Aspidistra elatior 3
Catalpa spps. 7–8
Decaisnea fargesii 5

Eriobotrya spp. 6
Fatsia japonica 4–5
×Fatshedera lizei 4
Ficus carica 5–6
Firmiana simplex 6–7
Galax urceolata 2
Gaultheria shallon 3
Gymnocladus dioica 8
Hamamelis mollis 5
Hydrangea arborescens 3
Hydrangea macrophylla cvs. 3
Hydrangea quercifolia 4–5
Idesia polycarpa 7
Kalopanax septemlobus 8
Leitneria floridana 5–6
Magnolia acuminata 8
Magnolia ashei 6
Magnolia campbellii 7
Magnolia fraseri 7
Magnolia grandiflora 8
Magnolia hypoleuca 7–8
Magnolia macrophylla 7
Magnolia pyramidata 6
Magnolia sargentiana & hybrids 7
Magnolia sprengeri 7
Magnolia ×thompsoniana 7
Melia azedarach 6
Morus spp. 6–8
Paulownia tomentosa 7
Picrasma quassioides 7
Platanus spp. 8
Populus deltoides 8
Prunus laurocerasus 4–6
Pueraria lobata 1 & 3
Rubus odoratus 4
Rubus parviflorus 4
Sambucus spp. 5
Smilax megalantha 1
Styrax obassia 6
Styrax grandifolium 6
Tetrapanax papyrifera 5
Tilia americana 8
Toona sinensis 6–7

40. Plants with Otherwise Distinctive Foliage

Abies spp. (part) 7–8
Acer buergerianum 7
Acer palmatum 6
Acer circinatum 6

Akebia spp. 1 & 2
Albizia julibrissin 6
Ampelopsis brevipedunculata 1
Araucaria spp. 8
Asarum spp. 2
Asimina triloba 6–7
Aspidistra elatior 3
Calocedrus decurrens 8
Chamaecyparis obtusa cvs. 3–7
Choisya ternata 5
Comptonia peregrina 2
Cryptomeria japonica 8
Cunninghamia lanceolata 8
Dirca palustris 4
Daphniphyllum spp. 4–6
Eleutherococcus sieboldianus 5
Epimedium spp. 2
Eucalyptus spp. 6–7
Galium odoratum 2
Gardenia augusta 4
Holboellia coriacea 1
Hylotelephium spp. 2–3
Hypericum spp. 2–4
Idesia polycarpa 7
Ilex spp. 4–7 (part)
Kerria japonica 4
Ligustrum japonicum 5–6
Lindera obtusiloba 6
Liquidambar spp. 6–8
Liriodendron spp. 8
Liriope spp. 2
Lonicera fragrantissima 5
Myrica spp. 4–5
Nandina domestica 4–5
Nerium oleander 6
Ophiopogon japonicum 2
Orixa japonica 5
Osmanthus spp. 4–6
Pachysandra spp. 2
Parkinsonia spp. 6
Passiflora caerulea 1 & 2
Pinus aristata 4–6
Pinus flexilis 8
Pinus palustris 8
Pinus parviflora 'Glauca' 7–8
Pinus strobus 8
Pinus wallichiana 8
Pittosporum tobira 4–5
Podophyllum peltatum 2
Podocarpus macrophyllus 5–7
Populus tremula 6–8

Populus tremuloides 6–8
Populus alba 8
Potentilla tridentata 2
Prunus laurocerasus 4–6
Prunus lusitanica 5–6
Pterocarya spp. 8
Quercus imbricaria 8
Quercus frainetto 8
Quercus phellos 7–8
Rhododendron schlippenbachii 5
Rhododendron vaseyi 5
Rhododendron yakushimanum 3–4
Rhodotypos scandens 4
Rubus tricolor 2
Sabal spp. 3–7
Sapium sebiferum 7
Sciadopitys verticillata 6–7
Sedum spp. 2
Sempervivum spp. 2
Serenoa spp. 3–4
Smilax megalantha 1
Stauntonia hexaphylla 1
Stephanandra spp. 4–5

41. Plants with Colorful or Interesting Fruits in Fall or Winter

Ardisia spp. 2–4
Aronia arbutifolia 5
Aucuba japonica 5
Berberis darwinii 4–5
Berberis koreana 4
Berberis ×stenophylla 5
Berberis thunbergii 4
Callicarpa spp. 4–5
Celastrus spp. 1 & 2
Chionanthus virginicus 6
Cornus alba 5
Cornus amomum 5
Cornus canadensis 2
Cornus florida 6–7
Cotoneaster spp. & cvs. 2–6 (part)
Crataegus spp. & cvs. 5–7 (part)
Danaë racemosa 3
Decaisnea fargesii 5
Elaeagnus angustifolia 6
Elaeagnus umbellata 5
Euonymus spp. & cvs. 1–6 (part)
Gaultheria spp. 2–3
Heptacodium miconioides 5
Ilex spp. and hybrids 3–7 (pistillate plants)

Ilex decidua 6
Ilex laevigata 5
Ilex serrata 5
Ilex verticillata 5
Juniperus virginiana 5–8
Koelreuteria spp. 6
Lindera benzoin 5
Lonicera maackii 6
Malus cvs. 5–7 (part):
  'Adams'
  'Adirondack'
  'Bob White'
  'Chrishozam'
  'Coral Cascade'
  'David'
  'Donald Wyman'
  'Indian Magic'
  'Indian Summer'
  'Inglis'
  'Jewelberry'
  'Jewelcole'
  'Kelsey'
  'Molozam'
  'Ormiston Roy'
  'Prairiefire'
  'Professor Sprenger'
  'Ralph Shay'
  'Robinson'
  'Snowdrift'
  'Sutyzam'
  'Weepcanzam'
Melia azedarach 6
Mitchella repens 2
Nandina domestica 4–5
Parthenocissus spp. 1 & 2
Photinia davidiana 6
Pistacia chinensis 8
Punica granatum 4–6
Pyracantha spp. & hybrids 3–5
Rhodotypos scandens 4
Rhus chinensis 6
Rhus copallina 5–6
Rhus glabra 6
Rhus typhina 6
Rosa multiflora 5
Rosa rugosa 4 and hybrids
Rosa virginiana 4
Rosa wichuraiana 1 & 2
Rosa cvs. 2–4 (few)
Sapindus drummondii 7
Sarcococca spp. 3–4

Sesbania punicea 5
Schisandra spp. 2
Skimmia japonica 2–3
Smilax megalantha 1
Sophora japonica 8
Sorbus spp. 6–8 (most)
Symphoricarpos × chenaultii 3
Symphoricarpos × doorenbosii 4
Symphoricarpos orbiculatus 3
Tetradium daniellii 6–7
Viburnum davidii 3
Viburnum dilatatum 4–5
Viburnum opulus 5
Viburnum sargentii 5
Viburnum setigerum 5
Viburnum trilobum 5
Viburnum wrightii 5

42. Plants with Colorful or Interesting Fruits in Summer or Early Autumn

Acer diabolicum f. purpurascens 6
Acer palmatum cvs. 6 (part)
Acer circinatum 6
Acer tataricum ssp. ginnala 6
Acer tataricum ssp. tataricum 6
Ailanthus altissima var. erythrocarpa 8
Ampelopsis brevipedunculata 1
Arctostaphylos spp. 2–5
Cornus alba 5
Cornus amomum 5
Cornus controversa 7
Cornus kousa 6
Cornus mas 6
Cornus officinalis 6
Cornus racemosa 5
Cornus stolonifera 5
Cotinus spp. 6–8
Cotoneaster adpressus 2
Cotoneaster apiculatus 3
Cotoneaster divaricatus 4
Cotoneaster horizontalis 3
Crataegus aestivalis 6
Crataegus brachyacantha 6
Crataegus ovata 6
Crataegus mollis 6
Elaeagnus commutata 5
Elaeagnus multiflora 5
Euscaphis japonica 5
Hovenia dulcis 7
Idesia polycarpa 7
Koelreuteria spp. 6

Lonicera alpigena 'Nana' 4
Lonicera × amoena 5
Lonicera × bella 5
Lonicera korolkowii 5
Lonicera morrowii 4
Lonicera tatarica 5
Magnolia spp. 5–8
Mahonia spp. 2–5
Oemleria cerasiformis 5
Prinsepia spp. 4–5
Prunus spp. & cvs. 4–7 (part)
Pyracantha spp. & hybrids 3–5
Rhus spp. 4–6
Ribes spp. 4–5
Sambucus spp. 5
Shepherdia argentea 5–6
Sophora japonica 8
Sorbus spp. 6–8 (part)
Symphoricarpos albus 3–4
Symplocos paniculata 6
Vaccinium spp. 2–6 (part)
Viburnum cassinoides 4
Viburnum dentatum 6
Viburnum lantana 6
Viburnum lentago 6
Viburnum nudum 5
Viburnum odoratissimum 5–6
Viburnum opulus 5
Viburnum plicatum f. tomentosum 5
Viburnum prunifolium 6
Viburnum × rhytidophylloides 5
Viburnum rhytidophyllum 5
Viburnum rufidulum 6
Viburnum sargentii 5
Viburnum sieboldii 6
Viburnum suspensum 4–5
Viburnum tinus 5
Viburnum trilobum 5
Vitis spp. 1
Ziziphus jujube 6

43. Plants with Otherwise Distinctive Fruits or Cones

Abies spp. 7–8 (some)
Aesculus spp. 6–8
Akebia spp. 1 & 2
Albizia julibrissin 6
Aristolochia macrophylla 1
Campsis spp. & hybrids 1
Carpinus spp. 7
Catalpa spp. 7–8

Cedrus spp. 7–8
Chaenomeles spp. & hybrids 3–4
Chilopsis linearis 6
Cudrania tricuspidata 6
Cydonia oblonga 6
Davidia involucrata 6–7
Decaisnea fargesii 5
Dipteronia sinensis 6
Ginkgo biloba 8
Gleditsia triacanthos 8
Gymnocladus dioica 8
Halesia spp. 6–8
Koelreuteria spp. 6
Liquidambar styraciflua 8
Maclura pomifera 7
Ostrya spp. 7–8
Paulownia tomentosa 7
Picea spp. 8 (part)
Pinus spp. 5–8 (part)
Platycarya strobilacea 7
Pseudocydonia sinensis 6
Pseudotsuga spp. 7–8
Ptelea spp. 6
Pterocarya spp. 8
Sophora japonica 8
Staphylea spp. 6
Tsuga spp. 6–8 (part)
Wisteria spp. 1
Xanthoceras sorbifolium 6

44. Plants with Edible Fruits or Nuts

Actinidia spp. & cvs. 1
Amelanchier spp. 4–7
Asimina triloba 6–7
Carya spp. 8 (part)
Castanea spp. & hybrids 6–8
Corylus spp. 5–8
Cudrania tricuspidata 6
Diospyros virginiana 6–7
Eriobotrya spp. 6
Fagus grandifolia 8
Feijoa sellowiana 6
Ficus carica 5–6
Fragaria spp. 2
Juglans spp. 7–8
Malus spp. & cvs. 5–7 (few)
Morus spp. 6–8
Pinus edulis 7
Prunus spp. 3–8 (part)
Punica granatum 4–6
Rosa rugosa 4

Rubus spp. 2–5 (part)
Sambucus canadensis 5
Sambucus nigra 5
Shepherdia spp. 5–6
Vaccinium spp. 2–6
Vitis spp. 1
Ziziphus jujuba 6

45. Plants with Colorful or Interesting Twigs or Branches in Winter or Year-Round

Acer capillipes 7
Acer davidii 7
Acer rubrum 8
Acer rufinerve 7
Acer palmatum cvs. 6
Acer pensylvanicum 7
Acer rubrum 8
Acer saccharinum 8
Acer tegmentosum 6
Argyrocytisus battandieri 6
Chamaecytisus spp. 2–3
Cornus alba 5
Cornus amomum 5
Cornus sanguineum 5
Cornus stolonifera 5
Corylus colurna 7–8
Cytisus spp. 2–4
Euonymus alatus 5
Euonymus phellomanus 6
Fagus spp. 8
Fraxinus excelsior cvs. 8 (few)
Genista spp. 2–4
Kerria japonica 4
Liquidambar styraciflua 8
Magnolia spp. & cvs. 5–8
Malus 'Red Jade' 5
Malus 'Schmidtcutleaf' 6
Rhus typhina 6
Robinia hispida cvs. 5
Rosa virginiana 4
Ruscus spp. 2–3
Salix alba 'Britzensis' 4–8
Salix alba var. tristis 4–8
Salix alba var. vitellina 4–8
Salix matsudana 'Scarcuzam' 6
Salix matsudana 'Tortuosa' 7
Sorbus alnifolia 8
Spartium junceum 5
Stephanandra spp. 4

46. Plants with Twigs (or Foliage) Prickly, Spiny, or Thorny

Agave americana 4
Aralia spp. 6–7
Araucaria araucana 8
Berberis spp. 3–5
Chaenomeles spp. 3–4
Cunninghamia lanceolata 8
Crataegus spp. 6–7
Cudrania tricuspidata 6
Elaeagnus pungens 5
Eleutherococcus sieboldianus 5
Gleditsia triacanthos 8
Ilex aquifolium and hybrids 6
Ilex ciliospinosa & hybrids 6
Ilex cornuta & hybrids 4–6
Ilex opaca & hybrids 6–7
Ilex pernyi & hybrids 6
Kalopanax septemlobus 8
Lonicera spinosa 3
Maclura pomifera 7
×Macludrania hybrida 7
Osmanthus spp. 4–6 (part)
Parkinsonia spp. 6
Poncirus trifoliata 5
Prinsepia spp. 4–5
Punica granatum 4–6
Pyracantha spp. & cvs. 3–5 (most)
Rhapidophyllum hystrix 3
Robinia spp. 5–8 (part)
Rosa spp. & cvs. 2–5
Ruscus spp. 2–3
Shepherdia spp. 4–6 (part)
Smilax spp. 1
Yucca spp. 3–5
Zanthoxylum spp. 6

47. Plants with Interesting Bark Color or Texture

Acer buergerianum 7
Acer capillipes 7
Acer circinatum 6
Acer davidii 7
Acer griseum 6
Acer pensylvanicum 7
Acer rufinerve 7
Acer tegmentosum 6
Acer triflorum 6
Acer rubrum 8

Araucaria spp. 8
Arctostaphylos spp. (part)
Betula albo-sinensis 8
Betula alleghaniensis 7–8
Betula costata 8
Betula davurica 7
Betula lenta 7–8
Betula mandshurica 7
Betula maximowicziana 8
Betula nigra 8
Betula papyrifera 8
Betula pendula 7–8
Betula populifolia 6–7
Betula utilis 7–8
Calocedrus decurrens 8
Carpinus spp. 7
Carya laciniosa 8
Carya ovata 8
Celtis spp. 7–8
Chamaecyparis spp. 7–8
Chionanthus retusus var. serrulatus 6
Cladrastis lutea 7
Cornus coreana 7–8
Cornus florida 6–7
Cornus kousa 6
Cornus officinalis 6
Corylus colurna 7–8
Cryptomeria japonica 8
Cunninghamia lanceolata 8
Cupressus spp. 7
Davidia involucrata 6–7
Diospyros virginiana 7
Eucalyptus spp. 6–7
Fagus spp. 8
Franklinia alatamaha 6
Halesia spp. 6–8
Heptacodium miconioides 5
Juglans nigra 8
Juniperus virginiana 6–8
Laburnum spp. 6
Lagerstroemia spp. & cvs. 3–7
Liriodendron tulipifera 8
Metasequoia glyptostroboides 8
Nyssa sylvatica 8
Parrotia persica 6–7
Phellodendron amurense 7–8
Pinus bungeana 6–7
Pinus densiflora 7–8
Pinus nigra 8
Pinus palustris 8
Pinus sylvestris 8

Pinus taeda 8
Platanus spp. 8
Pseudocydonia sinensis 6
Prunus avium 6–7
Prunus maackii 7
Prunus sargentii 8
Prunus serotina 8
Prunus serrula 6
Prunus serrulata 6
Prunus subhirtella 6
Prunus × yedoensis 6
Pteroceltis tatarinowii 7
Quercus macrocarpa 8

Quercus pagoda 8
Robinia pseudoacacia 8
Sciadopitys verticillata 6–7
Sorbus alnifolia 8
Stewartia spp. 6–7 (part)
Syringa reticulata 6–7
Syringa pekinensis 6
Taxodium distichum 8
Taxus spp. & hybrids 4–6
Tetradium daniellii 6–7
Ulmus parvifolia 7–8
Vaccinium arboreum 6
Zelkova serrata 8

INDEX OF PLANT NAMES